Seamen's Missions

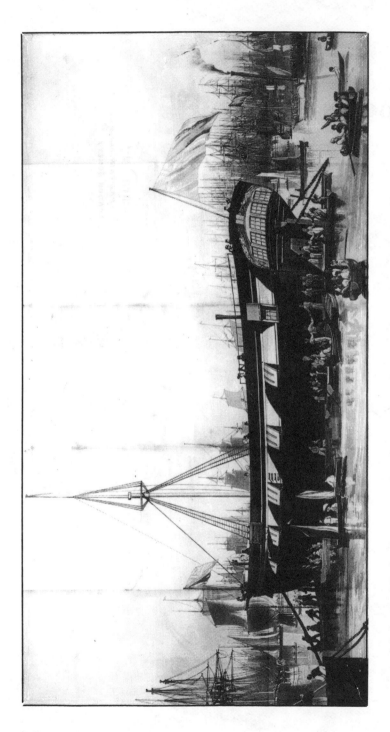

View of the world's first seamen's church, London's Floating Chapel for Seamen, dedicated May 4th, 1818. Dubbed the *Ark* by seamen themselves, the transformed warship *Speedy* from Nelson's navy is depicted here with signals flying for public worship, as she lies at her moorings off Wapping Stairs in the River Thames. (From a print published in 1819, based on a drawing by J. Gendall, engraved by D. Havell. Courtesy of the Bodleian Library, Oxford.)

Seamen's Missions
Their Origin and Early Growth

A Contribution to the History of the Church Maritime

By ROALD KVERNDAL

William Carey Library

P.O. Box 40129 • Pasadena, California 91104

Published by
William Carey Library
P.O. Box 40129, 1705 N. Sierra Bonita Avenue
Pasadena, California 91104
Telephone (818) 798-0819

Number 14 in the "Studies Series" of the Egede Institute for Missionary Study and Research, Oslo, Norway.

Publication partially funded by a major grant from the Norwegian Research Council for Science and the Humanities.

Cover and Part Leaf Illustrations by Ron Bomba.

Typeset by Dataprose, a Division of Bozotronics, Seattle.

Printed in the United States of America.

Library of Congress Cataloging-in-Publication Data

Kverndal, Roald.
    Seamen's missions.

    Bibliography: p.
    1. Merchant seamen—Missions and charities—Great Britain—History.
2. Merchant seamen—Missions and charities—United States—History.
3. Church work with military personnel—Great Britain—History. 4. Church work
with military personnel—United States—History. 5. Great Britain. Royal Navy—
Chaplains—History. I. Title.
BV2670.K94   1986   260   85-25508
ISBN 0-87808-440-1   (rev.)

TO RUTH

my beloved lifepartner,
unswerving companion in the faith

Contents

Abbreviations

A. Institutions

ABCFM	American Board of Commissioners for Foreign Missions
ABS	American Bible Society
ATS	American Tract Society
BFBS	British and Foreign Bible Society
BFSS	British and Foreign Sailors' Society
BFSFSBU	British and Foreign Seamen's Friend Society and Bethel Union
BFSSFS	British and Foreign Seamen and Soldiers' Friend Society
BMS	Baptist Missionary Society
BSFS	Boston Seaman's Friend Society
BSMRIP	Boston Society for the Moral and Religious Instruction of the Poor
BSRMIS	Boston Society for the Religious and Moral Improvement of Seamen
BSS	British Sailors' Society
BSU	Bethel Seamen's Union
BU	Bethel Union
CBU	Charleston Bethel Union
CCCS	Colonial and Continental Church Society
CMAS	Churchmen's Missionary Association for Seamen of the Port of Philadelphia
CMS	Church Missionary Society
CPAS	Church Pastoral Aid Society
CPS	Charleston Port Society
EFCS	Episcopal Floating Church Society
ICMA	International Christian Maritime Association
ICOSA	International Council of Seamen's Agencies
ILO	International Labour Organisation
LAMM	Lutheran Association for Maritime Ministry
LCM	London City Mission
LMS	London Missionary Society
MBS	Marine Bible Society
MBSNY	Marine Bible Society of New-York
MHS	Massachusetts Historical Society
MSABS	Merchant Seamen's Auxiliary Bible Society
MTS	The Missions to Seamen

NMBS	Naval and Military Bible Society
NYBU	New York Bethel Union
NYPS	New York Port Society
PBHS	Prayer Book and Homily Society
PECMSS	Protestant Episcopal Church Missionary Society for Seamen in the City and Port of New York
PHS	Port of Hull Society
PLBUS	Port of London and Bethel Union Sociey
PLS	Port of London Society
RNMDSF	Royal National Mission to Deep Sea Fishermen
RTS	Religious Tract Society
SAS	Seaman's Aid Society
SAWCM	St. Andrew's Waterside Church Mission
SCFS	Seamen's Christian Friend Society
SCI	Seamen's Church Institute
SGM	Scripture Gift Mission
SPCK	Society for Promoting Christian Knowledge
SPG	Society for the Propagation of the Gospel in Foreign Parts
SUBSB	Seamen's Union Bethel Society of Baltimore
TCM	Thames Church Mission
USS	United Seamen's Service
WSM	Wesleyan Seamen's Mission

B. Sources

ASMBUM	The American Sailor's Magazine and Bethel Union Messenger
BH	Bud og Hilsen
CC	The Chart and Compass
CH	The Christian Herald
CHSM	The Christian Herald and Seaman's Magazine
DAB	Dictionary of American Biography
DNB	Dictionary of National Biography
EM	The Evangelical Magazine
KLN	Kirke-Leksikon for Norden
MM	The Mariner's Mirror
MMNY	The Mariners' Magazine (New York)
MR	The Missionary Register
NSM	The New Sailor's Magazine
RR	The Religious Remembrancer
SML	The Sailor's Magazine (London)
SMNY	The Sailor's Magazine (New York)
SMR	The Scottish Missionary Register
WW	The Word on the Waters

Chronology

1779— Naval and Military Bible Society, world's first mission to seafarers.

1809— Naval Correspondence Mission instituted by Rev. G.C. Smith of Penzance (Baptist).

1812— Boston Society for the Religious and Moral Improvement of Seamen.

1813— Thames Union Bible Committee, world's first "Marine Bible Society."

1814— Thames shipboard prayer-meetings begun by Zebedee Rogers (Methodist).

1816— Naval Bible Society of Cronstadt (Port of St. Petersburg, Russia).

1816— "Seamen's Meeting" in New York begun by Rev. Ward Stafford (Presbyterian).

1817— Bethel Flag designed by Zebedee Rogers and hoisted on brig *Zephyr.*

1818— Committee for the Relief of Distressed Seamen; obtains seven "Receiving Ships" for unemployed seamen.

1818— Port of London Society (PLS) founded; opens first seamen's church, the *Ark.*

1818— New York Port Society founded; opens first *shore-based* seamen's church (1820).

1819— British and Foreign Seamen's Friend Society and Bethel Union (BFSFSBU).

1819— First sailing chapel mission to Norway by Carl von Bülow (Congregational).

1820— First Bethel Flag hoisted in North America at St. John, New Brunswick.

1821— Capt. Wm. H. Angas (Baptist) ordained as first "Missionary to Seafaring Men."

1821— Seamen's Hospital Society founded, with HMS *Grampus* as floating infirmary off Greenwich.

1822— Port of Dublin Society, first Anglican mission to seafarers.

1822— Calcutta Bethel Society founded with help of Dr. William Carey.

1822— Shipboard preaching in Whampoa, China, begun by Dr. Robert Morrison.

1822— Sydney Bethel Union Society founded by local Wesleyans and Anglicans.

1825— Rev. G.C. Smith acquires Danish-Norwegian Church in Wellclose Square as London Mariners' Church and headquarters of BFSSFS.

1825— Episcopal Floating Church Society founded in London; opens former HMS *Brazen* in 1829.

1826— American Seamen's Friend Society (ASFS) founded in New York; reactivated in 1828.

1827— Port of London and Bethel Union Society (PLBUS) established as merger of PLS and BFSFSBU.

1827— Merchant Seamen's Orphan Asylum opened in London by PLBUS.

1828— Destitute Sailors' Asylum opened in Dock Street, London (initiated by G.C. Smith).

1828— "Father Taylor" (Methodist) commences career in Boston; achieves world renown as seamen's preacher.

1830— Rev. David Abeel (Dutch Reformed Church) arrives in Canton as first ASFS "Sea Missionary."

1831— Havre de Grace British and American Seamen's Friend Society, first general seamen's mission organization in mainland Europe.

1831— Marine Hospital (willing to accept chronic/incurable cases) opened on Staten Island.

1832— Female Bethel Association of New York, later Mariners' Family Home, Staten Island.

1833— British and Foreign Sailors' Society (BFSS) organized in London, absorbing PLBUS.

1833— Seaman's Aid Society founded in Boston for help toward self-help of seafarers' families.

1833— Marine Temperance Society of New-York founded, initiating widespread emulation.

1833— Sailors' Snug Harbor opened on Staten Island for retired American seafarers.

1834— Young Men's Auxiliary Education and Missionary Society, precursor of PECMSS of New York.

1835— World's first "Sailors' Home" opened in Well Street, London (initiated by G.C. Smith).

1835— Dr. John Ashley (Anglican precursor) begins roadstead mission in Bristol Channel.

1836— American Bethel Society, pioneer organization for mission on "inland waterways."

1836— Rev. Augustus Kavel (Lutheran) becomes first BFSS "Thames Missionary" to foreign seamen.

1837— Rev. John Webster arrives as ASFS pioneer chaplain to seafarers in Cronstadt, Russia.

1841— First two ASFS "Sailor Missionaries" to Scandinavian port-cities remigrate to Sweden.

1842— Amsterdam British and American Seamen's Friend Society founded by BFSS and ASFS.

1844— Thames Church Mission (Anglican) for sailing chapel ministry on Thames (a precursor of RNMDSF).

1844— First in series of floating churches launched in New York by PECMSS (now SCI of NY/NJ).

1845— Methodists' Scandinavian Bethelship Mission to Nordic seafarers and immigrants, New York.

1846— Seamen's Christian Friend Society (SCFS) founded in London.

1846— Society for the Relief of Destitute Children of Seamen, New York (later Staten Island).

1849— Rev. William Taylor (Methodist) Pacific Coast pioneer chaplain in gold-rush San Francisco.

1856— The (Anglican) Missions to Seamen founded in London (facilitated by Wm. H.G. Kingston).

1856— London Sailors' Institute (BFSS) heralds a more comprehensive concept of mission facility.

1858— American Naval Awakening begins on board USS *North Carolina* in Brooklyn Navy Yard.

1864— St. Andrew's Waterside Church Mission founded in Gravesend, England, by Anglo-Catholics.

SOME SIGNIFICANT DATES AFTER THE PERIOD OF THIS STUDY

1864— Norwegian Seamen's Mission founded in Bergen, Norway.

1865— Bethel Union Register of Christian captains instituted in affiliation with BFSS.

1867— Danish Seamen's Mission founded in Copenhagen, Denmark.

1869— Swedish Seamen's Mission begun by Evangelical National Mission Society (ENMS).

1875— Finnish Seamen's Mission founded in Helsinki, Finland (then under Russia).

1876— Church of Sweden Seamen's Mission assumes co-responsibility with ENMS.

1881— Royal National Mission to Deep Sea Fishermen (RNMDSF) originated.

1886— Committee for Church Ministry to German Seafarers Abroad formed in Hannover (later: German Seamen's Mission).

1894— Société des Oeuvres de Mer founded in France as a Roman Catholic Mission to fishermen.

1899— International Seamen's Mission Conference in Boston, Massachusetts.

1905— Danish Domestic Port Seamen's Mission founded in Copenhagen, Denmark.

1920— Apostleship of the Sea (AOS) initiated by three Roman Catholic laymen in Glasgow, Scotland.

1932— National Group (later International Council) of Seamen's Agencies, for North America and Caribbean (ICOSA).

1955— Nordic Council of Seamen's Churches established.

1969— International Christian Maritime Association (ICMA) founded in Rotterdam.

1970— Pontifical Commission for the Pastoral Care of Migrants & Itinerant Peoples formed to include AOS and ministry to "People on the Move."

1974— Korea Harbor Evangelism founded for indigenous mission to international seafarers.

1982— Korea Seamen's Mission founded for indigenous mission to national seafarers and families.

1982— Center for Seafarers' Rights established in New York (affiliated with SCI of NY/NJ).

SOME SIGNIFICANT "FIRSTS"

First seamen's mission organization in the world (1779), p. 71
First organization exclusively for seamen's mission (1812), p. 412
First ongoing worship services for seafarers (1814), p. 156
First Continental seamen's mission organization (1815), p. 150
First Bethel Flag in the world (1817), p. 159
First publicly advertized seamen's service on shipboard (1817), p. 173
First full-time lay missionary to seafarers (1818), p. 145
First full-time ordained seafarers' chaplain (1818), p. 428
First seamen's church in the world (1818), p. 190
First Bethel Flag in North America (1820), p. 248
First shore-based seamen's church in the world (1820), p. 427
First ordination of a missionary to seafarers (1822), p. 253
First denominational (Anglican) seamen's mission (1822), p. 286
First shore-based seamen's church in the British Isles (1823), p. 236
First Christian seafarers' communion (1830), p. 488
First permanent Continental seamen's mission station (1831), p. 470
First institutionalized Christian seafarers' fellowship (1837), p. 368
First floating sanctuary in America (1844), p. 505
First indigenous Nordic seamen's mission organization (1861), p. 598
First R.C. worldwide coordination of "Sea Apostolate" (1920), p. 403
First interdenominational world assoc. for mission to seafarers (1969), p. 550
First indigenous Asian seamen's mission organization (1974), p. 581
First Christian coordinative body for seafarers' rights (1982), p. 585

Foreword

International Christian Maritime Association
General Secretary:
The Rev. Prebendary T.P. Kerfoot, O.B.E.
St. Michael Paternoster Royal
College Hill, London EC4R 2RL

I count it as a privilege to have been invited to write this foreword by my friend Roald Kverndal, whose contribution to Christian welfare in the maritime world has all along been marked by a constant devotion, understanding and vision.

In reading the manuscript of this unfolding "History of the Church Maritime," one became very conscious of the dedication of the author to the oneness of the ministry to seafarers in Christ, also to the reality of its great variety, rather like tributaries feeding the main-stream of God's love for "His seafarers." Such a concept gained substance in the final establishment of the International Christian Maritime Association in 1972, in which the author played an active part.

This is a work for which many of us have waited for a long time. It brings together in a scholarly way much research into the growth of Christian missions in the maritime world. It is factual. It is history made interesting and alive because the author dares to reveal what he sees as a definitive and providential pattern of growth. He goes further, and follows through the pattern of the past into that of the future, describing what he sees as its ultimate development, under God, in a chapter on "Maritime Missiology" — a much more practical chapter than its title might suggest.

Seamen's Missions: Their Origin and Early Growth is indeed a stimulative book. It fills a void which has long existed in maritime and church history. A careful study of its content will undoubtedly provide incentive for further research.

I write this foreword in my capacity as General Secretary of ICMA. After consultation with others in the Association, I commend it wholeheartedly as a reliable reference resource for those who are actively involved in maritime ministry. May God inspire all who read it, and give to them a new vision of their task in the building of His Kingdom amongst seafarers.

London, April 30, 1982   *Tom Kerfoot*

Preface

This book is the result of the most amazing discovery I ever made. No one had written the world history of the Seamen's Mission Movement. A well-known writer suggests that every author owes it to the reading public to explain why he should think fit to increase the torrent of publications pouring from the printing presses of the world every day. If this be so I have no problem justifying my endeavor. Another matter is, why should I be the one to write it? Two sets of circumstances may be relevant.

Centuries of seafaring heritage on both my mother's and father's side, centered around the seaport of Tvedestrand in Southern Norway, have been a natural, motivating factor. This form of filial incentive has been reinforced by a very personal sense of spiritual indebtedness. As a child, I belonged, with my family, to London's Norwegian Seamen's Church in the heart of the docklands of Rotherhithe, once the cradle of the worldwide Bethel Movement. As an adult, it was through the ministry of the Scandinavian Seamen's Church in Rouen, France, that the lack of commitment into which I had drifted was challenged, and I was reclaimed by the Gospel.

The other set of circumstances is of a vocational nature. A carefully considered career plan entailed the following: Seatime from cabin boy in the North Sea trade to fourth mate on the China Coast; apprentice at a shipyard in Oslo; shipbroking in London; consular service in France; and a degree in a branch of marine law. After my renewal of faith in Rouen, I received, much to my surprise, and the shock of family and friends, "new orders from the bridge." These orders were to prepare for the oldest ministry in the history of the church—mission to seafarers.

True, subjective involvement in any area of research raises questions of personal bias. On the other hand, there is the equally fundamental issue of rapport. Many years of service to men and women of the sea gave the personal affinity essential to identify and understand the issues involved.

After once casting off on this research endeavor, the history of its completion closely resembles a long sea voyage in the days of sail. It did not always proceed the way it was planned. The impluse to set sail in the first place was sparked by the Norwegian Seamen's Mission centenary. During all the focusing on this organization's historic orgin, as well as the challenge of change on the current shipping scene, many questions surfaced. Among them was the view of mission which impelled the pioneers. How far were they influenced by prior Anglo-American activities?

My original plan was therefore to research the prehistory of Nordic seamen's missions, with special reference to the impact of earlier organized endeavors elsewhere. It was as I searched in vain for comprehensive source literature on the latter that I found to my astonishment that none existed. The reason was simple. No one had so far taken up the task of a foundational study of the world-wide movement itself. Was I to abandon ship? Or head for a new port of destination? This book is the outcome of that quest.

The 15-year voyage, begun in Bergen, Norway, ended in her sister-city Seattle, in the Pacific Northwest. During the intervening crisscrossing of oceans and continents, discoveries were made in the archives, files and collections of libraries, museums, universities, seminaries, publishers, seamen's agencies, world mission and Bible institutes, municipal buildings, port authorities, shipping offices and private homes.

Probably the most dramatic examples of discovering primary source materials from the dawn period of the movement were: Gingerly opening mouldy paper packages in a dark, dank vault under the bank of the Thames. Also, making fascinating finds in the dusty, undisturbed stacks of two centuries old documents in a library on Boston's historic Beacon Hill. At every port of call along the way, I met people to whom I owe an infinite debt of gratitude.

Perhaps I can best sum up my hopes for the whole venture by responding to two questions which might be raised about the way I have dealt with my subject.

Why has this material not been organized so as to develop a specific thesis? The answer is because, with all the fragmentation and contradiction which has so far surrounded the subject, *the narrative itself* is the thesis. At an early stage, a professor gave the advice: "Do it so thoroughly that no one will have to redo it." However that may be, my hope is that it will stimulate and facilitate further academic research in all related disciplines. My hope is also that it will raise awareness of the potential role of seafarers as vital partners in Christ in his church's global outreach of witness and compassion.

Others might ask, as some already have, why allow a dissertation manuscript to become so "edifying"? The reason is — *the narrative itself* is precisely that. A seamen's mission leader from the pioneer era once wrote: "It is said of old time, the Spirit of God moved upon the face of the waters. A book might be written of how this self same Spirit moved upon the hearts of the men of the sea. . . ." To inspire, such a book need only be true to its subject. If that can be said of this book, it will have fulfilled its highest purpose.

Roald Kverndal
Seattle, September 1986

Acknowledgments

First and foremost, for their loyalty and encouragement, my loving thanks to my children, Olaf, Evelyn, Jeanette, Marianne. My warm thanks also to my brothers, Ole and John, as well as to God for my late parents, Olaf and Valli, and late brother, Erik.

For help, counsel and financial contributions toward many years of traveling, research and writing, also toward the academic defense of the dissertation and its publication at a purchasable price, my deep gratitude to each of the following, besides many more than I can list:

Johannes Aardal; Johan & Petra Arnesen; Steven & Isabel Austin; Walter Baepler; Nils E. Bloch-Hoell; Halfdan T. Bondevik; Kathleen Cann; Jim & Ethel Chandler; Alethe Clezy; Ingebrigt Dahle; T.K. Derry; Jim Dillenburg; Ray Eckhoff; Karl Eielsen; Lars Eklund; Charles W. Forman; Leif Frivold; Erik Fröiland; Johnny Glad; Rene H. Gracida; Ben Hansen; Arne Hassing; Elsa Hofstad; Lucille Johnson; Rolf & Ragnhild Kenback; John & Emily Kircheval; Reidar Kobro; Andrew Krey; Anders Kröger; Bernard Krug; Karl & Helene Lauvland; David & Sandra Lawley; Hans Chr. Lier; Jim Lindgren; Deryck Lovegrove; Sister Maria-Cecilia; Solveig Midtbö; Ole Modalsli; Ingunn Montgomery; Gerald E. Morris; Robert & Shirley Muntz; Olav G. Myklebust; Asbjörn Nilsen; Emil & Marit Nitter; Evert Olson; Onar Onarheim; Markku Pelane; Ray Rau; Gunnar Staalsett; Hans & Ella-Steensnaes; Kaare Stöylen; Leif Ström-Olsen; Olive Thompson; Johanna Thorsen; Hans Uittenbosch; Sverre Ulvestad; Dale Umbreit; Johnny Ursin; Gunnar C. Wasberg; Harold J. Williams; Christen & Liv Wroldsen; William J.D. Down; David Harries; James R. Whittemore.

Apostleship of the Sea in the U.S.; British Sailors' Society; Christianssands Skibsassuranceforening; Cross of Christ Men's Group; Danish Domestic-Port Seamen's Mission; Danish Seamen's Church in Foreign Ports; Finnish Seamen's Mission; German Seamen's Mission; Gerrards Rederi; Hansen-Tangen & Co.; International Transport Workers' Federation (ITF); O. Kverndal & Co.; A.I. Langfeldt & Co.; Lutheran Association for Maritime Ministry; Ministry to Seafarers of the Christian Reformed Church; The Missions to Seamen; Missions to Seamen, Thunder Bay (Ont.); New England Seamen's Mission; Norway's Shipowners' Federation & Seamen's Foundation of 1918; Norwegian Seamen's Mission; Torrey Mosvold & Co.;

Professor & Mrs. Hallesby's Legacy; Bendt Rasmussen & Co.; Einar Rasmussen & Co.; Sailors' Snug Harbor; Scandinavian Seamen's Mission Society of Seattle; Seafarers' & International House; Seamen's Church Institute of NY/NJ; I.M. Skaugen & Co.; Skibsassuranceforeningen i Arendal & Christiania; Peder Smedvig & Co.; C.H. Sörensen & Sönner; O.B. Sörensen & Co.; Southern Baptist Seafarers' Ministers' Fellowship; Swedish Seamen's Church, N.Y.; Tönnevolds Tankrederi A/S; Women's Seamen's Friend Society of Connecticut.

Also, for their professional skill and personal dedication in the production of this book, my sincere thanks to Ralph & Roberta Winter, David Shaver and their co-workers at the publishers in Pasadena, and to Everett Greiman of Seattle and the outstanding "crew" he mustered: Brenda Cann, Linda Mackey, Kate Robinson, William R. Carey, Mike Adair and Ron Bomba.

Finally, for their courage, compassion, comradeship and (in many cases) commitment to Christ, which make them such a privilege and joy to serve, I salute the seafarers of all nations.

SOLI DEO GLORIA!

Introduction

When a former man-of-war's man turned seamen's preacher launched, in 1820, the first *Sailor's Magazine* in the world, he was keenly conscious of the need for what he called "minute retrospection," in order to enable future historians to trace "the rise and progress of Evangelical Religion" among seafarers of his day. His writings remain, beyond dispute, the most valuable primary source material for any serious study on the germinal period of organized mission to seafarers.[1] However, he would have been amazed had he known that no such project would be carried out for the next century and a half.

This does not mean that the need was, in the meantime, entirely overlooked. In 1857, the editor of the New York version of *The Sailor's Magazine* wrote: "A history of the Seamen's cause is a desideratum." However, he had to acknowledge that if the importance and results of the work were to be presented "in anything like their just dimensions," the means were simply "not at hand."[2] Almost a century later (in 1952) Professor Elmo Hohman, a recognized authority on the maritime profession, referred to the record of ministry to seafarers by church-related voluntary agencies as still constituting "a little known but instructive chapter in the history of maritime labor." No "adequate sources of information" were available in print, and any real understanding could only be gained through personal visits in port-cities, and through the "patient collection of fugitive and often unpublished documents."[3]

True, some attempts had actually been made over the years. In 1835, that former man-of-war's man, the incomparable George Charles Smith (whose contribution to the cause will occupy a considerable proportion of this study) published the prospectus of a massive 24-part history of the Seamen's Cause entitled *The Bethel Flag*. Although his repeated retrospects make Smith's voluminous authorship a unique source, he never did complete any cohesive history.[4] Nor did his son, Theophilus, who optimistically announced a similar project in 1874.[5] Meanwhile, in 1858, Israel Warren, at that time Secretary of the American Seamen's Friend Society, actually published a 55-page overview entitled *The Seamen's Cause; Embracing the History, Results, and Present Condition, of the Efforts for the Moral Improvement of Seamen*. However, although the work includes important material of a more general nature, it is nevertheless appropriately styled a "sketch," being principally devoted to a summary of the year-by-year activities of the author's own society.[6]

In 1948, Peter Anson, puzzled that no writer had ever thought it worthwhile to make "a scientific investigation of the history and conditions of the apostolic action of the Church among seafarers," published a work in London entitled *The Church and the Sailor: A Survey of the Sea-Apostolate Past and Present.* However, although this, too, has obvious merit, and contains a well-researched section on sporadic ways in which the Christian Church sought to serve the seafarer, from the age of the Apostles to the time of the Reformation, the author is primarily concerned with the renewal of Roman Catholic seamen's mission through the founding, in 1920, of the *Apostleship of the Sea,* an event with which Anson was himself intimately involved.[7]

The fact remains that no comprehensive study has hitherto been made, on the basis of primary source materials, of the origin and early growth of the Seamen's Mission Movement, such as this emerged organizationally around the turn of the nineteenth century. Not surprisingly, therefore, encyclopedic articles attempting to summarize the leading events of such a history reflect this lack of research, and reveal, by and large, more inadequacies and inconsistencies than it would be practicable to list.[8]

Two major motives mandate a foundational study, based on primary source materials. First, there is the basic scientific need. A documentary history of the origin and early growth of the Seamen's Mission Movement has remained a missing chapter not only in church history, but also in secular history, especially maritime history and sociological history. (Since the Second World War, several valuable contributions have been made toward a science of maritime sociology. However, there has been a conspicuous lack of research in the maritime sociology of religion, not to speak of its historical background.)[9]

Secondly, there is a vital promotional need. Factors like radical technological change in the shipping industry, and mounting secularization in the world at large, have contributed to a very real identity crisis in maritime mission, and a sense of urgency in seeking authentic answers. What is valid Christian ministry to seafarers of today? With movements, as also with individuals, loss of identity may simply be the natural result of a loss of memory. Gustav Warneck, the great pioneer missiologist, points, at the close of the nineteenth century, to the acute need for a history of world mission, as a prerequisite for a theology of world mission. Since then, great strides have been made in world mission. However, in maritime mission, the corresponding need for a historical foundation has remained unmet, to the detriment of the whole enterprise. It is hoped that the present study might serve as a source of historical reference for a theology of maritime mission, and perhaps provide a stimulus toward further research in this fascinating field. Thus, it might help to avert what Latourette calls the "criminal waste" of neglecting the fruits of past experience, and instead perhaps contribute toward charting a viable course for the future.[10]

Having thus established the principal purpose of the project, the next question posing itself is one of fixation and formulation of theme. It would have been a tempting task to try to present, in one grand sweep, the entire tapestry of Christian ministry to seafarers, from the time of the New Testament Church to the critical challenges of our own times. However, this would have led to a sporadic, often superficial treatment of the subject. Since, then, selectivity is imperative, priority must be given to that era which must be presumed to have had the most fundamental impact on the emergence of modern-day maritime mission. It is, therefore, the "origin and early growth" of the movement, from which seamen's mission work of today directly derives, which forms the focus of this study, in other words, this movement's genesis and formative years.

The designation of the movement as "seamen's missions" in the opening words of the theme serves the practical purpose of providing easy identification in catalogs and elsewhere. But more importantly, "seamen's missions" is the *historical* designation. It was not the original term. In the early years of the movement, there was talk of the "Seamen's Cause," the "Seamen's Reformation," the "Bethel Movement," and "Sea Missions," to mention only a few alternatives. However, "seamen's missions" had, by the end of the movement's formative years, become by far the most widely accepted designation of the work. Used in the plural (as in the case of the accompanying "foreign missions" movement), the term "seamen's missions" identifies the movement as it actually emerged, organizationally, around the turn of the nineteenth century, employing as its vehicle the so-called "voluntary society" model. Collectively, it was these voluntary societies which made up the first institutionally organized form of the work. It is, therefore, the emergence of "seamen's missions" in this specific sense which constitutes the main theme of the study, not "seamen's mission" per se. (This does not, of course, prevent the use of the latter singular form, whenever the context makes the wider, more recent interpretation of the "mission" concept appropriate. A definition of the term "seamen's mission" in this generic meaning must be deferred, however, to be induced from the conclusions drawn in the final chapter of the study.)[11]

The subtitle, "A Contribution to the History of the Church Maritime," places the area of study within its wider context. Ever since the first generation of Christians, the body of believers has included at least some "that go down to the sea in ships, that do business in great waters." All too often, the

Christian seafarer would find himself an outcast, not only of society in general, but also of the institutional church. Nevertheless, none who know anything about the cost of consistent discipleship at sea would dispute his right to rank with fellow-members from shore in the Church Militant. At the same time, the unique vocational situation of the seafarer, with all its pressures and privations, fully justifies the designation of a sea-linked segment of that body as the "Church Maritime."[12]

Is it possible to determine, with any degree of accuracy, the time-frame covered by the theme? The answer to this question will depend on definitions. As to a *terminus a quo,* the task must be to establish which organization was first to fulfill the minimum requirements of a valid definition of seamen's mission. As will become evident in the course of the study, there is good reason to operate with the year 1779, even though a whole generation would elapse before the work could achieve the momentum needed to expand in any significant degree.[13] Likewise, a *terminus ad quem* must depend on a reasoned determination of what constitutes the completion of the movement's formative period. As George Charles Smith had rueful reason to comment, the early history of mission to seafarers was "like the ship in which Paul sailed . . . exceedingly tossed with a tempest."[14] However, by the early 1860's, years of turbulence had been succeeded by sufficient stability to give birth to a vigorous offspring. Thus in 1864, the founding of the Norwegian Seamen's Mission, as the first in a series of four Nordic seamen's missions, marks the end of Anglo-American hegemony and the beginning of what might be called a "Continental Phase" of the movement.[15] Although no attempt is made to enforce any rigid limitations, the main focus of the study is, therefore, directed toward an 85 year period, stretching from 1779 to 1864.

However, if meaningful research is to be pursued within a theme and time-frame such as indicated, careful documentation by means of primary source materials becomes a crucial concern. Fortunately, there has, so it proves, been no paucity of such materials. The problem has been their dispersed and fragmentary nature. Where the context requires reference to related disciplines such as, for example, missiology, church history, maritime history, or maritime sociology, a selection of secondary sources has been deemed sufficient. However, within the specific field of inquiry indicated in the theme, every effort has been made to search out relevant primary source materials.

If this study makes any claim to lasting value, it is rooted in the exhaustive examination of singularly scattered archives and repositories. (This is also a major reason for the high degree of detail in documentation.)[16] Such sources cannot, of course, be used without reservation. For promotional reasons, minutes may be edited and reports slanted. Likewise, periodicals can easily become a select vehicle for polemics (as in much of G.C. Smith's prolific authorship). Nevertheless, subjective sources are often the *only* source; and they do at least provide an indispensable immediacy.[17]

While eschewing an uncritical use of such data, it would be equally important to avoid a hypercritical attitude. It would, in fact, be gross injustice to discount the achievements of past pioneers simply because they were, in their day, portrayed in an overly pious hue. Again it would be sheer hypocrisy to brand the bias of those who were obviously children of other times, while ignoring the secular prejudice of one's own sophisticated age.[18]

In terms of methodology, the selection and treatment of source materials have not been dictated by a preconceived principle, other than the intention of presenting a fundamentally "phenomenological" study. Hence, the general structure of this project has had to be determined by models and margins set by the movement itself. If the narrative seems dominated by personalities, it is, because so was the movement. (This was pre-eminently the case with George Charles Smith, whose lifespan stretches over almost the entire timeframe of the study. However, it also holds good for several other powerful, often prophetic pioneer figures from both Britain and America.)[19]

Again, if the story seems preoccupied with Protestants of "evangelical" orientation, it is because these were the activists of the movement. (The "High Church" element of the Church of England did not assert itself before the end of the period covered by the study, and the Roman Catholic Church, despite centuries of sporadic involvement, did not officially initiate its Apostleship of the Sea until the year 1920.)[20]

Finally, if the scene seems largely limited to the English-speaking world, it is because British and American Christians were, historically, the first to take up the work, and they remained virtually alone in the field throughout its formative years. (When, eventually, Christians of other nationalities began to organize, their work was partly inspired, partly even initiated by British-American predecessors.)[21]

In following a phenomenological principle of organization, the study places major emphasis on an integrated genetic-historical presentation of the rise of the movement. If sources are fragmentary, all the more reason to ensure that the structure of the study emerges as an organic entity.

Thus, an opening chapter sets the background by seeking to answer such questions as: Why did seamen's missions emerge where they did, when they did, and the way they did? First, reference is made to earlier, pre-organizational forms of ministry to seafarers, from biblical times to the Napoleonic War period. Then follows an examination of the Anglo-American context in which organized mission to seafarers was born, both in general terms and, more specifically, in terms of the seafarer's situation at this particular point in history.

In succeeding chapters, the birth-process is described, as the movement sees the light of day in late eighteenth-century England. At first, that birth seems almost premature. But gradually the movement gathers momentum, beginning with the metropolis, and expanding not only numerically and geographically, but also in diversification of ministry, until maturity is reached, and a new generation of seamen's missions enters the international scene. Because the birth-process itself, though of fundamental importance, has been least known, a more detailed treatment seems justified during the initial years of the movement, with a gradual tapering off toward the latter part of the period of the study. Likewise, because the movement emerged almost simultaneously in the United States, and then followed a remarkably parallel pattern of evolution, a degree of economization has been pursued in dealing with some aspects of the American narrative, in order to avoid duplication. Meanwhile, the very similarity of the two movements on either side of the Atlantic also necessitates an exploration of their interrelationship.[22]

A final chapter is devoted to conclusions of a systematic-historical nature, drawn from the preceding narrative. It would have been impossible, for reasons of space, to combine in one volume both a genetic and systematic treatment of the theme in anything approaching an adequate manner. However, the task would seem lamentably incomplete if no attempt were made to include at least the historical rudiments of a sorely-needed "maritime missiology." While a major portion of the project is, therefore, allocated to a descriptive and interpretive study of the growth-process itself, sufficient space has been reserved for finally focusing on the principles (motives and objectives) and practice (impediments and methods) of seamen's missions during their first formative years. The study closes with brief allusions to two significant questions—concerning *results,* as compared with expectations, and *relevance,* as applied to present-day issues.[23]

A brief addendum entitled "The Emergence of Organized Nordic Seamen's Missions" seeks to show how early impulses (already in part included in the main narrative of the study) converge to set the stage for the subsequent Continental Phase of the Seamen's Mission Movement. Although this addendum therefore transcends the formative focus of the study, its inclusion has been deemed desirable for the reasons given, thus enhancing the value of the entire project as a reference source.

PART I

"THE SET TIME
TO FAVOUR SAILORS"

The Background of a
New Missionary Enterprise

Chapter 1

The Prelude:
Early Forms of
Ministry to Seafarers

"No man will be a sailor," insisted Dr. Samuel Johnson, "who has contrivance to get himself into a jail; for being in a ship is being in a jail, with the chance of being drowned."[1] Harsh though they might seem, those words, uttered in 1759, were nevertheless an understatement. Having once embarked upon a "life on the ocean wave," a British sailor in the late 1700's would normally know that the danger of drowning was only one of many hazards he would have to face.

Nowhere were those hazards more horrendous than in the flourishing West African slave trade. And no-one did more to ferret out the facts of it than a dedicated deacon of the Church of England named Thomas Clarkson. As he traveled the waterfronts of the nation, it did not take him long to discover that the mortality rate among seamen engaged in this barbarous traffic in human flesh was even higher than that of their captive cargo. On an average voyage via West Africa and the West Indies, fully one-fifth of the sailors themselves would perish, of sickness, suicide and brutalization, and even more would desert or be discharged before the ship returned home.

Such staggering statistics found officialdom shocked, and many who stood to gain enraged. In fact, so successful was the young deacon that his life was frequently in jeopardy. On one occasion, nine infuriated slave-ship captains were within one yard of pushing him over a pier to his death when— with typical resoluteness—he charged straight through them and escaped.[2]

As will be seen, the tenacity of Thomas Clarkson and the rude awakening he caused clearly contributed to the coming of organized Christian outreach to seafarers. However, it may be asked, why should it have to take so long? Where was the church in all the intervening years since it was first founded?

3

A natural point of departure would seem to be the question: how was the seafaring vocation viewed in Scripture? Regarding its rating in the Old Testament, the overall attitude to seafaring in ancient Israel was not unlike that reflected in Dr. Johnson's definition. The Hebrew held the sea in fear, at best in awe. With Passover as an annual reminder, he knew his nation owed its very existence to a divine manifestation of mercy by means of the sea. He could exult that God had his pathway in the great waters. But he showed little wish to make his own path on that element. Among his countrymen, only one Old Testament figure of note is recorded as having voluntarily put to sea; and Jonah did so only because he saw no other avenue of escape. For her sea-borne commerce, Israel was, in great measure, content to rely on her Phoenician neighbors to the north.[3]

From her Master, the Christian church inherited a more positive attitude toward the world of the seafarer. It was men of the sea whom Christ called to be his first followers; it was in the port city of Capernaum that he made his home during much of his three-year public ministry; and many events in the Gospel narratives expressly link the Lord with the sea. True, the Sea of Galilee was land-locked, and those who plied it were fishermen. But they were seafarers, nonetheless, with characteristics like courage, commitment and compassion in common with seafarers the world over.[4]

Nor was it long before the great "Western Sea" was included. Christ's commission to go with the Gospel to "the uttermost part of the earth" (Acts 1:8, cf. Matthew 28:19) left his followers with no option. Among those of his Apostles who, in response, literally launched forth into the deep, Paul is conspicuous. Born in the busy Mediterranean seaport of Tarsus, Paul was familiar with the maritime world from early life. Later, in obedience to his call, he recalls how, "in journeyings often," he was frequently in peril at sea, adrift a whole day and night, and shipwrecked no less than three times (2 Corinthians 11:25-26). It seems certain that he who admonished others to seize every opportunity to preach, both in season and out of season (2 Timothy 4:2), would not himself have neglected the many opportunities which sea-travels gave him to bring the Gospel to seafarers.[5]

This could hardly have been more graphically portrayed than in the 27th chapter of the Acts of the Apostles. Paul's words of witness for his Lord and encouragement for passengers and crew, as they face the foundering of their ship, show him as "the only man on board who kept his head and knew what to do."

In one sense, it was Christ himself who, during his life on earth, initiated a Christian ministry to seafarers. However, following the founding of the Christian church, the first whom the biblical record depicts as filling the role of a ship's chaplain is the Apostle Paul, bound for Rome on a storm-tossed grain ship from Alexandria around the year 60 A.D. In so doing, he became a pioneer of the earliest form of mission to men of the sea.[6]

The shipwrecked
Apostle Paul, marooned
on Malta after
ministering as ship's
chaplain during the
dramatic voyage
described in Acts 27.
(Gustav Doré:*The
Bible in Pictures.*)

MINISTRY AT SEA THROUGH THE CENTURIES

It seems only fitting that a "church maritime" should first have manifested itself at sea. Sources are scant. However, it is safe to assume that those pioneer missionaries who, during the earliest era of the church, put to sea in order to spread the faith beyond their own borders used the opportunity while on shipboard to share the Gospel with sailors and fellow-passengers alike. Probably there were those among them who, after arriving at their destination, would seek in various ways to reinforce the link thus forged with the seafarer.

By the Middle Ages, a rich flora of legends had blossomed around the names of several seafaring saints (such as St. Clement, St. Christopher, St. Nicholas of Myra, St. Elmo, St. Columba and St. Brendan the Navigator). Whatever their core of historicity, these legends at least bear witness to a widespread veneration among men of the sea for servants of the church who were held to have identified themselves with the world and welfare of the seafarer.[7]

Bearing in mind the manner in which almost every aspect of the life of medieval man was permeated by the piety and paternalism of the Roman Catholic Church, it comes as no surprise that ways were also sought to safeguard the spiritual life of those who spent much of their life at sea. Thus, it was required that provision be made for mariners to observe days of fasting and abstinence while in service. Also, it became a common custom for ships to carry with them to sea some sacred object, crucifix, image, picture or other form of church symbol. This could be connected to the mast. In this case, the foot of the mast would become a common place of prayer, and William Tyndale, the English reformer, informs us that "shipmen in peril of death, if a priest be not by, shrive themselves unto the mast." However, the object of veneration could also be fastened to the poop, or housed in a shrine astern. (It is thought that the tradition of saluting the quarter-deck in the Royal Navy may have its origin in the medieval mariner's obeisance to such a shrine.)[8]

In some cases, a ship could carry an altar, even a small chapel.[9] This presupposed the presence of seagoing priests as part of the ship's complement. The earliest English naval chaplain known by name is, according to Waldo Smith, one Odo, a Christian priest of Danish parentage, who, before he became Archbishop of Canterbury, served in the Saxon navy of King Athelstan, in the tenth century.[10] A priest is recorded as having accompanied the Norseman Leif Erikson on his epic voyage of discovery to the North American continent around the year 1000 A.D.[11] When, during the reign of King Stephen, a great expedition left Dartmouth for Lisbon in 1147 in order to fight the Moors, it was among the foremost articles of agreement that there should, on board each ship, be "a priest, and the same observances as in parishes on shore."[12]

By then, the Crusades were well under way, with Franciscan friars following the ships and sharing the incredible privations of those who manned them. Priests and monks also sailed on the many ships transporting pilgrims to shrines on the Continent as well as to the Holy Land. Eventually, with the advent of the Age of Discovery, Catholic clerics accompanied the galleons of Portugal and Spain across every ocean, seeking to plant the church wherever they went, while at the same time ministering to the crews with whom they sailed.[13]

Even with a priest on hand, it would not always be practicable to celebrate mass at sea. In heavy weather, a form of "Dry Mass" (*Missa Nautica*) would, therefore, take its place. Where, instead, the sacrament was simply "reserved" on board, the hierarchy of the church found it necessary to protect "God's body" from being touched by unhallowed hands, "upon pain of being drawn and hanged."[14]

By somewhat milder means, the medieval church also strove to protect the seaman from himself. Ancient European maritime codes like the Laws of Oléron (published in the twelfth century, but based on customs going back to the maritime ascendancy of Rhodes) give evidence of having evolved under the powerful influence of the church. Through statutes such as these, she would seek to circumscribe the conduct of her seafaring sons, and

Leif Erikson was accompanied by a priest, serving in effect
as ship's chaplain, on his epic voyage of discovery to the
American continent c. 1000 A.D. (From the original painting
by Christian Krogh, a reproduction of which hangs in the
Capitol, Washington, D.C. Courtesy of *Western Viking*, Seattle.)

promote their moral welfare. Varying punishments were prescribed for such
vices as drunkenness, blasphemy, theft, fighting and insubordination.

Preventive measures were also adopted. The *Black Book of the
Admiralty* (compiled in the early fifteenth century) would, for example,
admonish the medieval mariner, when in port, to be "no common frequenter
of taverns," but flee "the company of women unhoneste." As to virtuous
women, widows and maidens, the sea codes would command the sailor to be
"serviceable and true," and proclaim "that no man be so bold as to ravish
any woman upon pain of death." For such nefarious pursuits as piracy,
wrecking, or carrying contraband to the Saracens, the Pope, who at this time
claimed a kind of universal control over the high seas, could do no less than
order excommunication.[15]

The Reformation resulted in many reappraisals. At sea, the "heretic"
crews of Protestant nations automatically qualified as pirates. Hundreds
disappeared in the dungeons of the Inquisition. The religious vendetta which
ensued contributed directly to the rise of British sea power during the reign of
the Tudors. The Plymouth privateersman, no less than his counterpart from
Cadiz, saw himself as engaged in a crusade for the purity of the faith.
Another major impulse of expansion was the founding of the great trading
companies, in a belated but determined effort to reduce the long lead of the
Catholic countries in commerce and discovery.[16]

Certainly, for the mariners of England, this was no time for spiritual
lethargy. Whether war or trade were contemplated, the favor of God was

seen as crucial to the success of every enterprise. Hence, high priority was attached to the inclusion, if possible, of at least one cleric for every squadron of ships; and each captain would be expected to ensure some form of lay chaplaincy where an ordained "preacher" was not available.

Thus, for example, the instructions given in 1553 by the Governor of the Company of Merchants Adventurers, Sebastian Cabot, to his captains, before casting off for Cathay, state:

> That Morning and Evening Prayer, with other common services appointed by the King's Majestie, and lawes of this realm, to be raid and saide in every ship dayly by the Minister in the admirall, and the Marchant or some other person learned in other ships, and the Bible or other Paraphrases to be raid devoutly and Christianly to God's Honour, and for His Grace to be obtained and had by humble and heartie Praier of the navigants accordingly.[17]

Ordinances for Elizabeth's expedition against Cadiz in 1596 commanded captains to take special care to serve God by having Common Prayer said twice a day, by ensuring that the Lord's Prayer and "some Psalms of David" be sung when setting the watch for the night, and by suppressing all "swearing, brawling, dicing and such like disorders" in their ships, the express purpose being to avoid God's displeasure and win his favor.[18]

No one was more conspicuous in combining "moods of most reckless daring" with "a childlike faith that Heaven was listening to his Prayers" than Francis Drake, himself the son of a naval lay reader under Edward VI.[19] Like his celebrated contemporaries, Walter Raleigh, Richard Hawkins and Martin Frobisher, Drake was well aware of what rampant mischief might result from unrestrained cursing and gambling, under the tremendous stress of living in small, overcrowded ships for months on end. But more than that, he—like them—knew that no venture could possibly succeed by thus provoking the wrath of the Almighty.[20]

It was this kind of pragmatic piety which, in 1653, found expression in the British Navy's *Articles of War.* Seeking to replace the inconsistencies of earlier regulations, as well as the whims of individual commanders, they gave the force of law to two traditional concerns of the medieval maritime codes: (1) the "public worship of Almighty God" on board; and (2) the punishment of all profanity, drunkenness, "uncleanness" and "other scandalous actions."[21] It would be the lot of a later generation to call church and state to task for allowing the law to lapse.[22]

Meanwhile, in 1626, naval chaplains were, after centuries of improvisation, formally established in the British Navy, with an order by Charles I "for preachers to goe in every of his ships to sea."[23] Again, two centuries of subsequent naval history would show that commendable intentions were far from fulfilled; and even in the rare cases where chaplains were actually appointed, their competence could be questioned to a disturbing degree. True, there were, as Robinson reminds us, "staunch Christians" among them.[24] This was no less true in naval units of other European nations; and nowhere was it more graphically illustrated than in the heroism of Rasmus Jensen, Danish chaplain on the ill-fated Jens Munk Expedition, as he ministered with his last breath to his Scandinavian shipmates, dying in the Arctic wastes of Western Hudson Bay in the winter of 1619-20.[25]

Nevertheless, the high endeavor of the Elizabethan era gave way, at least in the British Navy, to a strange "slump in morale" under the Stuarts, and soon the scurrilous wit of an Edward Ward was lampooning the typical sea-chaplain as "much better at composing a Bowl of Punch than a Sermon." However exaggerated, his gibes contained—in all too many cases—an element of truth. Not till the close of the Napoleonic War would requirements for a radical reform of British naval chaplaincy be fulfilled.[26]

For much of the history of the Honourable East India Company, with its huge, heavily-armed merchantmen, the quality of chaplaincy service was hardly more impressive. Although, again, there were those who ministered faithfully under incredibly demoralizing conditions, the chaplaincy provisions of the Company's charter were, in general, "scandalously neglected."[27]

Turning to other nationalities, chaplains of the Dutch East India Company are credited with a significant role in early Protestant world missionary enterprise.[28] However, there is evidence that Scandinavian East Indiamen could be served by clerics conspicuous for conviviality rather than commitment to the pastoral office.[29]

While such forms of official and semi-official ministry were, during the seventeenth and eighteenth centuries, far from consistently effective, sources show how others could occasionally provide a viable alternative. There were, here and there, captains who assumed a paternal responsibility for the spiritual welfare of their crews.

Of those who commanded the greatest respect, many were Quakers.[30] Captain Thomas Chalkley, for example, a native of Southwark who sailed from American ports during the early eighteenth century, was known to hold frequent religious meetings on board, inviting visitors both from other ships and from shore.[31] In the 1750's, Captain Clunie of Stepney, another seafaring shepherd of souls, became the instrument of "much spiritual profit" at a critical juncture of the odyssey of faith of a famous fellow-captain, John Newton.[32] Scottish-born Captain Torial Joss, whose homiletical gifts led sailors to nick-name his ship *The Pulpit,* reluctantly left the sea in the 1760's, and became an eminent Independent minister in London.[33] Around the turn of the century, a Presbyterian, Captain Obadiah Congar, born in the

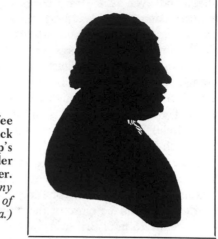

Paul Cuffee
(1759-1817). Black
Quaker ship's
captain, shipbuilder
and shipowner.
(From *Ebony
Pictorial History of
Black America.*)

State of New York, was extensively known as a seafaring sabbatarian, one who would willingly incur the displeasure of his owners by refusing to sail on the Lord's Day, while, wherever he happened to be on that day, consistently calling his crew together "to attend religious duties."[34]

Born near New Bedford, Massachusetts, Captain Paul Cuffee (1759-1817), son of an African slave and his American-Indian wife, won wide esteem for working his way from poverty and prejudice to a position of shipmaster, eventually shipowner. Cuffee was himself a convinced Quaker, and the crews under his command, sable yet free, were always conspicuous for their Christian bearing. (Ever eager to promote the welfare of fellow-blacks, Cuffee provided transportation for those willing to return to Africa when freed, thereby becoming a pioneer of the American recolonization movement.)[35]

An important, if sporadic, form of unofficial chaplaincy would, as in pre-Reformation times, be clerics or missionaries traveling as passengers overseas.

The Society for the Propagation of the Gospel (SPG), founded in 1701, included in sailing orders to its clergy instructions to "prevail with the Captain or Commander, to have Morning and Evening Prayer said daily; as also Preaching and Catechizing every Lord's Day." Although some were, at first, "cursed and treated very ill on board," the Society persisted in its policy, and soon met with a more general, positive response.[36] It was inevitable that John Woolman, that "quietest radical in history," with a true Quaker's love for the disadvantaged, should, on his voyage to England in 1772, discover the physical and moral misery of "poor wet toiling Seamen."

Having himself refused an offer of cabin accommodation, he had elected to share the overcrowded steerage space with them. Feeling a "fervent concern" that they might "come to experience salvation through Christ," he held many meetings and "weighty" conversations among them. He was particularly agitated over the corruptive impact of sea-life on the very young.[37]

Towards the close of the eighteenth century, and at the beginning of the new, the religious press carried frequent accounts of missionaries from various denominations seeking, during their sea voyages, to "improve" opportunities to share the Gospel with seamen. Particularly "happy effects" were reported from the labors of men of the London Missionary Society, as they divided their time between prisoners and crew, while traveling with convict transports to New South Wales, en route to assignments in the South Seas.[38]

Although originating ashore, the many maritime devotional aids which emerged among the Protestant seafaring nations following the Reformation were, basically, alternative means of ministry at sea. As such, they served a significant purpose. However widely the availability and quality of personal ministry might vary, here was a reliable method of spiritual self-help, always at hand. Technically, the production of such materials in realistic quantities had now been rendered feasible through the recent discovery of the art of printing. Theologically, the demand for manuals of moral guidance and devotion was stimulated by the Reformation's rediscovery of the principle of the priesthood of all believers. The "mutual responsibility" of members of a community of faith for one another's welfare of body and soul, occasionally interpreted as "religious individualism," was,

Official seal of the Society for the Propagation of the Gospel, depicting natives calling for help (Acts 16:9), shown arriving in the shape of a British warship carrying a clergyman in her bow. (John Haverstick: *The Progress of the Protestant.*)

in the view of others, no less than a revival of the spirit of New Testament Christianity.

Though in some respects indebted to Roman Catholic precedent, popular spiritual guides had, by the seventeenth century, become a characteristic feature of Protestantism everywhere. Consciences had been aroused by vigorous preaching, and troubled by new issues in a fast-changing world. This led to a "theology of conscience," characterized on the one hand by meticulous self-examination as a means of avoiding inadequate repentance.[39] Especially in an age where death seemed to be intruding everywhere, there was on the other hand great concern for practical guidance in the "art" of dying—*ars moriendi*. (One attempt to meet this need was, for example, John Kettlesworth's *Death Made Comfortable: Or, the Way to Die Well*, published in 1618.)[40]

In the isolated world of the seafarer, constantly confronted with moral and physical hazard to an extreme degree, the need for this kind of counseling and edification by media was seen as especially acute. Many have since overlooked the importance, even existence, of this pioneer form of seamen's ministry. In 1852, one major seamen's mission society deplored the fact that no-one, prior to themselves, had entertained "the idea of writing a book of devotion for their [seamen's] use, or of sermons for their edification."[41]

In actual fact, there emerged, from the close of the sixteenth century, a wide variety of mariners' manuals, written with a view to both private use and public services at sea. An early English example is a work by Dr. Samuel Page entitled *Divine Sea-service: Containing Sundry Necessary and Usefull Formes of Prayer and Thanksgiving for the Helpe of Such as Travaile by Sea, Fitted to Their Severall Necessities,* published in Deptford, 1616. Here were, besides Bible-based maritime meditations, a series of casuistic prayers, for morning and evening use, for deliverance from dangers of disease, enemies and storms, even for intercession on behalf of a ship's "Adventurers and Owners at home" (an interesting testimony to the closeness of industrial relations in that era).[42] In 1662, the (re-established) Church of England, provoked by an initiative in the Long Parliament's *Directory for Public Worship,* included *Forms of Prayers to be Used at Sea* in the *Book of Common Prayer.*[43] Both Church and Nonconformist divines continued to publish "sea-sermons." (Especially popular was John Ryther's series on the Book of Jonah, in *The Seaman's Preacher.*) At the same time, they continued giving out manuals of meditations and prayers for the seafarer. (Conspicuous were John Flavel's *Navigation Spiritualized,* and *The Seaman's Monitor* by Josiah Woodward.)[44]

In the American Colonies, Cotton Mather, controversial "keeper of the Puritan conscience" in New England Congregationalism, proved himself

John Flavel, 17th century
English divine and author of
"Navigation Spiritualiz'd" and
other popular devotional aids
for seafarers. (John Flavel:
Navigation Spiritualiz'd.)

a pioneer in maritime devotional literature on that side of the Atlantic. In the
midst of an authorship of over 450 books, he found time to publish both *The
Religious Marriner* (1700) and *The Sailour's Companion and Counsellour*
(1709), not to mention discourses on subjects ranging from gratitude for a
successful whaling season to lessons to be learnt from the tragic end of 26
pirates. On completion of his *Sailour's Companion* of 1709, Mather wrote
that he had already made a practice of "lodging *Books,* which may be
instruments of Piety, in all vessels of any Burden, that may sail out of these
Colonies." His hope was now that the *Sailour's Companion,* being published
especially for the "unregenerate Sailour," might henceforth be distributed
through naval officers on every vessel clearing a Colonial port. Cotton
Mather's concern for the spiritual welfare of seamen makes him a precursor
of the first seamen's mission organization in America, founded in his home
city of Boston, one century later.[45]

      Meanwhile, other American authors followed in Mather's literary
footsteps, through the eighteenth and the nineteenth century.[46] Furthermore,
several successful British manuals were republished in America, and found
a ready readership there.[47]

      As in other areas of early outreach to seafarers, such methods of
ministry were not restricted to the English-speaking world. In Scandinavia, a
brief mariner's manual entitled *En liden ny Skibsbog udaff den hellige
Bibelske Schrifft* ("A Small New Ship's Book, Based on the Holy Scriptures")
was published as early as 1580 by Tilemannus Henningius, a Lutheran state
church pastor in the Danish seaport of Marstrand. With characteristic
Lutheran emphasis on an ethic of vocation, the author is at pains to prove
seafaring a Christian, God-pleasing profession, while warning against the
shoals of vice on which seafarers may so easily suffer shipwreck, pointing to
Christ as the only true captain of the ship of the church, and ending with

Cotton Mather (1663-1728), New
England divine and pioneer
author of Christian literature
for seamen. (H. Shelton Smith:
American Christianity.)

powerful admonitions against piracy and pillage.[48] His book inspired the
Rev. Hans B. Fridag of Bergen, Norway, to publish an expanded version in
1601.[49] Other maritime devotional literature followed in Sweden, too.[50]

However, by far the most popular mariner's manual in Scandinavia
was the work of a Christian seafarer from North Norway, one Captain Johan
H. Heitman. His *Besværede Söe-Mænds söde Siele-Roe* ("Troubled Seamen's Sweet Peace of Soul"), with meditations, hymns and prayers for
practically every conceivable occasion, all filled with a certain unmistakable
flavor of maritime authenticity, was originally published in 1730, and went
through about a score of editions during the following 150 years.[51]

The celebrated Dutch lawyer-theologian, Hugo Grotius, wrote his
principal religious work, *De veritate religionis Christianae* ("On the Truth
of the Christian Religion") especially with seamen in mind. Originally
published in 1627, and subsequently translated into many languages, it
sought to help sailors not only overcome the wiles of "evil-disposed persons,"
but also refute the claims of both "pagans and Mohammedans," in their role
as voluntary foreign missionaries.[52]

In 1635, Adam Westerman published in Amsterdam his *Groote
Christelyke Zeevaart* ("Great Christian Navigation"), a manual of sea-
sermons, songs and prayers, which went through several editions. It was
followed by a rich flora of devotional aids for Dutch seamen and fishermen
through the years.[53]

In Germany, too, there are records of early efforts in this field. In
1662, for example, M. Mauritius Rochels, availing himself of the same
familiar nautical imagery of life as an ocean voyage, published his *Geistlicher
Seekompass* ("Spiritual Sea-Compass').[54]

OTHER FORMS OF EARLY MINISTRY TO SEAFARERS

Centuries before the printed word could accompany the seafarer on his travels to distant climes, the Roman Catholic Church sought by word of prayer to support him from shore.

Churches, chapels and chantries along the coasts of Christendom were frequently dedicated to maritime saints or the Virgin Mary (known also as "Stella Maris" or "Star of the Sea"). Their intercession on behalf of seafarers would be eagerly invoked.[55] The prayers of the church would especially be sought at the launching of a new vessel, or on embarkation for sea.[56] In gratitude for merciful deliverance, mariners would make model ships or other *ex voto* offerings for sanctuaries with which they sensed a special bond.[57]

Pious hermits would spend their lives in solitude on rocky headlands, praying for the souls and safety of seafarers, while at the same time tending a beacon or bell to warn them of imminent danger. Thus these lone servants of the church became, in effect, the pioneers of modern-day lighthouse and coast-guard services.[58] The towers of many monasteries could serve a similar purpose. In major ports, a monastery might also provide a *maison-dieu,* a hospice or hospital where travelers could find rest, and where mariners who fell sick or suffered injury could be provided for (as laid down in the Laws of Oléron). Such institutions were considered an important opportunity for both "prayers and gode werkes," and proved that the church was by no means oblivious to the bond between the Great Commission and the Great Commandment in relation to the seafaring world.[59]

In the Sailortown district of Rome, there was, before the Reformation, not only hospice accommodation, but also an oratory available for seafarers.[60] Elsewhere, too—for example in Amsterdam (with its fifteenth century Sint Olofs Kerk, dedicated to the patron saint of the Norsemen)—special worship facilities were provided for sailors in port.[61] In the post-Reformation era, seafaring Protestant nations (notably Great Britain) established chapels in connection with embassies or "factories" (overseas trading communities). Here seamen, too, would be invited to hear the Gospel in their mother tongue, as also in the seaport churches of emigrant countrymen.[62]

It is impossible, on the basis of available source materials, to form a precise picture of the degree of response to such sporadic endeavors. However, during the three hundred years which elapsed from the Reformation of the Church to what came to be called the Seamen's Reformation, there were some who sensed a very specific concern for the evangelization of seafarers, and whose preaching evidently made a very profound impact on them. Among these "Reformers before the [Seamen's] Reformation," three were conspicuous. All three were active during the Restoration period of seventeenth century England, and all three were persecuted for their Nonconformist faith.[63]

John Flavel (c. 1630-1691), an Oxford-educated Presbyterian who was characterized by a celebrated successor as the "greatest friend British Seamen ever had in former days," ministered for many years at the busy Devonshire seaport of Dartmouth.[64] John Ryther (c. 1634-1681), born in Yorkshire of Quaker parents, became immensely popular among sailors, who thronged his Congregational chapel at Wapping, on the north bank of the Thames. He was known simply as "the seaman's preacher" by his seafaring friends (who successfully shielded him from arrest for his Nonconformist stance).[65] James Janeway (c. 1636-1674), son of a Hertfordshire curate, preached to seafarers and their families in his chapel at Rotherhithe, on the south side of the same river. (When it was wrecked by a band of troopers, his people responded by simply rebuilding on a larger scale.)[66] Besides ministering by means of the spoken word, all three of these pioneer seamen's preachers published devotional literature for seafarers which went into numerous editions over the years.[67]

The eighteenth century produced no comparable examples of seamen's preachers. On the other hand, there were some remarkable instances of seamen becoming preachers. John Newton, the former slave-ship captain, became a clergyman in the Church of England and one of her greatest hymnwriters. Torial Joss, once master of a merchant-ship (whose prowess as a preacher has already been noticed), won renown as George Whitefield's trusted associate at the London Tabernacle for twenty years. Also, Samuel Medley gave up promising prospects as a naval officer to become the minister of Byrom Street Baptist Chapel in Liverpool. The new vocations of such men did not necessarily prevent them from further communication with seafarers; there is ample evidence to the contrary.[68] Moreover, there are examples of clergy of the established church serving waterfront parishes who would voluntarily visit nearby shipping, and celebrate holy communion on board—"long before any missionary Society [for Seamen] existed."[69]

Nevertheless, prior to the nineteenth century, there was little consistency, much less permanency, about ways in which churches and chapels might seek to serve the seafarer. Not surprisingly, seamen would sometimes take the initiative themselves, as they did in earlier days in the case of the maritime guilds. These made up an institution of far-reaching importance for both the social and spiritual welfare of the medieval seafarer.

Like other craft guilds, confraternities of seafarers were from the outset intimately related to the church. Among spiritual benefits they bestowed, the provision of mass for the souls of members lost at sea was evidently held highest. They would maintain chantries, supply votive candles, and pledge participation in funerals. Through processions, pageants and plays, they could contribute to a rudimentary Christian education of the masses. Dispensing relief and maintaining almshouses for disabled, sick or indigent members and dependents of deceased members were also important concerns of these "Shipmen's Gilds." The powerful Hanseatic League, which, for much of the Middle Ages, maintained a virtual trade monopoly in many North Sea and Baltic port cities, worked with its various "Schiffergesellschaften" in close alliance with the church. So also did early maritime guilds in the Mediterranean. However, with Luther's elimination of the doctrine of purgatory (hence also mass for the dead), a primary purpose of many maritime guilds in pre-Reformation Europe was lost. Best known of such institutions which nevertheless survived in England was the Corporation of Trinity House (chartered under Henry VIII, with roots going back far further). Today, the Corporation is still responsible for lights and buoys, and the licensing of pilots.[70]

In the years which followed, the role of medieval maritime guilds in promoting the socio-economic interests of seafarers was, in some measure, assumed by secular organizations for mutual self-help. Membership in such associations was, however, frequently limited to merchant ship-masters or naval officers.[71] In America, for example, so-called Marine Societies were formed in several port cities (in Boston in 1742, then successively in other New England ports, as well as New York). Membership was, at first, generally restricted to commanders of vessels, and the primary purpose was the financial relief of needy members and their dependents.[72]

In Great Britain, a Liverpool Marine Society was founded in 1789, on lines similar to those in America ("for the benefit of masters of vessels, their widows and children").[73] A generation earlier, however, in 1756, a society simply called "The Marine Society" had been organized in London for a very different purpose. This was on the eve of the Seven Years' War, and the primary object of the society was to encourage volunteers to man the fleet, at a time when press gangs alone were proving incapable of meeting the urgency of the hour. By expanding the scheme to include boys abandoned to the miseries of street life in the cities, the society was also able to provide a partial solution to the critical rise in juvenile delinquency. So successful were these efforts that, by the end of the war, in 1763, over 10,000 men and boys had, through the agency of the society, been fitted out for sea, both in the naval and merchant service. In 1786, by converting an old merchantman, the *Beatty,* into a training ship, anchored in the Thames, the society became a world pioneer in this form of pre-sea schooling.[74]

Chiefly instrumental in the founding and early policies of the whole enterprise was that remarkable merchant-philanthropist Jonas Hanway (1712-86). Notorious as the man who braved public obloquy by introducing the umbrella on the streets of London, Hanway was ever ready to promote the welfare of the under-privileged, from prostitutes to chimney-boys. A voluminous writer, he infused into both the structure of the society and the manuals he authored for young seafarers his own particular combination of practical piety and unswerving patriotism.[75] It is worthy of note that the treasurer of the society during its earliest years, John Thornton, was a man destined to play a pivotal part in the founding of the first organization in history dedicated to bringing the Gospel to seafarers.[76]

Among the many hazards of seafaring in earlier times and right into the nineteenth century was the very real risk of being forced into slavery. Although the practice persisted in varying forms through the centuries, some attempt was also made from time to time to develop methods of ministry to the victims of maritime slavery.

Of course, from the era of the triremes of ancient Rome, untold numbers of Christian galley-slaves would have witnessed to their faith, both among fellow-slaves and their oppressors. Later, even parts of "Christendom" condoned this form of systematic torture of captives and criminals.

A notorious example from the mid-sixteenth century is that of Scotland's great reformer. Carried off into captivity in 1547 as a galley slave in the French Navy, John Knox endured both irons and lash for one and a half years. During this time, he staunchly rejected every inducement to renounce his understanding of the faith.[77]

Nevertheless, within the framework of the whole inhuman system, there were Catholic chaplains who did, in their way, seek to convey some solace. In this context, the work of St. Vincent de Paul was outstanding. Captured by Barbary pirates as a young priest in 1605, he too tasted life as a galley slave. Having made good his escape in 1607, one of the works of charity to which he then devoted his life was the spiritual and bodily relief of those condemned to the galley bench. Eventually, as Royal Chaplain General of the Galleys under Louis XIII, he was able to improve chaplaincy services and establish, for the first time, a hospital for galley slaves at Marseilles.[78] For non-Catholics, too, the situation presumably improved in some degree. In 1705, it was reported that the influence of the recently-founded Society for the Propagation of the Gospel had been enlisted "with a view to ameliorating the condition of the galley slaves in France."[79]

A well-intentioned yet somewhat short-sighted method of maritime ministry was the provision of ransom for the release of crews captured by the corsairs of the Barbary Coast. For the Mohammedan "Barbary States" of Northern Africa (Tripolitania, Tunisia, Algeria and Morocco), plundering the ships of Christendom and carrying their crews off to slavery had, ever since the Middle Ages, developed into a major source of national income. By 1634, there were, according to Father Dan, who worked tirelessly among them for many years, no less than 25,000 slaves of Christian background in

Jonas Hanway (1712-86), merchant, philanthropist and founder of The Marine Society. An opponent of impressment, he pioneered programs of voluntary recruitment and pre-sea training. (Painting by the Rev. P.M. Peters, RA, Courtesy of The Marine Society.)

the port city of Algiers alone. Although punitive expeditions were occasionally organized, the political disunion of Europe inhibited any concerted action. For the most part, governments chose not to suppress the pirates, but to buy off their victims. However, the terms of such treaties were easily evaded, once tribute had been duly paid. Enslaved seamen who (with the majority) resolutely refused to turn renegade, could then only hope against hope for individual ransom, with demands differing widely, according to rank, skills and connections. Those who did manage to return spread the most gruesome tales of torture at the hands of their turbaned taskmasters.

From the end of the twelfth century, with the founding of the Order of the Holy Trinity and Redemption of Slaves, Catholic Fathers of the Redemption worked fearlessly for the victims of this variety of white slave-trade. Following the Reformation, collections for the redemption of sailors in slavery were regularly made in the churches of Protestant seafaring nations. Predictably, this whole policy of appeasement prompted only an expansion of such lucrative activities, to the point where Barbary pirates actually penetrated into the North Sea, even carrying off men and women from the coast of Iceland. Not even the organization of protective convoys could offer adequate security. Only after the defeat of Napoleon was the evil eventually eradicated, following a series of spectacular naval engagements by Britain and America, and a final *coup de grâce* by France—with the capture of Algiers in 1830.[80]

A third form of enslavement of seamen was that of naval impressment. The practice of "pressing" a people's own citizens into public service, or compelling compliance where volunteers would not suffice, seems to have been both ancient and universal. As a method of naval recruitment, it was, in an island nation like Great Britain, largely looked upon as a dire necessity and practiced in varying forms at least from the time of the Saxon kings. However, it was only after the deep decline in conditions of service and morale which set in during the time of the early Stuarts that officially condoned kidnapping by means of press gangs became the (Admiralty) order of the day. For the following two centuries, tales could be told of incredible cruelty and corruption, especially in times of great national emergency. When a "hot press" was out, grooms would be whisked away from their brides at the very door of the church, long-absent merchant seafarers would be forced into naval tenders before they even had a chance to set foot ashore, and the most desperate efforts would be made to avoid detection or gain exemption.[81]

Apologists for the underlying principle have, right up to the present, pointed to the performance under fire of men who nevertheless, in their hearts, accepted the inevitability of impressment. The fact that life on the lower deck was ever allowed to become so utterly intolerable has been identified as the root cause of the evil. How, one has asked, could anyone expect free-born citizens to volunteer for a form of enslavement characterized by bad food, miserable pay, savage discipline, and the repeated denial of due leave for fear of desertion?[82]

However, critics of the whole system would counter that cruel conditions afloat were largely an effect, not a cause, of impressment and all the vicious circle it spawned. With mounting fervor, they focused on four fundamental arguments against impressment: on the grounds of humanity (none could effectively deny its capricious cruelty); of legality (it had never been expressly enacted by Parliament); of morality (it was intolerable to hear those plead for it who were themselves not exposed to it); and finally of

General James Edward Oglethorpe (1696-1785), "Founding Father" of Georgia and eloquent opponent of impressment. (Phinzy Spalding: *Oglethorpe in America.*)

A press gang in action. (Note the apprehensive adolescent
in the foreground, and the distraught women in the
background.) (Roy Palmer, ed.: *The Valiant Sailor.*)

reality (history proved, for example in the mutinies of 1797, that one could
not with impunity dump "indiscriminate sweepings" of streets and jails into a
service on which depended the very existence of the nation).[83]

In the forefront of those agitating for the abolition of impressment
were men motivated by Christian conviction and compassion. Among these,
General James Edward Oglethorpe, famous as founder of the colony of
Georgia, philanthropist and opponent of oppression in any form, was a
pioneer figure. In 1728, he published a pamphlet entitled *The Sailor's
Advocate,* protesting vehemently against the inhumanity of impressment and
its open violation of both Magna Carta and the Petition of Right. Oglethorpe's
work, which went through many editions, helped to keep the cause alive until
1777, when it received new impetus through the enthusiastic support of
Granville Sharp, Christian scholar and original "father" of the Slave Trade
Abolition Movement in England. That year, with the cooperation of Sharp,
there appeared a new and enlarged edition of *The Sailor's Advocate.* Sharp
then followed up with a pamphlet of his own, in 1778, and took the whole
question to court. Although neither Oglethorpe nor Sharp lived to see the
close of the Napoleonic War and, therefore, the last of the press gang, their
combined efforts did help to create a climate rendering repetition unthinkable.[84]

One might speculate as to whether the War of 1812 (with British impressment of American seamen as a primary pretext) could have been averted, had the voices of Oglethorpe and Sharp been heeded earlier. However, there is no room for speculation as to their impact on the emergence of organized mission to seafarers. These men were not content merely to mitigate the suffering of victims of injustice. The concept of confronting established power structures, in order to redeem the basic human rights of seafarers, was not only novel, but radically prophetic. Just as both Oglethorpe and Sharp ardently denied the necessity of black slavery for reasons of national economy, so, too, both refused to accept the need of this form of white slavery—for alleged reasons of national security. Precisely this combination of concern for the plight of African slaves on the one hand, and that of seafarers on the other, was destined to play a significant role within the general context in which organized maritime mission would eventually emerge.[85]

Chapter 2

The Context:
Factors Heralding a
New Missionary Enterprise

Despite the many ways in which the Christian church did, with time, respond to her Master's call to serve the seafarer, that call was seldom, if ever, heard clearly and had, even after seventeen centuries, certainly led to no organizational structure for ongoing Gospel outreach to men of the sea. Why, then, should the picture alter so dramatically at the time it did—within just one more century? Again, why should the work assume the particular form it did—as a network of voluntary societies?

In seeking answers to these basic background questions, it will be natural to focus first on the general scene—on major forces of change in church and society, and ways in which these impringed upon the seafaring class. Following this, it will be necessary to analyze the special context of the seafarer's situation in life—viewed from a variety of perspectives at this particular point in time.

THE GENERAL CONTEXT: CONTRIBUTORY
INFLUENCES ON THE CONTEMPORARY SCENE

It was no mere matter of chance that the earliest efforts to promote systematic maritime mission were organized around the turn of the nineteenth century. The time was right. This new avenue of missionary advance was able to reap rich benefits from the religious and humanitarian awakening in eighteenth century Great Britain and America.

Britain's Evangelical United Front

True, in more ways than one, this could have been called the very worst of times. As far as England was concerned, she was at this juncture exposed to no less than three distinct forms of revolution. The close of the eighteenth century saw sweeping changes developing in the nation's socioeconomic structure, as the *Industrial Revolution* gathered momentum, ushering in the factory system with all its urbanization, exploitation and social ferment.[86] The last quarter of that century also witnessed the "high noon" of the Enlightenment, essentially an *intellectual revolution,* seeking to emancipate the mind of man from patterns of thought accepted since St. Augustine, and only tentatively challenged by the Renaissance. The autonomy of human reason was now openly supplanting the authority of divine revelation, and radical skepticism was taking the place of scriptural faith. The result was widespread secularization, leading among clergy of the Church of England to the predominance of "Latitudinarianism," a movement marked by a dispassionate doctrine of deism and moderation.[87] Again, in the American Colonies and later in France, it was men of the Enlightenment, infused with rationalistic critique of established authority, who played a leading role in engineering *political revolution.* The convulsive effect of both the American and French revolutions could hardly have been expected to promote missionary enterprise, at least not in England, and especially not after the French version escalated into the Reign of Terror in 1792.[88]

Nevertheless, despite circumstances—which together seemed tantamount to a total repudiation of the Gospel, not to speak of any urge to spread it—these also proved, paradoxically enough, to be the very best of times. They formed, in fact, the threshold of "The Great Century," as Latourette characterizes the next hundred years of unprecedented missionary expansion. Precisely when prospects for even survival of the faith seemed so dim, there emerged around the turn of the century a veritable upsurge of voluntary societies in the English-speaking world, founded for the express purpose of propagating the Gospel both at home and abroad.[89]

The origin of these societies may, in some degree, be traced back to the so-called "Religious Societies" of Restoration-era England. They emerged during the late 1670's, in direct protest against the licentiousness of the age and the spiritual barrenness of the National Church. Made up of groups of devoted young churchmen, they sought to edify their own members through disciplined, Bible-centered fellowship, while at the same time encouraging concern for the underprivileged. Largely instrumental in their founding was the popular preacher at the Savoy Chapel in London, Dr. Anthony

Horneck (1641-97). However, he himself seems to have been deeply influenced by the German Pietist Movement, itself a reaction against the rigidity of seventeenth-century Lutheran orthodoxy, but with roots going back to medieval monasticism. Spener's *Collegia Pietatis* and Horneck's Religious Societies were both conceived as *ecclesiolae in ecclesia,* nucleal growth-groups within the local congregation, intended as spiritual leaven in the lump of the institutional church. Their essential concern was to seek the source of spiritual life itself in the Scriptures, as a means of encountering the Savior and nurturing their consecration to him. However, in both cases, stress was laid on loyalty to their respective established churches. In both cases, too, the movement gave motivation for missionary outreach both at home and overseas.[90]

Within the Church of England, it was these small church renewal groups which set the stage for the formation of two great voluntary societies, both organized around the turn of the century, at the instigation of Dr. Thomas Bray, the zealous Ecclesiastical Commissary of the Bishop of London for the Colony of Maryland. The Society for Promoting Christian Knowledge (SPCK), founded in 1698, became the vehicle for supplying Christian literature and means of education on a world-wide scale. The Society for Propagation of the Gospel in Foreign Parts (SPG) was founded in 1701, to supplement the SPCK with a so-called "living" agency, by providing Anglican clergymen and missionaries for the Motherland's "Plantaceons, Colonies and Factories beyond the Seas."[91]

Both the more informal Religious Societies and these two major missionary organizations were closely identified with the Established Church of England. However, during the last decade of the seventeenth century, Dissenters, too, would freely join with Churchmen in forming so-called "Societies for the Reformation of Manners" in an effort to enforce the law of the land against various forms of manifest vice.[92]

In theory, therefore, there existed—a whole century before the organizational upsurge already indicated—models for both small-group lay involvement, and major voluntary societies, also along undenominational lines. Nevertheless, the time was not ripe. In the midst of the spiritual doldrums of the early Hanoverian Church, both the Religious Societies and Reformation Societies gradually declined. At all events, it was obvious that no form of voluntary association then in existence (not even the SPCK or the SPG, which have remained active to the present day) was capable of generating the degree of zeal or breadth of support needed to undertake a whole new area of missionary enterprise, such as the miserable plight of men of the sea. For that to happen, a powerful national revival would first have to enlighten and energize the people of God.[93]

John Wesley (1703-91).
Founder of Methodism,
which was to play a key
role in the dawn of
organized mission to sea-
farers. *(Journal and Year
Book of the Norwegian-
Danish Conference of the
Methodist Church, 1943.)*

The "watershed" event which was to herald a new era occurred on May 24, 1738. That day, a dedicated but deeply depressed clergyman of the Church of England entered the meeting of one of the surviving religious societies, assembled in Aldersgate Street in the City of London. John Wesley (1703-91), acknowledged leader of a group of eager Anglican ascetics dubbed "Methodists" by their critics, had recently returned from a disastrous mission to Georgia, undertaken in conjunction with Oglethorpe and the SPG. It was while listening to Luther's "Preface to the Epistle to the Romans" at that meeting that Wesley's heart was "strangely warmed." From that moment he himself counted his personal conversion. His tortuous quest for self-achieved holiness was replaced by the joyous assurance of "trust in Christ alone for salvation," and energies hitherto consumed in searching for self-justification could be released in seeking the salvation of others.

Although, in his rediscovery of the Reformation doctrine of justification by faith alone in the atoning death of Christ, Wesley was deeply indebted to friends among the missionary-minded Moravians, he separated from them for fear of antinomianism. Again, although (at the urging of his colleague George Whitefield) the scholarly Oxford don "submitted to be more vile," and, in 1739, commenced a life-long career of itinerant open-air preaching, he could not accept Whitefield's Calvinist doctrine of election. Instead, Wesley went his own way, combining Arminianism with a distinctive form of perfectionism, and welding awakened souls by the thousand into a nation-wide network of carefully disciplined lay "societies" (in essence only a large-scale renewal of those earlier Religious Societies).[94]

In the course of those quarter of a million miles which Wesley covered (at a conservative estimate), he was, like the Apostle Paul before him, both reviled and respected, both physically abused and virtually worshipped. In retrospect, historians, too, have drastically disagreed in their assessment of the revival he led. Some maintain that it was Methodism which, by attracting the working classes to the Christian faith, saved England from the excesses of a French Revolution. Some insist that other factors were decisive.[95]

At all events, it would be difficult to dispute that when John Wesley, in 1739, set forth on his mission to the masses, backed by his hymn-writing brother Charles, and his great fellow-evangelist George Whitefield, there was, behind a thin veneer of upper-class elegance, an incredible quantum of coarseness, cruelty and crime throughout the nation. Extensive poverty was considered an economic necessity, and drunkenness a legitimate opiate. Meanwhile, the National Church had entered her "glacial epoch." Though by no means dead, she was most certainly slumbering. Place-hunting and pluralism were commonplace. Multitudes were deprived of any form of regular ministration whatsoever, while the rest might well hear moralistic messages so meager in central, scriptural substance that one could almost wonder "whether the preacher were a follower of Confucius or Mahomet, or of Christ." Nothing was more universally feared than "enthusiasm" (as any form of zeal for the Gospel was quickly labeled).

There were, of course, many clergymen who quietly and faithfully tried to follow their vocation. However, the worldliness of the Hanoverian Church was so widespread that Montesquieu, commenting on the pagan ignorance of the people prior to Wesley's campaign, came to the conclusion: "In England, there is no religion, and the subject, if mentioned in Society, excites nothing but laughter." Nor were the Dissenters, delivered from danger but not from disabilities, in a more promising position. English Presbyterians were drifting into Unitarianism. Baptists and Independents were, in the main, embedded in their rigid, Calvinistic orthodoxy.[96]

In 1791, when Wesley died, almost literally in the saddle, after 53 years on the road, immorality, infidelity and injustice were still rampant in the land. Nevertheless, on the national and religious scene, it was everywhere evident that the forces of reform were gathering momentum. Much of that momentum was traceable to the Methodist Revival. True, Wesley was himself politically a Tory, and his avowed aim was to make "saints not citizens." At the same time, one of his fundamental axioms was: "The Bible knows nothing of a solitary religion." In his preaching, Wesley was resolute in rebuking whatever he recognized as social abuse. (Of particular interest to this study is, for example, his ceaseless campaign against not only the lawlessness of wrecking and smuggling, but also the tyranny of impressment.)

However, it was the matrix of his movement, the "society" structure, subdivided into "class-meetings," which was destined to become the most effective long-term catalyst of change. Here were not only personal growth groups, where individual converts could find spiritual nurture and moral encouragement (a model eventually to be followed by early lay ministry at sea). But here, too, were nurseries of political, economic and social reform, fostering in the poor and disadvantaged a sense of self-respect, a passion for loftier ideals, and the ability to articulate and exercise communal responsibility. (From this cell-group movement may be traced—in some degree—the eventual birth of the British trade union and cooperative society movement. There is, in fact, considerable justification for the statement that the British Labor Party "owes more to John Wesley than to Karl Marx.")[97]

Meanwhile, of more immediate significance was the immense impact of the Methodist Movement on church life in England, especially that of the National Church. As to his personal position, Wesley left no room for doubt. "I live and die a member of the Church of England," he wrote in 1790, "and none who regard my judgement or advice will ever separate from it." At first, his mission was, in fact, entirely a Church of England movement. Nor was the doctrinal difference between Wesley's Arminianism and the moderate Calvinism of most of his fellow-clergymen any insurmountable obstacle. But his liberal interpretation of Anglican church order most decidedly was. For John Wesley, his highest priority was to confront as many as possible of the neglected, brutalized masses of his day with the claims of the Gospel. Where local clergy condemned itinerancy and denied him their pulpits, he considered himself exempt from normal parochial niceties, and promptly preached in the open air. ("I look upon all the world as my parish," was his response to those who preferred to make the parish their world.)

When the work grew so fast that ordained clergy could not possibly cope with every call, he appointed laymen as "local preachers." Again, when anti-conventicle legislation prevented his societies from freely meeting in their own chapels, he reluctantly took advantage of exceptions applying to Dissenters. Finally, in 1784, he responded to the exigencies of the situation across the Atlantic by ordaining a bishop for the American Methodist Church.[98]

With that, Wesley had "crossed the Rubicon." In actual fact, if not by formal resolution, his organization had now separated from the State Church. Both bishops and clergy had long since railed against the "emotionalism" and "unchurchliness" of John Wesley and his colleagues. However, with time, many clergymen were themselves caught up in the revival. Of these, some identified themselves wholly with the movement. Others would endorse the evangelistic zeal of Methodism, yet refuse to rebel against their own church order, choosing rather to remain as a "rear-guard" of revivalism within the National Church. None were unaffected. As Lecky puts it, "the movement transformed for a time the whole spirit of the Established Church."[99] Thus, although the Methodist Revival played a predominant part in what has become known as the "Evangelical Revival," it was never identical with it.

There were evangelically-minded clergymen in the Church of England who showed signs of "seriousness" even before the Methodist Revival. (Clergy and laymen who shared fundamental evangelical convictions with the Methodists, but continued within the context of the Established Church, are in this study capitalized as "Evangelicals.") Conspicuous among early Evangelical clergy were William Romaine and John Newton, both of whom were to take a deep personal interest in the first organized missionary enterprise for seafarers.[100]

The Methodist Revival also had a marked revitalizing effect on the Dissenting church bodies, calling many within "Wide Dissent" back to the Gospel colors, and kindling among the ranks of this "New Dissent" a powerful missionary spirit.[101] Thus, toward the end of the century, there emerged three distinct groups, each in their way involved in the Evangelical Revival: Methodists, (Anglican) Evangelicals, and evangelical Dissenters.

Despite individual divergence (as, for example, in the sensitive areas of polity and predestination), all three groups shared a basic belief in the Bible as the sole, authoritative norm of faith and life. On this common ground, certain theological tenets held high priority, and constituted an informal, yet very real joint confessional stance. These were, primarily, man's total incapacity to save himself (in vivid contrast to the optimistic notions of the Enlightenment), God's total provision of salvation through the vicarious, atoning death of Christ, and, consequently, the need for an individual appropriation of that provision by turning in faith to Christ as Savior (conversion), in order to grow in grace and serve Him as Lord (sanctification). In such service, strong emphasis was placed on witness and mission, an obligation (and privilege) resting on the principle of the priesthood of all believers.

None of these doctrines were new. They were to be found, in essence, both in the Bible and the Book of Common Prayer. But the men of the Evangelical Revival believed them—and applied them—with a new seriousness and single-mindedness. As Gladstone said of the Evangelicals (but it applies equally as much to Methodists and evangelical Dissenters), "they preached Christ largely and fervently where, as a rule, he was but little and coldly preached before."[102]

William Wilberforce (1759-1833),
acknowledged leader of the Slave
Trade Abolition Movement, was
also an ardent advocate for
the early Seamen's Mission
Movement. *(Christianity Today.)*

Evangelical clergy of the Established Church were generally not deeply concerned with liturgical worship; and most of them showed, at this point in time, no great appreciation for the corporate nature and life of the church. Instead, with their Dissenting and Methodist fellow-evangelicals, they chose to throw their energies into one, overriding objective: winning to the lordship of Christ both their own nation and the whole world. As will be seen, this did not prevent but actually motivated pioneering efforts to combat many of the most shocking social evils of the day. However, given the socio-political realities of the times, all three groups were faced with awesome impediments: Dissenters, because they were outside the pale (and privileges) of the National Church; Methodists, because their membership was mainly among the unenfranchised "lower orders"; and Evangelicals, because they were still so few. It is against this background that the conversion of William Wilberforce in 1785 assumes a significance comparable only to that of John Wesley about half a century earlier.[103]

As the eighteenth century drew to a close, it became increasingly evident that the (largely Methodist-inspired) first fine flourish of the Evangelical Revival had spent itself. There were unmistakable signs of widespread relapse into the practical heathenism of former years. That this trend was arrested could, at least in some measure, be attributed to a "second spring" of the Evangelical Revival, this time the result of a resurgence of life among those who had remained loyal to the Establishment. So marked was the movement that its adherents have since been seen as constituting a distinct "party" within the Church of England.[104]

This nascent "Evangelical Party" drew, around the turn of the century, its direction and inspiration from two centers—Cambridge and Clapham.

Cambridge provided the party's clerical leadership through two powerful personalities: Charles Simeon (1759-1836), whose preaching and teaching steered the next generation of Evangelical clergy towards a new, vigorous churchmanship; and Isaac Milner (1750-1820), whose presidency at Queen's transformed that college into a veritable stronghold of Evangelicalism at the university.[105]

Meanwhile, the party's lay leadership centered around Clapham, then only a village some three miles southwest of London. Here were, however, the homes of a band of brethren "whose brains and brilliance could not be denied even by those who sneered at their religion." Nicknamed the "Clapham Sect," these "Saints" (as they were also derisively called) were wealthy enough, yet elected to live in almost monastic self-discipline. In a spirit of extraordinary unanimity, nurtured by Bible-study and weekly worship at their newly-erected parish church, this remarkable fraternity of philanthropists, politicians and professional men would meet in regular "Cabinet Councils" to discuss strategies to overcome whatever they saw as the major spiritual, moral and social evils of their day.

Henry Thornton (Member of Parliament for Southwark) was recognized as the "dean" of the brotherhood. Other distinguished members were Zachary Macaulay (Governor of Sierra Leone), Charles Grant (Chairman of the East India Company), Lord Teignmouth (Governor-General of India), James Stephen (the eminent lawyer), together with those two tireless champions of victims of the African slave trade, Granville Sharp and Thomas Clarkson. Of singular significance was, however, the acquisition of William Wilberforce (1759-1833), conspicuously gifted Member of Parliament for Hull, hailed by both Burke and Pitt as the greatest orator in England.[106]

At the time of Wilberforce's conversion (during a continental tour in the company of Isaac Milner), prospects for the cause of Anglican Evangelicals seemed, to say the least, unpromising. Although High Churchmen and Low Churchmen might be polar opposites in other respects, in one area they were in total agreement—their intense intolerance of Evangelicals. Caught in this continuous crossfire within their own church, there were, among Evangelical clergymen in 1785, none above the rank of a parish incumbent, only two who held London livings, and Evangelical laymen of means and standing were few and far between. They had no organization, no program, no political power. Moreover, they had no leader. But then, in 1785, it was "clear that God had provided one." Though seldom an originator, as animator and agitator Wilberforce was peerless. In addition, he was financially independent and an intimate friend of Prime Minister Pitt. In other words, he had both those indispensable ingredients of influence—wealth and connections.[107]

It was to the immortal credit of the Wesleys and Whitefield that, "by keeping alive a religion of the heart that had died in the rest of the church," they laid the essential foundation for a new generation of reformers, who were then in a position to bring to their task a radically different approach. Wilberforce and his fellow-Claphamites had access to circles of the ruling class which were completely closed to the Methodists; and they knew only too well that, without winning over a substantial number of that ruling class, their own efforts to reform the nation would be foredoomed to failure. It was with this in view that Wilberforce, in 1797, published his "religious manifesto," *A Practical View of the Religious System of Professed Christians Contrasted with Real Christianity,* a work which immediately became a best-seller, and exerted a profound influence on precisely the people who "counted."[108]

However, the basic vehicle they relied upon, the voluntary society, was, in essence, by no means new. Those early personal growth groups, the Religious Societies of the post-Restoration era, had already led to the founding of voluntary societies for both mission and morality. In like manner, Methodist societies from the mid-eighteenth century now became the forerunners of voluntary societies in new ventures of mission and reform. However, between the situation in the 1690's and that in the 1790's there were important differences. Needs were greater, in the wake of the infant Industrial Revolution, and new contact with vast, non-Christian segments of the earth's population. Motives were stronger, now that the deism and decadence of the age had been confronted with a nation-wide revival, still in progress. Finally, methods were more compatible with the recent "laicization" of organized religion, thus bypassing both political and clerical control, and filling the vacuum where bonds between church and state had loosened after the "glorious revolution" of 1688. By refining, multiplying and coordinating the voluntary society structure, men of the Revival, with Claphamites in the forefront, managed to bring this form of voluntaryism to an unprecedented level of effectiveness.[109]

In point of time, molding of the minds of the young was one of the earliest concerns of the "Sect." In 1785, five years after Robert Raikes' pioneering effort in Sooty Alley, they helped to organize the Sunday School Society, eventually capturing the cause for the Evangelicals by themselves founding the Sunday School Union, in 1803. However, it was world mission which became the primary power factor of the movement.

The awakening of the missionary idea was no doubt traceable, in some degree, to the pioneering endeavors of Pietists and Moravian precursors. It also owed much to Wesley's insistence that Christ died for all mankind, not only for the elect. Most importantly, missions became an inevitable consequence of the strong soteriological concern of the whole Evangelical Revival. Impelled by William Carey's momentous *Enquiry* of 1792, the founding of the Baptist Missionary Society that same year is generally held to mark the opening of the modern world missionary enterprise. The London Missionary Society was, at the time of its founding in 1795, intended as an interdenominational endeavor, and endorsed by Anglican Evangelicals. However, in church-planting activity such as this, the Claphamites came to the conclusion that the cause would be better served by organizing, in 1799, a Church Missionary Society, of avowedly Anglican affiliation. Then, after a long struggle, Wilberforce and his colleagues managed, in 1813, to force the East India Company to allow Christian missionaries into British India.[110]

The Clapham Sect also had a high regard for the power of the printed word. Wesley had made extensive use of the brief, popularly-written books at that time known as "tracts." From 1795, the "consecrated pen" of that close coadjutor of the Clapham Sect, Hannah More, produced a series of incredibly successful "Cheap Repository Tracts," in open competition with the "infidel" press. Her efforts to provide wholesome Christian reading-matter for the masses were followed up by the founding, in 1799, of the Religious Tract Society, as an evangelical, nondenominational enterprise, but with strong Claphamite endorsement. (The SPCK, like the SPG, was by this time decidedly High Church oriented, agitated openly against "enthusiasm," and remained for a while severely critical of the Evangelicals.) Then, in 1804, Claphamites cooperated enthusiastically with Dissenters in creating that giant of the Evangelical Movement, the British and Foreign Bible Society.[111]

In their endeavors to promote "the reformation of manners," the Saints encountered predictable opposition. Nevertheless, through the so-called "Proclamation Society" of 1788 and its successor, the "Society for the Suppression of Vice" of 1802, determined efforts were made to combat drunkenness, duelling, pornography, prostitution, gambling, blasphemy, brutal sports and violation of the Sabbath.[111]

Meanwhile, although "respectability" rated high in Clapham consciousness, they proved their concern for more than personal morality by their pioneering efforts for *social* reform. Thus they fought for the removal of election abuses, the support of penal reform, the abolition of the press-gang, the relief of chimney-boys, the emancipation of Roman Catholics, the improvement of factory conditions, and introduction of elementary education. The crowning achievement of Wilberforce and his Clapham colleagues was, of course, their leading role in the abolition of the Slave Trade in 1807 (to be followed in 1833 by the elimination of slavery itself in all British possessions).[113]

In the galaxy of benevolent societies for these and many other causes which sprang up during the decades following the French Revolution, Anglican Evangelicals—while warmly rejecting any attempt to confuse them with Methodists or Dissenters (for fear of circumscribing their "usefulness")— were more than willing to cooperate with them, wherever vital considerations of church discipline did not preclude it. In fact, scholars of this eventful era of Anglo-American church history have identified the deliberate development, during these years, of an "Evangelical United Front," whereby evangelicals of every persuasion might the more effectively consolidate their efforts to reform the nation. The voluntary society system, conceived as a contractual union of individual Christians (not church bodies), lent itself admirably to such a strategy. Here, denominational differences could be purposely under-played in the interest of unity. Published lists of patrons, office-bearers and subscribers gave tacit testimony to the success of the Clapham campaign to overcome social ostracization, and enlist men of means and position in the cause. Such lists also showed how effective control of this burgeoning "benevolent empire" could, by means of "interlocking directorates," be concentrated in the hands of a relatively modest number of key evangelicals (with Clapham almost invariably well represented).[114]

From Sydney Smith's biting sarcasm in contemporary columns of the *Edinburgh Review* to the present times, that generation of evangelicals in general, and Wilberforce with his fellow-Claphamites in particular, have been attacked for this whole "industry in doing good" on two main counts: first, because of self-seeking motives; secondly, on account of superficial methods.

As to their *motives,* they have been accused of mounting concerted crusades as an ideological counter-attack against revolutionary sympathies, in order to "buttress the stratified social structure" in which they themselves occupied such a privileged position. True, the revolutionary movement did assail Christianity as "a principal prop of the established order"; in common with the vast majority of their fellow-countrymen, Evangelicals did, in fact, consider England's class-structure to be God-ordained; and both Wilberforce and his Clapham colleagues did, in the wake of the French Reign of Terror, endorse the Tories' overt repression of civil liberties. Nevertheless, no one has produced one shred of evidence that their primary motive was ever anything less than they always acknowledged it to be: a consistent, uncom-promising concern for the salvation of their fellowmen.

Again, as to *methods,* they have been represented as reactionaries, blinded by their own paternalism and other-worldly piety, concerned more with alleviating the symptoms than eradicating the causes of human suffering. Undeniably, the Saints did (again, reflecting the temper of their times) work "*for* rather than *with* the poor." However, their piety, though other-worldly centered, was indisputably down-to-earth in its implications. "My business is in the world," wrote Wilberforce, and threw himself against the most titanic inequity of his time, one which, by then, had permeated the entire social and economic fabric of the nation. In so doing, he and his colleagues allied themselves gladly with liberals and humanitarians outside the church.

To reproach Wilberforce that he did not abolish factory slavery as well as African slavery would be to criticize Leif Erikson because, after discovering America, he did not go on to discover Australia!

In any case, the actual record of the Clapham Evangelicals in a broad spectrum of social reform, at a time when social activism was almost synonymous with sedition, reveals them as radical, rather than reactionary. Moreover, where they failed to deal directly with any specific evil themselves, their efforts elsewhere helped to sensitize those who eventually would (a circumstance relevant also to future reforms in the world of the seafarer). In short, there are valid reasons for the statement that it was men of the Evangelical Revival who first made modern England aware of her social obligations.[115]

AMERICA'S EVANGELICAL UNITED FRONT

Not surprisingly, the vigor of Britain's Evangelical United Front soon spread to the New World. In certain aspects, the situation was, of course, radically different in the former Thirteen Colonies, wrestling, around the turn of the century, with the formidable tasks of achieving a degree of national identity while claiming and taming the vast wilderness of the West. Nevertheless, the religious scene in America had, by then, developed into a particularly fertile field for the kind of coordinated spiritual strategy presented by the Evangelical United Front.

That scene bore all the marks of a two hundred-year encounter between an Old World heritage and a New World environment. When Martin Luther nailed his 95 theses to the door of the Castle Church at Wittenberg in 1517, only 25 years had elapsed since Christopher Columbus set foot on the Bahamas. The proximity of those two epochal events, the one igniting the Protestant Reformation, the other initiating the European colonization of America, was destined to have a profound impact on the character of American Christianity. Although Columbus was sponsored by Spain, at this time a bastion of Catholic colonialism, it was the British who gradually gained the ascendency along the Atlantic Seaboard, thus paving the way for centuries of Protestant predominance.[116]

However, this was "Protestantism with a difference" (Hudson). Though largely English in origin, it was by no means Anglican in essence. The Mayflower Pilgrims who landed at Plymouth (in what is now Massachusetts) in 1620 were Separatists from the Church of England, and their fellow-countrymen who followed in 1630, and formed the Massachusetts Bay Colony, were predominantly Puritans. These were radicals, of Calvinistic convictions, who had tried to resume (as they saw it) England's "arrested

Reformation." For years, they had sought to "purify" the National Church from within, despaired under the Laudian repressions, and decided instead to establish a "true" Church of England in New England. Eventually, they absorbed the Plymouth group, as they pursued their vision of building a Congregational theocracy, stretching from Connecticut through Massachusetts to New Hampshire.

Only in the oldest colony of Virginia, where the first settlers arrived in 1607, was there any serious effort to make Anglicanism an established religion from the start. A similar establishment was subsequently attempted, at least in name, in the other southern colonies. However, these endeavors were effectively inhibited by the post-Reformation influx of "dissenting" Quakers, Baptists and Presbyterians, coupled with other factors. There, and especially in the middle colonies, religious heterodoxy was further bolstered by waves of immigrants from Continental Europe, as men and women of Reformed, Lutheran and other backgrounds sought escape from religious, social and economic oppression in their homelands.[117]

A certain religious radicalism was typical of those for whom religious freedom formed a major motive for emigration. The very fact that they chose to emigrate was in itself an overt act of protest. But their radicalism had a ring which was basically positive. The aim of those pioneers was not simply to secure release and relief. They were borne by a sense of divine destiny. Here, at last, was the opportunity for a new beginning in a new land. For them, those wide open spaces were, in a very special sense, "God's own country." From the God-ordained "errand into the wilderness" of those New England Puritans, to Pennsylvania's "holy experiment" in total toleration, the great goal was to provide the world with the working model of a godly society. That hope could later, on occasion, be "subtly secularized," and restated in political terms. Nevertheless, in its original form, it imbued the churches of America with a unique sense of mission, and gave them, despite their indebtedness to European rootage, that restless pragmatism and openness to experimentation which has since been their strength. It also became intimately linked with two of the most characteristic features of American Christianity—pluralism and revivalism.[118]

Denominational pluralism was a natural consequence of the Protestant Reformation. That event shattered what remained of the *Corpus Christianum* concept, the medieval ideal of church and society constituting one homogeneous entity throughout the territorial extent of Christendom. By 1648, the Treaty of Westphalia had achieved grudging recognition of a confessional status quo among the warring nations and the different denominations they stood for. But within each individual state, there was no question of denominational diversity. There, the word was religious uniformity, ardently enforced by civil authority. In essence, this was also the dominant attitude transplanted to the American Colonies. However, seminal ideas of genuine religious freedom were also transplanted, as witnessed in Maryland, Rhode Island, and most spectacularly in Pennsylvaina. Even more significant than individual cases of idealism was the weight of sheer necessity. As immigrants from varied backgrounds kept coming across the ocean, religious pluralism simply became an inescapable fact of life; and whatever traditions of antagonism might persist in the Old World, mutual self-interest, if nothing else, called for coexistence on equal terms in the New. In America, disestablishment was inevitable, long before a "wall of separation" between church and state was officially enacted by the Constitution of 1787.[119]

The building of that wall may well have been America's "greatest national contribution to religious history" (Marty). At all events, the important role of the laity in American church life has been attributed, at least in part, to the absence of governmental paternalism. Also, the preclusion of state-support has underscored the need for self-support and the development of a vigorous spirit of voluntaryism. As voluntary associations based on uncoerced assent, America's "gathered churches" found themselves increasingly dependent for both self-perpetuation and growth on various practical techniques. Of these, none has engendered greater enthusiasm—or controversy—than that second fundamental characteristic of American Christianity, revivalism.[120]

By revivalism is understood the planned promotion of revival, that quickening of the spirit whereby noticeable numbers of non-Christians are brought to a personal and conscious relationship of trust in Christ as Savior and obedience to Him as Lord, or whereby lapsed or nominal Christians are brought to repentance and renewed commitment. Revivals, as such, were, of course, no new phenomenon of eighteenth-century America. They formed an integral feature of the faith, dating back to that first revival which, according to the biblical record in Acts, chapter two, gave birth to the Christian church itself. Since then, the spirit of revival had pulsated through the whole history of the church, more powerfully at some periods than others, but always there, and manifesting itself in a rich variety of ways, for example in monasticism, mysticism and a host of reform movements, often branded as heretical, and culminating in the Reformation. At its core lay a quest for authentic personalization of the faith, whenever institutionalization reached the point of quenching spiritual life. As already noted, the Pietist Movement, which emerged in Continental Lutheranism toward the close of the seventeenth century, erupted as a reaction against the dead formalism of contemporary Protestant orthodoxy. In so doing, it became the precursor not only of the Methodist-Evangelical Revival in eighteenth-century England, but also of its counterpart in Colonial America.[121]

There were good reasons why the British Colonies of North America were ripe for revival at the outset of the eighteenth century. Sociologically, the people had become what succeeding generations would long continue to be—a society in motion. A society in motion is, as Sweet points out, always an individualistic society. In a static society, group interest can assert itself and institutions take hold. In a mobile society, only a religion able to appeal to the individual, his needs, his aspirations and his sense of personal responsibility could expect to gain a hearing. The peopling of the North American Continent consisted of a continuous transplanting of society from older to newer regions. It was essentially a "frontier" society—with all the restlessness and rootlessness which that entailed. In the older communities, poverty was rife and church membership only for a privileged few. On the frontier, the twin-headed hydra of barbarism and infidelity was seen as an ominous threat. Surrounded by the wild men, beasts and terrain of the wilderness, frontiersmen were commonly exposed to an incredible coarseness of manners and morals. Since (in most cases) immigrants came from countries where church membership was "co-extensive" with citizenship, and since (also in most cases) the motive for emigration was not primarily religious, only a minority would identify themselves with any church whatever, even if they happened to have one within access. (In fact, contrary to frequent assumption, the average ratio of churched to unchurched in Colonial America was at no time more than one to twelve.)[122]

By the beginning of the eighteenth century, organized religion in the Colonies was obviously on the wane, painful proof that European patterns of religious life, when applied without major modification on the American scene, had not met New World needs. It was, as one contemporary commentator put it, a time of "extraordinary dullness" in religion. Then came the Great Awakening. As in every genuine revival, the question of how it originally ignited, and then reached the proportions of a general spiritual conflagration, remains the mystery of its Divine Author. However, certain aspects are readily accessible to the historian. At a time when the experiential piety of the pioneer generation of New England Puritans had been diluted to the level of the so-called "Half-Way Covenant," pietistic emphasis on a "religion of the heart rather than the head" was reintroduced (especially in the Middle Colonies) through a growing tide of German immigrants, many of whom belonged to the Mennonites, Moravians and other left-wing groups. It was also a time of warfare with the French, frequent forays by marauding Indians, and consequently widespread insecurity and unrest. Then, in the 1720's (over a decade before the beginning of the Wesleyan Awakening in England), revival broke out in New Jersey.[123]

It was an ardent young German-born pastor, one Theodore Jacobus Frelinghuysen, who, in the words of no less an authority than Whitefield, became the "beginner of the great work." Already deeply influenced, before his arrival, by European pietism, he had, in 1720, taken charge of four Dutch

Reformed congregations in the Raritan Valley of central New Jersey. His bold, frontal attack on the comfortable Calvinist orthodoxy of his congregations, combined, as that orthodoxy was, with deep-rooted Dutch ethnicity, created a furor of protest—but also conversions. By 1726, the revival had reached a peak and spread to other Dutch communities.

That year, another young pastor, Gilbert Tennent, was called to the Presbyterian church of nearby New Brunswick. Encouraged by Frelinghuysen, he, too, systematically stripped his hearers of their false spiritual security, as he strove to prove to them that "no one ever became a Christian without first being subjected to the terrifying realization that he is *not* a Christian." Again, many among the Scotch-Irish immigrants, who made up the congregation in his case, took offense; but many, too, took hold of the Gospel. Reinforced by the efforts of his father, William Tennent, and zealous graduates of the latter's ridiculed "Log College," the fires of revival spread, and Presbyterian congregations throughout the Middle Colonies began to throb with new life.

Then, in 1734, Jonathan Edwards, the brilliantly endowed pastor of Northampton, Massachusetts, alarmed by all the licentiousness and complacency he saw around him, preached a series of sermons on justification by faith alone. With chilling logic, he also held forth on the eternal consequences of rejecting that offer. The effect was electrifying. Multitudes were converted, and lives dramatically changed. Revival had also reached the staid Congregational churches of New England.[124]

Nevertheless, this was only the beginning. It was not until 1740 that the many local revivals merged into one "Great Awakening." The instrument in this case was that colleague of the Wesley brothers from Oxford "Holy Club" days, George Whitefield (1714-70), the tavern-owner's son who became the greatest preacher of the century. Landing in late 1739, on this second of his seven tours to America, Whitefield preached his impassioned message of new life in Christ from Georgia to New England, indoors, outdoors, wherever people would hear him. They did, in incredible numbers, as the waves of revival swept up and down the Atlantic Seaboard. (His life-long admirer, Benjamin Franklin, calculated on one occasion an open-air congregation of 25,000.)[125]

The Awakening proved itself "great" not only in geographic extent, but also in degree of impact. Again, the response was by no means only positive. From the very first stirring, congregations were split wide apart, between those who supported and those who resented the characteristic methods of promotion, particularly the pointed preaching of the revivalists, as they sought to convict and convert. Meanwhile, many ministers decried cases of excessive emotionalism, railed against reductionistic disregard for doctrine and tradition, and warmly rejected allegations that they themselves might stand in need of conversion. Nevertheless, with time, exaggerations were curbed, and far-reaching benefits recognized. Among the latter were a massive membership growth in virtually all denominations, a manifest improvement in public morality, a powerful impulse toward higher education (exemplified by the founding of Princeton and several other colonial colleges), and a renewal of missionary concern (typified by David Brainerd's heroic dedication to Indian missions). However, within the context of this study, the most significant consequence of the Great Awakening was the foundation it laid for a distinctly American arm of the Evangelical United Front.[126]

That an evangelical front should emerge from this awakening was not immediately apparent. Evangelicalism has often been understood as a revolt against orthodox Calvinism; and Jonathan Edwards, the theological giant of the Great Awakening (and, indeed, eighteenth-century America), was strenuously Calvinistic. However, he sought, at the same time, to bridge the gap between traditional Puritan theology and the individualism of the age, so as to reconcile his own Calvinistic presuppositions with the revivalism he helped to promote. As the incisive apologist for experiential Christianity, he proceeded. to reformulate Calvinism in terms of Edwardsian "New Divinity." In so doing, he became the founder of so-called "New England Theology," a school which, without wishing to take farewell with Calvinism, was nevertheless destined to make mounting concessions to freedom of the will.[127]

Nor did the Awakening at first seem to have any unifying effect, rather the contrary. Liberals among New England's Congregationalists, especially in and around Boston, reacted strongly against Edwardsian retention of "outmoded" Calvinist concepts of original sin and predestination, as well as against any endorsement of revivalism. This led to the defection of the Unitarians, although the breach did not become final until the first quarter of the next century. On the opposite wing, many who deplored the decline of revival fire in the Congregational churches separated from these and formed Baptist churches. It was Separatist Baptist preachers from these churches who fanned out into the newer frontier regions and, in the decades leading up to the Revolution, prompted an amazing growth of Baptist congregations in the South.

Nevertheless, the Awakening did create new bonds of unity, too. Basically, it brought to the majority of American Christians "a common understanding of the Christian life and the Christian faith." This was largely facilitated by the Awakening's emphasis on personal religious experience, not merely inherited religious tradition. It was also fostered by the consistent catholicity of its foremost promoters, particularly that of the "Grand Itinerant" himself. (Anglican-ordained George Whitefield "did not have a denominational hair on his head.") Eventually, most orthodox ministers originally opposed to revivalism, both among Middle Colony Presbyterians and New Congregationalists, were won over to a more positive position. Revivalism was well on its way to becoming "a constituent part" of an American form of Christianity, molded to meet the needs of the New World.[128]

One further consequence of the Great Awakening deserves mention at this point. Because it was not only interdenominational, but also inter-colonial, the unifying effect of the Awakening reached into the political sphere as well, thus helping to promote a national consciousness, of crucial importance for the impending struggle for independence. That struggle found the churches (with the partial exception of the Anglican and certain pacifist groups) increasingly identified with the Revolutionary Movement. Given the dissenting, Puritan character of the religious substratum in Colonial America, this was hardly surprising. However, for American church life, the whole eight-year period of warfare (1775-83), including the years immediately preceding and following, was an era of decline. This "religious depression" was not entirely due to the distracting demands of war and political upheaval. There was also the debilitating effect of an intellectual climate dominated by deistic devotees of the Enlightenment, both among the Founding Fathers of the new nation and its more radical publicists.[129]

As soon as the exuberance of victory had subsided, the churches—most of them reduced in numbers, resources and evangelistic zeal—were confronted with the sobering realities of an entirely new situation. In the immense, unchartered expanse which was now the United States, would the religious freedom guaranteed by the Federal Constitution become freedom for religion, or (as some hoped) freedom *from* religion?

Most pressing among the "institutional housekeeping chores" await-ing American Christians in 1783, was the need for independent, nationally-structured church organizations.

The Congregationalists (destined to dissipate much of their energies in an unsuccessful rearguard action to preserve their privileged status in New England) joined their Presbyterian fellow-Calvinists in a "Plan of Union" in 1801, in order to provide for joint churches in frontier areas. The Anglicans, stripped of their privileges and depleted by defecting Tories, became the greatest casualty of the Revolution. However, now that local resistance to a native episcopacy had subsided, a new generation of gifted bishops would eventually lead the reorganized Protestant Episcopal Church of America towards an impressive recovery. The Methodists, who had barely begun to establish themselves before the Revolution, confounded skeptics by being the first to form a national organization (now, after 1784, independent of the Anglicans). By means of native, circuit-riding lay-preachers, their flexible society-structure, and their inherent missionary fervor, they were uniquely equipped to respond to the challenge of America's ever westward-moving frontier, and became, within four decades, the nation's numerically greatest denomination. The Baptists, toughened by (and now respected for) years of bitter persecution, simply continued the amazing momentum they had developed shortly before the Revolution; while consolidating their gains in the East, they were, with their farmer lay-preachers, also able to meet much of the critical need in the new frontier settlements. The Lutherans would only reach appreciable numbers when waves of German and Scandinavian immigrants began arriving well into the next century. Roman Catholics, too, would only experience significant growth when the flood of European immigration began to build up through the nineteenth century.[130]

However important structural considerations might appear, no organizational efficiency could take the place of Spirit-imbued motivation. Since the Great Awakening, although much of its energy seemed to have been drained off by the Revolution, the fires of revival had never been completely extinguished, especially in the South. In one sense, therefore, it is true to say that the Second Awakening, or Second Great Awakening, as it is also called, grew out of the original Great Awakening. At all events, there were many who, toward the turn of the century, saw a resurgence of revivalism as the only hope of evangelizing the nation, and making this truly a people "under God."[131]

In actual fact, when a renewed awakening came, it came with such power that in one way or another, it continued to manifest itself across the country for two whole generations. Precisely how it originated is still a matter of debate. However, from the start there were two focal points: college campuses and frontier camp-meetings. As early as in 1787, revival came to the campuses of two Presbyterian colleges in Virginia. Candidates for the ministry from these colleges brought an immediate quickening of spiritual life into the New West, as they fanned out among the frontier settlements beyond the Alleghenies. It was also the Presbyterians who originated the enormously popular camp-meeting method of frontier evangelism, culminating at Cane Ridge, Kentucky, in 1801. A rich source of revivalism among the Congregationalists resulted from the student awakening prompted by the preaching of President Timothy Dwight at Yale, in 1797. However, while revivalism among Presbyterians and Congregationalists was normally more restrained, Methodists and Baptists became the unabashed protagonists of radical frontier evangelism. In fact, it was not long before camp-meeting revivals became a regular Methodist institution. Meanwhile, these frontier phenomena exerted a profound influence in the East, by promoting urban revivalisn in the settled communities along the Atlantic Seaboard.[132]

This is not the place to attempt to follow the continuing course of the Second Awakening. However, one consideration is of paramount importance in our context. What the "second spring" of the Evangelical Revival was for

England, the Second Awakening was for America. It rejuvenated the spiritual and social life of the entire nation, reinforced a sense of universal "moral stewardship" and generated a virtual "empire" of voluntary societies in the New World, too, bent on benevolent and missionary activity both at home and abroad.[133]

Although the founding of a national American Bible Society in 1816 is regarded as the official launching of the Evangelical United Front in the United States, the English "folk-pattern" of response to urgent needs by forming a "voluntary society" of like-minded friends had already become a familiar feature of life in the Colonial era. From the dawn of the new century, however, several factors combined to give the American society-movement fresh momentum.

First, there was a model. The population of the new nation being still predominantly British and Protestant by background, the "evangelical machinery" of the British "united front" served as a natural object of emulation.

Secondly, there was a well-adapted theology. While practical leadership of the American benevolence front would eventually devolve on one of Dwight's outstanding students, Lyman Beecher, two other spokesmen for Yale's "New Divinity," Samuel Hopkins and Nathaniel Taylor, provided the necessary theological rationale by drafting a doctrine of "disinterested benevolence." (Conversion was not the end but the beginning of Christian life, and evidence of genuine conversion was a life characterized by a shift of personal preference, from self-interest to disinterested benevolence.)

Thirdly, there was a positive psychological attitude in the land. The legacy of the Enlightenment, with its optimistic view of man's potential, added to the high sense of national destiny pervading the young republic; both of these factors combined to provide an atmosphere particularly favorable to benevolence activity.[134]

Understandably, the Evangelical United Front, as it developed on the American side, was required to be "naturalized" to serve American purposes, with an initial emphasis on home mission societies, in order to supply the crying needs in the frontier regions. Nevertheless, the American front followed the same basic pattern as the British original, with societies formed across denominational lines wherever considerations of polity did not militate against this. Thus there emerges, around the turn of the nineteenth century, the picture of a surging tide of evangelical Christianity, sweeping through the entire English-speaking world, supplying the dynamic to nerve the churches of both Britain and the United States to Christianize their own population and join forces in a vast mission to the whole of the non-Christian world.[135]

Factors Focusing Public Attention on Seafarers

At this point in time, there were already indications that mission might at last include the world of the seafarer. There were, in fact, in the midst of the wave of religious and humanitarian awakening in Britain and America, five factors focusing public attention especially on seamen. The recent voyages of exploration in the Pacific Ocean, the dawn of the era of Romanticism in the Western world, the awakening of Protestant world missionary endeavor, the gathering momentum of the anti-slave-trade movement, as well as lessons learnt from protracted warfare at sea, all served to direct at least some of the sensitivity and energy generated by the general awakening into a new concern for the sorely neglected seafarer.

The era of great oceanographical discoveries was by no means over with the "Age of Discovery" of the late fifteenth and early sixteenth centuries. It was the epic voyages of Captain James Cook, from 1768 to 1779, which brought Australia, New Zealand, and the vast expanse of the "South Seas" definitively within the bounds of the known world, in other words, approximately one third of the earth's surface. The excellent published narratives of Captain Cook's journeys served to create, in incredibly short time, an intense interest in these remote regions. In a sense, they symbolized the enlarged vistas of that new world which was breaking in upon the turbulent scene of human history at the close of the eighteenth century. Meanwhile, more scientific methods of navigation, new shipbuilding materials, and above all the harnessing of steam power to new means of propulsion, were fast approaching on the horizon, portents of a promising new age in ocean transportation. Visions of commercial enterprise, political gain and the spread of Western civilization could hardly help but stimulate an awareness of public dependence on the seafarer for their fulfillment. Moreover, as the misery of the seaman's true situation became more widely known, there were hopes that a sense of public indebtedness—even indignation—might prompt improvement.[136]

In the sea-conscious populations of Great Britain and much of the United States, public interest in the life of the seafarer would also tend to be enhanced by the new romantic mood which was, towards the turn of the century, fast supplanting the Age of Reason in almost every area of human activity. As sentiment was accorded new and vigorous validity in the mounting wave of romantic reaction against the restraints of the Enlightenment, there was widespread fascination for the past, the distant and the bizarre. This would, quite naturally, attract interest in the colorful life of the deep-sea sailor, as attested by the popularity of the hapless but heroic "tar" in contemporary writings.[137]

Without doubt, an element of romanticism also reinforced the hold of the "Great Missionary Awakening" which erupted within Protestantism during the closing years of the eighteenth century. As the doors to distant parts of the world were providentially flung open, the newly awakened life of faith was almost inevitably given "a missionary direction" (Warneck). Roman Catholic missionaries had long since occupied the new frontiers opened up by the great navigators of Spain and Portugal. Now, as Roman Catholic world mission experienced a lull, a great English navigator unwittingly awakened Protestant Christians to claim unknown climes for Christ. It was after carefully studying the journals of Captain Cook's Pacific voyages that William Carey published his famous missionary manifesto in 1792. Again, it was under the inspiration of Carey's example that Samuel Mills, at the so-called "Haystack Prayer Meeting," dedicated himself to world mission, and with his fellow-students prompted the founding of the pioneer American missionary organization, the "American Board of Commissioners for Foreign Missions" (1810).

Both the Methodist Revival in Britain and the Colonial counterpart in America had, in essence, been mission-oriented from the start. Now, as specific societies for world mission multiplied on both sides of the Atlantic, it was inevitable that zealous missionaries should "discover" the men on whom they must rely for both transportation and communication. No sooner had bridgeheads been established overseas, however, than missionary societies sensed an even more urgent stimulus. Seamen coming from supposedly "Christian" countries could, with one drunken spree ashore, effectively nullify any positive impact that months of patient missionary endeavor might have made on the local native population. Here, surely, was a missionary challenge of the highest priority: the evangelization of the seafarer.[138]

Another area of missionary concern, which contributed towards greater awareness of the seafarer's plight, was that of home mission. Mission to non-Christians abroad was accompanied by a new sensitivity towards the spiritually destitute at home. Thus, as organizations for domestic mission multiplied, and "urban missionaries" sought out underprivileged segments of society, they, too, could hardly avoid "discovering" the seafarer and his systematic victimization in the Sailortown slums of the port cities.[139]

Yet another form of missionary endeavor which helped to focus attention on the seafarer was that of media mission. The publication and distribution of literary media, such as the Scriptures and religious tracts, was seen as an essential adjunct to both world and home mission. As societies for

JOHN NEWTON
CLERK.
ONCE AN INFIDEL AND LIBERTINE
A SERVANT OF SLAVES IN AFRICA.
WAS.
BY THE RICH MERCY
OF OUR LORD AND SAVIOUR
JESUS CHRIST.
PRESERVED, RESTORED, PARDONED,
AND APPOINTED TO PREACH THE FAITH
HE HAD LONG LABOURED TO DESTROY.

HE MINISTERED
NEAR XVI YEARS AS CURATE AND VICAR
OF OLNEY IN BUCKS.
AND XXVIII YEARS AS RECTOR
OF THESE UNITED PARISHES.

ON FEB' THE FIRST MDCCL. HE MARRIED
MARY,
DAUGHTER OF THE LATE GEORGE CATLETT
OF CHATHAM KENT.
WHOM HE RESIGNED
TO THE LORD WHO GAVE HER,
ON DEC' THE XV° MDCC XC.

The above Epitaph was written by the Deceased
who directed it to be inscribed on a plain Marble Tablet
He died on Dec' the 21 1807. Aged 82 Years
and his mortal Remains
are deposited in the Vault
beneath this Church.

John Newton's self-written epitaph, on the north wall of St. Mary Woolnoth Church, Lombard Street, London. (Courtesy: St. Mary Woolnoth Church.)

these purposes proliferated, both in Britain and America, it was the under-privileged who were given priority. Thus, the "poor sailor" would become a natural object of their concern, the more so because, by providing the means of transportation, perhaps even actual distribution, he constituted a basic precondition for overseas media outreach.[140]

Even before this wave of world, home and media mission began building up towards the turn of the century, public awareness of the pitiable situation of merchant seamen was already on the increase as a result of the efforts of evangelical Christians involved in the Slave-Trade Abolition Movement. In sheer, selfless devotion to the abused Africans themselves, it is doubtful whether any surpassed that "Apostle of the Negroes," Peter Claver (1581-1654), the Jesuit missionary, later canonized, who, for over forty years, went out to meet incoming slave-ships in the harbor of Cartagena in order to minister to the desperate needs of surviving "cargo." Nevertheless, despite his moral heroism in the face of bitter opposition, he was still working within the system. It remained for the eighteenth-century abolitionists, spurred on by the Quakers, to assail the system itself, wisely choosing to wait until strong enough to attack slavery as such, and meanwhile concentrating on the crucial question of supply. In so doing, they had to contend with two

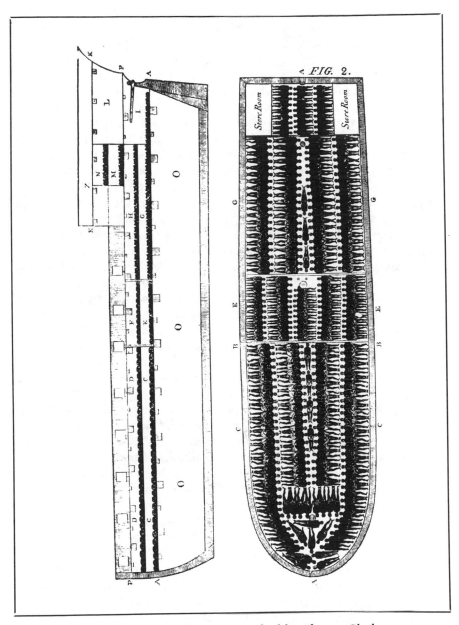

Sectional view of a slaver, researched by Thomas Clarkson, and used by Wilberforce in his campaign. (Oliver Warner: *William Wilberforce and His Times.*)

powerful arguments, both regarded as matters of vital national interest.[141]

In the first place, the slave trade had, by mid-eighteenth-century Britain, been accepted with "unquestioning cordiality" as an economic necessity. Protected and promoted by charters, treaties, even acts of Parliament, the "Triangular Trade" (shipping manufactured goods to West Africa, slaves across to the West Indies, and molasses, rum and tobacco back to England) was, as the second half-century progressed, bringing in fabulous fortunes, and the most natural ambition of any man in the street was to own an interest, however small, in a "Guinea cargo." As England continued consolidating her command of the seas, she gained unrivalled leadership in an enterprise which led to the enslavement of up to 100,000 fellow-humans per year. However, the general public refused to regard them as a part of the human race at large. They were "property," pure and simple. As a source of cheap, effective labor on colonial plantations, African slaves were looked upon in the Aristotelian sense of "living tools." So ingrained was this type of "slave complex" in the national consciousness that even a John Newton, after a radical conversion, could continue in command of a slave ship without "the least scruple" as to the lawfulness of the trade. By the time the self-styled "African blasphemer" had made full atonement by his zeal against an institution he eventually learned to hate, even a man of Nelson's stature could still say that never would the "just rights" of his nation's West Indian possessions be infringed while he had an arm to fight in their defense or tongue to launch his voice against "the damnable doctrine of Wilberforce and his hypocritical allies."[142]

In the second place, promotion of the slave trade was seen as indispensable to national security. It provided hard but healthy opportunities for the training of tough British seamen, so the nation believed. Indeed, in the words of one well-known naval historian, "admiral after admiral" raised the same argument, as the abolition debate wore on: the great number of vessels engaged in the slave trade made it an invaluable "nursery of seamen," on whom the Navy was utterly dependent in times of national emergency. To destroy such an institution was tantamount to national suicide.[143]

The economic argument was, in itself, irrefutable. The story of how the abolitionists nevertheless succeeded in making it a matter of national conscience to set aside economic self-interest and finally, from conspicuously Christian and humanitarian motives, outlaw the slave trade in 1807, remains almost without parallel in the history of mankind.[144] However, in their search for evidence to illustrate the incredible callousness of this traffic in human flesh, they inadvertently uncovered facts which proved the complete fallacy of the "naval nursery" argument.

Of particular significance were the "herculean labors" and meticulous research of a young deacon in the Church of England, Thomas Clarkson

This advertisement appeared in a Charleston newspaper
of 1766. (From *The Observer,* October 17, 1965.)

(1760-1846). After writing a prize-winning university essay *On the Slavery and Commerce of the Human Species,* he discovered his life's calling, helped, in 1787, to form a "Committee for the Abolition of the Slave Trade" and, for the next two decades, became a one-man fact-finding commission for the committee, scouring the waterfronts and hunting down facts and figures for use by Wilberforce and his Clapham colleagues.

Sensitive to the damaging implications of the "naval nursery" argument, Clarkson also gathered evidence with which he was able to prove, by careful documentation: (1) The frequently fatal physical effect of the slave trade, leading to a staggering annual loss of over half the seamen employed in Guinea ships; those who did not die from fever or pollution would succumb, desert, or be marked for life, as a result of the savage brutality which seemed endemic to slaver captains and their mates. (2) The

Thomas Clarkson
(1760-1846). Pioneer maritime sociologist and advocate
for victims of the slave
trade, both black and white.
(Oliver Warner: *William
Wilberforce and His Times*.)

consistently corruptive effect of a traffic where, during the dread "Middle
Passage" (from the Guinea Coast to the West Indies), men were ordered to
torture, mutilate, even jettison alive their fellow human beings; small wonder
that Guinea sailors would say they were all drunkards, because none of them
could do it sober. By demonstrating, with convincing methodology, that the
entire dehumanizing enterprise was not a nursery but a graveyard for the
nation's seamen, Thomas Clarkson proved himself a pioneer maritime
sociologist.[145]

As Clarkson's conclusions were corroborated by the evidence of
others and duly reported to Parliament, this new dimension of a diabolical
traffic began to dawn on the public at large. Thus, the men who, in the name
of Christ and humanity, devoted their lives to combat the white man's crime
against Africa made a contribution toward the early history of mission to
seafarers which has not been adequately recognized in the past. By their
agitation against "white" slavery, too (both the impressment of naval
seamen, noted earlier, and now this raw abuse of slave ship crews), slave
trade abolitionists also focused the attention of church and public on one of
the most neglected sectors of society—the men of the sea. Furthermore, by
confronting the establishment of their day, this embattled band of eighteenth-
century evangelicals actually pioneered an important prophetic function of
ministry to seafarers. In other words, contrary to popular belief, the dawn of
organized seamen's missions was heralded by ministry to the seafarer's

social needs to be followed in due time by a ministry of his spiritual needs—not vice versa.[146]

Finally, a fifth factor focusing public attention on the seafarer was the period of protracted warfare at sea, which began with the French Revolutionary War (1793-1801) and continued through the Napoleonic War (1803-1815). The outbreak of the French Revolution in 1789 has been acknowledged as pivotal in the history of human thought. Thus, one effect of the upheaval across the Channel (already introduced by its counterpart across the Atlantic) was the spread of a spirit of humanitarianism, which provided much of the motivation in the early phase of the Slave Trade Abolition Movement. Then in 1792, widespread revulsion over the news of the Reign of Terror paved the way to public acceptance of political repression, and postponed by fifteen years the final abolition of the traffic in slaves. However, this event had precisely the opposite effect on the incipient missionary society movement. It prepared the soil for a new spiritual "seriousness" in the propertied classes, induced Dissenters to close ranks with other evangelicals, and gave the movement sufficient momentum to overcome the anti-missionary bias of Latitudinarianism and establish the necessary network of societies.[147]

That the organization of societies for *seamen's* mission did not develop with equal rapidity is due to a variety of circumstances. A major war, with its calls to concentrate on the all-important issue of national survival, would tend to have retarding influences on initiatives in other spheres. In addition, any attempt to evangelize specifically seamen would have to contend with two particular forms of public prejudice. Many, not least in evangelical ranks, saw seamen as totally irredeemable; having been beyond the pale of church and society for centuries, they were now, as a class, considered to be utterly impervious to spiritual or moral impressions. Others, especially in "professional" quarters, held that a converted sailor would, by definition, make an inferior sailor; anything more than lip-service to religion would simply soften the "hardy tar," and rob him of that diligence and discipline which was indispensable to the commercial interest—and especially the defense—of his country. (Dealing with these so-called "hopeless" and "harmful" charges would become an important apologetic task for early advocates of mission to seafarers.)[148]

Nevertheless, the mere fact that the island nation was in time of war so completely dependent on seamen—in order to keep her overseas life-line open and man the "wooden walls" of her main line of defense—meant that the seafarer (especially in his naval role) was very much in the public eye. When Nelson's fleet at Trafalgar in 1805 sounded the death-knell to any revival of Napoleon's invasion plans, it brought the British Tar to his very pinnacle of popularity. Although, as Wilberforce and others had reason to remind, the resulting mood was one of general relief rather than moral obligation, a mounting proportion of evangelically awakened citizenry did sense a degree of indebtedness which would not be satisfied with tragicomical tributes to Jack in popular ballad and drama. Instead, that sense of debt would provide important potential motivation for future seamen's missions. Moreover, during the decade which followed Trafalgar, dramatic developments in the Royal Navy were destined to demonstrate that seafarers were very far from spiritually "hopeless," likewise that the effect of the Gospel on them was anything but "harmful." (Ironically, it was Methodists, among whom press gangs often felt they had a kind of franchise, who were to constitute the most convincing evidence of this.)[149]

Although on a much more modest scale, American naval exploits (during the Revolutionary War, the Quasi-War with France, the War of 1812, and the expeditions to the Barbary Coast) also fired the public imagination and created a corresponding enthusiasm for the American seafarer. This was reinforced by both the upsurge of American trading activities following the Peace of 1783 and the rising spirit of nationalism in the early years of the new century.[150]

On the whole, therefore, despite certain retarding influences, there were, by the turn of the century, many factors on the contemporary scene which seemed to converge to create a climate favorable to the launching of organized missions to seamen. Nevertheless, one final queston remains: did the overall situation of the seafarer of the day demonstrate a legitimate need for particularized missionary endeavor? In seeking an answer to that question, it seems natural to examine the seaman's situation from four different viewpoints—his physical, social, moral and spiritual situation at that time.

THE PARTICULAR CONTEXT: THE SEAMAN'S SITUATION AROUND THE TURN OF THE NINETEENTH CENTURY

Turning first to the physical conditions with which the seafarer had to contend, it must be observed that the period under study, from just prior to the turn of the century to the mid-1860's, was essentially "the heyday of sail and wood." True, steam propulsion did, during the first decade of the new century, move from fumbling experimentation to two epoch-making events. In 1802, the stern paddle-steamer *Charlotte Dundas,* powered by a steam engine designed by William Symington, started towage service on the Forth and Clyde Canal, thus becoming the first vessel in the world to put steam-power to commercial use. Only five years later, in 1807, the side paddle-steamer *Clermont* (built by Robert Fulton, and dubbed by skeptics "Fulton's

Folly") negotiated the Hudson River between New York and Albany, thereby inaugurating the first steamboat passenger service in history. Then, in 1820, the steamship *Aaron Manly,* carrying passengers from London to Paris, became the first to demonstrate the feasibility of iron as shipbuilding material, instead of wood. Nevertheless, progress by both steam and iron was slow and fraught with frustration. While steamships were widely despised, especially by veterans of sail, as ugly, noisy "steam kettles," wooden wind-ships with their graceful pyramids of sail continued to dominate the scene right up to the American Civil War.[151]

Reverting, then, to the period around the turn of the nineteenth century, who were the men who manned those sailing ships? In Britain, there had never been any basic distinction between naval and merchant seamen. The distinction lay between seamen and landsmen. The British seafaring community was, as it always had been, a people apart, self-conscious, suspicious and even scornful in relation to the "lubberly" land community. Together, seafarers made up a "common pool," which would normally suffice to meet all the nation's nautical needs. The average "seafaring person" was, quite simply, expected to man a merchant or naval vessel wherever he happened to be most needed. In times of national emergency, the government would enlist and, if need be, impress a sufficient proportion of the pool into its fighting fleet. Then, when peace returned, it would lay its ships up "in ordinary" and leave the men to seek re-employment in the merchant or fishing fleet.

At the turn of the century, there were about 145,000 men in the merchant service and some 125,000 in the Royal Navy, making a total of approximately 270,000. Until 1793, the entire seafaring population was hardly half that number. However, from that year, Britain became involved in the longest of her wars. To make up the balance now needed to man the fleet, the government found it had to look to landsmen and resort to drastic measures, including a Quota Act (of 1795) and a series of "red-hot presses." By such means, jails were emptied and the fleet infiltrated by a costly element of insubordination and incompetence.[152]

Across the Atlantic, what was, in 1783, still only a loose confederacy of thirteen poverty-stricken former colonies began building and manning merchant ships at a rate unparalleled anywhere, passing the half-million mark in deep-sea registered tonnage well before the turn of the century. With Salem, Massachusetts, conspicuously in the lead, resourceful shipowners along the North Atlantic Seaboard opened up immensely profitable trade routes to the Far East, and competed lustily elsewhere with England and other maritime powers, while the "pick and flower" of young American manhood vied with one another to provide officers and crews. From 1796 to

1812, there were reportedly enregistered some 140,000 American seamen. Meanwhile, under the combined threat of Barbary corsairs and a French fleet resentful of American neutrality, the nucleus of a United States Navy was born in the late 1790's. Despite its minute size, its remarkable success in both the Quasi-War with France (1798-1800) and the Tripolitan War (1801-1805) won for it world-wide respect.[153]

Although it would, as Lewis puts it, be "a monstrous calumny" to insinuate that the seamanhood of Britain was completely corrupted by the influx of undesirable elements when manpower needs were desperate, there can hardly be any doubt that, during the first years of the nineteenth century, the overall situation of the American seaman was conducive to higher morale than that of his British counterpart. Nevertheless, in many respects, their conditions of life and work were essentially similar. In fact, as confirmed by contemporary sailors' narratives from both sides of the Atlantic, there would seem to have been no mean justification for Dr. Johnson's negative cnclusion. A ship could, in a sense, be compared to a jail; and there was, most assuredly, a very good chance of being drowned, or at least maimed for life.[154]

Anyone shipping out on an ocean-going sailing vessel, at the complete mercy of wind and wave, could hardly expect life to be less than hard and hazardous. At the turn of the century, however, conditions were such that it might seem strange that any survived. A whole combination of causes, some incongruously classified as "Acts of God," others more obviously attributable to the aberrations of man, all seemed to conspire against the health and physical safety of the seafarer. As the number of merchant ships and lives lost at sea continued mounting during the early decades of the nineteenth century, statistics shocked the British public into demanding a Parliamentary Inquiry. The resulting Select Committee, appointed in 1836, identified as major causes of unseaworthiness and shipwreck: overloading, undermanning, defective construction, lack of repairs, inadequate equipment, unsafe harbors, faulty charts, unqualified shipmasters and drunkenness among officers and crews.[154]

Of course, such conditions did not prevail universally. Nor did the majority of vessels actually founder. However, even though the average sailor might, more likely than not, escape shipwreck, his physical well-being was under constant threat from other quarters. To be washed overboard by breakers, torn from a precarious hold in storm-rent rigging, or maimed in a cargo-handling accident, was just part of life. Caught between the competing claims of speed and revenue-bearing space, crew quarters were incredibly cramped. (A man's allotted living space was, even in the late nineteenth century, in the words of Andrew Furuseth, "too large for a coffin and too small for a grave.")

Cooped up in the dark, dank dungeon of a heaving forecastle, sailors succumbed all too easily to consumption, as well as other infections. His work-place also being his home—in fact, for weeks on end, his whole world—a seaman would be subject to the most severe stress and, all too frequently, mental illness. Malaria, typhoid, yellow-fever, venereal disease, as well as miscellaneous ailments related to alcohol abuse, were rampant. Captain Cook's success in dealing with scurvy, the disease which had traditionally taken the greatest toll of seafarers, was still very recent. At all events, poor provisions and prolonged voyages continued to make malnutrition and semi-starvation commonplace.[156]

One of the greatest physical and mental hazards which seamen had to face was the savage system of shipboard discipline. This was again linked with the low level of the seafarer's social status through the ages. In nations bordering on the sea, society would have a natural and vital interest in the supply and efficiency of its seafarers, out of concern for both commerce and defense. At the same time, the seafarer's distinctive conditions of life, cut off from society at large, and exposed to overwhelming physical and moral hazards, reinforced an image of the seafarer as one incapable of safeguarding either his own or society's interests. Hence, he had always been recognized as a "ward of the state." As such, it was assumed he would need both coercion and protection.

On the other hand, the need for coercion, in the shape of strict, unquestioning discipline, was seen as paramount, since the safety and success of any maritime enterprise would depend very largely on the reliability of each individual crew member to fulfill his alloted role in a responsible manner. On the other hand, the possibility of abuse of authority on shipboard and vulnerability to exploitation ashore would also necessitate measures for the protection of the seafarer. From time immemorial, the first of these concerns had predominated, to the point of virtually excluding the second.

In the fleets of the ancient world, centered mostly around the Mediterranean, the status of the seafarer was virtually one of chattel slavery. In the Middle Ages, a modicum of freedom was introduced by the Nordic concept of individualism. However, shipping codes continued to concentrate mainly on the rights of shipowners and the authority of shipmasters. The seaman's sins of omission and commission brought down upon him a brutality which defies description. Only as a more humanitarian spirit began to assert itself, in the wake of the Enlightenment and the Evangelical Awakenings, did emphasis on punishment and repression slowly swing over towards paternalism and emancipation, until the twentieth century brought its present preoccupation with the health, safety and general welfare of the seafarer.[157]

Much of the seafarer's hardships must be seen against the background of inhuman working conditions which society, in the wake of the

A study in reluctance: American seamen complying with the
order "All hands on deck to witness punishment." The
public knew little about such "standard procedures," and
seemed to care even less. (Bernard Raskin: *On a True Course.*)

Industrial Revolution, also condoned ashore. Nevertheless, the isolated
nature of shipboard society inevitably made a seaman's opportunities for
redress more limited than those of landsmen. Just how slowly the seafarer's
lot did improve is illustrated by the fact that, as the twentieth century
dawned, his status was still legally defined as one of "serfdom." Certainly,
around the year 1800, and for decades to come, both British and American
seamen were treated very literally like slaves; and no romantic myth in the
minds of landsmen about the glorious freedom of the "sons of the waves"
could alter that fundamental fact.

Compared to his counterpart in the Navy, where flogging, that
"hellish holdover from the days of barbarism," was still practiced, the
merchant seafarer was not necessarily better placed. His situation was also
in large measure military in character, and the Draconian discipline to which
he, too, was subjected was even more arbitrary. However, there was at least
a relatively limited term set on the merchant seaman's bondage—the period
of the voyage (as opposed, for example, to the duration of war). But bondage
it was. From the moment he signed articles (or found himself shanghaied on
board), he was kept in a constant state of involuntary servitude. If he
deserted ship in a foreign port, imprisonment was automatic (and remained
so through the century), regardless of reason. Meanwhile, many cases were
known of unscrupulous captains driving their men to despair and desertion,
simply to save the wages the men would then have to forfeit.[158]

The systematic dehumanization of the seafarer was only possible
because of his age-old social alienation. The story is told of a philosopher of

antiquity, who found it difficult to compile comparative statistics of the living and the dead. He felt that seafarers could not rightly be ranked with either, but made up "a third sort of persons . . . suspended between both."[159] This concept of the seafarer as a being *sui generis,* a species by himself, persisted through the centuries. "A wanderer on the face of the deep," he was "no less a wanderer upon the land." The sailor's pea-jacket was, quite simply, "an insurmountable barrier between himself and society." Well into the nine-teenth century, his fellow-countrymen could still not agree whether the hapless, homeless mariner belonged to the "lower class of society" or instead possessed "no rank in the social scale" whatsoever.[160] Such notions would, of course, prevail more particularly where a strict stratification of society was accepted by many as preordained.[161]

True, a vague idea did persist that the sailor "might possibly, at some future period, perhaps not before the millennium, become a more respectable member of society." Some enterprising mariners might even prefer not to wait that long, and try, in those early, pre-union days, to better their own lot, especially their miserable wages, by occasional bouts of "collective bargaining by riot." In Liverpool, armed merchant seamen, exasperated over wage grievances, managed to hold the city hostage for three whole days, in August 1775. In the Royal Navy, the mass mutiny at Spithead in 1797 actually led to improvements in both pay and conditions of service.[162]

But despite sporadic attempts by officialdom, too, to provide some form of patronizing protection, the seafarer's subhuman socio-economic situation remained basically the same, with chronic under-employment (due to the casual, voyage-based nature of his work-contract) included with his many other trials. Society, uneasily aware of the superhuman hardships and hazards of the seafaring life, remembered, on occasion, the sailor's feats, but all too frequently forgot the sailor himself, thereby consigning him to a subhuman destiny, cast off as unfit for human society, abandoned to abuse and extortion, and marked accordingly. This low public image naturally had a significant negative impact on the sailor's self-image; and both were destined to become important impediments to missionary motivation and implemen-tation, respectively.[163]

If life could be "hell afloat" under the belaying-pin of "Bucko" masters and mates, it was normally no less than purgatory ashore under that highly organized form of Sailortown extortion known as the "crimping system," to which sailors were consistently abandoned by "respectable" society. How hordes of human predators, aptly called "landsharks," managed to fleece seafarers by the thousands of their hard-earned wages, and (by discounting so-called "advance notes") even lure from them pay as yet not earned, will be the subject of a subsequent, more detailed study. However, in the present context it is necessary to note that successive Sailortown sprees, into which the men were led by those well able to exploit their social isolation, naturally had a cumulative, corruptive effect on the sailor's sense of morality. (The Dutch designation for the crimp as a *zielverkooper* or "soul-seller" was certainly very close to the mark.)[164]

Nevertheless, the average sailor's moral status was not normally regarded as uniformly reprehensible. Plato preferred to see all people avoid the sea, for, as he put it, the sea is "the Schoolmaster of all Vice and Dishonesty." That quiet eighteenth century Quaker "radical," John Woolman, saw seafaring life as "so full of Corruption" that he appealed to fellow-Christians to forgo luxuries and non-essential merchandise so as to reduce, as far as possible, the numbers exposed to the necessary evil of sea transportation. At the outset of the nineteenth century, there were still those who insisted that "every vicious propensity" was inseparable from the character of the sailor.

However, there were others who reacted against categoric statements about the universal depravity of seafarers. It was only as might be expected that, for example, the patriotic *Gentleman's Magazine,* in 1809, printed a eulogy to "the high excellence of British Seamen," in an effort to place their character "in a more favourable light" than was often the case. Again, that immensely popular poet of the British Tar, Charles Dibdin, was untiring in his praise of his hero's positive attributes.[165]

Against those who saw the sailor as totally irredeemable, early seamen's mission advocates, too, were quick to call attention to traits in the seaman's professional character which could only claim the unequivocal admiration of his fellow-countrymen on shore. These could be classified under four heads, as the proverbial maritime virtues: bravery, loyalty, honesty and generosity.[166]

In the words of no less an authority than Christopher Lloyd, "every vice seems to have flourished in the ships of the old navy except that of cowardice." Bravery, in the face of the elements or the enemy, was basic to sheer survival; again and again, it was the "brave tar's" cool courage, when confronted by fearsome odds, which would have to carry the day. Loyalty, closely akin to bravery, was also typical of the true sailor; he detested change, loved tradition, and showed intense, full-blooded attachment to his family (whom he seldom saw), to his shipmates (of whom he saw too much), to his country (by whom he was so deplorably neglected), and to his fellow-seafarers throughout the world (to whom he was bound by the powerful bond of the Brotherhood of the Sea). Honesty thrived in a context of close-knit solidarity and interdependence, such as in a ship's crew; "Honest Jack" earned his name because, by and large, he was frank, open and artless, with a

THE JOLLY JACK TAR OF FICTION   THE POOR JACK TAR OF REALITY

(Bernard Raskin: *On a True Course.*)

healthy hatred of hypocrisy and falsehood in any form. Generosity in the
midst of deprivation, compassion in the midst of inhumanity; this, too, was
learned in the harsh school of the sea—and nowhere was it more evident than
in the genuine sailor's chivalry and warm-hearted tenderness toward children
and the disadvantaged.[167]

Not surprisingly, such qualities, reinforced by both an aura of
romance and a sense of national indebtedness, made the deep-sea sailor a
popular figure with the general public, both in Britain and America. Again,
not surprisingly, there would, among the general public, be a tendency to
excuse Sailortown sorties as an understandable form of release from long
periods of unnatural restraint; and whatever immoral attributes such habits
might indicate would be dismissed as mere "foibles" in an age which still
tolerated an incredible degree of decadence and brutality. However, as
maritime historians have pointed out, the bold, breezy, rollicking sailor of
story and song was very far from the real, morose, maltreated mariner of the
turn of the century, a man who, when sober, was "always laboring under a
sense of burning injustice"—and for good reason.[168]

Although there was, undeniably, a strong element of boisterousness
in the sailor's humor, the "jolly tar" of popular fancy was, just as certainly,
grossly overdrawn. Instead, pioneer advocates of maritime mission showed
sufficient realism to reckon with the recurring duality of the sailor's life. It
was almost as if Jack afloat and Jack ashore were two totally different

persons, because the former would always, so it seemed, leave behind his good qualities before stepping ashore. At all events, the pioneers' efforts to steer a middle course in their assessment of the sailor's character would serve them in good stead when dealing with future critics of organized outreach to him. Those who saw the sailor as morally and spiritually hopeless would be reminded of his commendable characteristics. Meanwhile, those who saw mission to the seafarer as unwarranted could be confronted with drastic descriptions of his habitual entrapment by rapacious landsharks.[169]

Some have, both then and later, reacted against what they conceived as a condescending, judgmental attitude toward seafarers as a class, on the part of meddlesome, moralistic "activists."[170] Nevertheless, the nature of the evidence is irrefutable. No eyewitness accounts of vice and immorality among seafarers were more forthright than those of their most popular pioneer preachers, themselves former seafarers, and therefore hardly chargeable with paternalism.[171]

Later generations have identified many plausible reasons for impaired moral sensitivity among seafarers of that day and age, such as a general lack of education, illiteracy, boredom, anonymity, loneliness, stress, brutalizing discipline and a tremendous peer pressure, generated within the isolation of a floating "total institution." At all events, they have had to agree that the "noble tar" of those times did, despite all his sterling qualities, display certain characteristics which were most decidedly ignoble. Constant causes of moral shipwreck were held to be the twin shoals of drunkenness and promiscuity. To these were added the sailor's notoriety for profanity and Sabbath-breaking (both of which were, despite the permissiveness of the times, seen by many as highly reprobate).[172]

A more detailed study of these four particular "maritime vices" will be necessary in another context. A fifth charge was also levelled against the sailor with great insistence: that of recklessness. To many, he seemed so thoughtless, so improvident, so gullible. However, this was more accurately a general condition, born of the blind obedience and unquestioning solidarity of shipboard life. Recklessness would, therefore, reinforce the flaws already listed, rather than constitute a new addition to them. Nor would all agree that recklessness was necessarily bad. Because a high hazard to life and limb was held to be endemic to seafaring, a powerful professional school of thought insisted it was the non-reflective, devil-may-care attitude of the typical tar which was precisely what was called for. It was to become an urgent task of early advocates of mission to seafarers to prove that they were totally wrong.[173]

Meanwhile, the fact that sailors seemed so easily led could be put to good purpose, too. Ashore, the under-socialized sailor was totally "out of his depth." As a class, seamen would instinctively "recoil from the sense of their solitude," and therefore "ransom themselves, even at the price of their souls," an easy prey to the "spurious sympathy" of any who professed to befriend them. Should they instead be met by genuinely Christian "seamen's friends," what consequences might not this have for their true moral and spiritual welfare?[174]

Turning, then, to the spiritual status of the seafarer around the turn of the nineteenth century, there was keen sensitivity to the intimate relationship between moral and spiritual welfare as such. Abandoned morals hardened the heart to the call of God; correspondingly, a "low ebb" of genuine faith led to moral decline.[175] Hence, prospects might in many ways seem equally unpromising for the sailor's religion as for his morality.

An attempt to identify elements hostile to the Gospel in the spiritual life of seafarers of this epoch reveals two kinds of causes: on the one hand, directly deviant forms of religiosity; on the other hand, the obstruction posed by powerful inhibitive factors.

Seemingly at the mercy of awesome whims of wind and wave, the sailor might understandably seek by some sort of self-effort to influence the powers beyond his control. Such endeavors must theologically be classified as "legalism." In its most primitive form, legalistic religiosity could include a substantial admixture of superstition. Just as credulity, defined as uncritical readiness to believe, had, justly or unjustly, been associated with the mentality of seafarers for centuries, so too, in the sphere of the supernatural, he was held to be incurably superstitious. True, in the days of sail, superstitious beliefs were also rife among landsmen. However, on an element as vast and treacherous as the ocean, to be steeped in sea lore was almost a condition of survival.

The sea itself could be regarded animistically as a living being, endowed with a personality of its own; or the power of the sea could be vested in a sea-god of varying identity. At all events, the sea, or sea-god, would resent as intruders all who traveled across the deep. Propitiation and circumspection were, therefore, mandatory. As seafarers through the ages sought to come to terms with the arbitrary forces of the sea, there grew up a rich flora of maritime folklore, with local variations, but basically as international as seafaring itself.

Besides the sea-gods proper, there was a whole hierarchy of merfolk. There were elaborate initiation rites for both ships and men (among which launching libations and customs connected with crossing the Equator are, of course, still widely practiced). There were sailors' taboos (forbidden days, numbers, animals, etc.). There were weather portents, wind-raising witches, awe-inspiring Finns, scapegoat Jonahs and perilous passengers (women, clergy and lawyers). There were monsters, sea serpents, ghost ships, and a whole host of maritime folktales and legends to supply the need for "yarning,"

VOLUNTEERS.

G. R. III.

God Save the King.

LET us, who are Englishmen, protect and defend our good
KING and COUNTRY against the Attempts of all *Republicans* and *Levellers*, and against the Designs of our NATURAL
ENEMIES, who intend in this Year to invade OLD ENGLAND, *our happy Country*, to murder our gracious KING as they have
done *their own*; to make WHORES of our *Wives* and *Daughters*; to rob us of our Property, and teach us nothing but the *damn'd Art*
of murdering one another.

ROYAL TARS
Of OLD ENGLAND,

If you love your COUNTRY, and your LIBERTY, now is the Time to shew your Love.

REPAIR,

All who have good Hearts, who love their KING, their COUNTRY, and RELIGION, who hate the FRENCH,
and damn the POPE,

T O

Lieut. W. J. Stephens,

At his Rendezvous, SHOREHAM,

Where they will be allowed to Enter for any SHIP of WAR,

AND THE FOLLOWING

BOUNTIES will be given by his MAJESTY,
in Addition to Two Months Advance.

To Able Seamen, - - - -   *Five Pounds.*
To Ordinary Seamen, - - - *Two Pounds Ten Shillings.*
To Landmen, - - - - *Thirty Shillings.*

Conduct-Money paid to go by Land, and their Chests and Bedding sent Carriage free.
Those Men who have served as PETTY-OFFICERS, and those who are otherwise qualified, will be recommended accordingly.

LEWES: PRINTED BY W. AND A. LEE.

This recruiting poster from the Napoleonic War period
illustrates the religious chauvinism to which seafarers of the
day were exposed. (Roy Palmer, ed.: *The Valiant Sailor.*)

for expressing hopes and fears, and for explaining the inexplicable.[176]

A very significant subject of sea lore was, of course, death and after-life. According to widespread belief, sailors would, if they possessed at least some redeeming quality in the eyes of fellow-seafarers, end up in a fairyland, under-sea paradise called "Fiddler's Green." The rest would be consigned to "Davy Jones' Locker," a euphemism for hell.

One of the most common versions of legalistic self-redemption amounted to a kind of salvation by deprivation. To quote Richard Dana, sailors would "almost all" believe that their suffering and hard treatment, in pursuit of a hazardous but essential vocation, would be "passed to their credit in the books of the Great Captain hereafter." Or, as one seafarer himself put it,

> Do you think ... after a sailor has been knocked about ... now under a burning sun, and then off the Icy Cape, with hard usage and salt grub all the days of his life ... that he's not going to have some fun and frolic [in Fiddler's Green] after he slips his wind?[177]

Closely akin was a concept of salvation by dedication—in this case, to duty in the heat of battle. It was widely believed, with a fervor of faith "not unlike that of the Mahometans," that if a sailor died fighting for his country, his soul would go "straight to heaven." George Charles Smith, an able-bodied sailor in Nelson's fleet at the Battle of Copenhagen in 1801, recalls the ritual of bravado calculated to stifle fear of sudden death, as men worked their guns and shouted amid the carnage and cannon-roar: "England for ever!" "Fight for king and country!" A further means of morale-raising would be the adulation of their admiral, a practice which could almost reach the point of idolatry ("Nelson was considered our Saviour and our God," says Smith quite simply).[178]

Alongside all these elements of religious self-help, there existed, in the average seafarer, a strong streak of fatalism. This would express itself not so much in resignation to the inevitable as in reckless indifference to imminent danger, as well as apparent ingratitude following divine deliverance. An old source speaks of how death and danger only armed the sailor with "a kind of dissolute security." With only "the breadth of an inch-board ... betwixt him and drowning," he would, it was alleged, still swear and drink "as deeply as if hee were a fathom from it." Providentially delivered from the very jaws of death, he would normally neglect to pay the merest mite of gratitude to the Lord. A sailor would simply remain, as Michael Lewis puts it, "a cheerful extravert ... a fatalist to the last."[179]

Apart form such overt deviations as superstition and fatalism, the spirituality of the seafarer was also under attack by powerful inhibitive factors. As one Napoleonic War naval officer pointed out, British seamen, bereft as they were of means of grace, had for centuries been suffering from "spiritual famine." The different "disruptive factors" isolating the seafarer from normal sources of spiritual nourishment, both at sea and on shore, will be dealt with in a later context as important "impediments to maritime mission." So, too, will "corruptive factors" tending to obliterate whatever foothold the Gospel might nevertheless secure. Thus, among the so-called "Christian public," there was, in the words of the Psalmist, seemingly no one who cared for the sailor's soul. With many, one reason would be that the sailor was assumed to have no soul. Nor was the sailor's spiritual self-image materially better. As one well-intentioned tar replied when asked by a seamen's chaplain whether he was a Christian, "No, I am a sailor." In a mood of more serious reflection, a seaman might not deny he had a soul. But he would likely believe that seafaring could never be reconciled with sincere Christianity, and therefore choose to trust in the tenuous hope of a "death-bed repentance."[180]

Impelled by such a series of negative forces, some filling him with false security, some robbing him of legitimate hope, some even preventing him from thinking for himself and recognizing the difference, the seafarer might seem so impervious to the Gospel that it would indeed be "idle and futile" to seek to reach him with it.[181]

Nevertheless, the outlook was in reality far from hopeless. True, the anomaly was freely conceded: sailors seemed capable of reconciling "the grossest excesses" with reverence for the Being who forbade them.[182] However, that reverence was incontestable and almost universal. One observer recalls how when "apostles of infidelity," influenced by radical ideas from revolutionary France, threatened the British nation with "anarchy and blood," his own consolation was that they could have no hope of support among seamen. He goes on to say:

> Jack knows but little, but he believes in the existence of a God; he believes that it is by God's providence the world was created, and that by the same it is governed and sustained . . . . I have some-times thought of one of these infidel philosophers, as going on board a ship, and there endeavoring to preach infidelity. I have supposed one of these unhappy creatures standing by the helms-man, and telling honest Jack . . . that there was no First Cause, but that the world had made and still governs itself . . . . And, from what I know of Seamen, I have always felt confident . . . that the philosopher would stand in great danger of being thrown overboard.[183]

The very vocation of the seafarer constantly confronted him with "the works of the Lord, and his wonders in the deep." Isolated from all else, he had, as another seafarer put it, "a better chance to reflect upon God than a Landsman," for example "during the long dreary look out." In other words, with the handiwork of the Lord "spread out as a map before him" and with the voice of conscience within him, the seafarer had by no means been left without a divine witness. Certainly, this was not the Gospel, with its message of saving grace through Christ. This went no further than faith in God's providence, as Creator and Sustainer. Nevertheless, it was a faith in basic accord with the First Article of the Apostles' Creed. As such, it also served, as a fruit of general revelation, to prepare the heart for the acceptance of God's special revelation, through His word.[184]

In a sense, therefore, it might be said that God, in speaking to the seafarer through "the grandeur of the great deep," actually "schooled him for Christ."[185] Of course, true repentance as a negative condition of conversion to Christ required more than mere reverence before the reality of God. However, here the seafarer's natural aversion to any suggestion of sham or hypocrisy would stand him in good stead. He would need no repeated reminders of the hopelessness of man's lost condition. He knew himself to be a sinner, if only by bitter experience of the consequences.[186] In fact, when once exposed to a biblical message of sin and grace, he seemed far more easily convicted of sin than willing to accept forgiveness and salvation by grace.[187]

Nevertheless, the seafarer's undisguised sincerity, coupled with some of "that child-like simplicity with which the Saviour said the Gospel must be received," could—under the influence of the Holy Spirit—enable him to embrace that positive condition of conversion: faith in the sufficiency of Christ's sacrifice on the Cross. In fact, there were indications that man's need of a Gospel of free grace might well be grasped more clearly by men of the sea than by any other vocational group. As one seafarer finally came to see it, referring to the vain hope of salvation by deprivation, or by dedication to duty in battle:

> Dreadful sentiment; invented by devils, and propagated by mad-men! Can the fire of an enemy introduce a soul to heaven; or a mere act of duty to the country atone for the sins of an abandoned life? Then indeed had Christ died in vain. What refuges of lies will sinners rest in, rather than come to Christ that they might have life![188]

Long before the turn of the nineteenth century, there are scattered examples of how seafarers could, in their unostentatious but whole-hearted way, respond to the faithful communication of the Gospel. The fortitude with which Christian seafarers, since Tudor times, kept the faith as they faced both the terrors of the Inquisition and the horrors of Barbary slavery, aroused the unstinted admiration of their fellow-countrymen ashore.[189] Seventeenth-

The missionary ship *Duff* and Captain James Wilson,
Commander of the *Duff.* (C. Silvester Horne:
The Story of the L.M.S. / London Missionary Society.)

century Quaker captains, with their controversial yet quietly consistent form
of Christianity, made a deep impression wherever they went.[190] From the
moment the *Duff,* the pioneer mission-ship of the (London) Missionary
Society, weighed anchor one August morning in 1796 and sailed down the
Thames, the conduct of Captain James Wilson and his hand-picked Christian
crew caused amazement among onlookers all the way to Tahiti and back; in
Canton, the sobriety and general bearing of the sailors were such that
astonished observers re-christened the ship *The Ten Commandments.*[191] As
the world missionary movement gathered momentum, sensational reports
were published of sailors (even entire ship's companies) converted under the
ministrations of missionaries traveling to their fields overseas.[192]

Nevertheless, the candid observer, willing to face the harsh realities
of the seafarer's overall situation around the turn of the nineteenth century,
could hardly escape the conclusion that drastic steps were called for if there
was to be any prospect of meaningful change for the better. In fact, in some
respects, the whole context of life in which the seafarer found himself during
this so-called "heroic" age of sail seemed so dark that it might well have
been considered utterly hopeless. However, here too the picture appeared
darkest just before dawn; and it was the seafarer's *spiritual* situation which
was to be most manifestly affected by the first faint rays of that dawn.[193]

Landsmen had long since been reminded by British seamen, anxious
to affirm their national loyalty, that they were by no means bereft of
spirituality either. "Be pleased to understand," they had written on one

occasion, "although we have no churches, we say our prayers as well as you, and the same God you have on shore, is ours at sea . . . ."[194] Then, as Britain's two final wars with France wore on, incredible rumors began circulating about spiritual stirrings among the men of the Royal Navy. Seamen still had no churches in the sense of sanctuaries they could call their own. However, gathering in a small group on shipboard in the Savior's name was surely as scriptural a church as any.[195] As already seen, there was a mounting spirit of missionary awareness throughout the English-speaking world at this point in history; and several factors were converging to concentrate a portion of that awareness on the plight of the seafarer. After centuries of neglect by the institutional church, relieved only by sporadic and entirely inadequate forms of maritime ministry, the scene was finally set, so it seemed, for the inclusion of the seafarer in the ongoing, organized mission of the Christian church. But was the *time* set, too?[196]

Caught up in the dramatic aftermath of those spiritual stirrings in the British wartime navy, a merchant seaman exclaimed, in 1817, with words borrowed from the 102nd Psalm: "Surely, Lord, the time, yea the set time to favour sailors is come." If this were so, it was closely connected with a modest endeavor set afoot by two Methodist laymen, walking the streets of London one autumn evening in the year 1779.[197]

PART II

"FLOATING HELLS AND FIGHTING METHODISTS"

The Naval Awakening

Chapter 3

The Precursor:
The Naval and
Military Bible Society

THE ORIGIN
(1779)

The forerunner of seamen's missions in Great Britain—and, indeed, the world—did not originally have in view seamen in general, but strictly naval personnel. Moreover, those who provided the immediate incentive were not even in the navy, but in the army. Nevertheless, the claim of the Naval and Military Bible Society to the title of precursor of organized maritime mission appears to be indisputable. Whether this society (which is still in existence) also merits recognition as the first seamen's mission organization in the world, is another matter. A verdict on this issue must be deferred until the claims of others—on both sides of the Atlantic—can be adequately assessed.

The declared object of what was to become the Naval and Military Bible Society was recorded, together with the date "8th of November 1779" on the front page of the first minute-book of the infant Society:

> For purchasing Bibles to be distributed among the British Soldiers
> and Seamen of the Navy, in order (by the blessing of God) to
> spread abroad Christian knowledge and reformation of manners.[1]

True, this definition gives the Society, at best, only a claim to being the first institution known to have had the spiritual welfare of any category of seafarers as a part of its primary aim. However, this in itself provides ample justification for more detailed verification.

In assessing the validity of the above assertion, the first question posing itself is that of availability and reliability of source material. Several writers have, through the years, undertaken to examine the origin of the Society. The earliest initiative, to the knowledge of the present author, was taken by none other than Dr. Adam Clarke, the renowned Methodist minister, recognized as one of the most brilliant scholars of his day. The fact of his inquiry is recorded in the memoirs of George Cussons, one of the originators of the Society. In this source, it is expressly stated that Dr. Clarke "requested Mr. Cussons to furnish him with such particulars of its formation and progress, as he could recollect." There follows a quotation of the account of George Cussons addressed to Dr. Clarke.[2] The exact date and purpose of Dr. Clarke's investigation is not mentioned, nor what may have resulted from it. However, the strong Methodist ties of this pioneer Bible Society, at the time of its origin, coupled with Dr. Clarke's own involvement in the early activities of its rapidly expanding successor, are facts which render his interest at least plausible.[3]

The archives of the Naval and Military Bible Society (NMBS) no longer contain the early minute books of the Society. Nor do the earliest available reports provide significant details of its origin.[4] However, an *Appeal* published by its committee in 1834 purports to present a "Brief View of the Origin and Progress of the Society." While throwing no new light on the subject, this confirms some basic elements of the Cussons narrative.[5]

In 1861, three years after his appointment as clerical secretary to the NMBS, Charles P. McCarthy (a clergyman with several years' prior sea experience) published a book containing the substance of a public lecture delivered during extensive travels in his official capacity. This includes a number of statements regarding the origin of the Society, based on the author's claim to have "carefully examined the documents containing its history."[6]

However, the most comprehensive nineteenth-century account of the origin of the Society appears to be that contained in an article entitled "The First Bible Society," published in 1874 by the Religious Tract Society.[7] This 1874 author, while expressly quoting from the McCarthy version, adopts a distinctly critical attitude to its historicity. Meanwhile, the same author produces detailed results of his own personal research, "having obtained permission to examine the early records of the Society, which have been carefully preserved from the beginning." There is, however, no indication of any dependence on the Cussons version. On the contrary, there is strong evidence that the 1874 author has both had access to more complete archive materials, and provided a more authentic transcription.[8] Moreover, he seems to have been motivated by a relatively impartial spirit of inquiry,

The Wesleyan West Street
Chapel, Seven-Dials,
which was closely linked
with the origin of the
NMBS. (Courtesy: Naval,
Military and Air Force
Bible Society.)

independent of possible organizational or personal considerations (in contrast
to McCarthy and Cussons.)[9]

For these reasons, in spite of the later date of the 1874 investigation,
the following outline of events connected with the origin of the NMBS builds
primarily on evidence reproduced in the 1874 version.[10]

The scene was the London of 1779. One Friday evening on September tenth, two close friends, both Methodists and in their forties, were
making their way home after the "Leaders'–Meeting," following a service at
the Wesleyan West Street Chapel, Seven-Dials. By the time they reached
the vicinity of Soho Square, one of them, John Davis, a marble-cutter by
profession, had turned the topic of conversation to the condition of "that
numerous body of men, our common soldiers."[11]

These were troubled times. In America, a costly revolutionary war
was fast approaching its climax. During the summer of 1779, the combined
fleets of France and Spain had, at times, cruised at will in the Channel. The
nightmare threat of invasion could no longer be ignored.[12] The soldiery was
much in evidence, but what provisions were being made for the spiritual
welfare of these men?

With a combination of evangelical concern and practical approach
which had already come to characterize the Methodists, John Davis did not
content himself with pious generalities. As he walked on with his friend,
George Cussons, he unfolded a simple plan of action: in order to promote
"the genuine fear of God among the soldiers," he could wish "to distribute
some small pocket Bibles to a few private men in every company of Regulars
and Militia." This distribution was to be gratuitous, but by no means indiscriminate. Only such recipients were contemplated as indicated, upon inquiry,
that they would "receive such a gift thankfully, and perhaps use it to profit."

Moreover, if these could be induced to read to their comrades, the benefit would, of course, be multiplied. At all events, each Bible should be accompanied by "a small printed paper, showing the good-will and intention of the giver."[13]

In order to implement the plan, no organizational structure was specified. But George Cussons, a Yorkshire man by birth, who had set up a modest plate-chest-making business in Wardour Street, had a valuable connection. He was on sufficiently familiar terms with "that most benevolent gentleman," John Thornton, to have become one of the almoners through whom he channeled his philanthrophy to deserving cases. Davis suggested that Cussons could communicate the proposal to Thornton. If Thornton should then approve, Davis had no doubt that success was assured. And if further plans were to include a subscription, he (Davis) would be happy to contribute his mite, according to ability.[14]

Cussons asked Davis to give him his thoughts on the subject in writing, whereupon the contents of this letter (dated September 13, 1779) were transmitted to Thornton. The choice was well made. John Thornton of Clapham (1720-90), a successful merchant in the Russian trade, was known both for his personal frugality and his munificent support of the first generation of Evangelicals. He was a man who also put to good effect the opportunities for literary evangelistic outreach which his particular position gave him. (By the end of his life he had "circulated immense quantities of Bibles and religious books in all parts of the world, and printed many at his own expense.")[15]

Thornton's reaction was swift and characteristic. In a letter to Cussons dated September 17, 1779, he simply states: "Friend Davis I know not; but I suppose you do, and his abode, which he does not mention; and I should join with him in contributing if he can get a subscription. The times are not such as to allow looking back; I therefore inclose twenty pounds to go forward . . . ."[16]

Subsequent records testify that John Thornton honored his pledge in liberal manner. He provided numerous Bibles for distribution among men of the forces, both through the resulting Society and privately. Moreover, the collecting book could show that on at least three occasions he gave donations of £100.[17] However, available sources give only the sparsest information on the actual foundation of the Society and, indeed, on the first quarter century of its history.

All that can be established with any degree of certainty is that, after the initial approach to John Thornton, the subject was discussed with others, and "about twelve of them formed themselves into a society for promoting the object." Business meetings were held at the house of a Wesleyan friend

of Cussons, a Thomas Dobson, of 427 Oxford Street. Preparatory arrangements were made, and subscriptions solicited.[18]

These events are presented by one of those participating in them
(Cussons) as quite clearly having taken place before the close of 1779. This
is significant, since the Society itself for many years published 1780 as its
official year of origin.[19] However, the record of the first minute-book of the
Society corroborates the Cussons dating. The Society is here specifically
stated to have been "instituted November, 1779."[20]

THE FIRST QUARTER CENTURY
(1779–1804)

There is good reason why, for posterity, 1780, and not 1779,
became the year most intimately associated with the emergence of this novel
institution. Seventeen-eighty was the year of the "Gordon Riots." This
alarming event served in a memorable, if indirect, manner to underscore the
acute need for the new Society.

Liberal leaders had long been accustomed to regard the threat of
public disorder in the metropolis as a convenient weapon against the political
establishment. The excesses of ten traumatic days of mob violence in early
June, 1780, changed all that. In this case, the original incitement had come
from a quite different quarter, that of reactionary religious intolerance. The
central figure was the current champion of anti-Catholic extremists, Lord
George Gordon (1751-93). And the immediate objective was the repeal of
the Catholic Relief Act of 1778.

What began as a public procession supporting the presentation of a
petition to the Commons soon escalated into an orgy of mass terrorism which
caught the authorities completely unprepared. In vain, the young lord tried to
stem the flood which his own impetuous rhetoric had released. At one point,
widespread arson threatened to burn down London. Only when sufficient
troops had been mustered and finally ordered to use force, was a semblance
of law and order restored to the dazed metropolis.[21]

Despite this dramatic demonstration of the "pitiful inadequacy" of
the existing system, it was not until 1829 that Sir Robert Peel's Metropolitan
Police Act established Britain's first regular police force.[22] Nevertheless, the
riots served to demonstrate another kind of need for which a solution already
existed. Multitudes of militiamen were now encamped in Hyde Park and at
the center of London, in order to guard against a resurgence of public
disorder. However, immoral behavior within their own ranks became suffi-

The ill-fated
Royal George.
(Courtesy: National
Maritime Museum, London.)

ciently manifest to cause concern among serious-minded citizens. This would naturally provide both publicity and stimulus for an institution formed with the spiritual welfare of the soldiery as its specific object.[23]

The NMBS has never relinquished its responsibility for Scripture distribution in the British Army. For the purpose of this study, however, it will be natural to concentrate attention, as far as possible, on the *maritime* aspect of the Society's activities. Although the precise date is not known, it cannot have been long before British tars were also able to benefit from the benevolence of the infant Society. One event which won early publicity for the naval distribution of the Society was the notorious sinking of the *Royal George* in the summer of 1782.

The first news of the calamity was brought to the Admiralty by express the same night, August 29, 1782.[24] While refitting at Spithead, preparing to go to the relief of Gibraltar, the ship had been given a heel to repair a minor leakage. According to the contemporary press version, "a sudden gust of wind overset her," whereupon, in a matter of seconds, she went to the bottom. It was estimated that with her perished at least 800 souls, half of whom were crew, the remainder visitors (women, children and tradesmen). Included among the lost was Admiral Richard Kempenfelt, one of the most brilliant naval commanders of his day. Only some 300, mostly crew, survived.[25]

The loss of the *Royal George* became a legend. In actual fact, it was a scandal. (She was the oldest first-rate in the service. The subsequent court martial established that her hull, decayed through years of official "economy," literally fell apart under the strain of careening; but this incriminating report was suppressed.) At all events, the public was aghast. Cowper commemorates the disaster in his "Loss of the Royal George." "From my earliest days in the navy," writes George Charles Smith (in 1821) of the late 1790's, "I have been accustomed to hear constant allusions to the dreadful fate of the Royal George."[26]

An added trial of relatives and friends of the victims was, in the view of one commentator, that they were denied the consolation of that touch of "brilliancy" left behind "when the brave die in battle . . . ."[27] However, there was one circumstance so mitigating that the NMBS still found reason to revert to it publicly nearly a century later. When she went down, the *Royal George* had 400 Bibles on board, supplied under the auspices of the Naval and Military Bible Society. It was, therefore, possible to remind the public at large, and Christians in particular, that an offer of the Gospel of salvation had, at least in this way, been attempted before so many were suddenly "precipitated into eternity."[28]

This consideration was bound to commend the efforts of the still little known Society to the support of the religious public. At the same time, it gave to both committee and subscribers providential proof of the timeliness of this outreach. From now on, naval seamen had established an equal claim on the concern of the Society. Though not yet in name,[29] it had at least in fact and in public consciousness become the Naval and Military Bible Society.

The great paucity of records leaves one with only a very incomplete picture of the development of the Society up to about 1804. However, it is evident that the volume of work had, by the summer of 1781, increased sufficiently to require regular weekly committee meetings. At these, accounts were audited and applications for Bibles (already "very numerous") dealt with.[30] True, the decade of peace following the American War of Independence led to a reduction in the armed forces.[31] But the work continued.

A particularly interesting illustration of the latter is provided by a

Rowlandson's rendering of life on the middle deck of a British warship in port: HMS *Hector*, in 1782. (National Maritime Museum, London.)

subsequent allusion to the mutiny on the *Bounty*. In 1814, 25 years after that notorious event, two British frigates stumbled on Pitcairn's Island, and were able to verify the incredible report of an American merchant captain's discovery six years previously. To their utter amazement they found a small, thriving, English-speaking colony, well versed in the precepts of the Bible, under the benign authority and venerable countenance of the sole remaining ex-mutineer, Alexander Smith, who now called himself John Adams.[32]

The publication, in 1817, of a narrative of this eventful voyage, with all its romantic appeal, rapidly required new editions and called forth a rousing response from religious societies of the day.[33] The Committee of the NMBS, commendably alert to publicity potentials, were quick to point out in their 1817 report that the Bible which had "proved such a blessing to that little community established in primitive simplicity in the midst of the Pacific Ocean" had, in all probability, been furnished by their Society (prior to the sailing of the *Bounty* from England in 1787).[34]

In July 1789, less than three months after Captain Bligh had been cast adrift in the Pacific, events erupted in Europe which again moved that continent inexorably into the maelstrom of war. This, however, was a war with a difference. The ragged French Army of the Revolution was a People's Army, supplanting the "Professional War" of yesteryear with the ominous image of "Total War." This was a whole nation's mobilization of men and means, which could only be countered on a correspondingly national scale.

As before, it was first and last to her navy that Britain looked for hopes of success, and—very soon—survival itself. Never before had the manpower demand of the Navy reached such a peak. As the average naval peace establishment of less than 20,000 men leapt up to 100,000 and more, the nation's "natural reserve" of peacetime merchant seamen and fishermen threatened to run dry. For Britain, the War of the French Revolution (1793-1802) became more than once, in a very real sense, "the Navy against the World."[35]

In the Island nation's total dependency on her "Wooden Walls," during a decade of protracted crisis, the committee of the NMBS had vivid motivation in appealing for funds. And—in the ever increasing thousands needed to man them—they had an ample and urgent field of activity. Again, actual documentation is modest; however, the committee could, when looking back in 1804, say:

> For several years the Institution was amply supported, by liberal contributions, numerous subscriptions, and various collections at different churches and other places of worship; which enabled the Society to distribute Bibles very extensively, in consequence of the constant applications received from Naval and Military Officers, expressing their earnest desire to have the Bible put into the

John Newton (1725-1807). Former slave-ship captain, later staunch supporter of Wilberforce and the Anti-Slave Trade Movement. (The Mansell Collection.)

hands of their men, and engaging to use their influence to promote the views of the Society therein.[36]

Foremost among the Society's early ministerial supporters must be mentioned Rev. William Romaine (1714-95), then established as rector of St. Anne's, Blackfriars. Besides transmitting handsome donations from John Thornton,[37] this learned, leading Evangelical made, for several years, a point of preaching collection sermons for the Society, both in London and on his many preaching engagements in the provinces. As early as 1782, he identified himself so completely with the object of the work that he conceived of himself as a voluntary chaplain to the Society.[38]

Rev. John Newton (for whom John Thornton had obtained the rectory of St. Mary Woolnoth, London, in 1780), was, to begin with, Romaine's only Evangelical colleague in the metropolis. Newton showed a natural interest in these early organized efforts to bring the Gospel to his brother seafarers, and became a very warm friend of the Society.[39]

Two years after becoming rector of Clapham, Rev. John Venn preached a collection sermon for the Society (1794), after which the sanctuary of the Clapham Sect was repeatedly employed for this purpose. The widely renowned Rev. Rowland Hill, for whom the Surrey Chapel was built in 1783, became an ardent supporter of this as well as later forms of seamen's mission work. Among prominent lay supporters, William Wilberforce followed the example of John Thornton's interest in the Society and became an annual subscriber in 1794. He later became a vice president, which he remained to his death in 1833. In his active support of the NMBS, Wilberforce was joined by other key figures in the Slave Trade Abolition Movement, such as Granville Sharp, Thomas Clarkson and Zachary Macaulay.[40]

The lack of records of grants precludes any exact asessment of the extent to which needs were met.[41] However, there are indications that the Society's naval distribution of Bibles in the latter war years prior to the Peace of Amiens was, to say the least, far from adequate. Rev. Richard Marks, himself a former naval lieutenant, speaking at the NMBS anniversary in 1820, gives a vivid impression of Scripture scarcity in the "old school" Navy. More than three years elapsed after he entered the navy (which was in the year 1797), before he "saw a single copy of the Holy Scriptures." True, he did once or twice hear rumors about some society supposedly sending Scriptures on board ships, but that was all. Only on his return to England in 1805 from the Battle of Trafalgar did he, "by mere accident," come across an advertisement of the NMBS offering to send a portion of Scriptures to ships applying for them.[42]

This dearth of Scriptures in Britain's fighting ships around the turn of the century is confirmed by the celebrated Rev. George Charles Smith. His naval career (1796-1802) coincided very closely with this period. And his many retrospects describing spiritual and moral conditions in the men-of-war of his day are most explicit. But about Bible distribution by the NMBS at this time he is quite categorical: "When I served in the navy, we heard of no such exertions for our souls."[43]

REASSERTION YET INADEQUACY (1804–11)

The Rev. Marks suggests a simple explanation of the drastic discrepancy between supply and demand of Bibles at this juncture: "For want of funds, its [the Society's] hands had been tied up."[44] This is also the gist of the Society's own public statement in 1804, which goes on to offer three reasons for faltering finances: (1) Waning popularity during "successive intervals of peace" (a source of worry which was destined to become far more acute in the post-1815 era). (2) The decease of "many of the most liberal supporters" from the Society's earliest years. (3) The establishment earlier that year of the British and Foreign Bible Society (a fact which had already led some of the older Society's surviving friends "to conceive, that its continuance was less necessary," now that its particular objects were absorbed by the new, all-embracing organization).[45]

In 1803, the uneasy interval of peace flared into the Napoleonic War and, for two years, the Corsican's immense invasion preparations posed an alarming and very real threat.[46] Thus the first cause of anxiety for the Society was at least postponed. Still, the founding of the British and Foreign Bible Society (BFBS) in 1804 presented the NMBS with a challenge of

almost ultimatum force: either resignation (to absorption, possibly liquidation), or reassertion (of its own independent mission). Which was it to be?
The Society's published *Account* of 1804 was designed to leave no doubt as
to its decision.

In the first place, the NMBS was indisputably first on the scene
(having been instituted a quarter of a century earlier). In fact, the NMBS
remains the oldest Bible Society in the nation. In the England of 1779, there
existed no other institution "for the express and sole purpose of distributing
the Holy Scriptures."[47] (True, the full publicity potential of this fact did not
impress itself on the Society until later.[48] But there was already a keen
awareness of its antecedent status in relation to the BFBS.)

In the second place, the newcomer had revealed no wish to monopolize the scene. On the contrary, "the sole object" of the BFBS was, as
adopted on May 2, 1804, "to encourage a wider circulation of the Holy
Scriptures without note or comment." In so doing, the BFBS pledged to
"add its endeavours to those employed by other societies for circulating the
Scriptures." Obviously, supplementation, not usurpation, was to be the
watchword. In an essay published the previous year to promote these plans,
respectful mention is made of the earlier Society, observing that "as its
exertions are confined to the Army and Navy, the two plans will never
interfere." In appreciation of this policy, the committee of the NMBS could
soon note that "some very respectable and active members" of the BFBS
had lately thought it proper to assist the NMBS with voluntary contributions.[49]

Since its inception in 1779 and as the first in the field, the earlier
Society had simply borne the name of "The Bible Society." In consequence
of the foundation in 1804 of the far more extensive BFBS, the older institution realistically recognized the need for a name more expressive of its own
deliberately restricted purpose. That same year, it adopted the prefix "Naval
and Military."[50]

It would have been considerably less realistic had the committee
assumed that every doubt had been dispelled as to the relevance of the
Society as an independent institution. For several years to come, the NMBS
found it necessary to make official statements in response to persistent public
misgivings on this score.[51]

Was the Society's separatist stand entirely well-founded? So long as
the Society only offered the formal argument of having been first, there were
bound to be some for whom material considerations counted more. While
not wishing to trespass against tradition, they would nevertheless want valid
assurance on the score of efficacy. Finally, in their report of 1812, the
committee transmitted two "weighty reasons" to those who "are not satisfied
as to the necessity for the continuance of a separate society:" (1) Greater
aggregate support—Amalgamation might mean jeopardizing many "bene-

factors who do not unite with institutions engaged in the distribution of the Scriptures to other classes of society;" (2) Greater potential outreach. Must not the efforts of the Society elicit a warmer response from sailors and soldiers who, in the midst of danger and disease far from their native shores, are reminded "that there is a distinct Society of their Countrymen at home, peculiarly alive to their religious interests, and providing for *them exclusively* the best source of instruction and consolation?"[52] Here was genuine psychological insight, and appreciation of particular sensitivity to special attention, born of prolonged deprivation and neglect. (Within a few years, a corresponding compensatory mechanism was to provide one of the strongest arguments in favor of sanctuaries and servants of the Lord distinctly set apart for seafarers.)[53]

Unwillingness to risk alienating substantial supporters of the Society was understandable in 1812, but hardly relevant in 1804. Receipts from subscriptions and donations in 1804 amounted to £183.13s.10d. The number of naval or army officers appearing on the list of contributors totalled two.[54] Clearly, conditions were critical. However, the Society doggedly refused to "give up the ship." And although records are still sparse, they do indicate some subsequent improvement in the average annual distribution of Bibles and New Testaments (from 2,000 in 1794-1804 to 3,300 in 1804-10).[55]

Nevertheless, it might well have been said, "But what are they among so many?" The demand, expressed in forces in the field and on the ocean, was staggering. True, insofar as the navy was concerned, Nelson's epic victory off Cape Trafalgar in 1805 seemed to seal any hopes Napoleon might have had of ever reviving his invasion plans. But for Britain, *maintenance* of her mastery of the sea was equally vital. As the war settled into a grueling trial of endurance between land and sea power, the navy was needed to counter the Continental System, enforce a blockade stretching from the Baltic to the Mediterranean, safeguard Britain's own far-flung trade and overseas life-lines, and secure supplies for diversionary European expeditions (the Peninsular campaign, launched in 1808, and the abortive Walcheren attempt of 1809). Later, the War of 1812 with America was to add to the pressure. Small wonder, then, that never before had Britain had so many of her sons serving her forces at sea.[56]

It would be wrong to suppose that the spiritual nurture of these seamen was restricted to the bounty of the NMBS.[57] However, the overall impression—especially as regards Scripture distribution—was one of serious inadequacy. This situation called for considerable restraint on the part of the BFBS not to enter bodily into the breach. With annual receipts of well over £5,000 (even before the auxiliary system caused income to soar after 1809), there were certainly the means to pursue the Society's published object, and "add its endeavours to those employed by others" serving the Royal Navy.[58]

Instead of supplementing the NMBS distribution to men-of-war in general, however, the BFBS chose to concentrate its early naval endeavors on particular categories.

Foreign prisoners of war, many of whom were seamen, were frequently jammed into old hulks anchored in naval harbors around the coast. The first captives, survivors from the shattered Franco-Spanish fleet at Trafalgar, had barely been brought aboard their dismal dungeons when the committee of the BFBS took up the question of what could be done for them—two days before Christmas, 1805. The French and Spanish New Testaments then voted were the first step in a rapidly expanding prisoner-of-war outreach which was to continue, with great effectiveness, throughout the war. Soon Dutch and Scandinavian seafarers, too, figured largely among the grateful recipients.)[59]

But this was not all. The navy also had charge of convict transports to Australia, the latest "solution" to Britain's overflowing jails, after the loss of her Transatlantic expedient. In 1808, 100 Bibles were gratuitously distributed to "Convicts, sailing for New South Wales." From then on, the BFBS continued providing involuntary emigrants with consolation from the Scriptures.[60] Two further forms of government vessels claimed the attention of the BFBS committee. In 1809, twenty *H.M. Revenue* Cutters, with a crew of 618, were supplied at the request of two inspecting commanders. And in 1809-10, 35 post office packets based on Falmouth were supplied.[61] The sick, maimed, or dying in naval and military hospitals were also included. Donations to these are recorded as early as 1808-09.[62]

The BFBS reported in 1808 that it had supplied its corresponding committee in Bengal with a stock of Scriptures "for sale or gratuitous distribution to the Army and Navy, and other poor Europeans."[63] (The adjective "other" is noteworthy.) But this was an exception justified by circumstances. Normally, the BFBS participated only indirectly, at this juncture, in general naval distribution. For example, Bibles in sheets were voted for use by the NMBS at cost price in 1808.[64] It seems to have been standard practice up to this time, that Scripture applications from naval commanders, if addressed to the BFBS, were forwarded to the NMBS for action.[65]

However, the BFBS report for 1809-10 gave fair warning that this Society was sensing an increased need for direct naval involvement. Included under the list of grants for the past year were: a sloop-of-war, the receiving ships at Greenock, a guardship at the Nore, servicemen at "Plymouth Dock" (or Devonport), and large numbers of soldiers and seamen at Portsmouth.[66] Finally, prompted (at least in part) by the concern of their Wesleyan colleague, the well-known bookseller and philanthropist Joseph Butterworth, the committee of the BFBS took a decisive step. On February 5, 1810, it was recorded:

> Resolved that Agents be appointed at all the principal Military and Naval Depots, for selling Bibles and Testaments to the Soldiers and Sailors at the Reduced prices, on the Account of this Society. That Messrs. Pritt, Reyner & Steven be a Sub Committee to enquire for suitable Agents and to Report thereon. . . ."[67]

The continuing inability of the NMBS to cope with manifest needs had compelled the BFBS to revise its policy of relative passivity. However, it seems reasonable to assume that their active entry into general naval distribution was not envisaged as a permanent measure.[68] Rather, the ultimate objective appears to have been to provoke the self-styled specialists to more effective action. If this interpretation is correct, developments during the next half decade were to prove the plan abundantly successful. The year 1811 was to mark a turning point in the history of the NMBS.

RESURGENCE AND CONSOLIDATION (1811–15)

At all events, the BFBS was apparently anxious to maintain relations of mutual goodwill with the older Society. Only little more than a year had elapsed since the launching of the depot agency plan when William Henry Hoare, a well-known Fleet Street banker, submitted a paper to the committee of the BFBS on May 20, 1811, "on the subject of supplying the Army and Navy more generally with Bibles and Testaments." Mr. Hoare, one of those of the original BFBS committee who simultaneously supported the MNBS, had also presented his paper to the latter Society. The BFBS appointed him, together with the members of the 1810 Sub-Committee, "to confer with the Naval and Military Bible Society on the best means for effecting the above object."[69]

This deputation attended a special general meeting of the NMBS on May 23, 1811, at which the means of a more general Scripture supply in the forces underwent "much discussion." In reporting back to the BFBS, the deputation stated that they had:

> . . .offered such suggestions as appeared to them likely to forward the end mutually proposed by the two Societies, and tendered to the Naval & Military Bible Society every degree of friendly cooperation on the part of the British & Foreign Bible Society, it being understood on both sides that the two Societies were to continue to act independently of each other excepting so far as related to an amicable communication between them on points

relating to that object which they have in common.[70]

No details of the exact nature of the "suggestions" made by the BFBS deputation at this special general meeting have been discovered. But the younger society was certainly in a strong position to offer advice. Within seven years, the vitality of the BFBS had amazed all Christendom, and fostered a widespread spirit of emulation. An examination of the report issued by the NMBS for the year 1811-12 reveals that the new measures adopted since that meeting in 1811 were all such as had proved their worth in the brief life of the BFBS.

First among these new moves was a reassessment of actual needs. A special committee, appointed at the 1811 meeting, issued a circular letter dated "Committee Room, 190, Picadilly, July, 1811," and addressed to all officers commanding ships or regiments on home stations. Here, their assistance was requested in affording information on the following points:

1st. The number of Men under your command who can read.
2nd. The number who at present possess either Bibles or Testaments.
3rd. The further number of Bibles or Testaments with which you would wish the men under your commmand to be supplied, in consequence of a desire to that effect *actually expressed* by the individuals.[71]

In these early years of the rapidly spreading Bible Society Movement, statistical inquiries in the field, in both the Old World and the New, were repeatedly confounding optimistic assumptions as to how many possessed the Scriptures, or were able to read them if they obtained them.[72] The NMBS inquiry proved no exception. Results were overwhelming. Out of 31,340 sailors and soldiers reported capable of reading, only 5,465 had either a Bible or New Testament. 21,420 men (more than four out of five, based on the balance) made individual requests. This figure had increased to 26,327 by the date of publication. The committee was forced to admit their "utter inability" to supply other than such ships and regiments as were altogether or almost without a single Bible ("as several were"). A general compliance would have required ten times the Society's current average income of little more than £500 per annum. And so far only the needs of home stations had been taken into account.[73] (At home and abroad, it was estimated that Britain had, at this time, 560,000 men under arms.)[74]

For the purpose of this study, it is significant that approximately two thirds of the individual requests for Scriptures came from sailors. Unfortunately, the statistics do not show the total number of servicemen approached, nor the relative proportion of sailors and soldiers among them. However, the committee found reason to emphasize the fact that this "anxious desire to be possessed of the Holy Scriptures" had been imparted "amidst all the impediments to religion attending a life engaged in warfare, especially in the navy. . . ."[75]

The second measure adopted by the NMBS in 1811 was spurred by the results of the first. There was, "in this extremity," an obvious need for a reorganization of promotional methods. It was at once recognized that the traditional method of individual solicitation of donations and subscriptions, however necessary, would never suffice. a "General Address" was therefore prepared and sent to clergymen and ministers throughout the kingdom. The purpose was a special appeal for congregational collections to be read, if possible, from the pulpit on the day appointed for a general fast on February 5, 1812. The committee was astounded by the result. The total £2,042.16s.4½d., was "far exceeding the produce of any former effort of this kind."[76] For three years, as long as the critical final phase of the war offered widespread and powerful motivation, annual congregational appeals continued to provide the Society's principal source of income.[77]

In this case, such success would have been virtually impossible without due regard to public relations, especially as concerned the Established Church. The Society was still (as it has always remained) basically nondenominational. Church Evangelicals had, however, taken active part since its inception.[78] The "Clapham Sect," which had taken the new, broader Bible Society under their aegis in 1804, remained loyal supporters of their predecessor.[79] It was in complete conformity with their spiritual strategy when the sanction of influential prelates was enlisted on behalf of the NMBS. This would, as in the case of the BFBS, accomplished "that decided connection with the Established Church, which was a condition essential to the prosperity of the project."[80] The Archbishop of Canterbury appears as president as early as in the period of the 1806 Account. In 1811-12, the Bishop of London was enlisted as a vice president and expressly endorsed the 1812 *Address*. By 1818, the Society's Church patronage counted two archbishops and eight bishops.[81] Clearly, such strong commendation by the National Church was calculated to broaden both the base of public support and the Society's outreach in the nation's armed forces.

This emphasis on ecclesiastical endorsement was accompanied by a corresponding drive for secular patronage. These efforts met with such signal success that when meeting on the eve of Waterloo, the Society could report that it now possessed "almost without exception, the patronage and support of the distinguished Personages at the head of the several departments of the state in immediate connection with the Army and Navy . . . , together with that of other Noblemen and Gentlemen of the highest respectability in the community."[82] The 1815 list of officers of the Society proves this to have been no exaggeration.[83] Royal recognition was, by 1818, accorded by four princes, simultaneously serving as Patron and Vice Patrons.[84]

Under the theme "reorganization of promotional methods," brief mention must also be made of the advent of the auxiliary society system. Again, the example of the BFBS is discernible. Its introduction of this form of decentralization of initiative and support in 1809-10 rapidly resulted in an astonishing multiplication of revenue.[85] However, in the case of the NMBS, the auxiliary method only really gathered momentum in the 1820's. After an unsuccessful attempt in 1815 to form "Local Committees" closely tied to the parent society, Scotland showed the way, with its Glasgow "Auxiliary Society" and "Female Association," both founded in 1817.[86]

Reverting again to the question of areas in which renewal is noticeable in the post-1811 history of the NMBS, a third group of such measures concerns revision of the Society's Scripture distribution policy. Changes ensued as regards the object, the channels and the terms of distribution.

The only alterations in the Society's object of distribution after 1811 were of a technical nature. In order to obviate complaints sometimes received "respecting the smallness of print for common readers, and especially on board ship," steps were taken after that date to ensure supplies of Bibles and Testaments "of a good size and type for the use of the Navy and the Hospitals" (where, under current conditions, reading light was frequently poor). Likewise, arrangements were made to render copies of Scripture "much less liable to injury, when stowed in the Seaman's chest," by making certain improvements in the binding and by adding clasps.[87]

However, no alteration in principle was ever permitted regarding the object of the Society's distribution. This continued to be solely "the Holy Scriptures, without note or comment."[88] The exclusive status thereby accorded the Scriptures is, in the first place, evidence of faith in the efficacy of the Word as the primary means of grace. In pleading the Society's cause, successive committees constantly stressed the circulation of the Scriptures as the most effective method of dealing with both moral laxity and unpreparedness for death among sailors and soldiers.[89] In the second place, a restriction to Scripture only, was regarded as an absolute condition for broad, multi-denominational support. Nor can it be doubted that the inclusion of tracts, commentaries, homilies or prayer books in the distribution of the Society would, while meeting with the approval of some, have completely alienated others.[90]

True, when the first package of Bibles was issued by the infant Society from the vestry of West Street Chapel, "a large number of religious tracts" was, in actual fact, sent with them.[91] However, this was, according to one of the founders, a unique exception. Henceforth, the sole object of distribution was the Holy Scriptures. Had it been otherwise, the NMBS would have forfeited its claim to being "The First Bible Society"—in the nation.[92]

To an institution so wholly concerned with one single aim, the question of the most effective channels of distribution was vital. Rapid response to legitimate demands was, in 1811, still severely hampered by a slow-moving, over-centralized structure. The appointment of separate gratuitous secretaries for the Naval and Military Departments in 1811-12 achieved at least some differentiation. (Captain C.M. Fabian became the first Naval Secretary in 1821.) But much was yet to be desired. Some improvement was made by doubling the number of Bible depots at naval and military stations, thus reaching fourteen by 1812. All were on the coast, near the sea. In charge of them were gratuitous agents (a medley of mostly ministers and tradesmen).[93]

In 1814, the committee also recorded their "peculiar gratitude" for the exertions of some "female Correspondents" who, in keeping with the temper of the times, remained discreetly anonymous.[94] Despite this, the committee complained (in 1815) of "the almost insurmountable difficulties" encountered in ensuring a satisfactory supply to ships whose movements were so unpredictable.[95] With time, the emerging auxiliary societies also established depots and undertook responsibilty for local needs.

On the whole, the elaborate system whereby "applications" for Scriptures were "received" gives an inevitably static impression.[96] The day of the "Colporteur" had not yet dawned, and anyway, naval restrictions of access had to be respected. On the other hand, the changing post-war pattern of terms of distribution displayed a slightly more dynamic trend. In 1811, the Committee was "empowered to sell Bibles at reduced prices, as well as to distribute them gratuitously."[97] Before then, there is no indication that the gratuitous basis of Scripture distribution was even questioned. The Report for 1813-14 records, with satisfaction, "occasional Contributions of one day's pay from Ship's Companies on their being paid off."[98]

By now it was becoming generally appreciated in the NMBS, as in the BFBS, "that sale, at however reduced a price, was invariably to be preferred to gratuitous donation."[99] First, there were the spiritual advantages. A sailor or soldier who had paid for his own Bible or New Testament would be more likely to read it and help in spreading it.[100] Secondly, there were obvious financial advantages involved.[101] There was, however, never any question of "profit." Whereas a subscriber to the Society could obtain Scriptures at cost price, a special "reduced price" applied to the underpaid serviceman (the Society's funds bearing the deficit).[102]

There were, on the other hand, still cases where there was no question of any purchase-by-preference rule. In 1815, the Society confirmed that it would continue on a gratuitous basis, to deposit Bibles and Testaments "permanently in such situations as would render them at all times accessible to large numbers of Sailors and Soldiers at their leisure hours." This would include crew's quarters on board and wards in naval hospitals.[103]

The post-1811 period brought no immediate policy changes regarding the field of distribution. This remained basically the same until 1825: "Sailors and Soldiers . . . in the British Navy and Army."[104] Two proposals, both from Scotland, involving a significant extension of the maritime field, were however, publicized before that year.[105]

AN ASSESSMENT

After the close of the Napoleonic War, a small segment of the missionary minded Christian public on both sides of the Atlantic began to "discover" the seaman, in his merchant as well as his naval role. Organizational consequenses were soon to follow. To what extent had the NMBS— directly or indirectly—contributed? In order to assess this, the following are two of the questions which naturally pose themselves.

On the one hand, how far had they actually gone to meet the demand? The sole declared object of the NMBS being like that of the BFBS—expressed in strictly quantitative terms—it should have been a relatively simple matter to establish a rough ratio between potential demand and actual supply.[106] However, as the committee of the NMBS points out:

> In bodies so uncertain in their movements and so fluctuating in their numbers, as the Military Establishments of this country, it would be difficult, if not impossible, to ascertain the precise difference which at any given time exists between the number of men in employment and the quantity of the Scriptures in actual circulation.[107]

Nevertheless, available statistics do provide interesting information, especially regarding trends. Here too, the year 1811 marks the turning point. In 1810-11, the annual number of Bibles and Testaments issued to both services had fallen to 1,873. After the 1811-12 congregational collections had boosted the Society's flagging finances, the 1812-13 total reached a record 7,254. Of these, 1,820 went to naval ships and hospitals. (Up to 1818-19, the total Scripture issue remained above 9,000 per annum: of these, over 2,500 copies annually were sent on board naval ships and packets.)[108] The number of men voted for the Royal Navy in 1810 is given as 145,000 for 976 ships, of which 212 in ordinary. These figures do not alter appreciably before the end of the war. By 1818, however, the peace establishment voted had been run down to a fairly stable 20,000 men. These statistics show how the first years of peace were characterized by a marked improvement of the Scripture to manpower ratio.[109]

On the other hand, what beneficial results may reasonably be attributed to these activities? When the BFBS deputation, which had been appointed to confer with the NMBS in 1811, reported back concerning their lengthy discussions, they ventured to trust that "no unconsiderable good would result."[110] Were such hopes justified—in so far as results could be registered? Quite apart from inevitable human limitations in assessing what would be seen as the work of the Spirit, the NMBS recognized that opportunities of ascertaining "beneficial effects" resulting from the distribution of the Scriptures among sailors were necessarily restricted.[111] Such opportunities did, nevertheless, present themselves. To this, a series of extracts of correspondence from naval officers chaplains, and others bear manifest witness in the appendices of the Society's Reports from 1811 on. Moreover, there are several such allusions in the text of the reports, and especially in the recorded speeches of invited speakers at the Society's anniversary meetings. This material leaves an impression of astonishing, almost universal avidity for possession of the printed Word in the British Navy of the late Napoleonic War era, coupled with increasing evidence of an elevation of moral tone wherever it was read.[112]

These sources, as supplemented by collateral evidence, merit closer examination. They could provide more than purely chronological justification for giving the Naval and Military Bible Society first and honorable mention in a history of seamen's missions.

Chapter 4

The New Scene: Spiritual Stirrings in the Napoleonic War Navy

EVIDENCE OF CHANGE: BEFORE AND AFTER AMIENS

Two of the most articulate observers of the spiritual state of the "old school" British Navy leave no room for illusions. Both Richard Marks and George Charles Smith were serving in different ships of war around the close of the eighteenth century. "You, Sir," says the former—addressing His Royal Highness, the Duke of Gloucester, in the chair of the NMBS 1820 Anniversary— "can have no conception of the real state of things under what is thus called the old school. . . . I believe for more than three years after I entered the Navy [in 1797] I never saw one copy of the Holy Scriptures, and I do not recollect meeting with one character who even pretended to fear or love God. . . ."[113] On another occasion, the former naval lieutenant sums up the general attitude which he, too, then shared, in the following uncompromising manner:

> Many a seaman and many an officer scarcely ever gave eternity one thought. It was matter of doubt with us, whether the soul outlived the body; at all events, most of us endeavoured to persuade ourselves that we were not to be judged and dealt with as other men, but that, as a matter of course, all *our* troubles would end with the present life. The grand aim of all ranks then at sea was to forget a future judgment, to expend life in the indulgences of the flesh and of the mind, to brave death with brutal unconcern, and to dread nothing so much as thinking, and reading, and praying.[114]

The Rev. G.C. Smith found frequent occasion—through the years— to revert to the way in which, during the war of the French Revolution,

Lord James Gambier, Admiral of the
Fleet and pioneer advocate of the
Seamen's Cause. (Courtesy: British
Library.)

"darkness covered nearly the whole navy."[115] Even at the close of his long
life, he vividly recalls conditions on board his own ship just prior to the Battle
of Copenhagen, 1801: "We had no bibles, and no religious book or tracts
given to us before we left England, and no minister or religious man came on
board before we left Yarmouth to warn us, and direct us to the Lord Jesus
Christ for salvation if we should be killed...." Referring to the gross
spiritual ignorance prevalent among all ranks, he adds, "We were told it was
all right fighting for king and country, and God was merciful to sailors. Such
was the state of thousands in our fleet...."[116]

The general tenor of such statements is amply affirmed by numerous
naval officers speaking at post-war seamen's mission anniversaries.[117]
"Nevertheless," as the Rev. G.C. Smith was the first to concede, "God left
himself not without a witness in the darkest period...." Most prominent by
far, among exceptions to the general rule, was Captain James Gambier,
R.N.[118]

Born in 1756, of Norman-Huguenot stock, Gambier's naval career
commenced at the early age of 11. As an officer, he strove with "Luther-like
firmness" to practice those evangelical principles which he warmly embraced.
Under his command, largely dormant naval regulations prohibiting profanity
and promoting public prayers on shipboard were revived and systematically
enforced. Such notions were not calculated to win widespread approval in
the navy of the day. When he took over the *Defence,* 74, at the outbreak of
hostilities in 1793, it was freely questioned by colleagues whether what then
had become notorious as "a praying ship" could conceivably be counted on
as "a fighting ship."

Such doubts were put to shame—dramatically and convincingly—the following year. Serving under Earl Howe in the Battle of the Glorious First of June, Gambier achieved nation-wide fame as the first to cut the enemy's line, fighting with dogged fury under the galling fire of Frenchmen on all sides. At the end of the action, the *Defence,* heavily damaged, all her masts shot away, was hailed by Captain Pakenham of the *Invincible,* calling to his colleague across the waves with characteristic Irish wit: "I see you've been knocked about a good deal: never mind, Jimmy, whom the Lord loveth, he chasteneth." (Later, this friendly gibe was to provide useful ammunition in combating professional prejudice against religion in the navy.)[119]

Promoted five years afterwards to flag rank, Admiral Gambier figured prominently in public life for many years. During his long connection with the Board of Admiralty, Gambier was in command of the navy forces which reduced Copenhagen and carried off the Danish fleet in 1807 (an event which earned him a peerage), he was in command of the Channel Fleet at the controversial Battle of Basque Roads in 1809, and he was at the head of the British commission which negotiated the Treaty of Ghent with the USA in 1814. Lord Gambier's public perseverance in Christian witness, as high-ranking naval officer in exactly that era, would be reason enough to place him in the van of seamen's mission pioneers. But as an unashamedly Evangelical Churchman, he was destined to play a unique role in the post-war establishment of the first organized British seamen's mission societies. Lord Gambier's wholehearted patronage and active chairmanship of successive public meetings—until shortly before his death in 1833—were to give to the Seamen's Cause invaluable prestige and encouragement during its struggling start in the metropolis.[120]

Although Gambier's dauntless adherence to evangelical tenets was quite exceptional in the pre-Amiens navy, this does not mean that other naval commanders were always adverse to every aspect of the Christian faith. On the contrary, several showed—by both precept and practice—faith in divine providence and concern for divine service. Thus, we find that gigantic Scotsman, Admiral Duncan, faced in 1797 with the mutiny of all his ships save two, exhorting his remaining men to trust in "allwise Providence," and pray "that almighty God may keep us in the right way of thinking." In October that same year, as the British and Dutch fleets took up position off Camperdown, he assembled his officers on deck, knelt down, committed their cause, their families and themselves to God, rose up, and gave orders to attack.[121]

Admiral Nelson seems to have shown—both before and after his much-debated estrangement from his wife—a sincere sense of dependence on his Maker. As the *Victory* carried him to his last encounter, he left a spiritual legacy in the form of a personal prayer of commitment to God.[122]

Other instances might be quoted. But despite such examples of faith in the providence of a Creator God, one searches almost in vain for records of concern among any ranks for the Gospel of salvation through faith in the atonement of his Son. In that sense, there seems to have been good ground for Gambier's own summary of the spiritual status of the pre-1803 navy: "Among seamen religion was hardly a word that they understood."[123]

Against this bleak background, developments during the Napoleonic War present a dramatic difference. Contrasting with conditions in the pre-Amiens armed forces, the Rev. G.C. Smith comments on how, during the ensuing Napoleonic War, "religion shone forth with primitive simplicity, splendour and power among our maritime and military population." Whereas seamen in particular had, at the outset of the preceding war, come to be called "the most abandoned of men," there were, on board King's ships in the late war, "many who dared to serve the Lord. . . ."[124] By this he meant such as gave evidence of the current evangelical interpretation of personal conversion.

Here, statistics would, of course, be impossible to obtain. But the fact that a profound spiritual and moral transformation took place in the lives of a noticeable number of officers and men in the Napoleonic War navy is beyond dispute. For many years to come, this was to be the perennial theme of numerous naval officers speaking from personal observation at public meetings of the NMBS, as well as other societies seeking to promote the spiritual welfare of seamen. To some of these statements there will shortly be occasion to refer in more detail.[125]

Meanwhile, it seems natural to pose the question: to which cause or causes was this spiritual awakening in the British Navy primarily due? Did such influences as can be traced emanate principally from "official" quarters, or from various forms of private initiative?

NAVAL CHAPLAINCY DURING THE FRENCH WARS (1793-1815)

In principle, the official provision of permanent pastoral care by ministers of religion on shipboard would seem sufficient grounds for substantial spiritual returns. In practice, this would be conditional upon at least two factors—adequacy of supply and quality of service. What was the position on these two all-important scores during the French Wars?

With regard to chaplaincy supply, by 1790 Admiralty Regulations did, it is true, call for one chaplain per fifth-rate, or higher, in commission. But whereas it was unthinkable for a ship of war to be commissioned without a surgeon or a purser, it was the rare exception rather than the rule to find them accompanied by their clerical fellow civilian officer. In fact, even as late as 1814, when there were 713 ships in commission, only 58 chaplains appear on the official Navy List, and of these only 31 were actually in ships. In other words, the favored few (mainly 74's) which carried a sea-going chaplain, were precisely one in 23.[126] It is, therefore, no surprise that not only men like Richard Marks and G.C. Smith, but many more of those who have left records of their service in the war-time navy, comment on the complete absence of an officially appointed naval chaplain on board for years on end.[127]

On the score of quality of service, the widely publicized judgment of a fellow Anglican clergyman some sixty years later seems, at first glance, harsh and categorical:

> Towards the end of the last century and the beginning of the present, one great obstacle to religious progress in both services was, not alone a careless body of Chaplains, but, in some instances, of godless and wicked men, who in no sense felt the responsibility of their office.
>
> In many cases the Chaplains considered their duties completed on going through the formalities of Divine service, and adding thereto a written moral essay, without one word of the Gospel. This was supposed to compose the major portion of a week's duty, which was oftentimes interspersed with . . . drinking in the mess and ward rooms, and the whole occasionally seasoned with oaths and cursing.
>
> What could be expected from the ministrations of such a class of Clergymen . . . ?[128]

The author hastens to assure his readers of "the happy contrast which the present [1861] state of the Navy and Army exhibits in this respect, after many years of gradual reform."[129] But was this general condemnation of their predecessors justified? Contemporary sources show that the scene afloat cannot have been uniformly dark.

In a published farewell letter to his former shipmates, a chaplain who served during the whole of the French Revolutionary War thinks with gratitude of the consistent "kindness and civility" of both officers and crew, recalls times spent "in the sickbay or between the hammocks of the wounded," and concludes with a forthright appeal to his friends on shipboard not to forfeit their immortal destiny, but shun the shoals of temptation—such as profanity, drunkenness and debauchery.[130] Whatever temptations chaplains themselves might be exposed to, at least that of indolence would be reduced where (as often) secretarial and educational duties were added to the strictly pastoral.[131] During the French Wars, as previously, there are stirring exam-

A contemporary print of "church" on board a British
man-of-war during the French Wars around the turn of the
19th century. (Courtesy: British Library.)

ples of chaplains bodily identifying with the men, in the face of both the
violence of the enemy and the dangers of the deep.[132]

It would be gross injustice to deny all long-term spiritual significance of the ministry of naval chaplains of this period. Nor would it be
correct to assume that there were no cases of conspicuous conversion directly
attributable to them. The testimonies of two naval officers, alluding to their
own wartime experiences at subsequent public meetings, may serve as
examples. Captain Packenham quotes the case of a faithful Evangelical
clergyman who left a comfortable "living" in order to serve as chaplain on a
man-of-war. Here he preached usually three times a day. And such were his
exertions that two successive captains, profoundly impressed by the exemplary conduct of his converts, were forced to concede: "The Methodists are
the best men, after all."[133] Likewise, Lieutenant J.F. Arnold provides a
pertinent example of the success of a "pious Chaplain" on the *Repulse*—his
own conversion.[134]

Nevertheless, it would be idle to argue that the general standard of
service by naval chaplains of the French Wars was anywhere near satisfactory. True, evidence that much was amiss is not immediately apparent from
the entries in the navy's "Black Book." From 1790 to 1805, only six
chaplains are listed as dismissed from the service for alleged scandalous
behavior (certainly no sensational figure in times when clerical lassitude was
no rarity ashore).[135] More may be surmised from such a document as the

Miscellaneous Essays of Alexander Duncan, one-time chaplain with Admiral Duncan in the Battle of Camperdown. Dealing with the responsibilities of naval chaplains, he found conditions among his colleagues such as to warrant the following admonition:

> It is not enough to read prayers and to preach with elegance and grace to his audience on the Lord's Day, if he takes the name of God in vain, makes too free with his cup and employs much of his leisure hours through the week with cards and dice. . . .[136]

Reports to the Admiralty from highly respected naval commanders about the same period throw revealing and unflattering light on the conduct of "roué parsons who really should not hold their situations" (to use Lord St. Vincent's words).[137] A rare literary representative of the lower deck, Robert Hay (a Presbyterian), has recorded his reactions against the chaplain of the *Culloden,* on which he went to sea in 1804. His charges are on the scores of indolence, discrimination and formalism.[138] A veteran of Trafalgar, now retired after 23 years in the service, had the following to say, on entering the vestry (after the service) at the new Mariners' Church in London, some ten years after the war:

> This was the first time he had been in any place of worship, but one, for these seventeen years. He confessed he was utterly unacquainted with every thing relative to religion, and what he had seen in Chaplains [during his seafaring years] was not at all calculated to inspire him with any reverence for it, but quite the reverse. For his own part, he was obliged as Boatswain to swear so much, that when the hands were turned up to church, where a Chaplain was, he never attended himself for that reason.[139]

In a series of dialogues between British seamen in the 1803-15 navy, particularly caustic comments are made by a boisterous boatswain's mate on the only type of chaplain he had encountered. His views are significant because the publication, commenced in 1812 and based on eye-witness accounts, quickly achieved an amazing circulation and influence:

> I've served my country in the navy 15 years, and never saw a chaplain yet who said, "Bob, repent, and cry for mercy!" Seldom have we ever had one in the . . . , and when we had, he was like a chaplain at Guernsey, the soldiers told me of when I was sitting in the sternsheets as cockswain of the captain's gig.—"He preaches," says one, "52 sermons every year from this text—Soldiers, be content with your wages!" I love good old king George! and I have bled for my country: I want no chaplain to spin out a long story about that; I know my duty in the fore-top a great deal better than he can tell me; so I want none of his palaver there: and as for thieving, and obedience to my officers, and all such things, I hear

enough of that from the articles of war every time a poor fellow's spread out on the hatchway grating to get an odd dozen. I want to know, if I have a soul, and am not like the cook's dog, that dies and there's an end of it, I want to know how I am to be saved, and what's to become of my soul after the sharks have finished my body. Poor Jack what a state he's in on board a man-of-war: the devil within him . . . and the chaplain, like a fair-weather sailor . . . pockets 2d. a head; gabbles away some Oxford gibberish, about commodore Plato and old admiral Socrates, . . . and laughs to think he's done his duty.[140]

A twentieth-century professor of history at the Royal Naval College, Greenwich, sums up the situation at this period by saying that not only were parsons rarities afloat, but good ones were almost nonexistent, tending to be among "the dregs" of the clerical profession. At best, they could, it seems, only be characterized as "a mixed bag."[141] At all events, there appears to be ample reason to ask for underlying causes. Why was the naval chaplaincy of the French Wars period so unimpressively represented? Some clue may be provided by the following two facts.

In the first place, the policy of admission was one of ecclesiastical exclusiveness. Access to naval chaplaincy was restricted to the National Church.[142] Whatever plausible arguments might be advanced in justification of this policy, it had at least two inescapable consequences. On the one hand, the standard of naval chaplains would be largely determined by the degree of clerical quality available in the Church of England as such. As noted, the latter was at a notoriously low ebb in the eighteenth century.[143] On the other hand, officers and men of the navy were automatically deprived of chaplaincy services, however beneficial, from Methodist and Nonconformist quarters. Apart from the institutionalized discrimination involved, this would inevitably isolate existing Church chaplaincy services from needful supplementation. (For example, available records of sermon themes indicate that Anglican preaching in the navy of that era was largely *legalistic* in emphasis.)[144]

In the second place, adverse conditions of service presented a formidable impediment to improvement. By tradition, the British naval chaplain was bereft of basic employment requirements. On the one hand, he had never had the benefit of effective ecclesiastical supervision. True, Samuel Pepys had made the approval of the Primate—or (in practice) the Bishop of London—a condition of appointment. But although the latter did attempt to fill the breach, it was physically impossible for him to meet the continuing need for surveillance and support.[145] On the other hand, the naval chaplain had for generations been the victim of a degrading and demoralizing shipboard status.

Despite the level of his education and responsibilities, the pay itself was still wretched, and the manner of payment humiliating—frequently fraudulent. In matters of rank and social recognition, a similarly nebulous position prevailed. Though officially a "warrant officer," his acceptance as such, his personal welfare, and indeed his opportunities of exercising his primary office on board were entirely at the whim and fancy of whosoever happened to be the commanding officer.[147] The "padre" has always eschewed rank for its own sake. But with service conditions so abjectly discouraging, instead of providing some compensation for privations and hazards inherent in sea service, the wonder is not that the quality of candidates was questioned, but that any offered for duty at all, even as a "last resort."

At length, in 1812, a brighter day dawned for the British naval chaplain. By Orders in Council, which have since become known as "the Chaplain's Charter," vast improvements were introduced in areas of salary and status. Also, a permanent ecclesiastical supervision was established. The office of "Chaplain-General of the Navy" was combined with that of "Chaplain-General of the Army," already held by Archdeacon John Owen. Naval chaplaincy was still strictly a Church of England monopoly. But, as such, it was at least given a fairer opportunity of functioning effectively. A "constant correspondence" was introduced with every chaplain in the Royal Navy. And, a program of distribution of select religious literature was actively sponsored.[148]

Prior to 1812, the gradual improvement in the general spiritual and moral tone of the Established Church was also becoming evident among naval chaplains.[149] Moreover, the 1812 reforms undoubtedly meant a material contribution toward higher standards. But by then the war was nearly over. And as post-war evidence could attest, it took time to make up the leeway.[150] While it would be wrong, therefore, to ignore the potential for good which naval chaplains represented, their numbers were nevertheless too limited and their efforts too constrained for them to have been a really major factor in promoting a spiritual awakening in the British Navy of the War of 1803-15.

DISTRIBUTION OF RELIGIOUS LITERATURE IN THE WARTIME BRITISH NAVY

In the early years of the Napoleonic War, voluntary corporate measures, with a bearing on the spiritual benefit of seafarers, were indeed few and far between. But in one particular area—that of the maritime distribution of religious literary media—the first crumbs of spiritual bread had long since been deliberately cast upon the waters. Among the pioneers in this field, the Naval and Military Bible Society occupies the unique position of being the only voluntary agency specifically designed for seamen. True, prior to the 1811 rehabilitation measures, the Society's activities were manifestly inadequate.[151] Nevertheless, the paucity of extant records of demonstrable results must not lead to underestimation of the cumulative effect of a quarter-century of Scripture circulation in the British Navy. By 1804, a total of 43,000 Bibles and New Testaments had been distributed to servicemen, including the crews of 240 ships of war.[152] Such efforts cannot have left that navy unmarked.

By the close of 1810, a further 20,000 copies of Scripture had been issued to seamen and soldiers.[153] And from 1811 on, the far more satisfactory records of activities indicate an amazing eagerness, in the navy of the day, to be supplied with the written Word. Undoubtedly, the 1811 circular to naval and military commanders on home stations meant much in making needs manifest, not only to the Society but, where necessary, to the men themselves.[154] However, such needs must have been at least latently pre-existent.

A scrutiny of the many extracts of correspondence appended to the Society's *Reports* from the four final war years sheds interesting light on various aspects of this avidity for the Scriptures among naval seamen.[155] Several such extracts of correspondence are from commanders of vessels. Some seem spontaneous: the writer referring perhaps to seeing himself as responsible for "immortal souls" committed to his care, and likely to pass their lives "in hourly jeopardy."[156] Others are in response to a specific initiative from the Society. There is evidence that a commander, thus placed in a position of unexpected spiritual trust, might be "led to consider the inconsistency of giving a book to others, with a view to their benefit, which he practically disregarded himself."[157]

Not infrequently, a naval commander would, in his request for copies of Scripture, refer to "the most happy effects" he himself had already observed of such distribution among seamen under his command.[158] It would, however, be quite erroneous to assume that the demand for Scripture supply in the navy of the Napoleonic War was mainly on the part of commanders primarily concerned about side-effects, such as the counteraction of intemperance and insubordination in their crews. There is striking evidence of genuine and independent interest among the men themselves. Some would, for example, allot a day's pay, or otherwise make donations from their miserable mites, to the Society's funds. Others might lose all in shipwreck, yet make sure they salvaged their Bibles.[159]

The efforts of the NMBS, intensified as they were from 1811 on, were by no means the only form of religious literary outreach in the navy of this period. The supplementary naval activities of the British and Foreign Bible Society have already been noted.[160] Of major importance, however, was distribution during the French Wars by the Society for Promoting Christian Knowledge. With its close connection with the National Church, and its long-standing tradition of service to the Royal Navy, this Society was, even in the early 1790's, receiving frequent applications from naval commanders for gratuitous consignments of books. The Society's minute-books record how the committee itself dealt with each individual request according to a rough quota system based on the ship's complement. Grants would include, besides a more limited supply of Bibles and Books of Common Prayer, several Psalters and generally copious stocks of carefully selected religious tracts. The favorite, by far, was still Woodward's *Seaman's Monitor.* (A few *Maxims for the Poor* were also deemed a most appropriate item.) Occasionally, books for ship schools were provided.[161] Among SPCK applicants were such celebrities as Sir Edward Pellew (later Lord Exmouth, who also joined the Society), and Nelson himself (who made a personal practice of soliciting grants from the Society to supply successive ships under his command).[162]

Naval chaplains, too, figured occasionally among SPCK correspondents during the war of 1793-1802. However, the appointment in 1812 of Archdeacon John Owen as Chaplain-General of the Navy provided them with fresh stimulus and, indeed, appeared to open up a new chapter in official responsibility for the supply of religious literature to naval personnel. While accepting a vice presidency in the NMBS,[163] Owen made it quite clear where his churchman's heart belonged. Working in close cooperation with the SPCK, in both his naval and military capacity, he could, in March 1812, convey to the Committee news of a remarkable grant of £1,500 by the Admiralty, "for the purpose of supplying his Majesty's Ships with Bibles, Testaments, & prayer Books." It was expressly left to Owen to communicate with the SPCK "as to the best method of distribution."

The grant (for 1812-13) was repeated the following year (for 1813-14) before being diminished, and disappearing again in 1817.[164] As far as it went, the gesture was undoubtedly a financial relief for the SPCK. As regards methods of distribution, however, the experiment of treating Bibles and Prayer-Books allocated to each mess as purser's stores (to be recalled at the close of each voyage) proved unsuccessful. Understandably, there were definite reactions against Holy Writ being "made a slop of."[165]

For churchmen—also of Evangelical mold—the distribution of the Book of Common Prayer to Anglicans was important. Charles Simeon set the priorities straight with the statement: "The Bible first, the Prayer-Book next, and all the other books in subordination to these."[166] From 1812 on, the Prayer-Book distribution of the SPCK was supplemented by that of the Prayer-Book and Homily Society, founded in that year by Zachary Macaulay and colleagues of the "Clapham Sect."[167] Among the reasons assigned for this new organization was expressly mentioned the lack of "any adequate provision made for the supply of the long-subsisting and still increasing wants of the Navy and Army." With the dual purpose its name implies, this Society was destined to fill a highly important need in post-war literary missions to seamen, especially from the mid-twenties.[168]

Of more material relevance to a spiritual awakening in the wartime navy, however, was the foundation in 1799 of the Religious Tract Society. Again, the SPCK were the pioneers, both in general tract distribution and in naval outreach in particular. Nevertheless, the enthusiastic founders of the new nondenominational agency had other notions of the purpose of a religious tract than their Anglican predecessors. True, both attacked the same moral evils. But the doctrinal emphasis was different. As their early "packetts of Books" show, the SPCK aim was clearly catechetical—to inculcate the orderly religion of the Prayer-Book.[169] (In the latter half of the eighteenth century, it was deemed advisable to add works specifically warning against the evils of "Enthusiasm.")[170] The object of the RTS was emphatically evangelistic: to present to all men "the way of a sinner's salvation." (The Society insisted, therefore, that all its tracts, however subjects might vary, should include unerring guidance on this score.)[171]

Whatever benefits might otherwise accrue from the tract distribution of the SPCK, the tracts of the RTS—itself a fruit of evangelical revival—were more likely to promote a spiritual awakening in the navy. Pledged, as the Society was, to compete with purveyors of infidelity and immorality in the race to provide reading matter for the underprivileged masses now being brought within the orbit of literacy, the pioneers' attention was readily roused to the plight of seafarers. Tremors from the upheavals at Spithead and the Nore could still be felt in 1799. How secure was Britain's naval shield? Who cared for the souls of the men who manned it?

Up to 1805, naval distribution by the RTS was sporadic but immensely encouraging. In 1802, a naval lieutenant reported to the Society how, on board his ship two years ago, religious tracts led to a marine collecting his comrades for Bible reading. Soon they were nearly 30, those who could not read "singing along with the others."[172] Another naval officer described how "aged seamen read the Tracts with great attention, then put them into their bosoms, and poured upon me a thousand benedictions for them."[173] Spurred on by the many reports of ready response among servicemen, the committee states in their *Seventh Report* (1806) that they were led to adopt more systematic measures. An advertisement in the *Evangelical Magazine* resulted in a host of voluntary agents who, in little more than a year, had already supplied seamen and soldiers with nearly 100,000 gratuitous tracts.[174]

As in the case of the British and Foreign Bible Society (to which the Religious Tract Society had recently given birth), a keen concern was also felt for the spiritual welfare of foreign prisoners of war and convicts in hulks and transports. The RTS, too, employed seafarer "missionaries," in order to distribute translated tracts to the inhabitants of foreign ports. Among these evidently grateful recipients were also "Galley Slaves in the Mediterranean."[175]

From the outset, the RTS took as its model the Wesleyan tract tradition, combining rational argument with deliberate emotional appeal, calculated to provide a point of decision at which the reader could cast himself upon the mercy of the Lord.[176] Successive reports could confirm how such decisions became increasingly manifest in the navy, and naturally led to an increased demand for personal possession of the Scriptures.

In short, it is evident that the British Navy of the French Wars became the object of a general campaign of Christian literature distribution, for long sporadic and wholly inadequate, by no means cohesive, and yet rising at length to impressive intensity and effect. The efforts of such literary agencies ashore must, however, have necessitated "animators" afloat, willing and able to promote the use of these media. By whom was such collaboration undertaken, and what forms did it assume?

THE LAY WITNESS OF
RICHARD MARKS AND OTHERS

The notorious naval run-down, ordered as part of Addington's retrenchment policy in the interval of Amiens, resulted in a manpower reduction from (approximately) 130,000 in 1802 to 50,000 in 1803.[177] However short-sighted this measure may have been strategically, in terms of spiritual significance it was to prove a blessing in disguise. Thousands of discharged officers and men were suddenly "cast on shore" amid mushrooming religious societies and a general spirit of revival in the land.[178] When hostilities broke out afresh, and hundreds of ships of war had to be re-manned in desperate haste, many—both veterans and newcomers—had meanwhile been marked, positively or negatively, by personal contact with the "newly-enlightened and revived population" of Britain.[179]

Large numbers—both officers and men—were ostensibly negative in their immediate reaction. On shore, they might well have imbibed some of the popular prejudice and confusion concerning Methodism and evangelicalism in general. On board, they would readily reinforce a group cohesion already adversely disposed to active religious individualism.[180] For the more positive elements, there would be a manifest need of some form of counter-cohesion. The timid or uncommitted would otherwise easily succumb. There was, therefore, a demand for some sort of supportive spiritual cell system, capable of serving the dual purpose of nurture and outreach, in other words—those two fundamental features of the faith: fellowship and mission.

To this latent need, the Methodist movement admirably lent itself. Its system of "classes," presided over by lay "class leaders," could easily be applied to shipboard conditions. Its emphasis on personal evangelism gave it a dynamic dimension. Severe opposition could render this a dire necessity. With traditional Anglican stress on church order, the Chaplain-General (John Owen) reacted sharply against what he saw as Methodist infiltration into the forces: "When men in the ranks undertake to preach and pray extempore they become shocking coxcombs and think all knowledge and religion centered in such as themselves. . . ." He offered ready advice to his chaplains on how to keep the men from these and other forms of "enthusiasm and methodistical self importance."[181] Exactly how far their superior's attitude was the rule among naval chaplains of the day is difficult to prove. He was certainly not alone with it.[182]

At the same time, it must be borne in mind that—apart from antagonism against Methodism as such—there was widespread popular confusion of Methodism with evangelicalism in general. Quoting scoffing fellow officers, Marks offers the following definition of the general misconception:

> "Methodists" [was] a term which, in their vocabulary, comprised individuals of all sects, parties, ranks, and ages, who feared God, and endeavoured to work righteousness.[183]

This more general use of the term could gain recognition from unexpected quarters. One case was given great publicity. A captain had complained to his admiral about a number of his men, who disturbed the rest of the ship's company by "frequent noises." At the inquiry, they were formally charged with being "Methodists," habitually meeting for Bible reading, social prayer, and hymn singing. This statement having been proved against them, the admiral made careful inquiries about their professional conduct. Such were the superlatives used regarding their skill, discipline and courage in battle that the admiral promptly dismissed the case, with the fervent hope that, if such men were "Methodists," *all* his crews might be "Methodists."[184]

Normally, a naval captain would deal with such matters himself. His authority was almost absolute. Hence, his potential influence for spiritual good—or evil—was immense.[185] Conditions would, therefore, vary according to the caprice of a captain. A few actively suppressed any semblance of religious devotions on board.[186] Not a few simply neglected their duty, as laid down in the Articles of War, to provide for divine service at sea.[187]

As signs of spiritual awakening spread through the Royal
Navy during the Napoleonic War, some doubted that
"religious" seamen would show the caliber of courage
called for in sea battle in the days of sail. Others,
like Nelson, recognized that the contrary was the case.
The above picture shows the carnage on board the
Victory at the time of Nelson's death at Trafalgar
in 1805. (P. O'Brien: *Men-of-War.*)

But it would be well to remember that there had long been many
commanders who recognized the moral—particularly the disciplinary—value
of religion.[188] As signs of awakening appeared, some would (as Nelson is
known to have done) take steps to prevent the molestation of crew members
meeting for prayer and hymn singing.[189] More and more would, in the
absence of a chaplain, hold divine service or prayers themselves, or at least
appoint one of their officers to do so. Commanders like James Hillyar,
George Keith, and C.M. Fabian became particularly well known for their
evangelical zeal and promotion of shipboard religion. (Captain Fabian was
at first ridiculed by his men with the epithet "Old Lazarus." But the crew in
their turn underwent such a transformation that not one of them required
punishment for over thirty months—a quite incredible phenomenon in the
navy of those days.)[190]

As regards naval officers in general, it is noteworthy that a very substantial proportion of them had, as in the case of Nelson, been nurtured in the homes of clergymen.[191] However, the positive effect of this kind of background was likely to vary. At all events, a more immediate spiritual impact would be made by the daily Christian witness, in word and deed, of a committed fellow officer. Thus it was generally acknowledged that many naval officers, who became active in post-war seamen's missions, "owed their first [decisive] impression of a religious nature" to Gambier's conduct at sea.[192]

Among openly evangelical naval officers of the Napoleonic War years, exceptionally wide influence was exercised by Lieutenant Richard Marks (1778-1847). This was largely due to the extraordinary demand for his maritime authorship from the time after his ordination. But while still on active naval service, his personal witness affected the lives of many. No history of the dawn of organized seamen's missions would be complete without due credit to the moral courage of this unassuming yet persevering pioneer spirit.

The main events of Marks' maritime career are found in his widely read collection of naval reminiscences, *The Retrospect.* (Published in book form in 1816, under the pseudonym Aliquis, "formerly a Lieutenant in the Royal Navy, and now a Minister in the Established Church," the work went through numerous editions on both sides of the Atlantic.)[193] In February 1797, at the age of eighteen, "ignorant of the world and impatient of control," young Richard Marks decided to join the navy, and "embarked on the great deep, in pursuit of honours and fancied happiness."[194] Two hair-breadth escapes from harrowing shipwrecks in successive ships only seemed to confirm him in a life he openly describes as deliberate rebellion against God.[195] After three years of sea service, when hospitalized in Minorca, he records his first serious misgivings, while recovering from a fever which had brought him to the brink of eternity.[196]

Continuing on the Mediterranean station, he sought spiritual clarity through religious reading. Isolated from pastoral care and Christian fellowship, he failed, however. After altogether six years of sea life, finally as midshipman and master's mate, he briefly returned home (June 1803).[197] In his next ship, the *Defense,* he fought with such distinction at Trafalgar that he was one of the first to receive promotion from Collingwood after the close of the battle.[198] For more than two years he had now vacillated between unsuccessful attempts to please his Maker and evade the ridicule of man.[199] At length, after transferring to the *Conqueror,* 74, a period in the Channel service gave opportunities to attend the preaching of the Evangelical rector of Stoke Church. The young lieutenant sought further counsel at the rectory, and finally found liberation, "both doctrinally and experimentally." Further futile attempts at self-justification were "swept away," as he now "cast his burdens" upon an all-sufficient Savior.[200]

Having himself at last found the "key," he sensed the urge to share it with others. The opportunity was soon provided. The *Conquerer's* commander, impressed by Marks' effective rejoinder to unscriptural statements by fellow officers during a dinner table discussion on religion, promptly ordered him to "turn parson" and read prayers next Sunday. This being the first instance of Sabbath observation on board in nearly eight years since the vessel was commissioned, the news that Lieutenant Marks was to preach ran through the ship "like lightning." To "preach" signified the reading of set prayers. But the lieutenant obtained advance permission to add a brief discourse from his copy of Burder's famous *Village Sermons*. The following Sunday, while cruising off Brest harbor, orders were duly given to "rig Church." And although "six hundred bare heads and attentive looks" seemed at first "more terrible than the muzzles of so many fierce cannon," thus began the public ministry of a great seafarers' preacher.[201]

An impressive expansion of shipboard religious activities ensued. Sunday morning services for all hands were continued. But Marks also obtained permission to read Sunday evening prayers (again—with a sermon) between decks to those who chose to attend, "generally about two hundred." He cheerfully made light of a common term of derision for pious shipmates ("Psalm-singers"), and organized a ship's choir, aided by some of the ship's band. The next concern was the supply of sufficient literary media. On arrival at a home port, Marks obtained Bibles (from the NMBS) for every mess, and several hundred tracts for distribution. (Henceforth, he seldom went between decks "without seeing some of the crew reading them.") He also organized a ship's library of evangelical books, with over 150 subscribing members. For the benefit of the ship's boys, he established a successful sea school.[202]

From the choir practices, a form of evening fellowship meetings developed. Those who met for singing felt a need for further mutual edification. Marks encouraged them by regular readings and explanations. Several others joined, including some from the quarter-deck. Soon 30-40 of the 640 on board attended.[203] Six months later a reaction set in. Officers raised the cry of "Methodism." The men stigmatized their comrades as "Wingers" (from the fact of their canvas-screened retreat being below in one of the "wings" of the vessel). Nevertheless, facts spoke for themselves. Cases of manifest conversion in notoriously "abandoned characters" eventually amazed the whole crew, and officers had to admit to a marked improvement of the general moral tone on board. Absurd allegations of "mutinous assemblies" were effectively met by the provision that Lieutenant Marks was always to be personally present.[204]

The decisive influence of a captain's individual attitude to religion was dramatically demonstrated when a change of command eventually took place. The newcomer's violently negative notions led to a successive suppression of practically all forms of social religion on board. Sunday services were, of course, eliminated. The boy's school was broken up as "a mistaken idea." And fellowship meetings were forbidden on pain of flogging. To the credit of the other officers, these arbitrary measures produced a wave of sympathy for Marks, and several of them would henceforth meet privately in one another's cabins, "for serious conversation and reading the Scriptures."[205]

After more than four years on the *Conquerer,* and the accumulated strain of thirteen years of almost unremitting active service, Marks was directed to take a passage home, arriving at Portsmouth in 1810. Influential friends ashore were ready to promote his continued career. However, God had, as he puts it, meanwhile given him "another mind." In viewing "this span of time" on the one hand against "the concerns of eternity" on the other, he realized that God would henceforth have him devote his "whole life and exertions exclusively to his service in the established church." After completing his studies at Cambridge, he was ordained and, following an initial seven-year curacy elsewhere, served for over a quarter of a century among the humble cottagers of Buckinghamshire, as vicar of Great Missenden.[206]

No man could justly accuse Marks of having quitted the navy and entered the church from lack of personal prospects. In the former, he had that all-important prerequisite of advancement—good "interest."[207] In the latter he had—and sought—none other than "to labour amongst a poor and plain people for the honour of God and the good of souls."[208] But it would be no less unjust to interpret his decision as lack of sympathy for the men of his former profession. The concept of a full-time seamen's chaplaincy had, at the close of the Napoleonic War, simply not yet dawned on the Christian Church.[209]

However, there are many proofs that the Rev. Richard Marks never forgot his brother seafarers. On the contrary, as one of them, he evidently sensed "a double responsibility" for them. He had not been long ashore before he applied his literary talent and sea experience to a series of remarkably popular publications, expressly designed for their spiritual benefit. (His seamen's tracts alone are estimated to have reached eventually one million copies.)[210] Subsequently, as specific seamen's mission societies appeared upon the scene, Marks was to become one of their most zealous advocates.[211]

Reverting to the Napoleonic War period, a lay ministry at sea was not dependent on an officer's status (however useful this might be). Writing in 1810, John Hubback records how he, on two occasions, succeeded in getting on board the *Conquerer* to attend Marks' fellowship meetings, and was "uncommonly blessed." By then, Hubback had himself three years of arduous naval lay ministry behind him. Born in Sunderland in 1774, he was the mate of a merchantman when seized by the press gang in 1807 and drafted as a common sailor to *HMS Elizabeth*, 74. His character and conduct were such, however, as to procure his rapid promotion to the rank of chief master's mate. Meanwhile, he had succeeded in forming a small fellowship group, which met three evenings a week in the starboard wing, "to converse, and sing hymns and pray." The captain, ultimately hearing of this, was incensed. Alluding to Hubback's promotion, he raved: "And now, Sir . . . in return for all my kindness, you have brought Methodism into my ship!"[212]

Threats of flogging for mutinous assembly forced the group to be more circumspect, and prevented them "enjoying the pleasure of psalmody" (though others might freely "sing the most obscene and reprobate songs as usual"). As often, however, persecution of religion led to its promotion. Meetings continued privately, and numbers increased. They were even joined by the midshipman who had informed on them. Hubback himself served briefly in two further ships (finally as master), before this ever cheerful, widely respected lay leader was drowned, in November 1810.[213]

Sources indicate that much of this naval lay ministry followed a pattern of genuine, organized Methodism. Hubback was in touch with a society on the *Ganges*, 74, which met in two "classes," sanctioned by the captain.[214] The *Victory* was known to have a society of this "psalm-singing gentry," who acquitted themselves admirably at Trafalgar.[215] A Methodist local preacher from Kidderminster, who joined the frigate *Phoebe* as a marine in 1806, was roundly ridiculed for his repeated reproofs of shipboard vice. However, some three years later, that well known Evangelical, James Hillyar, took command, bringing with him a host of Bibles, prayer books and religious tracts. This gave the "Methodist Parson" (as he was scornfully called) greater scope. After a while, a main-top captain, notorious as one of the most vicious characters on board, became so convincingly converted, and showed such courage when killed in a subsequent action, that "the thoughtless became thoughtful" and a general change of attitude became evident. By 1812, the Methodist marine was, in actual fact, pastor of an organized floating society 20 strong (refusing to leave them when offered promotion elsewhere.)[216]

In 1812, George Charles Smith commenced publication of a series of marine tracts called *The Boatswain's Mate*. They rapidly achieved enormous popularity. As a single source of reference on the British Naval Awakening of the Napoleonic War period, there has been nothing to rival them, except Marks' *Retrospect*. Although presented in the form of a

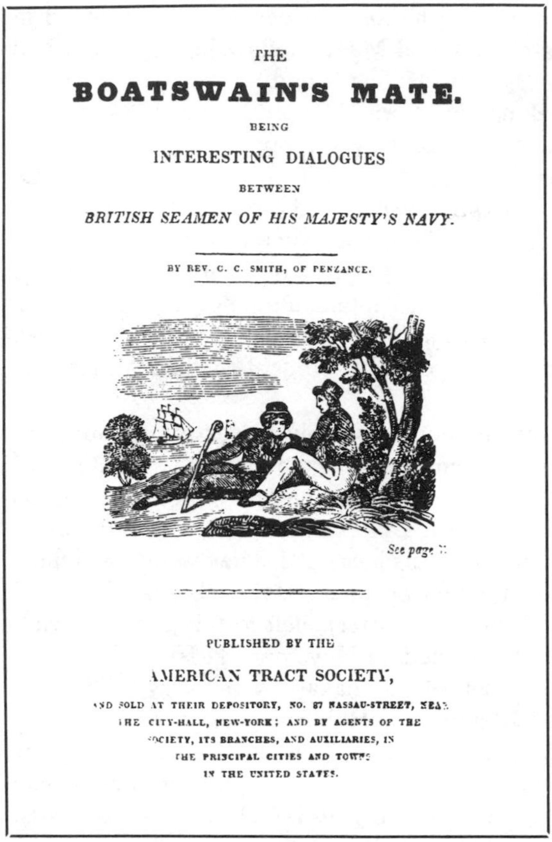

THE

BOATSWAIN'S MATE.

BEING

INTERESTING DIALOGUES

BETWEEN

BRITISH SEAMEN OF HIS MAJESTY'S NAVY.

BY REV. G. C. SMITH, OF PENZANCE.

See page :

PUBLISHED BY THE

AMERICAN TRACT SOCIETY,

AND SOLD AT THEIR DEPOSITORY, NO. 87 NASSAU-STREET, NEAR
THE CITY-HALL, NEW-YORK; AND BY AGENTS OF THE
SOCIETY, ITS BRANCHES, AND AUXILIARIES, IN
THE PRINCIPAL CITIES AND TOWNS
IN THE UNITED STATES.

Title page of G.C. Smith's incredibly popular seven-part seamen's tract, incorporating copious autobiographical materials. (Here in an American edition.)

dialogue between British naval seamen, and not conforming to the requirements of a strictly historical narrative, there can be no doubt as to the basic authenticity of both the background and general pattern of events.[217] The remarkable repercussions of a case of unexpected, obviously genuine shipboard conversion, and the emergence of another unit in the naval cell group movement, are strikingly reproduced in the nautical and religious terminology of the times.[218]

Besides evidence of a mounting spiritual awakening afloat, accounts eventually emerged of corresponding manifestations among British prisoners of war in France. As the War of 1803-15 progressed (and French privateers continued their marauding), such prisoners came to include increasing numbers of seamen, particularly (though not exclusively) from the merchant navy. Subscriptions at Lloyd's helped to eke out the men's miserable food rations.[219] Others—notably the British and Foreign Bible Society—strove to procure spiritual nourishment. The BFBS shipments to the eleven prisoner-of-war depots in France commenced with 100 Bibles and 500 New Testaments dispatched in August 1811, the result of a remarkable form of cooperation between the Transport Board and Ministry of Marine of the two warring countries. This distribution was subsequently continued on a larger scale.[220]

As on board, the collaboration of committed lay leaders was a *sine qua non*. In the midst of the acute hardships and high mortality of this prolonged confinement, "a few pious men (chiefly Sailors) were made instrumental in the conversion of many of their companions."[221] Again, Methodists assumed a leading role. Conspicuous among these was J. Cavanagh, an Irish-born naval officer, who already had several years' experience of founding Methodist societies in men-of-war, before his capture on a transport in 1810. Continuing in like manner ashore, he launched a broad program of spiritual and material relief for the benefit of his fellow prisoners. Undaunted by initial opposition (to which he was well seasoned on board), he saw his society at Cambrai rapidly grow to 80 intensely active members. Here he received welcome assistance, in 1811, from a black American Methodist fellow preacher, also at that time a prisoner.[222] A Sunderland sailor, Jeremiah Taylor, provides another outstanding example of a mariner turned Methodist minister during seven grueling years in French prisons.[223] Besides the many Methodist societies which evolved, there were also Baptist and Independent groups. As to Anglicans, the exertions of the Evangelical Rev. Robert B. Wolfe and his naval coadjutor, Captain Jahleel Brenton, were particularly noteworthy.[224]

According to one estimate, "nearly eight hundred souls were converted to God" among British naval and merchant officers and men in war-time French depots. An indication of the spiritual hunger which could exist is provided by the fact that Dr. Rippon's and the Wesleyan Methodist hymn books were laboriously copied by prisoners, in order to relieve the scarcity of hymnals. Sermons and Scriptures were also transcribed and circulated.[225]

A study of the many accounts of the eruption of evangelistic concern among naval personnel, afloat and ashore, in the Napoleonic War era, reveals a constant repetition of certain salient features:[226] (1) The fundamental role of literary media (particularly the Scriptures) in both awakening and sustaining spiritual life. (2) The widespread development of cellular fellowship groups as a means of preserving and multiplying converts. (3) The involvement of officers and men of all ranks in both leadership and participant roles. (4) A frequent transition in the reaction of the remaining majority, from initial ridicule and persecution to subsequent restraint and respect.[227]

Chapter 5

The Coadjutor:
George Charles Smith and the
Naval Correspondence Mission

QUALIFICATION: EARLY YEARS (1782-1807)

Fellowship meetings within one and the same ship were not the only means of counteracting the erosive effect of spiritual isolation in the navy of the Napoleonic War. A stay in port or at anchor might give welcome opportunities of inter-ship visitation.[228] Again, every transfer of a mature member of an existing fellowship group by inter-ship drafting meant a new possibility for spiritual proliferation.[229] However, external pressure and internal frailty still made acute the need of some coordinating pastoral agency. This requirement was, at least in some measure, to be filled by the efforts of a former man-of-war's man. In fact, for Rev. G.C. Smith, this was to be the first phase of a trail-blazing, life-long ministry to seafarers.

Musing on the manner in which "the Lord leads his people to see his providence in everything, Robert Ralston, famous Philadelphia merchant and warm advocate of mission to seafarers, wrote enthusiastically to Smith in 1821. Like many others, he was deeply struck with the latter's checkered early career, and could, in retrospect, only see this as an unpremeditated yet perfectly indispensable preparation for his later pioneer role. Both in view of the pivotal position of this remarkable man in the origin of organized seamen's missions, and in the absence hitherto of a cohesive account of his early years, this would seem an opportune occasion to attempt to meet the need.[230] (For supplementary biographical data, reference is made to the Notes.)

George Charles Smith was born in London, March 19, 1782, in Castle Street (now Charing Cross Road), near Leicester Square.[231] Both his parents came originally from Yorkshire, but had settled in London in the early 1770's, and became converted there. "Neither elevated by rank, nor

The Rev. George Charles Smith (1782-1863). Once a sailor
himself under Admiral Nelson in the British Napoleonic
War Navy, and destined to become "father" of the
modern-day Seamen's Mission Movement.
(Courtesy: British Sailors' Society.)

distinguished by wealth, but struggling through life, with a numerous and a
very disobedient and trying family," his parents are frequently the subject of
grateful reminiscence in the authorship of the Rev. G.C. Smith. His father, a
tailor by profession, became a member of (the Independent) Surrey Chapel
in Blackfriars Road. Here young George was enrolled as a Sunday school
boy, after his family had moved to nearby Boundary Row (then called St.
George's Row). At this stage his infant ardor attracted the attention of that
chapel's renowned minister, the Rev. Rowland Hill.[232]

When, as a mere twelve year old, the lad lost his father, he
commenced work as "shop boy assistant" with a big bookselling and
publishing concern in Tooley Street, Southwark. Thus, for two years, he had

"daily intercourse with Paternoster Row," the hub of the metropolitan publishing world. More important still, his position opened the opportunity to satisfy an extraordinary thirst for knowledge. Day or night, sometimes until three in the morning, he read—histories, more popular works, all he could come by. The future author of upwards of 80 publications, and for more than 50 years sole editor of the world's first seamen's mission periodical, had good reason to reflect, in later life, "Here I was literally trained up for all my present work. . . ."[233]

But here, on the very shores of the Thames, near London Bridge, he also came into close contact with ships and "hosts of sailors." The call of the sea became too strong.[234] Finally, despite all his mother's remonstrances, he succeeded in getting her to bind him apprentice at Tower Hill to a Captain Clark, master of an American merchant-brig. Thus it was, in the spring of 1796, that a 14-year-old cabin boy sailed from Cherry Garden Stairs, Rotherhithe, in the *Betsey* of Salem, bound for Boston via the Caribbean.[235] Another decisive step had been taken in the equipment of George Charles Smith as future seamen's mission pioneer.

The young cabin boy never reached Boston with *Betsey,* however. *HMS Scipio,* 64, finding herself short of crew while involved in blockading the Dutch at Surinam, resorted to the deeply resented yet usual expedient of helping herself from an American merchantman. George Charles Smith was duly impressed from the cabin of the *Betsey,* and abruptly introduced to the brutal realities of life in the British wartime navy.[236]

On board the *Scipio,* a great number, including Smith, were soon struck down by a wave of that deadly disease to which seamen were constantly exposed in the Tropics, yellow fever. At Martinico, many died. Smith recovered, though still so debilitated that he was drafted to a convoy escort, *HMS Ariadne,* for repatriation.[237] On arrival at Spithead, after barely surviving severe winter storms, the impressionable young lad was initiated into a tradition of permissive pandemonium, which was later to become the subject of constant crusading. As soon as the ship had anchored, "boat loads of sea harlots, with bladders of strong drink concealed about their persons, were scattered all around the ship, so that for a week or ten days His Majesty's ship *Ariadne,* became . . . the greatest floating hell in the world."[238]

When the ship finally arrived at Sheerness, he was able to add another harrowing experience, later to be put to good purpose. Discharged and "left upon the beach there to perish," without any clothes but what he had on, and without the money to pay his fare home, he learned what it meant to become "a poor forlorn destitute sea boy. . . ." Somehow he struggled back to Boundary Row, and an anxious mother, just before Christmas 1796.[239]

Somehow, too, he could not resist the call to return. This time, however, better provision was made. Through "family interest," exercised on his behalf by the Rev. Rowland Hill, it was as Admiralty-midshipman that the young fifteen year old traveled back to Sheerness in March, 1797. Here he joined *HMS Agamemnon,* 64, the ship he was destined to continue with, "during the heat of war," for his remaining five years in the navy.[240] In her, he experienced the Mutiny at the Nore, in May 1797, confined to his cabin, at the height of the crisis, like the rest of the quarterdeck.[241] In her, he served under Duncan at Camperdown in October 1797[242] and, with particular distinction, under Nelson at Copenhagen in April 1801. (His detailed descriptions of the latter engagement provided valuable insights into the psychology of seamen before, during and after a major action in the days of sail.)[243]

Long before the Battle of Copenhagen, however, Smith had fallen into disfavor with his commander. Apparently he had signed some petition in favor of an officer-messmate, whom the captain was "determined to have tried by a court-martial." At all events, he confirms that in the spring of 1798 he was, while at Hull, disrated (allegedly "by cruelty"). At Copenhagen he refers to himself as "second captain of the foretop," a responsible, highly exposed, but decidedly "lower-deck" position. (The statement that he held, at this time, the rank of "master's mate" is, therefore, erroneous.)[244]

After returning from the Baltic expedition, Smith continued, he says, on his "old course of sin" wherever he landed and "knocking about a great part of the winter in the North Sea." Suddenly seized with a violent fever, he was confined critically ill for three months in Yarmouth Naval Hospital, and finally invalided out of the navy, "a few weeks before the peace" (of Amiens, March 27, 1802).[245] This did not prevent him, after settling in London again, from immediately engaging in a round of riotous living, together with a set of former naval shipmates. (The climax was reached in a mad meleé at the Surrey Theatre, subsequently immortalized in *The Boatswain's Mate.*)[246]

As he later looked back on this period of his life, Smith felt that here, in the motley course of his naval career, was a divinely ordained plan:

> I was now training up to begin God's work among sailors, as a sailor myself, who had been in storms and battles, and hells afloat and on shore, ... neglected and left to perish; and therefore I could not forget the heart and life of a sailor, as God said, by Moses, to Israel, "Ye know the heart of a *stranger,* seeing ye were *strangers* in the land of Egypt"; Exodus xxiii.: and thus, I firmly believe, God was *preparing me* for the work. It was not a minister from the University, ... but one who had been "nursed in the wind and cradled in the storm."[247]

The Battle of Copenhagen Roads, April 2, 1801, in which
George Charles Smith distinguished himself as second
captain of the fore-top on HMS *Agamemnon*, 64.
(O. Eidem & O. Lütken: *Sömakts Historie*—
History of Our Naval Power.)

The picture Smith generally paints of the seaman's life and environment is so
dark as to be rivaled only by his frequent, Newton-like insistence on his own
utter depravity in pre-conversion sea years.[248] But it would be unjust to
interpret such exposés as expressions of disloyalty to brother seamen, or
moral masochism in himself. On the contrary, here in six years' intimate
experience of the seamy side of sea life lay a powerful potential for success in
the two main roles of a seamen's mission pioneer: (1) As advocate of the
cause, he could provide relevant, realistic motivation for the work.[249] (2) As
active missionary among the men, he now had the requisite rapport for
effective preaching and counseling.[250]

    The next phase of George Charles Smith's colorful career is con-
cerned with the events which culminated in his conversion. For Smith, the
brief interlude of international peace became one of spiritual turbulence.
Having obtained "a situation of respectability," as "superintendent of whare-
houses and cellars" with a large firm of wholesale wine and spirit merchants
in the city, he made a practice of attending chapel and visiting his ailing
mother every Sabbath.[251] (In true sailor tradition, his mother-attachment was
strong and unswerving, as evidenced in countless tender allusions to her
throughout his long life.)[252] He describes himself as still "wild and unregen-

erated," seeking his pleasure where he could. However, on a spiritually starved sailor, who had "never had a chaplain since 1797," the combined impact of regular attendance to a Gospel ministry and the prayerful admonitions of a dying parent were not without effect.[253]

By March 1803, it was obvious that the precarious peace was crumbling. A "hot press" was the inevitable result. Advised by his employers to take to the country for a fortnight until the press gangs had "cooled," Smith made for Reading to visit his closest shipmate from *Agamemnon* days.[254] Here he was, as he puts it, "stopped in his mad career, like Saul of Tarsus." Laid low by a sudden, virulent fever, he was rapidly reduced to a state of physical extremity and spiritual despair. "Afraid to die, yet . . . indifferent to life," he seized upon "a small ray of hope," instilled into his mind by his pious nurse: "He [the Lord] does not despise prayer, sir . . . the Lord can save your soul."

Through the counseling of the minister of an adjoining chapel, Smith relates how he shortly afterwards obtained assurance. The pastor could remind him that the Lord was not only able to save him—he was also willing, as he "died on the cross to prove it." Only then could the afflicted man say: "Light broke into my heart."[255] But to George Charles Smith, the decisive date was when that nurse had given him the first faint glimmer. This date, March 19, 1803, his 21st anniversary, was to be constantly recalled as his "natural and spiritual birthday."[256]

The nature of Smith's conversion experience was destined to influence radically his subsequent method of ministry. But first it is natural to ask: When and how did George Charles Smith enter the ministry?

Smith's mother had long since cherished a hope that her erring son would one day become a second John Newton. He himself had then only "laughed heartily at the idea."[257] However, after five weeks of illness at Reading, such prospects seemed already somewhat less incredible. The "report of *Nelson's sailor* had gone through all the streets," so that "when he was able to crawl to the chapel, crowds of people came to hear him tell, from the pulpit, what the Lord had done for his soul."[258]

In the autumn of 1803, he was recommended to a promising situation as cellar superintendent at fashionable York House Hotel in Bath.[259] Here he soon became restless, however, and found himself praying for "deliverance from the worldly pleasures" of his present environment and "an open door for preaching the Gospel to the poor somewhere." Finding fellowship at nearby Somerset Street (Baptist) Chapel, he was befriended by a well-known merchant and deacon there, Opie Smith, of Westfield House. Finally, in the autumn of 1804, Opie Smith, after promoting occasional preaching excursions by the former seafarer to neighboring villages, proposed that he should study for the ministry.[260]

Acting as ringleader in a sailortown spree, G.C. Smith
actually led a "boarding party" of shipmates in a leap from
the gallery into the pit of a local theatre, as "an act of
drunken bravado." (From *The Boatswain's Mate,* Part II.)

From this connection with his merchant namesake may be traced
George Charles Smith's long association with Devon, Cornwall and particularly the port of Penzance. Opie Smith had, by 1804, already begun sponsoring, with zeal and success, the establishment of Baptist chapels in this
relatively destitute corner of the kingdom.[261] It was through his patronage
that George Charles Smith obtained his "open door" —three years' private
theological tuition under the Rev. Isaiah Birt, minister of the Baptist Chapel
in Morice Square, Devonport (as yet still known as "Plymouth Dock").[262]
Then, in 1807, he was elected pastor of the Octagon Chapel, in Chapel
Street, Penzance (a Baptist church originally built by the Independents in
1789, bought from them by Opie Smith in 1802, and renamed the Jordan
Chapel in 1822). Here George Charles Smith was ordained on October 28,
1807, his former tutor giving the charge.[263] And here, then, was the flock of
which, for the next eighteen years, he was to be the intensely active but
increasingly absent shepherd.

VOCATION: THE "DOLPHIN" INCIDENT: 1809

During his tutorship term, 1804-07, George Charles Smith occupied lodgings in Prince's Street, Devonport, in order to "attend upon Mr. Birt for daily instruction." At the same time, however, he was, as his tutor's assistant preacher, entrusted with regular preaching responsibility for the Baptist Chapel at Saltash (four miles up the River Tamar, recently founded by Birt). Also, besides assistance at the main chapel at Devonport, Smith had occasional preaching assignments at Plymouth, Dartmouth, Brixham and Torquay. Inevitably, this meant mixing with a largely maritime population, and ministering to "many maritime hearers." Here were "sailors, dockyard-men, fishermen, and watermen," as well as their families. After being settled as pastor at Penzance, in 1807, he by no means limited his labors to his local chapel, but "began preaching to fishermen and sailors all around the coast to Land's End," whenever the occasion offered.[264]

Thus, by 1809, the Rev. George Charles Smith could justly claim that he had ministered to seafarers and their dependents "during five years from Torbay to the Lands End, on the South Devon and Cornwall coast."[265] Yet he is the first to emphasize that, in principle, "there was nothing extra-ordinary in it, as other ministers in coastal districts did the same." True, his "natural energies and constitutional activity" impelled him to exceptional exertions. Moreover, "as a converted sailor" himself, he gained understand-able satisfaction from sailors' families forming a substantial part of his hearers. Nevertheless, he insists that, until 1809, his ministry to seafarers was—like that of his coastal colleagues—essentially only an integral part of his general ministry. He was, in other words, like his predecessors from the eighteenth century, Joss, Medley and Newton, still only a *sailor minister,* not yet a *sailors' minister.*[267]

Then came one memorable afternoon in early 1809. Smith has himself recorded how, as he was walking down Chapel Street, he was "hailed" by some seamen, eagerly waving their hats to him, while making their way up to town from the quay:

> "Will you please to come on board our vessel, and preach a sermon to us?" "Preach a sermon! How came you to think of asking me?" "Why, sir, we belong to the Dolphin revenue cutter, and we have been out in such a dreadful gale of wind that every soul expected to perish; our captain is brought on shore very ill, and we thought to have a sermon on board when we came in." "Where does your vessel lay?" "In Guavas Lake, sir, here out in the Bay." "Will your officer allow me to come on board and

preach?" "O yes, sir, he told us to ask." "Well this is very
singular. I have often wished to preach on board a ship, but have
never done such a thing: however, if you will bring your boat on
shore for me to-morrow afternoon, I will very gladly go off with
you to preach." "Thank you, sir, we'll be ashore depend upon
it."[268]

Apparently the crew, appalled by their narrow escape, had begun to
talk of their need for "a little religion." A seaman from the neighboring
fishing village of Newlyn (where Smith had often preached) had then
proposed inviting on board "a preacher at the Octagon Chapel, in Penzance,
who had been a sailor." The plan had met with approval.[269] Still "perfectly
astonished" at the novelty of this initiative, Smith was duly rowed on board
the next day. Here he was received "with great kindness" by the chief
officer, and led below to where an open space had been cleared and all hands
assembled. Preaching from the appropriate text, Jonah 1:6, his soul was
"deeply affected" as he shared his own recollections of "storms and tempests
at sea, and sins and snares on shore" when he himself had been "a thoughtless
sailor in a ship of war." The service was closed with prayer by Smith's
student-assistant at that time, Mr. Shell, who had accompanied him on
board.[270]

As they were being rowed back from the anchorage across the bay,
Smith "conversed with the boat's crew very freely about religion," observing
that he had met only one "real religious" sailor during his years in the
navy.[271]

> Immediately the man pulling with the stroke or first oar cried out,
> in his Cornish dialect, "Maester, I know one of thy religion in a
> man-of-war now." I was so much surprised, that I asked what he
> meant by *my religion?* His answer was, *"Why, one of your
> Methodie men."* As this was the general term for a religious
> person, ... I entreated him to get me his name, and the ship to
> which he belonged, and where she was.[272]

The stroke oar (one Hannibal Curnoe from nearby Marazion, soon
to become a "most zealous" member of Smith's church) obtained the address
forthwith, from an acquaintance ashore.[273] Smith lost no time:

> I wrote immediately to Portsmouth, and received a kind and
> affectionate answer, begging I would correspond with him. I wrote
> again to ask if he had any more sailors on board who loved our
> Lord Jesus Christ. His reply informed me, there was a pious
> marine on board. I then wrote to the marine, and inquired if he
> knew of any other religious sailors in the navy. He informed me
> concerning the Royal George, 100 guns: I wrote to this ship, and
> the sailor corresponded with me, and informed me of the Royal
> Oak, 74: I wrote here also, and heard of the Zealous, 74, and the

Elizabeth, 74. I addressed some sailors of these ships, and had then information of the Ganges, 74. My correspondence with this ship directed me to the Tonnant of 80; and here I heard of the Repulse, 74, the Conquerer, 74, and some frigates and sloops of war, and tenders and cutters.[274]

Amazed, but delighted, the former man-of-war's man "determined to prosecute a correspondence with all naval ships where a pious sailor was to be found." Thus was George Charles Smith "brought into this great work" —the cause which was to be his life's calling. Thus, too, began a new, potentially vital phase in the emergence of organized outreach to seafarers, later to be designated the "Naval Correspondence Mission."[275]

COORDINATION: THE NAVAL CORRESPONDENCE MISSION: 1809-14

Confronted with this unexpected challenge, the 27-year-old pastor of Penzance committed himself to the task with characteristic energy and enthusiasm. Nevertheless, in view of the far more conspicuous role he was to play in the next two decades, it might seem surprising that Smith should, in later years, refer to this correspondence ministry as "the greatest work in all my life."[276] However, compelling pastoral and publicity considerations both contributed to make the need for some such agency at this juncture particularly urgent.

First, there was the directly supportive, pastoral purpose. Here, indeed, was a flock "scattered abroad, as sheep without a shepherd." The problem of dispersion, due to disintegrating forces inherent in both sea life and war conditions, was aggravated by the varying forms of discrimination to which naval "Methodists" were often exposed. Biased officers might, for example, deliberately "select three or four religious men, when they were required to send any away" (in routine drafts). True, they would thereby unwittingly favor "the advancement of religion, as the persecutions of old." Such transfers would cause dismay in like-minded officers on men-of-war with "not one religious man," who, as the newcomers won adherents, "heard, to their utter astonishment, that their ship was tainted with Methodism."[277] Nevertheless, it meant an increase in the already inevitable degree of disruption.

Added to this, there was the stress and strain of persecution itself. This could, on some ships, go beyond both ridicule and excessive drafting. Letters spoke of cases where "petty officers were broke, midshipmen disrated, men were selected, on the slightest pretence, and flogged."[278]

Clearly, conditions called for some form of concerted pastoral care. These men "greatly needed the advice, and encouragement, and countenance of some minister on shore." For such a task, the Rev. G.C. Smith had at least two important assets: (1) A status "totally independent of government and the navy." (2) A personal acquaintance with the "language, temptations, propensities, and peculiarities of officers and seamen."[279]

Through the system of counseling by correspondence he developed, Smith sought to fulfill three functions. First, he wished to stimulate self-examination, by posing probing questions about the foundation of his correspondent's faith. (In a situation of prolonged pressure, a faith grounded in the sufficiency of free grace alone was seen as doubly indispensable.)[280] Secondly, he provided scriptural encouragement to persevere. (Replies reveal how warmly such words were welcomed, likewise his intercessory prayers and those of others ashore. Tracts that he enclosed were also gratefully acknowledged.)[281] Thirdly, he supplied specific advice in answer to concrete "cases of conscience, of trial, of doubt, and of enquiry." (In certain instances of persecution, he went so far as to write to an officer on board, and respectfully request freedom of worship for a victimized seaman.)[282]

At first, as the correspondence mission began to gather momentum, Smith speaks of the sheer thrill he felt at the news he was now "daily receiving from converted sailors."[283] However, his meticulous methods of inquiry about further potential correspondents added continually to the list.[284] Again, the volume of mail increased further, says Smith, "as the sailors learned from my letters that I had been a sailor and an officer in ships of war, and therefore well understood their phraseology and their comparisons in nautical terms, which I used for their religious instruction."[285]

At length, such "hosts of letters" arrived, that he was faced with serious physical and financial problems. The former were partly overcome by means of teams of volunteers, helping to duplicate new batches of letters to be sent out.[286] The latter reached formidable proportions. Expenditure for stationery and writing materials was heavy; but for postage it became unbearable. A resultant debt of £50 drew protests from Smith's young wife, and introduced him to a problem which was to plague him throughout his long career.[287]

True, it pleased Smith that the first contribution he could recollect, "subscribed to promote religion generally among sailors," was an unsolicited gift from a seaman. (He had enclosed a one pound note with his letter, to help the postage account.)[288] In fact, however, the gesture only served to underscore the urgency of an issue with far wider implications: how could the church serve seamen without adequate promotional provision? Again, how could such provision be expected without the communication of relevant information and motivation? However important the new ministry might be in its directly pastoral bearing on seamen, was this to be its only use?

The Naval Correspondence Mission must also be made to serve a secondary but vital publicity purpose. This became increasingly apparent to its originator. He frankly admits that at the outset, in 1809, he had not "the most distant idea whereunto all this would grow."[289] His immediate involvement had been a spontaneous response to the totally unexpected news of the Christian cell group movement which was already emerging on ships of war:

> I certainly knew what was Admiral Gambier's general character, and one or two other officers, but beyond this I was as much in the dark as my [ministerial] brethren in general [regarding signs of a spiritual awakening in the navy]. . . . Great good was doing, but it required to be known through the kingdom, that good men might aid this work by their prayers and by their exertions.[290]

A painful realization of just how acute was this publicity need, dawned on the dismayed Smith as he attempted to share his exuberant joy with such as lacked his particular motivation:

> I was indeed like the woman of Samaria—I could not contain this good news, but ran around . . . with those letters, reading them for weeks to all descriptions of persons, and expressing my amazement that God should begin such a work as this in the navy. . . . [But] I found many ministers and persons, to whom I mentioned these things, said very calmly, "Ah, it is all very well if they last," and then turn off to something else quite irrelevant; . . . others actually declared, "It's all empty profession, we don't believe there can be any religion in a man-of-war." Some even laughed at me, and for a considerable time not a soul would encourage me. . . .

Members of Smith's own congregation in Penzance censured him, saying, "We can hear nothing now at that chapel but about sailors. . . ." There were even dark insinuations of subversion by "sectarians."[291]

Nevertheless, after a while, Smith realized he was not entirely alone. There were other shore coadjutors in the naval awakening. In addition to the efforts of the NMBS, BFBS and SPCK, many ministers and laymen had already responded to the 1805 appeal of the Religious Tract Society, and provided volunteer agents at ports with dockyards and naval stations.[292] Smith found specific reason to commend the concern of Dr. Robert Hawker at Plymouth, the Rev. J. Hitchins, Isaiah Birt and J. Steadman at Devonport, as well as the Rev. Daniel Miall and John Griffin at Portsmouth and Portsea. Also mentioned are the Wesleyan ministers at both the major naval ports of Portsmouth and Devonport. These are said to have greatly encouraged "officers and sailors from refitting-ships" with whom they came into contact in their respective ministries.[293] After quitting the Navy, and commencing his preparations for the ministry, Richard Marks, too, continued to correspond with fellow Christians still in active service at sea.[294]

Among the laity, Smith makes well-merited mention of Sir George and Lady Mary Grey. From the appointment of (then) Captain Grey as Commissioner of the Naval Dockyard at Portsmouth in 1806, these two were in a singularly strategic position to promote the spiritual welfare of seamen. While the Commissioner remained loyal to his evangelical convictions and readily lent his patronage to the NMBS and other seamen's mission endeavors,[295] his wife was, in this field, destined to play an even more prominent part. Lady Mary Grey (1770-1858) deserves to be remembered as the first seamen's mission pioneer of her sex of whom we have definite records. Accompanying her husband on active service, she had already seen "the grievous neglect of religion and morality which prevailed in the navy." With the willing cooperation of her husband, she now transformed the Commissioner's House in Portsmouth Dockyard into a hub of Christian benevolence.[296]

Besides showing a constant concern for the employees of the dockyard and their families, Lady Grey cared for sick sailors and sailors' orphans. Of particularly far-reaching effect, however, was her systematic circulation, for over two decades, of immense quantities of Scripture and religious literature among active naval personnel (as well as merchant seamen, embarking soldiers, prisoners of war and convicts). The NMBS, BFSB and RTS all claimed her as a valued collaborator. She made a special point of prevailing on officers leaving for sea "to attend to the welfare of their own immortal souls, and to seek the spiritual good of their ship's company."[297]

An example of what this could lead to has been recorded by an officer serving on the *St. Alban's,* 64, during the years 1807 to 1810. (The conversation was enacted between two "tars," as they settled down in a quiet corner on deck, to read a religious tract, distributed by a captain who practiced public prayers on shipboard.)

> Dan says: "I wonder where the Captain got all these pretty books; for the more we read, or hear them read, the more we want. . . ."
> Jem made answer, "Why don't you know that Lady Grey, the Commissioner's Lady, sent them on board at Portsmouth?"
> *Dan.*—"God bless her, she is as good a woman as our Captain is a man, and I'm sure, Jem, if we don't go to heaven we ought to be ashamed of ourselves. . . ."[298]

Having mastered "the art of laying under contribution the talent of others," Lady Grey's influence was remarkable. She became, in fact, a Lady Huntingdon of early seamen's missions. With officers who became converted, she maintained correspondence, and continued to "cheer and animate to the most extensive usefulness." It is, therefore, not surprising to find her a warm supporter of the Rev. G.C. Smith and the Naval Correspondence Mission, when his work came to her notice. He has gratefully recorded how, in 1812, she provided both new names for his list and sorely needed support for his expense account.[299]

By then others, too, had begun to show an active interest in this new missionary endeavor. The very first seems to have been another lady coadjutor, Mrs. Selina Wills (widow of the widely reputed Rev. Thomas Wills and a niece of the Countess of Huntingdon).[300] Indispensable financial aid was rendered by William Henry Hoare, during his two-year residence in Penzance,[301] followed by similar support from J. Anstey.[302] Besides practical cooperation from his ministerial colleagues in Plymouth, Portsmouth and Devonport, Smith also emphasizes the encouragement of the Rev. Andrew Fuller of Kettering, the Rev. Samuel Greatheed of Newport Pagnell, and Dr. Charles Stuart of Edinburgh.[303]

What support Smith received up to 1812 in his correspondence mission was, in great measure, the fruit of a two-fold publicity plan. In the first place, he had begun to send a selection of his seamen's letters to the religious press for publication, and some to brother ministers for use in sermon illustration or otherwise.[304] Smith also supplied the committee of the BFBS with such material.[305] A letter from the ill-fated *Saint George* was published as a tract and circulated also among sailors in large numbers.[306]

The frank piety and "almost apostolical" vein of these letters produced "the most wonderful effects," particularly in London and Edinburgh. The incredible fact was being brought home to increasing numbers of the religious public that the British sailor was, after all, redeemable.[307] It was this reception which induced Smith to launch forth on a second endeavor, the compilation of his nautical religious tract, *The Boatswain's Mate,* embodying, as it did, not only his own naval experience, but also events drawn from his subsequent naval correspondence.[308]

The literary precedent had already been set by the Evangelical vicar of Charles, Plymouth, Dr. Robert Hawker, with his didactic biography, *The Sailor Pilgrm* (published in two parts, 1806 and 1810). Though well received, the idea required a George Charles Smith to give it that smell of tar and taste of salt water which made *The Boatswain's Mate* such a success.[309] (The first two parts of the latter were originally published jointly, in the *Instructor* religious newspaper, 1811-12.)[310]

Although of particular interest to seamen, *The Boatswain's Mate* also proved of great promotional value. It was, in fact, the combined impact of Smith's sailors' letters and sailors' dialogue which paved the way for what was now to become a third channel of publicity: the first public presentation of the the "Seamen's Cause" from metropolitan pulpits, in 1812.[311]

The primary purpose of Smith's visit to London was to make collections in order to discharge a debt on the Octagon Chapel in Penzance. Among those he was directed to call upon was John Wilson, influential Cheapside merchant and chapel manager. Asked if he were not the author of the much-discussed "Dialogue about Bob and James in the *Instructor,*" Smith was immediately engaged to preach at Whitefield's well-known Tabernacle (Moorfields) and Tottenham Court Road Chapel. Here he seized the opportunity to present to crowded, awe-struck audiences the "progress of evangelical religion" in the navy, quoting liberally from his seamen's correspondence.[312] Similar opportunities were afforded at Lady Huntingdon's Silver Street and Islington chapels, by an introduction from his Land's End patron, Mrs. Wills, to the minister, the Rev. J.E. Jones.[313]

Through these well-frequented chapels, Smith obtained access to a far wider circle of metropolitan religious society than his fellow Baptists. In fact, he had—in relation to an entirely new field of mission—begun to raise the consciousness of popular evangelicalism—in other words, the rank and file who made up "the hidden base of the evangelical movement" (Lovegrove). In so doing, he made many valuable potential contacts.

Among these latter, Smith's friendship with Thomas Thompson (1785-1865) was to provide the Seamen's Cause with one of its "first and warmest" advocates. At that time an active young layman of Islington Chapel, Thompson had already acquired a sizable fortune in business and was determined to devote his means to the service of the Gospel. As a twelve year old, he had learned shorthand in order not to miss a word in his private notes of John Newton's sermons. (Finally, he was privileged to serve as the old sailor-preacher's pulpit boy.) To Smith's account of the Naval Correspondence Mission he responded at once (with ten guineas toward expenses), and henceforth the concern of this widely respected Congregationalist for the welfare of seamen was to prove both powerful and persistent.[314]

It was, however, one of the leading Baptist divines of the day, Dr. John Rippon (1751-1836),[315] who was to furnish the culmination point of Smith's entrance on the London scene by what was claimed to be the first sermon to seamen "by general public advertisement," in the autumn of 1812. The Rippons, with a son in the navy as midshipman, were particularly gratified by all Smith could recount of signs of an awakening afloat. Then Dr. Rippon hit upon a plan. He well knew, from the location of his own chapel in a notorious sector of London's "Sailortown," what concentrated vice seamen came up against ashore. Without further ado, he announced publicly, at the Baptist Chapel, Carter Lane, Tooley Street, that the Rev. G.C. Smith from Penzance would be preaching there to sailors the following Lord's-day evening.[316]

The decision once made, nothing was left to chance. Dr. Rippon had a host of bills published and posted, on board in the tiers of shipping, and along both banks of the Thames. On the evening itself, torchbearers were stationed to direct the men. The response was extraordinary. Every part of the chapel was "crowded to excess," and the capacious gallery, especially reserved for sailors for the occasion, was "completely wedged up" with officers and men, from both the merchant service and the navy. In front sat none other than the captain of the Tower Hill press gang himself, in full uniform, surrounded by his officers and men. (He had kindly taken care to circulate that, "on such an important religious occasion," no mariner would be molested going to or coming from the chapel.)[317]

Smith, overwhelmed with what was "for that day truly an amazing scene," discoursed from Scripture, from sailors' letters, and from his own six years at sea. Such, it was said, was the effect, that "hundreds of sailors were in tears," while the people from shore, in the aisles below, "wept for sympathy." At the close, the captain of the press gang came into the vestry, and summed up the significance of the occasion with the following words (addressed to the surprised Smith):

> My dear sir, I was once standing on a course for hell, but blessed be God he has brought me round by his grace. . . . I rejoice indeed that God has raised up a brother officer and sailor to hail our poor fellows on their way to perdition; you see I am in an awkward berth for religion, but I am ordered to this post and I must make the best of it. Thank God that you are press-master for Jesus Christ. Good night!—take all hands to heaven, if possible.[318]

True, the Carter Lane Chapel seamen's service led to no immediate organizational consequences. Nevertheless, its long-term significance was noteworthy in at least two aspects: (1) As public demonstration of positive response to seaman-oriented preaching (and therefore manifest motivation for organized maritime evangelism); (2) As early evidence of spiritual concern for the seaman in his *merchant* navy role (and therefore an indication of transition to a new post-war phase of the work). Hence it was not entirely unjustified for Dr. Rippon to claim, at the establishment of a permanent sanctuary for seafarers in 1818, that in this field it was a Baptist chapel on the south bank of the Thames that had taken the lead, in 1812.[319]

On his return to Penzance, Smith continued his correspondence mission, in the midst of his many other activities, until early 1814. Then he launched forth on a new, brief, but eventful enterprise: a voluntary continental chaplaincy, in the wake of Wellington's Peninsular Army. In the autumn of 1813, a British transport, repatriating French soldier-prisoners from San Sebastian to Brest, was forced into Penzance by a storm. Impelled by their avid reception of French-language tracts, Smith armed himself with a great stock of Bibles, Testaments and tracts, and in early March 1814 embarked for Pasajes, near the Franco-Spanish border.[320]

Smith's purpose was two-fold. On the one hand, this was a Christian literature mission to Spain and (particularly) France, ravaged by war, and ridden with the "infidel" writings of Voltaire and Rousseau. On the other hand, here was an opportunity to minister to British soldiers in the field and British sailors in foreign ports. By his mission to France, Smith became instrumental in introducing the Lancastrian school system to that country, and in prompting the post-war French Methodist Mission.[321] In his ministry to wounded soldiers, he received the personal approbation of Wellington;[322] his work among sailors at Pasajes, Marseilles, Bordeaux and Calais was in practice limited, but in principle a prelude to later foreign-port seamen's missions.[323]

By the time of Smith's return to Penzance, at the end of July 1814, Bonaparte had been banished to Elba.[324] The advent of peace marked the termination of the Naval Correspondence Mission. What had this five-year form of follow-up work actually achieved?

Statistically, pastoral contact had, by 1814, been established with approximately 70 ships of war.[325] On these, the number with whom Smith was in touch could vary from one single man to groups of ten to twenty, in exceptional cases even twenty to thirty. (In all, there were, by the end of the war, Christian fellowship groups on board some 80 men-of-war.)[326]

Strategically, the Naval Correspondence Mission was to be of far-reaching significance, in both of the aspects already indicated. From a pastoral standpoint, it gave to many an isolated, hard-pressed Christian seaman sorely needed nurture and a sense of spiritual cohesion. In so doing, this individualized form of maritime pastoral counseling represents a new departure, in relation to the more general guidance provided by published devotional aids for seafarers.[327] (The continuing relevance of a coordinative correspondence agency to the spiritual needs of seamen is evidenced by its counterpart in the follow-up work of modern day seamen's missions.)[328]

From a publicity standpoint, too, the Naval Correspondence Mission (coupled with the publication and pulpit activity which ensued) was highly significant. It meant that a small beginning had been made toward reinforcing sporadic local initiative with motivation for concern on a national scale. George Charles Smith was, as already seen, by no means the originator of the first form of organizational seamen's mission activity. But there is good reason to consider him as the pioneer advocate of the Seamen's Cause, at all events in Great Britain. For there that cause, though far from ready for sea, had, by 1812, in actual fact been publicly launched.[329]

Seen in a wider context, therefore, the Naval Correspondence Mission played a unique part in consolidating the results of the Naval Awakening, and thus enabling this diffuse phenomenon to fulfill its post-war destiny.

EPISODE OR ERA?

Reviewing the stirring events leading to the recent founding of the first general seamen's mission societies, the 1821 *Report* of the British and Foreign Seamen's Friend Society and Bethel Union left no doubt as to the fundamental importance it attached to the Naval Awakening. It had this to say:

> When the future historian shall retrace the rise and progress of Evangelical Religion [amongst the seamen of Great Britain] . . . he will refer to the war of 1793, for the preparation of the materials for this work, and to the subsequent war of 1803, for the seed scattered in our Navy . . . , from which such abundant crops are now gathering, by the various religious societies, in connection with the great bulwarks of our country.[330]

Before attempting to assess the results of this movement, however, it would first seem natural to summarize its apparent causes. To what factors was the Naval Awakening chiefly attributable?

More than one commentator has emphasized the role of the Holy Spirit as the original, transcendental factor. Having "begun on the bosom of the ocean, on board of a few ships of war, where neither chaplain nor spiritual guide was found," this kindling of new life was manifestly "the work of God alone."[331] In terms of human instrumentality, the main, immanent factor proves to have been an intimate interaction of literary media and lay ministry. Between the latter, it would be arbitrary to attempt any fine distinctions; sources show how each mutually promoted the other. (However, among literary media, the dominant role of Scripture distribution, and particularly that of the NMBS, is very apparent.)[332] Finally, the Naval Correspondence Mission forms the posterior, consolidatory factor, providing essential pastoral and promotional aid.[333] There will be reason to refer to three precisely parallel factors in tracing the course of the post-war merchant navy revival.

Some indication of the influence of the Naval Awakening on the post-war scene may be gained by attempting to answer the following question: How far did this movement meet the preconditions for the development of general, organized seamen's missions? Basically, these would consist of manpower needs and motivational needs.

It was no mere coincidence that the year 1814 marked both the advent of peace and the commencement of the movement culminating in the formation of the first British societies for general seamen's missions. This movement, in order to succeed, required not merely manpower as such, but men qualified to meet exacting demands. Of such there were many, among the thousands now returning from ships of war and French prison depots.[334]

Afloat, in the post-war merchant service, the precedent of self-help set by the lay ministry of the Naval Awakening was of paramount importance. (However zealous the chaplains of the wartime navy might have been, they would still have been hopelessly too few to meet actual pastoral needs. For the post-war merchant service, organized professional ministerial provision was non-existent.) Among the multitudes seeking employment in merchant ships were many who now knew how to nurture their faith with Bible reading and Christian fellowship, and whose potential for witnessing had become well-weathered in recurring bouts of ridicule and persecution.[335]

It would be unforgivable to imply that only such genuine Christianity as expressed itself in cell groups existed in the wartime navy. (It would be equally unpardonable to assume that membership in such a cell group guaranteed sincerity of faith.) Yet whatever reason some might have for reacting against "enthusiasm" or "conventicles" on shipboard,[336] it was the considered opinion of others that what was achieved during the first post-war decade of seamen's mission endeavor was principally the work of officers and men who, in living their faith, had "dared to be singular, and to encounter the frowns of their superiors."[337] Certainly, without men of this caliber and this background, that mainstay of the pioneering era, the essentially lay-oriented "Bethel Movement," would have been unthinkable.

Ashore, in the post-war organization of seamen's mission societies, there was an urgent need of particularly qualified personnel. Again, the Naval Awakening proved to be an indispensable source.[338] For direct "missionary" work, professional rapport with the men was invaluable. For supportive work, in a new field replete with prejudice and indifference, firsthand experience of the impact of the Gospel at sea was vital, both as an incentive to personal perseverance, and in providing motivation for others. Several of the most successful pioneer chaplains and agents among the men,[339] and literally scores of the most zealous public advocates of the cause,[340] were, in fact, men who had served in the wartime navy, and who had, therefore, personally experienced, or at least witnessed, the awakening there.

The availability of these men for collaboration was, in part, a result of the retention of nearly 90 percent of the naval officer corps as unemployed, on half-pay, in the years following the 1814-17 run-down. In 1818, there were some three and a half thousand unemployed lieutenants; by 1832, this redundancy had only been reduced by one thousand.[341]

In meeting motivational needs, the Naval Awakening provided early advocates of the Seamen's Cause with irrefutable arguments in two important areas. Against professional apprehension of the alleged "injurous" effect of religion on seamen, countless cases could be quoted where Bible-reading seamen, once the laughing-stock of the navy, were now acknowledged as "sheet-anchor men."[342] Against the apathy of such church- and chapel-goers as held seamen to be occupationally immune to religious response, examples of evangelistic heroism in converted seamen could put even the most prejudiced to shame.[343] Thus, successive speeches at post-war seamen's mission anniversaries sought to emphasize that Christian seamen were not only the best seamen, but also the best Christians.[344] (The "harmful" and "hopeless" charges, and their positive counterparts—the political-commercial and evangelistic-missiological motives, are dealt with in detail in Part VIII.)[345]

Sufficient has already been said to show that here—in the Naval Awakening of the Napoleonic War period—was no fleeting episode. Here was the dawn of a new era.

PART III

BIRTH OF THE BETHEL MOVEMENT

Toward a British Metropolitan Society

Chapter 6

The Marine
Bible Societies

EARLY MERCHANT MARINE BIBLE DISTRIBUTION
(FROM 1805)

In the year 1800, an aggregate of 126,192 men is stated to have
been borne in ships of the Royal Navy. Available records show that the
number of men employed that same year on merchant vessels, registered in
the British Isles, was almost exactly the same (126,674).[1] Among the
former, efforts had, for several years, already been made by both the NMBS
and SPK to distribute the Word of Life. Among the latter, however, no
corresponding concern had yet become manifest. Was this disparity bound
up with the more conspicuous wartime role of the naval seaman? However
vital her commercial life-lines were to the island nation, her seamen somehow
symbolized more obviously the basic political motive of national survival.[2]

It fell first to the British and Foreign Bible Society (of 1804) to
assume responsibility for Scripture distribution to the seaman in his merchant
navy capacity. However, during most of the Society's first decade, there was
no question of any general outreach to the British merchant seaman as such.
The sporadic cases which can be traced appear to have concerned largely
foreign seamen. Just as concentration on naval (not merchant) seamen in the
pre-1804 period demonstrates the potency of *political* motivation, so the
restriction of nascent merchant distribution to mainly foreign (not British)
seamen in the first post-1804 period could indicate the operation of an
additional, *romantic* motive.[3]

At all events, Scripture distribution among foreign seamen proved
one of the earliest ways in which the new Bible Society justified its global
self-designation. The individual situation of such seamen could, however,
vary widely. Many of them belonged to the category already noticed under
the treatment of the Society's naval outreach, prisoners of war, thousands of

whom were incarcerated in old naval hulks.[4] Of particular interest in the present context is the fact that many of these internees were merchant seamen, the crews of foreign privateers and trading vessels seized as prizes. The majority of them were French. (Altogether 27,613 French privateersmen were captured from 1803 to 1814.)[5] However, large numbers of Scandinavian and Dutch seafarers suffered the same fate, as did also many Americans, after the outbreak of the War of 1812 with the United States.[6]

These seamen shared in the liberal grants of Bibles and Testaments to war prisoners, made annually by the BFBS from 1805 on.[7] Conspicuous in alerting the Society to the spiritual straits of their seafaring countrymen in captivity were the pastors of the Scandinavian and Dutch resident congregations in London.[8] Besides the BFBS, and the loosely affiliated Edinburgh Bible Society, the RTS maintained a substantial distribution among maritime prisoners of war.[9] Members of the Society of Friends showed, through visitation work, their customary concern for victims of warfare.[10]

Apart from internees, other categories of foreign seafarers also figure in the wartime distribution of the BFBS. In London, Samuel Allen maintained supplies to a wide variety of foreign seamen from 1811 to 1815, through a depository in his St. Katherine's warehouse.[11] German seamen are particularly mentioned in several English ports. Here, the Rev. C.F.A. Steinkopff, pastor of the German Lutheran Chapel of the Savoy, and foreign secretary of the BFBS, was largely instrumental.[12] Among other beneficiaries were British and foreign seamen calling at Portsmouth (where Lady Grey maintained copious supplies) and the crews of Portuguese Brazil ships and merchantmen at Lisbon during the Peninsular War.[13]

Scripture copies also found their way to merchant seamen through another channel. During its first years, the BFBS relied solely on gratuitous agents for general distribution purposes. In the foreign sector, several such volunteers were seafarers. In fact, these so-called "agents afloat" form a fascinating chapter of the Bible Society's pioneer period. Some were naval officers, such as Admiral Sir Charles Penrose and Captain John Gourly of the Mediterranean Fleet. Others could be masters of merchant vessels. At all events, the committee was only too grateful to utilize both the transportation facilities and the invaluable foreign contacts which these men afforded.[14] (The RTS also gave grateful recognition to what they called "pious masters of trading vessels, who are in the habit of distributing Tracts in various parts abroad.")[15]

Prominent among such merchant captain collaborators was Francis Reynalds of Hull. In a series of letters from the year 1810 on, Reynalds reports distribution of Scripture in French, Spanish, Portuguese, Italian, German, Dutch, and Danish, to the inhabitants of ports of call as far apart as the Mediterranean, the Baltic and Caribbean. (Grateful recipients included even the President of Haiti.)[16] Reynalds remembered especially his seafaring brethren, however, both British and foreign. Soliciting Scripture on their behalf before leaving again for Malta, he writes to Assistant Secretary Joseph Tarn in 1811:

> . . . and when the exortation in Isa 42,10, with the promises recorded in Isa 24,24, and 60,5 is considered, I have no doubt but the Committee will continue to remember that class of men who seams to be neither numbered with the Living or the Dead. I expect to sail in a short time. . . .[17]

Another merchant Captain, George Orton, writes of his joy at having been the first to circulate the BFBS Modern Greek Testament in the Mediterranean.[18] Like Captain Reynalds, he later involved himself with enthusiasm in early post-war seamen's mission activity ashore.[19]

Captain Anthony Landers of Sunderland forms a further example. It was he who, in 1812, offered to carry to Halifax the supply of Scriptures which was to gain such unexpected publicity on both sides of the Atlantic, after its capture by an American privateer.[20] Like his fellow "agents afloat," he seems to have been willing to "bear a hand" wherever needed in the Kingdom Cause (and was, shortly after the peace, instrumental in a remarkable multiplication of Sunday Schools in New York).[21] But Landers looked with impatience to the dawn of general missions to seafarers. As he put it, "so long as one of the greatest of all [missionary institutions] is wanting, I mourn & lament, tho' not without continuing to use my feeble efforts to rouse the Religious Public to the Condition of the Sailors."[22]

This was written in 1816, in a letter to the BFBS, giving details of recent foreign distribution on their behalf. At the same time, Landers underlines the importance of a ministry to seafarers being particularly oriented:

> One thing I am certain of by experience, that a Sailor will read what is particularly addressed to him, . . . and would the Ministers of the Gospel at Sea port Towns Invite them, particularly with sermons adapted to them, they would attend, for tho' He is so easy to be lead to a bad thing, yet you may also lead him to that which is good. I could get Captains to go with me to hear the late Capt. J. Newton, who would afterwards go themselves, & ministers who only recollect the Sailor in their Prayers, they will go to hear, when they will not others, so that I am persuaded the Means must be aim'd at them, & *for* them to do them good.[23]

On the most effective means of communicating the Gospel to seafarers, Captain Landers did not content himself with offering advice to others. In 1815, he published in New York "a Sermon Solely for Sailors," entitled *Sailors Wanted! Officers and Men, on a Voyage with the Captain of Our Salvation: Bound from the Harbour of Destruction to the Haven of*

Eternal Rest. Dedicated to Lord Gambier, the sermon sets out, in forthright nautical terminology, what were to become the customary components of many a subsequent sermon to seafarers. (Such components will be the object of a later analysis.)[24]

About this time, Landers also published a circular *Letter to Captains*, which achieved wide publicity. It was originally addressed to and (as it states) "occasioned by about forty Captains of British Ships, lying at a port in the West Indies, not attending Church on the Lord's Day, though the Minister was truly respectable." Here he hammers home a theme which was to be constantly repeated by ordained successors: the inescapable responsibility of a ship's captain, by the force of his example, for the spiritual welfare and eternal destiny of his crew.[25]

METROPOLITAN MARINE BIBLE SOCIETIES (FROM 1813)

Although Captain Landers and others still had to wait in 1816 for the foundation of a *general* seamen's mission society, three years had then already elapsed since the advent of a new form of literary precursor. For in 1813 was born the first British organization seeking to promote the spiritual welfare of specifically merchant seafarers.

It was a member of the Southwark Auxiliary Bible Society who took the initiative. Charles C. Dudley, of Addington Place, Camberwell, was a man of exceptional organizing ability (a talent which later led to his appointment as the first full-time "Domestic Agent" of the BFBS).[26] In his own written account of this new endeavor, he tells how, toward the close of 1812,

> [he] had occasion to visit some merchant ships lying in the Thames; and the result of his casual inquiries induced a belief, that an unexpected and deplorable dearth of the holy scriptures existed among the British and Foreign sailors resorting to the port of London. In order to ascertain the fact, eleven ships were indiscriminately visited by him, and only *one* Bible found, and this on board a *Swedish* vessel. A subsequent and more extensive investigation followed; which led to a conviction, that, of the ships that entered the Thames, *not one in twenty* was furnished with a Bible. In pursuing this investigation, more than three hundred vessels were visited; and in no instance whatever were the inquiries treated with disrespect. . . .[27]

The drastic way in which Dudley describes his discovery of Scripture scarcity among merchant seamen in general, and the British in particular, confirms the impression already noted, that the futility of ministering to this class had simply been taken for granted. During the winter, Dudley devoted himself, with the assistance of a colleague in the Southwark Auxiliary, Benjamin Neale, MP, to a plan for meeting the need now so dramatically disclosed. Basically, the plan recognized the obligation of BFBS auxiliaries bordering on the waterfront of a port, in this case the banks of the Thames, to join in union to supply the Bible to visiting seafarers, and for this purpose form a particular committee.[28] Dudley's proposal for such a "Thames Union Bible Committee" was enthusiastically and unanimously adopted by the Committee of the Southwark Auxiliary, meeting on May 12, 1813.[29] The sensation caused by G.C. Smith's successful seamen's service the previous autumn in the same south bank borough must have been fresh in the memory of members of the committee.[30] That event would have conveyed some realization of the potential spiritual hunger of the merchant seaman. Now they had been brought to see how pitifully he was bereft of a basic means of satisfying this hunger.

Copies of the plan, sent to three auxiliaries in a similar situation, met with "cordial approbation." On June 21, 1813, at the Three Tuns Tavern, Southwark, the organization held its first, constitutive meeting, Dr. O. Gregory of Woolwich in the chair. After receiving a report from Dudley, the four deputations unanimously adopted the following as their first resolution:

> That it appears to this meeting highly expedient that measures should be adopted for the distribution, *by sale,* of the Sacred Scriptures amongst the crews of several ships, British & Foreign, resorting to the River.[31]

It was agreed to form a joint committee, consisting of four representatives from each of the four participating auxiliaries: Southwark and Blackheath on the south side of the river, City of London and East London on the north. Distribution was to be channeled through depositories, established "in convenient situations," and supplied with Bibles and Testaments in proportionate quantities by the respective auxiliaries. Furthermore, Dudley was requested to prepare an *Address to Mariners,* to be published in English, French, Spanish, Portuguese, German, Dutch and Danish. (Danish would be intelligible not only to Norwegians, but also to Swedes and some Finns.) The purpose was to provide visiting seamen with both address lists of depositories and motivation to apply.[32]

The address, duly drawn up and circulated, put the provocative question: "While the rich and the poor, the high and the low, are thus coming forward . . . will *you* [seamen] be the last in supplying yourselves with this teacher of the way to heaven, and in sharing the happy privilege of conveying it to foreign lands?"[33] Whatever such arguments may have contributed (or not), first reactions were recorded as positive. At the depositories, nearly twenty of which were eventually established on both banks of the Thames, from London Bridge to Woolwich, "numerous applications" were received. These "speedily and amply confirmed the melancholy estimate which originally prompted the formation of this establishment." (Secretary of the Thames Union Bible Committee was, as late as 1815, Joseph Shewell of Deptford, a Quaker, who was also secretary of the Blackheath Auxiliary Bible Society.)[34]

In spite of initial encouragement, it was nevertheless not long before two major problems posed serious threats. First, there was the financial aspect. Funds placed at the disposal of the committee by the four sponsoring auxiliaries proved "utterly inadequate." This was largely due to the inability of foreign seamen to pay even greatly reduced prices for Scripture copies, thereby necessitating costly gratuitous distribution.[35] Secondly, as initial curiosity wore off, the problem of motivation became increasingly apparent. Time consuming person-to-person work among the men was largely out of the question for committee members. (However enthusiastic in the cause, their opportunities to serve were severely limited by normal every-day avocations.) Hence, it is hardly surprising that, by 1815, those members had to report "deep regret that the results of the Thames Union Bible Committee have fallen very far short of our expectations."[36]

The need for some form of restructuring was painfully manifest. Was Captain Reynalds' initiative, as early as the summer of 1813, the answer? In a letter to the BFBS, dated off the Mother Bank, June 24, 1813, this enterprising pioneer could report the formation among his crew of the first floating "Marine Bible Association" on record. After a meeting of all hands, convened by the captain, the men had, according to the accompanying report of proceedings, unanimously agreed as their first resolution:

> That the crew of this vessel do form themselves into an Association for the purpose of contributing towards the circulation of the holy scriptures, both at home and abroad, and that this Association be denominated 'The Ship Vigilant (of Hull) Bible Association.'[37]

Ashore, Richard Phillips, a philanthropist and member of the BFBS Committee, had, in 1811, produced a plan for nationwide Bible Associations. Affiliated to BFBS Auxiliary Societies, these were grassroots units, intended to provide both information on needs among the poorer classes, and—by minimum penny-a-week subscriptions—stimulus to self-help. By 1813-14, "astonishing results" had been achieved (and nowhere more "brilliantly illustrated" than in the Southwark Auxiliary).[38] Prompted, perhaps, also by the news of Captain Reynalds' original shipboard version, Phillips now suggested a general plan for Marine Bible Associations throughout the merchant service. In cooperation with C.S. Dudley, he prepared a *Code of Rules* and an *Address to Owners and Commanders* which were widely circulated by the BFBS.[39] Like its shore equivalent, the Marine Bible

Association was based on members pledging to subscribe "not less than One Penny a week." The primary purpose was self-supportive (providing individual Scripture copies for the ship's own crew). Any balance could be applied to purchasing supplies for distribution abroad, or to supporting the general funds of the Parent Society.[40]

At the close of 1814, shortly before the official publication of these rules, the commander of a King's packet based at Falmouth established a Marine Bible Association on a foreign voyage. Although it is erroneous to state that this was the first Marine Bible Association, the example was followed by others.[41] Optimistically believing that here, at last, was the answer to both its financial and motivational problems, the Thames Union Bible Committee voted in 1815 to adopt the title "Thames Marine Bible Association Committee."[42] The formal change of name reflected a deliberate transfer of focus from shore-based depositories to shipboard associations.

Hopes that this alone would provide the panacea for organizational worries proved in vain, however. In early 1816, the Thames Marine Bible Association Committee could only admit that "associations onboard ship to any great extent were not so practicable as was thought." The committee asked leave of its sponsors to reopen its shore depositories.[43] A year later, with results still "not equal to the wishes of the Committee," it became obvious that some far more radical change was called for. Efforts hitherto had proved the design itself to be not only practicable, but "too important to continue merely as an appendage to other institutions." After a series of consultations, the committee, meeting with merchants, shipowners and others connected with shipping, resolved, on December 30, 1817, at the Jerusalem Coffee-House, Cornhill, to publish an *Address,* call a public meeting, and merge into a new organization on a far more extensive scale.[44]

The *Address* is significant for its early and eloquent presentation of a whole series of persuasive motives (both specifically Christian and commercial) for active support of seamen's mission measures in general, and the projected Society in particular.[45] It also realistically recognizes both disruptive and corruptive factors frustrating the influence of Christianity at sea, but refuses to regard seafarers as occupationally debarred from positive response to the Word of God:

> Is not the Seaman . . . formed by the same Hand with ourselves? . . . Does the volume of Divine Truth appeal so forcibly to all other men; and is he alone, by some law of creation, or by some hard condition of his lot, to be regarded as excluded from the common range of his Maker's bounty, and as inaccessible to the influence of his word and Spirit?[46]

After the address had been duly circulated, a public meeting was held in the Egyptian Hall of the Mansion House on January 29, 1818, and a new, widely conceived seamen's mission endeavor was launched under the designation "The Merchant-Seamen's Auxiliary Bible Society" (MSABS). In the chair was the Lord Mayor himself, and among those who moved the motions were Admiral Lord Gambier, William Wilberforce and the Rev. Richard Marks. The First Lord of the Admiralty, Viscount Melville, headed the long list of distinguished vice presidents. As joint (gratuitous) secretaries were elected Edward Suter and Joseph Trueman. (The former was to continue in this capacity throughout the 37-year life of the Society.)[47]

While it was also hoped to benefit *foreign* seamen (as in the case of its predecessor), it was specifically stated that the new Society was founded "for the purpose of supplying British Merchant Ships with the Holy Scriptures."[48] Quite naturally, the founders saw the society as "more immediately occupied in supplying the wants of the Seamen belonging to the Port of London." However, there is no doubt that, as originally conceived, this purported to become a *national* society ("to provide Bibles for at least about 120,000 British Seamen, now destitute of them"). It was, therefore, resolved "to encourage the formation of Branch Societies at the principal Out-ports of the British Empire" by immediately opening a correspondence with these.[49]

At the outset, matters seemed promising enough. The stocks of the Thames Marine Bible Association Committee were transferred to the new Society.[50] A first supply of Scriptures to the value of £1,061 was voted by the committee of the BFBS.[51] But in the first place, despite the stimulus provided to others, the Society never became more than a *London* Merchant-Seamen's Auxiliary Bible Society.[52] In the second place, despite determined efforts to promote a more general response from metropolitan merchants and shipowners, the MSABS met with the same financial frustrations as its predecessor, only on a larger scale. Dudley provides an interesting yet debatable reason for this condition of affairs:

> The nature of that connexion which subsists between seamen and
> their employers, particularly in the port of London, is too transient
> and uncertain to create or cherish an interest on the part of the
> latter, in the spiritual welfare of the former.[53]

Nevertheless, within weeks, such signal success was registered in one vital aspect, that there could be no shadow of doubt as to the fundamental justification of the new Society. At last a workable method of motivation of the men had been discovered. The general spiritual ignorance of seamen, combined with the necessity of addressing "this singular but valuable class of men" in "their own way," had inevitably led to the "failure of every measure founded on the presumption that seamen would *apply for Bibles,*" however many depositories were placed within their reach.[54] A radically new principle of approach was wanted, and finally found. The Thames Marine Bible Association Committee had begun, early in 1817, to search for a suitable agent at Gravesend who could visit outward-bound ships and "strive to prevail on all crews to make the Scriptures the companion of their voyage."[55] That committee could hardly have been more gratified by the result of their search. In human terms, Lieutenant John Cox, R.N., was, without question, the new Society's greatest asset during its first critical years.

In the Bible Society's team of early gratuitous co-workers, Lieutenant John Cox had long since come to command a key position. Scripture shipments to foreign fields in the midst of Napoleonic War conditions could have confronted the young Society with formidable physical and financial impediments. But in this enterprising officer, the BFBS found a combined "Lloyd's List" and shipping agency, exactly where most acutely needed.

As early as 1806, when serving on H.M. Frigate *Woolwich* on the Thames, Cox had already come to the notice of the Society by his pioneering concern for Scripture distribution among convicts on board the prison-ships in Woolwich Roads. (A vast number of them, he had found, were chained not only by the leg, but, he feared, "in greater bondage, being bound and fetter'd with their sins, and perishing for lack of knowledge. . . .")[56] From the period immediately following, numerous letters bear witness to Cox's constant alertness for convenient and gratuitous opportunities to serve the shipping needs of the BFBS. Men-of-war, transports, supply-ships bound for Gibraltar, Malta, Rio, the Cape, Port Jackson—any sailings he thought might interest were systematically reported, and frequently made use of.[57]

Writing to Joseph Tarn in 1809, when on the tender *Tower* fitting out at Deptford, Lieutenant Cox evinced keen awareness of the realities of personal relations in a missionary context, coupled with Methodist partiality— and humor:

> [Two officer-acquaintances in the Transport Office] are both stationary there [at Deptford], and tho' (I fear) not of the common-wealth of Israel are like Mr. Cuthbert of Woolwich very civil, and ready to give every information. . . . P.S. I shall not fail to look out for those who savour of Methodism as bearers of your commands and you know the stronger they smell the better.[58]

At all events, the impression made by this resourceful naval lieutenant was fresh in the minds of Bible Society leaders when, in the midst of post-war officer redundancy, a choice had to be made for the Gravesend agency of the MSABS. In Cox, the committee was given reason to expect "the zeal, activity, intelligence and discretion, which the situation required," and he "fully justified their confidence." Confronted with this novel call, Cox proved willing to commence without a day's delay, on February 26, 1818.[59]

Detailed instructions had been prepared for the Society's Gravesend agent. It was to be his "main business" to visit every foreign-bound ship which brought up at Gravesend. (This they would normally have to do, in order to obtain final clearance.) On boarding, he was to ascertain how many Bibles and Testaments there were in relation to the number of crew and, if deficient according to a minimum scale, leave a corresponding gratuitous ship's supply "as a part of the ship's furniture" for the joint use of successive crews. At the same time, Scripture copies were to be offered at half cost-price for individual use. He was to encourage those who could read to help those who could not; they might both read aloud for them, and teach them the art of reading.[60]

In order to furnish the committee with a means of continuing reassessment of needs and methods, the agent was expected to maintain minute records. By Cox, both instructions and records were kept "with a singular degree of regularity." His weekly reports quoting (anonymously) countless conversations illustrating the response of captains, mates, and men met during his daily visitation program, were publicized and eagerly read throughout the country, even across the Atlantic.[61]

The published reports from Cox's first year provide interesting examples of such ship-visiting dialogue: "One poor fellow . . . ,having no money, offered to barter a pair of good trowsers for a Bible." "O, Sir, do leave us a Bible!" shouted the men, as the "Bible-Boat" was shoving off from a ship which seemed too busy weighing anchor. (The captain promptly delayed departure to allow a supply.) "We sailors have been swearers quite long enough; it is now high time we begin to pray. Let me have a Bible." (Such was the candid confession of an "honest tar" on another vessel.) Two Testaments given to a Spanish crew induced them to follow the agent with thanks "a thousand times," even after he had left their ship far behind.[62]

Reports from ships systematically revisited confirmed the beneficial effect of the work: on questioning crews on a whole series of ships (without the master present), all asserted that the Scriptures left with them had been read on every suitable occasion. A Scotsman had risked his life to rescue a New Testament during shipwreck on the last voyage. A passenger on a ship previously supplied, seeing several of the crew at pay-off buying Bibles they could "call their own," marveled at what was indeed "an uncommon sight, but a very comely one."[63] While owners, pilots, customs officials and captains continued to commend the sobriety and sense of responsibility instilled by the work of the Society, the men, too, had their spokesmen. "God forbid that I should go to sea without a Bible," said one who had now learned its worth. "What is man without a Bible? What is a ship without a compass?"[64]

A seamen's missionary offering Christian literature to
his evidently interested dockland congregation.
(A contemporary print.)

On completion of Cox's first year of intense activity at Gravesend, it
transpired that 1,681 vessels (British and foreign) carrying 24,765 men had
been supplied with 6,370 copies of Scripture. Some 600 of the ships supplied
had proved to be completely devoid of the Scriptures, and only 2,200 (solely
private) copies had been found on the remainder. Apart from "a very few
cases," the agent had been welcomed on board with "a gratifying cordiality."[65]

Despite—or rather on account of—this great initial distribution, the
new "Auxiliary" became financially a direct liability during the first years of
its existence. (The proportion of Scripture copies sold was, the first year,
little more than one tenth of the number given gratuitously. Not before the
fourth year was parity achieved, to be eventually succeeded by a reversal of
the original picture.)[66] In principle, however, the appointment of a Gravesend
agent by the MSABS proved another new departure of epoch-making
significance in the history of seamen's missions. Lieutenant John Cox was
presumably the world's first full-time seamen's missionary and ship's visitor.

In this dual capacity, he convincingly showed the ultimate necessity of the former, and the key role of the latter.[67]

PROVINCIAL MARINE BIBLE SOCIETIES (FROM 1814)

In contrast to the painful process of protracted experimentation in the metropolitan area, the organization of merchant marine Scripture distribution in provincial ports met with far more rapid success. The ground had, here too, been prepared by an existing local auxiliary of the BFBS. (In typically maritime districts, enterprising spirits in the auxiliary would soon be alerted to Scripture "destitution" among seafarers, and sense this as a challenge to organized action.) Conspicuous among the various agencies which thus emerged were those in the Northern Counties.

First was the "Tyne Union Bible Committee." Modeled on the earlier Thames version, it was founded in 1814 as a joint venture by the Tyneside Auxiliary Bible Societies at Newcastle and Shields. A partial survey of ships entering the Tyne revealed that here, as in London, "not more than one in twenty was furnished with a Bible." An *Address to Ship Owners* was drawn up and liberally circulated. True, "such was the general insensibility on the subject of religion, which then prevailed among sea-faring people," that the pioneers had first to contend with both indifference and sneers, even on board. But they persevered, the BFBS supplemented limited local supplies and, after a while, the committee's visits on board were "hailed with pleasure." (The Tyne Union Bible Committee was still actively surveying and supplying needs in 1829.)[68] Immediately to the south, Sunderland ships were systematically supplied by a special sub-committee appointed in 1817 by the Bishop-Wearmouth &c. Auxiliary Bible Society.[69]

Particularly impressive, however, were the results of the three "Marine Bible Associations" at Whitby, Hull and Aberdeen. (Dudley's orderly mind would have preferred to see their designation confined to *shipboard* usage, but he has only unstinted praise for their achievements.)[70] The "Whitby Marine Bible Association" was founded early in 1816 and quickly flourished, thanks partly to "a munificent donation of 50 guineas" from Captain Scoresby of the *Mars,* a Greenland ship.[71] The "Hull Marine Bible Association" was established February 13, 1817, with Captain Francis Reynalds playing a leading role, and 700-800 seafarers taking part.[72] The "Aberdeen Marine Bible Association" was instituted in February 1818 and also achieved a rousing response.[73] A statistical comparison between the record of these northern societies and their London counterpart underscores the ascendancy of the former.[74]

It is significant how, in the case of each of these three ports, two common features seem to have combined to ensure success: (1) The active involvement of shipowners, merchants and captains in subscribing and supplying. (Especially fruitful was the practice of consigning a supply of Scripture to the captain for sale during the ensuing voyage.)[75] (2) The confrontation of crews with cooperative responsibility. (Instead of making seamen the objects of charity, distribution by sale was made the rule; also, shipboard Marine Bible Associations here proved eminently successful, and promoted concern beyond self.)[76] Other factors may have contributed. Whitby and Hull were both strongholds of Methodism, and there was a large proportion of evangelical-spirited Greenland fishing captains from these ports. Also, "seamen were uniformly disposed to purchase Bibles if their captains wished them to do so."[77] Finally, here were mostly so-called "home crews," with what positive spiritual potential this form of social cohesion could entail.[78]

In other ports, too, societies were founded with a similar purpose in view (normally in conjunction with the local Auxiliary Bible Society). On March 23, 1818, a thriving society based on Lerwick in the Shetland Islands was established under the name of the "Zetland, Davies' Straits, Greenland Fishery, and Marine Bible Society" (in this case, in connection with the Edinburgh Bible Society). The Shetlands had recently been evangelized by both Baptists and Independents.[79] On October 14, 1818, the "Liverpool Marine Bible Society" was reorganized on the pattern of the London MSABS (after having been originally founded January 13, 1818). This society soon found it necessary to employ two agents.[80] Shortly afterwards, a "Bristol Marine Bible Association" emerged from the pioneering activity of a zealous Bible Association collector in the Auxiliary of that city, John James Beard.[81]

Before leaving the subject of early British Marine Bible Societies, mention must be made of similar efforts for the benefit of bargemen and boatmen. At the close of the Napoleonic War, it was stated that:

> The number of persons employed in navigating the boats on the Grand Junction and other canals, is estimated at about 6,000; including their wives and families, the number is probably not less than 20,000. These may be said almost to *live* upon the water; and, by the peculiar nature of their occupation, are precluded all opportunity of attending public worship on the sabbath-day. For this deprivation, no remedy offers itself, equal to that of providing them with copies of the holy scriptures. . . .

Such was the conviction of the founders of "The Grand Junction and General Canal Bible Association" established at Paddington, March 20, 1816, under the patronage of the Bishops of Durham, Norwich and Gloucester.

First reactions were encouraging. Bibles and Testaments, granted by the BFBS and offered at cost or reduced prices, were "speedily and gratefully purchased by the boatmen." (Among the association's "collateral benefits" was a "Canal School" shortly afterwards established at Paddington for upwards of 150 sorely underprivileged boatmen's children.) The Uxbridge Auxiliary Bible Society had, as early as 1812, taken the initiative among this class by alloting a large-print Bible to each barge navigating between Brentford and Rickmansworth. However, the 1816 association was apparently the first organization specifically founded for the spiritual welfare of crews on inland waterways. As such, it deserves mention in a study of the origin of seamen's missions, even though—as in the case of other peripheral categories —early efforts among canalmen and rivermen cannot here be treated in detail.[82]

CONTINENTAL MARINE BIBLE SOCIETIES (FROM 1815)

The lofty vision of Britain's home-port Marine Bible Societies was thus formulated by one of their number:

> If, by means of such institutions, an interest first, in favour of the possession, and then in favour of the dispersion of the Scriptures, can be created on board of every vessel that leaves a British port, there is, perhaps, no measure which may ultimately be productive of more powerful effect in promoting the distribution of Scripture abroad.[83]

In a few ports abroad, the efforts of such seafaring collaborators were—in so far as marine distribution was concerned—eventually supplemented by *foreign* Marine Bible Societies.

As in the case of the home-port agencies, beginnings abroad were closely connected with the existing network for *general* Bible distribution.[84] The latter was again largely traceable to the influence and support of the ever-expanding Parent Society. (The rapid development of Marine Bible Societies in the USA is a subject requiring separate attention.)[85]

The first Continental marine Bible agencies had as their object Scripture distribution among principally *naval* personnel, together with their (generally impoverished) dependents. They were nevertheless classified as "Marine Bible Societies" by the BFBS.

The earliest example seems to have been a small auxiliary of the Swedish Bible Society, established in 1815 in Stockholm, in "the Admiralty Parish of Shipsholm" (Skeppsholms Auxiliaire Bibel-Sällskap).[86] A similar but far more extensive society was founded February 2, 1819, at the naval base of Carlscrona, "the Portsmouth of Sweden." The initiative was here taken by the Rev. Ebenezer Henderson, whose offer of a £200 grant from the BFBS laid the financial foundation. This was expressly referred to as the "Swedish Naval Bible Society" (Svenska Orlogsflottans och Carlscrona Stads Bibel-Sällskap). It soon became the means of spreading Scriptures in large numbers among seamen, naval employees and their families in this predominantly maritime district.[87]

Before this, a so-called "Naval Bible Society" had also been founded in Russia at the key commercial and naval port of Cronstadt on October 22, 1816, at the instigation of Henderson's colleague, the Rev. John Paterson. (Captain Francis Reynalds seems to have helped to prepare the way.) Officially an auxiliary of the Russian Bible Society, the new endeavor was warmly supported by Vice-Admiral Korobka (as chairman) and numerous other naval officers. Its directors were highly cosmopolitan, including both resident foreign clergymen and consuls. Besides the effect of the Society's foreign distribution, its domestic influence was such that Prince Galitzin could, in 1819, assert that Russian sailors had now "learned to value the Scriptures, and the use of them was becoming general. . . ."[88]

In 1820, what was termed a "Marine Bible Society" for seamen in general was established in Copenhagen by the Danish Bible Society. A depository (Bibel-Oplag for Sömænd) was opened in the Master-Mariners' Guildhouse and supplied with Scripture in Danish, German and English, partly through the BFBS. The founders were inspired by the earlier example set not only by London, but also by other ports.[89]

Among these other ports, mention is made of Hamburg-Altona. (In this major port area, the Hamburg-Altona Bible Society had been founded in 1814 with substantial aid from the BFBS.)[90] Also mentioned is Amsterdam. Here, too, a Marine Bible Society had been established in 1820 under the local Auxiliary of the United Netherlands Bible Society. With a number of "retired Captains of pious character" as directors, a wide and vigorous program of distribution was undertaken among the Dutch and foreign seamen. Scriptures in "Dutch, English, Swedish, Danish, German, French, and even Hebrew and Malay" were supplied, chiefly through the local BFBS depository. The success of the Society led to the formation of a similar agency in Rotterdam the following year.[91]

AN ASSESSMENT

An evaluation of the significance of the Marine Bible Society Movement as a whole must take into account the fact that a substantial proportion of Scripture distribution to merchant seamen, both at home and overseas, continued to go through other channels. These could be concerned individuals (seafarers, ministers and men employed in the shipping industry, or others). They could also be the local organization for *general* Scripture distribution (especially in harbor or coastal districts).[92]

Where such concern found expression in specific organization, the resultant "Continental Marine Bible Societies" are noteworthy not least because they constitute the first (and hitherto largely ignored) type of Continental seamen's mission organization. The fact that a hiatus of half a century was to elapse before societies with more diversified seamen's mission activities were to emerge on the Continent, should in no wise be permitted to detract from the significance of their modest predecessors.[93]

Of more immediate interest, however, is the role of BFBS home-port Marine Bible Societies as the earliest form of seamen's organization for specifically *merchant* seamen in Britain. Dudley saw, even in 1821, the possibility of Marine Bible Societies becoming "the principal instrument" of effecting the seaman's reformation.[94]

Although this was to prove an overestimation, Marine Bible Societies did nevertheless fulfill a highly important threefold purpose: (1) They provided, in some measure, the primary means of grace for the merchant seaman, just as the NMBS had sought to reach the naval seaman with it.[95] (Significantly, the strongest initial response came from the Northern Counties, whose collier crews were destined to play a vital part in ensuing events on the Thames.)[96] (2) They inaugurated the concept of institutionalized lay collaboration on shipboard with the introduction of seagoing Marine Bible Associations. (In so doing, they carried the cell group movement of the Naval Awakening a stage further. Again, the societies in the Northern Counties took the lead.) (3) They confirmed the necessity of a particularly oriented structuring of seamen's mission activity.[97] (This was to prove of fundamental importance for the development of differentiated patterns of seamen's ministry in the years immediately ahead. The obligation of the Christian Church to bring the Gospel to seafarers could not be adequately met by only utilizing *established* methods and media.)

Chapter 7

The Thames Revival

The Rotherhithe Methodists

Even as late as in 1820, a British officer stationed at Gibraltar found himself compelled to advise the committee of the BFBS that any immediate attempt to found a regular auxiliary there would be doomed to failure:

> The methodists are the only people willing to assist, but there are very few of them of any respectability, and the very name is held so generally, though unjustly, in detestation that any of their body coming forward to promote it *ostensibly* would only mar the attempt. . . .[98]

The argument is illuminating and typical of the times. Would it be unreasonable to link this lack of respect for an emerging Christian denomination with early Methodist involvement in precisely *seamen's* missions? The seafarer was, at the close of the Napoleonic War, socially and spiritually still subject to the stigma of belonging to a pariah caste.[99] The Methodists, with so little to lose in general estimation themselves, were least likely to be deterred by the current public image of seamen.

At all events, G.C. Smith, himself a Baptist and intimately involved with the development of organized seamen's missions, is quite categorical about where denominational credit is due in this particular field. Writing some fourteen years after the beginnings of what was to become the "Bethel Movement," he states:

> [It is] notorious that it began, as most good things that require active zeal do, among the *Wesleyan Methodists;* and that *three years* before any member of [any other] . . . denomination had been permitted to put his hand to the work, it was zealously and nobly promoted and advanced by the Wesleyan Methodists, at Rotherhithe. . . . God was pleased to honour their denomination to commence this great work, . . . an honour as justly their due, as it

is to the Baptist denomination that they were appointed specially
of God to give the first grand impulse to missions throughout the
world. . . .[100]

The pioneer figure in this new missionary movement, Zebedee
Rogers, was, like William Carey before him, a shoemaker by profession.
(His first name has occasionally but incorrectly been rendered as Zebulon,
or Zachariah.)[101] Rogers' domicile is significant. Rotherhithe has ancient
maritime traditions going back at least to the Saxon era. (According to one
theory, the name is derived from "Redhra-hythe," Saxon for "Sailors'
Haven.") Among the many mementos of Rotherhithe's maritime past at the
parish church of St. Mary's is also the grave of Captain Christopher Jones,
master of the *Mayflower*; his epic voyage in 1620 actually began from here.
At the turn of the nineteenth century, the township of Rotherhithe still
consisted mainly of London's longest street, hugging the south bank of the
Thames from Dockhead roughly a mile below London Bridge, along the
whole length of the Lower Pool, and down Limehouse Reach to the east.
Seafaring together with its many allied occupations continued to dominate
the Rotherhithe scene.[102]

As the son of a coal-measurer, Rogers had, during his boyhood,
frequently accompanied his father on board North Country collier brigs.
These crowded the river, especially along the Lower Pool (where they were
moored in tiers in such numbers that they looked like whole "forests of
masts").[103] In this way, Rogers received early impressions of the hard life to
which seamen were exposed.

The "poor shoemaker from Rotherhithe" has himself recorded the
unforeseen train of events which resulted from impressions he received in a
quite different sense:

> Having had to labor much under strong convictions for sin
> during some months, and but little attention being paid me by
> professing christians, from that day to the present, I have en-
> deavoured to assist any persons I saw under similar religious
> impressions. In 1814, I beheld a person weeping under a sermon
> in the Wesleyan Methodist Chapel, at Silver-street, Rotherhithe.
> When the service was concluded, I went to the chapel door, and
> spoke to him with much tenderness and sympathy, taking him by
> the hand. I found his name was captain Simpson, of the *Friendship*
> brig. We soon became well acquainted together; and I took him to
> our class-meeting. He came on shore, and invited me on board his
> vessel, the next voyage. I asked him if he thought his people would
> come into the cabin and let me pray with them. The captain said,
> "go and ask them." I went to the half deck, and told them they
> were all wanted in the cabin. "Cabin, sir!" they said with surprise.

Old Rotherhithe waterfront, with the parish
church of St. Mary's in the background.
(From a print by J. Carter.)

"Yes, all of you." They all came. I read and prayed with them,
and got the captain to pray also. We had one more prayer-meeting
that voyage; and the next voyage, when he came up, we had
another. The *Hammond* brig laid at the *Friendship's* quarter, and
the captain invited me on board her to hold a meeting. From that
time I went on until now [1827].[104]

That first informal prayer-meeting on the Shields collier brig
Friendship was said to have taken place on June 22, 1814.[105] The date was
in the future to be celebrated as the day on which the mustard seed of the
Bethel Movement was first sown.[106] It seems natural to ask, therefore, who
was this shipmaster friend of the shoemaker from Rotherhithe? Little is
known of the personal background of Captain David Simpson beyond the
fact that he was domiciled in North Shields.[107] After his 1814 conversion,
however, there is frequent evidence of his consistent zeal in sharing the
Gospel with brother-seafarers wherever he sailed, both in the coastal coal
trade, and later overseas. Pioneering the cause in Archangel, as late as 1831,
this "first Bethel Captain" maintained close ties with G.C. Smith and his
seamen's mission societies throughout.[108]

The example of the *Friendship* spread further than to the *Hammond*
(of Harley). Gradually other names were added to the list of North Country
collier brigs whose captains opened their cabins for social prayer. Specifically
mentioned are: the *Venus,* the *Robert and Margaret,* the *Amphitrite,* the

Zeno, and the *John* (all from the Tyne ports of Newcastle and North and South Shields). As arrivals rotated, two meetings a week were generally held on board. The captains of such ships were considered to be committed Christians, with their firm shoemaker friend from shore providing stimulus and a continuing connecting link. In this way, the meetings progressed some two and a half years, towards the close of 1816.[109]

What manner of men were these collier captains and their crews? Primarily, they were professional, thoroughbred seafarers. As such, they were by no means exempt from the foibles and frustrations of their fellows.[110] Nevertheless, it was with good reason that the North Country collier fleet was known as the "Nursery of the British Navy."[111] As seamen from the north in general, these men were regarded as "remarkable not only for being sober, steady, and orderly men, but also for being more thinking" than seamen from elsewhere. Despite an initial show of indifference, even contempt, they often displayed a remarkable degree of religious receptivity. This, combined with the North Countryman's traditional independence of spirit, could produce a particularly "strong sturdy faith in Christ."[112] No more convincing proof of this could be provided than the history of the Thames Revival, and the Bethel Movement to which it gave birth.[113]

However decisive the perseverance of Zebedee Rogers proved to be, he did not continue entirely alone. He had the encouragement and increasing cooperation of fellow-members of the Silver Street Methodist Chapel. Rotherhithe folk had a tradition of rugged piety.[114] This had been renewed through repeated visits by John Wesley and his colleagues. (After preaching again in Rotherhithe in 1790, he records "a remarkable revival of the work of God" there.)[115] Nor was the zeal of the congregation which eventually emerged in Silver Street likely to be dampened by the appearance of sailors in their midst. For that, the sea was already too much a part of their lives. It was, therefore, only natural that Rogers, soon after the positive response to his first shipboard prayer-meetings, should follow up his visitation by inviting the men ashore to services at the chapel.[116] Situated off Rotherhithe Street on the eastern side of the peninsula (where Silver Walk Flats now stand), Silver Street was easily accessible from the Lower Pool. (The "Pool" of the Thames was generally divided into the Upper Pool, from London Bridge to the London Docks, and the Lower Pool, from the London Docks to Limehouse.)[117]

Among local Wesleyans who lent Rogers their support, Samuel Jennings, a successful Rotherhithe timber merchant, was to play a unique role. Jennings had a spiritual history very similar to that of Rogers. Weighted down in early life with an acute sense of personal sin, he had suffered long from lack of Christian concern and counseling. After removing across the river from Wapping to Rotherhithe, he turned to the Methodists and at Silver Street Chapel "found peace to his soul." Having learned by experience the value of Christian fellowship, he was soon appointed "Class Leader." A practical man, he saw that Sunday-school facilities at the chapel were far from satisfactory. Instead, at his own expense, he fitted up a stable in his garden as Sunday-school for the children. His home and business were on the river-side of Rotherhithe Street (where Enthoven's Lead Factory has since been constructed), only a short walk north of the chapel. Here what came to be known as "Mr. Jennings' Sunday-school" continued to flourish until after his death.[118]

For the emerging organization of seamen's missions, this particular Sunday-school was to have a singular significance. Samuel Jennings, whose timber trade brought him into constant contact with ships and seamen, must have sensed something of the sensation inherent in those colliermen's response to a shoemaker's initative. At all events, sources show that Jennings gave Zebedee Rogers early encouragement and made sure he should not lack waterage-money for his ship visitation.[119] However, Rogers' activity soon posed a problem. Space at Silver Street Chapel was, of course, limited. Meanwhile captains, mates, seamen and boys found their way there in increasing numbers. "Mr. Jennings' School-Room" became the solution.[120]

At his transformed stable, Samuel Jennings could provide room not only for hundreds of Sunday-school children, but also for the many from ship and shore who came to his class- and prayer-meetings. As the proportion of seamen at these meetings continued to mount, he was compelled to enlarge and rebuild "the Tempel," as he called it, both in 1815 and again in 1816. At the same time, he found it necessary to provide a program more particularly adapted to their needs. On Sundays, besides an afternoon service, he invited them to a special dawn service prior to the early morning prayer-meeting. Thus,

> winter and summer, he was always up on the Sabbath morning at six o'clock, and expounded the Scriptures to the sailors, one hour before the prayer-meeting commenced. It was the delight of his soul to to see the school-room full of sailors.[121]

A regular mid-week meeting was also instituted on Wednesday evenings. (So popular did this eventually prove among seamen in the Lower Pool that Wednesday evening came to be called simply "Mr. Jennings' Night." It became an unwritten law among them that no meeting afloat should ever be arranged that night.)[122] It was while Jennings was preaching at a Wednesday night service for seamen that the Circuit Superintendent, Rev. Joseph Sutcliffe (who happened to hear him), was so profoundly struck by his talents that he promptly appointed him a "Local Preacher."[123]

Meanwhile, in his shipboard activities, Zebedee Rogers was for long largely alone. However, in 1815, a young black seafarer, called Frederick Sanderson, was "awakened by God on board a ship," joined the Wesleyans, and became, together with Rogers, a zealous co-worker among the collier crews in the Lower Pool. (He later became a "most useful" Methodist minister in Jamaica, where he ultimately died.)[124]

At an early stage, Rogers had cheerfully placed his activities afloat under the superintendence of his merchant co-religionist.[125] For this role, Jennings evidently had the zeal and the status required. Thus, the picture of the first phase of the Thames Revival emerges as a "combined operation," based primarily on the sustained efforts of two dedicated Methodist laymen. On the waters of the Lower Pool was the shoemaker, wending his way between the tiers of North Country collier brigs, sharing his experience of Christ and knowledge of the Scriptures, leading prayer-meetings in the cabins of cooperating captains, and inviting the men to the meetings on the Rotherhithe shore. By his wharf at the Pageant Stairs was the timber merchant, leading, "like a father among them," the seamen's meetings in his school-room sanctuary.[126] Many of these seamen joined Jennings' class as formal members.[127]

The whole continued, with increasing help from local preachers and others, but always at Jennings' entire expense, into the 1820's.[128] An indication of the love and veneration in which the name of Samuel Jennings came to be held by seamen of his day was the way in which they received the news of his death, January 26, 1828. Afloat and along both banks of the Thames, flags were hoisted half-mast high, and the London Mariners' Church was thronged by the many who came to hear a special memorial sermon preached by G.C. Smith.[129]

Although Smith could, with some justification, refer to Mr. Jennings' School-Room as "The First River Thames Bethel Station," it was not exclusively a seamen's mission station.[130] Nevertheless, it is important to note that here, in the coordinated efforts of Zebedee Rogers and Samuel Jennings, was developed, during 1814 and the years immediately following, the first organized, ongoing program of preaching known to have been established especially for seafarers.

THE BETHEL FLAG

As the year 1816 drew to a close, there were unmistakable signs of spiritual renewal on the Thames. However, the number of ships and seamen directly involved was still strictly limited. The sequence of events which resulted in these more modest manifestations rapidly reaching revival proportions was introduced by another Tyneside collier captain.

The Early Bethel Flag.
(*Chart and Compass*, 1914, p. 55.)

Although generally referred to as a captain, Anthony Wilkins (stated to have been a native of South Shields) was, in actual fact, still a mate at the time. He is described as having already "joined the Wesleyan Methodists, as a subject of Divine grace, through the instrumentality of Mr. Boyden, a king's pilot of North Yarmouth."[131] On the Thames, his evangelistic ardor combined with a particularly powerful voice soon made him "a sort of Boanerges" of the Bethel Movement.[132] In 1820, as master of the *Hannah,* Wilkins provides the following recapitulation in a letter to G.C. Smith:

> When I was mate of the ship Zeno, of North Shields, December 13, 1816, I was walking the deck, reflecting with great pleasure on the privileges we enjoyed in our bark, and a sudden desire powerfully starting up in my mind, that meetings for prayer were more general among Sailors, I instantly determined to make the experiment, and went on board the Juno, North Shields, to ask for the cabin for that evening. Captain M[ortin] gave his consent, and we met accordingly. ... We had about sixty persons present, and eleven engaged in prayer. This was a time ever to be remembered.[133]

When Wilkins, "without consulting flesh and blood" (as he puts it), took his boat and rowed over to the *Juno* that evening,[134] his brief trip marked a decisive new departure in the development of seamen's missions. His plan was, out of genuine missionary concern for his "much neglected brethren of the deep," to solicit henceforth the use of any convenient ship, irrespective of the spiritual standpoint of whoever happened to be the captain. Here was, then, a definite transition from relatively isolated conventicles to a dynamic principle of itineration. Proof of the timeliness of the venture was provided by the conversion of the captain of that first experimental host-vessel.[135]

The continued success of itinerant shipboard prayer-meetings would now depend on the adoption of effective media of communication. Here again, Wilkins rose to the occasion. Resuming his narrative of that first meeting on the *Juno*, he states:

> I told the Sailors we should meet again the following evening, and that a lantern would be hoisted, as a signal. — Captain M[ortin] very kindly offered his ship for the next night; I thanked him, but thought if we could get a fresh ship every night, it would be the best. We obtained next the Happy Return, and had about seventy present. — Then we had the Joseph and Mary, of Newcastle, quite crowded with Sailors: many could not get below. — A pious Merchant from Rotherhithe [Samuel Jennings] came on board, and gave an exhortation. ... We met the next night in the Prosperity, of Sunderland, our pious friend came off from the shore. ... We now held meetings every night in the week, but we found Saturday evening, being thus engaged, the sailors and cabin-boys were forced to clean shoes, &c. on Sabbath mornings. This we considered wrong, and have ever since given up the Saturday evening, that they may have time to prepare for the Lord's day. Our ship was now ready to leave London. ... Such a parting, I have never since witnessed. As we sailed down the Thames — tack and half-tack — the numbers that waved and shouted Farewell, completely overpowered me.[136]

Clearly, by Christmas 1816, revival had reached the merchant seaman. As the winter progressed, prayer-meetings in the Lower Pool continued to multiply. Zebedee Rogers was still intensely active, aided by Samuel Jennings and others from the Silver Street Chapel. At the same time, new faces were seen at the sailors' meetings in the School-Room ashore.[137] On the *Zeno's* return, Wilkins, this time as captain, again threw himself wholeheartedly into the fray. Though conscious of being an "unpolished instrument" for so great a work, he and others like him felt that "enthusiasm" was justified. "The wind bloweth where it listeth." When God sent them "a fair wind" they knew as sailors it was their duty to take advantage of it, spread all their "canvas," and "press" all hands for the heaven-bound voyage. As captains, mates and men gave evidence of conversion, Wilkins, with his fellow-laborers, was awe-struck: "Who could have thought of Sailors, wicked, depraved, and daring Sailors, returning to the Shepherd and Bishop of their souls, with weeping and supplication!"[138]

A lantern hoisted at the main top-gallant masthead proved an easy and effective means of giving advance notice of the host vessel for the evening in the darker part of the winter. But as spring approached and days lengthened the colliermen and their colleagues from Rotherhithe realized that their "winter signal" was becoming useless. They discussed an alternative. "A flag was then thought of," writes Captain Wilkins, without specifying which of them happened to voice the thought first.[139] The all-important question was: What kind of flag? The answer has been recorded in all its unadorned simplicity:

> Zebedee Rogers, the poor shoemaker of Rotherhithe, who attended all these meetings, now began to think, and talk, and pray about this religious signal it was proposed to have hoisted in a ship, and to his great surprise, one evening, the word "BETHEL" was deeply impressed upon his soul, and he thought that would be a very pretty *bible-word,* but he could not imagine what could be the meaning of that *outlandish* word, as he called it; but having one day sent to his sister, . . . he enquired of her whether she had ever heard any person tell the meaning of the word "BETHEL." His sister, to his great surprise, returned this answer, that some time hence she had heard a preacher from the pulpit declare that the word "BETHEL," in the Old Testament, signified the *House of God.* Zebedee Rogers was so delighted with this information, that he went to work as soon as possible to collect a few shillings on shore and afloat, to buy the blue and white bunting, and have a flag made with the word "BETHEL," and to have it hoisted as soon as possible at the masthead of a ship in the Lower Pool . . . [to] signify that a prayer meeting in the evening would be held in that ship, and neighbours were invited, afloat and on shore, to go on board. Thus the work began. . . .[140]

Certainly, the introduction of this banner began a phase of the work which opened up horizons hardly envisaged by those humble harvesters in the vineyard of the Thames. For decades to come, the Bethel Flag was to circle the globe and become the great symbol—even a pre-condition—of expanding seamen's mission outreach.[141] This fact, coupled with the inconsistency of accounts hitherto current concerning the origin of the flag, call for a closer scrutiny.

Captain Wilkins evidently helped to collect for the materials, a sailor (one Peter Hunt) cut out the letters "B-E-T-H-E-L," and Zebedee Rogers' sister sewed the first flag together.[142] This flag is stated to have been hoisted for the first time on Sunday afternoon, March 23, 1817, by Captain T. Hindhulph of South Shields, on the collier brig *Zephyr.* The event attracted an attendance "more numerous than on any preceding occasion."[143] (Captain Hindhulph was, like Captain Wilkins, a staunch Methodist, co-operating closely with him in promoting continued "Bethel operations" on the Thames and in supporting the meetings at Mr. Jennings' School-Room ashore.)[144]

The word "BETHEL" in large letters on a blue ground, as in the original device, was to remain the essential feature of the Bethel Flag.

Dove with olive branch
symbolizing the peace
of God, as depicted by
the Early Church in the
catacombs of Rome.
(J. Ursin: *"Kristne
Symboler."*)

Shortly after the first version had been taken into use, however, two further features were added to it. Captain Wilkins gives the following summary of the circumstances:

> In July [1817] our converts had so increased, that it was necessary to divide ourselves into two bands, — another signal was now necessary. We therefore collected a few shillings amongst ourselves, and got a second Bethel flag. To this flag, we added the star, and the dove. We could now therefore occupy two tiers, five times a week, making the ratio of ten services per week.[145]

Although the original, simpler version was also occasionally employed in the decades ahead,[146] the inclusion of the star and dove met with immediate approval, and had obviously come to stay. The most generally used pattern seems to have become the word "BETHEL" horizontally across the center of the blue ground, a star at the top of the hoist, and a dove (with an olive branch in its beak, as in the narrative of the biblical Ark) at the base of the hoist, flying towards the center.[147] The relative position of the individual components could occasionally vary.[148] With time, all three came to be represented in white; but sources indicate that in earlier years this was not consistently the case.[149]

There appears to have been basic consensus as to *interpretation* of the symbols, however. As one later leader of seamen's missions put it: "A more significant, scriptural flag could scarcely have sprung from the brain and heart of man."[150] Here were the Star of Bethlehem, the Dove of Peace and the House of God. The first two symbolized the incarnation and the atoning death of Christ; since "BETHEL" signified the church, the three components could, therefore, be said to represent the three major festivals of the Christian year: Christmas (the star), Easter (the dove), and Pentecost (the word "BETHEL"). (A later trinitarian interpretation, however, is not supported by available sources, nor by the traditional significance in Christian symbolism of an olive branch in the beak of the dove.)[151]

Although there quickly developed a kind of "common consent" on both sides of the Atlantic as to the general appearance and significance of the Bethel Flag,[152] there was never any question of rigid, universal uniformity. The history of the origin of this emblem, preceding, as it did, the emergence of the major seamen's mission societies, made it the potential property of all, and the monopoly of none. As the flag assumed a steadily more predominant role, some of these societies came to identify themselves with it to a marked degree. (Not a few based their own institutional emblem on elements of the Bethel Flag.)[153]

However, considerable confusion as to the historical origin of the flag was to result from the controversies which for some years beset certain of these societies on the British scene.[154] These controversies, as far as they influenced the course and pace of seamen's mission development, will be the subject of a later analysis. Nevertheless, certain facts require to be emphasized at this stage. They concern the relative roles of Captain Wilkins and Zebedee Rogers in the introduction of the Bethel Flag.

Zebedee Rogers was, for approximately fifteen years, first a voluntary collaborator then later an employee with the Rev. G.C. Smith in his seamen's mission endeavors.[155] Captain Wilkins cooperated closely with both Rogers and Smith during the early years of the Bethel Movement,[156] but after the organizational upheavals of 1832-33, we find him identifying himself with a society which for many years disassociated itself with Smith.[157] This organization, while initially ignoring the pioneering work of G.C. Smith, and (with his) also that of Zebedee Rogers, found itself overstating the early contribution of Captain Wilkins. At all events, its spokesmen (themselves of a later generation) drew conclusions which have proved both unsupportable from other sources and mutually inconsistent, but which have nevertheless been reproduced as factual in many subsequent publications. According to these spokesmen, Captain Wilkins is supposed to have invented the Bethel Flag, with or without the aid of his wife, at dates alternating between 1818, 1816 and even 1814.[158]

No evidence has been traced which could confirm any of this, or reduce Rogers' role as already represented. Nor do available early sources show any instance of the word "Bethel" used in connection with shipboard prayer-meetings before Rogers' innovation in 1817.[159] The first seamen's mission society to adopt and officially promote the use of the Bethel Flag continued for years to place its orders with "Mr. Van's, Ship-chandler, in Tooley-street," on the basis of the original pattern which Rogers had been requested to submit to him.[160] When Zebedee Rogers was finally laid to rest, it was as publicly recognized originator of the international emblem of the Seamen's Cause. "He was brought to the Mariner's Church, and buried with all the Bethel flags and honours that grateful hearts could procure, amidst a vast host of spectators."[161]

This banner was designed and distributed in 1914, in order
to mark what was believed to be the "Bethel Flag
Centenary." Recent research proves the year to have
been 1817 (not 1814); the originator Zebedee Rogers
(not Captain Wilkins); and the symbolism Christmas,
Easter and Pentecost (not the Trinity). (*The Chart
and Compass*, 1914, p. 117.)

As for Wilkins, it is significant that, while otherwise willing to
communicate details of his involvement in the Bethel Movement, he nowhere
contradicts the contribution of Zebedee Rogers.[162] Captain Wilkins gives the
consistent impression of an uncomplicated, generous-hearted seaman, whose
great passion in life was purely and simply the spiritual welfare of his brother
seafarers. His place in history is in any case assured. From that memorable
move in December 1816, and through at least a quarter century of indefatigable service as "Bethel Captain" both in coastal and foreign trade, Anthony
Wilkins, too, proved himself one of the great pioneer spirits of early seamen's
missions.[163]

Following the basic pattern of spiritual revivals, the transition
during the winter of 1816-17 from relatively private prayer-meetings to a
system of deliberate missionary outreach, resulted in negative reaction, too.
Writing some two years later, G.C. Smith saw this as evidence of the
authenticity of the new movement:

> It was not to be imagined that Satan would view with in-
> difference such an assault on his kingdom as was now making by

converted sailors. Persecution, therefore, the natural consequence of a revival in religion, raged furiously for a time. . . . Ungodly captains and sailors poured forth the most dreadful oaths; even cabin boys joined in throwing coals at those who were seriously disposed; and the watermen united in the general clamour against this work of God [by splashing with their oars and shouting their derision].[164]

Such were the eye-witness accounts of the gauntlet which had to be run by those who responded to invitation and rowed to shipboard assemblies "for singing and prayer, after their wearisome day's work in discharging the ship." In some cases, owners themselves "forbade their captains allowing such meetings on board their ships," and certain "broken-down merchants and unprincipled insolvents . . . joined the world's dread laugh."[165] That such descriptions were no exaggeration was attested by others.[166] Small wonder that many saw a parallel to similar phenomena familiar from the recent Naval Awakening:

[It was] like the religious societies in King's ships last war, who met every evening for prayer between the guns on the maindeck, while their enemies sent in prostitutes to interrupt them, threw various things at them, and rolled shot in among them. . . .[167]

Understandably enough, opposition found a focal point in the means by which the meetings were publicized. The lantern winter signal came up for questioning first. This unorthodox "new light" had not been shown long before it "became the subject of debate and controversy." Some simply dismissed it as a sign that the captain was ashore for the evening. As others discovered its connection with the "psalm singers," dark insinuations about a "Radical Light" and "seditious meetings" were set on foot.[168] No sooner had the first Bethel Flag been introduced than similar suspicions were circulated and it became generally styled the "Radical Flag."[169]

In one case at least, opponents of "Methodistical" religion actually succeeded (as also in the Naval Awakening) to prey on the apprehensions of hypersensitive officialdom. Reports reached the Thames Police that "sailors were turning radical," that "large companies" were meeting on shipboard at night "to plot treason" and that secret signals were conveyed by means of "a certain flag, containing some Masonic emblem in the day-time, and a dirty ship's lantern at night."[170] Different sources record the "utter astonishment" of the police officer in command of a cutter-full of men which had quietly tied up alongside a brig where a mysterious meeting was said to be in session. Having taken up his position at the companion, so as to cut off any means of escape, he was amazed to hear nothing but hearty hymn-singing and fervent, orderly prayer. Shouting "Below, there!" he called the captain up on deck for interrogation.

Captain Wilkins recalls the conversation which ensued:

"Well, sir, are these your meetings?" "Yes, sir, ... we meet to
return thanks to God, for bringing us safe to port, while others
pray for protection on their passage." "Well, sir, these meetings
have been differently represented to our office; — it has been said,
that you meet together for treason, and conspiracy, against your
sovereign." One of our pious sailors cried out, "GOD BLESS
THE KING! ... tell him we won't hurt a hair of his head, but
we'll pray for him, master!" "Well, sir, if these are your meetings,
go on, and may the Lord prosper you." "Amen and amen," cried
our sailors; "let us have the old hundredth."[171]

With that, the police boat cast off, "while the solemn sounds of the far-famed
tune broke the stillness of the night on the river, and seemed to keep pace
with the oars of the police cutter," as she slowly passed the tiers of North
Country collier brigs in the Lower Pool. In the stern-sheets sat the police
officer "wondering to think that sailors, who were so notorious in the pool for
swearing, should have exchanged it for *praying.....*"[172]

The incident is significant in at least two aspects: (1) It provides an
interesting insight into relations between seamen and the political establishment of the day. For such meetings to raise suspicions of sedition, though
perhaps ludicrous to a later generation, was by no means unthinkable in the
England of 1817. No Peel had yet brought an end to "the system of
espionage and repression exercised by Government against the Radical
working men."[173] Moreover, strikes and economic unrest among North
Country colliermen had become commonplace.[174] (2) The episode also
provides vivid evidence of the power of the public image of seamen still
current at this stage. Well might seamen who became "serious" ruefully
reflect "that when they called for damnation with every breath—when they
wallowed in uncleanness, and pressed forward to destroy body and soul, then
they were applauded; but now that they wished to seek the salvation of their
souls, the comfort of their families, and the glory of God; they were accursed
of men, and bitterly persecuted."[175]

However, the "Bethel Men," as they came to be known, persevered.
So, too, did their persecutors for the present.[176] Nevertheless, the Thames
Police posed no further problem and "Bethel Meetings" were soon to receive
a powerful stimulus from a new quarter. Hitherto, the Methodists had striven
alone. Now the Baptists entered the scene, first in the form of Thomas
Phillips, master-lighterman of the Upper Pool.

Thomas Phillips lived in Potter's Fields, a pleasant lane by the
south bank of the Upper Pool, at Horsleydown, Southwark. Here he was an
active member of Carter Lane Baptist Chapel.[177] His office premises were on
the opposite side of the river at a wharf near London Bridge, just above

Billingsgate Fish Market.[178] His business naturally involved him in constant intercourse with seamen and rivermen. This fact, together with a particularly warm, spiritual concern for his fellow-men, combined to fit him for a key role in the Thames Revival and subsequent seamen's missions.

It was in November 1816 that Phillips took the first major step in a series of ways in which he harnessed his shipping activities to the furtherance of God's Kingdom. He refused to accept lighterage fees from the Bible Society for a foreign shipment via Gravesend, stating he would be honored if they would permit him to be, in the future, their gratuitous lighterman.[179] For fifteen years there are records of substantial savings to the BFBS on this account. He considered himself "amply repaid" by occasional grants of Bibles and Testaments, which he could distribute to deserving cases among the seamen he met.[180]

Then in May 1817, he was told by a friend who was Collector at the London Dock, that there was "much good going forward among the sailors on board the Colliers in the river."[181] Summoned by a blue flag with "the significant motto, *Bethel*" hoisted at twelve noon, boat-loads of seamen from different tiers converged "almost every evening in the week" on a floating "House of Prayer." Determined to discover the truth of such incredible news, Phillips records the following in a letter to the Religious Tract Society shortly afterwards:

> On Thursday afternoon, I had occasion to go down the river, and, in the midst of a number of colliers, saw the signal, and rowed silently alongside. The quarter-deck was covered with an awning—one of the sailors was engaged in prayer: on his concluding, another immediately began. Their expression of gratitude for mercies received, and sorrow on account of the depravity of their hearts; their humble trust in a crucified Jesus for salvation, and prayers for each other that they might be kept from the evil of the world, and all the temptations to which they were exposed, evidently shewed that they had set their faces towards Zion. . . .[182]

On introducing himself to the captain after the service, Phillips was warmly invited to join in the next meeting, and also entreated to bring with him some tracts. Thus, armed with a supply from the RTS depository, he returned on Friday, this time with his wife and son. The captain carefully distributed the tracts to eager recipients, with a few spares for absent shipmates. The service had gathered some 30 in all (two or three captains, the rest mates and men). It lasted from 7:15 to 9 p.m., and consisted of hymn and prayer alternately, with altogether nine or ten who engaged in prayer. The Phillips family was especially affected by the men's fervent prayers "for *strangers,* whom nothing but Christian love could have induced to come and visit a parcel of poor sailors," as they put it. (These prayers, coupled with the men's "unanimous wish" that they should repeat the visits, and bring with them "some pious friends" from shore, throw interesting light on the seamen-landsmen relationship. From the seaman's frequently misinterpreted viewpoint, not segregation but respect was the real desideratum.)[183]

The master-lighterman's discovery of the Lower Pool Bethel Meetings had two consequences of immediate importance: (1) Nation-wide publicity was achieved for the sensational news of the Thames Revival. (The RTS continued to publish far and wide copious details of Phillips' reports.)[184] (2) New impetus was given to Christian literature distribution among merchant seamen by the vivid accounts of their receptivity to tracts offered by Phillips. In order to assess the significance of this, it becomes necessary to examine what had been achieved in this field prior to 1817.

Scripture distribution among merchant seamen during the first two decades of the nineteenth century has already been dealt with.[185] Sporadic efforts to reach them with tracts, too, were made by the RTS. Here, up to the end of the Napoleonic War, a roughly parallel pattern to that of Scripture distribution is discernible. Tracts were liberally distributed among foreign (often merchant navy) prisoners of war, and also sent abroad with "pious Masters," while the ordinary British merchant seaman, though not entirely overlooked, received far less attention than his naval counterpart.[186]

Nevertheless, a number of publications independent of the RTS gave evidence of individual concern for seamen in general at this period. Some were new editions of the "classical" seamen's devotionals by Janeway, Flavel and Ryther.[187] Others were scattered examples of more recent sermons or spiritual guides especially addressed to seafarers.[188] Of these, *A Christian Exhortation to Sailors* (1813) by the "emphatically evangelical" Quaker minister, William Forster (brother-in-law of Elizabeth Fry), was sufficiently popular to go through several editions. New editions of John Newton's autobiography and the naval surgeon James Meikle's meditations also attained wide circulation.[189]

However, despite a spirited appeal by "W.F." in *The Evangelical Magazine* for 1806, "On the Distribution of Religious Books among Seamen,"[190] supplies as far as the merchant service was concerned remained modest indeed throughout the war. Apart from the lack of concerted distributive action, the range of tract literature calculated to appeal particularly to seamen was severely limited. True, such universal favorites as *The Swearer's Prayer* and *The Dairyman's Daughter* seemed equally popular on land and sea.[191] Moreover, one specifically maritime tract did achieve a perfectly amazing circulation: *An Account of the Bravery and Happy Death of James Covey, a British Seaman,* by the Rev. John Griffin of Portsea. (Dealing with the dramatic conversion of one who could count it his most "precious loss" to be bereft of both his legs at the Battle of Camperdown, this tract, originally written in 1807, soon traversed the seas in a series of translations.)[192]

James Covey was originally an exception, however. Not until after the peace of 1815 was there a noticeable change. The man who not only recognized, but went far to fill, the need for tract literature "expressly intended for Seamen," was Richard Marks. Familiar with Jack's disgust for "lubberly" misuse of nautical terminology, he set himself to write, from 1816 on, seven seamen's tracts for the RTS. Within a decade their distribution had passed the half-million mark.[193] After the publication of his widely read naval reminiscences in *The Retrospect* (1816), his first two tracts were both in the seamen's dialogue form: *Conversation in a Boat* and *The Shipmates* (1816-17).[194] Next came *The Seaman's Friend* and *The Seaman's Spy-Glass* (1817-18), the former a forthright treatment of "traditional" maritime vices, the latter a nucleus for his later "essay" collection, *The Ocean* (a virtual masterpiece of nautical-scriptural imagery).[195]

When Thomas Phillips in 1817 took upon himself the task of volunteer tract distributor on the Thames, he could, therefore, already include with his supplies the first of Marks' products. As these proved their worth, Phillips made sure to reorder exactly such as were "particularly calculated" to appeal to and benefit sailors.[196] Combining common sense with fervent faith, Phillips showed equal discriminaton in his method of distribution. As successive reports show, the degree of demand could captivate, but not carry him away. Rather than scatter tracts wherever he could, he used them selectively, as an incentive, to attend forthcoming Bethel Meetings, or as an instrument in the hands of seamen concerned for their fellows. Swearing coal-heavers were reduced to tears by reading them, and idle colliermen crowded into prayer-meetings in the hope of obtaining them. Both East and West Indiamen soon came within the compass of Phillips' activities, as also did a number of outports in the United Kingdom.[197] After eighteen months, he confirmed his conviction on the efficacy of marine tract distribution in these words:

> For such as will neither enter a place of worship, nor read the scriptures, *Religious Tracts,* freely distributed, appear to be the only way to get at their consciences: these they *will accept* and *read. . . .*[198]

His tenacity matched his enthusiasm. For over a decade Phillips found sufficient encouragement to persevere, as undisputed "chief gratuitous agent of the Religious Tract Society for the Thames."[199] However, there were other pioneers in the field. One was a "worthy Custom House officer," who believed in prompting his recipients to become tract missionaries themselves in foreign ports to which they traded.[200] Another was Lieutenant Francis Collins, who, after being severely wounded under Nelson in Egypt, was invalided out of the navy, and became, during many years, a zealous depository for the RTS. In this capacity, he cooperated warmly with Thomas Phillips, and—as he, too, now entered the scene—George Charles Smith.[201]

"The gentlemen go by . . ."
In the impoverished
villages of Southwest
England, smuggling had,
by the early 1800's,
become almost socially
acceptable. G.C. Smith
preached against it with
fervor but little success.
(Drawing by Paul Hardy
in Charles Harper:
The Smugglers.)

THE SEAMEN'S PREACHER

Although still primarily pastor of the Baptist Church in Penzance, G.C. Smith had, since returning from his 1814 chaplaincy on the Continent, by no means restricted himself to tending his local flock. On the contrary, records reveal three years packed with restless activity in widely dispersed fields. In the autumn of 1814, he is in London again, providing pulpit supply at the Church Street Chapel, Spitalfields, and busy also with school plans for French Protestants in conjunction with the British and Foreign School Society.[202] In 1815, he embarks upon a dramatic mission of spiritual and material aid to the impoverished inhabitants of the Isles of Scilly.

By the end of the war this island society, situated some 26 miles west of Land's End, was, from a variety of causes, rapidly approaching complete economic collapse. One of the more immediate reasons was the efficiency of the new Preventive Service. Fast coastguard cutters clamped down on all contraband trade with France, thereby depriving the islanders of what was maintained to be their "chief means of support."[203] G.C. Smith responded to disquieting reports by launching a fact-finding mission and having one of his student-preachers, J.T. Jeffery, placed as home missionary there.[204] Both preaching-places and Sabbath- and weekday-schools were established; but crop failures rapidly aggravated the situation, particularly on the off-islands, to the point of famine and despair. Today, Smith is credited with having been the first to bring the real degree of distress home to the public on the mainland.[205]

Frustrated for long by the repudiations of local authorities anxious to avert an open scandal, Smith nevertheless managed—with the support of men like Thomas Thompson, Opie Smith, and eventually Richard Phillips (of the Bible Society) and his Quaker connections—to ship sufficient cargoes of food, clothing, blankets and medicine to ward off a catastrophe. At Hugh Town on St. Mary's, he succeeded in founding an "Industrious Society" in order to stimulate the women of the island to self-help. After the veracity of Smith's published reports had been vindicated, a national relief committee for Scilly was established in the metropolis with the help of two evangelical naval officers, Lieutenant J.E. Gordon and Captain (later Admiral) Edward Hawker.[206] William Wilberforce (with whom Smith also had contact concerning the Naval Correspondence Mission and the improvement of the naval chaplaincy service) gave active support; and royalty afforded patronage.[207]

The hard-pressed islanders themselves had never been in doubt as to the name of their greatest benefactor. As he stepped ashore at the pierhead of St. Mary's on one of his visits to superintend the distribution of necessities, G.C. Smith was welcomed by the cheering populace with a lit tar barrel and a flag inscribed "SMITH FOR EVER!"[208] Apart from the direct value of this early form of fishermen's missions, Smith's Scilly Islands Mission from 1815 on certainly gives evidence of a remarkable modernity of method in approaching a complex social problem. Here was an instinctive realization of the need for: (1) preliminary field research, (2) a deliberate P.R. campaign, and (3) systemic change, where necessary, not solely benevolent relief.

The spiritual and social straits of seamen of his day were soon to provide Smith with ample opportunity to put this experience to wider purpose. As he himself said shortly afterwards: "This business of Scilly taught me such a lesson concerning the importance of *perseverance* and *public opinion,* as I shall never forget."[209] Unfortunately, however, he neither then nor later learned the additional lesson of keeping accurate accounts.[210] (This failing, though there was never the slightest evidence of personal dishonesty, was destined to cause him endless embarrassment in both public and private affairs.)[211]

On the mainland, too, G.C. Smith was, between 1814 and 1817, involved in an expanding program of "Home Missions." On the local level he continued supplying some twelve preaching missions in villages surround-ing Penzance. To assist him, he normally had a team of four student-preachers at one and the same time. In this way, "nearly twenty plain zealous young men" were in due course trained for the ministry. As a further result, several new chapels were built in the area. The program was strongly supported by subscriptions from Opie Smith and Thomas Thompson.[212]

In 1816, while again in London providing pulpit supply, Smith conferred with Thompson and Lieutenant Francis Collins on some drastic reports of moral and spiritual destitution in the villages of Southwest England, particularly North Devon. The outcome was the "North Devon Sea Coast Mission" in the spring of 1817.[213] Taking one of his assistant preachers, James Heath, as his companion, Smith set off with the horse and spring cart he kept for his local village preaching, loaded down with a huge supply of tracts from Collins and faithfully backed by Thompson. Wending his way through "the darkest villages and sea-ports" along the north coast of Devonshire, he eventually arrived at Minehead and Watchet on the Bristol Channel. Following in the footsteps of Wesley and Whitefield, Smith found himself forced to rely chiefly on open-air preaching in order to reach the unchurched masses. Like his predecessors, too, he harvested a pitch of persecution which could have made many a courageous man capitulate. Mob violence more than once caused imminent danger to life and limb.[214]

However, Smith also met with sufficient encouragement to make him a leading protagonist of open-air preaching to the end of his days. With his "stentorian voice" and forceful rhetoric, this was a role for which he was admirably equipped. (Within a decade no less a judge than *The Times* was hailing him as "The prince of field preachers.")[215] The tour was gratifying, too, for Smith's sponsors. Thomas Thompson later conceded that it was the itinerant preaching of George Charles Smith which "led to" the founding, in 1819, of the "Home Missionary Society" (which again, seven years later, contributed to the formation of a similar and even larger society in America). Thompson, who was subsequently for 40 years the treasurer of the (Congregationalists') Home Missionary Society, also gave Smith's example, as pioneer home and city missionary, the credit for the foundation of the "Christian Instruction Society."[216]

His preoccupation with home missions, from 1814 to 1817, did not mean that Smith had forgotten his brother seafarers. In the first place, there is evidence that he showed constant concern for Christian literature distribu-tion among British and foreign seamen with whom he came into contact; for this purpose, he made repeated applications to both the BFBS and the RTS.[217] Moreover, his home mission activity was, in one sense, also a seamen's mission activity. Itinerant preaching in coastal villages brought large numbers of seamen and fishermen directly under the sound of the

Gospel. Also, Smith showed keen awareness of the environmental influence of such villages as nurseries of "paganism" for future generations of seafarers.

Others had already pointed to links between seamen and *foreign* missions; it seems to have been G.C. Smith who first emphasized the interrelationship between seamen and *home* missions.[218] Closely connected with this conviction was Smith's oft-repeated insistance, in years to come, that a concept of seamen's missions which did not squarely face and deal with the network of organized vice which comprised a normal sailortown environment was an amputated and utterly inadequate form of ministry to seafarers.[219]

However, despite the fact that "sailors and villages" had both so often been the subject of consultation and correspondence with Thompson and others during recent years, Smith had still not arrived at any specific plan for general missions to seamen.[220] (At the close of his North Devon Mission, he did travel via Bristol, he states, "hoping to begin a Seamen's Society" in some unspecified form; but he was "advised to wait another year.")[221] On arriving in London from his tour in the summer of the same year (1817), Smith was amazed to discover that seamen themselves, without the help of a single ordained minister, had already improvised a scheme for their own evangelization.

It was through Thomas Phillips that G.C. Smith was introduced to the Thames Revival, when some months had already elapsed since the Bethel Flag was first unfurled. Smith had become acquainted with Phillips while supplying Dr. Rippon's pulpit for one month the previous year. On his arrival now, in order to supply the Carter Lane pulpit again (as well as others), Smith had been invited to lodge at Phillips' home at Horsleydown. Phillips, of course, informed his guest of the prayer-meetings he had recently discovered on the North Country colliers. "Struck with this intelligence," Smith at once determined to see this for himself.[222]

In a tract written later the same year, G.C. Smith has recorded his impressions from the memorable evening, when he took part in his first Bethel Meeting. Accompanied by Thomas Phillips and his family, he was rowed downriver at the earliest opportunity which presented itself. That evening, it proved to be none other than the *Zephyr* which flew the flag, with Captain Hindhulph there to welcome them on board.[223] Warmed at the sight of the Bethel emblem for the first time, Smith continues:

> I had requested of my friends not to inform him [the Captain] that
> I was a minister, in order that I might hear, as quite a stranger, the
> spontaneous effusions of seamen's hearts before the Lord. At
> seven o'clock, a person [Zebedee Rogers] came on board from
> Rotherhithe. — I have since learnt that he generally attends to
> conduct the worship at these meetings. The cabin became soon

filled with captains and seamen. — It had been cleaned up for the occasion, and some bars of wood were laid across different chests to serve as seats. It was interesting to see how curiously and willingly the seamen stowed themselves away on the lockers, coiling up their legs to make as much room as possible. I stood behind, up in a corner; and while unobserved, I noticed attentively their method of proceeding; the person who had come off from the shore, gave out three verses of a hymn and then prayed. Several captains and seamen successively followed with a short hymn, or prayer. The singing was very lively and animated; and the prayers of these good men were at once simple, copious, and energetic. They did not consist in a relation of circumstances, but they had a continued succession of fervent supplications. . . . The phraseology . . . was singularly interesting, often technical, but always solemn, expressive, and appropriate. I was much impressed with the following . . . "O thou, that didst call the seamen of Galilee, make bare thine arm and pour down thy blessings on all the captains and mates, seamen and cabin boys, now lying in the river. . . ."[224]

This proved too much for Smith. "Associating the heart of seamen with the feelings of a christian minister," he could no longer resist the urge to beg leave to address them and offer a word of encouragement. Such was his emotion, however, that after advancing to the table in the center of the cabin, words at first failed him. Recovering his voice, he introduced himself as one who had once "sailed out of this river as a cabin boy" and was now, through divine grace, "a minister of the Lord Jesus Christ." Considering the temptations abounding on either shore of that river, calculated to lead sailors to ruin, he confessed his astonishment at what God had wrought. He felt it "an honour" to stand among them, and counted it one of the "happiest circumstances" of his life to be thus able to mingle his prayers and praises with theirs. At the close, "tears rolled plentifully down their weather-beaten cheeks" (a reaction which appears to have been typical of even the hardiest seamen of those times, when gripped by the Gospel). Then, after sharing out tracts and agreeing about a ship for the next night, they shook hands all around, and slipped over the side.[225]

In his brief address Smith had offered to return and preach a sermon for them, if they wished. "As a brother sailor," both the preacher and his proposition met with obvious acceptance. The following week, he preached on the quarter-deck of the *Zephyr* to a great gathering from different ships. He closed by preparing his hearers for more of the ridicule and opposition they had already met, exhorting them not to be more ashamed to serve Christ on the river than others were to serve sin at Wapping or Rotherhithe: "You have, for the first time in the history of our country, raised a standard for Christ on the river Thames — May that flag never be struck to any of the enemies of the cross!" The many who followed with prayers for the preacher proved that the pastor from Penzance had won the hearts of those Bethel pioneers. That they had won his became increasingly manifest in the weeks which followed. The *Dolphin*-call had been renewed — this time for life.[226]

During his three months' stay in the Phillips home on the south bank of the Upper Pool, there is no record of how far Smith succeeded in one of the original objects of his London visit—to collect for his chapel funds back in Cornwall. On the other hand, there are several references to how he during these weeks continued to attend meeting after meeting on the Thames, preaching to the seamen "on crowded decks." Enthusiastically assisting him with their attendance and support were particularly Thompson, Phillips and Lieutenant Collins.[227]

Meanwhile, G.C. Smith—conscious, as ever, of publicity potentials— conceived the idea of the first publicly advertised seamen's service on shipboard, in other words a floating counterpart to the memorable seamen's service ashore, at Carter Lane Chapel in 1812.[228] Since Bethel Meeting activity had so far centered mainly around Rotherhithe and the south side of the river, Smith was anxious that such a service should be arranged on the north side, preferably at some centrally situated spot near the Sailortown district of Wapping. His chance came when he was invited to preach at the Cotton Street Baptist Chapel, in the hamlet of Poplar, near the West India Docks. Here, as elsewhere, he seized the opportunity to publicize the news of the seamen's Bethel Meetings on the Thames. A great number of seamen thenselves had responded to the opportunity of hearing their preacher friend in a chapel ashore. At the close, he made an appeal to any owner or merchant present for the loan of a ship, suitably placed, on the deck of which a public seamen's service could be arranged. Immediately afterwards a Wapping shipowner, Captain Hill, entered the vestry and offered the gratuitous use of his ship, the *Agenoria*, Captain Posgate.[229]

The *Agenoria* was ideally placed near the London Docks, moored on the inside of a tier, just off the Wapping shore. A great publicity campaign was launched. Hand-bills and placards were printed and distributed along both banks of the Thames. Invitations were extended throughout the tiers of shipping.[230] When the agreed day arrived, the response, from ship and shore, was even more overwhelming than five years previously at Carter Lane:

> The evening was exceedingly fine. . . . Boats from all parts were soon seen approaching, and it was feared that the deck would not accommodate all who might attend; a large lighter [evidently provided by Thomas Phillips] was therefore made fast alongside, on which some hundreds of persons could stand within hearing. The windows of houses on shore were filled with people, the beach was crowded, and people drew nearer as the tide ebbed;

watermen waited alongside in their wherrys—the rigging of the
ships [on the off-shore side] were filled. . . . Three casks were
fixed on the hatchway [for a speaker's platform].[231]

The service started at six o'clock with two Baptist brother-ministers
assisting (the Rev J. Edwards and the Rev. W. Shenstone). As the Bethel
Flag waved aloft, "some thousands of hearers" heard the powerful voice of
George Charles Smith, preaching a heart-searching revival sermon from
Acts 27:27-29. Both the novelty of the scene and the interpretation of the
text (applied as an illustration of sinners suddenly awakened to their
imminent danger) made a visible impression on the vast audience.[232]

Smith's publicity purpose could hardly have met with more signal
success. The event assumed the character of a religious sensation. The
practicability of preaching to seamen on their own element, and their rousing
response to the attempt, had now been publicly demonstrated by experimentation. The press produced headlines about "Aquatic Preaching," and
the "religious improvement" of seamen became a topic of general conversation.[233] For good measure, the message was, a few weeks later, brought
home again, as G.C. Smith acceded to the request of his collier friends, and
delivered a public sermon to another crowded audience of seamen and
landsmen, this time on the *John*, Captain Robinson. The autumn evenings
were now becoming darker, and a great awning had been stretched over the
deck with lanterns hung on the companion and the capstan. The text was
from Matthew 14:30-31, and the combined effect of the sermon and the
prayers of seamen which succeeded it was such as to reduce to shame "some
infidel young men," who had come to scoff.[234]

The immediate significance of Smith's summer stay in London, in
1817, was twofold: (1) George Charles Smith became indisputably "The
Seamen's Preacher" of his age. Acclaimed eventually as "the most popular
preacher in the kingdom," his status among his brother-seamen remained
unique.[235] The title "Boatswain Smith," by which he became universally
known, was, from their side, a token of jovial but deeply genuine affection.[236]
(2) Smith established itinerant shipboard preaching as a new feature of the
Bethel Movement. Shipboard *prayer*-meetings had commenced in June 1814.
Itinerant shipboard prayer meetings followed from December 1816. Itinerant
shipboard *preaching* only became an established practice as from Smith's
sermon on the *Zephyr* in the summer of 1817 (although Samuel Jennings
may well, by then, have introduced the idea when he occasionally accompanied Zebedee Rogers on the colliers).[237] G.C. Smith was, at all events, the
first ordained minister to take part in these activities; he was to be by no
means the last.

Chapter 8

The Floating Chapel

THE PLAN (AUTUMN 1817)

When John Ryther, the Nonconformist divine who settled in Wapping around 1669, became known as "The Seaman's Preacher," it was because he identified himself with them and learned to address them "in a style so much adapted to their situation and taste."[238] His successor, one and a half centuries later, may be said to have earned the title in a double sense. George Charles Smith was not only a preacher to seamen. He was also pre-eminently a preacher for seamen. It was as the pioneering, untiring advocate of the the Seamen's Cause that George Charles probably made his greatest and most enduring contribution to the evolution of seamen's missions.[239] Here lies the long-term significance of Smith's summer visit to London in 1817, especially the impact of the *Agenoria* service. From then on, he could focus his advocacy of the cause on concrete objectives, primarily the provision of suitable seamen's sanctuaries in London and elsewhere.

It is possible that the thought of a floating chapel struck others, too, among the ministers and concerned laymen who witnessed that soul-stirring scene off the Wapping shore.[240] However, G.C. Smith was certainly the first who went to work on it. He recollects that it was while watching the boat-loads of seamen converging on the *Agenoria* that the thought suddenly occurred to him for the first time in his life, "what an excellent plan it would be to have a ship converted into a chapel afloat and moored in the Thames for constant preaching to sailors." From that time on, he states, the thought never left him. He was convinced that "this was from God." For the remainder of his stay the subject of a "permanent pulpit" in the river was "continually brought forth" wherever opportunities were afforded him, afloat or ashore, in "the pulpit, the vestry, and the parlour."

Was the notion of a floating sanctuary entirely novel? As far back as during the reign of Mary Tudor (1553-58), a persecuted Protestant congregation in the metropolis had occasionally made a ship on the Thames their clandestine floating chapel.[242] In 1812, *The Evangelical Magazine* carried the headline "A Floating Church" when reporting the activities of a Christian fellowship group on a 74-gun man-of-war.[243] By 1817, transformed ships of war had long since become a familiar sight not only as floating dungeons, but also—off Deptford—for benevolent purposes, as the training ship of the philanthropic Marine Society.[244] Nevertheless, none of these could provide any direct precedent for the concept of a floating chapel, permanently moored and exclusively appropriated to regular public services for seafarers. Here was an innovation of significant dimensions.

For Smith, anxious to win wide enough support for the plan, prospects seemed promising. Influential brother-ministers, like Dr. John Rippon, Dr. W.B. Collyer, Dr. Alexander Waugh, and the Rev. J.E. Jones, gave him every encouragement. Members of the Thames Marine Bible Association Committee "manifested a lively anxiety that the attempt prosper." Among the many church- and chapel-goers from the metropolis, as well as "surrounding villages" like Greenwich, Rotherhithe, Limehouse and Poplar, who thronged to the *Agenoria* service, Smith had won numerous potential spokesmen for the cause.[245] These and others who had been accustomed to thinking of seamen as utter stangers to places of worship . . .

> remarked with what alacrity and delight they had pulled up alongside the ship where a sermon was to be preached, or a prayer-meeting was to be held — leaping from the boat by the chain plates, a rope, or a ladder to the deck, and taking their stations on the rigging or gangways, where they felt more at home than they could be in the most elegantly cushioned pews on shore. A ship is their dwelling—their delight—their boast—and almost their all.[246]

Another source of encouragement was the fact that new faces were seen at services ashore. Following the first "preaching experiments" afloat,

> sailors were afterwards observed for weeks attending with deep seriousness at some places of worship in several parts of London; and, when spoken to in a way of enquiry, said they had been hearers of the sermons on board the ships in the Thames.[247]

Undoubtedly, many more would have made an appearance if these briny visitors had sensed a sincere and universal welcome. As things were, they were deterred both by pewing restrictions and all who took offense at the "smell of tar."[248] So much more reason was there to hope that seamen would support a sanctuary they could call their own. In fact, as the subject of a floating chapel was discussed with them, regular attendants at Bethel Meetings on the Thames gave ground to believe that seamen would warmly sanction "a plan so congenial with their habits."[249]

However, as the time approached when he would have to return to his duties in Penzance, Smith sensed increasing impatience. "All approved but no one came forward" who could head a promotional campaign on the spot, now that he himself would be far removed from the metropolitan scene. He felt satisfied that adequate support was potentially present, "yet there wanted some person of sufficient zeal and influence to bring the subject before the public, and become the main spring . . . around whom others might rally."[250]

G.C. Smith was familiar with the "evangelical piety" of the widely respected Surveyor General of the London Custom House. Colonel Burgess was a warm supporter of home missions not only in the Falmouth area, but throughout the Southwest. Was he the man? During a two-hour interview, accompanied by Thomas Thompson, Smith presented the case and discussed ways and means. Burgess entered enthusiastically into the scheme, but felt it called for a leader less encumbered and less advanced in years. Nevertheless, much of the practical advice he was able to give was duly followed and proved its worth by leading to the goal in only a matter of months.[251]

At the moment, however, the situation seemed critical. Then, one day shortly before his departure, Smith was being directed by his host, Thomas Phillips, to houses in the City where he might apply with his Penzance "chapel case." So far, results had been disappointing. Having arrived at America Square in the Minories, and feeling somewhat at a loss, Phillips noted that they were close to the counting-house of Mr. Marten, the shipbroker, and suggested trying there. Smith always remained, despite later turbulent relations, keenly conscious of the divine providence which led to this totally unforeseen meeting. He is, therefore, at pains to record how, even while waiting in the outer office, he was still "without the most distant idea" of discussing any floating chapel plan with this gentleman. It was then that his companion, Thomas Phillips, whispered, as they looked at all the bills posted along the walls advertising ships for sale: "Here is your man for a floating chapel."[252]

Robert Humphrey Marten, who for fifteen years was to remain a central figure in the first, formative period of British seamen's missions, was, like G.C. Smith, a Dissenter. (In his case, he was a Congregationalist, deacon of the Independent Chapel at Plaistow.) Unlike the impulsive, boisterous "Boatswain" from Penzance, Marten was meticulous and cautious by nature. This became apparent in their first conversation. However, it also became clear that here was more than a well-connected businessman, commanding considerable respect and influence in commercial circles. Marten quite evidently also had the capacity for "ardency," when once convinced of sagacity.[253] Recalling their meeting, less than three years after the event, Smith states that after dispatching his first business, he entered on

the subject of the Bethel Meetings on the Thames and his own participation
by preaching:

> He [Mr. Marten] said he had heard of it, and could not approve of
> it, fearing it would draw improper characters on board, who would
> rob the vessels. I then informed him of the plan, that had been so
> long agitated, to establish a Floating Chapel. He listened attentively
> . . . to this, repeatedly observing, there was something very feasible
> in the idea. . . . [At length] he proposed, that we should get some
> person to . . . draw up a prospectus, which might be submitted to
> different friends who would assist at a preliminary meeting, when
> the scheme could be fully developed, and an institution established
> to carry it into effect.[254]

"Can we find such a one as this . . . ?" was Smith's immediate
reaction; he urged the shipbroker to write the prospectus himself. To this
Marten readily consented, sending the result a few days later to Smith and
his friends for comment. At a second interview immediately before his
departure, Smith assured Marten of their unanimous approval, entreating
him to pursue the project through the winter in every way possible. Smith
had, from his friends, already obtained pledges for the first £100 toward the
plan, and he promised to promote publicity by writing, at the first opportunity,
a tract about the *"Ark,"* as he now called it. Meanwhile, as he also pointed
out, Phillips was familiar with Smith's thinking on the subject. Thompson,
too, was to prove a valuable link during Smith's absence.[255]

Understandably relieved, Smith returned to Penzance. Soon afterwards, Marten went into print, in the *Public Ledger,* with a spirited appeal
for a floating sanctuary on the Thames.[256] The prospectus itself he presented
in *The Evangelical Magazine* for December, 1817, under the title: "Suggestions for the More Effectual Religious Instruction of British Seamen while in
Harbour." Here he emphasizes again the priority of a *preached* Gospel,
quoting especially from Romans, chapter 10. (For "faith cometh by hearing,"
but "how shall they hear without a preacher?") He laments the gross
ingratitude and inconsistency which can send the Gospel to "the darkest
villages of our own island" and to "the sable sons of Africa," while neglecting
"the meritorious defenders, under God, of all the invaluable blessings of our
sea-girt land."

In his appeal in the *Ledger* Marten pointed to the example of Christ,
who "preached to the multitudes from a ship." Here he adds three somewhat
more forceful arguments for the feasibility of a floating chapel: the successful
experimentation (of G.C. Smith's ship-preaching in the Pool), the psychological factor (of a ship being "the seaman's house," whereas he feels "out of
his element" on land), and the financial saving (of buying an old ship, rather

than raising a new brick building ashore). Further notice of a preliminary public meeting to effectuate the plan would follow in the new year.[257]

Meanwhile, toward the close of the year 1817, Smith was able to dispatch the manuscript of his promised tract, *The Ark,* to Marten. The latter prefixed the word "British" and made other minor additions, whereupon he instantly published it. Here Smith sets forth, as the subtitle announces, "A Brief Narrative of Facts, Leading, by Divine Providence, to An attempt to Obtain a Floating Place of Worship. . . ." The tract traces the sequence of events from the summer of 1817, as experienced by Smith, from his first visit on board the *Zephyr* to his interview with R.H. Marten. (Names of ships and persons are, understandably enough, omitted, and the author only refers to himself as: "A Minister of the Everlasting Gospel; once in the Humble Station of a Cabin Boy.")[258]

Marten made sure that *The British Ark* served its purpose. It rapidly made the rounds of the Exchange and the strategic City coffee houses such as Lloyd's, John's, the Jerusalem and the Jamaica. Results followed. As he himself published, this tract was, from the moment it first appeared, "so eagerly demanded, and so widely distributed" as to contribute substantially to rousing the interest required to launch specific seamen's mission measures. (It went through several editions.)[259] At the same time, Smith could confirm the great attention excited, both in commercial circles and elsewhere, by Marten's own appeal and prospectus. In short, as this eventful year ebbed out, there seemed reason to conclude that the fulfillment of the floating chapel plan had begun to "bear features of probability."[260]

THE PORT OF LONDON SOCIETY (FOUNDED MARCH 18, 1818)

With the advent of 1818, two events in January contributed further to focus public interest on the welfare of seamen. The publicity achieved by the founding, on the 29th, of a new metropolitan society for maritime Scripture distribution (the MSABS), has already been noticed.[261] Before this, however, an organization had also been formed for the relief of *temporal* destitution among seamen. Economic disruption following the Napoleonic War, coupled with continuing manpower redundancy after the return to a peace-time naval establishment, culminated in a crisis during the winter of 1817-18, when great numbers of unemployed seamen roamed the streets of London in obviously desperate straits.[262]

The driving force behind relief measures was particularly J.E. Gordon, the ardent naval lieutenant who had recently been so successful in promoting NMBS expansions in the Glasgow area.[263] At a public meeting, January 5, 1818, at the City of London Tavern, Bishopsgate Street, a "Committee for the Relief of Distressed Seamen" was founded. William Wilberforce and R.H. Marten both played a prominent role at this meeting (as also at the founding of the MSABS later the same month). Lieutenant Gordon became Honorary Secretary and, in this capacity, received active support from Lieutenant Collins of the RTS.[264] Impressive results were achieved. A substantial subscription was rapidly raised. Shelter was secured in the shape of seven receiving ships in the River, provided by the Government. Here, hundreds were given clothes, food and rudimentary medical treatment until employment could be obtained. At the same time, provision was also made for the spiritual welfare of the men. In cooperation with the BFBS and RTS, Scriptures and tracts were distributed. The Rev. James Rudge of Limehouse preached on board the receiving ships with great effect. Other clergymen followed suit. (The "decorous deportment" and spirit of devotion of the seamen on these occasions caused widespread comment.)[265]

The immediate success of these relief measures induced a "Merchant Seaman's Friend" (Jeffery Dennis) to publish the same year *An Address,* to the Committee for the Relief of Distressed Seamen. This voluminous publication (which soon appeared in a second edition) contained, among various proposals intended to remove the current "radical defects" of the Merchant Service, an ambitious plan for a shore-based "British Merchant's Seaman's Institution," as well as reforms in nautical education, pay and apprenticeship.[266] Although such suggestions proved to be before their time, the efforts of the committee did lead directly to the founding, in 1821, of the (still active) "Seamen's Hospital Society."[267] Of special significance is the fact that those who took the principle initiative in this type of social action were evidently impelled by Christian motivation. The leaders were evangelically minded Churchmen and Dissenters. The work of the Committee for the Relief of Distressed Seamen must, therefore, be seen as an early example of organized maritime diaconal concern.[268]

There seemed reason to hope that "the solicitude thus excited for the temporal interests" of seamen could, in some sections of the public, be extended to their "spiritual concerns."[269] At all events, both Smith and Marten continued, through January, 1818, to work on exactly this. From Penzance, Smith maintained a lively correspondence about the floating chapel plans with contacts in the metropolis. He also "employed a sailor draftsman to draw out a sketch of a ship's interior, fitted up as a floating chapel," and sent this, together with other communications, to Marten. In London, Marten meanwhile prepared for the preliminary meeting, at which it was hoped to take the first step towards forming an organization.[270]

A Distressed Sailor
by Thomas Rowlandson,
depicting one of the
many thousands of
discharged and destitute
seamen roaming the
streets and highways of
England in the aftermath
of the Napoleonic Wars.
(Courtesy: British Library
Print Room.)

Accordingly, on Thursday, February 5, 1818, pursuant to public
notice, a preliminary meeting was held at twelve noon at the City of London
Tavern, "to consider of the best means of affording religious instruction to
British Seamen while in the port of London." Here, the drawings which had
been prepared were duly exhibited. As Marten could afterwards report to
Smith, the meeting accomplished its primary purpose—to form a provisional
committee which could "mature a plan to be laid before a future public
meeting." A motion to this effect was made by the Rev. Mr. Fleming, a
missionary bound for Malacca. (His participation on this occasion is of
interest as an early indication of that sense of interrelationship between
foreign and seamen's missions which was to become such a marked feature
of the early years of organized Christian outreach to seafarers.) As provisional officers, R.H. Marten was appointed treasurer, the Rev. N.E. Sloper
and Thomas Thompson were made honorary secretaries.[271]

The committee itself was—like those who had taken the most active
initiative toward its foundation—composed of ministers and laymen of predominantly Congregational and Baptist affiliation. Recognizing the realities
of church polity involved, Marten, who had been requested to take the chair,
stated at the preliminary meeting that—in addition to plans for an interdenominational floating chapel—

> suggestions had been conveyed to some members of the Govern-
> ment, that a frigate fitted as a church ship [i.e. under the care of

> the Established Church], could not but be beneficial to those
> sailors who would prefer the worship according to the ritual of the
> Church of England, and would cetainly be consistent with the
> recent recommendation from the Throne to provide more churches,
> to meet the wants of a greatly increased population. . . .

He added that he had been "assured that the subject should be considered."
In order to make sure it reached all concerned, he also wrote to the Archbishop of Canterbury and the Bishop of London, suggesting "off the Tower"
as an admirable location for such a vessel. This initiative, originating with a
Dissenter, is significant as the first in a long series of requests from different
quarters through the years for more direct Church of England involvement in
seamen's mission activity.[272]

Meanwhile, the Provisional Committee appointed at the preliminary
meeting of the projected Society was faced with two pressing problems: first,
finding a suitable ship; secondly, preparing plans for running her as a place of
worship. Meeting weekly (at the King's Head Tavern, in the Poultry), and
delegating details to a series of sub-committees among their own number, the
Provisional Committee proved during the following five weeks that they "did
not sleep at their posts."[273]

A key role was entrusted to the "Sub-Committee for enquiring the
best size for a Vessel—how the same might be obtained—and what would be
the probable expense." This group included, besides the shipbroking provisional treasurer, two men whose qualifications in this capacity were
obvious: George Green, the well-known Blackwall shipbuilder and owner,
and Benjamin Tanner, a leading shipwright in the Ratcliffe Highway district.[274]

By March 4, 1818, the Ship-Enquiry Sub-Committee was able to
report the results of their investigation of a promising possibility. HMS
Speedy, a veteran of the Napoleonic War, was now offered for sale. A sloop-
rigged, three-decked bomb-ship of 379 tons, she was originally built at
Newcastle in 1803 as a merchantman (the *Georg Hibbert*), but purchased
by the Admiralty at the time of the renewal of war. The sub-committee
estimated that she "might be made to hold from 5 to 700 Persons." (In
actual fact, she was, after refitting, capable of holding "nearly 800.") She
was copper-fastened and should with caulking last up to fifteen years, it was
thought; with a new sheathing, she should last a further fifteen. The price
asked, as she lay, was £700.[275]

The proposition duly approved, it was resolved: "That the Gentlemen be appointed to engage the Vessel and to commence the fitting." When
the Provisional Committee met again the following week, it could be confirmed that purchase papers had, in fact, been signed for this price.[276] With
only £100 so far subscribed, Marten wrote to Smith that he nevertheless had
"no fear for the money." An anonymous well-wisher (in fact, George Green)

What did HMS *Speedy* took like as an active sloop-
of war? The above is a painting of an almost
identical vessel, the HMS *Serres,* about to set sail.
(Courtesy: National Maritime Museum, Greenwich.)

made an unsolicited loan of £500 toward the purchase money, without
security or repayment term. It was optimistically anticipated that collections
and subscriptions at the intended public meeting for the official establishment of the Society would go far to provide a firm financial foundation. The
original minutes give evidence of minute preparations for the event.[277]

As it happened, Liverpool almost anticipated London. Early March,
1818, found G.C. Smith actively exploiting a visit to the Northwest, to whip
up support for similar efforts in Britain's second-largest port. Here, he seized
every available opportunity to publish "the glad tidings of an Ark for sailors
to be launched on the Thames, and the Sailor's Prayer-Meetings from
whence it originated." Chapel preaching and consultations culminated in the
first publicly advertised service to seafarers in Liverpool, in Byrom Street
Baptist Chapel. The spacious sanctuary (raised by Smith's sailor-preacher
predecessor, Samuel Medley) was filled to capacity. Seamen, especially
invited by handbills in all the docks, soon jammed the gallery and "multitudes
could not get in." The response to the rhetoric of G.C. Smith was such that

the time seemed opportune for forming an organization. In company with a deputation of brother ministers, Smith obtained an interview with Samuel Hope, the Liverpool merchant and philanthropist. The result was a decision to postpone further plans, however, pending the outcome of the proposed public meeting in London.[278]

Shortly afterwards, Smith made his way to the metropolis to take part in the great occasion. As originator of the whole enterprise, he had, despite his distance from the daily scene, been appointed to the Provisional Committee.[279] Marten had also invited him to give the important closing address on the day, thereby hoping that Smith would, as the treasurer put it, "enliven the meeting, and promote the subscription."[280]

In good time, the following notice had been sent to the *Public Ledger,* the *Philanthropic Gazette* and *The Times:*

> British Merchant Seamen in the Port of London &c. A Public Meeting of Persons desirous to promote Religious Instruction among Seamen will be held at the City of London Tavern Bishopsgate Street on Wednesday the 18th of March 1818 for the purpose of forming a Society for procuring more easy and ample means for their attending Public Worship.[281]

Thus, on March 18, 1818, at a "numerous and respectable" meeting, was formally founded "The Port of London Society for Promoting Religion among Merchant Seamen." Benjamin Shaw, M.P., was called to the chair, and R.H. Marten "powerfully urged" the purpose of the meeting. Marten thereupon introduced the first resolution, proposing the formation of the new Society. He was warmly seconded by Dr. John Rippon. In all, a series of seven resolutions were passed, specifying motives, objectives, methods, officers and regulations.[282]

By way of motivation, attention is concentrated on the "moral" motive of political and commercial indebtedness to seamen. The object of the Society is presented as being to supplement the hitherto almost exclusive attention to seamen's "temporal interests" by promoting "their religious instruction, their moral reformation, and their eternal happiness." Among methods, "the Ministry of the Gospel," preached on board a floating chapel, on a completely non-sectarian basis, is emphasized as the prinicipal means; however, "other plans" are also envisaged (especially the religious instruction of young sea-trainees).[283]

In accordance with the rules of the new Society, a committee of 40 was listed in a resolution moved by G.C. Smith (roughly half consisting of ministers, half laymen). Of these, R.H. Marten continued as treasurer, while the Rev. N.E. Sloper, Thomas Thompson and William Cook were appointed honorary secretaries. The rules otherwise follow the contemporary pattern of

At a General Meeting of Persons desirous to promote the Religious Instruction of Seamen held pursuant to Public Notice at the City of London Tavern Bishopsgate Street on Wednesday the 18th of March 1818

Benj.n Shaw Esq.re M.P. in the Chair

It was
 On the Motion of R.H. Marten Esq.re
 Seconded by the Rev.d Dr. Rippon
Resolved
 That it appeared to this Meeting that Britain owes much of its national Security Political independance, and Commercial greatness, to the Instrumentality of its numerous and intrepid Seamen; who have therefore an urgent claim upon the benevolence of those who enjoy the fruits of their adventurous and toilsome Services —
That while a laudable and liberal attention has been shewn to their temporal interests, no direct and adequate means have been employed to promote their Religious instruction, their moral reformation and their Eternal happiness — a neglect in the British Christians which appears the more astonishing, as well as culpable when viewed by the side of those exertions which are made on every hand, to diffuse Spiritual Knowledge, and Religion among other Classes of the Community —
and that for the purpose of supplying this acknowledged and lamented defect there be now formed an Institution to be called — 'The Port of London Society for Promoting Religion among Merchant Seamen'

Entry for March 18, 1818, in the Minutes
of the Port of London Society.

religious voluntary societies, in basing committee and society membership on degrees of financial support.[284] (In view of the unique nature of these proceedings, a transcript of the original minutes for March 18, 1818 is included as an Appendix.)

Since the new Society so utterly disclaimed all intention and inclination to promote "sectarian views and party feelings," it seems natural to ask: how far was the Port of London Society successful in pursuing this "United Front" policy?[285] Well might the Society publish (as in the fourth resolution at its foundation) "an intended union of all denominations of Christians," and "leave the forms and mode of worship to the Ministers appointed" on each individual occasion; but practical implications of church polity imposed serious impediments.

At all events, the Congregational-Baptist Provisional Committee felt the need for a formal resolution, on March 4, 1818, to assure "the Body of Wesleyan Methodists" that their attendance at the founding and cooperation in the future would be gladly received. Samuel Jennings responded by taking part at the founding and joining the committee for its first year. To what extent the Methodists' centralized Conference structure or other factors influenced events is difficult to say; but their official involvement in the PLS remained modest.[286] As far as the Established Church was concerned, Anglican Evangelicals, both ordained and lay, felt free to endorse the Society at public meetings, but balked at clerical cooperation in public worship. No resolution by a Dissenting society could alter the prevailing fundamentals of Anglican church order.[287]

It would be unrealistic to assume that the committee was not motivated by the publicity value of a broad, non-sectarian appeal. But it would be uncharitable to discount at least a simultaneous wish for actual interdenominational cooperation. Be that as it may, there was ample reason for "grateful rejoicing." The Port of London Society (PLS) had become a fact. Public "excitement" had been achieved. A "liberal collection" had been made.[288] The most immediate concern was now to make the recently-acquired vessel ready for her novel role.

The "Ark" (dedicated May 4, 1818)

To superintend the transformation of a veteran warship into a floating sanctuary was obviously no task for any enthusiastic amateur. Benjamin Tanner, as master shipwright, had all the expertise needed; he had also acquired the motivation. After, glancing at a tract he had received from Martin (*The British Ark*), Tanner found it "spoiled his night's sleep." Recollecting that he, like the author, had commenced his career in the

Interior view of the Thames Floating Chapel,
the former HMS *Speedy,* rebuilt and
dedicated May 4th 1818 as the world's first
fully appropriated seamen's church, popularly
known by seafarers as the *Ark.*
(From a contemporary print, British Sailors' Society.)

humble station of a cabin boy, he was moved to offer his gratuitous services
for planning and supervising the refitting of the *Ark.* [289]

As a result, captains and seamen had "high praise for the ingenious
and comfortable accommodation" which was provided:

> ... the gun-deck has been cut fore and aft, so as to leave the sides
> the whole length of the ship, and which are converted into galleries,
> while a platform has been laid at a suitable height above the
> keelson for seats to go round the entire hold. The pulpit and desk
> are built near to where the step of the mainmast was, and the
> ship's cabin affords an excellent vestry and committee-room. The
> main-deck has a long sky-light and grating, and under the counter
> and under the larboard bow are entrance ports from permanent
> stages, on which the ships' boats deliver their companies. [290]

This arrangement allowed a free height from the platform to the under-side of
the upper-deck of sixteen feet. The gun-ports made good windows around the

gallery. At the head was placed "a well cut bust of the venerable George III., 'the father of his people.' " On the stern was painted "The Port of London Society's Chapel for Seamen." (The ship was nevertheless widely known as the *Ark*, the name originally used in Smith's popular tract.)[291]

The minutes of the infant Society during these first weeks show that the project had sufficient appeal to prompt many to contribute in kind. A new mast, rigging and fittings for it, signal colors, deck-lighting gear, chain cables for mooring and a handsome Pulpit Bible were among items donated by tradesmen and others. Dr. Rippon provided copies of his hymn book, the RTS gave tracts, the MSABS furnished Scripture copies, and the British and Foreign School Society supplied school materials.[292]

All was not plain sailing, however. The Navy Board declined to provide gratuitous ballast for the ship.[293] The Committee for the Relief of Distressed Seamen refused to channel any proportion of their (very considerable) funds through the PLS, even though the object was "the promotion of the welfare of Seamen destitute of Religious Instruction."[294] Nor did the fact of it being a floating place of worship exempt it from the discriminatory legislation still enforced against non-Anglican religious assembly; investigations proved that, as "Protestant Dissenters of the denomination of Independents and Baptists," the committee had to go through the process of applying for registration of the sanctuary by the Bishop of London.[295] (A transcription of this interesting document is also included as an Appendix.)

Nevertheless, officialdom also gave encouragement. The Harbour-Master raised no objection to the mooring of such a vessel "in any part of the Harbour."[296] The Committee for Improving the Port of London, though unauthorized to remit canal dues, sent a personal donation of double the amount, "as a token of their cordial approbation of the objects of the Society."[297] The magistrates of the Thames Police made an unsolicited offer of protection against possible interference or injury to which worshippers might be exposed.[298] Moreover, liberal donations were received from the Bank of England, the East India Company and the Royal Exchange, among others.[299] The Watermen's Company offered special terms and services, to facilitate access to the vessel.[300]

As the work of refitting progressed, and investment value increased, it became necessary to secure satisfactory insurance coverage. (It was decided to insure the *Ark* for £1,500.)[301] As she approached completion, there were also personnel problems to be solved. First, a suitable "Ship-Keeper" had to be found to take up residence on board and attend to the many maintenance duties involved, including the regulation of boat traffic to and fro, and keeping a ship's log of "daily occurrences." (A Mr. Joseph Church was eventually appointed at £60 per annum.)[302] Next, a "Preaching

Roster" had to be prepared, in order to secure pulpit supply for coming months. This task was entrusted to a sub-committee of ministers.

It is noteworthy that there is, at this stage, no traceable suggestion of any full-time seamen's chaplain—even as a desideratum. On the other hand, the committee makes it quite clear that "the list of Supplies, should be of those Gentlemen only who are exclusively occupied in Ministerial Duties." While this principle would militate against part-time Methodist Local Preachers, the committee gratefully accepted the offer of students of the Hoxton and Homerton Academies "to supply the Pulpit, at a moment's notice," in case of emergency. (The Society's *Minutes* record continuing difficulties in assuring a steady ministerial supply, while the performance of the youthful student volunteers could create critical comments.)[303]

By the end of April, the *Ark* was ready for her new use. (Across the Atlantic, the religious press joined in commending the "singular promptitude" and "ingenuity" of the operation.) G.C. Smith, unable to remain in London that long, had already visited the vessel while she was fitting out in Limehouse Dock. Here, with typical impetuosity, he had called the shipwrights and their men from their work for a short devotion. Thus, as they gathered around, Boatswain Smith offered the first public prayer on board, for the future mission of the floating chapel. The impromptu consecration ended with all hands singing the Doxology.[304]

On May 1, 1818, the ship was towed up-river to her mooring. Zebedee Rogers had already alerted ships in the Lower Pool, and flags were hoisted to honor the occasion. While the crews of ships she passed and crowds along the banks who witnessed the scene cheered the *Ark* on her way, boatmen attending her gave resounding cheers in response, and "the gentlemen on board answered by taking off their hats." Finally, she was brought up at her station at the London Docks Buoy, off Wapping New Stairs. The spot had been carefully selected. Immediately below the chief entrance of the busy, recently constructed London Docks, it was both midway between the Upper and Lower Pools and close to north-bank Sailortown. (Even that notorious neighbor, Execution Dock, scene of many a maritime malefactor's final fate, could serve a positive purpose; here, in close juxtaposition, were the *Ark* and the *Gibbet*, striking symbols, for all to see, of the way of life and the way of death.)[305]

As soon as the ship had been moored, a spontaneous service of "prayer and praise" took place among the many who had accompanied her. Then, on May 4, 1818, the Floating Chapel was formally opened by a memorable service of dedication. To underscore the interdenominational invitation of the new place of worship, the service was opened by the reading of prayers from the Anglican Liturgy. Dr. John Rippon followed with

The Rev. Rowland Hill,
who was G.C. Smith's
childhood pastor at the
(Independent) Surrey
Chapel and preached the
dedicatory sermon at the
opening of the *Ark.*
(C. Silvester Horne:
The Story of the L.M.S.)

extemporaneous prayer. The Rev. Rowland Hill, already known for his
warm sympathy with seamen, preached the dedicatory sermon. Speaking
"with his usual animation," he took as his highly appropriate text: "But the
dove found no rest for the sole of her foot, and she returned unto the ark. . . ."
(Genesis 8:9), In the afternoon, a well-known Baptist minister from Bristol,
bred to a seafaring life in early boyhood, the Rev. Thomas Roberts, delivered
a sermon which the PLS Committee later decided to publish. The historic
day closed with an evening service by Dr. William B. Collyer in Albion
Chapel, Finsbury, where he "addressed a very numerous and interested
assembly" from Psalm 142:4, "No man cared for my soul."[306]

The opening of the *Ark* as the world's first fully appropriated
seamen's church proved that now some, at least, had commenced caring for
the long-neglected soul of the seafarer. As the secretary of a Society which
traces its origin to that unique event put it, practically a century later: "The
Thames from the first day it began to flow, never witnessed a greater day in
its history than this."[307]

DIVINE STRATEGY? "FROM THE RIVER TO THE ENDS OF THE EARTH" (ZECH. 9:10)

"The very incipiency of the mission to the sailor marks its heavenly
origin." Such was the conclusion of the leading American Society in 1860,
when looking back over 80 years to the humble beginning of the Naval and
Military Bible Society. "God is come into the camp," is quoted as the
message (from 1 Samuel 4:7) preached at the first service in aid of that
Society.[308] By the same token, "God is come into the cabin," could have

been said of that first seamen's prayer-meeting on board the *Friendship* in 1814.[309] At all events, Captain Wilkins was not alone in openly attributing the origin of the Thames Revival to the Holy Spirit himself.[310] Others, too, emphasized divine intervention as the fundamental factor: the Spirit of God had once more "moved upon the face of the waters." Confronted with centuries of "manifest indifference" by organized Christianity towards the seafarer, God had "remembered mercy, and revived his own work ... through the instrumentality of mariners themselves."[311] Repeated references to the "discovery" of seamen's prayer-meetings, during the years 1814-17, underscore the divine source attributed to these manifestations.[312]

As previously noted, a precisely parallel pattern is traceable in factors affecting the course of each of the two distinct phenomena we have referred to as the Naval Awakening and the Thames Revival.[313] In both cases there was first the *transcendental* factor, mentioned above. The Thames Revival, though not exactly (as the Naval Awakening) begun "on the bosom of the ocean," was worked on the waters of the Thames, as "a wonder of sovereign grace."[314] A second common feature was the *immanent* factor of close interaction between literary media and lay ministry. On the one hand, there was the marine Bible and tract distribution in London and on the North Country coast; on the other, there was the type of lay-promoted prayer-meeting and preaching which characterized the early Bethel Movement.[315] A third similarity was the operation of a *consolidatory* factor, centered in the particular role of G.C. Smith. On the Thames, his emergence as the Seamen's Preacher was preceded and supplemented by the coordinative activities of the Rotherhithe Methodists, especially Samuel Jennings and Zebedee Rogers.[316]

It would, however, be an oversimplification to regard the Naval Awakening of the Napoleonic War era, and the Thames Revival of the immediate post-war period, as merely a case of repetition of structural similarities inherent in certain spiritual phenomena. The whole train of events, from that conversation between two concerned Methodists in Soho Square in 1779[317] until the opening of the *Ark* off Wapping New Stairs in 1818, constitutes a continuous progression of one and the same basic movement — towards the emergence of organized seamen's missions.

The two successive phases of this single movement are closely interrelated by a process of transplantation.[318] The many thousands discharged from naval service or returned from French prisons who, as from 1814, sought employment in the coastal and foreign trades, had witnessed— and been in varying degrees affected by—the Naval Awakening.[319] Here in the merchant service, the Marine Bible Societies could continue on the foundation already laid in the navy by the NMBS. Thus, it was largely the potentials present in embryo in the Naval Awakening which saw fruition in the Thames Revival and the birth of the Bethel Movement. The Naval Awakening would have been only an episode, destined to dissolve with the war-time navy itself, had it not been channeled into the Thames Revival; and the Thames Revival might never have developed the dynamic force of the Bethel Movement, which again laid the foundation for future seamen's mission organization, had it not been infused with the rugged vitality of the Naval Awakening.

As the first organizational fruit of the new-born Bethel Movement, the establishment of the Port of London Society and the opening of the *Ark* might well be hailed, by Richard Marks, as evidence of "a new era" in British maritime history.[320] This first place of worship in the world wholly and solely appropriated to the seafarer had not yet provided him with a permanent preacher; but at least he now had a permanent pulpit. In thus providing for stated preaching for seamen in a sanctuary dedicated to their particular use, the Port of London Society represents an epoch-making new departure in relation to the only prior form of organization for the spiritual welfare of seamen: the marine Scripture distribution societies (the NMBS, the Marine Bible Societies and the MSABS).

In this sense, the PLS supplements its predecessors in a vital function. Similarly, over a century earlier, the SPG had been formed to supply, through the Gospel ministry of its missionaries, that "living agency abroad" which the literary media distribution of the SPCK still needed.[321] Referring to the prospects anticipated from the combined effect of the MSABS agent at Gravesend and now the PLS Floating Chapel off Wapping, a contemporary correspondent of *The Evangelical Magazine* felt constrained to exclaim: "Where is the discernment of the enemies of all righteousness that they cannot observe 'the signs of the times?'"[322]

Nevertheless, the growth potential of the Bethel Movement was by no means exhausted by the launching of the *Ark*. As its name implied, the PLS was—despite everything—a local emanation, expressly limiting its scope to British seamen, in the Port of London. The Bethel Movement was born for greater things yet—and George Charles Smith was not the man to let it die in infancy.

The secretary of a successor of the PLS could later confirm that it was "chiefly through the labours of the Rev. G.C. Smith, of Penzance," that the growing revival movement in the Royal and Merchant Navies up to 1818 "found a centre in the establishment of this Society, with its floating chapel on the Thames."[323] Otherwise, the whole seamen's revival would, in the words of another general secretary, "without doubt have been extinguished from want of planning and cohesion."[324] However, the immediate future was to prove that, just as Smith had been the dominating figure in the first phase

Hoisting the Bethel Flag, worship-signal and rallying point for lay-led promotion of seamen's missions in both domestic and foreign ports. Here, the simpler version, without the dove and star. (*Chart and Compass*, 1882.)

of British organized seamen's missions, so too—in his continued promotion of the potentials of the Bethel Movement—he was to play a decisive role during the second, post-1818 phase.[325] His influence during these years becomes all the more impressive when it is borne in mind that he was, until the mid-twenties, formally still the pastor of a congregation in one of the most remote corners of England.

However, human instrumentality was not all. Smith, in common with other pioneers of the Seamen's Cause, was keenly conscious of the fact that the Bethel Movement was, ultimately, not only divine in origin; it was also divine in direction. Not only the birth but also the growth of the Bethel Movement were both seen as part of one and the same divine stategy for the reclamation and rehabilitation of the long-neglected seafarer, meeting basic koinonial and kerygmatic needs, while also leading into a mounting diaconal involvement.[326] Although the opening of the *Ark* in 1818 marks the beginning of a transition toward institutionalizaton, the Bethel Flag was yet to see its greatest glory, as the symbol of a movement which was to encompass the globe, promoting or improvising for institutional seamen's missions wherever it went.[327]

PART IV

PEACE AND WAR

Toward A British
National Society

Chapter 9

Metropolitan Expansion

Prelude to a National Society

In the history of the evolution of organized British seamen's missions, the year 1818 marks, as seen, a transition from a preliminary pattern of almost exclusive concentration on maritime literary media distribution to a form of more general seamen's missions, centered around the preaching of the Gospel. How wide was the field to which these new, expanding efforts were endeavoring to minister? Apart from approximately 20,000 men retained in the navy of that period, some 150,000 men were employed in the merchant ships of the British Isles. As to the metropolis, it was estimated that some 45,000 men frequented the Port of London annually on board vessels of different descriptions and that there were some 7,000 seamen on the River at any given time.[1] Certainly, the harvest seemed plenteous, and the laborers few.

However, as the old warship off Wapping went into the first year of her novel commission, the immediate queston was: How would the average seaman respond to a Gospel ministry of which he was the particular object? Critics characterized the whole project as "eccentric." Pessimists prophesied that it would be impossible to excite sufficient interest among seamen "to bring ten of them to the place." A passer-by was heard to comment wrily that "these Methodists . . . have no need to make such a stir about the sailors, for they will never hear them."[2]

In actual fact, seamen's worship attendance was, at the outset, far from impressive. The early *Minutes* of the Society indicate that attendance figures averaged, at that time, somewhat less than 100 (in a sanctuary capable of holding close to 800).[3] A major factor in achieving increased momentum was the return of George Charles Smith, in August 1818, for another round of three months' preaching engagements in the metropolis. Under the headline "GOOD NEWS FOR SEAMEN!" Jeffery Dennis announced in the second edition of his *Address:*

The Floating Chapel, fitted by the Port of London Society, was crowded on Sunday (the 16th of August, 1818,) beyond all former precedent, on the occasion of the first Sermon on board her by the Rev. G.C. Smith, of Penzance. It was this Gentleman who preached last summer on board several vessels in the River Thames, to sailors, for whom he has naturally a strong affection, having commenced his career at sea, and served for many years on the ocean, and the Society owes its origin to the hopes of success arising from his labours. Between thirty and forty ship's boats were made fast to the ship, to wait the conclusion of the service to which they had brought the crews of the ships to which they respectively belonged. The centre of the Chapel was filled with seamen, and the side seats and galleries with masters of merchantmen and their families, and a very respectable number of ladies and gentlemen from the shore. The standings between the seats were perfectly crowded, and even the upper deck was filled with attentive listeners to the voice of the preacher, as it ascended through the opened windows of the skylights. Mr. Smith preached both morning and evening, and a liberal collection was made. . . .[4]

The Rev. G.C. Smith was, during his London stay, repeatedly requested to preach on board the *Ark,* constantly to crowded congregations. After his departure, the committee could report a "progressive increase" in the attendance of seamen; by February 1819, it had reached five times the initial average.[5] The *Ark* had, at length, been adopted by the seafarer. Pleasing proof of this sense of identification was provided by reports, even from the Pacific, of how seamen would speak with obvious pride of "their" chapel on the Thames.[6]

This increasing popularity of worship services in the *Ark* was intimately connected with the more informal Bethel Meetings in the tiers of the Lower Pool. These continued to thrive, both stimulating and supplementing activities on the Floating Chapel. Here, too, Smith was, by frequent preaching and counseling, able to provide a powerful impulse during his London stay, faithfully supported by the ever-zealous Zebedee Rogers.[7] Drawing on his recent home mission experience, Smith compared the relationship between the *Ark* and itinerant preaching in neighboring tiers to "a town surrounded with villages." The way to fill a central sanctuary was systematic exertion at the local level.[8]

The vitality inherent in the Bethel Meetings could not be confined indefinitely to the Lower Pool. As Thomas Phillips emphasized, it was important that sailors in this part of the River "should not have all the good things to themselves."[9] Largely due to Phillips' initiative, Bethel Meetings were, before the close of 1818, also firmly established in the Upper Pool.

Here he was on "home ground." At Chamberlain's Wharf (immediately below London Bridge, on the south side), he obtained the *Ocean* of Hull, Captain Foster. In her, one dark and wet early winter night, was held the first Bethel Meeting in the Upper Pool. G.C. Smith preached in a packed cabin, while "several sailors stowed themselves away on the half deck."[10]

With the arrival of winter, Smith had to return to his pastoral duties in Penzance. Upper Pool meetings went on, however, "from London Bridge to Pickle Herring Stairs," generally three nights a week, under the enthusiastic encouragement of Phillips and his friends from shore. As news of these meetings traveled down-river, an important innovation was introduced:

> The Sailors in the Lower Pool rejoiced at the work of God being thus extended and it was proposed to have a monthly prayer-meeting alternately in each Pool; thereby forming a union among those who were unacquainted with each other. One month would be seen the captains and Seamen coming up from the Lower Pool to join their brethren near London Bridge, and the next month our Sailors from the Upper Pool would be seen on board the colliers in the Lower Pool.[11]

The sense of spiritual union, fostered by fellowship experienced especially at these joint "Monthly Bethel Meetings," was to find institutional expression before the end of the following year. The precise circumstances, however, cast the first foreboding shadows across a scene which had hitherto become only progressively brighter. Their source was not external opposition. Although many captains were still averse to lending their ship for a meeting, and large numbers of sailors still refused "with oaths and contempt, to join their pious shipmates," each week brought fresh proof that the Bethel Movement was, nevertheless, going from strength to strength.[12] The first portent of serious storms ahead were of a quite different character.

Although the PLS (with the *Ark*) was historically the organizational first-fruit of the Bethel Movement, circumstances surrounding the Society's establishment and constitution had already indicated the possible presence of widely differing trends. Here were potentials for polarization between a lay and an ordained ministry, between a "united front" and a denominational orientation, between a local and a national structure, between a revival and a nurture emphasis. A year after the foundation of the Society, the pattern of inherent tensions was still by no means manifest. Only the subsequent public eruption of controversy, from 1827 on, brought to light evidence of the dramatic developments which were enacted as early as 1819.[13] Here again, the powerful personality of George Charles Smith was to play a predominant role.

When Smith arrived at Horsleydown in August 1819 in order to lodge with the Phillips household during another three months of metropolitan preaching engagements, he was prepared to devote much of his time and energy to preaching both in the *Ark* and in the tiers of shipping. As soon as he entered the London scene, however, he was made forcibly aware of "a kind of religious war" which had developed on the River during recent weeks.[14]

Two lay members of the Port Society Committee, Benjamin Tanner (the master shipwright who had supervised the rebuilding of the vessel) and John Francis (a ship's slop-seller of Ratcliffe Highway), had been appointed as chief and assistant managers, respectively, on board the Floating Chapel. At the first opportunity, the two stated their case to the Rev. G.C. Smith in the vestry of the *Ark* after Sunday service. In addition to the regular Sunday program, the PLS had advertised a week-night service every Thursday. In order to promote attendance, the managers had requested captains of vessels in the Pools to renounce their Bethel Meetings in the tiers that night. This the captains and their crews had been unwilling to do. The managers, aware of Smith's unique prestige with the Bethel leaders, urged him, therefore, to add his moral support to what was represented as the Society's standpoint.[15]

A deputation of captains from the Lower Pool confronted Smith with a radically different picture, however. During the preceding winter Bethel Meetings, especially in the Lower Pool where the majority of the shipping was, had flourished to such a degree that up to nine such meetings could be held simultaneously on week-nights, with signal lanterns hoisted from tier to tier and assemblies of well over 100 in a single ship.[16] They had themselves long since volunteered to surrender Wednesday night in deference to Mr. Jennings' Rotherhithe mid-week meeting.[17] That they should abandon all opportunity of meeting in the tiers the following night seemed to the Bethel leaders an arbitrary demand. Particularly was this so when presented in the form of a prohibition. Messrs. Tanner and Francis were alleged to have "used all their influence with the ship-owners" with whom they had professional contact, in order to enforce their will. The captain of the *Brotherly Love* was, ironically enough, the first who, as a result of instructions received from his owners, had to obey orders from the Floating Chapel Committee to "strike the Bethel Flag." Other similar cases followed.[18]

Thus Smith found himself the unwilling umpire between two conflicting parties, neither of whom he could decide for without the risk of alienating the other. Placed in this tortuous dilemma, he consulted with friends both afloat and ashore (particularly his close colleagues, Phillips, Thompson and Collins). Their reactions confirmed his own. After continuing, for a while, to preach "for all parties," both on board the *Ark* (to greater crowds than ever before) and at Bethel Meetings in the tiers, Smith's mind was made up. Convinced that infinitely more was at issue than a case of colliding programs, he felt the situation called for far more than mere "moral support." Deliberately staking all his "now opulent and influential connections," the former man-of-war's man determined, in true Nelson tradition, to throw himself "in the breach at whatever risk" and launch a new seamen's mission society.[19]

In arriving at what was to prove perhaps the most far-reaching decision of his career,[20] Smith seems to have been guided by two basic considerations: (1) A sense of solidarity with the claims of his brother-seafarers on the Thames; (2) A vision of the vocation of the Bethel Flag on a global scale.

First, with regard to the local situation, Smith had no difficulty in identifying with Bethel captains and crew members who sensed a threat to their freedom of assembly or the validity of a lay ministry. Symptomatic of the sentiments of these men was the reaction of those whom Thomas Phillips had spoken to, when visiting an early Bethel Meeting in 1817. His offer of providing for a minister to preach to them was, on that occasion, "civilly declined."[21] Men of such independence of spirit were not likely to stomach the dictates of a committee denying them "any meeting but theirs." This they saw as no less than an assault on "their religious privileges as British subjects."[22]

Here the Bethel Flag adherents on the Thames could be assured of the whole-hearted sympathy of their Seamen's Preacher friend. To Smith, the value of itinerant religious meetings consisted not only in promoting attendence at a central place of worship. As in the case of village meetings in the country, Bethel Meetings in the tiers had an independent value in their own right.[23] From an evangelistic or *kerygmatic* viewpoint, only a fraction of the field could find accommodation within the walls of the *Ark;* and the stubborn, who would never bestir themselves anyway, could only be brought under the sound of the Gospel if they were "sought out" and efforts were made "to carry religion on board to them."[24] From the viewpoint of Christian fellowship, or *koinonìa,* the needs of the committed would, in many cases, not be satisfied with only the formal worship services of the Floating Chapel; more informal meetings would for some be a preferable alternative, for many a necessary supplement. At all events, Smith saw a fundamental need for Bethel Meetings on shipboard as a means of "domesticating" religion in the seaman's situation.[25]

However, in arriving at his decision, Smith was motivated by more than the local, immediate need of providing protection against intimidation by such as seemed "determined to monopolize all the religious meetings to the floating chapel." Without organizational coordination and support, he saw little prospect of the Bethel Flag fulfilling a long-term destiny which he knew to be not only metropolitan, but national, even world-wide. "If Bethel flags could be extended through the nation and the world," Smith maintained, "the cause of God, among sailors, would be most efficiently . . . promoted in all parts of the globe."[26]

As for the Port of London Society, the very name reflected a self-imposed restriction of outreach. The treasurer's words of general disapproval of Bethel Meetings were still fresh in Smith's memory. He had noted how the Bethel Flag had so far never been sanctioned on board the Floating Chapel, or otherwise been associated with the Port of London Society.[27] In fact, the Floating Chapel Committee had, in what others, too, interpreted as an attempt to "annihilate the Bethel Flag," gone to the trouble of inventing and sponsoring a "new flag with the word *Ebenezer* in the room of *Bethel*." True, the experiment was short-lived. (As one observer put it, "It would not do. Jack refused to be trifled with.") Nevertheless, the episode only confirmed Smith's suspicion of some fundamental hostility to both the principle and the possibilities of the Bethel Flag.[28] This was reinforced by what he saw as "not the least intention to promote any efforts in the out-ports, at home or . . . abroad."[29]

In short, the dynamic potential of the Bethel Movement could not, it seemed to Smith, hope to find scope within the static structure of the existing Society. Hence it was imperative to establish an alternative.[30]

BRITISH AND FOREIGN SEAMEN'S FRIEND SOCIETY AND BETHEL UNION (FOUNDED NOVEMBER 12, 1819)

The momentous decision once made, George Charles Smith went to the task of carrying it into effect with typical vigor. He first called a consultative meeting with "captains, mates and friends" on board the *Ocean*, lying at Chamberlain's Wharf again, in the Upper Pool. Here, the procedure of the Floating Chapel Management Committee was strongly censured by those present. Smith's proposal to form a society to protect the cause met with spontaneous approval, and his suggestion for a title was forthwith agreed: The Bethel Seamen's Union. The name evinced the purpose—with the "Bethel" emblem as rallying point, to encourage "Seamen" to join in a "Union" of Christian fellowship and mission. In practice, the title became, "for brevity sake," the "Bethel Union," a term soon to be adopted by similar organizations on both sides of the Atlantic. However, it is noteworthy that what seems to have been the first specific "Seamen's Union" in history was founded by Christian seafarers, for the spiritual welfare of their fellows.[31]

There is reference to a similar meeting on a ship in the Lower Pool.[32] His decision thus endorsed by brother-seafarers, Smith felt he could now devote himself to preparations for the official establishment of the Society. These included two publications and two public meetings.

The first of the two tracts, published in the autumn of 1819, bears the title: *Bethel: or, the Flag Unfurled. Containing a Correct Statement of Interesting Facts Respecting the Prayer Meetings among Sailors on the River Thames.* This leads up to the announcement of two forthcoming public meetings.[33] The second tract is called: *English Sailors: or, Britains Best Bulwarks. Being the Substance of Various Addresses to Seamen.* Here, Smith concentrates on "the Claims of Sailors to more general attention," with all the Scripture quotations and comments he manages to muster. This work, which was also given wide circulation, concludes with a report of the proceedings of the first of the two public meetings.[34]

As in the case of the PLS, the Bethel Seamen's Union, too, was made the object of a two-phased foundation. First, a preliminary public meeting was called for Friday, October 22, 1819, at Horsleydown, Southwark. Here, Thomas Phillips had obtained the loan of the School Hall in White's Grounds, owned by the British and Foreign School Society. Amid a large assembly of captains, mates, seamen and concerned members of the public, invited by printed bills, G.C. Smith took the chair. Above the platform hung three Bethel Flags.[35]

A motion to form a Bethel Seamen's Union was made by Captain Edward Smith, a naval lieutenant who, like so many others, had entered the merchant service after the Peace. (He had recently become agent of the MSABS for the Metropolitan Thames area.)[36] Other naval officers who moved and seconded resolutions were Lieutenants J.F. Arnold and Francis Collins. Besides both Thomas Phillips and Thomas Thompson, the Rev. A. Brown of South Ockendon, as well as the Rev. Mr. Allen of Warminster, also warmly advocated the cause. With a characteristically keen eye to emotional effect, G.C. Smith had invited a veteran sea captain, George Orton, pioneer "agent afloat" of the BFBS and RTS, now "a venerable grey headed man" with 48 years of sea service behind him. He likewise introduced "a pious Sailor," Cuthbert Ward, a hero from the *Robert and Margaret* (whose recent dramatic rescue of three crews off Memel had thrilled the nation). The general response to their account was tremendous.[37]

A provisional committee having been appointed, with Thomas Phillips and Lieutenant Collins as secretaries, the meeting was adjourned. Finally, on Friday, November 12, 1819, at a general public meeting held at the City of London Tavern, the new Society was officially established. On the advice of Dr. W.B. Collyer, Captain Sir George Mount Keith, Bart., R.N., a decided Evangelical, was obtained as chairman. The meeting was widely advertised, and "an immense assembly" gathered, with several naval officers, merchants and gentlemen connected with shipping on the platform, and numerous captains and mates of merchantmen, as well as some 200 seamen and cabin boys also in attendance. In addition to speakers from the preliminary meeting, a number of "the most pious and zealous sea captains," including Anthony Wilkins, took an active part and made a deep impression on the public. The Rev. William Ward, the pioneer missionary from Serampore, also warmly advocated the object of the Society.[38]

The meeting was the first occasion on which Ward's close friend and fellow Baptist, George Fife Angas (1789-1879), appeared before a metropolitan public on behalf of the Seamen's Cause. Ultimately best known for his key role in emancipating the slaves of Honduras and founding the colonies of South Australia and New Zealand, George Fife Angas rapidly won wide respect as merchant and shipowner for his strict adherence to Christian ethics in business. In the development of British seamen's mission organization, he was destined to take an increasingly active part, particularly after his removal, in 1824, from Newcastle to London.

Characteristically alert to global and ecumenical perspectives, it was G.F. Angas who proposed an important addition to the title of the Society. It was now to be known as "The Bethel Seamen's Union, British and Foreign." Angas shared with Smith the vision of a seamen's mission society with pretensions equal to those of the British and Foreign Bible Society, the sphere of one to be separated from the other only "by the margin of a water-line."[39]

Within a year, the position of this addition was moved forward and the title changed to "The British and Foreign Seamen's Friend Society and Bethel Union" (BFSFSBU).[40] This was to remain the official title until the merger of 1827, although frequently abbreviated (for example to "British Seamen's Friend Society" or "The Bethel Union"). By 1820, benevolent societies of "Friends" of the deprived or discriminated were no novelty.[41] There was also the precedent of a very similar wording in a few seamen's manuals.[42] Now, the Bethel Union Movement (apparently spurred by a Scottish initiative) adopted the combination "Seamen's Friend" as the suggestive title of kindred seamen's mission societies. Among all the false "friends," anxious to exploit the seamen the moment he reached port, here was, by implication, one on whom he could depend. Like the "Bethel Union" combination, the words "Seamen's Friend," as a designation for seamen's mission societies, was to achieve wide and durable popularity on both sides of the Atlantic.[43]

What were, in effect, the distinctive objects and means contemplated by this first national seamen's misson society? A transcription of the brief prospectus of the Society as projected in the autumn of 1819, together with

George Fife Angas,
younger brother of
William Henry Angas,
shipowner, philanthropist
and from 1819 on a
pioneer promoter of
seamen's missions in
Great Britain and
overseas.
(G. Holden Pike: *Among
the Sailors.*)

the revised constitution as presented the following year, are included as
Appendices.[44] From these and other available sources, though not in themselves strictly systematic in composition, it is nevertheless possible to
distinguish certain basic structural features.

The fundamental purpose of the new Society could well be summarized in one overall objective: the promotion of an evangelical union of
seamen, supra-denominational in basis and supra-national in scope.

A spirit of "Christian Candour," willing to throw overboard every
vestige of denominational demands, was regarded as fundamental.[45] Recognizing, in effect, the inevitability of the seamen's socialization process, with
attendant separation from "land-life" attitudes, the Society saw nothing
more alien to the mentality of a typical "Tar" than narrow, religious
sectarianism.[46] It was stipulated that sailors must be left "fully at liberty to
follow on shore the Church or Meeting, as seemed most agreeable to
themselves." At sea, a sufficient basis of spiritual unity was assumed to exist
in the broad bond of evangelical consensus. (This was expressly interpreted
as being "agreeable to the articles and homilies of the Church of England.")
At this early stage, the concept of a particular "Church of Seamen," as a
corporate community, was not yet a conscious issue.[47]

The scope of the new Society was to be not only national, seeking to
benefit the British seafarer wherever he might be, but, as G.C. Smith put it:
the limits of the Society were to be "the circumference of the Globe."[48]
Besides ministering to foreign seamen in British ships or the crews of foreign

flag vessels calling at British ports, the aim was to be "instrumental in awakening the attention of foreign nations, and promoting every plan which might be adopted in the same way as the British and Foreign Bible Society."[49] In this orientation, there was an appeal akin to that contained in the vision of the Rev. Joseph Hughes when the Bible Society was conceived in 1802: ". . . if for Wales, why not for the Kingdom, and if for the Kingdom, why not for the World?"[50] Reports of the progress of the two societies during their first years show how much wider support the new Society achieved than the PLS, with its constricted scope.

Although sources show some terminological confusion of objectives with methods, the BFSFSBU clearly intended to rely on four principal means in achieving its ends: (1) The Bethel Flag, as the universal rallying point of religious assemblies for seafarers. (These might quite simply meet on shipboard, at sea or in port, relying largely on lay leadership; but where practicable they might lead to the establishment of permanent sanctuaries, afloat or ashore, with stated ministerial supply.) (2) Literary media, such as Scripture and tracts. The "itinerating system" would naturally facilitate a wider distribution. A "Sailor's Magazine" was considered an object of primary importance, as a monthly medium of both missionary outreach and promotional motivation. (This, under G.C. Smith's editorship, was to prove a phenomenal success.) (3) Foreign correspondence, in order to promote similar efforts throughout the world, and "stimulate mutual co-operation." (4) Miscellaneous other means, calculated to promote the overall object of the Society. (Expressly mentioned was the provision of "suitable boarding-houses for Sailors on their arrival from foreign voyages.")[51]

How did the Port of London Society react to the appearance of a new interdenominational seamen's mission society on the metropolitan scene? Such contemporary sources as were available to the public could scarcely give cause for alarm. In his prospectus, G.C. Smith had published that whatever plan might be adopted would "keep the Floating Chapel in view," and actively promote attendance there.[52] At the preliminary public meeting, October 22, 1819, Thomas Thompson (then honorary secretary of the PLS) emphasized that supplementation, not competition, was the motivation for a second society, as "both Institutions went hand in hand, and each filled up its separate department."[53] Nevertheless, publications dating from the eruption of public controversy between metropolitan seamen's mission societies (after 1827) reveal strong reactions within the PLS against the projection of a new society in the autumn of 1819. This impression is borne out by contemporary entries (and significant silences) in the PLS *Minutes* from that period.[54]

In the first place, the committee of the PLS thwarted attempts by the new Society, both before and after its official foundation, to join forces. The former was made by G.C. Smith at an interview with R.H. Marten. To "avoid giving unnecessary offence," Smith suggested that the proposed Bethel Union should become an auxiliary of the PLS, and that the projected "Sailor's Magazine" should be transferred to this institution. The offer was "politely declined."[55] On the latter occasion, half a year after the foundation of the Bethel Union, a six-man deputation (including G.F. Angas) presented the committee of the PLS with a "Proposition for uniting the 2 Societies under one common designation." Again the offer was rejected, with the uninformative comment that, "under existing circumstances, an Union would not be productive of equal benefit to Seamen. . . ."[56]

Furthermore, certain circumstances connected with the foundation itself left no doubt in the minds of the projectors of the new Society as to the attitude of leading elements in the old. On the eve of the general public meeting at which the Bethel Seamen's Union was to be founded, a significant advertisement appeared in the *Public Ledger,* seeking to "apprize the public" that this meeting did "not emanate from" the committee of the PLS, and that it would be "distinct from" the one which they had the pleasure and honor to conduct. Even after alteration in deference to a dissenting member of the committee, its intention of "warning the public" against the newcomer was still considered to be sufficiently clear.[57] The treasurer of the PLS had already refused an invitation to take the chair;[58] and when the day arrived, it was apparently only a powerful and well-timed plea on behalf of his Bethel brethren by Captain Wilkins which overwhelmed the intended opposition of two ministerial members of the PLS Committee.[59]

It would be unrealistic to deny that a conflict of personalities contributed toward the rift which arose in early metropolitan seamen's missions. Two specific episodes in the year 1819 undoubtedly helped to exacerbate relations. Both involved the Rev. G.C. Smith. In the so-called "Guinea" case, he was mistakenly criticized for accepting a fixed honorarium to which he was perfectly entitled.[60] In the "Founder" issue, his pioneer role in the establishment of the Floating Chapel was eclipsed by a somewhat misleading tribute to R.H. Marten.[61] In both cases, the vehemence of Smith's reaction gave fair warning to those directly involved, of troubled times ahead.[62]

Nevertheless, the conflict which commenced in 1819 was in its origin not one of personalities as such, but basically, one of principles for which conflicting personalities stood. Against that which not only Smith, but men like Thomas Thompson and Thomas Phillips, considered to be an overt attempt to restrain revivalism and lay collaboration among seafarers, the Seamen's Preacher from Penzance was prepared to do battle, whatever the cost.[63]

The cost was formidable. Smith traced all the "open warfare," which developed between metropolitan seamen's mission societies for a generation to come, to the founding of the Bethel Union in November 1819.[64] Some might see this event as "a schism or a secession," resulting in a "rival Institution."[65] To the founders themselves, it was a question of saving the Bethel Flag and all it stood for. They took heart from the thought that this was not the first case of a sign which should be "spoken against," and yet prevail.[66] Their conviction was confirmed as they saw the Bethel Flag unfurling over successive new horizons, the symbol of both expanding metropolitan efforts, and promising beginnings in provincial and foreign ports. In the years immediately ahead, the story of the *Seamen's* Cause was to become, in Britain, as also in America, largely the story of the *Bethel* Cause.[67]

ORGANIZING FOR VICTORY

"But we have a flag. . . ." In its 1822 *Retrospect,* the BFSFSBU compressed into five simple words the difference between its own modest assets with those of the PLS. The Port Society was, despite its "noble and appropriate Seamen's Chapel on the Thames," inevitably limited, tied, as it was, to one single ship and one specific location. The Bethel Union Society could boast a banner calling on both seamen and their friends to unite in "personal exertions throughout the world."[68]

The secret of the Bethel Movement's astounding success was, perhaps, more than anything, its fundamental simplicity. This, again, accounted for its economy and flexibility—both vital factors in rapid expansion. Granted a few pieces of blue and white bunting comprising the recognized emblem, a convenient ship and a cooperative captain, an improvised seamen's chapel could be "rigged" no matter where. Should there be "seamen's friends" ashore with sufficient concern, a local Seamen's Friend Society and/or Bethel Union could result. (The two components were, as in London, combinable or interchangeable.) This society would then, in principle, be free "to promote the moral and religious instruction of Seamen, in every lawful, prudent, and possible way" (to quote Richard Marks' interpretation of the characteristic feature of adaptability of method).[69]

The fundamental need for this mobile concept of seamen's missions was outlined by Marks in the following manner. Seamen, he maintained, generally required

> the active and zealous exertions of good men to rouse them— to visit their ships—to address them in the streets—and, in fact, to carry religion home to those who would not or could not go forth to find it for themselves.

This strategy of mobility, embodying the dual principles of visitation and itineration, inherited as a distinctly Methodist trait and transplanted to the

Thames Revival, was to remain a basic feature of future seamen's missions.[70]

Who were the men in the metropolis who took upon themselves the crucial task of ensuring the application of these principles in the course of the first phase of Bethel Union organization? The Rev. George Charles Smith was, without comparison, the central figure. True, he was still officially pastor of a congregation at Land's End. (In fact, so far did the work there flourish, that his Penzance chapel had to be enlarged both in 1818 and again in 1822, when it was renamed Jordan Chapel.)[71] However, he was at the same time the undisputed architect of the new, metropolitan-based Society; and he continued to be intimately involved in the early progress of the work, both in London and elsewhere.

As editor of the world's first, immensely popular seamen's mission periodical, *The Sailor's Magazine, and Naval Miscellany* (published as from January 1820, under the patronage of the BFSFSBU), Smith's influence —both nationally and soon internationally—became prodigious. His distance from the daily scene precluded him from a general secretaryship in the Society; but he filled the strategic position of foreign secretary. During his annual autumn preaching engagements in London, he took an active part in the Society's committee meetings, at its offices at 18, Aldermanbury (occasionally as chairman). He drew up the Society's *Annual Retrospect*, and played a leading role at its annual meetings (which in this case were held in the autumn). On his travels elsewhere in the country, he took the initiative toward the foundation of numerous provincial societies, some of which, in certain respects, managed to outmatch the metropolis.[72]

Referring in retrospect to the early officers and committee of the BFSFSBU, G.C. Smith found reason to commend their willingness to work.[73] The Minutes of the Society certainly indicate an impressive range of "personal exertions" (administrative, promotional and missionary), in which committee members were individually expected to engage.[74] Besides G.C. Smith, the committee included those other veterans of the early Bethel Meetings in the Pool, Thomas Phillips (now a corresponding secretary), Lieutenant Francis Collins and Captain George Orton. (Thomas Thompson, himself a warm Bethel supporter, remained a conciliatory influence within the committee of the PLS.) Captain Charles Allen, R.N., of Camberwell, also a corresponding secretary, frequently served as chairman at the Society's committee meetings; the *Minutes* of the committee prove him to have obtained an increasing influence over its decisions. George Fife Angas was joined on the committee by his elder brother, Captain William Henry Angas (of whom more was soon to be heard).[75]

The high proportion of naval officers in the leadership of the BFSFSBU (practically half the committee membership) reflects the stronger involvement of Church Evangelicals in this Society than in the PLS. Admiral Lord Gambier accepted the office of president in 1820, and normally chaired the Society's annual meetings. The 1821 Committee includes the name of the Rev. William Gurney, Rector of St. Clements Danes; the Rev. Richard Marks, as well as several other Evangelical clergymen, became warm advocates of the Society, both at successive anniversaries and in other ways. In the absence of an Anglican alternative at this stage, Evangelical Bethel Union sympathizers evidently felt with Gambier that "whoever supports this cause is not a dissenter from the cause of Christ."[76]

The Rev. A. Brown, Congregational Minister of South Ockendon, himself a former seaman and naval officer, became the Society's zealous "Seamen's Minister," continuing for several years with great apparent success to preach on a part-time basis at Bethel Meetings in the River.[77] For a brief period, the Rev. J. Heafford shared in his responsibilities. However, although the need for full-time seamen's missionaries was forcefully put in *The Sailor's Magazine* and constantly pressed by G.C. Smith, limited funds compelled the Society to rely mainly on a roster of volunteer preachers for stated Bethel Meetings in the Upper and Lower Pools. Among these, Methodist ministers in districts bordering the Thames were prominent in "going afloat," as far as they had opportunity.[78]

The mainstay of the Society was lay collaboration, however, captains mates and men personally, unashamedly committed to the Bethel Cause wherever they went. It was their right of assembly that had become the original *casus belli,* setting the scene for the founding of the new Society.

BETHEL OPERATIONS ON THE RIVER

The stimulation and coordination of Bethel Meetings on the River remained a primary concern of the BFSFSBU in the metropolis. As the meetings progressed, conversions multiplied and praying sailors continued to voice their amazement at the transforming power of the Gospel. As one astonished convert put it, simply and vividly:

> O Lord, we bless Thee we are not at a *brothel,* but a *Bethel!* We praise Thee we are not now rolling on shore as staggering drunkards, but down on our knees in this cabin. . . .We used to kick at the Bible and the gospel, but now we love them. . . .[79]

The Bethel Flag proved to possess the appeal necessary to create in Christian seamen a strong *esprit de corps.* As one of them exclaimed in prayer:

> Lord, we rejoice to see the Bethel flag flying on the Thames; Oh may it never be doused [that is, struck to the enemy], but may it fly to invite sailors to prayer in every roadstead, or bay. . . . Lord,

> we have been champions for the Devil, oh make us champions for
> Christ.[80]

Pervading their piety, as one of its predominant features, was the fervor of
their missionary concern for the fate of fellow seafarers. One captain
expressed this as follows:

> Lord, . . . if a man has been to sea he will ever after love sailors
> . . . if he does not, he is not worthy the name of a sailor. Lord, thou
> knowest how we love to see sailors coming to Christ. O Lord,
> increase their number . . . we pray that there may be ten flags
> flying every night in the Upper Pool, and double the number in the
> Lower . . . [where there were generally more ships].[81]

This last prayer seemed at times to come close to literal fulfillment.
In the course of two to three years, the situation had changed radically in
terms of general reactions. In the June 1820 number of *The Sailor's
Magazine,* the editor notes:

> Formerly there was considerable difficulty in obtaining a ship for
> the evening meeting, but now, captains and owners frequently
> intreat that the Bethel flags may be hoisted on board their ships,
> . . . they consider their vessel honoured when this flag is at the
> masthead. A respectable ship-owner who has retired from business,
> and sold his interest in some vessels, particularly stipulated with
> the purchaser for permission, that these signals of prayer should
> be allowed, as usual, on board, which was complied with.[82]

Lightermen now stated a definite preference for dealing with Bethel
Ships, since there they were assured of "such civil treatment from the master
and crew." Watermen no longer pelted the Bethel men, but competed for
their custom, some confounding the world by purchasing hymn books and
attending worship services themselves. Slop-sellers on the waterfront, used
to sailors descending on them just before sailing, "drunk, obscene, and
profane," had only unstinted praise for the wonders worked in their behavior
by the advent of the Bethel Flag. Publicans, on the other hand, complained of
hard times, their premises "not half so full of Sailors as they used to be."
Street-walkers, too, were dismayed that seamen, formerly always "sure
prey," could now frequently pass them "unallured by their temptations."[83]
    It was too early to speak of any general reformation; but a change
had obviously begun. In noticeably many, their whole appearance was
evidence of an "improvement of manners." Whereas, earlier, a seamen
could be unfailingly recognized by "the silk handkerchief carelessly tied, the
[blue] jacket loosely hanging about the shoulders, and the stockings falling
over the shoes," many were now examples to landsmen of "cleanliness,
decency, and respectability."[84] Attitudes among the majority of seamen

towards Bethel Meeting participants were also undergoing change. There were fewer open attempts to interfere, such as, for example, by methodically beating a drum nearby, or systematically trying to smoke out the assembly. (In one such case, two sworn enemies of Bethel Meetings had refused to stow away their hammocks, but "continued loading their pipes and smoking most furiously." At length, they gave up and joined in prayer themselves!)[85] In fact, so evident were the signs of transformation that Smith found reason to comment:

> Thus will the kingdom of Heaven suffer violence, while Seamen
> under the influence of almighty grace are pressing into it. . . .
> Blessed be God! Satan's reign among our poor depraved seamen
> is diminishing. His kingdom is assailed, his throne totters. . . .[86]

The burgeoning of Bethel Meetings on the Thames was able to benefit by the coordinative influence of the Bethel Union Society. While the men themselves arranged the normal nightly meetings consisting of prayer, song and perhaps a brief exhortation, the Society was able to procure and publicize preachers at stated times and places.[87] In order to assist all who were willing but unable to attend, a transportation system was worked out. (The initiative came from the men; the Society ensured publicity.) Signal boats, rowing within hailing distance of the different tiers, brought the men to one or more stationary "receiving ships," where all hands were "mustered," and thence transported collectively to Bethel Ships on which meetings were scheduled.[88]

A special "high day" with the seamen was the joint monthly Bethel Meeting, alternating between the two Pools. Here, more than 200 could converge on the assigned ship and assemble in the hold or on deck, according to the season. When the "Monthly Meeting" was held in the Upper Pool, London Bridge could be lined with spectators marveling at the sight of boatloads of sailors "making melody unto the Lord" as they rowed up-river and joined their brethren on board the Bethel Ship for the evening.[89]

SAILORTOWN EVANGELISM

Striking evidence of the missionary zeal engendered by the meeting on the River is provided by the manner in which the Bethel Movement virtually "overflowed" the banks of the Thames in a remarkable form of Sailortown evangelism by sailors themselves. Both the "Screw Bay Mission" and the "Stepney Mission" were phenomena with wide implications for the development of the Christian ministry to seafarers.[90]

Screw Bay, notorious as "the worst neighbourhood in Rotherhithe," was deliberately "fixed on" as a suitable scene for evangelistic enterprise by participants in the Lower Pool Bethel Meetings as early as March 1817.

Screw Bay, notorious as "the worst neighbourhood in Rotherhithe," was deliberately "fixed on" as a suitable scene for evangelistic enterprise by participants in the Lower Pool Bethel Meetings as early as March 1817. After attending evening service at the local Methodist chapel, a team of six to nine "pious sailors" would make for the "Bay" sector of High Street and hold a prayer-meeting "for the guilty inhabitants" of the area, in a room obtained for the purpose. At the close of each meeting, another room in the vicinity was solicited for the following Sunday (on the same itinerant principle as already adopted on the River). Despite determined initial opposition, the sailor evangelists persevered and reaped the reward of seeing the district transformed within two or three years. "Depraved watermen and abandoned women" were converted, a Sunday morning prayer-meeting was well attended, and all was allegedly "tranquil" — where "shameless immorality" had previously prevailed.[91]

By the beginning of the 1820's, Zebedee Rogers, who evidently played a leading role in the Screw Bay venture,[92] had removed across the River to Stepney. Here we find him, in 1821, deeply involved in an even more ambitious project of Sailortown evangelism, this time aimed at both seamen and landsmen. Whatever may have motivated his choice of Stepney, he could hardly have settled at a more strategic spot.

Hitherto, evangelistic endeavors among seamen in the Port of London had, through the agency of the PLS and the BFSFSBU, centered chiefly around the shipping in the Lower and Upper Pools. However, much of the East and West India trade was concentrated in the docks bearing these names, to *the east* of the Pool. Here, in the vicinity of Poplar and Blackwall, lived large numbers of deep-sea sailors between voyages. Stepney lay astride their main thoroughfare as they went, especially on the Sabbath, "crowding backwards and forward," between Poplar and Limehouse to the east and Shadwell and Wapping to the west, sometimes as far as the Tower. En route, many would be only too easily "allured to the snares of sin," surrounding them on every hand, ready to relieve "the poor thoughtless sailor" of his hard-earned wages.[93]

Zebedee Rogers lived in a house of which the lower part was "a large coal-shed." These primitive quarters the zealous shoemaker managed to fit up as a relatively spacious meeting place and, with the aid of "a few pious Sailors," commenced a Sunday evening religious meeting "for the good of the inhabitants" in the area. Thus began the so-called "Stepney Mission." One "wicked waterman," now converted, voiced his enthusiasm in the following vein: "O Lord! We have heard thou hast blessed the hoisting of the Bethel Flag from ship to ship. O Lord, I pray thee, bless it from house to house. . . ."[94]

The original "home mission" object was not lost from view. However, the main thrust of the Mission came to be directed toward seamen ashore. Here, Rogers and his seafaring friends sensed a dual obligation: (1) In view of the concerted competition of Sailortown specialists in vice, it was unrealistic to expect seamen to come to a place of worship unless one were willing to obey the command of Christ to go forth and "kindly compel." (2) They well knew that none were "more capable of attracting the notice and prevailing on the minds of seamen than seamen themselves." The solution was a sort of religious "Impress Service," based on Bethel "press gangs," which soon achieved remarkable results.[95]

The plan adopted was simple and effective, centered around a Sunday full of intense, almost incredible activity. Zebedee Rogers, busy, as usual, leading prayer meetings in the Lower Pool, would call for volunteers toward the close of the week. A handful of intrepid tars would then muster under the Bethel Flag at the "Bethel Mission-House" (as it was called), early Sunday morning.

After a dawn prayer-meeting at the local Methodist chapel, and a brief breakfast at the Mission-House, they would disperse on a round of neighborhood visitation, knocking at doors, offering tracts, and inviting residents (many of whom "scarcely ever entered the house of God") to the evening "Sailors' Meeting" at Stepney. Armed with a copious supply of tracts, they would then for the rest of the day concern themselves principally with brother seamen. Hailing them in streets and fields, hunting them up in boarding houses and brothels, countering scoffing and swearing with cheerful rejoinders in genuine, nautical argot, they pushed and pulled, both figuratively and literally.

If a morning sermon was to be preached "professedly to sailors" at a Stepney or Shadwell chapel, they would descend upon the congregation with a motley haul of mariners. Heading for the East and West India docks after lunch, they would take large numbers "in tow" to a recently established Sunday afternoon seamen's service, held under the Bethel Flag and rotating monthly between chapels cooperating in the Blackwall, Poplar and Limehouse Auxiliary of the BFSFSBU.

A final foray on the way back to Stepney would result in a crowded climax to the day at the evening Mission-House meeting. Here, under the leadership of Zebedee Rogers, the program would consist of hymn-singing, alternating with up to a dozen masters, mates and men engaging in turn in extemporaneous prayer, before the astonished eyes of those they had "pressed." With a hearty handshake as they left, seamen present were invited to follow up by attending the coming week's program of evening meetings on the River.[96]

The results of these aggressive tactics caused considerable comment. Milkmen and shoemakers, infidels and prostitutes, local landsmen who at first insisted they had nothing to do with "Sailors' Meetings," were surprisingly converted. Seamen, hauled in from neighboring "dens of iniquity" and suddenly confronted with brother-bluejackets pouring out their souls in prayer, were often overwhelmed by the shock of such an "unexpected transition." Torn between the condemnation of a guilty conscience and the portrayal of a dying Savior's love, they would labor in vain to repress the upsurge of emotion, until their sleeves became "wetted through with the briny flood." Before they left for sea again, many had given evidence of at least "an outward reformation."[97]

In a tract publicizing the Stepney Mission, aptly called *The Press Gang,* G.C.Smith shows critical awareness of the pitfalls of emotionalism, while warmly contending for the basic legitimacy of revivalism in seamen's missions:

> Thus is he [the conscience-stricken seaman at a Sailor's Meeting] *softened,* if not converted, and though no dependence can be placed on emotions so suddenly raised, and perhaps as rapidly quelled; yet he will not easily forget the scenes that occasioned them, or the violence of their impression while they lasted. Like the greatest storm, or the utmost danger to which he was ever exposed, they will leave. . . . [But] in the stillness of the midwatch at sea, when far far removed from land and noise, while his shipmates are sleeping round him, he will silently stand at the helm, . . . until "busy meddling memory" will revive them all afresh in his mind, the starting tear shall hide the compass from his view, and he shall be ready to fall upon his knees before the binnacle. . . . And should Almighty Grace breathe on his soul the heavenly gales of mercy, he will, under the convictions of the Holy Ghost, retire to his hammock when the watch is over, and . . . exclaim, "Jesus, refuge of my soul—Let me to thy bosom fly. . . ."[98]

Whether these zealous Bethel Men were filling the role of "Home Missionaries" or (as Smith called them) "Sea Missionaries," they produced ample proof of their resourcefulness. Worried at what he had witnessed in recent weeks, a "gentleman of the neighbourhood" stopped a seaman eagerly leading a fellow seaman along to the evening meeting. Reminding him that this was a free country, and that, since the war was over and men were no longer wanted for the navy, no man could be "forced any where against his will," he demanded to know what he meant to do with these men. The reply was to the point: "Sir, there is an everlasting war proclaimed against the kingdom of darkness, and we are on the impress service for the king of kings. . . ." Utterly amazed, the gentleman could only wish God's blessings

upon such novel yet noble endeavors. Although persuasion was only administered "in a smiling friendly way," a swearing constable demanded an
explanation on a similar occasion. He was duly silenced by a tract (*The
Swearer's Prayer*) deftly thrust into his hand by a pious sailor.[99]

In order to succeed, this friendly form of "Religious Impressment"
had to follow a carefully tested methodology. "Lines of communication"
were established to Sailors' Meetings by means of "conductors" and
"receivers" (corresponding roughly to the system of signal boats and receiving
ships on the River). Protestations were countered with cheerful dexterity, and
seamen's natural curiosity was deliberately encouraged. Finally, one such
blue-jacket, hearing the hearty strains of an introductory hymn, would leap
into the meeting with an air of reckless bravado, exclaiming: "Here goes to
have a chaunt with them." Another would say to his straggling shipmates:
"D— me . . . we all came out together; let us go together. . . ." In this way
the phenomenon of group cohesion would be put to a new, positive purpose.[100]

An important extension of outreach was achieved by transforming a
large Wapping public-house into a second Bethel Mission-House on Sunday
evenings. The landlord of "The Royal Oak" refused to sell liquor on the
Lord's Day, but readily agreed to religious meetings instead. The Stepney
Mission assigned a particular "press gang" for this venture, hoisted Bethel
Flags from oars stuck through the windows of the building "fore and aft," and
managed to fill it to excess with seamen and neighboring landsmen. Although
some would belatedly discover another kind of meeting than they had
anticipated in a public-house, none would normally leave before the close.[101]

Until the autumn of 1821, the Stepney Mission had been "solely
conducted" by Zebedee Rogers and his alternating seamen volunteers.
"Deeply impressed with a conviction of the great importance of those
efforts," a few friends of the Bethel Cause sought to secure sufficient support
and permanency by organizing, on September 28, 1821, the "Stepney and
Wapping Bethel Mission Society." Its principal object was the provision of
funds for the activities of the mission (including "wateridge" and Bethel
Flags and lanterns for weekday work in the Lower Pool). G.C. Smith, who
took the chair at the public meeting in Mr. Fitch's Academy, became a
member of the committee. The Rev. J. Lockyer of Shadwell, who had
cooperated closely with Zebedee Rogers and the Stepney Mission, was also
elected. Thomas Phillips, another enthusiastic supporter, was appointed
treasurer. Six of the ten-member committee were Bethel Captains (including
the pioneers Simpson, Wilkins and Hindhulph). Rogers himself was appointed
a secretary.[102]

This work was wholly according to the heart of George Charles
Smith; and it is to him that posterity is indebted for most of the scant and

scattered data which makes it possible to reconstruct the role of Zebedee Rogers. The contribution of that "obscure individual" to the emergence of organized seamen's missions was, despite his "lower sphere" in station-conscious England, unique. Not the least important part of this contribution was that Rotherhithe shoemaker's leadership of the Stepney Mission in the early 1820's.[103]

The general significance of the Stepney Mission was at least threefold: (1) In the history of the Bethel Flag, this enterprise marked the systematic adoption of the Bethel emblem as a symbol for the religious assembly of seamen not only afloat, but also ashore.[104] (2) It vindicated the validity of lay collaboration (with seafarers) in seamen's missions, both as a powerful (evangelistic) motive, and as a virtually indispensable method.[105] (3) In conjunction with the Screw Bay Mission, it introduced the amelioraton of Sailortown environment as an important function of a ministry to seafarers within the context of human ecology.[106]

METROPOLITAN AUXILIARIES

The Stepney and Wapping Bethel Mission Society was, despite its vital operational role on the waterfront, hardly an "auxiliary" in the wide sense of the word. Financially, it was a liability rather than an asset. However, auxiliary societies with both promotional and operational functions were, from the outset, recognized as a basic condition of growth for the BFSFSBU. In the metropolis, the first was established barely a fortnight after the parent society itself.[107]

The "Camberwell Auxiliary" was established November 21, 1819, with Captain Charles Allen, R.N., in the chair and G.C. Smith ardently supporting. The initiative had sprung from Captain Allen and a number of retired naval brother-officers, who lived in the villages of Camberwell, Walworth and Peckham. Their primary object was "to obtain Subscriptions and Donations to assist the funds of the 'Parent Institution.' " In this, they freely acknowledged the quite invaluable aid rendered by the "pious and active ladies" of their "Ladies' Committee" (who took upon themselves "the laborious task of visiting from house to house, and employing their successful oratory in favour of their gallant countrymen"). Although resident at a distance from the south bank of the Thames, and therefore finding regular operational activity impracticable, several of the Auxiliary's officers did, nevertheless, encourage by active participation the Bethel Meetings on that side of the River.[108]

Other metropolitan auxiliaries of the BFSFSBU represented districts bordering on the Thames; these accepted an active operational responsibility along their own respective sections of the riverside. Hard on the heels of their Camberwell precursor came the "North-East London Auxiliary." Here, too, women played a prominent part. Founded January 4, 1820, at Albion Chapel, Moorfields, with the warm support of its minister, the Rev. Alexander Fletcher, and with Captain C.M. Fabian, R.N., in the chair, the Auxiliary owed its origin to "the piety and zeal of a respectable female and her friends." Seeking to cover the waterfront on the north bank, from London Bridge down to the Scotch Wharves, the Auxiliary consisted chiefly of members of the Tabernacle, Hoxton Chapel, and other chapels in the vicinity.

The women concentrated their main efforts on maintaining an adequate ratio of Bethel Meetings on the north shore of the Upper Pool. (In this, they also obtained the regular assistance of Wesleyan Methodist preachers.)[109] However, within their bounds lay, just below the Tower, the parish of St. Katharine's or, as G.C. Smith characterized it, "Satan's Sailortown Seat." To the notorious haunts of what ranked as "the *very lowest* sink of iniquity in London," a seaman would only too often steer his course "the moment he could leave his ship." On exactly this most strategic site, the Auxiliary chose to raise a standard of defiance. On February 13, 1823, they opened "a convenient place" as a Seamen's Chapel, at 42 Lower East-Smithfield. Here, in addition to the provision of regular Sunday evening services, a Sea-boys' School was established for 60 to 70 children of seafaring families, "sought out of the immoral sewers of St. Katherine's."[110] (In the mid-1820's, stated preaching to seamen was also instituted in Shakespeare's Walk Chapel, Shadwell, and Pell Street Chapel, Ratcliffe Highway.)[111]

Further east, on the Isle of Dogs, a "Poplar Auxiliary" was founded April 23, 1821, at a public meeting held in the Mast-House at Wigram and Green's famous Blackwall shipyard. George Green himself was elected treasurer and president. The area one sought to cover is indicated by the full title: "The Blackwall, Poplar, and Limehouse Auxiliary Seamen's Friend Society and Bethel Union." Dissenting chapels in this district combined to provide Sunday afternoon services (in monthly rotation) and Friday evening prayer-meetings (at the School Room, High Street, Poplar), both specifically for seamen, under the emblem of the Bethel Flag. (The success of the former, in cooperation with the Stepney Mission, has already been noted.) Here, too, there is evidence of the eagerness of women to be of assistance to the parent society.[112]

Further downriver, on the opposite side, a "Woolwich Auxiliary" was established February 14, 1821, at Union Chapel, with the minister, the Rev. Thomas Sharp, as chairman (and zealous future promoter). A similar system of weekly services and prayer-meetings, rotating between local Dissenter chapels, was adopted here as in Poplar. However, with the Arsenal and large numbers of soldiers and marines within the area, it was natural to extend the ministry of the Auxiliary to these on an equal footing with seamen. The title adopted was, accordingly: "The Woolwich Auxiliary Seamen and Soldiers' Friend Society and Bethel Union." In 1823, a small "Bethel Chapel," as it was called, was opened for seamen, watermen and their families, near the "Ship and Half-Moon" Stairs.[113]

Also serving the south bank was a "Greenwich Auxiliary," founded April 24, 1822, at London Street Chapel. An important responsibility was here the evangelization of nearly 3,000 "decayed" naval pensioners, a task for which more hope was entertained now that the Bethel Flag "waved to the stately domes of Greenwich Hospital." (Conspicuous in this field was Jeremiah Lacy, naval veteran from the American Revolutionary War, who became a local Methodist class-leader and for many years a devoted evangelist among his fellow pensioners.)[114]

A society which was not formally affiliated with the BFSFSBU, yet intimately connected with it, was "The Cambrian Union Society, for Promoting Religion among Welch Seamen." Normally, there would be in the River, at any given time, some 20 to 30 Welsh ships (mainly coasters), with from 200 to 300 crewmen. Trained up from boyhood in the villages of the Wales to a marked "respect for religious duties, and especially to the observance of the Sabbath," yet, while in London, prevented by their language barrier from deriving any real benefit from the Bethel Meetings and services on the *Ark,* they "felt a little jealous." Finally, on Friday, July 7, 1820, at "a numerous Meeting of Captains of Merchant Vessels, and of others connected with the Welch Trade," held in the River on board the *Betsy* of Cardigan, a society was formed under the above title, with Captain James Morse in the chair.[115]

Welsh shipmasters, known for their "greater influence over their men," had, as already noticed, shown paternal concern for their apprentices through the provisions of "The Maritime Cambrian Society." The committee of the new Society, comprising fourteen Cambrian captains and a minimum of ten London residents, saw it as its first object to establish "preaching the Gospel." Following the Bethel pattern, they solved the problem of a suitable sanctuary by obtaining the use of whatever hold happened to be empty among vessels in the Welsh Tier (located off the Southwark shore by Pickle Herring Stairs opposite the Tower). This would then be fitted out with pulpit and forms "in the most respectable manner" by the master, preaching being provided by a voluntary roster of different denominations of Welsh-speaking ministers in the metropolis. The vessel appointed was distinguished by a red flag with the inscription "PREGETH" (Preaching), hoisted at the mast-head from early morning.[116]

Cambrian Union services became an immediate success, with congregations frequently 200 strong. By the autumn, weekly Welsh prayer-meetings on ship-board had also been introduced, warmly urged by G.C. Smith. These, too, were announced by a distinctive flag, in this case with the words "CYFARFOD GWEDDI" (Prayer-meeting) in white on a blue ground, together with the traditional Bethel star and dove. (The first of these was presented by Smith, in a ceremony on the *Hope* of Aberystwith, November 5, 1820, on behalf of the BFSFSBU, to "their Brethren" of the Principality.)[117]

An ultimate goal had, from the outset, been the establishment of a *Welsh Ark* on the Thames. This plan was, however, relinquished in favor of a solution ashore. In 1821, the committee of the Cambrian Union Society managed to purchase the lease of a wool warehouse (previously used as a Quakers' meeting) in Fair Street, Horsleydown, adjoining Tooley Street. This was fitted up at a total cost of £170 and, as winter approached that same year, opened by Dr. Waugh as "The Cambrian Chapel." This Welsh Seamen's Chapel off Tooley Street thus became one of the first shore sanctuaries in the United Kingdom established primarily for the use of seafarers.[118] (As from February 1822, at the invitation of the Cambrian Union Society, the Bethel Union Society was able to make use of this strategically situated chapel for instituting a Sunday afternoon service for rivermen and their families.)[119]

Scotch and Irish vessels visiting the Thames posed no parallel problems. Captain George Orton and some friends from shore established Bethel Meetings in 1820 among the Scotch smacks on the north side. The Rev. W. Shenstone, Smith's colleague at the famous *Agenoria* service three years earlier, helped with preaching. The same year, the Bethel Flag was also hoisted aboard Irish ships in the Thames. Zealous captains of Scotch, Irish, as well as Welsh ships introduced to the Bethel Union Movement in the metropolis thus became (like their provincial English colleagues) the means of spreading the system to their respective home ports elsewhere.[120]

Chapter 10

Provincial Beginnings

A PARALLEL PATTERN

The formal organization, in November 1819, of a metropolitan society with avowedly national aspirations gave natural stimulus to the proliferation of Bethel Union organization throughout the British Isles. As news of "Bethel operations" in London spread to the provinces, both by word of mouth and through the religious press (particularly *The Sailor's Magazine*), a roughly parallel pattern of two-phased growth is discernible throughout the British Isles. (1) First would come the establishment of local prayer-meetings and preaching "under the Bethel Flag." (Frequently, the ground had been prepared through the marine distribution of pioneering agencies of the BFBS and the RTS.)[121] (2) Such measures might, sooner or later, develop into a local Seamen's Friend Society and/or Bethel Union. This process requires closer scrutiny.

Provincial societies were not characterized by any closely-knit, organizational uniformity. Nevertheless, besides a clear identity of nomenclature, certain structural similarities are easily distinguished: high priority was attached to a permanent place of worship, ashore or (at this stage preferably) afloat. However, financial or harbor restrictions might make it necessary to confine aspirations to a Bethel Loft or Room, near the waterfront. Provisions were generally made (in the constitutive resolutions) for not only the continuation of itinerant shipboard prayer-meetings, but also a systematic tract and Scripture distribution, marine library services, rudimentary schooling for seafarers and their children, and reliable lodging facilities. (Details of the development of such services, both in the metropolis and in the provinces, are dealt with under "Differentiation of the Maritime Ministry.")[122]

Chronologically, the year 1822 denoted a transition from an initial period marked mainly by the emergence of formally independent societies in five major British ports to a subsequent period of numerous new societies, generally on a smaller scale and often with a more professedly "auxiliary" status.

SCOTLAND TAKES THE LEAD

The first two major societies outside the London area were both established north of the border, on the Firths of Clyde and Forth, respectively. The "Greenock Seamen's Friend Society," the first seamen's mission organization known to have adopted the self-designation "Seamen's Friend," was founded at a public meeting in the New Church, January 6, 1820. This was largely the result of the enterprise of a member of the newly formed "Bethel Seamen's Union" of London, Captain Edward Smith.[123]

Engaged by George Fife Angas (on the strength of a recommendation by G.C. Smith), Captain Smith had, after resigning his appointment as agent of the MSABS, left for Greenock in December 1819, in order to take command of the Angas ship *Robert.* As soon as he arrived, he obtained the wholehearted approval of local ministers for his plan of hoisting the Bethel Flag over his ship, and holding a public service on board. The event caused a sensation. The press estimated that there must have been some 600 seamen and landsmen jamming the decks that evening, as "head rose above head on the bulwarks and in the rigging," to witness the novel scene. As a result of the interest thus created, over 2,000 crowded the meeting at which the Society was founded shortly afterwards.[124]

Initial manpower problems were quite simply solved by dividing the "Committee of Directors" (consisting of ministers of different denominations and directors of the local Marine Society) into eight sub-committees; each of these was then charged, in weekly rotation, with personally carrying out the ship visitation and other activities specified in the objects of the Society.[125] During its first year, the Greenock Society succeeded in fitting up as a floating chapel a ship presented by the Clyde Marine Society. (Originally granted to that body by the Admiralty as a floating nautical school, she had long since been disused.)[126] The vessel was to form the hub of this pioneer provincial Society's manifold activities for many years to come (including the provision of new and considerably more successful school facilities).[127]

Only a month behind Greenock, the "Edinburg and Leith Seamen's Friend Society" was officially founded at the Assembly Rooms, Leith, February 7, 1820. In this case, it was George Fife Angas who personally provided the original impetus. On leaving London in December 1819, as committee member of the newly established Bethel Seamen's Union, Angas undertook to publicize the plan of the London Society on a tour he was making through North England and Scotland. On his arrival in Edinburgh, he found, in a minister of Leith, a ready response to the idea of similar exertions in the outport of the capital. Thus, largely through the "indefatigable perseverance" of the Rev. W. Henry, the new Society was shortly afterwards launched at what was reported to have been "one of the most numerous and respectable assemblies" ever witnessed in those parts.[128]

True, the Society faced two frustrating problems at the outset; but both were ultimately overcome. Although public patronage was at first reduced by rumors of total Dissenter control, publication of the fact that two thirds of the committee belonged to the Established Church of Scotland helped to turn the tide. (The Lord Provost of Edinburgh and the Admiral of Leith became president and vice president, respectively.)[129] Secondly, the current high price of ships delayed the attainment of "the primary object of the society," the provision of a floating sanctuary for seamen. However, with the aid of a leading promoter of the Greenock Society, they were able to buy, in October 1820, a fir-built "Russian brig" lying in that port, its owners "considerably diminishing the price" on hearing the intended purpose. While this vessel (formerly the *Vine* of Glasgow) was being fitted out, the Society maintained Sunday preaching for congregations varying from 150 to 400 seamen on ships in port lent and "rigged" for the purpose.

Finally, on March 18, 1821, the Leith Floating Chapel, now moored at the west end of the Second Wet Dock, was officially opened under the Society's original "Seaman's Friend" flag. She then proved capable of holding "upwards of 380 Seamen."[130] Successive reports show attendance to have remained steady into the 1830's under the voluntary preaching of ministers of different denominations. In fact, despite dismal prophecies— also by some seamen themselves—that it would be hopeless "ever getting Jack into the hold of a preaching ship," the Leith "Ark" was found to be too small to contain the crowds pressing in (even when enlarged by one third, after some two and a half years' service.)[131]

Meanwhile, the Edinburgh and Leith Seamen's Friend Society earned early recognition for their determined experimentation in areas of social concern. Their exceptionally well-developed educational programs (with differentiated nautical, elementary and Sunday schools), as well as their portable marine libraries, their reading room provisions, their seamen's savings bank, their distress fund for seamen's widows and orphans, their emergency employment measures for workless seamen, their sponsorship of a "Seamen's Register," and their promotion of new life-saving methods at sea, finally also their appointment of a full-time "Home Missionary" for social and spiritual ministry to the many sorely neglected local seamen's families, such measures were, in their day, little short of revolutionary and placed the Leith Society in the very van of fledgling maritime social reform efforts in the 1820's.[132] Although setbacks, too, were encountered, the parent society in London felt, in 1824, they had reason to hail the pioneers in Leith as "the noblest of Seamen's Friend Societies," and their "astonishing results" were commended the following year even from across the Atlantic.[133]

THE AVON

In the founding of the first provincial society in a major English port, it was George Charles Smith who played the decisive role. Prior to the establishment of the Bristol Seamen's Friend Society and Bethel Union August 4, 1820, the country's third seaport had already shown signs of spiritual concern for the seafarer. Although Smith met with hesitancy when he broached the subject on his 1817 visit to Bristol,[134] the purchase of a floating chapel for the Thames in March 1818 stimulated the Wesleyans in this western stronghold of Methodism to attempt something similar on the Avon. (Available sources show that a provisional Bristol Ark was, in fact, opened by the Wesleyans in May of that year in a merchantman moored in the harbor.)[135] The ground in Bristol was further prepared by the early marine Bible distribution in that port, already noticed.[136] However, it was the introduction of itinerant ship preaching under the Bethel Flag by G.C. Smith, in the summer of 1820, that provided the immediate impulse for the formation of a permanent society.

Invited to supply for his Baptist colleague, the Rev. Thomas Roberts at Old King Street Chapel, Smith seized the opportunity to summon thousands on the decks of ships in port, many of them large West Indiamen, in a five-week series of sermons to seamen under the Bethel banner. Despite the initial "censure of many," he persevered until the response was such as to warrant a preliminary meeting to prepare the formation of a society. With the enthusiastic cooperation of the Rev. Thomas Roberts, himself a former seaman, a meeting for this purpose was convened on July 27, 1820.

Finally, by August 4, 1820, at a general meeting in the Great Rooms, Princes Street, public interest had reached a point where hundreds were unable to obtain entrance. Here, with a large blue flag inscribed "The Bethel Seamen's Union" floating behind the chair, the Society was officially established. As joint secretaries were chosen two naval officers, Captain John Banks and Lieutenant Edward Sewell, together with John James Beard, the zealous Bristol Marine Bible Association pioneer. Admiral Sir James Saumarez, Bart., shortly afterwards accepted the office of president.[137]

The "most essential" object of the new Society was here, as in Scotland, the provision of "a suitable place of Worship for Seamen, either afloat or on shore." After months of fruitless search, a large Swedish ship, so damaged as to necessitate her sale, providentially arrived in Bristol and was, in April 1821, bought "in faith" for £300. In the process of fitting the vessel up for her new role, a soon famous figure-head was added, depicting "the sacred Bible open at that portion where Sailors are reminded of 'the wonders of God in the deep,' " (Psalm 107:23-24).

At length, on Wednesday, August 29, 1821, the "Seamen's Chapel," as it was called, with accommodation for up to 1,000, was officially opened; the Rev. Thomas Roberts (by now widely known for his effective advocacy of the Bethel cause) the morning sermon. Strategically moored by the Grove, in Bristol's recently created "Floating Harbour," the Seamen's Chapel continued to be well attended for many years to come, with her pulpit voluntarily supplied by local ministers.[138] In addition to a "Sunday Afternoon Reading Society" on board the "Chapel," the Society also sponsored a separately organized Marine School ashore, which proved highly successful.[139]

The positive response of large numbers of seamen to the program offered in this second English floating chapel was, in great measure, attributable to Bristol's "Bethel Companies," a novel means of mobilizing lay landsmen in direct waterfront evangelism. It was G.C. Smith who, before leaving Bristol in August 1820, organized the four first Bethel Companies as an integral function of a Seamen's Friend Society. Consisting of twelve (male) members each recruited from local congregations of different denominations, the main activity of these groups was the maintenance of itinerant shipboard prayer-meetings, rotating through weekday nights, under the Bethel Flag.[140]

Particularly prominent in this work was one J. Parker, naval veteran and correspondent of G.C. Smith from the Naval Awakening era.[141] A fifth company was soon added for the Cumberland Basin shipping. Subsequent annual reports of the Society continue to confirm the consistent success of the Bethel Companies. By this means, assemblies of frequently up to 50 (occasionally nearly 100) seamen and "trowmen" could be collected for social prayer, hymn-singing and scriptural exhortation throughout the week in various parts of the port.[142]

Striking evidence of the vitality of the Bethel Union Movement on the Avon was the fact that Bristol became the first port to provide two floating chapels. The second, moored a short distance downriver, at the Hotwells, was owned by a distinct society, the "Clifton, Hotwells, and Pill Seamen's Friend Society and Bethel Union." Again, G.C. Smith was there to give both impetus and guidance. Prompted by local concern, he publicized the idea from the pulpit of the Bristol Seamen's Chapel during his summer visit in 1823. A provisional committee was formed, a suitable vessel secured (the 350-ton *Mary* of New York), and a preliminary meeting called on board, August 15, 1823. The following month, a general meeting, confirming the establishment of the new Society, was held at the Gloucester Hotel, Hotwells.[143]

In planning the transformation of the American merchantman during the following winter, the shipwrights were able to reap the benefit of Smith's experience of deficiencies in her forerunners. Finally, when the so-called *Clifton Ark* was officially opened June 2, 1824, her many improvements made her "a Model for all future Floating Chapels." Despite due deference to contemporary social discrimination in seating arrangements, it was nevertheless possible to provide (relatively) well-ventilated accommodation for assemblies of up to 1,000.[144] (Many impoverished families of seafarers in the Hotwell Road area, hitherto unchurched, had "strained every nerve to contribute their mite towards her," and afterwards formed a faithful congregational core.)[145]

THE MERSEY

In 1821, a year after Bristol's lead, England's rapidly expanding second seaport saw the foundation of a "Liverpool Seamen's Friend Society and Bethel Union." However, the prelude to organization went back to at least 1818. In that year, the Liverpool Marine Bible Society had been founded.[146] During his Liverpool visit the same year, G.C. Smith had proved, at the sensational Byrom Street service, how positively seamen could respond to evangelistic initiatives on their behalf.[147] This impression had already been confirmed through the pioneering perseverance of a Scottish-born Congregational minister. The Rev. Robert Phillip (1791-1858), later known on both sides of the Atlantic for his prolific religious authorship and not least his inveterate opposition to the white man's opium traffic in China, took the charge of Newington Chapel, Renshaw Street, in 1815. Here, he had introduced a series of Sunday evening "lectures" for seafarers, stated to have been maintained for "near four years" before the Liverpool Society was organized. He was thus "the first to bring Seamen of the Port under a regular course of religious instruction."[148]

These facts, coupled with news of Bethel Union advances elsewhere, prompted, in 1820, a group of concerned Liverpool ministers and merchants to form a provisional committee. Sensing a special concern for the seafarer's dependents, their first action was to establish a day school for seamen's children. (This proved so popular that they soon had to exchange their modest quarters in Blundell Street for larger accommodation in the American Hotel, Sparling Street.) They also endeavored to promote preaching stately for seamen, both on ships in the docks and in chapels ashore, where such could be secured. (In these sporadic early efforts, the Methodists were typically prominent.)[149]

By 1821, the provisional committee felt the time was ripe for the foundation of a formal institution. Conversant with the recent role of the Rev. G.C. Smith as "mainly instrumental" in the formation of Bethel Unions elsewhere, and confident that he would be the man to "set in motion the moral machinery" to meet the case on the Mersey, too, they sent him an invitation. In the words of the resulting Society's first *Report,* Smith "obeyed their summons with cheerful alacrity."[150]

However, instead of merely preaching in two or three chapels, Smith asked leave to follow the formula successfully adopted in Bristol. Hoisting the Bethel Flag first on board the *Merope* in the Queen's Dock August 28, 1821, he launched forth in a spectacular series of open-air shipboard sermons to seamen in the heart of Liverpool's Dockland. The response is reported to have been such that the rigging of every vessel in the vicinity was crowded to the tops.

Meanwhile, with the cooperation of local ministers, Smith formed six Bethel Companies of lay landsmen capable of promoting prayer-meetings and then arranged a massive, interdenominational rally at Dr. Raffle's spacious Congregational Chapel in Great George Street. Here, crowds of seamen followed the proceedings with fixed attention, as the Bethel Companies were formally inaugurated and each publicly presented with a Bethel Flag. It was when confronted with this scene that Dr. Thomas Raffles—Liverpool's leading Nonconformist minister and for years to come an active advocate of seamen's missions— turned to Smith and exclaimed: "This is going to heaven too fast!"[151]

Finally, the moment was deemed opportune. On Wednedsay, September 12, 1821 (not 1820, as later widely misunderstood), at a public meeting in the crowded courtroom of Liverpool's Town Hall, the new Society was formally founded.[152] The scene, according to the press, was such "as Liverpool had never yet beheld." Surrounded by three new Bethel Flags, Admiral Robert Murray (who subsequently—as vice president—became a steadfast patron of the Society) took the chair.[153] Two merchants, both among the most active early promoters of the work, Samuel Hope and Nicholas Hurry, introduced the first resolution.[154] Captain William Scoresby, of Artic fame and destined soon to make his own outstanding contribution to the Seamen's Cause, made the motion proposing the founding of the Society.[155] Among the many prominent speakers, G.C. Smith made a particularly profound impression with his drastic details of sailors' immorality. Seamen themselves (of whom there were many present), so far from reacting negatively to this, "cheerfullly told out the whole contents of their pockets" into the collection which followed.[156]

The Liverpool Seamen's Friend Society, though organized late in relation to major sister-societies, made remarkably rapid progress once underway.[157] Of significant importance was the acquisition of Admiral Viscount Exmouth as president.[158] (Immensely popular after his liberation of the Christian slaves of Algiers in 1816, Exmouth, as also his illustrious yet sterner contemporary Admiral Earl St. Vincent, publicly endorsed the Bethel Cause in later years.)[159]

The Society was fortunate, too, in securing the support of particularly adept ministers. As clerical secretary, the Rev Robert Phillip, with his experience as a pioneer preacher to seamen, was uniquely qualified. (His collection of seamen's sermons, *The Bethel Flag,* published in 1823, was destined to achieve wide circulation.)[160] The Rev. Cleland Kirkpatrick, Methodist minister of Macclesfield, put his personal naval background to positive purpose, responding willingly to frequent invitations to preach both directly to as well as on behalf of brother-seafarers in Liverpool.[161] Besides Dr. Thomas Raffles, the Rev. Moses Fisher (of Byrom Street Baptist Chapel) was also elected a life member of the Society, "in consideration of Important Services."[162] In addition to such personal factors, the early appointment of special sub-committees for public worship, school superintendence, boarding house supervision and finance made for an effective division of labor.[163]

The immediate concern of the new Society was to compile a preaching roster for Sunday afternoon Bethel services. Pending the purchase of a permanent place of worship, these were held on board ships in port whose captains were willing to cooperate. (Dr. Raffles commenced September 16, 1821, on the deck of Captain Scoresby's Greenland whaler, the *Baffin,* with reportedly vast crowds attending.)[164]

Like their predecessors in the Bethel Union Movement, the Liverpool Society also found that "the great additional expense of purchasing or erecting a building on shore" coupled with "the Sailor's known predilection for a ship," favored a floating sanctuary. Finding the 447-ton former slave ship *William* "exactly suited to their purpose," they bought her on October 6, 1821 and had her converted, in the course of the winter, to accommodate a congregation of at least 1,000. On May 16, 1822, she was formally opened with a service by the Rev. Thomas Roberts of Bristol.[165] Moored first in the Salthouse Dock, by Canning Place (not far from notorious Paradise Street, the hub of South End Sailortown), she was, in 1827, transferred to the King's Dock, a little further south, where she' remained in service for many years.[166]

As in Bristol, the key to much of the Society's early success proved to be those dedicated groups of waterfront volunteers, the Bethel Companies.

Not the least important of their objects was, in the view of the committee, to provide the means "whereby the impression created by the Sabbath services might be continued and deepened" through the ensuing week. (Otherwise, it was feared "one opportunity in a week of worshiping God, was too little from which to expect any permanent beneficial consequences.") The number of companies soon increased to eight, with over 100 zealous members and a "Bethel Loft" (in Pool Lane, abreast of the Old Dock) as a rendezvous for nightly meetings. Extracts of their activities were published by the Society and widely circulated in the religious press of the day.[167]

THE HUMBER

Some months before the foundation of the Liverpool Seamen's Friend Society, the Bethel Union Movement had also reached the Humber. Here, too, the ground was far from unprepared. In addition to a mounting Baltic and North Sea trade, Hull had by now a substantial share in the Greenland whale fishery. According to well-established tradition, special farewell services were held in the city's churches and chapels the Sunday before the whaling fleet set sail. Hundreds of Hull's hardy mariners would then flock to attend "the last sermon that many of them would hear."[168] The impressive founding and first-fruits of the Hull Marine Bible Association had proved that such response could not be dismissed as mere emotionalism.[169] Recently, preaching on shipboard under the Bethel Flag had been introduced in the harbor, spurred on by Captain Foster of the *Ocean*[170] and Captain Reynalds, the Bible Society's veteran "agent afloat."[171] The Rev. J. Morely had spoken with signal success on such occasions.[172]

At length, a group of ministers and laymen, many of whom were connected with the shipping, agreed to call a public meeting in the Boy's School Room, Salthouse Lane. Here, on April 19, 1821, was founded the "Port of Hull Society for the Religious Instruction of Seamen."[173] Tactically, the time seemed inopportune. Caught in the midst of post-war economic upheaval, the commerce of Hull was just then at a particularly low ebb. The meeting was, in fact, "so very thinly attended," that many advised postponement. Nevertheless, the promoters persevered under the chairmanship of William Rust (a deacon of Fish Street Congregational Chapel, and celebrated author of *The Swearer's Prayer*, one of those days" most widely circulated tracts). An Anglican layman was chosen as treasurer, William H. Dykes, the shipbuilder. Captain Francis Reynalds was elected a gratuitous secretary.[174]

Although, in the first part of their official title, the originators decided to follow the example of the Port of London Society, they had also secured detailed advance information from the BFSFSBU, and both constitution and pattern of procedure show the new organization's close kinship with Seamen's

Friend Societies and Bethel Unions in general.[175] Ignoring both sneers of "fanaticism" and pessimistic prophecies, the committee evidently preferred "setting their shoulders to the work." They immediately prepared an address, canvassed the town for subscriptions, obtained the offer of a prospective floating chapel and, undismayed by soaring costs, sent deputations successfully soliciting funds—even far inland. Conspicuous in their aid were members of the Society of Friends. William Wilberforce, too, readily supported the purchase of a seamen's sanctuary in the city of his birth.[176]

The outcome was that, on October 3, 1821, the Port of Hull Society's "Seamen's Chapel" could be opened at her centrally situated moorings in Queen's Dock, with a crowded congregation and a rousing sermon by Dr. Raffles of Liverpool. He was followed by the Rev. Thomas Smith of Rotherham (another Methodist naval veteran).[177] Like her "sister-ships" in other ports, Hull's floating sanctuary had her secular history; in her case, she had been an armed Dutch merchantman of 361 tons, captured as a prize of war in 1803, and ultimately, as the *Valiant,* employed by Hull shipowners in the Baltic trade. Successive reports confirm the consistently good attendance of seamen and their families. The vessel could accommodate 550 "comfortably," and 650 "when crowded." With time, she was transferred to Prince's Dock, close by.[178]

Among the many cases quoted of positive results, is one of a swearing seaman, whose curiosity was first roused by the flag hoisted on board the Chapel. Just then a landsman (who had evidently hoped to enjoy a free pew) came down the gangway, exclaiming in disgust: "They wont let any person go in but Sailors." This settled the question for the shellback. In he went, and became roundly converted.[179]

As with floating chapels elsewhere, however, maintenance expenses became onerous with years. Eventually, the old huld leaked so severely that the committee was torn between the choice of disturbing the peace of the services with the clanking of pumps, or alarming the audience by allowing the water to rise above the floor. They chose the former. (It was not until 1849 that they felt compelled to abandon her to be broken up.)[180]

Although unable to reach Hull for the reopening of the Floating Chapel in 1821, G.C. Smith maintained for years a particularly close connection with the Port of Hull Society. His recurring participation in their anniversaries became the talk of the town. (In 1823, over 3,000 crowded onto the deck of the chapel, on adjacent ships and on the shore, to hear him preach from atop the companion. The same Sunday afernoon at least 5,000 milled around to hear a second sermon.)[181] As editor, he readily made room in his magazines for stirring stories of Bethel exploits from Hull. In winter, zealous friends of the Society, refusing to be thwarted by lighting restrictions in the docks, hoisted the Bethel Flag at alternative localities ashore, so as to

The Port of Hull Society's floating
"Seamen's Chapel," the former
Baltic Trader *Valiant,* opened for
service in 1821. (From a contemporary print.)

ensure the unimpeded continuation of week-day evening prayer-meetings.[182]
Bethel Captains from Hull won wide renown for their enterprise in promoting
divine services on shipboard, both at sea and in foreign ports.[183]

Four major naval bases

Concurrently with the formation of five major "Bethel Union
Societies" in British home ports, the London *Sailor's Magazine* could,
during 1820-21, report constantly new cases of "Bethel exertions" around
the coast. In fact by the close of 1821, it was calculated that "Societies had
been formed or flags hoisted in more than 60 different ports of Great
Britain."[184] Nevertheless, a closer study reveals that, in the majority of these
cases, little more had so far been achieved than sporadic attempts at
providing prayer-meetings (some places also preaching) under the Bethel
Flag. Of the societies actually founded, several did not survive for long.[185]

Four Bethel Union Societies, formed in late 1820 at major British naval bases, were, however, able to play a relatively important role.

The more significant of these societies were two on the South Coast. The "Portsmouth and Portsea Seamen's Bethel Union" was publically founded, October 30, 1820, after "a pious officer of the navy" had already launched a provisional Bethel Union in the early summer. From the "Bethel Chapel," which the Society acquired, determined competition was offered to the sordid attractions of Portsmouth's "Point." Initial prejudice among "some persons of respectability" was eventually overcome by the acknowledged "utility" of the work. Presumably, too, the patronage of not only Sir George Grey, the Dockyard Commissioner, but also Admiral Earl Northesk and Admiral Gifford, carried weight.[186]

Corresponding patronage was accorded the "Plymouth, Plymouth Dock, and Stonehouse Soldiers' and Seamen's Friend Society and Bethel Union," founded November 24, 1820, at Stonehaven, after the ground had been prepared by G.C. Smith the previous spring. Vigorous evangelistic activities were based on three Bethel Lofts, one at each town, and manned by zealous Bethel Companies.[187]

The inclusion of soldiers in the ministry of a Seamen's Friend Society, as in Plymouth, was not entirely novel. During a "Bethel tour" in Kent a few weeks previously, G.C. Smith had, in company with the part-time minister of the "Parent Society," the Rev. A. Brown, succeeded in founding an "Auxiliary Seamen and Soldiers' Friend Society and Bethel Union" at each of the Thames-mouth naval bases of Chatham and Sheerness (on October 12 and 20, respectively). In his colorful report from the tour, Smith states how—impressed by the strong attendance of soldiers at the meetings—he "thought it would be unnecessary to multiply societies, and, therefore, proposed that soldiers be included." (As already seen, a Woolwich Auxiliary adopted the same principle the following year.) In all four societies, both at the Thames Estuary and on the South Coast, naval (partly also military) officers of different ranks provided support in remarkably large numbers.[188]

PROVINCIAL AUXILIARIES

As the Chatham and Sheerness Societies demonstrate, it would be arbitrary to assume that the close of 1821 denotes any definitive demarcation line in British seamen's mission organization between "independent" and "auxiliary" societies. However, the year 1822 does mark the introduction of a new emphasis on auxiliary society support, not only by the BFSFSBU, but also by at least three of the other major societies.[189]

As for London, the "Parent Society" had, at their very first (1820) Anniversary, passed a resolution recording:

To Sailors, Watermen, and others.

The Committee for the

Bethel Union Society,

Anxious to promote the present and eternal Welfare of their Fellow Subjects employed in the Seafaring Line, beg to acquaint them that, for their better Accommodation,

ROOMS ARE OPENED

For the Performance of Divine Worship

At the following places and times, which may be known by a

Flag, having the Word " *Bethel*" in it,

Flying at a Staff on shore, or at the Mast-head when the Services are performed on board of a Ship.

Mutton-Cove, and North-Corner Dock,

SABBATH DAYS, half-past Two and half-past Six, P.M.
TUESDAYS and FRIDAYS, half-past Six, P.M.

Stonehouse, New Slip, near the Point,

SABBATH DAYS, Nine, A.M. and Six, P.M.
TUESDAYS and FRIDAYS, Six, P.M.

Plymouth, Fishermen's Steps, near the Barbican,

SABBATH DAYS, half-past Two, and Six, P.M.
WEDNESDAYS and SATURDAYS, Seven, P.M.

Attendance will be given from Nine to a quarter-past Ten every Sabbath Morning, to instruct those who may wish to learn to read.
Bibles and Testaments sold to Seamen and Soldiers at a Reduced Price.
January 31st, 1822.

—o—

Provincial Bethel Unions: an example from
Plymouth in 1822.

> That it is exceedingly desirable that Auxiliary Societies be
> established in every sea-port of the United Kingdom, and that a
> moiety of their funds be devoted to the Parent Institution, to aid its
> general efforts both at home and abroad.[190]

None of the "major five" were founded as auxiliary societies. Nor did they,
in their official pronouncements, go beyond (1) a clear acknowledgement of
London's leading example and (2) a desire to establish an "active correspondence" with especially the BFSFSBU, in order to promote mutual goals.[191]
Even in the case of the Chatham and Sheerness Societies, expressly
designated as "Auxiliary," there was apparently no advance undertaking of

any specific financial responsibility for the "Parent." They had at least one plausible reason in common—an inadequacy to meet their own exigencies, let alone contribute to those of others.

Nevertheless, in 1822, the Committee of the BFSFSBU, anxious to discharge the Society's debt and promote further expansion, decided to address an "Appeal to Seamen's Friend Societies throughout Great Britain." Writing "as a Central Committee in the United Kingdom," they point out:

> We have not yet called on our Christian friends in the country to aid us, but we do now, for the *first time,* most respectfully solicit whatever trifling assistance any of our "Seamen's Friends Societies," as collective bodies or individual members, may think fit to grant. . . . Shall we also venture to recommend to any new Societies that may yet be formed, that they be pleased to incorporate with their arrangements "that some small portion of their funds be annually voted" to this Metropolitan Society for general purposes?[192]

By the time this appeal was published, news had already arrived of the highly successful auxiliary-founding tour by the Rev. William Henry Angas in the summer of 1822. The circumstances leading to his ordination as a seamen's "missionary," May 11, 1822, and the pioneering efforts with which his name was to be especially connected, will be dealt with in the following sub-section, under "Early foreign outreach."[193] First, hovever, almost immediately after his ordination, Angas dedicated himself to an intense, home-port organization-building commission for the BFSFSBU (with which he was associated). Applying himself in characteristic, methodical manner, he worked his way around a substantial part of the English coast in the course of the next months.[194]

Dividing his assignment into two phases, Angas first followed the East Coast northwards from London, visiting (during June-August) Colchester, Harwich, Ipswich, Great Yarmouth, King's Lynn, Wisbech, Boston, Hull, Bridlington, Scarborough, Whitby and Newcastle; thence he promptly "steered" west to Maryport, Workington and Whitehaven on the Cumberland Coast. During an interval in Newcastle in late August, the Rev. W.H. Angas laid the foundation of a society in his home town. (The "Newcastle-upon-Tyne Bethel Union, Seamen's and Watermen's Society" was officially founded December 23, 1822, with his brother, G.F. Angas, as president.)

The second phase of Angas' itinerary (during the month of September) took in Blyth, North and South Shields, Sunderland and Stockton. After embarking at Hull (September 18, 1822) for Hamburg, he exploited a brief opportunity, while wind-bound off Grimsby, to join a jolly-boat ashore, and stimulate merchants and ministers to form a society there too, as soon as possible.[195]

What were the evident results of this mariner-missionary's first arduous assignment? At both North Shields and Hull, societies had been established in 1820 and 1821 respectively; here, Angas' brother-seafarers were already being provided for, and he could limit himself to preaching to them in their own chapels. (The North Shields station, fitted up during the winter of 1820-21 in a transformed sail-loft, was presumably one of the earliest seamen's chapels ever opened ashore in the United Kingdom.) At the majority of ports visited, Angas succeeded in forming Seamen's Friend and Bethel Union Societies before resuming his journey; these were all on the same, strongly evangelistic pattern (with interdenominational preaching and prayer-meetings under the Bethel Flag as the primary concern, often assisted by a local Bethel Company). At Harwich, Ipswich, Kings' Lynn, Newcastle, South Shields, Sunderland and Stockton, Angas at least laid the necessary foundation by forming provisional committees. Of the societies which soon afterwards resulted, those at Sunderland and Newcastle proved to be of particular significance.[196]

Although these societies could provide little prospect of assuming anything beyond strictly local financial obligations, there are nevertheless frequent allusions to an unspecific auxiliary-parent relationship with the BFSFSBU, coupled with many expressions of indebtedness for the timely aid of its one-man deputation. The "Sunderland Auxiliary Seamen's Friend Society and Bethel Union" summarized it thus (in terms similar to those of the corresponding Whitby Auxiliary):

> . . . It is but justice to state that the spiritual interests of Seamen, who form so large and important a part of the population of this town, had not been previously overlooked nor altogether neglected. . . . Still, however, there was abundant room for increased and combined exertion, and we hope the Seamen of this port will have reason eventually to bless God for the visit of Mr. Angas, whose voice first called forth the ministers and friends of religion here to unite in forming a Society exclusively for their benefit.[197]

Despite all this encouraging confirmation of the continuing vitality of the basic Bethel Union concept, some of the major independent societies achieved greater strictly financial returns from their "auxiliary"-founding activities, than did the original London Bethel Union. This applied particularly to the promotional efforts of the societies in Hull, Liverpool and Leith.

As already seen, the committee of the Port of Hull Society, unable to finance the purchase and fitting of their prospective floating chapel from local sources, sent out deputations elsewhere during the summer of 1821. Concentrating mainly on inland towns, "in the principal manufacturing districts," they had two powerful arguments: (1) The commercial dependence of these towns, at least in part, on the port of Hull. (2) Their responsibility for the spiritual welfare of the sloopmen (and their families), who linked many of them with Hull by river and canal. Committee members traveled to towns as wide apart as York, Leeds, Sheffield, Bradford, Manchester and Blackburn, winning widespread response.[198]

Although formal auxiliaries did not result at first, several emerged later as both Liverpool and London, too, discovered opportunities for support from towns unencumbered with direct operational obligations. Dr. Raffles was prominent in advocating the claims of the Liverpool Seamen's Friend Society in Manchester (from 1822 on). G.C. Smith, too, preached with great effect in these parts, jointly on behalf of the Liverpool Society and the BFSFSBU. In 1825, the BFSBSBU launched a general publicity campaign for the formation of auxiliary societies in inland towns throughout the kingdom, pledged to assist the funds of Bethel Union Societies in port areas, as well as to promote the spiritual welfare of rivermen and canalmen in their own vicinity.[199]

FURTHER SOCIETIES IN
SCOTLAND, WALES AND IRELAND

In Scotland, the initial financial straits of the Edinburgh and Leith Seamen's Friend Society led to an early significant extension of the work. A naval lieutenant on the committee volunteered, in 1821, to undertake a collection tour on the Society's behalf, in order to relieve them of their onerous floating chapel debt (over £300). Starting in October 1821, he covered 648 miles in 135 days returning with £305 gross. However, he also fulfilled the committee's hopes that something less "narrow and selfish" than mere financial gain would result; in fact, in what they termed the Society's "first exertions in the nature of a *Home Mission,*" their agent became directly instrumental in the formation of Seamen's Friend Societies in three significant Scottish ports: Aberdeen, Dundee and Glasgow.[200]

The "Aberdeen Seamen's Friend Society" was founded January 2, 1822. The committee, forced to abandon hopes of procuring a floating chapel for want of a suitable mooring place, proceeded to erect, by the quay, a Mariners' Church—the first shore sanctuary known to have been built specifically for seamen in the British Isles. It was opened on January 8, 1823. (The committee then promptly turned to Edinburgh and Leith to relieve their debt—with great apparent success.)[201]

In Dundee, as in Aberdeen, local concern for the spiritual welfare of seamen had already found expression in Marine Bible Society activity and occasional special sermons for seamen. However, it was the visit of the naval lieutenant from Leith which gave the impulse for a "Dundee Seamen's Friend Society."[202]

In Glasgow, where concerned Christians were conscious of the efforts already made at Greenock and elsewhere, the Leith Society's agent helped to promote a preliminary meeting with a view to forming a similar society. As a first attempt to stir public interest, two seamen's services were announced for Sunday, March 17, 1822, on board the American brig *Morning Star.* Captain Stevens gladly fitted up his hold for the purpose, and seamen readily responded. The following Sunday, the experiment was successfully repeated. Then the hold was needed for cargo. However, the point had been proved. On May 13, 1822, the "Glasgow Seamen's Friend Society" was formed, with the Lord Provost himself as chairman, and henceforth president. On March 27, 1825, the Society, having resigned to the impracticability of a solution afloat, could finally open a new, land-based "Seamen's Chapel," built on a strategic site in Brown Street, off the Broomielaw. (Here, worship services for seamen, which had meanwhile been maintained in provisional premises ashore, have been carried on since.)[203]

Elsewhere too, throughout the British Isles, new Seamen's Friend Societies and Bethel Unions emerged as from 1822. In Wales, the "Milford Haven Seamen's Friend Society and Bethel Union" was established on April 15, 1822, having received a Bethel Flag from the "Parent Society" in London.[204] Next month, on May 9, 1822, the "Cardiff Bethel Union Society" was founded, in this case after regular preaching under the Bethel Flag since January 1821 (principally by Welsh Baptist ministers).[205] In July 1822, the "Carnarvon Seamen's Friend Society and Bethel Union" reported their formation as an auxiliary of the BFSFSBU, soliciting reports and rules from London.[206] During a South Wales "Bethel tour" in 1824, G.C. Smith was instrumental in founding a similar society in Swansea, which succeed in opening a "Seamen's Chapel" ashore the following year.[207]

From Ireland, there was news of shipboard Bethel Meetings in various ports as early as 1820. In Dublin, a correspondent of the London Bethel Union promoted what was apparently the first such sermon (by a "Church Methodist") on board the *Joseph* in October 1820, with about 300 present. In late 1822 and 1823, there are reports of the Rev. George Lilly actively engaged in visitation and preaching under the Bethel Flag among the shipping in Dublin; he is described as having been appointed by the Irish Evangelical Society as a Seamen's Missionary for Ireland. (A regular, interdenominational society did not materialize before 1826, however, when G.C. Smith promoted the founding of a "Dublin Mariners' and Rivermen's Bethel Union." The delay was no doubt partly due to the emergence meanwhile of the Anglican "Port of Dublin Society," dealt with on pp. 285-6.)[208]

In Belfast, after Methodist and Dissenting ministers had already established regular shipboard preaching in rotation, a "Belfast Seamen's Friend Society" was founded in September 1822, with the added support of

Anglican clergymen; a large quayside warehouse at the Limekiln Dock was fitted up as a Seamen's Chapel (with accomodation for over 400).[209]

The same year (1822), similar societies were stated to have been formed in each of the southern ports of Cork, Youghal and Waterford.[210] In Limerick, the Bethel Flag was reported hoisted by "a pious captain" in 1820; by 1823, the Rev. William Thomas, a resident Baptist "Missionary," had established preaching under the Flag on the decks of both British and foreign ships, with local landsmen joining in.[211]

A TRULY NATIONAL SOCIETY?

Thus this strange, unwieldy movement gathered momentum as society followed society around almost the entire coast of the kingdom, even to the Shetland Islands in the north, and the Channel Islands in the south.[212] In view of the varying mutual and metropolitan relationships of these societies, could the British and Foreign Seamen's Friend Society claim to constitute a truly "national" society? From a purely structural viewpoint, such a claim might seem debatable. (Even societies which employed the self-designation "Auxiliary" retained complete independence of management and undertook no formal financial responsibility toward any "Parent Society.") Nevertheless, there are other legitimate criteria. Despite the absence of closely-knit organizational fabric, the many Seamen's Friend Societies mushrooming around the kingdom sensed a powerful bond of spiritual kinship, not only with one another, but especially with the original Seamen's Friend Society in London. They were, in a deeper sense, only local manifestations of the same basic Bethel Union.[213]

Practically, this fundamental sense of union expressed itself in the adoption of essentially similar constitutions. Aims and means were (virtually or specifically) "in support of the plan of the Parent Society."[214] Symbolically, this cooperative fellowship found expression in a fervent enthusiasm for by far the most indispensable of these mutual means—the Bethel Flag.

In no case was this more dramatically illustrated than in the so-called "Minehead and Watchet Affair" in the spring of 1823. The customs officers at these adjacent Bristol Channel ports had, in an overt attempt to intimidate local Bethel Union pioneers, prevented the hoisting of the Bethel Flag on shipboard, on pain of seizing any offending vessel and fining the captain £500. Only after personal intervention by Lord Gambier, as president of the parent society, was the order finally rescinded (and characterized by higher authority as "highly improper"). G.C. Smith promptly seized on the incident to produce a spirited, 64-page tract, whereby he achieved new, world-wide publicity for the story of the origin of the Bethel emblem, and astonishing progress of the movement for which it stood.[215]

Chapter 11

Early Foreign Outreach

HOME-PORT MINISTRY TO FOREIGN SEAFARERS

The Bethel Flag represented more than a national movement. It symbolized an international, global dimension, as expressed in the official name of the London Bethel Union.[216] To what extent could the British and Foreign Seamen's Friend Society claim to be not only "British," but also, in actual fact "Foreign"? A study of the Society's early minute-books and magazines, as well as other available sources, reveals far less formally organized activity abroad than in home ports. In practice, much of what was achieved was the fruit of individual initiative, and lacked permanent structure. Nevertheless, such efforts were warmly acclaimed and encouraged by the parent society which, within severe financial limitations, showed, through the 1820's, a deliberate, sustained concern for various forms of foreign outreach.

Naturally, such foreign outreach was centered in the more heavily-frequented ports overseas. Equally naturally, it sought first and foremost the benefit of English-speaking seafarers (including a mounting proportion of Americans). There is, however, evidence of genuine concern for foreign-language crews also. Such concern was not limited to ports abroad. Examples have already been noted of foreign-language Scripture and tract distribution in home ports as early as during the Napoleonic War.[217] While Christian literature distribution continued,[218] efforts to provide preaching, too, for foreign seamen in British ports, became a feature of the 1820's, under the auspices of both the BFSFSBU and kindred societies. (Although examples were quoted where foreign seamen derived real benefit from an English-language ministry, such cases were nevertheless recognized as exceptions.)[219]

Particular significance was later attached to a sermon in Bengali, preached by the Rev. William Ward in the winter of 1819-20, to a crowd of Lascars at West Ham Abbey. The desperate plight of these Indian sailors, arriving in large numbers on East Indian ships, had already aroused the

239

concern of the London Mission Society. (The West Ham service was the result of an initiative by Thomas Phillips, as secretary of the Bethel Seamen's Union, the foundation of which the Baptist missionary pioneer had just attended.)[220]

As early as December 1819, William Henry Angas advocated floating chapels in all major British ports, with regular alternate preaching "in the languages of all commercial nations." Although this remained a remote ideal, Angas himself (completely conversant, as he was, with German, Dutch and French) exploited occasions offered during his 1822 home-port tour, as well as later, to minister to foreign seafarers in Britain in their own languages.[221]

A colorful Danish-born evangelist called Carl von Bülow also undertook a ministry under the Bethel Flag to foreign seamen in British ports, especially Scandinavians and Germans. During 1824-26, he preached to them and distributed Scripture and tracts in their own language, chiefly on the Thames, but also in ports along the North Sea Coast.[222] From the mid-1820's, there are reports of the Hull and Leith Societies employing their floating chapels for special services for foreign seafarers, with the aid of both Von Bülow and others. (A "pious Dutch captain" preached to a large congregation of his seafaring countrymen in the Hull Chapel, and at both places German ministers in Britain were invited to officiate.)[223]

ROLE OF THE BETHEL FLAG ABROAD

The primary sphere of foreign outreach was, however, the seafarer *overseas,* whether British or foreign. Here, it was natural for the Parent Bethel Union to sense a special responsibility. Faced with even more formidable manpower demands than at home, the only course open to the BFSFSBU abroad was to encourage voluntary coadjutors, afloat and ashore. Afloat, hopes were pinned to the ingenuity and intrepidity of a lengthening list of Bethel Captains. Ashore, cooperation was sought with resident missionaries, ministers and merchants. In the latter case, the aim was, where possible, "to promote similar Establishments" to those in Great Britain. In practically every instance, the indispensable instrument and universal rallying point was, just as at home, the Bethel Flag.[224]

In fact, the Bethel emblem proved itself even more indispensable abroad. There was, in foreign ports, less prospect of obtaining a permanent station, hence greater dependence on the deck or hold of a suitable ship as an improvised sanctuary. The *Minutes* of the BFSFSBU reveal each presentation of a Bethel Flag to an individual or institution as having been a carefully-

**An artist's impression of a Bethel Meeting aboard
a ship at anchor. (Courtesy: The Bodleian Library.)**

considered committee case. By recipients, to have a flag "voted" in this
manner was prized as a high privilege. The committee, however, held themselves responsible for both guarding the virtually sacred emblem against
misuse, and husbanding the sorely restricted resources of the Society. (The
committee was charged £3 per flag; by 1824, their shipchandler debt had
reached the point where they could only make a partial payment.)[225] In some
cases, the committee would offer credit terms. (One captain, however, his
savings swept away by sudden sickness, was allowed to retain his flag free of
debt, the committee having received a report of "the good use he had made of
it.")[226] There were also more indirect methods of cutting cost, as exemplified
by the following minute-entry in 1823:

> Mr. Conder a Ship Owner from Teignmouth waited on the
> Committee reporting that his vessels had opportunity of hoisting
> the Flag for Prayer at several Foreign Ports solicited that a Flag
> be presented to him promising if possible his aid on a further day.
> Resolved. That a Flag be presented to Mr. Saml. Conder of
> Teignmouth Devon for the use of his Shipping at home and
> abroad, and two Collecting Boxes.[227]

The Bethel Captains

Just as the North Country collier captains had heralded the dawn of organized seamen's missions at home, it was primarily the lay initiative of deep-sea Bethel Captains in the 1820's which laid the foundation for foreign port seamen's missions. A precondition for such initiative was the unique authority of the sailing ship captain. With final, sole responsibility for the welfare of ship, cargo and crew, he had acquired the status of not only a professional commander but also a *paterfamilias*. A paternal solicitude for the well-being of one's crew was not considered as sentimentality, but simply sound sense.[228] However, in a converted captain, such concern would take on a spiritual dimension (not merely as a matter of formal duty, but with that irrepressible enthusiasm which was characteristic of the Bethel Movement). With whatever devotional aids he could muster,[229] he would minister to the souls committed to his care, becoming both "priest and instructor—the father of the family," in the deepest sense. The mounting number of masters maintaining daily devotions and some form of Sunday services with their crew while at sea, was noted with warm commendation by Seamen's Friend Societies ashore.[230]

On arrival at a foreign port, a Bethel Captain would be confronted with wider opportunities of ministry. Motivated by concern for "brethren by profession" in other ships too, he would hoist his Bethel Flag and, by means of this religious status factor, put both traditional and charismatic authority to extended use.[231] Thus, for example, an eye-witness could relate how, in Spanish waters, a Bethel Flag had been "answered by five or six Union Jacks, and there was a contention among the captains in port, which of them should have the prayer-meeting on board his ship."[232] A typical instance of the resourcefulness of these men was provided by a captain visiting Trieste:

> . . . he lamented much the want of a Bethel Flag, as there were several ships lying here. This good man recollected that he had an old English ensign on board, and having cut off the fly, or blue field of it, he went on shore to a pious English lady who resides there; she kindly placed the letters and the dove complete on the flag, and returned it to the captain, who hoisted it as the first Bethel Flag that had ever appeared in the port. . . . [For Sunday worship, in which he included extracts from the Church Service and a read sermon, he gathered] Masters, Mates, Seamen, and also several Gentlemen from the shore, some of whom were Roman Catholics. . . . The inhabitants of Trieste were astonished. . . .[233]

Emulating in some respects the example of the early agents afloat of the Bible and Religious Tract Societies, Bethel Captains could, in their concern for native populations, too, assume "the character of a Christian Missionary." (Conspicuous, here, were the so-called Missionary Captains of G.F. Angas.)[234] Among these pioneers of foreign-port seamen's missions, captains from North Country ports such as Leith, the Tyne ports, Sunderland and Hull were particularly prominent; several of them were Methodist veterans of the Thames Revival.[235]

By the end of the 1820's, the first seeds of institutionalization had already been sown. In 1828, the leading London Society at that time published a list of 48 Bethel Captains considered as acting in union with the Society.[236] In 1829, Captain Anthony Landers, now as earlier keenly alert to new methods of maritime evangelism, pledged himself, together with ten fellow-masters and two mates, at a meeting on board the Bristol Floating Chapel, to adhere to a thirteen-point *Bethel Chart.* Here was set forth a concentrated code of maritime ethics dealing with the Christian captain's relations to his crew, his owners and others.[237]

In their persistent preoccupation with the response of captains, seamen's mission societies were showing not blatant discrimination, but keen appreciation of sociological realities. The grand vision of the Bethel Movement was that every ship on the seven seas should become a veritable "Bethel." But owing to his pivotal position in the social system of a ship, a Christian captain was considered the precondition for Christian seamen. As one Bethel Captain put it to a hesitant fellow captain whom he was trying to "press" to the meeting on board his ship, ". . . if we get you, we shall have your men too." Exactly this resulted.[238] The wide scope for personal initiative and involvement which the Bethel Movement afforded them, gave to Bethel Captains an *esprit de corps* reminiscent of Nelson's invincible "Band of Brothers."[239] To seamen's mission societies of their day, seeking to serve overseas on hopelessly inadequate budgets, they proved invaluable.

OTHER OVERSEAS COADJUTORS

While Bethel Captains accounted for much of the first phase of foreign port outreach, some form of cooperation with resident coadjutors was essential to any prospect of permanancy. Among these, foreign missionaries were conspicuous in their aid. Their contact with seafarers was inevitable; and there are numerous accounts of how missionaries, through preaching and counseling, responded to the opportunities for ministry which their sea travels opened to them. Here, they would be motivated by general, evangelistic concern, enhanced by this sudden confrontation with the grim hardships and hazards of the seafarer's life.[240]

Where mission fields were situated on the coast, the spiritual destitution of these men would continue to call on the compassion of the missionary. Here, however, an additional, specifically missiological motive would operate. Seamen from professedly "Christian" countries would, all according to their conduct, create either a negative or a positive image among the native population, thereby forming a powerful deterrent or opportunity for the Gospel. (This fact was to provide major motivation for seamen's missions in general, and will be dealt with in detail in Part VIII.)[241]

The committee of the BFSFSBU, aware of the breadth of potential support from foreign missionaries, made early attempts at coordination. In November 1820, they could report that it had already become the practice for foreign-bound missionaries first to be "schooled" in the Bethel system by taking part in Bethel Meetings on the Thames.[242] On May 15, 1822, with the Rev. W.H. Angas in the chair, it was resolved, "that a circular letter . . . be sent to every Missionary stationed in the coast abroad, with suitable documents, requesting their exertions in the cause."[243] During his ensuing Continental tour, Angas also enlisted the cooperation of the Missionary Institutions at Basle and Berlin, obtaining assurances from the authorities that each missionary should, on leaving his college, have "instructions also to preach the Gospel to Seamen," on board such ships as might be "accessible," wherever they settled.[244]

Reports during succeeding years from missionaries in all quarters of the globe confirm that, by many of them, opportunities to minister to seamen on this voluntary basis were eagerly embraced. (The Methodist, London, Baptist and Church Missionary Societies are all mentioned in this connection.)[245] The term "missionary" was also used of a wider range of activity, however, from evangelistic endeavors in European Christendom to church-building among the voluntary and involuntary settlers of far-off Australia.[246] In addition to cooperation from such quarters, help was occasionally rendered by clergymen and ministers serving British residents abroad,[247] as well as by lay coadjutors here and there, such as naval officers and merchants.[248]

As foreign secretary of the BFSFSBU, as well as editor of *The Sailor's Magazine,* G.C. Smith was initmately involved in the Society's endeavors abroad. As corresponding secretary, Thomas Phillips, too, played an important part (particularly in communications with the USA). Concrete aid to correspondents overseas was normally a committee case, and took the form of a Bethel Flag, together with a variety of printed matter. The latter could consist of a complete set of *The Sailor's Magazine* (from January 1820), several copies of the latest number, the *Reports* of the parent society, a few *Sailor's Hymn Books,* and perhaps such additional items as a number of *Bethel Tracts, Boatswain's Mates* and *Marks' Sermons.* (Direct financial aid was normally out of the question.)[249] In some cases, corresponding members were elected.[250] There is evidence of the immense importance of *The Sailor's Magazine* as well as personal correspondence, in stimulating and maintaining efforts abroad, especially where spiritually isolated groups were, "separated from their friends by a distance of half the globe."[251]

EARLY BETHEL UNION SOCIETIES IN BRITISH EMPIRE PORTS

A review of activities in the various ports of the world during the 1820's reveals that such general seamen's mission societies as emerged at this juncture were within English-speaking areas. The American side of the story requires separate treatment. However, apart from those originating in the USA, early Bethel Union Societies were founded in several ports of the British Empire, specifically in the Mediterranean, India and Australia.

First, largely through the initiative of an enterprising naval lieutenant, came the "Gibraltar Seamen's Bethel Society," established in September 1821. As "Resident Agent for Transports," Lt. John William Bailey was strategically placed, and had the warm cooperation of especially the Rev. William Croscombe (the local Methodist "Missionary"), in preaching under the Bethel Flag on successive British (often also American) merchant ships in the Bay. Despite both restrictions and direct opposition, the work flourished.[252]

At Malta, after a "Wesleyan missionary on his way to Palestine" had kindled interest by two months' preaching under the Bethel Flag on board different ships, the provisional committee of a "Malta Bethel Union" was formed May 16, 1824. Dr. Pinkerton, of Bible Society fame, took part at the time. Missionaries of various denominations (including Anglican) cooperated in maintaining worship services for seamen, while Admiral Richard H. Pearson, on his return from that island to England in 1825, launched a spirited fund-raising campaign in conjunction the the BFSFSBU, to procure a floating chapel for Valletta.[253]

In addition to these two key stations, there were, by 1825, also reports of pioneer preaching under the Bethel Flag at the Mediterranean ports of Malaga, Messina, Leghorn, Trieste, Constantinople, Smyrna and Alexandria.[254]

In India, the Gospel had been given new opportunities, both among the native population and the white man in those parts, since the passing, in 1813, of the East India Bill. Here, too, there emerged two early seamen's mission societies.

Baptist missionaries were largely responsible for the founding of the first of these societies in Calcutta. On his return from England in 1821, the Rev. William Ward, fresh from his involvement with the Parent Bethel Union in London, took the initiative.[255] A first experiment failed. Competing against all the sordid allurements of Calcutta's Sailortown, an attempt in the

William Carey (1761-1834),
renowned as the Baptist
pioneer of the modern
missionary era, was also in
the forefront of the earliest
organized seamen's mission
efforts in India.
(*Eerdman's Handbook of
the History of Christianity.*)

autumn of 1821 to institute Sunday afternoon services for seamen at the Bow
Bazaar Chapel proved abortive. However, Ward persevered. At a public
meeting, June 4, 1822, it was resolved to form a "Calcutta Bethel Society."
Itinerant shipboard preaching was now launched, but this also met with
"obstacles" (evidently captains who "hung back"). Still undaunted, the
provisional committee managed to purchase a brig-rigged pinnace and fit her
up as a floating chapel capable of seating 150, the whole financed by local
donations and subscriptions. Finally, on July 27, 1822, this *Calcutta Ark*
was inaugurated, with "the venerable Dr. Carey" preaching the opening
sermon. (Dr. Carey, together with his colleagues Dr. Marshman and William
Ward, continued on the committee, and personally promoted Christian
literature distribution among seamen sailing from Calcutta.)[256]

In an effort to curb the hitherto unchallenged sway of Calcutta's
notorious "tavern-keepers," a Bethel Lodging House was shortly afterwards
opened for seamen ashore.[257] Despite great difficulties, the Society also
sought means of ministering to the many local Lascars. (At one time, the
Gospel was preached to "about 1,000 Lascar Sailors on the beach.")[258]

Although reports could speak with refreshing candor of the peculiar
"indifference and listlessness" with which the work was continually confronted in Asian waters, it was not abandoned.[259] In Calcutta, where foreign
missionaries of different denominations supplied preaching in rotation, the
work went on, from 1827 under the name of the "Calcutta Seamen's Friend
Society."[260] In Bombay, at the close of 1824, an incipient Bethel Union

stimulated the establishment of an Anglican floating chapel, under the superintendence of the resident senior chaplain. A laid-up frigate, the *Hastings*,
was granted by the Governor. (In deference, the interdenominational group
then disbanded.)[261] At the close of the decade, a "Bombay Seamen's Friend
Association" was formed to continue the work, under the presidency of the
Bishop of Bombay.[262] As also in the case of both Calcutta and Bombay, the
BFSFSBU had, in 1823, sent a Bethel Flag and suitable literature to
concerned missionaries in the east coast port of Madras. Here, too, "Bethel
operations" resulted.[263]

Further east, the father of Protestant Missions to China, Dr. Robert
Morrison, became the earliest pioneer figure of seamen's missions in those
parts. However, his persistent efforts in the 1820's are so closely tied with
the establishment of the first American foreign station, that they will more
conveniently be dealt with under this head.[264]

In the early 1820's, Australia had barely begun to emerge from the
narrow concept of a penal settlement in the corner of a continent, when the
Bethel Movement also reached those remote shores. *The Sydney Gazette* for
September 27, 1822, featured "An Appeal to the Friends of Religion, in
Behalf of Seamen," to provide "a floating sanctuary" for sailors in Sydney.
The proposal, subscribed "A Well-wisher to Seamen," led to a memorable
service on board the brig *Lynx*, Sunday afternoon, November 17, 1822.
With the Bethel Flag hoisted at the main-top masthead, 100 seamen heard a
Wesleyan "missionary," the Rev. Erskine, preach from the text "Prepare to
meet thy God!" This again led to a meeting of "Friends of Seamen" at the
Gazette office, Monday, December 23, 1822, and the founding of a "Sydney
Bethel Union Society."[265] News of the latter was greeted in the 1824
Retrospect of the BFSFSBU as of great potential significance for the
furtherance of the Seamen's Cause, not only in "the island called Australia,"
but throughout "the vast Pacific Ocean."

While Anglican senior chaplains of the Colony presided at the
meetings at which the Society was constituted, Wesleyan missionaries
continued to play a major role, bearing the brunt of the waterfront work, and
preaching on shipboard in Sydney Cove. Meanwhile, a subscription for
procuring a floating chapel was launched, with the Governor, Sir Thomas
Brisbane, personally contributing £100 for the purpose.[266]

Soon the example of Sydney spread to Hobart Town, in the newly-
established sister-colony of Van Diemen's Land (Tasmania). Here a
"temporary" Bethel Flag was hoisted for the first time on the *Persian*,
December 16, 1827, with the Rev. W. Scholfield preaching. On January 29,
1828, the "Van Diemen's Land Seamen's Friend and Bethel Union Society"
was organized at a public meeting at the courthouse. The Society's agents
continued with preaching and prayer-meetings under the Bethel Flag on

board different ships. Meanwhile, a promise was obtained from the Lieutenant-Governor that a hulk, currently serving as a floating powder-magazine in the harbor, could be taken over as soon as it became disposable, as a floating chapel. The narrative of further developments on the Australian scene belongs to a later phase.[267]

In the various island groups in the Pacific Ocean there could, during the 1820's, be no question of formal societies. Here, however, the need for a ministry to seafarers was felt to be particularly acute. Especially did this apply to the British and American whaling crews in these waters (reputed to number some 10,000). Cut off from home, as they were for periods of up to three years, these men would be exposed to recurring opportunities for sheer, unbridled license. The BFSFSBU, therefore, gave great publicity to the early efforts of the pioneer missionaries in these parts who responded to the need, particularly two prominent representatives of the LMS, William P. Crook and William Ellis. Both established preaching for whalers under Bethel Flags received from this Society in 1823, the former in Wilks' Harbour, Tahiti, the latter at Oahu, in the Sandwich Islands (Hawaii).[268] Remarkable evidence of positive response to such efforts was provided by the text of two public pledges intended to combat the twin temptations of intemperance and promiscuity, drawn up and signed on the initiative of masters and men of vessels calling at the Sandwich Islands in 1824.[269]

Turning to the other principal whaling grounds off the Arctic coast of Greenland, the *Annual Retrospects* of the BFSFSBU during the 1820's gave warm credit to Bethel pioneers among captains and crews of Hull and Liverpool whale-ships in "these comfortless climes." Stirring scenes were reported of Sundays in Baffin Bay and Davis Strait, with "three or four hundred Sailors marching across the ice" from different directions, all converging on a ship where the Bethel Flag was hoisted for worship.[270]

By then, the Bethel Movement had already reached the mainland of Canada. In fact, available records indicate that it was in St. John (New Brunswick) in 1820, that preaching under the Bethel Flag was first established in North America. The Rev. Mr. Scott, Baptist minister from Lyme, Dorsetshire, had emigrated there in March of that year. His enthusiasm had already been roused when invited to a Bethel Meeting on the Thames, shortly before leaving his homeland. He had "never witnessed such a scene in his life, and . . . could not help addressing the Sailors, and declaring his determination . . . to establish similar meetings in America." G.C. Smith, happening to meet him on the point of embarkation from Devonport and finding he had no Bethel Flag, offered him his own. Thus it was, that, at the close of a crowded Bethel Service led by Smith in the hold of a vessel on which the emblem had just been used, a Baptist minister publicly "took possession of the Bethel Flag for America."[271] Subsequent reports could

Quebec harbor, where (as in several other Canadian port-
cities) organized seamen's missions began in the early
1820's with improvised services under the Bethel Flag.
(*Chart and Compass,* 1884.)

confirm that Scott put the flag to good purpose, as "great numbers" of
seamen continued to gather under his preaching on board ships in the harbor
of St John.[272]

By the mid-1820's beginnings had also been made in other Canadian
ports. Bethel Flags were entrusted with local correspondents of the BFSFSBU
in St. Johns (Newfoundland) in 1823 and Quebec in 1823-24.[273] In 1825,
the Society appointed the Rev. Thaddeus Osgood (destined to become a
seamen's mission pioneer in Montreal), as their "gratuitous agent in British
North America," sending him a Bethel Flag and other materials.[274] In
Halifax (Nova Scotia), John L. Starr, an "eminent merchant," had already
given convincing proof of personal dedication to the spiritual welfare of
seamen, when he was granted a flag, tracts, magazines and reports, in
1826.[275]

Calling attention to Bethel progress in British possessions further
south, the BFSFSBU could, in its 1822 *Retrospect*, hail the establishment of
"a most important line of communication" from Bermuda to Berbice, where
British and American seamen could now count on being greeted by the
Bethel Flag.[276] First in point of time was the Central American port of
Belize, by the Gulf of Honduras. Here, as early as June 1820, Lieutenant
Edward Smith, in command of the Angas vessel *Robert,* had already followed
up his pioneering role at Greenock by effectively introducing ship-to-ship

preaching under the Bethel Flag. (The Rev. Armstrong, "clergyman of the Bay of Honduras," enthusiastically embraced the opportunity to continue this form of ministry under the flag which Smith left behind him.)[277] In 1822, the BFSFSBU could consign Bethel Flags to zealous correspondents at both Barbados[278] and Berbice (in eastern British Guiana).[279] Meanwhile, Bermuda and the Bahamas were supplied by the New York Bethel Union, a gesture which was warmly acknowledged in London.[280]

SOUTH AND CENTRAL AMERICAN PORTS

Still further south, enterprising Bethel Captains undertook to introduce the flag and the cause it symbolized into one major South American port after another. In Rio de Janeiro, it was Captain Stephenson (in command of another Angas vessel), who took the initiative in April 1821. Here, before sailing, he was able to commit his emblem to "a religious merchant" from shore who, amazed at the sight of "seamen from every vessel in the harbour" eagerly taking part in meetings of this nature, offered to do his utmost to promote their continuation. (So far did he succeed, that the tradition of resident British merchants unfurling the flag and conducting shipboard Sunday services in Rio harbor was still reportedly unbroken at the close of the decade.)[281] Captains of the same category could report on corresponding activities in Montevideo and Buenos Aires, in 1823 and 1824, respectively.[282] In 1824, similar news arrived from such ports as Valparaiso and Lima on the Pacific coast.[283] Many of these reports indicate a mounting involvement by *American* captains in this area.[284]

Among British Bethel Captains who played pioneering roles in Caribbean and South American ports, several belonged to the dedicated company of so-called "Missionary Captains" purposely employed by the firm of Angas & Co. on this particular coast. Caleb Angas Senior had opened an extensive import trade in mahogany, dye-woods and other products from British Honduras. To his youngest son, however, the firm's agency in Belize was simultaneously a beach-head for the Gospel. Incensed at what he found of abject slavery and spiritual deprivation among the aboriginal Indians, George Fife Angas launched an attack on both in the early 1820's. He was so successful that he earned the whole-hearted hatred of the slave-holding merchants of the settlement. In England, he built up the necessary political pressure, enlisting the aid of Zachary Macaulay and other anti-slavery champions.[285] Locally, he pursued the personnel policy of appointing captains and agents imbued with the same missionary spirit as himself. Reports from such captains could tell not only of Christian literature distribution among native Indians and Negroes ashore, but also of how these latter were included in the fellowship of Bethel Meetings on board. These captains also had the courage to try to redress glaring cases of social injustice they came across among the blacks, both slaves and free.[286]

WILLIAM HENRY ANGAS: FIRST ORDAINED "MISSIONARY TO SEAFARING MEN"

G.F. Angas' elder brother, William Henry, had earlier, for several years, commanded ships in the firm's Caribbean trade. However, it was in certain key ports on the continent of Europe that William Henry Angas was destined to make a unique contribution to the development of seamen's missions. In reverting to the European scene, therefore, it becomes necessary to examine briefly the background and qualifications of this pioneer personality.[287]

Descended from a branch of the Scottish clan of Angus, which had long since settled in Northumberland, William Henry Angas was born in the major port-city of Newcastle-on-Tyne, October 6, 1781. His father, Caleb Angas, a successful coach manufacturer, merchant and shipowner had brought up his son in the tradition of personal integrity and Baptist piety for which the family had been known for generations. William was originally educated with a view to the legal profession. However, he had "heard it was extremely difficult for an honest man to pursue that calling." Instead, he declared his preference for a seafaring career, completely underestimating (as he later admitted) the particular privations and temptations to which he now exposed himself.[288]

As in the case of his contemporary, G.C. Smith, the maritime life of W.H. Angas was dramatic to the extreme.[289] After being bound apprentice, he experienced several narrow escapes, culminating in his capture off the Naze of Norway by a French privateer. During a twenty-month incarceration in France, he managed, shortly after an unsuccessful escape bid, to purchase the remains of a pocket edition of *Dr. Watts' Hymns*, which a French Hussar on guard duty had been using to light his pipe. This was made the means of reviving the decision of faith he had made as a schoolboy. Released in an exchange of prisoners, he had no sooner regained his native shore when he was seized by a press gang, and forced into a man-of-war about to sail. However, through the last-minute intervention of his father, he was discharged. Then, around the turn of the century, at the age of nineteen, he was made captain of the first in a series of ships he commanded in the Angas trade on the Caribbean. Finally, in the early part of the Napoleonic War, after battling through shipwrecks, attacks by both privateers and mutineers, as well as bouts of yellow fever, his health became so severely reduced that he decided to retire from active seafaring and take over the work of a ship's husband, in the family partnership in Newcastle.[290]

Captain Angas could later attest how, in the midst of these trials, he had experienced a decisive deepening of his Christian faith. These trials included the loss (in 1803) of an elder brother, who became for a while his spiritual counselor at sea. He had already realized that the "true source" of all the erosion of spiritual life he had suffered at sea lay not in that profession *per se,* but in his own heart. Thus he was led to a fundamental reassessment of priorities: "The things which had appeared so good . . . I seemed beginning to count loss."[291]

With the new opportunities for spiritual fellowship offered by his settlement ashore, Captain Angas sensed "an increasing desire" to live more wholly than hitherto for the glory of God and the good of his fellow-men. Having, however, since boyhood been "acquainted with the abandoned condition of seafaring men in general," he felt this original, more diffuse sense of vocation mature into a "corresponding desire of becoming in one way or another instrumental" in the salvation of "that class in particular." This impulse came, as he himself states, "a little prior to the event of last peace" (1815).[292] His biographer records how Captain Angas would make use of intervals of business by "visiting various seaports, for the purpose of promoting the cause of God amongst sailors, by the establishment of Sunday-schools, the distribution of Bibles and Tracts, and occasional addresses. . . ."[293]

Such activities, novel as they then were, could as yet only be sporadic. However, at the close of the French Wars, the simultaneous loss of two of the firm's three ships signified for Captain Angas a providential release from his obligations to the partnership. In 1816, with the concurrence and material support of his father, he commenced an intense course of studies at Edinburgh University in preparation for the ministry. In August 1817, he was "regularly called to the exercise of the Christian ministry," by the Baptist Church in Carter Lane, Southwark (where he had been baptized by Dr. Rippon December 3, 1807, during a stay in London, and where he had since retained his membership).

His church recommended him, however, "not to enter at once upon public labours, but to devote himself for a time to pursue preparatory studies. . . ." Taking the hint to heart, he left the following month for the Continent, where he continued linguistic and theological studies in Brussels (1817), in Rotterdam (1818) and at Zeist, a German Moravian settlement near Utrecht (1819). Here he not only received rich ecumenical impulses, but acquired a fluency in French, Dutch and German which he purposely planned as a means of ministering to foreign seamen in their own tongue.[294]

Angas was thus prevented from taking any personal part in the stirring scenes in the metropolis in 1818 and 1819. However, he heard of them with enthusiasm. To the newly-formed Bethel Seamen's Union, he wrote from Zeist in December 1819 to offer not only far-sighted practical advice, but himself as a future collaborator, if the Society should honor him with "a place in their ranks." Specifically, he would then, when duly qualified, hope to visit the chief German-, Dutch- and French-speaking seaports on the Continent, "and there form lines of co-operation with the London Union."[295] Although he agreed to a promotional assignment during 1820 among the Mennonite churches of Holland on behalf of the Baptist Missionary Society, he kept his original intention of bringing the Gospel to his "brethren on the on the seas" steadily in view. Finally, after a year of further theological study, 1821-22 (this time in London at the College of Stepney), he was ready. Receiving "an unanimous call" from his church in Carter Lane, he "immediately made arrangements for his public designation."[296]

On board the Bristol Floating Chapel, May 11, 1822, William Henry Angas became the first in history known to have been officially ordained to a ministry to seamen, or—to use the exact words on that occasion—"to the work and office of a Missionary to Seafaring Men." To this was added the further qualification: "in connection with the British and Foreign Seamen's Friend Society and Bethel Union." At the interdenominational service which took place that Wednesday evening, the Rev. Thomas Roberts requested the candidate first to relate "the Lord's dealings in bringing him to the knowledge of the truth, and how he had been led to the work in which he was now formally and solemnly about to be set apart." In answer to a second question, he gave an outline of "the leading doctrines he professed to believe and desired to proclaim." These proved to be "briefly the same as distinguished the body of Protestant Evangelical Christians." Dr. John Ryland then delivered the charge from the text: "The love of Christ constraineth us."[297]

What was the specific significance of the designation under which the Rev. W.H. Angas presented himself? The term "missionary" was, as already noted, by no means tied to a ministry beyond the bounds of Christendom.[298] An anonymous article entitled "The Seamen's Missionary" in the first (1820) volume of *The Sailors Magazine* advocates the adoption of both the principle and practice of the "missionary" concept in relation to seafarers.

The argument of the article underlines the two basic attributes attached to the term by common contemporary usage: (1) Total commitment. (A missionary must, both in heart and time, be "wholly devoted to the work.") (2) Itinerant exertion. (A missionary must, as already practiced in

William Henry Angas (1781-1832), Newcastle-born
Baptist sea-captain and "Missionary to Seafaring Men,"
the first in history known to have been ordained
specifically for ministry to seafarers. (Picture thanks
to extensive research by Reverends David Harries and
Norman Parkes, both affiliated with the BSS.)

both "home" and "foreign" missions, embody the principle of "constant
motion" and "seeking out," in this case "among ships and seamen.")[299] The
qualification "to Seafaring Men" was defined by Angas himself as signifying
"to foreign Seamen as well as our own."[300] The further addition "in connection with the British and Foreign Seamen's Friend Society and Bethel
Union" indentified the commission as a corporate undertaking. (Significantly,
however, the sending forth of this first ordained "seamen's missionary" was

only financially feasible at this early juncture because he happened to be a man of independent means, able and willing to serve gratuitously.)[301]

ANGAS' PIONEERING MINISTRY
IN KEY CONTINENTAL PORTS

What could have been the motivation behind the priority given by this pioneer seamen's missionary to *foreign* outreach? Apart from a global outlook which had become second nature, an indication is given in a letter he wrote on board a brig bound for Hamburg, just after leaving Hull, September 18, 1822. He had then devoted the time he felt he should to the home-port tour he undertook for the committee of the BFSFSBU immediately after his ordination.[302]

> . . . the Seamen's cause being already in a flourishing state there [at Hull], I judged it of higher importance for me to push on to those parts where the message of love and mercy has not yet reached, much as it would have delighted me to meet our Hull friends around a throne of grace, and given them the parting hand. The less, however, must give way to the greater in all matters of such moment as the great salvation of our brethren of the sea.[303]

To William Henry Angas, the question was simply this: where was the current need greatest? The answer seemed obvious: among British seamen abroad and foreign seamen in general. In literally launching forth on that principle, he proved himself a missionary in more than name.

Hamburg would seem to have been well chosen as the first field of the newly-ordained seamen's missionary's labors. Considered second only to London in importance as a European seaport (with more than half the annual shipping under British or American flag), Hamburg had a Sailortown notorious for its "sanctioned profligacy."[304] Since the seizure of the city's last remaining *Wachtschiff* by the French in 1811, the accompanying *Schiffspredigerstelle* (in other words, the only native preaching ministry specifically for seamen) had also disappeared.[305]

The first recorded Bethel Meeting in Hamburg harbor was reported in early 1821. The 22-year-old captain of a Hull trader, for want of a more "regular" version, made his own improvised worship-signal by painting the word "ARK" on his bed sheet and hoisting it from the masthead. There were negative reactions. Some labeled it a "Radical Flag." One merchant cancelled his freight offer on account of it. However, another took his place, commending the captain for serving "a good Master"; and seamen responded well.[306] The first service under an official Bethel emblem was reported held in June the same year, with the Rev. George D. Mudie of the local Evangelical English Reformed Church preaching, and German friends joining him on board.[307] As meetings multiplied, evidence of their positive impact was provided by remarks such as those of a captain from Hamburg on seeing a Bethel Flag in Liverpool: "I know dat flag do all de vonder—is done much goot at Hamburg dat goot flag."[308]

On reaching Hamburg in October 1822, after a stormy 24-day crossing from Hull during which the brig had actually been reported lost on the Hamburg Exchange), the Rev. W.H. Angas applied himself to the task of consolidating the Bethel Cause in this key port with characteristic thoroughness and vigor. Incessantly hoisting the flag on board British and American ships through the rigors of a particularly severe winter, he preached to "overflowing audiences." (The frozen surface of the Elbe made access easy.) He was unremitting in his visitation of sick and afflicted seamen. He procured and distributed great quantities of Scriptures and tracts in English, German and other languages. (Several of the English "sea-tracts" he took upon himself to translate and print in German; he also published in German a book called *Good News on the Sea*, which was "greatly circulated," and excited considerable "concern for Sailors.") He founded a Sunday school primarily for seamen's children, which eventually grew to great proportions and, incidentally, stimulated the institution of Sunday schools elsewhere in Germany. He even obtained the sanction of the City Senate for the establishment of a floating chapel for Hamburg.[309]

The Senate Syndicus was, however, careful to include the priviso "for English Seamen in our port." Mindful of such national sensitivities, Angas avoided unnecessary provocation. By restricting his preaching to non-German ships, he remained unmolested by the Harbor Police. However, he could not—and would not—escape the hostility of many of the merchants in regard to the Bethel Flag. On the contrary, his sailor-like response to his personal portion of their odium was simply: "Lord, grant that I may be covered with such odium all the days of my life!"[310]

Angas had warm collaborators, however. Prominent among these were the Rev. T.W. Matthews (Mudie's successor), as well as his "excellent partner in life." Moreover, Matthews zealously continued the work (as far as other duties would permit), when Angas, in late April 1823, moved on to new fields.[311] In so doing, Matthews received ready cooperation from one of Angas' "sons of the faith," Johann Gerhard Oncken (1800-84). This young German-born evangelist (destined to play a decisive role in the organization of German and Scandinavian Baptists), had only recently arrived as a "missionary" of The Continental Society.[312] On Sunday afternoon, March 21, 1824, he preached on board a German vessel a message which was held to be the first public sermon in German under the Bethel Flag in a German port. The event became an ongoing tradition as Oncken persevered with a flag granted him by the BFSFSBU. Attendance could vary from 50 to 100. Oncken also preached under the flag to Prussian bargemen on the Elbe, and distributed large quantities of Christian literature among both German and other seamen.[313]

A floating chapel remained only a desideratum, for want of funds. However, some form of alternative (at least for British and American seamen) did become available when a new English Reformed Church was opened in July 1826, not far from the shore. Here, Matthews had incorporated a 200-seat Seamen's Gallery.[314] Nevertheless, news of the seamen's response reaching W.H. Angas on a home-port tour in 1829 was far from satisfactory. He sailed at once for Hamburg, soon succeeded in filling the gallery accommodation with British and American seamen, formed a local society for their benefit, and established seamen's Bible classes there. In 1831, "many sailors" were still reportedly attending from time to time.[315]

W.H. Angas originally conceived of himself as being "wholly devoted" to a ministry to his brother-seafarers, and there is ample evidence that this remained his "chosen and beloved work" throughout his life. However, his sensitivity to providential guidance led him also to undertake promotional assignments among scattered Mennonite congregations for the Baptist Missionary Society, wherever this could be combined with "seafaring labours" on the Continent. Thus, for example, on leaving Hamburg in the spring of 1823, he visited scattered Mennonite congregations in Germany, Poland, Prussia, Switzerland and France. However, at such times he once wrote: "I long to be upon the sea-coast again, within the smell of pitch and tar. That's my nosegay!"[316]

In June 1823, Angas took the opportunity to hoist the flag in the busy Baltic port of Danzing. Here, despite initial setbacks (both on account of uncooperative captains and local restrictions) he eventually obtained the familiar *Agenoria* for English language preaching; meanwhile, he was able to visit German and Dutch shipping, conversing and counseling with the crews, and circulating Christian literature among them.[317]

Returning to England again in July and August of 1824, Angas made a point of "shaping his course" via Antwerp, and securing valuable contacts for future endeavors in this rapidly expanding port.[318] Resuming his work on the Continent, Angas revisited Antwerp in early 1825, following up with an intense round of preaching under the Bethel Flag (this time especially on American ships); "familiar conversation, on religion" with captains and crews of ships of different nationalities (as usual in their own tongue); and (not least) encouraging a concern for seamen among local "eminent christians."[319]

Angas then spent a large part of the year 1825 on a concentrated tour of Dutch ports, including Rotterdam, St. Gravendeel, Dort, Zealand and Flushing, following a similar pattern of activity as in Antwerp.[320] In Holland, the ground had been partially prepared by that country's relatively rich tradition of Christian maritime literature, coupled with the influence of the recently-founded Marine Bible Societies.[321] Angas spoke highly of the warm collaboration of Captain Van Zeuglan Nyevelt of the Netherlands Navy (who also became a subscriber to the BFSFSBU). Before leaving, Angas sought to stimulate further national effort by drawing up a *Memorial to the Dutch Nation,* in behalf of their seamen, intended for circulation "in all the sea-ports in Holland."[322]

After his return to England in 1826, the Rev. W.H. Angas devoted himself henceforth to a series of significant home-port activities (from 1827, in connection with the newly-merged Port of London and Bethel Union Society). Independent of both financial and family ties, he was free to select what he considered to be areas of particular need or strategic importance. "Cruising" (as he put it) round the coast, he endeavored to "form new or restore declining societies." (On the Isle of Wight, the Channel Islands, and among smugglers and windbound sailors on the coast of Kent and Sussex, he made particularly long stays.)

In order to succeed in "shaking Satan's empire on the sea," Angas was convinced that preaching and circulating Scripture and tracts, however basic, was not enough. Wherever he could, he sought to supplement this by promoting Sunday schools for seamen's children, Bible classes for adult seamen and depots for marine libraries. Always, he proved particularly alert to the needs of foreign seamen, eagerly embracing opportunities to minister to them in German, Dutch and French. (When working in Liverpool in 1828, he published brief hymnals in German and Dutch for his Floating Chapel services with seamen from those countries.)[323]

The year 1832 found Angas ministering to seamen along the Tyne and providing urgently-needed ministerial supply at the Baptist Chapel at South Shields. Suddenly struck down with cholera (which was then raging in those parts), he died in a matter of hours, on September 7, 1832, hardly 51 years old.[324]

The loss was widely lamented. Unlike G.C. Smith (his tempestuous contemporary), W.H. Angas, with his irenic unobtrusive nature, possessed no "extraordinary eloquence" as a public speaker.[325] Yet his personal influence was remarkable, and his contribution to the Seamen's Cause at a critical period proved both profound and lasting.

Apart from filling a very vital consolidatory role, William Henry Angas was in two important aspects a genuine pioneer: (1) As the first

In Memory of the
LATE WILLIAM HENRY ANGAS.

BEING MADE EARLY ACQUAINTED WITH THE
SAVIOUR OF SINNERS,
HE WAS DEEPLY IMPRESSED WITH THE DESIRE OF
CONSECRATING ALL THE ENERGIES OF HIS LIFE
TO THE SPIRITUAL INTERESTS OF HIS FELLOW MEN.
THE LAMENTABLE STATE OF HIS BRETHREN ON THE SEA
ENGAGED ALL SPECIAL ATTENTION ;
AND FOR THEIR SAKES
(AFTER ENDURING MANY HARDSHIPS, IN FRENCH PRISONS,
IN SHIPWRECKS, IN TEMPESTS, & IN UNHEALTHY CLIMATES,
DURING WHICH
HE ZEALOUSLY LABOURED FOR THEIR MORAL
AND RELIGIOUS WELFARE)
HE GAVE UP ALL SECULAR PURSUITS, AND VISITED
THE PRINCIPAL SEA-PORTS OF GREAT BRITAIN & JAMAICA,
AND THE CONTINENT OF EUROPE ;
WHERE HE
SUCCESSFULLY LABOURED TO BRING SAILORS UNDER
THE SOUND OF THE GLORIOUS GOSPEL OF THE BLESSED GOD.
IN THIS WORK
HE WAS ENGAGED AT SOUTH SHIELDS,
WHEN SUDDENLY CALLED TO QUIT HIS LABOUR
AND TO ENTER INTO THE JOY OF HIS LORD.
HE DIED, DEPLORED BY ALL,
SEPTEMBER 7TH, 1832, AGED 51 YEARS
AND WAS INTERRED BENEATH
THIS MEMORIAL OF FRATERNAL AFFECTION.

His record is on high : the stone we raise
Exalts the Saviour—not the servant's praise.
He loved the sons of Ocean ; and he bore
The sound of heavenly grace from shore to shore,
He fix'd his anchor firm within the vail,
And blessed the Refuge that could never fail :
The billows rose—he smiled, with Heaven in view,
And dying, proved his living witness true.

E. R.

Memorial marking the grave of William Henry Angas
in the New Cemetery in Newcastle-on-Tyne, where
he was buried September 8, 1832. (Edward W.
Matthews: *The King's Brotherhood.*)

specifically ordained seamen's missionary in history, he showed the necessity of henceforth providing both personnel and funds for a full-time ministry to seafarers. (In thus living out the concept of seamen's missionary, he also, in effect, promoted the recognition of the concept of "seamen's missions" as a Christian ministry in its own right, before this idea had actually become current.)[326] (2) As the first minister to leave his native shores expressly to undertake foreign-port missions to seamen, he gave convincing proof of the need for permanent stations—as well as indigenous societies—abroad. (In so doing, he pursued a policy of "interdenominational approach" as a condition for interational outreach.)[327]

The dominant idea that took such early hold of William Henry Angas—and never left him—was that every Christian on the seven seas should become that which none other could be with equal effectiveness: a missionary to his brother-seafarers.[328] Of the validity of his argument, his own consecrated life gave vivid evidence.

CARL VON BÜLOW'S
SAILING MISSIONS TO NORWAY

Whereas Angas' concern for foreign seamen led him to seaports in Germany, Holland and Belgium, the spiritual welfare of *Scandinavian* seafarers became the special burden of von Bülow. Also known under the Christian name "Carlos," his full name was, in fact: Carl Gustav Christopher Ditlev von Bülow.[329] Born September 29, 1787 in Svendborg, Denmark, he was descended from German nobility (and therefore occasionally—though erroneously— referred to as "Baron" von Bülow). Moving with his family to Drammen, Norway, when two years old, he later returned to Denmark and was educated as an army officer. Serving in the Napoleonic War during 1807-15, first in the Danish Calvary, subsequently in the Würtemberg Army, he was at length seriously wounded. Spiritually awakened through the testimony of a Christian nurse and personal Bible study, he ultimately decided to resign his military commission and become a full-time warrior for Christ.[330]

Having arrived in Edinburgh in 1818, von Bülow left for Norway in 1819 with a stock of Danish Bibles and Testaments from both the Edinburgh Bible Society and the BFBS. He also secured large supplies of tracts from the RTS, some of which he had himself translated into Danish. Thus equipped, the lone evangelist traveled in a fishing craft along the coast of Norway, distributing literature and holding religious meetings among the largely seafaring inhabitants. Evidently, the results of the experiment fully confirmed von Bülow's faith in the necessity of this novel form of maritime evangelism.[331]

After remaining in Norway and Denmark until 1824, von Bülow left for London in that year.[332] Here, he systematically sought sponsorship for what was in one sense a "Scandinavian Seamen's Mission." Shortly after his arrival, he offered his services to the British and Foreign Seamen's Friend Society as a preacher to foreign seamen. Undeterred by the Society's current "want of funds" for such purposes, he persevered; was voted a Bethel Flag by the committee; and preached on board foreign ships on the Thames, particularly those of Norwegian registry. At this period, von Bülow was in close touch with the Rev. G.C. Smith.[333]

Von Bülow's Bethel activity in the metropolis was, however, expressly subordinate to his principal plan—namely that of sailing chapel mission to the coastal population and the shipping in the ports of the three Northern Kingdoms, Norway, Denmark and Sweden.[334] Here, another society proved better placed to provide significant support. "The Continental Society for the Diffusion of Religious Knowledge over the Continent of Europe" had been founded in London in 1818, under strong impressions of the spiritual "darkness and superstition" prevalent in post-war Europe. Supported by both Church Evangelicals and Dissenters, the Society disclaimed any attempt at proselytism, limiting its support to select "Native Preachers," and professing only to "recover the people to the faith once delivered to the saints."[335]

It was thus essentially a Continental Home Missionary Society which, in 1825, not only embraced the plan presented by von Bülow, but also appointed its originator to carry it into effect.[336] The BFSFSBU signified their participation, too, by providing publicity, a Bethel Flag and financial assistance (toward the purchase of a vessel "to promote Religion among Foreign Sailors in the ports of Sweden and Norway").[337]

After a preaching and promotional tour up the British North Sea coast,[338] von Bülow finally embarked in the spring of 1826 on his so-called "Norway Mission." On his arrival at Kristiansand in April 1826, he purchased a six-ton oak-built sailing vessel, able to accommodate "a congregation of twenty persons on the deck." He loaded her with great quantities of Scripture and tracts (from the BFBS and RTS). Then he launched forth with the Bethel Flag aloft.

Von Bülow's *Journal* of his coastal voyages between Kristiansand and Trondheim, from April 1826 to January 1827, records vivid details of his evangelistic activities among landsmen and seafarers alike. To the latter he ministered by Bethel Meetings, counseling and literature distribution, whether the crews were local, British or foreign; and whether they were sailing in traders, lobster-smacks or fishing craft. As opportunity offered, he would visit their vessels or gather them on board his own. Although opposition and indifference were also encountered, the general response was evidently encouraging.[339]

Carl von Bülow
(1787-1867), Danish-born
German cavalry officer,
who became the Congre-
gational-ordained British
pioneer of the sailing
chapel concept of
seamen's missions on the
coast of Norway in 1819
and 1826. (Aage Holter:
*Det Norske Bibelselskap
gjennom 150 aar / The
Norwegian Bible Society
through 150 years.* Vol. I.)

        Recalled in January 1827 in order to take part in further promotional
activity, von Bülow was ordained a minister of the Gospel at the (Congregational) Poultry Chapel in London. However, despite the support of the Rev.
Edward Irving and the formation of a special committee in Hull for the
purpose, funds still proved insufficient for the larger vessel for which von
Bülow pleaded.[340] Returning to Norway in May 1827, he continued evangelistic activities ashore, until compelled to leave in May 1828. (His sweeping
statements on the spiritual destitution of "that benighted country," coupled
with scathing criticism of the State Church, had antagonized the clergy.
Charged with unlawful conventicle and heretical activities, he was finally
served an official expulsion order.)[341]

        Von Bülow's mission has since been recognized as the earliest major
confrontation of the rigid Lutheran Church Establishment of Norway with
society-sponsored Anglo-Saxon revivalism; his name is also famous for his
leading role in the founding of a local missionary society in Stavanger
(December 5, 1826), destined to become the forerunner of the Nowegian
Missionary Society.[342] However, in a history of seamen's missions, Carl von
Bülow deserves credit primarily as the pioneer of sailing chapels, a method
of maritime ministry which became the key to the successful Anglican
endeavors which began a decade later.[343] He was also the first of those
seamen's missionaries from British and American societies who, during the
following generation, were to carry the cause to the coasts of Scandinavia.[344]

        Although von Bülow was forced to abandon the original plan of
continuing his sailing chapel mission to the other Scandinavian countries,

there were reports of early efforts by others to minister to seafarers in these parts (in addition to the Marine Bible Society activities previously noted).[345]

In Gothenburg, there was news of Bethel Meetings in the harbor in 1822.[346] At Wisby, in the Baltic island of Gothland, a Swedish minister, the Rev. J.C. Laurin, offered, in December 1821, to carry out "any commissions" for the BFSFSBU among the many local seafarers.[347]

In the Russian port-city of Cronstadt, a Captain Higgins successfully pioneered Bethel Meetings in 1822. After that, other Bethel Captains continued them, to the amazement of local Russian residents. A key role in the Cronstadt work was played by Dr. Ebenezer Henderson of the BFBS. From 1822 until shortly before he left St. Petersburg in 1825, he traveled to Cronstadt to provide English-language Sunday preaching on shipboard under the Bethel Flag. He found seamen to be "the most attentive congregations" he had ever addressed. Preparations were even under way to obtain a Russian man-of-war as a floating chapel for Cronstadt (only to be frustrated by the sudden reversal of Emperor Alexander's religious policy in the mid-1820's).[348]

On board ships in the busy Latvian port of Riga, the Bethel Flag was hoisted in the summer of 1821. The work here was coordinated by a Mr. Hiron, who also fitted up a large Bethel Room "for Religious Worship among Sailors."[349]

Among timber-traders in the Prussian port of Memel, those pioneers of the Thames Revival, Captains Simpson, Wilkins and Cowie, were conspicuous in promoting Bethel Meetings during the 1820's. Again, incredulous inhabitants became not only spectators but active participants. Similar scenes were enacted near the Arctic Circle, in the White Sea port of Archangel in Northern Russia.[350]

AIMS FULFILLED — AND PENDING

Such is the evidence of foreign outreach during the first decade of the Bethel Movement. To what extent were original aspirations actually fulfilled? One of the declared "Foreign objects" of the parent Bethel Union in London was, by force of example, to stimulate the formation of indigenous societies of a similar nature throughout the world.[351] How far the corresponding movement in the USA was a result of British influence remains to be seen. Within the British Empire some societies did result, as already noted. Beyond this, however, the organization of foreign seamen's mission societies (in a more comprehensive sense than literature distribution) remained unrealized until the second half-century. Despite the determined efforts of an Angas and a von Bülow, the British and Foreign Seamen's Friend Society had no network of foreign agencies even remotely comparable to that of the British and Foreign Bible Society.

Greater success could be registered in providing for British (and American) seamen abroad. True, at this stage, the modest rate of income of the parent Society precluded any direct sponsorship of regular stations overseas, staffed with full-time personnel.[352] Nevertheless, in a substantial number of major foreign ports, both on the Continent and beyond, an improvised, yet surprisingly effective, form of maritime ministry had, through the potentials of the Bethel Movement, been established.

Although this ministry was, inevitably, of more immediate benefit to English-language seafarers, it was carried on in full view of both foreign crews and local landsmen. Hence there was every possibility of positive long-term influence in these quarters, too. Meanwhile, many might well appreciate that now, after the war, Englishmen were (as G.C. Smith put it) no longer setting out to destroy foreign sailors, but to bless them, under the Bethel banner of peace.[353] Some might even find reason to respond like the foreign seamen who said—after attending a British Bethel service: "Good God bless the Anglis-man — the Sailor's best friend. . . ."[354]

Chapter 12

Conflict in the Metropolis

A SECOND METROPOLITAN ESTABLISHMENT: THE LONDON MARINERS' CHURCH (1825)

By the mid-1820's, public statements by a wide range of observers were bearing witness to the radical improvement in the religious response and general moral standard of British seamen since the beginning of the Bethel Movement. At Bethel Meetings, seamen who "came to scoff, remained to pray." Their uniformly "attentive demeanour" under the preached word compared favorably with landsmen. It was widely held that at least 5,000 British seafarers had so far given evidence of personal conversion. A perceptible decrease in profanity, drunkenness and debauchery was generally acknowledged. In fact, some seriously maintained that seamen of the day seemed, by comparison, "a different species of men."[355]

Nevertheless, both the pace and scope of British seamen's mission endeavors to date convinced their warmest advocates of serious inadequacies. They saw the need for (1) a more vigorous metropolitan leadership; (2) a more direct Anglican involvement; and, (3) a more differentiated maritime ministry. The most persistent spokesman for renewal and restructurization in the first of these areas was the Rev. G.C. Smith.

Smith had soon seen a "Second Metropolitan Marine Establishment" (or seamen's mission facility) as a pressing priority, if London's leadership in the cause was to be commensurate with her maritime significance. In detail, plans progressed through three distinct phases. The original idea called for a shore chapel on the south side of the Upper Pool. The plan was to procure a "Sailors' Tabernacle" in the notorious Tooley Street district (a project which Smith had, as early as 1819, included in the prospectus of the parent Bethel Union).[356]

By the autumn of 1822, several important considerations had induced Smith to abandon this plan in favor of a "New Floating Chapel" on the north side, off the Tower. A shore-based facility (especially if it were to keep pace with changing needs for a more differentiated maritime ministry) would entail an "immense" outlay, compared with a transformed hulk. Also, the density of seamen congregating on the Tower-side of the River had now increased to a ratio of more than ten to one, compared with the Southwark side.[357]

Faced with a public statement by the PLS denying the necessity "at present" of any facility beyond their own Floating Chapel, Smith provided the BFSFSBU with potent arguments to the contrary. The average number of seamen on ships lying in the Pool at any given time, estimated at 7,000, was practically ten times as many as the *Ark* could hold. To these could be added another 9,000 watermen and lightermen.[358] Experience had already proven that, for the large proportion of this floating population lying in the Upper Pool, the distance itself was an impediment (especially against the tide).[359]

Implementation of the new plans was voluntarily arrested, however, both in 1823 and again in 1824, in deference to attempts by a group of Evangelicals in the Established Church to obtain an "Episcopal" floating sanctuary for the Thames.[360] Finally in 1825, with the latter project apparently nearing fruition, Smith sponsored plans for a "Mariner's Church" ashore, on the north side near the London Docks. In thus reverting to the concept of a land-based facility, Smith could claim three convincing arguments in his favor: (1) The "perfect ease of access" compared with a floating chapel. (2) The greater permanancy and lower long-term maintenance cost of a shore structure. (3) The need to carry the contest to the enemy, and stand by the seaman where he was most likely to founder—on shore, in the midst of the vice-haunts of Sailortown.[361]

While plans for an Episcopal "Church Ship" suffered further delay, a nondenominational London Mariners' Church did, thanks to the dogged perserverance of G.C. Smith, become a reality before the close of 1825. During one of his north-bank Sailortown field surveys, in the summer of 1824, Smith had come across the old disused Danish Church in Wellclose Square. Closer scrutiny led him to commend it to the committee of the BFSFSBU before he left London again for the winter. On his return in the summer of 1825, Smith found that nothing had been done. Exasperated at this apparent inertia, he decided to act independently.[362]

Accordingly, Smith now launched a series of seven o'clock Sabbath-morning services in the open air on Tower Hill. Huge crowds gathered and the subject of a mariners' church near the London Dock Gates was "continually pressed upon their attention." The campaign culminated in a pre-advertized Sabbath-evening open-air meeting, August 1825, when "at least 5,000 souls" heard the Seamen's Preacher publicize plans from a stand opposite the flag of the Naval Recruitment Rendezvous. A "capacious building" was already in view, where sailors might be "arrested in their fatal career to destruction," while the "hardened plunderers of their property" would learn that no longer could they "destroy Mariners with impunity."[363]

Before the end of August, Smith entered into direct negotiations with the trustees of the Danish Church and eventually contracted to rent the building, when duly repaired, at £50 per annum.[364] Meanwhile, he created the necessary organizational nucleus by collecting "a few friends" into a provisional committee, who, at a public meeting at the City of London Tavern on September 6, 1825, founded the "Mariners' Church Society." The public was informed that the new Society was to be considered "a distinct Institution," since the concerns of the BFSFSBU were "so extensive now." However, the Mariners' Church Society (MCS) wished, at this point, also to be considered a "Branch Society" of the BFSFSBU.[365] Smith freely acknowledged the term "Mariners' Church" to be "in imitation" of the United States, where it had long since become familiar.[366]

At the outset, there seemed "nothing to depend upon but the goodness of the cause." Nevertheless, the first contribution was published as a promising portent, "because it came spontaneously from a British Sailor's heart." (Hearing of the intended Mariners' Church at the close of one of Smith's open-air services, a passing "Tar" had reportedly called out, "Clear the gangway there, I've got a shot in the locker yet, I'll help any thing that does good to poor Jack. . . . Here, shipmate, here's my sixpence to begin with.")[367] Smith's faithful friend Thomas Thompson forwarded fifty guineas, with warm encouragements to persevere.[368] At length (in December 1825) repairs were ready and Britain's first, shore-based "Mariners' Church" was publicly opened.[369]

Such was both the building and its location, that George Charles Smith would wax eloquent for years to come, when reverting to what he saw as nothing less than "a sort of divine arrangement." The edifice of the Danish Church answered eminently to its new purpose; it was also already steeped in maritime tradition. Completed and consecrated in 1696, this impressive *Templum Dano-Norvegicum* had served as the Lutheran place of worship of both resident and seafaring Danes and Norwegians. With the dissolution of the union between those countries in 1814, the congregation disintegrated and services were discontinued. Nevertheless, the structure was still basically sound and capable of holding about 1,000 people.[370]

The situation of the church, in the center of the green in Wellclose Square, could hardly have been more strategic. Known formerly as "Marine Square" (from the large numbers of merchants, shipowners and captains then living there), the locality had recently undergone a radical change. With the construction of the London Docks (southeast of the Square) in 1805, and the St. Katherine's Docks (southwest of it) about to follow in 1828, this

The London Mariners' Church, Wellclose Square, for two
decades, 1825-45, the metropolitan hub of G.C. Smith's
manifold maritime ministries.
(Contemporary print by E. Duncan.)

previously genteel quarter was now being taken over by the poverty-ridden
families of seamen and waterfront workers. Leading up to it was notorious
Ratcliffe Highway, and surrounding it was a network of courts and alleys of
such ill-repute as to form the very hub of London maritime vice.[371]

Here, where great crowds of seamen would converge from as far
afield as Blackwall, Boatswain Smith determined to raise his Master's
standard and transform what he saw as the "Sodom and Gomorrah of
Sailors" into a "marine Jerusalem."[372] On the front of the building he
inscribed: *The London Mariners' Church and Rivermen's Bethel Union.*
On the roof he erected a mast and yard and hoisted a huge Bethel Flag. He
then set to, trying to translate into action the blueprint of comprehensive
"Marine Establishment," for the basic elements of which he had agitated
since 1823. Having "an eye to the Sailor's temporal as well as his spiritual
interests," he published plans embracing not only a regular preaching ministry
to British and foreign seafarers, but also day-schools for the children of
seamen and rivermen, a marine academy, a seamen's portable library,
reading-rooms for both officers and enlisted men, a marine book depot, a
seamen's register, a seamen's savings bank and a boarding-house referral
service.[373]

Further schemes for the benefit of fellow-seafarers were to follow,
several of them novel, some even revolutionary.[374] At all events, 30 years of

subsequent service as a major "Metropolitan Marine Establishment" was sufficient vindication of Smith's lone enterprise in originally securing the site. However, in so doing, he simultaneously set the scene for inter-organizational friction of far more serious consequence than that which had already developed in 1819.[375]

THE 1827 MERGER:
THE PORT OF LONDON AND BETHEL UNION SOCIETY

"There is, my Lord, one favourite motto of mine . . . *Go forward.*" These words, addressed to the chairman (Lord Gambier) at the 1820 anniversary of the BFSFSBU, aptly express the great categoric imperative of George Charles Smith's restless soul.[376] In the Seamen's Cause, once convinced of a course of action, to remain passive was for him impossible. Nor was he without encouragement. In the sensational success of the early Bethel Movement, both in the outports and abroad, no single man had played a more prominent part than Smith himself. (This was freely admitted by even his severest critics).[377] So much the keener was his sense of frustration at the continuing "low state of things in London." What with Bristol's second floating chapel, Liverpool's thriving Bethel Companies, Leith's successful social innovations, why was the great marine metropolis of London lagging behind?[378]

The annual income of the parent Bethel Union had never exceeded £500. To those of the committee of the BFSFSBU who ranged themselves behind Captain Charles Allen, caution was the watchword. Plans to "enlarge the sphere of the Society" must wait until debts had been cleared.[379] To the publicity-minded Smith, here was a vicious circle; and this could only be broken by demonstrating to the public "a real demand for funds" in the shape of what he never tired of terming a "tangible source of expenditure."[380] This was precisely what the new Marine Establishment represented.

From the moment the original contract was signed for the hire of the church in Wellclose Square, events moved inexorably toward the point of rupture. At the outset, Smith had quite evidently no intention of removing from Penzance, but published plans for pulpit supply in the Mariners' Church on the customary "Tabernacle System" (with a roster of visiting ministers alternating every six weeks).[381] However, "in a most abandoned neighbor-hood, with an empty church," Smith had virtually no choice. Pressed by practical concerns which only continued to "grow upon his hands," he realized that this would demand his all. Returning to Penzance in March 1826, he saw it as his duty "to yield up the Church and salary" there, in order to devote himself henceforth "entirely to the cause of Christ among sailors." Then, with no prospect of a penny beyond what he brought in himself, he moved, with his wife and five children, to Wellclose Square. In so doing, G.C. Smith became the first full-time resident seamen's minister in Great Britain.[382]

In actual fact, Smith had already published the basic rationale of this new concept of maritime ministry, after an 1824 field survey in the vice-haunts of Wapping:

> No good will ever be done to *the mass of Sailors* in London, until we have settled among them (like missionaries among the heathen). ... They must be *among* the Sailors to be affected with their miseries.[383]

His Penzance pastorate was, however, not the only office which Smith was now compelled to resign. Under his dynamic leadership, the new Mariners' Church Society soon took on national proportions, and rendered his official ties with the BFSFSBU increasingly problematic. Having first declined an offer of cooperation in using the building of the London Mariners' Church the committee of the BFSFSBU found themselves reduced to the role of spectators, while their foreign secretary forged ahead in the service of what was now a totally independent organizaton.[384] Although originally conceived as a *metropolitan* facility ("to cultivate all the Marine wilderness around it"), the Mariners' Church—with its many planned appendages—needed nation-wide support. The resident minister of the MCS—with all his provincial contacts and tremendous prestige—also became traveling secretary of the new Society.[385] The situation was obviously untenable. In a letter dated May 9, 1826, G.C. Smith resigned his secretaryship in the BFSFSBU.[386]

On the surface, all was still well. Both Smith's letter of resignation (underlining the pressure of his present concerns), and the committee's resolution of good wishes (for success in his "new sphere of action") were duly published in *The Sailor's Magazine*.[387] However, the continuance of Smith as editor of the latter created a situation which could not be equally easily resolved.

The committee of the BFSFSBU (under whose patronage *The Sailor's Magazine* appeared) were well aware of Smith's exceptional qualification for the task, and at the same time anxious to eliminate the risk of a rival publication. By way of compromise, a half-sheet in small print entitled *The Semaphore*, devoted entirely to the interests of the MCS, was (during 1826) included with the monthly numbers of *The Sailor's Magazine*. This arrangement proved too restrictive for the MCS, however. At the close of the year, this Society decided to publish a separate, low-priced monthly, *The Mariners' Church Steam Packet and Naval Chronicle*. The Committee of the BFSFSBU promptly retaliated by "discontinuing" (as from January 10,

1827) the editorial services of G.C. Smith in *The Sailor's Magazine*. As originator and (for seven years) sole editor of what had become an indispensable medium, Smith reacted warmly and commenced instead the publication of *The New Sailor's Magazine*. (This periodical he continued—under varying titles, but with few interruptions—from 1828 until 1863.)[388]

Simultaneously with the aggravation of relations between the BFSFSBU and the new metropolitan society, a radical realignment took place in relation to the old. The Port of London Society had reason for concern. Unwilling to follow the example of New York and appoint "a stated Minister" to the Floating Chapel, their committee had witnessed a discouraging decline of attendance over the years.[389] There were also unmistakable signs of disaffection within the ranks, coupled with a disheartening public response.[390] Nevertheless, the PLS had hitherto shown no wish to alter its official stance of respectful but complete separation from the BFSFSBU.[391]

On the other hand, by the mid-1820's, the BFSFSBU, too, seemed decidedly "in a declining state."[392] Finally, faced with the fact of a rapidly expanding third nondenominational "Seamen's Society" in the metropolis, the committee of the BFSFSBU resolved that the time was ripe for a new initiative. With the Angas brothers playing a conspicuous part in the preliminaries, a meeting was arranged for December 19, 1826, at John's Coffee House in the City, between deputations from the BFSFSBU and the PLS, in order to discuss a possible merger.[393] Here it was agreed:

> [That] many persons of note & the voice of the Public generally were desirous of a union the public mind being distracted and divided by so many Societies for the same object. That a lessening of expence & strength to carry forward the good object was desirable. . . . That Mr. Marten be Treasurer of the new Society, to be called Port of London & Bethel Union Society, for the promotion of Religion amongst British & Foreign Seamen United 1827. To be understood by the Committees as taking place from the 1st of January.[394]

Accordingly, a public meeting was held February 15, 1827, at the Argyle Rooms, Regent Street, to provide public recognition of the union and confirmation of the founding of the "Port of London and Bethel Union Society" (PLBUS). Admiral Gambier took the chair and became president of the merged Society. The "most lively satisfaction" was felt that "needless rivalry" was now at an end, thus eliminating both operational duplicaton and promotional ambiguity.[395]

As a "stationary token of the Bethel Cause being identified with the Port of London Society," a Bethel Flag was, for the first time in history, hoisted on board the Floating Chapel.[396] In several major British ports, the successful combinaton of floating chapel and Bethel Union in one and the same society had long since proved the non-existence of any inherent conflict between these two forms of seamen's mission activity. However, tension between the two metropolitan societies was now openly admitted to have been such, that it had "frequently threatened the destruction of both."[397] The question arises, therefore, what new circumstances could have prompted the PLS to this complete reversal of policy?

In the first place, the committee of the PLS had harvested powerful reasons to regret their original attitude towards the parent Bethel Union. (Their isolationism had cost them much of that subtle but vital asset in all forms of maritime ministry, the goodwill of seamen;[398] it had also deprived them of the public appeal of a movement with so much "bolder flight and wider range.")[399] In the second place, the termination of G.C. Smith's official connection with the BFSFSBU removed what was felt by influential members of the PLS Committee as a major impediment to uniting.[400]

Nevertheless, despite auspicious appearances, time would soon show that disunion was far from eliminated on the metropolitan scene. On the contrary, the union of 1827 was destined to become only the signal for open warfare.

THE ERUPTION OF PUBLIC CONTROVERSY: DISSOLUTION OF THE BRITISH AND FOREIGN SEAMEN AND SOLDIERS' FRIEND SOCIETY

In dealing with the fateful hostilities which erupted between the metropolitan seamen's mission societies in 1827, the future historian would, according to G.C. Smith, be faced with a formidable task, in trying to "sift and investigate for truth amidst rubbish of reports, speeches, circulars, and resolutions."[401] Certainly, the record of this religious civil war was for years to fill both periodicals and newspapers with masses of unedifying print. Apart from other considerations, mere limitations of space forbid elaboration. (Sources of reference for further details are indicated in the notes for this chapter.) However, the course and cost of the conflict were to affect so fundamentally the development of British seamen's missions, that an analysis in outline becomes indispensable.

Pervading the whole controversy seem to have been two basic causes of contention. There was (1) a distinct polarization of principles. Was organizational monopolism or pluralism to dominate the interdenominational ministry to seafarers on the metropolitan (and national) scene? (The PLBUS was evidently unwilling to concede any real justification for the latter.)

Added to this, there was (2) a mounting conflict of personalities. To leading elements in the PLBUS, cooperation with the free-spoken, strong-willed Seamen's Preacher had already become unthinkable. At all events, the situation soon escalated into a veritable "war of extermination."[402]

The immediate pretext for war was provided shortly after the union, in February 1827, of the two original London-based societies. In order to promote the rapidly expanding program of the MCS, Smith continued to develop a deliberate nationwide appeal, traveling personally an average of a fortnight a month, also engaging assistant traveling secretaries, preaching collection sermons and forming auxiliaries, in inland towns and wherever possible.[403]

Since the PLBUS had virtually "abandoned" the major part of the title of the former BFSFSBU, Smith felt free to appropriate this for his own Society, including with it an allusion to a new outreach to soldiers. The MCS was, therefore, officially renamed "The British and Foreign Seamen's and Soldiers' Friend Society" (BFSSFS), with the occasional addition "or Mariners' Church and Watermen's (Rivermen's) Bethel Union."[404]

The PLBUS thereupon delivered what Smith and the BFSSFS interpreted as a formal declaration of "open warfare." In April and May of 1827, circulars were published warning the public against a "mistaken appropriation of funds," due to a "completely distinct Society" assuming organizational and magazine titles which both closely resembled those of one of the recently-merged societies.[405] Dr. John Styles, a Congregatonal minister with a reputation as a pungent polemic, had just been engaged by the PLBUS as editor of *The Sailor's Magazine*; he was now entrusted with the task of following up the attack.[406] This he began by publishing the following assertion:

> We [the PLBUS] cannot possibly imagine a necessity for the establishment of any similar *independent* Institution within the territories of the three kingdoms. Separation from such a Society deserves no milder epithet than that of schism. . . ."[407]

Added to this formulation of uncompromising monopolism were unveiled allusions to "low cunning, . . . bearing our colours, but making war on our resources." Smith immediately took up the challenge with typical over-reaction. If it was an open fight this "fresh water sailor" from Brixton wanted, one who had "stood the fire of the hottest battles" was not now likely to be "afraid of squibs and crackers."[408] To intermittent attacks from Styles and his committee, Smith replied with a whole series of literary broadsides, mainly in the shape of warmly-worded tracts, written during 1827-28. Their primary purpose was, by reference to the course of past events, to demonstrate the need for the new Society and justify the nature of Smith's personal involvement.[409]

Smith's continued success, coupled with their own diminishing support, caused the committee of the PLBUS obvious alarm. Their editor (now also appointed traveling secretary) was commissioned to deal a decisive blow. In the course of 1828, Dr. Styles prepared a scathing 144-page denunciation of their opponent, published early 1829 in the name of the committee, and entitled *An Appeal to the Public, Being an Answer to the Misrepresentation and Calumnies of the Rev. G.C. Smith.* Although it was systematically circulated and allegedly intended to "blast and destroy" Smith's reputation "all over the kingdom," the injurious effect of all this invective was largely neutralized from an unexpected quarter.[410]

Those two veterans of the Seamen's Cause from Thames Revival days, Thomas Thompson and Thomas Phillips, had continued as honorary secretaries of the societies which merged in February 1827. The following year, these widely-respected lay leaders caused a sensation in the religious world, by tendering their resignations from the PLBUS, in September and December, respectively.[411] Having failed in a final peace-bid, they published jointly, in April 1829, a 40-page pamphlet called *Refutation: Being a Reply to the "Appeal" of the Port of London Society.* Here they both give, as their reason for resigning, persistent intransigence and inactivity by the PLBUS. Then, by powerful, factual argument, they successively refute the imputations of the *Appeal* against the character of G.C. Smith. While unwilling to exonerate him on every score (notably his warmth of temperament), they convincingly vindicate hs personal integrity.[412] As to his unique contribution to the cause, Thompson makes this prediction:

> The records of history which shall tell of a Howard for prisoners, a Wilberforce and Clarkson for slaves, ... shall also tell of George Charles Smith as the unwearied, disinterested, faithful, laborer for seamen of the world.[413]

Whereas Thompson and Phillips could, as secretaries in each of the two original societies from their very foundation, write from first-hand knowledge, Styles, as a newcomer, exposed himself to both omissions and contradictons. Nor could his subsequent *Reply* alter the public impression, that the *Refutation* remained unrefuted.[414] This conclusion was clearly reflected in the relative status of the PLBUS and the BFSSFS at this juncture. The former had to face a continued falling off in attendance at the *Ark,* and an obviously fatal financial trend. (Total receipts of the PLBUS equalled barely half the former meager incomes of the merging societies.)[415] The BFSSFS, on the other hand, could, in May 1829, show four times the income (over £3,000), a well-frequented Mariners' Church, with several subsidiary stations, new branch activities of great promise and a truly impressive list of patrons and officers.[416]

The stormy start of the British and Foreign Seamen and Soldiers' Friend Society thus culminated in endorsement on a scale hitherto unprecedented. For George Charles Smith personally, the early summer of 1829 marked the very zenith of his public prestige. Heading the list of naval patrons of Evangelical affiliation, Admiral Gambier showed Smith warm, personal solicitude.[417] One of the Evangelical clergymen on the committee, the Rev. Richard Marks, had, after careful investigation of the facts of the interorganizational feud, severed connections with the PLBUS; he now gave Smith his unstinted public support, as "one of the most persecuted men in this kingdom."[418]

Speaking at the triumphant 1829 anniversary of the BFSSFS, Smith's colleague from the *Agenoria* service twelve years previously, the Rev. W. Shenstone, expressed the pious hope that his friend would henceforth have to fight with "no other foe than the prince of darkness."[419] As it proved, the early summer of 1829 brought no lasting peace, only a respite. However, in this second phase of the conflict (1829-31), the PLBUS abstained from further direct assault; instead, Smith and the BFSSFS were subjected to two distinct waves of indirect attack, this time from individuals.

First came the so-called "Philo-Veritas" controversy, a veritable poison-pen campaign launched in August 1829. A misinformed ministerial secretary of the PLBUS, signing himself Philo-Veritas, circulated a host of defamatory letters charging Smith with gross embezzlement, in connection with the new Sailors' Home, then being projected. The charges caused commotion in both press and pulpit, far and wide, before being exposed as utterly unfounded, and followed, in November, by the public apology of the author. (The fact that Smith refrained from publishing his calumniator's name was the only redeeming feature of this tragic tale.)[420]

Next, in 1831, came the so-called "Voice" controversy. Boatswain Smith had no mercy with stowaways among his hardworking crew. In the spring of 1831, he dismissed "some worthless servants," among them his recording secretary, one Joseph Mead (for "excessive indolence"). Young Mead retaliated by publishing, in the summer, a 68-page tract entitled *A Voice from Wellclose Square,* purporting to give a narrative of the BFSSFS, including a "complete exposure of the conduct of the Rev. G.C. Smith." Representing the Society as "distinguished only by defraud," the book "sold fast all over the kingdom," and succeeded in closing hundreds of pulpits against Smith and his coadjutors.[421] The Rev. John Sibree, a leading Congregatonal minister in Coventry, also gave credence to the contents, and, without any apparent attempt at first-hand investigation, published, during the autumn, a series of virulent attacks on Smith and his Society in the *World* newspaper.[422]

By the close of the year, this new campaign of calumny, coordinated by a "confluence of discarded agents," employing both anonymous letters and defamatory pamphlets, had brought the Society to the brink of ruin.[423] Although receipts for the past year had reached a record of over £5,000, they could not keep pace with the daily demands of the Society's widespread activities. Six years of accumulated debts had already passed £2,500 and continued to mount. Creditors clamored. Both Smith and his colleagues were in serious arrears of salary. Despite a debt fund launched with the Lord Mayor himself as treasurer, it was clearly a losing battle.[424]

At length, in December 1831, Smith struck upon a plan which seemed to offer hope. In order to "stem the torrent of obloquy," the BFSSFS instituted a public inquiry into all the affairs of the Society, to be carried out by an interdenominational twenty-member committee of well-known ministers and laymen. After four days of exhaustive examination of facilities, staff and accounts (January 17-20, 1832), this committee published its report. Here, Smith and his colleagues were "completely exonerated . . . from any misappropriation or want of integrity." While warmly commending Smith's general conduct of the Society and all its "highly-adapted" activities, the report did, however, make certain recommendations, among them the formation of a board of directors.[425]

After protracted negotiations, a provisional board of directors, consisting of metropolitan Dissenting ministers, was eventually appointed in June 1832, with Dr. Francis Augustus Cox (Baptist Minister of Hackney) and the Rev. John Clayton, Jr. (Congregational Minister of the Poultry) as leading members. To this body, Smith willingly transferred the entire management of the Society, with the exception of the Mariners' Church and one magazine (which it was agreed he would continue independently).[426] On July 23, the Directors advertized in the *Patriot* newspaper their readiness to apply any income in excess of current expenses to the liquidation of the Society's debts (which had now passed £3,000). Then, only a week later, on August 1, the *Patriot* carried a sensational notice, announcing the complete withdrawal of half the board, headed by Clayton. Cox and the remainder followed suit a fortnight later.[427]

Smith had no illusion as to the significance of this fateful event. Left with overwhelming debts, his treasury empty and his committee dissolved, he knew full well—as from August 1832, the British and Foreign Seamen and Soldiers' Friend Society "was no more."[428] This was bound to have far-reaching repercussions.

To George Charles Smith, there was only one explanation of the disastrous turn of events of the summer of 1832. By their "desertion," the newly-appointed directors had dealt a deliberate "deathblow" to the greatest "Seamen's Society" in the kingdom.[429] His indignation knew no bounds.

Was his reaction justified? Specifically, was he correct in assuming the complicity in this connection of his personal antagonists in the "Port Society?"[430]

With an "almost deserted" Floating Chapel and receipts only a fraction of those of the BFSSFS, the Port of London and Bethel Union Society, too, faced a crisis situation at the outset of 1832.[431] However, their troubles were of a diametrically opposite nature to those of their rival. Instead of being plagued by the consequences of over-activity, they were, on their own admission, "getting becalmed." Or, to quote their debt-ridden adversary, "If they had done more work, they must have spent more money."[432]

Certainly, as the year progressed, the Port Society presented a sorry picture indeed. In February, they boycotted a reconciliation meeting proposed by the BFSSFS. Speeches at their annual meeting in May were remarkable for their frank pessimism. In July, it was members of the committee of the PLBUS who allegedly interceded with the Rev. Clayton to take the lead in the mass-resignation of BFSSFS directors, resulting in the ruin of this Society. Shortly afterwards, they launched an advertising campaign in order to prepare their transformation into a far more comprehensive Sailors' Religious Society, but found they had to abandon the attempt in November. Finally, at the close of the year, The (Old) Sailor's Magazine (which Smith had always considered "violently torn" from him in 1827) was given up, for the time being, after disastrously dwindling sales.[433]

Whatever pressure there may or may not have been from the fast-sinking Port Society, published documents indicate that Clayton and his colleagues at one point had hopes of effecting a "cordial union" of the two rival societies, and that they resigned when they realised that certain unspecified "obstructions" were "insurmountable." Foremost among these was no doubt Smith's refusal to abstain from another (and separate) organization, thus rendering a union pointless, and prolonged polarization inevitable.[434]

From Smith's viewpoint, there seemed no alternative. His sense of vocation was as strong as ever: "I dare not leave the work. I should as soon think of drowning myself in the Thames. I am chained to the oar."[435] In order to pursue this calling, there were two means he consistently considered as indispensable—his church and his magazine. If the BFSSFS were to be united with a society in which he had long since lost all confidence, Smith felt compelled to safeguard these two basic resources by securing some form of independent organizational framework.[436]

Faced with the dissolution of the BFSSFS, the embattled "Bosun" saw a new organization as an even more dire necessity. Dazed, but by no means defeated, he decided forthwith to "arraign all the directors at the bar of public opinion," advertising in the following vein:

> To save the cause from the most fatal shipwreck and the most
> lubberly pilots, the London Mariners' Church Society will be
> publicly established at the City of London Tavern, Bishopsgate-
> street, on Wednesday, October 10th, in the presence, it is hoped,
> of many blue jackets, who will nail their colours to the mast and
> go down with the ship, sooner than strike to any letter of marque
> on the ocean.[437]

The response was, indeed, encouraging. The meeting was "crowded
to excess," and a new body, the "London Mariners' Church Society, or
Bethel Flag Union" was duly formed.[438] True, the debts of the BFSSFS
rebounded onto Smith (posing a constant threat of imprisonment), the situation of the former Society's agents was distressing in the extreme, and it was
bereaved of all its branch activities.[439] Nevertheless, with his reduced band
of coadjutors, Smith set about systematically "reconquering all the ground
lost by the late destroyed Society." Within half a year, the new Society's
receipts had already exceeded those of its rival for a full year. As a result, in
April 1833, the Society publicly adopted a new national title, as the "British
and Foreign Sailors' and Soldiers' Bethel Flag Union."[440]

However, among those who during 1832 had striven in vain to
reconstitute a united, national seamen's mission society, there were some
who were obviously not content to remain passive. Conspicuous among
these was Dr. F.A. Cox. This influential metropolitan minister had earlier
identified himself with G.C. Smith and the BFSSFS, and it was only "with
regret" that he had later followed the Rev. John Clayton's lead and resigned
his directorship in that Society—in mid-August 1832.[441] The next year, Dr.
Cox decided the time was ripe for a new initiative, entirely independent of
Smith. In this, his fellow-Baptist, George Fife Angas, readily concurred.
Angas was entrusted with the important task of first "sounding the friends of
seamen throughout the country."[442] Then, on May 6, 1833, at a public
meeting held at the London Tavern, with the Lord Mayor (Sir Peter Laurie)
in the chair, a new national nondenominational seamen's mission society,
called quite simply the "Sailors' Society" came into being.[443]

In the words of the constitutive resolution (moved by Dr. Cox,
honorary secretary of the new enterprise), a major motive was, "by avoiding
sectarian distinctions, party prejudices, and personal hostilities," to make it
possible to "associate the energies of all Christians in one united effort."[444]
There is no record of any endeavor to come to terms with G.C. Smith and
the British and Foreign Sailors' and Soldiers' Bethel Flag Union. With the
Port Society, on the other hand, the position was quite different. At the
annual meeting of the PLBUS (also held May 6, 1833, there was ample
evidence of a continuing fatal trend in this Society's affairs. However, the

Rev. John Clayton, Jr. undertook to attempt to "resuscitate" the PLBUS, whereupon negotiations were opened for merging with the new Sailors' Society.[445]

These negotiations culminated in the absorption, on July 3, 1833, of the Port Society into the Sailors' Society, under the designation "British and Foreign Sailors' Society, for promoting their moral and religious improvement." The public meeting consumating the event was held at the City of London Tavern. Lord Henley, already widely known for his warm advocacy of organizational reform in the Church of England, took the chair. As honorary secretaries were elected Dr. F.A. Cox and the Rev.Thomas Timpson (a Congregational minister in the village of Lewisham by Blackheath). After fifteen years' treasurership in the PLS and PLBUS successively, R.H. Marten now retired, while Alderman John Pirie and (shortly afterwards) G.F. Angas became treasurers of the new Society. As board of directors were elected 70 of "the most influential merchants and ministers in London" (largely Dissenters of Congregational and Baptist affiliation). Angas procured the premises which, for more than two decades, were to be the offices of the Society: 2 Jeffrey Square, St. Mary Axe.[446]

A comparison between the aims and means of the Sailors' Society and those of the British and Foreign Sailors' Society (BFSS) reveals close identity, affirming that the PLBUS was, essentially, absorbed into the new Society, not merely united on equal terms.[447] Even the acquisition of the Port Society's Floating Chapel was of no major consequence; this was very evidently already ripe for replacement (by a chapel ashore).[448] Nevertheless, it was the inclusion of the Port Society in 1833 which enabled the BFSS to claim 1818 as its earliest origin,[449] and (in due course) George Charles Smith as its earliest pioneer.[450]

Thus, the turmoil of the 'twenties had, by 1833, resulted in the emergence of two distinct metropolitan seamen's mission organizations, each purporting to fill the role of a nondenominational national society, the Smith-sponsored British and Foreign Sailors' and Soldiers' Bethel Flag Union and the powerfully-patronized British and Foreign Sailors' Society.[451] Before attempting to assess the significance of this situation and tracing its eventual outcome, it will be necessary to examine the distinct differentiation of the maritime ministry which emerged concurrently with and in spite of the society-strife in the metropolis. This process led to an extensive diversification in terms of denominational participation, categories of coadjutors, field of mission and diaconal ministry.

PART V

CRIMPS AND CRUSADERS

Early Differentiation of
British Maritime Mission

Chapter 13

Early Anglican Endeavors

THE ANGLICAN DILEMMA

During the period under review (1818-33), prior to the advent of the Oxford Movement, spiritual activism in the Church of England was still largely limited to the Evangelical Party.[1] In the field of foreign missions, the latter had long since responded to the need for a separate society within the Established Church (1799). However, by the beginning of the 1820's, there was still no "Church *Seamen's* Missionary Society."

True, the concept of a society organized for the specific purpose of promoting the spiritual welfare of seamen was by then not entirely novel in Anglican circles. Even as early as 1805, a naval commander signing himself "R.J.N." published in *The Christian Observer* a well motivated proposal for a so-called "Naval Religious Society." The Society would have the object of "encouraging morality and piety" among seamen (presumably primarily in the navy). This it would do by seeking to reward "virtuous conduct" and check "prevailing vices" among them. An essential adjunct was the provision of "pious books" to every ship (Scriptures, religious tracts and Common Prayer Books). Although the writer's simultaneous suggestions for the reform of the naval chaplaincy service met with more rapid results, the plan for an organized society of the nature described was in itself remarkable at this early juncture.[2]

Fifteen years later, *The Sailor's Magazine* featured an article entitled "Church Ship," where an anonymous naval officer, commending the initiative of the Dissenters, puts the question: "Have Churchmen no obligation to do good among British Seamen also?" Strongly stressing the indebtedness of the nation (and, therefore, the National Church) to her "brave tars," he urges the immediate establishment of an "Episcopal Ark" in the Upper Pool, off the Tower of London. Moored here, it would be "sufficiently distant from the Floating Chapel [at Wapping] and in the center of a vast body of seamen on both banks of the river." Dr. Thomas Scott, renowned commentator and veteran advocate of the Church Missionary Society, wrote the same year (1820): "I should rejoice if a *Church Ark* could be formed, and respectably supported. . . ."[3]

Nevertheless, these were lone voices in the wilderness. Numerically Evangelical clergymen in the Established Church were, in 1820, still outnumbered by something like twenty to one; and the chances of any initiative on their part being "respectably supported" (at least ecclesiastically) were critically curtailed by the fact that they had as yet only one avowed adherent on the Episcopal Bench.[4] The early efforts of such Dissenting pioneers as R.H. Marten and G.C. Smith, to motivate the mobilization of "the *wealth,* the *piety,* and the *influence* of the Establishment" in the cause, seemed even less capable of affecting the inertia inherent in a state church structure.[5]

Anglican "friends of seamen" were, therefore, faced with a frustrating dilemma: either to remain passive pending the ultimate emergence (if ever) of specifically Anglican seamen's mission societies, or actively to support existing nondenominational societies, within the confines of Anglican church order. Despite evident High Church disapproval, Evangelical clergy and laymen chose at first the course of such "united front" action. Their position was eloquently put by one clergyman, preaching on behalf of a nondenominational seamen's mission society in an Anglican church:

> Perhaps, however, someone may say. How far is it consistent for you, as a Minister of the Church of England, to call upon us who are members of that Church, to contribute to the support of a Society, the operations of which must, under existing circumstances, be almost entirely conducted by Dissenting agents; and the places of worship opened by which, must be licensed or registered as Dissenting places. . . . Were there any Society conducted by Churchmen for these especial objects, the question would be entirely different. . . . [I would then have] devoted the little property or talent I could employ exclusively to what appeared to me the more excellent way. But while no such society exists, . . . I stand forth and call upon my fellow Churchmen . . . to come forward in this great work. The question is not whether our Sailors shall be Churchmen or Dissenters: it is one of infinitely more importance—it is, whether they shall be Christians or heathens. . . . To me it has ever appeared, that the way to make Churchmen is to make Christians.[6]

To a degree, this battle had already been fought and won by the British and Foreign Bible Society.[7] At all events, from the very outset, British nondenominational societies, both those specializing in marine Christian literature distribution and those involved in more comprehensive seamen's mission programs, came to depend heavily on the financial support of members of the Established Church. Some clergymen and (consequent on the Naval Awakening) a whole host of naval officers of Anglican affiliation served on the committees of these societies; such naval officers also frequently assumed important promotional and operational responsibilities.[8] Their spirit of uncomplicated, seaman-like cooperation was aptly epitomized by one Evanglical Admiral. What the situation called for, he said, was simply "a long pull, and a strong pull, and a pull altogether."[9]

However, despite Dissenters' reiterated readiness to unite with their Evangelical "brethren of the Establishment" in unsectarian societies serving seamen,[10] and despite considerable positive response, there were factors exerting powerful pressure in the direction of separate Anglican societies. Two of the strongest such factors were: (1) Circumscription of the potential participation of the Anglican clergy (who were canonically prevented from ministering in chapels not "episcopally consecrated and governed"). (2) Discrimination against the needs of the seafaring Anglican laity (who were exposed to constant confusion through lack of uniformity of doctrine, and whose "predilections for the ritual and service of Episcopacy" were widespread).[11]

Attempts were made to justify delay of official involvement by the Church of England in this area. In the words of the Evangelical Bishop of Chester (1828):

> If it be said, that the Established Church has moved slowly [compared with the Dissenters] . . . , let it be remembered, that it is not only natural, but necessary, that such a body should, in these matters, move with great caution and deliberation, and not till after due enquiry. . . .[12]

However, the general mood among Evangelical supporters of the Seamen's Cause was one of mounting self-incrimination for past lethargy, coupled with unstinted praise for the achievements of the Dissenters.[13] At length, demands for independent Anglican action gave results, although (significantly) not first in London.

PROVINCIAL BEGINNINGS: THE FIRST ANGLICAN MARINERS' CHURCHES

The first seamen's chapel in the Church of England was opened for service as early as March 1823, in the the port of Dublin. This fact has hitherto been largely overlooked.[14] However, that the capital of Ireland should thus lead the van is not surprising. Here Evangelical clergy were both strongly embedded and particularly militant.[15]

The Port of Dublin Society ("for promoting the religious instruction of Seamen, agreeable to the constitution of the Established Church") was founded September 25, 1822. The original initiative was attributed to "a few Naval Officers and other Gentlemen," impressed with the fact that exactly those most exposed to the stroke of death were "least apprehensive of the consequences. . . ." The endeavor met with the "entire approbation" of the Archbishop of Dublin, and the active support of Admirals Rowley and Oliver.[16]

Freely acknowledging the commendable example set by Dissenters elsewhere (including the key role played by G.C. Smith), these Anglican pioneers purchased a Danish vessel, the *Prince Christian* of about 250 tons; this was transformed to accommodate some 400 persons, and moored in the River Liffey ("at the basin near Ringsend"). A "blue flag with the dove on it" was hoisted as signal for worship. Results were eminently encouraging. Whereas the reformation of seamen had previously been regarded as "chimerical," it was reported that they in fact responded to the invitation to attend services "with avidity." The Rev. Thomas Gregg, who had, shortly after the opening, been appointed chaplain on board, became so popular with the men, that they entreated him to sail with them on their voyages. For several years to come, the Dublin Floating Church continued to flourish.[17]

By the close of 1825, however, no place of worship for the specific benefit of seamen had as yet been established by the National Church itself. It was against this disturbing background that the Rev. Richard Marks at length instigated the first comprehensive publicity campaign on behalf of the Seamen's Cause by a Church of England spokesman. With the warm encouragement of G.C. Smith (who had, as editor of *The Sailor's Magazine,* continued to advocate official Anglican involvement in the service of seafarers), the former naval lieutenant, now Vicar of Great Missenden, published "An Appeal to the Christian Public in behalf of British Seamen." This took the form of a series of five strongly-worded letters printed, as from January 1826, in a widely-read Church of England periodical, *The Christian Guardian.*[18] Spurred by the "extraordinary" interest aroused by these letters, and brought up to date as to current conditions in London's dockland by G.C. Smith (who took him on a guided tour of "Satan's undisturbed and favourite kingdom"), Marks followed up with a new series of five articles in the same vein and in the same publication, entitled "The Seamen's Friend" (1826-27).[19]

Marks made his position quite clear. Aware, as he was, of the unsuccessful attempts hitherto made in the metropolis, he was prepared that "many years" would yet elapse before "the Bishops and Clergy of the Established Church in general" could be expected to sanction anything approaching a national Anglican seamen's mission society. There were still "a thousand difficulties in the way."[20] Beyond commenting on the inevitably "irregular" nature of a Church ministry to seafarers, Marks refused to elaborate on immediate impediments.[21] Instead, he warmly encouraged (and

personally negotiated) individual Anglican financial support for existing
nondenominational societies.[22]

Nevertheless, Marks' powerful plea for a more general Anglican
involvement in the Seamen's Cause served to fan his fellow Churchmen's
spirit of emulation; and he left no doubt as to their loyalty where an
"episcopal establishment for seamen" proved practicable.[23] By the close of
1826, there was tangible evidence of the latter not only in Dublin but also in
Liverpool.

Liverpool had, in common with many other ports, a parochial church
of Medieval origin, dedicated to the patron saint of seafarers. In practice,
however, St. Nicholas' Church, Liverpool, was—like its namesakes elsewhere
—largely a church for regular resident parishioners, with neither the staff nor
the facilities for an Anglican ministry to the estimated 10,000 seamen and
port workers normally in the area.[24] Awakened to this challenge by the
example recently set by the Nonconformists, a number of concerned clergymen and laymen consulted together "on various occasions, during the years
1822 and 1823," formed themselves into a provisional committee, and
commenced negotiations for the grant of a redundant warship to be transformed into an Anglican Mariners' Church.[25]

Despite delays, plans progressed to the point where, on April 26,
1825, at a public meeting in the Town Hall, the "Liverpool Mariners'
Church Society" was established ("for promoting the religious instruction of
seamen, agreeably to the constitution of the Established Church").[26] At
length, largely as a result of the persevering cooperation of the Diocesan, the
Bishop of Chester, and the "ready compliance" of the First Lord of the
Admiralty, Viscount Melville, HMS *Tees* was loaned by the Government on
particularly generous terms. A 40-gun frigate which had once seen service
under Nelson, the *Tees* had latterly (1825-26) been commanded by the
subsequently famous naval novelist, Captain Frederick Marryat. Arriving
from Plymouth under tow in November 1826, she was fitted up in the course
of the winter for her final commission. Moored in the southwest corner of
George's Dock (by the present Pier Head), the former warship was opened
on May 17, 1827, as "the first place of worship in Great Britain, under the
Establishment, for the use of seamen."[27] (The committee adopted the
designation "Mariners' Church," as used by G.C. Smith in London.)[28]

The choice of chaplain was well-founded. Born at Cropton, near
Whitby, William Scoresby the Younger (1789-1857) had already made a
rapid and brilliant career as both whaling-ship captain and Arctic scientist.
(His pioneering achievements in the latter field eventually earned him international recognition.) Subsequent to a conversion experience around 1817,
Scoresby made a practice of holding regular religious services on all ships
under his command and became known as a strict Sabbatarian. Having
moved to Liverpool in 1819, he co-operated whole-heartedly with G.C.

Dr. William Scoresby, the
Younger (1789-1857), arctic
explorer, scientist and first
full-time Anglican seamen's
chaplain in Great Britain.
(R.E. Scoresby-Jackson:
The Life of William Scoresby.)

Smith and others in the founding (1821) and early promotion of the Liverpool
Seamen's Friend Society and Bethel Union. Then, in 1823, at the height of
his professional career, he acted upon what had become a "deeply-rooted
desire for the work of Christ's ministry." After intense studies at Queen's
College, Cambridge, he offered himself for ordination in 1825 to the modest
curacy of Bessingby, near Bridlington Quay.[29]

It was at Bessingby, toward the close of 1826, that Scoresby was
now approached by friends on the committee of the newly-formed Liverpool
Mariners' Church Society. Sensing a strong personal obligation through his
"intimate acquaintance with the sailor, his habits of thought, prejudice,
language, and prepossessions," Scoresby saw here the hand of Providence,
was unanimously appointed, and thus became the first full-time Anglican
seamen's chaplain in Great Britain. Duly licensed by the Bishop of Chester,
he entered on his Merseyside ministry in May 1827, the day the Floating
Church was opened.[30]

Evidently, expectations were amply fulfilled. An average of 800, the
majority of them seafarers, crowded into the services during the first year,
the consistent "sobriety and fixed attention" of the seamen serving to
confound every sceptic. For five years, Scoresby continued his unremitting
labors in Liverpool's docklands. A key factor in the "remarkable success"
attending his ministry was the regular program of ship visitation which he
maintained from week to week. On these occasions, he made a particular
point of cultivating the friendship of fellow-captains, "both with a view,
under the Divine blessing, to the promotion of religion among them personally,
and through their instrumentality, among the sailors under their command."[31]

It is possible that Scoresby's chaplaincy at the Liverpool Mariners' Church would have continued many years yet. By 1832, however, his wife's health made a change imperative; moving to the more congenial climate of Exeter, he succeeded to the incumbancy of Bedford Chapel.[32]

Nevertheless, the Rev. William Scoresby (who in 1839 was created a Doctor of Divinity) retained a deep concern for the spiritual welfare of his fellow-seafarers, and continued his significant contributions to their devotional literature. As early as 1822, before leaving the sea, he had published a *Seamen's Prayer Book*; this was based on the Book of Common Prayer, but partly abridged, partly supplemented, so as to become better adapted to the needs and sensitivities of seamen. Intended to stimulate services and devotions on shipboard, the book became a notable success and was extensively used on both Greenland vessels and merchantmen.[33] In 1831, he published *Discourses to Seamen,* a selection of fifteen sermons preached in the Mariners' Church, reminiscent of Richard Marks' authorship in their strongly evangelical content and their striking use of nautical imagery.[34] Then, in 1835, came his *Memorials of the Sea,* with its powerful plea for consistent Sabbath observance on shipboard; this was partly republished fifteen years later.[35]

The floating Mariners' Church on the Mersey continued in service for many years following Scoresby's pioneering efforts.[36] Meanwhile, corresponding endeavors on the Humber led to the erection of the first *shore-based* Anglican mariners' church in the kingdom, in Hull.

Much of the credit was due to the churchbuilding zeal of the renowned Rector of St. John's, the Rev. Thomas Dykes, and his son, William Dykes, of shipbuilding fame. Both had, with other Evangelical Churchmen, already been intimately involved in the foundation (1821) and expansion of the nondenominational Port of Hull Society.[37] Nevertheless, the need for an additional specifically Anglican seamen's church in Hull had become increasingly apparent. As in other ports, G.C. Smith had cordially encouraged this concern (even enlisting, during a lengthy interview in 1824, the active support of the Archbishop of York).[38] Finally, after a provisional committee had been formed and preliminary plans laid (1827), the "Mariners' Church Society" was officially established at a public meeting at the Mansion House, January 28, 1828, for the "religious instruction of the seamen of the Port of Hull, conformably to the principles of the Church of England."[39]

Although the Admiralty was willing to provide a dismantled warship for a floating church, the provisional committee had already abandoned this thought for three reasons: (1) heavy anticipated maintenance costs, (2) lack of convenient mooring place, (3) winter lighting restrictions on the docks.[40] Providentially, a spacious, disused Dissenting Chapel in Dagger Lane was available, strategically situated on Prince's Dockside. This was leased, licensed by the Archbishop as Hull Mariners' Church, and opened February

The Liverpool Mariners' Floating Church, formerly
HMS *Tees,* moored in George's Dock (by Pier Head)
and opened May 17, 1827, as the first Anglican church
for seafarers ever established in Great Britain.
(M.R. Kingsford: *The Mersey Mission to Seamen, 1856-1956.*)

Interior view of the Liverpool Mariners' Floating Church,
showing seamen and their families gathering for service.
(M.R. Kingsford: *The Mersey Mission to Seamen, 1856-1956.*)

17, 1828. The Rev. John Robinson was ordained as its first minister (and also became chaplain to the local Trinity House).[41] From the outset, as in Liverpool, a spirit of mutual goodwill and respect was evident between the two societies now operating in the same port. Extension—not competition—was the watchword.[42] As the work progressed, it was decided to pull down the original building, and erect on the same site a new, brick Mariners' Church. Opened June 15, 1834 this remained in use for some seventy years.[43]

Well ahead of Hull, the building of a shore-based Anglican mariners' church in Plymouth was initiated before the close of 1826 by the Rev. John Hatchard, Vicar of St. Andrew's. Scarcity of funds hampered the completion of the project, however.[44]

In Cork, a public meeting with the Dean of Cork in the chair endorsed in 1830 the initiative of local Churchmen, who had recently fitted up a suitable vessel as an Anglican floating chapel, and duly appointed a chaplain.[45] From far-off India came news of the erection in Calcutta of an Anglican mariners' church opened May 16, 1830. The project was promoted at the outset by the SPG, as a counterpart to the work of the nondenominational Calcutta Seamen's Friend Society.[46] In January the following year, the Anglicans were able to open a floating chapel in Bombay.[47]

THE METROPOLITAN SCENE: THE EPISCOPAL FLOATING CHURCH SOCIETY (FOUNDED JULY 20, 1825)

Meanwhile, what had come of the proposals from as far back as 1820, for the establishment of an "Episcopal Ark" in the metropolis? After abortive attempts both in 1823 and 1824, the summer of 1825 seemed at length to Anglican advocates of the plan to be the auspicious time. In fact, they felt justified in presenting a project with a vastly wider scope than originally conceived.[48]

The promoters, a provisional committee composed of "noblemen and gentlemen of the Establishment," believed they had good grounds for optimism. Besides the successful initiative of the Dissenters in several ports, two years' experience by Anglicans in Dublin had produced "almost incredible" results. A similar society had recently been organized in Liverpool. Apprized of the plans for a metropolitan society in connection with the National Church, Viscount Melville had now, on behalf of the Government, promised to provide: (1) the gratuitous loan of as many vessels, duly altered and fitted out, as might be required for "the principle Ports of the Empire," and (2) the salary of their chaplains, where local resources proved inadequate.

Important, too, was the fact that "all the Episcopal Bench had concurred in the measure."[49]

Accordingly, a public meeting was convened at the City of London Tavern, with the Lord Mayor in the chair. Here, on July 20, 1825, the "Episcopal Floating Church Society" (EFCS) was duly founded, "for Promoting the Diffusion of Religion among Seamen of the Empire, agreeable to the Doctrines and Discipline of the Church of England."[50]

The event was remarkable in at least two aspects. On the one hand, no apology was offered for a militantly denominational motive. ("The minds of the sailors should not be allowed to wander from the doctrines of one church to those of another. . . .") On the other hand, here was the first deliberate effort to form an Anglican seamen's mission society of Empire-wide scope. (It was the declared intent of the Society to promote the establishment of floating churches wherever they might be "of service to the object," together with facilities for the education of apprentices and the distribution of literary media similar to those contemplated in London.)[51]

The new Society was able to take over ground which had already been prepared by G.C. Smith and the provisional committee of the BFSFSBU, while these were working for a new floating chapel in the Upper Pool, 1823-25. (The latter committee even ceded to the new Society their office premises, the Religious and Charitable Society House, at 32 Sackville Street, Piccadilly.) The new committee could count among its members such names as Zachary Macaulay, Alderman Key and the Hon. Captain Walde-grave. Lord Gambier was elected a vice-president.[52]

The committee of the EFCS set as their goal to build up a "Chaplains' Salary Fund" sufficient to avoid having to surrender the right of nomination to the Admiralty. Despite an ominous economic recession in 1825, initial subscriptions proved immensely encouraging.[53] Nevertheless, a series of setbacks were destined to dog the steps of the Society, throughout the two decades of its existence.

In the first place, so far from expanding elsewhere, nearly four years elapsed before the EFCS could open its first (and only) floating church on the Thames. The Society's key positions were entrusted to men of great promise. The Rev. Horatio Montagu, like Richard Marks a former lieutenant of the Royal Navy, was appointed chaplain. From 1825 to 1828, he main-tained a tireless ministry of ship visitation between London Bridge and the Pool.[54] Another naval lieutenant, long known for his persistent zeal in the Seamen's Cause, James Edward Gordon, became the Society's secretary. Nevertheless, despite the latter's ardent efforts to enlist the support of his many connections among "pious noblemen and ladies of rank," the imple-mentation of the Society's plans was constantly frustrated from unspecified "unavoidable causes."[55]

Not until 1828 did matters change. Then, in its February number, *The New Sailor's Magazine* was able to announce that HMS *Brazen* had now been "cheerfully given to the National Establishment, to be converted into a floating church for the Thames." Thus it fell to the Duke of Clarence (the future "Sailor King"), during his brief tenure of office as Lord High Admiral (1827-28), to honor the pledge made by Melville. A 26-gun sloop-of-war of the frigate-built class, launched in 1808, of 422 tons, the *Brazen* had latterly served as a convict ship. Lying in the Royal Dockyard at Deptford in January 1828, she was first closely examined by none other than the Rev. G.C. Smith, accompanied by two naval captains, George C. Gambier and Robert J. Elliot (both of whom had recently assumed a leading role in the EFCS). The celebrated Seamen's Preacher, after having "offered up the first prayer in her," also offered, on the basis of his long experience, valuable advice and plans for adaption of the vessel for her new purpose.[56]

On completion of her reconstruction, the new Anglican *Ark* (now capable of accommodating 500 hearers) was towed up to the position allocated by the harbor-master, and moored off Rotherhithe Parish Church, on the south side of the Lower Pool, almost exactly opposite the original, nondenominational *Ark*.[57] The Rev. James Hough (late of the "Madras Establishment") was selected as chaplain by the Archbishop of Canterbury, and duly licensed by the Bishop of Winchester. A resident ship-keeper was appointed by the Government. Finally, on the morning of Good Friday, 1829, the so-called "Episcopal Floating Church" was opened, and divine service performed for the first time. All seemed well.[58]

However, it was not long before discouraging developments became only too apparent. Despite "immense patronage," the Society was continually plagued by financial deficits, resulting in recurring arrears of salary to its hard-pressed chaplains.[59] Another source of frustration was the chronic paucity of attendance on board the Floating Church. So far from turning the trend, a new chaplain, the Rev. John Davis, appointed in late 1830, felt compelled to publish a virtual ultimatum after only six months, addressed to "the Seamen of the Port of London." Here, threatening to resign unless response improved, he concludes with the following forceful logic: "I cannot, my dear brethren, preach without a congregation."[60]

Two years later, the work came close to disaster from a totally different cause. During remooring operations in the summer of 1832, the Floating Church suddenly capsized at low water.[61] However, there was no loss of life, the vessel was duly repaired and by 1834, after being compelled to relinquish her Rotherhithe moorings, was accommodated in a presumably favorable location in the Admiralty Tier off the Tower.[62]

Nevertheless, the same disheartening picture prevailed, both in terms of finance and attendance, at this new station on the north side of the

The "Sailors' (Episcopal) Floating Church," the former
sloop-of-war *Brazen,* had also served as a convict ship
before she was refitted for her new purpose. Opened in
1829 on the Rotherhithe side, she was moved in 1834
to the Admiralty Tier off the Tower (as depicted here).
(From a contemporary painting. Courtesy: The
Missions to Seamen, London.)

Upper Pool. Two reasons for this state of affairs were repeatedly advanced:
(1) The neglect of far too many captains in their duty of inculcating sound
devotional habits in their crews. (2) The "awful desecration of the Lord's
Day" on the Thames (by cargo-handling, sailing, or simply "pleasure-
seeking" on the Sabbath).[63] A somewhat disillusioned G.C. Smith had other
theories, however, primarily: (1) The alleged "Irvingite" leanings of certain
leaders in the EFCS (resulting in the disaffection of others). (2) The
involvement of elements of the EFCS in the general warfare between the
metropolitan seamen's mission societies (resulting in the alienation of both
public support and seamen's sympathies).[64]

However negative the experience of the promoters of this first
independent Anglican seamen's mission endeavor in the metropolis (compared with both their own original aspirations, and the relative success of
Anglican efforts elsewhere), it would be unfair to ignore obviously positive
results. Foremost among these was the maintenance of an active Anglican
"presence" on the metropolitan waterfront until the dawn of happier days,
with the adoption (in the 1840's) of other methods of ministry, both ashore
and afloat.[65]

Chapter 14

New Coadjutors and a Wider Field of Mission

The period under review, from the foundation of the first general, metropolitan seamen's mission society in 1818, to the emergence of a reconstituted national society in 1833, is characterized by a pattern of developing differentiation. This applies to various aspects of this still very novel ministry, for example in the area of manpower.

In the operational sector, the 1820's witnessed a growing appreciation of the need for not only voluntary and part-time ministerial involvement, but the full-time services of chaplains specifically set apart for the maritime ministry. Several examples have already been noted.[66]

On the promotional side, these early years saw several efforts to channel the vast supportive potential of "the Christian fair" into Ladies' Auxiliary Societies. Here, as in other respects, the BFBS had cleared the way. The first "Female Associations" for promoting Scripture circulation among the poorer classes had been launched well before the end of the Napoleonic War, and had to contend with wide-spread male prejudice. The claims of "domesticity, propriety, and decorum" were energetically urged, but—fortunately for this and so many other areas of Christian concern— such arguments proved in vain. Those persistent pioneers simply proved themselves indispensable; and the prevalent "Oriental conception of the Christian status of womanhood" had to be drastically revised.[67]

In the area of seamen's missions, a spirited appeal was published in *The Sailor's Magazine* of 1821, with a seaman from Nelson's *Victory* loudly "hailing" British womenfolk to take up the cause and form ladies' auxiliaries. Invoking the moral obligation of his "fair countrywomen" toward seamen on a variety of accounts, he asks:

> What are the ladies about? . . . Now, Mr. Editor, I have heard of
> Ladies Associations for Bible, and Missionary, and School

Societies, but I ask—what are the Ladies of Great Britain doing to promote the Salvation of our Navy and Army, and Merchant Seamen?[68]

In actual fact, a beginning had already been made in April 1817, with the formation of the "Glasgow Female Association, in aid of the Naval and Military Bible Society" (with Lieutenant J.E. Gordon as its zealous promoter and first secretary).[69] London followed in 1821, with the foundation of the "Ladies' Association in aid of the Naval Military Bible Society, and Merchant Seamen's Auxiliary Bible Society."[70]

It would, at this point, have been unthinkable to involve the fair sex in the leadership of any parent society, or in any operational capacity (save in exceptional cases directly concerned with women and children).[71] However, in the early 1820's, with the rapid spread of Seamen's Friend and Bethel Union Societies, there are frequent records of Ladies' Auxiliary Societies formed in order to assist in fundraising. Besides securing subscriptions and donations, these resourceful coadjutors would, for example, arrange sales of work.[72] For them, the provision of Bethel Flags was a cherished responsibility. At the close of the decade, a number of "Ladies' Associations" were formed for the purpose of providing clothes for destitute seamen and their families.[73]

Nor was the ability of children to cooperate in the cause entirely neglected. Some would emulate adults in collecting substantial sums in so-called "Bethel Boxes" (or, as in the case of Thomas Phillips Jr., in a model "Bethel Ship").[74] G.C. Smith effectively enlisted the aid of orphans attached to his Mariners' Church organization as an ambulating children's choir, both in his open-air activity and on his frequent indoor speaking engagements.[75] The earliest available record of a children's society. specifically organized in support of the Seamen's Cause, is the foundation, on February 28, 1821, of a "Sailors' Children's Bethel Union" at Newlyn (adjoining Penzance), by Sunday school teachers of the Newlyn Sailors' Chapel.[76]

What segment of society comprised the sphere of responsibility envisaged by early British seamen's mission organizations? Impelled, at least in part, by the expansive vision of G.C. Smith, pioneers of the movement found themselves preoccupied with a progressively wider field of mission. There was, however, no general consensus. Not all societies would adopt every category of responsibility assumed by others. Moreover, some such categories were, in time, destined to lapse altogether.

NAVAL PERSONNEL

It seems natural that naval personnel should be considered first. Naval seamen had been the object of the very earliest organized British seamen's mission endeavor, and provided the prelude to the Thames Revival. Nevertheless, the Port of London Society did not feel it necessary to mention them specifically in their 1818 constitution. True, the term "sailor" or "seaman" was, through the 1820's, still being used indiscriminately of men in both the Merchant and Royal Navy. However, G.C. Smith, himself always keenly conscious of his naval past, constantly criticized this society for neglect of the naval seaman,[77] while leaving no shadow of doubt as to the comprehensive concern of his own. At the Constitutive Meeting of the original Bethel Seamen's Union in 1819, he expressly included, as an object of the Society's activities, "British Seamen in every port throughout Great Britain in the Navy and the Merchant Service."[78]

As naval officers became increasingly prominent in post-war seamen's mission organization, and as many of the men came under the influence of newly-formed Seamen's Friend Societies, both in major naval ports and elsewhere, G.C. Smith was quick to stress a significant implication. Should a return to war once more swell the naval establishment, this could become as respectable for "morality and piety" as it had formerly been notorious for a "total disregard of all the principles of our Christian faith."[79]

Credit for any amelioration which might be registered must also be attributed to improvements in the supply and standard of naval chaplaincy in the reduced peace-time establishment. However, the Royal Navy of the 1820's still provided ample room for reform, both in terms of religious toleration and social welfare. In these areas (generally designated "Naval Mission," and dealt with in detail below), Smith was conspicuously active, both in personal visitation and in agitatory publication.[80]

SOLDIERS

In regard to soldiers, George Whitefield could testify to the existence at Gibraltar of a "Religious Society of soldiers," fully fifty years prior to the foundation of the Naval and Military Bible Society (1779).[81] As from the establishment of that Society, soldiers were expressly linked with seamen as objects of organized Christian literature distribution.[82]

With the advent of societies for more comprehensive seamen's missionary endeavor, G.C. Smith pioneered similar efforts on behalf of soldiers. Deeming it "unnecessary to multiply societies," he strove for several years to unite seamen's and soldiers' missions in the same organizational structure. In 1814, during his Continental chaplaincy, Smith had already demonstrated a combination of these concerns in his own dual role at that time.[83] In 1820, he promoted the founding of the first combined Seamen and Soldiers' Friend Societies, at Chatham and Sheerness. That same year he secured the following addition to the official objects of the parent society (the BFSFSBU): ". . . this institution considers it desirable to promote the spiritual improvement of Soldiers in every town and city, where it may be found practicable."[84] By 1822, similar combined societies had been established at the naval-military arsenals of Woolwich, Plymouth, Devonport and Stonehouse. Meanwhile, reports were published of soldiers even joining the seamen in Bethel Meetings on the Thames.[85]

Nevertheless, the structural union of seamen's and soldiers' missions proved ultimately unfeasible. This was no doubt largely due to a certain professional incompatibility, bound up with deep-rooted psychological factors. True, the BFSFSBU could, in 1822, report with satisfaction that a Soldiers' Friend Society had been established (at Knightsbridge), with preaching provided in the proximity of various barracks.[86] However, there is no evidence of any response (either among the soldiery or the public) comparable to that engendered by the Seamen's Cause. Although G.C. Smith made a point of inserting the word "Soldiers" in the title of both his societies and his magazine, from 1827 on this branch of the work suffered from an evident lack of continuity.[87] The only manifest, permanent fruit of this combined concern for both soldier and sailor seems to have been the Soldiers' Chapel which Smith opened in Tothill Street, Westminster, in 1830. This eventually promoted the formation of the "Army Scripture Readers' Society" (today the "Soldiers' and Airmen's Scripture Readers Association.")[88]

TRANSPORTEES

Closely connected with the armed services were the mounting number of transportees to Australia. Their brief but brutal contact with shipboard life also aroused the concern of seamen's mission workers. Wilberforce himself was instrumental in sending a chaplain with the first shipment of convicts to Australia in 1787. From the closing years of the Napoleonic War, there is frequent evidence of efforts to promote the spiritual welfare of those luckless thousands, bound for Botany Bay and Van Diemen's Land. This found expression through the distribution of Christian literature, as well as agitation for regular chaplaincy services en route.[89]

As from 1818, the particularly pitiable lot of female transportees, among whom abuse and prostitution were rampant, promoted the pioneering (and remarkably successful) efforts of Elizabeth Fry and her colleagues. Systemetic attempts were made to supply not only devotional, but also educational and recreational needs. A "Convict-ship Committee" was formed to give continuity to the work.[90] (Although the transportation of convicts to New South Wales was officially abolished in 1840, it was not entirely eliminated in the Continent as a whole until 1868.)[91]

Aboard the convict transport *John Calvin*, in the
NE trades, en route to Australia in the 1840's.
(Painted by one of the convicts, Kanute Bull; in Charles
Bateson: *The Convict Ships 1787-1868.*)

An emigrant sailing packet about to be towed out into the River
Mersey, 1850. (*Illustrated London News*, July 6, 1850.)

EMIGRANTS

Representing a category of voyagers voluntarily sharing, for a while, the fate of the seafarer, emigrants also attracted the early attention of societies involved in seamen's mission. Again, the original emphasis was on Christian literature distribution. In its *Report* for 1816-17, the BFBS records Scripture supplies to "20 Free Women" (besides 100 female convicts) bound for New South Wales. In 1817-18, the Society supplied "200 German Emigrants, proceeding to Canada."[92]

There was, at this period, some discussion behind the scenes, since the mounting numbers of "poor distressed passengers" (which emigrants indisputably were) could not "with any propriety be considered as forming part of the 'Mercantile Marine.' "[93] Nevertheless, to many who sought to alleviate the lot of the seaman, the need was plain to see, and through the 1820's efforts were, indeed, made to maintain a distribution of religious literature among emigrants of different nationalities embarking at British seaports.[94] Their numbers reached new heights in the early 1830's. But the really great wave of emigration (primarily westwards toward North America) did not set in before close to mid-century.[95]

BOATMEN

Seamen's mission pioneers were also inevitably confronted with the miserable plight of a class intimately connected with the shipping industry, and collectively referred to as "boatmen." They were regarded as virtually "an entirely distinct people," embracing all employed on lighters, barges and passenger-craft in harbor areas, navigable rivers and the rapidly expanding network of canals. (Of the corresponding individual designations: lightermen, bargemen and watermen, the last of these could also be used synonymously with the general term "boatmen.") Common to them all was a particular notoriety for profanity, licentiousness and Sabbath-breaking. Among bargemen (or canalmen), whose families frequently functioned as crew, illiteracy and spiritual deprivation was almost universal.[96]

Here again, it is G.C. Smith who stands out as the conspicuous pioneer figure. Although preceded in time by the Scripture distribution efforts already alluded to among bargemen at Uxbridge and Paddington,[97] Smith was the first to launch a comprehensive scheme of evangelization among boatmen in general. Undeterred by assurances that "he might as well run his head up against a post, as ever think to do good among so depraved and hardened a race of men," he set forth on a "River Mission" during the summer of 1821, along both banks of the Thames above London Bridge.

Boatmen (watermen, lightermen, bargemen and their
families) were neglected by the institutional church, but not
by early seamen's missionaries. Here one of them is seen
offering pastoral counseling to a waterman while
visiting ships in the readstead. (Contemporary print, courtesy
Methodist Seamen's Mission, London.)

Preaching in the open air at the different river-stairs, Smith found
the response of the spiritually starved boatmen and their families sufficiently
encouraging to repeat the plan the following summer. Largely as a result of
these efforts, coupled with the constant cooperation of Smith's master-
lighterman friend, Thomas Phillips, a society was formed September 18,
1822, as a "sister institution" of the BFSFSBU, entitled the "Watermen,
Lightermen, and Bargemen's Friend Society and Bethel Union."[98]

The new Society, generally abbreviated to the "Thames Rivermen's
Society," sought to minister to the needs of more than 30,000 rivermen, or
such as were constantly occupied on the surface and banks of the River
Thames. In this figure were included not only boatmen, but also porters,
coal-whippers, ballastmen and similar marginal-income river occupations.
With the addition of their equally unchurched families, the figure could be far
more than doubled.[99] Funds proved quite inadequate for the implementation
of the expansive plans of the Society (including such items as a free-school
for boatmen's children and an asylum for "worn-out Watermen"). True, the
services already instituted at the Cambrian Chapel (mentioned earlier) were
continued, and progress at the various meeting-stations along the banks of

the Thames was (in 1824) reported to be "gradual, but useful." Nevertheless, the Society as such seems to have succumbed shortly afterwards.[100]

However, when G.C. Smith established himself independently in Wellclose Square in the mid-twenties, he transferred his concern for boatmen to his new church and society, including in the extended title of each the words "and Rivermen's (Watermen's) Bethel Union."[101] In 1828, Smith's current organization, the British and Foreign Seamen and Soldiers' Friend Society, acting through its North London Auxiliary, built and opened (in Macclesfield Street, City Road) what was held to be the first "Boatmen's Chapel" ever erected as such in the kingdom. Simultaneously, the Society could report that chapel facilities for boatmen and their families were available at three further stations: Paddington, Lambeth and Southwark (at the Cambrian Chapel).[102]

Meanwhile, there were reports of similar endeavors in the provinces. Barge-preaching had been undertaken at Reading and Ware at the beginning of the decade, while the Port of Hull Society stimulated concern for sloopmen on the inland waterways within a wide radius.[103] Following the appeal made by the BFSFSBU to inland towns in the mid-twenties, where these were expressly reminded of responsibilities for local boatmen,[104] several societies reported specific efforts among this class (for example in Birmingham, Leicester, Nottingham, Wakefield and Bath).[105] However, by the beginning of the 1830's, G.C. Smith still had reason to challenge churches situated near rivers and canals to make Boatmen's Missionaries and Boatmen's Friend Societies something more than mere exceptions to a norm of neglect.[106]

FISHERMEN

Although, like boatmen, fishermen were not necessarily considered "seamen properly so called,"[107] they were often expressly included as objects of early seamen's mission endeavor. Again, this took, to begin with, primarily the form of Christian literary media distribution. The large numbers of whaling crews reached by Marine Bible Societies in the Northern Countries and the Shetlands have already been noted.[108] Further efforts on behalf of whalers, especially in the so-called "South-Sea Fishery," were to become the particular object of American seamen's mission outreach in the 1830's.[109] Meanwhile, fishermen nearer home were not entirely overlooked. They might (as in Barking) become a major concern of the local Seamen's Friend Society;[110] they might be expressly included in activities on behalf of boatmen;[111] or they might benefit from the coastal activities of agents of the BFSSFS (such as in Brighton, where preaching on the beach by G.C. Smith resulted in the formation of a "Brighton Fishermen's Friend Society").[112] However, more than half a century was to elapse before British fishermen were to have their own specific national society (the "Royal National Mission To Deep Sea Fishermen," which traces its origins to 1881).[113]

Fishing vessels, here seen flying the Bethel Flag, were
the concern of the BFSS long before the founding of the
Royal National Mission to Deep Sea Fishermen (1881).
(G. Holden Pike: *Among the Sailors.*)

were to have their own specific national society (the "Royal National
Mission To Deep Sea Fishermen," which traces its origins to 1881).[113]

SPECIAL CATEGORIES

A limited (mainly literary) outreach also developed for the benefit
of special categories of seafarers serving in an official capacity. By the end
of the 1820's, early Scripture distribution efforts among the crews of Post
Office Packets and H.M. Revenue Cutters[114] had been supplemented by
sporadic attempts to reach the men manning lightships and lighthouses with
Christian literature.[115] Nor were pilots altogether ignored.[116]

SEAFARERS' DEPENDENTS

Last but not least, there emerged, around the 1820's, the first
significant diaconal concern for seafarers' dependents. This was prompted by
the dawning recognition of a specific moral obligation as such, while also

promoting the total well-being of the seafarer himself.[117] (Examples of Christ-motivated social action for the benefit of seamen's families will be dealt with below, under "An Emerging Maritime Diaconate.")[118] Time would show that here, at least, was a widening of the early field of mission which had come to stay.[119]

Chapter 15

Expanding Literary Media Distribution

The supply of Christian literature, as the first form of society-sponsored ministry to seafarers, was not superseded by the development, after 1818, of more comprehensive seamen's mission organizations. On the contrary, literary media remained an indispensable method of mission in virtually every emerging society. In fact it became even more intensified and more diversified during the ensuing decade.

At least three significant reasons could be advanced for this turn of events: (1) With full-time salaried "seamen's missionaries" for years still a rarity (under existing financial frustrations), the printed word represented a relatively reasonable avenue of expansion.[120] (2) In any event, the efficacy of preaching in port presupposed a literary follow-up at sea (in order to "keep those impressions on the heart" of the seafarers).[121] (3) The current nation-wide circulation of "impious and seditious publications" (by Richard Carlile and the like), to which seafarers, too, were increasingly exposed, called for a vigorous "anti-infidel" counter-influence.[122]

THE SCRIPTURES

As the two major societies committed exclusively to supplying seamen with the Scriptures sought to meet this challenge, the older, the Naval and Military Bible Society, found it necessary to undergo a radical reorganization, in two important aspects.

In the first place, it was during the 1820's that the auxiliary society system became the structural backbone of the NMBS. The initiative had already been taken by Scotland in 1817, with the founding of the Glasgow Auxiliary (thanks largely to the dynamic drive of Lieutenant J.E. Gordon again). By 1830, the Society could list 36 auxiliary societies, scattered throughout the British Isles.[123]

Secondly, with the commencement of Captain J.W. Bazalgette's long secretaryship, a far-reaching expansion of the field of mission was decided upon. As from 1825, the constitution of the Society was altered so as to embrace (under its "objects") "all Mariners, whether connected with inland or general navigation." Both fishermen and crews of East Indiamen were also specifically included.[124] As in the case of the Society's Glasgow Auxiliary (which had made a similar provision eight years previously), a contributory motive was undoubtedly the return of the post-war armed establishments to "their present reduced scale." Moreover, among the far fewer naval seamen who remained, a limited supply of Bibles and prayer-books was reintroduced as official ship's stores.[125] Faced with such a severe curtailment of its own quantitative usefulness, what could be more natural for the NMBS than to follow the seafarer in his peace-time role?

On the other hand, was not the mercantile marine the particular province of the Merchant Seamen's Auxiliary Bible Society? Officially, the NMBS felt justified by the consideration that here was "a body of men already partially connected with it, and not adequately provided by any other specific institution."[126] In actual fact, contemporary manuscript sources show that relations with the MSABS shortly after 1825 were by no means free from friction.[127] Nor did it help matters when, in 1831, in the heat of the "Trinitarian Controversy," the NMBS repudiated the Bible Society's hard-won "principle of catholicity" in Scripture distribution, by introducing an orthodoxy test into its membership clause; at one point (around 1832) there were even allegations of Irvingite heresy among certain members of the Society's committee.[128]

Nevertheless, the NMBS weathered the storms. Successive annual reports up to and into the next decade give evidence of massive (predominantly Anglican) patronage, and of continuing usefulness, a fact repeatedly attested by such supporters as Captains Sir John Franklin and Sir Edward Parry, both of Arctic discovery fame).[129] "Extracts from the Correspondence" underscore the breadth of response to the 1825 measure among seafarers of every description.[130] By 1830, the NMBS had built up a list of 62 "Gratuitous Agents and Correspondents" through whom its distribution was channeled, thus covering a substantial number of British home ports, a few also in the Colonies.[131]

Meanwhile, the Merchant Seamen's Auxiliary Bible Society had been limiting its distribution exclusively to the Thames. Here, however, this Society's system of full-time colportage clearly showed its superiority.[132] In the early 1820's, John Cox, the pioneering Gravesend Agent of the MSABS (now a Captain R.N.) was supplemented by a Mr. Percival as London Agent. A decade later, the tireless Cox with his "Bible-boat" was relieved by a Lieutenant Petley at Gravesend, and joined Percival in the upper reaches of the River.

The concerted efforts of these men bore very evident fruit. Copious extracts of their reports quoted case after case of incredible eagerness for personal possession of the Scriptures. A comparison made at Gravesend showed that, whereas nearly 600 ships had been found completely destitute of the Scriptures in the first year of the Society's history (1818-19), this was the case with only four in 1829-30, "and these four were all foreigners."[133] (The Society's concern for the latter category is illustrated by the fact that, in the same year, 40 percent of all Bibles and Testaments supplied by the MSABS to seamen in the Port of London were in foreign languages, sold at drastically reduced prices.)[134]

As to the British and Foreign Bible Society, its archives reveal throughout the period under consideration a concern for seafarers far beyond the immediate responsibility of its maritime auxiliary, the MSABS. Its activities could range from opening depots of foreign language Scriptures in major home-ports, to supplying South Sea missionaries with the means of making distributions among whaler and merchantmen in those distant ports.[135]

The Edinburgh Bible Society also continued its involvement in various forms of maritime Scripture distribution, including through its eminently active agent in Hamburg, the Rev. J.G. Oncken.[136]

RELIGIOUS TRACTS

Concurrently with these endeavors, the Religious Tract Society, building on its initial success among seafarers, maintained an expanding supply of both specific "sea-tracts" and other popular titles.[137] The Rev. Richard Marks completed his series of the former;[128] and the (Congregational) founding father of the Society, the Rev. George Burder, supplemented them with a collection of twelve *Sea Sermons* of his own (1821).[139] Grants by the RTS for maritime distribution were channeled largely through the different seamen's mission societies (both in the metropolis and in the outports), by whom they were warmly acknowledged.[140]

The high estimation of these "silent monitors" is reflected in the priority attached to them in the constitution of practically every seamen's mission society at this period. In short, they simply considered the distribution of the Scriptures and "moral and religious tracts" as methodologically mandatory.[141] Some of the major societies occasionally went ot the expense of publishing their own.[142] Efforts were likewise made, both in home ports and abroad, to meet the need of foreign seafarers for tracts translated into their own languages.[143]

SAILORS' MAGAZINES

January 1820 saw the publication of the world's first religious periodical specifically designed for seamen and their present or potential "friends."[144] Published under the patronage of the BFSFSBU, *The Sailor's Magazine, and Naval Miscellany* rapidly proved itself indispensable. Its originator and sole editor, G.C. Smith, steadfastly stressed its dual missionary and promotional purpose. Large quantities were distributed gratuitously, by way of tracts, both ashore and on shipboard. At home and overseas, parcels of back numbers became an invaluable medium of communication, stimulating existing societies and motivating new.[145]

Although the magazine developed a chronic inability to pay its way, it was eagerly emulated by the USA, and endorsed even by the editor's inveterate enemies at home. After finally ousting Smith in 1827, the PLBUS was anxious to retain both the name and the good-will of the magazine he had pioneered. But the breezy, briny style of a Boatswain Smith proved non-negotiable. Under the PLBUS (and subsequently for a whole generation under the BFSS), the magazine never recovered its early popularity. Reduced to a quarterly, and characterized by a self-admitted "sameness," it was finally given up in 1869.[146]

Meanwhile, Smith's *New Sailor's Magazine* (started in 1827 as *The New Sailor's Magazine and Naval Chronicle*) began to forge ahead. However, as its editor became more and more enmeshed in personal polemics, the character of the contents—once so refreshingly diversified—inevitably suffered. Rambling retrospects and financial frustrations were to fill an increasing proportion of Smith's magazine during the remainder of his life.[147]

MARITIME DEVOTIONAL AIDS

The Bethel Movement, with its renewed emphasis on the priesthood of all believers, created an acute need for maritime devotional aids. Since this could not be adequately met by reprints of earlier manuals,[148] the two metropolitan seamen's mission societies each undertook an important project for mass publication. The PLS was first, with *The Seamen's Devotional Assistant,* written by "an officer of the Royal Navy." Conceived as a prayer-book and worship manual, and intended to stimulate not only personal devotions, but especially public services on shipboard, it was, in 1821, in great demand.[149] In 1822, the BFSFSBU followed with *The Sailors' Hymn Book,* compiled by the Rev. G.C. Smith. This was a time when hymnody

THE

SAILOR'S MAGAZINE,

AND

Naval Miscellany.

PUBLISHED UNDER THE PATRONAGE

OF THE

BRITISH AND FOREIGN

SEAMEN'S FRIEND SOCIETY,

AND

Bethel Union.

" The abundance of the sea shall be converted to Thee."

VOL. I.

LONDON:

Printed by T. Hamblin, Garlick Hill;

Published by W. SIMPKIN and R. MARSHALL, Stationers' Court,
Ludgate-Street :

And sold by Whittemore, Paternoster Row ; Robins, Tooley-street ; Rubidge, ditto ;
Van, ditto ; Delahoy, Deptford ; Richardson, Greenwich ; Hardcastle, Wool-
wich ; Richardson, Bristol ; Clark, St. Michael's Hill, Bristol ; Kaye, Liverpool ;
Harris, Duke-street, Dock ; Dodd's, South Shields ; and all Booksellers in the
Ports of Great Britain.

1820.

The world's first seamen's mission magazine, launched and
edited by George Charles Smith (at that time a
Baptist pastor in Penzance.)

was successfully breaking the hegemony of psalmody in church music. It contained no less than 345 hymns, topically arranged, of both maritime and general content, by such authors as Watts, Charles Wesley, Newton and Cowper, besides several original contributions by Smith himself. The book proved a resounding success. (As late as 1881, the BFSS found reason to add to a long series of intervening editions yet another revised version.)[150]

Within a few years, other maritime hymnals appeared, for example *The Christian Sailor's Companion, or Hymns for Seamen,* by Robert Joyce, a minister of the PLBUS,[151] and *The Naval, Military, and Village Hymn Book,* by Captain Richard Weymouth, R.N.[152]

During the same period, the popular maritime homilies of men like Marks, Burder and Scoresby (already noticed)[153] were supplemented by others, such as *The Bethel Flag, or Sermons to Seamen,* by the Rev. Robert Philip of Liverpool,[154] and *The Christian Mariner's Journal,* by an anonymous naval officer.[155]

As in the case of seamen's mission endeavor in general, the main bulk of Christian maritime media distribution was, at this stage, on a non-denominational basis. However, the 1820's also saw the beginnings of a specifically Anglican involvement in this area. Prompted on the one hand by the zeal of the Nonconformists, and on the other by the inadequacy of the SPCK during this period, it fell to the "Prayer-Book and Homily Society" to take up the challenge.

At the time of its establishment in 1812, the maritime concern of the PBHS was restricted to naval seamen.[156] By 1824, however, the plight of the merchant seaman had been "long pressed on the attention of the Society." In June of that year, the assistant secretary (Mr. Seaward), personally commenced an experimental program of ship visitation among the 100,000 seamen estimated to be annually employed on the Thames. A separate fund was started to finance the venture.[157] Although opposition, even of the "grossest character," was also encountered, the general response was sufficiently encouraging to make "Labours among Seamen" a permanent and henceforth widely publicized feature of the Society's work.[158]

The rationale of the endeavor was clear. The Society was confident that that "Daughter of the Bible," The *Book of Common Prayer,* would "commend itself in an especial manner to that feeling of nationality which distinguishes the English Sailor." It was also anxious to promote the "godly and wholesome doctrine" of those "plain good old Sermons of the blessed Martyrs and Reformers of our English Church," the *Book of Homilies.*[159] Hence it sought, through a special *Address to Seamen* (1825), to alert the seafarer to his personal need of particular aids to spiritual self-help.[160] At the same time, its agents worked incessantly to further the "grand object" of the Society, to secure the cooperation of captains in maintaining regular worship

NAVIGATION SPIRITUALIZ'D:
OR, A
NEW COMPASS
FOR
SEAMEN;

Confifting of **XXXII** Points.

Of {
Pleafant OBSERVATIONS,
Profitable APPLICATIONS, and
Serious REFLECTIONS.

All concluded with fo many Spiritual POEMS.

Whereunto is now added,

I. A Sober Confideration of the Sin of Drunkennefs.
II. The Harlot's Face in the Scripture-Glafs.
III. The Art of Preferving the Fruit of the Lips.
IV. The Refurrection of buried Mercies and Promifes.
V. The Seaman's Catechifm.

Being an ESSAY toward their much-defir'd Reformation from the horrible and deteftable Sins of *Drunkennefs, Swearing, Uncleannefs, Forgetfulnefs of Mercies, Violation of Promifes,* and *Atheiftical Contempt of Death.*

Fit to be ferioufly recommended to their profane Relations, whether SEAMEN or Others, by all fuch as unfeignedly defire their eternal Welfare.

And they faid, Come, let us caft Lots, that we may know for
whofe [Caufe] this Evil is come upon us.   Jonah i. 7.
Knowing therefore the Terrors of the Lord, we perfuade Men.
2 Cor. v. 11.

By JOHN FLAVEL, *Minifter of the Gofpel.*

The EIGHTH EDITION.

L O N D O N:
Printed for C. HITCH and L. HAWES, J. BUCKLAND, J. WARD, G. KEITH, T. FIELD, and E. DILLY. 1760.

The burgeoning Bethel Movement created the need for
a wide choice of maritime devotional aids. But
for classics like Flavel's *Navigation Spiritualiz'd*
there was still a strong market.

services with their crews, by reading prayers, preferably also a homily, at all events every Sabbath.[161]

For this purpose, the Prayer-book was sold to crew-members at reduced price, while a ship's copy of the *Book of Select Homilies* would be entrusted gratuitously to the care of the captain. As the demand became apparent, agents were appointed in several provincial ports. Homilies printed as tracts were also channeled through the two metropolitan seamen's mission societies.[162] These efforts bore tangible fruit. By 1830, the number of captains of foreign-bound ships holding "Divine Worship on board ship on the Sabbath, weather permitting" had reportedly risen to fully two-thirds of the total.[163] The following is a typical example of the type of pressure which adept agents found highly effective with diffident shipmasters:

> The master . . . said, "He had never called his crew together for prayers; but confessed the great impropriety of neglecting this duty." The crew having been asked whether they were willing to unite with their captain in prayers when at sea, unanimously consented. . . . Two sailors bought a book each, to be prepared for the captain's call. . . .[164]

Voluntary services were also rendered by clergymen stationed abroad. For example, the Chaplain of the British Embassy Chapel in Constantinople found the Prayer-book "very acceptable indeed to the sailors." Correspondents both in Hamburg and Calcutta undertook ship visitation on behalf of the Society.[165] Furthermore, a demand was discovered for translations of selections from the Prayer-book and the Homilies among foreign crews. Thus, both on the Thames and in the out-ports, cases could be quoted of Anglican formularies and homilies eagerly accepted by German, French, Dutch and Scandinavian seamen.[166] Nor were other categories connected with seafaring entirely overlooked. Naval seamen, boatmen, fishermen, emigrants, convicts on board their hulks, even lighthouse personnel, all became objects of the Society's concern.[167]

Although serving a specific denominational need, the strongly Evangelical Prayer-Book and Homily Society maintained cordial inter-denominational relations.[168] In 1827, however, a more militantly Anglican interest (emanating from a quite different quarter) began to assert itself, at least among naval seamen.

OFFICIAL REACTION

On May 28, 827, the Duke of Clarence (later King William IV), acting as Lord High Admiral, sent out an order prohibiting "any tracts or religious books" from being "received" on board any naval vessels, unless duly "approved and pointed out" by the Senior Chaplain of Greenwich Hospital, the Rev. Samuel Cole, D.D. Dr. Cole, notorious as "the only chaplain proscribed by the mutineers of 1797," was known to be "by no means favourable to evangelical sentiments."[169]

The order provoked an immediate and intense protest. One religious newspaper (*The World*) flatly denied the right of any authority to "dictate" to a free-born British seaman what religious books he should read.[170] *The Christian Guardian* (itself Anglican) challenged the Duke's advisors rather to rid His Majesty's ships of all the obscene literature and abandoned women with which they were still so "grievously infested."[171] G.C. Smith published an indignant protest against any Greenwich-based "Pope of the Navy," in an address to King George IV entitled *Windsor.*[172]

As a result of this restrictive policy, the naval outreach of the BFSSFS, the BFSS, the NMBS, even the PBHS, was materially affected.[173] Any attempt to alter social tradition in the Royal Navy was bound to be confronted with an almost insurmountable barrier of resistance. Such was the fate of what was felt to be undue zeal in Christian literature distribution. It was also the lot of repeated efforts to eradicate shipboard prostitution. The latter will be dealt with under the following examples of early maritime social concern.[174]

Chapter 16

An Emerging
Maritime Diaconate

The pioneer spirits of an organized Christian ministry to seafarers set about their task with no preconceived doctrine of "diakonia." On the other hand, nor were they restricted by any narrow, exclusively spiritual concept of mission. Although a soteriological motivation and objective were clearly primary, the seaman's social and cultural needs were by no means ignored.[175] In fact—despite common assumptions to the contrary—there was, even at this early stage, ample evidence of genuine Christian concern for the legitimate needs of the whole person, in other words—a "holistic" approach. Furthermore—even though a policy of "personalistic answers to public problems" was still typical of the times[176]—there were also remarkable examples of efforts to uncover and combat root causes of social ills.

Library Services for Seamen

Intimately related with the mounting literary media distribution of the 1820's were endeavors to establish library services for seamen. Here was a means of increasing the effectiveness of maritime literary outreach (more books becoming available for more people). Here, too, was a means of widening the seafarer's cultural horizon (as not only religious books, but also an increasing number of other "profitable" subjects, such as travel, history and biography, came to be included). In short, here was an undertaking with dual diaconal dimensions, both educational and recreational.

A "Marine Library," or (as it also came to be called) a "Seamen's Library," was established as early as 1820, on the newly acquired Greenock Floating Chapel.[177] Similar provisions were successively made on board the floating chapels of Leith, Hull, Dublin, London and Clifton.[178] Following the example of Lady Mary Grey in mission by media, a number of ladies of rank took a corresponding initiative with regard to libraries. Most prominent in this field were the Duchess of Beaufort and her daughter (who, in 1821, established a "Seamen's Library" at West Cowes), and Lady Thompson of Fareham (who, in 1823, founded a "British Seamen's Library" in Genoa). G.C. Smith warmly commended their efforts, advocating a "Metropolitan Seamen's Library" in the Tower Hill area as a further goal for "British Ladies."[179] At length, after establishing himself in Wellclose Square in the mid-twenties, he succeeded in organizing his own "Sea-Book Depository," incorporating a seamen's library.[180]

In addition to such stationary libraries, a need was soon recognized for *portable* libraries. A so-called "Ship's Library" was seen as a means of both literally and figuratively defeating the "Doldrums." In order to relieve the tedium and attendant temptations of especially long voyages, seamen now had means that might "not only rationally amuse, but also tend to Christianize their minds."[181]

The circulation of tracts and books (from the SPCK) by early eighteenth-century naval chaplains was the forerunner of subsequent ship's libraries in the British Navy.[182] The pioneering achievement of Richard Marks, in successfully establishing a library of religious books on the *Conqueror* during the Napoleonic War, has already been noted.[183] In the merchant navy, W.H. Angas became an early, persistent advocate of not only seamen's libraries ashore, but also ship's libraries afloat.[184] Here, as in so many areas of social and cultural concern for the seafarer, Leith led the way (in 1822-23); by 1827, that Society had some 30 library-boxes in circulation.[185]

Meanwhile, other seamen's mission societies followed suit.[186] The procedure was simple. A box of books was entrusted to the master for the ensuing voyage. The response was remarkable. One captain reported that his ship was now unrecognizable, having become "like a little Heaven." From a ship which was foundering in the Atlantic, the library-box was the first object to be saved. When boxes were returned, they were frequently accompanied by voluntary contributions from grateful crews.[187] Concurrently with the distribution of the first ship's libraries, portable libraries were also allocated to the more reputable boarding-houses for seamen.[188]

RECREATIONAL FACILITIES FOR SEAMEN

Where a stationary library was made available in port, the nucleus of recreational facilities for seamen was already functioning. As early as 1820, the Committee of the Greenock Seamen's Friend Society made it clear that the seamen's library on board their recently dedicated Floating Chapel was intended for seamen who, while unemployed between voyages, might "choose to spend part of the day in the improvement of their minds."[189] The Port of Hull Society emphasized the benefit obtained by seamen's families, as they, too, frequented the library of the local Floating Chapel.[190]

It was from one of these early shipboard seamen's libraries that the first shore-based "Sailor's Reading Room" originated, an institution destined to become a permanent feature of future seamen's missions everywhere. The committee of the Edinburgh and Leith Seamen's Friend Society, in common with others of their social standing, held the conviction that, for the laboring classes, protracted leisure-time (if "unimproved") was courting moral (perhaps also political) disaster. Hence, as they reported in 1823, they had often viewed "with feelings of regret" the crowds of seamen wasting away their days ashore, particularly while their vessels were laid up during the months of winter. As they put it:

> Supposing that these habits of idleness and neglect might possibly proceed from want of access to proper books, or a convenient place for the accommodation of Seamen, it was resolved to endeavour to give those Seamen who might be inclined to improve their leisure hours by reading, a convenient place for that purpose. Suitable premises, at the entrance to the docks, being at that time unoccupied, your Committee took them, and had them fitted up as *The Sailor's Reading Room*. The room was opened three hours every night, and supplied regularly with a charge of books from the library on board the Chapel. Comfortable seats, with fire and candle, were provided, and a free admission was granted to every Seaman who desired it.[191]

Seamen evidently availed themselves of such opportunities with enthusiasm, wherever offered. G.C. Smith incorporated into his "Mariners' Church Establishment" in Wellclose Square both a general seamen's library (where "decent sailors" were at liberty to read) and a "reading-room for captains and sea-officers."[192] Toward the end of the 1820's, he was advocating plans for more commodious reading-rooms, open all day, with "warm fires by night," magazines and newspapers (both religious and general), writing facilities, a "Marine Museum" (with sea curiosities, ship models and nautical prints), even the provision of refreshments.[193] The turbulent events of Smith's continuing career prevented him from carrying through these and other laudable projects. But time would vindicate their validity.[194]

MARITIME EDUCATION

Closely connected with the provision of library and reading-room facilities, were ways in which seamen's misson pioneers sought to promote maritime education in the widest sense. The need was nothing short of desperate. In England of 1819 (despite the mounting impact of the monitorial system of primary education, recently introduced by Bell and Lancaster), the number of children attending school amounted to only one-fifteenth of the population.[195] Among seamen, the position was further aggravated by two severe vocational impediments, both affecting them at their most impressionable age: (1) Their deprivation of whatever positive influence might have been conveyed by home, church and school. (2) Their exposure to the many moral and physical hazards of seafaring life.[196]

However sporadic, efforts had been made, even before 1818, to provide some semblance of elementary education and catechization of seamen. In the British Navy, there were instances of commanders or chaplains establishing some form of school for the boys on board their ship (often with the aid of the SPCK, latterly also the NMBS).[197] With the former frigate *Solebay,* moored off Deptford, as its current training ship (1815-33), The Marine Society continued to provide general, nautical and religious education for the boys it sent into the Royal Navy, the East India Company's fleet, and the merchant service.[198] At the same time, aboard the former ship-of-the-line *Lancaster*, moored at Blackwall (and also loaned by the Admiralty), merchants and shipowners interested in the West India trade provided likely lads with a "West India Naval School."[199]

Nevertheless, these were exceptions. The average first-voyager of the day frequently found himself forced by sheer poverty to ship out without any formal education whatever, "unskilled and unguarded, the easy prey of . . . every home and foreign shark."[200] It was an age when overt opposition to demands for popular education had barely begun to subside,[201] and nautical schools, as such, were still largely a thing of the future. However, there is evidence that contemporary seamen's mission pioneers both identified important issues and sought serious solutions. True, they developed no national blue-print for maritime education, or any comprehensive maritime catechumenate. (Local needs and resources would vary widely; so, too, would the degree of inter-agency communication.) However, three thrusts are distinctly discernible in the course of the 1820's, in the areas of Christian, general and vocational education, respectively.

Since its effective origin, in 1780, the Sunday-school Movement had become both a spearhead of elementary education, and an indispensable asset in the evangelical cause. By 1820, it had gathered such momentum, that Sunday-schools in England and Wales numbered some half a million scholars.[202] Nothing was now more natural, than to adapt them to the needs of the long-neglected seafaring community. Practical considerations, too, made Sunday-schools for seamen and seamen's children an early feature of organized seamen's missions.

Emblem of The Marine Society, London (f. 1756).
(The Marine Society: *213th Annual Report.*)

Scene at the Seamen's Office at the Royal Exchange
where the Marine Society would meet in earlier years
to interview street boys and begin transforming them
into young sailors. (Cipriani's engraving, courtesy of
The Marine Society.)

Such schools were relatively easy and economical to operate. With Scripture-reading and catechization by voluntary teachers as their fundamental function, they could cater to a varying range of participants, from active seamen and apprentices to children (boys and girls) of both seamen and others connected with the waterfront.[203] Since illiteracy was still widespread, reading lessons formed an integral feature of the work. (On board the Bristol Floating Chapel, a regular "Sunday Afternoon Reading Society" was formed for this purpose in 1821, and soon proved its worth.)[204] Similar efforts were persistently promoted by W.H. Angas during his coastal travels.[205]

Concurrently with these endeavors, there developed a corresponding concern for *general* education, specifically by way of day-schools for seamen's children. "So-called Sea-boys' Schools" would, in practice, belong to this category, since they consisted largely of sons of seamen, themselves bent on (or abandoned to) a seafaring life. G.C. Smith published as early as 1820 a national plan, proposing a "Poor Sea-Boys' Society" (and school) in every major port-city.[206] In London, the proprietors of the *Ark* did not respond.[207] But the North-East London Auxiliary of the BFSFSBU did; their "Poor Sea-Boys' Day School," originally in Lower East Smithfield, [208] was later enlarged to include girls, too, and continued at Wapping under the auspices of the PLBUS.[209] After setting up his own organization in the mid-twenties, Smith soon secured both a "Sea-Boys' School" and a "Mariners' Girls' School," in connection with the London Mariners' Church.[210]

First in the field was Liverpool, however, with a day-school for seamen's children, established (as already noted) shortly before the official founding of its parent society, in 1821.[211] Other ports followed suit.[212] Tuition was either free or at a nominal fee. A complete set of clothing was often a dire necessity. The subjects taught were primarily the "Three R's" (reading, writing and 'rithmetic), together with religious instruction (which for boys would have "a special bearing on the maritime profession"). Senior "sea-boys" might also be taught "the elements of Navigation."[213]

Although day-schools for seamen's children could (for those of their pupils who eventually embarked) go far towards filling the need for pre-sea training, their primary purpose was a ministry to seafarers' families.[214] A more specifically *vocational* education was provided by a number of nautical (often called "marine") schools.

The Scots (who at this time were far in advance of the English in the field of popular education) took the lead. On January 16, 1823, the Edinburgh and Leith Seamen's Friend Society opened a "Seamen's Academy" for seagoing men of every category: cabin boys, apprentices, ordinary seamen, mates, even masters. The school was organized in two departments, first general education, then maritime subjects such as navigation, geography and astronomy.

The initial response was such as to evoke emulation in other ports.[215] In Bristol the following year, a "Marine School" was opened which, besides offering an evening school for active seamen leading up to navigation requirements, also incorporated a sea-boys' day-school (with pupils, principally the sons of seafarers, admitted at the tender age of eight).[216] Also in 1824, the Port of Hull Society opened a "Marine School"; this was restricted to the winter months, but was to flourish for years to come.[217]

With what arguments did these early seamen's mission societies seek to justify their involvement in such strictly vocational endeavors? On the one hand, there was the social benefit, of providing "the advantage of scientific Seamenship" to many who would, under existing conditions, otherwise have been bereft of them. On the other hand, there were important religious and moral considerations. Not only were seamen thus diverted from "idleness and dissipation," but—through the religious instruction always included in their curriculum—they would come to recognize the "God of Nature" also as the "God of Grace." Thus they might learn to navigate not only their ship to her port of destination, but also "their own souls into the haven of everlasting rest and peace."[218]

CARE OF SEAMENS' ORPHANS

In striving to salvage Sailortown youngsters by educational means, those who sought them out were impressed by the high proportion and pitiful plight of seamen's orphans. Thus the Leith Society found that, by the mid-twenties, more than one-fourth of those attending their day-schools belonged to this category.[219] Before the end of the decade, the need for specialized institutions had been recognized. G.C. Smith (himself, as he put it, once a fatherless, destitute sailor orphan) listed eight reasons why these children had "most peculiar and pre-eminent claims" on public benevolence.[220]

In 1827, on the initiative of Smith's associates, Phillips and Thompson, a "Merchant Seamen's Orphan Asylum" was founded in connection with the PLBUS.[221] In 1829, Smith himself promoted a somewhat more comprehensive "Sailors' Orphan House Establishment," as a branch of his BFSSFS, open for the orphans of naval, revenue and merchant seamen alike.[222] Also in 1829, a "Sailors' Orphan Girls' School" was established as a specifically Anglican undertaking, in connection with the Episcopal Floating Church Society.[223] Such institutions, concerned not only with the education of the children, but also with their clothing, lodging and eventual placement, were inevitably costly, and therefore, as a rule, separately funded.

RELIEF OF DISTRESSED SEAMEN AND
THEIR DEPENDENTS: SAILORS' ASYLUMS, ETC.

The situation of seamen's orphans, however serious, was never-theless only one among many areas of need calling for special measures for the benefit of distressed seamen and their dependents. In addition to the hazards of shipwreck or enemy action, the seafarer (and his normally impoverished family) had to face the hardships of frequent unemployment, disease and disability, as well as the particular problems of old age, if he survived thus far. In keeping with the temper of the times, public concern focused more readily on the relief of symptoms of distress, than on the eradication of their causes. However, in such attempts as were made to alleviate the manifold miseries of the distitute mariner, a major role was played by the seamen's mission pioneers of the 1820's, with G.C. Smith again in the forefront.

As already noted, there did, even before the turn of the century, exist opportunities, however limited, of participating in certain maritime mutual benefit societies.[224] With the rapid growth of "friendly societies" in general, toward the close of the eighteenth century, this mode of mutual protection was able to find a firmer foothold within the seafarer's precarious profession. The relaxation, in 1824-25, of Pitt's harsh Combination Acts may have provided further stimulus.[225]

At all events, in the late 1820's the formation of many more maritime mutual benefit societies could be reported, particularly among North Country seamen. A characteristic feature of this type of association or "club" was their strong ties with local "Bethel operations." At Sunderland, for example, the secretary and steward of a flourishing "Seamen's Loyal Standard Association" cooperated closely in the opening of a mariner's church there in 1828; the Association itself maintained by means of graduated fines a strict moral code, including an unswerving loyalty to crown and constitution. (The latter could be of significance in countering any confusion with the determinedly militant maritime "Combination Societies" referred to below.)[226]

However, only a modest minority were at this point able to make use of such means of self-help. To what extent did emerging seamen's mission societies involve themselves with the desperate need of the remainder? G.C. Smith left no doubt as to the Bethel Union standpoint. No longer (in the 1820's) could seamen say that no man cared about their souls. Now, he declared, it would be tragic indeed, if seamen should have to ask: "Why do you attend to our souls and neglect our bodies?"[227]

Shipwrecked sailors desperately clinging to the shrouds, as
they await rescue. (G. Holden Pike: *Among the Sailors.*)

As the toll of post-war marine disasters steadily mounted, Smith
seized upon the drastic case of two destitute seamen, miraculously preserved
after 22 months' shipwreck on desert islands, only to be literally left to starve
in the streets of London. This was in November 1823. Systematically
stirring up public excitement both from chapel pulpits and in the daily press,
he also pleaded their case—and the need for organized counter-measures—
before the Lord Mayor himself. In the wake of all the interest aroused, both
by this and other means, the "Royal National Institution for the Preservation
of Life from Shipwreck" was duly established, early 1824. Providing lifeboats
around the coast of the British Isles, together with such incentives as rewards
for their crews, and relief for the wives and children of those lost in rescue
attempts, the Society became an immediate success. It still continues as the
"Royal National Life-boat Institution."[228]

Smith was nevertheless far from satisfied with the scope of this or
other agencies for the benefit of distressed seafarers. What of the seafarer's
bereaved dependents, or, for that matter (if he survived), the seafarer
himself? Later the same year, December 9, 1824, Smith succeeded in
establishing a "Shipwrecked and Distressed Sailors' Family Fund," as a
"distinct branch" of the BFSFSBU. Its primary purpose was to grant

"prompt temporary aid" to the dependents of seamen perished in shipwreck or on shore, or incapacitated by sickness. But relief might also be afforded the seaman himself, if (as was all too often the case) he were reduced to utter destitution while seeking re-employment.

The Fund sought "scrupulously" to avoid cases comtemplated by other benevolent institutions. In practice, the risk of overlapping was, among strictly merchant seamen, minimal; the Merchant Seamen's Society reached relatively few, the Royal Hospital at Greenwich virtually none. The fund achieved remarkable results with limited resources, and became the precursor of the more comprehensive present-day "Shipwrecked Fishermen and Mariners' Royal Benevolent Society," founded in 1839.[229]

Any seamen's mission society was liable, from time to time, to receive desperate appeals from destitute seafarers or their families. Some would, therefore, include the establishment of a specific "Distress Fund" in their constitution.[230] In Leith, one went further. A full-time "Missionary" (the Rev. Matthew Kirkland) was appointed by the local Seamen's Friend Society as from 1830. Besides preaching on the Floating Chapel and at the Society's schools, his duties included systematic weekday visitation of all seamen's families (in "cordial co-operation" with the North Leith parish minister), "inquiring into their circumstances, temporal and spiritual, and administering the relief and instruction which these seemed to require." This form of maritime "home mission" proved eminently successful.[231]

In cases of manifest distress, aid did not necessarily take the form of monetary support. Toward the close of the 1820's, Smith organized, in connection with his new headquarters in Wellclose Square, a "Destitute Sailors' Clothing Department." For this purpose, he established several "Ladies' Maritime Associations" during his travels, and thereby secured the support of a number of ladies of nobility.[232] At the same time, he enlisted the aid of local "pious females" to form a "Mariners' Infant Friend Society," expressly "to visit and relieve, by a small donation and the loan of a box of useful Linen, the distressed Sailor's wife during the month of her confinement."[233]

By this time, Smith had found the steady stream of half-starved seamen around the Mariners' Church "exhausting all our funds and wearying all our energies."[234] Hence he had come to see some form of "asylum" activity as indispensable. A precedent had already been provided during the critical winter of 1817-18, by the seven receiving ships—or "floating asylums"—of the Committee for the Relief of Distressed Seamen.[235] The need for similar but more permanent facilities was finally brought home to Smith in a dramatic way, exactly a decade later.

It was New Year's Eve, 1827, in Wellclose Square, " a cold frosty night, with hail and sleet." A crowd of famished seamen, picked up from the surrounding streets, had been taking part in a Watch Night service at the Mariners' Church, climaxed by a free meal of bread and cheese. It was past 2 a.m., Smith recalls, when, after a closing prayer, the men reluctantly withdrew.

> But there being a long pavement from the church doors, . . . the sailors lined themselves along both sides . . . , and, as I walked from the church to the gates, they sighed, and cried most piteously that these cold nights they had no lodgings, no shelter, no food, no clothes but the rags about them; . . . as I passed to my home . . . I was truly shocked, and filled with horror, to think that I and ministers and members had comfortable rooms and fires and beds, but those poor sailors, unto whom he owed all, . . . were left to perish. Therefore, I resolved to have a shelter provided . . . and, if possible, a biscuit and basin of plain soup in the morning, and another in the evening, and then out in the day to look for a ship that wanted men, and that there should be preaching to them every evening. . . .[236]

Within the remarkably brief space of one week, Smith's vision had been translated into action, and the first so-called "Destitute Sailors' Asylum" was a reality. After sending his schoolmaster-coadjutor, George Woolcott, on a reconnoitering mission, Smith was made aware that an old deserted warehouse was available in Dock Street (then "a dirty narrow lane," particularly notorious for all its brothels, running parallel to the west side of Wellclose Square). Though, as usual, bereft of funds, Smith saw the potentials of the place, and promptly engaged to rent it. Providentially, two naval captains, as soon as they heard of the plan, offered to take personal responsibility for the venture.[237]

It was in November 1827, that Captain George Cornish Gambier (a nephew of the Admiral) and his friend, Captain Robert James Elliot, had first been confronted with that hectic hub of maritime mission which was Wellclose Square in the late 1820's. Their curiosity originally aroused by the polemic publications of Smith's opponents, they had come all the way from Piccadilly to find out for themselves. Profoundly impressed, they offered to lighten the load of Smith's Society, by opening in his "Mariners' House" (at No. 19 Wellclose Square) an office for the relief of destitute seamen. Through Smith, they obtained the daily services of a Methodist ship's mate, Thomas Sargent, as agent, in order to deal with individual cases of distress.[238]

Overwhelmed by the mounting misery they had witnessed during preceeding weeks, the two naval officers eagerly embraced Smith's plan for the new asylum. The lower floor was fitted up as a mess-room (for serving a staple diet of soup), and the loft was covered with straw for sleeping quarters. On January 8, 1828, the building was opened (not in 1827, as assumed in subsequent publications). The place was rapidly filled, with room for 160 when jammed closely enough together. Sargent was made superintendent. Captains Elliot and Gambier (helped by the latter's elder brother, Robert, likewise a naval captain), undertook the directorship of the institution.[239]

Until the summer of 1829, Smith and his organization (the BFSSFS) remained closely affiliated with the Destitute Sailors' Asylum.[240] However, for reasons which will be dealt with below, this relationship came to an abrupt end in the autumn of that year. The original asylum continued, for the present, as a private charity, under the personal charge of Captain Elliot.[241] Meanwhile, as another winter set in, shivering seamen, shelterless, shoeless, even shirtless, continued to converge on the Mariners' Church and its offices, from "all parts of the kingdom," pleading for the barest necessities of life. Wellclose Square had quite simply become known as the "Mecca" of metropolitan maritime welfare. And Smith was not the man to betray his fellow-seafarers' trust. He determined to found a so-called "New Sailors' Asylum." (The "Old" was at all events incapable of coping with more than a minute fraction of all the continuing cases of distress.)[242]

A beginning was made in temporary accommodation in Wellclose Square, even before the close of 1829. Delapidated but more extensive premises were soon secured, in Cannon-Street Road, St. George's-in-the-East (five minutes' distance), calculated to accommodate up to 300 nightly. Opened in the spring of 1830, the institution came to be called the "Sailors' Rest Asylum," as the first phase in Smith's major maritime social welfare project of that period. It was run on precisely the same lines as proposed by Smith for the original asylum in Dock Street: simply ensuring physical survival while seeking re-employment, with a strong simultaneous emphasis on a rigorous regimen of "religious instruction."[243] Falling victim to the 1832 organizational debacle, the new asylum was transferred at the close of that year to the care of a neighboring clergyman (the Rev. Thomas Bodington), Subsequently continuing in Anglican hands as the "Shipwrecked and Distressed Sailors' Asylum."[244]

In promoting public appeals for funds, pioneers in this work cited shipwreck, seasonal unemployment, ill-health, disability and advanced age as common causes of "maritime distress."[245] However, in addition to such vocational hazards and unavoidable facts of seafaring life, a major reason for ruin was held to be the sailor's personal "proneness to the vices of the lower orders," notably "drunkenness and debauchery," powerfully promoted by both his own improvidence and the imposition of others. Despite the unsavory social bias of the times evident in such formulations, no discrimination was permitted on the score of individual culpability. To those who criticized asylums as indirect encouragement to indulge in riotous living, their promoters replied:

The Destitute Sailors' Asylum, originally opened in a
deserted warehouse in Dock Street, January 8, 1828,
is depicted here in its subsequent form. (From a report
of the asylum dated June 1, 1855.)

We are not set to judge of evil actions, but to relieve distress. . . .
Reject men under any circumstances at the Asylum, and we see
little hope for them but to live by begging, or to die of starvation;
receive them, and we know not a condition of misery and evil,
however deep or degraded, from which, by the blessing of God,
they may not by reclaimed.[246]

ANTI-CRIMPING MEASURES:
SAILORS' HOMES, ETC.

Well might the combined effect of material relief and spiritual care
provide reason for encouragement. Such efforts at rehabilitation were nevertheless bound to prove inadequate, unless accompanied by attempts to come
to grips with root causes in contemporary society and provide preventive
solutions. To George Charles Smith belongs the credit for initiating the first
integrated scheme for Christian maritime social reform.

True, Smith was unable to implement every element of his expansive
plans. But he was the first to focus general attention on the sociological
realities of that "universal system of maritime plunder" known as the
Crimping System. By so doing, he (1) identified the fundamental cause of

much of the seafarer's self-inflicted misery, (2) brought this monstrous but hitherto widely-ignored social evil into public notice, and (3) supplied a strategy for its eventual elimination.

This was the result not of detached theorization, but of sustained close combat on the battlefield of London's Sailortown. It was in grappling with the grim fate of the destitute seafarer that Smith was confronted, dramatically and decisively, with the enormities of crimping. The mere fact that "at least fifty thousand persons" were estimated to be engaged in this livelihood along the north bank of the Thames alone, says something of the sheer dimensions of the problem.[247]

The Crimping System was destined, in years to come, to rank as the most notorious international impediment to the spiritual and social welfare of seamen.[248] By the 1820's, the "crimp" was already only too well established on the British waterfront, as a species of seaport parasite whose sole profession was to separate the sailor from his hard-earned wages by fair means or foul, normally foul. His method consisted in attaching himself to his victim from the earliest possible moment, and thereupon exploiting every peculiarity of the seaman's situation and character to serve his mercenary end.

For this purpose, a successful crimp would organize a whole hierarchy of helpers. Himself often a weathy publican or boarding-house owner, he could be in league with any or all of the following, as listed by G.C. Smith: "Runners," "brothel-keepers," "pot-house bullies," "cheating slop-sellers," and "pettyfogging sea-lawyers." With their aid, the crimp would establish a virtual monopoly, in meeting those two basic needs of any homecoming seafarer—relief from the privations and stress of sea-life, and re-employment when no longer willing or able to remain ashore.[249]

The resultant system of "marine slavery" (as Smith called it) seemed completely fool-proof. By devious means the seaman was duly fleeced, both of what he had earned on his arrival, and of any advance (generally two months' wages) obtainable on his departure. Meanwhile, the crimp cunningly contrived to make the shipowner dependent on him for supplying new hands when and where needed. Incredible as it may seem, this unscrupulous gangster was, in fact, the principal "shipping agent" of his day, a position he reinforced by impressive expertise in legal evasion. Nevertheless, G.C. Smith refused to resign to the prevalent attitude of *laissez-faire*. Having once "sighted the enemy," he proved himself relentless in pressing the pursuit.[250]

While still pastor at Penzance, Smith published dramatic exposés of this whole system of condoned extortion. With brutal realism, he showed how naval seamen, too, were habitually lured into the clutch of the crimp. Most explicit, however, were his accounts of conditions in the metropolis. The voracious land-sharks of London were, he alleged, "a thousand times

The ruins of New Brunswick Theatre on Well Street on
the morning of Thursday, February 28, 1828, when
the iron roof caved in, killing the proprietor and
several of the company during a rehearsal.
(A contemporary print, courtesy of BSS.)

worse than sharks at sea." (A sailor might at least be fortunate enough to
avoid the latter.)[251] After he had himself settled in the center of London's
Sailortown (1825), his anti-crimping agitation was intensified, and his
projects for "sailor-emancipation" became constantly more comprehensive.

The strategy developed by Smith and his fellow-pioneers in their
warfare with the crimp was basically a system of substitution. Every
"service" rendered by the crimp, from the very first "ship-visit" by his wily,
well-trained runners (methodically plying their prey with drink, before Jack
even had a chance to set his foot ashore), must be countered by positive
alternatives at every juncture.

A particularly crucial need for the deep-sea sailor was the provision
of boarding and lodging facilities during the time between voyages. Here, in
so-called sailors' boarding-houses, was the main stronghold of the Crimping
System. Here, therefore, was the logical place to commence competition.

This was already recognized in the constitution of the original Bethel
Union, which expressly called for: "The providing of suitable boarding-
houses for Sailors on their arrival from foreign voyages."[252] In 1821, the
BFSFSBU did, in fact, open the first of what was hoped would be a series of

Society-owned sailors' boarding-houses, at 52 Great Hermitage Street, Wapping. Here seamen could be "comfortably lodged and boarded at a moderate expense, under the superintendance of a pious brother-seaman" (a Captain Baker). After two years, the experiment was abandoned, however, owing to "expenses increasing so rapidly and weakening the funds of the Society." Instead, the committee decided to adopt the "Liverpool plan."[253]

The Liverpool Seamen's Friend Society had made their position perfectly plain. They regarded Society-recommended sailors' boarding-houses as "next in importance" only to the provision of the means of grace. Confronted with all the ramifications of the Crimping System, that Society saw no other prospect of "giving permanency" to whatever good they might otherwise do. By 1822, only a year after the formation of the Society, its "Sub-Committee for Lodging-Houses" could report twenty duly-approved lodging-houses for seamen, also eight for captains and mates, all under "vigilant inspection."[254]

In actual fact, the method had already been launched as early as 1820, by the Seamen's Friend Societies in Greenock and Leith respectively. Bristol soon followed suit. The principle was the same. Lists of boarding-houses, meeting the Society's standard for comfort, cleanliness and fair-dealing, were systematically circulated among the men on arrival. Library-boxes were allocated to each address, as at least some degree of counter-attraction to more sordid Sailortown entertainment.[255]

Sources indicate that surprisingly many seamen responded positively. Certainly, the crimp's monopoly was broken. But he was by no means beaten, least of all in London, where all the society-strife of the 1820's had left him relatively unmolested. During the first weeks of 1828, as forlorn seafarers clamored daily for admittance to the recently-opened Destitute Sailors' Asylum in Dock Street, G.C. Smith was acutely aware that their numbers would only continue to swell, unless seamen could, before they became enmeshed in the crimping net, be met with some concrete, competitive alternative on a significant scale.

Then—like a bolt from the blue—came the sensational fall of the Brunswick Theatre on Well Street, in the morning of February 28, 1828. Despite all the immediate human tragedy (which he, too, deplored), Smith could not, to the end of his days, help but see the whole as an awe-inspiring manifestation of both divine judgment and providence.[256] Certainly, the consequences for the Seamen's Cause were far-reaching.

The Brunswick Theatre had been opened only three days previously. But Smith and his colleagues had no illusions as to its anticipated impact. On the same site (in this parallel street, separating Wellclose Square from Dock Street) had stood the old Royalty Theatre, until its destruction by fire in

1826. In an age when even a better-class playhouse was a place where prostitutes openly plied their trade, the Royalty had achieved noteriety as a veritable hotbed of vice. Set in the center of "the largest maritime neighborhood in the world," it had become a focal-point for crimps, thieves and harlots, and, according to Smith, an annual source of ruin for thousands of gullible tars.[257]

On that fateful February morning, from the moment one of his agents thundered at his door, shouting that the new theater had collapsed, Smith reacted with a resolution worthy of one of Nelson's men. Arriving as one of the first on the scene, he at once took command of the situation. A rehearsal had been in progress when the huge roof caved in, and scores were buried in the rubble. Smith immediately sent for every available man at the Destitute Sailors' Asylum (in adjacent Dock Street). Then, for nine hours, he personally superintended the work of digging out the dead and wounded.[258]

Standing amidst the ruins, Smith was suddenly seized by a vision. Only shortly before, he had published the desperate need, as he saw it, for some large "Sailors' Depot," with facilities for both receiving and reshipping discharged (as opposed to destitute) seamen. Had not now God himself providentially pointed out the place? The disasters of 1826 and now 1828 had surely proved: "God will not have a sailors' playhouse in Well Street." Originally, this had been the site of a chapel. What could be more appropriate than to "restore" the ground to God, for the rescue instead of the ruin of seafarers? With all the "determination of his soul," Smith sallied forth to achieve exactly that.[259]

In attempting to wrest the ground from those who were anxious to raise yet a third theater on the site, Smith had the benefit of personal publicity from a massive press coverage of the disaster. The following Sunday, he preached to vast crowds of credulous sightseers, both by the ruins and in the grounds of the Mariners' Church, with 4,000 and 5,000 hearers, respectively. For March 6th, Smith had already arranged a public meeting at Freemasons' Hall, in order to launch a subscription for the relief of the wounded, widowed and orphaned from the recent Battle of Navarino. This gave him a golden opportunity of publicly presenting his depot-plan for the first time, and of securing initial pledges of support. Public feeling was further fanned by a series of six tracts, simultaneously rushed off the press by the enterprising Smith.

By August, Smith's efforts had led to an agreement for the purchase of the leasehold of the ground. On September 10, 1828, to the "astonishment and horror" of onlooking crimps, Smith held a historic public meeting on the site itself, where this was solemnly dedicated to its new purpose. Officers were elected "pro tempore."[260]

At length, again on Smith's initiative a public meeting was held on January 8, 1829, at the City of London Tavern. Here, organizational machinery was finally established, and the "Sailors' Home, or Royal Brunswick Maritime Establishment" officially founded. The first part of the title, only recently coined by Smith, was destined to become a universal, generic term. The latter original designation, recalling the former use of the site, was eventually abandoned. As confirmed by subsequent events, the year 1829 (later widely misrepresented as 1830) is significant as marking the founding of the first "sailors' home" (in the modern sense) in the world.

After further promotional activity, the freehold was finally purchased on May 29th. On June 22nd, exactly the fifteenth anniversary of the traditional origin of the Thames Revival, hard-hit seamen from the Dock Street Asylum helped lay the first bricks of this haven of hope for fellow-seafarers. With such a turn of events in a district notorious as the very "Sodom and Gomorrah of Sailors," friends of the Seamen's Cause optimistically felt the kingdom of the crimp had at long last been dealt a "death-blow."[261]

Who were the men willing to join with Smith, during the critical first phase of this epoch-making venture? The list of officers elected in January 1829 includes, among sixteen directors, such early friends as Opie Smith, Thomas Thompson and Thomas Phillips. The Rev. Richard Marks became (with Smith himself) an honorary secretary. However, in a special category came the two naval captains already involved in the superintendance of the neighboring Destitute Sailors' Asylum.

After Smith had publicized his plans, George Gambier and Robert Elliot were among the first to offer their aid. The former became, for a short while, the conspicuously active treasurer of the enterprise, the latter an honorary secretary for whom the Sailors' Home in Well Street developed into an all-consuming life-work. Captains Gambier and Elliot, themselves already intimately involved in the manifold activities of the Religious and Charitable Society House at 32 Sackville Street, brought with them several Evangelical colleagues from the Naval and Military Bible Society and the Episcopal Floating Church Society into the sponsorship of this new endeavor.[262]

Nevertheless, later events should not be permitted to obscure (as they largely did)[263] the fact that it was the Rev. George Charles Smith who first conceived the idea of the Sailors' Home, who secured its highly strategic site, and who bore the full weight of the intense publicity campaign needed to reach the point where work on the building actually began. Through his magazines, tracts and speeches, he kept elaborating on a three-point plan, which, in some of its implications, was nothing short of revolutionary.

A "Receiving and Shipping Depot" was to be the first and major facility of the new facility. Here, on the invitation of agents (who would

THE LONDON CRIMPING SYSTEM,—With a view to the exposure and annihilation of this nefarious and destructive system, bv which British and Foreign Sailors are ruined on the banks of the Thames, the GENERAL PUBLIC MEETING of the SAILORS' HOME, or Royal Brunswick Maritime Establishment, will be held at the Freemasons' Hall, on Thursday, May 14, for the ERECTION of a BUILDING, on the site of the late Royal Brunswick Theatre, for the reception, lodging, and protection of the persons and property of sailors, the improvement of their morals, saving them from the crimps of London, and regularly shipping them on outward bound vessels to all parts of the world, for His Majesty's Navy, the Coast Guard or Revenue Service.

The Right Hon. Lord Viscount MANDEVILLE, R.N., M.P., Perpetual Chairman, will preside.

The chair will be taken at 12 o'clock precisely.

The Leasehold of the Ground, and all the materials of the Theatre, have been purchased, and £1,000 are now in the hands of the treasurer for the purchase of the freehold, in order that the ground and buildings which shall be erected on it shall be the exclusive property of sailors for ever.

Tickets may be had of Capt. G. Gambier, R.N. ; Capt. R. Elliott, R.N. ; J. Chippindale, Esq., jun. ; Nisbett, Berners-street ; Hatchard, Piccadilly ; or at the office, 17, Wellclose-square.

Notice of a public meeting to be held May 14, 1829,
to secure the purchase of the freehold of the
Brunswick Theatre site in Well Street (as it
appeared in *The Times,* May 1, 1829.)

The world's first "Sailors' Home," commenced in 1829
on the initiative of the Rev. George Charles Smith
on the site of the Brunswick Theatre ruins in Well
Street, and completed in 1835, largely due to the
perseverance of Captain Robert James Elliot, RN.
(*Chart and Compass,* 1884.)

accost crews on arrival with boats and carts belonging to the Home), the sailor could, at a reasonable rate, and in relative comfort and perfect safety, find board and lodging for himself, and safe-keeping for his sea-chest.[264]

Besides a museum and library for recreation purposes, a "Seamen's Saving Bank" was projected, in order to encourage wage deposits, and facilitate family remmittances.[265] (Others, as well as Smith, had for several years advocated this method of evading the grasp of the crimp. Such a bank had, in actual fact, been opened by the Edinburgh and Leith Seamen's Friend Society as early as 1823.)[266]

Even more potentially disastrous to the Crimping System was the proposed "Seamen's Register Office." Here, seamen residing in the Home (or transferred for want of room to approved boarding houses) would be recorded, so that ship's husbands, captains and naval officers could henceforth cover their shipping needs through this agency. A system of character references was also proposed, where earlier all that counted was whether a man could "hand reef and steer."[267] (A register of this nature had for some years been planned by both the BFSFSBU and others. Again, that enterprising Society in Leith was the first to put it into practice, in the mid-1820's.) Otherwise, seamen's mission societies in general had, from the very outset, found themselves involved in an employment agency role, whether in consequence of educational, orphanage and relief programs, or simply because they were there, while seamen's unions and official shipping offices were still far into the future.[268]

Another facility included in Smith's Sailors' Home plan was a so-called "Sailors' Refuge." Smith distinguished between three categories of seamen seeking shelter: the monied (capable of paying their own way for a while), the middle-class ("decent but distressed," though not to the point of having sold or literally lost everything), and the miserable ("starving, houseless, wretched," in other words utterly destitute). If a seaman of the second category were to be saved from slipping into the third ("soup and straw") group, with attendant loss of self-respect, it was "absolutely necessary" to provide an alternative to the existing Asylum, a place where he could hang his hammock, and "ride out his temporal storms," leaving it to his own integrity to repay on his next return from overseas.[269]

A third facility featured in Smith's Sailors' Home plan consisted of a junior department entitled the "Sea Boys' Rendezvous." This was intended as a means of mass pre-sea training, simultaneously solving the problem of parents of spirited offspring smitten with the "rage" for a seafaring life, as well as magistrates seeking to divert the rising tide of urban juvenile delinquency by constantly crying "Send them to sea!" (The scheme could, it was pointed out, also help to obviate the blight of impressment, in the event of future naval hostilities.)[270]

The "great fundamental principle" of the Sailors' Home enterprise was the pervasion of every activity with "Christian discipline." Where "men of the world," in despair over all the derelicts of society around them, would say they had "tried the hulks," the supporters of the Home could reply, "We will try religious instruction." As to the crimping fraternity, these were (in early 1829) reportedly terrified at the prospect of an establishment in their midst, whose inmates would "enjoy the important advantage of morning and evening domestic prayers," and where "a religious observance of the sabbath" would be taught. It was emphasized that such instruction would be based on "the general principles of Christianity, without reference to particular tenets of faith."[271]

Neither this decidely nondenominational basis nor several other features of the plan saw final fruition. In the latter part of the summer of 1829, a sudden crisis among leaders of the venture led to both modifications and half a decade of delay. Simply stated, G.C. Smith had "excited the displeasure" of George Gambier. The immediate bone of contention was easily eliminated. (From two charges leveled by Gambier, both of a minor nature, yet nevertheless liable to injure Smith's public character, he was completely exonerated.)[272] The underlying cause of conflict was not so readily resolved. Smith adamantly refused to tolerate Gambier's Irvingite ideas.

The Rev. Edward Irving (1792-1834), brilliant Presbyterian preacher of the Scotch Church in London, who had in recent years been taking that city "by storm," had long since shown a personal interest in the Seamen's Cause. (He had, for example, preached at the inauguration of services afloat in Glasgow, in 1822.) By 1829, his mounting millenarian radicalism had already alienated many. Nevertheless, restless spirits within the Church of England, among them Captain Gambier, responded enthusiastically to Irving's urgent message of Christ's imminent return.[273] The more practical-minded Smith, on the other hand, constantly importuned by Gambier, had no patience with apocalyptic speculations. Gambier persevered, condemning Smith for resorting to such "worldly means" as the fund-raising methods currently in vogue among religious societies, protesting against such normal precautions as estimates and contracts. The Home must be built entirely "by faith."[274]

The two were clearly on a collision course. The outcome was Smith's resignation as honorary secretary (in August 1829), and Gambier's as secretary (in September the same year). Thereupon Smith, exasperated also by the concurrent "Philo-Veritas" poison-pen campaign, decided to launch a separate, far more comprehensive project: "The Sailors' Rest, or Maritime Guardian Establishment" ("for lodging, relieving, protecting, and improving the sailors of all nations"). This was publicized at a preliminary public meeting at the Mariners' Church October 29, 1829.

Meanwhile, Gambier's close companion Elliot, though at this period holding Irvingite sympathies, had proved himself of milder mould, and had taken no part in stigmatizing Smith. This fact opened the way for a conciliatory meeting at the City of London Tavern, November 24, 1829, under the chairmanship of the Rev. Richard Marks. Here, Smith's role as founder and principal promoter of the original Sailors' Home was publicly recognized, and supporters of this institution were set at liberty to transfer their subscriptions to the new Sailors' Rest project. Many evidently did.[275]

The situation for the Sailors' Home seemed unpromising. Nevertheless, the fact that many of those who withdrew were Dissenters opened the possibility for Captain Elliot and his friends to make this an entirely Anglican institution, and thereby seek support from circles which had hitherto held back. By spring 1831, efforts had progressed to the point where the Bishop of London accepted the office of Patron of the Home, provided the chaplain were Church of England, and approved by him. However, with the outcry against Irvingite "heresy" culminating shortly afterwards, public uneasiness about the involvement of Elliot and his Sackville Street associates brought building operations (already badly delayed) to a complete standstill.[276]

Meanwhile Smith, after opening his New Sailors' Asylum in Cannon-Street Road, early 1830, [277] continued on his separate course, publicizing plans for further phases of an impressive scheme of maritime social welfare. "No half measures will do to destroy the crimping system," he insisted. Besides the features originally planned for the Well Street Sailors' Home, the prospectus of the "Sailors' Rest, or Maritime Guardian Establishment" called for several important innovations.[278]

The need for specifically maritime medical care had been dramatically demonstrated during the first years following the peace of 1815, when "vast numbers" of merchant seamen in the metropolis were known to have died, simply through lack of hospital treatment. This was again ascribed to the combined effect of two causes in the seafarer himself: (1) His powerful prejudice against having to "repair to a Hospital on shore," often preferring to perish on board or in the streets. (2) His general "ignorance of the proper mode of obtaining admission," even if he wanted it. Both impediments were taken into careful consideration with the founding, on March 8, 1821, of the "Seamen's Hospital Society for the Relief of Sick and Diseased Seamen arriving in the Port of London" (already noted as evolving directly from the 1818 Committee for the Relief of Distressed Seamen).

The same year, the 50-gun *Grampus* was granted by the Government, fitted out as a "Floating Hospital," and permanently moored off Greenwich. Here the radical practice was introduced of immediately accepting "every sick seaman, on presenting himself alongside," without regard to

The hospital ship *Dreadnought,* Collingwood's former
flagship at Trafalgar, moored off Greenwich as a floating
hospital for international sailors, 1831-57. The Dreadnought
Seamen's Hospital eventually "went ashore" in 1870.
(*Chart and Compass,* 1884.)

nationality or recommendation (other than "his own apparent condition").
Replaced after a decade by the larger three-decker *Dreadnought* (of Trafalgar
fame), the Seamen's Hospital off Greenwich had long before then established
itself as an indispensable "Christian Charity," including in its regular staff
the ministrations of a Church of England chaplain.[279]

The provision of seamen's hospital facilities as such was not seen as
a direct function of seamen's mission societies. However, the latter would
warmly advocate an enterprise such as the Seamen's Hospital off Greenwich,
as being vital to the general wellbeing of seafarers. They also voiced a
natural concern for the availability and quality of pastoral care wherever
seamen were hospitalized.

In certain ways, seamen's mission societies even sought to provide
supplementary medical care. The asylum in Well Street and Cannon-Street
Road would give sorely-needed convalescence opportunities to seamen
discharged from the hospital hulk. In his Sailors' Rest project, G.C. Smith
published plans for both a "Convalescent Haven" (for those discharged from
hospital, but still "utterly unfit for ship's duty"), and a "Sailors' Infirmary"
(for those with minor afflictions, not admissable as hospital cases, yet
jeopardizing re-employment).[280]

An area in need of even more radical reform was the care of aged
and disabled seafarers. The plight of seamen stranded ashore owing to

advancing years or physical handicap was not merely pitiful, but little short of ridiculous. A seaman who had contributed his sixpence per month as obliged by law to the funds of Greenwich Royal Hospital, during a whole life-time in the merchant service of his country, would normally "never derive one penny of advantage" from it, but be left, when "decayed" or disabled, to perish in the streets or in the parish workhouse. In practice, the Royal Hospital had room for *naval* veterans only.[281]

In order to remedy this "unpatriotic and unchristian" condition of affairs, Smith projected, as part of his Sailors' Rest plan, a vast "Merchant Seamen's Hospital" (or "Infirm and Aged Sailors' Moorings"). Intended to provide "peace and piety" for 2,000 to 3,000 "disabled and worn-out Mariners," this was to be an institution remarkable for its enlightened geriatric principles. It would seek to (1) eliminate the "dreadful vacuum of mind" evident at Greenwich Royal Hospital, by providing well-stocked reading-rooms, (2) defeat demoralizing idleness by suitable light employment, and (3) combat "gross immoralities" resulting from lack of married quarters. In close proximity to this asylum was planned what was thought to be the first "Sailors' Cemetery" in the world. Proposals for financing the project included a transfer of the merchant seamen's controversial "Greenwich Sixpence." Petitions were presented to Parliament. Smith even headed a deputation to Downing Street, and "reasoned with his lordship [Earl Grey] for nearly an hour."[282]

Meanwhile, Smith became increasingly convinced that, for the sea-going sailor, the situation called for nothing short of a total remedy. The original Sailors' Home could not (even if building operations were recommenced) effect more than a partial solution. There must be one "general maritime depot," large enough to accommodate all seamen seeking lodging in London. Furthermore, a New Sailors' Home of this nature (from 1831 on referred to as the "Sailors' Anchorage") must, in order to succeed, leave easily-led seamen no choice. For this purpose, Smith suggested a twofold strategy: (1) that shipowners voluntarily agree to ship seamen from no other place, and (2) that the Government pass stringent anti-crimping laws, making it penal "to buy a sailor's wages, or to take . . . advantage of his inexperience or his vices."[283]

Among further innovations proposed by Smith, was the provision of sorely-needed legal aid for seafarers. A seaman assailed by land-sharks, and arrested for some ficticious debt, would normally not even attempt to obtain legal redress. As Smith pointed out, "when he [the sailor] got into what he called the *bilboes,* his only anxiety was, how to get out as quickly as possible, even at the sacrifice of a large sum of money." Henceforth, a "respectable solicitor" would be employed and made available to seamen who had been exposed to extortion ashore, or, for that matter, cruelty on shipboard. (Similar services were recommended for the outports.)[284]

Providing slop-chest stores was also indispensable to a seaman. The wry comment of one shirtless sailor, "all drift" after a shore spree, is understandable: "I must look out for a ship again, and it's no use without some rigging over my mast-head. . . ." In order to combat the tactics of the "crimp slopseller," who, on the strength of an advance-note, would sell substandard sea-gear to stranded seamen at exorbitant prices, Smith proposed patronizing a list of "upright tradesmen," whom seamen could frequent without fear of imposition. (His Society actually promoted, in 1829, the settlement of one Mr. Coleman in Grace's Alley, by Wellclose Square, as providing a dependable "general warehouse for seamen's clothing.")[285]

Another significant service to be sponsored by the New Sailors' Home was their provision of maritime lectures, in rooms espressly allocated for the purpose. Here,

> . . . scientific lectures should be delivered to sailors on navigation, geography, astronomy, hydraulics, steam, history, health, climate, and useful resources in times of extremity, . . . and our sailors would thus rise in mental intelligence as labouring men in Mechanics' Institutes from the low brutified sensualities which now unhappily constitute all their paradise.[286]

The great goal for Smith's program of maritime social action was that every single seamen should, before shipping out, pass through the process of a sort of "moral hospital," eventually resulting in the raising of a whole "new race of seamen."[287] However, the demise of the British and Foreign Seamen and Soldiers' Friend Society, in the summer of 1832, proved fatal to almost every aspect of his ingenious Sailors' Rest project. (By that time, only the Asylum in Cannon-Street Road had materialized.) Nevertheless, Smith had uncovered desperate, basic needs, in an age not yet prepared to meet them; and he had charted a course in maritime social reform, which future generations could no more afford to ignore.

Meanwhile, the disaster of 1832 left Smith's original scheme, the Sailors' Home in Well Street, virtually alone in the field, thereby opening new hope for this far more modest enterprise. True, a new threat was posed, in 1832, by the defection of Thomas Sargent and a number of disillusioned promoters of the Well Street Home. A rival institution was actually opened, in a large warehouse in the same street. The attempt was abandoned the following year, however, and Sargent was reconciled with Captain Elliot.[288] So, too, was G.C.Smith, eventually. Smith had never found the slightest reason to question the personal piety and integrity of Elliot (or, for that matter, Gambier).

After the culmination of the Irvingite alarm, Captain Elliot and his friends made good their opportunity to re-establish loyalty to the Church of England, and to make use of a more acceptable society structure. With restored public confidence, and renewed interest on the part of shipowners, work on what had long been only the "carcass" of a building was at last resumed. On May 1, 1835, the Sailors' Home, Well Street, could finally be opened, more due to the dogged determination of Captain Robert Elliot, than probably any other human factor.[289]

Attacking the maritime vices: prostitution, intemperance, profanity, sabbath breaking

In maritime devotional literature through the centuries, warnings against four particular vices recur with such remarkable regularity, that they might well be designated the cardinal maritime vices: promiscuity, drunkenness, swearing and desecration of the Lord's Day. All four were held to have profound social as well as strictly spiritual implications. Hence, combating them was considered by seamen's mission pioneers a matter of high priority, calling for not only verbal admonition by also drastic and systematic countermeasures.

An early argument in favor of a London Sailors' Home had been that outward-bound seamen seemed predestined to go only "from the brothels of Wapping to the brothels of Calcutta." G.C. Smith was keenly aware of the close connection between Sailortown prostitution and the Crimping System. He became an ardent pioneer of the "Maritime Anti-Prostitution Movement."[290]

Motivated not only by concern for his hard-pressed fellow-seafarers, but also by compassion for the "poor sea-harlots" themselves, Smith counseled them in their hovels and preached to them in the streets. However, he realized that more drastic means were called for, if these miserable maritime "Magdalenes" were to be rescued from the real criminals, the "Crimping Brothel-Owners" and their notorious host of "Procuresses," "Teachers," and "Watchers."

The impulse came from seven sea-harlots who, in the autumn of 1829, responded to tracts and invitations to attend services at the Mariners' Church. Overjoyed, Smith had a special pew screened in for their use. Soon, up to thirty would come, "without bonnets" (in token of their trade). However, they also presented a problem. Conscious-stricken, the hapless girls complained they had no place to go, but back to "walk the streets, and roll in infamy for a night's lodging, or a loaf of bread."[291]

The outcome was a preliminary public meeting at the Galilee Chapel, January 4, 1830. Here was established the "Maritime Penitent

Young Woman's Refuge" ("for the rescue, abode, employment, and restoration to society, of Thirty Females from the Seafaring District"). Located in Wellclose Square, and organized as a branch of the BFSSFS, it was (like the Sailors' Orphan House Establishment) operated partly by the fair sex of Smith's own immediate family, and supported by ladies' associations in different parts of the country. Results were both "painful and pleasing." At all events, the enterprise (then renamed the "Maritime Female Refuge") proved sufficiently robust to survive the debacle of 1832, and move to Hackney Road, as an independent institution.[292]

Smith was well aware that existing facilities for the rehabilitation of penitent prostitutes, besides being grievously overtaxed, were inadequate in principle. As in the case of seamen's lodgings, rescue measures required supplementation by preventive action. In the battle for the abolition of the Sailortown branch of this continuing "Female Slave Trade," Smith underscored the prophylactic effect of virtually every form of seamen's mission activity, including general Sailortown evangelism, and the relief of distressed seamen's families. Nor did he omit to point out the long-term impact of "pious females" as coadjutors in seamen's mission work, or of pupils from the Society's girls' school as future seamen's wives. These would promote a Christian counter-image of true womanhood, as compared to that projected by prostitutes. In fact, he maintained, speaking of the magnetic pull of the mariners' vice-dens in the metropolis:

> Let marriage be recommended and promoted among sailors, and
> in a few years the mass of seamen who visit London, would return
> as regularly to their homes, their wives and children, as our
> coasting sailors now do.[293]

Against a form of condoned promiscuity which Smith characterized as the "brothelization" of the Navy, he was merciless and ultimately victorious. The Articles of War were unmistakable in condemning any act of "uncleanness" on His Majesty's ships. But, "in order to keep the Seamen contented on board," and supposedly suppress mass desertions in port, an attitude of official permissiveness had prevailed since Stuart times. The target of Smith's incessant attacks was, therefore, not the "fleshmongers" of Portsmouth or other naval stations, the bumboat-owners who brought out prostitutes by the hundreds on the arrival of ships of war, but the Lords Commissioners of the Admiralty, who refused to prevent the admission of unmarried females on vessels under their jurisdiction. Did they believe that "God winks at such things as the Lords of the Admiralty deem necessary for the indulgence of the ship's company?"

Smith pointed in his own writings to the urgency of eradicating this evil before a new war would multiply it, by drawing into the vortex "*twenty thousand* young females, in addition to those already in the paths of public vice." He simultaneously published a series of lurid descriptions of lower-deck orgies, based on recollections from his own years in the Navy, as well as observations during his later travels. Vividly portraying the effect of such scenes on the impressionable minds of young midshipmen, Smith showed how the sanctioning of debauchery on demand was enough to nullify evangelical endeavor on any given ship, whether by her own chaplains or others.[294]

Deliberately emulating the strategy of the slave trade abolitionists, Smith mounted a continuous campaign, by articles, tracts and petitions, to rouse the general public to the actual extent of these "naval enormities." An exposé entitled *Portsmouth,* published in 1828 and addressed to the Bishop of London, was presented to the Duke of Wellington; it achieved particularly wide publicity.[295] Others, too, eagerly quoted by Smith, helped to unmask the double morality of an embarrased but obdurate officialdom. Richard Marks spoke out boldly and eloquently; a well-argued *Statement* by Admiral Hawkins, first circulated privately in 1821, but published openly in 1822, caused nation-wide consternation; an *Address* published in Dublin shortly afterwards by a veteran naval surgeon added further dramatic documentation.[296] But at mid-century, the fact that the practice had by then been "done away with" was—in human terms— credited mainly to the unflagging perseverence of G.C. Smith.[297]

From time immemorial, drunkenness had, especially for the seafarer, been regarded as the twin temptation of debauchery.[298] For him, powerful sociological factors (to be dealt with later) would conspire to compound these problems.[299] Thus, the conventional attitude to intoxication was to think of it not as "sin, harm, or disgrace," but rather as the very "acme of sensual bliss," to be loyally and liberally shared with shipmates.[300]

The British Marine Temperance Movement, like the nineteenth-century Temperance Reformation as a whole, owed much to the drive and initiative of transatlantic temperance pioneers. (Smith writes in retrospect of the reciprocation by which the Bethel Movement was brought from Britain to America, and the Marine Temperance Movement from America back to Britain.) A major catalyst in this case seems to have been a letter dated May 16, 1829, addressed by the Rev. Joshua Leavitt, at that time General Agent of the American Seamen's Friend Society, to G.C. Smith:

> The most absorbing topic of enquiry on moral subjects now agitated in the United States, is the question of "Temperance". I send you some pamphlets, but they will give you no idea of the interest which the subject is exciting here. Many ships are now navigated without grog. . . . I wish you would turn your attention to this subject, you might commence a reformation in England as great as we have now going on here.[301]

"The Jolly Tars of Old England on a Land Cruise."
A favorite form of revelry for naval seamen on an all too
rare shore leave. (Peter Kemp: *The British Sailor.*)

Exactly that was what Smith set out to accomplish. In September 1829, he published a 94-page pamphlet through the BFSSFS entitled *Intemperance,* embracing much of the material sent by Leavitt. The book ("designed to lay the foundation for the general establishment of Temperance Societies throughout the kingdom") aroused great interest, especially among concerned Quakers. In 1831, the "British and Foreign Temperance Society" was formed. Meanwhile, Smith continued to "agitate" the cause through his magazine, particularly in relation to seafarers.

Finally, on June 14, 1832, a public meeting was held at the Mariners' Church, with Smith in the chair, at which a maritime temperance society was founded, under the title "Riverside Temperance Association," as a distinct branch of the BFSSFS. From the autumn of that year, a growing list of captains signed the Society's "Temperance Book," following the American example of declaring their ships "temperance ships," and allowing no ardent spirits on board. With Admiral Sir J. Brenton as president, and with Smith's son, Theophilus, and Edmund Fry Jr., as its enthusiastic secretaries, the Society survived the summer storms of 1832, and merged into a general "Sailors' and Soldiers' Temperance Union," in January 1833.[302]

The sin of swearing was another vice to which seafarers were considered especially susceptible. In Wesley's England, coarseness and

This later flag illustrates the convergence of the Bethel and Temperance Movements, promoted by G.C. Smith from 1829 on. (*Chart and Compass,* 1884.)

blasphemy had become the vogue. A servant could, for example, say of a visitor: "She swore so dreadfully, I knew she must be a lady of quality."[303] At sea, however, where sudden stress situations were commonplace, swearing had, for centuries, been a general tradition. Here, as with sexual permissiveness in the Navy, a strange dualism was quite evident. On the one hand, "profane oaths, cursings, execrations" were proscribed by the Articles of War, and punishable by court-martial. On the other, swearing was justified by high and low, even encouraged as a kind of vocational necessity. Officers had to curse to command respect. The men would compete to become a "leading hand" at swearing; or they might object to sailing with missionaries as passengers, for fear of having the privilege of cursing curtailed![304]

Reaction to this situation converged in a "Marine Anti-swearing Movement." Such as took the scriptural consequences seriously sought to protect both swearer and hearer, whether by forcible suppression or by subtler means of persuasion. Lord Gambier, as commander of the *Defence*, cured culprits by reviving the old penalty of wearing a weighted wooden collar. Others might employ flogging or fines.[305] Seamen's devotional literature, tracts and magazines were liberally supplied with examples of "awful visitations," where thoughtless imprecations were answered as requested by an offended Almighty.[306] On one ship, swearing simply ceased when each man secured his own Bible.[307] In Liverpool, an evangelical dockmaster promoted the founding of a so-called "Swearing Society," during the winter of 1830-31. Ship's officers subscribing to it would only ship crews on the understanding that no swearing would be allowed on board.[308]

The inimitable Rev. Rowland Hill has recorded a priceless example of how plain good humor could carry the day:

> Once when I was returning from Ireland, I found myself much
> annoyed by the reprobate conduct of the captain and mate, who

were both sadly given to the scandalous habit of swearing. First the captain swore at the mate—then the mate swore at the captain—then they swore at the wind—when I called them with a strong voice for fair play. "Stop, stop," said I, "if you please gentlemen, let us have fair play, it's my turn now." "At what is it your turn, pray?" said the captain. "At swearing," I replied. Well they waited and waited until their patience was exhausted, and then wanted me to make haste and take my turn. I told them, however, that I had a right to take my own time, and swear at my own convenience. To this the captain replied, with a laugh, "Perhaps you don't mean to take your turn?" "Pardon me, captain," I replied, "but I do, as soon as I can find the good of doing so.". . . I did not hear another oath on the voyage.[309]

The fourth of the maritime vices, deliberate "desecration of the Sabbath," was considered fateful and frustrating to a particular degree. In the first place, Sabbath-breaking was the *crucial* sin, looked on as "the inlet to every other sin" (such as indolence, bad company, drinking, dissipation and "ultimate ruin of both soul and body"). In the second place, here was a sin to which the seafarer was frequently *forced,* by his own superiors. The wry humor of the so-called seamen's version of the Fourth Commandment (widely known as "The Philadelphia Catechism") was far from unjustified:

"Six days shalt thou labour and do all thou art able,
And on the seventh holystone the deck and scrape the cable."[310]

The basic premise of the "Maritime Sabbath Observance Movement," which emerged during the 1820's, was the prevalent Sabbatarian "substitution theory," which saw the Christian Sunday as simply replacing the Mosaic Sabbath. However, for seamen's mission advocates, four factors made rigorous Sabbath observance a matter of particular urgency: (1) The "deadly influence" in the impressionable minds of young sailors of the example of Sabbath-violating seniors. (2) The "fearful stigma" of Sabbath-breaking seamen undermining the message of missionaries to the heathen, by their negative image. (3) The severe vocational limits on a seaman's Sabbath opportunities, emphasizing the need to "value and improve them the more," whenever available. (4) The advent of steam-propulsion, with heavier capital investment and the demand for faster "turn-arounds." (The first two factors would apply equally as much to the three vices already dealt with.)[311]

The strategy adopted in order to promote respect for the Lord's Day would vary according to the source of violation. As individuals, seamen were exhorted, by word of mouth and literary media, to make the best of whatever opportunities were available—in port or at sea—for spiritual edification and physical rest.[312] In practice, however, such opportunities might be at the complete mercy of masters and shipowners. For fishing and whaling crews,

Sunday catching developed into an early controversial issue.[313] In the case of
merchant ships, putting to sea on Sunday became the target of a continuous
crusade of opposition by seamen's mission societies of the day. "Only alive
to their temporal interests, . . . insensible to all divine authority or divine
displeasure," merchants and shipowners who forced crews to sea on the
Sabbath were warned that, in so doing, they were victimizing not only the
seamen themselves, but also their families, and hosts of people in allied
occupations.

      The Greenock Seamen's Friend Society was particularly vocal. In
1827, they published an animated *Address to the Owners of Vessels
belonging to, and sailing from the Clyde*, to which was attached a petition
signed by "upwards of 300 Sailors, Pilots, Riggers, and Jobbers." The
forthrightness of these Clydeside Scots inspired similar demands in other
major ports, such as Leith, Liverpool and London.[314]

      Although the champions of the seamen's Sabbath seemed to be
fighting a losing battle against the claims of "progress" and profit, their
efforts were far from futile. As a result of their campaigning, "several shipowners made a point of not allowing their vessels to go to sea on the
Sabbath." By 1833, it was nevertheless recognized that "voluntary means"
had not sufficed, and hopes were pinned to statutory safeguards (such as Sir
Andrew Agnew's Sabbath Observance Bill).[315]

      For maritime Sabbatarians, one source of frustration was a super-
stitious notion among seamen themselves, that to sail on a Sunday was good,
since it was to "take the prayers of the church with them" (alluding to the
petition in the Anglican Litany for "all persons traveling by land or by
water").[316] More serious, however, was the opposition within the industry
itself. Seamen's mission societies sensed they must forfeit their claim to be
"The Seamen's Friend," were they unwilling to plead for his "temporal and
spiritual welfare" as they saw it, despite the "hazard of being reproached for
doing so." It took no mean moral courage to confront an establishment on
which they were themselves in no small measure dependent. But in so doing,
these seamen's mission pioneers by their persevering prophetic ministry,
helped promote "one of the first forward steps in modern social progress" (as
the liberation of the laborer's Sunday has since been called).[317]

POLITICAL AND INDUSTRIAL ACTION

      In essence, the battle for the seafarer's Sabbath was, in its confronta-
tion with the economic establishment, and in its resort to legislative action, a
significant manifestation of maritime diaconal concern in the field of politics
and industrial relations, an area where early advocates of seamen's missions
have hitherto received little recognition.

However, it is a fact of subsequent history that nearly all the projects already presented, as part of an emerging maritime diaconate, preceded—and in some measure prompted—ultimate government action. (This applies to such concerns as maritime educational and recreational facilities, relief of destitute seamen and their dependents, provision for sick, disabled and retired seafarers, as well as a variety of anti-crimping measures.) Furthermore, as already noted, seamen's mission pioneers were stimulated by the revelations of the anti-slave trade campaign to agitate against both of those notorious forms of officially condoned abuse against the individual liberty of seafarers: the threat of impressment, and disciplinary cruelty at sea.[318]

Among those who, in the post-war period, revived the earlier outcry against impressment with particular vehemence, was G.C. Smith. He argued that, precisely in a period of precarious peace, one had to eradicate a practice which violated the British seaman just as much as the "home-wrested Negro." He prepared petitions, and gladly gave magazine coverage to those who, like J.S. Buckingham, M.P., would agitate to remove a paradox that sought to enslave the defenders of Britain's liberty. Were the press gang to be revived in time of war, every improvement in the "moral condition" of British seamen would be set at nought. Many would again "expatriate themselves," or, by going into hiding, "become the prey of the crimp." Once more, boys, beggars, convicts and foreigners would be forced to fill their place.

In 1835, two years after the abolition of slavery in British colonies, it was seen as a similar victory, when Parliament acceded to the reformers' long-standing demand for a General Register Office of Merchant Seamen. Naval impressment, though not expressly eliminated, was never again found feasible.[319]

There was an obvious and intimate interrelationship between impressment and disciplinary cruelty at sea. That brutal and arbitrary methods of maintaining naval discipline went back to antiquity, and that they were also widely applied in the merchant service, only underscored the magnitude of the problem.[320] Although the barbarous torture of "flogging round the fleet" was still practiced in the Royal Navy, it was the capriciousness of corporal punishment on East Indiamen which caused greater public concern around the year 1830. Matters were brought to a head that year by the arrival of the *Lowther Castle* and the *Inglis* with crews driven to the verge of mutiny. G.C. Smith championed the cause of the goaded men with fervor and flair, spoke up for them at the Police Court, published an *Appeal to the British Nation* on their behalf, and organized an impressive protest march through the metropolis.

Quoting these and other cases, he demonstrated the desperate need of a "Maritime Code of Laws," which could determine duties and disciplinary action in the Merchant Service, in the same way as the Articles of War in the Navy. With this he persevered, petitioning King and Parliament, and continuing to publish both his own arguments and those of others.[321]

However, while attempts were being made to alleviate certain forms of physical abuse, no redress seemed in sight for dehumanizing working and living conditions to which seamen were still subjected as a matter of course. In this regard, they shared the fate of the laboring masses ashore. The national conscience had yet to be roused. The battles of Shaftesbury and Plimsoll were still to be fought.

One proposal for improving the seaman's miserable wages was more well-intentioned than realistic. The development of docklands had, it was alleged, been "exclusively calculated to benefit the merchant or ship-owner." Crews were now summarily turned ashore on arrival, unloading was left to "lumpers," traditional loyalties to both ship and shipowner were destroyed, and seamen suffered a serious loss of income. However, pleas for renewed crew participation in cargo-handling proved futile.[322] One writer to *The Times* (presumably no seaman himself) conceded that seamen's wages were too low, but argued that any increase would only benefit the crimp.[323]

On a spiritual level, the Bethel Movement was, in its strong lay orientation, essentially democratic. However, in relation to the seafarer's socio-political situation, friends seeking his welfare took, quite without question, the prevalent paternalistic approach. Nowhere was this more dramatically demonstrated than in Leith, in the turbulent mid-twenties.

In their classic history of trade unionism, the Webbs show how difficult it has been for later generations to comprehend "the naive surprise with which the employers of that time regarded the practical development of working-class solidarity."[324] When the repeal of the Combination Acts (1824) changed the status of trade unions overnight from criminal conspiracy to complete legality, the middle and upper classes were shocked at the enthusiasm with which the long-repressed lowest strata of society seized their opportunity. Trade union societies sprang up on all sides, many of them openly militant. A strong combination of seamen on the Tyne and Wear brought the shipping trade on the Northeast Coast to a temporary standstill. Parliament reacted by passing a new act in 1825, which all but rendered trade unions illegal again. Only a vestige of the right to collective bargaining was salvaged.[325]

In this situation, evangelical Christians saw the specter of sedition no less vividly than the rest of middle-class society, where they had their main strength. This applied equally as much to the directors of the Edinburgh and Leith Seamen's Friend Society. In their reports both in 1825 and 1827, they express their unfeigned gratitude for having been the means of saving

"All hands to witness punishment." A dramatic moment on
board a British man-of-war, as the real culprit comes forward
just before an innocent shipmate, already "seized up" on a
grating, is to be flogged by the boatswain's mate with a
cat-o'-nine-tails. (A widely publicized picture by George
Cruikshank, as published in *Greenwich Hospital,* 1825.)

some 1,700 seamen of Leith from "the temptations to combination." On
both occasions, traveling delegates from a Seamen's Union had almost
induced the men to join, and take part in a general "rising for wages." But the
directors "reasoned" with the seamen, their advice was "kindly taken," and
"the scenes of disorder exhibited at many other ports—attended at one port
of England with cases of manslaughter—were prevented. . . ."[326]

Many years were to pass, before the right of seafarers to join hands
in order to better their lot was to be universally recognized. However, it is
worthy of note, that the man who, toward the close of the century, emerged
as the great champion of maritime unions, Andrew Furuseth, the "Seafarers'
Abraham Lincoln," was motivated by a clear, self-professed Christian
commitment.[327]

Moreover, it would be both an over-simplification and an injustice to
assert that early promoters of seamen's missions sought solely to mitigate
suffering, not change the system which created it. True, a divinely-ordained
"stratifiction" of society, and the myth about the "contented poor" were
widely accepted. But these were men unversed in any modern theology of

social ethics. Consequently, their conformism was not necessarily hypocrisy. Nor did it have to imply heartlessness. Those mission leaders in Leith, who harangued against "combinations," were the very men who set in motion a program of social self-help for seafarers which could, as already seen, only be characterized as revolutionary.[328]

As in the evolution of maritime evangelism, so too in the development of a maritime diaconate, it is the personality of George Charles Smith that predominates. Despite the clearly paternalistic temper of the times, he surmounted the temptation to seek purely particularistic solutions. His merciless exposé of the Crimping System and his master plan for its eradication were not "the recipés of a moral and social atomism." They were nothing short of epoch-making. In his constant quest for underlying causes, and his agitation for adequate answers, Smith moved beyond the bounds of maritime philanthropy and proved himself a precursor of maritime sociology.[329]

Social services to seafarers have traditionally been thought of as a relatively late development in seamen's missions, representing a shift of emphasis from what was for long an exclusive preoccupation with the salvation of "the isolated soul," and only by way of the Word.[330] Sources have shown that several forms of social maritime ministry had already been launched by the beginning of the 1830's. These sources also indicate that such social ministry was neither relegated to a mere means to an end, not elevated to the highest end. Rather, it was simply an unpremeditated response to challenges not envisaged at the outset, but (to quote Smith) experienced as "leadings and stimulants of Divine Providence."[331]

In short, the diaconal concern of these pioneer personalities displayed something of the spontaneity of that urge which the Bible calls the constraining love of Christ.[332] Through their ministry — with all its shortcomings — these men played a vital role in ensuring that what began as a revival could eventually take on the dimensions of a reformation.

PART VI

FINAL FORMATIVE YEARS

Toward British Multi-Denominational Maritime Mission

Chapter 17

Continuing Nondenominational Activity

The Situation in 1833: "Peace" — at a Price

In more ways than one, the early 1830's appeared to herald a new era of general peace and prosperity, after the mounting social and political unrest of the immediate post-war period. On the Continent, the July Revolution of 1830 had evidently dealt a mortal blow to the concept of a feudal monarchy. At home, Earl Grey's Reform Act of 1832 went far toward weakening the power of the aristocratic oligarchy. However, subsequent events were to prove that tremendous tensions remained unresolved, both at home and abroad. The same might be said of the status of British seamen's missions, at this point still basically nondenominatonal.

A comparison between British involvement in the Seamen's Cause in 1818 and 1833 provides an overall picture of progress, both quantitatively (in terms of general outreach) and qualitatively (in terms of differentiation of ministry). Even on the controversy-ridden metropolitan scene, the situation seemed somewhat more promising in 1833 than in recent years. Here, the new, widely-endorsed British and Foreign Sailors' Society symbolized a fresh determination that "the centre must be strengthened and the circumference reached."[1]

Nevertheless, with G.C. Smith's reorganized British and Foreign Sailors' and Soldiers' Bethel Flag Union making equally wide, if somewhat less realistic pretensions, metropolitan peace prospects were, in 1833, at best precarious. Moreover, they had been bought at a tragically heavy cost. True, organizational feuds in metropolitan religious societies had been no rarity in recent years. (The "winnowing process" of controversy had already rent asunder both the Bible Society and several leading missionary societies.)[2] It must also be borne in mind, that religious polemics of that day and age could reach a pitch of virulence seldom seen since. (In large segments of Protestantism, the tongue and pen of *odium theologicum* had simply replaced the rack and stake of the Inquisition.)[3] However, all of this conveys small comfort. The fact remains, that constant conflict had a debilitating effect on British seamen's missions at their potentially most expansive period.

The cost of conflict manifested itself primarily in the stunted growth of maritime ministry in the metropolis and abroad. What Smith had seen, in the mid-1820's, as a division of labor, calculated to promote the "natural, but friendly competition of Seamen's Societies," had rapidly degenerated into a state of religious civil war. Reported at great length in such religious newspapers as *The World* and *The Record*, details were quoted and commented upon by the "infidel" press, thereupon making the rounds of the kingdom.

The national notoriety thus achieved by the two major metropolitan seamen's mission societies resulted in widespread public disaffection. Thousands decided to "stand aloof" and support neither.[4] At the same time, repercussions retarded both the development of Anglican endeavors in the metropolis, and a more effective meeting of the severe social needs of seamen there.[5] Finally, relatively meager metropolitan ministry resulted in a frustrated foreign outreach, otherwise an area of natural responsibility for societies claiming national support in the mother country of a world-wide empire. That the USA was destined to take a decided lead in this aspect in the early 1830's, was directly attributable to the continuing controversy on the British side.[6]

Leading seamen's mission personalities on the American scene, while deploring the disgrace and delay suffered by the Seamen's Cause in general, through the "dreadful dissensions" in London, showed early apprehension of another costly consequence: the virtual isolation of G.C. Smith and subsequent sacrifice of his unique capabilities.[7] The following phase of the narrative provides convincing proof that such fears were well justified.[8]

George Charles Smith: Isolation and Rehabilitation

Existing biographical sketches of G.C. Smith practically bypass the last three decades of his long life (1833-63). However, he continued, in the face of enormous odds, to publish his *New Sailor's Magazine* (under varying titles) until the time of his death; and although (as already noted) it deteriorated dramatically over the years, it does—used critically, and in conjunction with other sources—make it possible to piece together a picture of the more significant events of his later career.[9]

Despite the overwhelming problems he faced in 1832-33, Smith remained for a few more years very much a force to be reckoned with. Indeed, the remarkable fact is not that Smith's new national society ultimately sank, but that it was ever launched, and for a while even held the hegemony. Published figures for 1833-34 showed the British and Foreign Sailors' and Soldiers' Bethel Flag Union as having four times the income of the British and Foreign Sailors' Society.[10] Meanwhile, from Smith's fertile imagination flowed an incessant stream of schemes for the spiritual and social betterment of his brother-seamen, projecting the image of a society eminently alive to the issues of the day.

In 1833, the *Royal William* became the first ship to cross the Atlantic by steam alone; five years later, Smith's Society became the first to found a religious organization specifically for the benefit of the rapidly growing new class of seamen known as "steamers" (the "British and Foreign Steamers' Friend Society").[11]

In 1835, the crusade of Samuel Plimsoll was still a generation ahead. But already Smith was publicly protesting against "Sea coffins, or frail ships, built cheap, to be lost to gain the insurance."[12]

Also in 1835, spurred by the American example, Smith and his associates initiated a radicalization of the marine temperance movement, on the principle of "total abstinence from all intoxicating drinks." Accordingly, the earlier, more moderate "Sailors' and Soldiers' Temperance Union" was, in 1838, succeeded by a "Sailors' and Soldiers' Evangelical Temperance Society," formed on teetotal lines. Among its objects was the promotion of temperance coffee houses, and the sensitive issue of abolishing grog in the Royal Navy. Powerful arguments were provided by the recent findings of the Parliamentary Select Committee enquiring into the causes of drunkenness.[13] Through these endeavors, a warm relationship developed between G.C. Smith and Father (Theobald) Mathew, Ireland's "Apostle of Temperance."[14]

Through a series of petitions and public statements, Smith also involved himself (and thereby his Society) in promoting the social emancipation of that ill-used class of Thames-side stevedores known as coal-whippers;[15] in opposing Britain's part in the inglorious Opium War of 1839-42;[16] and in exposing the alleged perils of "infidel" political radicalism.[17]

At the same time, Smith continued his pre-1832 campaign for an adequate Merchant Seamen's Hospital for the disabled and aging, as well as more effective anti-crimping measures.[18] He also formed a "Female Protection Society" (1837), for the reformation of penitent "sea-harlots" and the relief of destitute "sea-women." (Included among the latter was the widow of notorious Richard Parker, ringleader of the mutiny at the Nore.)[19]

Futhermore, Smith agitated for the formation of a "Heathen Land Seamen's Missionary Society." This was to be run by foreign mission societies themselves, in order to counteract the negative impact of carousing seamen in port areas of foreign mission fields.[20]

Nevertheless, in the midst of all this impressive activity, ominous clouds were gathering on the immediate horizon. As the 1830's progressed, it became all too apparent that Smith's Society was in serious financial straits. He changed the title — back to "British and Foreign Seamen and Soldiers' Friend Society."[21] But he could not change the trend. Debts from the 1832 disaster remained unpaid, and new debts were steadily making matters worse. Smith soon ceased publishing annual accounts, only acknowledgements of contributions.

Meanwhile, Smith made matters no easier for himself, by the persistent vehemence of his reaction against the powerfully patronized British and Foreign Sailors' Society, for what he alleged to be both subversion of his own Society, and exaggerated claims on behalf of theirs.[22]

For their part, the BFSS donned a cloak of offical silence. However, from the close of 1834, a handful of embittered individuals launched a new campaign of calumny against Smith and his colleagues. Most vocal were John Harding (a "discarded agent" of Smith's Society); the noted Fleet Street atheist Richard Carlile (who undertook to lampoon Smith in his weekly *Scourge*, quoting liberally from sources like Styles, Mead and Sibree); as well as John Stephens (editor of the *Christian Advocate*, notorious in the mid-1830's for its religious sensationalism). After the embattled "Boatswain" had been duly "hung, drawn, and quartered . . . and the ashes scattered to the four winds," extracts from Stephens' columns were put together in book-form, and circulated under the title *G.C.S. Unmasked.*[23]

Not satified with literary onslaughts alone, Harding contrived to have Smith arrested in March 1836, for an alleged debt of £70. On a promotional tour of Buckinghamshire at the time, Smith was compelled to abandon the group of singing seamen's orphans who frequently accompanied him on such occasions, and subject himself to three months' incarceration in the County Prison at Aylesbury. After a short while, he managed to obtain a tansfer to the Fleet Prison in London, so as to be nearer his headquarters. Here he remained until his release six weeks later.

It was scant consolation that the arbitrary Law of Imprisonment for Debt, then in force, quite commonly committed clergymen, officers and gentlemen of standing to indefinite periods of mental and physical torture in debtors' jails. Nor could it avail that Harding himself was imprisoned shortly thereafter. For Smith, this was the first of a series of four disastrous prison terms, all connected with clamoring creditors, and culminating in a catastrophe only comparable to that of 1832. Behind the bars of the Queen's Bench Debtors' Prison, he was to spend a further five months in 1840, seven months in 1843-44, and five months again in 1845. Finally, he lost his church.[24]

No. 3088.   JUNE, 1842.   Vol. 30

Please to lend your Magazine after you have read it ; and aid the Cause by promoting its Circulation, and collecting ONE SHILLING *for the General Cause, or for the Orphans, or for the Naval and Military Temperance Society, or Open Air Preaching Missions.*

THE

Mariners' Church

GOSPEL TEMPERANCE

SOLDIERS' AND SAILORS'

MAGAZINE.

Published for the Temperance British and Foreign Seamen Soldiers', and Steamers' Friend Society and Bethel Flag Union, to promote Religious Instruction, and Temperance Moral Reformation.

THE LONDON MARINERS' CHURCH, WELLCLOSE SQUARE,
For Sailors, Soldiers, Fishermen, Watermen, and their Families.

Published at the Naval and Military Office, Bethel House, 17, Wellclose Square and by W. Brittain 11, Paternoster Row, and may be had of all Booksellers.

⁎⁎ We beg to repeat that any Bookseller, in any Town, can order this Magazine, Monthly, in London, and throughout the United Kingdom.

PRICE 6*d*.

C.G. Smith's Magazine, as published during his turbulent terms in debtors' prisons, 1836-45.

Until one fateful February morning in 1845, Smith had stoutly refused to "give up the ship" (in other words, his church). Already, by then, thrice imprisoned by different adversaries for what he claimed to be "false debts," he had persevered against all odds, editing his magazine from within the walls, and (with the help of family and friends) directing general operations in Wellclose Square. Spurred by the spiritual neglect and human degradation he discovered during his prison terms, he even managed to found and personally promote a "Prison Howard Bethel Mission Society."[25]

It was then that the lawyers charged with enforcing the terms under which the Mariners' Church was rented delivered their decisive blow. After protracted and fruitless negotiations, they descended on their luckless debtor on February 13, 1845. Armed with an order of ejection, they forced an entry into the church, had the minister arrested for non-payment of their expenses, and negotiated a new contract of rent with his arch-rivals at that time, the British and Foreign Sailors' Society. When Smith emerged from his final five months in the Queen's Bench, all he had left was his magazine. The other indispensible asset—his "Metropolitan Maritime Establishment"—was, after twenty years of continuous ministry, lost forever.[26]

What can have been the fundamental cause of the calamity of 1845? A major factor was undoubtedly the structural vulnerability of Smith's Society. It was totally dominated by one single personality—that of himself. Had that same personality been perfect in every respect, the task would still have been far beyond the capacity of "solitary individuals, however endowed and zealous."[27] But Smith's personality, in many senses commendable, in some incomparable, was far from perfect.

Again, the response from "the humbler portions of society" had been consistently remarkable. But in England of Smith's day, no minister could expect to defy the demands of "respectability" with impunity. Dispensing with committees, and arraigning all the "high mightinesses of dissent," Smith alienated himself in the post-1832 period from both fellow-ministers and every other source of patronage. Though his most inveterate enemies conceded that he never enriched himself, his chronic inability to keep regular accounts only served to compound his problems.[28]

For three years after his release, Smith remained in the metropolis, contending with an "ocean of troubles." His house at No. 19 Wellclose Square collapsed in ruins shortly after his return. But he battled on, taking temporary lodgings here and there, as he preached and admonished on the waterfront, in barracks and in the streets. He even managed to minister from a makeshift seamen's chapel, in Ratcliffe Highway, during 1846-47.

However, in reality Smith's Society was now little more than a name. He lived in a state of permanent poverty. Finally, his health became

The familiar figure of "Bosun" Smith, here jovially depicted in silhouette in later years. (Courtesy of Seamen's Christian Friend Society.)

so seriously undermined, that, in the spring of 1848, he accepted what he saw as a providential call to return to the milder climate and relative peace of Penzance, as pastor again of Jordan Chapel.[29]

For the remaining fifteen years of his life, Smith made his home in Penzance. But the call of the waterfront in the great port cities was irresistible. Many months were regularly spent each year on so-called "Summer Missions" to London and along the sea-coast. These lengthy periods of absence, coupled with other problems, prompted him finally to resign his pastorate in 1853, make his private home ("Jordan House") his headquarters, and improvise a seamen's chapel on the ground floor.[30]

Frustrations followed Smith incessantly during his declining years. Yet there were also positive developments. In the first place, there were signs of genuine reconciliaton. This applied to Smith's immediate family. Intolerable stress had culminated in his wife's separation during Smith's third prison term.[31] However, an initiative on Smith's side in later years resulted in mutual forgiveness.[32]

Meanwhile, a more conciliatory tone also became evident in Smith's attitude to the British and Foreign Sailors' Society. This was particularly so after they had vacated his former London headquarters, and, in 1856, opened a Sailors' Institute which he, too, found ample cause to commend.[33] Only, it seems, in relation to the Tractarians was Smith completely implacable. After "Puseyite priests," later in 1856, had taken over the old Mariners' Church in Wellclose Square, he made repeated, though futile, attempts to have the building restored to seafarers.[34]

In the second place, there were, even before the close of Smith's calumniated career, promising prospects of personal rehabilitation. In later years, Smith sensed an overwhelming urge for "usefulness" overseas. His offer to ship for Constantinople, and serve as a voluntary chaplain in the heat of the Crimean conflict was not accepted.[35] Likewise, his 1858-59 "Scandinavian Mission," with projected preaching "on the coast of Denmark and Sweden," foundered from lack of funds.[36] However, Smith's "American Sailors' Mission," in the summer of 1861, turned into a triumphal tour.

Besides the pro-American bias of British Baptists in general, Smith had many personal ties with the United States. Recently, he had been stirred by news of the 1857 Revival, and its impact on seamen.[37] On the invitation of the New York Port Society, the aged veteran, now in his eightieth year, eagerly embarked from Liverpool by steamer, arriving in New York June 5, 1861.

In the course of a six-week stay, Smith was the honored guest of seamen's mission societies in six major sea-ports along the East Coast (New York, Philadelphia, Boston, Salem, Portland and New Haven). More ready to accept his eccentricities than his own countrymen had been, Smith's American hosts hailed him everywhere as the "Originator and Founder of the whole scheme of Bethel Union operations among Sailors." After he had visited, lectured and preached his way back to New York, his tour was climaxed by the presentation of a commemorative medal on the eve of his departure. The presentation was made by Chaplain Charles J. Jones, on behalf of all "Friends of Seamen" in that port.[38]

Toward the close of 1862, there were indications of Smith being rediscovered by the religious community of his own native land. Letters appeared in the press, deploring that after "such services to his fellow-countrymen," he should be found "in circumstances of grinding poverty." A public subscription was launched for the relief of this "octogenarian veteran . . . in the army of Emmanuel," and a petition for a pension was delivered on his behalf to the Prime Minister, Lord Palmerston.

However, before Smith could benefit by either, his "last watch upon deck" (as he himself called it) came to an end. After being bed-ridden for some while with dropsy, George Charles Smith, now almost eighty-one, died peacefully in his sleep Saturday morning, January 10, 1863, at Jordan House, Penzance.[39]

G.C. Smith's American Commemorative Medal. (Custody of Seamen's Christian Friend Society.)

Like his childhood pastor, Rowland Hill, Smith had long since made up his mind to "die in harness." That wish was fulfilled. Only ten days earlier, he had, on his own insistance, been carried downstairs, to hold Watch-night Service in his ground-floor seamen's chapel. His magazine did not expire before he did. According to a local obituary, he was "to the last full of active zeal for Christ, and the salvation of souls."[40]

The funeral on January 16th in Penzance Cemetery gave an indication of the degree of attachment Smith enjoyed in his adopted home-town. Preceded by five flags and detachments from both the Coastguard and Naval Reserve, an estimated two thousand people attended. Several ministers of different denominations took part.[41]

On a national and international level, revived recognition of G.C. Smith's fundamental role in the evolution of seamen's missions was prompted partly by the persistent efforts of an American fellow-chaplain, Charles J. Jones, the man who played a major role in arranging Smith's 1861 tour to the United States. Besides all he publicized on his own account, Jones warmly endorsed, in the American version of *The Sailors' Magazine,* the earlier testimony of an influential English minister:

> I connect with the name of Smith the commencement of one of the
> greatest moral revolutions England ever saw; he was the Morning
> Star of the Sailor's Reformation.[42]

Does the historical record bear out the validity of that designation? It would be futile to deny a degree of truth in some of the allegations against G.C. Smith. But among "all the shiploads of calumny landed on every shore," many charges were obviously unfounded, others grossly exaggerated, and dishonesty was never among them. Nevertheless, on two scores Smith would seem to have been vulnerable.

First, there can be no doubt that Smith's "oceanic tempestuous nature" made many enemies in his day. But the burly Boatswain's belligerence was not all bad. Once convinced of the righteousness of a cause, the veteran man-of-war's-man would, true enough, hurl himself into the fray, without the slightest regard for whom the "enemy" happened to be, or however impossible the odds. Yet it would be unjust to dismiss his vehemence as pure pugnacity, or love of war for its own sake. A certain "temperature of soul" was seen by a prominent fellow-minister as indispensable, where spiritual innovation was called for in the face of obdurate opposition. Smith's combination of the choleric and the sanguine was perhaps precisely what was required to effect "that which the whole Christian world feared to attempt."[43]

Secondly, Smith's evident ambitiousness exposed him to censure. Yet this trait, too, need not have been only evil. His was a tremendous sense

The Rev. George Charles Smith as octogenarian, seen here wearing the medal presented to him in New York in July 1861. (Courtesy Seamen's Church Institute of NY/NJ.)

of vocation, nurtured by a realization of providential preparation, and stimulated by the virulence of those intent upon his ruin.[44]

Smith's many personal foibles, coupled with a steady refusal to be bound by convention, gave his critics cause to compare him with an erratic comet, rather than a morning star.[45] Nevertheless, eccentricity and ingenuity are often close companions; and degree of infallibility is no yardstick of true greatness. Thus, history was to prove (as predicted publicly as early as in 1830), that posterity would "not willingly allow either detraction or demerit to erase from the scroll of christian worthies the name of the reverend G.C. Smith of Penzance."[46] Ultimately, the British and Foreign Sailors' Society, too, openly acknowledged Smith's unique role, not only in the origin of their own Society, but also in the dawn of the whole seamen's mission enterprise.[47]

That role might perhaps best be summarized as a "John the Baptist of the Seamen's Cause." To rouse the Christian church from the lethargy into which it had lapsed through centuries of neglect, and sensitize it to its responsibility for the evangelization of the seafarer and the humanization of the maritime industry, this was the task of a *prophet*, with vision, courage, and perseverance akin to that of the rugged precursor who cried in the wilderness. In contrast to the Baptist of Bible times, however, his seafaring successor "outlived his generation," as one commentator observed.[48] Thus, that restless catalyst of reform became the unwilling witness of how others appropriated the part of the *priest,* as they transformed the new into the conventional.

Indisputably, George Charles Smith was a rough diamond, but—withal—a diamond. The massive evidence presented in this study can only confirm the conclusion: here was a pioneer personality who so towered above all others, that he richly merits the title of Founding Father of organized Christian mission to seafarers.[49]

BRITISH AND FOREIGN SAILORS' SOCIETY: THREE DECADES OF TRIAL AND TRIUMPH

How did the British and Foreign Sailors' Society fare during the declining years of Smith's career? Reverting to the metropolitan scene of the mid-thirties, it soon became apparent that this new endeavor was—despite all its impressive patronage—having serious difficulty in gaining support commensurate with the Society's great goals.

True, the times were not propitious. Mounting Chartist agitation was symptomatic of the continuing social and political tensions in the nation. An "almost unparalleled depression of trade" was followed by the economic upheaval of the Irish Potato Famine of 1845-46.[50] However, such adverse circumstances, with which every contemporary charity had to contend, were undoubtedly aggravated in the case of the BFSS by more proximate causes. Foremost among these were: (1) public disaffection due to the continuing societal fratricide (already noted),[51] and (2) a manifest lack of dynamic leadership.[52]

At all events, the trend was unmistakable. The Society's Treasurer, G.F. Angas, put it bluntly at its Annual Meeting in 1839 (as quoted in the Society's own published *Report*):

> They should be ashamed of themselves for having done so little in this department of the cause of Christ. . . . The paltry sum of £2,600 was all that had been placed in their hands, for the evangelization of the seamen of the world! Why, it did not exceed the amount of a single ship's freight, for bringing home a cargo from the East Indies.[53]

Coupled with a perennial picture of restricted resources, reports from these years reveal only too clearly how retrenchment rather than reaching out became a characteristic feature of the Society's policy.[54]

On the metropolitan scene, the Society was constantly frustrated by the lack of a satisfactory station. In 1834, after sixteen years' service, it was decided to abandon the *Ark*. With the original note of novelty gone, attendance had for long been flagging, attempts to secure easier access by means of a mooring-place along the shore had failed, and maintenance repairs had become excessive.[55]

The grave of George Charles Smith in Penzance Cemetery.
For inscription, see Note No. 49. (Photograph by
Leonard M. Richards, Madron near Penzance.)

However, the alternative proved hardly preferable. A disused distillery, located at Bell Wharf, in an obscure section of Lower Shadwell, was rented and opened May 29, 1834, as the Society's "new" Sailors' Chapel. After dragging through a decade of discouragement, with the Society's directors freely admitting that accomodation was "of the worst description," richly deserving the disgust of seafarers themselves, the premises were finally given up in 1844. They were exchanged for part-time access to nearby Ebenezer Chapel.[56]

Beyond the metropolis, the Society's early record seems to have been barely any more impressive. Again and again, their Minutes show how appeals to the Society for financial aid, in order to establish stations elsewhere, were refused for lack of funds. Especially evident was this in the foreign field, where the directors acknowledged, with commendable frankness, the utter inadequacy of the Society's involvement.[57]

Nevertheless, this is not to say that nothing noteworthy was accomplished during the first decade or so of the new Society's existence. On the contrary, through Bethel Meetings on the River, and Bethel Captains on the seven seas, significant achievements were registered both at home and in a long list of foreign ports.

Despite the disheartening scene on the Shadwell shore, there ministered among the docks and tiers of the Thames a Cornish-born captain of exceptional caliber: the first of a singularly successful series of so-called "Thames Missionaries" maintained by the BFSS.

The concept of a former merchant captain employed full-time as "missionary" among the shipping on the Thames was by no means new. Apart from the personal example set by William Henry Angas, G.C. Smith had long since promoted the idea in his magazines; and the BFSSFS had sponsored it in practice.[58] However, the BFSS gave the project top priority, by making a "Thames Missionary" one of the primary objects of their 1833 constitution; and the Society's treasurer, G.F. Angas, knew where he was to find the man (even personally providing his first year's salary).[59]

Benjamin Prynn seemed predestined for the task. Born at Penryn, Cornwall, March 17, 1781, a direct descendent of the persecuted Puritan William Prynne, the future seamen's mission pioneer was not nine when he went to sea, and not quite twenty when he became captain. Of Wesleyan Methodist affiliation, he credited his actual conversion to the counseling of a fellow-captain. With him (Captain Banks), and others (such as Captain Wilkins and Hindhulph), he became actively involved in the very beginning of the Bethel Movement. After helping to pioneer the early Bethel Meetings in the Upper Pool, he appears to have been the first to hoist the Bethel Flag not only in numerous ports around the British coast, but in no less than 23 foreign sea-ports, as far apart as Northern Europe, the Mediterranean and Canada.[60]

During the 1820's, Captain Prynn developed strong ties with G.C. Smith and his Society (finally as member of the committee of the BFSSFS). Only on the "urgent counsels" of the renowned Dr. Raffles, was he induced to quit the sea, after 44 years, and accept the position of Thames Missionary for the BFSS.[61] However, having once commenced in this capacity, from New Year 1834, he brought all his personal charisma and a tremendous enthusiasm into the work, rapidly becoming the new Society's most indispensable asset. For 22 years, until he died in 1856, as a result of injuries while ship-visiting, Captain Benjamin Prynn's published reports were widely read, and their stirring contents did much to redeem the early image of the struggling Society.[62]

For more than three years, Captain Prynn labored alone. Then, spurred by his prodigious efforts, the Society appointed a "Junior Thames Missionary" to share the load. These two Thames Missionaries, in addition to their own intensive program of shipboard evangelism, secured ships for an annual aggregate of over 1,000 Bethel Meetings, led by four part-time stipendiary "Thames Agents."[63]

Abroad, on the other hand, attempts at direct involvement by the Society resolved themselves into repeated frustrations. Normally, no greater liability would be assumed than the granting of a Bethel Flag and books (only in rare instances also a modest monetary grant). The Society's *Third Annual Report* (1836) could list thirteen such recipients, or voluntary "Foreign Directors and Agents."[64] When the Society, from 1838, took on "something entirely new," by directly employing a full-time seamen's chaplain (the Rev. John Pears) at Cape Town, the whole enterprise fell through the following year, on his accepting a pastoral charge in the interior.[65]

At Cronstadt and Le Havre, even Sydney,[66] all of which were frequented by thousands of British seamen annually, responsibility for full-time seamen's chaplaincy was left largely to the corresponding American Society. As late as the 1850's, the BFSS could only admit that they were "without a stated agency in foreign ports."[67]

Nevertheless, the Society was, during these bleak years abroad, able to point to encouraging achievements by two categories of coadjutors, with whom it became closely associated: foreign missionaries and foreign-trade Bethel Captains.

With the powerful expansion of foreign missions during the 1830's, came a correspondingly urgent accentuation of the missiological motive for maritime evangelization (a motive already noticeable in the preceding decade).[68] In December 1833, this was especially evident in the Pacific, where an upsurge in missionary activity coincided with the burgeoning whaling industry.

Hardly half a year after its foundation, the BFSS received, in December 1833, a strongly-worded appeal from the London Missionary Society, deploring the fact that American and British sailors had, besides ravaging the native womenfolk, opened grog-shops on the South Sea Islands, and induced the local native chieftains to become "traffickers in rum." Their call for "prompt and efficient exertions," to combat the "baneful influence" of such behavior on foreign mission-fields, was reiterated in similar statements by both the Church and Wesleyan Missionary Societies.[69]

In their reply, the BFSS followed the pattern already provided by the societies with which G.C. Smith was associated in the 1820's. The only available manpower was that of the missionary societies themselves. But to missionaries willing to make use of them, the BFSS gladly sent Bethel Flags, books, tracts, even whole "Sailors' Libraries."[70]

Many responded. The *Annual Report* for 1836 could list among "Foreign Directors and Agents of the Society" missionaries not only in the Pacific (on Tahiti and the Samoan Islands), but also in the Caribbean (in Jamaica, Demerara, Honduras and Berbice).[71] John Williams, the "Apostle of the South Seas." consistently encouraged cooperation with the BFSS, and himself became an enthusiastic "Foreign Director" for Raratonga.[72]

"Seizing" (as it was said) an hour from their other duties, these volunteer chaplains would hoist the Bethel Flag and take their stand, "with a ship as their sanctuary,—the heavens as their canopy,—the capstan as their desk, and . . . beseech the sailor to be reconciled to God." Where a chapel had been erected, seafarers were invited, and frequently responded.[73] Nevertheless, the aid of missionaries was admittedly limited and intermittent. Their obligation to the native population must "necessarily absorb the far greater proportion of their time and energies."[74]

An alternative and probably more effective volunteer ministry was that of the deep-sea Bethel Captains. In the course of the 1830's, the seeds of institutionalization sown in the preceding decade showed visible growth. In terms of mutual relationship, Captain Landers' experimental "Bethel Chart" of 1829 was replaced by a more widely conceived "Bethel Covenant" of 1837. In terms of official affiliation, the early Bethel Captains' solidarity with the BFSFSBU and the BFSSFS was now (with the organizational eclipse of G.C. Smith) succeeded by close indentification with the BFSS.[75]

The far-sighted treasurer of the BFSS, G.F. Angas, played a key role in the founding phase. On March 26, 1837, he headed a preliminary planning meeting at the Society's Sailors' Chapel, together with 27 veteran Bethel Captains. On June 15th, he chaired another meeting of Bethel Captains, also at the Sailors' Chapel, where the Bethel Covenant was agreed upon. The subscribers pledged close cooperation with the BFSS, "special exertions" among their own crews, and consistent intercessory prayer.[76]

In April 1838, one hundred signatories published a powerful plea entitled *A Voice from the Ocean* (reminiscent of an earlier American publication).[77] Here, headed by none other than Captain Anthony Wilkins of Thames Revival fame, Bethel Captains call on the pastors and churches of Great Britain to awaken from their "lukewarmness and apathy," and help seek the salvation of 290,000 British brother-seamen, "yet in moral darkness and death . . . hastening to an unchanging eternity."[78]

The precise impact of the new organization is impossible to assess. However, the demand for the *Voice* was such, that it had to be republished (by the BFSS) two years later; a translation into German was also published. By 1844, about 500 captains were enrolled in the Bethel Covenant. The BFSS published frequent accounts of consecration services on the Thames, whenever the ship of a new member was "set apart" as a Bethel Ship, before putting to sea again. The exploits of these intrepid allies in foreign waters followed the same pattern as their precursors in the 1820's. Meanwhile, their numbers continued to increase. The concept of a voluntary "cooperative union" of seafaring lay collaborators had come to stay (although its form was destined to change with years).[79]

The BFSS summed up its evaluation of these gratuitous coadjutors with the following words:

If the Society had accomplished nothing more than the organization of the Bethel masters into a confederate body of holy and
active labourers in the cause of Christ, it would have been no
common achievement.[80]

These years also saw the dawning of concern for cohesion among
"Bethel Men," in other words committed Christians of other ranks. Spurred
by the American example, the BFSS could announce in 1842 the formation
of a "christian Society, composed of pious seamen of all denominations,"
connected as communicant members with the Sailors' Chapel, and "pledged
in every way possible to promote the kingdom of Christ among their brethren
of the deep." By next year, nearly 200 had been enrolled.[81]

A powerful impetus was provided in 1845, when the BFSS was
offered the lease of the well-established Wellclose Square Mariners' Church,
re-opened April 30th as the (British and Foreign) Sailors' Church.[82] With
this unanticipated answer to the Society's critical need for an acceptable
metropolitan station, the fortunes of the BFSS began slowly but surely to
improve.

There were other factors, too. On the national scene, the repeal of
the Corn Laws in 1846 introduced "the great period of mid-Victorian
commercial and industrial expansion."[83] The previous year, one Thomas
Augustus Fieldwick, a gifted young man who had attracted attention as
Junior Thames Missionary, was promoted to the secretaryship of the Society.
The fact that the British and Foreign Sailors' Society, in the course of the
next two decades, achieved (and has since retained) such a prominent
position in British and world ministry to seafarers, must in some measure be
ascribed to this man's skillful leadership during a decisive phase of the
Society's history.[84]

It had, by the mid-1840's, become only too apparent that more than
mere verbal motivation was needed before the Society could expect really
significant support. The BFSS had, in 1837, selected and published a prize-
winning essay entitled *Britannia; or, the Moral Claims of Seamen Stated
and Enforced,* by the Rev. John Harris. It was also published in the USA,
and even translated into Swedish. However, for all its eloquence, it failed to
remove what was characterized as the "culpable apathy" of the British
public toward the Seamen's Cause. Some more manifest rallying-point
seemed requisite.[85]

Fieldwick came to the conclusion that the Sailors' Church, however
much of an improvement on the past, was in itself no permanent solution.
The Society must have "a residence, nobly and truthfully its own," with such
appearances and facilities as could stand forth as an irrefutable "argument
with the public."[86] Further stimulation came from an unanticipated source.

Around mid-century, the directors of the BFSS felt called to campaign against a rash of "Counterfeit Seamen's Societies," with bogus collectors begging through the length and breadth of the land, for objects "never properly attempted," or simply posing as agents of the BFSS. Available evidence indicates that there were, indeed, questionable characters involved in this type of "travelling mendicancy."[87]

However, there were also competitors of another caliber, who genuinely sought alternative structures, in order to serve important needs as yet not adequately met. Such was the group which convened a public meeting on June 29, 1849 in the Hall of Commerce. Bound by a common concern for the mariner's total needs, they proposed the establishment of a "Merchant Seamen's Institution," dedicated to serving not only religious, but also educational, recreational and social needs of seafarers.[88]

Fieldwick, who had himself "for some time" had in mind a broader base of operations in the BFSS, seized on this challenge to motivate his Society to invite the provisional committee of the projected Institution to join forces with the BFSS under a new, more comprehensive constitution. As a result, the object of the Society was henceforth formulated as "the religious, intellectual, and social elevation of British and Foreign Seamen." A public meeting was held on December 12, 1849, to consolidate the merger.[89]

Although the Society had, in some measure, already involved itself in day-schools, navigation classes, boarding-house promotion, temperance work and loan library circulation, the directors readily admitted that the BFSS had hitherto concentrated very largely on the "strictly religious" aspect of the work. Nevertheless, they were anxious to point out that, however "valuable" they now deemed the "intellectual and social improvement of seamen," they would "never for one moment" weaken the efforts of the Society towards "the religious welfare" of seamen as its "primary and paramount design."[90]

Finally, plans were adopted, in April 1854, for the erection of a so-called "Sailors' Institute," designed to effectuate the Society's new, differentiated statement of purpose, and strategically situated in Mercers' Street, close to Ratcliffe Highway. The original concept was that of G.C. Smith, a quarter of a century earlier; the name was suggested by John Harris in the 1837 Prize Essay; a modified version was opened by the Port of Hull Society December 12, 1842; but realization on a grand scale must be credited largely to the tenacity of T.A. Fieldwick, in the early 1850's.[91]

The time seemed auspicious. The outbreak of the Crimean War, in March 1854, had brought British seamen back into public focus. A special "Building Fund" was launched, and the patronage of the Prince Consort, even that of the Emperor of France, was secured. On November 1, 1855, the Lord Mayor could lay the foundation stone, while an ailing Captain Prynn

The London "Sailors' Institute," opened in 1856 in Mercers' Street, Shadwell, by the British and Foreign Sailors' Society. It was soon popularly know as the "Sailors' Palace," and became, with its diversified facilities, a model for similar institutions worldwide. (Courtesy British Sailors' Society.)

proudly hoisted the first Bethel Flag over the site. In less than eight months, on July 23, 1856, the new Institute was offically opened.

With its stately facade "in the Italian style of architecture," its highly appropriate observation tower, its impressive dimensions and diversified facilities, the London Sailors' Institute achieved a status among seamen which was hitherto unparalleled. Here was offered, for the specific use of seafarers, and for the first time under one roof, a spacious public hall (for popular weekly lectures, on "science, temperance and topics of general interest," as well as regular worship services), a reading-room, library, refreshment-room with "temperance bar," seamen's savings bank, and class-rooms for both day and navigation schools (the latter in close conjunction with the Board of Trade).[92]

Destined to remain the headquarters of the BFSS for almost half a century, the building became the "mother and model for all other Sailors' Institutes throughout the world" (including the "Seamen's Church Institutes" of the American Episcopalians). In this way, the BFSS gave a socio-religious connotation to a term which had hitherto been used only in a secular sense (as, for example, in the case of the many "Mechanics' Institutes" around the nation).[93]

Prior to preparation for this remarkable achievement, progress had already been made, during the first years of Fieldwick's secretaryship, in a limited but significant area of outreach to foreign seafarers. Although the voluntary efforts of foreign missionaries and Bethel Captains continued, there could at this time, be no question of directly financing foreign-port activities. However, by means of a "Thames Missionary to Foreign Seamen," thousands could nevertheless be reached, at relatively modest expense, in the very midst of the metropolis.[94]

A precedent had been set ten years previously, in the person of one Augustus Kavel, a Lutheran pastor who in 1836 sought asylum in Great Britain from unionistic coercion in his native Prussia. For two and a half years, he ministered zealously to foreign, especially German seamen on the Thames, sponsored by George Fife Angas, and in affiliation with the BFSS. Before finally leaving for South Australia with a party of fellow-refugees, he even managed (in 1837) to form "an auxiliary to an intended German Sailors' Society . . . to be established in Germany itself."[95]

By the mid-1840's, the large number of Continental vessels, especially Scandinavian and German, berthed on the south side of the River, in the docklands of Rotherhithe, convinced the committee that special staff was called for on a more permanent basis. Accordingly, the Society considered itself fortunate in securing the services of one who was so conspicuously "not a novice," the Rev. Carl von Bülow.[96] Since his dramatic exploits in the 1820's, that restless precursor of Scandinavian Seamen's Missions had continued his labors, partly in Hamburg (and North Germany generally), partly in England.

Duly installed as "Thames Missionary to Foreign Seamen" in the Sailors' Church, Wellclose Square, November 24, 1846, von Bülow reported regularly on his many evangelistic exploits, mainly among seafarers of North European origin, but frequently also of Latin background. On shipboard, in church, in boarding-houses, on the hospital ship *Dreadnought*, von Bülow persevered, until failing health finally forced him to resign in 1850.[97]

His successor, a German minister called Steinitz, was only able to serve for six months (1851), before he, too, found the physical strain too

Example of an early "Sailors' Institute," such as
opened by the Port of Hull Society in 1842.
(From a contemporary print.)

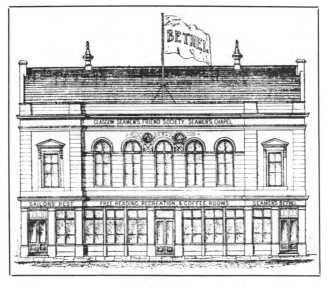

The Glasgow Seamen's Bethel, a typical example of
integration of the "Institute" concept into an old
building. The original 1825 Bethel was reconstructed
in 1860 and again later. (*Chart and Compass*, 1884.)

"Father Neptune"
(the Rev. Edward W.
Matthews) piloted the
BFSS as General
Secretary from 1878 and
for nearly four decades.
(*Chart and Compass,*
1914.)

severe.[98] A German-born layman, Joseph D. Hahn, served as "Colporteur of Foreign Scriptures, Tracts, &c." from 1852 to 1855.[99] Then, the critical phase of the financing of the new Institute forced a cessation.

However, in 1857, the Rev. D.A. Herschell, a converted Jew of Congregational affiliation, formed an "Association for Supplying the Scriptures to Foreign Sailors" ("at the various Ports of the Kingdom"), which sought to some extent to fill the void. This Association offered to contribute toward the support of a new Thames Missionary for Foreign Seamen. The BFSS, who had considered their metropolitan staff significantly "incomplete" during the intervening period, found the man—one August Thiemann, a German-born evangelist of extraordinary talent.[100]

Appointed in the summer of 1860, Thiemann was destined to play a fundamental role in the founding (four years later) of the Norwegian Seamen's Mission, first of a new era of Continental societes. His stay in Norway during the winter of 1860-61 (in order to improve his Norwegian, and thereby better serve Scandinavian seamen on the Thames) resulted in nationwide publicity there for the hitherto unknown work of the BFSS. His return to Norway the following winter led to the formation of a local forerunner of the national society, also to indelible impressions on the mind of its ultimate founder.[101]

Meanwhile, the BFSS established, in 1861, a "Rotherhithe Sailors' Institute," for the particular benefit of the mounting numbers of Scandinavian seamen in that area. This proved an invaluable asset for Thiemann's work

(1860-62),[102] likewise for that of his highly commended successor, Conrad Schelling (1863-69).[103]

In 1868, a chaplain from the new Norwegian Seamen's Mission arrived to establish a station in London, thereby releasing the BFSS from one area of responsibility.[104] In the field of direct foreign-port involvement, however, there were by then already signs that the Society's long "moratorium" was coming to and end. A start was made in 1860, in the port of Alexandria, where the Pasha himself gave a "magnificent" iron ship, fitting her up as a floating chapel at his own expense.[105] At Malta, the Society opened a station in 1866-67.[106] In the early 1870's, permanent work was taken up in Antwerp, Hamburg and Genoa.[107]

By now, however, the Society had entered on a new chapter of its history, which belongs beyond the scope of the present study. Nevertheless, it is worthy of note, that the man who for nearly four decades was to pilot the British and Foreign Sailors' Society, as it continued to go from strength to strength, was once a seventeen-year old sailor-lad, converted on board that floating Bethel in Alexandria Harbor in 1863.[108]

OTHER NONDENOMINATIONAL ORGANIZATIONS

Although it was indisputably the British and Foreign Sailors' Society which, by mid-century, had come to dominate the scene of British nondenominational ministry to seafarers, this was nevertheless shared in varying degrees by a diversity of other organizations.

Prominent among these was the "Seamen's Christian Friend Society" (SCFS), founded January 14,1846, for the promotion of "Missions to Ships &c. in the Port of London, and on the Sea Coasts, to Barracks, Prisons & the Poor in general." The Society was expressly formed to fill the void following G.C. Smith's organizational eclipse in 1845. A leading figure in the founding of the new venture, the Rev. George Teil Hill, had been a close colleague of G.C. Smith during the last years preceding his eviction from the Wellclose Square Mariners' Church. There is also evidence that Smith was, in some measure, involved in the early development of this new metropolitan mission. Thus, through G.C. Smith, the SCFS could claim a personal, if not strictly formal, link with the pioneer period of the Bethel Movement.[109]

Like the BFSS, the SCFS adopted a modified version of the Bethel Flag as its emblem, appointed Thames Missionaries (including to foreign seamen); held frequent Bethel Services on board; and could, in 1854, report the successful establishment of a "Seamen and working Men's Educational Institute" (with weekly lectures in practical science, philosophy and navigation). From the beginning, the Society's headquarters and "Seamen's Chapel" were established in a former sugar warehouse opposite the London Dock Gate, right on Ratcliffe Highway.

Though operating on a more modest scale than the BFSS, the SCFS has, right up to the present, been characterized by a particularly strong evangelistic emphasis. Under the successive superintendency of the Rev. George Teil Hill, and (from 1867) his son, the Rev. George John Hill, the Society steadily expanded, so as to include "Seamen's Institutes" and other facilities in several provincial ports, especially along the West Coast.[110]

Though not having for its original purpose a specifically maritime ministry, the nondenominational "London City Mission" (LCM), formed in 1835 in order to evangelize the metropolis and its masses of unchurched poor, found itself involved with seafarers from the very start. Relying primarily on personal visitation and Scripture distribution, urban missionaries of the LCM have, until now, consistently sought out seamen (especially foreign seamen) and canal crews, as well as both their dependents and their exploiters.[111]

In the area of maritime Christian literature distribution during the post-1833 period, the Naval and Military Bible Society held its own up to the 1860's, it provided numerous grants to the various seamen's mission societies, and at one point (in the mid-1840's) it was represented by "Gratuitous Agents and Correspondents" in eight world ports. (Although the Society suffered a severe decline in the latter part of the century, it secured the means of continuing usefulness by amalgamating in 1910 with the "Scripture Gift Mission." In 1961, It adopted the name Naval, Military and Air Force Bible Society.)[112]

Meanwhile, the British and Foreign Bible Society found itself, from the 1830's on, more and more involved in Scripture distribution among the mounting tide of emigrants to North America and Australia, which reached a new peak in the "Hungry Forties." From London and Gravesend, this work was handled through the Merchant Seamen's Auxiliary Bible Society, which continued its general maritime colportage on the Thames until 1855.

By then, "various reasons" had indicated the need for restructuring; as from August 1, 1855, the MSABS was dissolved, and its functions taken over by a "River Colportage," under immediate administrative control of the parent Society. Reports from the two colporteurs entrusted with this work indicate the importance attached to distribution among foreign seamen, commend Scandinavians as the "most willing" to deal with, but candidly admit occasional opposition. (Ultimately, the BFBS decided to eliminate direct distribution, and rather subsidize that of the specialized seamen's mission societies.)[113]

Adverting to the general scene beyond the metropolis, the period under consideration produced two promising new nondenominational endeavors in Scotland. The "Scottish Sailors' and Soldiers' Bethel Flag Union," founded in Edinburgh in 1835, sought no less than the evangelization

The Liverpool Sailors' Home, on far-famed Paradise
Street, an example of the proliferation of these facilities
in provincial port-cities, following the successful completion
of the London Sailors' Home in 1835. (From the
Liverpool Journal, August 1, 1846.)

of every sailor, soldier, fisherman and boatman in Scotland; within a decade, however, the Society was obliged to discontinue for lack of funds.[114]

The "Scottish Coast Missions" were established during the years 1850-58, in order to "occupy definite portions of the coast (of Scotland) with evangelising agencies," among seamen, fishermen and their families; by 1862, more than 30 coastal missionaries were employed in an enterprise which was to bear evident and lasting fruit.[115]

Otherwise, in major provincial ports such as Liverpool, Bristol, Hull, Glasgow and Leith, reports from these years show that nondenominational endeavors initiated in the early 1820's continued to develop—with local variations—along broadly parallel lines. With evangelism still the primary priority, sources underscore a simultaneous concern for the socio-cultural needs of seafarers, as evidenced in a consolidation of the "Institute" concept, with the provision of reading-room, refreshments, library and educational facilities. But beyond this, the diffuse differentiation of the maritime ministry which was characteristic of the preceding phase was succeeded by a trend toward stricter selectivity, born of necessity. Limited resources nourished the conviction that it were better to do certain central tasks well, than many superficially.[116]

However, publicity and moral support were willingly accorded the efforts of others to provide help, including, for example, curbs on cruelty and exploitation. Especially was this the case with any measures calculated to combat the continuing ravages of the Crimping System. Thus, seamen's mission societies warmly welcomed (even though they felt they could not directly finance) a distinct feature of this period—the proliferation of sailors' homes.

In London, the very success of the Well Street Home (finally opened in 1835) seemed at first only to provoke the crimps to redoubled competition.[117] However, it also encouraged emulation by an enlightened evangelical shipowner.

In 1841, George Green of Blackwall opened a new, model 200-bed sailors' home at 133 East India Dock Road, Poplar, built basically for the benefit of crews of his family fleet. Here, "East India sailors, white and black," found facilities for unmolested accomodation and vocational self-improvement, which made "Green's" (as the home was popularly known) a by-word for the best in mercantile marine personnel policy.[118] This form of racial integration was not normal at this time.

With the cooperation of the London City Mission, a so-called "Coloured Sailors' Home" (officially "The Strangers' Home") was opened in 1857, in nearby West India Dock Road, Limehouse. Intended for "Asiatic seamen and others," it did render at least real physical relief, especially for Lascar seamen (many of whom had, during past winters, literally died in the streets of London from sheer neglect).[119]

In 1852, an enterprising naval officer with a remarkable flair for public relations, Captain (later Admiral) William H. Hall, founded in London a "Sailors' Home Institution," for the promotion of sailors' homes throughout the British Empire. The Institution itself was short-lived. Nevertheless, by 1856, some twenty sailors' homes had been opened in different ports in Great Britain and Ireland, with at least seven more under preparation. Their establishment was recognized as largely the result of Captain Hall's initiative and perseverance. His most active coadjutors were also naval officers, who had had "seamen's wants forced upon their notice." In a sense, their response represents another long-term after-effect of the Naval Awakening.[120]

Turning to developments overseas, remarkable achievements were reported from the "East Indies" in the late 1830's. The Calcutta Seamen's Friend Society (revitalized through the enthusiastic leadership of the Rev.

An 1853 view of Sydney Harbor from Fort Macquarie.
(By Fleury, courtesy: Société de Géographie, Paris.)

The Port of Melbourne just prior to the founding of the
first seamen's mission there in 1857. (Courtesy:
Port of Melbourne Authority.)

Thomas Boaz, G.C. Smith's convert and former coadjutor) opened a Sailors' Home in July 1837. Others followed suit. Within twelve months, thanks again to the concern of local foreign missionaries, sailors' homes had been established in Bombay, Madras and Penang. Shortly afterwards, similar institutions were opened in Singapore and Cape of Good Hope.[121]

In Australia, sailors' homes were as yet hardly an issue during the decades under review. However, with increasing immigrants and the opening up of natural resources, shipping filled the harbors, and spurred regular Gospel ministries to seafarers.

Thus in Sydney, the barely surviving Sydney Bethel Union was revived with the arrival in 1841 of its first full-time chaplain, Matthew T. Adams, a Scottish-born Presbyterian, sent out from New York by the American Seamen's Friend Society. In 1856, a Mariners' Church was erected on Lower George Street, which came to be considered "an ornament to that flourishing colony," and gained a great reputation among seafarers. (Transferred toward the end of the century to the Anglicans, it still provides the main structure of the current Missions to Seamen facility in Sydney.)[122]

During the 1840's and 1850's, there are references to floating chapels or Bethel Ships, "served by a Dissenting Minister," both in Hobart and Launceston, Tasmania.[123] In Port Adelaide, a former Thames Agent of the BFSS, J. Barclay, commenced preaching under the Bethel Flag in 1838, and was instrumental in the erection of a Sailors' Union Church in 1839.[124]

In the new colony of Victoria, leaping to the forefront with the discovery of gold there in 1851, the "Victorian Bethel Union and Sailors' Mission at Melbourne" was founded in 1857, to promote the "Temporal and Spiritual Welfare" of seafarers and immigrants, then arriving in their thousands there. With the Rev Kerr Johnston as Chaplain, and under the patronage of the Governor, a Floating Church in Hobson's Bay (the former hulk *Emily*) was inaugurated on July 1st that same year, as the first headquarters of the Mission.[125]

From nearby New Zealand came reports of a preaching ministry to seafarers under the Bethel Flag, established in Wellington in the mid-1840's. In 1859, there was also news of the founding of an "Aukland Bethel Union" in that major port city.[126]

While seamen's mission endeavors without specific denominational affiliation continued to progress, the Established Church of the Mother Country had, at mid-century, still not developed any effective strategy for world-wide ministry to her own seafaring sons. However, by then, events in England were giving real reason for hope.

Chapter 18

New Denominational Organizations

AN ANGLICAN NATIONAL SOCIETY: "THE MISSIONS TO SEAMEN" (1856)

On the threshold of the Victorian Era, prophets of doom were pronouncing the imminent end of the Established Church. No less a figure than Dr. Arnold of Rugby wrote: "The Church as it now is, no human power can save."[127]

However, England's threatened ecclesiastical revolution was, as Trevelyan puts it, "side-tracked." While Radicals and Dissenters alike anticipated that, before long, the reformed Parliament of 1833 would have to disestablish and disendow the National Church, the opposite happened. An Ecclesiastical Commission, appointed in 1835, rapidly removed some of the most glaring abuses, in a series of sorely-needed reforms. Thereupon Evangelical clergy, already rescued from any general drift into Dissent by the pervasive preaching of Charles Simeon, rallied enthusiastically to the colors of the Establishment. Meanwhile, John Keble had, in 1833, delivered his stirring sermon on "National Apostasy," thereby ushering in the Oxford Movement, and both providing a powerful High Church challenge, and stimulating even greater exertions by Evangelical (now "Low Church") adherents.[128]

In the period of mid-century denominational self-assertion resulting from these and other factors, was born the Church of England's global ministry to seafarers. Its original conception, however, may be traced back to exactly those crucial times in the 1830's. The place, too, is worthy of note. Despite its declared Empire-wide object, the Episcopal Floating Church Society had (for reasons already touched upon) failed to consolidate itself even in the metropolis.[129] Instead of strife-torn London, it was the Bristol Channel which was to set the scene for an Anglican enterprise destined to reach out to the seven seas.[130]

When would the National Church develop a national
ministry to her own seafaring sons? British sailors at
mid-century, in a rather romanticized depiction by
G. Thomas. (*The London Illustrated News,* 1854.)

Well might the immediate circumstances surrounding the origin of
that enterprise by characterized as "at once providential and remarkable." A
young Church of England clergyman, recently returned with his family from
Ireland, in order to seek a new parish, was staying during the summer of
1835 at Clevedon on the coast of Somerset. One day, according to the
traditional version of events, the clergyman stood gazing from a headland
across the Bristol Channel, together with his little son, with whom he
happened to be taking a walk. Midway between the coasts of England and

Wales lay two lonely islets. The one called Steep Holm, was clearly visible against the horizon, and gave the impression of being nothing but a barren, desolate rock.

Suddenly a glint of sunlight reflected in some windows caught the couple's attention, and confirmed the fact that there must be people living there after all. The little boy, wondering with natural curiosity what kind of lives those lonely inhabitants were living, then turned to his father and asked, "How can those people go to church?" The father was unable to give a satisfactory answer, at least not one which could satisfy his own conscience. Accordingly, it was that innocent question which started the train of thoughts which were to bear such unforeseen fruits.[131]

The historicity of the role played by the clergyman's son has been questioned. Be that as it may, the Rev. John Ashley, a man intelligent enough to acquire a doctoral degree, and obviously possessed of a deep personal commitment to the evangelistic responsibility of his church, was quite capable of harboring his own apprehension as to the spiritual status of those isolated island-dwellers. At all events, he decided to ascertain for himself, hired a boat and cast off.

On his arrival at Steep Holm, he was given a cordial reception by the lonely fisherfolk. Continuing on to the nearby islet of Flat Holm, with its lighthouse and larger population, he expereinced the same warm welcome. In both cases, it was quickly confirmed, however, that these island-folk were altogether "shut off from the ordinary means of grace," and they gladly accepted his offer to provide them with services during the remainder of his stay in the area.[132]

Having finally received the offer of a parish he felt he was to accept, Ashley was, after three months of constant voluntary ministration, on a farewell visit to his isolated flocks. Then while walking along the beach on Flat Holm, he caught sight of a particularly large fleet of sail anchored off the coast of Wales, waiting for a favorable wind, just as he had seen others do during his island visits. The following is from a report quoted in 1853:

> Addressing himself to the fisherman by his side, he said, " ... does any one go to them?" "No more, sir, I believe than came to us before you first came to us."—was the simple answer of the fisherman. These words made such an impression on his mind that after service on the island, instead of returning home to the Coast of England, he engaged his boat to take him to the fleet off the Coast of Wales. He reached the fleet the next morning at ten o'clock. Here were 400 vessels. ... Boarding the first vessel he arrived at, and addressing himself to the Captain he said, "I have seen you here ever since I came out into the Channel to visit the little islands yonder. I believe your men have little or no ship's work to do. Tell me, what do they do with themselves?" "Do with

The Rev. John Ashley, L.L.D., whose single-handed
response to the plight of windbound sailing ship crews
in the roadsteads of the British Channel during a summer
vacation in 1835 resulted in the founding of the Bristol
Channel Mission in 1837. His epic 15-year ministry
led to the organization in 1856 of the Church of
England's worldwide network "The Missions to Seamen."
(Mary L. Walrond: *Launching Out Into the Deep.*)

themselves," he replied, "curse and swear, and lounge about my
deck morning, noon, and night, not knowing what to do with
themselves—tired of life, Sir." "Captain," said Dr. Ashley, "has
no one been appointed to visit this immense fleet. — Here it is, as
a great floating city. . . ." Then, looking at him, as Dr. Ashley
describes it, "with a look of sovereign contempt," the captain
answered, "Visit us, Sir? No Sir, as long as they can get anything
by us poor seamen, I believe they leave us to perish like dogs." . . .
Feeling strongly impressed that under these circumstances he
could not possibly withdraw, he, [Dr. Ashley] turned to the

Commander of the vessel and said, "Then Captain, all I can say is, I will go on shore, and decline the Church which I was about to take, and, God willing, give myself up to the work."[133]

That, in a very literal sense, was precisely what he proceded to do. Besides what he had witnessed off Penarth Road, he soon discovered that there was "fleet after fleet in this immense channel," in exactly the same state of spiritual and physical neglect. For fifteen years (1835-50), Ashley maintained a ministry of intensive visitation, counseling and preaching among windbound ships anchored in the busy roadsteads of the Bristol Channel (off places like Avonmouth, Portishead, Cardiff and Penarth).[134]

In this highly "irregular," non-parochial capacity, Ashley labored alone, seeking neither recognition nor remuneration. The latter was possible because family property in the West Indies made him financially independent. However, after two years, he bowed before the force of his friends' arguments: with lack of public recognition, "the field thus singularly discovered" would be bound to die with him. He sought the guidance of the Archbishop of Canterbury, and the same year, 1837, a society called the "Bristol Channel Mission" was formed as a framework for the venture.[135]

A new era in the whole endeavor opened up with the launching in 1841 of a mission cutter, the *Eirene,* built at Pill, specifically for the work.

The mission cutter *Eirene,* specifically built for
Dr. John Ashley's roadstead ministry, was launched in 1841.
With chapel accomodations below deck for 60-70 men,
she became the precursor of a whole series of Anglican
mission vessels in different ports. (Courtesy:
The Missions to Seamen.)

Hitherto, Ashley had to use open boats for his roadstead visitation, and make himself dependent on the goodwill of captains for opportunities to hold services on shipboard. The new cutter, however, besides being a fine sailer, had a chapel fitted up below deck, with accommodation for 60-70 seamen. Making a practice of anchoring to windward of the fleet, so that crews could return rapidly to their ships in case of a sudden gale, Ashley would run up his special signals to announce the times of services.

Time and again, his journals from these years record his utter amazement at the response from the men. Scoffing and hostility could occur, but rarely. Despite "such tremendous weather as ... was sufficient to thin every congregation on shore," still they came. Often over a hundred would somehow stow themselves into the sailing sanctuary. (Once he forced his way forward, only to find two men squeezed into his own pulpit-chair!) The explanation cannot have been only boredom on board their own ships. Ashley's enthusiasm, his sense of humor, his powerful voice and his personal gift of preaching combined to produce a particularly "manly type of Christianity," commanding the genuine respect of this "hardy breed of parishioners."[136]

However, public support was still meager. In 1845, the Society was reorganized and its title expanded to the "Bristol Channel Seamen's Mission." Nevertheless, no fundamental improvement could realistically be expected, so long as the Society's whole existence centered so exclusively around one over-burdened individual, however gifted and dedicated. Whenever he withdrew, under pressure from friends in order to advocate the cause on shore, Ashley experienced such severe conflicts of conscience over the resultant interruption of the work afloat, that he preferred making himself personally responsible for much of the Society's annual expenses.[137]

At the close of the year 1850, two factors finally forced a change. His health, never robust, at length gave way under the strain of incessant exposure. (At one time, he had been compelled to resort to crutches, and still not given up.) Meanwhile, the ruin of his family's estate in the West Indies removed his personal means of livelihood. Reluctantly, Ashley brought the *Eirene* to her moorings, and a heroic pastor and friend of seafarers went ashore for good. By then, it was calculated that he had visited upwards of 14,000 vessels of different nationalities, at sea or in open roadsteads, sold some 5,000 Bibles and Prayer-books, and circulated ship lending-libraries to every part of the globe.[138]

Dr. John Ashley had, with his pioneering form of roadstead evangelism, uncovered a vast and hitherto almost totally neglected field of maritime ministry. Must it now, after fifteen fruitful years, simply be abandoned? To the few who had followed developments at close hand, it was evident that at the root of the problem lay some serious communication gap. Although

The Rev. Thomas Cave Childs, who helped pave the way for the emerging National Church Society through his brief but far-reaching ministry as "Chaplain to the English Channel," 1855-57. (Mary L. Walrond: *Launching Out Into the Deep.*)

direct missionary activity was now at a standstill, the Society somehow struggled on, while Ashley (still officially its Chaplain) agreed to plead the cause from pulpits and at public meetings around the country.[139]

The effort was not in vain. Typical and widely publicized was the reaction of the Bishop of Llandaff: "We will never let it drop." Eventually, stimulated also by patriotic fervor engendered during the Crimean War, "something like a national spirit" was evoked on behalf of the Mission. The Society was once more reorganized, this time, in 1855, as the "Bristol Missions to Seamen." When this renewed Society, despite its debts, made the daring decision to expand activities to the English as well as the Bristol Channel, this in itself was a significant step in the direction of a national society.[140]

So too, as it proved, was the appointment that same year of the enthusiastic, gifted young Vicar of St. Mary's, Devonport. The Rev. Thomas Cave Childs had already attracted wide attention for his six-year volunteer ministry to emigrants sailing from Plymouth Sound. As "Chaplain to the English Channel," strategically based at Ryde on the Isle of Wight, Childs adopted Ashley's precedent. Fitting out a cutter as his "movable Church," and naming her the *Eirene* like her Bristol Channel predecessor, he systematically visited windbound shipping from Plymouth to the Downs. His ministry was brief (1855-57), but incredibly influential, a fact reflected in the way he managed to motivate others to key leadership roles in the work.[141]

Especially was this the case with William Henry Giles Kingston. To Chaplain Childs' alert mind, it soon became obvious that no provincial project, however well intentioned, could effectively meet the case. The needs of British seafarers called for no less than a boldly comprehensive, centrally coordinated, National Church organization. And in Kingston he knew he had the kind of "consecrated layman" qualified to launch such an enterprise.

Here was a loyal Churchman, unequivocally evangelical, though by no means bigoted; by background *persona grata* with both sections of the nautical community—naval and merchant; well-traveled and multi-lingual; nationally known as one of the most popular writers of sea stories and adolesent literature of his age, as well as a brilliant propagandist for organized emigration within the Empire. In this latter capacity, he had cooperated closely with the Rev. T. Cave Childs, whom he greatly admired. In response to Childs' "urgent appeal," Kingston took up the challenge.[142]

With his characteristic combination of drive and flair, Kingston lost no time in collecting co-workers and setting up organizational machinery. A preliminary meeting of six laymen sympathetic to the cause was held in Fenchurch Street on February 20, 1856. Here it was resolved "that a provisional Committee should forthwith be formed to carry out the object in hand." At a meeting April 5, 1856, rules and regulations were agreed upon, also the title, which for the first two years remained the "Society for Promoting Missions to Seamen Afloat at Home and Abroad." Lord Shaftesbury, the leading Evangelical layman of his day, was enlisted as president. He and the Bishop of London were consulted before the following was finally written into the constitution:

1. The object of the Society is the spiritual welfare of the seafaring classes at home and abroad.
2. In pursuance of this Object, the Society will use every means consistent with the principles and received practice of the Church of England.
3. The operations of the Society shall for the most part be carried on afloat, and for this purpose its Chaplains and Scripture Readers shall, as far as possible, be provided with vessels and boats for visiting the ships in Roadsteads, Rivers, Harbours.[143]

Future reports would make it clear that by "seafaring classes" was meant not only British and foreign merchant seamen, but also naval personnel, fishermen, boatmen, lighthouse and lightship men, emigrants, even general ship's passengers. Likewise, the strongly spiritual goal of the original constitution, while remaining the "first object" of the Society's solicitude, was soon to be supplemented by a serious concern for "bettering his [the seafarer's] temporal position."[144]

Kingston himself assumed the role of honorary secretary for the Society's first year, and secured the Rev. Theodore A, Walrond as a full-time secretary (a position he was to fill with distinction from 1856 until his

William Henry Giles
Kingston, empire-builder,
churchman and nautical
author, the man who
master-minded the
organization of The
Missions to Seamen in
in 1856. (M.R. Kingsford:
*The Life, Work and
Influence of William
Henry Giles Kingston.*)

death in 1873). The predominantly lay committee, with naval officers forming
a large segment, reflected Kingston's high evaluation of practical experience
and nautical expertise.[145]

In order to create a truly national society, a primary object was "to
amalgamate any [Church of England] work already in progress." In the
course of the first year, Kingston visited various ports, and in several cases
local Anglican activities were brought into association with the new Society.
In Liverpool, the subsequently far-famed "Mersey Mission to Seamen" was
established (November 24,1856), through a visit by Kingston at that time.

At the first public meeting of the London Society, in March 1857, Kingston
could report that five chaplains were already at work, in "the Mersey, the
Bristol Channel, the Isle of Wight, Milford and Swansea, and Cork River."
"Scripture Readers" had been appointed to the Tyne, Great Yarmouth,
Plymouth and Portsmouth. And so far six honorary chaplains were willing to
serve on the Sussex Coast, the Tyne, at Great Yarmouth, Plymouth, Malta
and on the Elbe.[146]

Having seen the infant organization through most of its early "growing pains," Kingston now felt free to resign. First, however, he left a powerful plea with the Society's Bristol predecessors to join forces. After some vacillation, a union was consumated, May 19,1858. The Bristol Society's name, "The Missions to Seamen," was adopted by the joint Society (as being "shorter, more free and open than the London Society's").[147] In practice, the Society soon came to be known as "The Flying Angel." Kingston's wife and sister composed an 1856 a banner, which became the emblem of the Society. Depicting the Angel of Revelation 14:6, flying with "the everlasting gospel" to every nation, it soon gained great popularity.[148]

That W. H. Kingston played a fundamental role in the formation of The Missions to Seamen, as now known, is indisputable. His biographer

The original "Flying Angel" from 1856.

Today's more modern version.

"There must be something in religion . . ." was the distinctly heard comment of one of those who watched the Rev. Thomas Treanor (Anglican) Missions to Seamen "Chaplain for the Downs," hazarding his life to make a pastoral call during a storm in the 1880's. There could, at any given time, be over 500 ships windbound in the Downs anchorage off the coast of Kent. (Thomas S. Treanor: *The Log of a Sky-Pilot.*)

even makes out a strong case for his right to the title of "Founder," taking issue with those who bestow this honor on Dr. John Ashley.[149] However, the fact that the Bristol Society merged with the London Society in 1858, gives the latter the same formal right to refer to the founding date of the Bristol Channel Mission (1837), as the British Sailors' Society of today has to trace its origin to that of the Port of London Society (1818).[150] Perhaps it would conform closest with the facts to designate Dr. Ashley the "Originator," and W.H. Kingston the "Organizer."[151]

At all events, Ashley established the method of mission which was to become the mainstay of not only the Bristol Society, but also the London Society, as originally conceived. Strictly speaking, "Mission Afloat" (in the sense of employing sailing sanctuaries, and/or focusing especially on windbound ships in roadsteads) were no absolute novelty in 1835.[152] However, it was to the credit of Ashley and his early followers that a field of mission with such vast potential was, after years of neglect, made the object of concerted and consistent action.

In fact, so intensely did The Missions to Seamen, during the Society's first years, believe in the importance of "anchorage work," that alternative methods of mission were not only omitted in the original title, but expressly dismissed as irrelevant in practice.[153] It was the Rev. Robert B.

The Rev. Robert Buckley Boyer, who took over the Missions to Seamen Bristol Channel chaplaincy in 1862. He was conspiciously successful in fighting the crimp, and soon proved to his Society the validity of shore-based ministry. (Mary L. Walrond: *Launching Out Into the Deep.*)

Boyer who, after taking over the Bristol Channel Chaplaincy in 1862, was to convince the Society of the validity of simultaneous shore-based activity.

Best known for his success in combating the crimp (comparable only to the feats of Chaplain Fell of 'Frisco), Boyer brought, in 1863, the Admiralty frigate *Thisbe* to Cardiff, where she was destined for decades to serve as the Society's popular "Church and Institute." The Tyne followed suit — with HMS *Diamond,* then others — with various forms of shore facilities. Finally, with the completion of the transition from sail to steam, the need for roadstead work, once the Society's primary purpose, was radically reduced, while other activities flourished, both at home and abroad.[154]

These latter developments in the continuing expansion of The Missions to Seamen lie beyond the scope of this study. However, an issue which claimed early attention was the appropriate role of the laity in the operational work of this avowedly Anglican enterprise. From the outset, the employment of "Scripture Readers" (or "Lay Readers," as they were later called) was considered essential, not only from a manpower standpoint, but also from psychological considerations. Himself frequently a seafarer by background, a lay coadjutor would be able to share the Gospel "with even more effect than the regular clergyman."

For the Low Church evangelically-oriented organizers of The Missions to Seamen, this presented no problem. However, in promoting a national society, they were anxious to obtain wide endorsement by the episcopate. "The Church Pastoral Aid Society" (founded in 1836) had already borne the brunt of the battle for greater lay participation in evangelism.

The Admiralty frigate *Thisbe*, which served as Missions to Seamen
Church and Institute in Cardiff Docks from 1863 to 1891.
(Mary L. Walrond: *Launching Out Into the Deep.*)

An early Missions to Seamen Bethel worship service.
(Kathleen Heasman: *Evangelicals in Action.*)

But care was still called for, to prevent the activities of Scripture Readers from infringing on the authority of parochial clergy.[155]

Somehow the Society continued to find scope for its lay workers, pointing out that, in practice, the work must frequently be done by a lay helper—or not at all. This was just as true of ministry at sea as on the waterfront. The Society's officers, sought assiduously to promote "service on the high seas," exhorting ship's officers and sending forth "Service Boxes" by the hundreds. In the 1860's, Secretary Walrond launched the "Missions to Seamen Helpers and Associates," as an Anglican counterpart to the Bethel Union Register. Consisting of officers and foremast-seamen respectively, these pledged themselves, as active Churchmen, to afford help and witness to fellow-seafarers afloat and ashore.[156]

Significantly, Walrond's modern-day successor, the Rev. Prebendary Tom Kerfoot, predicted in 1975 that the Missions to Seamen would, in order to fulfill their task in a new age, have to become a partnership, "with by far the greater part of the effective pastoral and missionary work being done by seafarers themselves at sea."[157]

OTHER CHURCH OF ENGLAND ENDEAVORS

In the early 1860's, feelings in Anglican circles were running high concerning the eligibility of laymen to perform pastoral functions. The rising tide of Anglo-Catholicism engendered by the Oxford Movement was not content to continue leaving "Church" ministry to seafarers at the mercy of a polity which was poles apart from their own. The emergence, in 1864, of "St. Andrew's Waterside Church Mission," though taking place at the termination of the period covered by this study, supplements a picture of hitherto almost exclusive Evangelical involvement.[158]

Churchmen of Anglo-Catholic persuasion obtained an ardent and eloquent spokesman in the Rev. C.E.R. Robinson. As Vicar of St. James's Ryde, he had watched with deep interest the ministry of Chaplain Childs on the Channel Coast (1857). On becoming Vicar of Holy Trinity, Milton-next-Gravesend, he found himself faced with an impoverished waterside parish ashore, and offshore—a constant stream of ships, many of them filled with anxious emigrants, pausing at anchor before putting to sea. Unwilling to ignore the need at his door, and yet unable to reconcile his High Church convictions with the lay-orientation and extra-parochial organization of a society like the newly-established Missions to Seamen, Robinson resolved to go his own way.[159]

In January 1864, Robinson established a "Church Mission" in connection with his waterfront parish. A former public-house was rented for the purpose, and a young clergyman was ordained to the work by the Bishop of Rochester. Emigrant ships, merchantmen, colliers and coal-hulks were visited, likewise homes and hovels ashore, and great quantities of Christian literature were distributed. In 1871, a Mission Church (St. Andrew's) was completed, built right on the wharfside.[160]

Meanwhile, Robinson eagerly advocated the national dimensions of the new Mission. The basic premise was simply stated: "The Mission work of the Church can best be done by consistently enabling responsible clergy to do it." It viewed itself, therefore, as nothing more than "a mediary, ministering between the seafaring classes and the rest of the Church," channeling the resources of the Church at Large so as to enable parochial clergy in underprivileged port districts to undertake a local maritime responsibility.

However, the argument did not stop there. Promoters of parochial mission publicly denied the legitimacy of any organized Anglican alternative.[161] Understandably, The Missions to Seamen reacted, claiming that maritime ministry required a degree of expertise and flexibility which the parochial system alone could not possibly provide. As their secretary, Commander W. Dawson R.N., put it (quoting the Bishop of Durham):

> The sailor has his own ways, his own times, his own resorts. He is
> a migratory being. You would throw the parochial machinery out
> of gear if you would try to adapt it to sailors.[162]

Nevertheless, the St. Andrew's Waterside Church Mission had, in so far as it sought to promote parochial involvement, presented a valid viewpoint. In fact it did, in the years ahead, manage to moblize a concern for seafarers not only among parish clergy in home ports, but also among a mounting number of Consular and Resident Chaplains overseas.[163]

However, it proved impossible to refute the right to life of the specialized form of vocational ministry represented by The Missions to Seamen as they continued to forge ahead through the remainder of the century and into the next. At length, in a 1939 merger between the two organizations, years of polerization terminated with a warmly welcomed intergration of both concerns. (The Missions to Seamen are today organized as an independent association linked with the Church of England through representation on the Missionary and Ecumenical Council of the Church Assembly, and through a system of "Liaison Bishops.")[164]

Two other Anglican endeavors on the Thames waterfront, both of considerably earlier origin, and both of decidedly Evangelical allegiance, claim attention. In a sense, they were, each in their own way, a logical outcome of the eclipse of the only Anglican seamen's mission until then in existence on the metropolitan scene—the Episcopal Floating Church Society, whose *Brazen* was, in the mid-1840's, ripe for abandonment.[165] However, whereas one of the two successors took the shape of a sailortown church in the mainstream of all the allurements of shore life, the other (earlier) alternative was launched as a sailing church in the midst of the Thames shipping.

The concept of a sailing "Thames Church," as it came to be called, was the result of a routine lightship inspection in the Bristol Channel by "Elder Brethren" of London's Trinity House. They were here able to witness at first hand the successful roadstead ministry of Dr. John Ashley, and returned to London inspired with the thought that at last they had found the solution to the deteriorating situation on board the *Brazen*.[166]

Thus it happened, that on February 23, 1844, seven seafarers (three naval captains and four Trinity Brethren) assembled at the City offices of the Seamen's Hospital, under the chairmanship of the Hon. Captain W. Waldergrave R.N., and founded the "Thames Church Mission" (TCM). All of them were men of known Evangelical affiliation. Several of them had served on the Committee of the EFCS, and were anxious to profit by painful past experience. The object of the Society, originally "to afford Pastoral Superintendence to the Colliers and other Shipping on the Thames," was, a few weeks later, elaborated as follows:

> To promote the spiritual welfare of the Seamen in the River Thames, especially between the Pools in London and the anchorage at Gravesend, as well as to visit emigrants and others on board vessels about to leave Gravesend.[167]

Although clergy members were invited to supplement the seven sea officers who first launched the venture, the object of the Society was such as to necessitate nautical expertise. After deciding for a sailing vessel rather than a steamer, the committee entrusted to Captain R.J. Elliot, R.N., the promoter of the Well Street Sailors' Home, and now joint honorary secretary of the new Society, the vital task of obtaining from the Admiralty the loan of a suitable naval vessel, and then fitting her up for her new commission. Accordingly, a redundant, 144-ton cutter from the Napoleonic War years, the *Swan*, was made seaworthy, rendered capable of accommodating a congregation of 120, and officially opened April 21, 1845, under the patronage of the Archbishop of Canterbury.[168]

The position as "Resident Chaplain" had also been a subject of solicitude for the committee. Candidates who lacked "power" in their preaching, or the necessary "energy of manner," were rejected as not likely to "sufficiently interest the Seamen." In the Rev. William Holderness, however, who took over in 1846, the Committee's hopes were "more than realised." His incessant visitation on board the shipping in the different reaches of the river resulted in remarkably responsive audiences in his "cruising Church," as he called it.

As the century progressed, the mission fleet and personnel were expanded, in order to cope with an ever widening outreach to merchantmen,

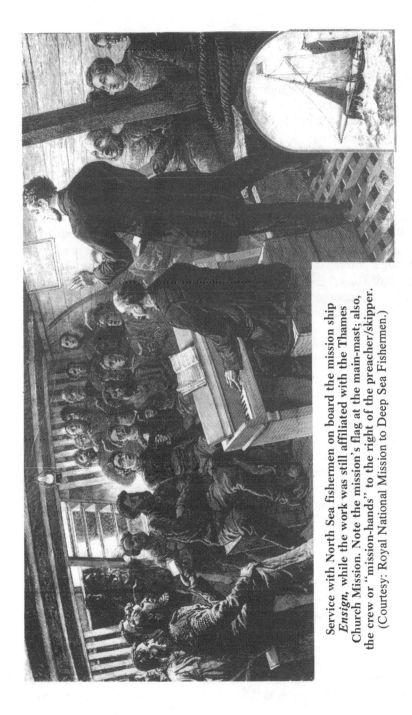

Service with North Sea fishermen on board the mission ship *Ensign*, while the work was still affiliated with the Thames Church Mission. Note the mission's flag at the main-mast; also, the crew or "mission-hands" to the right of the preacher/skipper. (Courtesy: Royal National Mission to Deep Sea Fishermen.)

colliers, convict ships, emigrant ships, training ships and even fishing craft in the North Sea (where the Society became the forerunners of the Royal National Mission to Deep Sea Fishermen).[169]

With the firm foundation laid during Holderness' ministry, it was not surprising that Churchmen, who in the mid-fifties were endeavoring to establish a national society based in London, thought first of making this successful Anglican enterprise (the TCM) "the basis of a work to be gradually expanded" throughout the kingdom and the world. Although early merger negotiations foundered, The Missions to Seamen took care, during the decades which followed, to avoid denominational duplication on the Thames. Their forebearance was rewarded in 1904, when a union was finally achieved.[170]

While preparations were afoot in the early forties for the establishment of a Thames version of Ashley's roadstead work, plans were also maturing for a "more stable" successor to the fast failing Floating Church in the Admiralty Tier off the Tower. As early as in 1836, the *Annual Report* of the EFCS had proposed the opening of an alternative "Episcopal Chapel on shore." Here, too, Captain Elliot was "mainly instrumental" in both promoting patronage and actual implementation. In 1847, following the final abandonment of the *Brazen*, the stately spired sanctuary of "St. Paul's Church for Seamen" was consecrated, with accommodation for some 800. The site, adjacent to the Destitute Sailors' Asylum in Dock Street, and close to the Sailors' Home in Well Street, was chosen with a view to benefiting both.[171]

A sound basis for future work was laid by the vigorous ministry of the Rev. Charles B. Gribble, a former chief officer in the East India Company, who simultaneously acted as chaplain to the two neighboring institutions. It was during the unique 35-year incumbency of the Rev. Dan Greatorex, who took over in 1862, that the former Mariners' Church in nearby Wellclose Square was acquired and replaced by a social ministry dedicated to the education of Sailortown children and the rehabilitation of victims of vice, which has since continued.[172]

The successful establishment of St. Paul's Church for Seamen was partly attributable to the pastoral zeal of the Rev. W.W.Champneys, Rector of the huge Thames-side parish of Whitechapel, 1837-60. This brilliant, Evangelical Churchman had already involved himself in the committee of the Thames Church Mission. St. Paul's was one of four Whitechapel churches raised during Champneys' incumbency, and maintained with significant help from the Church Pastoral Aid Society.[173]

Founded in 1836, as an evangelical home misson project, primarily to supply curates and lay-workers for the most neglected parishes, the CPAS had as one of its earliest concerns the wretched conditions prevailing among

St. Paul's Church for
Seamen, Dock Street,
consecrated 1847,
adjacent to the Destitute
Sailors' Asylum.
(From a contemporary
print.)

the boatmen's families, who manned the many barges on Britain's 3,000 miles of inland waterways. It was largely the support of this Society which enabled the Rev. John Davies (Rector of St. Clement's, Worcester, and affectionately styled "The Apostle of the Watermen") to establish, in the early 1840's, an effective ministry to bargees, later also deep-sea mariners, on the River Severn.[174]

Abroad, the "Colonial and Continental Church Society" assumed a corresponding responsibility. Organized by Evangelical Churchmen in 1838, in order to promote Anglican church extension overseas, the CCCS gave significant support to Anglican chaplains in port cities in the Colonies and on the Continent, many of whom involved themselves in part-time voluntary service to seafarers. (An outstanding example was the maritime ministry of the Rev. M.J. Mayers in Marseilles.)[175] The Crimean War signaled a new period of participation on the Continent of Europe by the older Society for the Propagation of the Gospel, through grants to chaplaincies both in Constantinople and other ports where there were "large numbers of British sailors."[176]

The efforts of the various Anglican societies involved in ministry to seafarers were supplemented during the middle decades of the nineteenth century by continuing grants from both the Prayer Book and Homily Society and the Society for the Promotion of Christian Knowledge. The maritime distribution of the PBHS was for years a stable and major Evangelical avenue of Anglican outreach among seamen.[177] The SPCK cooperated with the SPG in various port cities, including an extensive ministry to emigrants, leaving Liverpool and other home ports for the Colonies.[178]

In the Royal Navy, a quiet but powerful impact was made by the "Royal Naval Scripture Readers' Society," founded in affiliation with the Church of England in 1860. Pledged to prove "by word and deed that it is possible to live a Christian life" despite the many adverse pressures of life at sea, it is now known as the "Royal Naval Lay Readers' Society." Readers have generally been former naval personnel, working under the direction of naval chaplains.[179]

A Methodist enterprise: Wesleyan Seamen's Mission (1843)

While Baptists and Congregationalists, with their independent church polity, continued to cooperate in the nondenominational BFSS, the Methodists followed the lead of the Anglicans, from whom they had sprung, and established their own, denominational mission to seafarers.[180] To this end, they had long been urged by G.C. Smith, who never tired of publicizing the fact that it was the Methodists who had pioneered the whole seamen's mission movement.[181]

The "Wesleyan Seamen's Mission" (originally known as the "Wesleyan Seamen's Missionary Society") was founded in 1843, on the initiative of "a few godly men connected with the shipping interest." After initiating a powerful program of visitation and Bethel Meetings, the Society, seeing the need for a suitable shore facility, too, purchased the lease of a stately columned building on Commercial Road called the "Eastern Institution," and opened it March 14, 1849 as the "Wesleyan Seamen's Chapel." The choice was sufficiently successful to warrant retaining these commodious premises as headquarters of the work for almost half a century.[182]

The emphasis was vigorously evangelistic, but by no means fanatic. A spacious reading-room offered seafarers a sorely-needed "place of their own," for social fellowship and recreation. Here, a "Sabbath Afternoon Social Meeting," with free tea included, provided a blending of "social and religious elements" in the kind of informal atmosphere which held "an irresistible charm" for the seafarer, so it was claimed. In actual fact, it really

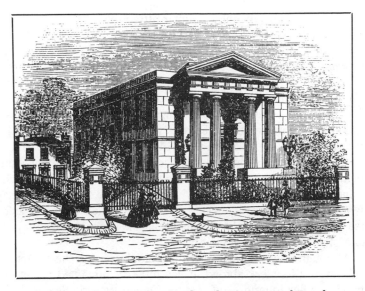

The Wesleyan Seamen's Chapel, Commercial Road,
London, opened 1849. (*Wesleyan Seamen's
Mission Reports, 1847-1860.*)

A Wesleyan "Sailors' Bible Woman" encouraging seafarers
to seek out the truth in the Scriptures.
(*Wesleyan Seamen's Mission Reports, 1847-1860.*)

did prove a remarkably popular counter-attraction to the gin-palace — a gateway for the Gospel.[183]

Another innovative feature of this Wesleyan waterfront endeavor in London was the introduction of women in direct ministry to seafarers. In the summer of 1860, the first "Sailors' Bible Woman" (herself a "Sailor's widow") was commissioned to "visit seamen in their lodgings and places of resort," seeking to engage them in religious conversation and distribute Christian literature among them. Results were evidently rewarding, proving seamen to be "peculiarly susceptible to the influence of a good woman."[184]

A third feature of the work was the practice of appointing committed crew members as volunteer coadjutors, referring to them as "Ship Missionaries," and supplying them with Christian literature. Reports of chaplains and lay agents quoted dramatic cases of their usefulness. (The concept was, of course, as old as the Bethel Movement, but the formal designation, as well as certain other aspects, were new.)[185]

Although it was the "wish of the Founders" that the Society should ultimately extend its work abroad, it has hitherto remained a metropolitan institution (with headquarters today at the Queen Victoria Seamen's Rest, in East India Dock Road, Poplar).[186] An independent Methodist ministry to seafarers was, nevertheless, undertaken in several overseas ports during the nineteenth century, including in Dublin, Hamburg and Gibraltar.[187]

THE ROMAN CATHOLICS:
PRELUDE TO A NEW APOSTOLATE

During the evolution of (Protestant) seamen's mission organizations, early reports seldom mention Roman Catholic seafarers except as objects of mission. It would, however, be unfair to attribute this attitude solely to what was still a harsh Protestant-Catholic climate.

On the one hand, there is no reason to doubt the overriding concern of the average nineteenth-century "seamen's missionary," for seafarers—regardless of nominal church affiliation—to appropriate a saving faith in Christ. On the other hand, there was the added motivation which lay in the fact that the numerically greatest denomination in Christendom had so far not established any organization for maritime mission even remotely comparable to that of the Protestants.

Describing the situation toward the close of the nineteenth century, Peter Anson (1889-1975), co-founder and historian of the future "Apostleship of the Sea," writes:

> There was no co-ordinated Catholic sea apostolate to set beside
> the multifarious non-Catholic activities distributed all over the

Peter F. Anson (1889-1975) fisherman, author and
Oblate of the Benedictines of Caldey (an island off
the south coast of Wales), was co-founder of the
Apostleship of the Sea and designer of their world-famous
emblem. (Francis S. Frayne: *What is the
Apostleship of the Sea?*)

world. . . . Just why the Church of Peter the fisherman-apostle had
neglected this particular field of apostolate is difficult to explain.[188]

However, there are many examples of sporadic attempts by Catholic
individuals and groups to minister to the spiritual needs of seafarers during
the latter half of the nineteenth century. The earliest Anson himself lists, is
the appointment in 1856 by Cardinal Wiseman of the Rev. William Woolett
as the first Catholic chaplain to the Royal Navy. The next is the work of two
French priests, the Abbé Bernard and the Abbé Beaudouin, ministering in
Iceland in 1860 to fishermen from Brittany and Normandy.[189] It is interesting
to note that "the first Catholic Sailors' Club in England" (later commonly
known as Stella Maris Clubs) was opened in 1893 at 18 Wellclose Square,
precisely the scene of Boatswain Smith's hectic hey-day, two generations
previously.[190]

Despite promising beginnings on both sides of the Atlantic in the
1890's,[191] it was not until October 4, 1920, that a handful of concerned
Catholic laymen met in Glasgow, to found what finally became the world-
wide Apostleship of the Sea.("Apostolatus Maris"). The event is reminiscent
of the role of the laity in the origin of the Thames Revival a century earlier.

Since then, the Apostleship of the Sea (AOS) has witnessed a truly
remarkable rate of growth throughout the world. Today, the AOS cooperates
closely with other denominations through the International Christian Maritime Association (ICMA). Details, however, fall far beyond the horizon of
the present study.[192]

The Catholic Maritime Club in Brooklyn, New York, one of the best-equipped seafarers' centers in the world when opened in 1943, symbolizing the vigorous expansion which has characterized the brief history of the worldwide Apostleship of the Sea. (Picture by Peter F. Anson in his book, *The Church and the Sailor.*)

On the other hand, the evolution of an American ministry to seafarers constitutes an integral part of the early nineteenth century seamen's mission movement. In fact, the record of American efforts form a fascinating parallel to patterns of maritime ministry developed more or less concurrently in Great Britain. However, these transatlantic endeavors also include indigenous traits and initiatives of such significance as to warrant a separate study of the specifically American contribution to the work, together with an analysis of the nature of British-American interaction.

PART VII

"A SORT OF SIMULTANEOUS MOVEMENT"

The New World and the Seamen's Cause

Chapter 19

Toward an American
Metropolitan Society (1812-18)

THE AMERICAN PRECURSOR:
THE BOSTON SOCIETY FOR THE RELIGIOUS AND
MORAL IMPROVEMENT OF SEAMEN (FOUNDED 1812)

By the year 1812, when the United States of America entered the scene of organized Christian ministry to seafarers, her overseas-trade tonnage had, during the first generation of her history as an independent nation, increased more than seven-fold to near the million mark. However, Europe was embroiled in the final phase of the Napoleonic War, and America's position was precarious. In 1809, Madison had inherited, from Jefferson, severely strained relations with the two major belligerents, Great Britain and France, both of whom had been making repeated inroads on the upstart republic's sea-borne commerce. By 1811, Napoleon had, by deceitful diplomacy, managed to extricate France from economic retaliation, and instead bring Britain and America to the brink of war.[1]

Meanwhile, in the midst of all the clamor over continuing British infringements of "Free Trade and Sailors' Rights," a handful of Bostonians began raising the issue of the complete spiritual neglect of those same sailors by their own countrymen. Nor was it by accident that such concern should manifest itself exactly here. Boston was the major port city of the largest shipowning state in the Union, and her citizens had a heavy stake in her seafarers. Moreover, Boston had for nearly two centuries been the citadel of New England Congregationalism.[2]

However, the original initiative did not come from the ranks of the orthodox. This was a Boston whose progressive moneyed and intellectual classes found the Calvinist doctrine of human depravity increasingly repugnant, and whose parochial clergy were, in their dread of revivalism, moving more and more toward a Unitarian position. Division did not come

**Boston's busy early nineteenth century waterfront, seen
here from the South Boston toll-bridge. (J. Milbert:
Itineraire pittoresque du Fleuve Hudson. . . .)**

to the surface before 1815.[3] But among those destined to become prominent
among Boston Unitarians in the decades ahead was the Congregational
pastor who, in 1801 had settled in the obscure village of Chelsea, a little to
the northeast of the city.

Joseph Tuckerman (1778-1840), born of English immigrant stock
from the early years of the Bay Colony, is cited as an outstanding example of
"the early rise of the Unitarian social passion."[4] His life-long friend and
fellow-graduate from Harvard, the renowned Dr. William Ellery Channing
had this to say of the way in which the young country pastor became
involved in plans for a ministry to seafarers, during the winter of 1811-12:

> His strength did not lie in abstract speculation. . . . His heart
> yearned for active life. . . . His study window looked on the sea;
> and the white sail, as it skirted the horizon, reminded him of the
> ignorance and moral perils of the sailor; and accordingly, he was
> the first man in the country to make an effort for the improvement
> and instruction of this class of men.[5]

The latter statement is not quite correct. As already noted, others
had made earlier, sporadic efforts.[6] However, it is true to say that Tuckerman
took the initiative to found the first *organization* for this purpose.

We are indebted to the Boston Marine Society for details. According to the *Records* of this venerable body, a communication was read at the Society's meeting January 7, 1812, from "a number of Clergymen of Boston and the neighborhood," whose support Tuckerman had enlisted. The letter sought the Society's cooperation on the question of "ameliorating the moral and religious condition of Seamen." A committee of members was forthwith appointed to confer with them. The outcome was a vote that the Society would "cheerfully lend their aid in support of the benevolent design of the Clergy in reforming the Seamen."[7]

As a result of this mutual concern among ministers, merchants and shipmasters, subscription lists were laid out, inviting membership on the basis of an annual payment of two dollars. Finally, on May 11, 1812, a meeting was held in the hall of the Branch Bank in Boston where the "Boston Society for the Religious and Moral improvement of Seamen" (BSRMIS) was founded, and a constitution unanimously adopted. This document contains no elaboration on the purpose of the Society beyond that expressed in the title. Nevertheless, the choice of the word "Improvement," though not unique, would reflect a characteristic Unitarian preoccupation with the ethical dimension of the faith and with social reform.[8]

Among the initial membership of some 70, what kind of men were most actively involved in the project? The list of officers elected to serve for the year 1812 gives a good indication. Apart from the originator, the Rev. Joseph Tuckerman who was appointed secretary, the list includes the names of three merchant sea-captains, all delegates of the Marine Society: Captains Gamaliel Bradford (elected president),[9] Jonathan Chapman,[10] and Tristam Barnard.[11] The executive committee numbered four ministerial members, each of them subsequently eloquent spokesmen for "classical" Unitarianism: William Ellery Channing (their "princeps inter pares"),[12] Joseph Stevens Buckminster,[13] Charles Lowell,[14] and Horace Holley.[15] Richard Sullivan, prominent lawyer and later State Senator, was chosen as treasurer.[16]

In an *Address to Masters of Vessels*, written by Tuckerman and dated June 1812, the Society seeks to enlist the active cooperation of shipmasters, as it specifies the means whereby it hoped to promote its stated aims: (1) To distribute "tracts of a religious and moral nature, for the use of seamen," (2) to establish "a regular divine service on board of our merchant vessels," (3) to open "a school for the instruction of lads for the sea" (or at least provide the means of "assisting in their education"), and (4) to promote "whatever can contribute to the advancement of the best interests of seamen."[17]

Curiously enough, the two last-mentioned "objects" have hitherto been overlooked in standard references to the Society. Both are none the less significant. The third may well have been inspired by news of the pre-sea training sponsored by the Marine Society in London. The fourth evinces openness to expansion and methodological differentiation. At all events, the Society was concerned, as they expressed it, about "those who become sailors at a very tender age, and pass from the salutary restraints of domestic discipline, into a society, in which they are exposed to early and confirmed depravity. . . ."[18]

However, within six weeks of the launching of the new endeavor, an event took place which threatened its very existence. With large segments of public opinion fanned to fury by repeated reports of British impressment of American crews on the high seas, the "War Hawks" of Washington secured a slim majority for a declaration of war, June 18, 1812.

New Englanders however, hoisted their flags at half-mast on receipt of the news. For them, this Second War with Great Britain (or, as they contemptuously called it, "Mr. Madison's War") was a potential commercial catastrophe. And true enough, despite lucrative American privateering and blockade-running, the British bottled up the Seaboard States so effectively, that some 250 ships remained rotting in Boston Harbor, and soup kitchens had to be opened for starving seamen in the streets of neighboring Marblehead.[19]

Obviously, this was no season to seek support for a novel ministry among the dwindling ranks of merchant seafarers. As the Society's first *Annual Report* ruefully remarks, the Society was "instituted at a time, very unfavorable to its extensive operation." Nevertheless, Tuckerman and his friends refused to abandon what they knew to be a legitimate cause, and chose to carry on in anticipation of "brighter and happier days."[20]

Undeniably, an effort was made to pursue the first of the Society's objectives, and supply seafarers with appropriate religious reading-matter. Thus, a whole series of nautical "tracts" (as these brief, popular books were called in America, too) were produced during the years 1812-17.

They were, in the main, original (the classic *James Covey* constituting a notable exception). Many were written by the Society's president, Captain Gamaliel Bradford, a man widely respected as the one-legged hero of a successful action in the Quasi-War with France. Some were authored by Tuckerman himself. Several of them dwell on the role of prayer in providential rescues from shipwreck; there are various maritime versions of the Prodigal Son; and almost all contain vivid warnings against the power of evil example, and against each of the traditional "Maritime Vices."[21]

At the same time, a deliberate attempt was made to implement the second of the Society's avowed aims, the promotion of devotional life at sea. As stated in the Society's original *Address to Masters of Vessels* (1812),

> A few masters, independent enough to act only from a sense of
> duty, and not to be afraid either of the ridicule or the censure of

the frivolous or the base, might effect an extensive and most desirable reformation. . . .

With the return of peace, renewed efforts were made in an *Address to the Master of a Vessel* (1815), to confront ship's captains with their paternal responsibility for the spiritual welfare of their crews. In conjunction with this, a collection of *Prayers, Social and Private, to Be Used at Sea* was published that same year. (Captain Bradford, who was intimately involved in the production of these aids, had here, until he quit the sea in 1809, consistently "practiced what he preached.")[22]

Looking back over the years, after having removed to Boston and pursued his pioneering "ministry-at-large" among the urban poor, Tuckerman recalls that "the enterprise was begun with much spirit," but "soon declined," and that in 1817 the Society published its last tract.[23] Why? Several causes could be assigned for the early demise of this maritime version of the current "Moral Society" Movement.

Among the more manifest of such reasons was first the immediate outbreak of the War of 1812. This had the effect of not only severely reducing the number of merchant seamen capable of receiving any benefit from the new Society, but also of diverting public attention into other, more pressing concerns.[24]

Secondly, the lack of experience of the founders led to serious errors of judgment. On the one hand, without personal visitation, simply sending out a series of tracts, all heavily laden with legalism and moralism, could not establish any real rapport with seafarers. ("About this new fangled society . . . what the devil are they going to do with us . . . make us all saints and deacons?" Such was evidently the reaction of the skeptical.) On the other hand, underestimation of the need for powerful promotional activity precluded effective public support, and therefore, prospects of expansion. (The establishment of a "Marblehead Auxiliary Society for the Religious and Moral Improvement of Seamen" remained a solitary exception. The Society as such continued to be "upperclassish.")[25]

A third factor finalized matters. The breakdown of Tuckerman's health (never robust) removed the Society's single, very part-time staff person. (He went to Europe in 1816 in hopes of recovery.)[26]

Tuckerman's close colleague, Channing, referred in retrospect to the whole endeavor as a "failure." His modern-day biographer echoes that judgment.[27] However, such a categorical conclusion would seem unwarranted.

In the first place, the Society, besides boosting its membership to 150 within a year, attained a distribution of its publications which was by no means negligible. Naval personnel provided an unexpected and gratifying alternative, in the midst of all the wartime "embarrassment of commerce." (For example, "about 300 were sent to Commodore Bainbridge, when he commanded the Constitution.") Tracts were also entrusted to a variety of individuals and institutions in touch with seafarers, including selected slop-shops. Some were sent to provincial ports even out of State (for example to Newport, Rhode Island). There are indications that the response was far from uniformly negative.[28]

In the second place, lessons were learnt which might be of great potential value in a situation which was more mature, at the same time hastening that day by raising public consciousness concerning the plight of a particularly destitute category of the "neglected poor."[29]

Finally (although the Society was ignored in early American presentations of the movement),[30] none can now deny the Boston Society for the Religious and Moral Improvement of Seamen its rightful and unique place in the history of seamen's missions. In contrast to its 33-year-old British predecessor, the Naval and Military Bible Society, with its dual objective, this was the earliest organization in the world known to have been founded for the exclusive purpose of promoting the spiritual welfare of seafarers.[31]

Whatever the relationship between this Bostonian precursor and its successors on the American scene, it remains an interesting fact that the first comprehensive seamen's mission society in New York (also, eventually, the first such society in Boston) was organized by men who, like that unorthodox pioneer of the American City Mission Movement, Joseph Tuckerman, were deeply concerned with the spiritual and moral misery of the urban poor.[32]

As in the United Kingdom, however, so too in the United States, the commencement of comprehensive seamen's mission societies was preceded by the seemingly spontaneous emergence of Marine Bible Societies.[33]

THE AMERICAN MARINE BIBLE SOCIETY MOVEMENT

As Admiral Lord Gambier subcribed his signature to the Treaty of Ghent, on Christmas Eve 1814, that pioneer patron of the Seamen's Cause in England was unwittingly removing a major impediment to the expansion of seamen's misson organization in the United States as well.[34] For the church in America, the cessation of hostilities with Great Britain had at least two significant consequences.

First, the advent of peace meant a resumption of the revivalism of the Second Awakening, as the "suspended animation" of the war years gave way to the nationalist and missionary fervor of the so-called "Era of Good Feelings."

Secondly, peace meant a renewal of British example and inspiration, as voluntary, nondenominational societies for an ever-widening variety of benevolent causes proliferated in post-1815 America, too.[35] (A striking example of the tenacity of such transatlantic ties was the action of the Massachusetts Bible Society in compensating the British and Foreign Bible Society, both in 1813 and again in 1814, for Scripture consignments lost with ships captured by American privateers. For, if Americans were at war with England, they were "not at war with her pious and benevolent institutions.")[36]

Both of the above factors were to have a profound impact on the development of an American ministry to seafarers. Just as revivalism was fast becoming the "typical religion of the frontier," and the English voluntary society model its vehicle, so too, among that *other* category of "continually migrating folk." For, while concerned Christians throughout the nation (caught up in the current concept of "Manifest Destiny") were seeking to possess for the Lord the Promised Land of the West, some were beginning to discern an entirely new frontier—that of the sea, and its long neglected toilers.[37]

It was in Philadelphia, the "religious capital" of the nation, and birthplace of American independence from Great Britain, that the "first public link of alliance" was forged between the two nations, at least in the realm of Bible distribution. The "Bible Society of Philadelphia" was founded December 12, 1808. The following year, it was emulated by six others in neighboring states. Like the Philadelphia Society, they were founded on a strictly nondenominational basis. They acknowledged their obligation to the British and Foreign Bible Society, as both "parent" and "example," and from that quarter they received prompt and effective aid. (Within eight years, the BFBS was able to present £3,122 to sixteen similar societies in the United States.)[38]

As in Great Britain, so too in the United States, it did not take Bible society pioneers long to discover that few were more destitute of the Scriptures than that "most interesting and valuable class of fellowmen," the men of the sea. Reports from societies along the Eastern Seaboard during these first years recount how the Scriptures were, in devious ways, "cast upon the ocean."[39] With the outbreak of the War of 1812, attention was especially focused on the needs of naval personnel and privateersmen; and just as captive American sailors at Dartmoor and on board prison hulks became the object of "bounty" by the BFBS, so too would British maritime prisoners of war in the USA benefit by such gestures of "religious brotherhood . . . amidst the calamities and desolations of war."[40]

From the first decade of the century, the American religious press had carried colorful quotations from British publications illustrating the "Value of Bibles on Board Ships," and similar themes. From copious consignments of BFBS *Reports*, news had reached America of the early maritime distribution of that Society. Finally, with the return of peace in the winter of 1814-15, American Christians learned of the founding of the Thames Union Bible Committee, and similar endeavors elsewhere, specifically structured for seafarers.[41]

Whether the idea "leapt the Atlantic," or was simply motivated by the obvious inadequacy of general Bible distribution, the first Marine Bible Society in America was ultimately launched in the same city as the nation's first Bible Society. Robert Ralston (1761-1836), prominent merchant and shipowner of early nineteenth-century Philadelphia, and a pioneer of the Bible Society Movement in America, had throughout been in direct personal correspondence with the BFBS. In a letter to them, dated March 8, 1816, Ralston wrote that a few weeks ago a "Marine Association" had been established, with the support of "some of the most respectable and distinquish'd of our Naval Officers."[42]

The 8th *Report* of the Bible Society of Philadelphia (read May 1, 1816) gives further details:

> The little done [previously, in supplying ships with Bibles] ... served but to show how much could be effected in the good work. The managers therefore, determined to attempt the formation of a Marine Bible Association of the Port of Philadelphia, to consist of gentlemen who are of rank in the navy of the United States, or who have been, or now are, masters or mates of vessels, for the purpose of encouraging small stated contributions on the part of mariners, and the general circulation of the scriptures amongst them. . . . The attempt, through the blessing of God, has succeeded.[43]

The following year's *Report* revealed that the "Marine Bible Association of Philadelphia," with Commodore Richard Dale, naval hero of the Revolutionary War, as president, now counted 103 members, all (with one or two exceptions) active or former ship-masters. In addition to supplying their own crews, some would assume responsibility for distribution aboard other vessels in port, including local steamers. Others would, in emulation of British "Agents Afloat," take Scripture supplies to distant ports, such as Canton or Calcutta, for local distribution, both among American crews and others.[44]

One enterprising member (Captain William B. Osman of the *Pacific*) was, in 1817, warmly commended for having "judiciously invested" in Chinese silks the sum of $100, the major proportion of a subscription he had solicited among American merchants in Canton. The silks, solemnly accepted by the treasurer, "largely increased the funds of the association."[45]

Again, the initiative of Philadelphia was followed elsewhere, first in the neighboring port of New York. Here too, the ground had been prepared by the marine distribution of the local Bible society pioneers, in this case the

Commodore Richard
Dale, President of
America's pioneer
Marine Bible Society,
founded in Philadelphia
in 1816. (Donald Barr
Childsey: *The Wars
in Barbary.*)

New York Bible Society. Like their friends in Philadelphia, they became
convinced of the feasibility of a specialized society for seafarers on seeing
examples of seamen voluntarily "consecrating a portion of their earnings" to
the existing Society's funds.[46] Thus was founded, March 14, 1817, at the
City Hotel, the "Marine Bible Society of New-York."

The sole purpose was simply "to encourage the circulation of the
Holy Scriptures, without note or comment, among Seamen." In contrast to
its neighbor on the Delaware, however, the Society stipulated that membership should be open to all who subscribed "not less than one sixteenth of a
dollar per month." With the well-known New York merchant, Jonathan
Little of Pearl Street, as president, the list of officers contains names destined
to become familiar in the forefront of future seamen's mission organization in
that port.[47]

The Marine Bible Society of New-York developed a distribution,
influence and longevity well beyond their peers. This could be partly
attributable to a more democratic, less paternalistic approach, apparent in
their initial *Address to Seamen.* "There is on foot a glorious enterprise . . ."
the men are told, and a powerful plea is made to enlist them in global misson,
by bringing that "treasure of heaven," the Bible, to "the perishing heathen,"

not only in their holds, but in their hearts. Thus they will "share in the profit and glory of this undertaking."

> For the sum of six cents a month, a sum not one third as large as that which you pay for the relief of your sick companions in the Hospital, you may become a Member. . . . Let it not be forgotten, that it is an Institution of our own, formed by Merchants, Masters of Vessels, and Seamen. . . . Let us all embark in this noble ship, whose Captain is the Prince of Peace.[48]

Immediate response was encouraging. Fifty sailors on the USS *Hornet*, desirous (as they write to the Chaplain of the New York Navy Yard, in a letter dated February 1, 1818) of "uniting with our Christian Brethren in the dispersion of the gospel of that Jesus to whom we all look as our common Saviour," signed subscriptions for two years. At the other end of the social scale, Daniel Tompkins, Vice President of the United States, and Governor De Witt Clinton of New York, both became "Life Subscribers." After four years, the Society could count not far from 1,000 subscribers from sea and shore. At the same time, it was reported that "few Captains" were now willing to go to sea without Bibles.[49]

To sailing members, a "certificate of membership" was issued. Since this would serve as a testimonial when competing for employment, there was always the possibility of abuse. However, "to the devoted Christian in any country," they would normally identify the bearer as "a brother, embarked on the grand enterprise of extending to the whole human family the precious blessings of the Gospel." At all events, such a token of membership was, by seamen, "highly valued," and could, in a sense, be considered a precursor of the Christian seafarers' associations of later years.[50]

The success of the Society was in no small measure due to the zeal and rapport of its "principal mover," Boston-born Captain Christopher Prince (1751-1832). A midshipman in the Royal Navy in earlier years, he served as a lieutenant in an American privateer during the Revolution, finally quitting the sea as a merchant captain in 1797. During the last eighteen years of his life, he was "United States Hospital Agent," constantly involved with the admission of sick seamen for hospitalization. It was in his home that merchants and shipmasters were invited to meet on February 12, 1817, "to take into consideration the subject of forming a Marine Bible Society." When the Society was finally organized the following month, Captain·Prince was elected a vice president.

Subsequently, instead of the Society relying on the variable volunteer services of the managers, their 1819 *Annual Report* could relate that "an agent" had now been appointed, who could devote "a considerable portion" of his time to examining and supplying Scripture needs among the shipping. For this important post, the leadership found none better qualified than their own 70-year-old vice president, Captain Christopher Prince. (Significantly, the Society had recently become familiar with the striking success of Lieutenant Cox, the new full-time agent of the Merchant Seamen's Auxiliary Bible Society at Gravesend, England, and had begun to reproduce his reports.)[51]

Another whoses services were both fundamental and far- reaching, was an ardent young Presbyterian minister by the name of Ward Stafford. Fired with missionary fervor from his years at Yale during the presidency of Timothy Dwight, this was the man with whom the Society entrusted the office of corresponding secretary. In this capacity, he performed several journeys during the early years of the Society, to "awaken public attention" for the cause. One of these was nothing short of sensational. On a nine-week tour of New England during the autum of 1820, he founded, on his own initiative, no less than 23 Marine Bible Societies, in ports ranging from Connecticut to Maine. His argumentation was simple yet powerful:

> Seamen, of all others, should be furnished with the Bible, since, by
> their profession, they are, a great proportion of the time, deprived
> of other means of religious instruction.[52]

Among societies organized prior to this, was one in New Haven in July 1817, likewise one in Charleston, S.C., in April 1818. With the founding at this time of an "Albany Marine Bible Society," a beginning had been made on the "Inland Waters"—that vast network of rivers, canals and lakes in the Great Interior. By 1820, several such Inland Waters societies had been formed, including on Lake Champlain and Lake Erie. Though delayed due to "a prevailing sickness" on the Baltimore waterfront, a Marine Bible Society eventually resulted there, too, from a visit by Stafford in 1822.

Some societies, like that in Philadelphia, preferred an independent status. Most, however, followed New York's example, and became auxiliaries affiliated with the American Bible Society, the new, national organization established in New York in 1816.[53]

Not all Marine Bible Societies continued for long. But many did, some for several decades. Eventually, as in Great Britain, distribution would be channeled chiefly through general seamen's missions societies. However, as an initial phase in the evolution of organized seamen's missions, the Marine Bible Society Movement in the New World showed, during those crucial early years, a vigor appreciably greater than that of the Old.[54]

In all of this, the Rev. Ward Stafford played a unique role. In addition to his remarkable achievements in promoting Marine Bible Societies, however, he became the key figure in the transition from mere media distribution to a more comprehensive American maritime ministry. His entry on the scene in this capacity dates back to as early as the year 1816.

The first comprehensive endeavor:
The Society for Promoting the Gospel Among Seamen in the Port of New York (founded 1818).

"The efforts to do good evangelically among seamen in this country originated in New-York . . . in the year 1816." So stated, fifteen years later, *The Sailor's Magazine*, for long America's leading advocate of seamen's missions.[55] The statement has been repeated up to the present.[56] Since the Boston Society of 1812 was, despite its Unitarian leanings, far from devoid of evangelical emphasis, there is no justification for entirely ignoring it in this context. Nevertheless, there did exist a significant difference between the situation in Boston in 1812 and that in New York in 1816: The 1812 endeavor was launched abruptly—in a kind of "vacuum-like isolation" (to quote Tuckerman's biographer).[57] New York of 1816 presented no picture of motivational void.

On the contrary, the wave of renewed revivalism which swept the country after the conclusion of peace had, by 1816, already made a powerful impact on the religious life of the nation's leading seaport, then a city of some 120,000 resident inhabitants. It was May 12, 1816, the eve of the founding of the American Bible Society, that great triumph of emerging evangelical ecumenism in America. For young men, and a rapidly increasing number of young women, participation in Christian benevolence was fast becoming a social fad. Several such women's societies, belonging to different Calvinist denominations, had decided to take up the challenge of the unchurched masses of urban poor. That day, some banded together to form "The Female Missionary Society for the Poor of the City of New York and its Vicinity."[58]

Dedicated to supplying "the ignorant and the destitute" of the city with "the ordinary means of salvation," they appointed the Rev. Ward Stafford as their "Missionary." Nine months later, he wrote a remarkable report entitled *New Missionary Field* (1817). Here he describes, in graphic detail, the despair and the depravity of the under-privileged. He then goes on to present recommendations which were to become "a foreshadowing of much that was to be done in American cities during the next twenty years."[59]

Although the maritime section of the population was not a pre-meditated object of his ministry, Stafford states that, employed as he was, it was impossible not to observe "another class of the destitute," namely seafarers, a people whose problems were compounded by "their having no permanent place of residence." It was estimated that there were, at this time, constantly at least 6,000 or 7,000 seamen in port. He points out:

> By associating with them, and appointing some evening lectures in
> the neighbourhood of their lodgings, it was discovered, that they

were deplorably destitute of religious instruction, and that it would be easy to give them that instruction, provided proper measures were adopted.[60]

Stafford goes on to provide a remarkable far-sighted three-point blueprint for such measures. This proved to be a prediction of much that would be implemented on American (and British) waterfronts in the years to come: (1) Marine Schools, with opportunities for elementary and navigational instruction while in port, and the encouragement of continuing education, in group sessions with "more knowing companions," while at sea. (A library should be connected with each school, to counteract want of employment and consequent frequenting of "haunts of vice" when ashore.) (2) Bible Societies where seamen should constitute "the active members," each obtaining his own copy of the Scriptures "by his own industry." (3) Churches "erected expressly for their accommodation" in all "large seaports."[61]

To what extent, if any, future marine schools and libraries owed their origin to Stafford's suggestions cannot be documented.[62] Also, Marine Bible Societies were already emerging at the time the report was being published.[63] However, the concept of expressly erected, shore-based "Mariners' Churches," destined in time to become the standard form of facility internationally, appears to have been originated by none other than that enterprising young urban missionary in early nineteenth-century New York, the Rev. Ward Stafford. Certainly, it was first effectively publicized by him. (In so doing, he was, incidentally, also one of the first to formulate an explicit missiological motive for maritime evangelism. As he put it, "Let our seamen and others who visit the heathen become pious; and instead of contradicting the glad tidings which our missionaries publish, . . . they will become a powerful weapon in their hands.")[64]

Even before the end of the year 1816 (in other words, prior to the publication of the *New Missionary Field*), an organizational nucleus was actually established, as a direct result of Stafford's initiative, with a "New York Mariners' Church" in view. A public appeal was launched with the following wording:

> A number of gentlemen, who are known to be men of respectability and property, in December, 1816, formed themselves into a Committee, and agreed to hold and appropriate whatever sums of money might be lodged in their hands, for the purpose of erecting, in the city of New-York, a house of worship for the gratuitous accommodation of Seamen. They engage, that, if money enough shall be subscribed, within two years, to warrant the undertaking, they will superintend the erection of the building, and have it completed by the 1st of December 1820. . . . Those who are disposed to aid in carrying into effect this benevolent design can

forward their donations to Capt. Gabriel Havens, Harbourmaster, No. 35 William-street; or to Mr. Henry Eckford, Shipbuilder, Clinton-Street, who are members of the Committee.[65]

In the meantime, a provisional place of worship was acquired, in the shape of "a school-room in the rear of No 37, Cherry street." Here, on December 20, 1816, Stafford started a so-called "Seamen's Meeting." In years to come, this was generally referred to as "the first religious meeting ever held in America, for the special benefit of sailors."[66]

This characterization is not quite correct. There were, as in Great Britain, early, sporadic cases of preaching specifically for seafarers in American ports.[67] Moreover, in the summer of that same year (1816), special prayer-meetings for seamen had been established in New York's Sailortown, originally as an outreach ministry of the Presbyterians' historic "Brick Church." This latter initiative calls for closer scrutiny.

The so-called "Brick Church" of that day, dating from 1768, and described as "a dignified colonial structure built of red brick with a white wooden spire," was situated on Beekman Street (by Nassau), not far from the present City Hall, and within easy walking distance of the wharves. Restored from near ruin, when used as a military hospital by the British during the Revolutionary War, the church had only recently been saved from certain destruction by the heroism of a passing seaman:

It was members of the Presbyterians' historic Brick Church in Beekman Street, Manhattan, who established New York's first prayer-meetings for seamen in the summer of 1816. (From a contemporary print.)

Dr. Gardiner Spring
(1785-1873), for 63 years
pastor of New York's
Presbyterian Brick
Church, and a pioneer
figure in the seamen's
mission movement in that
city. (From a
contemporary print.)

One Sunday afternoon in May 1811, the congregation . . . gathered
for prayer when a fire broke out in a waterfront warehouse three
blocks away. A burning spark carried by the wind fell on the
wooden steeple, bursting into flame. While the disheartened
congregation watched expecting to see their church destroyed, a
young seaman pushed his way through the crowd and climbed the
lightening-rod. Using his jacket he beat out the fire and saved the
church. His name was Stephen McCormack. The grateful congregation voted him a reward of $100 but he disappeared and
never returned to claim it.[68]

Only one year previously, the young and gifted Gardiner Spring had
taken up a ministry there, which became remarkable for both its power and
duration (of 63 years). It has been assumed that his deep interest in the
welfare of seamen was, at least in part, prompted by the heroic action of that
seafaring passer-by. There is also reason to believe that the reward, which
was sailor-like left unclaimed, may have constituted the original endowment
of the Port Society founded a few years later. At all events, both pastor and
congregation of the Brick Church were to become heavily involved in the
city's ministry to seafarers, as developed during the decades ahead.[69]

In fact, at the very outset of that ministry, those Brick Church
Presbyterians were to play a role reminiscent of that of the Rotherhithe
Methodists in the Thames Revival. In the summer of 1816, a number of
zealous Brick Church laymen launched a series of prayer-meetings in
different houses in nearby Water Street, "in the hope of benefiting such

classes of the population as did not frequent public worship." To their evident surprise, these laymen discovered that, not only sailors' boarding-house keepers and others "connected with the shipping," but also seamen themselves were finding their way to these prayer-meetings.

In order to encourage others to follow suit, a prayer-meeting was appointed "specifically for sailors," and first held in a house strategically situated at the corner of Old Ship and Front Street, by the East River. The attempt proved a success, similar meetings were organized on an ongoing basis, as interest was aroused in wider circles, and "brethren in other churches and denominations" came to the aid of the Brick Church pioneers. (Among the latter was, no doubt, Captain Christopher Prince, during these years "an exemplary member" of the Brick Church.)[70]

Available sources do not make it clear at what point Ward Stafford, who, during the summer of 1816, had "preached at the ship-yards on Manhattan Island,"[71] actually joined hands with the promoters of these prayer-meetings for seamen. On the other hand, it becomes very evident that Stafford soon came to symbolize a sorely-needed coordinative influence at this time. His introduction of the concept of stated preaching for seamen by an ordained minister (December 1816) represents a significant step toward the realization of a genuine Mariners' Church. Although it soon became apparent that the way was "not then prepared for such considerable an undertaking" as the erection of an appropriate building, Stafford sought to promote such activities as were within reach, specifically Marine Bible Societies and "Seamen's Meetings" in provisional locations.[72]

Meanwhile, Stafford never permitted the ultimate objective to be lost from view. A second edition of the New Missionary Field was prepared. The report it contained was reviewed at length in the religious press. The maritime parts were extracted and also published separately, under the heading Important to Seamen.[73] In this way, Stafford's arguments in favor of specific mariners' churches continued to prepare the ground. Those arguments were forceful:

> They [seamen] regard themselves, and they are regarded by others as an entirely separate class of the community. . . . When in port they . . . have no places of resort, except those which frequently become the grave of their property, their morals, their happiness, and their souls. . . . When they enter a church, they are known and marked as sailors. . . . Most of them would sooner face the cannon's mouth than the [congregation's] thoughtless, supercilious gaze. . . . Pews have been closed against them—and they, in some cases, have been informed, that there was no room for sailors. Such was not the manner in which they were treated by the Son of God.[74]

At length, by early 1818, the time seemed ripe to form a firmer foundation for a New York Mariners' Church. On Stafford's initiative, a preliminary meeting of interested merchants and shipmasters was convened at the house of Jonathan Little. Under his chairmanship, a vigorous publicity campaign was launched, in order to present in the press the "deplorable" current condition of seamen, and future benefits contemplated. Furthermore, Stafford was commissioned to write an *Address* (1818), which was then "extensively circulated."[75] This emphasizes how seafarers have hitherto been not only neglected, but positively rejected by the Christian Church, while also elaborating on the case for a mariners' church, as already published in Stafford's *Report* of 1817.[76]

After an adjourned meeting (May 22,1818), a constitution was adopted, and a society was finally founded on June 5, 1818, bearing the cumbersome yet self-explanatory title "The Society for Promoting the Gospel among Seamen in the Port of New York," with Jonathan Little as president, Heman Averill as secretary, and a board of directors belonging to "several of the principal denominations."[77]

With a New York Mariners' Church now a realistic prospect, the establishment of the "New York Port Society" (NYPS), as it came to be called, marks the transition to a new era in the evolution of American seamen's missions, just as did the founding of the Port of London Society in England less than three months earlier.[78] This parallelism poses an important question, however. Was the first "Port Society" in the New World a uniquely American creation, or is a modern historian justified in claiming that "the impulse came from Britain"?[79]

The introduction of the British voluntary society model, as a means of extending the Evangelical United Front in America, has already been noted.[80] However, primary sources do not disclose any direct dependence on British initiative in the emergence of America's first society for a comprehensive Gospel ministry to seafarers.

On the contrary, although no definitive society was founded at the time, the opening of a public subscription as early as December 1816 by a group committed to erecting a "Church for Seamen" in New York, preceded by many months any similar, clearly defined movement in Great Britain.[81] Moreover, this group followed an entirely independent course in planning for a shore-based as opposed to a floating sanctuary.[82] Finally, news of the "daring" involvement of the gentle sex in promotional activity, such as in support of Stafford's endeavors, even aroused a cry of envy from across the Atlantic: "Might not the example of the ladies and females of America be imitated with advantage by the hosts of well disposed females in Britain?"[83]

Although some degree of British influence is discernible in the origin of Marine Bible Societies on the American side of the ocean, both the Boston Society of 1812 and the New York Society of 1818 bear the marks of genuine American initiative. In short, the facts, as far as can be traced, all tend to confirm the conclusion of those authors of early retrospects, who saw seamen's missions on both sides of the Atlantic as having commenced "simultaneously and without concert," thereby evincing, as one of them put it, "an origin in both countries evidently Divine." [84]

However, with increased communication, Britain's basic ascendancy and prestige in matters evangelical were bound to assert themselves in this "new missionary field," too. To what extent did, in fact, British influence become manifest during the decade to come, as the work now under way in New York, began to expand and eventually lead to an American national society?

Chapter 20

Toward an American National Society (1818-28)

NEW YORK EXPANSION:
THE MARINERS' CHURCH AND
THE NEW YORK BETHEL UNION

In early 1818, New York's position as America's premier port city was already well assured. Governor Clinton's "Big Ditch," the Erie Canal, was under way, bringing water-borne communication with the Great Lakes and the West within relatively easy reach. Significantly, the launching of the New York Port Society coincided with the inauguration of transatlantic liner traffic. When the Black Ball Line square-rigger *James Monroe* set sail from New York on January 5, 1818, she left on pre-scheduled time, "full or not full," thereby pioneering a concept of ocean transportation which was to capture for American packets the North Atlantic premium trade for years to come.[85]

As it proved, the spirit of relentless perseverence needed to "drive" a packet ship across the ocean, whatever the weather, was no less wanted when it came to raising a mariner's church in New York of that day. Stafford showed he had that spirit. Appointed by the new Society "both as a pastor and preacher for seamen," he found himself faced with a host of "difficulties" and "prejudices," coupled with the "general embarrassment" of the national economy.

Undaunted, Stafford hired a hall (the upper room in Mr. Lindon's Academy in Cherry Street), capable of holding 400 persons. Here he instituted a ministry of public worship for seafarers which was to be "regularly maintained" until May, 1820. The "cordial approbation" of his hearers was evidenced by the fact that,

> In the course of six months, more than 800 seamen called upon Mr. Stafford, either to converse on religious subjects, to take leave of him, or to solicit Bibles and Tracts.[86]

Meanwhile, a "Marine Missionary Society" was organized, "to furnish preaching to seamen until the church should be completed." This Society immediately charged itself with raising Stafford's salary. (It later merged into the NYPS.)[87]

Having thus secured the Society's capacity to function on an interim basis, Stafford and his friends followed up with further measures in logical sequence as minimal funds became available. A suitable site was selected on Roosevelt Street near the East River wharves, and purchased February 17, 1819. On April 13, 1819, the Society was legally incorporated in the State of New York. In October, construction came under way. Finally, after eight months, the edifice was ready.

Described as "a neat, brick building . . . finished in a plain chaste style," the new Mariners' Church measured 59 by 58 feet, was fitted with galleries, giving it accommodation for up to 1,000 people, and included a basement "for a lecture and school-room."[88] The building was offically dedicated on Sunday, June 4, 1820.

The event was a deliberate demonstration of ecumenicity. "For the first time, the novelty was presented to the world, of a church knowing no sectarian denomination." Accordingly, a Presbyterian minister presided, while sermons were delivered in turn by Protestant Episcopal, Reformed Dutch, and Methodist Episcopal clerics.[89] As recorded in the religious press of the day,

> The Church was filled at an early hour, and the aisles were crowded with those who stood during the whole service. . . . The Hon. Mr. Thompson, Secretary of the Navy, Commodore Evans, and several other Officers of the United States' Navy, were present. The seats on the lower floor of the Church were principally occupied with Masters of merchant vessels, and with sailors, and among them a company of the Unitied States' Marines, in uniform. There was something deeply impressive in the appearance of so large a number of sailors, well dressed, decent, and devotional in their demeanor. . . .[90]

A curious feature on the background of the denominational integration of the Mariners' Church was a careful segregation of the sexes during the services. The lower floor of the sanctuary was to be for the sole use of "seafaring persons and the male friends of the institution," leaving the galleries for female members of seafarers' families. This arrangement would, it was hoped, remove the barrier of "backwardness" thought to typify a Tar's attitude to a "mixed assembly." Whether from social conditioning or from other causes, seafarers evidently acquiesced, since results after one year were reported to have "surpassed the most sanguine expectations of the board."[91]

The original New York
Mariner's Church on
Roosevelt Street,
dedicated June 4, 1820.
(*The Christian Herald
and Seaman's Magazine*,
New York, August 2,
1823.)

Having thus planned and promoted the erection of the first shore-based mariners' church in history, the Rev. Ward Stafford felt free to resign his position with the Society half a year later (November, 1820), only to devote himself again to raising a sanctuary for the spiritually destitute—this time among the derelicts and deprived in the Bowery.[92] Before so doing, however, Stafford succeeded in initiating yet another form of seamen's mission enterprise of great future significance.

The Rev. G.C. Smith, shortly after having discovered, to his amazement, the existence of both a Port Society and Mariners' Church in New York, wrote a letter to the Society, dated February 7, 1821, warmly recommending "an American Sailors' Magazine." Already aware of the success of *The Sailor's Magazine* in London, Stafford responded by proposing the appropriation of eight pages of *The Christian Herald*, a bi-monthly evangelical magazine founded in 1816, which had already carried much of interest to the Seamen's Cause from both sides of the Atlantic.

From May 1821 to December 1824, this *Seaman's Magazine* appeared as a regular portion of *The Christian Herald and Seaman's Magazine* (the whole henceforth published "under the Patronage of the Society for Promoting the Gospel among Seamen"). From this eventually evolved *The Sailor's Magazine* of New York, a full-fledged American counterpart of the original British model.[93]

In less than five years, the Rev. Ward Stafford had thus proved himself a pioneer in many modes of maritime mission. Especially significant, however, was his role as the first in history known to have been specifically appointed to a full-time pastoral office among seafarers. As such, he fulfilled a function hitherto "unknown in ecclesiastical history" (to quote the exuberant G.C. Smith). In contrast to a maritime ministry centered around the distribution of literary media, Stafford signifies the emergence of a "living ministry," providing the interpersonal dimension of preaching and pastoral counseling.[94]

Following Stafford's resignation, the directors of the Society were confronted with a difficult decision. With annual subscriptions too few, and weekly collections too modest to meet current expenses, together with a heavy mortgage on the building, the Society was steeped in severe "pecuniary embarrassments." It was tempting to try retrenchment. From November 1820, the pulpit was supplied by a ministerial roster of volunteers from different denominations.

However, the directors acknowledged that "something more" was essential to even a minimal ministry. In March, 1821, they engaged a young Methodist minister, the Rev. Henry Chase (1790-1853), to undertake pastoral duties on a part-time basis. Although primarily employed as teacher at the Wesleyan Seminary in New York, Chase managed to visit boarding-houses, and homes of seafarers and "along-shore-men," distribute Scripture and tracts, lead prayer meetings, counsel those in conflict, and occasionally preach on the Sabbath.[95]

Nevertheless, the obvious inadequacies of this intermittent ministry finally prompted the Society to appoint a full-time "stated" minister, in hopes that he would at least pay his own way. Accordingly, in January, 1822, they invited the Rev. John Truair to become combined pastor and soliciting agent of the Mariners' Church.[96] Already known as a remarkably successful revivalist preacher in the "burnt-over district" of rural New York, Truair came to the port-city from Presbyterian pastorates in turbulent Oneida and (latterly) Cherry Valley. Described as well-educated, talented and of English birth, John Truair was destined to make an impact on emerging American maritime ministry comparable only to that of Ward Stafford.[97]

Before discussing Truair's spectacular contribution, however, it will be necessary to trace the introduction of the Bethel Flag in New York, and the early spread of seamen's mission enterprise elsewhere, from Maine to the mouth of the Mississippi.

In his letter to the NYPS in February, 1821, G.C.Smith not only writes of the need for an American Sailors' Magazine, but recommends "most forcibly ... the early adoption of the Bethel Flag," as "a simple and cheap means" of multiplying the blessings of the Society. Adding that a flag

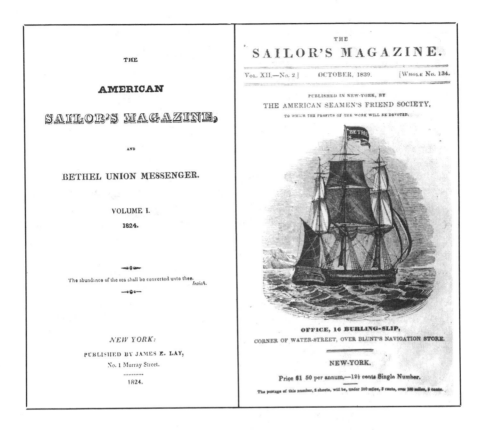

The American version of *The Sailor's Magazine,* before and after the founding of the American Seamen's Friend Society.

would be on its way from London, he offers detailed practical advice, and sees great prospects for an American branch of the Bethel Movement.[98]

The flag referred to was, in actual fact, entrusted by the British and Foreign Seamen's Friend Society and Bethel Union to one John Allan, an American Presbyterian minister, who happened to be visiting London in the winter of 1820-21. Having heard of the work on the Thames as far away as in his home state of Tenessee, he entered enthusiastically into preaching both on the Floating Chapel and at Bethel Meetings on the River. Before leaving, he publicly pledged to honor the Society's request "that with his *own* hands, on the first suitable occasion, he would hoist it [the Bethel Flag] on board some American vessel."[99]

An opportunity soon presented itself—on Sunday, March 11, 1821, nine days out of Liverpool, bound for New York, on none other than the

pioneer packet of the Black Ball Line, the *James Monroe*. After running up
the flag, he "gazed on it with delight," and then—under a cloudless sky out
on the Atlantic—conducted public worship under the first Bethel Flag of the
United States.[100] (Reference has already been made to the first such flag
known to have been hoisted on the North American continent, specifically at
St. John, New Brunswick, the preceding year.)[101]

"Animated" by G.C. Smith's letter, by the many reports of "Bethel
operations" in Britain, and now by the arrival of a genuine Bethel Flag from
its port of origin, leading personalities in both the Port Society and the
Marine Bible Society of New York decided the time had come to attempt an
American transplantation. On Sunday, June 3, 1821, the eighteen-foot flag
was flown for the first time in the United States from a staff especially
erected atop the Mariners' Church. Services to mark the occasion were held
morning, afternoon and evening, conducted by Baptist, Dutch Reformed and
Presbyterian preachers, respectively.

The following day, June 4, 1821, "a number of merchants and other
gentlemen" met at the house of Jonathan Little. Under his chairmanship,
they founded a "New-York Bethel Union," discarding (like their British
forerunners) "all sectarian jealousies." As president was elected the Scottish-
born merchant and Presbyterian philanthropist Divie Bethune (already vice-
president of the NYPS). Captain Christopher Prince was elected treasurer,
and Horace Holden secretary.[102]

Shortly afterwards, an occasion presented itself to raise the emblem
on its intended element:

> On Friday, the 22d of June, 1821, for the first time in America,
> the Bethel Flag ... was hoisted at the mast-head of the ship
> Cadmus, Capt. Whitlock, lying at the Pine-street Wharf. In the
> morning of the day, the committee were apprehensive that they
> would have no hearers. The experiment here was novel .... They
> were told by several, who are "wise in worldly matters," that a
> guard of constables would be necessary to preserve order. At first
> it was thought adviseable to hold the meetings in the cabin to
> prevent the possibility of disturbance. On arriving at the vessel,
> the deck was found cleared, an awning stretched, and all necessary
> preparations for holding the meetings there. At 8 o'clock the
> President opened the meeting. ... The Mariners' (107) Psalm
> was sung with great animation ... and seamen were immediately
> seen pressing in from all quarters. After prayer by an aged sea
> captain [Christopher Prince?], Dr. Spring addressed the seamen—
> other appropriate exercises followed. The vessel and wharf were
> crowded—order and solemnity prevailed throughout—every ear
> was open, every eye was fixed. Tracts were distributed among the
> seamen, who received them with gratitude. Every circumstance

was calculated to inspire the Board with courage and confidence to go forward.[103]

And forward they went—from ship to ship, coasters, deep-sea traders, British too, even naval vessels. On August 21, 1821, a memorable meeting was held on the USS *Franklin*, 74, Commodore Stewart, lying off the Battery, and about to sail on a long cruise. A congregation of 800, mostly seamen, gathered under the Bethel Flag, while Dr. Spring and "Father" Eastburn (celebrated "Seamen's Friend" of Philadelphia) were among those who "conducted the exercises." Several seamen came up to Eastburn afterwards, and thanked him for the "good things he had told them."[104]

Soon the positive impact of these Bethel meetings became evident in the ministry of the Mariners' Church, thus fulfilling an important purpose of the founders of the New York version of the Bethel Union concept. Although they had, after much discussion, found it best to organize "independently of the Port Society," their hope, as expressed in the constitution, was that the Union would fill both a supplementary and a stimulatory role:

> The object of this association shall be to encourage and conduct prayer meetings among seamen on board of vessels, and to render assistance to the "Society for promoting the Gospel among Seamen."[105]

Despite a "flourishing" Sunday School and other promising features of the Mariners' Church, service attendance by seafarers themselves had, initially, been far from satisfactory. As the Union's first *Report* points out, "a class of people so long excluded from the sanctuary, seemed to require that the messages of mercy should be brought to their very cabin doors." This they achieved by assigning all members to specific committees responsible for conducting meetings on the different evenings, and by adhering to their published policy of "short prayers," "short addresses," and "few verses." A large lantern was donated for hoisting at the masthead as a night signal. With winter coming on, meetings were continued ashore in the homes of cooperative keepers of sailors' boarding-houses, or others in sympathy with the work. Stirring descriptions of those Bethel Meetings were made by Captain Christopher Prince in his popular "Journal of the Bethel Flag," appearing regularly in the *Seaman's Magazine*.[106]

Undoubtedly, a typical Bethel Meeting, with "mariners breaking through the ordinary restraints of habit and custom," and standing up to pray aloud, or to tell their fellows what the Lord had "done for their souls," bore some similarity to the so-called "camp-meetings," then current in the frontier settlements. In America, as in Great Britain, Bethel Meetings were clearly a kind of "spiritual grassroots movement," providing opportunities for both spontaneity and emotional release. However, there was normally no ecstatic excess; instead—a spirit of "solemn awe" and the "utmost propriety" was the rule.[107]

Both of the Port Society chaplains during these years, Chase and Truair, were enthusiastic participants in the meetings of the Bethel Union (the former in his new capacity of full-time "Missionary to Seamen," 1823-24).[108] Eminent evangelical churchmen, such as Dr. Gardiner Spring and Dr. James Milnor, were also in evidence at Bethel Meetings. Dr. Milnor (at one time, perhaps the most influential evangelical Episcopalian in America) developed, like Dr. Spring, a life-long interest in the Seamen's Cause. In 1822, the Port Society published his book, *The Seamen's Devotional Assistant* ("intended to aid masters and seamen in the daily worship of Almighty God, on board their vessels at sea"). Emulating the example of the Port of London Society's original, the manual was warmly endorsed by the Bethel Union.[109]

Both the Port Society and the Bethel Union cooperated closely with the Marine Bible Society of New York in Scripture distribution.[110] Moreover, they made grateful use of tracts, granted by the New York Religious Tract Society (who reprinted *The Boatswain's Mate*), and the American Tract Society (who, from 1825, also reprinted many well-known British originals).[111]

True to the expansive potential of the Bethel concept, the NYBU sought to implement its published plan of opening "a correspondence with

A Bethel Prayer Meeting at night, sponsored by the
New-York Bethel Union on board a ship docked alongside
a Manhattan warf in the early 1820's. (*The Christian
Herald and Seaman's Magazine,* New York, Dec. 6, 1823.)

An American packet carrying a New York version of
the Bethel Flag back to Britain, as she approaches
Liverpool in the late 1820's. (*The Sailor's Magazine,*
New York, January 1830.)

the different ports in the U.S. and foreign nations, to promote similar institutions." From the outset, "benevolent ladies" were encouraged to sew Bethel Flags, using the gift-flag from London as a pattern. Only a few days after the Bethel Union had been formed, one such lady "presented an elegant 'Bethel Flag,' which she had made during the day, to the committee, with the desire that it might be sent ... to the merchants in Bermuda, for the use of the shipping there." In a short while, flags were donated to "friends of seamen" in seaports such as Boston, New London, Richmond (Virginia), Savannah, New Orleans, as well as the inland port of Albany. In some cases, a resultant Bethel Union became the nucleus of a local maritime ministry; in others, the gift gave fresh impulse and new dimensions to work already under way.[112]

At length, the New York Bethel Union was discontinued. In contrast to the case in London, however, this was no result of "society warfare,"[113] but, on the contrary, a consequence of sheer success. Locally, intimate coordination of the lay-oriented Bethel Union with the work of the Port Society had led to "greatly improved" attendance at the Mariners' Church, and to a vital extension of its ministry during crucial years of consolidation; finally, as one retrospect records, "two organizations seemed no longer necessary."[114] Nationally, the New York Bethel Union, though local in name, found itself in practice projected into a leadership role, thereby paving the way for another, professedly national society—formed in 1826.[115] Internationally, the New York Bethel Union introduced an era of transatlantic partnership in mission, where England and America were now, as Admiral Lord Gambier put it in 1822, "once more united under the same flag."[116]

BOSTON AND DR. JENKS

Beyond New York, Boston is the port it is natural to turn to first, in following the further expansion of early American maritime ministry. Chronologically, it was here it all began. But was the work which was to continue in Boston a direct derivative of the Society of 1812? Within a generation, precisely this was being seriously asserted. In 1833, a missionary historian claimed, on behalf of a local society still in existence today, that "its first organizaiton was in 1812."[117] The statement was subsequently repeated by others, in varying forms.[118] Does primary source material confirm this claim?

On Tuesday, August 11, 1818, *The Recorder* of Boston carried the following notice under the title "Sermons to Seamen":

> In pursuance of a design long since contemplated, to provide for Seamen, free of all expence, (other than they may *voluntarily* contribute,) a Place of Public Worship, and a Preacher, exclusively for their benefit, a *Sermon* was delivered at the *Hall over the Centre Arch of the new Stores on Central Wharf,* in this town, on Sunday last, at 10 o'clock, A.M. by the Rev. WILLIAM JENKS. "The Sermon (says the Boston Gazette) was such as might be expected from this learned divine," and was delivered "in presence of a large concourse of the Mariners of Boston, and those attached to coasting vessels now lying in our port." This meeting [was intended] . . . as the commencement of a regular course of *Sermons,* to be delivered for the future, on every succeeding Sabbath, at the above named hour and place. . . .[119]

Such was, following the publication (in 1817) of the last tract of BSRMIS, the first form of public ministry to seafarers on the Boston waterfront. This initiative in 1818 was directly related to a visit to Boston by the Rev. Ward Stafford in 1816. His impassioned plea that year, on behalf of the urban poor, such as he had met in New York, prompted some of his hearers to make a social survey of their own. The result was the founding, on October 9, 1816, of the "Boston Society for the Moral and Religious Instruction of the Poor" (BSMRIP). This was the Society which, on August 9, 1818, succeeded in its long-standing "design" of initiating a "Seamen's Meeting," in that sail-loft sanctuary under the observatory on Central Wharf.[120]

Dr. William Jenks,
Congregational scholar,
and pioneer seamen's
chaplain in Boston,
from 1818. (J. Leslie
Dunstan: *A Light to the City.*)

Who, then, were those city fathers whom Stafford stimulated to action in 1816? So far from having the least leaning toward Unitarianism, these men were, like Stafford himself, indisputably evangelical, and the two churches in which he addressed them (Old South and Park Street) were known as "the only Trinitarian Congregational churches" in Boston of that day. Among them were men who, in 1810, had banded together to form the "American Board of Commissioners for Foreign Missions." The new "Poor Society" was their response to the dramatic discovery that "the heathen were at their doors. . . ."[121]

While it has not proved possible to point to any formal ties between the Society of 1812 and the Society which eventually emerged from the Seamen's Meeting of 1818, there does exist some element of credibility in the statement that the efforts of the former "touched a chord in the heart of the Christian community" in Boston, on behalf of the seafarer. Some of those in the BSMRIP who supported the 1818 endeavor must have been at least aware of the existence of the Society of 1812. However, Tuckerman himself refused, in later years, to speculate in this regard.[123] Moreover, Stafford's speeches and the ensuing survey in the field were, in themselves, more than sufficient to motivate the Society's early concern for the seafarer. The reason for the two-year delay was "primarily because neither funds nor personnel were available."[124]

By August, 1818, however, the Poor Society had consolidated itself. Also, a willing and widely respected preacher had been found. William Jenks (1778-1866), whose English immigrant ancestors hailed from Hammersmith in London, had—after graduating from Harvard—served thirteen years as Congregational parish pastor in Bath, a port-city on the coast of Maine with rich shipbuilding traditions. After volunteering as chaplain in the War of

1812, Jenks took up teaching, proving himself an outstanding biblical and oriental scholar (eventually receiving the recognition of a doctorate of divinity). A strong adherent of the New England theology of Jonathan Edwards' successors, he was an equally strong spokesman for the human right of private judgment. His compassion for the oppressed was to embrace the American Indian, the Jew, the black, the poor and the seafarer alike. Such was the richly-endowed 40 year old, who in 1818 returned to the Boston scene, primarily to open a private school there.[125]

Having once agreed to integrate the highly unconventional assignment of seamen's preacher into his well-filled weekly work schedule, Jenks took up the task conscientiously and methodically. Attendance soon increased "from one hundred to three or four hundred." However, in October 1818, he had to report on two major areas of concern:

> I think but of one objection to the place—& that respects the formation of a Church among our seafaring friends. If a Church be formed, it should grow out of the family relation, or consist with it, & must hence admit both males & females, as they appear qualified. But the wharf is not a fit place for females—& on this account a house for publick worship seems desirable. ... Nor have I, from the nature of my engagements during the week, had opportunities of private conference with my hearers. It is obvious, that on such opportunities much of a minister's usefulness must depend.[126]

With regard to the follow-up aspect, Jenks did eventually manage to set aside one evening a week, "for the purpose of religious inquiry." Moreover, he found that Scripture distribution, in conjunction with the "Marine Bible Society of Boston" (founded in the Central Wharf "chapel," August 29, 1820), gave frequent opportunities for "conversatons of a religious tendency." Tracts supplied by the New England Tract Society and the Massachusetts Society for Promoting Christian Knowledge (who also furnished free copies of their reprint of Ryther's *Seaman's Preacher*) were regarded as an indispensable adjunct to preaching and counseling, and "invariably received with apparent eagerness." A Bethel Flag for shipboard meetings in the harbor, presented by the New York Bethel Union in July, 1821, led to another form of extended ministry (continued until 1824, when Jenks' precarious health compelled him to curb his participation).

Meanwhile, at the Marine Hospital at Charlestown, Jenks maintained a visiting chaplaincy with the aid of his colleague in the Poor Society, the Rev. A. Bingham and, during their vacation, students of Andover Theological Seminary. (The latter would also occasionally help with ship-visiting.)[127]

In a far further field, Jenks proved himself a genuine pioneer. As he himself wrote (as secretary of the BSMRIP, in their 1822 *Annual Report*): "While provision is made at home for the religious benefit of Seamen, it has seemed important that measures should be in operation to prepare the same privileges abroad." Accordingly, the Bethel Flag received from New York was, in 1822, reconsigned to the American Mission recently established in the Sandwich Islands, as a means of meeting the pressing need for a maritime ministry there. (Ladies of "known benevolence" in Boston soon secured a substitute.)[128] In response to an earlier appeal by Dr. Robert Morrison for chaplaincy provision at Canton, Jenks could, also in 1822, report that he had been able to "commence a correspondence on the subject" with American merchants there.[129] Again, in 1824, he was in touch with missionaries of the ABCFM, who initiated a preaching ministry among the shipping at Buenos Aires. In this connection, he publicized a plan (recently renewed in the present post-World War II era) for:

> . . . the placing of suitable persons, as Missionary Chaplains on board our vessels frequenting foreign ports, where the privileges of the Gospel are not enjoyed, whose labours shall be devoted not only to the Seamen on board their own vessel, but to the benefit of others in the harbours they visit.[130]

Meanwhile, although hundreds would continue to hear him on Sunday mornings at Central Wharf, Jenks kept constantly before the public the need for a sanctuary "in strictness a Mariner's Church," where seamen when home could resort with their relatives, and where those won for the faith could be protected from backsliding by belonging to a communion fellowship in Christ. A temporary solution was in fact achieved, with the official organization on December 3, 1823, of a congregation comprised of a few who frequented the Seamen's Meeting at Central Wharf, and some who congregated at the Mission House built by the Society in 1821 in Butolph Street, an impoverished part of West Boston, which was also served by William Jenks. By "taking the name of *Mariner's Church,*" this congregation (henceforth based at the Mission House) became the first formal Christian congregation in the world so designated.

With the sacrament of the Lord's Supper now regularly administered, "many a wandering son of the ocean here joined Christ." However, the congregation consisted essentially of landsmen, and when Jenks, in 1826 was called to the pastorate of a new parish church built in Green Street, the majority joined that congregation while the remainder "dropped its designation."[131]

Nevertheless, the concept of a genuine mariners' church for Boston did not die. When Jenks held his farewell service at Central Wharf on October 22, 1826, a modest financial foundation had already been laid. Two of the donations were given particular publicity. In 1823, the directors had reported the receipt of the dying bequest of a Norwegian-born sailor, one William Bender. Bender had expired as his ship, the *Galatea* of Boston, was rounding the Cape of Good Hope. He had willed all he had in the world to the Seamen's Meeting on Central Wharf, to which he (like so many other seamen of Scandinavian background) had become "attached." The sum, "somewhat short of fifty dollars" in wages due, was appropriated as the commencement of a "permanent fund" for the erection of a mariners' church, when deemed "expedient."

Then, in 1825, the Society had received five "Napoleons" towards the same purpose, from a "fellow-labourer" in Antwerp, the Rev. W.H. Angas. While ministering to American shipping there, he had, in a copy of the American version of *The Sailor's Magazine*, read about the work and aspirations of Chaplain William Jenks, a man with whose background he happened to bear a remarkable resemblance.[132]

Events were to prove that more than money was needed. Ministry to the seafarer, though intrinsically related to home mission (as also to world mission), required to be recognized as a mission in its own right. The catalyst in the case of Boston was the work initiated in New York by the Rev. John Truair, for the creation of a national society (see later).[133] The Seamen's Meeting on Central Wharf had not been abandoned after Jenks' resignation. On the contrary, under the Rev. Stephen Bailey from Nantucket, who took over from 1827 to 1828, the work flourished to a degree which convinced leaders of the Poor Society that their seamen's work must have a separate status. Acting on an earlier invitation from New York, transmitted by Truair, they decided, on December 13, 1827, to form a "Boston Seaman's Friend Society," to be considered a "Branch" of the American Seamen's Friend Society (established in its original form in New York in 1826).[134]

With time, a program was developed, which has, in varying forms, continued ever since.[135] Although not formally linked with its precursor of 1812, the Boston Seaman's Friend Society had solid justification for tracing its origin to 1818, and the beginning of William Jenks' eight-year maritime ministry.[136] The fact that this man's ministry should have such far-reaching results, underscores how divergent were the characteristics of those who became the great pioneer personalities of the Seamen's Mission Movement. Of them all, perhaps none presented a less likely candidate than that mild-mannered, diminutive divine, Dr. Jenks of Boston. He frankly admitted he could record "no unusual excitement" among those who gathered under his pulpit, and certainly he had none of the briny boisterousness of Britain's Boatswain Smith or Boston's own immortal Father Taylor.[137]

Why, then, did seamen keep coming? Apart from the natural appeal of Dr. Jenks' personal humility, they doubtless also recognized the moral courage of one who would, on their behalf, confront callous crimps and materialistic merchants with equal determination.[138] Perhaps they felt flattered that one with such immense learning was willing to devote his time and talents to wayward sons of the ocean. At all events, in common with the greatest of his colleagues, Dr. Jenks' love for both the Savior and seamen ran clear and deep. This they knew.[139]

Father Joseph Eastburn (1748-1828), Philadelphia's legendary pioneer seamen's chaplain, called by George Charles Smith "The Apostle of Sailors in the United States." (Courtesy: Presbyterian Historical Society, Philadelphia.)

PHILADELPHIA AND FATHER EASTBURN

Just as the name Dr. Jenks became inseparably linked with the history of the early maritime ministry of New York's northern neighbor, so too that of Father Eastburn came to be intimately interwoven with similar endeavors on the Delaware waterfront to the south. In terms of academic achievement, Eastburn was Jenks' polar opposite. But what he lacked in formal education was counterbalanced by an exceptional degree of natural endowment and spiritual maturity.[140]

Joseph Eastburn (1748-1828) was born in Philadelphia, as the youngest of six children, whose father had become actively involved in Presbyterian revivalist circles following the Great Awakening.[141] Joseph Eastburn's personal awakening came, so he relates in his private journal, when out with fellow-apprentices on a Sunday morning skating trip on the Schuylkill River. The chime of church bells suddenly struck his conscience, whereupon he ran back, hid his skates, and "went to meeting." Eastburn then describes how, after "protracted spiritual conflict," he experienced conversion. Having himself at length found assurance of salvation in the "all-sufficiency of Christ," Eastburn sensed an overpowering urge to share this discovery with others, and began holding weekly meetings in his father's house.[142]

Impressed with the young man's gifts as an "exhorter," his Presbyterian pastor encouraged him to study for the ministry. Eastburn's efforts to obtain a classical education foundered, however, as he studied "day and night," finally pushing himself to the brink of a breakdown. But if the intricacies of Latin grammar evaded him, his Bible knowledge was remarkable. He committed large sections of Scripture to memory. This was to serve him in good stead. Especially was this the case during the city's yellow fever epidemics in the 1790's, when, as coffin-maker, Eastburn was in constant contact with hundreds of the distressed and dying.[143]

Providentially, Eastburn was, as a result of the urgent demand for coffins during these years, able to acquire sufficient capital to forego a salary in his future ministry among seafarers. But how, in the education-conscious denomination to which he belonged, could he hope to obtain the necessary ministerial standing? Providentially again, Quakers in control of Philadelphia's jail, hospital and alms-house, who were unwilling to accept an ordained minister for the sorely needed services of a chaplain there, would, it was understood, warmly welcome a Joseph Eastburn.

Hence, on May 14, 1805, Eastburn was officially licensed by the Presbytery of Philadelphia, to assume the chaplaincy of these institutions. Their action was enthusiastically endorsed by Dr. Ashbel Green (then pastor of Second Presbyterian), for whom Eastburn had served as lay-preacher for nearly six years. Owing to the "defects" of his education, and his doctrinal "deviation" on the subject of baptism, it was expressly stipulated that Eastburn's licensure did not qualify him for ordination to "the pastoral office."[144] With this, Eastburn himself appeared perfectly content. However, his position and prestige became such, that he was accorded the epithet "Reverend" both in Presbyterian publications and by "general and cordial suffrage of the religious public."[145]

Eastburn's license left him free to speak also to "collections of people in other places, on the concerns of their souls." Indeed, it conveyed all the ecclesiastical authority he would need for the rest of his life. The record of how he made use of that authority provides almost incredible reading. For fourteen years, he visited, counseled and preached among the hapless inmates of his chaplaincy charge and far beyond. Both in Philadelphia and elsewhere, he was in constant demand, and not only in Presbyterian circles, but among almost every denomination, including Black Methodists and German Calvinists. From 1811, on the death of his wife, he abandoned his "mechanical occupation," and devoted himself entirely to the ministry. Whatever the need, Eastburn had by then become "a kind of common property of the whole religious community."[146]

Then, in 1819, the historic link between city and seamen's mission, already noted in New York and Boston, emerges again. Together with a few friends, Eastburn "determined to have a meeting for the dear mariners." As one who loved to labor "especially for those for whom others had not sufficiently cared," Eastburn was, in a major port-city like Philadelphia, almost predestined to discover the destitute state of seafarers. He had already ministered to them on occasion, for example at the hospital and the navy yard. Eastburn's biographer also assumes that his concern for the seafarer was "increased by the remembrance of his son," who, after having risen to the rank of captain, lost his life during the Quasi-War with France. At all events, from that first seamen's service in October 1819, the roving chaplain became "in a measure" more stationary. At 71, well past the retirement age of many, Joseph Eastburn had, as "stated preacher" to seafarers, finally found the vocation which was to become his crowning life-work.[147]

Who had, however, actually taken the first initiative toward establishing Philadelphia's form of "Mariners' Meeting" (as Eastburn called it)? Undoubtedly, the way had, to some extent, been prepared by the founding of the local Marine Bible Society three years previously. It was that Society's co-founder, Robert Ralston, who earlier in 1819 had addressed an inquiry to Boston, in order to obtain information about the "progress and state" of the seamen's work there. This was cordially provided by Dr. Jenks.[148] Later, a notice was inserted in the press, addressed to the "Mariners of the Port of Philadelphia and all others . . . transiently in port," announcing the commencement of morning and afternoon services, for their benefit, as from Sunday, October 24, 1819.

As in Boston, the site selected was a strategically situated sail-loft, in this case capable of holding some 700, and located at "No. 6, fronting the water, and the second wharf north of Market street." Accommodation was gratuitously provided by the proprietor, Jacob Dunston, a well-known sail-maker.[149]

It was stated in the initial press notice that this meeting was meant "to be continued as a permanent Mariners' place of worship," until a church could be erected "for the special purpose."[150] No organization was announced; but others, besides Dunston, were, from the outset, involved together with

Eastburn. Prominent among them was Robert Ralston (an active Presbyterian),[151] evidently also Commodore Richard Dale (the Episcopal President
of the Marine Bible Society),[152] as well as Samuel Archer (a prominent
merchant of Quaker affiliation).[153] These latter three were all to become
actively involved in promoting plans for a permanent mariners' church.

However, the major cohesive force during the decade ahead was
only too obviously the personality and style of ministry of Father Eastburn
himself. This was evidenced from that very first meeting in October 1819,
when, in his own words,

> We hung out a flag [from the sail-loft]. As they [the sailors] came
> by they hailed us—"Ship ahoy!" We answered them. They asked
> us "where we were bound?" We told them, to the port of New
> Jerusalem; that we sailed under Admiral Jesus, a good commander;
> that we wanted men; that we had several ships—that there was the
> ship Methodist, the ship Baptist, the ship Episcopalian, the ship
> Presbyterian, &c.; that they might have choice of ships and of
> under officers, but that they would do well to go in the fleet.
> "Well," said they, "we will come in and hear your terms."[154]

Sailors continued to come—in their hundreds, until the old sail-loft
at length became "too confined and uncomfortable." Then, in July, 1822,
the meeting was moved to the session-room of Eastburn's own church on
Cherry Street (Second Presbyterian). Here too, the attendance was generally
"crowded." Nevertheless, the distance from the Delaware was problematic.
Eastburn was anxious that seamen should not be ousted by residents, and
that the waterfront should not be abandoned to the enemy. (He felt strongly
that, in a seamen's church, seamen must always have first priority. His goal
was to "bring the church as close to the landing place of the seamen as the
grog shop, the gambling den and the palace of lust.") He was, therefore,

Father Eastburn preaching to sailors in 1822, in Jacob
Dunstan's sail-loft on the second wharf north of Market
Street, Philadelphia. (Photograph of an engraving made in
1822, courtesy of Presbyterian Historical Society, Philadelphia.)

Philadelphia's stately Mariners' Church, built by William Strickland and dedicated October 16, 1824. Located at what would now be 129-133 South Water Street, it could seat 1,200. (*The Sailor's Magazine,* New York, November 1835.)

relieved when, in June, 1823, an ideal site for a permanent structure was secured on the east side of South Water Street, between Chestnut and Walnut, "in the very centre of the shipping business."[155]

Philadelphians, though not the first to build a mariners' church, eventually did so with characteristic independence. There was no formal society structure, nor any organized church, only a trio of trustees consisting of Eastburn's faithful friends, Ralston, Dale and Archer. But these brought to their task both acumen and drive. In the incredibly short space of a few weeks, the sum of $10,000 (half the total budget figure) was subscribed; William Strickland, the famous Philadelphia architect, was commissioned in April, 1824.

Finally, Sunday, October 16, 1824, saw the dedication of a uniquely conceived mariners' church. With accommodation for 1,200, it ranked as one of the largest churches in the city. It was also one of the most handsome, built of brick, covered with slate, and topped by a 20-foot observatory, with encircling colonade, and a flag-standard uppermost. The sanctuary occupied the upper story, with a number of stores at street level bringing in an annual income of over $800 in rent. As this impressive edifice quickly consolidated its position with seafarers and their families, its income was further augmented by "mariners' monthly contributions," voluntarily made at sea by crews with Philadelphia as home-port.[156]

In relation to the Bethel Union Movement, too, Philadelphians followed their own course. No separate society was organized. But in

January, 1821, an emblem reminiscent of the Bethel Flag was raised at the sail-loft, showing two stars, a dove, an anchor and the words "Mariners' Church." During 1821, Eastburn promoted a number of prayer meetings on shipboard, although cases also occurred, where a captain found he could not cooperate "on account of the sentiments of his owner." When Bethel Meetings in the regular sense were ultimately introduced, it was as a result of a direct impulse from England, not New York. On April 25, 1822, a Bethel Flag, sent by the BFSFSBU as a "token of their respect for a venerable fisher of men" (Father Eastburn), was hoisted at the masthead of the brig *Junius*. From then on, weekday evening Bethel Meetings were frequently held aboard ships in port, often with the participation of prominent preachers, such as Doctors Ely, Brodhead and Janeway.[157]

Not surprisingly, there developed a bond of deep mutual sympathy and respect between Joseph Eastburn and George Charles Smith, a connection traceable to the constant correspondence of Robert Ralston with British Bible and seamen's societies. Eastburn would often read a part of *The Boatswain's Mate* or *The Sailor's Magazine* at the close of his address. Smith would gladly quote intelligence of Eastburn's activities in his magazines. On Eastburn's death in 1828, Smith and his Society spoke of him as "the apostle of sailors in the United States."[158] The designation was not unjustified. As preacher, pastor and person, he left an indelible impression on literally thousands of seafarers during the last decade of his life.

As preacher, Eastburn reached the very pinnacle of popularity in his day. He was experiential yet scriptural, extemporaneous yet eloquent. His delivery was fervent, but never ranting, above all deeply sincere. It was said that frequently, as he spoke, his whole body would sway, as tears rolled down his wrinkled cheeks. In addressing seamen, he believed in "plain short discourses, interspersed with anecdotes," and worded "in their own style," as far as this was genuinely familiar to the preacher.[159]

As pastor, his orientation was intensely practical. Where a Dr. Jenks would theorize about innovations in church organization and foreign-port outreach, Father Eastburn dealt differently with both. Those who wished to commune, he would accompany to a church of their own choosing. Abroad, he himself became a pervasive influence in the lives of seamen wherever they sailed; from the Atlantic and the Pacific came constant requests from whole crews to be remembered in his prayers.[160]

As a person, he was only a friendly, sprightly and courteous old gentleman, "a little below the middle size," neatly dressed in a Quaker coat. And yet (to quote his biographer) he was filled with a "force of piety" so transparantly honest that, again and again, even the most hardened individuals he encountered as preacher or pastor simply "resigned himself" to him, and the message of salvation he brought.[161]

In Joseph Eastburn's case, it is no exaggeration to say he became a legend in his lifetime. Within two years of his first meeting in the sail-loft, a ship had been named after him,[162] and "a genuine reformation" among seafarers was being publicly attributed to him.[163] He was credited with consolidating the work in New York, and with originating that in Baltimore, after appearing as guest preacher on the waterfronts there.[164] His funeral, on February 2, 1828, gave vivid evidence of how widely he was beloved and revered. It was such as Philadelphia had never seen since its foundation. Up to 20,000 were estimated to have attended, as his body was carried through the crowded streets by twelve seafarers, preceded by the Bethel Flag, and a cortege consisting of a host of seamen from ships in port, children of the Mariners' Church Sunday School and clergymen of every denomination.[165]

Significantly, Joseph Eastburn was the first seamen's chaplain given by common consent the epithet "Father"; and certainly, to many a "prodigal son of the ocean," he had, in a very real sense, become a spiritual father.[166] Half a century later, *The Sailor's Magazine* of New York could say that the name of Father Eastburn was still "spoken with love by converted seamen in the four quarters of the globe."[167]

CHARLESTON AND ELSEWHERE

The different methods of maritime ministry already familiar from Boston, New York and Philadelphia emerge as basic elements in the origin of the work in other American ports, too. However, the precise composition of such elements in the total picture in each case would vary from port to port.

Charleston, South Carolina, was known as post-Revolutionary America's major seaport in the South. The city of Charleston, with its awakening concern for those destitute of the Gospel, had also become "Boston's spiritual twin." Here, city missionaries of the "Female Domestic Missionary Society of Charleston," founded in June, 1818, commenced, evidently that same year, a successful sail-loft "Seamen's Meeting." They also instituted regular visitation at Charleston's Marine Hospital.[168]

Meanwhile, members of the local Marine Bible Society, also founded in 1818, were so impressed with the "strict decorum" and positive response of the seafarers to this improvised form of stated preaching ministry, that they resolved, "at a regular meeting" of the Society, to provide a permanent structure for the work. Committees were formed, and ultimately the Old Baptist Church on the east side of Church Street was bought. On February 10, 1822, the building was publicly opened as a Charleston Mariners' Church.[169]

In order to give the church a corporate body, a "Charleston Port Society for Promoting the Gospel among Seamen" was established on January 4, 1823, with the declared object of furnishing seamen with "the regular Evangelical Ministrations of the Gospel, and such other religious and intellectual instruction as . . . practicable." The following month, the roster of preachers (from different denominations supplying the pulpit) was replaced with the appointment of the Rev. Joseph Brown as full-time pastor of the Mariners' Church. Thus began an outstanding, innovative, nine-year ministry on the Charleston waterfront.[170]

Spurred by the enthusiasm of their new chaplain, and "provoked" to further action by recent reports of Bethel Union achievements in London and New York, "friends of seamen" met on March 26, 1822, in the Mariners' Church, and resolved to form a "Charleston Bethel Union." Patterned closely on New York's example, the Charleston Union, with Chaplain Brown as corresponding secretary, soon shot ahead of its parent. In fact, in the words of none other than G.C. Smith, these newcomers "seemed determined to out-rival England in doing good to seamen."[171]

Certainly, the record makes remarkable reading. At Bethel Meetings on board, an attendance of 400 to 500 was not uncommon. Also, the Union introduced a novel series of shipboard "free discussion" meetings, between members and ship's captains in port, in order to identify issues and seek solutions. This resulted in the world's hitherto widest form of organized international action for the welfare of seafarers. In January, 1823, the Union sent out a circular addressed to "all Bethel Unions, Port Societies, and Ship Masters," on both sides of the Atlantic, seeking cooperation in establishing, in all major world ports, (1) Register-offices, based on a system of service reference, calculated to stimulate self-betterment, and (2) Boarding-houses, meeting minimal standards in both freedom from imposition and provision of "rational entertainment and solid improvement."[172]

The argument seemed simple enough. A sailor, deprived of the positive stimulus of proximity to family and friends, needs "some other motive," besides religious instruction, to seek self-improvement; and, "if the sailor needs such a motive in one port, he needs it through the world."[173] There is evidence that the appeal was given wide coverage in both Britain and America.[174]

Meanwhile, its authors set about translating words into at least *local* action. A register-office was actually opened in East-Bay, during the winter of 1823-24, a Charleston pioneer achievement of wide significance. (The office, which simultaneously served as "Marine Bible and Tract Depository," was entrusted to one Captain Horace Utley, who was also Notary Public.)[175] Also, the Board of the Bethel Union decided, in 1823, to take a particularly "regular and orderly" sailors' boarding-house (John Carnighan's in North Elliott Street) under its official patronage. A sailors' reading-room was opened there, and supplied with a library by the Board. (Similar facilities for officers were provided at the register-office.)

The Baltimore Seamen's Bethel of the Seamen's Union
Bethel Society of Baltimore, built on the corner of Philpot
(later Block) and Will's Streets on Fell's Point, and
dedicated November 19, 1826. (*The Sailor's Magazine,*
New York, January 1836.)

Criticism for deliberate competition was countered by the Board offering to extend the same patronage to any boarding-house masters, who "entered into their views." Few did. However, the Bethel Union persevered, eventually gaining the collaboration of a "Charleston Female Seamen's Friend Society." By year's end, these zealous ladies had founded and furnished the first avowedly "religious" sailors' boarding-house in the country.[176]

In Baltimore, that "nest of pirates," whose clippers had castigated the British during the War of 1812, "Bethel operations" began, curiously enough, aboard a British brig. It was on the *Union* of Liverpool, lying alongside Prince's Wharf at Fell's Point, the historic hub of Baltimore's Sailortown, that about 30 people from ship and shore (including clergy) gathered on Sunday, May 11, 1823, for a brief morning service.[177] After this modest trial effort, more elaborate preparations were made for the following Sunday. Newspapers carried notices, handbills were "circulated through the Point," James Conner's spacious sail-loft in Ann Street was loaned, and a "large blue bunting flag," with "Seamen's Bethel" in white letters, was hoisted above it. "Upwards of 400 precious souls" responded. A "Seamen's Meeting" had also been established in Chesapeake Bay.[178]

Although Bethel Meetings (in the strict sense of weekday prayer-meetings on shipboard) had not yet evolved, services continued to be regularly held on Sundays, on shipboard or in sail-lofts, under the Bethel emblem, with visiting or local ministers of varying church affiliation preaching to throngs of "hardy shellbacks." During the summer of that year (1823), a "Seamen's Union Bethel Society of Baltimore" was organized to perpetuate the work. The response was still such that "three-fourths of the seamen in port at any one time" were reportedly reached through the Society's meetings. However, without "some particular, stated preacher," here as elsewhere, individual "cases of conviction" could not be "followed up successfully" with appropriate pastoral counseling.

It was a great day, therefore, when—in 1824—the Rev. Stephen Williams was appointed full-time "Chaplain to the Seamen." It was also a great day, when—on November 19, 1826—a new Seamen's Bethel, built at Fell's Point, corner of Philpot (later Block) and Will's Streets, at a cost of $4,000, was "solemnly dedicated to the service of God." Fittingly, it was the voice of the venerable Father Eastburn of Philadelphia (who had "greatly cheered" the Society with a ten-day preaching visit in 1824), which was "first heard to reverberate around its walls" that day.[179] Locally, the loyal support of the Rev. John P.K. Henshaw (a brilliant speaker and future Protestant Episcopal Bishop of Rhode Island) was likewise important, during the Society's early struggles.[180]

Not many months after the beginning of Bethel Union organization in Maryland, Maine followed suit. Portland, though still with her back to the wilderness, had her face turned toward the sea-lanes of the North Atlantic; and her rapidly expanding maritime trade filled the waterfront with seafarers. Again, it was a local media-mission which first sought them out, in this case the "Portland Marine Bible Society" (founded September 12, 1820, during Stafford's tour that autumn). However, that Society derived much of its immediate impact from its association, from the very start, with a preacher considered "second to none in New England."[181]

The Rev. Edward Payson, 38-year-old pastor of Portland's orthodox Second Congregational Church, had witnessed many scenes of revival. But this was different. It was the evening of October 28, 1821. Payson, an ardent advocate of popular Bible distribution, was to speak on behalf of the Marine Bible Society. All seamen in port were invited; and almost all of them came—in a long procession through the streets, headed for "Old Jerusalem" (as Second Church was nicknamed), and solemnly led by a well-known, one-legged boarding-house master. The building was packed. No less a body than the prestigious British and Foreign Bible Society joined in publishing the result: "In the two following days, one hundred and fifty seamen applied to be furnished with the Scriptures, and eighty became members of the Society. (Payson's *Address to Seamen* on that occasion was translated into several languages, and printed in a number "past computation.")[182]

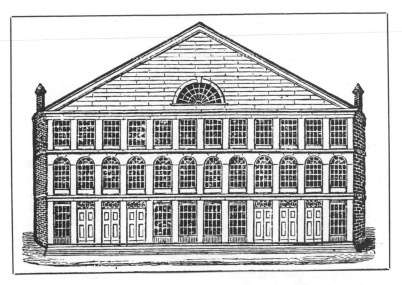

Portland's uniquely comprehensive Mariners' Church, with
facilities calculated to meet a whole spectrum of spiritual,
social and cultural needs. Located between Commercial
and Long Wharves, facing Fore Street, it was dedicated
June 14, 1829. (*The Sailor's Magazine,* New York, May 1829.)

A valid need had been dramatically demonstrated. Dr. Payson (as
he became) continued, on occasion, to preach to seamen, even though he
was, as pastor of Portland's largest congregation, already heavily over-
burdened.[183] Then, in 1823, a Bethel Flag received from the New York
Bethel Union became an incentive to concerted action. On December 4,
1823, a group of Christians connected with the shipping met to form a
"Portland Bethel Union," a sail-loft was fitted up, and a regular preaching
ministry was launched. For two seasons, the Union had the benefit of no less
a personage than Jotham Sewall, the itinerant "Apostle of Maine." He was
followed by local ministers of different denominations, supplying the pulpit
as best they could.[184]

By 1826, it was felt that a permanent structure had to be raised. The
outcome was the incorporation, on February 16, 1827, of sixteen "Trustees
of the Mariners' Church." These conceived, and in the course of two years
carried out, a plan of hitherto unparalleled dimensions. Selecting a site
between Commercial and Long Wharves, facing Fore Street, they raised a
granite-front three-storied edifice, which became the biggest building in
town. With lower stories devoted to commercial use (for renting out as
stores, offices, even a market-house), the uppermost story was reserved for
not only a large chapel and a comprehensive nautical academy, but also a

reading-room, library and maritime museum (suitable for "daily resort and rational amusement"). The complex even included a savings bank for seamen, a registry and intelligence office , as well as rooms for Portland's Marine Society.

Dedicated June 14, 1829, the Portland Mariners' Church became an evident success among the men, with their own stated preacher (the Rev. Robert Blake), three services on the Sabbath, and "generally full to over-flowing." [185] With a total cost of some $35,000, time would show that the Trustees had over-extended themselves. However, their courageous attempt to meet under one roof such a spectrum of legitimate seamen's needs—spiritual, social and cultural—was hitherto unique. The New York-based editor of *The Sailor's Magazine* could only cry with obvious envy: "Can nothing [comparable] be done in the marine capital of America?" [186]

Something comparable was, in fact, done in the Gulf of Mexico. But here, too, the pioneers proved over-optimistic. In 1823, New Orleans, fascinating French "Queen City of the South," had only been part of the United States for two brief decades. Besides being the "most foreign-flavored" city in the nation, however, she was probably also the most notorious. Below Canal Street, on the Levee, seamen were, in the words of those concerned with their welfare, confronted with a veritable "battery of hell." [187]

At nearby New-Market, on Sunday morning in mid-March, 1823, a number of local seamen's friends decided to provide a service particularly for "that long-neglected class." Seats were prepared, and some 200 solemn-faced seamen responded. The experiment was, therefore, repeated. The arrival of a Bethel Flag from the New York parent society gave the impetus for the foundation, on March 1823, of a "New Orleans Bethel Union." On

Nineteenth-century New Orleans, "Queen City of the South."
(Painting by W.J. Bennett, in Alexander Laing, *American Sail.*)

The New Orleans Mariners' Church, built by the Mariners' Church Society of New Orleans in the Custom House Square on the Levee, and opened thanks to seafaring volunteers on December 20, 1829. (*The Sailors' Magazine,* New York, February 1830.)

April 20, 1823, the flag was hoisted by the new Society on the schooner *George.* From then on, both Sunday and weekday meetings continued on shipboard under the Bethel Flag, with the cooperation of various ministers, and on the same nonsectarian basis as in other ports. The scene caused constant astonishment among newly-arrived captains and crews, amazed "that such a thing had been started in New-Orleans."[188]

In New Orleans, as elsewhere, these improvised meetings manifested the need for a permanent structure ashore. A meeting of masters and local friends of the cause was held on board the ship *Grand Turk* on the evening of March 11, 1825, and a "Mariners' Church Society of New Orleans" was formed, with this end in view.[189] The following winter, the Rev. William Shedd, who had himself frequently preached on board in New Orleans, made a promotional tour in England, as agent of the new Society. The largely Catholic Creole citizenry could hardly be expected to support such a plainly Protestant venture. Moreover, those 10,000 seamen who annually visited the port did not come from New Orleans. They were, as Shedd reminded his hearers, "principally natives of Great Britain and the Northern States of America." His efforts on behalf of the "dark and hitherto neglected waters of the Mississippi" were reportedly well rewarded. "Several thousand dollars" were donated by British Christians. Americans in Northern States also contributed.[190]

In early 1829, the Trustees felt justified in launching forth. By the Federal Government, they were given a "very conspicuous" site, in the

Custom-house Square on the Levee, "between the shipping and steam-boats." Here, a building was begun, in concept "the most elegant and costly ... ever dedicated to the sons of the ocean." The walls were erected, the roof covered and the basement fitted up for stores. By now, $15,000 had been expended. Then funds failed; and matters came to an ignominious halt. Before year's end, however, seamen themselves, in a very literal sense, stepped in. They removed the staging, cleared out the rubbish, collected two hundred dollars among the shipping, fitted a few windows, erected a temporary pulpit, and put up a hundred plank benches. Thus, on Sunday, December 20, 1829, the church was opened, with the Bethel Flag flying, and at least 500 present, two-thirds of them seamen.[191]

The years immediately ahead would show that obtaining a full-time chaplain was no easy matter, and completing the projected building proved altogether impossible.[192] Nevertheless, the feat of those indefatigable sea-farers in late 1829 was unforgettable.

In Savannah, the busy cotton exporting seaport of Georgia, con-cerned Christians rented a room "on one of the wharves" as early as the summer of 1821, and established a Sabbath seamen's meeting. On January 18, 1822, *The Georgian* could report a rare instance of direct *Lutheran* involve-ment in ministry to seafarers at this early period. Captains and crew members in port were invited to attend "the Lutheran Church (Court-House square)," now "opened as a Permanent place of Worship for Seamen, and ... designated by the Bethel flag ... displayed in front of the building."

In actual fact, such efforts were sporadic and far from permanent, until a bequest by a noted silversmith provided the financial foundation for a regular ministry. On his death in 1828, Josiah Penfield, known as a warm "seamen's friend" and deacon of Savannah's First Baptist Church, left the balance of his property "in trust for the erection of a House for the religious worship of seamen in the city of Savannah." The result was the erection and, in December 1832, consecration of a "very commodious and handsome brick building," named in his memory the "Penfield Mariners' Church" (popularly known as "the Bethel on the Bay").[193]

In Richmond, state capital of Virginia, situated astride the James River, a preaching ministry to seamen was started the same year as in Savannah. Prompted by a packet-captain who had brought a Bethel Flag with him from New York, a "Richmond Bethel Union" was founded November 16, 1821. Bethel committees were organized; but after a brief blossoming, the work waned owing to increasingly dispersed shipping. A decade later, there are records of renewed efforts at nearby Rocketts.[194]

In Virginia's principal port-city, a "Norfolk Seamen's Friend Society" was first formed January 31, 1825, for the purpose of "propagating the gospel among Seamen in that port and its vicinity." (This adoption of the denomination "Seamen's Friend Society" in early 1825 antedates by a whole year the future American national society's use of the name.)[195] The Society was evidently organized on a more permanent basis February 14, 1826. The Baptist minister, Noah Davis, who had been chairman of the former, became the secretary of the latter, gladly "surrendering" to it the Bethel Flag previously given for the work on the Norfolk waterfront by the New York Bethel Union.

A Sabbath afternoon seamen's meeting was then commenced in a conveniently located sail-loft, and Wednesday evening prayer-meetings were held at a seamen's boarding-house. In 1827, subscriptions were sought for the erection of a Norfolk mariners' church. (Applications were also made to American ships in port, and "several hundred dollars were thus collected.") There were to be long delays, however, before plans could be put into practice.[196]

Reverting to the New England scene, a media ministry had been maintained by the "Marine Bible Society of the Port of New Haven" since its foundation July 4, 1817. A decade later, however, the Society saw a need for "enlarging the sphere of its operations . . . to make provision for the preaching of the gospel on the Lord's Day." In the spring of 1828, therefore, the Society altered its constitution accordingly, at the same time changing its title to the "Seamen's Friend and Marine Bible Society of New Haven." Instrumental in this transformation was one Henry Lines, a Baptist and former seafarer, who had already "a few years since" preached to seamen "in the street, near the shipping." (Now a seamen's tailor, he would, when selling his wares, secretly slip "a tract or two" into a jacket or trouser pocket.) Hiring a loft at the head of Long Wharf, capable of holding some 200, The Society provided regular Sunday preaching with the help of local clergy and "gentlemen connected with the theological department of Yale College."

Although fluctuations in foreign seamen arriving in New Haven led to a discontinuation of the Society in a few years, so long as the Bethel Flag waved over the improvised seamen's chapel at the wharf-head, "most of the sailors in port" would attend. The same Society also did commendable pioneer work in placing "Marine Libraries" on board. Since 1859, the work has been continued by "The Woman's Seamen's Friend Society of Connecticut."[197]

Salem, proud pioneer of the prosperous American China Trade, was in 1820 not yet eclipsed by her deep-water rivals on the East Coast. Spiritual concern for the city's seafarers, stimulated by Stafford's promotional visit at the time, found expression in the founding, on September 1, 1820, of a "Marine Bible Society for the District of Salem and Beverly." However, here as in Boston, it was a local "Poor Society" (the Salem Society for the

Moral and Religious Instruction of the Poor, founded in 1819), that first assumed responsibility for a preaching ministry to seamen in port. In 1824, this Society, through its agent, established a "Seamen's Meeting" in a store on Derby Wharf, and "a Bethel Society" was formed to support the work. In this way, a modified Gospel ministry was maintained until a permanent seamen's chapel could be opened at the wharf-head seven years later.[198]

In the 1820's, New Bedford was fast becoming the whaling capital of the world. Legendary "Father Taylor" of Boston rode the Methodist circuit of Fairhaven and New Bedford in 1822-24, and pioneered a preaching ministry among the thousands of whalers shipping out from these parts. In 1825, a Marine Bible Society was formed in New Bedford. For the following five years, it remained the only institution specifically seeking the spiritual welfare of the local whaleman and his family. Then, from 1830 on, a more comprehensive ministry was taken up. Strictly speaking, however, this falls beyond the period at present under consideration.[199] The same applies to the various forms of maritime ministry organized during the early 1830's in a series of other seaports, from Eastport, Maine, to Mobile, Mississippi.[200]

TRUAIR'S VISION AND THE AMERICAN SEAMEN'S FRIEND SOCIETY

While local endeavors continued sporadically through the 1820's, plans for a coordinative "National Society," too, came to fruition before the close of the decade. The British, headed by the Rev. George Charles Smith, were the first to formulate the concept and attempt its prosecution. Likewise, it was the British-born Rev. John Truair who was to be the primary and persistent spokesman for the idea in America. Was this only a coincidence?

In March 1823, it was a little more than three years since Smith had founded the first *British* national society (the British and Foreign Seamen's Friend Society and Bethel Union). That month, before starting on his summer preaching tour, Smith wrote to Truair as follows, one year prior to Truair's installation as pastor of the New York Port Society's Mariners' Church, and editor of their *Seaman's Magazine:*

> I think the Seamen's Society at New-York will never be able to do so much good, and be so extensively sanctioned by its local, as by a more general name. Mankind will have their little prejudices and prepossessions [sic]. They will love their own towns, their own districts, and every thing connected with them, better than others, in which they have no local interest. ... Make it *American,* and every American citizen will feel more or less that it is *his* Society, and demands his aid. ... Call it the American Seamen's Friend Society and Bethel Union, and then go forth with your righteous claims. ...[201]

By 1823, the reciprocal exchange of reports and magazines between major seamen's mission societies in Great Britain and America had become customary. Hence, Smith was well informed about the financial straits of the New York Mariners' Church; also about Truair's 1822 collection tour to New England states, in imitation of Smith's own policy. In his report, Truair had quoted the suggestion of two college professors he met at Hanover, New Hampshire, that the NYPS should be converted into "a kind of national society," answering to the British and Foreign Seamen's Friend Society and Bethel Union, with auxiliaries throughout the country, rather than resembling, as now, the Port of London Society. Thereby he would remove the objection raised, for example, by Bostonians who believed they should support solely their own institution, since the New York Port Society was "local," at least in name. (The fact that the New York Mariners' Church ministered to many New England seafarers, a key point in Truair's argumentation, was for them evidently insufficient motivation.)[202]

Tenaciously, Truair tried to keep in view some kind of *conversion* of the Society he had already served. However, Smith had intimated an alternative, that of *supplementation*. "Two great National Institutions" (the British and Foreign and the American Seamen's Friend Societies), and "two noble local Societies" (the Port of London and the New York Port Societies), would present "an interesting parallel," and be more likely to promote "the universal dominion of Jesus Christ on the Ocean."[203]

Truair ultimately agreed. After having tirelessly traveled, preached and published for three whole years, he believed the time had finally come for the realization of Smith's suggestion. in March, 1825, under the combined patronage of the NYPS and the NYBU, he launched as his first step *The Mariners' Magazine*, a separate 18-page weekly, dedicated wholly to the Seamen's Cause (thereby replacing the *Seaman's Magazine* supplement to *The Christian Herald*). For Truair, this was a logical prelude. He saw the British *Sailor's Magazine* as the chief reason for Britain's current pre-eminence in this field of mission; for, as he put it, "we will not believe, till it be proved to us, that a British Christian is more ready to do his duty to seamen than an American Christian, when the latter is equally well informed."[204]

Then, in a forceful magazine editorial, dated July 23, 1825, Truair presented his grand project. While Christianity had "reigned on shore, and spread her triumphs over Europe and America," the ocean had "never been brought under her sway." True, some societies had been created locally. But they were now "nearly overlooked," amidst all the "splendid machinery" of the major *national* societies for mission and media distribution. Hence, he would herewith "throw out" the plan of an American Seamen's Friend Society and Bethel Union, in the hope that "editorial brethren" would come with their comments, and create a concern in wider circles.[205]

Evincing a determination worthy of a George Charles Smith (whom he continued to hold in undisguised admiration), Truair pressed on during the weeks which followed. With the friends of other institutions successfully urging their claims on the Christian public through nation-wide organizations, when would the friends of seamen wake up? Blissfully ignorant of the civil war brewing at precisely that time in British metropolitan societies, Truair tried to goad America's "few" and "feeble" societies, with their "snail-like pace," into emulation of England's, which he ruefully represented as "nearly half a century in advance."[206]

Despite such obvious hyperbole, Truair's proposal received a remarkably favorable response from the press, evidently enhanced by his own strongly ecumenical stance. He also obtained wide publicity for a powerful appeal entitled *Voice from the Sea,* bearing the signature of 100 masters and fourteen mates, dated New York Harbor, September 1825, and published in *The Mariner's Magazine* for October 1, 1825. Warmly endorsing the proposed organization "on the principles of the British and Foreign Seamen's Friend Society," these men maintain—

> . . . that the efforts of individual Societies, without concert of action, or correspondence of labour, . . . will not be able to accomplish the great end in view, with the same ease, or in the same period, that the uniform and increased operations of a general institution would.[207]

Finally, three months after the appearance of Truair's initial editorial, the time had, it seemed, arrived for formal action. This had the apparent approval of not only Truair's own Port Society, but also that of the New York Bethel Union (with whose semi-national role he had constantly identified). On October 25, 1825, a preliminary meeting was held in New York's City Hotel, at which spirited speeches endorsing the project were delivered by ministers of different denominations. As a result, it was decided to proceed with the drafting of a constitution, and the invitation of delegates from all major commercial cities in the Union.[208]

At length, on January 13, 1826, at the same place and in the presence of "a very large auditory," the American Seamen's Friend Society (ASFS) was officially founded, the proposed constitution unanimously adopted, and officers elected. As president was chosen former Secretary of the Navy, the Hon. Smith Thompson of New York. (He had chaired both public meetings.) Fifteen vice-presidents were elected, among prominent men in port-cities from Portland, Maine, to New Orleans, also 30 directors (not less than thirteen to be from the city of New York). Societies established for similar purposes on a local level were invited to become auxiliaries, on the understanding that any surplus funds would be annually paid over to the parent society.[209]

The Hon. Smith Thompson, the first president of the American Seamen's Friend Society, both at its foundation in 1826 and at its resuscitation in 1828. (Courtesy: The American Seamen's Friend Society.)

Perhaps even more significant than this attempt at national co-ordination, was the integrated concept of mission of the new Society, apparent in Article 2 of its constitution:

> The object of this Society shall be to ameliorate the condition, and improve the moral and religious character of seamen, by the establishment of well-regulated boarding-houses, and suitable libraries and reading-rooms, when practicable; Savings Banks, Register Offices, Schools of elementary and nautical instruction, by the employment of agents for carrying into effect the operations of the Society in different parts of the United States, and by the use of such other means as may seem calculated to promote the designs of the Institution.[210]

The statement of purpose articulates a clear concern for the total (not merely spiritual) welfare of the seafarer.[211] The accompanying statement of methods recognizes a corresponding need for "other expedients, auxiliary to the simple preaching of the gospel." These methods had been repeatedly listed by G.C. Smith, during his agitation in 1823-25 for a more differentiated maritime ministry by the British national society, and its American counterpart now gladly acknowledged its indebtedness.[212]

The religious press responded with enthusiasm. "This," comments one editor, "is the brightest ray of Millennial glory that has ever beamed upon this benighted world. . . ." Truair himself, in trying to translate vision into reality, struck a more sober note. As agent and corresponding secretary of the new Society, he published in their name a 34-page pamphlet entitled *Call from the Ocean, or an Appeal to the Patriot and the Christian,* setting forth a systematic motivation and methodology of maritime mission. The work was widely circulated and highly acclaimed. During the early part of 1826, Truair also traveled to "some of the southern ports," zealously advocating the cause and raising funds. Meanwhile, members of the Society's executive committee were reported actively engaged in the duties assigned to them. Said Truair, "The public will probably soon hear from them." [213]

Shortly afterwards, Truair resigned. For long, virtually nothing was heard from the Society or its leadership. Why, when prospects seemed so promising, should the Society become so dramatically dormant? Available sources are unspecific, and much remains shrouded in mystery.

The following may, however, well have been contributory causes: (1) Premature birth: Although it is simply not in accordance with the facts to allege that "no one was enthusiastic but the agent," [214] the space of six months from first suggestion to formal foundation of such a comprehensive undertaking was certainly short; the *Call* could have meant more if published before the founding. As it was, other important concerns came "crowding upon the public mind," just at this juncture. [215] (2) Personality-related reasons: Truair's bold tone of authorship 1822-26, and the unorthodox nature of his subsequent ministerial career, indicate an independence of mind and impatience of spirit which could easily produce frustration in himself, or jeopardize cooperation with others. At all events, his early resignation deprived the new, struggling Society of its most indispensable asset—a conspicuously capable and diligent general agent. [216]

Nevertheless, the society structure was never dismantled. Its existence was "precarious," but a "pulsation" remained. "A small number of individuals," it was stated, "retained the form of the society, in hopes to resuscitate it at a favourable opportunity." This, they felt, had arrived by the spring of 1828. Sensing the need for reactivating the Society "daily growing more and more imperious," they convened a meeting on May 5, 1828. Here, elections were held, and "some vacancies" supplied among the Society's officers. Most important, the general agency was again filled, now on a more permanent basis.

First, the Society obtained, for a few months, the loan of one who had long since ardently endorsed its concept, the Rev. Joseph Brown of the Charleston Port Society. Ater a strenuous summer, during which Brown launched *The Sailor's Magazine* as the official monthly organ of the ASFS, the Rev. Joshua Leavitt, a brilliantly endowed Congregational clergyman from Stratford, Connecticuit, was appointed as the Society's first "Permanent Agent" (and magazine editor) from November 1828. [217]

That here was a case of *resuscitation* rather than any radical *reorganization,* is evident from a study of the list of officers, which retains many of the same names; also from the wording of the constitution, which

New York's waterfront in 1828, at the time a reinvigorated
American Seamen's Friend Society was getting underway.
Here, South Street, from Maiden Lane. (Engraving by
R. Varin, courtesy of Seamen's Church Institute of NY/NJ.)

reveals changes chiefly of an editorial nature only. The most obvious
difference is the revised wording of Article II:

> The object of the Society shall be to improve the social and moral
> condition of Seamen, by uniting the efforts of the wise and good in
> their behalf; by promoting in every port, Boarding Houses of good
> character, Savings Banks, Register Offices, Libraries, Reading
> Rooms, and Schools; and also the ministrations of the Gospel,
> and other religious blessings.

Here, too, however, the fundamental content of the 1826 version has been
retained.[218]

The essential identity of the Society of 1828 with that of 1826 is
acknowledged in the very first line of the *Annual Report* for 1828: "The
Society was first instituted in January 1826." Why, then, has the American
Seamen's Friend Society over the years preferred to recognize 1828, rather
than 1826, as the Society's official founding year? It seems reasonable to
assume that this whole tendency to minimize 1826 and maximiize 1828 has
had at least some relevance to the anticlimax of those two years of
embarrassing dormancy.[219]

Nevertheless, nothing can rob the Rev. John Truair of his rightful role in history. He was by no means the father of American Seamen's missions. There, Ward Stafford has an indisputably prior claim. But Truair caught the vision of a national society for America, raised public consciousness of the need for it, and saw it through to its first fruition. Thus, he undeniably did initiate a nation-wide enterprise destined, during the following phase of the work, to lead the world: The American Seamen's Friend Society.

Chapter 21

Toward American Multi-Denominational Maritime Mission (1828-64)

FOREIGN OUTREACH AND THE AMERICAN SEAMEN'S FRIEND SOCIETY

It has been said, "From the Evangelical point of view, an unchristian nation elected Jefferson; an uncivilized nation chose Jackson." As already noted, with the continuing westward move of the frontier, America's Christians saw the twin specters of mass infidelity and barbarism looming on the immediate horizon. At all events, when America's first "frontier president" assumed office in 1829, the Evangelical United Front found the time opportune to mount a new general offensive.

Much of the spiritual dynamic derived from the remarkable revival touched off in upstate New York in the mid-1820's by that amazing lawyer-evangelist, Charles G. Finney. By the turn of the decade, its waves had "burst all bounds and spread over the whole nation." In an intimate union of revivalism and reform, converts carried the combined cause of redeeming the people and reshaping their society into constantly new fields. One such field, which clearly stood to benefit, was "the reformation of the seafarer."[220]

On the American scene, as in Great Britain, it was the eventual establishment of a national society which more specifically marked a transition from Bethel Unions, and other forms of early evangelistic endeavor, to an era of more diversified maritime ministry. This was characterized by not only a deliberate denominational orientation and increased diaconal concern, but also systematic involvement on inland waterways and overseas.

Turning first to the last of these, foreign port ministry was soon to become the most distinctive feature of the American Seamen's Friend Society. Among the positive results of that "unnecessary" War of 1812 was, from the viewpoint of the United States, the nautical ingenuity developed

In 1830, the American Seamen's Friend Society moved into
their first more "permanent" office in front of South
Baptist Church on Nassua Street, Manhattan, "midway
between the two rivers." (*The Sailor's Magazine,*
New York, November 1830.)

during her time of testing, and the wholesome international respect it
engendered. True, in 1819 America missed the (steam-) boat, by failing to
exploit her epic achievement in sending the *Savannah* to Europe, the first
vessel to make a partly steam-powered Atlantic crossing. However, during
the four following decades of the final glory of sail, Yankee packets and
clippers reigned supreme in their respective trades. In 1828, therefore, the
merchant fleet of the United States was in the midst of a period of rapid
expansion. As a result, masses of American seamen were already then
milling around in foreign ports, with "no Gospel provision." This situation in
itself constituted a clear claim on Christians who called themselves "American
Seamen's Friends."[221]

However, sources show that three main motives were more particularly influential in the Society's overseas involvement. They may
conveniently be classified as (1) psychological, (2) missiological and (3)
promotional.

From a *psychological* standpoint, the average sailor was seen as subject to more "unrestrained exposure to temptation," when far removed from family, church and native land. At the same time, he was regarded as more ready to respond to "missionary labours" on his behalf in such a situation.[222]

Several factors provided a powerful *missiological* motive for foreign-port ministry. Concern was widespread at this time over the need to alter the negative impact on "pagan" minds of dissolute seafarers (or merchants) from reputedly "Christian" countries. Reiterated by Truair in his *Call*, this "image" argument had long been one of the most familiar themes among advocates of the cause on both sides of the Atlantic. It was also pointed out that a seamen's chaplain, raising the standard of the Cross at the waterfront, might well become a "bridgehead" for either (1) infiltrating avowedly "heathen" countries closed to conventional missionaries, or (2) bringing "the pure Gospel" to bear where "a corrupt Christianity, supported by intolerant laws," had the ascendancy.[223]

However, it was undoubtedly *promotional* considerations which gave to this avenue of missionary concern much of the requisite relevance and weight. In retrospect, foreign-port outreach would seem only a natural task for a national organization. Nevertheless, this particular mode of ministry was not articulated in either the 1826 or the 1828 version of the Society's constitution. Nor was it expressly projected in the preceding press discussion. Meanwhile, there was, in the months immediately following the Society's (May 1828) resuscitation little external evidence that her prospects were any brighter now than two years earlier. *The Sailor's Magazine* remained "the only instrument" the Society so far possessed. Public support was positively disappointing. There existed an obvious need for a banner, behind which Christians across the country could be rallied.[224]

Such a banner had already been raised. As Charles I. Foster observes, foreign missions were fast becoming "the primary power factor of the whole Evangelical movement," with a mighty surge of missionary enthusiasm sweeping through the entire East Coast of America.[225] What could be more timely than to remind the Christian public that, for the success of such missions, the evangelization of seamen was utterly indispensable?

Accordingly, in February 1829, the Executive Committee of the ASFS resolved, since no "general reformation" of seamen was possible by means of "domestic operations alone,"

> That it is the appropriate province of the American Seamen's Friend Society, to institute missions, and send out sea missionaries to those principal foreign ports, frequented by American seamen, which are not furnished with gospel institutions accessible to our sea-faring brethren.[226]

The resolution marks a milestone in seamen's mission history. Whereas an Angas and a Von Bülow had made earlier, sporadic forrays out to foreign ports, none had so far made it a major matter of policy to establish permanent stations abroad, and then—not only in "Christendom," but in "heathen" countries of special concern to world missionary strategy. In this regard, the ASFS was positively a pioneer on the international scene.[227]

The Society was fortunate in the caliber of man who at this time had taken hold of the helm, and held it firmly for the first four critical years. Joshua Leavitt (1794-1873), Yale-educated lawyer and pastor, combined both the revivalist and the humanitarian. (He went on to pursue a distinguished career as editor, social reformer and anti-slavery leader.) It says something of his commitment, that he accepted the call of a Society known to be "without a dollar for his support," owning only "a Magazine without any subscribers." As "General Agent," Leavitt had the help of an outstanding evangelical Episcopalian, the Rev. Charles P. McIlvaine (later Bishop of Ohio), who acted as corresponding secretary during the same period.[228]

Launched under Leavitt's leadership, the first phase of "foreign operations" (1829-37) provides ample proof of the Society's determination to identify with the world missionary enterprise. This is especially evident in the selection of foreign "sea missions." The Society's first choice could hardly have been better calculated to fire the enthusiasm of the missionary-minded public: Canton, China.

It is not generally known that the first seamen's chaplain in China was none other than Protestantism's pioneer missionary in those parts, Dr. Robert Morrison (1782-1834), himself a Presbyterian, affiliated with the nondenominational London Missionary Society. From his first, circuitous voyage to Canton in 1807, he evinced a keen and constant compassion for

Dr. Robert Morrison
(1782-1834), renowned as
Presbyterian pioneer
missionary to China, was
also the first known to
have initiated missions to
seafarers in Chinese
waters in 1822.
(C. Sylvester Horne: *The
Story of the London
Missionary Society.*)

Dr. Joshua Leavitt
(1794-1873), the
brilliantly endowed
Congregational
clergyman who as new
"General Agent" steered
the ASFS through its first
critical years from 1828.
(George S. Webster:
The Seamen's Friend.)

men of the sea. There is every indication that this remained his foremost motivation. But, coupled with that compassion, was an acute awareness of how effectively a seaman could either, by unrestrained indulgence ashore, expose his religion to "the scorn of the Pagan Chinese," or, contrawise, by making Christ the captain of his soul, become a "missionary in a degree," wherever he went.

Hence, despite the tremendous missionary burdens he already carried, Dr. Morrison preached for visiting seamen, counseled them, ministered to their sick, and helped them in innumerable practical ways. In 1822, he dedicated to them the first English-text tract ever published in China. The same year, he published a proposal for a "Floating Hospital" and a "Floating Chapel," both to be stationed at Whampoa (Canton's deep-sea anchorage). Before the close of the year, on November 10, 1822, he preached the first sermon ever believed to have been held under the Bethel Flag in Chinese waters (on board the *Pacific*, a Ralston ship registered in Philadelphia). Finally, from the mid-1820's, Dr. Morrison launched a series of spirited appeals, both in the United Kingdom and the USA, in order to secure at least a full-time seamen's chaplain.[229]

To the London-based societies, currently embroiled in debilitating domestic strife, a new level of involvement, and at such a distance, was unthinkable. To the American Seamen's Friend Society, the plea of this revered man of God became a "Macedonian Call" it could not ignore.

Leavitt listed two major reasons for his Society's ready response: (1) For the evangelization of seafarers, there was "probably no place in the world so favorable" (with up to two thousand British and American seamen in port for weeks on end). (2) For bringing the Gospel to the hitherto inaccessible Celestial Empire, and thus to "one fourth of the human race," a ministry to the seamen and foreign residents in the semi-open port-city of Canton offered a fascinating, far more immediate point of penetration than the only hope hitherto (that of kindling a light of evangelical truth in Russia, which could one day "shine over the *great wall,* and illumine the darkness of China"). Here, on the waterfront of Whampoa and in the "hongs" of Canton, a consistent Christian bearing before the eyes of the natives would, it was alleged, excite reverence for such a religion, and predispose the people to receive the Bible, as the revelation from God responsible for bearing such "blessed fruits."[230]

Finally, the Society found their man, a 25-year-old graduate from the New Brunswick Seminary of the Dutch Reformed Church. The Rev. David Abeel (1804-46), son of a United States naval captain of Amsterdam ancestry, was weak in body, but strong in spirit. After over four months at sea, he arrived in Canton on February 25, 1830, as the first foreign-port "sea missionary" of the ASFS. Warmly welcomed by Dr. Morrison (who handed him his own Bethel Flag for use among the shipping), Abeel alternated between the seamen at Whampoa and the foreign residents at Canton. Despite awesome impediments, he even succeeded in ministering to individual Chinese.

With "an empty treasury," the Society had thus (in the words of its *Second Annual Report*) plunged into "the greatest and most difficult enterprise, remaining for the church before the millennium," that bringing the Gospel of Christ to the "vast population of China and Japan." Predictably,

The Rev. David Abeel, D.D. (1804-46), a graduate of the Dutch Reformed Church's New Brunswick Seminary, who arrived in Canton, China, Feb. 25, 1830, as the first foreign-port "sea missionary" of the ASFS. (George S. Webster: *The Seamen's Friend.*)

The ship anchorage of Whampoa, China, around 1830.
Note the Bethel Flag hoisted at the main top of the
American ship anchored second from the left.
(George S. Webster: *The Seamen's Friend*.)

churches, societies and individuals responded enthusiastically. The American Seamen's Friend Society was under weigh at last.[231]

However, after barely a year, Abeel exercised a previously agreed option of transferring to the employ of the American Board of Commissioners for Foreign Missions, investing the balance of his brief lifespan in a series of brilliant missionary endeavors in various parts of Southeast Asia. Nevertheless, he remained an eager advocate of the missiological motive for "foreign sea missions" as long as he lived. (As he put it, "Convert the sailors—send pious merchants— and you will reach the world through them!") Above all, foreign-port chaplaincy had proved its practicability as a permanent method of maritime ministry. Encouraged by the outcome of their experiment, the committee of the ASFS determined to lose no time in finding men "of the right stamp," both to fill Abeel's place and respond to the most pressing needs elsewhere.[232]

Despite their "most assiduous endeavors," however, the committee were compelled to confess their failure the following year to motivate one single "suitable" seminary graduate to offer himself for foreign-port chaplaincy. Then, in the spring of 1832, Leavitt, before leaving his post for new areas of ministry, was able to publish that no less than "three gentlemen" had been secured and duly appointed to serve in different overseas ports, each considered highly strategic for those dual objects of "preaching to seamen" and "helping forward the grand enterprise of the world's conversion."[233]

To resume the work already commenced at Canton, a highly gifted Yale-educated Congregationalist, Edwin Stevens, was ordained at New Haven in June 1832, arriving at his station in October the same year. Here he continued "with encouraging success" until March 1836, when he, too, availed himself of a previously agreed liberty to enter the service of the American Board. However, he persevered in preaching at Whampoa in a voluntary capacity until shortly before his untimely death (January 1837). For a brief period, his predecessor, Abeel, was able to afford assistance on the same basis.[234]

The second of those three candidates of 1832 was designated for the Sandwich Islands (as Hawaii was then still called). In the decision to establish a station here, missiological arguments were quite particularly relevant. Still in fresh memory were the outrages of 1825-27, when bands of rampaging, rum-drunk sailors, enraged at missionary-inspired anti-prostitution legislation, had attacked mission stations under the Black Flag, pressing home their demands on at least one occasion with live cannon-shot! The ASFS, like their British counterparts, received repeated appeals. Local missionaries had, since the early 1820's, pioneered a part-time ministry to the whaling crews. However, overburdened as they were with other demands, they were unable to devote to seamen the time they knew they needed. Honolulu, principal port of Oahu and the whole island group, had become notorious as the "Wapping of the Pacific." Here were frequently gathered as

If life for a 19th century whaler could be wild ashore, it was no less wild at sea. Scenes such as this were not uncommon while whales were still hunted with whaleboat and hand-harpoon. (Old Dartmouth Historical Society: *Whale Fishery of New England.*)

A "View of the Village of Honolulu" which appeared in
the first issue of Chaplain Samuel Damon's "Marine
Temperance" newspaper *The Friend,* January 1843.
Note the Seamen's Chapel at the center, surrounded
by grass-covered native dwellings.

many as 1,000 seamen, most of them British and American whalers. Here,
therefore, the Society decided to take its stand.[235]

From the outset, however, the Honolulu station was, more clearly
than Canton, conceived as a *seamen's* mission. In relation to foreign mission
interests, it was seen as supportive, but in no way subservient. The distinction
is significant. As Stevens pointed out, a seamen's mission station in the
"remote corner of Canton" offered a unique opportunity for foreign missionaries to be "trained up for service" in the "vast and dark prison-house" of
China (an opportunity for which he and his predecessor had both been
grateful). In Hawaii, on the other hand, the first American missionaries had,
in 1820, stepped straight into a spiritual vacuum. By the early 1830's, New
England Calvinism (and culture) had already made an indelible impression.
Here was no need to establish a beachhead in hostile territory. Hence the
committee of the ASFS felt justified in instructing their young chaplain: "In
your appointment, support, and field of labor, you are entirely distinct from
the missionaries." They even requested him to secure, before he sailed, his
own prefabricated church![236]

John Diell, a native of Cherry Valley, New York, and a Princeton-
educated Presbyterian, went to his task with determination. For weeks, he
traveled up and down the New England coastline, visiting what was at that
time the various "villages" engaged in the whale fishery, and collecting for
"their" chapel in the Sandwich Islands. When, after a five-month voyage, he
finally arrived in Honolulu on May 1, 1833, he had with him not only

materials for his chapel, reading-room and residence, but even two carpenters to set them up, also a seamen's library worth over $500, contributed by Diell's fellow-students at the seminary.

Diell was warmly welcomed by "the king and his principal chieftains," and lost no time in beginning building operations on a site ceded by the king himself. Able to accommodate some 500 souls, the edifice was said to have been raised "without the use of ardent spirit" (at that time evidently a sensation). On November 28, 1833, the Honolulu Seamen's Chapel was officially opened, with the Bethel Flag unfurled from its tower. Here Diell served diligently for five years until his health broke down in October 1838.[237]

The third of that 1832 trio of chaplains was assigned to France, a land well *within* the bounds of Christendom. However, here again, missiological motivation was conspicuous. This nominally Catholic country was regarded by British and American evangelicals as spiritually speaking engulfed in "thick darkness." What "salutary influence" might not a Bible-based seamen's ministry have on the native population precisely at this "critical and interesting" hour of history?[238]

Earlier evangelistic endeavors among French seafarers had already been begun by the British. The distribution of Scripture and tracts among French maritime prisoners of war in Britain was followed up after the war by sporadic Protestant efforts in France itself (including among the galley slaves).[239] During the 1820's, a humble form of "Reading-Room for Sailors" was actually established, partly through the instrumentality of the Rev. Mark Wilks of Paris, partly with the help of "benevolent British ladies," in four French seaports: Honfleur, Le Havre, Marseilles and Bordeaux.[240] On October 31, 1830, Captain Benjamin Prynn preached in the docklands of Le Havre, under his own Bethel Flag, said to be the first hoisted in that port.[241]

Finally, the Rev. G.C. Smith (who had demonstrated deep concern for French seafarers, ever since his personal contact with them during his 1814 "Continental Chaplaincy") made a fact-finding tour of Northern France in the spring of 1831. He failed to form a "Paris Seamen and Soldiers' Friend Society." However, he did succeed in founding the first permanent seamen's mission station on the mainland of Europe, so far as is known. On April 23, 1831, he launched the "Havre de Grace British and American Seamen's Friend Society," in affiliation with his own British and Foreign Seamen and Soldiers' Friend Society in London. A young Baptist minister from Lancashire, the Rev. Thomas Harbottle, served as the station's first chaplain through the winter, 1831-32. (In 1831, there were also reports of a "Toulouse Seamen and Soldiers' Friend Society," auxiliary to Le Havre.)[242]

Virginia-born Flavel S. Mines, like Diell a Presbyterian from Princeton, was originally appointed for the Mediterranean port of Marseilles.

The Rev. John Diell,
Presbyterian pioneer
seaman's chaplain in
Honolulu for the ASFS,
who arrived May 1, 1833,
complete with pre-
fabricated seamen's
chapel. (Courtesy:
Honolulu Sailor's Home.)

The Honolulu Seamen's Chapel, eventually called the Bethel
Church, was dedicated November 28, 1833, at the corner of
what became known as Bethel and King Streets. Honolulu's
famous present-day Central Union Church at the corner of
Beritania and Punahou Streets traces its origins back to the
old Seamen's Bethel. (George S. Webster: *The Seamen's Friend.*)

The Rev. Samuel C. Damon (1815-85), who was seamen's chaplain in Honolulu for 42 years. Following his arrival in 1842, he was also widely known as newspaper editor and temperance advocate. (George S. Webster: *The Seamen's Friend.*)

However, by the summer of 1832, Smith's Society had agreed to "resign" Le Havre to the Americans. (With the British Society on the verge of collapse, it was less an act of "Christian magnanimity," than one of sheer necessity.) Arriving in Le Havre in August 1832, Mines managed, by December, to establish a church organization styled "The American English Mariners' Church of Le Havre." Composed of resident and seafaring members alike, it even assumed an evangelistic responsibility for the native population, by engaging "a French city missionary" for that purpose.

Mines, released in 1834 to serve a Protestant congregation in Paris, was succeeded in October of that year by the Rev. David De Forest Ely. Ely added a ministry to the America-bound European emigrants, now embarking at Le Havre in increasing numbers.

In July 1836, Ely was himself succeeded by an exceptionally talented Presbyterian cleric, the Rev. Eli Newton Sawtell (1799-1885). A native of New Hampshire, Sawtell was already recognized as an outstanding evangelist during his ministry in America. No sooner had he commenced on French soil than both seamen and landsmen "thronged" to hear him, as the miserably inadequate "chapel" on Quai de l'Ile became the scene of a sustained, powerful revival.[243]

Meanwhile, the ASFS managed to establish their long-planned station in Marseilles by moving Sawtell's predecessor south. Arriving amidst the "forest of shipping" there in August 1836, Chaplain Ely succeeded in opening a shore chapel in December of the same year.[244]

Again in 1836, the Society opened its first South American station, by placing the Rev. Obadiah M. Johnson in Rio de Janeiro. Here he was able to revive those Sunday shipboard services under the Bethel Flag, which had been conducted by resident British merchants continuously for thirteen years (1821-34).[245]

Also in the mid-1830's, the American Society voted support for part-time ministry to seafarers by foreign missionaries stationed in such widespread ports as Smyrna (Izmir), Calcutta, Singapore, Batavia and Lahaina.[246]

Such was the picture of steady expansion under Leavitt's successor, the Rev. Jonathan Greenleaf, when suddenly the great financial panic of 1837 burst upon the American scene. Among the many benevolent causes which could not escape its repercussions was that of American seamen's friends. Faced with a budget for 1837-38 of $16,000, and an income for 1836-37 of little more than one half of that figure, the committee found retrenchment forced upon them. With a "feeling somewhat like that of a surgeon who amputates a limb to save life," they recalled their two most recently appointed foreign chaplains (from Marseilles and Rio), and curtailed their newly allocated aid to foreign missionaries.[247]

Thus, despite the continuing depressed state of the national economy, the Society managed, by a cautious husbanding of funds, to weather the storm, consolidate the position at its three original stations, and even enter a new phase of foreign expansion (1838-64).

At Canton-Whampoa, the work suffered an initial setback as a result of the Opium War of 1839-42. In January 1848, however, Chaplain George Loomis revived public interest by landing in New York in dramatic style, at the head of 26 stray Chinese sailors. These, after being cared for by the New York Sailors' Home, all enrolled themselves in the Marine Temperance Society of that city.[248] On his return to China, Loomis obtained further funds from visiting seamen and foreign residents. Finally he had a handsome floating Bethel constructed at Whampoa, complete with a Gothic-style sanctuary seating 300, a reading-room, library and chaplain's residence. Then, after six years' service, this conspicuous symbol of Western "civilization" became a casualty of the Second Opium War (1856-60), and was burned at the outbreak of hostilities.

However, the new chaplain, James C. Beecher (son of the renowned Dr. Lyman Beecher) managed to escape to Hong Kong and there complete another floating Bethel (November 1857). Meanwhile, as early as 1850, efforts were also initiated in Shanghai, where Dr. E.C. Bridgman of the American Board began preaching on shipboard, under a Bethel Flag sent out by the ASFS. Thanks largely to the zeal of A.L. Freeman, a young merchant from Boston, a floating Bethel was built there too. Resembling "an abridged Noah's Ark," it was opened in May 1857.[249] (It was the work of these

American pioneers which thus laid the foundation for the important British stations in Shanghai and Hong Kong which eventually evolved.)

In Honolulu, Diell's death at 32 led to the appointment of a young Andover graduate named Samuel C. Damon (1815-85). Arriving in October 1842, and remaining at his post for 42 years, "Father Damon" (as he was known) became inseparably linked with Honolulu in the minds of multitudes from sea and shore. (His "marine temperance" publication *The Friend*, launched in 1843, became a pioneer newspaper in those ports, and eventually a unique source of Hawaiian history.) During the 1840's, the ASFS expanded their work in the Sandwich Islands by appointing a full-time chaplain at Lahaina, and making the American Board missionary at Hilo their agent. At both of these ports, American missionaries had already built Bethel churches.[250]

At the third of the American Seamen's Friend Society's original stations, Sawtell successfully completed a new "American and English Seamen's Chapel" on Rue de la Paix. Built with substantial support from England, it was dedicated November 27, 1842. During a second term in Le Havre (1855-63), Sawtell launched a personal crusade against the more blatant forms of cruelty on shipboard, something which gave his ministry an impact far beyond the borders of France.[251] From 1847, the Society was able to assume partial responsibility for Protestant chaplaincies in both Marseilles and Bordeaux.[252]

In their *First Annual Report*, ASFS pioneers had piously hoped that if they only entered boldly into "Sea Missions" abroad, the British

Dr. Eli Newton Sawtell (1799-1885) became, as seamen's chaplain in Le Havre, from 1836 on, widely known both as a brilliant evangelist and an indefatigable advocate of justice for seafarers. (Eli N. Sawtell: *Treasured Moments.*)

The American Seamen's Friend Society's impressive new Seamen's Chapel in Le Havre, opened on Rue de la Paix in 1842. (Eli N. Sawtell: *Treasured Moments.*)

would "undoubtedly bear their part." Frustrated at first by the fratricide between Britain's metropolitan seamen's mission societies, such hopes were revived as the British and Foreign Sailors' Society seemed to consolidate its position towards the close of the 1830's.[253]

Not surprisingly, Cronstadt, the seaport of St. Petersburg, became the scene of the two societies' first mutual endeavor. Aspirations ran high. Russia was regarded by both British and American Christians alike as destined to become "a mighty engine in the conversion of the world." Cronstadt, besides being visited by over 1,000 ships of different nationalities annually, might provide opportunities "to be useful also on board the [naval] ships of the Czar." The ASFS provided chaplains (John C. Webster, 1837-38, and Ezra E. Adams, 1840-42), while the BFSS shared in their support. The Emperor Nicholas had actually approved the erection of a "Cronstadt Seamen's Chapel," when ill-health in Adam's family, together with other obstacles, virtually ended the joint venture.[254]

An "Amsterdam British and American Seamen's Friend Society," formed in affiliation with the English Reformed Church of that city, commenced activities in May 1842. Its visitation program for the benefit of British and American shipping secured support for a few years from both the BFSS and the ASFS.[255] In neighboring Antwerp, a cooperative involvement emerged at the close of the period under study.[256]

However, the Cronstadt and Amsterdam ventures were exceptions. Where the American society saw a need for English-language overseas chaplaincy during the 1840's and 50's, they would generally have to proceed without significant help from their British counterpart. This even applied to ports of the British Empire. Nowhere was this more dramatically illustrated than in the so-called "Sydney Case," connected with the ministry of Matthew T. Adam, the ASFS full-time pioneer chaplain in that port during the early 1840's.[257] In such Empire ports as Cape Town, Calcutta, Singapore, St. John (New Brunswick), Caribou Island (Labrador), even the Island of St. Helena, it was, in the main, the American Society which came to the aid of local endeavors in the hour of need.[258]

Understandably, North American seamen's friends sensed a special concern for the seaports of their sister-continent to the south. Demands made on the Society's waterfront workers in South and Central America were heavy, however. Sources show how, right up to the Civil War and beyond, these had to do battle with three formidable foes: rampant disease, varying degrees of religious persecution, and an impossible work-load (rendered even more so by the conflicting claims of quickly growing resident congregations).[259]

In Brazil, Rio remained "unrepossessed" until the early 1850's, and even then—despite an annual influx of over 20,000 seamen—chaplaincy services were for long only sporadic. More satisfactory was the work in Valparaiso, Chili. This vital South Pacific link in the blossoming California trade was well served from 1846 on by the renowned Dr. David Trumbull and his successive colleagues. Determined efforts were also made in Peru's port-city of Callao, where one young pioneer chaplain lost his life on arrival (in 1854), and his successor was laid low for five months with fever. In Buenos Aires, a Methodist Episcopal minister serving the local "Templo Americano" took up, in 1858, a part-time commission from the ASFS.[260]

Cuba's capital was considered a key port-city. However, Havana's officialdom surpassed the zeal of all others in obstructing the activity of "heretic" seamen's chaplains. After two vain earlier attempts, the American society succeeded in placing a chaplain there in 1848, only to have their man virtually deported in 1851. On another West Indian Island, St. Thomas, they were more fortunate, and managed to maintain an active chaplaincy from 1848 on (thereby reaching many in the Puerto Rico trade, too).[261]

As the California Gold Rush gathered momentum at mid-century, the Society saw the vast importance of the Isthmus of Panama, that great "gateway of the nations," through which the world was rushing, "some to

The Rev. Fredrick Olaus
Nilsson, later anglicized
to "Nelson" (1812-1903),
Swedish-born pioneer
"Sailor Missionary" to
Nordic seaports in the
service of the ASFS, from
1841. (George S. Webster:
The Seamen's Friend.)

riches, more to ruin" (to quote their *Annual Report* for 1851). A Panama
Canal was at this point only a dream, not to be realized until 1914. However,
in 1850, the Panama Railroad Company had begun building toward the
more readily reached goal of linking by locomotive the Atlantic with the
Pacific. At the two termini of Aspinwall (Colón) and Panama, where ship
arrivals rapidly rose, it was said with good reason: "Men die fast." Here, the
ASFS posted one chaplain at each port during the critical years 1852-56,
under conditions that could hardly have put them to a severer test.[262]

"Saving the Norsemen"—thus reads a remarkable chapter-heading
in a brief historical overview of the American Seamen's Friend Society.[263]
Certainly, the Society's so-called "Scandinavian Missions," with native-
born "Sailor Missionaries" stationed in significant Scandinavian seaports,
became a major concern during some 75 years of the Society's history. It
seems legitimate, therefore, to ask: Why such a heavy investment in this
particular form of "Foreign Operations"?

At least two probable reasons present themselves: (1) The rapidly
rising proportion of Scandinavian seamen, not only in world trade in general,
but in American-flag ships in particular.[264] (2) The relative receptivity of
Scandinavian seamen to the Gospel as attested in countless contemporary
reports. In fact, many of the sailor missionaries were themselves Scandinavian
seamen, converted through American agencies.[265]

The situation which confronted these men called for all the courage
and resourcefulness associated with seafarers at their best. In all three of the
Scandinavian kingdoms, the Society saw the "icy fetters of state control over
the Church." It was to Sweden, where state-enforced Lutheran conformity
was at its most rigid, that the first of these nautical emissaries was assigned.
In 1841, two converted Swedish sailors, Fredrick Olaus Nilsson and Olof

Pettersson, were commissioned to "labor in the seamen's cause" in Gothenburg and Stockholm, respectively. The appointment was the outcome of an initiative by that catalyst of nineteenth century Swedish revivalism, the Wesleyan Methodist minister in Stockholm, George Scott.[266]

At first, these two Methodist mariners were, as lay-preachers, placed under Scott's supervision. However, the following year, mounting religious repression combined with personal provocation forced Scott to return to Britain. An even harsher fate was reserved for Nelson (as he came to be known in English-speaking circles). Having sought baptism by immersion in 1847, and thereupon laid the foundation of the Baptist Church in Sweden, he found himself fined, beaten, stoned, imprisoned and finally banished for life from his native land, in 1851. The resultant uproar, both in Britain and America, has been represented as a significant factor in the ultimate achievement of religious liberty in Sweden. (Lord Palmerston himself was among those who protested against the treatment meted out to Nelson.)[267]

Meanwhile, the ASFS continued undeterred. By now, the Society had sailor missionaries in Stockholm (where Anders Martin Ljungberg succeeded Pettersson), on Gothland (John Lindelius) and in Gothenburg (where Erik Eriksson took the place of F.O. Nelson). Before returning to America, Nelson helped to pioneer seamen's work in Copenhagen, 1851-53. As his successor there, the Society appointed a fellow-Baptist, P.E. Ryding. Yet another Danish Baptist, F.L. Rymker (like Nelson, a converted seamen) carried the cause to Norway, arriving in 1857, and laboring among seafarers and their families until 1862 (chiefly in Porsgrunn and Larvik). He then returned to Odense and continued his maritime ministry from there. Even the setback of the Civil War back in America did not seem to affect the momentum of expansion. By the late 1860's, the Society had a team of no less than twelve sailor missionaries stationed in Scandinavian seaports (three of them by then in Norway, at Kristiansand, Kragerö and Porsgrunn).[268]

However, the kingdoms of Scandinavia were more massively Lutheran than their intended benefactors believed. Missionary endeavor in the employ of a nation so unashamedly republican and religiously pluralistic as the United States of America could not escape opposition, especially when performed by men with Methodist and Baptist loyalties. Even after the relaxation of more blatantly intolerant legislation, the efforts of these emissaries were inevitably curtailed by sociological and denominational realities. Nevertheless, there is good reason to believe that their very presence provided powerful ecclesiological motivation for action by the existing established churches, spurring them to assume responsibility at last for their own seafaring members, both in foreign and (eventually) home ports.[269]

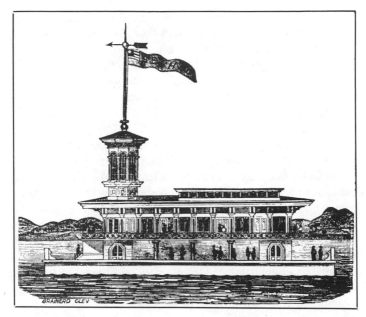

The Floating Church of the Western Seamen's Friend
Society, stationed on the Ohio River off Cincinnati in
the mid-1850's. Note the "different" kind of Bethel Flag.
(From the Society's *Annual Report,* 1856.)

INLAND WATERS AND THE
AMERICAN BETHEL SOCIETY

In the early nineteenth century America, the pioneer could go West
one of two ways, by wagon or by water. Roads were few and poor. Wherever
available, waterways were the obvious answer. The 1820's saw the beginning
of the great steamboat days on the Mississippi, Missouri and Ohio rivers.
They also saw the commencement of "the craze for canals," spurred by the
spectacular success of the Eric Canal, opened in 1825, between Albany and
Buffalo. (Although it was in 1825, too, that John Stevens built his experimental steam locomotive in Hoboken, New Jersey, canals continued to
dominate the scene until the big break-through of the American railroad in
the 1850's.)[270]

As originally conceived, the American Seamen's Friend Society
was to embrace not only salt-water seafarers, but also the men employed on
the navigable rivers, lakes and canals of the "Western Waters." Like foreign-
port ministry, the task of reaching the "friendless wanderers" of the inland
waterways seemed natural for a national organization. Here was a segment

of society believed to number more than 100,000, who had hitherto been almost totally ignored. Moreover, time was short. At issue was whether these rapidly expanding "natural and artificial channels of inland commerce" were to become a moral blight or blessing. Would they let loose a "flood of iniquity" over the vast virgin territory of the interior, or would they become highways of healing and health? In taking up this challenge, the ASFS was able to capitalize on the urgent concern within the "Benevolence Empire" for the evangelization of the West.[271]

In 1824, even before the official opening of the Erie Canal, a Bethel Society was founded at Albany. Though this attempt proved premature, a permanent Bethel station did eventually emerge (1843). Then, in the spring of 1830, a Lieutenant Page of the U.S. Navy set forth, in the spirit of his British counterparts, on a voluntary one-man expedition along the Ohio River, seeking to stimulate interest in the cause. That same summer, the ASFS dispatched their first missionary to this wide-open field, the Rev. Gordon Winslow. Like his predecessor Page, Winslow was able to stir sufficient interest to begin Bethel Unions here and there, in this case along the Erie Canal and the shores of Lakes Ontario and Erie. (At Oswego, on "a beautiful autumnal Sabbath morn," he held a Bethel service on board the schooner *Winnebago*, believed to have been the first time the Bethel Flag was unfurled on the waters of the Great Lakes.) However, these societies were largely local in character. Some survived, and struggled on. Others succumbed.[272]

By the mid-thirties, it was realized that such sporadic support as the distant, New York-based ASFS was able to give would not suffice. As with "Ocean Sailors," so too, ministry among these "Inland Sailors" called for "concert of action." Finally, their more zealous friends, meeting at Buffalo, on June 10, 1836, founded the "American Bethel Society," to superintend, aid and extend nationwide "Bethel operations upon the inland waters," and constitute a kind of "bond of union" between them. This society, henceforth based in Buffalo, voted in 1846 to become a branch of the ASFS.[273]

With the continuing westward movement of population, the "Western Seamen's Friend Society," prematurely born in Cleveland in 1830 (through Winslow's instrumentality) and resuscitated as a branch of the American Bethel Society in 1847, eventually outgrew her "parent." By the eve of the Civil War, this virile society had eighteen chaplains and missionaries in its employ, at stations serving some 200,000 men, from Pittsburg in Western Pennsylvania to the upper and lower reaches of the Mississippi.[274] Lakes Michigan and Superior, a quarter century earlier "almost unknown," were by now both navigated by "thousands of vessels"; and the rapidly growing port of Chicago, with a "Marine Temperance Society" dating from 1842, and a "Seamen's Bethel Church" from 1844, had become one of the Society's "most important fields of labor."[275]

The Gospel Ship *Glad Tidings* of Chicago, a sailing
sanctuary on the Great Lakes upon which God, in the
words of her missionary captain, "let down his blessings
from truck to deadeye." (From the *Annual Report* of
the Western Seamen's Friend Society for 1887.)

Despite much initial discouragement among men deemed destitute
of the "noble and generous characteristics" which distinguished the salt-
water sailor, slow but steady progress was reported over the years. Contributions were also made toward social betterment, by such means as boatmen's
libraries, as well as Sabbath and Free Schools for boatmen's children (many
of whom also had to be clothed and fed). Nor were boatmen's friends afraid
to speak a word in season against oppressive work conditions, publishing
abroad that "the very *mules* on a Kentucky corn plantation" were treated
with "better accommodations and more consideration than many of these
men."[276]

HOME PORTS AND NEW DENOMINATIONAL SOCIETIES

Whereas foreign-port chaplaincy and inland waterway ministry
were, in the post-1828 period, essentially new areas of outreach on the
American scene, sources also show how American domestic-port ministry
already well-estalished, now entered into an era of renewed expansion and
diversification. Such diversification was also destined to develop along
denominational lines. First, however, it seems natural to trace the continuing
evolution of *nondenominational* seamen's work.

The American Seamen's Friend Society had, from the outset, seen itself in a basically *coordinative* capacity. To what extent did that Society, in actual fact, contribute during the coming decades to increased growth on the domestic scene? In 1829, The ASFS published its disappointment over the frustration of its hopes for a nation-wide "bond of union." None of the existing "local institutions" (save one) had "seen fit to give an official proof of confidence and respect by the form of declaring themselves auxiliary."[277] The solitary exception was the Boston Seamen's Friend Society, which retained a "branch" status until 1888. On January 1, 1830, that Society succeeded in opening a commodious Mariners' Church in Purchase Street, Fort Hill, the first in a series of facilities leading up to the present.[278]

With time, however, the American Seamen's Friend Society significantly increased its influence in the domestic sector. With the New York Port Society, although it never formally became auxiliary to the ASFS, close ties were developed both financially and in practical outreach.[279] Meanwhile, the Roosevelt Street Mariners' Church became a veritable beacon-light of sustained evangelistic endeavor, during the 27-year tenure of its Methodist pastor, Henry Chase (who took over from Truair in 1826 and continued unremittingly until he died at his post in 1853).[280]

In 1855, during the pastorate of Chase's Presbyterian successor, Charles J. Jones, 1854-63, the Mariners' Church was removed to a more desirable location at the corner of Madison and Catherine Streets.[281] Here, under the powerful ministry of this British-born, Princeton-educated veteran seafarer, the revival which erupted in New York in the wake of the 1857 financial crisis found a remarkable maritime counterpart.[282] Among hosts of awakened seafarers of different nationalities were noticeably many Scandinavians, constantly counseled and encouraged by Jones' Norwegian-born Methodist coadjutor, Ole Helland.[283] The revival also radically affected the United States Navy on the eve of the Civil War.[284]

An even closer relationship developed in New Orleans, with the National Society virtually playing the part of a lifesaver. The ASFS, recognizing the Crescent City as "the most important place in the United States, after New York" for ministry to seafarers, sensed a special responsibility here, From 1830 on, the Society sponsored a series of chaplains on the New Orleans waterfront. After the government-ordered demolition of the uncompleted Mariners' Church (1835), a less pretentious "Seamen's Bethel" was opened in January 1837, and a "New Orleans Seamen's Friend Society" was organized, auxiliary to the ASFS. With the help of the parent society the work continued, despite severe setbacks right up into the present century.[285]

At neighboring Mobile, Alabama's major cotton-exporting port-city, it was the ASFS who, in 1835, took the initiative to appoint a chaplain and, there too, form an auxiliary society—originally the "Mobile Port Society," later changed to the "Mobile Bethel Society." Besides establishing a "Bethel

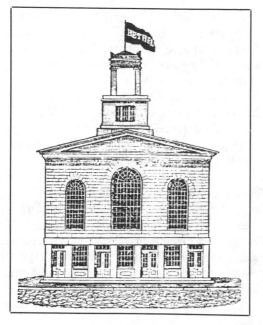

Boston Mariners' Church, opened on Jan. 1, 1830, by the Boston Seaman's Friend Society, and located in Purchase Street, Fort Hill, fronting the harbor. (*The Sailor's Magazine,* New York, August 1830.)

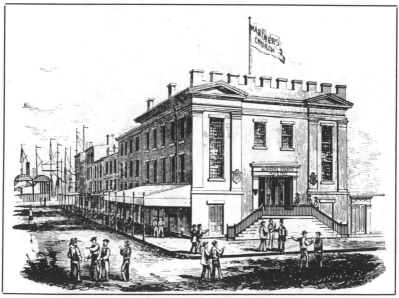

The New York Mariners' Church of the nondenominational New York Port Society, in the new, improved location it occupied from 1855 at 46 Catherine Street, at the corner of Madison. (From the Society's *Annual Statements,* 1855.)

Church" ashore, the Society also opened, with the help of the ASFS, a "Floating Bethel and Hospital" in a wrecked British sailing ship, anchored in the busy Bay area (1853). Here, a unique series of chaplain-physicians sought—by Scripture and scalpel—to "save both the souls and the bodies of the sailors." This model of "holistic" ministry was continued with evident success until the vessel sank in a storm in September 1860, after which contact with the South was cut off by the outbreak of the Civil War.[286]

Reverting to the East Coast, the work in Portland, Maine, was given a fresh impetus in 1849, with the formation of another ASFS auxiliary, the "Maine Seamen's Union." This Society succeeded in opening a new "Seamen's Bethel" the following year, to replace the resplendent former edifice, which had to be forfeited for lack of funds.[287]

The year 1849 also marked the onrush of gold-hungry "forty-niners," and the start of significant settlement along the coastlands of the Pacific. The American Seamen's Friend Society was well aware of the region's reputation for being enveloped, spiritually and morally, in "more than Egyptian darkness"; and as early as May 1849, they were able to report that a corrsepondence had already been opened with "missionaries" in San Francisco, with a view to securing a Gospel ministry for the seafarers suddenly arriving there in their thousands.

As the vessels freighting the forty-niners to San Francisco
dropped anchor in the Bay, they were frequently
abandoned by crews and captains alike, leaving at one
time 500 ships rotting in the mud. Some, however, would
be reincarnated as hotels, restaurants, warehouses, a jail,
an asylum and (as in 1851) a Seamen's Bethel Church.
(Courtesy: San Francisco Maritime Museum.)

Hoisting a "shanghaied" (doped or drunk) seaman on
board, a widely accepted method of overcoming crew
shortage, not least on the west coast of the USA.
(*The Lookout,* January–February 1980.)

Whether as a result of that particular initiative or not, the Methodists
were, true to tradition, quick to respond to new needs. The first full-time
seamen's chaplain on San Francisco's notorious waterfront was one William
Taylor, appointed in 1849 by the local Methodist Conference. By 1851, he
had fitted up the *Panama*, one of the many hundreds of ships abandoned in
the Bay, as a "Seamen's Bethel Church." This reportedly "flourished." This
other "Father Taylor" was a genuine brother-in-arms of his namesake in
Boston, and holds the honor of having opened up the long and bitter local war
against "shanghaiing" (as he called the Crimping System on the Barbary
Coast).

In 1855, "Frisco's Father Taylor" was succeeded by George E.
Davis, a ship's mate, who "came to get gold, but found a Savior," became a
Baptist minister, and built a Bethel on the piles of a Clark Street water-lot.
Davis was in turn succeeded by the Rev. Joseph Rowell (1820-1918), who
arrived in July 1858. Sent out under the sponsorship of the ASFS, Rowell
also received the support of a "San Francisco Port Society" (from 1859),
and saw the consecration of a new, much-improved Mariners' Church (in
1867). He remained at his post in San Francisco's Sailortown for more than
half a century, loved and revered by seafarers everywhere as the great
"Pioneer Apostle of the Pacific Coast."[288]

Meanwhile, in the vast virgin territory north of San Francisco, specifically the ports of the Columbia River and the Puget Sound, Bethel services appear to have been initiated by an unnamed sailor who, having "swallowed the anchor," had settled in Oregon City and sent a sum of money to Father Damon, in Honolulu, in order to secure from him a genuine Bethel Flag. As the lone pioneer put it, if no one else was willing to preach the Gospel of Jesus Christ under the emblem, he was. However, there is no record of really ongoing services to seafarers in the Pacific Northwest prior to the epic ministry of Chaplain Robert Sherwood Stubbs (1823-1925).

Stubbs, also a former seafarer of British background and Methodist affiliation, was, in 1877, commissioned by the American Seamen's Friend Society as their chaplain to the ports of the Columbia River and Puget Sound. How this man founded a "Portland Seamen's Friend Society" (in 1877), pioneered the work in Seattle and Tacoma (in 1878), and devoted the rest of his long life to serving the seafarer and battling the crimp in those parts, goes far beyond the scope of this study. (However, the fact that San Francisco and Oregon City were, at mid-century, both listed by the ASFS under "Foreign Operations," is a vivid reminder of the remoteness of West Coast activities to East Coast Americans of those days, and reveals a reason for their relatively late start.)[289]

While existing auxiliary societies were primarily committed to maintaining a Gospel ministry in their own respective port areas, the mounting annual deficits of the parent society gave dramatic evidence of the need for a network of auxiliaries principally concerned with fund-raising. Small wonder that the ASFS was "happy" to report, in May 1834, a sharp increase in the number of such societies. The list now counted no less than 42. Many of these were so-called "Female Auxiliaries," which would, when located in a port city, also assume responsibility for alternative seamen's lodgings, perhaps even a full-scale sailors' home.[290]

A significant area of expansion during the period under review was, in America as in Britain, that of maritime literary media distribution. In Scripture work, the American Bible Society continued playing a dominant role, making substantial grants to the ASFS, individual seamen's and boatmen's societies, naval ships and establishments, often through their own local auxiliaries in coastal districts.

As for other forms of Christian literature, the American Tract Society, founded in 1825 (eight years after the BSRMIS had sent out their last seamen's tract), gave high priority and publicity to "marine distribution." Merging much of the local work already in existence, the Society assumed in this field a role very similar to that of the new national Bible society in Scripture circulation.

The Rev. Robert Sherwood Stubbs, (1823-1925), a British-born former seafarer of Methodist affiliation, who became the indefatigable pioneer of seamen's missions in the Pacific Northwest. (G.S. Webster, *The Seamen's Friend.*)

The Port of Seattle, the Pacific Northwest's "Emerald City," located on scenic Puget Sound. This lithograph by C.L. Smith, with stately Mt. Rainier in the distance, gives an overview from 1884, 33 years after the first settlers had arrived. (J.R. Warren, *King County and its Queen City: Seattle.*)

In 1830, the ASFS followed up on James Milnor's successful *Seamen's Devotional Assistant* (1822) with a *Seamen's Devotional Assistant, and Mariners' Hymns,* compiled by Joshua Leavitt. This was, over the years, succeeded by a series of similar devotional aids (of native American origin—in contrast to many of the "tracts").[291]

In a category for itself came the American Seamen's Friend Society's periodical, *The Sailor's Magazine* (New York). Under its early editors, the magazine soon came to be recognized as an indispensable medium of communication, "assisting, encouraging, and continuing" the efforts of otherwise isolated bodies of fellow-workers. A frequent topic of discussion in the columns of the magazine during its early years was the question of a "Seamen's Communion" or a "Christian Church" organized specifically for seamen. (In fact, the issue had already been agitated in 1825, in the columns of *The Mariners' Magazine.*)[292]

Why should Christian seamen be left spiritually "homeless," bereft of both the sacrament of holy communion, and that "bond of brotherly love" which could by acquired by belonging to a church made up of seafaring fellow-believers? The "little jealousies of the sectary" must be prevented from "parceling out and labeling converted seamen. . . ." Some suggested organizing an international Christian fellowship of seafarers. However, the situation was evidently not ripe for a structure of world-wide dimensions. Instead, there emerged a form of *localized* communion, based on individual mariners' churches. Admission would generally be open to seafarers and residents who (1) gave "satisfactory evidence of a change of heart," and (2) agreed to a confession of faith and form of covenant of broadly evangelical and nonsectarian content. Boston began—in 1830. Afterwards, a parallel pattern of church organization was adopted by mariners' churches elsewhere, for example in Philadelphia (later in 1830), Baltimore (1837) and Portland, Maine (1840). Abroad, the same model was followed, for example in Le Havre (1832) and Honolulu (1837).[293]

Although the Mariners' Church in New York followed suit in 1856, and then San Francisco in 1858, powerful denominational winds of change had by then already swept across the nation. During the latter part of the Jacksonian administration (1829-37), it became apparent that America's first-generation "era of nationalism" was yielding to a second-generation "era of sectionalism." As on the political scene, so also on the religious, there appeared evidence of mounting denominationalism, accompanied by corresponding signs of disintegration of the Evangelical United Front.

Among contributing factors were, on the one hand, the prevailing mood of romanticism in western culture with its emphasis on history and tradition; this led in America, as in Europe, to renewed interest in the nature of the church and the credal heritage of its denominations. On the other

The original Methodist Bethel Ship *John Wesley* (ex *Henry Leeds*), a rebuilt brig moored at Pier 11 on Manhattan's North River side, which served as a Gospel-centered haven of hospitality and help for countless Nordic seafarers and immigrants entering New York in 1844-57.
(V. Witting: *Minnen fraan mitt lif.*)

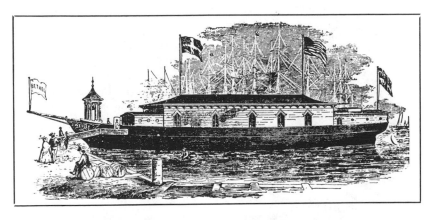

The Bethel Ship *John Wesley II* (ex *Carrier Pigeon*), a reconstructed bark which succeeded the original Bethel Ship 1857-79, from 1876 at the foot of Harrison Street, Brooklyn. (V. Witting: *Minnen fraan mitt lif.*)

hand, the reformism of the age became more and more absorbed with that "peculiar institution" of the South (slavery), creating a cleavage in the three major Protestant churches long before the political rupture of 1861. One result was an added concern for denominational mission, as new church divisions vied with each other in both zeal and efficacy.[294]

Beginning with the largest of America's three major Protestant churches of that time, the Methodist Episcopal Church had already suffered secession in 1843, when the perfectionistic "Wesleyan Methodist Church of America" was formed (in opposition to episcopacy as well as slavery). Then, in 1844, came the decisive disruption of the major body. The same year, on the 31st of October, the northern division opened a "Mariners' Methodist Episcopal Church" in the port of New York. Located on Cherry Street between Clinton and Montgomery, it soon found itself outstripped by the *original* Mariners' Church on the same side of Manhattan.[295]

An almost simultaneous undertaking, in this case on the Hudson shoreline, met with a more favorable fate. It began with the Wesleyan Methodists, who, on November 21, 1844, inaugurated a battered old brig (formerly the *Henry Leeds*) as a floating chapel at Pier 11, North River, the first seamen's sanctuary ever established on Manhattan's west side. Despite evident initial success, the Wesleyans willingly transferred their Bethel Ship *John Wesley* (as they named it) to the "Asbury Society" of the Methodist Episcopalians, who were at that time anxious to commence an outreach to Scandinavian crews now arriving in that part of the port in increasing numbers. Thus began the famous "Scandinavian Bethelship Mission," with

The Rev. Olof Gustaf Hedstrom (1803-77), Swedish-born pioneer of the Methodists' "Scandinavian Bethelship Mission." C.F. Eltzholtz: *Livsbilleder.*)

The Rev. Ole Peter
Petersen (1822-1901),
Hedstrom's Norwegian-
born associate in the
Scandinavian Bethelship
Mission, and founding
father of the Methodist
Church in Norway, 1856.
(A. Hardy: *O.P. Petersen*).

a Swedish-born circuit-rider at the helm, the Rev. Olof Gustaf Hedström, or Hedstrom (1803-77).[296]

Contemporary sources show Hedstrom's opening service to have been held on Sunday, June 8, 1845 (not May 25, 1845, as historians have hitherto assumed).[297] Assisted in part by two former seafarers, fellow-countryman Peter Bergner as colporteur, and Norwegian-born Ole Peter Petersen as his "mate" on the Bethel Ship, Hedstrom continued at the helm for most of three hectic decades.

To the pioneers of the project, it was a clear case of providence, that such a strategically situated mission should be established so briefly before immigration from Scandinavia began on a new and massive scale. As they poured into New York, with all that city's host of waterfront swindlers and sharpers, many a dazed and destitute immigrant family found in the Bethel Ship a welcome haven of hospitality and ethnic identity, securely moored in the midst of a very alien environment. As the need arose, their ever-friendly factotum would fulfill the functions of employment agency, post office, interpreter, missing persons bureau and travel agency.

Meanwhile, Scandinavian seafarers were converted on board the Bethel Ship by the hundreds.[298] In fact, nowhere could be found more striking vindicaton of the oft-repeated contention that seamen committed to Christ would make the world's most effective missionaries. Many followed the immigrants west and helped found Scandinavian-American Methodism. Others—by a process of re-migration—brought their new faith back to their fatherlands, and became directly instrumental in introducing Methodism to the Nordic nations.[299]

An indication of the superlative success of this first "Nordic Seamen's Mission" in history was the reaction of those who regarded it as rivalry. Sources show how the mounting "defections" of nominally Lutheran seamen and immigrants into the ranks of the Methodists provided Scandinavian Lutheran leaders with sufficiently powerful ecclesiological motivation to found Scandinavian-language churches in New York for both immigrants and seafarers.[300]

Reverting to the mid-1840's, in Philadelphia, a "Methodist Episcopal Mariners' Bethel" was dedicated on November 13, 1845. Erected close to the waterfront at Penn and Shippen (later Bainbridge) Streets, the building became a base for Methodist maritime mission on the Deleware for years to come. (The origin of the work, however, goes back to a preaching visit by far-famed "Father Taylor" of Boston in the summer of 1831, which inspired a group of young men to hire a sail-loft and launch a Methodist ministry to seafarers on the local waterfront.)[301]

In 1846, Baltimore Methodists, who had started a Sailor's City Bethel Society five years earlier, had an old hulk lying in the harbor, the *William Penn*, converted into a "Church Ship," moored her along the pier at Light and Lee Streets, and ordained her former captain (Samuel Kraemer) as minister. As on board her Methodist sister-ship in New York, hundreds of sailors (many of them foreigners) were converted, and "a great number" went on to become zealous ministers of the Gospel. When the vessel was condemned in 1852, the work was continued from a succession of shore Bethels.[302]

"Baggage smashers," separating a newcomer from his belongings. Only one of the many hazards facing mid-19th century immigrants entering New York.
(*Yankee Notions,* New York, 1853.)

The Rev. Edward Thompson Taylor (1793-1871), Boston's
legendary "Father Taylor," as sailor preacher rivaled only
by Britain's "Bosun Smith." He was revered and beloved
everywhere by weather-beaten sailors and the literary elite.
(Engraving by T. Johnson, courtesy of Boston Port Society.)

From New Orleans, too, came reports in 1846 of a "Methodist
Bethel." This was for several years located at the Levee Buildings in the
Third Municipality, with a Mr. Trippet as chaplain.[303]

Among Methodist ministers to seamen, however, none could ever
emulate "Father Taylor" of Boston. In November 1828 (not in 1829, as
often assumed), "a company of members of the Methodist-Episcopal Church"
formed themselves into a "Port Society of the City of Boston and its
Vicinity," ("for the moral and religious instruction of seamen"). According
to a contemporary report published in *The Palladium,* it was their intention
"to employ the Rev. Edward T. Taylor, formerly a mariner, to officiate as
their minister."[304]

To many who knew him (and they already numbered thousands) the appointment appeared divinely ordained. Edward Thompson Taylor (1793-1871) believed he was born in Richmond, Virginia, and that he was only three when he became an orphan.[305] At all events, at seven he ran off to sea, without taking farewell with either fostermother or friends. Ten years later, as a bronzed and weather-beaten young "tar" complete with sailor-jacket and tarpaulin-hat, he happened to be on shore leave in Boston. While drifting down Bromfield Street, he recalls how he heard an evening revival meeting in progress at the local Methodist church. His curiosity aroused, he decided to go in—not, however, like ordinary mortals, by the door.

> I crept in through the porthole and stowed myself away upon the gundeck, when a broadside from the pulpit stove me to pieces, and, in a sinking condition, I hauled down my colors and cried for quarter. . . .[306]

Such, in his own words, was the conversion of the man destined to become one of the greatest sailor-preachers of all time. This was in the autumn of 1811. Presumably during the same stay, the young mariner also experienced his call to *the ministry*—this time conveyed in a Congregational context. Again, only his narrative can do justice to the event:

> I was walking along Tremont Street, and the bell of Park-street Church was tolling. I put in . . . made for the gallery . . . and came to anchor. . . . I tell you, the old ship Gospel never sailed more prosperously. The salt-spray flew in every direction; but more especially did it run down my cheeks. I was melted. Every one in the house wept. Satan had to strike sail; his guns were dismounted. . . . I said, "Why can't I preach so? I'll try it."

He did try—before an utterly unforeseen auditory. As crew member of a Boston privateer (the *Curlew,* according to recent research), he was captured in July 1812, and imprisoned in the British fortress of Melville Island, near Halifax, Nova Scotia.[307] Here his shipmates and fellow-prisoners petitioned to have Taylor take the place of an unappreciated (British) chaplain. Though at this time totally illiterate, the twenty-year-old sailor-preacher swept all before him with his ardor and vivid nautical imagery.

Back in Boston after an exchange of prisoners, he won a Methodist lay-preacher's license in the late spring of 1814. With this, he preached and peddled through the villages of Vermont and Massachusetts with such success that, despite his almost complete lack of formal education, he was at length ordained into the ministry (1821). Serving circuits along the Massachusetts and Rhode Island coast, he prepared the ground for the "Whalemen's Bethel" at New Bedford (1822-24), and pioneered shipboard preaching on departing whaleships at Martha's Vineyard (1824-25). Every-

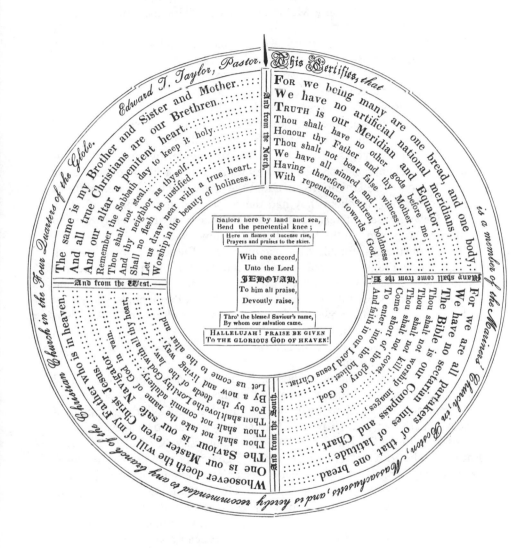

Father Taylor's novel Mariners' Church membership certificate, constructed like a catechetical compass. (David L. Holmes: *The Early Career of Father Taylor.*)

where, seamen and seamen's families flocked to his pulpit. Small wonder that the Boston Port Society Methodists made Taylor their first choice in November 1828.

They also obtained the use of the old Methodist (later Hanover) Alley Chapel as a Bethel. However, this "cradle of Boston Methodism" became too confined for the crowds coming to hear the gifted young sailor-preacher. The same could be said of the Society's support-base. However, it was never envisaged as an exclusively Methodist institution. On the contrary, though the founders were predominantly Methodist, they expressly disavowed the slightest sectarian interest. As the Society's flagging finances during its first two or three years brought it close to foundering, its basic, non-denominational character opened the way for the city's well-to-do merchants, many of whom were Unitarians, to adopt the cause and build a Bethel fit for a Father Taylor (for whom they had the most unstinted admiration). In a sense, they represent a resurfacing of the concern of those early Boston Unitarians who came to the aid of Tuckerman in 1812.

Nonetheless, for his own personal part, Father Taylor remained, throughout his life, a firm, free-spoken member of the Methodist Episcopal Church (which he considered "not a whit behind any, for moral worth and Christian purity"). He told his Unitarian friends that they "might as well try to heat a furnace with snowballs," as seek to save sailors' souls with their "skimmed-milk sermons." But he loved them, and as he moved into his spacious new Seamen's Bethel in 1833, no one knew better than he to whom the credit was mainly due.[308]

The site was carefully chosen. As Father Taylor himself put it: "I set my Bethel in North Square, because I learned to set my net where the fish ran." But no building alone could account for Father Taylor's phenomenal success. As one admirer (Edward Everett) aptly expressed it, he was himself a "walking Bethel." Graduated from the "university of wind and wave," Father Taylor took orders from no man. "I go on my own hook," he would say with wry humor. His pulpit rhetoric was always extemporaneous, replete with both briny wit and evangelical pathos. He could turn tears to laughter at will, or bring his whole congregation leaping to their feet in sheer suspense.[309] The unlettered sailor-preacher quickly became a living landmark in nineteenth-century Boston. Charles Dickens, Hariett Martineau and Jenny Lind were among the many foreign celebrities who sat under his pulpit. Emerson, Channing, Webster, Whitman and Longfellow were among his American admirers.[310]

Nevertheless, Father Taylor was at pains to prove that none could usurp the seafarer's first claim on his love and labor. Others came, but were admitted only on sufferance. As the captain of the Bethel, short, stocky, with spectacles pushed up high on his forehead, paced his "quarter-deck" before

Father Taylor's famous
Seamen's Bethel in
Boston's North Square,
erected in 1833 by the
Boston Port and Seamen's
Aid Society. (G. Haven
and T. Russell:
Father Taylor.)

beginning a service, he would watch with eagle eye that no sailor was left to stand while landsmen sat. Nor did he aim at anything less for his "sailor boys" (as he called them) than a genuine, Methodist-style conversion. This they knew—and counted on.

The story is told of two Bethel-bound seamen one Sunday morning, who had lost their bearings in the winding streets of Boston's North End. Seeing the Bethel Flag aloft, one of them who could read a little spelled out slowly for the benefit of his shipmates: "B-E-T, beat. H-E-L, Hell. This is where the old man beats hell. That's the place we want."

Just as Father Taylor could be full of compassion for both drunkard and prostitute, he was merciless toward their seducers. He would pray publicly that both "Bacchus and Venus might be driven to the ends of the earth—and off it." In order to combat the crimp, he started, in May 1837, a sailor boarding-house at 226 Ann Street, for a while unaided by others. (This was to become a forerunner of the present "Mariners' House," completed in 1847.)[311] By promoting a Bethel Temperance Society, and by whatever means he found, Father Taylor remained to the end of his days a sworn enemy of those he regarded as "rum-murderers."[312]

For forty years, the Captain continued in command of his Bethel, insisting he would never abandon ship so long as there was one single "shot in the locker." At his side strove his loyal helpmeet, Debora Millet of Marblehead, a woman whom he openly worshiped and whom the sailors loved. When "Mother Taylor," as they dubbed her, died; her husband, whose health had long been undermined, followed less than two years later, on April 6, 1871. His seafaring flock was quick to note he left on the ebb tide—as a sailor should.[313]

Among the many testimonials of Father Taylor's standing among seamen, is that of Richard Henry Dana. In his *Two Years Before the Mast,* he records how, on arrival in far-off San Diego Bay in 1835, he was visiting with seamen long separated from home; their very first inquiry was for Father Taylor.[314] One sailor said he had been to places where they had never heard of the United States, but never where Father Taylor was unknown.[315] As with Boatswain Smith of Penzance, Father Taylor of Boston was seen by seamen as one of their own.

Both of these celebrated sailor-preachers were rough diamonds. But in some respects, they presented striking contrasts. While Smith was a prolific writer, Taylor—like his Master—wrote nothing. While Smith was not only an outstanding orator, but a man of vast vision and organizing talent, Taylor threw all his energies into his unique facility for piercing the heart of the seafarer with the preached Word of God. While Smith's belligerence antagonized so many, Taylor's tolerance and overflowing sympathies endeared him to the refined intellingencia and forecastle roughnecks alike. In short, Taylor may have been no pioneer, either in time or in type of ministry.

New Bedford's far famed
Seamen's Bethel, built
and opened in 1832 by
that historic whaling
city's Port Society.
Immortalized by Herman
Melville's *Moby Dick,*
the chapel still stands on
Johnny Cake Hill.
(Courtesy: New Bedford
Port Society.)

"Mother Taylor,"
formerly Debora Millett
of Marblehead. Father
Taylor's faithful partner
in life and ministry,
whom he openly
worshiped and sailors the
world over loved.
(G. Haven and T. Russell:
Father Taylor.)

But in the magnetic power of his personality and pulpit rhetoric, Boston's Father Taylor remains unsurpassed in the annals of maritime mission.

Another, if somewhat less conspicuous case of a new, nondenominational mariner's church served by a Methodist minister, was that of New Bedford, Massachusetts. Here, in 1830, a "New Bedford Port Society for the Moral Improvement of Seamen" was founded. In 1832, the Society was able to open its new "Seamen's Bethel" on Johnny Cake Hill. The church still stands, long since immortalized by Herman Melville's epic whaling novel, *Moby Dick*. It was faithfully served for its first twelve years (1832-44) by Father Taylor's close friend and co-religionist, the Rev. Enoch Mudge. Though the salty speech and dramatic air of Melville's "Father Mapple" point to Taylor as his prototype rather than the milder Mudge, there is ample evidence that the latter's less ostentatious ministry bore rich fruit.[316]

By the 1830's, that other dynamic denomination of the American Frontier, the Baptists, was close to the Methodists in numerical strength. They might well differ sharply in polity and doctrine, but their history of internal cleavage and denominational assertiveness developed along very similar lines.[317]

In seamen's ministry, the Baptists began their first independent endeavor at precisely the same time and place as the Methodists—in Philadelphia in the year 1831. It was on the 6th of June in that year, that a few Baptist landsmen covenanted themselves together to constitute the "First Mariner's Baptist Church of Philadelphia." Hiring a hall in North Water Street that same summer, the church secured the services of the Rev.

Thomas Porter as its first pastor, eventually obtaining a more permanent "Baptist Bethel" on Front Street, below Christian Street.[318]

In New York, a decade later, Baptist friends of seamen succeeded in initiating a work which was, in many respects, to become a remarkable counterpart to the Scandinavian Bethelship Mission. It was the "New York Domestic Missionary Society" who conceived the original idea of a Baptist outreach to seafarers in New York, hiring a hall in 1841 as a "Baptist Seamen's Bethel," at the corner of Catherine and Cherry Streets. For the continuation of the work however, major credit was clearly due to their "sisters of the Baptist Churches" in the city. Forming themselves that same year into a "New York Baptist Female Bethel Union," they continued tenaciously for 25 years to "aid in the support of the gospel among seamen."

As a result, the "First Baptist Mariners' Church" was successfully organized on December 4, 1843. The Rev. Ira R. Steward, of Mystic, Connecticut was called as its first pastor. Described as a man of "sterling qualifications," he served the seafarer tirelessly for twenty years, until at length his health broke down. But he lived to see a long succession of maritime candidates for baptism "put on Christ" and sally forth, as fervent missionaries to fellow-seafarers and frontier settlers alike. In the same spirit as those eager emissaries from the Methodist Bethel Ship, men like Fredrick L. Rymker (also known as "Hendrickson"), Gustavus W. Schroeder and Fredrick O. Nilsson, sailed back to their native lands, and made the First Baptist Mariners' Church of New York "mother church" of the Baptist churches of Scandinavia. Finally, Steward succeeded in securing a more satisfactory site for his sanctuary, taking over in 1863 the former Oliver Street Baptist Church at the corner of Oliver and Henry Streets (still known as the "Mariners' Temple").[319]

In Boston, Baptist waterfront work began with the pioneer ministry of Charles W. Denison. On June 16, 1843, he held his first Bethel Meeting in a hired hall on the corner of Commercial and Lewis Streets. In August of that year, Denison was instrumental in establishing a "Boston Bethel Union," and shortly afterwards a "Female Bethel Union." He also organized a "Boston Marine Total Abstinence Society," through which "thousands of seamen" were induced to sign pledges.

On Denison's departure, the work was, in June 1845, reorganized as a "Boston Baptist Bethel Society" with the help of local Baptist churches. A highly-regarded young Baptist minister in New Haven, Connecticut, the Rev. Phineas Stowe, was then called to lead the work. Like his British fellow-Baptist, G.C. Smith, whom he deeply admired, Stowe possessed a fertile imagination for new projects for the benefit of both seafarers and the under-privileged at large. A rehabilitation center for young offenders (the "Quincy Home"), a soldier's home, a seamen's recreation center (or

"Maritime Exchange"), and a sailors' burial ground (at Woodlawn) all originated with Phineas Stowe. In 1864, he acquired the former Universalist Church in Hanover Street as a sorely-needed, new Baptist Bethel Church. From here, he continued his ministry with unabated enthusiasm, until his mind gave way under the strain, and he died in 1868.[320]

Turning to the third largest body of churches at the time, no denomination was destined to supply a more impressive succession of individual seamen's mission pioneers than the Presbyterians. Names such as Stafford, Eastburn, Truair, Diell, Sawtell and Jones have become inseparable from the early history of the movement. However, not until after the half-century mark was the denomination officially indentified with any particular station.

In Philadelphia, the Presbyterians had, from the outset, provided both support and supply for their local Mariners' Church. Despite the danger of disarray after the disappearance of Father Eastburn from the scene he dominated so completely, fellow-Presbyterians—though without his charisma —did follow in his spirit. Eventually, as similar institutions entered the field under denominational pennants, their precursor elected, in 1854, to align itself officially with the Presbyterians. Finally, in 1859, it merged into what is now "Third, Scots' and Mariners' Presbyterian (or 'Old Pine Street') Church."[321]

Not before the Civil War was an independent Presbyterian ministry undertaken in New York. However, in the autumn of 1864 a group of concerned Presbyterians commenced worship services at the Sailor's Home in Cherry Street, then hired and fitted up their own hall, at 52 Market Street (home of the late Rev. Henry Chase). On December 29, 1864, they organized the "Church of the Sea and Land" (numbering 32, mostly "Presbyterian families and seamen recently converted to God"). Among the estimated over 100,000 seamen annually calling at New York, many were known to be Scotch or Scotch-Irish, who would "prefer the church of their fathers." Largely through the munificence of one shipping merchant (Hanson K. Corning), the church was, in 1866, able to take over the old Dutch Reformed Church at the corner of Market and Henry Streets. Here it was to flourish under the twenty-year pastorate of Dr. Edward Hopper (author of the well-known hymn "Jesus, Savior, Pilot Me"). Here the Church of the Sea and Land still stands, like the Baptists' Mariners' Temple nearby, preserved as an official New York City landmark.[322]

Although the record of systematic *Lutheran* movement in mission to seafarers falls beyond the limits of this study, it is noteworthy that the Bethel Hall at 52 Market Street, vacated by the Presbyterians in 1866, was taken over that same year as the original sanctuary of a "Norwegian Evangelical Lutheran Congregation in New York," whose ministry to immigrants and

Dr. Edward Hopper (1816-88), who for two decades
pioneered the seamen's ministry of the Presbyterian Church
of the Sea and Land in New York, founded in 1864 and
(since 1866) still located at the corner of Market and Henry
Streets. Dr. Hopper is the author of the internationally-
known nautical hymn, "Jesus, Savior, Pilot Me."
(F. Brückbauer: *The Kirk On Rutgers Farm.*)

seafarers from Norway was to become the forerunner of the present
"Norwegian Seamen's Church" in New York.[323]

In Boston, the involvement of the *Congregationalists* (as a denomination) followed much the same pattern as that of the Presbyterians in
Philadelphia. The Boston Seaman's Friend Society, as also the pioneering
work of its precursor, Dr. William Jenks, was essentially a Congregational
undertaking. Especially was this manifest as maritime missions were later
launched by other denominations. (However, formal denominational recognition was not achieved until 1904).[324]

Between Congregationalists and Presbyterians of the 1820's, the
partnership in mission initiated by their "Plan of Union" of 1801 was still
largely in effect. By this time there had emerged, at several seminaries and
colleges of the two denominations, a form of missionary involvement called
"Societies of Inquiry Respecting Missions." Here information was gathered,
motivation fueled, and plans discussed. In the forefront of this movement,
itself a forerunner of the "Student Volunteer Movement," were the students
of Andover Theological Seminary, spiritual successors of the "Haystack
Meeting" pioneers.[325] In August 1829, some members of that Seminary's

Society of Inquiry felt prompted to form a special "Seaman's Committee" (thereby continuing the tradition of concern for seafarers already shown by those student helpers of Dr. Jenks in the early 1820's).[326]

The *Records* of Andover's Seaman's Committee make fascinating reading. Among early subjects of debate were: "Difficulties to be surmounted in the conversion of Seamen." "Is it practicable for Seamen's Preachers to have the care of Nautical Schools?" "How can ministers of the Gospel in our sea port towns best promote the cause of Seamen without doing injury to their respective congregations?" In February 1831, the committee even appointed a sub-committee "to investigate the causes of the inefficiency of the General Seamen's Society." (Such radical fervor did not prevent that "General" Society from shortly afterwards employing a member of the same sub-committee as its first chaplain in Honolulu.)[327]

Sources indicate that other East Coast seminaries followed suit. Theological students at Yale took an active concern in the waterfront work at New Haven. Also, at Princeton, students not only supplied personnel for promotional activity on behalf of the ASFS during their vacations, but sponsored co-called "floating libraries" for the benefit of seafarers.[328] The availability of such highly motivated candidates for foreign chaplaincy as the ASFS found in the spring of 1832 was, at least in some measure, related to the activity of these Societies of Inquiry and their maritime committees.[329]

The *Episcopalians'* contribution to denominational involvement in American maritime ministry was, in some respects, unique. By 1830, the American branch of the Anglican Communion was well on the road to recovery as the "Protestant Episcopal Church of America." Suddenly orphaned (and suspect) in 1776, "Churchmen" had, by loyal participation in the War of 1812, purged themselves of every vestige of unpatriotism. Meanwhile, the aggressive high-churchmanship of Bishop John H. Hobart of New York, though at variance with the spirit of evangelicalism then predominant among American Episcopalians, had helped lift them to new levels of denominational morale. The watchword was: "Episcopal agencies for Episcopal mission!"[330]

Not surprisingly, it was in New York that the first Episcopal agency for seamen's mission was organized. In 1834, the New York version of *The Sailor's Magazine* could report that the Anglican Bishop of Quebec had just consecrated a "St. Paul's Chapel," erected by subscription in that key Canadian port-city, expressly "for the use of Mariners."[331] That same year, a group of young men of Episcopal affiliation banded together in New York to launch a missionary endeavor from which was eventually to emerge the world's largest church-related facility for seafarers' welfare.

There is no evidence that those young men realized at the time that specifically *seafarers* would ultimately become the beneficiaries of their enterprise. It was a "Young Men's Auxiliary Education and Missionary Society" they formed, on that 6th day of March, 1834. Their avowed aim was to provide means for the education of candidates for the ministry of the Protestant Episcopal Church, and for the support of its missionaries, whether in the wilds of New York State, in the frontier region of the West, or overseas. Although they did, in fact, achieve noteworthy results over the years, sources indicate that a deeply committed nucleus among them was by no means satisfied. In March 1842, in an effort to achieve "greater efficiency," the Society dropped its educational involvement, and reorganized itself as the "Young Men's Church Missionary Society of New York," auxiliary to the (Episcopal) City Mission Society.[332]

It so happened that the City Mission Society had already had the needs of the sailor in mind, but had so far met with no success. Their concern served to sensitize the restructured Young Men's Society, however, who seized the opportunity to focus their efforts henceforth on a neglected yet fascinating field of mission at their very doorstep. At a joint committee meeting of these two societies on November 24, 1842, they succeeded in obtaining a resolution to establish an Episcopal "Seamen's Mission" (as it was called) in the port of New York, employing (preferably) a floating chapel, and a "missionary" nominated and supported by the Young Men.[333]

The year 1842, therefore, marks the effective adoption of maritime mission by an arm of the Protestant Episcopal Church of America. For, committed to the cause as they now were, the Young Men lost no time making the necessary preparations, and seeking out a suitable candidate for the position they had in mind. The man they finally found was already equipped with motivation not unlike that of Britain's John Ashley. Harvard-educated Benjamin Clarke Cutler Parker (1796-1859) had, in the autumn of 1841, been windbound off Martha's Vineyard, on the way from Boston to New York, for the General Convention of his church. Struck with the thought of the "spiritual destitution" that must prevail among the men on board those "nearly fifty sail" gathered there, he arranged for Sunday services in a nearby public house. At the close, many of the 150 who had come "wept like children," and were unwilling to let him leave. There, in a tavern in Tarpaulin Cove, America's first Episcopal "Seamen's Missionary" had heard his Macedonian Call.[334]

Parker was, according to those who knew him best, "not the man to let the grass grow under his feet." Once appointed, he immediately took up his task, on July 3, 1843, and hired on faith "an unattractive room over a grog shop" as a temporary chapel. Located on the East River side at the corner of Pike and South Streets, it was to be opened on July 10, 1843. With this as his base, Parker brought to the waterfront a zeal that personally provoked others to redouble their own efforts. He was preeminently the

The Rev. Benjamin
Clarke Cutler Parker
(1796-1859), from 1843
the zealous pioneer of
the seamen's mission arm
of the Protestant
Episcopal Church of
America. (*The Lookout,*
Oct./Nov. 1982.)

priest, urging the seafarer to request intercession, prepare for confirmation, and receive communion. But he was also the earnest evangelist, seeking out his men wherever they could be found, addressing them "as if they were hearing their last sermon on earth" (as well they might), and following up with offers of both Bibles and Books of Common Prayer.[335]

Meanwhile, the Society signed a contract for the building of the nation's first floating sanctuary. In breaking the American tradition of shore-based Bethels, the Young Men argued the (debatable) advantages of "less original cost in building, less annual expense in . . . maintenance, and far greater attraction." If those American Episcopalians were swayed by British precedent in insisting that the sailor must be allowed to worship "on his own element," they also showed remarkable independence, in introducing a completely novel form of ecclesiastical marine architecture. A pinnacled, Gothic-style church, complete with 70-foot steeple and capable of accommodating 500 "with comfort," was simply planted onto a deck stretched across the divided hull of a former ferry-boat (the *Manhattan*). Moored in the midst of the shipping at the foot of Pike Street on the East River, the "Floating Church of Our Saviour" was duly consecrated on February 20, 1844, by the Bishop of New York. No longer, said the Society, did the seamen need to look at the tall spires of New York's numerous churches and exclaim: "No man cares for my soul!"[336]

Having finally found a focal point for their fervor, the Young Men decided the time had now come to operate independently of any parent society with wider interests. Hence, they reorganized themselves accordingly and, on April 12, 1844, obtained a charter as the "Protestant Episcopal Church Missionary Society for Seamen in the City and Port of New York" (PECMSS) From that year, the Society commenced counting its corporate existence.[337]

How did the Society's innovative form of sanctuary fare? Despite published assurances that worshipers should experience no inconvenience beyond "a little undulation," there were reasons for scepticism. In his diary, Parker could confide that, during high winds, the motion could become so violent, that "many were seasick and went out." At communion, he sometimes found it hard to keep his balance. More than once, ships actually collided with the church, while maneuvering in the river; and in 1853 she actually suffered the indignity of sinking at her moorings (rendered top-heavy under masses of snow).[338]

Nevertheless, both seamen and landsmen converged on that ingenious structure in such numbers that a sister-ship, slightly smaller in size, had to be built for the North River side. Called the "Floating Church of the Holy Comforter," she was towed to the foot of Dey Street, and opened on October 11, 1846. Much of the shipping here was of foreign registry, yet many of their crews responded. The young "missionary" in charge, the Rev. Daniel Van Mater Johnson, was evidently a man of vision and enterprise. In 1851, with a sensitivity to the seafarer's intellectual and social, as well as spiritual needs, he set up a modest reading-room and home for his charges, at 2 Carlyle Street. This was, owing to the limitation of the charter then in force, organized as a private venture, in cooperation with three laymen on his board. But it became the seed from which great things would one day grow.[339]

In 1852, a "missionary-at-large" was appointed to an arduous open-air ministry by the boatmen's terminal at Coenties Slip. In 1856, a room was rented here, as a kind of combined base for the missionary and meeting-place for the men, eventually also an improvised shipping office, in competition with the crimp.[340] The two floating churches on the East and North Rivers saw stalwart service until they had to be abandoned, in 1866 and 1868, respectively.[341] But through the succeeding decades, the Episcopal presence on the New York waterfront continued to expand, culminating in the present century in the multi-faceted ministry of the Seamen's Church Institute of New York and New Jersey.[342]

In Philadelphia, a group of Episcopalians, fired by reports of the brethren in New York, founded on December 30, 1847, a "Churchmen's Missionary Association for Seamen of the Port of Philadelphia" (CMAS). Early in 1848, a deputation was sent to their sister-society in New York in order to benefit by experience there. As a result, a floating church was constructed at Bordentown, New Jersey, and towed to its moorings at Dock Street Wharf on the first anniversary of the Society. It was the sight of that

The Episcopalians' Floating Church of Our Saviour,
moored at the foot of Pike Street, on Manhattan's
East River side, and consecrated on February 20, 1844.

Interior view of the Floating Church of Our Saviour. The
"crew" consisted of the missionary, a sexton, and a boy to
blow the organ bellows. (*The Lookout,* Oct./Nov. 1982.)

seagoing Gothic church, making her way majestically down the Delaware with banner flying from her 75-foot steeple, that inspired one spectator, Bishop George Washington Doane, to write one of the most stirring missionary hymns, "Fling out the Banner!"

At the consecration of this "Floating Church of the Redeemer" by Bishop Alonzo Potter, on January 11, 1849, New York's Chaplain Parker proclaimed her the most beautiful floating church in the world, her interior (embellished with magnificent fresco paintings, and capable of holding some 600) even excelling her exterior. However, despite the ardent efforts of her chaplain, the Rev. R.S. Trapier (a former lieutenant of the United States Navy), her history afloat was brief. In August 1850, she sank due to defects in the twin hulls on which the church had been erected. Refloated, she was forced from one mooring to another by the "exigencies of commerce," until finally, in 1853, she was towed across river, and the sanctuary set ashore to become the Parish Church of St. John's, Camden. But the work went on, first from a rented loft at Dock Street, later located in a series of more sophisticated facilities, and today still continuing through the "Seamen's Church Institute of Philadelphia."[343]

In Boston, besides the three maritime ministries already referred to, there developed, during the 1840's, two more. One, the "Marine Mission at Large," initiated by Captain Thomas V. Sullivan in 1848, was based on

The Seamen's Church Institute of New York and New Jersey built and occupied this magnificent multi-service skyscraper at 15 State Street, Manhattan, from 1968 to 1985. (Courtesy: SCI of NY/NJ.)

The Floating Church of the Redeemer, built by the
Churchmen's Missionary Association of the Port of
Philadelphia in emulation of her "sister-ship" in New York,
dedicated January 11, 1849 and moved to Dock Street
Wharf. (From the 4th *Annual Report* of the Society.)

Long Wharf, and worked on an "unsectarian" basis.[344] The other, the "Free
Church of St. Mary for Sailors," was unequivocally Episcopal, and owed its
existence largely to the zeal of its rector, the Rev. John P. Robinson. In
February 1845, he leased a loft on the corner of Ann and Ferry Streets as a
temporary "Episcopal Chapel," secured the support of a diocesan "Board of
Missions for Seamen" and, in 1851, organized a regular "Parish for Sailors,"
taking over the more commodious (yet still free-pewed) St. Mary's Church in
Richmond Street. Robinson continued to respond with compassion and
determination to the needs of seafarers and the neighborhood poor.[345]

The initiative of those New York Episcopalians was undoubtedly a factor in the founding of the work in Philadelphia, perhaps in Boston, and very probably in New Orleans, too.[346] An Episcopal "mission to seamen" in New Orleans was taken up on April 19, 1846, employing as a base an "Episcopal Bethel" in Conde (Esplanade) Street, opposite the United States Mint. The Rev. C.W. Whitall served as chaplain during the early years, and support was secured in part by a "Young Men's Seamen's Mission Society of the Protestant Episcopal Church." In the course of the 1850's, the work grew into a regular waterfront parish (St. Paul's Church), with the center pews appropriated to seamen, with the Rev. Amos D. McCoy as rector, and with the rectory basement as a reading-room for seamen, boatmen and longshoremen.[347]

In 1853, a bequest by Harriott Pinckney (daughter of the famous Federalist general of that name) brought Episcopalians into the picture in Charleston, South Carolina. Under the terms of the trust, a Protestant Episcopal Church was to be erected on the property bequeathed (on Market Street and East Bay), "for the free use of seamen frequenting the Port of Charleston." Eventually, in 1915, the nondenominational Charleston Port Society merged its resources with the Episcopalians to make possible the consecration the following year of a new, combined institution called "The Church of the Redeemer and the Harriott Pinckney Home for Seamen," under the charge of an Episcopal clergyman.[348]

In one port after the other, the Episcopalians were to continue their expansion. Two factors undoubtedly contributed to the mounting momentum of their ministry to seafarers through the second half-century and into the next. On the one hand, the denomination kept to its tradition of all-comprehensiveness and escaped anything more than quite minimal disruption over slavery and the Civil War. On the other, there was the obvious advantage of being the American counterpart of that national church to which the majority of the world's largest body of seafarers officially belonged.[349]

AN AMERICAN MARITIME DIACONATE

Just as American sail reached its "golden age" toward mid-century, so, too, American ministry to seafarers attained a high-point at that time, not only in denominational but also diaconal involvement. The times were propitious. The spirit of soul-searching, which had animated the Second Awakening, carried with it "a dynamic social significance." Moreover, the need was overwhelming. Among seafarers, the picture of social alienation and systematic exploitation was, in many respects, similar on both sides of the Atlantic.[350]

"Runners," pushers and intimidators in the employ of Sailortown dens, relaxing between boats on the New York waterfront. (*Harper's Weekly,* June 26, 1858.)

Hence, it is not surprising to find friends of seamen in both Britain and America adopting similar strategies. This was perhaps most manifest in the provision of alternative lodging and shipping facilities. The infamous Crimping System was, on the wild waterfronts of the New World, even more than in Europe, "the Moloch of Seamen." Like their British counterparts, American seamen's chaplains soon saw anti-crimping measures as basic to bringing lasting benefit of any description.[351] As already noted, Charleston's pioneers pointed the way as early as 1823.[352] Other American port-cities would eventually follow their lead. But it required the powerful impulse of a national society, and its medium of communication, to achieve the necessary momentum.

The American Seamen's Friend Society was, from its first inception, committed to the promotion of satisfactory sailors' boarding-houses as a primary purpose. As Truair pointed out in his *Call,* the need was indisputable:

> "Show us," say they [the sailors], "a house where we can go, and find pious shipmates and landlords who will care for us, and then we will attend to religion; but as soon as we get home, our messmates, the landlord, and the girls, are all ready to board us at once, and we cannot think seriously. . . ."[353]

The great question was which system to adopt: to establish one's own model sailor's boarding-houses in open competition with the rest, or follow the previously noted "Liverpool Plan" of endorsing existing boarding-houses meeting certain minimum standards. In New York, the latter course was followed at first, and in 1830 nine keepers could be reported to have agreed to provide no bar, gambling, "or other immoral practices," currently customary in sailor boarding-houses.[354]

However, this was to prove impracticable in some ports (for example in Norfolk, where there were "27 sailor boarding-houses—all groggeries").[355]

Even in New York, positive results from the endorsement experiment were so meager, that the ASFS resolved to raise a "Sailors Home" on a scale grand enough literally to dwarf the opposition. Limited funds forced a postponement during which a building was leased at 140 Cherry Street (1837), and another in James Slip (1838). Placed under the superintendence of seasoned shipmasters, the two houses had a total capacity of 120 boarders.

Then, in May 1842, the Society succeeded in opening its long-projected five-story "Sailors' Home" at 190 Cherry St. (between Market and Pike). Capable of accommodating some 300 boarders, the building also embraced a chapel, reading-room, maritime museum, even a "noble bowling-alley." Among the many testimonies to its success were repeated donations from New York's marine underwriters, coupled with the alarmed reaction of local boarding-masters. (Some, in desperation, resorted to intimidation and violence; others adjusted to new realities, by transmuting to temperance.)[356]

During the 1830's and following decades, society-sponsored boarding facilities for seafarers continued to multiply in America's major seaports. As in New York, earlier involvement with moderate-sized boarding-houses would sooner or later be superseded by a more commodious sailors' home. Sometimes (as, for example, in Charleston and Boston) this would be combined

The New York Sailors' Home, built and opened in 1842 by the American Seamen's Friend Society at 190 Cherry Street, between Market and Pike. (G.S. Webster: *The Seamen's Friend.*)

The Boston Sailors' Home (left) and the Portland Sailors'
Home (right) were built shortly after their New York
predecessor for the Boston Seaman's Friend Society
and the Maine Seamen's Union, respectively.
(I.P. Warren: *The Seamen's Cause.*)

with a register-office, where seamen would be shipped in direct competition
with the crimps. Providing support for such a home-from-home for the
"tempest-tossed tar" would understandably become the particular province
of a local Female Bethel Society or Female Seamen's Friend Society.
Providing shelter for shipwrecked or otherwise destitute seafarers "with
nothing but their wretchedness to plead" became a financially burdening but
sorely-needed adjunct of these institutions.[357]

A sailors' home would normally also be a local stronghold of the
"Marine Temperance Movement." This again was one manifestation of that
"American phenomenon," the Temperance Reformation, which, in the
United States of the early 1830's, had risen to the head of the surging tide of
humanitarian reform, reaching such proportions that it even swept across the
Atlantic. (In 1829, there were 1,000 temperance societies nationwide; by
1833, these had increased to 6,000, counting over 1,000,0000 members.)[358]

In the American merchant fleet there were, during the late 1820's,
an increasing number of ships which, in the words of Joshua Leavitt, now
"navigated without grog."[359] Perhaps the earliest attempt at voluntary
organization was the sensational case of eleven whaling captains who, in
1824, formed a union in the Sandwich Islands "for the suppression of
intemperance."[360] From 1828 on, in practically every issue of *The Sailor's
Magazine*, the ASFS kept up a constant crusade against this "besetting sin"
of the sailor, whether in the merchant or the naval service.

In 1830, The Society published a letter from a Captain Edward Richardson of the ship *Salem*, deploring that shipmasters and owners could not see they were destroying both body and soul of seamen by continuing "the worse than useless practice of putting on board their vessels an article that never has any other tendency that to cause confusion, sickness, and death." He then goes on to propose the formation of a "Seaman's Temperance Society," citing his own experience of two years without ardent spirits on board, except half a gallon as medicine, and even that, he was "decidedly of opinion, did more hurt than good." (As to crew reactions, almost to a man, they had re-engaged on the same ship.)[361]

The following year, the magazine published a plan by "A Sailor's Friend," expanding Captain Richardson's proposal so as to include marine temperance societies in every port-city, with auxiliaries on every ship trading from them. At length, on February 21, 1833, in the Roosevelt Street Mariners' Church, a formal beginning was made with the successful founding of a "Marine Temperance Society of the Port of New-York." Captain Richardson (later a widely-respected superintendent of the New York Sailor's Home) was elected president, and Chaplain Henry Chase (who had played a leading role in organizing the Society) assumed the secretaryship.[362]

In a circular sent out shortly afterwards, the Society shared a strategy based on sound sociological principles. The example set by captain and officers would be crucial. Also, just as drinking had become "a social custom," so, too, *liberation* from drink must become "a social or combined effort."[363]

The years following gave proof of incredible success in pursuing precisely that purpose, as similar societies spread both in domestic ports and overseas. Nor did momentum abate with the radicalization of the movement to total abstinence. If anything, it appeared to increase, as shipowners discovered that alcohol was not, after all, "indispensable as an article of ship's stores," and were able to pocket sizable insurance savings on every vessel sailing as a so-called "cold water ship." Membership certificates of those who had signed total abstinence pledges at the New York Sailors' Home soon covered the chapel walls. In little more than a decade, over 40,000 had signed the pledge, and joined marine temperance societies located along the Eastern Seaboard. (By the beginning of the Civil War, the New York society alone had almost reached this figure.)[364]

Such statistics do not reflect either cases of backsliding or willful deception, both of which undoubtedly occured.[365] However, there is abundant evidence that the American Marine Temperance Movement was far more than a fad. Rather, it represents a positive expression of group cohesion, in modern mission terminology perhaps best described as a maritime "people"

PLEDGE

...OF THE...

Marine Temperance Society

...OF THE...

Port of   New York.

MARINERS' CHURCH,   WEST SIDE BRANCH,
NO. 46 CATHARINE STREET,   NO. 128 CHARLTON STREET,
                    NEW YORK.

_____ President.   _____ Secretary.

Believing the use of intoxicating drinks to be not only unnecessary, but injurious to the social, civil, and religious interests of men: I do hereby agree, looking to God for help, that I will not use them myself, nor provide them as an article of entertainment for my friends, and that I will make special efforts to promote habits of temperance among seamen.

SIGNATURE,

_____

ATTEST:

_____

A temperance pledge form as circulated by the New York
Port Society's Mariners' Church at 46 Catherine Street.

movement.[366] Given the obstacles it had to overcome, in the subhuman circumstances of a seaman's life in the age of sail, the wonder is (as Langley aptly puts it, addressing conditions in the American Navy of the day) "that the temperance movement ever made any headway at all. . . ."[367]

Among the most demoralizing conditions of life for the average American merchant seamen was the pitiful inadequacy of provisions for health and family care. However, in this area, as in that of temperance reform, friends of seamen in the New World could at least attack their problems unhampered by the conventions of a highly stratified tradition-bound social system. Moreover, they had, at any rate in New York, the advantage of an ideal location for multi-faceted social ministry to seafarers and their dependents.

Staten Island, now the southernmost of New York's five boroughs, was in the 1830's, felt to be far removed from "the temptation and expense incident to a city," and celebrated for its "salubrity of air" and rural environment. At the same time, easy access by steam ferry from Manhattan was already well established. Moreover, the water-girt community had strong, historic ties with the sea, and many of its inhabitants were involved in shipbuilding, boating and seafaring. Such was the setting of this unique Staten Island sanctuary of maritime diaconal ministry.[368]

First on the scene was the nucleus of what was to become internationally known as "New York's Marine Hospital." By an act of Congress

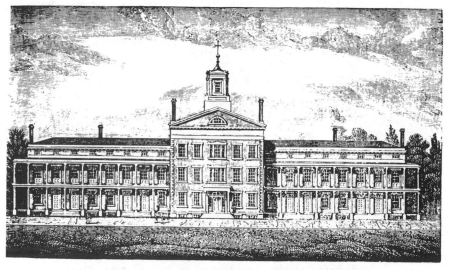

This so-called "Seamen's Retreat" was added in 1837 to
the 1831 nucleus of New York's Marine Hospital at
Stapleton, Staten Island. (*The Sailor's Magazine,*
New York, November 1837.)

Old salts at Sailors' Snug Harbor, Staten Island, New York,
spending their scheduled time each day in the dormitory
workroom, as shown in this scene from the 1880's, making
mats, hammocks, baskets and ship models.
(Barnett Shepherd: *Sailors' Snug Harbor.*)

in 1798, every seaman on any American ship arriving from foreign ports was
docked twenty cents per month toward a "Marine Hospital Fund." From
time to time, funds were thus made available for erecting hospitals especially
for seafarers. By 1802, marine hospitals had been established in Norfolk,
Boston and Charleston. Others would eventually follow. However, chronic
or incurable cases were not accepted. Moreover, the rest usually found
themselves "farmed out" to the lowest bidder among local hospitals, private
boarding-houses, even poor-houses.[369]

Such was still the situation in the nation's largest seaport, when the
ASFS, through *The Sailor's Magazine* (1829) appealed for "needful
buildings" and more adequate services. Finally, in 1831, the New York state
legislature acted. A "Seamen's Fund and Retreat" was established, a new
local system of contribution was introduced, and a site was secured—at
Stapleton, fronting the bay. The first buildings were erected and, on October 1,
1831, 34 patients were transferred from the Quarantine Hospital at nearby
Tompkinsville. A large new unit of this "Seamen's Retreat" (as it was
called) was completed in 1837. Here, as in other port-cities (with the brief
but notable exception of Mobile), local seamen's mission societies did not
see it as their task to assume direct responsibility for marine hospital care.

But from year to year they gladly provided supplementary chaplaincy services to sick or disabled seafarers, here as elsewhere.[370]

Seamen's friends were also concerned about the desperate plight of many whose sea-life lay behind them. By 1833, there was new hope for these, too, or at least for such as were fortunate enough to find a haven at "Sailors' Snug Harbor" on the north shore of Staten Island. Briefly before he died in 1801, Captain Robert Richard Randall, one-time privateer, merchant and member of New York's Marine Society, had bequeathed the better part of his great fortune, once harvested from exploits at sea, to the welfare of men of the sea, or, in the words of his will, to build an asylum "for the purpose of maintaining and supporting aged, decrepit and worn-out sailors."

The philanthropic bachelor's bequest was hotly contested, but in vain. A generation of court battles only served to multiply the amount eventually available. After the official opening on August 1, 1833, some 450

Bird's-eye view of Sailors' Snug Harbor in 1898, by then seen as the "haughtiest and richest" charitable institution in the world, housing nearly a thousand men. The earliest eight-pillared, cupola-covered main building (from 1833) is seen at the center fronting the shoreline, the Randall Memorial Church (somewhat reminiscent of a miniature St. Paul's Cathedral) to the left, and the huge hospital/sanitorium complex to the rear right.
(Barnett Shepherd: *Sailors' Snug Harbor.*)

Sarah Josepha Hale
(1788-1879), pioneer
maritime sociologist and
originator of the
innovative, Boston-based
Seamen's Aid Society.
(From the Society's 4th
Annual Report, 1837.)

"old salts" were safely moored within the walls of those stately Greek revival buildings overlooking the shoreline of Kill Van Kull. A condition for eligibility was that one had sailed at least five years under the American flag. Board and lodgings were free. Among many other provisions were a chapel and resident chaplain.[371] In 1852, a more modestly conceived Sailors' Snug Harbor was also established at Duxbury, Massachusetts.[372]

The fate of female dependents of distressed or deceased seafarers might be more tragic than any. So felt the "Mariners' Family Industrial Society." This institution (now the "Mariners' Family Home," on Staten Island) continues to count its founding from the year 1843.[373] However, as early as in 1832, over a hundred "wives of shipmasters" had banded together to form a "Female Bethel Association of New-York," in order to "afford relief to the distressed families of seamen." Meeting in the lecture-room of the Mariners' Church, they continued their well-meant work from year to year, "preparing and distributing articles of clothing, receiving calls from the needy, and visits from any of their Patrons. . . ." But there was perhaps also a mounting feeling of frustration. At all events, the receipt of a number of annual reports from a sister-society in Boston broke upon them like a revelation from above.[374]

The "Seamen's Aid Society," founded in Boston in 1833, was the brainchild of that brilliant Christian sociologist, Sarah Joseph Hale (1788-1879). This Boston-based benevolence was well aware that seamen's families were almost predestined to destitution. But whereas almsgiving was seen as a legitimate province of private charity, when made the policy of a benevolent society it could only aggravate pauperism by fostering dependence, indolence and all too often intemperance. Instead, Sarah Hale and her sisters in the cause substituted a so-called "Charity of Wages." Women willing to work were organized to make articles of apparel for sale in the Society's seamen's clothing store in competition with other (often highly unreliable) "slop shops."

The experiment proved an enormous success. In 1836, the Society opened a "Free School for the Daughters of Seamen." (Illiterate wives were equally welcome.) Then, in 1839, they undertook the support of Father Taylor's Ann Street "Mariners' House." Finally, in 1847, these indefatigable ladies took over the lease and management of his *new* "Mariners' House," built by the local Port Society, directly opposite the Seamen's Bethel on North Square.[375]

Meanwhile, New York's Female Bethel Association, now duly "converted," resolved to reorganize on the basis of the Boston model, starting afresh on December 3, 1843, as a "Mariners' Family Industrial Society of the Port of New York." They, too, opened their own clothing store, and in 1847 a "Mariners' Home" (for homeless, shipwrecked juveniles and seamen), both located in the city. Then, on June 9, 1855, on a six-acre site ceded by the Marine Hospital on Staten Island, they were able to dedicate a five-story "Mariners' Family Asylum," for the benefit of "Aged Women of the Sea."[376]

A fourth kind of marine casualty for whom nineteenth-century Staten Island provided protection was the habitually underprivileged children of seafarers, whether orphaned, half-orphaned or otherwise deprived. It was on April 2, 1846, that a number of "benevolent ladies" met in the lecture-room of the Presbyterian "Brick Church" (then still in Beckman Street), and listened intently as the Rev, B.C.C. Parker (of the nearby Episcopal Floating Church of Our Saviour) described in graphic detail "the needy condition of the families of sailors and the necessity of providing for their destitute children."

The outcome that day was the formation of a "Society for the Relief of Destitute Children of Seamen," in New York and its vicinity. This they purposed to do "by providing an Asylum for them, with proper arrangements for their health, comfort and education." Strong emphasis was to be placed on the inculcation of "religious instruction and habits of industry." The management was placed entirely in the hands of ladies (among whom were such prominent names as Stuyvesant, Kissam, Morgan, Aspinwall and Decatur); but they elected males (including Chaplain Parker) as "Advisers." Again, there was ready consensus that, for the planned home, Staten Island "presented advantages over every situation in the neighborhood of the city."

After renting temporary quarters elsewhere, the Society obtained a lease of land from Sailors' Snug Harbor, where their "Sailors' Orphan Home" was opened in 1852, with accommodation for upwards of 100. Here,

The Mariners' House at 11 North Square, Boston, erected by the Boston Port Society in 1847, closely affiliated with Father Taylor's ministry, and still actively serving seafarers. (G. Haven and T. Russell: *Father Taylor.*)

during the decades ahead, the Society sought to provide a better start in life for these "Little Snugs," as they were popularly called.[377]

Each facet of Staten Island's fourfold maritime diaconate has (with some modification and relocation) survived up to the present. In each case, the concern and cooperation of societies already involved in evangelical ministry to seafarers was apparent from the start. Sources also indicate consistent, active support by members of the Marine Society of New York.[378]

In other areas of maritime social concern, the picture emerging on the American scene was very similar to that already traced in the United Kingdom, with such variations as local conditions would induce. In the field of educational facilities, for example, "Sabbath Schools" soon became an integral part of virtually every domestic American Bethel or mariners' church (so much so, that this kind of community involvement often facilitated subsequent transition to a landsmen's church). Although they never became a consistent and integrated feature of the work, "Schools of elementary and nautical instruction" were specifically included in the original objects of the ASFS, and were, with the endorsement of local mariners' churches, attempted, with varying success, in Baltimore, Boston, Portland (Maine) and Charleston.[379]

The need for "rational" recreational facilities was, as already seen, recognized by those Charleston pioneers as early as 1823, when they

provided a reading-room and library in their first society-sponsored sailors'
boarding-house. As "temperance" boarding-houses and eventually sailors'
homes became a familiar form of ministry to seafarers, these would include
reading-room and library facilities as a regular feature. This was also true of
American seamen's churches both at home and abroad. (As early as in
1829, the ASFS sent library books to the sailors' reading-rooms then
recently opened up in four French port-cities.)[380]

From 1828 on, there were sporadic reports of "friends of seamen"
in New Haven and other ports placing ship's libraries on board ocean-going
vessels before departure. In 1837, the ASFS entered the field in earnest,
sending out ship's libraries with some 60 vessels, the intention being that
they were to remain on board, "there to be worn out." This system was later
changed to the circulation of *loan* libraries, and eventually expanded to
become one of the Society's main projects, supplying, in some measure, that
"missing link" of maritime ministry—the sailor's long periods of "seclusion
on the sea."

From 1859, drawing on the fruits of the recently commenced revival
among seafarers, the Society started so-called "Sea Missions," entrusting
their loan libraries to converted seamen, and encouraging these to "hold
religious services, or institute Bible classes" among their shipmates. Remarkable results were reported following this reorientation from cabin to forecastle.[381]

The American sailor, no less than his British counterpart, was
widely regarded as "naturally improvident." ("Jack's money always burns in
his pocket," was the comment of one current editorial.)[382] However, in the
early 1820's, the leaders of New York's Bethel Union and Port Society
reasoned (like their colleagues in Leith and Liverpool) that much might be
diverted from the clutches of the crimp, by means of savings banks especially
established for seamen. Warmly endorsed by the ASFS, the idea finally
came to fruition on May 11, 1829, when a "Seamen's Bank for Savings"
was opened at 149 Maiden Lane, corner of Front Street, with well-known
New York merchant Najah Taylor as president, and prominent men in the
city's maritime trade as trustees.

It was the "era of wildcat banks." But this bank had come to stay.
Founded on a strictly philanthropic basis, it gradually overcame the wariness
of suspicious seamen and stevedores, moved to Wall Street in 1831,
accepted non-maritime depositors from 1833, and continues today as a
modern multi-million dollar banking concern with several branches.[383]

In 1833, a "Savings Bank for Seamen" was also opened in Boston,
with the active endorsement of the local Port Society and Seamen's Friend
Society, and the special blessing of Father Taylor. By the end of the decade,

The first office of New York's Seamen's Bank for Savings,
opened May 11, 1829, at 149 Maiden Lane, close to the
shipping along South Street on the East River. The
American Seamen's Friend Society warmly welcomed the
event. (By E.P. Chrystie, courtesy: Seamen's Bank for Savings.)

similar institutions were available in Portland (Maine), Warren (Rhode
Island), New Haven and Mobile.[384]

Apart from specialized professional facilities, family remittances for
seafarers became a standard service of seamen's missions, in America as
elsewhere.

To the seafarer (and his family), a "watery grave" was an occupational hazard one had learned to accept. But the prospect of an obliterating
burial ashore could cause much mental anguish. Seriously sick seamen
would even refuse to enter the New York Hospital, for fear of being
consigned to a pauper's grave in Potter's Field. Eventually, the Trustees of
Brooklyn's Greenwood Cemetery donated to the ASFS a plot of land
especially for seafarers. During the winter of 1852-53, the Society was also
instrumental in securing a Seamen's Cemetery in beautiful Evergreen's
Cemetery on Long Island. "Seamen's friends" were involved in the allocation
of seamen's cemeteries in other major seaports too, such as Boston and
Philadelphia.[385]

Reverting to early efforts to improve the quality of the seafarer's life
on this side of the grave, American seamen's mission organizations were far

from indifferent to political and industrial action as a means towards humanization of the seafaring vocation. They were well aware of abuses "which Bethels and religious societies might mitigate, but which they could not remove." Hence, they sought to motivate those who could, by wielding the power of pen and pulpit. Especially was this true of the ASFS, with its national status, national magazine and national connections.[386]

The struggle to protect the seamen's Sabbath was no less intense in America than in Great Britain. Sunday sailing was subject to sustained attack despite mounting (and eventually successful) counter-pressure from the industry.[387]

More permanent results were finally achieved by repeated revelations of cruelty at sea. When Richard Henry Dana published, in 1840, his graphic exposé of abused authority in *Two Years Before the Mast*, the book was eagerly distributed by the British Admiralty as a deterrent for would-be deserters to the American merchant marine. The ASFS, too, however, sought to capitalize on the book's immense impact, constantly publicizing cases of "quarter-deck absolutism," and requesting their exceptionally articulate chaplain in Le Havre, Dr. Eli Sawtell, to submit detailed reports of verified atrocities.[388] By also publicizing periodic accounts of "Marine Disasters," the Society helped to highlight the need for drastic changes to ensure greater safety at sea.[389]

Nor did the ASFS avoid the sensitive issue of the seamen's wages. To his utterly "inadequate compensation," must be added the insecurity of his status as a casual laborer, rendered systematically unemployed by being discharged after every voyage. Moreover, he was seldom honorably paid, but instead subjected to that "sailor's bane"—the misuse of advance payment. In a bold blueprint for social reform of the merchant service, published in their *Annual Report* for 1856, the Society sought to show how shipowners themselves were "the chief obstacle" to improvement. Instead of condoning intolerable conditions, they were admonished to employ humane masters, disavow the crimp, provide livable crew quarters, good healthy fare, and a wage able to motivate better (also family) men. They even had the courage to call for the conversion of shipowners themselves, not only those who manned their ships.[390]

There were reminders that the era of unions must eventually dawn.[391] Meanwhile, two factors continued, it was held, to "depress the service," by making "better" elements leave, and the rest "deteriorate." First, it was all the physical abuse (already mentioned). Secondly, it was the high proportion of foreign seamen. Of the 200,000 men in the merchant service of mid-century America, four-fifths were seamen of foreign origin. (Of a total of 50,000 just one generation earlier, most had been of New England origin.) Whether from considerations of national security or narrow nativism, this

Graphic illustration of the natural hazards of life on board
a square-rigger. While hoisting in the upper main topsail,
the topman shouts to the helmsman to luff the ship so as
to reduce the wind factor. (By Oswald Penningten in
Jean Randier, *Men and Ships Around the Horn, 1616-1939.*)

situation, together with a parallel picture in the American Navy, gave cause
for concern in wide circles.[392]

Certainly, in relation to black ("colored") seamen, racial prejudice
was all too evident. Freed (or so-called "manumitted") slaves did not, as a
rule, get equal pay for equal work; they were severely restricted when their
ship called at southern ports; and there was always the risk of re-enslavement.
By sponsoring a series of "Homes for Colored Seamen" in New York's
sailortown (beginning in 1839), the ASFS simply acquiesced in current
patterns of discrimination. The same may be said of their organization of
special "prayer meetings for colored seamen," as well as the fact that they in
1863 endorsed the appointment of a black Episcopalian, Prince Loveridge,
as "Missionary to Colored Seamen" in New York. In so doing, they sought,
they said, to compensate for "past supineness" toward the white seafarer's
"darker-skinned, but likewise immortal brother."

There were, by the time of the Civil War, some 3,000 blacks sailing
from New York, and an estimated 35,000 in the combined merchant and

navy service. Despite the undermining effect of "black land-sharks" and numerous "anti-temperance" boarding-houses for "colored seamen," it is interesting to note that blacks were generally considered more spiritually receptive than their so-called "Gospel-hardened white fellow-travelers to the same judgment bar."[393]

Meanwhile, during the decades preceding the outbreak of hostilities in 1861, Congress was, as one American sailor-author put it, being bombarded with petitions for the abolition of slavery in the Southern States, while willing to tolerate that the men who manned their Navy were subjected to conditions allegedly worse than those suffered by "the swarthy brood of Africa."[394] At all events, redress of such grievances became the goal of a reform movement which culminated in a belated but remarkable counterpart to the British Naval Awakening.

THE AMERICAN NAVAL AWAKENING

At the head of the movement for social reform in the United States Navy was the American Seamen's Friend Society. In the midst of those decades of decline which that service suffered during the years following the War of 1812, the ASFS had lofty visions of the vocation of these men, as the highest class of public representatives of the only modern state whose institutions had ever been "based upon the oracles of God."[395]

For the image and general efficiency of the Navy, the Society saw the provision of an adequate naval chaplaincy as crucial. Hence, they hailed with joy hopeful signs, in 1829, that the new government would no longer make that office "a retreat for debauchees of broken fortune" (of which there had, in the past, been repeated examples).[396] Certainly, in his dual capacity as pastor for the entire ship's company and schoolmaster for its midshipmen, the naval chaplain's potential influence was wide and deep. The Society lost little time, therefore, in launching a campaign to help upgrade the service from its low level of public esteem.

In pursuing its purpose, the Society had significant assets. As president, it had secured an ex-Secretary of the Navy (Smith Thompson), and two of the latter's successors served as vice presidents. Naval representation in the Society's general membership also grew perceptibly as the organization gained stength.[397]

In early 1831, the Rev. Joshua Leavitt left for Washington with a memorandum signed by the Society requesting radical reforms in the quantity, instructions and salary of naval chaplains. The memorandum was received by the Secretary of the Navy "in a very respectful manner." An interview was also obtained with President Andrew Jackson himself. As Leavitt laid forth the objects and plans of his Society, the President seemed, it was said, "much interested."[398]

Numerical advances were not immediately forthcoming. (Not until 1841 was an average of nine naval chaplains increased to twenty.) However, inadequate in number, zealous candidates of high caliber did, nevertheless, offer themselves for service during the ensuing years, cooperating both directly and indirectly with the ASFS. Some managed to reach a wide readership through travel books which revealed a less romantic view of shipboard life, thus helping to sensitize the general public to conditions calling for reform.[399]

By far the most controversial issue of social reform in the United States Navy of this period was what many considered the vicious circle of grog and flogging. The sequence was significant, since it was widely believed that the former led to the latter. The prescribed daily "dips" of government-sponsored grog (in the United States Navy, a half-pint of whisky, diluted with a quart of water) created a craving, it was felt, for further (in this case illicit) liquor, leading to drunkenness, deterioration of discipline, and a need for drastic punishment. This would usually take the "time-honored" form of flogging. Then, under the steady stimulus of grog, the same cycle of events would all too often continue repeating itself. In his recent, meticulously researched study of *Social Reform in the United States Navy, 1798-1862*, Harold D. Langley shows how humanitarians of varying backgrounds, consistently encouraged by the ASFS, eventually secured sufficient support in Congress to achieve the abolition of both officially administered liquor and lash.[400]

The anti-grog crusade was fought in two phases. First came a campaign to promote a policy of voluntary abstention. Included in the memorial presented by Leavitt to the Secretary of the Navy in early 1831, was a plea for the government to hold out "every inducement in the power of the nation, for seamen to renounce voluntarily the use of intoxicating liquor."[401] True enough, in June of that same year, a decree was issued by the new Secretary of the Navy authorizing the voluntary commutation of grog into extra pay at the rate of six cents per ration.[402] Soon, the columns of *The Sailor's Magazine* could carry encouraging reports of the response in various units of the fleet. As the Temperance Movement ashore gathered momentum through the thirties, there was also news of entire ship's companies "refusing their grog."[403]

Nevertheless, misuse was still too widespread to satisfy the reformers. Fired by the elimination of the spirit ration in the Army, they mounted a campaign for total abolition of "legalized drunkenness" in the Navy. However, their arguments about the "baneful" effect of the spirit ration, especially on boys and young men, were not sufficient to convince Congress, where many were concerned that abolition would cause deep discontent and compound already serious recruiting problems. Instead, in 1842, a compromise was reached whereby grog was forbidden for minors and halved for others.[404]

While by no means giving up their goal, the reformers found they should now focus on flogging. (It had been discovered that sailors who might have preferred money in lieu of grog, continued to draw their spirit ration, as "insurance" against leaving their commander with no alternative but flogging for offenses where he would otherwise have stopped their grog for a while!) The reformers found a powerful argument in the Navy's perennial problem of recruitment and the steadily mounting proportion of foreigners in the fleet. How could one hope to attract free-born native Americans to a service where they would likely be both tortured and degraded by being flogged "like a convict"?

In vain, conservatives contended that such "false philanthropy" ignored the "bone and sinew" of the Navy, veteran tars who knew flogging was necessary for naval discipline. In vain, too, they sought its restoration after flogging was, in 1850, officially abolished, both in the Navy and the merchant service. By then, it had become impossible to withstand the pressure of public opinion, aroused both by a series of literary exposés (culminating in Melville's *White Jacket*), and by mounting anti-slavery sentiment in the North.[405]

In a final test of endurance, naval reformers could now concentrate their undivided energy on eliminating that "manufactory of drunkards," the grog-tub. From a national "Convention of Chaplains and other Friends of Seamen" held in New York in 1859, a respected, reform-conscious naval captain, Andrew H. Foote, forwarded a strongly worded memorandum to Congress, protesting against the injustice of allocating funds contributed by "the religious and temperance people of the country" toward further financing of naval grog.

The anti-grog cause (like that of anti-flogging) had now become a sectional rather than a party issue, with naval reformers tending to be identified with Northern abolitionism in the minds of Southern politician. With the outbreak of Civil War, the source of opposition was removed, therefore. In June, 1862, Congress was reminded that the whisky ration was one of the strongest reasons why parents were "unwilling that their minor sons should enlist in the naval service." One month later, the abolition of grog and the prohibition of "distilled spiritous liquors" on board American ships of war was signed into law by President Lincoln.[406]

A major factor in delaying reform had been the susceptibility of the Senate Committee on Naval Affairs to the scepticism of tradition-minded veteran officers. However, a dedicated core of reform-minded colleagues destroyed any assertion that all naval officers thought as one. (One of their number, Captain Robert F. Stockton, "father" of the first screw-driven naval vessel in the world, resigned his commission and took up the fight against flogging as a United States Senator.)[407] It was among such men that the naval distribution of Christian literature and maintenance of lay-led shipboard worship found their most ardent supporters.

A Bethel Meeting on the quarter deck of the receiving ship
Fulton in the New York Navy Yard, July 18, 1828.
(*The Sailor's Magazine,* New York, September 1828.)

These latter activities did not reach revival proportions until the late 1850's. However, their history goes back to the War of 1812, when both naval personnel and privateersmen could benefit by the sporadic distribution of early Bible and tract societies, as well as that of the Boston Society for the Religious and Moral Improvement of Seamen.[408] Then, in 1817, the newly-founded American Bible Society made its first naval grant, comprising 65 Bibles "to the United States Navy ship *John Adams* for its crew." This marked the commencement of a continuing commitment to meeting the needs of the nation's armed forces. In 1820, the Society's offer to "furnish Bibles annually, for the use of the Seamen and Marines of the Navy" was accepted with thanks by Secretary Smith Thompson. (Some 3,500 were needed the first year, and after that—considerably more than the Secretary's modest estimate of 300 annually.)[409] From the mid-twenties, that other national society involved in media distribution, the American Tract Society, also assumed responsibility for supplying "national vessels" with Christian literature.[410]

Sources do not indicate that naval mass meetings under the Bethel Flag, like that in 1821 on the 74-gun *Franklin* off New York's Battery, became a regular feature of Bethel Union activity during that decade.[411] Nevertheless, by the 1830's, the ASFS could report that the number of "pious officers" had increased to the point where they were conducting worship on board "several of the United States sloops of war," attending to the distribution of "large packages" of Scripture, books and magazines

Charles J. Jones, London-born former seafarer and senior chaplain at the New York Mariners' Church, played a key coordinative role during the American Naval Awakening, only comparable to that of G.C. Smith during the earlier British counter-part. (*Chart and Compass,* 1884.)

(provided by the ABS, ATS and ASFS), and teaching "Sabbath Schools and Bible classes" among the men under their command. In some cases, the commander would officiate and, in the words of Melville, make "a far better chaplain for his crew than any clergyman could." In others, seamen them-selves (including "some methodist brethren") would gather shipmates in fellowship groups on board, and, where there was an official chaplain assigned, "second" his efforts in other ways, too.[412]

Although such phenomena were, at this period, by no means general, they could not easily be ignored. Doubtless, too, their effect was reinforced by the impact of concurrent efforts toward social reform. From the ranks, there was never any serious attempt to impede the anti-flogging campaign. On the contrary, there were several signs of sincere gratitude. The anti-grog campaign could hardly be expected to create equal enthusiasm. Yet the remarkable response to the Temperance Movement in the pre-Civil War Navy bears tacit testimony to a general realization that Christian reformers were, in this regard, too, seeking the genuine best interest of the naval seaman.[413] In fact, the ongoing media distribution and lay witness, combined with all the goodwill (or at least respect) engendered by reform efforts on behalf of the men of the Navy had, by the late 1850's, effectively prepared the ground for revival.

The "cradle" of the American Naval Awakening proved to be the U.S. Receiving Ship *North Carolina*, stationed at the Brooklyn Navy Yard, and capable of carrying over 1,000 recruits. When a seasoned 47-year-old Swedish-born man-of-war's-man named John A. Morris re-enlisted into the Navy, and found himself on board the *Old North* (as she was familiarly known), it was not the first time a prayer-meeting had been organized at that unlikely location.[414] But this time the consequences quickly became a sensation in the religious press.

After having long lived the life of "a hardened sinner," and recently having "cast himself unreservedly on Christ," Morris determined to share the light which, as he said, had now broken in on his soul. He found three fellow-believers among his shipmates, two Baptists and an Episcopalian. With these as a nucleus, he obtained permission to hold a prayer-meeting in the forward part of the orlop-deck. Many came, but "a large number" only to scoff and "skylark." Refusing to heed his friends' advice to "abandon ship," the big Swede instead dropped to his knees in the midst of the uproar and began to pray. The effect was electrifying. When Morris rose to address them, the men listened in awed silence. The date was November 21, 1858. Revival had reached the Navy, this time that of the United States.[415]

Briefly before this, Morris had been enrolled as a member of the New York Mariners' Church, where the Rev. Charles J. Jones was already involved in stirring scenes.[416] When he arrived on board the *North Carolina* on the 25th of November, Jones found Morris' meeting "in full blast." From then on, Chaplain Jones became a dominant figure in the revival, preaching, counseling, corresponding and finally recording the history of those amazing years.[417] However, Ira R. Steward, pastor of the First Baptist Mariners' Church, Charles S. Stewart, former ABCFM missionary to the Sandwich Islands, now a veteran naval chaplain, and Joseph Stockbridge, chaplain on the *North Carolina*, all played important supportive roles. Meetings were now held several times a week, with normally hundreds present. Within weeks, scores of converted seamen had been received into membership in the Madison Street Mariners' Church, and many others into the mariners' churches of the Baptists and Methodists.[418]

While persecution diminished on the *Old North,* the genuineness of these sailors' new-found faith was subjected to another, perhaps equally severe trial, that of dispersion, as drafts were selected and sent to various units of the fleet far and near. But this fragmentation of fellowship proved only a precondition of mobility and growth. Within six months, "little bands of sailor missionaries" had been planted in a score of widely scattered United States ships. And with remarkably few exceptions, the caliber of their Christianity withstood the test. From the beginning, the revival had been characterized by an "absence of all mere excitement or self-assertion." Rather, there was a "humbled dependence on God, in Christ," coupled with an earnest "eagerness to secure the salvation of their companions." These were "young men from eighteen to thirty years of age," often "of more than ordinary intellectual ability," and generally "the hardiest of the ship's company." In short, even in the estimate of officers not themselves professing the faith, they were, quite simply, "the best men" in the Navy.[419]

In its origin, this was essentially a movement among "the foremast men." They had to be prepared for not only "the slanders of the slaves of the tub," but also intimidation by many a "petty despot of the quarter-deck." However, more and more officers became sympathetic, and soon not a few assumed active leadership responsibilities in the revival. Conspicuous was the case of the steam frigate *Niagara*, at one time reputed to be "the largest man-of-war afloat," where over 70 of the ship's company, including the commander and fourteen other officers, were "converted men." But this was by no means unique. On the steam frigate *Hartford*, flagship of the China Squadron, there were soon some 40 "active Christian men," including the Commodore, who hoisted the Bethel Flag at the main every Sabbath. In due course, the spirit of revival was "carried by renewed hearts through all the squadrons of the U.S. Navy."[420]

It was the Rev. Charles J. Jones who first took upon himself the important task of providing some kind of cohesion and communication between the many scattered cells making up the movement. Jones was, as already noted, a great admirer of G.C. Smith, and set up a pastoral correspondence system very similar to Smith's "Naval Correspondence Mission."[421]

Another major method of follow-up and consolidation was that of "Sea Missions," the system of individually entrusted loan libraries launched by the ASFS in 1859. By this means, the Society sought (1) to enlist active cooperation with committed Christian naval personnel as "Librarians," and (2) to enlighten the mind and motivation of untold others who might benefit from the libraries' carefully selected volumes of varied religious and cultural content. The response to this form of extended chaplaincy was, if anything, even more overwhelming than in the merchant service. "Yellow-covered literature" gave way to good books and the Bible—and countless conversions followed. At the end of the Civil War, the Society saw this as "the largest field in the country" for naval outreach, centers of distribution being by then established at navy yards and bases from Portsmouth, New Hampshire, to New Orleans, even Chicago.[422]

In assessing the significance of the American Naval Awakening, it would be necessary to bear in mind the diversity of background of the many converts, and "converts of the converts" of that revival. Here were not only native Americans, "from Maine to Wisconsin," but also men from almost every country in Europe, especially Scandinavia. This gave the work, as Chaplain Stewart put it, "a most interesting missionary aspect," reminiscent of the ripple effect of the concurrent Methodist Bethelship Mission in New York harbor.[423] Of more immediate relevance was, from the Unionist standpoint, the fact that the revival came on the eve of the "Rebellion," thereby—despite the inadequate official chaplaincy—kindling in the hearts of men of the Navy both "the fires of loyalty to country and fidelity to God."[424]

But the awakening also had an impact which reached far beyond the years of fratricide. While the Civil War was to mark the end of the Golden Age of the American Merchant Marine, her Navy had her time of greatest growth yet to come. Who could measure what it would mean for the men who would man America's future Navy that, during seven years of spiritual awakening (1858-65), "thousands," in the estimate of that revival's historian, had been transformed by the "quickening power" of the Gospel?[425]

However, those were mistaken who declared that the American Naval Awakening was "without parallel" in the "religious annals of the sea."[426] It is impossible to study sources bearing on the British Naval Awakening without being impressed by the striking parallelism of pattern, even though separated in time by half a century.[427] These, as well as other considerations, confirm the need for a brief comparison of the origin and early growth of seamen's missions in general, in Great Britain and America.

TRANSATLANTIC TIES:
EMULATION AND COOPERATION

William Wilberforce, writing shortly after the War of 1812, expresses the hope that the new institutions for ministry to seafarers now beginning on both sides of the Ocean, "will bind us together in bonds of love, which may prevent all future differences."[428] Certainly, between a war-weary England and an America tired of sectional strife, the stage seemed well set for such a prospect.[429] The question remained, in what way, if any, did the seamen's mission endeavors, which eventually emerged in the two nations, actually relate to one another?

In the first place, sources show the powerful impact of a mutual spirit of emulation. This was especially evident in the extraordinary importance attached to the so-called "question of firsts." The emotionally charged issue of who was, in fact, first in the field calls for clarification for reasons more significant than sentimentality. In a study purporting to present the genesis of the seamen's mission movement, it becomes a matter of paramount importance to compare conflicting claims to precedence and establish factual causal connections.[430]

Inevitably, the answer to the question of the first seamen's mission organization in the world must be a matter of definition. Based, then, on contemporary criteria as evolved during the formative phase of the seamen's mission movement,[431] the honor must be accorded the Naval and Military Bible Society of 1779. Here was not only a forerunner. Here was, for the first time in history, an association for the purpose of evangelizing seafarers. However succeeding societies varied in other respects, bringing the Gospel to the seafarer became their common constitutive characteristic. Neither the circumstance that the NMBS was not *exclusively* involved with seafarers, nor that those seafarers were, at the outset, not in the *merchant* navy, can alter the fact that this society stands, in the words of one (American) successor, as "the very incipiency of the mission to the sailor."[432]

At length, when efforts to organize a systematic outreach to seafarers were resumed in the second decade of the nineteenth century, significant innovations followed in rapid succession on both sides of the Atlantic.

In 1812, the Boston Society for the Religious and Moral Improvement of Seamen became the first organization in the world to seek the spiritual welfare of seafarers exclusively; it was the first to employ, as a means to that end, not only the distribution of literary media, but the promotion (albeit modestly) of divine worship among seafarers; and finally, it ranks as the first seamen's mission organization founded in the New World.[433]

In 1813, the Thames Union Bible Committee became the first in a long succession of marine bible societies in both Europe and America.[434]

In 1818, the Port of London Society became the first organization ever established for the stated preaching of the Gospel to seamen, dedicating a floating chapel as the first specific seamen's sanctuary in the world.[435]

Also in 1818, the New York Port Society appointed the Rev. Ward Stafford as the first full-time seamen's chaplain in history; in 1820, the Society could open a "Mariner's Church," as the world's first specifically built shore-based seamen's sanctuary.[436]

In 1819, the British and Foreign Seamen's Friend Society and Bethel Union was the first society publicly to promote the Bethel Flag as a seamen's mission emblem; it became the first to adopt a national, as well as international role; in 1820, the Society's founding father, the Rev. George Charles Smith, assumed the editorship of the world's first seamen's mission magazine; and in 1822, Captain William Henry Angas became, in affiliation with the same society, the first on record to be ordained to a ministry to seafarers.[437]

From the above, it becomes evident that here was no case of America simply endeavoring to "follow the example . . . proposed to them in England."[438] Instead, it would, as already noted, be more correct to view the origin of at least the Boston Society of 1812 and the New York Society of 1818 as spontaneous expressions of the same missionary and humanitarian revival then evident in both Britain and America.[439] Or, as G.C. Smith saw the situation in 1820:

> Here is a sort of simultaneous movement of hearts and hands in
> the Sailors' cause, by brethren in origin, habits, and language,
> separated by the vast Atlantic, and the work must be of God.[440]

Once an initiative had been taken, news was carried across the
ocean, both ways, by such means as "fraternal correspondence" between
societies, the exchange of periodicals and reports, and "living links," such as
seafarers themselves committed to the cause, or delegates occasionally
attending annual meetings overseas.[441] However, improved bonds of transatlantic communication conveyed more than the stimulus of a spirit of
emulation. From the early 1820's, there emerged specific areas of direct
cooperation between societies on either side.

Such cooperative efforts emerged first in the form of seamen's
tracts, mainly British, republished in America (although there were also
instances of the opposite).[442] Maritime devotional aids were considered
common property.[443] No sooner had America, too, launched a seamen's
mission magazine, than they both began quoting at length from annual
reports and other "intelligence from transatlantic brethren."[444] However, no
kind of common endeavor engendered more enthusiasm than the Bethel
Flag, once it had also reached the waterfronts of America. The impetus
which this emblem gave to the cause throughout the world has already been
described.[445] So, too, has cooperation in foreign-port chaplaincy (by joint
funding, reciprocation of ministry, and the avoidance of duplication).[446]
Finally, it would be an omission to ignore American efforts to mediate in the
warfare between early British seamen's missions, or their invitation to British
brethren to join in systematic intercessory prayer for seafarers everywhere.[448]

In any comparison between early seamen's mission history in the
United Kingdom and that in the United States, one can hardly help seeing
some striking similarities in the general pattern of development. Both movements are preceded by precursors, with a largely indirect impact on subsequent developments. Then, through the second decade of the nineteenth
century, follows a first phase of experimentation, with media missions and
seamen themselves playing a prominent role, leading up to the launching of
the Bethel Movement and the emergence of metropolitan port societies. In a
second phase, covering the third decade, centralizing factors lead to the
establishment of national societies. Finally, in a third phase, there follows a
generation of denominational and diaconal differentiation, thereby rounding
out the formative years of the movement. Though at quite opposite times,
both nations did experience a remarkable Naval Awakening, both very
similar in pattern.[449]

Despite such similarities, distinct *differences* are also discernible.
During the first quarter of the nineteenth century, there was, in mission to

seafarers as in other sectors of the Evangelical United Front, a clear British ascendency (though by no means a monopoly).[450] But by the time of the founding of the American Seamen's Friend Society (1826), an indigenous "American" type of seamen's mission, congruent with that of American Christianity as a whole, was beginning to take shape. Characteristic ingredients (such as revivalistic preaching, strong lay participation, and assertive, self-perpetuating strategies) contributed toward a vitality in seamen's work, which eventually resulted in an American hegemony in at least two important fields.[451] In marine temperance (as well as other areas of diaconal concern) and in foreign-port ministry, the Americans gradually gained an impressive lead, unencumbered by organizational feuding such as in Great Britain.[452]

Among the many pioneer personalities of emerging British and American seamen's missions, none had more powerful overall impact than George Charles Smith; and although in England he was at the very core of that controversy which clouded the scene for so long, in promoting Anglo-American harmony and cooperation in mission to the seafarer, none was more zealous or consistent than he.[453] It seems symbolic, therefore, that— just as Smith's turbulent voyage of life drew to its close (in 1863)—so, too, did the Formative Phase of that world-wide movement with which he had, for over half a century, been so intimately identified.[454]

The titanic struggle which was just then engulfing America marked almost the eclipse of that nation's proud merchant fleet. Devastating shipping losses, the flight of capital and manpower to America's great western "Inland Empire," coupled with a general failure to adjust in time to the transition from sail to steam, were all contributory causes.[455] Nevertheless, America's national society would continue to serve the seafarers of the world. So, too, would the two major British societies. In fact, despite both inadequacies and setbacks, time would show that a foundation had now been laid for a "maritime missiology," which would serve the rapidly expanding merchant fleets of the northern continent of Europe in good stead during the coming Continental Phase of the seamen's mission movement.[456]

Tracing the history of that Continental Phase lies clearly beyond the scope of this study. Identifying the shape of a maritime missiology based on the formative years of the seamen's mission movement remains just as clearly an indispensable task (which will be the subject of Part VIII).

PART VIII

MARITIME MISSIOLOGY

Toward a Theology
of Maritime Mission

Chapter 22

Motivation for Maritime Mission

This is not the place to attempt a full-orbed, systematic and normative theology of maritime mission. There can be no question here of any really comprehensive treatment of such a project, nor of departing from the strictly empirical intent of the present study. However, by seeking to systematize certain conclusions that may be drawn from the preceding narrative, as well as other sources, it is hoped that this part may, in some measure, contribute toward a historical foundation for maritime missiology.

The term "missiology" has hitherto been primarily associated with world mission as such. Is it, therefore, appropriate to apply it to the maritime world? In so far as seafarers had ties, however tenuous, with any Christian church, ministry among them might well be considered a form of *home mission* activity.[1] Nevertheless, there have always been ship's crews which were professedly non-Christian.[2] Moreover, sources have consistently confirmed how, from its inception, organized outreach to seafarers was intimately linked with the *world mission* enterprise.[3] Fundamentally, this is still the case.[4] Hence, in this study there seems to be justification for focusing on four basic themes of missionary theology: motives, objectives, impediments and methods.[5] These display not only a mutual organic relationship, but the two first and the two last also reflect major concerns of missionary principle and practice, respectively.

In seeking to identify the historical roots of maritime missiology, the following must, however, be borne in mind. The early Christian church had no explicit "theology" of mission. Historians have been unable to provide any satisfactory explanation for the amazing rate of conversion during those dramatic years, other than "spontaneous expansion" from local centers of Christian life, with laymen (like soldiers and slaves, merchants and travelers) acting as catalysts. The ultimate cause could, as Latourette points out, only be ascribed to the Founder of their faith.[6] Based on the findings of this study, the same holds true for the early expansion of Christianity *afloat*, during the first decades of the nineteenth century.[7] This does not relieve succeeding generations of their obligation to promote research. Rather, it reminds them that some factors may be beyond the bounds of human rationality.

NEGATIVE ASPECT: REFUTATION OF OBJECTIONS

As in the case of world mission, the first and fundamental question with which a theology of maritime mission must contend is that of motivation, raison d'etre, "Begründung," in short the "why" of mission to seafarers. However, besides presenting positive motives for mission, early advocates of the Seamen's Cause were confronted with a particular task of missionary apologetics: the refutation of popular objections.[8] These were, at one point, powerful enough to constitute a very real impediment. Nevertheless, such allegations are dealt with here, rather in the subsequent chapter specifically on "Impediments to Maritime Mission." Historically, the refutation of objections became a *promotional* issue; in other words, an integral part of advocating the cause and motivating support.[9]

Initial antagonism (or indifference) toward "seamen's missions" centered around three indictments, already familiar from the field of "foreign missions." First, there were those who put forth an "unnecessary" charge. The cause had to struggle, at the outset, through both obloquy and opposition, as "uncalled for" and "superfluous." Critics would contend that seamen were neither so "morally destitute" as to require special "missions," nor incapable of availing themselves of existing worship facilities ashore. In short, why should seamen, among the many vocations of society, be singled out for such special treatment?[10]

In reply, advocates of the cause would, in vivid colors, portray the depths of depravity to which the seafarer could sink. But this, they were quick to add, was precisely because, for nearly 1,800 years, he had been "cut off from the prayers and privileges of the church," and become virtually "an outcast of society" (Leavitt).[11] Experience had proved, for all to see, that existing facilities were not meeting the need. None were more exposed or deprived, on sea or land, than "the poor tempest-tossed mariner"; such special conditions of life called for correspondingly special counter-measures, including sanctuaries where he would not risk being ostracized. None were more vehement or persistent in publicizing that point than George Charles Smith.[12]

In vain, a rare voice, like that of Nathaniel Ames, would continue to complain about the "sweeping and undiscriminating" statements of the sailor's so-called vices, by "saints" who sought to do him good; the weight of other evidence (including that of seafarers themselves) was too heavy.[13]

Nevertheless, if the picture they painted was dark, seamen's friends found no reason to accept the widespread objection which, instead of understating, went to the opposite extreme. According to the "hopeless" charge, seamen were "beings of a different race" compared with humanity at large, "a *caste*, who, if not by cruel law, yet by a stern necessity, were doomed to live and die like the brutes that perish."[14]

This was not merely the view of worldly cynics, but also a popular myth among professing Christians who, in the words of Richard Marks, saw, sighed, sometimes shuddered, and then—like the priest and the Levite—hurried on, leaving the abused sailor "to perish on the high road of an evil and unfeeling world."[15] The tar-smelling, drunken, blaspheming "son of the ocean" was a stereotype, considered socially, morally and spiritually irredeemable, both in his own eyes and in those of the world around him. Hence, hopes of effecting his radical reformation were labeled "quixotic," "utopian," and a sheer "moral impossibility." As one captain himself put it, "You might as well preach to the mainmast, as to Sailors. . . ."[16]

So deeply embedded was this belief at the outset of the seamen's mission movement, that advocates of the cause found it necessary to assemble a whole battery of counter-arguments, "to prove the sailor [nevertheless] susceptible of imbibing religious sentiment." Logically, they pointed to the "strange inconsistency" of lauding the "noble tar" to the skies for his bravery, honesty and generosity, and yet assuming him to be otherwise incorrigible; to portray him thus was "a palpable falsehood," inferring that, whereas "wild Indians" could be transformed into "heralds of the cross," sailors were utterly unconvertible.[17]

Psychologically, no class was more receptive to the Gospel than that typical "creature of feeling," the seafarer, with his particular "warmth of attachments" and spirit of "religious dependency."[18] *Sociologically,* seamen caught up in the Bethel Movement were able to offer a new, positive alternative to the negative group cohesion of their own ship's crew (the only form hitherto available).[19] *Theologically,* none who put their faith in the prophecies of Scripture, who claimed to follow the Christ who came "to seek and to save the lost," or who believed in the life-transforming power of the Gospel, were entitled to make exemptions for seafarers, nor were they "authorized to stand aloof from any man," however "desperate his spiritual condition," and however "unquestioned sway" Satan seemed to hold over the seas. Seamen were men, and the Gospel of Christ was "designed to save *men.*"[20] *Experientially,* the evidence was irrefutable; even "infidels" were "abashed" by the countless cases of genuine "reformation," where the Gospel was effectively communicated. Among emerging seamen's mission organizations there was one common conclusion: no portion of Christ's vineyard promised and actually produced "such immediate, and valuable, and permanent fruits from the same amount of labor."[21]

Finally, there were those who realized only too well that seamen were receptive to the Gospel, deplored the fact, and warned that the consequences would be disastrous. The argument behind this "harmful" charge was, particularly in sea-girt Great Britain, stated with more emotion than insight: conversion, or personal appropriation of the Gospel, would undermine exactly those traits of character which were considered indispensable to sound seamanship. Officers (especially, it seemed, the young and less experienced) maintained that giving the Gospel to seamen was "calculated to sap their energies, and to damp their courage"; they would, in effect, become "mere driveling poltroons," in other words, so "mopish and timid," that they would be unable to fire a gun in battle, or reef sail in a storm. Authorities worried that evangelization would erode the seamen's "native spirit," breed insubordination, and reduce recruitment. Even some clerics claimed that missionary efforts among seafarers would foster "fanaticism." Finally, seamen themselves would easily imbibe the idea that conversion was an unforgivable breach of shipboard solidarity.[22]

The threat posed by such polemics was taken seriously by advocates of the cause. Among the most articulate in his repeated refutation of the "harmful" charge was none other than William Wilberforce. Speaking of the notion that seamen should lose "any thing of their manliness and vigour by their becoming religious," he asserted that such a "foolish idea" came "not from above." He would refrain from elaborating on "where else it came from," but emphasized the radical difference between that "blind impulse" which would make a sailor rush into danger without knowing what he was doing, and true "moral courage." How could one better fortify against the fear of death, than by exciting "a hope full of immortality"?[23] As early as in 1815, the Boston Society for the Religious and Moral Improvement of Seamen argued forcibly for the rejection of every negative insinuation. Promotion of religion at sea was the best means of ensuring a reliable, well-disciplined and well-provided crew.[24] Captain Angas compared prejudice against the evangelization of seafarers to early opposition against the education of the poor; both attitudes were equally reactionary.[25]

A doctrine of inherent incompatibility between Christianity and seamanship was, of course, a very real potential impediment to faith among seamen themselves. Not surprisingly, its refutation became an important theme in maritime homiletics and pastoral counseling.[26] The most convincing counter-argument was, therefore, incessantly invoked, both in print and at public meetings—that of factual experience. Admirals of national renown, merchant navy captains, underwriters, police officers and other civil authorities were willing to provide professional testimony that the Christian seafarer had, in fact, proved himself the *best* seafarer, and thus both the best security and the best investment.[27]

POSITIVE ASPECT: ANALYSIS OF MOTIVES

While great efforts were made to meet every negative argument in direct confrontation, the persistent presentation of positive motives for mission was significant as a supplementary form of refutation. However, the *primary* importance of such presentation lay elsewhere. The Seamen's Revival of the first two decades of the nineteenth century posed the same problem as every genuine outpouring of the Spirit since Pentecost. During the first phase of "charismatic immediacy," motivation for mission was both spontaneous and strong. Then, with the advent of institutionalization, came a corresponding demand for articulation in order to perpetuate motivation, where organization had succeeded spontaneity. Thus, by the mid-twenties, there had developed a need for an informed presentation of the "real character and claims" of seafarers.[28]

In a brief analysis of early arguments advanced in "pleading the Seamen's Cause," there can be no discussion in depth of intricate issues such as the purity or priority of motives.[29] An attempt will, however, be made to identify the intended address of individual incentives, as well as their basic interrelationship. Throughout, it must be borne in mind that motives which are here treated separately, seldom, if ever, appeared independently in practice. Moreover, the motives examined are "communal" motives, impelling collective support, rather than the individual motives of those who sensed a personal call to participation.

Widest in its potential appeal was the so-called "self-interest" motive (also termed the "prudential" motive). Van den Berg points out how, at the dawn of the nineteenth century, the "new Evangelicalism" brought with it "a certain purification of the missionary motives," restoring "religious" motives to their rightful centrality.[30] Nevertheless, evangelical seamen's friends, who might well espouse "disinterested benevolence" as an ideal, saw no realistic reason why multitudes, for whom the utilitarianism of the Enlightenment was still a strong stimulus, should not be encouraged to contribute liberally to the cause. In contrast to the "sleepless activity" of those whose "sordid self-interest" was promoted by plundering the seafarer,[31] efforts to elevate him could, in the case of maritime countries, be a question of national self-preservation. Such corporate self-interest could assume political, commercial, societal, and even religious character.

From the viewpoint of *political* self-interest, it was tempting, in the case of an island nation, to conjure up colorful comparisons of how, but for the "wooden walls of old England," the enemy would have murdered their gracious king, as they had done with their own, and made whores of their wives and daughters.[32] Still, the future of Britain's far-flung Empire was in the hands of her navy, and G.C. Smith, for one, believed that one Bethel

Flag could do more in terms of creating the caliber of seamen needed, "than all the cannon a ship could carry."[33] There could be no stronger safeguard against seditious "combinations" or mutiny, than Christian respect for "legitimate authority."[34] It was also pointed out that the Gospel, by promoting patriotism afloat, would discourage the defection of native-born seamen.[35] In short, ministry to seafarers soon became a point of national honor.[36] It could also, under the international emblem of the Bethel Flag, foster fellowship across the barriers of race and culture, thereby promoting peace and goodwill among the nations of the world.[37]

    The *commercial* self-interest of both Britain and America in evangelizing "that valuable class" was no less enthusiastically urged. "Poor" as the argument admittedly was, it was nevertheless considered quite "legitimate" to remind the commercial community of their stake in the sobriety and subordination of those to whom they entrusted their property. W.H. Angas proposed that "Underwriters at Lloyd's" reduce their rates for ships commanded by Bethel Captains, since these were known to be especially conscientious with cargoes in their custody. Others compared the whole seamen's mission enterprise with one "grand insurance office," where the wise would "re-insure their riches," by making generous contributions. Nor can there be any doubt that this line of thinking did, in fact, provide a major motive for both reductions of premium for "temperance ships," and the substantial sums donated to seamen's mission societies by merchants and marine insurance companies. If Christian seamen were better seamen, they were also a better business investment.[38]

    As overall tonnage increased and steamer explosions occurred with more disturbing frequency, marine disasters were publicized and "improved" to provide a powerful motive of *societal* self-interest. Father Taylor was quick to point out that, "when we consider the alarming loss of property by shipwreck at sea ... the effects only of abominable drunkenness and unhallowed society," investing in temperance boarding-houses for seamen would, for merchants, be "cheap at almost *any* rate." As more people traveled by sea, it was not least the loss of life which appalled the populace. Besides anxiety about public safety, there was also considerable concern over the "contageous example" of unregenerate seafarers in seaport communities ashore and among emigrant passengers afloat. However, under the refining influence of the Gospel, the sailor could bring into society those "noble elements" of character which he undeniably had, and which society so sorely needed. Every seafaring Christian could contribute toward crime prevention at home and improved national image overseas, as well as "the general improvement of the race." (It was unnecessary to add that for such seamen "smuggling, piracy, and similar asocial activities" could be entirely discounted.)[39]

Two further aspects of self-interest in mission to seafarers should not be overlooked, although they could only be expected to carry weight with "the Christian public." In terms of transportation, missionary, Bible and tract societies were largely dependent on reliable seamen.[40] Moreover (despite the legalism and even materialism inherent in such thinking), it was believed by some that concern for the spiritual welfare of seamen must be the "most effectual way" to invoke divine favor upon commercial transactions, just as neglect in this regard must inevitably invite divine retribution.[41]

Just as the motivating power of self-interest had almost universal application, so, too, its "higher," altruistic corollary, the "indebtedness" motive, by appealing to conscience, could claim a general, nationwide hearing. Revelations of the horrors of the slave trade had already aroused a spirit of public remorse, calling for some form of restitution. This "growing sense of collective debt" the advocates of foreign mission managed to put to positive purpose.[42] In like manner, friends of the Seamen's Cause would hold forth about the centuries-old exploitation of the seafarer, compounded by an incredibly callous neglect of his personal welfare. G.C. Smith stressed these arrears even further. Society had, by demanding a degree of gullibility in the seafarer (seen as essential for ship's discipline) rendered him "quite incompetent to guide himself." Instead of filling that need, the nation had blatantly betrayed its paternal trust, and left the seafarer a piteous prey to every temptation ashore.

However, eager advocates of the cause could also carry matters beyond the bounds of credibility. For example, they might well laud the "sacrificial" selection of vocation of those who would willingly "commit themselves to the perils of the deep . . . for the purpose of supplying delicacies for our tables . . . and decorations for our dwellings."[43]

In each of the four areas of self-interest already listed, the sailor's debtors were summoned to make amends. In post-Trafalgar Britain, the nation's *political* indebtedness was especially evident. Sailors had fulfilled England's expectations and done their duty in her hour of need. Now they had a right to expect England to do her duty—to them. It was not enough for her people to behold the blood-stained timbers of her battleships and feed her future seamen with the same false gospel, that heaven would be the reward of dying for Old England. . . .[44]

Again, who had more cause for *commercial* indebtedness, than those whom Napoleon, with more reason for envy than scorn, had named a "nation of shopkeepers"? Of course, Americans, too, were reminded of how her merchants had harvested "the spoils of continents" at the expense of "the sweat and sinew of poor sailors."[45]

Society's indebtedness to seamen was brought home to Britons by asserting that, but for them, they would all have "remained under the cruelties of barbarism," still separated from those lands where "the arts and sciences first flourished." On the world scene, seamen supplied an indispensable bond of communication between "all the scattered portions of the earth." In short, the seaman's service to the total community placed a corresponding obligation on the total community.[46]

Finally, the indebtedness of the *Christian church* was fundamental. Seamen had brought both the Bible and the "first heralds of salvation" to British and American shores. Now there seemed to be more concern for the fate of far-off Hindus and Hottentots, than for the prevention of "human sacrifice" among the sharks of one's own waterfront. And yet, without sailors, the British and Foreign Bible Society would simply have to erase "Foreign" from its title. Moreover, who else could fulfill the prophecy of the repatriation of the Jews?[47]

Although the "natural" (and scriptural) order was for charity to begin at home, the obligation of both church and society to seafarers was, nevertheless, not charity, but a debt of honor, or, in the words of Albert Schweitzer, "not benevolence, but atonement."[48] Again, although the most important means by which that debt could be paid was to give seamen the Gospel, this was not escapism—into "other-worldliness," but a clear question of priorities. (The genuine social concern of seamen's mission pioneers has already been well documented.)[49]

There might be more justification for seeing an element of escapism in an occasional "romantic" motive for mission to seamen. Just as it is common to speak of "that valuable class" in a context of self-interest, calling sailors "that interesting class" might well reveal a romantic admixture in missionary motivation. Once "hopeless-harmful" charges had been duly refuted, the post-Enlightenment public felt free to indulge a fascination for the "peculiar charm" of the seafarer. Pitted in a popularity contest with the (likewise voluntary) foreign mission societies and their original notion of the "noble savage," small wonder that seamen's friends felt they had to make the most of their "noble tar." In this way they were helped by his many endearing traits of character, his frequent exposure to superhuman trials and hazards, and his aura of far-off, exotic climes.

Meanwhile, in an age bereft of modern-day media, the lurid descriptions of depravity to which seamen could also descend would meet a need for sensation, and might well be tinged with romantic exaggeration. Nevertheless, as in foreign missions, so, too, in seamen's missions, the romantic stimulus, with its strong strain of subjectivity, was never dominant, at most ancillary.[50]

More realistic in character, was the "cultural" motive often advanced on behalf of missions to seamen. True, their advocates were not exempt from the uncritical attitude to western culture then current among evangelicals, too; they saw no reason to question the notion that their own culture was infinitely superior to any other.[51] However, three facts transpire: (1) Those advocates did not (unlike the English eighteenth-century Latitudinarians before them) confuse "cultural elevation" with Christian conversion; rather, they saw the former as an important adjunct, or concomitant blessing, of the latter.[52] (2) The world was undoubtedly indebted to seafarers for the genuine expansion of civilization (for example, in such cases as geographical discovery, international communication and overseas commerce).[53] (3) There was undeniable validity in the oft-repeated statement that seamen would, with their bearing abroad, inevitably make a positive or negative influence on their own nation's image, wherever they went. They were, for better or for worse, their country's "first culture carriers."[54]

Though the savor of societal self-interest and nationalism might be strong in such reasoning, there was also room for real concern for the sailor's own sake, specifically that he should assume his rightful and respected place in society. Just as the "poor native" needed to be liberated from his bondage of barbarism, so, too, must "poor Jack" be lifted up from his depths of ignorance, induced, all too often, by his early removal from "parental restraint and instruction." This compassionate concern for the *diakonia* of education linked cultural considerations closely to the "humanitarian" motive.[55]

In so far as societies also sought the seafarer's "temporal welfare," they would expect support from those of a philanthropic disposition who might be moved by the mariner's pitiful privations and constant exploitation.[56] For genuine Christians, there were deeper, more specifically biblical motives for seeking justice and humanity for the seafarer. They were not only bound by the Great Commandment, to love their fellowmen, and therefore fill the role of the sailor's Samaritan. Through their existential Spirit-born relationship with Jesus Christ, they would sense themselves impelled by a "reflex of faith," or (quoting Charles Wesley's paraphrase of 2 Corinthians 5:14-15) "constrained by Jesus' love, to live the servants of mankind." The indwelling Spirit of Christ could demand no less (Gal. 2:20, 5:22).[57]

Social concern for the seafarer and humanization of the industry will be the subject of further study under "Objectives of Maritime Mission."[58] Meanwhile, just as empirical knowledge of the sailor's hardships would engender concern for his "present happiness," theological reflection on his "eternal fate" gave a compelling *spiritual* dimension to the motivation of compassion. In fact, as also in emerging missions to the heathen, the "sotoriological" motive of seeking the salvation of the lost was to become, without comparison, the great consuming passion of evangelical friends of the seafarer. (It will be evident, from the nature of this and subsequent motives, that these addressed themselves primarily to people who would respond positively to biblical argument and authority, in Kraemer's view the only "valid and tenable" source of missionary motivation.)[59]

Reacting against the shallowness of earlier sporadic "benevolence," based on the apparent assumption that seamen had soulless bodies, some went to the opposite extreme and spoke as if they only had bodyless souls.[60] Most, however, would recognize the obligation of ministering to the seamen's "temporal needs," while nevertheless attaching "incalculably greater moment" to his "everlasting felicity." For this order of priority, as well as their own accountability before God, they found scriptural endorsement in passages like Matthew 16:26 and Ezekiel 3:18.[61]

Two further factors which contributed to the sense of urgency surrounding the soteriological motive were, on the one hand, the precariousness of the sailor's profession (separating him from certain death by "but a few inches") and, on the other hand, the sheer enormity of the need (with world-wide some "two millions of unbefriended seamen, sinking into an eternity of which they had scarcely heard").[62] Marks made the most of this motive in words which convey, with vivid intensity, the theological thinking of colleagues in the cause:

> The stormy waves may, indeed, wash the profane seaman from his vessel's deck, but waves cannot wash away his sins. The enemy's cannon may at once dash the seaman's body to pieces, but it cannot let out the defilement of the heart. He must be born again, or never see the kingdom of God. As the tree falls, so it must lie. There is no repentance in the grave.[63]

Whereas social and spiritual aspects of the motive of compassion could each become both anthropocentric and subjective,[64] this would be counterbalanced where integrated with a "theocentric" motive. The latter might assume the character of both obedience to the command of Christ, and promotion of the glory of God.

On the world mission scene, the "imperative" motive, based on the explicit command of Christ, had been brought into new prominence by William Carey in his epoch-making *Enquiry.*[65] When quoted by friends of seafarers, this "Great Commission" was generally rendered in the version of Mark 16:15, "Go ye into all the world, and preach the gospel to every creature." However debatable that particular text might be, both the basic content and the universal aim of Christ's missionary command were well documented in Scripture.[66] There was, therefore, validity in the oft-repeated argument, that the Savior could never have meant to exclude men of the sea, especially since it was among them he chose his first followers and performed "some signal miracles."[67] By both precept and example, the sovereign will of the Master was manifest.[68] Hence, his nineteenth-century followers had but one response—in loving obedience toward him who loved first, to make every mariner a disciple of the Lord.[69]

Since this concept of mission was, fundamentally, a mission of God ("Missio Dei"), its furtherance would, essentially, promote the glory of God ("Gloria Dei"). Always a major concern in Calvinistic theology, seeking the glory of God became an important stimulus in evangelical motivation for maritime as well as world mission.[70] In fact, in the view of men like Marks, to glorify God was nothing less than the "chief end of man" (1 Corinthians 10:31), hence, this principle must be given decisive priority in the choice of vocation, be it maritime or ministerial.[71] It must also undergird all mission support. ("Without the conversion of seamen, nearly two-thirds of the surface of this globe would be dumb as to the praises of God.")[72] Friends of seamen were reminded that the Lord himself began this work; now transferred into human hands, it must be continued to the greater glory of that same Lord.[73]

Together, these "theocentric" motives (focusing on the command of Christ and the glory of God) and the previously mentioned motives of compassion (expressing concern for the temporal and spiritual welfare of seamen) would reflect the duality of the response of regenerate Christians to the Gospel of salvation: motivated not by legalistic servility, but by gratitude toward him who died for all, they would seek to live no longer for themselves, but in obedience to him and to his glory (2 Corinthians 5:15). However, Christ made it clear that they could only love and serve him in a valid way by loving service to fellowmen (Matthew chapter 25, John chapter 14); and in order to be biblical, the scope of that loving service, that compassionate concern for the temporal and spiritual welfare of fellowmen, must encompass the maritime "stranger within the gates," the seafarer.[74]

In contrast to these latter motives, the "ecclesiological" motive of promoting the life and growth of the Christian church was not prominent, especially at the outset of the seamen's mission movement. Early advocates of mission to the seafarer did not have the benefit of more recent theological insights into the biblical nature of the church as the body of Christ, and the role of mission as an essential function of that body.[74]

Nevertheless, the nondenominational nature of early seamen's missions, with its emphasis on individualistic revivalism, did not necessarily imply *indifference* toward the corporate nature and responsibility of the church as such. Again and again, the church of Christ was reminded that no class of humanity was, by reason of vocation, more "virtually excluded" from her ordinances than that of the seafarer, and none had been more grossly neglected in the past. The seamen's "singular" form of spiritual deprivation placed on the Christian church, as trustee of the only authentic remedy, a corresponding responsibility to provide a particularized ministry of evangelism and pastoral care, through societies of Christians banded together on broad evangelical principles.

In so far as such efforts sought to benefit fellow-countrymen with at least a nominally Christian background, they could be classified as "home mission" activity.[76] In the following phase of the work, with mounting emphasis on denominational concerns, a corresponding element of self-interest became bound up with this kind of ecclesiological stimulus. Besides the positive priority of providing "especially" for one's own (1 Timothy 5:8), some spokesmen, particularly for the more privileged "established" churches, pursued a policy of deliberate denominational protectionism. True, there was "no Bishopric on the ocean, no parish on the sea." Yet, by means of a maritime extension of the ministry of the home parish, even nominal members could and should, it was urged, be guarded against the dangers of dissent, not least in regard to sacramental theology.[77]

In maritime mission, as in other areas of Christian enterprise, it was not easy to reconcile the right to contend for confessional convictions with a biblically-based "ecumenical" motive. However, while the work was still promoted on a consistently nondenominational basis, many would be able to endorse the hopes of a person, signing himself "Anti-Sectarian," and writing in *The Mariners' Magazine* in New York, July 1825. Here he points to the probability of seamen being "greatly instrumental in bringing about that happy state of the church, when her members shall be one," thus removing one of the major stumbling-blocks to faith for the watching world of unbelief (John 17:21).[78]

There seemed to be sound reasons for believing that the Church Maritime would fulfill its rightful role in the ranks of the Church Universal: (1) The seafarer was naturally unsectarian; his soul had, like God's mercy, something of "the wideness of the sea"; his inherent largeness of heart created in the Christian seafarer a strong sense of catholicity and brotherhood toward "all Christians, always and everywhere."[79] (2) The transitory nature of the seafarer's vocation, incessantly on the move, and constantly confined to the company of crew-members of varying convictions, made "binding down to particular church connexions" seem absurd.[80] (3) The emblem and aims of the Bethel Movement created a "common ground" of cooperation between "Christians of every evangelical denomination"; this, it was claimed, was "Bethel Union indeed!"[81]

Later, as denominational emphasis increased, ecumenical concern seemed to recede. Nevertheless, it never gave way to purposeful proselytism.[82] On the contrary, it survived to flourish afresh in a new form. In the present-day "Ecumenical Phase" of maritime mission, Protestant delegates deliberate with Roman Catholics under the auspices of the International Christian Maritime Association (founded in 1969). Here, the impetus toward ecumenicity always present in genuine Christian social concern (Bloch-Hoell) has recently been reinforced by a concerted campaign for "Seafarers' Rights." Meanwhile, the concept of chaplains of different denominations operating from a joint base in the form of an "International Seamen's (or Seafarers') Center" has become a familiar feature in an increasing number of world ports.[83]

If the incentive of self-interest had the widest appeal, and soteriological concern carried most weight with evangelicals, the most spectacular of the seafarer's "claims" on the Christian public has already been identified as a so-called "missiological" motive. Basically, this rested on a recognition that the cause of world mission was, in large measure, dependent upon the successful evangelization of seafarers. Hence, spokesmen for seamen's missions felt free to enlist the aid of those who were already actively supporting world mission, and their argument was essentially the same on both sides of the Atlantic.[84]

In practice, it was the *negative* aspect of the missiological motive which gained the greater publicity. Such was the impact on pagan minds of so often "seeing Neptune's bravest sons delighting in . . . drunkenness, lust, and blasphemy," that even a George Charles Smith, perhaps their greatest friend, felt constrained to concede that they must "*inevitably* become the greatest curse" to the missionary cause, counteracting by their negative image the very validity of the Gospel. Missionaries themselves could be quite candid too. "Convert your seamen," they cried, "for they now pull down, as fast as all your missionaries can build up."[85]

Certainly, the facts appeared irrefutable and were stated with dramatic force. Just as, a thousand years earlier, the sight of Viking sails would strike terror into the hearts of inhabitants of foreign coasts, so now the approach of a British or American ship had become "more dreaded on a distant shore, than pestilence itself." Spreading disease, destruction and despair, such vessels were notorious among the natives as, quite simply, "the wickedness of the sea." Some, out of sheer compassion, would seek to convert these sailors to their own idolatrous religion. Others would say to the missionaries, in so many words, "Physician, heal thyself!" Many, therefore, expressed no interest in reaching a heavenly home, where they ran the slightest risk of sharing forever that kind of company.[86] As already noticed in connection with the choice of those first foreign stations of the American Seamen's Friend Society, the injury inflicted on the missionary cause by the negative image of supposedly "Christian" seamen, could even, on rare occasions, flare up in the form of open hostilities.[87]

Nevertheless, there were at least three mitigating circumstances. First, if seamen were, as a class, considered to be "depraved," it was only because they had been so shamefully neglected. Secondly, though seamen were those most in evidence, white traders, with far less excuse, had gone to greater excess. Thirdly, the fact that the conduct of seamen from the "Christian" West was confused with the Christian faith was unfortunate, but hardly the prime responsibility of those seamen. Nor was it entirely chargeable to romantic unrealism among contemporary missionaries, for whom the finer implications of concepts like "cross-cultural communication" and "contextualization of the Gospel" were far beyond the immediate theological horizon.[88]

At all events, though it might seem, on the surface, as if foreign and seamen's mission societies were simply vying with each other in rehearsing scandals perpetrated by seamen overseas, the purpose was by no means to slander the seafarer, but rather to awaken the church. This was quite evident from the emphasis persistently placed on the *positive* aspect of the missiological motive. Among seamen's friends, there was wide consensus that, just as seamen had hitherto, alienated from the ordinances of the church, become a "mighty agency of evil," so they would, when once effectively evangelized, become an equally "mighty agency of good." Their spokesmen felt they had sound reasons for optimism. In selecting men of the sea as his first followers, the Savior must have taken into account those "traits of nautical character" which would particularly fit such men for "rugged and perilous service." Like the sons of Zebedee of old, the Christian seafarer would still "leave all to follow the Master."[89]

Added to "the fearlessness, fidelity and fervour of the converted sailor," was the itinerant character of his vocation. This made him—in a day when the concept of mission on six continents was unknown—a natural "connecting link between the Christian and the heathen world" (Stafford).[90] "Foreign" missions were already indebted to seamen for the fact that Bibles and missionaries could freely "traverse the trackless ocean." Now, as incessantly mobile, self-supporting emissaries of the Gospel, "only bound by the limits of the globe itself," seamen might themselves become both the best and the cheapest missionaries imaginable.[91]

This they could accomplish in two ways, corresponding closely to the nature of their negative impact on world mission. First, as "living epistles, known and read of all men," seamen would, by their very bearing, be preparing the ground for the Gospel in every port of call, or validating it wherever it had already been preached. The heathen's susceptibility to a sincerely devout image was well known, and examples of Christian seamen causing that kind of astonishment were eagerly recounted.[92]

Secondly, seamen could, by exploiting opportunities for direct missionary activity, do much to promote world mission. Again, cases could be quoted from life. Some had become "Agents Afloat," maintaining a widespread voluntary distribution of Scripture and tracts in foreign ports;

others had, in various ways, rendered invaluable service as close coadjutors of missionaries in the field. (An early and noteworthty example was the way in which a number of shipwrecked sailors had, during the furious internecine struggles on Tahiti in the year 1802, made common cause with the missionaries in barricading and defending the mission house.)[93]

However, the crucial question remained: how could a sufficient number of seamen be won for the Gospel, to make a real and substantial impact on the progress of world mission? Here, too, seamen's friends found reason for optimism, pinning their principal hope on the seafarer's proven potential for "peer evangelism." Elaborating on what might be characterized as a subsidiary "evangelistic" motive, they underscored how the seafarer's "strong fellow-feeling" would, upon conversion, express itself first in an overwhelming concern for the salvation of his fellow-seafarers. Safe from shipwreck himself, he must instinctively "stop to give all the aid and assistance he can to his perishing shipmates." Thus, as the Bethel Movement had made so manifest, converted seamen had already become "the best of missionaries to their own class."[94] More than that, by both general image and direct action, they would soon be exercising a beneficial influence on the whole waterfront environment of port-cities, not only at home, but also abroad, where there had hitherto only been "sinks of pollution," perverting particularly the juvenile population.[95]

Closely connected with the ecumenical, and especially the missiologcal motive, was a further and final incentive for maritime mission. If the evangelization of seafarers could make them instruments in God's hand to both "still the tumults of his people," and carry the Gospel to the ends of the earth, it would thereby also hasten the "blissful era" of the church's latter-day glory.[96] The "eschatological" motive for mission goes back to the words of the Master himself where, in Matthew 24:14, he makes the evangelization of the world a decisive anticipatory sign ("signum præcursorium") of his return ("parousia"), and the end of the age.[97]

With the great political, social and spiritual upheavals of the eighteenth and nineteenth centuries both in Europe and North America, this "inescapably biblical" concept of Christ's Second Coming became linked with widespread Millennialism. Based on a literalistic interpretation of the visions of John the Apostle in Revelation 20:1-10, the belief in a utopian prelude to the end, consisting of a precisely 1,000-year reign of Christ over a perfect world-order on earth, has never been universally accepted by Bible scholars. However, by the beginning of the nineteenth century, the millennial theme was part of the religious vocabulary of almost every denomination, on both sides of the Atlantic. Although radical, apocalyptic forms of pre-millennialism did appear (as in English Irvingism and American Millerism), it was the milder, more progressive post-millennial position which dominated the scene, looking to the return of Christ after—rather than before—the Millennium.[98]

As the world mission enterprise gathered momentum, spokesmen for the seafarer reminded that the evangelization of seamen had hitherto been largely neglected. "And," as they emphasized, "until this is done, the latter-day glory cannot be ushered in." Not only were seamen themselves a part of the world which must be evangelized before the Millennium, but, as a vital part of "the new eschatological community" (Barth), they were destined to be one of the "principal means" of reaching the rest of the world with the Gospel.[99]

Throughout the period under study, from the literary debut of George Charles Smith and on, the eschatological motive was maintained with remarkable consistency.[100] As late as in 1872, *The Sailors' Magazine* of New York pointed out that the evangelization of seamen was not "something to be done if convenient," with what "left-over energy" the church might muster at the end of the Millennium. It was to antecede the Millennium, as "one of its introducing causes," and until the church ("not the church on the sea-board, but the Church Universal") heeded the call to help, the glory of the Coming Kingdom would "continue to tarry."[101]

One may hold to a literal Millennium, or, with Augustine, Luther and others, interpret it symbolically, as the era of the Gospel, in other words the present "interim period" between the Resurrection and the Second Coming.[102] Nevertheless, world mission — and therefore also maritime mission — is still at the center of what Van den Berg calls "the drama of eschatology." This is so both because its objective remains a decisive sign of the coming of the end, and because it solves, at least in some measure, the mystery of the postponment of that end.[103] A concept of mission to seafarers claiming to be true to a biblical concern for evangelism can never neglect the dynamic urgency inherent in the motive of the impending return of the Lord, and the apocalyptic consummation of human history.[104]

Chapter 23

Objectives of Maritime Mission

EMPIRICAL OBJECTIVES

The foregoing attempt to identify some significant motives for maritime mission does not dispense with the need for an analysis of objectives. Logically, the distinction between power and purpose is as valid here as elsewhere. In practice, however, the two could be so closely correlated that it would be largely repetitive to deal with both in the same degree of detail. Instead, it seems reasonable to examine objectives from the perspective of the one overriding issue in this area—the relationship between "vertical" and "horizontal" dimensions in maritime mission or, as it was then called, between "spiritual" and "temporal" goals.[105]

During not only the earliest years of the seamen's mission movement, but throughout the formative phase of the work, "spiritual" objectives were consistently accorded the highest priority. Among these objectives, "incalculably greater moment" was attached to the task of maritime evangelization, than to any other. By "evangelization," contemporary evangelicals meant much the same as evangelicals of today: the communication of the biblical Gospel of a crucified, risen, reigning and returning Christ, "with a view to persuading people to come to him personally and so be reconciled to God."[106]

This intent could, for example, be reflected in the title of a society ("The Society for Promoting the Gospel among Seamen in the Port of . . .");[107] it would normally be included in a society's constitution (". . . to lead [Seamen] to the one foundation of human life revealed in the Scriptures");[108] it could find expression in speeches and reports ("The great object . . . [is that Seamen be] soundly converted");[109] it would likewise lie implicit in the selection of methods of ministry (the marine distribution of Scripture and tracts, also the provision of worship facilities and stated preaching for men of the sea).[110]

555

Although the soteriological aim of individual conversion and salvation remained the primary spiritual objective in seamen's as in foreign missions, there is ample evidence of awareness of the consequent need for "after-care" and "discipling," including integration into the "common life and mission" of a worshiping and witnessing community, thereby furthering "God's final purpose for the world." Thus, one would not only encourage the spiritual growth and "moral improvement" of new converts, but also advance important ecclesiological, missiological and eschatological objectives. This comprehensive focus has been aptly characterized as a "missionary-pastoral" approach (Uittenbosch)[111]

Occasionally, the priority of "spiritual" goals would be emphasized so strongly that social or "temporal" objectives virtually disappeared from view.[112] Nevertheless, a closer scrutiny of sources lends no support to the popular stereotype of early evangelicals as exclusively interested in capturing "spiritual scalps." True, they were, with Matthew 16:26, well aware it would not profit the seafarer, if the whole world were humanized, and he were to "lose his own soul." Yet their unwillingness to transform their segment of the Christian church into a service or goodwill agency (Kraemer), did not necessarily imply social insensitivity.[113]

Where, for example, the promoters of the Port of London Society in 1818 formulated only "spiritual" objectives, it was against a background of earlier concern for seamen (by others) which had hardly moved beyond "their temporal interests." (That they envisaged what they called a "wider purpose" in due course, was proved both by their original plans and subsequent history.)[114] A year earlier, in 1817, an Auxiliary Bible Society bordering on the Thames, with no trace of social concern articulated in their constitution, had, in a sensational case of shipwreck, quite as a matter of course, cared first for the "outward circumstances" of the needy (with bedding, clothes, soap and tobacco), and only then ministered to their spiritual needs (by distributing scores of New Testaments).[115] George Charles Smith, a man who could speak of the aim as quite simply "to rescue the maritime slaves of Satan from the torments of Hell," was the same who launched, long before its time, a truly revolutionary program of maritime social reform.[116]

Genuine diaconal concern was, in other words, present from the early years of the movement, even where no corresponding objective was actually verbalized. In a large number of cases, however, it was explicitly stated from the start that the object of the society would be "to promote the spiritual and temporal welfare" of the seafarer.[117] At times, one might wonder whether such social responsibility was viewed only as a means to an end (for example, where maritime social service was made "subservient" to the "one aim" of evangelizing seamen).[118] Nevertheless, there is solid documentation that, for most, diaconal involvement in a widening range of legitimate humane needs was, if not a primary aim of mission, at least a natural, integral, indeed essential expression of faith in one and the same Gospel.

The Great Commandment (Matthew 22:36-39) was no less valid than the Great Commission (Matthew 28:19-20). There may not have been a clear concept of every aspect of human wholeness (or "holistic" ministry), nor of every implication of a biblical doctrine of incarnation. Be that as it may, in practice, there was no narrowed-down Gospel, no unscriptural spiritualization of the faith. It was in order to promote a holistic approach, a ministry to the total man, that fellow-workers were warmly admonished not to neglect "the soul's temple," but love both sailors' bodies and souls.[119]

Nor did those pioneer spirits limit themselves to supplying "the ordinances of the Gospel," in seeking to *implement* that love. True, they had unflinching faith that the Gospel could not only lead to final fulfillment in a life to come, but decisively influence for good "the life which now is."[120] Yet, as already seen, concern for the sailor's "bodily" needs could also take new and (in their day) radical directions. In ways which will be summarized under the section on "Methodology," friends of seamen sought, by word and deed, both the social-cultural elevation of the seafarer himself, and the humanization of the context within which he worked and lived: the maritime industry as such. (Admittedly, the pursuit of a prophetic purpose, by means of political and social critique, was never powerful; but men like G.C. Smith and Joshua Leavitt proved it was by no means ignored.)[121]

An early spokesman for the Seamen's Cause formulated the following three "grand objects" for the work: "To raise the seamen from the ruins of the fall; to reinstate him in his proper station in civilized society; and never leave him till he was landed on Canaan's happy shore." Those words were uttered in 1829.[122] In times more attuned to subjectivism and secularism, such thoughts might well be construed as "paternalism" and "pietism."[123] But they are in undeniable harmony with a concept of love deep enough and broad enough to see a fellow human as an integrated totality of body, soul and community.[124]

ELEMENTS OF A DEFINITION

Just as the rudiments of maritime missiology form a natural conclusion to a narrative of the formative phase of organized Christian outreach to seafarers, so, too, the elements of a definition of maritime mission may be discerned from the foregoing presentation of principles. Again, the purpose is not to attempt a normative formulation to be applied uncritically to current-day conditions. Rather, it is hoped to induce a historical concept of seamen's mission, such as this eventually evolved; one which, for precisely that reason, should be of basic and continuing interest to succeeding generations seeking to serve the seafarer from a Christian motivation.[125]

The precise formulation "seamen's missions" does not appear to have been in general use before the latter years of the period under study.[126] However, the basic concept was alive long before. As already noted, the first "Missionary to Seafaring Men" was ordained in England in 1822,[127] and in 1823, Editor Truair referred to "the Mission to Seamen" of the New York Port Society.[128] The American Seamen's Friend Society spoke of "Sea Missions," in connection with their early overseas stations. (This latter designation could have constituted a logical parallel to "foreign" or "world" missions, but it never became general.)[129]

The term "seamen," specifying the scope or field of mission, calls for clarification first. Exactly what was meant by a "seaman"? Throughout the centuries of sail, and right up to recent times, seafaring was—with few exceptions—a male vocation.[130] However, the term could conceivably cover a wide range of activities. From the preceding history of the evolution of seamen's missions, a gradual trend toward specialization becomes apparent, both in Britain and America.

At one extreme stands G.C. Smith, with his expansive schemes taking in every conceivable category connected with water-borne activity. Here were not only merchant seamen, but naval personnel (for that matter the army too), fishermen, boatmen, coastguard crews, people temporarily at sea (passengers, emigrants, convict transportees, prisoners-of-war in hulks), and diverse representatives of Sailortown "allied industries" (from dock laborers to boarding-masters, crimps, publicans and prostitutes). Smith's concern embraced not only the breadwinner, but also his dependents, the orphaned, the disabled and the elderly. Though showing sensitivity to the interdependence of members of the maritime industry, many of his plans were, as already noted, well before their time; some never proved practicable.

The majority of "seamen's societies" tended to give priority to active merchant seamen. However, the precise boundary would depend on factors like financial feasibility and the extent to which others became concerned for special categories (such as naval personnel, fishermen, boatmen, would-be seamen, ex-seamen and seamen's families).[131]

Against this historical development, there are signs indicating the renewal of a wider concept in more recent years. Two specific examples are the current-day concern for pastoral care for off-shore oil-drilling personnel and more effective advocacy for seafarers' human rights. Monsignor Francis Frayne, at the XVth World Congress of the Apostleship of the Sea in 1972, offered the following definition:

> Today [in contrast to fifty years ago, when the Apostleship of the
> Sea was barely founded] the concept of seafarer has widened to

include all those who, through being on board ship in any waters, are habitually or temporarily deprived or cut off from the normal and ordinary mission of the Church. The concept also includes the family of the seafarer because he is one with his family and his problems are closely tied up with his family relations. In the same way we now realise that our thinking about seafarers must embrace their environment, especially those aspects of it which contribute to their problematic situation.[132]

Whereas major Anglo-American missions would minister in both domestic ports and overseas, also—not only to their own nationals, but to foreign crews as well, the Nordic societies emerging with the Continental Phase of the work from the mid-1860's were to represent the exactly opposite extreme. Largely limiting their efforts to foreign-port ministry among their own ethnic group, Nordic seamen's missions were nevertheless destined to achieve impressive results.[133]

Finally, since seafaring was seen as essentially a male vocation during the period of this study, the male connotation of the term "seamen" was never really at issue. The wide use of the more inclusive term "seafarer" in more recent years is the result of both increased active participation by women in sea-related careers and greater public awareness of the need to counteract sexism in the work-place.

Having considered the intended beneficiary, it remains to establish the nature of the activity itself. Over the years, the use of the term "mission(s)" in connection with outreach to seafarers, has been the subject of some debate. This can, at least in part, be attributed to the traditional meaning of "missions" (in the plural form), signifying the promotion of the Gospel among non-Christian, "unevangelized" peoples.[134] However, despite this linkage with the "heathen" (or—as in America—the derelict), the world-wide Church of England organization, "Missions to Seamen," has retained the word, likewise several continental societies, while the Roman Catholic "Apostleship of the Sea" has kept the New Testament Greek equivalent of the Latin word "missio," both basically meaning "sending."[135]

Although the psychological image evoked among seamen themselves must weigh heavily, there can be no doubt that the word "mission," in the singular form and the modern, more inclusive meaning, does describe the activity here envisaged. If—based on the words of the Master in John 20:21—"mission" may be understood to mean "everything which God sends his people into the world to do" (Stott), it must be perfectly legitimate to speak of a "mission to seamen," or, for example, "maritime mission." Here is an obvious need for that "crossing of frontiers," which is so fundamental to a true concept of mission, bringing to the normally neglected seafarer, whether at home or at "the ends of the earth," the message of the Gospel by word and deed.[136]

It is this special vocational situation of the seafarer which gives to this area of mission its unique identity, its character of a mission *sui generis*. Through the years, seamen's or maritime mission has been variously categorized as world mission, home mission, industrial chaplaincy and social service. However, although it may well include elements of each, it cannot rightfully be identified with any.

Ultimately, it remains the particular vocational situation of the seafarer which forms the frame of reference in such (generally German) definitions of the work as have hitherto been published. These state it is precisely the universal alienation and exploitation of the seafarer which obligate the church to cross the "sea frontier," and seek him out in a ministry corresponding as closely as possible to the pressures and perils surrounding him. (Elaboration on these latter forces forms the subject of the subsequent chapter on "Impediments to Maritime Mission.")[137] Meanwhile, most enclyclopedic articles make no attempt at any comprehensive definition, but confine themselves to a brief history and methodology.[138] Mission cannot, however, be adequately defined in terms of methods, much less results, both of which may vary radically.[139]

Otherwise, sources make it abundantly clear that, in maritime as in world mission, it is the church, those who profess the lordship of Jesus Christ, who constitute the visible subject of mission. Although missionary motives which might move "the worldly" were willingly presented, and although the work was, in practice, promoted by a bewildering variety of voluntary societies, there was evidently no doubt in the minds of early pioneers of the movement, that seamen's mission was preeminently the obligation of those who individually knew the constraining love of Christ, and who corporately functioned as "the steward of God's mission in the world."[140]

Nor do sources leave any doubt that the message to be proclaimed was anything less than that joint evangelical understanding of the Gospel, which comprised all the doctrines "essential to salvation."[141] Again, although the primacy of personal conversion was not at issue, the seaman's total welfare was simultaneously sought, however limited the means might be, especially in the pioneer period of the work.[142]

In fact, few "friends of seamen" would have found cause to disagree with the following adaption of a well-known mid-twentieth-century slogan: The whole church bringing the whole Gospel to the whole seaman.[143] However, if justice is to be done to the rich diversity of primary sources, a more detailed definition would be the following:

> Seamen's mission, as conceived by the pioneers of the movement, embraces everything people professing the lordship of Christ understand he would have them do, as he sends them forth to

serve seamen, in their special vocational situation, with word and deed, in order to promote their total welfare, in body, mind and spirit, above all providing each of them with the opportunity to become a new creation in Christ, incorporated into his church, and effective as a witness in the world for him. (In this context, the scope of the word "seamen" would not be rigidly restricted to active merchant seamen, but could, as far as feasible, also encompass their dependents, together with a wide range of related categories, including those preparing for sea, or no longer at sea.)[144]

Having thus attempted to identify certain principles of maritime missiology, as developed during the early decades of the work, it remains to examine the means by which pioneers in mission to seafarers sought to translate principles into practice. First, however, it becomes necessary to analyze the most significant impediments which would have to be taken into account. By "impediments" are meant not simply "problems" (of which many have already been encountered), nor theoretical "objections" (which have been dealt with under "Motivation for Maritime Mission"), but practical obstacles ("Hindernissen") of a dimension capable of frustrating fundamental objectives of the work.[145] Friends of seamen found these men to be "placed in the mixed extremes of social solitude and of solitary society."[146] Hence, those seeking to minister to them were compelled to contend with two complemctary categories of impediments, the first associated with isolation ("disruptive factors"), the other with exposure ("corruptive factors").

Chapter 24

Impediments to Maritime Mission

DISRUPTIVE FACTORS:
SOCIAL AND SPIRITUAL ISOLATION

Although seafarers were not until relatively recent years classified as "transients," it was recognized from the very dawn of the seamen's mission movement that "the principal difficulty" in the way of an effective ministry to them arose from the transitory nature of their vocation ("their having no permanent place of residence").[147] Their "ever-changing circumstances," tied to an ever-wandering working-place, which was also their home, would virtually isolate them from the outside world, cutting them off from "the moral influence of all those checks and charities which restrain and humanize landsmen."[148]

Deprived of such basic "primary relationships" as close family and friends, the sailor would be habitually homeless;[149] and, as Wilberforce as well as other advocates of the Seamen's Cause underscored, domestic deprivation could only be compounded in the case of sons of absent seafaring fathers, who, already half-orphaned, were removed from the care of the one remaining parent, as they themselves left for sea at a notoriously early age.[150] Meanwhile, on shipboard, the degree of depersonalization would increase even further in a mixed crew, where ethnic and linguistic barriers enhanced the seafarer's sense of loneliness.[151] To make this picture of privation complete, the sailor would, cut off from society at large with all its positive and negative sanctions, easily fall victim to the vicious spiral of an "undersocialization syndrome," making him only more and more maladjusted to mankind in general.[152]

As already intimated when discussing the background for the origin of the work, the seafarer's social isolation, entailing "a wide variety of atypical conditions and relationships with normal society," resulted in a largely negative *public image.*[153] With his conduct and character "every where reprobated," this had, by a process of self-fulfilling prophecy, inevitable consequences for his *self-image.* As one seamen's mission society said with commendable candor (in 1823):

> We withheld from our marine brethren the means and motives to self-respect, and then affected to be shocked at their want of self-control. To this may be attributed chiefly that moral deterioration of character which all have deplored, but few attempted to prevent.[154]

Although a seamen could seek to salvage a degree of self-esteem by affecting a corresponding contempt for "land-lubbers,"[155] his constant estrangement from society might seriously affect his mental health, leading to a high incidence of psychoses, alcoholism and suicides, a fact which more recent research has clearly documented.[156] But even over a century ago, there were friends of seamen who saw that if it was not good for "unfallen" man to be alone, it must be "vastly worse for fallen man" to be abandoned to a life in continuous isolation.[157]

Although *social alienation* could create formidable barriers between the seafarer and those who sought to help him, his *spiritual isolation* would have no less fatal consequences. Sociological studies of seafarer's norms and needs have (except in connection with superstition at sea) so far focused little attention on the very real spiritual aspirations and privations of this vocational group.[158] By contrast, the few who sought to better the seafarer's lot by early organized efforts to minister to him, showed keen awareness of the issues involved as they identified individual reasons for his spiritual isolation.

At the pre-sea stage, there was a conspicuous lack of positive selection (as well as prior provision) for the awesome stress and strain of a seafaring life; all too often it was the lad least mentally and morally fit for sea-service who went into it, and — prematurely deprived of parental protection — he would have slim chances of redeeming those handicaps later.[159] Once out to sea, in his own "watery world," together with others in literally "the same boat," he would normally be effectively isolated against any impact by the traditional means of grace; so complete was this isolation, that it gave credence to an old saying that it was self-imposed (outward-bound sailors simply laying any semblance of religion behind on a certain island, where it would quietly remain until they picked it up again, on their return from the sea).[160]

Moreover, on reaching home shores, whatever remnants of religion the sailor might still possess would avail him little; here, every effort would be made to "hurry him into the grossest sensuality" in the dens of the local Sailortown ghetto, without a single Christian place of worship willing to welcome him. (One waterfront minister frankly admitted that, until recently, the mere sight of a sailor entering his church would have caused universal alarm, and made everyone "anxious to get him out again. . . ."[161] With no provisions for follow-up, since seamen were interminably transient, "here today, and gone tomorrow," how could any spiritual light, even if it were ignited ashore, avoid being just as soon extinguished at sea?[162]

Even after the advent of shipboard and shore-based Bethel activities, with the opening of so many means of breaking the seafarer's spiritual isolation, certain stumbling blocks might nevertheless inhibit their usefulness. Any person involved in mission to seafarers, whether voluntary or professional, lay or ordained, was still subject to human frailty, and therefore liable to convey not only the "offense" of the cross, but also personal offense. Pride, worldliness, belligerence, hypocrisy, lack of zeal, even apostasy, all were within the bounds of possibility, and (so sources show) sometimes also within those of reality.[163] Societies, too, could corporately become obstacles to their own objectives, such as when they lapsed into lethargy, became overly competitive, or (in rare cases) involved themselves in counterfeit activity.[164] Where seamen's mission societies (justifiably or not) became identified with shipowners' interests and therefore an "employer-bias," this could also alienate them from the men they sought to reach, and whose confidence they would have to win.[165]

Clearly, there were many factors tending to isolate the seafarer from sources of spiritual nourishment. That in itself was ominous enough, since seamen, as partakers of the "fallen nature" common to all men, were just as lost as others, without the redeeming grace of the Gospel.[166] However, the seafarer's predicament was not only his privation. The very fact that he was constantly deprived by disruptive forces from satisfying deep, legitimate needs, rendered him so much the more vulnerable to the many *corruptive* factors to which he was simultaneously exposed, both at sea and in port.[167]

CORRUPTIVE FACTORS:
ADVERSE GROUP COHESION — SAILORTOWN
EXTORTION — VOCATIONAL DEHUMANIZATION

In order to assess the forces exerting a corruptive influence on the early nineteenth-century sailor, it becomes necessary to analyze first the nature of the social system to which he belonged. If modern-day sociologists find (with Goffman) reason to regard the ship as a "total institution," comparable (in a structural sense) to prisons, military barracks, mental hospitals, monasteries and boarding schools, the concept would be no less applicable to the days of sail. Used of people working and living within narrowly prescribed confines in a sort of self-contained society-in-minature, a total institution would entail a radical resocialization and demand a degree of depersonalization typical of the treatment of a greenhorn.

On the one hand, there would be the social weaning, or *disculturation,* of separation from "land-life" (with its attendant "mortification of self"). On the other hand, there would be pressures to procure conformity with a system of norms and values considered essential for shipboard socialization (in other words, a form of nautical *enculturation,* which could be summarized as "sailorization"). This would include the rich "under-life" developed within any total institution, in order to safeguard self-esteem and individuality in the face of bureaucratic authority, in this case that of the ship hierarchy.[168]

In this maritime version of a total institution, there would be a high degree of "social cohesion." True, the "lack of affective ties" in a typical ship's company, composed of fellow-transients, unrelated by blood or background, with only their vocation in common, made them by no means a genuine "primary group." The seaman was, essentially, a lonely man. Nevertheless, at least two factors, one physical, the other psychological, helped create a unique sense of community. First, the mere fact of being compressed into such close contact with others on a 24-hour basis for weeks, perhaps months on end, meant that a seaman was never alone. Secondly, there was an acute awareness of interdependence, bred by being joined in a common enterprise and exposed to common perils.

Hence, as Tuckerman observed, seamen believed strongly in "the principle of combination," or, in more modern terms, they acknowledged the demands of "group cohesion." Norms regulating the role of the seafarer rigidly ritualized and hallowed by centuries of tradition would provide a pattern of behavior covering virtually every situation in life, whether at work or leisure. These norms and the values on which they were based would again be safeguarded by a set of sanctions, calculated to discourage deviation and ensure conformity.[169]

Being so "total" in its demands, the force of group cohesion would, in any given ship, present a major impediment to the individual adoption of a faith recognizing another, higher authority, and requiring in some respects a radically different life-style. The psychological pattern applying here bears a striking resemblence to a basic principle of "church growth."[170] As long as, for example, public worship on shipboard was "harmless" enough to leave men free to follow the prevailing peer-pattern, there would be no reason for real "role-conflict" on that account. However, a totally different situation was created as the Bethel Movement gathered momentum, with its emphasis on conversion as a personal appropriation of the faith (Matthew 18:3), and on witnessing as a commitment to share that faith in word and deed (Mark 8:38).

Despite the many positive aspects of a sailor's sense of solidarity with his shipmates, there could be no basic compatibility between a Christian walk of faith and a model of manhood which had to prove itself by bouts of "confirmed depravity" (to quote the Boston Society of 1812). Thus, a freshly converted shipmate, who now refused to run with the rest "in the same excess of riot" (1 Peter 4:4), would immediately be labeled as a sociological "deviant," and have to take the inevitable consequences.[171]

Such consequences could consist of varying degrees of negative sanctions, like ridicule, ostracization, even physical abuse. Instances of persecution kept recurring from the very beginning of the British Naval Awakening; and backsliding could conceivably result. To be constantly reminded that religion was "only another name for cowardice and lubberly character" might tax the tenacity of any man.[172] However, Christ had himself predicted persecution for those who would attempt to follow him consistently (John 15:20), and cases of direct defection "under fire" were rare. A professing Christian crew member would, in a sense, have to develop his own "under-life," alongside that of the crew in general.

A greater hazard than so-called "roasting" was the contagious effect of incessant negative example. While out at sea, there would be little opportunity for "drunkenness and debauchery"; safety considerations, coupled with the fact that a ship was essentially "a man's world," saw to that. However, in an environment of prolonged close confinement, other opportunities for mutual corruption were continually presenting themselves, such as so-called "yarning" (as a verbal re-enactment of past sprees on shore), the circulation of blasphemous or obscene reading-matter (described as "books of superlative abomination"), profanity employed as a professional necessity, systematic "Sabbath-breaking," gambling and a host of other inducements to abandon the faith. Moreover, such practices were customarily condoned and frequently promoted by the ship's officers.[173] On arriving in port, pressures to re-conform would become markedly more severe, emanating, as they did, from an entirely different source.

As soon as he set foot on shore, often even before, the sailor would be confronted by a virtual "industry," exclusively focused on fleecing him. This form of sailortown extortion, for years notorious as the "Crimping System," has already been the subject of detailed study in connection with early lodging facilities for seamen.[174] In the present context however, there is a need to examine more specifically in what way that infamous fraternity could constitute such a formidable impediment to mission.

It was only to be expected that, after long weeks at sea, confined to cramped quarters, his nerves frayed by boredom, brutal discipline and bad food, the seafarer yearned for the release of reaching land with all its opportunities for relief and recreation. A "vacation psychology" is hardly an adequate description; it was more like an "escape from prison." However, stripped of his power of personal volition on shipboard, and now so literally "out of his element," he was hardly prepared for the sudden change "from a state of self-surrender on the ship, to a condition of temptation on shore," where self-surrender (to the land-sharks lying in wait) could only spell self-ruin.[175] Deprived of decision-making opportunities at sea, sailors ashore would all too often "exercise suspicion where they should be most trustful and confidence where they should be most cautious."[176]

The very name "Sailortown" (generally located on or near the waterfront) would underscore the careful segregation of that sector of town in relation to the remainder of the community. It was not least the development of dock systems which made maritime ghettos feasible and gave the local population a convenient means of averting contact with an unwelcome, alien element of society. Here, covered by a cloak of anonymity, sailors could find free play for their pent-up emotions and be left to their fate. Thus, the luckless shellback, hurried off with his shipmates in a crimp's cart on a Sailortown "cruise," was really only exchanging one form of social isolation for another. From this evolved the saying: "Sailors go round the world without going into it."[177]

True, a sailor would be "free," as long as his hard-earned wages lasted, to worship the waterfront's twin deities, Bacchus and Venus.[178] But basically, even the "best" bar in Sailortown was a sad symbol of home, its keeper a feeble father-image, and its clientele too transitory to be "a true primary group" (as Sherar aptly observes).[179] Again, he could hardly expect to encounter anyone who would fulfill a sailor's habitually high woman-image and deep "belongingness need," at least not among the "brothel Mothers" and the "poor Magdalenes" he met on the waterfront; a typical prostitute would leave him with no money, with a burdened conscience (unless already insensitive in that regard) and, frequently, with a terrible price to pay in terms of venereal disease.[180]

Genuine "seamen's friends" were wide awake to the tremendous obstacle posed by port-life habits which had for so long governed "the great marine republic" of the world. The force of those habits would leave no one unaffected. Although a committed Christian seafarer would be more motivated toward sobriety and self-restraint, the temptations which took such toll of his shipmates, together with powerful pressures to conform, made him by no means immune.[181] Again, there has been ample evidence of the tenacity of traditions of Sailortown extortion. Although the Crimping System as such eventually crumbled, others would continue to wield its weapons wherever seamen ashore sought solace from the isolation of frustration inherent in sea-life.[182]

G.C. Smith, who devoted so much of his turbulent career to combat the crimp, pointed also to ways in which Sailortown vice was intimately connected with various forms of "sordid seafaring." It was the most "sin-hardened" victims of the Crimping System who, not satisfied with becoming "the greatest curse to the inhabitants of every country" they visited, would readily desert, instigate mutiny, or "join piratical crews."[183] Mutineers and pirates were regarded as irredeemable, at least in theory, by both church and state in the Anglo-American world.

The 1723 edition of Dr. Josiah Woodward's widely-distributed devotional, *The Seaman's Monitor,* included "A Kind Admonition to All Seafaring Persons, against Mutiny & Pyracy, Shewing the Great Sinfulness as well as Danger thereof." The former was felt to be the forerunner of the latter, and that was the heyday of both. However, an 1812 edition still spoke of this admonition as "seasonable." The great mutinies of Spithead and the Nore were then in fresh memory; and piracy was still rife, not only in Chinese water, but especially in the Caribbean.[184]

Whether privateering was to be looked upon as "legalized piracy" or simply semi-private naval warefare would depend on the side on which one was involved. G.C. Smith supported the prevailing British view and suggested, in 1833, the formation of an "Anti-Privateer Society." (This category of commerce-raider, the strategic predecessor of the submarine, was, in fact, outlawed by international agreement in 1856.)[185]

The Slave Trade was another form of maritime pursuit which, though for long officially condoned (even promoted), came to be regarded as a very real impediment to mission. Historically—through centuries of marauding by the Mediterranean Barbaresque States—there developed a close connection between piracy and traffic in human flesh. When the British, who, during the eighteenth century, carried more human cargo from the Guinea Coast than all other nations combined, outlawed the slave trade in 1807, they placed on it, in practice, the stamp of piracy. Then, as other nations offically followed suit, it was again the British who, with their West African Squadron and other units of the Royal Navy, were the foremost in carrying the abolition into effect. However, as the next half-century would prove, prohibition provoked only greater exertions—and greater atrocities.

By the mid-1830's, the annual "export figures" from the African Slave Coast had reached 135,000, well beyond the average before the traffic was illegalized. The Portuguese, who had originally pioneered the trade, were the last to relinquish it. However, they were joined by ships from France, Spain and, not least, the United States. Thus, many who manned the faster type of slave-ship were American, some British. Hence, both American and British societies found reason to remind that, for the sailor, the "Torrid Trade" was certainly no less demoralizing and dehumanizing now than when the traffic was openly tolerated.[186]

Smuggling was another form of illicit maritime pursuit which proved both immensely profitable—and correspondingly hard to eradicate. During the eighteenth century, smuggling had, in some poverty-stricken districts along the English coast, become a local industry, recognized by virtue of dire economic necessity, occasionally with "the church itself as depot for contraband goods."[187] During the French Wars (1793-1815), smuggling saw a resurgence which prompted vigorous intervention by Preventive Service cutters, as well as renewed evangelical efforts to influence a public opinion which frequently accepted the need for clandestine commerce.

Thus, the Religious Tract Society sent out large quantities of a tract called *The Smugglers* (written by the Rev. Richard Marks). However, the Rev. William Henry Angas found the practice so "corrupting" around the coast of Kent and Sussex, that in these parts he "could obtain little or no attention to things of everlasting moment." G.C. Smith, on the other hand, while intimately familiar with the degenerative effect of smuggling along the Cornish coast, showed, at least in the case of the Fishermen's Famine on the Scilly Islands, a striking sensitivity to local socio-economic realities.[188]

The notorious Opium Wars of the 1840's and 1850's provided examples of sailors becoming accomplices (in fact if not by intent) to smuggling on a national scale. In prophetic vein, Smith's *New Sailor's Magazine* carried warnings of righteous retribution upon purportedly Christian peoples, who would permit poison to be thrust down the throats of a non-Christian nation at the point of the bayonet. Seamen themselves may quite well have sensed no personal conflict of conscience, but the negative image they conveyed could hardly escape the Chinese.[189]

To no form of sea-related occupation could more odium attach than to the age-old practice of wrecking. In maritime law, a vessel would not qualifiy as a wreck if anyone escaped alive. Not surprisingly, the temptation to ensure that this condition was duly fulfilled could easily prove too powerful, at least where the local level of poverty had descended to desperation point. Thus, dangerous coastlands the world over could provide tales of how some would stoop to luring ships ashore with false lights, refraining from rescuing survivors, even adding murder to pillage. Such stories (like those of the "Mooncussers" of Cape Cod) would be hotly denied, and much may doubtless be classified as fantasy and folklore. Yet, that many did, in fact, follow that ghoulish trade, is irrefutable.

In the Middle Ages, papal bulls would simply anathematize anyone guilty of such practices. In early nineteenth-century England, the Bishop of St. David's found wrecking still so prevalent that he had to direct the clergy of his diocese "to preach an annual sermon on this horrid sin." Wreckers, who often combined their nefarious profession with that of smuggling, were also the subject of vivid tracts by G.C. Smith and Richard Marks. (Smith at one point even appointed a "missionary" among the wreckers on the Cornish coast.)[190]

Although desertion has, from time immemorial, been the subject of general censure and severe punishment, motivation could vary widely from criminal irresponsibility to a seaman's only recourse in the face of utterly inhuman conditions on board.[191]

On some ships, conditions would, of course, be more tolerable than others. But by and large, dehumanizing conditions at sea were simply a vocational fact of life in the days of sail. The degree of deprivation inherent in sea-life led all too easily to the seafarer's devaluation in public esteem, which again opened the door to his dehumanization by the industry as such. The sailor belonged, as noted earlier, to a race apart, a species consigned to a level of life lower than the rest of humanity.[192] This was for long true of the naval service. It was even more true of the merchant service. Here, his employers appeared, at that point in history, to overlook entirely a primary factor in the earning capacity of their ships: "the physical condition and morale of the crews" (Straus).[193]

By the 1860's (the end of the period under study), important improvements had been made in the seafarer's overall life-situation.[194] Generally speaking, however, his living and working conditions remained just as dehumanizing as already described at the turn of the nineteenth century.[195] In some respects, conditions were worse. In 1872, Samuel Plimsoll published *Our Seamen,* a momentous indictment of the so-called "coffin-ships," grossly over-insured vessels sent to sea in such unseaworthy condition that their likely loss would bring rich rewards to their owners. ("Murder for gain," was Captain Marryat's biting comment.) Meanwhile, there was also a heavy investment in larger, sleeker ships, which meant that crews would be couped up in even closer quarters, yet driven with even more diabolical insistence on speed.[196]

In 1874, two reports were issued which, each in their way, gave graphic evidence of the shocking conditions of life and work to which seafarers were still exposed. In his report entitled *Among Our Sailors,* Dr. J. Grey Jewell, former United States Consul at Singapore, provides massive documentation of both maiming and murder in the name of "discipline," and of both starvation and exploitation in the interests of "economy."[197] In his annual report that same year, the Supervising Surgeon of the American Marine Hospital Service estimated the average length of a sailor's life after going to sea to be no more than twelve years.

Sources such as these lay bare that blend of avarice, cruelty and fear by which the luckless seafarer of the day was deprived of his true humanity. More than that, the seafarer was also deprived of much of his receptivity to a Gospel to which many of his oppressors obviously paid only lip-service.[198]

Not all impediments to mission, depicted as "inherent" to the vocation of the seafarer, could be accepted as such by societies responding to the call to serve him. Impediments which could be shown to be only *apparently* inherent were (as noted under "Motivation for Maritime Mission") dealt with as an important task of missionary apologetics.[199] Where impediments proved to be genuinely inherent (such as social isolation, environmental stress, and moral exposure), stategies would need to be worked out to counter them, or at least compensate for them. How did, in fact, such societies seek to promote the objectives they had set themselves—despite the very real impediments in their way?

Chapter 25

Methodology of Maritime Mission

ANALYSIS OF INDIVIDUAL METHODS

Considerations of space preclude any exhaustive study of individual methods at this juncture. Nor should this be necessary, since a detailed treatment has already been incorporated at various points in the main narrative. Instead, it is more appropriate to summarize and systematize such methods, adding a number of general observations where called for.

Compared with categories like motives, objectives and impediments, methodology signifies the *dynamic* dimension of maritime missiology, as the church seeks to "become all things" to all seafarers, by constant reassessment of means by which it may, in any given situation, best pursue its biblical objectives.[200] In so doing, the pioneers pledged, in the paternalistic terminology of the day, "to save the sailor from himself." At the outset, the measures they adopted were simple and sorely limited. But diversification seems to have been delayed more by lack of funds than by lack of vision. Moreover, as new areas of need were discovered, they realized that, rather than railing over the sources of the sailor's temptations and privations, more could be achieved "to counteract such baneful influences" by positive, systematic countermeasures.[201]

This policy is reflected in the very names adopted. For the exploited, friendless seafarer, seamen's friend societies were founded. For the uprooted, homeless mariner, sailors' homes were established. For the aging, restless wanderer of the deep, sailors' rests were built. Again, for the socially ostracized shellback, the monopoly of the gin-palace could be broken by the opening of an institute entitled "The Sailors' Palace" (as in Shadwell, London).[202]

In the following review of individual methods of mission, sequence does not necessarily reflect priority. That methods of maritime evangelism precede methods of maritime diaconal ministry, is due to the circumstance that such was (with some significant qualifications) the general order in which needs of the seafarer were, in fact, discovered and met, as elements of an expanding, increasingly diversified ministry.[203]

Historically, the earliest organizational expression of Christian concern for seafarers on both sides of the Atlantic, took the form of a maritime media ministry.[204] Before long, it was recognized that the distribution of literary media must not remain the *only* method of maritime ministry. However, in at least two respects, media distribution answered needs which are no less valid today. From a purely quantitive viewpoint, *literary* media (those so-called "printed heralds of the cross") could cover a far wider field than *living* media (such as particularly appointed preachers).[205] From a pastoral viewpoint, the printed word could provide a vital means of follow-up during the sailor's long periods of sea-life, and thus "keep those impressions on the heart," which a chaplain might have left during an encounter in port.[206]

Among the different types of media, the Scriptures occupied a unique place. They were both inspired by the Spirit at the outset, and employed by the Spirit as a fundamental means of grace. Sources show how the pioneers of the Marine Bible Society Movement were sensitive to at least two forms of potential abuse: an indiscriminate and therefore harmful mode of distribution, and a superstitious, almost idolatrous attitude to the Bible-book as such. However, where there was discriminating distribution, there was overwhelming evidence of positive, effective response.[207]

Nor were religious tracts intended to be indiscriminately "scattered." Used in the sense of brief books with a purposely popular appeal (corresponding to modern-day paperbacks), tracts were highly rated in contemporary mission strategy. Religious tracts were considered a crucial antidote against the mounting flood of "impious and seditious" literature which was now invading the waterfront. At the same time, they were seen as virtually the only means of reaching the consciences of those "not awakened to a proper sense of their guilt," or who simply evaded the hearing of the preached Word. One British authority gave the successful distribution of tracts credit for being "mainly instrumental" in the Seamen's Revival of the early nineteenth century. At all events, marine tract and Scripture distribution was destined to become both the first and the most durable method of maritime mission.[208]

However, other forms of media ministry were also in early use, and have since secured a permanent place in outreach to seafarers. These include maritime devotional aids (which gained surprisingly wide acceptance when authentically relevant to the seafarer's situation);[209] maritime pastoral correspondence (a form of follow-up which, with the advent of modern means of duplication and communication, now has even wider application);[210]

sailor's magazines (which, besides being a promotional "mainstay" could— where the nautical flavor was genuine—hold a strong appeal for seafarers);[211] and marine libraries (which would, by making both classics of Christian literature and select books of more general content available to seamen, serve not only spiritual but also important educational and recreational needs).[212]

Although the written word was taken into use prior to the preached word as a method of organized seamen's mission, the movement had not progressed far before the priority of preaching was firmly established. Thus, the committee of the Port of London Society, while "rejoicing" in earlier exertions by the major Marine Bible Societies, felt (in 1821) bound to remind the Christian public that the preaching of the Gospel was still "the principal instrument" appointed by God in his Word "for the salvation of men" (1 Corinthians 1:20-25). Hence, it would be primarily by the so-called "foolishness of preaching," that they now looked for the light of the Gospel to "shine into the hearts of Seamen."[213] G.C. Smith put it more bluntly:

> God has not said, Go, disperse prayer-books, homilies, and tracts, although there can be no question of the duty and the blessing of such activities; but, He has positively said, "Go, preach the Gospel to every creature."[214]

A logical consequence of the high evaluation of preaching was the early concern for a "stated" ministry. This would be important for the chaplain, it was believed, if he were to learn the "peculiarities" of his hearers, and for seamen, if they were to sense any real devotion toward their preacher, confide in him, and develop a "father-image" of him (one that could contrast with that of local Sailortown extortionists).[215]

Just as preaching the Gospel became the "leading feature" of corporate efforts to benefit the seafarer, so, too, it was made the "main business" of the individual chaplain.[216] One of those who had himself experienced the inadequacy of literary media alone, the Rev. Richard Marks, was among the first to share with would-be seamen's-preachers some basic elements of maritime homiletics. Marks points to the following theological presuppositions for preaching to seafarers: (1) The totality of man's depravity and the universality of Christ's atonement as the objective aspects of salvation. (2) The need for personal repentance, and faith in that atonement, as corresponding conditions of the subjective appropriation of salvation.[217]

Corresponding to that form of broad, evangelical agreement on the theological *basis* of preaching to seafarers, there also appeared to be complete consensus about its primary *purpose*. In contrast to a former focus on duty to God, king and country, typifying the legalistic naval preaching of the preceding century,[218] the overriding aim was now to bring seamen to conversion, by enabling them to see their sins, confess them, and "come to

Christ for pardon" (1 John 1:8-9), thereby, through the power of his Spirit, becoming "born again," and partakers of "everlasting life" (John 3:3-7, 36).[219]

The greater the number of conversions which such preaching could lead to, the more powerful, of course, would be the "counter-cohesion" which would result in any given ship community. The impediment of a monolithic "group cohesion" which sensed individual conversion as blatant disloyalty could best be countered by the norms and values of an alternative (Christian) form of fellowship, a fact which became especially evident during the Thames Revival in England, as well as during the Marine Temperance Revival in America.[220]

A further purpose of preaching to seafarers would be to encourage the spiritual growth of those already converted, both for their own sake, and in order to make them "living epistles of commendation to the gospel," in other words—effective witnesses for Christ (2 Corinthians 3:2-3). Thereby they would, it was hoped, not only become invaluable partners in mission among their peers, but also "bear a large part in the conversion of the world." (However, since any given audience of seafarers would normally be made up of mainly unconverted men, a sanctification emphasis would not be dominant.)[221]

Turning to the question of sermon-content, the "voyage-of-life" concept proved by far the most popular theme in preaching to seafarers.[222] The "reigning sins of Sailors" would be graphically described as "shoals, against which they would be in mortal danger of foundering."[223] Despite occasional allegations to the contrary, sources in no way indicate any taint of anti-nominianism.[224] On the other hand, "if a system of self-righteousness were necessary to save a man," seamen would be "beyond its reach." Hence, few would be more receptive than they to a plain, straightforward Gospel of free grace. Nor would they need any of the "shiboleths of a religious sect," or the "refined speculations in modern theology."[225]

Reports of literal shipwrecks and other "marine disasters" were habitually "improved" to bring home the reality of the seafarer's constant confrontation with the alternatives of eternity.[226] Since they were preceived as no less misinformed about their true situation than the general public, sermons to seafarers would often include elements of the kind of maritime apologetics used in refuting popular objections to seamen's missions. (There were, for example, repeated references to the high estimation of their vocation by him who "made a ship his first pulpit, and seamen his first converts.")[227] For sermon-texts, efforts were persistently made to capitalize on such Scripture passages as refer to ships, seafarers and the sea.[228]

As to sermon-form, two considerations were regarded as paramount. In the first place, the message must be brief and readily comprehensible; it must not be childish, and yet be perfectly plain. Seamen had little patience with "long-winded" sentences or "jaw-cracking dictionary words."[229] Again, they would react with disgust, and label as "lubberly" any arbitrary effort by landsmen to address them "in the technical language of their profession." Such attempts at better "cross-cultural communication," however well-intentioned, would, where misapplied, only divert attention and inhibit acceptance of the Gospel (as Secretary Greenleaf of the American Seamen's Friend Society repeatedly reminded).[230]

This need not mean that a landsman should never, on occasion, follow the example of the Bible and make judicious use of nautical imagery. However, great caution was advised.[231] On the other hand, where the preacher was himself a former seafarer and therefore "knew the ropes," the situation would be completely reversed. Here, his hearers would recognize one of their own, and sense that powerful bond of the brotherhood of the sea. In this case, the use of not only nautical imagery but also nautical terminology, would ring true, thus "indigenizing" the message and enhancing its acceptance (as evidenced by the striking success of a Smith, Angas, Scoresby, Taylor and Jones).[232] So strongly was this felt, that some would warmly recommend sea-experience as one of the most important formal qualifications of any seamen's chaplain.[233]

In the second place, the message must be sufficiently forceful to convey the need for an immediate and personal response. It was as true of seamen as of landsmen, that they were "lost" unless awakened from the spiritual slumber of an unregenerate life. They, too, needed an actual invitation "to be reconciled to God, and not merely an attempt to announce to them that they were already reconciled."[234] However, in the case of seamen, a note of urgency was, if anything, even more mandatory. Seamen were "a short-lived race" of transients. Moreover, nowhere was it more true that the harvest was plenteous, but the laborers were few. Hence, many would "hear the Gospel but once."

Just as every address, however brief, must therefore include the essential contents of the "way of salvation," so, too, it must be delivered as to "one who hears it for the first and last time." It must leave him "without the shadow of an excuse" if he should choose to reject it. This he would respect. A seaman was trained to be "professionally prompt," always alert to translating impulse into action. "Baby simplicity," "effeminate softness," or "vapoury harangues" would never win the manly mind and heart of the sailor. But "strength of style and manner" could.[235]

In this connection, extemporaneous preaching was considered indisputably "the best." Seamen were noted for "eyeing the preacher," and would soon lose both interest and respect if they noticed he was "only reading to them." However, extemporizing would be no license for lack of prayerful preparation; rather, by "leaning on the Spirit of all grace for guidance," the well-prepared preacher would be "at liberty" to exploit to the full any providential opening for sowing the Word, both "in season" and "out of season."[236]

The opportunities for verbal witness open to the average seamen's chaplain were by no means limited to the pulpit. In common with colporteurs and other lay workers in waterfront ministry, he would find ample scope for both the spoken and the written Word in a wide range of "maritime visitation." The rationale for this method of mission was formulated thus, as early as in 1824:

> *We must go to them.* We have lost their confidence and friendship by our indifference and wicked neglect of them; and we can never gain it, but by going after them, and convincing them, by our own unwearied efforts to do them good, that we seek not theirs, but them. . . .[237]

In addition to this psychological reason why the sailor should be systematically "sought out," there was also a very practical consideration. The seaman's friends were locked in relentless conflict with his enemies. In many cases, the only way to "outcrimp the crimp" would be to be the first to gain a foothold on board an incoming ship. At all events, the visitation of seamen in their own environment, whether on shipboard or in their boarding-houses, or, for that matter, in hospitals or prisons, soon became a regular, virtually indispensable feature of the work.[238]

Although the aim of maritime visitation, especially so-called "ship-visiting," has recently become a subject of debate,[239] it was, in the early years of the work, never at issue. During the first, media-centered phase, the primary purpose was self-evident: an invitation to accept the Gospel. (There were as yet no facilities to which to invite.) However, even when "Bethels" began to appear, the essential focus of ship-visitation would still be to share the Gospel, there and then (or, to quote Marks again, "to carry religion home to those who would not or could not go forth to find it for themselves").

With literary media distribution continuing to fill a vital role in maritime mission, reports of the various societies show how colportage would consistently create opportunities to "engage in religious conversation."[240] This would generally take the form of conversational evangelism, where the immediate goal would, without apology, be the conversion of the unregenerate. Though decidedly directive in approach, this form of dialogue could evidently be combined with genuine willingness to listen and identify. (Marks, for example, would have no part in "cramming religion down men's throats.") Scoffing, however, was generally taken seriously, and met with brisk counter-attack. Otherwise, the themes of visitational dialogue would vary, just as those of maritime homiletics.[241]

In relation to the spiritually awakened or converted seafarer, such dialogue would assume the character of "maritime pastoral counseling." In this case, the proximate purpose would be to encourage commitment and growth.

Special concern was shown first-voyagers. Otherwise, responsibility would rest largely with the seafarer himself, to avail himself of such sparse opportunities for counseling as existed, whether by responding during visitation, seeking personal counseling later, or acquiring counsel through correspondence or devotional literature.[242] At all events, it was recognized that, among such highly transient hearers as seafarers, isolated sermons would never meet the whole need. Individual cases of conviction, or those manifesting a deep concern for their soul's welfare, would require more, if they were to be "followed up successfully, and the nail riveted in a sure place." As early as 1823, it was urged that "something allied to pastoral service must also be furnished."[243]

By then, a voluntary source of supply (for both pastoral and other needs) had already begun to manifest itself—the Christian seafarer. Where methods like media distribution, proclamation and visitation led to personal conversion, the task would be not only one of edification, but also "the equipment of the saints for the work of the ministry" (Ephesians 4:12). That work was undertaken with sustained determination. It would be impossible to study, with any degree of impartiality, the sources of early seamen's mission history without acknowledging the pivotal part played by various forms of "maritime lay ministry."[244]

By this term is meant, not the work of salaried employees of societies, nor that of promotional helpers, but voluntary lay partnership in direct maritime mission. Though not then formulated as such, the issue was essentially one of "indigenization." The Bethel Movement was basically an implementation, in the seafarer's world, of the Reformation principle of "the priesthood of all believers." As such, it also acknowledged the "Church Growth" theory that, ideally, "witness should follow the natural lines of kinship" (the so-called "Homogeneous Unit Principle"). There was already a brotherhood of the sea. The task was now to build a brotherhood in Christ.

Peer-group pressure need not, therefore, be seen solely from a negative viewpoint. Peer-group *contact* could offer unique opportunities for the genuine Christian's most powerful witness in any peer-group situation— his daily life. In short, it was recognized that, in maritime as in world mission, the work of evangelizing an ethnic or vocational group must be done chiefly by those indigenous ("native") to that group.[245]

With its powerful emphasis on lay collaboration, the Bethel Movement was able to counter the current spirit of paternalism with an invigorating reliance on partnership. That partnership would be equally evident in both of those basic needs of spiritual life—mission and fellowship. If mission is "never effective unless it results in a new missionary," the Bethel Movement may be said to have been effective indeed.[246] As the movement gathered momentum, more and more converts proved by their missionary zeal that no truly Christian seafarer would ever be "satisfied to go to heaven alone." They also proved that in no way could organized societies hope to evangelize the merchant seamen of the world without wide participation by those already won for the faith.

Hence, such societies would seek ways in which to render the efforts of seafaring partners in the Gospel even more effective.[247] With or without the aid of local "Bethel Companies" of lay landsmen, they would promote the "domestication" of religion on the men's own ships by helping to hold Bethel Meetings on board during a ship's stay in port (in addition to inviting to "Bethel" facilities ashore).[248] They would encourage committed Christian seafarers to see a continuing seafaring career as not only perfectly compatible with their faith, but also as an indispensable opportunity for witness during those long periods when shipmates would be beyond the reach of societies ashore.[249] They would animate such seafarers to undertake responsibility for regular Scripture-reading and prayers on board, as well as to superintend loan libraries; and they would seek to help them become both adroit as apologists and capable as counselors.[250] In particular, they saw clearly how Christian captains (to some degree also other officers) were a key factor in the development of a viable lay ministry afloat.[251]

Meanwhile, just as the church of Jesus Christ had to be "sent forth" into the world ("Sendung"), she must also be "gathered together" from the world ("Sammlung"). Bonhoeffer speaks fervently of the need for God's people, as "the seed of the Kingdom," to "remain scattered," willing to forego the "incomparable joy and strength" of visible fellowship with other Christians, held together "solely in Jesus Christ."[252] Societies for seamen's mission were, from the earliest era of the work, sensitive to the special problems preventing seafarers from normal access to the power and inspiration of physical fellowship in the faith. They would, therefore, gladly promote such manifestations of Christian community as might nevertheless prove possible.

However, here (as in the case of early outreach endeavor) first efforts were uniquely a *lay* initiative. It was seamen's mission societies which grew out of early forms of Christian seamen's fellowship, not vice versa. It was only after those informal cell groups of the British Naval Awakening and the Thames Revival had, with the help of the Bethel Flag, blossomed into the vibrant fellowship of the early Bethel Movement, that seamen's mission societies came into their own. (This is, of course, just another example of the historic interdependence between free movements of "sodalities" and institutional structures or "modalities," which has been the object of recent research.)[253]

During this period, there was no serious attempt at formal organization. Then came those two dramatic appeals by a hundred "Bethel Captains" on either side of the Atlantic, both in conjunction with major nondenominational seamen's mission societies: (1) *Voice from the Sea,* published in New York, 1825, in support of the proposed American Seamen's Friend Society;[254] (2) *A Voice from the Ocean,* published in London, 1838, on behalf of the British and Foreign Sailor's Society.[255] The British captains had then already begun a process of institutionalization, by uniting, in 1837, to form a "Bethel Covenant;" organization was carried a step further with the founding, in 1865, of the "Bethel Union Register" (renamed the "Bethel Union Association"), also in affiliation with the BFSS. By the turn of the century, over 1,000 shipmasters had enrolled.[256]

Although strictly speaking beyond the period of study, it is worthy of note that, in 1908, with the merging of this association into a "Seamen's Christian Brotherhood," sponsored by the British and Foreign Sailor's Society and the American Seamen's Friend Society in unison, the concept of Christian seafarers' associations was widened to include all ranks, regardless of nationality. The Brotherhood adopted from its precursor two features which have become characteristic of such associations: an emblem, incorporating elements of the original Bethel Flag, and a "rule of life," undertaking personal responsibility for one's own walk of faith and witness to fellow-seafarers. A significant purpose of these associations was that seamen should present a positive image to "natives of the countries they [would] visit."[257]

Although both ecclesiological and practical considerations were destined to inhibit any spectacular growth,[258] the fundamental concept has, in varying forms, lived on.[259] With recent radical changes in the shipping industry and the acute need for maritime lay ministry, the International Christian Maritime Association has made the organization of a strong, ecumenically-based world-wide Christian seafarers' fellowship, and the promotion of self-propagating, "cellular Christianity" on board ship, a major concern. (A recent and promising venture to help fill this need is the so-called "Ministering Seafarers' Program," a system of pastoral follow-up and lay ministry at sea launched in 1979 by the Tacoma Seamen's Center, computer-coordinated from there, and already the object of extensive inter-agency cooperation. Included are the two major indigenous Korean seamen's mission organizations—Korea Harbor Evangelism and Korea Seamen's Mission founded in 1974 and 1982, respectively.)[260]

From the earliest phase of the work, a vital area of lay ministry had been that of "maritime intercessory prayer." The very emergence of the

seamen's mission enterprise (like that of world mission), was attributed to
the fact that it had, from the outset, been "undergirded by intercession."[261]
The cell groups of the British Naval Awakening and the Thames Revival, as
well as the shipboard Bethel Meetings which evolved world-wide, were,
essentially, prayer-meetings; and the theme was not only one's own personal
welfare, but the salvation of all brother-seafarers, blessings upon all seamen's
friends, and the promotion of the Seamen's Cause throughout the world. The
prayers of seamen themselves, always so "well seasoned with salt," were
held to be especially effectual, as they "ardently importuned a Throne of
Grace" (Hebrews 4:16).[262]

Others were also involved, however, and among landsmen, the
example and leadership of the clergy was considered crucial. With fellow-
clerics who failed to pray for seafarers, G.C. Smith was merciless. He
desired no communion with "selfish monopolizers of prayer," who could
forget it was from "the sailors of Galilee" that all "bishops and clergy, and
independent, methodist and baptist ministers," had sprung; he even admonished their congregations to issue them with an ultimatum if they
persisted.[263] Meanwhile, many ashore did, in fact, begin to pray systematically for seamen, both in Britain and in America. Seamen's friends in the
United States, inspired by similar endeavors in "foreign" mission circles,
actually succeeded in maintaining, for many years, a "Concert of Prayer for
Seamen," held every third Monday in the month.[264]

In a historical overview of the methodology of maritime mission, the
evolution of well-adapted "operational facilities" is significant as providing
the prerequisite for a regular preaching and pastoral ministry to seafarers.

Four phases may be discerned over the years: (1) Separate
sanctuaries, with "seats free," and a name symbolizing "a standing
invitation" to seafarers were soon seen as both physically and psychologically necessary. (Normally, church and chapel seats were already
"pewed out;" and even where "sailors' pews" were, occasionally, provided,
the seafarer was sufficiently sensitive to his own "peculiarities of dress and
manner" to save himself the embarassment of seeking to "stow away"
among "dressed up folks" from shore.[265] (2) Land-based stations eventually
became the rule, as representing a sound, long-term solution. (But early
floating sanctuaries called for less initial outlay, and held a powerful appeal
for the sailor; he had a "known prediliction" for worshiping "on his own
element.")[266] (3) Diversification of facilities followed the widening of the
concept of ministry. (While lodging needs were met by separate "sailors'
homes," the sanctuary building was adapted to meet other, social, recreational and cultural needs, culminating in the multi-ministry "institute"
model.)[267] (4) Increased emphasis on mobility has, in more recent years,
become the order of the day, corresponding to the radical structural changes

in the shipping industry itself. (The earlier Church of England "roadstead" ministry has, in a sense, re-emerged, only on wheels instead of keels.)[268]

It is the origin and early growth of *organized* mission to seafarers which forms the focus of the present study. Hence, it would seem relevant to examine, however briefly, in what ways early leaders of the movement sought to coordinate their ministry and give permanence to its fruits. What were, in other words, the "organizational policies" pursued by the pioneers?

Focusing first on personnel policy, and in particular on the recruitment of chaplains, there was never any question of uniformity. However, importance was consistently attached to such qualities as evangelical zeal, spiritual maturity, general resourcefulness and robust health. Advanced age was considered no hindrance, and a high premium was placed on "solid sea experience."[269]

In their promotional policy, seamen's mission societies on both sides of the Atlantic followed the general "voluntary society" pattern of the Evangelical United Front. They thought highly of the public relations value of annual reports, annual meetings, and annual sermons (while concern for patronage remained, for sociological reasons, a more specifically British phenomenon). They also adopted much the same methods of fund-raising, soliciting donations, annual subscriptions, bequests and church offerings, with or without the aid of traveling agents and auxiliary societies.[270]

In relational policies, they followed largely liberal lines. Although a period of *denominational* emphasis did, to some extent, succeed the original era of nondenominational endeavor, denominational relations have, more recently, entered a new ecumenical phase.[271] Apart from the debilitating controversy in the British capital during the second quarter of the nineteenth century, inter-organizational relations were generally positive.[272] So, too, were relations with *residents*. Where seamen's families, former seafarers, or other local inhabitants made up the congregational nucleus of a seamen's church, however, care would be needed to maintain a judicious balance between the relative claims of seafarers and residents.[273] Nor did *race* relations develop into any major issue during the period under study. Although there were disturbing indications of discrimination against American blacks and Lascar crews from British India, both British and American societies showed genuine and consistent concern for foreign seafarers in general.[274]

In the area of "maritime education," sufficient has already been said of early efforts to confirm the contention that here was a field of social and cultural endeavor where seamen's mission leaders were indeed pioneers. Through "Sabbath schools," "Sea-boys' (or Day) schools" and "Nautical (or Marine) schools," they were able not only to provide for the catechization of large numbers of seamen and their children, but also to contribute toward the elementary education of the poor, and the vocational training of an important segment of society.[275] After an intervening period of secularization in vocational maritime education, there is now, once more, a growing concern that such training should serve the total needs (not only physical and mental, but also spiritual and moral) of young seafarers.[276]

As in world mission, so, too, in maritime mission, education could be classified as more than a method of evangelism; it was also a means of social service.[277] As noted previously, methods of "maritime diaconal ministry" were not regarded by the pioneers of mission to seafarers as merely a means to an end. Nor were they seen as essentially of lower priority, even though they did, in the main, emerge somewhat later. However primary the soteriological objective of the work, in methodology *kerygma* and *diakonia* belonged basically to each other as equivalent and complementary partners.[278] This was, for example, quite evident in Father Taylor's view of social action as an indispensable corollary to evangelistic endeavors:

> We should not consume metals by frequent heating, unless with a design of putting into useful shape. But, for want of good "Boarding-Houses," in the first part of my ministry, this was not the case. My people were attracted to church by hundreds, and melted into a resolving and vowing tenderness of conscience, and then thrown out into the chilling and paralyzing effects of rum-selling boarding-houses. . . .[279]

Just as, on the world mission scene, "the printing press, the school and the hospital alongside the church became identifying marks of Protestant mission stations," so, too, in maritime ministry, sea libraries, marine schools and sailor's homes came to be intimately identified with seamen's mission stations. This close connection between maritime social service and evangelism endowed such service with the quality of testimony to Christ. It ensured that degree of verbalization so necessary for a communication of the content of the Gospel with needful precision.[280]

Methods of ministry devised during the early decades of the work to meet the seafarer's "temporal" needs were wide in range. Sorely limited funds would, therefore, place severe restrictions on the degree of involvement, and in almost every area, secular agencies would eventually adopt major responsibilities. Nevertheless, it remains a fact of history, that those who first identified and initially met the immediate social needs of seafarers were men and women moved by the constraining love of Christ.[281]

As already seen, certain appalling aspects of sea-life were uncovered by concerned Christians even before the first societies for the evangelization of seafarers were established. However, at the beginning of the Bethel Movement, with the inhumanity of impressment and slave trade already exposed,[282] the pioneers now pooled their resources in a sustained onslaught against the system they saw as the sailor's deadliest menace, the clutch of the crimp. Alternative boarding-facilities were provided in forms varying from modest "recommended" lodging-houses, to huge, specially-constructed "Sailor's Homes."[283] Such facilities were supplements by other measures, all calculated to undermine the empire of the crimp. These would include seamen's register offices, savings facilities and reading-rooms, as well as a remarkably successful Marine Temperance Movement.[284]

Through such additional means as marine libraries and museums, maritime education opportunities and lecture series, societies sought to elevate the seafarer culturally and economically, thereby redeeming not only his public image, but also his self-esteem.[285] Though sporadic and wholly inadequate, some efforts were nevertheless made to relieve the pitiful plight of seafarers' dependents, both by direct benevolence and by elementary education and vocational training.[286] Pioneering initiatives were also taken in various crisis situations with which seafarers themselves were constantly confronted, such as shipwreck, prolonged unemployment, sickness, disability and (for the few who survived thus far) the grinding problems of old age.[287]

Finally, although the general working and living conditions of the average seafarer were, at the end of the formative years of the seamen's mission movement, still deplorable, the pioneers of the work were far from indifferent toward humanization of the industry as such. Some have been quick to discount as futile any efforts by "sky pilots and devil dodgers" to better the lot of the seafarer. The fact of the matter is, they fulfilled no mean "prophetic" task over the years. Through the printed and spoken word, they were (as seen in several instances) able to alert the public to many exploitive practices and glaring inequities, contribute towards a climate of reform, and even participate in political action.[288] While trade unionism and international labor organization lie well beyound the boundaries of this study, there can be no doubt that much of the ground for their major achievements was prepared by those who had long since, from clear Christian motives, devoted themselves to the spiritual, moral and social welfare of the seafarer. It is this latter legacy of Christian concern for the human dignity of seafarers which has, since 1982, been so brilliantly revived by the new "Center for Seafarers' Rights" of the Seamen's Church Institute of New York and New Jersey.[289]

QUESTIONS OF RESULTS AND RELEVANCE

Shortly after the establishment of the New York Sailors' Home in 1842, there were some who worried that seamen were now placed in circumstances "so favorable to their comfort and independence," that they would be "unfitted for the mean accommodation of the forecastle, or for the

servile subjection imposed upon them at sea."[290] Such words add credibility
to the statement that seamen, after the Civil War, were one class of "slaves"
still awaiting emancipation.[291] At the same time, they accentuate the success
of at least some social reforms attempted on their behalf. These were duly
publicized by seamen's mission societies as tangible results of efforts to
advance the "temporal" welfare of seafarers.[292]

To what extent did methods calculated to promote also their moral
and spiritual welfare prove effectual? That societies were deeply concerned
about visible fruits of the work is understandable. Reliable results would
constitute an important means of ascertaining how far the methods adopted
were, in actual fact, serving set objectives. Again, the publication of results
was an accepted means of quickening concern, and encouraging the zeal to
persevere.[293]

In practice, however, the question of identifiable individual results
posed serious problems. What criteria could be used? The mere fact that
seamen comprised such a "circulating auditory" precluded any form of
individual control. Nevertheless, the whole issue was considered so crucial,
that continual efforts were made to provide at least some indication of the
impact of the work in the lives of intended beneficiaries.[294]

Certainly, if one could judge by the tenor of published reports
bearing on the "general deportment" of sailors (after the launching of the
Bethel Movement), it would be difficult to deny at least some degree of
"moral improvement." Magistrates, custom-house officials, merchants and
others in close contact with the seafaring class, would frequently attest to the
remarkable "reformation" among them. No more was the word "seamen"
synonymous with "swearing, drunkenness, and rags." Converted tars told of
their own astonishment, as they "knocked off" one overt sin after the other.
Seamen's savings accounts went up, and marine insurance premiums (on
"temperance ships") went down. Resident churchgoers were no longer
alarmed if seamen came; they were disappointed if they did not. It was freely
admitted that much remained unredeemed. Maritime vice was partially
"smothered," but by no means extinguished. Yet evidence of change seemed
irrefutable. One Lloyd's surveyor gave it as his considered opinion, that
sailors were now (in 1826) simply a "different species of men."[295]

Whereas "moral melioration" would be relatively discernible, how
could any human agency hope to keep accurate accounts of personal
conversions? After all, genuine spiritual life could only result where created
by the Spirit, and was, therefore, beyond exact empirical verification
(John 3:13, 1 Corinthians 2:11). However, just as the Spirit would work
through visible instruments, so, too, there would be at least some visible
indications of spiritual response. These might assume a wide variety of
forms, for example: tales of "tearful eyes" and "fixed attention" among

"hardy sons of the ocean," when exposed to the preaching of the Gospel; testimonics of incredible attachment to the Scriptures and Gospel literature; reports of warm collaboration by both officers and men, as lay evangelists in the ranks of the Bethel Movement; and (at least initially) predictable persecution for so doing.[296]

On the basis of these and other indications, some would seek to set up "spiritual statistics." By 1825, for example, among 15,000 men regularly engaged in the British coal-trade, some 5,000 were estimated to have become "reformed and praying men" during the eight years following the unfurling of the first Bethel Flag (in 1817). Also by 1825, a further 5,000 seamen were believed to have "become pious" among British and American seafarers in general, making at that time a total of some 10,000 seamen "hopefully converted" (out of an estimated 600,000 seamen in the British and American merchant fleets combined).

Such statistics would not take into account the number of seamen "under serious impressions," and therefore potentially close to conversion. However, an interesting indication of receptivity to the Gospel was the observation that, in a typical American major seaport like Baltimore, it was, in the mid-1820's, customary to find "about three-fourths of the Seamen in port attend upon religious exercises under the Bethel Flag." Another significant item of information was the fact that, by 1828, some 500 captains would engage in the weekly prayer meetings then regularly held on the Thames. (Subsequently, the membership figures for Christian captains' associations could provide important though by no means comprehensive statistics.) A half-century later, it was reported, of 350,000 American-born seamen, one-tenth were known to "honor the claims of Christ" in their lives.[297]

Societies involved in maritime mission readily recognized that all such statistics were at best only estimates. They knew that personal manifestations of faith could vary, that there were aspects "known only to God," and that the ultimate record of spiritual life was with him alone, who had created it. Nor should later generations feel at liberty to ridicule the "romanticism" of the pioneers, because they were, occasionally, tempted to overdraw the prospects for the future. In their eagerness to see new life in Christ among men of the sea, they were at least evincing a concern for what is, according to the Word of God, still the one thing needful. Meanwhile, they were not oblivious to their Master's prediction, that a personal commitment to him would, in the present age, not be made by the majority.[298]

The truth is, those early pioneers were by no means devoid of biblical realism. On the contrary, they consistently refused to reduce the tension between God's universal will to save, and the necessity for man's individual appropriation of that salvation. They were, in fact, well aware that the measure of their "success" was not the degree of response to their ministrations, much less any personal popularity rating as a result, but quite simply their own obedience to one overriding missionary mandate: that of bringing, by word and deed, the Gospel of Christ to the seafaring world. It lies in the very nature of authentic mission that its validity can never be judged by results.[299]

How, then, can the outcome of 85 formative years of organized maritime mission best be summarized? Perhaps it would be, in the words of one who was a seafarer himself: "Thanks—for giving us an alternative!"[300] By 1864, it was recognized that the mission of the Christian church to seafarers of the world was largely an unfinished task.[301] However, a beginning had been made. In a growing number of world ports, where previously the seafarer would be welcomed only by those intent on exploiting him, he could now count on an alternative, on the fact that there were some who would seek his best interest in the name of Christ, and provide him with at least some semblance of personal choice.

Today, over a century later, the task of securing an adequate Christian ministry for seafarers of the world is still far from completed. It is true that, in the intervening years, great strides have been made in raising their socio-economic status, with a variety of secular organizations assuming wide responsibilities. Many church-related agencies, too, have become increasingly preoccupied with the seafarer's physical and social needs. Such needs can quickly become acute, whenever the increasing transfer of national tonnage to "flags of convenience" leads to the violation of seafarers' rights. Has this, however, for the Christian church at large, led to less concern for the seafarer's continuing *spiritual* needs? If so, a renewed study of the past might prompt a reappraisal of priorities, and reduce the risk of polarization.[302]

Certainly, the "Maritime Industrial Revolution," which has emerged in international shipping since World War II, has confronted the church with awesome challenges. Such technological changes as automation, containerization and "mammothization" have pointed to the need for new, updated versions of well-tried methods of maritime ministry.

As far as the social aspect of such ministry is concerned, there will doubtless be a continuing need. Many hardships and deprivations can still be eradicated. Others that are intrinsic to seafaring may be better alleviated. Moreover, the present era of new, ecumenical patterns of inter-agency cooperation, such as the worldwide "International Christian Maritime Association" (ICMA) and the western hemisphere "International Council of Seamen's Agencies" (ICOSA), in close cooperation with the Center for Seafarers' Rights in New York, make it possible for a collective, prophetic voice to be heard in the fora of the maritime world, where issues are at stake affecting the lives and welfare of seafarers. However, while strides in social progress made in one generation will not normally need to be repeated in the next, the most ultimate human needs will remain the same. Hence, each new generation of seafarers will need to appropriate the Gospel anew, as church-related agencies, through a specifically missionary-pastoral ministry, continue to do what they, and they alone, are called and equipped to do.[303]

Meanwhile, there are also signs of rapidly increasing *ethnic change* on the international shipping scene, as Third World (especially Asian) and Communist countries man a mounting proportion of the world's merchant tonnage. There are already strong indications that the next phase of the continuing history of maritime mission will be an era of increasing non-Western participation. What implications should this have for not only the younger but also the older churches?

An observer, who, in the mid-1820's, was struck with the remarkable readiness of seafarers to embrace the Gospel, found their case resembling "that of the first converts to Christianity." Whereas landsmen would, through the influence of habit, "too often hear the words of salvation as though they heard them not," for seafarers, secluded for so long from "religious advantages," such words were, so to speak, a "strange thing."[304] There is much in the present-day picture to indicate that history is repeating itself, where seafarers of non-Christian religions and ideologies (whether Muslim, Hindu, Buddhist, Shintoist, animist or atheist) are being confronted with a valid, holistic presentation of the Gospel on the waterfront. The consequences for Christian global mission could be nothing short of overwhelming. As one modern-day missiologist (Bloomquist) has put it:

> Our seaports are "gateways" through which fellow-humans from all over the world come to us by *centripetal* movement, after which they are "spun back" to all parts of the world again by *centrifugal* movement. What a unique, God-given opportunity to give them the Gospel—just where these two movements intersect![305]

The classic "missiological" motive for maritime mission, so central at the beginning of the Bethel Movement, is, therefore, as relevant as ever.[306]

So, too, is a principal perspective emerging from this entire study—the crucial role of peer ministry in evangelizing and discipling within an isolated social group such as that of the seafarer.[307] As one who knew them well put it at the close of the period of the study, there was nowhere any nobler evidence of "warm, generous, self-forgetting consecration to Christ" than in the Christian seafarer. Despite drastic technological and social change, basic factors affecting the seafarer's life and personality remain the same today as then. According to Scripture, Christ, the source of Christian faith, is also the same. The potential for effective lay ministry by Christian seafarers to fellow-seafarers is, therefore, as powerful as it ever was, a fact clearly demonstrated by the dedication and witness of current-day Christian seafarers from Asia.[308]

The saga of the seamen's mission movement began with the New Testament record, culminating in the pioneering ship's chaplaincy of the Apostle Paul on his epic voyage to Rome, as described in chapter 27 of the Acts of the Apostles. Then the Book of Acts ends—abruptly, as if unfinished, by the banks of the Tiber. Though scholars may be baffled by the historic reason, what could be more symbolic? The book ends, but the work continues—through the acts of every succeeding generation of apostles, on land and sea.

Since the seafaring side of that apostolate experienced such a dramatic blossoming by the banks of the Thames in the early 1800's, a factor has arisen which gives to both the global and maritime mission enterprise a new note of urgency. In recent years, the doors have been closed to traditional forms of Christian mission in a mounting number of nations. Nevertheless, there is one door which has not been closed—that of seafarers committed to Christ, serving wherever they go as "non-professional missionaries." [309]

In fact, just as seafarers were once the first means of bringing the Gospel to the non-Christian world, they may one day prove to be the ultimate. [310]

Addendum

The Emergence of Organized Nordic Seamen's Missions

In the preceding study the founding of the first Continental seamen's mission society (that of the Norwegian Seamen's Mission in 1864) marks a transition from the Anglo-American hegemony of the *Formative Phase* of the seamen's mission movement to the ensuing *Continental Phase,* incorporating the other seafaring peoples of Northern Europe: the Nordic nations, followed by the Germans and the Dutch.

Although this Continental Phase falls strictly speaking beyond the scope of this study, an addendum on the emergence of Nordic seamen's missions would seem justified for at least three reasons: (1) Historically, it is the founding of these Nordic seamen's missions which constitutes the bridge between the beginning of the movement and all that follows. (2) Recently, there has been some question as to the present-day legitimacy and relevancy of "nationally orientated seamen's missions," in an age of increasing emphasis on multi-national and multi-denominational cooperation. (3) From the viewpoint of equity, too, it seems only fair to include the origins of that Nordic branch of the work which provided both the original funding and incentive for the whole study.[1]

The three Scandinavian countries, Norway, Denmark and Sweden, share with Finland and Iceland a strong seafaring tradition. *Sociologically,* the basic significance of seafaring in the national economy of the Nordic nations has resulted in the Nordic seafarer enjoying a relatively high social status. *Ecclesiologically,* the powerful patriotism of the Nordics is reflected in the evolution of monolithic state church structures, of identical (Lutheran) denominational allegiance. To these national churches the vast majority of the respective populations still subscribe, at least in name. (The symbol of the cross in each of the national emblems bears tacit testimony to close historic ties between church and state.) Not surprisingly, therefore, the seamen's mission organizations of this particular population group are easily identifiable as a distinct Nordic "type," with certain common characteristics within the wide spectrum of international Christian ministry to seafarers.

The earliest roots of organized Nordic seamen's missions go back to the same sporadic church-related ministries as preceded Anglo-American seamen's mission organization. Thus, long before specific mission to seafarers was organized in the Nordic countries, their crews could, in common with those of the other seafaring nations of Christendom, derive benefit from varied efforts on their behalf by the (Catholic) Medieval Church. These would, as noted in chapter 1 (under "Early Forms of Ministry to Seafarers"), include the ministrations of missionaries during passage overseas, the facilities of hospitals and hostels connected with monasteries and churches in coastal districts, the promotion of church-related maritime guilds, the invocation of seafaring saints, and the provision of mass for those in peril on the sea or the souls of those lost there.

Then, in the wake of the Reformation, there emerged in the Nordic nations, as in other Protestant seafaring states, a whole series of devotional aids for seafarers containing homilies, meditations and casuistic prayers, covering almost every conceivable situation at sea. As elsewhere, ship's chaplains would be appointed to major naval units and East Indiamen. In Nordic churches, too, offerings would be collected for the ransom of seamen enslaved by the pirate states of the Barbary Coast.[2]

A significant avenue of early maritime history to Nordic seafarers was furnished by Nordic emigrant churches and embassy chapels in foreign ports. Here, seafarers from home would naturally be invited and be ministered to. Examples are: the Danish-Norwegian Church in London (opened in 1696), the Swedish Church in London (opened in 1728), the Swedish Embassy Chapel in Constantinople (opened in the 1750's and rebuilt a century later), the German-Danish Chapel in Bordeaux (opened in 1838). The extensive seamen's ministry maintained by Nordic emigrant congregations in American ports during the second half of the nineteenth century had, as precursors, the pioneer churches of New Sweden on the Delaware River more than two centuries earlier.[3]

Apart from such endeavors originating from native Nordic instrumentality, a vital ministry to Nordic seafarers was developed by British and American agencies during the half-century they were alone in the field. These efforts go back as far as to the Napoleonic War era. For the edification of Norwegian and Danish seamen incarcerated in British prison hulks from 1807 to 1814, the British and Foreign Bible Society, with the help of the minister of the Danish-Norwegian Church in London, the Rev. Ulrik Frederik Rosing, printed and donated 5,000 Danish New Testaments. Likewise with his assistance, the Society for Promoting Christian Knowledge provided 2,250 copies of the Danish Hymnal. Imprisoned seamen, converted through the ministrations of English Quakers during these years, became,

SEBULON (Gen. 49.13.)

Eller

For De

Aandelige Søe-Farende/

Som seiler i dette Liv paa

Verdens Hav/

VEJEN dertil vises efter Compassets Maade med XXXII

Linier eller Lignelser/

Som lærer/

Hvorledis et hvert Christen Menniske lyckeligen og vel kand fare igiennem

Verden til Himmelen/

At hand ikke skal

Enten støde an paa Forargelsers blinde Skiær og Klipper/
Eller kuld-seile af Syndens og Sorgens Storm-Vinde/
Ikke heller druckne i Dødens dybe Hav/
Men først med Siæls og siden med Legoms heel og holden Vahre
komme efter sit fuldendte Livets Reise

Fra Fare til Frelse/
Fra Havet til Havnen/
Fra Verden til Himmelen/

Tillige med nogle Aandelige Vers og Sange i adskillige Tilfælde/

Skrevet paa Hans Kongl. Majests. Orlogs-Flode/ og sammenskrevet i Brøndby Vester Præste-Gaard Ao. 1719 den 9 Novembr.	Eenfoldig oprettet af JENS COLDING Med-Tiener i Ordet til Brøndby Vester og Øster Meenigheder.

Kiøbenhavn/ Trykt i Kongl. Maj. privil. Bogtrykkerie paa Amager-Torv/ 1720.

Title-page of a typical Nordic devotional manual for
seafarers. Here, the 1720 edition of the Danish Rev.
Jens Colding's "Zebulon: or, Sea-port for Spiritual
Seafarers, who Sail on the Ocean of Life, Demonstrated
according to the Compass by 32 Points or Parables. . . ."

The Rev. Ulrik Frederik
Rosing (1776-1841),
Norwegian-born
benefactor of Norwegian
and Danish seafarers
incarcerated on board
British prison hulks,
1807-1814. (J. Smidt:
Fotefar.)

The prison ship *Bahama* anchored off the British
naval base at Chatham, 30 miles east of London, one
whose luckless Norwegian-Danish inmates were
regularly visited by the Rev. O.F. Rosing during
the Napoleonic War years.

with the advent of peace, the means of transplanting the Quaker faith to Norway.[4]

Meanwhile, as Dr. John Paterson recalls in his *Memoirs* while ministering to English-speaking seamen in Stockholm in 1808-09, how he put that extraordinarily popular seamen's tract *James Covey* into the hands of Count Lagerbjelke, Admiral of the Swedish Fleet. The latter was "so much pleased with it that he translated it with his own hand into Swedish and 30,000 copies of it were published and nearly all circulated in a few months."[5] The Religious Tract Society in London made sure that many more of its most successful tracts were translated into Swedish and Danish (which at that time was also the written language of Norway). These were widely distributed among Scandinavian seamen via various channels.

One of the earliest of these distribution channels was the so-called "Agents Afloat," a handful of committed Christian sea-captains who, during the first struggling years of the BFBS and RTS, circulated Scripture and tracts on a voluntary basis in many foreign ports including Nordic. Harwich fishermen, too, zealously scattered translated tracts among the reportedly "dreary inhabitants of the rocks of Norway" during the lobster season.[6]

Following the British example, and with enthusiastic support from the BFBS, "Marine Bible Societies" were, as noted in chapter 6 of this study, established in port-cities like Stockholm (1815), Carlscrona (1819) and Copenhagen (1820), for distribution among both naval and merchant seamen.[7] Also, during the 1820's, the Prayer Book and Homily Society took up the distribution of translated homilies among Scandinavian seamen.[8]

From 1818 on, with the establishment of regular seamen's mission societies in Britain and America, Nordic seafarers inevitably came within the orbit of their activities. Almost all would have some smattering of "Seamen's English." Many actually sailed on British and American ships. Through the ensuing decades sources indicate that seamen from the Nordic nations responded in surprising numbers to the general English-language ministry of the major British and American agencies. This applied not only to regular shore-based activities but also to floating chapels, mariners' churches, and (eventually) sailors' homes. As elsewhere, so too along the coasts of Northern Europe, the volunteer sea-going arm of these societies, the so-called "Bethel Captains," hoisted the Bethel Flag and held shipboard services for whoever cared to come from ship or shore. Eventually, there evolved *Scandinavian* versions of the flag.[9]

Impressed, however, with the relatively large numbers and religious receptivity of Nordic seafarers, the major British and American seamen's mission societies sought to supplement these activities with a special native-language ministry for their particular benefit, both on British and American waterfronts and in the seaports of Northern Europe.

BRITANNIA,

ELLER

Sjömäns Moraliska Anspråk,

FRAMSTÄLLDE

af

REV. JOHN HARRIS.

Prisskrift utgifven i London.

Öfwersatt

efter Femte Upplagan, med bifogade anteckningar

öfver

Sjöfolkets belägenhet vid Handels-Flottan

i Sverige;

AF

A. G. Oxehufwud.

Title-page of Harris'
prize-winning 1837 essay
translated into Swedish
by that colorful naval
officer Adolph Göran
Oxehufwud (1799-1852).
His advocacy of the
Bethel Flag introduced
its adoption in modified
form in Scandinavia.

A pioneer example of the latter was the colorful career of that Danish-born cavalry officer called Carl Gustav Christopher von Bülow. His efforts to launch a "Scandinavian Seamen's Mission" by means of those one-man evangelistic sailing tours along the coast of Norway (in 1819 and again in 1826-28) have already been described in detail in chapter 11.[10] Then, from the other side of the Atlantic, the American Seamen's Friend Society commissioned, in 1841, the first in a rapidly lengthening list of "Sailor Missionaries" to the various port-cities of Norway, Denmark, Sweden and Finland, culminating in no less than twelve at one time in the late 1860's. (Details of their activities form part of the narrative of chapter 21.)[11]

Such attempts to penetrate the Nordic Lutheran establishment by seafaring emissaries of Methodist and Baptist affiliation, although they actually succeeded in transplanting these denominations to Nordic soil, also met with predictable resistance. No comparable difficulties were encountered by efforts to provide a Scandinavian-language ministry on the waterfronts of religiously pluralistic Britain and America. The most notable example of such ministry in the New World was without doubt the Swedish-born Rev. Olaf Gustaf Hedstrom and the Methodist Bethelship Mission of New York (inaugurated in 1845 and dealt with in chapter 21 of this study).[12]

An international version of
the Bethel Flag as depicted in
Folkevennen (Oslo) in 1861.

A Swedish version adopted by the
Marine Societies of Gothenburg
and Stockholm in 1838.

Emblem adopted by the
Norwegian Seamen's Mission
in 1865.

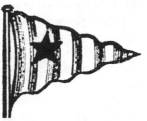

The blue star burgee of the
BFSS-related Bethel Union
Register founded in 1865.

The "Dove Flag" of the
Norwegian and Danish seafarers
fellowships of 1885 and 1899.

Emblem of the Seamen's Christian
Brotherhood of the BFSS & ASFS,
founded in 1908.

Emblem of the Swedish seafarers'
fellowship of 1884, highlighting
the invitation in Genesis 24:31.

The BSS has retained the star
and dove symbols of the original
Bethel Flag.

Meanwhile, the British and Foreign Sailors' Society expanded their staff of so-called "Thames Missionaries" to include, in 1846, the Rev. Carl von Bülow, with responsibility for foreign (principally Nordic) seafarers. After a lapse, due to financial frustrations, this form of outreach was revived in June 1860 with the appointment of August Thiemann. Of an amorphous Lutheran-Reformed background, this German-born evangelist was destined to play such a pivotal part in the evolution of independent Norwegian (and so also Nordic) seamen's missions, that a more detailed treatment is called for here than accorded in chapter 17 of this study.[13]

Thiemann spent the winter immediately following his appointment in Norway, in order to improve his knowledge of Norwegian and thereby better serve Scandinavian seamen on the Thames. While there, Thiemann and the Society he represented were given unprecedented publicity. Eilert Sundt, Norway's pioneer sociologist and influential leader of "Selskabet for Folkeoplysningens Fremme" (The Society for the Promotion of Popular Enlightenment) was fired by enthusiasm as a result of his encounter with Thiemann. Through the length and breadth of the land Sundt circulated detailed information on the work of the British and Foreign Sailors' Society in general and on its activities on behalf of Nordic seamen in particular. He launched a nation-wide appeal for books and funds for the Society and exhorted Norwegian shipmasters to copy the custom of hoisting the Bethel Flag as a signal for services on shipboard.[14]

At the same time Thiemann himself started a school for seamen's children in Oslo and visited the ice-bound shipping in the fjord. On a return visit the following autumn, he was even instrumental in founding, in Stavanger, on November 19, 1861, the first seamen's mission society in Norway, "Selskabet til befordring af Religiösitet og Kundskab blandt Söfolk" (The Society for Promoting Religion and Knowledge among Seafarers). Organized expressly on the lines of the London Society, it succeeded in opening a local seamen's reading-room the following year.[15]

Nevertheless, no indigenous *national* society was the outcome, at least not in Stavanger. Although several State Church clergymen responded positively to Thiemann's efforts, the *Norwegian Church Times* was quick to question "un-Lutheran doctrine" when this became apparent in his preaching. Thiemann was not invited back.[16]

Yet his efforts had not been in vain. The accumulated impact of half a century of British-American endeavor, climaxed by Thiemann's visits to Norway in the early 1860's, had laid the task squarely before the door of the National Church. What the situation now called for was a caliber of leadership from within its own walls capable of taking up that task.

However, before pursuing that matter further, another question calls for an answer: why should half a century have to elapse between the founding of the first major British and American seamen's mission societies (in the second and third decades of the nineteenth century) and the Nordic societies (in the seventh and eighth)?

Undoubtedly *economic factors* played a part. Not before the second half-century did the Nordic merchant fleets (and their crews) reach proportions substantial enough to make the need pressing. Nor was there earlier the level of national income required to develop and maintain effective organization overseas.

At least equally decisive was a combination of *ecclesiological factors*. In denominationally more diversified Britain and America powerful revivals had, around the turn of the century, already led to a proliferation of religious voluntary societies. Meanwhile, the governments of the Nordic Lutheran bloc felt called to conserve the religious stability and homogeneity of their peoples. Consequently, they resisted the inroads of revival or dissent. Historically, too, Lutheranism had a legacy of quietism as contrasted with the more activist Reformed stance.[17]

However, as the second half of the nineteenth century set in, the winds of change became more and more apparent. Religious revival in varying forms had reached the North. Anti-conventicle legislation (limiting the freedom of religious assembly) had by then been repealed, religious toleration had made significant progress, and voluntary societies for both foreign and home missions were developing within the framework of the national churches.

The times were propitious. Moreover, the catalyst was now at hand. It seems only fitting that it proved to be none other than that enterprising Thames missionary, August Thiemann, who unwittingly conveyed the call. After the founding of "The Seamen's Society" in Stavanger Thiemann had, in late November 1861, left for Bergen. Here, too, he held a public meeting to stir up local interest in the cause. Although he did not succeed in establishing any corresponding port society for that city, his visit was destined to be far from fruitless. While there, he visited with a young, recently graduated theologian, and laid the need for mission outreach to seafarers so heavily on his heart that the impression never left him. This was, late in life, readily affirmed by Johan Cordt Harmens Storjohann himself, universally acknowledged as the "Father of Nordic Seamen's Missions."[18]

To what manner of man was the Herculean task of initiating this movement entrusted? The Rev. J.C.H. Storjohann (1832-1914) was quite evidently endowed with rich natural gifts. A man of eminently fertile imagination, he had both the boldness of vision and organizing talent to translate vision into reality. True, traits of intransigence and impulsiveness could encumber cooperation in the long run. Nevertheless he had, through the new, so-called "Johnsonian" school of theology, imbibed a fervent missionary zeal, linked with an unflinching loyalty to Lutheran state church orthodoxy. Moreover, he possessed a personal charisma which made him one of the most powerful preachers of the day. His restless, combative spirit may not have made him the man to maintain momentum. But Storjohann certainly combined the characteristics needed to overcome an ecclesiastical inertia which had hitherto blocked a beginning.[19]

However, Storjohann needed yet another impulse himself before he was finally ready for action. What Thiemann had told him two years previously, about the pitiful plight of the average seafarer, he could confirm from vivid first-hand experience in the autumn of 1863. He had barely arrived in Scotland, in order to pursue theological research, when he found himself prompted to preach for the spiritually starving Scandinavian seamen he saw in Leith. The mate of a Norwegian sailing-ship in port (one Jörgen Johansen) was so moved by the message that he sought Storjohann out in neighboring Edinburgh next day in order to secure pastoral help. For Storjohann this man's plight and perseverance became the Nordic mariner's Macedonian Call: "Our seamen must have their own pastors!"[20]

His mind made up, Storjohann set to with dogged determination. This being the period when Norway was united with Sweden (1814-1905), he obtained financial support from the Swedish Church in London in order to prolong his stay in Great Britain. In this way, he was able to harvest vital personal experience in waterfront ministry, promote the concerns of resident Scandinavians (especially in Leith), and develop valuable contacts in British seamen's missions. In London he found Thiemann's Swiss-born successor, Conrad Schelling, zealously serving Scandinavian seamen from his base at the so-called "Rotherhithe Institute." Before Storjohann's return to Norway in the early summer of 1864, the Rev. George Scott welcomed him to the pulpit of his Methodist Chapel in Newcastle-on-Tyne (where Scott had long since put to good use language skills acquired during his years in Sweden and maintained a successful native-language ministry to Scandinavian seafarers and residents).[21]

Back in Bergen, Storjohann's strategy was to integrate seamen's missions into the already established foreign mission structure. However, the Norwegian Missionary Society, founded in 1842 as a voluntary society in affiliation with the National Church, was unwilling to accept such a substantially increased liability. This apparent rebuff was soon seen as a blessing in disguise. It compelled those concerned with the spiritual welfare of seamen to build up an independent organization, strong enough to stand on its own feet. Storjohann succeeded instead in collecting a committee of clergymen, merchants and sea-officers which in Bergen, on August 31, 1864, founded "Foreningen til Evangeliets Forkyndelse for skandinaviske Sömaend

The Rev. Johan Cordt Harmens Storjohann (1832-1914),
Norwegian-born "Father of Nordic Seamen's Missions."

i fremmede Havne" (The Society for the Proclamation of the Gospel to
Scandinavian Seamen in Foreign Ports). This cumbersome title, though
illustrative of the primary purpose, was eventually replaced by "Den norske
Sjömannsmisjon" (The Norwegian Seamen's Mission).

As the infant Society's secretary during its first struggling months,
Storjohann established a series of local auxiliaries around the coast of
Norway, while an appeal for financial support was circulated through every
parish in the land. The response was sufficiently encouraging to enable the
Society to send out its first three seamen's chaplains the following year, to
Leith, Newcastle and Antwerp, respectively. In 1866, Cardiff was added. In
1868, Storjohann himself came as pioneer pastor to the docklands of London.
That year also, Leith saw the completion of the first Norwegian seamen's

church specifically built as such. (In Leith, as elsewhere, these pioneer chaplains would have to make use of ships in port, or the existing shore facilities of colleagues in the host country, until they were able to move into their own.)[22]

As demands from all quarters poured in and promotional methods improved, the work expanded rapidly. By the Society's fiftieth anniversary (in 1914), activities were based on 35 shore facilities (or "stations") abroad. At the Society's centenary (in 1964), it was represented in exactly the same number of foreign ports, but stations were more satisfactorily staffed, more adequately equipped, and more widely dispersed (taking into account not least the needs of Norway's mammoth tanker fleet).

From the very outset, the Society's principal source of income has been a national network of auxiliaries, closely followed by voluntary support from seamen themselves as well as residents abroad. Shipowners have accounted for approximately one-tenth. Following the Society's centenary, the State agreed to defray a proportion of chaplains' salaries. (This now accounts for one-eighth of the annual budget.)

The Society has always seen itself as essentially only "the extended arm of the Church of Norway." Hence, its personnel are bound by the doctrine, liturgy and laws of the National Church. This position provided powerful ecclesiological motivation for expansion in ports where nominally Lutheran seamen were particularly exposed to denominational defection. (In New York, for example, Methodist and Baptist success with seamen was cited as a major motive for the establishment of an "orthodox" Norwegian station.)[23] A corresponding concern eventually led to the formation in 1885 of a national, Lutheran counterpart to the British-sponsored "Bethel Union Register," a 20-year-old association of Christian shipmasters which carried on the traditions of the early Bethel Captains. (Similar associations were formed in Sweden and Denmark.)[24]

The close affiliation between the Norwegian Seamen's Mission and the established Church of Norway also resulted in a special sense of affinity with the corresponding society of the Church of England. Historically, clergymen of the Church of Norway had, as already noted, earlier ties with the British and Foreign Sailors' Society. However, this was inevitable since the Church of England Missions to Seamen were not definitively organized until 1856, just eight years before the Norwegian national society.

The Norwegian Seamen's Mission had, in 1978, 32 stations of its own in foreign ports throughout the world, with a total staff of some 190, a home base of about 3,000 auxiliaries and a budget around 20 million Norwegian Kroner. Few, if any, forms of church activity in Norway are the object of more widespread goodwill.

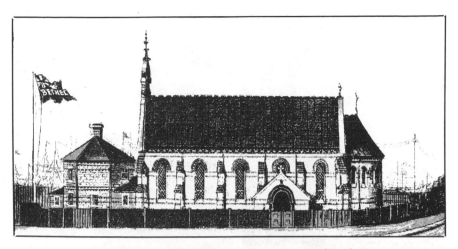

The Norwegian ("Eben-Ezer") Seamen's Church in
London, built by Storjohann in 1872, and strategically
located in the midst of Rotherhithe's huge Surrey
Commercial Docks. Note the novel Norwegian-
Swedish version of the Bethel Flag.
(K. Helle: *Broderkretsen paa Havet 1885-1985.*)

Within a decade after Norway had sent out her pioneer seamen's
chaplains, her Nordic neighbors had established their own national seamen's
mission organizations. In each case the key role of Storjohann is clearly
evident.

First came Denmark, culturally closest to Norway. Here, the part
played by Storjohann was more indirect. A powerful appeal on behalf of
Scandinavian seafarers had already been launched in 1862, and repeated in
1863, by that untiring advocate of Danish foreign missions, the Rev. Jens
Vahl of Aarhus. War with Prussia (1864) intervened. Nevertheless, Storjohann encouraged Vahl to persevere; and finally, in Copenhagen, on
November 12, 1867, the ground was ready for the foundation of "Den
danske Forening til Evangeliets Forkyndelse for skandinaviske Sömaend i
fremmede Havne" (The Danish Society for the Proclamation of the Gospel
to Scandinavian Seamen in Foreign Ports).[25]

The Danish Society made the Norwegian, projected principally by
Storjohann, its model, as a voluntary organization closely identified with the
National Church, with a network of local auxiliaries. Within two years,
chaplains had been sent to Hull, St. Petersburg and London. However, the
most impressive expansion took place in the period of reconstruction following World War II. In 1978, what is now known as "Dansk Sömandskirke i

The Danish (St. Nikolaj)
Seamen's Church in Hull,
dedicated in 1871 as the
first established by the
Danish (Overseas)
Seamen's Mission.
(H. Henningsen:
Sömand og Sömandskirke.)

fremmede Havne" (Danish Seamen's Church in Foreign Ports) had eleven
stations of its own. Of the total budget over one-half is now covered by State
sources.

Meanwhile, a vigorous Danish "Indenlandsk Sömandsmission"
(Domestic Port Seamen's Mission) was eventually established in Copenhagen
in 1905, largely as a result of the groundwork laid by a Danish-born seamen's
missionary called Andreas ("Andrew") Wollesen (1845-1910). Sent there
in 1876 by the American Seamen's Friend Society, he pioneered a preaching
ministry to seafarers in the capital, from 1881 with a permanently moored
"Bethel Ship" as floating church. The Society currently maintains over 20
seamen's homes in Denmark, two in the Faroe Islands, five in Greenland, as
well as a seafarers' center in Grimsby (England).[26]

In the case of Sweden, Storjohann was more directly instrumental in
establishing the first national endeavor. Shortly after the founding of the
Norwegian Society, Storjohann was in Sweden, seeking the support of the
Rev. H.J. Lundborg. As the founding father of the "Evangeliska Fosterlands-
Stiftelsen" (The Evangelical National Missionary Society, or literally,
Evangelical Fatherland Foundation), Lundborg was a key figure. Established
in 1856 as a result of the revival then gathering momentum within the State
Church, the Society sought to promote both home and foreign missions.
Together, both Storjohann and Lundborg established in Gothenburg a
"Committee for Seamen's Missions" (1866). This attempt proved abortive;
but instead of despairing, Storjohann succeeded, on a return visit in 1869, in
bringing the challenge home to the Evangelical National Missionary Society
in Stockholm. On his personal appeal, at a board meeting on June 25, 1869,

Andreas ("Andrew") Wollesen (1845-1910), the Danish-born American immigrant, who, after a radical conversion during D.L. Moody's Chicago crusade in 1872, arrived in Copenhagen as seamen's missionary for the American Seamen's Friend Society in 1876. (W. Larsen: *Ret Kurs.*)

The "Bethel Ship" moored at Kongens Nytorv in Nyhavn, Copenhagen. It was Andrew Wollesen who, familiar with the Methodist Bethelship Mission in New York, rescued a condemned Norwegian brig (the *Fortuna*) from being scrapped, and had her fitted for her new role in 1881. (*Redningsbaaden,* December 1981.)

the Society finally decided to adopt seamen's missions as an integral part of its foreign mission outreach.

The Society promptly appointed two of its own freshly-trained foreign missionaries to pioneer the work in Constantinople and Alexandria respectively. The purpose was partly to promote mission work among native Mohammedans. In the long run however, greater success was achieved where the Society's chaplains could concentrate exclusively on seafarers and resident Scandinavians. Within a decade, the Society had taken up activities in ten foreign port-cities. One of them was New York. Here, the arrival of the Rev. Per Johan Svärd (also spelled "Swärd") in 1873 from a four-year ministry in Constantinople marks the official origin of both the Swedish Seamen's Church in New York and the present twelve-story Lutheran sailors' home there (called "Seamen and International House," with rich roots in Augustana Synod history).[27]

Another eminently successful Swedish sailors' home enterprise was the massive multi-service "Scandinavian Sailors' Temperance Home" raised in 1888 in London's docklands by that indomitable Swedish-born seamen's missionary Agnes Welin (née Hedenström). This is only one conspicuous example among several of Scandinavian non-Lutheran free churches, too, accepting responsibility for mission outreach to seafarers.[28]

Meanwhile, the efforts of the Lutheran but strongly lay-oriented "Fosterlands-stiftelsen" roused a spirit of emulation among Swedish State Church clergy. In 1876, the National Assembly, on the recommendation of the General Synod of the Church, voted funds for seamen's chaplains to take up activities in both West Hartlepool and Kiel. However, the subordination of seamen's work under the Mission Board of the National Church retarded

Dr. Per Johan Svärd, (1845-1901), pioneer pastor of the Seamen's Mission of the Swedish Evangelical Missionary Society, in Constantinople (1869-73), and in New York (1873-77), subsequently president of the Augustana Synod. (*Svensk Sjömanskyrka 100 aar, 1869-1969.*)

The Swedish (Gustaf Adolf) Seamen's Church in Liverpool, built in Park Lane in 1884, at the peak of Nordic mass emigration via that port-city to North America. (*Svensk Sjömanskyrka 100 aar, 1869-1969.*)

the growth of these "official" seamen's missions. Not before 1933 was "Svenska Kyrkans Sjömansvaardsstyrelse" (The Church of Sweden Seamen's Mission Board) established as an agency in its own right, directly under the chairmanship of the Archbishop of Sweden.

Since then, while the Evangelical National Missionary Society has (after World War II) all but wound up its seamen's mission activities, the involvement of the National Church has reached impressive proportions, by 1978 operating some 20 stations of its own. Affirming ecclesiastical responsibility for *resident* nationals, but also prompted by a wish to eliminate any suspicion of paternalism in relation to the seafarer, the Board changed its name after 1976 to "Styrelsen för Svenska Kyrkan i utlandet" (The Board of the Church of Sweden Abroad).[29]

With the eventual inclusion of Finland in the Nordic family of seamen's missions, Storjohann was at least as intimately concerned as in the case of Sweden. For five years (1869-74), he maintained a virtual barrage of admonitions, appeals and proposals, many addressed to the Rev. K.J.G. Sirelius, Director of the Finnish Missionary Society. In 1872, the latter

Agnes Hedenström, the Swedish Free Church missionary candidate who, instead of going to Asia as originally planned, found her calling in the docklands of London (1875). Here she became a pioneer woman sea-farers' missionary, preaching, counseling, caring for the thousands who flocked to hear her, and filled the lodgings she provided for. (E.J. Ekman: *Illustreret Missionshistorie.*)

The great five-story Scandinavian Sailors' Temperance Home which Agnes Welin (now married) eventually erected in 1887, close to the West India Docks. Here, with the help of her husband and others, she continued to lead the work until her death in 1928. (E.J. Ekman: *Illustreret Missionshistorie.*)

launched a separate mission fund for outreach to seafarers. But not before 1874, when Storjohann succeeded in making a personal visit to Finland, was a distinct society structure agreed upon. Storjohann spoke at the anniversary of the Missionary Society in Helsinki, won the whole-hearted support of the Finnish clergy there, traveled the length of the land, and took the country by storm. After parliamentary approval had been duly secured, the new society was officially founded on September 30, 1875, organizationally independent of the Missionary Society from which it had sprung but in close affiliation with the Church of Finland.

The original title clearly revealed the priority aim: "Föreningen till beredande av själavaard aat finska sjömän i utlandska hamnar" (The Society for the Provision of Pastoral Care for Finnish Seamen in Foreign Ports). Following Storjohann's suggestion, the Society's first chaplain was sent to Grimsby (1880). Progress was slow but steady. The Society survived the national crises of Civil War (1918) and World War II. In 1978, the Society, now known as "Finska Sjömansmissionssällskapet" (The Finnish Seamen's Mission), had eight stations of its own in foreign ports and nine in home ports.[30]

In 1979, Iceland, as the fifth of the Nordic family of nations, established its own Icelandic Seamen's Mission as an integrated "Sjomann-arstarf Kirkjunnar" (Church Seamen's Work) of the National (Lutheran) Church of Iceland. The Rev. Helgi Hrobjartsson was called to pioneer this new endeavor, working in close cooperation with the other Nordic seamen's mission organizations. A relatively high proportion of Iceland's population of a quarter of a million is involved in seafaring, mostly deep sea fishing.[31]

In retrospect, it is interesting to note how advocates of foreign missions were, in varying degrees, involved in the historic origin of all the major foreign-port Nordic seamen's missions. Nevertheless, as in the case of their British and American predecessors, these missions all fought, and eventually won, recognition for maritime ministry as an autonomous area of mission. Nordic seafarers, however nominal their personal commitment might be, would normally have been both baptized and confirmed by their own national church as a prerequisite for shipping out. It was, therefore, seen as unsound, both psychologically and in principle, to identify them with "heathens" who had never been confronted with the claims of the Gospel.[32]

One of the pioneer advocates of Nordic seamen's missions over a century ago advanced two arguments for national, denominational seamen's missions. First, it was impossible to sense "unmitigated joy" at foreign endeavors to seek the spiritual welfare of Nordic seamen, since this meant exposing them to non-Lutheran and therefore "erroneous" doctrine. Secondly, however well one might understand a foreign language, "the Word of God nevertheless gains far easier access to the heart when it is communicated to us in our mother tongue."

A stronger spirit of ecumenicity in our day has modified much of the denominational exclusivism evident in the first argument. The second still seems valid. In fact, to it might well be added the obvious human value to any uprooted seafarer of access to an environment genuinely reminiscent of home.

However, two factors have, in recent years, been radically affecting the number of Nordic seafarers able to benefit by such ministry, however beneficial per se: (1) the post World War II "Maritime Industrial Revolution" with its greatly reduced manning requirements, and even more (2) the massive transfer of national Nordic tonnage to "flags of convenience" with cheaper non-Nordic maritime labor taking over.

As the numbers of Nordic merchant seafarers have, in consequence, decreased dramatically, Nordic seamen's missions have been faced with a hard choice: Either to sell stations, where the level of Nordic ship arrivals no longer justifies retaining them. Or, to maintain them as a means of enhanced ministry in other directions, especially to expatriate communities of Nordics living in substantial numbers within any given port area. However, where resident fellow-ethnics are relatively few, it has been suggested that the historic national orientation of these societies might be broadened to include *international* seafarers.[33]

Since the early 1980's, a number of American Lutheran initiatives in cooperative maritime ministry may well prove to have a significant bearing on the possibility of this kind of "internationalization." In 1981, American Lutheran seafarers' chaplains and laypersons serving international/ interdenominational seafarers' agencies in United States port-cities founded a "Lutheran Association for Maritime Ministry" (LAMM), conceived as a grassroots organization committed to the expansion and enhancement of cooperative Lutheran outreach to seafarers, in America and beyond, regardless of ethnic origin. The resulting heightened awareness of Lutheran co-responsibility for mission to seafarers of the world led to the establishment of a "Maritime Ministry Consultancy" by the Lutheran Council in the USA (LCUSA) in 1984, which was joined by the Lutheran World Federation (LWF) in 1985. This combined consultancy has already resulted in inter-Lutheran maritime ministry consultations in America, Asia and Europe, with the active participation of representatives of Nordic seamen's missions.[34]

What significance all of this may have in terms of the future direction of Nordic seamen's missions, and their relationship with the worldwide community of Christian outreach to seafarers, remains to be seen. Hopefully, however, these new opportunities for dialogue, combined with a deeper understanding of the historic origin and current role of both nationally and internationally oriented mission to seafarers, will contribute toward a climate of mutuality which will enable the total human needs of seafarers, *whatever* their background, to be met ever more effectively.

Appendices

NOTE: These appendices have been selected because they provide authentic documentation which is not easily accessible, yet offers important insights into both background and personalities connected with the early seamen's mission movement. As such, these materials reflect priorities and presuppositions which are, in part, at variance with more modern-day concepts of social awareness and cultural sensitivity.

APPENDIX NO. 1

AN EARLY AMERICAN EXHORTATION TO SEAFARERS BY REV. COTTON MATHER OF MASSACHUSETTS

Excerpts from the Rev. Cotton Mather's widely distributed sailor's devotional entitled *The Sailour's Companion and Counsellour: An Offer of Considerations for the Tribe of Zebulun; Awakening the Mariner To Think and to Do Those things that may render his Voyage Prosperous.* The work was first published in Boston, Massachusetts, in 1709. (See pp. 12-3.)

From the Introduction, addressed "To the Commanders of Our Vessels," concerning their opportunity and obligation to maintain divine worship for the "poor Sea-faring People" under their charge:

> When, when shall we see the Spirit [once again] moving on the face of the Waters! It is a matter of the saddest complaint and wonder, That there should be no more Serious Piety, in the Seafaring Tribe.... Old Ambrose called the Sea, The School of Vertue. It afflicts all vertuous Men, that the Mariners of our Dayes do no more make it so.... The Company aboard with you is Your Family. Family-Worship is Expected from all that would not forfeit the Name of Christianity. For such a Society to Live without any Social Acknowledgment of a God would be a Practical Atheism....
>> "The World is the Sea. The Church is the Ship. Our Souls are the Passengers.
>> "Christ is our Pilot. The Word is our Compass. Faith is our Helm.
>> "Hope is our Anchor. Charity our Sails. Perseverance our Ballast.
>> "The Holy Spirit our Gale. And Heaven our Haven." (From Chrysostom.)

On the urgent need for the unconverted sailor to awaken from his "unregenerate state," based on a comparison in Proverbs 23:34 with one "that lies down in the midst of the Sea," or one "that lieth on the Top of a Mast."

> A Sleep on the Round-top.... To continue in a State of Unregeneracy, is to sleep on the Top of a Mast, in the midst of the Sea.... There are Two very grievous Things, in the condition of an Ungodly Sinner, which I must earnestly desire you to take Notice of.... First, the *Slumber* of the Sinner; And, Secondly, the *Danger* of the Sinner....

The Church-yards use [sic] to be called, Cemeteris [sic], or, Sleeping-places; But, let not our Churches themselves be so! ... *An Unregenerate Sinner is One fast Asleep;* yea, he has a Dead Sleep upon him. ... Dead in Trespasses and Sins. ... And, O my Hearers; If thou dost grow Sensible of these Demonstrations, and own that they are so, 'twil be a Sign that thy Sleep is happily going off. ... [But those who continue in spiritual sleep are] Speechless. ... "They have not called upon God" (Psalm 53:4). An unregenerate wants [is devoid of] the Spirit of Prayer. He can at best but *Say* Prayers. What he does at it is Playing rather than Praying; the Scripture says, Tis Howling. Tis a mere Formality. He is not in Earnest. ... [Instead] he dreams that Satisfaction is to be found in the Enjoyments of this World. He Dreams, That he shall Continue, if not Forever, yet a long while, in this World. ... That it will be Time Enough Hereafter to Turn unto God. ...

Thus the Sinner Sleeps in his Unregeneracy. But, *Where* does he Sleep? ... *On the Top of a Mast in the midst of the Sea.* ... How dismally art thou circumstanced. ... with so many Thousands of Sins, All Unpardoned! ... [For] he who Dies before he is Born again, will fall into a Wretchedness, that will make him wish, that he had never been born at all. This is the upshot of all. The Sinner Sleeping on the Top of a Mast is in hourly Danger of a Damnation that Slumbers not. ... Banished from God; Banished where he shall never see Light. ... [Therefore] my Brother, Examine thy self. ... Examine, Have I ever yet Mourn'd for, and Turn'd from all my Sins? Examine, Have I ever yet made my Flight unto a Glorious Christ, as my mighty and only Savior? ... Oh! Hearts harder than the Rocks, you are sometimes afraid of, if this consideration affect you not! ... You must either have Experience of a Conversion from Sin to God in Christ, or else Deny your Baptism. Oh! Do not make the Waters of your Baptism, send a cry after you, as a Deserter from the Banners of your Saviour, when you are going upon the Waters!

On the spiritually awakened mariner's need to be constantly "on Watch against all the Vices of the Sea; and Steer Clear of them," especially those of intoxication, fornication, profanity and gambling. (Cf. pp. 340-6.)

Methinks, there is no Mariner, but what should be taught by common Sense, to count it [Drunkenness] as bad as Drowning. My Friend, Six Foot Water in the Hold of the Vessel, would not more Endanger it, than thy pouring in the Cups of Intoxication will Endanger thy Soul. ... Every time a Sailor makes himself Drunk, the Devil Keelhauls him. ...

But then, the Helm; Look well to That. That is, *The Tongue.* The Ship Shears most wretchedly, when the Helm is under no Good Government. You will by no means allow the man at Helm,

to throw the Whipstaff carelessly out of his hand. . . . For a
Sailour to be a Swearer . . . is a thousand times more Loathsome,
than if they were Uttering their Vomit. . . . My Friend, if a Devil
hath thy Helm in his hand, [And by Wicked Speeches thou dost
Lodge it there!] Whither, Whither art thou like to bear away? . . .
Lord How can One who does Blaspheme and Deny his God,
Expect any Favour from Him! And why shouldest thou not be as
lothe to take any Obscene, Smutty, Baudy Talk, into thy Mouth,
as to Swallow so much Filthy Bildge Water!

Much more, does it concern the Sailor, to avoid all Practices
of *Unchastity.* It is mentioned among the Practices of the worst of
men; Rom. 1:24. . . . The Dead Sea was Produced as an Eternal
Monument of the Divine Vengeance on such Practices. Perhaps
many a Vessel has been lost in the Salt Sea, because there have
been Sodomites on board. . . . And when a Sailour comes ashore,
What Good will a Whore do unto him . . . [but] make him
Foolishly Squander away all his Wages, . . . or, if he be not
quickly hauled up with Rottenness in his Bones . . . he founders in
a Whirl-pool of Eternal Perdition (1 Cor. 6:19).

But I must not forget the *Mispence of Time*, which is too often
the Miscarriage of the Sailour. My Brother, Thou hast much
Leisure aboard. . . . Improve thy Leisure in the Service of God,
and for the Welfare of thy own Soul. . . . It is Doctor Josiah
Wood, who in the little book much dispersed in the British Navy,
and Entitled *The Seamans Monitor,* has the Words. ". . . The
Habit of Gaming Seldom knows Moderation, or Admits of Limits
or Rules. And it is therefore usually attended with Multitudes of
Mischiefs. It occasions Broils, and Quarrels, and sometimes
Blood-shed. It wastes Time, and consumes Wealth, and introduces
Sloth. . . . And, what is still Worse, it usually indisposes men for
their Devotions and all Serious Thoughts. . . ."

APPENDIX NO. 2

MEMOIRS OF "BOATSWAIN SMITH" AT THE BATTLE OF COPENHAGEN, 1801

Composed of memoirs of the Rev. George Charles Smith, when serving under Admiral Nelson at the Battle of Copenhagen in 1801, as a wild-natured British Tar of barely nineteen, on board His Majesty's 64-gun ship-of-the-line *Agamemnon*. Excerpted from the following volumes of Smith's own nautical periodical *The New Sailor's Magazine*, London: 1852, pp. 417-23; 1856, pp. 233-5; 1857, pp. 113-5; 1858, pp. 321-7; 1859, pp. 149-56, 159-68, 199-201, 387-8. The resulting narrative (also published in *The Mariner's Mirror* 1976, pp. 47-51) is replete with rare insights into the psychology of seamen, before, during and after a major naval action in the days of sail. Despite all its vehement subjectivity, its ring of authenticity and wealth of dramatic detail make it a significant source text in a largely unresearched area of maritime ethnology.

The year 1801 was one of the most perilous years for England, after the French Revolution. Our fleets were demanded, winter and summer, to blockade the Dutch fleet in Holland, the Spanish fleet at Cadiz, and the French fleets at Brest and Toulon, while ships of war were incessantly demanded to protect our colonies in the East and West Indies. But now, by some influence from France, it appeared that Paul, the Emperor of Russia, had lain an embargo on our English ships in Russian ports, and also prevailed upon the Baltic nations of Denmark and Sweden, to form a *Northern Confederacy* against England. Early in the year 1801 it was generally expected that war by the northern powers would be declared against England, and when the ice broke in the Baltic, about March, that the combined fleets of Russia, Denmark and Sweden would sail from the Baltic and invade England.

As something must be done, it was considered, to prevent invasion, an immense fleet should be collected. Although it was most dangerous to send out such a fleet through the storms of the North Sea at this time, yet this large fleet was collected and prepared, and Admiral Lord Nelson having been so celebrated at St. Vincent and the Nile, was commanded to join Admiral Sir Hyde Parker in command.

But alas! at this time, England cared nothing about the souls of her sailors. The country provided ships and wages for them at sea, and dens of vice for them on shore, but as to their immortal souls and eternity, they were supposed to be a people so unfit for heaven, that it would be idle and useless to direct them there. . . .

We sailed from Yarmouth Roads March 12th, 1801. One of our fleet, the *Invincible,* 74, was lost. We suffered most dreadfully for nearly a week in the North Sea. At length we reached the Scaw Point anchorage. [This became the] general rendezvous for the fleet, while Mr. Vansittart, from the English Government, should go up to Elsineur, and try negotiation, for permission to pass the Sound Channel, and sail up to Russia with all the fleet of war. This permission was refused, and the decision of our admirals was, that we now force the passage of the Sound Channel, and the first shot fired at our fleet would be considered a declaration of war by the Northern Confederacy. We were surprised at not finding the fleet of gunboats and ships we expected, but the Sound was protected on the Swedish side, at our left hand, by the fort of Helsingborg, and on that of Denmark by the Castle of Cronenberg.

No man not in a fleet can imagine the horrors of conscience and the emotions in such long delayed anticipations of war and bloodshed, and no religious preparation for it. Our battles generally had been by a sudden rush into action. But here all was deliberate and on the mind for days. O, what pale, agitated countenances I saw among the crowd of men on our forecastle, among the greatest drunkards, blasphemers, whoremongers. . . .Not a man but trembled, all ready for battle — yet not one soul ready for eternity! I was like the rest, only, having been a Sunday school boy at Surrey Chapel, and with a pious father and mother, in London, I knew more about sin, and hell, and shuddered with horror, so that officers' cry for *'King and country — fighting for king and country'* could not quell the risings of conscience, and the prospects of death and judgement.

It had long been considered impossible to force a passage through the Sound. But the signal was made by Lord Nelson, to *'Prepare for Action',* and early on March 31st, Nelson led the van, steering close over to the Swedish coast, risking all the shot firing from Helsingborg. We expected [this] to be very great, but not equal to the firing from Elsineur. We had heard much of the artilley and ammunition at Elsineur. . . .

We [in the *Agamemnon,* 64] were about the fourth ship in the line following him (Nelson). I was now one of the most daring, desperate men on board, doing duty as second captain of the foretop. I determined to run up the shrouds of our fore-rigging and narrowly watch Nelson the moment he was fired at from Elsineur, to see if he engaged Helsingborg as well as Elsineur; because then we would have the prospect of being cut to pieces on the upper deck and in the tops, as we were so near the Swedish shore.

The moment Nelson's ship arrived on a line with Cronenberg Castle, they opened the most tremendous fire. I saw the first broadside of Nelson's ship, to return this fire; and as the wind from Elsineur blew the smoke of Nelson's guns over the ship to leeward, the flash of his guns through the smoke deceived me, and I ran down the rigging, jumped on the forecastle, and cried out aloud, 'Clear away the guns! Nelson is engaged on both sides. We shall have hot work, if we live. . . .'

I have never been able to remember anything more, as all our men were at work with their guns, crying out amidst the roar of cannon, 'Hold on,' 'get ready,' 'England for ever,' 'cheer up,' 'if we are wounded we shall get down to the doctor,' 'good-bye, shipmates,' 'my turn next,' 'fight for king and country,' 'a good drop of grog when we are done,' with all such idle nonsense.

The shot at our right hand fell like showers of hail near us. But not one shot was fired upon us from the Swedish coast. We were all perfectly astonished at this amazing forbearance on the part of Sweden.

Having forced the Sound, [we] anchored at the entrance of the Baltic Sea, with Copenhagen in sight, with all the fleet of block ships, frigates, ships of the line, gun brigs, Crown batteries, and the Copenhagen sea coast batteries. All the beacons and buoys were removed by the Danes. But [while] our fleet were all at anchor, the boats were out attendant upon Nelson and Captain Riou, with their lead lines, and *sounded* through all the channel, as the men did in Paul's ship, Acts xxvii, 28. [Thus they] found out the channel, for all our ships to sail the next day [to] Draco Point, at the head of the roadstead that led down to the Danish fleet.

[Again we had] a long time for gloomy anticipation. My most intimate friend, John Lovegrove [and] I took our pipes to smoke and talk about the morrow, while most of the men were down below at their dinner and grog. I said, 'What do you think about to-morrow, John?' He shook his head and cried, 'The last day for many of us. . . .' We now could not avoid shedding a tear about home, and he said, 'I have aft a letter in my chest. If I should be killed, send it to my aunt at Reading, if you live.' I said, 'I have also left a letter; send it to my mother if I am killed to-morrow.'

We could not stand this; he fled to a corner, and I looked round, longing for some place where I could kneel and try to pray, as my father and mother [used to do]. But I was afraid and ashamed to be seen on my knees, as every man would have ridiculed me, and called out *Methodist* — which at that time was a most contemptable [sic] word, and meant *coward*. But looking up to our large foretop, I hastened aloft, where no man might see me, and I kneeled down before the head of the foremast, and in my ignorance, as an unconverted man, said, 'O God, please let me not be killed in battle tomorrow, but please let me live, and go home to see mother — and I'll never do anything bad again as long as I live.' And, with this ignorance, I hastened down on deck, all ready to fight now; because we were told it was all right fighting for king and country, and God was merciful to sailors. . . .

Such was the state of thousands in our fleet; and thus, with five hundred men in our ship. We had not one man that knew any better; but all were left in this ignorance, and sent out to fight by Christian England! Shame, shame on our country, thus to neglect us! With no Bible or minister, to warn us to flee from the wrath to come, by a just and righteous God. We never had a chaplain since 1797, and [even] then it was only reading and prayers, and telling us to be good. . . .

Friday, April 2nd, 1801, O what a gloomy melancholy morning, as this was the day of battle, and Nelson was to lead us on to blood and slaughter. It was our duty to fight for king and country. This was all — but no hope of heaven. Only, perhaps, we [might] not be killed, but conquer and take prizes. Then how happy, and how glorious we [should] be, shouting victory with Nelson, in Yarmouth, Sheerness, Portsmouth, and Plymouth. This was all the heaven we looked for; and Nelson was considered our Saviour and our God.

But now nine a.m. had passed, and as our ship was to be the second ship in the line, we who belonged to the tops hastened aloft, and the multitude to the guns. H.M.S. *Edgar,* 74, made sail to pass all the Danish line of ships, until she arrived opposite the ship numbered for her to engage. But as soon as she arrived opposite the first Danish ship of their line, [she] received a broadside from that ship, and heeled over as if she had been struck by a heavy sea. I well remember seeing the blood of the killed and wounded pouring out of her scupper holes and making the sea red with the victims' life-blood. . . .

Our ship, the *Agamemnon,* was to follow next. We had just made sail when, to our great astonishment, we could not weather a shoal or quicksand beneath, and, nothwithstanding all our exertions, she stuck fast. Thus the Danes were saved from one ship of the line that threatened the most destructive fire, as the *Agamemnon* had long been the favourite of Capt. Horatio Nelson, and in her at Bastia, where he lost his eye, he took the Island of Corsica. H.M.S. *Russell,* 74, and H.M.S. *Bellona,* 74, followed our ship across what was called the Middle Ground, but here they also struck, and were grounded so fast, that they remained here during all the battle.

It has long since been published that few ships of the fleet were more damaged by the shower of shot from ships and batteries than H.M.S. *Ardent,* 64, [and those] three line of battle ships [which had] struck upon shoals of sand in Copenhagen Roads. To relieve the *Ardent,* and to stimulate and excite to most extraordinary exertions, an officer on the quarter deck of the *Agamemnon* cried aloud, 'Fifty men must be sent on board the *Ardent,* to repair damages, and help the wounded, and supply the place of the killed there. Who will volunteer for the *Ardent* near the batteries?' I rushed aft, as belonging to the foretop, and therefore well acquainted with rigging, and exclaimed, 'I volunteer for the *Ardent.*'

Boats were ordered up and we were rowed on board. We hastened down to the after cockpit, hearing cries and groans of the wounded at the cable tiers, and we shovelled up the heaps of congealed blood to clear the deck, and cast it overboard, and then render all possible aid to the many who had arms or legs shot off, or who were dying of their wounds.

When Nelson saw three ships aground, and that Admiral Parker could not get up sufficiently, and when he anticipated the desperate havoc the Danes might produce at night by bombshells and fire-ships, he withdrew to the cabin of the *Elephant,* and wrote a letter 'To the brothers of Englishmen — the Danes,' addressed to the Crown Prince of Denmark, requesting a truce of twelve hours.

Having finished this letter, Nelson said to an officer in the cabin, 'Send a messenger down below, sir, for a lantern and sealing wax.' The officer sent one down immediately, but in a short time he returned, saying, 'My Lord, a shot came suddenly and struck off his head, as he was coming up the companion ladder to the quarter deck.' Nelson instantly replied, 'Send another, sir.' The officer said, 'Won't a wafer do, my Lord?' Nelson rejoined, 'No, sir, the wafer will be wet when the boat gets ashore. A wafer indicates hurry, [and that] we are asking a favour. Sealing wax is the work of time.'

It was the wisest thing that Nelson ever did to solicit a truce; and it was the most unaccountably humane, and generous, and wonderful act that the Danish government agreed to a truce; for had they continued to fire from the batteries that night, our ships would have been cut to pieces, and scarcely an officer or man left alive. What would Mr. Pitt, or George III, or the English government have said then, with the French flotillas that were ready for invasion at Boulogne? Had a righteous God permitted the Danes to have been obstinate, and to have refused a truce, and this night have taken all advantage of us, England might soon have beheld her palaces, churches, chapels, mansions, and shops in flames, amidst the most ruthless plunder and devastation, from French and Spanish forces. . . .

It was not Nelson, but God, who saved the country from all these horrors. It was not Nelson, but God, who graciously inclined the Crown Prince of Denmark, and the Danish government, to grant that truce, and cease firing. In gratitude to the Danes, we ought ever to remember this most extraordinary act of national kindness and humanity, and to testify our thankfulness whenever opportunity serves.

NOTE: Smith expresses similar sentiments for the Swedes, who, instead of immediately descending from their nearby naval base of Carlscrona upon the battered British fleet in Copenhagen, withheld, and also entered upon an armistice. Finally, Smith describes how peace proposals were received from Russia, too, on Alexander's timely accession to the imperial throne. Thus, according to Smith, was removed the ominous threat of the Northern Powers in the spring of 1801. Thus, too, was the future "Father of Seamen's Missions" able to acquire invaluable training in what he termed the university of the ocean. With a sense of commitment and power of persuasion closely linked to personal observation and experience, he went on to become a combination of Seamen's Preacher and Seamen's Advocate such as the world has never seen, before or since.

Appendix no. 3

An Early Advocate and "Agent Afloat" — Captain Anthony Landers of Sunderland

Letter to Mr. Joseph Tarn, Secretary of the British and Foreign Bible Society, from one of their pioneer "Agents Afloat," Captain Anthony Landers of Sunderland, dated Cork, October 4, 1816. Captain Landers was one of the most active and articulate of these early volunteer missionary partners of the BFBS. He was also one of the earliest and most ardent advocates of organized mission to his own seafaring class. (Letter in BFBS Archives: "Home Correspondence" Files. See also pp. 137-8.)

Dear Sir,

After writing you on my arrival was obliged to your favour of the 4th ult. Below you have a small statement of the Books I gave away myself, but except the Dutch Bibles sold at New York, the most of the others was sent into the Country from Halifax & as I did not expect my Voyages to turn out so disasterous, did not require a particular account to be sent me, how they were Disposed of, as it was my intention to make up at least the whole sum. However as I have been disappointed, if you please to pass to my Credit the amount of my Subscription, I shall be perfectly satisfy'd. I think it is two Guineas a year how many I am not certain; I rejoice to hear the Bible Society still prospers, it must, it will prevail, till the knowlidge of the truth shall cover the earth as the waters the place of the Sea. It is of God & therefore must ever stand.

I was in New-York when the National Bible Society was form'd. I have no dout but it will prosper. 10,000 Dollars from its worthy President was a good beginning. When last in London, I got several Sunday School Books & Tracts, before I sail'd to the West Indies last Voyage [and] gave them to a Public Spirited Lady, who before I got back to New York had fill'd the City with Sunday Schools, both for Children & Adults, of which there are Hundreds of Black people, so that the Seed of those Schools came from London & are growing & spreading all over the United States, so that I told her they had now begun at the right end to reform the land, every Protestant Congregation has a School, but the Committee is made up of the Whole & each School Visited by all with the funds the same;

For this & all the Institutions, having for their object the Salvation of Man & the Glory of God I rejoice, but so long as one of the greatest of all is wanting I will mourn & lament, Tho' not without continuing to use my feeble efforts to rouse the Religious Public to the Condition of the Sailors, could I but succeed in this, could they but know their Ignorant & Wicked state, while they Send the

Gospel to the Heathen & distant Nations, would first regard the Sailor who must carry the heavenly Harbinger, . . . to the Destruction of himself, his morals & Hundreds more, so that He only wants the Wisdom of those who feel for the Misery of Mankind.

I think you would serve the poor Sailor's cause if you would insert the inclosed in the Religious Newspaper or the Christian observer Magazine, with any improvement or alteration that you & my friend Collins or any other Gentlemen would suggest. I have wrote Mr. Collins on the subject by a Vessel bound to London the Hero Capt. Evans with a small parcel containing a few of my Narratives, those Letters & a few of the Sermons in a Corrected State. Correction of the Sermon as follows, Page 6, at the end of the 16 line after the word effects, add (See Leviticus 24th Chapter.) in the Second line from this, strike out the words (by Moses) in the Second line from this again strike out the word (Solomon) & Insert in its stead the word (Jehoshaphat) Page the 16 Bottom line put out the word praise & insert the word (race) with any other improvement the Committee may think proper.

One thing I am certain of by experience, that a Sailor will read what is particularly address'd to him, when He will not the Bible, nor any other Tract, and would the Ministers of the Gospel at Sea port Towns Invite them, particularly with Sermons adapted to them, they would attend, for tho' He is so easy to be lead to a bad thing, yet you may also lead him to that which is good. I could get Captains to go with me to hear the late Capt. J. Newton, who would afterwards go themselves, & Ministers who only recollect the Sailor in their Prayers, they will go to hear, when they will not others, so that I am persuaded the Means must be aim'd at them & for them to do them good.

Yours most Sincerely,

Anty. Landers.

	£	s.	d.	
23 Small Testaments at 7/8 ...	7 "	18 "	4	
12 Second Size ...... 2/4 ...	1 "	8 "	–	
6 Large Do. .... 3/6 ...	1 "	1 "	–	at Demerary
4 Second Bibles ..... 6/5 ...	1 "	5 "	8	
7 Small Do. .... 4/6 ...	1 "	11 "	6	
1 Small Testament		1 "	8	at Cartine
2 Large Do.		7 "	–	
together	7 "	18 "	2	

APPENDIX NO. 4

WARD STAFFORD'S 1817 BLUEPRINT FOR MULTI-SERVICE MISSION TO SEAFARERS

Excerpts from the promotional tract *Important to Seamen,* itself (as the sub-title indicates) a series of *Extracts from a Report entitled "New Missionary Field,"* an 1817 proposal for urban missionary endeavor in early 19th century New York by the Rev. Ward Stafford. His three-point plan for ministry to the most obviously deprived class of urban poor (the seafarer) calls for schools, Bible societies and church buildings, all expressly adapted to the needs of seafarers. Of these, Stafford's strong advocacy of shore-based seamen's churches is reproduced here, since it represents the first such systematic effort in the world. The closely related "missiological motive" which follows it is also reproduced, as a powerful pioneer presentation of this particular motive; the fact that Stafford's arguments were formulated long before current-day concepts of "internationalization" and "contextualization" in global mission detracts nothing from their validity in other respects. (See pp. 418-9.)

It is proposed . . . that in large seaports, churches be erected expressly for their [the seamen's] accomodation. This is conceived as the only way in which they can extensively enjoy a preached Gospel. It is said, that they may be accommodated in other churches, and in them may hear the Gospel. In answer to this, it may be observed, in the first place, that there is no provision for them. The few seats which are not occupied by private families, are occupied by the poor, whom we always have with us. No provision whatever has been made for seamen as a class of men by themselves. They have been either forgotten, or entirely neglected.

But, in the second place, were provision made for them in our churches, it would not remove the difficulty. They regard themselves, and they are regarded by others, as an entirely separate class of the community. They do not mingle with other people. Their very mode of life excludes them from all society, except that of their companions. With them they necessarily and exclusively associate while at sea.

When in port they have no other acquaintance, and have but little occasion or inducement to form any, except it be that, which, though very limited in its duration, is extremely pernicious in its consequences. They have no places of resort, except those which frequently become the grave of their property, their morals, their happiness, and their souls. . . . As they have generally become vicious in consequence of being neglected, and as no distinction is made between the sober and the profligate, they are strangers whom all feel at liberty to despise.

Those of them who are respectable, and such there are, notwithstanding all the disadvantages under which they labour, have a high sense of propriety, and will not be guilty of intrusion: hence they have a natural aversion to enter our churches.

Another barrier is their dress. Their dress is generally different from that of other people. When they enter a church, they are known and marked as sailors; they attract the notice of no small part of the congregation; and most of them would sooner face the cannon's mouth than that thoughtless, supercilious gaze. . . .

There is another reason why they do not more frequently go to church. It is a fact, and one at the recital of which the persons concerned ought to blush, that they have been virtually turned out of our churches when they have entered! They have received no invitation to take seats — the pews have been closed against them — and they, in some cases, have been informed, that there was no room for sailors. Such was not the manner in which they were treated by the Son of God. . . .

[On the other hand] it is the opinion of a large number of masters of vessels and seamen, who have been consulted during the past year, not only in this, but in some other ports, that this [plan of erecting churches in seaports expressly for their accommodation] is the only way in which the Gospel can be effectually preached to seamen. . . . Were it known to seamen, that, whenever they entered a large seaport they would find [such] a church, many would be induced to attend by the influence of early education, by curiosity, a desire to see their companions and to be like other people, or the pride which they would take in an institution of their own. . . .

The expense of such an establishment would, at first, be very considerable. But when we consider the number of seamen, and their unparalleled liberality, we cannot doubt, that they would, in the end, amply support, by their contributions, the preaching of the Gospel. . . .

Our cities have an intimate connexion with the Heathen, by means of our seamen. At present, seamen are a barrier to the spread of the Gospel; a screen which intercepts the ray of the Sun of Rightiousness. When they visit Pagan countries, as thousands of them do every year, they not not only join in all the wickedness of the Heathen, but teach them new vices. To their cuperior cunning the Heathen become an easy prey, and are not unfrequently robbed of their property, their children and their friends.

Sailors sometimes take up their abode in Pagan countries, that they may acquire wealth, and be free from the restraints of the Gospel. A part of the crew of the ship, which transported the first Missionaries to the South Sea Islands, settled there, and are supposed to have been the principal reason why their efforts were, for so long a time, attended with no more success. . . . It is owing in great measure to the same cause [the negative witness of white settlers], that the efforts to Christianize the aborigines of our own country have proved so ineffectual.

The influence of our seamen is not unknown to the men of the world. A master of a vessel which recently arrived, and which had visited one of our Missionary stations, triumphantly observed, that his sailors could, in a few days, undo all the work of our Missionaries. Though we do not believe this representation to be strictly correct, it is not without meaning. Let our sailors continue vicious, and wherever Christians send one Missionary, Satan will send a hundred to oppose his efforts.

Should our seamen become pious, not only would a great obstacle be removed, but the number of hands employed, and the amount of labour performed in the great Missionary field, would be augmented. Should a crew land on a Heathen shore, all pious; all deeply concerned for the salvation of the Pagan brethren; all anxious to tell them of that Savious, who is the only hope of lost men — to impart to them those treasures of knowledge and grace which they had received, how would the darkness retire before them?

That property, of which our seamen earn and receive no small quantity, and which is now squandered away, would, doubtless, be consecrated to the spread of the Gospel. No men are so liberal; none, whose hearts and hands are so easily opened; none, who have such a strong fellow-feeling; none, who are less careful to preserve their lives. Were all consecrated to God, what sacrifices would they not make; what hardships would they not endure; to what dangers would they not expose themselves, for the salvation of their fellow-men?

While, in consequence of actually witnessing the wretched state of the Heathen, they would feel more deeply interested than other Christians; they would communicate the same feeling to their brethren; they would become heralds, publishing glad tidings in every direction. Every vessel, which arrived, would add new fuel to the flame, and cause that flame to spread from our cities into the surrounding country. Who does not see, that thousands and tens of thousands of pious men constantly passing, and repassing, throughout the world: mingling, now with Christians, now with the Heathen, would give a new, and powerful, and lasting impulse to that great machine, which is to diffuse abroad the blessings of the Gospel? They form the connecting link between the Christian and the Heathen world; the channel through which the water of life must flow; the medium through which the light of the Gospel must shine. . . .

Though, in consequence of their being scattered over the world, the effect of labours in this, or in any other port, should not be known, may we not hope, that we shall see many of them at the last day on the right hand of Christ? May we not hope, that soon every flag will become a standard of the cross — every ship a temple, from which "incense and a pure offering" shall ascend to God — every seaman a herald of salvation; and that this long neglected class of men will be eminently instrumental in hastening in that period, when "the knowledge of the Lord shall cover the earth as the waters do the seas?"

APPENDIX NO. 5

THE FOUNDING OF THE WORLD'S FIRST COMPREHENSIVE SEAMEN'S MISSION ORGANIZATION

Although other organizations for the evangelization of seafarers preceded the founding of the Port of London Society in 1818, this latter did become the first organization in the world expressly established for promoting mission to seafarers in a comprehensive sense, with stated preaching and a specifically dedicated sanctuary. (See pp. 192, 534.) The extracts below are from the Minute Book (1818-28) of the "Port of London Society for Promoting Religion among Merchant Seamen." (In Archives of the British Sailor's Society, Ilford, Essex.)

Entry for 18 March 1818: Founding of the Society

At a General Meeting of Persons desirous to promote the Religious Instruction of Seamen held pursuant to Public Notice at the City of London Tavern Bishopsgate Street on Wednesday the 18th of March 1818. Ben' Shaw Esqr. M.P. in the Chair. It was

On the Motion of R.H. Marten Esqr.
Seconded by the Revd. Dr. Rippon

Resolved

That it appeared to this Meeting that Britain owes much of its national Security, and Political independance, and Commercial greatness, to the Instrumentality of its numerous and intrepid Seamen; who have therefore an urgent claim upon the benevolence of those who enjoy the fruits of their adventurous and toilsome Services — that while a laudable and liberal attention has been shown to their temporal interests, no direct and adequate mooves have been employed to promote their Religious instruction, their moral reformation, and their Eternal happiness — a neglect on the British Christians which appears the more astonishing, as well as culpable when viewed by the side of those exertions which are made on every hand, to diffuse Spiritual Knowledge, and Religion among other Classes of the Community — and that for the purpose of supplying this acknowledged and lamented defect there be now formed an Institution to be Called — *"The Port of London Society for Promoting Religion among Merchant Seamen."*

On the Motion of J. Cowell Esqr.
Seconded by the Revd. J.

Resolved

That this Meeting is sensible of the importance of an universal distribution of the Bible and rejoices in the establishment and exertions of the Naval and Military Bible Society, and the Merchant Seamen's Auxiliary Bible Society — at the same time recollecting that the Ministers of the Gospel is the principal Instrument which God has appointed and which he employs for the Salvation of Men — the Society now formed resolves to add this to the other means of Religion which Seamen enjoy, and that the addition may be made in a form most likely to ensure success — It determines to prove [sic] a Vessel, capable of accomodating from 600 to 700 Persons, to make such alterations as may be necessary to render it a convenient Chapel to station it in some public Part of the River Thames, and to make arrangements for the regular preaching of the Gospel, and the observance of Public Worship on Board, at least twice every Sunday, and once in the course of the Week.

On the Motion of S. Jenning[s], Esqr.
Seconded by the Revd. Thos. Hooper

Resolved

That altho' the Preaching of the Gospel is first adapted as the most direct means of accomplishing its desirable objects, this Society is nevertheless formed with the wide purpose of furthering, according to the extent of its funds, such other plans as shall appear upon mature consideration adapted to excite the more general attention of Seamen to the Momentous concerns of Religion and Eternity — and especially to promote the Religious instruction of Boys training to a Seafaring Life —

On the Motion of the Revd. W. Knowles
Seconded by the Revd. Dr. Collyer

Resolved

That in this important undertaking this Society utterly disclaims all intention and all inclination to promote Sectarial Views and party feelings. While it aims to lead the objects of its benevolence to the one foundation of human hope revealed in the Scriptures and to promote its consequences and appropriate moral effects — It proposes to accomplish these valuable objects by an extended Union of all denominations of Christians, and will therefore leave the forms and modes of Worship to the Ministers appointed to conduct it — Clergymen officiating according to the established nature of the Church of England, and Dissenting Ministers conducting their portion of the service according to the sentiments and Customs of their respective Churches —

On the Motion of the Revd. G. Smith
Seconded by the Revd. W. Sheaston

Resolved

That R.H. Marten Esqr. be Treasurer — The Revd. N.E. Sloper, Mr. Thos. Thompson and Mr. W. Cook be the Gratuitous Secretaries — and the following Ministers and Gentlemen the Committee for the ensuing Year

Revd. W. Chapman
" Dr. Collyer
" J. Edwards
" A. Fletcher
" Griffin
" R. Hill
" W. Hobes
" J. Hatcheys

Revd. Chas. Hyatt
" H. Lucey
" J. Leifchild
" Dr. Nicholl
" A. Reed
" Dr. Rippon
" W. Sheaston
" Dr. Waugh

Mr. W. Anderson
" A. Brown
" J. Cook
" Dr. Cox
" J. Dyer
" Francis
" Gibbs
" Green
" Jennings

Mr. J. Cowell
" Napier
" Phillips
" D.R. Munn
" Rist
" Robilliard
" B. Shaw Esqr. M.P.
" Stone
" Tanner

Mr. H. Teape

On the Motion of the Revd. D.R. Munn Esqr.
Seconded by the Revd. C. Hyatt

Resolved

[1st]   That this Society be under the superintendence of a Committee consisting of 40 Members with power to add to their Number one half of which shall consist of Ministers and the other half laymen chosen from the different denominations of Christians of which the Society is composed

2nd   One third of the Members who have least frequently attended the Meetings of the Committee shall go out at the beginning of every Year, but shall be re-eligible at the beginning of the Year following

3rd   Every Person proposed on the Committee must have the Votes of two thirds of the Members present before he can be elected; and the election shall not take place until two Meetings after that on which the Nomination has been made —

4th   The Treasurer and Secretaries shall be considered "ex officio" Members of the Committee. Five Members shall form a Quorum.

5th   Special Meetings of the Committee may be called at the written request of the same Member addressed to the Secretaries. And such Meeting must be summoned within 7 days after the requisition is delivered

6th   A Donation of Ten Guineas at one time, or a Donation of three Guineas accompanied by an Annual Subscription of two will entitle the doners to attend all Committees and Vote upon all questions

7th   Subscribers of One Guinea annually are Members of the Society entitled to vote at the General Meeting — Clergymen and other Ministers rendering service to The Society by Preaching, or promoting its objects any other way acceptable to the Committee shall be considered Members and are eligible to be chosen on the Committee

8th   The General Annual Meeting of the Society shall be held at a place and on a day to be fixed by the Committee —

The Chairman having left the Chair, it was
On the Motion of the Revd. G. Evans

Resolved unanimously

That the most cordial thanks of this Meeting be given to the Chairman for his obliging attention to the business of the day.

Entry for April 28, 1818: Application for Registration of Sanctuary

Copy of the Register:

To the Right Reverend Father in God, William, by Divine Permission Lord Bishop of London: We whose names are hereunto subscribed being protestant Dissenters from the Church of England, Do hereby certify that the Vessel formerly called the Speedy but now fitted for and appropriated as a place of worship on the River Thames, near Wapping new Stairs in the Parish of St. John Wapping in the County of Middlesex is intended to be used for the Worship a [sic] Almighty God by Protestant Dissenters of the denomination of Independents and Baptists, and we do hereby require that this certificate may be registered in your Court pursuant to the directions of an Act of Parliament made and Passed in the fifty second Year of the Reign of his present Majesty King George the Third, intitled "An Act to repeal certain Acts and amend other Acts relating to Religion, Worship and Assemblies and persons teaching and Preaching therein" as witness our hands this twenty first day of April one Thousand Eight hundred and Eighteen.

R.H. Marten	Henry Lacey
Anthy. Brown	T. Phillips
Thos. Hill	William Cook
N.E. Sloper	John Francis
John Cowell	George Evans
Chas. Birt	Benym. Tanner

This is to certify all whom it shall or may concern that on the twenty fifth day of April one Thousand Eight hundred and Eighteen this Certificate was Registered in the Bishop of London's Registry. John Shephard. Dy. Registrar.

Appendix no. 6

The Institutional Beginnings of the Bethel Union Movement

The Bethel Movement per se had already begun with the first informal prayer-meeting on the Thames June 22, 1814, and more specifically with the hoisting of the first Bethel Flag March 23, 1817. (See pp. 153, 159.) However, the institutionalization of the movement began with the founding in late 1819 of the first Bethel Union Society. The prime mover in all of this was the Rev. George Charles Smith, who was also principally responsible for the recording of the following reports: October 27, 1819; November 12, 1819; and October 6, 1820. (Quoted from *The Sailor's Magazine* 1820, pp. 22-5, 25-6, 426-7, respectively. Cf. George Charles Smith, *English Sailors,* London, n.d., pp. 26-36. See pp. 202-5.)

BETHEL SEAMEN'S UNION, BRITISH AND FOREIGN:
Preliminary Meeting October 22, 1819

The Preliminary Meeting of this Society was held at Horslydown, on Friday, October 22, 1819.

A hymn was sung by the Multitude assembled, a pious Sailor solemnly addressed the Almighty in prayer. After singing the following verse,

> "At anchor laid, remote from home,
> Toiling, I cry, Sweet Spirit, come!
> Celestial breeze, no longer stay,
> But swell my sails, and speed my way!"

the Rev. G.C. Smith [as Chairman] briefly stated the object of this Meeting; and explained the arrangement of the colours usually hoisted, as signals for prayer, by the pious Seamen.

The Rev. Mr. Allen, of Warminster, then moved a Resolution expressive of the satisfaction with which the present Meeting hailed the information just communicated. This gentleman offered many striking remarks on our obligations to Seamen, as conveying the produce of the world to England, and defending the country by their loyalty and courage, as instruments in the hands of God. He produced a fine effect on the Meeting, by pathetically stating, "he loved Sailors, for it was a ship that first brought the Gospel to England, and Sailors who conveyed the first Missionary to our native shores." He spoke of the benefits of this *"Seamen's Union,"* in uniting all hearts, and producing mutual prayers among sailors for each other, and pleasantly described the meeting of the two Sailors on shore, after a long voyage in different ships, who welcomed each other's return with a hearty shake of the hand, and a kind assurance that they had remembered each other in prayer, and all the exertions of the Bethel Union ever since they had been absent from London.

Lieut. Arnold, of the Royal Navy, seconded this Resolution. He rejoiced to see the interest Christians on shore were now taking for our brave Seamen. He had himself, for many years, been a poor wandering Sailor. far from God, and accustomed to love the distance well. He had endured many storms, fought various battles for his country, and been happily rescued from the paths of sin, through the instrumentality of a pious Chaplain, on board His Majesty's Ship Repulse. He had there been a living witness of the advantage of religion among officers and seamen, and was persuaded, that the influence of divine grace on a sailor's heart would make him a better man — a better Christian — and an heir of immortal glory.

The Rev. Mr. Brown, of South Ockenden, moved the second resolution, on the promoting of *morality* and *religion* among *Seamen,* being of the first importance to the commerce, the character, and the glory of this kingdom.

This gentleman had spent the earlier part of his life at sea, and the recollections this meeting produced, were of the most affecting description. He took shame to himself, that he had not, as a Minister of the gospel, paid more attention to the spiritual interests of his brother seamen. He welcomed every effort to promote those interests, and trusted the day would yet arrive when sailors in general should more generally love and serve the Lord Jesus Christ. Alluding to the British ensign, stretched as a canopy over the platform, above which three flags with the word "BETHEL" in them, (as the signals used in the Merchant ships) were suspended, he observed, it had long been the boast and glory of this kingdom, that the flag of Britain had never been struck to a superior power. He rejoiced now to behold it prostrate at the feet of Jesus, and struck to the flag of Immanuel. He dwelt long and forcibly on the dreadful immorality that prevailed among the seamen of his Majesty's Navy, when he belonged to it; and expressed his astonishment at the forbearance and mercy of God to them. He could scarcely describe his joy, when, sailing up the Thames, he beheld the *Bethel* flag flying, or, when looking to the floating chapel, he saw a refuge for seamen from the temptations on shore, a sanctuary where Christ Jesus was proclaimed as the only ransom for guilty sinners. With all his heart and soul would he join in the proposed Union, and doubted not but the best blessing of heaven would rest upon it. *(This address drew forth tears of joy and shouts of approbation.)*

Thomas Thompson, Esq, one of the Secretaries of the Port of London Society, welcomed this fresh proof of religious zeal for our neglected Seamen. He adverted to the objection, that there were societies enough already. He certainly rejoiced in every well-meant effort, but could not believe but there was still an abundant field for christian exertion. That noble institution, to which he had the honour to belong, had, by means of the Floating Chapel, been exceedingly useful to seamen; and he trusted that the *Bethel Union* would so prosper, that, while both Institutions went hand in hand, and each filled up its separate department, God would be glorified, and Sailors eternally benefited. He related a very pleasing circumstance of a sailor, awakened by divine grace in a French prison, and when restored to his native country, employing his time and talents, in some villages in the west of England, for the instruction of those who know not the value of salvation.

The Chairman, deeply impressed with the extraordinary unanimity — the concern manifested for seamen — and the interesting scene this meeting presented, addressed the assembly, and described a sort of grand triumphal entry of Lord Nelson and his Fleet into Kioge Bay, in the Baltic, after the Battle of Copenhagen, and the appearance of the Fleet off the Swedish Naval Arsenal. The Chairman well remembered the beauties of the summer's evening, the music of different bands, the majestic advance of the St. George, 98 guns, in which Lord Nelson's flag was, and the shouts of the people who came off from the shore to hail this renowned Admiral's approach. "But ah! Nelson, what were thy honours, and what were all thy glories, compared with this peaceful assembly — these bloodless banners — and this glorious Union to gather together in one the Seamen of my Country, and conduct them to honors and glories imperishable, and durable as eternity! Honors that will flourish in immortal vigour amidst

> *"The wreck of matter,*
> *And the crush of worlds."*

Lieutenant E. Smith moved that "THE BETHEL SEAMEN'S UNION" be now formed. He detailed with awful minuteness the sad lives of Seamen in general. He noticed, with the utmost energy of feeling, the state of the atmosphere during the dreadful wreck of the St George, and other line of battle ships, in the North Sea, when so many hundreds of our Seamen perished. He described the interesting scenes he had witnessed of pious Seamen holding Prayer meetings on board of King's ships in which he had sailed, and spoke to their good conduct and general character on board. As an agent for the Merchant Seamen's Bible Society, and accustomed to visit almost every ship on the Thames, he could form a pretty accurate opinion of the present state of Seamen; and he was confident that it demanded, in this time of peace, when sailors were so easy of access, the utmost exertion of every friend to Christianity.

Mr. Phillips, in seconding this motion, observed, that, as his business lay chiefly on the Thames, he had many opportunites of noticing the conduct of seamen. He had also been engaged with the Prayer meetings among the sailors, and witnessed with inexpressible satisfaction the improvement among the Colliers and Coasters that entered the Thames, though he deeply lamented the awful state of the crews of many foreign ships, particularly in the West India trade. As a resident in the vicinity of Tooley-Street, he had long contemplated with horror the many Seamen who were continually drawn from that street by the vilest creatures; and thus body and soul ruined for ever. He wondered at the indifference of Christians of this neighbourhood to this subject, and was persuaded, if a place could be opened for Sailors on a sabbath evening in

Tooley Street, and a few friends would, by mild methods, endeavour to draw the Sailors there, the greatest good might be effected. A Sailors' Magazine for moral and religious improvement in the Seamen would also be of importance; and *more than 200 Seamen* had already expressed their desire to take a Monthly Publication of this description.

A gentleman from the West Indies, who had been labouring in the Methodist connection, moved that Messrs. Phillips and Collins should be Secretaries.

This motion was seconded by *Captain Orton,* a venerable grey-headed man, (who had spent 48 years of his life at sea, and escaped innumerable dangers) with the most amiable and primitive simplicity; he exclaimed, "What shall I render unto the Lord for all his mercies to me! When I first went to sea, there was scarcely a praying Captain or Seaman to be met with; but now, O how it rejoices my heart, to see what is going forward among seamen! When I attend the Sailors' Prayer Meetings, I cry out, 'Surely this is the Lord's doing, and it is marvellous in our eyes.' My soul shall praise God, that poor seamen, whose lives are so much exposed, are now seeking salvation by Jesus Christ. I have for many years carried Tracts and Bibles to all parts of the world. I was the first person that had the honour to distribute Greek Testaments in the Archipeligo; I have carried them to Smyrna, Salonica, Thessalonica; and at Athens, I stood on Mars-hill, where Paul preached, and gave the Holy Scriptures, I have done the same at Constantinople, and also in the Black Sea. In my last voyage I sailed about 40,000 miles. Before I returned I visited various parts of the East Indies, conversed with the Missionaries, and in every part laboured to serve my Divine Master. O how good he has been to me! How many times I have been overboard, and preserved as by a miracle! — What shall I render to the Lord! I have prayed in the most fearful storms, and he has heard me; my port has appeared, and I have anchored, in safety, while thousands have perished around me. 'O what shall I render to the Lord!' Yes, Sir, he has been good indeed to me, and will be so, Mr. Chairman, to every one that trusts alone in him. I have grown grey in his service, and I can and will speak well of his name. I have tried his promises and faithfulness nearly half a century on the ocean, and never found one to fail. 'What shall I render to my Lord for all his mercies to me!' I do most heartily enter into all the plans of this Union. It shall have my feeble support. O that my God may touch the hearts of poor Seamen, that they may live, as I have lived, by faith in Christ Jesus. They will find, then, as I do now, that in old age religion will be their chief support." It is not possible to describe the effect produced by the address of this venerable Sea Captain. Every heart was melted, and every eye bespoke the emotions of the soul. There was so much of genuine simplicity, obvious sincerity, impressive gravity, and attractive piety, in all he said, that the assembly seemed to have but one sentiment; when the Chairman, evidently much affected, appealed to all, and enquired, "Could the cold cheerless system of Infidels produce any thing like the solid, the celestial enjoyments in which we had so bountifully participated this evening?"

Mr. F. Collins, Depository of the Tract Society, and who had been a Lieutenant in the Navy, moved the adjournment of this *preliminary* to a *general* Meeting at the City of London Tavern. Mr. C. from his situation in the depot of

the Tract Society; from his habits of visiting for sick societies; and from his
frequent attendance at the Prayer Meetings in ships, as well as from his early
life being spent at sea; was quite capable of entering, as he did most fully, into
the miserable condition of our Seamen, and the facilities that were now afforded
to improve their morals and become the honoured instruments of saving their
souls. He declared, his own mind was fully convinced, that Sailors were one
day to become most eminent instruments in the hands of God, to promote his
glory throughout the globe. Already they have carried our Missionaries and our
Bibles to every part of the world; but when they themselves become *"living
epistles,* known and read of all men,"* they might diffuse that "leaven" which "is
to leaven the whole lump."

The Chairman observed, it would be impossible for Christians to stand
unmoved on the banks of the Ganges, and see sharks bearing away the infatuated
Hindoo; and he would hope, for the credit of members of Christian churches in
the vicinity of Tooley-street, that they will no longer witness with indifference
abandoned prostitutes leading sailors to the vilest brothels, and thus hurrying
downward to perdition hundreds of our bravest and most useful men. Surely,
while we plead so strenuously the importance of alleviating the miseries and
removing the moral degradation of the Heathens in Asia and Africa, we ought
to be consistent, and not suffer our countrymen to perish eternally before our
eyes, while we have the means of administering to their relief. "Physician heal
thyself" is an ancient adage strictly applicable to England; and very justly might
the Pagan, the Mahometan, and the Papist interpret it, by saying, "before we
can admit the Protestant faith to be superior to our own, let us see its fruits
exemplified in the captains, mates, and seamen, you send to our countries."
The chairman begged now to introduce *C. Ward,* a pious Sailor, who was one of
the noble crew of the Robert and Margaret, and assisted in saving three crews of
stranded vessels on the bar at Memel. He was sorry to inform the ladies and
gentlemen, that this worthy Sailor had been shipwrecked on the North Coast,
about a fortnight since, and had only just arrived in London. C. Ward then came
forward, with great modesty and humility, bowing to the company, and observing
that many allusions had been made this evening to Lord Nelson, and he
recollected the commands of that great admiral were — *"England expects every
man to do his duty."* Over your head, Mr. Chairman, (bowing to the chair) is an
ensign bearing a red cross; may I not say now, that the cross of Christ expects
every man to do his duty? yes, Sir; when we volunteered, in the storm at Memel,
to go off in the boat to the stranded ships, it was the blood of Christ that
impelled us to do our duty, and risk our own lives, to save our fellow-seamen
who were perishing on the bar. (The blood of Christ still expects every man to
do his duty. We poor seamen, who have scarcely been thought of by Christians
on shore, we stand in need of your kind help, and we are much obliged to you for
thinking of us; we will in return pray for you.) When we were returning home
from Memel, we had such a gale, that all hands expected to perish. We all
bowed before the Lord, and cried for help; our prayers were not in vain; the gale
abated, and we were brought safe to our desired haven. "O that" all "men
would praise the Lord for his goodness" to poor seamen, who are so often

"tossed with tempests and not comforted." About a fortnight since, our ship struck, and we had scarcely time to hoist out the boat and leave her. It was night, and the sea ran high; I lost my all; but what affected me most was this, *"I lost my Bible!"* Every heart was affected at this artless and pious narration, and tears flowed abundantly, to hear a poor shipwrecked Sailor, *in these days of Deism and Infidelity,* exclaim, with an emphasis that showed how he valued the book, *"I lost my Bible."* He continued, "We pulled off from the shore to avoid the broken water. (the surging billows;) our situation was dreadful, in an open boat, at night, on a boisterous ocean, and the wind blowing furiously upon us. Our captain advised attempting the shore; we dreaded this, and cried, No, no. Then, said he, if you think it better to remain out at sea for the night, you should heave the boat too [sic]; we did this, and I fell upon my knees in the boat and cried, "O God, who hast the winds in thy fist, and the waters in the hollow of thy hand, O look in mercy upon us poor shipwrecked Sailors." A vessel passed us; we hailed her, we shouted our distress; but, O sir, there are some British Seamen who have no bowels of compassion; "she passed us, *and left us to perish." (He delivered this with a tone so mournful, and a manner so affecting, that every heart was ready to burst with pity for shipwrecked Sailors, and indignation at the unfeeling Levite-like crew that passed by, regardless of the misery of others; "Teach me to feel for another's woe" vibrated from soul to soul.)* We continued in this state (said he) for some hours, expecting to be engulphed every moment, until our God directed a vessel near us, and took us on board, and brought us safe to land. I stand now as a living witness of the goodness and mercy of God; O think of us poor Sailors, when we are far off at sea, and you are comfortable in your beds on shore.

Few can imagine the effect of this address on all present. It was now ten o'clock, but scarce an individual stirred from his seat. The Chairman had once been in a line of battle ship, that struck on some rocks of the French coast, and when all hands expected to perish, a frigate, to whom signals of distress were made, refused to bear down on the wreck, but held on her course. The tale of this worthy Sailor had so much affected him, therefore, that it was with difficulty he could sum up the business of the evening. He declared he had never attended any public meeting in his life, that had been so interesting, and so important, in his view, as this. He affirmed that this object had for some time deeply impressed his mind. He had made many sacrifices of his own concerns in the country to bring this forward. He had met with immense difficulties in the progress of this business, but he now felt satisfied that the work was of God, and therefore must prosper. He stated, that the Sailors in the Lower Pool had already begun to set an example of energy to Christians on shore. They had gone to the worst neighbourhood in Rotherhithe, every Sabbath evening, borrowed a different room, and eight or nine of then [sic] engaged in prayer. This had been the means of the conversion of many depraved watermen and abandoned women. He hoped pious Sailors would soon labour in the same manner in Tooley Street and Ratcliffe-highway. He dwelt on the necessity and importance of a *Sailors' Magazine.* He wished it clearly to be understood, that this Society had only in view the promotion of *Loyalty, Morality,* and *Religion,* among Seamen. It had nothing whatever to do with religious denominations. Sailors were left fully at liberty to follow on shore the Church or the Meeting, as seemed most agreeable to themselves. The great aim of the Society would be to improve the morals of the Navy, and promote every good work in the Merchant service, that had the glory of God for its object. Considerable expences would be incurred by the measures proposed, and he had therefore to solicit Subscriptions, and announce a Collection. He also begged to observe, that if any Lady present should feel disposed to present the shipwrecked Sailor with a Bible, he should be most happy to be the instrument of conveying her bounty to him. He hoped to have a full meeting at the London Tavern, and that many respectable persons would come forward to aid a design of real importance to the Seamen of Great Britain.

BETHEL SEAMEN'S UNION, BRITISH AND FOREIGN:
General Meeting November 12, 1819

On Friday evening, Nov. 12, a General Meeting of this Society was held at the City-of-London Tavern, *Sir Geo. Mount Keith,* Bart. Commander in the Royal Navy, in the Chair; supported on his right by *C.M. Fabian,* Esq. R.N. and surrounded by several Naval Officers, Merchants, Captains of Merchant Ships, and Gentlemen who had been engaged in various marine services for many years; about 200 Seamen and Cabin-boys were also present.

The gallant Chairman opened the business of the Meeting with a most able Address, urging attention to the immortal interests of Sailors. *The Rev. G.C. Smith,* of Penzance, explained the objects of the Society; first, To unite and extend the Prayer Meetings now established in various ships on the River Thames; secondly, To ascertain the state of British Seamen in every port throughout Great Britain in the Navy and the Merchant Service, and to adopt such measures in connection with friends in maritime towns, as may best conduce to their moral and religious interests; thirdly, To establish a Foreign correspondence, and solicit information and direction as to the best means of doing good to Foreign Sailors, so that the limits of this Society shall be the circumference of the Globe! fourthly, To publish *"A Sailors' Magazine"* (Monthly) for the improvement of Seamen, and the communication of general information, concerning this interesting portion of the human race.

The Rev. Mr. Irons, of Camberwell; *the Rev. Mr. Ward,* Missionary from Serampore; and *the Rev. Mr. Allen,* late of Exeter, deeply interested the Meeting. *Captain Fabian,* an officer of long standing in his Majesty's Navy, furnished a noble testimony of the value of pious officers and seamen, and added his hearty wishes for prosperity to this excellent Institution. He was followed by *the Rev. Mr. Brown,* formerly of the Navy, *Captain Orton, Lieutenants E. Smith* and *J. Arnold,* who powerfully advocated the cause of Seamen. *G.F. Angas,* Esq. Merchant and Ship-owner, from the North, considered the Society fully entitled to the countenance and support of every Gentleman interested in shipping. *W. Stevens,* Esq. strongly recommended the

Institution. *Mr. T. Phillips* related some interesting anecdotes. *A. Black,* Esq. who had been for many years at sea, added his testimony, and *Mr. Smith* closed by the relation of the most affecting anecdote concerning the humanity and heroism of the crew of the *Robert and Margaret;* one of the crew being present was requested to stand up, when the cheerings of a most numerous and respectable Meeting were astounding and protracted.

On the whole, this Meeting was conducted with an energy and interest that promise the most extensive usefulness to an Institution that contemplates the present and eternal welfare of all those who "Go down to the sea in ships," in Asia, Africa, Europe, and America.

BETHEL SEAMEN'S UNION, BRITISH AND FOREIGN:
Committee Meeting October 6, 1820

Resolutions unanimously adopted by the Committee of this Institution:-

I. *THE NAME.* — That this Society shall in future be designated *"The British and Foreign Seamen's Friend Society, and Bethel Union."*

II. *THE OBJECTS.* — To extend the Christian Religion, improve the Morals, and promote the general good conduct of British and Foreign Seamen; and, in consequence of recent measures adopted at Chatham and Sheerness in the formation of Auxiliary Seamen's Friend Societies, this Institution considers it desirable to promote the spiritual improvement of Soldiers in every Town and City where it may be found practicable.

III. *THE MEANS.* — First, Domestic and Social Worship of Almighty God, by the union of a ship's crew at sea, or the collection of various Captains and Seamen in Port under the Bethel Flag. Secondly, The distribution of Bibles and Religious Works published by the most respectable Institutions for Piety and Morality. Thirdly, The encouragement of Religious Assemblies, and preaching by suitable Ministers on various parts of the River Thames, particularly the Upper and the Lower Pools. Fourthly, The establishment of Bethel Signal Flags and Divine Worship on board of different Ships in every Seaport. Fifthly, A correspondence with Foreign Nations to promote similar Establishments throughout the World. Sixthly, The extensive circulation of the *"Sailor's Magazine,"* as a suitable mode of Instruction, a Monthly medium of Intelligence, and an interesting compilation of Anecdotes and Narratives from the correspondence of zealous Friends to the Temporal and Eternal welfare of Seamen. Seventhly, The providing suitable boarding-houses for Sailors on their arrival from foreign voyages.

IV. *THE SPIRIT.* — Christian Philanthropy, as expressed in the Gospel, "Glory be to God in the highest; Peace on Earth, and good will towards men;" Christian Candour, as displayed in the Apostolic Benediction, "Grace be with all them who love our Lord Jesus Christ in sincerity." The sentiments to be promoted will be agreeable to the articles and homilies of the Church of England, and the doctrines inculcated are, "Repentance towards God, and faith in our Lord Jesus Christ."

V. *THE CONSTITUTION*. — The most respectable and honorary patronage, and efficient Committee, British and Foreign Secretaries, Treasurer, and Collector.

VI. *THE RULES*.

1. That the following Gentlemen be members of the Committee, with power to add to their Number:-

Captain C.M. Fabian, R.N.	C.F. Angas, Esq.
Captain Sir G.M. Keith, R.N.	H. Ashley, Esq.
Captain P. Lamb, R.N.	Mr. G. Yeoland.
Lieut. E. Smith, R.N.	Mr. H. Parks.
Lieut. W.H. Nichols, R.N.	Mr. F. Collins.
Lieut. J.F. Arnold, R.N.	Mr. J. Congdon.
Lieut. J. Norris, R.N.	Mr. S. Cheeswright.
Rev. W.B. Collyer, D.D.	Captain G. Orton.
Rev. J. Irons.	

2. That the following Gentlemen be the Officers of the Society, viz.:-

Benjamin Shaw, Esq.	*Treasurer.*
Captain C. Allen, R.N.	*Corresponding Secretary.*
Lieut. T.G. Nichols, R.N.	,,
Mr. T. Phillips.	,,
Captain W. H. Angas	*Foreign Secretary.*
Rev. G.C. Smith.	,,
Mr. E.M. Sparkes	*Secretary.*
Rev. A. Brown.	*Minister for the Society to Address the Seamen in the Upper and Lower Pools.*
Mr. M. Clarke, R.N.	*Collector.*

3. The Committee to meet monthly for the transaction of business, and that five be considered a quorum.

4. A Subscription for carrying into effect the objects of this Society shall be opened, and a donation of 10 guineas or upwards constitute the donor a life member, and an annual Subscription of half a guinea, or more, a member of this Society.

5. That an Annual Meeting of this Society be held in the City of London; when a report of its proceedings will be read, and the audited accounts of its receipts and disbursements communicated to the public.

Donations and Subscriptions will be thankfully received by the Treasurer, Secretaries, and Members of the Committee; also, at the Banking-house of Sir John Perring, Bart. Shaw, Barber, and Co. 72, Cornhill.

Committee Room, 18, Aldermanbury, Oct. 6, 1820.

APPENDIX NO. 7

EXAMPLES OF THE RHETORICAL GENIUS OF FATHER TAYLOR OF BOSTON

America has had many great maritime pulpit orators, but none greater than Boston's inimitable Father Taylor (see pp. 493-9). However, no sermon of his is left, "for sermon there was none until it came to him in the pulpit" (Allan Macdonald). When a friend asked him what he was going to preach about on Sunday, he answered, "Don't know, don't want to forestall God." Nevertheless, glimpses of his rhetorical genius and saltwater theology, both in the pulpit and elsewhere, may still be caught in the reminiscences of his admirers, from which the following are a selection. (See sources listed under Part VII, Note No. 305.)

On last-minute conversions (when presented as a role-model): "I tell you boys, no man can calculate on serving the devil all his life and then cheating him with his last breath. Don't burn the candle down to the end in sin and then give God the snuff."

On arguments about finer points of doctrine (compared to controversy among the crew of a ship in distress, after sighting the sails of a vessel bearing down to the rescue): "Now what mattered it, whether she [the vessel coming to the rescue] was a ship, a bark, or a brig. She was a savior!"

On religious bigotry (when a fellow-minister refused Taylor's invitation to sit in his ample pulpit because another had recently sat there, with whose theology he deeply disagreed): "Lord, there are two things we need to be delivered from in Boston — bad rum and bigotry."

On self-righteous Pharisees (whom he knew to be present during a prayer-meeting): "[We pray] that every rag of their sails may be torn from their masts, and [that they may] scud under bare poles to Jesus."

On predestination (to a fellow-minister who insisted that the non-elect, no matter what they do, will be lost): "To exhort men to repent on those terms is like inviting a lot of gravestones home to dinner."

On denominational creeds (and their limited validity): "Blessed Jesus . . . let no man put blinkers on us, that we can only see in a certain direction; for we want to look all around the horizon."

On the limitless riches of the Gospel (as he gazed for the first time at the Niagara Falls): "Niagara is like the Gospel . . . you never come to it for water and go away with an empty bucket."

On worrying (when thinking of how his recent seafaring converts might backslide for want of spiritual nurture while he was absent from his Bethel for a while): "What am I doing? I am not believing that our God who gives the great whale a ton of herrings for his breakfast can take care of my boys while I am away."

On world mission (and ignoring the crucial role of Christian seafarers): "You might as well think of melting a mountain of ice with moonbeams. . . . But get the sailor converted, and he is off [with the Gospel] from one port to another, as if you had put spurs to lightning."

On intemperance (and Boston's toleration of "soul-destroying grog-shops"): "Your patriotic fathers could make a cup of tea for his Britannic Majesty out of a whole cargo, but you can't cork up a gin-jug? Ha!"

On preaching (quoting with evident approval the words of an honest tar): "When a man preaches at me, I want he should take something warm out of his heart and *shove* it into mine; that's what I calls preaching, sir. If you're goin' to *read* it, give me the book and I will read it myself."

On sermon interruption (by a religious enthusiast from shore, claiming to have special permission from the Holy Ghost to speak during the service): "You will please give my compliments to the Holy Ghost, and tell him I say you can't speak here today. Sit down."

On priorities in life (when he got tangled up in his grammar during sermon delivery): "I have lost the nominative case, but I'm on my way to glory!"

On angels (when, as life was ebbing out, a well-meaning sister in the faith tried to console him with the thought that the angels were waiting to welcome him home): "I don't want angels, I want folks."

Appendix no. 8

American Seamen's Mission Statistics in the Early 1850's

Table giving a summary view of the "Seamen's Cause" in the USA in the 1850's, as estimated from "the best data at hand" at that time. The table does not include "hospitals for seamen, and other establishments, charitable or otherwise, of a similar character." (From Israel P. Warren, *The Seamen's Cause . . .*, New York, 1858.)

SOCIETIES.	No. of Chaplains, Missionaries, &c.	Places of Worship	Average Attendance.	No. of Homes.	Average Annual Boarders.	Annual Receipts.
A.S.F. SOCIETY AND ITS CONNECTIONS.						
American Seamen's Friend Soc.,	Stations abroad			2	3,500	$20,000
Maine Seamen's Union,	1	1	150	1	600	600 †
Boston Seamen's Friend Society,	1	1	300	1	2,800	5,000
New York Port Society	4	1	400	-	-	4,000 †
Pennsylvania Sea. Friend Society,	-	-	-	1	1,200	1,000
Mobile Bethel Society,	2	2	250	1	1,200	2,000 †
American Bethel Society,	20	15	-	-	-	8,000
Western Seamen's Friend Society,	30	20	-	-	-	15,000
A.S.F. Soc'y and Connections,	58	40	-	6	9,300	$55,600

† Exclusive of amount received from A.S.F.S.

INDEPENDENT SOCIETIES						
Salem Bethel,	1	1	200	-	-	1,000
Boston Port Society	1	1	200	-	-	3,000
" Seamen's Aid Society,	-	-	-	1	1,800	2,000 †
" Baptist Bethel Society,	1	1	200	-	-	2,000
" Church of St. Mary's,	1	1	150	-	-	1,200
" Mission at large,	1	1	-	-	-	1,500

	No. of Chaplains, Missionaries, &c.	Places of Worship	Average Attendance.	No. of Homes.	Average Annual Boarders.	Annual Receipts.
INDEPENDENT SOCIETIES (cont.)						
New Bedford Port Society,	1	1	200	1	500	1,200
Episcopal Society for Sea., N.Y.,	3	2	300	1	800	5,000
Methodist Missions, N.Y.,	4	3	500	-	-	6,000
American Baptist Bethel Society,	1	1	250	-	-	1,500
Eastburn Bethel, Philadelphia,	1	1	220	-	-	2,000
Philadelphia Sabbath Association,	6	6	-	-	-	3,500
Episcopal Bethel, Philadelphia,	1	1	-	-	-	1,000
Methodist ” ”	1	1	-	-	-	1,000
Seamen's Union Bethel, Baltimore,	1	1	200	1	800	1,000
Sailor's City Bethel,	1	1	200	-	-	1,000
Alexandria Bethel,	1	1	150	-	-	1,000
Norfolk Seamen's Friend Society,	-	-	-	-	-	
Wilmington ” ” ”	1	1	200	1	700	1,200
Charleston Port Society,	1	1	250	1	600	2,000
Savannah Port Society,	1	1	200	2	1,000	2,000
New Orleans Sea. Fr'd Society,	1	1	150	1	500	1,200
San Francisco Sea. Fr'd Soc.,	1	1	150	1	600	3,000
Total Independent Societies,	31	29	-	9	7,300	$44,300
Am. Sea. Fr'd Soc. and connections,	58	40	-	6	9,300	55,600
Whole Amount, ...	89	69	-	15	16,600	$99,900

† Exclusive of sales of clothing

Notes

Introduction Notes

1. SML (edited by George Charles Smith) 1820, p. 214; 1821, p. 486; 1826, p. 46. Cf. NSM 1858, p. 567.
2. SMNY 1856-57, p 353.
3. Hohman 1952, pp. 283, 285; cf. p. 413.
4. NSM 1835, p. 443.
5. Smith 1874.
6. Warren 1858. See also SMNY 1876, p. 212. Yates 1851, however, provides less than the title would suggest, and includes several significant errors of fact.
7. Anson 1948.
8. For a lengthy list of erroneous statements on the origins of seamen's mission work, see Part VII, Note 430. Here, two typical examples must suffice: (1) The fictitious "Wilkins-version" of the origin of the Thames Revival with its many repercussions (infra, p. 161). (2) the omission of all organized seamen's missions prior to John Ashley's venture in the Bristol Channel in the mid-1830's (e.g.: *Svensk Uppslagsbok* 1957, c. 81. *Nordisk Familjebok* 1963 Vol. 19, cc. 291-2. Cf. infra, p. 384).
9. Pfeiffer 1920, pp. 203-4. Kverndal 1972, p. 38. Cf. Owen 1816, pp. 1-2. Matthews 1911, p. 174. Warneck Vol. 1, 1892, pp. 8-10. Infra, p. 50.
10. Pfeiffer 1920, pp. 203-4, 213-8. Latourette 1932, pp. 532-46. Seierstad 1947, p. 180. Hodgson 1968, p. 167. Toynbee 1969, pp. 30-2. Kverndal 1972, pp. 38-9.
11. Cf. Andersen 1955, p. 15. Beaver 1964, passim. Myklebust 1971, pp. 16-20. Note also the transition, in 1969, from *The International Review of Missions* to *International Review of Mission*. Although the word "ministry" is, where deemed appropriate, used interchangeably with the word "mission," this does not imply that the two words are regarded as identical. Cf. Verkuyl 1978, pp. 1-5. Infra, pp. 557-61.
12. Psalm 107:23. Infra, pp. 122-3.
13. Infra, pp. 90, 533-4.
14. Acts 27:18. NSM 1834, p. 225. Cf. Elliott-Binns 1946, pp. 506-7. Infra, pp. 269-79.
15. Kverndal (Bergen) 1978, pp. 103-34. Infra, p. 591.
16. Kverndal 1972, p. 41.

17. Cf. Davis 1961, p. v. Infra, p. 308.

18. Cf. Howse 1960, pp. 132-7. Infra, p. 556.

19. Infra, p. 536.

20. Anson 1948, pp. xi, 46, 98-9. Infra, p. 403.

21. Kverndal (Bergen) 1978, pp. 103-33.

22. Kverndal 1972, p. 41.

23. Anson introduces the concept of "maritime missiology" as early as 1948 (p. 103). Cf. Myklebust 1946, pp. 128-9, Infra, p. 539.

PART I — NOTES

1. Boswell 1953, pp. 246-7. Cf. Whitely 1938, pp. 80-2.

2. Infra, pp. 48-51.

3. New Schaff-Herzog, Vol. 8, 1910, pp. 88-90. Anson 1948, p. 6; 1954, pp. 3-8. Harper 1972, p. 20. *The New Bible Dictionary* 1974, pp. 1153, 1178.

4. Anson 1948, p. 6; 1954, pp. xiii-xvii, 11-98. SMNY 1832-33, p. 303. Infra, pp. 58-9.

5. SML 1824, pp. 171-2. Anson 1948, p. 6; 1954, pp. 101-8. *The New Bible Dictionary* 1974, p. 1240.

6. SML 1824, p. 171. Smith 1880, passim. SMNY 1897, pp. 363 ff. Robinson 1918, pp. 474-6. Anson 1948, pp. 6-7; 1954, pp. 131-48. Cf. Janeway on Acts 27:18-20 in "The Seaman's Preacher." *A Token for Mariners* 1708, passim. There has even been speculation that Paul celebrated the Eucharist on board that battered grain-ship (Acts 27:35-36). Cf. Taylor 1978, p. 1.

7. Anson 1948, pp. 8-37. Ursin 1965, pp. 145, 160-1, 170-1. Harper 1975, pp. 293-4. Infra p. 15.

8. Anson 1948, pp. 18, 20-2, Smith 1961, p. 2. Goldsmith-Carter 1966, p. 137. Wright 1967, pp. 12, 25-31. Cf. Taylor 1978, p. 13.

9. Burwash 1947, pp. 72-77.

10. Smith 1961, p. 1. Gordon Taylor, in his exhaustive study of chaplaincy in the Royal Navy, accords "seniority" to a priest named Utta, sent in 651 from Northumbria to Kent, in order to bring back, by sea, a bride for his king; to what extent this Utta also ministered to the spiritual needs of these crews is not mentioned, however (Taylor 1978, p. 1).

11. *Vinland the Good* 1970, p. 78. Kverndal (N.Y.) 1978, p. 5.

12. Walrond 1904, p. xi. Kealey 1905, pp. 3, 17. WW 1905, pp. 13-4. (MS) Curry 1956, p. 12. Smith 1961, p. 1. Taylor 1978, p. 3.

13. Anson 1948, pp. 13-30. Wright 1967, pp. 29, 120. Cf. Hakluyt, Vol. 4, 1903, pp. 340-1, 346. Froude 1926, pp. 249, 290. Taylor 1978, pp. 3-18.

14. Anson 1948, pp. 15, 20-1. Wright 1967, p. 18. Taylor 1978, pp. 12-3.

15. Hohman 1956, pp. 3-5. Wright 1967, passim. Lloyd 1968, pp. 23, 25. Ellacott 1970, pp. 48-9, 58-9. Kemp 1976, pp. 615, 700. Cf. Andrea 1982, pp. 203-9. Infra, pp. 568-71.

16. SMNY 1899, pp. 203-4. Walrond 1904, pp. xi-xii. Elias 1912, pp. 91-104. Froude 1926, passim. Trevelyan 1946, pp. 194-5. Kemp 1970, pp. 1-3. Taylor 1978, p. 19.

17. Walrond 1904, pp. xi-xii. *The Churchman* 1905, pp. 250-1. (MS) Curry 1956, pp. 14-6, quoting from Hakluyt, Vol. 12, 1903, p. 199.

18. Laffin 1969, p. 117. Cf. Wright 1970, pp. 330-5.

19. Corbett 1899, pp. 70, 392. (MS) Curry 1956, p. 16. Taylor 1978, pp. 23-4.

20. Smith 1961, pp. 3-10. Wright 1970, pp. 335-7. Cf. SML 1823, p. 127. (MS) Curry 1956, passim. Taylor 1978, passim. Miller 1980, p. 80. Hawkins went so far as to insist that all hands join him in prayer at the mainmast on bended knee, morning and evening, "under pain of twenty-four hours in irons" ([MS] Curry 1956, pp. 17-8). Cf. Muscat 1984, p. 394.

21. *A Collection* 1768, pp. 671-4. Procter 1951, p. 645. Kemp 1976, p. 42.

22. E.g., SML 1822, pp. 15-16. *The Christian Mariner's Journal* 1829, pp. 37-41.

23. *The Naval Chronicle* 1806, pp. 458-9. Robinson 1894, p. 337. Kealey 1905, p. 3. Smith 1961, p. 13. Taylor 1978, pp. 65-66.

24. Robinson 1894, p. 402. Cf. Powell 1922, Miller 1974, and Taylor 1978, passim.

25. Evjen 1916, pp. 376-83. Anderson 1920, pp. 306-29. Hansen 1970, passim. Kverndal 1975, p. 45. N.Y. 1978, p. 5. Lehane 1981, pp. 63-4. For an elevated concept of (Roman Catholic) chaplaincy in the French navy, see Fournier 1677, pp. 107-9.

26. Ward 1929, pp. 41-8. Smith 1961, pp. 10-1 and passim. Cf. Teonge 1927, passim. (MS) Curry 1956, p. 10. Infra, pp. 94-9.

27. SML 1820, p. 136; 1821, pp. 293-4. Kingsford 1947, p. 124. Cf NSM 1831, p. 58. ASFS *AR* 1878, pp. 75-76. Manwaring 1927, passim.

28. Beaver 1968, p. 114. However, Dutch lay *krank-bezoekers* (sick-visitors) were also known as *drank-bezoekers* (drink-visitors). See Miller 1980, p. 71.

29. Waltari 1925, pp. 36-41. Weltzer 1952, p. 10. Wallenberg 1967, passim.

30. Braithwaite 1961, pp. 563-4. Cf. Coxere 1945, passim. Lurting 1816, passim.

31. SML 1821, pp. 129-31. CHSM 1822-23, p. 57. NSM 1861, pp. 437-43.

32. EM 1808, pp. 57-8. SML 1856, pp. 185-6.

33. SML 1820, p. 441. NSM 1839, p. 282; 1841, pp. 44-6.

34. Cheever 1851, passim.

35. EM 1811, p. 366. Williams 1818, passim. SML 1826, pp. 168-75. Canwright 1973-74, pp. 5, 9. Carlisle 1975, pp. 198-99. *The Negro Almanac* 1976, pp. 169-70, 190. Atkin 1977, passim. In contrast to his New England colleagues, Cuffee, as captain and owner, renounced the profitable "Triangle Trade," and consistently refused to carry slaves or intoxicating liquor (*South Street Reporter* 1943-44, p. 9). Nor was Cuffee's case unique. Among the freed slaves of nearby Nantucket, Absalom Boston became a Quaker whaleship captain who in 1822 sailed out with an all-black crew. There is evidence that black Nantucket whalers commanded wide respect. (Gautier 1983, pp. 24-7.)

36. Pascoe 1901, pp. 12, 837-8.

37. Gummere 1922, pp. 289-303, 505-508.

38. E.g., EM 1799, pp. 38-9; 1801, pp. 490-1. CH 1818-19, pp. 413-4. Paterson 1858, pp. 1-2. Atkinson 1896, pp. 128-30. Clark 1958, pp. 5-6. Davies 1961, pp. 25-6. Cf. Danbolt 1973, p. 10.

39. Stranks 1961, pp. 13, 64. Macneill 1965, pp. 264-5, 284, 327-8.

40. Macneill 1965, pp. 157-8, 234-6.

41. SML 1822, pp. 245-6; 1852, p. 154. Cf. infra, pp. 563-5.

42. Page 1616, passim. Dr. Page is anxious to point out in his dedication that he does not wish to "preiudice the holy libertie of such as are able without these directions, to pour forth their hearts before God, to use their own formes, but to give helpe to such as cannot. . . ." Dr. John Wood, in a similar work, underscores even further the vital role of prayer. "The sea-man . . . being for the most part debarred of the spirituall food of his soule (that is, the Word of God ordinarily preached), should laboure to redeeme and recover that loss, both by reading the Word of God, and learned mens workes: but especially by having continuall recourse to God in prayer. For it is the end of our preaching to teach men how to pray. . . ." (Wood 1618, p. 37.)

43. Kealey 1905, pp. 18-9. Procter 1951, pp. 644-5. Smith 1961, pp. 140-1. Cross 1971, p. 1234.

44. Ryther 1806. Flavel 1760. Woodward 1723. (For dates of original editions, see Bibliography.) Madoxe 1581 provides a very early example of Protestant sea-sermons.

45. Mather 1700, 1709, 1717, 1723, 1724. DAB vol. 6, 1933, pp. 386-9. Holmes 1940, passim. Macneill 1965, p. 276. For an example of Mather's exhortations to seafarers, see Appendix No. 1, p. 612. Infra, p. 407-12.

46. E.g., Clap 1738, Smith 1771, Brown 1793, Emerson 1804, Abbot 1804 and 1812.

47. E.g.: Janeway 1715, Flavel 1796, Ryther 1806.

48. Henningius 1580, passim. Weltzer 1952, pp. 8-9. Aarflot 1965, p. 115.

49. Fridag's book bears the title *En liden Haandbog oc Tröstespeyel for Söfarne Folk* ("A Small Manual and Source of Comfort for Seafarers"). Aarflot 1965, p. 115; 1967, p. 465.

50. Weltzer 1952, pp. 8-11. Waltari 1925, pp. 32-5.

51. Heitman 1793, passim. Nerhus 1941, passim. Stöylen 1955, pp. 284-6.

52. CHSM 1824, pp. 639-40. NSM 1828, p. 253. Brauer 1971, pp. 380-1.

53. (MS) Nederlandsch Historisch Scheepvaart Museum 1970.

54. Thun 1959, p. 126.

55. Anson 1948, pp. 31-5.

56. Ibid., p. 35. Yarham 1972, pp. 214-6. Beck 1973, pp. 26, 305.

57. Anson 1948, pp. 34-5. Henningsen 1950, passim; 1952, pp. 294-300. Ursin 1965, pp. 138-44.

58. Anson 1948, pp. 36-7. Chase 1965, p. 23. Wright 1967, pp. 116-7.

59. Wright 1967, pp. 116-7. Lloyd 1968, pp. 22-4.

60. Anson 1948, p. 34; 1954, p. 160.

61. Wasberg 1964, pp. 21-2. Carlzon 1969, p. 166. Storli 1971, pp. 20-2.

62. Pascoe 1901, p. 740. Thompson 1951, pp. 32-3, 469. Kverndal (Bergen) 1978, pp. 106-7.

63. NSM 1839, p. 281. SMNY 1876, p. 47. ASFS *AR* 1878, p. 77.

64. Ibid. Aiken vol. 4, 1803, pp. 121-2. SML 1820, p. 420; 1822, p. 245; 1823, pp. 121-7. DNB vol. 19, 1889, pp. 253-4.

65. NSM 1839, p. 281. SMNY 1876, pp. 47-8. ASFS *AR* 1878, p. 77. DNB vol. 50, 1897, p. 70.

66. NSM 1839, p. 281. SMNY 1876, p. 48. ASFS *AR* 1878, p. 77. DNB vol. 29, 1892, p. 246. Beck 1907, pp. 165-7.

67. Flavel 1676; 1760; 1799. Ryther 1806. Janeway 1708; 1715; 1810.

68. Newton 1799, passim. SML 1820, pp. 1-3, 32-6, 73-6, 281-6, 321-3. NSM 1839, pp. 281-2; 1841, pp. 43-8. SMNY 1885, pp. 280-3. DNB vol. 9, 1887, pp. 398-9. Martin 1950, passim. Matthews 1911, pp. 174-83. Infra. pp. 79, 137.

69. Scarth 1889, p. 124.

70. Münchmeyer 1912, p. 91. Westlake 1919, pp. vi, 88, 131, 157, 193. Waltari 1925, pp. 302. Burwash 1947, pp. 71-2. Anson 1948, pp. 32-7. Thun 1959, p. 11. Lensch 1966, pp. 27-30. Wright 1967, pp. 121-3. Storey 1967, passim. *The Corporation of Trinity House* n.d., pp. 1-13. Cf. Smith 1870, pp. 22-3, 111-2.

71. Highmore 1810, Vol. 2, pp. 946, 948, 952-3. Mease 1811, pp. 268-70. Low 1850, pp. 265-7. SMNY 1828-29, pp. 214-5.

72. Jenkins 1952, pp. 1-6. Smith 1966, pp. 272-3. Cf. infra, p. 409.

73. Brooke 1853, p. 393.

74. Hanway 1757 and 1759, passim. The Marine Society 1809, passim; 1976, pp. 1-2. Highmore 1810, Vol. 2, pp. 786-818. NSM 1841, pp. 121-6; 1857, pp. 235-6. Lloyd 1968, pp. 184-7. Distad 1973, pp. 156-60. The Marine Society, which now (since 1975) administers the Sailor's Home Trust and Destitute Sailor's Fund, is today "mainly concerned with providing help to potential and serving seafarers" through the Seafarers' Education Service and the College of the Sea (The Marine Society 1976, passim). In 1979, the Society's new headquarters were opened at 202 Lambeth Rd.

75. Hanway 1763, 1778, 1779, 1788. Aiken Vol. 5, 1804, p. 49. PLS *Proceedings* 1821, p. 44. DNB Vol. 8, 1917, pp. 1196-1200. Distad 1973, pp. 156-60.

76. DNB Vol. 56, 1898, p. 301. Infra. p. 74.

77. Cowan 1905, pp. 81-7. Cf. Stackpole 1962, pp. 87-106.

78. Anson 1948, pp. 25-7. McColgan 1951, pp. 1, 6, 8, 15, 21-22. Apostleship of the Sea 1951, p. 22.

79. Pascoe 1901, p. 735. Cf. SML 1820, pp. 225, 349-50.

80. NSM 1832, pp. 177-89, 214-5. Daae 1880, pp. 51-8. Brooks 1899, pp. 149-55. Latimer 1893, p. 188. Montgomery 1902, p. 208. Gray 1905, pp. 39-41. Currey 1910, Ray 1911, and Olán 1921, passim. Gosse 1932, pp. 70-87. Lloyd 1942, pp. 32-4. Fairburn Vol. 1, 1945, pp. 658, 756. Thun 1959, pp. 11-2. Deutsche Seemannsmission 1966, pp. 32-3. Chidsey 1971, passim. Laing 1974, pp. 119-30. Kemp 1976, p. 58. For a more positive appraisal of the exploits of the Barbary corsairs, see Ireland 1976, pp. 271-83.

81. Latimer 1893, p. 322. Hutchinson 1914, passim. Whitley 1938, p. 159. Trevelyan 1946, p. 498. *Encyclopaedia of the Social Sciences* Vol. 7, pp. 614-5. Lewis 1965, p. 171. Lloyd 1968, pp. 16-7, 60, 83-6, 104-6, 124-49. Baynham 1969, pp. 4-8. Jones 1972, pp. 431-2.

82. Lewis 1960, pp. 100-1, 114; 1965, pp. 171-2. Baynham 1969, pp. 5, 9. Lloyd 1968, pp. 12-3, 150-72.

83. *A Dialogue* 1709, Defoe 1728, Oglethorpe 1728 and 1777, Phillips 1766, Sharp 1778, Urquart (to Melville and Wilberforce) 1824, passim. SML 1824, pp. 321-6. Crow 1830, pp. 3, 31-2. NSM 1833, pp. 105-6, 511. *The Life . . . of Adam Clarke* 1834, pp. 48-9.

84. Hoare 1820, pp. 160-71; 1828 Vol. 1, p. 238. DNB Vol. 51, 1897, pp. 401-4. Wright 1867, pp. 43-4. Lascelles 1928, pp. 92-5. Church 1930, pp. 25-31. Ettinger 1936, pp. 88, 309-10. (Carrol 1942, pp. 33-4, does not distinguish between impressment into the navy and shanghaiing into the merchant service.) Infra. p. 347.

85. In light of the intimate mutuality which emerged between early British and American seamen's mission endeavor, it is interesting to note that these two British precursors both identified themselves with the cause of *the colonists* during the American Revolutionary War (Ettinger 1936, pp. 306-7). Cf. Urquart (to Wilberforce) 1824, passim. SML 1824, pp. 321-6. Ettinger 1936, p. 310. Infra, p. 46-51.

86. Whiteley 1938, pp. 149-54. Howse 1960, p. 3. Halévy 1961, pp. 256-337. Erickson 1968, pp. 328-54. Toynbee 1969, passim. Briggs 1977, pp. 510-1. Cf. Latourette 1953, pp. 1064-5; 1970, Vol. 4, pp. 10-1. Israel 1966, pp. 589-99.

87. Latourette 1953, pp. 1003-8; 1970, Vol. 3, pp. 49-50. Cragg 1962, pp. 234-55. Langley 1967, pp. 43-44. Marty 1975, pp. 273-6, 297-8.

88. SML 1826, p. 280. Latourette 1953, pp. 1006-10; 1970 Vol. 3, pp. 455-6. Howse 1960, pp. 3-4, 45, 127. Halévy 1961, pp. 450-1. Marty 1975, p. 276.

89. Latourette 1953, pp. 997-1001; 1970, Vol. 3, pp. 454-57; Vol. 4, pp. 1-6. Around the turn of the century, signs of missionary awakening were becoming manifest in *Continental* Protestanism, too. Soon, there was evidence of a gradual recovery of missionary spirit in *Roman Catholicism,* after decades of decline. However, the missionary revival around the year 1800 was essentially a phenomenon of the churches of the *English-speaking* world (Latourette, 1953, pp. 1001-55).

90. Allen, 1898, pp. 7-9. Pascoe 1901, pp. 2-3. Woodward 1935, passim. Balleine 1951, pp. 27-8. Berg 1956, pp 30-2. Hogg 1961, pp. 103-4. Cragg 1962, pp. 61-2. Bullock 1963, passim. Neill 1965, p. 188. Cf. Moorman 1953, pp. 266-7. United Bible Societies *Bulletin* No. 19, 1954, p. 2.

91. Allen 1898, pp. 13-24. Pascoe 1901, pp. 3-9. Woodward 1935, pp, 8-9. Balleine 1951, pp. 126-7. Berg 1956, pp. 40-52. Bullock 1963, p. 139. Neill 1965, pp. 196-8. Latourette 1970, Vol. 3, pp. 48-9.

92. Allen 1898, p. 8. Woodward 1935, pp. 7-8. Berg 1956, pp. 36-8.

93. Woodward 1935, p. 14. Cragg 1962, pp. 117-40. Bullock 1963, p. 162. In its concern for "the moving multitudes," the SPCK did, however, from the beginning attempt a distribution, however sporadic, of the Scriptures, devotional literature, and the like, among both naval and merchant seafarers. ([MS]

SPCK *Minutes,* passim. Allen 1898, passim. Lane 1900, p. 467. Cf. supra, p. 12, infra, pp. 100-1.) Also, the SPG did, from the outset, instruct its emissaries, while traveling by sea, to assume responsibility for services and catechization for the benefit of both crew and fellow-passengers (Pascoe 1901, pp. 837-8).

94. Woodward 1935, pp. 11-5. Balleine 1951, pp. 1-9, 18-39. Moorman 1953, pp. 297-300. Berg 1956, pp. 31, 44, 73-5. Cameron 1961, pp. 32-40. Cragg 1962, pp. 141-52. Neill 1965, pp. 188-9. Winchester 1966, pp. 54-61. Latourette 1970, Vol. 3, p. 48. Marty 1975, pp. 289-93.

95. Whiteley 1938, pp. 374-5. Bready 1938, p. 14. Cameron 1961, p. 45. Halévy 1961, passim. Cragg 1962, pp. 148-9. Neill 1965, p. 194.

96. Russel 1915, p. 11. Whiteley 1938, p. 339. Balleine 1951, pp. 1-17. Moorman 1953, pp. 310-1. Berg 1956, pp. 66-72. Brown 1961, pp. 15-44. Cameron 1961, p. 29. Cragg 1962, pp. 117-40. Winchester 1966, pp. 71-6. Erickson 1968, pp. 349-52.

97. Warner 1930, pp. 56-9. Whiteley 1938, pp. 206-10, 374-7. Bready 1938, p. 398. Hennell 1947, pp. 192-3; 1954, p. 21; 1960, p. 61. Balleine 1951, pp. 23-32. Cameron 1961, pp. 31-80. Winchester 1966, pp. 76-7. Cf. infra. pp. 130-1.

98. Overton 1906, p. 76. Balleine 1951, pp. 33-9. Moorman 1953, pp. 300-1. Berg 1956, pp. 84-6. Cameron 1961, pp. 35-51. Neill 1965, pp. 188-93.

99. Overton 1906, p. 73. Lecky 1921, pp. 140-1. Balleine 1951, passim. Berg 1956, p. 113. Halévy 1961, p. 433. Cragg 1962, pp. 150-1. It is important to note, however, that significant contributions to the mid-century revival in Britain were made by both *Moravianism* and Whitefield's *Calvinistic Methodism* (Wood 1977, p. 448).

100. Russel 1915, pp. 1-10. Balleine 1951, pp. 40-106. Moorman 1953, pp. 306-8. Hennell 1954, p. 22. Berg 1956, pp. 76-7, 113-4. Neill 1965, p. 190.

101. Hennell 1954, pp. 21-2. Berg 1956, pp. 114-5. Halévy 1961, pp. 410, 417, 428. Vidler 1961, p. 40. Walls 1977, pp. 547, 549. See especially (MS) Lovegrove 1981, passim.

102. Though they did emphasize the *Christian life,* and contributed little to Christian scholarship, the evangelicals were far from indifferent to *Christian doctrine.* This was, in general, uncompromisingly conservative. (Russel 1915, pp. 7, 11-2. Balleine 1951, pp. 30-3, 106-7. Moorman 1953, pp. 302-3. Heasman 1962, pp. 15-6. Neill 1965, pp. 192-4. Hennell 1977, p. 512. *Christian Herald* July-Aug 1979, p. 61. Cf. Foster 1960, p. viii.)

103. Balleine 1951, p. 106. Moorman 1953, pp. 308, 315-6. Howse 1960, pp. 7, 10. Brown 1961, pp. 1-6, 46-7. Heasman 1962, pp. 19-20. Cf. Neill 1965, p. 194.

104. Russel 1915, pp. 21-2. Balleine 1951, p. vii. Berg 1956, pp. 113-4. Howse 1960, p. 6. Brown 1961, p. 45. The term "Evangelical Party" distinguishes this group from the "High Church Party" who, with their zealous assertion of episcopal authority, orthodox doctrine and liturgical traditionalism, were so called from the late 17th century and became forerunners of the 19th century Oxford Movement. Their opposites, the "Low Church Party," so called from the early 18th century, were identical with the Latitudinarian (liberal) clergy of that century, but became the "Broad Church Party" of the mid-19th century.

The term "Low" was from then on applied to Anglican Evangelicals. The latter were, at the turn of the 19th century, under constant attack by both the High Church Party (in *The Anti-Jacobin Review*) and the Low Church Party (in *The Edinburgh Review*). See Balleine 1951, pp. 40, 165, 173, 177. Moorman 1953, pp. 302-13. Neill 1965, pp. 190-94, 232-7. Cross 1971, pp. 199, 477, 636, 824. For the view that "Evangelicals in the Church of England have never been a party," see Neill 1965, pp. 190-1, 237.

105. Balleine 1951, pp. 100-4. Moorman 1953, pp. 316-7. Howse 1960, pp. 17-8. Halévy 1961, pp. 434-5. Neill 1965, pp. 235-6. Cf. Brown 1961, pp. 289-316.

106. Coupland 1923, passim. Balleine 1951, pp. 115-24. Moorman 1953, pp. 318-9. Howse 1960, pp. 10-27. Halévy 1961, pp. 435-6. Brown 1961, passim. Neill 1965, pp. 238-40.

107. Overton 1886, pp. 47-50. Russel 1915, pp. 29-32. Coupland 1923, pp. 32-43. Howse 1960, pp. 10, 25-6. Brown 1961, pp. 2, 72-8, and passim. Halévy 1961, pp. 440-50. Vidler 1961, pp. 38-40.

108. Russel 1915, pp. 21-2. Moorman 1953, p. 207. Brown 1961, pp. 4-11. Re. Wilberforce's *Practical View,* see Hennell 1947, p. 206; Foster 1960, pp. 52-5; Howse 1960, pp. 100-1; Brown 1961, pp. 115-22. Selina, Countess of Huntingdon, a zealous patroness of Whitefield's Calvinistic Methodism, did make determined efforts to carry the revival to higher society, but with very little success (Balleine 1951, pp. 45-7; Cragg 1962, p. 152; Wood 1977, p. 449).

109. Trevelyan 1946, p. 362. Foster 1951, pp. 49, 60. Berg 1956, pp. 33, 82, 111. Smith Vol. 2, 1963, pp. 66-7. Orchard 1970, p. 394. Marty 1975, pp. 273-4. Walls 1977, p. 549. Cf. Heasman 1962, p. 9. Andersen 1955, pp. 15-7.

110. Balleine 1951, pp. 110-2, 126-31. Hennell 1954, pp. 21-2. Foster 1960, pp. 63-8, 78-80. Berg 1956, pp. 126-37. Howse 1960, passim. Brown 1961, passim. Neill 1965, pp. 227-38. It should not be forgotten that, as early as 1786 (in other words, six years *before* Carey's great challenge), the Wesleyan Conference had officially adopted the task of overseas mission (Wood 1977, pp. 454-55).

111. Balleine 1951, pp. 121-3, 131-5, 142-5. Foster 1960, pp. 61-2, 68-78, 81-100. Berg 1956, pp. 136-7. Howse 1960, passim. Brown 1961, passim. Infra, pp. 99-103, 135-8. Just as the Evangelical Revival has as its precursor the Continental Pietistic Movement, so, too, the BFBS had as its forerunner not only the NMBS of 1779 (infra, pp. 80-1), but also the "Canstein Bible Institute," founded by the Pietist German nobleman Carl Hildebrand von Canstein, at Halle, in 1710. It is still active as the oldest Bible Society in the world. (See United Bible Societies *Bulletins,* No. 19, 1954, pp. 2-5; No. 43, 1960, pp. 102-4.)

112. Hennell 1947, pp. 195-6, 206. Howse 1960, pp. 118-24. Halévy 1961, pp. 450-3. Brown 1961, passim.

113. Hennell 1947, pp. 197-207. Howse 1960, pp. 28-64, 124-65. Halévy 1961, pp. 454-9. Brown 1961, passim.

114. Foster 1960, passim. Howse 1960, pp. 175-6. Brown 1961, passim. Heasman 1962, pp. 16-7. Smith Vol. 2, 1963, pp. 10-1, 66-7. Hudson 1965, pp. 150-4. The Claphamites were, by virtue of their cooperative stance, able to form a

vital link between middle-class Dissent and the government, an essential prerequisite of any national reform (Howse 1960, p. 175).

115. Hennell 1947, pp. 198-207; 1960, p. 59. Foster 1951, pp. 48-9; 1960, pp. viii, 3-118. Young 1956, pp. 28-32. Howse 1960, pp. 7, 116-37. Watson 1960, pp. 353-5. Brown 1961, pp. 376-83 and passim. Halévy 1961, pp. 437-9. Neill 1965, pp. 241-2. Vidler 1965, p. 37. Wood 1977, p. 455. Briggs 1977, p. 514. Cf. Hennell 1954, p. 20. Armstrong 1973, pp. 151-55.

116. Sweet 1950, pp. 8-9. Hudson 1965, pp. 3-7. Latourette 1970, Vol. 3, pp. 186-7.

117. Sweet 1950, pp. 8-126. Miller 1964, p. 11. Hudson 1965, pp. 5-58. Gaustad 1966, pp. 36-110. Ahlstrom 1975, Vol. 1, pp. 147-323.

118. Mead 1963, pp. 72-89. Miller 1964, pp. 1-15. Hudson 1965, pp. 12-22. Infra, p. 461.

119. Sweet 1950, pp. 26-116. Latourette 1953, p. 974. Berg 1956, p. 14. Mead 1963, pp. 1-37, 105. Hudson 1965, pp. 10-8, 99. Gaustad 1968, pp. 15-27. Marty 1975, pp. 271-5. Ahlstrom 1975, Vol. 1, pp. 459-63. Dowley 1977, p. xvi.

120. Sweet 1944, p. 19. Hudson 1965, pp. 12-6. Marty 1975, p. 285.

121. A revival was, in a sense, *a reaction,* erupting at the point where concern for corporate, objective dimensions of the faith (such as orthodox conformity in doctrine and practice) threatened to oust individual, subjective dimensions (such as personal experience of the Divine, and growth in holiness). See Sweet 1944, pp. 1, 24-6. Mead 1963, pp. 29, 121-9. Hudson 1965, pp. 53-9. Brauer 1971, pp. 659-60, 715-6. Marty 1975, p. 275. Dowley 1977, pp. xi-xx, 442-3.

122. Sweet 1944, pp. xi-xv, 1-21. Bloch-Hoell 1964, pp. 6-7. Brauer 1971, pp. 345-6.

123. Sweet 1950, pp. 127-8. Hudson 1965, pp. 59-61. Dowley 1977, p. xix. For a vivid, contemporary documentation of the course of *the Great Awakening,* see Heimert 1967, passim.

124. Sweet 1944, pp. 26-32, 44-85; 1950, pp. 127-42. Olmstead 1961, pp. 41-6. Burr 1961, pp. 121-37. Miller 1964, pp. 152-66. Hudson 1965, pp. 61-7. Ahlstrom 1975, Vol. 1, pp. 334-9, 346-9.

125. Like John Wesley, George Whitefield had read Jonathan Edwards' *Faithful Narrative* of the Northampton Revival, and been decisively affected by it. (Sweet 1944, pp. 32-4, 106-11; 1950, pp. 131-3. Olmstead 1961, pp. 42-3. Burr 1961, pp. 144-8. Hudson 1965, pp. 67-9. Ahlstrom 1975, Vol. 1, pp. 350-3.

126. Sweet 1944, pp. 140-61; 1950, pp. 127-71. Olmstead 1961, pp. 41-8. Burr 1961, pp. 148-55. Hudson 1965, pp. 59-82. Gaustad 1968, pp. 28-45. Ahlstrom 1975, Vol. 1, pp. 334-62. Supra, p. 34.

127. Sweet 1950, pp. 134-7. Olmstead 1961, pp. 47-8. Hudson 1965, pp. 78-82. Ahlstrom 1975, Vol. 1, pp. 363-84. Jonathan Edwards recognized the role of *emotions* in genuine religious experience, a theme he brilliantly defends in *A Treatise Concerning Religious Affections,* 1746 (Burr 1961, pp. 132-3).

128. Sweet 1944, pp. xii, 32-3; 1950, pp. 135, 149-52. Trinterud 1949, p. 197. Olmstead 1961, pp. 45-6. Hudson 1965, pp. 72-5, 80-2, 99-100, 114-7. Ahlstrom 1975, Vol. 1, pp. 357-62, 461-5, 471-7. Infra, p. 461.

129. Sweet 1950, pp. 137, 172-88. Olmstead 1961, pp. 49-55. Hudson 1965, pp. 76-7, 83-98. Ahlstrom 1975, Vol. 1, pp. 361-2, 437-46.

130. Sweet 1950, pp. 189-204. Littell 1961, pp. 117-8. Olmstead 1961, pp. 52-65. Hudson 1965, pp. 109-30. Ahlstrom 1975, Vol. 1, pp. 446-65.

131. Sweet 1944, pp. 117-8; 1950, pp. 223-5. Hudson 1965, pp. 115, 131-4. Cf. Griffin 1960, p. x.

132. Sweet 1944, pp. 119-34; 1950, pp. 225-31. Olmstead 1961, pp. 65-7. Burr 1961, pp. 155-72. Hudson 1965, pp. 134-41. Ahlstrom 1975, Vol. 1, pp. 469-70, 504-7, 521-40.

133. Sweet 1944, pp. 140, 152-4. Smith Vol. 2, 1963, p. 10. Hudson 1965, pp. 145-6. Ahlstrom 1975, Vol. 1, p. 469. Supra, p. 30. For the further record of American revivalism, and the great "reform crusades" of the "Sentimental Years" (1830-60), see, for example, Tyler 1944, Cole 1954, Griffin 1960, and Foster 1960. Cf. Burr 1961, pp. 155-85.

134. Foster 1951, pp. 48-50; 1960, pp. 115-8 and passim. Smith Vol. 2, 1963, pp. 10-5. Hudson 1965, pp. 135-6, 146-53. Ahlstrom 1975, Vol. 1, pp. 509-13. Cf. Youngren 1981, pp. 38-9.

135. Sweet 1950, pp. 243-57. Foster 1960, passim. Smith Vol. 2, 1963, pp. 10-65. Hudson 1965, pp. 59-60, 145-57. Ahlstrom 1975, Vol. 1, pp. 512-20; Vol. 2, pp. 70-83.

136. Williamson 1941 and 1947, passim. Berg 1956, pp. 70, 98, 109-10, 127. Neill 1964, pp. 246-7, 296. Warren 1965, p. 21. Ellacott 1971, Vol. 2, pp. 62-5. Infra, pp. 543-6.

137. Berg 1956, pp. 97-8. Foster 1960, pp. 42-3. Cragg 1962, pp. 172, 253-4, 283. Watson 1960, pp. 161-203. Laffin 1969, pp. 182-93. Ahlstrom 1975, Vol. 2, pp. 15-31. Cf. Olmstead 1961, p. 70. Infra, p. 546.

138. Warneck 1901, p. 74. Berg 1956, pp. 84-5 and passim. Foster 1960, pp. 63-9. Olmstead 1961, pp. 67-71. Warren 1965, p. 21. Syrdal 1967, p. 124. Phillips 1969, passim. Latourette 1970, Vol. 3, pp. 49-50; Vol. 4, pp. 65-88. Myklebust 1976, pp. 314-20. Andrew 1976, passim. Infra, p. 551. In the New World, the American Indian's presence meant that there had *always* been an immediate missionary challenge. The epic labors of John Eliot, Puritan pastor at Roxbury, Massachusetts, resulted in the incorporation of the first Protestant missionary society by the English Parliament in 1649: *Society for the Propagation of the Gospel in New England.* (Berg 1956, pp. 24-7. Ahlstrom 1975, Vol. 1, p. 207. Dowley 1977, pp. 471-2, 551.)

139. BFSS *AR* 1834, p. 7. NSM 1858, p. 545. SMNY 1878, p. 270. Cole 1954, p. 112. Foster 1960, p. 211. Burr 1961, pp. 158-9. Cf. Myklebust 1971, p. 22.

140. Hewitt 1949, pp. 17-8. Hudson 1965, p. 150. Infra. pp. 135-50.

141. Anson 1948, p. 30. Cross 1971, p. 1053.

142. Gray 1905, pp. 188-9. Bready 1938, p. 341. Whiteley 1938, pp. 31, 156-7. Lloyd 1949, pp. 3-10. Howse 1960, pp. 28-32. Sundkler 1966, pp. 148-9. Pope-Hennessey 1968, pp. 262-72. So literally were slaves regarded as private property that when the master of the slaver *Zong* (in 1781) jettisoned alive 132 sickly slaves in order to defraud the underwriters, the courts refused to entertain insinuations of murder or even manslaughter; slaves were simply

"chattels or goods." Granville Sharp made sure the blatant inhumanity of that conclusion was not missed. (Hoare 1820, pp. 236-47.)

143. Clarkson 1845, pp. 3-4. Lloyd 1949, pp. 10-11. Howse 1960, pp. 28-32. Howard 1971, p. 48.

144. Howse 1960, pp. 137-8. Denmark had (by royal decree effective from 1803) the honor of becoming the first European power to abolish the Slave Trade. The United States, like England, enacted prohibition of the traffic in 1807 (Religious Society of Friends 1851, pp. 6-7). Where there has been less appreciation for the impact of the Evangelical Revival on national morality, it has been suggested that the Slave Trade was abolished only when no longer economically or politically feasible (Pope-Hennessey 1968, pp. 248-9). However, the bitter 50-year battle to *enforce* the abolition argues powerfully against this view. (Coupland 1923, pp. 160-61, 391.) Cf. supra, p. 48. Infra, p. 569.

145. Clarkson 1788, passim; 1808, passim; 1845, pp. 3-6, 11. *The Evangelical Magazine* 1799, pp. 197-8. BSRMIS *True Friendship,* 1812, pp. 10-3. SML 1821, 197-8; 1826, p. 234. Truair 1826, p. 11. *The Christian Guardian* 1826, pp. 169-70. RTS *The Iniquity of the Slave Trade,* n.d. Elmes 1854, passim. Coupland 1923, passim. Dow 1927, pp. 155-66. Griggs 1936, passim. Mannix 1963, passim. Pope-Hennessey 1968, pp. 250-62. Howard 1971, pp. 48-67, 200. In 1786, Clarkson points out that, of approximately 5,000 seamen employed in the Slave Trade, only 2,320 eventually came home; 1,130 appeared on "dead list," and 1,550 deserted or were discharged in West Africa and the West Indies (Clarkson 1788, p. 55). On his first research tour alone, Clarkson accumulated, from the muster-roles of slave-ships, the names and fates of no less than 20,000 seamen (Pope-Hennessey 1968, p. 255). An early Quaker voice of protest against not only the horrors of the Slave Trade itself, but also its corruptive effect on seamen engaged in it, was that of John Woolman (Gummere 1922, pp. 296, 505). Cf. Hope 1969, p. 18.

146. Neill 1965, pp. 239-40. Supra, pp. 34-5.

147. Overton 1906, pp. 218-25. Russel 1915, pp. 35-6. Trevelyan 1946, pp. 492-7. Elliott-Binns 1946, pp. 22-4, 377-8. Berg 1956, p. 112. Howse 1960, pp. 3-4, 44-5. Vidler 1965, p. 34. Warren 1965, p. 37.

148. SML 1821, p. 419. Smith Vol. 2, 1963, p. 61. Foster 1960, p. 79. Cf. Williamson 1941, pp. 138-9. Infra, pp. 411-2, 541-2.

149. SML 1821, p. 146. NMBS *Report* 1828, p. 28. Milne 1851, pp. 4-5. Elliott-Binns 1946, pp. 11-2. Parkinson 1949, passim. Watson 1960, pp. 426, 433. Cameron 1961, pp. 54-5. Infra, pp. 109-11.

150. Denison 1944, pp. 78-93. Laing 1974, pp. 39-147. Cf. Brooks 1899, pp. 111-78. Paine 1919, pp. 18-135.

151. Further landmarks were achieved in 1819, when the American *Savannah* became the first steamship to cross the Atlantic using steam-power for at least part of the voyage, and in 1838, when the British *Sirius* was first to cross the ocean under steam alone. Apart from ingrained prejudice, major deterrents to the introduction of steam propulsion were both the far higher cost per ton of cargo, and the initial frequency of major mechanical breakdowns and accidents. (Lindsay 1876, Vol. 4, pp. 1-177. Writers' Program 1941, pp. 122-3, 158. Hohman 1956, p. 21. Course 1963, p. 215. Hobsbaum 1968, p. 92. Ellacott 1971, Vol. 2, pp. 62-8. Kemp 1976, passim.) Infra, pp. 461-2.

152. Moyse-Bartlett 1937, pp. 212-4. Lewis 1960, pp. 98-124, 139; 1965, pp. 170-7. Lloyd 1968, pp. 112-23, 289.

153. Brooks 1899, pp. 134-55. Marvin 1910, passim. Spears 1910, passim. Paine 1919, pp. 51-95. Bankers' Trust 1920, pp. 4-6, 9. Morison 1921, passim. Denison 1944, pp. 79-82. Carse 1964, pp. 203-55. Laing 1974, passim. In 1789, a total of 123,893 registered tons of American merchant shipping was engaged in foreign trade, in 1797 — 597,777 tons, in 1800 — 667,107 tons, in 1810 — 981,019 tons. (Brooks 1899, pp. 137, 179. Bankers' Trust 1920, pp. 7-8.)

154. During the second quarter of the century, the promise and freedoms of the frontier lured American young men away from the sea, foreign crews filled the forecastles, and conditions in American ships worsened considerably (Denison 1944, pp. 103-4). Examples of contemporary sailors' narratives: Nicol 1822; Watson 1827; McPherson 1829; Crow 1830; Ames 1832; Nasty-face 1836; Bechervaise 1839; McNally 1839; Hoxse 1840; Leech 1843; Sampson 1847. See also Marryat 1836; (MS) Lindgren 1961; Henningsen 1969. A rich and largely untapped source of nautical autobiography from the turn of the 19th century is, of course, the copious authorship of George Charles Smith (cf. Kverndal [London] 1976). Supra, p. 3.

155. Rawson 1934, pp. 216-7. Hohman 1956, pp. 6-7. The Ministry of Transport 1956, pp. 15-8. Davis 1962, p. 156. Course 1963, pp. 198-206. Hope 1969, pp. 18-9.

156. Rawson 1934, pp. 216-7. Whiteley 1938, pp. 79-83. Parkinson 1949, pp. 93-7. Straus 1950, p. 11. Hohman 1956, pp. 5-7, 25. Otterland 1960, passim. Dillon 1961, pp. 30-1. Sundby 1964, pp. 1240-43. Villiers 1967, passim. Henningsen 1967, p. 14. Weibust 1969, pp. 71-104. Miller 1980, pp. 64-80. Cf. Anson 1948, pp. 17-23. While it was said of British seamen that they were "often half drowned and always half starved," seamen on American ships were, in comparison, at least *better fed* (Rawson 1934, pp. 217-8). Infra, p. 571.

157. Marine Hospital Service 1873, pp. 131-2. ASFS *AR* 1878, p. 87. Johnson 1899, p. 1. Kelley 1940, p. 350. Hohman 1956, pp. 3-5, 20-1. Dillon 1961, pp. 10-1. Although there existed earlier enactments of limited scope, it was not until midway through the 19th century that the legislatures of Britain and America seriously embarked upon a series of maritime shipping acts aimed at effectively safeguarding life and property at sea, and protecting seafarers from abuse and exploitation on ship and ashore. (Rawson 1934, pp. 218-9. The Ministry of Transport 1956, passim. Hohman 1956, pp. 18-45. Course 1963, pp. 214-67, and passim.)

158. Nicol 1822, pp. 35-6. SML 1824, p. 308. Leech 1843, passim. Yexley 1908, passim. Millington 1935, pp. 42-3. Hohman 1952, p. 4; 1956, pp. 28-45. Weedfald 1956, pp. 95-7. Goldberg 1958, p. 13. Lewis 1960, p. 101. Dillon 1961, pp. 12, 50-5. Langley 1967, pp. 131-9. Laffin 1969, pp. 41-63. Kemp 1970, passim. Wilson 1973, "Introduction," n.p. Palmer 1973, passim. Miller 1980, pp. 80-1. Not until the passing of the La Follette Seamen's Act of 1915 was the American seafarer finally freed from his legal status of bondsman by the abolition of imprisonment for desertion. As Andrew Furuseth, the driving force behind the act, put it, "This finishes the work Lincoln began!" (Axtell n.d., passim. Dillon 1961, pp. 12-3, 300-51. Raskin 1967, pp. 1-6.) Infra, pp. 528, 571.

159. Flavel 1760, p. iii. NMBS *Report* 1825, p. 12.

160. SML 1823, pp. 122-3; 1825, p. 315. PECMSS *AR* 1848, Appendix. ASFS *AR* 1854, p. 8; 1878, pp. 76, 80, 202. Powell 1940, pp. 12-4. Straus 1950, pp. 12-4. Dillon 1961, pp. 54-5. Cf. Henningsen 1967, p. 13. Infra, pp. 563-4.

161. Whiteley 1938, p. 159. Cf. Foster 1960, pp. 44-5. Supra, p. 34.

162. Foner 1947, Vol. 1, p. 34. Aspinall 1949, pp. 11-4, et passim. Rose 1958, pp. 85-92. Davis 1962, p. 155. Hobsbaum 1968, p. 70. For a more detailed study of seamen's wages at this time, see Davis 1962, pp. 133-55. Cf. Woodward 1938, pp. 60-2. Hennell 1960, p. 59. Watson 1960, p. 593. Raskin 1967, pp. 2-3. Kemp 1970, pp. 173-4. Seymour 1976, pp. 39-40. Infra, p. 569.

163. SML 1820, p. 57; 1823, p. 219. CHSM 1824, p. 155. SMNY 1828-29, p. 3; 1834-35, pp. 298-99. NSM 1833, p. 509. CMAS *AR* 1850, p. 9. Marine Hospital Service *AR* 1873, p. 131. Johnson 1899, p. 1. Healey 1936, pp. 71-2. Dillon 1961, p. 26. Langley 1967, p. 77. Infra, pp. 540, 564.

164. Hohman 1952, pp. 270-1. Course 1963, p. 239. Miller 1980, pp. 62-4. Infra, pp. 511, 567-8.

165. Flavel 1760, p. v. *Gentlemen's Magazine* 1809, pp. 339-40. SML 1820, p. 57. SMNY 1851-52, pp. 642-3. WW 1858, pp. 3, 5. Gummere 1922, pp. 296, 302-3.

166. SML 1820, p. 354. PECMSS *AR* 1855, pp. 7-8. Larrouy 1927, passim. Lewis 1960, p. 122. Laffin 1969, pp. 11-21, et passim. Infra, p. 552.

167. SML 1820, pp. 144, 183, 350; 1825, p. 11. Marks 1826, pp. 227-8. NSM 1830, pp. 387-8; 1835, p. 426. Penn 1833, pp. 17-19, 64. Sullivan 1853, pp. 11-2. Murray 1857, pp. 95-6. WW 1858, p. 15. McCarthy 1861, p. 99. Esquiros 1868, pp. 198-200. ASFS *AR* 1878, pp. 89-90. Larrouy 1927, pp. 106-8. Lewis 1965, p. 173. Lloyd 1968, p. 221. Laffin 1969, pp. 12-21.

168. NMBS *Report* 1825, p. 25. NSM 1858, pp. 357-64. ASFS *AR* 1878, p. 76. Rawson 1934, p. 219. Trevelyan 1946, p. 499. Cf. NSM 1828, p. 197. PHS *Lifebelt* 1907, pp. 16-7. Brown 1961, pp. 15-24. Infra, pp. 543-6.

169. Rawson 1934, p. 219. Laffin 1969, pp. 11-2. Infra, pp. 541-2.

170. E.g. *The Christian Guardian* 1826, pp. 209-12. Ames 1832, pp. 40-8. Dillon 1961, pp. 12, 37-8, 65, 244-6. Davis 1979, pp. 49-50, 56.

171. Significant examples are: George Charles Smith, Richard Marks, William Henry Angas, William Scoresby, Jr., Edward Taylor (of Boston), and Charles J. Jones, all of whose reminiscences are replete with such descriptions. Cf. Chapel 1982, pp. 59-60.

172. Numerous examples of underlying reasons for moral laxity among seafarers of those times are to be found in the works of Norborg 1932, Rawson 1934, Healey 1936, Straus 1950, Hohman 1952 and 1956, Lewis 1960 and 1965, Dillon 1961, Carse 1963, Langley 1967, Lloyd 1968, Weibust 1969, Kemp 1970, Fricke 1973, Sherar 1973. On the low level of education and cultural interest in the British Napoleonic War navy, see also Richard Marks' assessment in SML 1826, pp. 233-4. Infra, pp. 340-6, 563-71.

173. Phillips 1776, pp. 61-2. SML 1821, pp. 333-5. Blackwoods 1821, pp. 416-7. Clarkson 1845, p. 6. Warren 1858, p. 46. Straus 1950, p. 9. Hohman 1956, p. 8. Lewis 1965, pp. 173-4. Laffin 1969, pp. 11, 15, 20. Infra, pp. 340-6.

174. (MS) BFBS *Home Correspondence*, letter from Anthony Landers to Joseph Tarn, Oct. 4, 1816. Cf. New Bedford Port Society *AR* 1867, pp. 7-8, Infra, pp. 567-8.

175. E.g. NMBS *Report* 1820, p. 40. SML 1820, p. 33. Stuart 1856, p. 108.

176. The Phoenicians had their Dagon, the Greeks their Poseidon, the Romans their Neptune, and the Vikings their Aegir. There is still, as attested by Beck, copious evidence that, though maritime folklore has *suffered* from the incursions of science, it has by no means *surrendered* to them. EM 1817, p. 186. SML 1826, pp. 190-1; 1827, pp. 367-8, 510. NSM 1841, p. 132; 1855, pp. 35-6. Martingale 1856, p. 14. Basset 1885, passim, CMAS *AR* 1889, n. p. Pascoe 1901, pp. 12, 837. Rappaport 1928, passim. Rogers 1934, passim. Whiteley 1938, p. 79 et passim. Shay 1951, passim. Goldsmith-Carter 1966, pp. 134-42. Henningsen 1966, 1967, pp. 5-10. Beck 1973, passim. Polley 1978, pp. 230-55. Thue 1980, pp. 202-7. For "Crossing the Line," see Lydenberg 1957, and (especially) Henningsen 1961.

177. Calcutta Seamen's Friend Society *AR* 1839, p. 19. SMNY 1847-48, p. 168. Williamson 1848, p. 73. WW 1859, p. 270. Paine 1919, pp. 183-4. Dana 1929, p. 44. Occasionally, a seafarer would speak of heaven and hell in terms of getting a "good berth aloft," and not being "clapped under the hatches." (NSM 1841, p. 79. SMNY 1847-48, p. 168.)

178. NSM 1859, pp. 162-3, 165. Hardy 1892, p. 734. Kverndal (London) 1976, pp. 48-9. Also seen as reminiscent of Islamic thinking was the despotic concept of God apparent in the ferocious punishments for blasphemy meted out to mariners in the Middle Ages. (Field 1932, p. 48. [MS] Curry 1956, p. 110.)

179. Richard Braithwaite's *Whimsies* of 1631, as quoted by Lewis 1965, p. 173. Cf. Mather 1709, pp. 57-61; 1717, passim. Flavel 1760, p. iv et passim. Hawker 1806, p. 35. NMBS *Report* 1813, pp. 16-7; 1818, p. 26. Marks 1818, p. 105. SML 1820, pp. 268-9, 355. NSM 1828, p. 446; 1841, pp. 132-3; 1858, pp. 363-4. Williamson 1848, pp. 73-4. G.C. Smith, *The Custom House* n.d., p. 6. (MS) Poppen n.d., p. 31.

180. Psalm 142:4. SML 1820, p. 168; 1822, p. 224; 1823, p. 306. CHSM 1824, p. 713. NSM 1830, pp. 297-8; 1834, pp. 203-4; 1859, pp. 152, 162, 165. CMAS 1848, p. 17. Pike 1897, pp. 285-6. PHS 1907, p. 23. Elias 1912, pp. 219-20. Cf. Parkinson 1949, pp. 117-8. Infra, pp. 563-72.

181. NSM 1859, p. 160.

182. "On the Probable Influence ..." 1821, p. 539. Cf. SML 1826, p. 158. PECMSS *AR* 1855, pp. 7-8. Downey 1958, pp. 76 ff. Villiers 1970, pp. 187-8.

183. NMBS *Report* 1820, pp. 44-5.

184. Psalm 107:24. Acts 14:17. Romans 1:20, 2:15. Downey 1958, pp. 76 ff. Cf. BFBS *Reports* 1811-13, p. 167. PECMSS *AR* 1855, p. 8. Hardy 1892, p. 732. Allen 1898, p. 456. Smith 1961, p. 33. The power and providence of the Creator, as manifested before the eyes of the mariner, is a constant theme of inspiration and exhortation in early maritime devotional aids (supra, pp. 11-4).

185. CMAS *AR* 1889, n.p.

186. Warren 1858, p. 46. WW 1859, p. 271. Cf. Bullen 1904, p. vii. Thompson 1952, pp. 4-6. Supra, pp. 58-9, 64-5

187. Note the many references, in early reports of preaching to seafarers, to how hardy, weather-beaten men could be quickly reduced to tears of contrition and joy. E.g. *Virginia Evangelical and Literary Magazine* 1820, pp. 194-5. SML 1845, p. 134. G.C. Smith *The Boatswain's Mate* n.d., passim. Infra, pp. 152, 172, 215.

188. SML 1820, p. 355; 1821, p. 424. PLS *Proceedings* 1821, p. 29. *The Christian Advocate* 1823, p. 38. Marsden 1847, p. 36. NSM 1861, p. 232. Smith 1961, pp. 142-3, 150. G.C. Smith *The Boatswain's Mate* n.d., Part III, pp. 22-3. Infra, p. 576. Strong attributes the spiritual receptivity of 19th-century seafarers to their comparatively high physical risk rate (1956, pp. 25-32). However, this explanation cannot easily be reconciled with their proverbial disregard for danger, regardless of religious conviction (supra, p. 63).

189. (MS) Curry 1956, pp. 35, 50-1. Infra, pp. 7, 18-19.

190. Supra, pp. 9-10.

191. The Missionary Society 1799, passim. Horne 1894, pp 23-9. From the mizzen top-gallant masthead flew a missionary flag consisting of "three doves argent, on a purple field, bearing olive-branches in their bills," an interesting precursor of the famous Bethel Flag (infra, pp. 158-61). Captain James Wilson, a former infidel of some notoriety, had been converted under the preaching of the Rev. John Griffin of Portsea; it was Griffin who also helped James Covey to the faith, the bold blaspheming veteran who was to become the subject of the most popular of all seamen's tracts, and whose simple, effective testimony was: "Tell them [other sailors], that since I have found mercy, none that seek need to despair." (The Massachusetts Missionary Magazine 1808, pp. 369ff. NSM 1834, pp. 187-9.) Infra. pp. 166-7.

192. E.g., *Virginia Evangelical and Literary Magazine* 1820, pp. 193-6. Supra, p. 11.

193. *The Christian Guardian* 1826, p. 171. Infra, pp. 91-2.

194. Kemp 1970, p. 30, quoting *The Seamen's Protestation,* London, 1642.

195. Cf. Matthew 18:20; Acts 2:42.

196. For the implications of this situation in terms of missionary strategy and church growth, see McGavran 1970, pp. 216-32. Also, Wagner 1979, pp. 83-5.

197. NSM 1841, p. 41; 1861, p. 517. Berg 1956, pp. 22-3. Infra, pp. 73, 89-90.

PART II — NOTES

1. "The First Bible Society" 1874, pp. 772-5. For a discussion of the reliability of this source, infra, pp. 72-3.

2. Middleton 1819, pp. 71-6.

3. DNB, Vol. 10, 1887, pp. 413-4.

4. This applies both to the *Account* of the Society, as presented 1804-11 (in the British Museum), and its *Report,* annually from 1812 (in NMBS archives, SGM London).

5. NMBS *Appeal* 1834.

6. McCarthy 1861, pp. 17-28.

7. "The First Bible Society" 1874.

8. Neither the *Cussons* version nor the *McCarthy* version refer specifically (as does the 1874 article) to personal perusal of the first NMBS minute-book. The Cussons version was, with slight variations, quoted in the current religious press (e.g., SMR 1823, pp. 506-7). However, the important letter from Cussons' friend, John Davis, dated September 13, 1779, appears in a less flattering, unedited style in the 1874 article, than in Cussons' briefer, more polished reproduction. John Davis' name is rendered in this study in the orthography of the 1874 article.

9. "The First Bible Society" 1874, p. 773.

10. This conclusion corresponds with the policy of the Society itself, which, from 1875 through the century, included the 1874 article unabridged as a recurring feature of its annual reports. (The article is constantly misdated, however; while it appears in the original under the date Dec. 5, 1874, NMBS *Report* for 1874, published in 1875, has Dec. 4, 1874, which is again replaced by Dec. 4, 1875 in later reports.)

11. Middleton 1819, pp. 72-3. Cf. SMR 1823, pp. 506-7.

12. Watson 1960, pp. 223-6.

13. "The First Bible Society" 1874, pp. 773-4. Cf. Middleton 1819, pp. 73-4.

14. Middleton 1819, pp. 29, 73-4.

15. DNB Vol. 56, 1898, p. 301. Among John Thornton's sons, Henry, the economist and philanthropist (1760-1815), was to become one of the most influential members of the "Clapham Sect" (ibid., pp. 301-3).

16. "The First Bible Society" 1874, p. 774.

17. Ibid. Cf. Middleton 1819, p. 75. John Thornton was doubtless largely instrumental in the founding and early growth of the Society. However, the title of "originator," as bestowed at the Society's centennial, would seem more justly applied to John Davis. (See NMBS *Report* 1880, p. 11.)

18. Middleton 1819, pp. 74-5. The circumstances detailed in the amazing McCarthy version (with its humorous dialogue between "Mr. Black" and "Mr. White") are such as to render an allegorical interpretation the most credible. In support of this conclusion, see "The First Bible Society" 1874, p. 773. (The critical comments of the author of the latter are, however, omitted, and the McCarthy version presented as fact in the official history of the Scripture Gift Mission, the institution with which the NMBS was merged in 1910. See Scripture Gift Mission 1961, pp. 66-9.)

19. The *Account* published by the renamed Society in 1804 refers in its title to "its institution in 1780." This dating is retained unaltered for several decades. Cf. McCarthy 1861, p. 21 (quoting NMBS *Report* 1860).

20. "The First Bible Society" 1874, p. 774. The authenticity of this evidence is confirmed in the NMBS Centennial Report for 1879, and continued through the century. Here, "Instituted 1780" has been substituted by "Instituted 1779." (See title pages, NMBS *Report* 1880 et seq.) Nevertheless, in more recent years, the Society has (as in Scripture Gift Mission 1961, p. 66) been widely represented as "Founded in 1780." This is also the case in the

Society's own recent-most publications (e.g., *Naval, Military and Air Force Bible Society,* a brochure current in 1980.) However, if an additional, more official act, whereby the Society was more formally "established" or "regularly organized" did, in fact, take place in 1780, it remains a mystery why an independent, critical examination of the Society's first minute-book, as carried out in 1874, revealed no record of this. An article entitled "The 200th Anniversary of Organized Seamen's Missions, 1779-1979" in MM 1979, pp. 255-65, reproduces the findings of this Author's personal research.

21. DNB Vol. 22, 1890, pp. 197-8. Watson 1960, pp. 234-9. *New Catholic Encyclopedia* Vol. 6, 1967, p. 631.

22. Chambers's Encyclopædia Vol. 11, 1950, p. 21. (The event motivated Jonas Hanway to write *The Citizen's Monitor: Showing the Necessity of a Salutary Police...*, London, 1780.)

23. Middleton 1819, p. 75. "The First Bible Society" 1874, p. 772. McCarthy 1861, p. 19.

24. *The Gentleman's Magazine,* 1782, p. 405.

25. Ibid. SML 1840, pp. 79-82. DNB Vol. 30, 1892, pp. 395-6. Kemp 1970, pp. 147-9.

26. Ibid. *The Gentleman's Magazine* 1782, p. 450. SML 1821, pp. 249-51. Callender 1934, pp. 176-8.

27. SML 1821, p. 249.

28. SML 1825, p. 263. Canton Vol. 1, 1904, p. 3. Howse 1960, p. 110. The figure 400 is remarkably high. (40 Bibles would have been nearer subsequent policy.) However, it is possible that the major part were intended for consignment to the naval and military station at Gibraltar. Cf. Brown 1961, pp. 21-2.

29. Infra, p. 81.

30. "The First Bible Society" 1874, p. 774.

31. Watson 1960, pp. 363-4.

32. DNB Vol. 1, 1885, pp. 18-9. Cf. Kennedy 1978, passim.

33. Shillibeer 1817. Quoted in SML 1821, pp. 81-4. Cf. DNB Vol. 1, 1885, pp. 7-8, 131-4. Dudley 1821, p. 308.

34. NMBS *Report* 1817, pp. 34-5; cf. 1843, pp. 22-3.

35. Lewis 1959, pp. 152-70. Lloyd 1968, pp. 194-5, 288-9.

36. NMBS *Account* 1804, pp. 3-4.

37. Supra, p. 74.

38. "The First Bible Society" 1874, pp. 774-5. McCarthy 1861, pp. 39-40.

39. DNB Vol. 40, 1894, p. 397. Besides employing his church for collection sermons for the Society, Newton became a personal subscriber (NMBS *Account* 1804, pp. 18-9, 23).

40. (MS) Fowler, passim. Re. Rowland Hill, see also Elliott-Binns 1946, p. 53.

41. By 1799, the Society is stated to have circulated (in two decades) some 30,000 copies of the Bible; but no details are provided. (Bullock 1963, p. 236.) By March 1803, a total of 214 ships of war were stated to have been supplied by the Society since its institution (NMBS *Account* 1804, pp. 10-2).

42. NMBS *Report* 1820, pp. 38-9; 1829, p. 20; 1833, p. 16. Marks even asserts that "for some years the Society suspended its operations altogether," and became "entirely paralyzed" (SML 1826, p. 235).

43. NSM 1857, p. 201. Cf. G.C. Smith *The Log-Book* Part I, pp. 7-8.

44. NMBS *Report* 1820, p. 40. SML 1826, p. 235.

45. NMBS *Account* 1804, pp. 4-5.

46. Lewis 1959, pp. 171-2.

47. NMBS *Appeal* 1834, p. 1.

48. McCarthy 1861, p. 19. Cf. NMBS *Report* 1817 (quoting press comments on "that most ancient of all Bible Institutions"), p. 61.

49. NMBS *Account* 1804, p. 5-6. Owen 1816, Part 1, pp. 19ff.

50. NMBS *Account* 1804, p. 3. NMBS *Appeal* 1834, p. 2.

51. The theme recurs consistently in the Society's *Accounts* 1804-11. See especially its *Account* 1811, pp. 17-9, also its *Report* 1812, pp. 33-4.

52. NMBS *Report* 1812, pp. 33-4.

53. Infra, pp. 137, 176, 198.

54. NMBS *Appeal* 1834, p. 2.

55. Ibid., p. 10.

56. Lewis 1959, pp. 180-4. The "peak" naval manpower demand in the Napoleonic War navy actually reached 145,000 men. (Lewis 1965, p. 175. Lloyd 1968, p. 289.)

57. Infra, pp. 100-3.

58. Canton Vol. 1, 1904, pp. 18-50.

59. BFBS *Reports* 1805-10, pp. 158-9. (Also, *Reports* for 1808 et seq.) (MS) BFBS *Minutes of Sub-Committees,* Dec. 26, 1805. Canton Vol. 1, 1904, pp. 123-8. Cf. infra, pp. 135-6. Cf. Johnson 1970, passim.

60. Canton Vol. 1, 1904, pp. 122-3. Cf. infra, pp. 298-9.

61. (MS) BFBS *Minutes,* Oct. 16, 1809. BFBS *Reports* 1805-10, pp. 396-7; 1811-13, pp. 177-8.

62. BFBS *Reports* 1805-10, p. 268.

63. Ibid., p. 174.

64. (MS) BFBS *Minutes,* June 6, 1808. BFBS *Reports* 1805-10, pp. 218-9.

65. (MS) BFBS *Home Corresp.* E.g., Letter dated July 31, 1808, from Captain Thomas Renwick, HMS *Combatant.*

66. BFBS *Reports* 1805-10, pp. 396-9.

67. (MS) BFBS *Minutes:* Jan. 15 and Feb. 5, 1810; Sept. 2, 1811. Brown 1961, pp. 351-2.

68. Infra, p. 135.

69. (MS) BFBS *Minutes,* May 20, 1811.

70. Ibid., June 3, 1811.

71. NMBS *Report* 1812, pp. 41-2.

72. Canton Vol. 1, 1904, p. 243.

73. NMBS *Report* 1812, pp. 22-3, 42.

74. Ibid., p. 35.

75. Ibid., pp. 42-3.

76. Ibid., pp. 23-4.

77. See "Abstracts of Receipts and Expenses" in NMBS *Reports* 1812-14.

78. Supra, pp. 74, 79-80.

79. Howse 1960, p. 112.

80. Canton Vol. 1, 1904, p. 44.

81. NMBS *Account* 1806, p. 13. NMBS *Report* 1812, pp. 3, 24, 44; 1818, pp. v-vi. (The 1829 *Report*, recording the death of the Archbishop of Canterbury, recalls his 23 years as president of the Society, as well as liberal contributor to its funds, p. 11.)

82. NMBS *Report* 1815, p. 21.

83. Ibid., pp. 3-4. As vice-presidents appear: The First Lord of the Admiralty, the War Secretary (Lord Palmerston), the Chancellor of the Exchequer, four admirals, four generals, and four earls. Cf. Warren 1858, p. 3.

84. NMBS *Accounts* 1804-11. NMBS *Reports* 1812 et seq. However low the contemporary image of the Royal Princes had fallen at this time, their patronage was still obviously considered a very worthwhile asset. Cf. Halévy 1961, pp. 6-8.)

85. Canton Vol. 1, 1904, pp. 50-1.

86. NMBS *Reports* 1813, pp. 13-4; 1814, p. 20; 1815, pp 54-8; 1816, p. 6; 1817, pp. 11, 25-7, 60-9. Cf. infra, p. 305.

87. NMBS *Report* 1812, pp. 27-8.

88. This formulation, corresponding precisely to that of the BFBS, was used for the first time in the 1815 edition of the "Laws and Regulations" of the NMBS (*Report* 1815, p. 9). The principle embodied was no innovation, however.

89. In short, "to fear God and honour the king." (NMBS *Report* 1812, pp. 4-7. See also e.g., 1813, pp. 16-7.

90. NMBS *Report* 1812, p. 7. Cf Canton Vol. 1, 1904, p. 17.

91. Middleton 1819, p. 75. In his letter to George Cussons, enclosing his first donation of £20 to the proposed society, John Thornton suggests that certain religious books (for example, "Baxters") be included with the Bibles to be distributed. Possibly these were among those sent out at the first West Street Chapel issue ("The First Bible Society" 1874, p. 774). Note, however, the declared object of the infant society as recorded in its first minute-book (supra, p. 71).

92. Both the Anglican SPCK (1698) and the interdenominational Society for Promoting Religious Knowledge among the Poor, known as "The Book Society" (1750), had promoted Scripture distribution in their activities, but not exclusively Scripture (Owen 1816, Part 1, pp. 19ff). It was the *exclusiveness* of the Scripture distribution of the NMBS which enabled enthusiastic advocates to claim for it some sort of "parent" status in relation to the globally-orientated BFBS. (E.g., NMBS *Report* 1817, p. 63. McCarthy 1861, pp. 18-20. "The First Bible Society" 1874, p. 772.) In the USA, the BFBS

came to be understood as "undoubtedly" owing its "parentage" to the NMBS. (Cf. Warren 1858, p. 3. Yates 1851, p. 5.)

93. NMBS *Account* 1811, p. 32. NMBS *Report* 1812, pp. 12, 14, 28.

94. NMBS *Report* 1814, p. 27.

95. Ibid., 1815, pp. 33-4, 54-8.

96. Ibid., 1812, p. 17.

97. NMBS *Account* 1811, pp. 32-3. Canton Vol. 1, 1904, pp. 53-5.

98. NMBS *Report* 1814, p. 22.

99. Canton Vol. 1, 1904, p. 54. Cf. NMBS *Report* 1814, pp. 26-7; 1815, p. 56.

100. NMBS *Report* 1813, p. 14.

101. Ibid., 1818, p. 48. By 1818, more than a quarter of the Society's aggregate income was being received from sailors and soldiers.

102. NMBS *Report* 1815, p. 60; 1827, p. 31.

103. Ibid. 1815, pp. 26-7, 56-7, 61. (The standard ration was to be one Bible and two Testaments to eight men.)

104. Included in the "Laws and Regulations" of the Society's *Reports* (as from 1815 under No. IV). See also the object of the Society, as recorded in its first minute-book (supra, p. 71).

105. NMBS *Report* 1816, pp. 42-3; 1817, pp. 61, 65-6. Infra, p. 306.

106. The wording "to encourage a wider circulation of the Holy Scriptures without note or comment" has remained exactly identical in the "Laws and Regulations" of both societies since this time.

107. NMBS *Report* 1819, p. 31.

108. See distribution lists in NMBS *Reports* 1813-19. NMBS *Appeal* 1834, p. 10.

109. Lewis 1965, pp. 64-66. Lloyd 1968, p. 289. A four-year special survey of NMBS issues of Scriptures to naval vessels, 1811-15, revealed that 2,697 copies were now "permanently" placed on board 60 ships still in commission (with crews of about 16,000 men in number). 56 ships had meanwhile been put out of commission, the 2,068 copies issued to them following with their approximately 13,000 men. (NMBS *Report* 1815, pp. 27, 44-6.)

110. (MS) BFBS *Minutes,* May 20, 1811. Cf. supra, pp. 54-5.

111. NMBS *Report* 1815, p. 26.

112. Infra, pp. 99-100.

113. NMBS *Report* 1820, pp. 39-40.

114. Marks 1826, pp. 218-9. Cf. SML 1826, p. 233.

115. NSM 1834, p. 226. Cf. Isaiah 60:2.

116. NSM 1859, pp. 152, 162.

117. See also supra, p. 63.

118. NSM 1934, p. 226. Cf. SML 1823, p. 428; 1826, p. 235.

119. NSM 1828, pp. 34-5; 1833, p. 233. "The Right Hon. James Gambier," in *The Annual Biography and Obituary* Vol. 18, 1834, pp. 233-41. Lewis 1960, pp. 74-5, 280. Gambier's consistent walk of faith earned him the nickname of "Sir Jemmy the Good" (Parkinson 1949, p. 116). J.K. Laughton's biography of Gambier in DNB Vol. 20, 1889, pp. 293-5, is marred by obvious partiality. He omits to note Gambier's refusal to accept a pension of £2,000 following the

success of the vital Copenhagen expedition. Nor has he one word to say of his invaluable services to the church, as testified by the published accounts of the proceedings of a wide range of religious and philanthropic societies during the first fifteen post-war years. Cf. SMNY 1876, pp. 70-5.

120. Ibid. NSM 1828, pp. 347-8. See also SML and NSM, under accounts of proceedings of the metropolitan seamen's mission societies, from 1818 and through the 1820's.

121. Smith 1961, p. 95; cf. p. 158. DNB Vol. 16, 1888, pp. 159-61. SML 1826, pp. 235, 273; 1827, p. 33. Cf. NSM 1828, p. 51.

122. Smith 1961, pp. 95-7. DNB Vol. 40, 1894, pp. 195, 197, 206.

123. SML 1821, p. 459. Note, in the case of Nelson, how Marks carefully distinguishes between his general spirit of humanity and religiosity on the one hand, and his apparent ignorance of the nature of the Gospel and salvation on the other (Marks 1818, pp. 160-1, 167-8, 182-4).

124. SML 1820, p. 353. NSM 1834, p. 226. Brown 1961, pp. 401-2. Marks uses the term "awakening" to characterize the spiritual situation of many in the late Napoleonic War navy (Marks 1843, p. 244).

125. Infra, pp. 96, 100-3, 108-11.

126. Lewis 1965, pp. 251-3.

127. NMBS *Report* 1820, p. 40. NMBS 1834, p. 162. Lewis 1965, pp. 251-3.

128. McCarthy 1861, pp. 42-3.

129. Ibid., p. 43.

130. Smith 1961, p. 154, quoting *The Old Chaplain's Farewell Letter* (1803). Cf. Laffin 1969, p. 118.

131. Smith 1961, pp. 108-12.

132. Robinson 1894, p. 402. Smith 1961, pp. 107-8. (Note the morale-raising effect of the action of the chaplain of HMS *Meander*, in stripping and taking his turn with the rest at the pumps.)

133. NMBS *Report* 1836, p. 24. ("Methodists" used here as synonymous with "converted men.")

134. G.C. Smith *English Sailors* n.d., p. 27. Possibly the Rev. Terrot, to whom the Rev. Richard Marks refers as "an honoured instrument in the hand of God of turning many from darkness into light," in contrast to the allegedly ineffectual ministry of many other contemporary naval chaplains. (SML 1826, pp. 235-6. See also NSM 1828, pp. 347-8; 1859, p. 441; and *The Christian Guardian* 1826. p. 171.)

135. Smith 1961, pp. 69-70.

136. Ibid., pp. 113-4.

137. Ibid., pp. 103-4.

138. Ibid., p. 102. Lewis 1960, pp. 254-5.

139. SML 1826, pp. 156-8.

140. G.C. Smith *The Boatswain's Mate* n.d., Part 2, pp. 8-9. The companion of the boatswain's mate points out that faithful chaplains do exist (such as in the *Repulse*). But he concedes that they are only honorable exceptions, and emphasizes the futility of thinking "that the iniquity of ungodly chaplains can excuse us." (Ibid., pp. 9-10.)

141. Lewis 1960, p. 252. Cf. SML 1820, p. 319; Lewis 1948, p. 267. A particularly searing critique, by a clergyman of the Church of England, is provided in *The Christian Guardian* 1826, p. 451. From his own service as a naval officer during this period, Richard Marks had this to say: "Few ships ever had a chaplain on board, and several which had them would have better without them; — with very few exceptions, they were the butt of the officers' jokes, and furnished too many sad subjects for their contempt and ridicule." (SML 1826, p. 235.) This dark picture is borne out by a fellow-clergyman, the Rev. Thomas Webster, in SML 1827, p. 1.

142. Robinson 1894, p. 450. Smith 1961, pp. 64, 103.

143. Supra, p. 9.

144. SML 1826, p. 160, is an example of a typical G.C. Smith reaction against the exclusion of Methodists and Dissenters from naval ministry. (Cf. G.C. Smith *The Boatswain's Mate* n.d., Part 5, p. 18.) See also Smith 1961, pp. 64, 133-5. (In illustration of legalistic sermon emphasis, note the consistent concentration on the theme of *duty* — to God and man, e.g., pp. 149-51, 165. Cf. Laffin 1969, pp. 118-9.)

145. Smith 1961, pp. 121-6.

146. After the 1797 mutinies, even the ordinary seaman drew a higher wage than the parson's pittance of 19 shillings a month. This was only augmented by the highly unpopular and often uncertain monthly levy of fourpence per head on board ("preacher's groat"). Cf. Lewis 1960, pp. 260-2, 266-9.

147. Until 1808, before a chaplain could draw his pay, or be reappointed to another ship, he had to submit to the humiliation of obtaining a certificate from three fellow-officers, stating that he had done his duty to their satisfaction. Thus, as Lewis points out, any one of the trio, who put so-called "good-fellowship" before godliness, might well refuse to sign simply *because* the clergyman had done his duty! (Lewis 1960, pp. 263, 266-9.) See also Kealey 1905, pp. 11, 19.

148. Improvements included a fixed salary (£150 p.a.), a schoolmaster "bounty" of £20, a superannuation scheme, a more specific status on board, etc. Kealey 1905, pp. 12-4. Lewis 1960, p. 269. Smith 1961, pp. 111-2, 126-9, 132-5. Taylor 1978, pp. 233-41.

149. Lewis 1948a, p. 269.

150. SML 1820, pp. 102, 319; 1826, pp. 56-7.

151. Supra, pp. 80-4.

152. NMBS *Appeal* 1834, p. 2.

153. Ibid., p. 10.

154. Supra, pp. 84-7.

155. Letters directly from naval chaplains do not appear until *after* the war, however. E.g., NMBS *Reports* 1818 (pp. 63-4), 1824 (p. 42), and 1825 (pp. 45-6).

156. NMBS *Reports* 1813, p. 52; 1814, p. 72.

157. Ibid., 1826, p. 21.

158. Ibid., 1812, pp. 59-60; 1813, pp. 54-5; cf. 1826, p. 11.

159. Ibid., 1812, p. 62; 1814, pp. 78-9, 89.

160. Supra, pp. 82-4.

161. Supra, p. 12. (MS) SPCK *Minutes* 1787-1816. Smith 1961, pp. 142, 152-4. The Society also supplied native-language church literature to Danish/ Norwegian sailor P.O.W.s, and Swedish/Finnish seafaring allies. (Owens 1816, p. 218. Allen 1898, p. 206.)

162. Ibid. It was evidently also Sir Edward Pellew who arranged with the NMBS for the supply of 400 Bibles to his squadron in Indian waters in 1808. In appreciation, he sent a subscription of 20 guineas to that society, with a request for further supplies. (NMBS *Account* 1809, pp. 22-3; 1811, pp. 23-4.) As to Horatio Nelson, an application to the SPCK is recorded, for example, February 26, 1793, when he wrote to them as commander of the *Agamemnon.* ([MS] SPCK *Minutes* 1792-95.)

163. NMBS *Report* 1814, p. 4.

164. (MS) SPCK *Minutes* 1811-13, pp. 169-70. Cf. "Receipts and Payments" in SPCK *Reports* 1813-18. (In contrast to these sources, Allen and McClure 1898, p. 456, represent the Admiralty grant of £1,500 as simply an annual allowance "during the great war with France;" in Smith 1961, pp. 154-5; it is stated to have been voted in 1814.)

165. Smith 1961, pp. 155-6. Cf. G.C. Smith *The Log-Book* n.d., Part 1, pp. 7-8.

166. Howse 1960, pp. 114-5.

167. PBHS *Proceedings* 1813, pp. ix-x, 21. Howse 1960, pp. 114-5.

168. Infra, pp. 305-6.

169. Allen and McClure 1898, pp. 166-89.

170. Ibid., p. 189.

171. RTS 1828, No. 1, p. 10. Hewitt 1949, pp. 18-9. Cf. Foster 1960, p. 70.

172. RTS 1820, pp. 43-4.

173. Ibid., p. 69.

174. Ibid., p. 74. EM 1805, p. 326.

175. RTS 1820, pp. 96, 151-2.

176. Hewitt 1949, pp. 19-20.

177. Lloyd 1968, pp. 194, 289. Watson 1960, p. 412.

178. Supra, pp. 33-4.

179. SML 1820, pp. 441-2. Cf. Marks 1821, pp. 69-73, 77.

180. Infra, pp. 104-11. Dramatic examples of the varying motives behind negative reactions to a shipmate's conversion are provided by G.C. Smith in *The Boatswain's Mate* n.d. (See especially Part 5, pp. 10-17.)

181. Smith 1961, pp. 133-4.

182. Lloyd 1968, pp. 237-9. Cf. G.C. Smith *The Boatswain's Mate* n.d., Part 5, p. 18. Also see McCarthy 1861, p. 43.

183. Marks 1843, p. 152.

184. SML 1822, p. 403. Cf. G.C. Smith *The Boatswain's Mate* n.d. Part 5, p. 24.

185. Lloyd 1968, pp. 230-1.

186. E.g., infra, pp. 108-9.

187. Marks maintained, from personal observation during most of the Napoleonic War, that "for a certainty, two thirds of our line of battle ships and nine-tenths of all smaller ships" completely neglected "hallowing the Lord's day." (Marks 1821, p. 95; see also 1818, p. 174.) Cf. *A Collection of the Statutes* 1768, pp. 671-4. SML 1821, pp. 120-6.

188. Smith 1961, pp. 71-2, 90-1.

189. SML 1826, p. 368.

190. RTS 1820, pp. 68-9. SML 1820, p. 230; 1821, pp. 461-2. Marks 1821, pp. 76-7. NMBS *Reports* 1837, p. 20; 1840, p. 21. Lewis 1960, p. 252.

191. In fact, in an analysis of the social status of R.N. officers' parents, 1793-1815, the Church represented the next-largest group of professional men, after the Navy (17.4% of the whole). See Lewis 1960, pp. 36-8; 1965, pp. 26-7.

192. SML 1821, p. 428. NSM 1828, p. 348.

193. In 1843, a third American edition was published in New York, from the seventeenth London edition. Despite the formal anonymity of the book, its author could not long escape recognition. By 1820, he had obviously abandoned the attempt. (See, e.g., NMBS *Report* 1820, pp. 39ff.; SML 1821, pp. 415-6. Cf. RTS 1820, p. 337.)

194. Marks 1821, p. 15. A Baptismal Certificate, based on the Parish Register Book of North Crawley, Buckinghamshire, states that, "Richard Son of Thomas and Mary Marks, was baptized January 17th, 1779." ([MS] PRO Adm. 107/30, f. 33.) A mural tablet on the south side of the Parish Church of St. Peter and St. Paul at Great Messenden, Buckinghamshire, states that the Rev. Richard Marks "was born at North Crawley in this county Dec. 31, 1778 and closed a life of piety, usefulness and honour in this village 22nd May 1847." A slab over his grave in the south aisle bears the simple inscription: "The Grave of Richard Marks — 1847 — 24 Years Vicar of this Parish." ([MS] Kverndal, 1976.)

195. Marks 1821, pp. 15-45.

196. Ibid., pp. 45-51.

197. Ibid., pp. 50-8. For Marks' naval service 1797-1803: (MS) PRO Adm. 107/30, f. 32.

198. Marks 1821, p. 61.

199. Ibid., p. 66.

200. Ibid., pp. 69-72. The fact that "the C—" was the *Conqueror,* of 74 guns, is often alluded to elsewhere (e.g., SML 1820, p. 156; 1821, p. 416).

201. Marks 1821, pp. 73-9, 95.

202. Ibid., pp. 79-81.

203. Ibid., pp. 81-2. SML 1821, p. 415. These evening fellowship meetings are, in *The Quarterly Christian Spectator* 1881, p. 255, stated to have commenced in 1809. This dating seems far too late, however. Moreover, Marks was on the *Defence* at Trafalgar, not the *Conqueror.* Cf. NSM 1828, p. 50.

204. Marks 1821, pp. 82-5.

205. Ibid., pp. 85-8, 91-3.

206. Ibid., pp. 94-9. *The Christian Guardian* 1826 (May), p. 176. Green 1828, p. 142. Marks (NY) 1843, pp. 223-5. Marsden 1847, pp. 30-2. Cf. SML 1826, p. 376.

207. Marks 1821, p. 175. Lewis 1960, pp. 202ff.

208. Marks 1821, p. 98. Marsden 1847, pp. 30-2.

209. In 1826, G.C. Smith, as editor of *The Sailor's Magazine,* exhorted in vain Anglican friends of seamen to make good the continuing absence of a particular Church ministry to seamen in the metropolis, by settling the Rev. Richard Marks in a London seamen's church (SML 1826, pp. 51-2).

210. RTS 1820, pp. 337, 369, 417. NMBS *Report* 1829, p. 20. Marks (NY) 1843, pp. 245-7. Marsden 1847, pp. 37-8. Richard Marks' literary production embraces a wide variety of popular devotional aids, books on "Village" themes, and publications bearing on the Trinitarian and Tractarian controversies. His works intended especially for seamen include: Seven tracts, entitled *Conversation in a Boat, The Shipmates, The Seaman's Friend, The Seaman's Spy-Glass, The Smugglers, The Wreckers, The Royal Review* (all published by the RTS); *The Prayer Book at Sea* (published by the Church of England Tract Society); *The Retrospect* (1st ed.: 1816); *Nautical Essays* (incorporating *The Seaman's Spy-Glass,* published 1818); *The Ocean* (incorporating *Nautical Essays,* published 1824); *Sea Sermons* (published 1843).

211. Note, e.g., Marks' early involvement on behalf of the NMBS (NMBS *Report* 1820, pp. 39-46; 1829, pp. 20-1), and the BFSFSBU (SML 1821, pp. 415-6), likewise his spirited promotion of the Seamen's Cause among fellow-Anglicans, and his public endorsement of the Rev. G.C. Smith in the latter's controversy with the PLBUS in the late 1820's. Infra, pp. 210, 275, 286-7, 307, 336, 342.

212. SML 1820, pp. 113-7, 154-60.

213. Ibid. See also Milne 1851, pp. 28-36.

214. SML 1820, pp. 116-7, 156. In 1809, Marks, too, was in touch with a society on the *Ganges,* then numbering 17-18, under the leadership of one John Clark, a seaman previously converted at Otaheite, or Tahiti (EM 1817, pp. 168-72).

215. SML 1820, p. 300.

216. NSM 1829, Part I, pp. 45-9. The name of this Methodist marine is given as "William M."

217. The reliability of *The Boatswain's Mate* as a source of information on the Naval Awakening rests primarily on the unique dual qualifications of the author: (1) his personal experience of naval life up to 1802; and (2) his "Naval Correspondence Mission" from 1809 (with which he himself specifically links this series of tracts). The individual elements of Smith's composite portrayal are in complete accord with the letters from contemporary sailors which appeared in the religious press. Nor do there appear to be any of its thousands of readers, themselves eye-witnesses of what actually took place, who ever seriously challenged the essential historicity of the work. The contents of the first two parts were published jointly in the *Instructor* 1811-12. In 1817, these were published separately, and followed successively by five further parts. By 1828, nearly 100,000 copies had been sold. The numerous editions include American editions (N.Y., n.d., also Newburyport, n.d.), and a London edition as late as 1883. (Cf. SML 1821, p. 131; 1837, pp. 435-40; 1860, pp. 187-90. CC 1881, pp. 19-20.)

218. The narrative traces the conversion of *Bob,* the high-spirited boatswain's mate of the *Dreadnought,* during shore leave at Plymouth Dock (Devonport), under the zealous counseling of *James,* the pious quartermaster of the *Royal George* (Parts I-IV). The story continues with the establishment of a spiritual fellowship

group, despite partial opposition on the *Dreadnought,* and includes an account of inter-ship visiting by Bob on the *Royal George* (Parts V-VII). In identifying himself with the person of James, the author has interwoven with the narrative a mass of autobiographical material, covering the life of George Charles Smith up to and including the time of his 1803 conversion. Occasional and less accurate items of such material (e.g., Part III, pp. 3-4) are linked with Bob, too, however. (G.C. Smith *The Boatswain's Mate,* London, n.d.)

219. SML 1827, pp. 142, 175.

220. Owen 1816, Part II, pp. 56-7. BFBS *Reports* Vol. 2, 1811-13, p. 204 (1812); p. 392 (1813). EM 1813, pp. 71-2.

221. SML 1827, pp. 45-6.

222. Ibid., pp. 45-8, 87-9, 140-2, 173-5. It is noteworthy that Cavanagh traces his original conversion to his own grudging curiosity about one among a number of Bibles alotted to his ship early in the French Revolutionary War. Taunted by his shipmates with "Methodism," he determined to become a Methodist indeed, and joined the Society at Portsmouth (pp. 46-7). See also SML 1825, p. 523; NSM 1828, pp 272-3.

223. After reuniting with his family on his release in 1814, Jeremiah Taylor resumed his seafaring profession, and was evidently made a blessing to many in the emerging Bethel Movement. (G.C. Smith *The History of a Sunderland Cabin Boy* n.d. Milne 1851, pp. 15-27.)

224. *The Methodist Magazine* carried, during the later war years, several letters from members of Methodist societies in French prison depots. The Rev. R.B. Wolfe has recorded his experiences in *English Prisoners in France . . . during Nine Years Residence in the Depots of Fontainebleau, Verdun, Givet and Valensiennes,* London, 1830. (NSM 1855, pp. 182-8. Cf MM 1973, p. 217.)

225. NSM 1834, pp. 189-91, 227. According to the Rev. George Burder, both his own *Village Sermons* and Flavel's *Sermons* were copied, besides the whole of *Dr. Watts's Psalms and Hymns,* and a "great part of the Scriptures" (SML 1822, p. 152).

226. Even *before* the Peace of Amiens, there are isolated examples of a Bible-reading seaman being instrumental in the conversion of a shipmate, and in the subsequent formation of a small Christian community on the lower deck. In this way, a society of 13 developed in a ship which took part in the Battle of the Nile. (SML 1820, pp. 14-5. Cf. BH 1880, pp. 80-5.) A regular society of 24 grew out of a similar start on another ship-of-war prior to 1802, according to NMBS *Report* 1812, pp. 63-4. See also *The Evangelical Magazine* 1798, pp. 467-8, 529-32. However, it was only during the Napoleonic War that a spiritual awakening in the Navy reached really significant proportions.

227. The following references provide additional examples: (1) *The Evangelical Magazine* 1813, pp. 390-1. RTS 1820, pp. 43-4, 111. G.C. Smith *The Boatswain's Mate* n.d., Part. III, pp. 3-5; Part VI, p. 5. (2) *The Evangelical Magazine* 1808, pp. 485-6. RTS 1820, pp. 43-4. G.C. Smith *The Boatswain's Mate* n.d., Part V, pp. 22-4; Part VI, pp. 5-7; Part VII, pp. 3, 18. (3) Self-evident (from these and previous examples). (4) *The Evangelical Magazine* 1812, pp. 345-6. SML 1820, pp. 111, 414; 1821, p. 267; cf. 1822, pp. 57-8. Marks 1821, pp. 114-5. G.C. Smith *The Boatswain's Mate* n.d., Part V, pp. 8-24; Part VI, pp. 3-5.

228. See, e.g., supra. pp. 108-9.

229. See, e.g., SML 1820, pp. 117, 356.

230. SML 1821, pp. 399-400. Cf. CC 1881, p. 20.

231. SML 1821, p. 287. (Cf. Boase 1882, p. 664. DNB Vol. 53, 1898, p. 42.)

232. SML 1821, pp. 285-90. NSM 1856, pp. 275-6, 333. *George Charles Smith* (or, to use his own abbreviation, G.C.S.) describes his father, William Smith, as "a plain man, a native of the city of York, and a taylor by trade, who, as a young man, removed to . . . Knottingley." In this small Yorkshire town, he met and married one Nancy Wilson, born there, and daughter of a local innkeeper. After having tried his hand as a publican himself, at Pontefract (also in Yorkshire), he gave up, removed to London (evidently around 1772), and settled in Castle Street. At George Whitefield's Tottenham Court Road Chapel, not far distant, he was converted. His wife, who also "became the subject of divine grace," was made chapel-keeper of Lady Huntingdon's Chapel in Westminster, near Tothill Street. This was thanks to the influence of the pious governor of Tothill Fields Prison, George Smith. It was after this family benefactor that George Charles Smith was named in 1882. (NSM 1839, p. 257; 1856, p. 333.) While his evidently more robust mother continued keeping "a respectable lodging-house" in Castle Street, his ailing, asthmatic father lived, for health reasons, on the south side of the Thames, in Dover Place, Old Kent Road (then considered "a sort of country place"). Here, during his early childhood, the boy was often left in his father's care. (SML 1820, p. 287.) According to the record of the Octagon (later Jordan) Chapel in Penzance, George Charles Smith "as a boy about seven, belonged to Bermondsey Parish School at Bermondsey Church . . . and after lived at Lant Street, in the borough of Southwark." (NSM 1857, pp. 121-2.) After a brief, renewed residence in Westminster, in York Street (where the infant George received early impressions of a future mission-field, the soldiery), the family settled on the south side again, this time in Boundary Row, Blackfriars Road (NSM 1856, p. 275). After her husband's death, the boy's mother continued living here until she, too, died in 1803. In the meantime, during her later years, she remarried, her second husband being a "Mr. Hayman, an organ builder, and deacon of the Baptist Chapel in Church Street, Blackfriars Road." (NSM 1856, p. 333; 1858, p. 364; 1861, pp. 309-10.) Much of the above biographical data is also to be found in a 24-page tract (G.C. Smith *Sailor's Visit to Surrey Chapel,* London, n.d.).

233. NSM 1855, p. 99; 1856, p. 275; 1859, p. 126. The location is stated to have been "near Chamberlain's wharf," but he was also "for awhile in the same employ at Dockhead" (NSM 1839, p. 448).

234. A contributory cause was no doubt the example of two elder brothers. Young George had already visited William, when the latter arrived in the Thames as chief mate on a West Indiaman. (This brother later became "chief mate or captain of a large American ship from Philadelphia, where he had a wife and family.") Thomas had "perished in a distant land, after losing both his legs in a desperate battle at sea," while in the naval service off Trincomalee, in the East Indies. (SML 1821, p. 286. NSM 1839, p. 448; 1861, p. 368. G.C. Smith *The Log-Book* n.d., Part I, pp. 10-4.

235. NSM 1857, p. 122; 1858, p. 210; 1859, p. 126; 1861, pp. 1, 363. Cf. SMNY 1861-62, p. 9. (Note variations in spelling: *Clarke, Betsy.*) The apprenticeship was for seven years. Captain Clark, whom Smith describes in warm, filial terms, though not exactly as "religious," held out the prospect of making Smith

a mate the last two years, and getting him the command of an American ship after that. Smith was evidently in complete agreement with his captain's plan to make him a United States citizen on his first arrival in America. (G.C. Smith *The Log-Book* n.d., Part I, pp. 14-20; Part II, p. 16.)

236. NSM 1861, pp. 1, 321. A graphic description of the traumatic effect of impressment on a fourteen-year-old London lad is contained in G.C. Smith *The Log-Book* n.d., Part. I, pp. 22-4; Part II, pp. 15-24.

237. NSM 1859, pp. 126-7; 1861, p. 321. Cf. Lewis 1960, pp. 405-9.

238. NSM 1859, p. 127.

239. NSM 1837, pp. 459-60; 1859, pp. 127, 198.

240. The Rev. Rowland Hill was related to Admiral John Holloway. To exercise influence through him on behalf of a promising, personally known youth, was only in keeping with long-standing officer-recruitment and promotion tradition in the Royal Navy. (NSM 1832, p. 222; 1855, p. 99; 1857, p. 122; 1861, p. 322. See also 1857, pp. 96-7. Cf. Lewis 1960, pp. 202ff.)

241. NSM 1828, p. 171; 1859, p. 127.

242. NSM 1858, p. 357.

243. In the midst of the carnage at Copenhagen, Smith was one of the party who volunteered to transfer temporarily to the heavily stricken *Ardent* (NSM 1859, pp. 166-7). In later years, when planning a Scandinavian tour, Smith published in his magazine frequent detailed reminiscences of the Baltic expedition of 1801, dwelling particularly on the various phases of the battle of Copenhagen (e.g., NSM 1858, pp. 321-7; 1859, pp. 150-6, 160-8). Colorful comments on this battle had long since also been included in *The Boatswain's Mate*, however (G.C. Smith *The Boatswain's Mate* n.d., Part III, pp. 9-14). See also Pope 1972; Kverndal (London) 1976. For Smith's dramatic description of the Battle of Copenhagen in later issues of his magazine, see Appendix No. 2.

244. NSM 1832, p. 222; 1857, p. 122; 1858, p. 324. Cf. 1837, p. 598. It was in order to avert such victimization that the system of signatures arranged in a circle (a *round robin*) was frequently adopted when setting up unpopular petitions. There has been some confusion as to the precise rank held by Smith at this time: Smith himself also refers to himself as having served as *captain* of the fore-top (SML 1820, p. 471; cf. NSM 1859, p. 163). This may well be; but the statement that he was "master's mate" at the Battle of Copenhagen (e.g., Mee 1947, pp. 174-5) is obviously incorrect. Nor has the Author discovered evidence proving that he had at any *other* time been promoted to that rank (as represented, e.g., by Boase 1882, p. 664; Boase 1965, c. 628; DNB Vol. 53, 1898, p. 42; and Langley 1967, p. 47). Dr. John Styles' statement in PLBUS 1829, that Smith never reached more than the rank of "boatswain's mate" is likewise quite incorrect (Thompson and Phillips 1829, p. 19).

245. G.C. Smith *The Boatswain's Mate* n.d., Part III, pp. 14-20, Part VI, p. 8. NSM 1832, pp. 222-3; 1859, p. 129.

246. G.C. Smith *The Boatswain's Mate* n.d., Part II, pp. 11-5. NSM 1858, pp. 358-64. Here, Smith provides interesting supplementary information on this astounding sailor's spree, when he—as ringleader—"madly attempted to jump out of the gallery into the pit, as an act of drunken bravado." (The actual scene of the affray is stated to have been the Surrey Theatre, not the Royal Circus.)

247. NSM 1859, p. 160. Cf. SML 1820, p. 471.

248. In point of fact, Smith's pious mother, during one of her Spithead visits to a son still in the midst of all his "sea wickedness and folly," gave him a copy of John Newton's *Narrative* (NSM 1829, Part II, pp. 349-51).

249. Infra, p. 126.

250. Infra, pp. 172-4, 198.

251. G.C. Smith *The Boatswain's Mate* n.d., Part VI, p. 8. NSM 1859, pp. 129-30. The firm, Messrs. Baxter & Noble, was located at St. Mary Hill, Billingsgate.

252. Concerning "mother-attachment" in seamen, see infra, pp. 497-9, 568, 608, *illus.*

253. NSM 1857, p. 122; 1859, p. 162. Before his mother became bed-ridden, Smith accompanied her not only to Surrey Chapel, but occasionally also to the nearby Baptist Chapel in Church Street, and the Wesleyan Chapel in Lambeth Marsh (NSM 1856, p. 276). Unable, as he says, to "give up a place of worship altogether," though it only filled him "with terror," he continued, after her confinement, to attend Surrey Chapel regularly throughout this period (G.C. Smith *The Boatswain's Mate* n.d., Part VI, pp. 8-10).

254. The sudden sight, one morning on St. Mary Hill, of "about fifty men walking two and two chained together, and forced on by the press gang to the Tower stairs" and into the tender there, was evidently more than fair warning. (NSM 1859, pp. 130-1. Cf. G.C. Smith *The Boatswain's Mate* n.d., Part VI, pp. 14-5.)

255. It was Smith's shipmate at Reading, John Lovegrove, who arranged for the transfer of his stricken friend from the inn "Jack of Newbury" to sick-lodgings in "a court at London Street." The minister, the Rev. Mr. Weller, came in response to a prayer note, which Smith's nurse ("Mrs. R.") had encouraged him to send to the adjoining chapel early on Sunday morning, March 30, 1803. (G.C. Smith *The Boatswain's Mate* n.d., Part VI, pp. 15-34. NSM 1861, pp. 309-10.) Note the erroneous account of this and other important events in Smith's life in Harms 1909, pp. 6-7.

256. See, e.g., NSM 1859, p. 99.

257. NSM 1829, Part II, p. 349.

258. NSM 1861, p. 310. His counselor, the Rev. Weller, had actually foretold, from the moment they met, "we shall see you in the pulpit yet." (G.C. Smith *The Boatswain's Mate* n.d., Part VI, p. 32.)

259. When sufficiently recovered at Reading, Smith left for London again, attended to the funeral of his mother at Tottenham Court Road Chapel ground (where his father, too, was buried), and obtained employment in the same capacity as before. Being now "converted by the grace of God," and becoming "accustomed to engage in prayer meetings, and some occasional public speakings in a humble way," duties demanded by his employer on Sundays caused a conflict of conscience. Hence his resignation and removal to a situation offering other prospects at Bath. (NSM 1859, pp. 131-2; 1861, pp. 104, 310.)

260. NSM 1839, p. 229; 1859, pp. 132-3; 1861, pp. 104-5.

261. Opie Smith's concern for Cornwall had been roused by accounts in Dr. Rippon's missionary periodical of the spiritual destitution in this "Druidical county ... where idol gods were originally so abundantly worshipped." Besides promoting the founding of Baptist chapels in Cornwall and Devon, he

also arranged, with Dr. John Ryland of the Baptist College in Bristol, for ministerial supply. (NSM 1857, p. 121; 1858, pp. 544-5; 1861, p. 106. Boase 1904, c. 1349.)

262. Smith was offered the choice, by Opie Smith, of enrollment at the Baptist College, Bristol, or private theological tuition, combined with assistant-preacher duties, under "some able minister." True to his impatiently activist nature, Smith chose the latter, but not without "much serious consideration and prayer." During his tutorship, he received £20 per annum from Opie Smith toward his support. (NMS 1861, p. 105.) On this background, it is interesting to note Smith's opinions of the strictly limited value of formal education (NSM 1839, p. 257; 1855, pp. 389-90; 1859, p. 160). Before his arrival at Devonport, Smith mentions having been given the "sanction" (call) to enter the ministry from the "humble" church to which he had belonged in London Street, Reading (NSM 1859, p. 134; 1861, p. 105).

263. Smith filled the vacancy created by the removal of the Rev. Samuel Saunders, Baptist minister in Penzance, from the acquisition of the Octagon Chapel in 1802. In the spring of 1807, Smith served a few weeks on probation. As a result, he was enthusiastically invited to take the pastoral charge of the church, in a letter of call dated May 6, 1807. ([MS] *Jordan Chapel Minutes,* May 1807. NSM 1834, p. 213; 1857, pp. 121-6; 1858, p. 545. Boase 1965, Vol. III, c. 628.) Rees 1956, p. 43, states that the Octagon Chapel was formerly Wesleyan. After it was sold by the Baptists again, it became "Central Hall," then the "Regal Cinema." (This has since been destroyed.)

264. NSM 1832, p. 225; 1855, p. 99; 1856, pp. 61, 391; 1861, p. 105.

265. NSM 1833, p. 233.

266. NSM 1832, p. 225; 1859, p. 429. Where Smith occasionally (e.g., NSM 1839, p. 448) alludes to his "ministry among sailors" having commenced in 1804, this must be construed as part of his *overall* ministry, 1804-9. He states, in 1821: "I confess I had not thought of it [a specific ministry to seamen] till a revenue cutter came into Mount's Bay [in 1809]" (SML 1821, p. 458).

267. NSM 1839, p. 449; 1855, pp. 97-9; Cf. infra, p. 16.

268. NSM 1832, p. 273. The *Dolphin* was apparently kept constantly on the alert about the Land's End, in order to prevent smuggling, one of the "notorious customs of Cornwall." (NSM 1859, p. 429; 1861, p. 50.)

269. NSM 1861, pp. 50-1.

270. NSM 1832, p. 273; 1859; p. 429; 1861, p. 51.

271. NSM 1832, p. 273. The name of this one "real religious" sailor is given as Thomas Doeg, quartermaster on the *Agamemnon* in 1797, when Smith was Admiralty midshipman on board (NSM 1861, pp. 51-2).

272. NSM 1859, p. 430. Cf. SML 1821, p. 458.

273. NSM 1857, p. 89; 1861, p. 52.

274. NSM 1832, pp. 273-4.

275. NSM 1832, p. 273; 1860, p. 186. This designation is adopted in this study, although—as in the case of many other names for Smith's expanding seamen's mission activities—it was not used consistently by its originator.

276. NSM 1859, p. 430.

277. Ibid., pp. 432-3.

278. "Staggered at the loss of so many servants, Satan stirred up" (as Smith puts it) more drastic measures. G.C. Smith *The Boatswain's Mate* n.d., Part V, p. 24. NSM 1859, pp. 433-4; cf. 1839, pp. 252-3.

279. NSM 1832, pp. 226-7.

280. See, e.g., NSM 1859, p. 436.

281. Ibid., pp. 435-41.

282. NSM 1832, pp. 226-7, 275; 1859, p. 440.

283. NSM 1832, pp. 274-6. Smith speaks of becoming so "infatuated" with the work, that he could willingly have laid down his life to promote it (p. 276).

284. NSM 1832, pp. 273-4; 1859, pp. 438-9. A good example of the way in which Smith enlisted assistance from his correspondents, in continually supplementing and correcting his list of contacts, is provided by the reply of a Midshipman J. Campbell, dated March 23, 1811 (NSM 1832, pp. 97-9).

285. NSM 1860, p. 186.

286. NSM 1832, p. 275. Smith's assistant preacher was also mobilized to help. Cf. NSM 1860, p. 186.

287. NSM 1832, pp. 275-7. Cf. Theophilus Smith 1874, p. 5. G.C. Smith was married in June 1808 to Theodosia, daughter of a "distinguished" Baptist, John Skipwith. (DNB Vol. 53, 1898, p. 43. Boase 1904, c. 907. Cf. NSM 1856, p. 334.) In a letter to the Author, dated London, Dec. 30, 1971, Frank N. Trumble, secretary of the SCFS, quotes confirmation of the spelling "Theodosia" by a surviving great-granddaughter of G.C. Smith, Miss Violet Maud Bosier, London. (Boase 1904, c. 907 has "Theodoria.") See also infra, p. 359.

288. NSM 1832, pp. 276-7.

289. Ibid., p. 275.

290. Ibid., pp. 225-6. Cf. Marks (NY) 1843, pp. 244-5.

291. NSM 1832, pp. 274-5. SMNY 1876, p. 131.

292. Supra, p. 102.

293. SML 1820, p. 442. NSM 1833, p. 233; 1859, p. 441; 1860, p. 187. Smith quotes interesting examples, from 1810-11, of the particular concern for naval personnel demonstrated by "the pious and most exemplary clergyman of Plymouth Dock," the Rev. J. Hitchins (SML 1820, pp. 67-8, 111).

294. Marks 1821, pp. 127-41. NMBS *Report* 1829, p. 20.

295. *George Grey,* descended from a famous Northumberland family, became a favorite captain of Sir John Jervis, and won distinction at the Battle of St. Vincent, 1797. In 1804, he was appointed Commissioner of the Dockyard at Sheerness; in 1806, he was transferred to the same office at Portsmouth, where he remained to his death in 1828. In 1814, he was made a baronet in recognition of his outstanding services. (Creighton 1901, p. 12. DNB Vol. 23, 1890, p. 183.) "The strong character of the wife deepened the seriousness of the husband," according to the family biographer (Creighton 1901, p. 12). His clearly evangelical stance drew unfavorable reactions both from the local chaplain, the Rev. T.C. Scott, and the Duke of Clarence, who visited Portsmouth as Lord High Admiral in 1827. (NSM 1829, Part II, p. 380; 1857, pp. 98-9; 1858, p. 534. Gates 1900, pp. 335-6.) There are many examples of

Grey's active support of early seamen's mission activities (e.g., NMBS *Reports* 1829, p. xci; SML 1820, p. 457; 1821, p. 16; 1824, p. 260. NSM 1829, Part II, p. 379; 1832, p. 226; 1858, p. 536).

296. *Mary Grey* was said to have "inherited the decided character of her mother" (sister of Lord Cornwallis of India), and "imbibed the religious teaching of her father (Samuel Whitbread, famous brewer and philanthropist). Married in 1795, she sailed with her husband to Gibraltar in 1798. Here, her calmness and fortitude under enemy fire impressed others, and corresponds well with her attitude under the anti-evangelical fire which later erupted in Portsmouth. At Gibraltar, in 1799, she gave birth to her future statesman son, George. (DNB Vol. 23, 1890, p. 183. Creighton 1901, pp. 4, 10-13. Cf. NSM 1858, pp. 534-6, quoting an obituary in the religious newspaper *Record* for May 26, 1858.)

297. Ibid. An indication of the extent of Lady Grey's activity is provided by the fact that she had, from 1810 to 1815, distributed 28,201 Scripture copies, in her capacity as Portsmouth correspondent of the BFBS alone. (*Report* 1815, p. 482; cf. 1811, pp. 165-6. See also Dudley 1821, p. 293.) The BFBS *Home Correspondence* files contain numerous letters from Lady Grey from 1808 onwards, giving a vivid picture of her tenacity and zeal in marine Scripture distribution. The NMBS, in making her an Honorary Governor for life in 1820, states: "Perhaps to no individual has this Society been more indebted for an extended distribution of the Scriptures in the Navy than to the Honourable Lady Grey" (NMBS *Report* 1820, p. 77). A typical example of her concern for foreign seamen, too, is contained in SML 1826, p. 463.

298. NSM 1828, pp. 271-2 (erroneously printed "571-2").

299. NSM 1829, Part II, p. 380; 1857, p. 98; 1858, p. 536. The well-intentioned but exaggerated claim made by the family biographer, the Rev. Mandell Creighton (later Bishop of London), must not mar the brilliance of the pioneering role of Lady Mary Grey, nor the value of her husband's consistent support. (The work of missions to seamen was, of course, not "practically begun" by them, but nevertheless materially promoted, during its first, decisive phase. Cf. Creighton 1901, pp. 12-3.)

300. NSM 1832, pp. 274-6; 1857, p. 99. DNB Vol. 62, 1900, pp. 46-7.

301. NSM 1833, p. 233; 1834, p. 227; 1860, p. 186. The BFBS *Home Correspondence* files give evidence of Hoare's concern for Scripture distribution among French Peninsular War prisoners during his Penzance stay. See also Owen 1816, Part I, p. 398. Cf. supra, p. 84.

302. NSM 1860, pp. 186-7. (*John* Anstey? Cf. DNB Vol. 2, 1885, pp. 39-40.)

303. NSM 1828, p. 533; 1833, p. 233; 1834, p. 227. Cf. BFBS *Reports* 1811-13, pp. 57-8.

304. SML 1820, pp. 466-7. NSM 1859, pp. 431-41; 1860, p. 186; 1861, p. 217.

305. (MS) *Home Correspondence,* letter from G.C. Smith, Feb. 3, 1812.

306. NSM 1859, pp. 436-8. The published letter from the *Saint George* was furnished with the following note by Smith: "The Minister to whom this letter was directed, will esteem it a most gratifying privilege to hear from any sailor, who is desirous of making inquiries respecting the salvation of his soul, and the religion of the Lord Jesus Christ."

307. NSM 1859, p. 431; 1860, p. 186. The editor of *The Evangelical Magazine* apologized in 1812 for not being able to quote more of the many letters from pious seamen, "from want of room" (Vol. for 1812, p. 346).

308. NSM 1860, p. 187; cf. 1833, p. 20. Supra, pp. 97, 109-10.

309. *Dr. Robert Hawker* (1753-1827), married to a naval officer's daughter, himself having served about three years as assistant-surgeon in the Royal Marines, became deputy-chaplain of the Plymouth garrison in 1797. He is reputed to have been "one of the most popular extemporaneous preachers in the kingdom." His prolific writing includes several biblical and devotional aids for "the poor man." (DNB Vol. 25, 1891, p. 201.) In the preface of *The Sailor Pilgrim*, the author shows keen awareness of the need of seamen to be *"amused,* while their *improvement* is principally aimed at." This he seeks to achieve by "divine truths mingled in the history" of an imagined seaman, with events largely from real life. (Hawker Part I, 1806, pp. iv-v. NSM 1861, pp. 510-2.) Compared with G.C. Smith's spicy dialogue, however, Hawker's sailor-autobiography seems conspicuously more involved, both in style and content.

310. NSM 1860, p. 187. The 13th London edition was published in 1888 (by the [Anglican] Thames Church Mission).

311. NSM 1856, p. 271; 1860, pp. 187-90.

312. NSM 1860, pp. 187-9.

313. NSM 1857, p. 99.

314. NSM 1857, pp. 99-100; 1860, p. 189. Luke 1868, pp. 5-6. Thompson's daughter, in her biography of her father, describes how his "extraordinary aptitude for calculation" contributed largely to his early success at the Stock Exchange. Smith's first acquaintance with and support from Thompson was in 1812, two years before the latter's entry into public life, not, as erroneously recollected by his daughter, in 1809. (Ibid., pp. 20-2.) The observation on reaching the rank and file of popular evangelicalism was made by Dr. Deryck W. Lovegrove, at the Author's disputation, June 2, 1984.

315. *John Rippon,* like the majority of his co-religionists a warm sympathizer with the Americans during their struggle for independence, had, in 1792, been created a Doctor of Divinity by the Baptist College of Providence, Rhode Island. Best known for his hymnal, which achieved great popularity, he also pioneered an early religious periodical, *The Baptist Annual Register,* 1790-1802. Rippon had become personally acquainted with Smith at an 1807 ministerial convention at Rippon's native Tiverton, Devonshire; a correspondence ensued, and the gift of a set of Rippon's periodical was to prove of "immense importance" to Smith. Rippon was also chairman of the board which had summoned Smith to London in 1812, and, at the Jamaica Coffee House, given him instructions regarding collection procedure for his "chapel case." (NSM 1856, pp. 270-1. DNB Vol. 48, 1896, pp. 318-9.)

316. NSM 1856, pp. 270-1; 1861, p. 218; cf. 1839, pp. 256-7.

317. NSM 1839, p. 256; 1856, pp. 271-2; 1861, p. 218.

318. NSM 1856, p. 272. The text was the same as on the *Dolphin* in 1809: Jonah 1:6. Later evidence was held to indicate that "scarcely less than thirty persons" were converted as a result of this service. On the initiative of Dr. Rippon, a handsome collection was received from the landsfolk as they left, in aid of Smith's continued work among naval seamen. (Cf. NSM 1834, p. 227.)

319. The occasion was the foundation of the Port of London Society for Promoting Religion among Merchant Seamen, March 18, 1818. (SML 1820, p. 216. NSM 1856, p. 272.)

320. NSM 1855, pp. 188-94, 235; 1857, pp. 100-2. Smith wrote at the time that he hoped to help the French "convert the energies of their ardent minds from the wild project of subjugating Europe, to the noble and sublime scheme of aiding Britain in . . . subduing the world beneath the feet of the 'Prince of Peace.' " In this, he was animated also by the "cheering accounts" of revival among British prisoners in French depots. (SML 1821, pp. 10-2. Supra, p. 111.)

321. Ibid. Cf. NSM 1828, p. 350.

322. NSM 1855, pp. 192-3.

323. NSM 1834, p. 228.

324. NSM 1855, p. 193.

325. NSM 1833, p. 233; 1857, p. 89. Estimates vary up to "eighty or ninety" (e.g., NSM 1834, p. 227).

326. NSM 1859, p. 431; 1860, p. 186. The Rev. W.H. Angas quotes a case of a society on a warship increasing from two to fifty members (SML 1822, pp. 152-3).

327. *The Massachusetts Missionary Magazine* 1808, pp. 386-7. NSM 1832, p. 97. Supra, pp. 11-4.

328. Cf. "The Seafarers' (Christian) Fellowship" of the Missions to Seamen and British Sailor's Society; the "Ministering Seafarers' Program" of the International Council of Seamen's Agencies (ICOSA); and "Sjömannsmisjonens Kontakttjeneste" of the Norwegian Seamen's Mission. Infra, pp. 579-81.

329. Supra, pp. 122-8. Cf. NSM 1828, p. 533. Warren 1858, p. 5.

330. SML 1821, pp. 486-7.

331. *The Christian Guardian* 1826, p. 171. NSM 1831, p. 216; 1832, p. 97. Cf. Milne 1851, p. 3. Also, ASFS *Report* 1860, pp. 5-6. It was the fact that so many had found Christ through Scripture reading, "without any of man's instruction," that evinced the initiative of the Holy Spirit. (Cf. EM 1798, pp. 467-8.)

332. Supra, pp. 100-1.

333. Cf. G.C. Smith's own comments: "I did not begin the work, the Lord alone began it in a few ships of war; when I first heard of it the Lord put it into my heart to commence the first general systematic land operation . . . to exhort, advise, console, and encourage pious officers and men in their holy progress" (NSM 1832, p. 97).

334. SML 1820, p. 165; 1826, p. 100; 1827, pp. 45-6. Milne 1851, pp. 4-5.

335. A conspicuous example was Lieutenant Edward Smith, R.N., in 1820 a zealous Bethel Captain. (SML 1820, pp. 105-6. Cf. NSM 1860, p. 69.)

336. "On the Probable Influence . . ." 1821, p. 517.

337. SML 1826, p. 55; cf. 1820, pp. 178-9.

338. SML 1820, pp. 442-3; 1821, pp. 486-8.

339. Typical examples were: Lt. Francis Collins (RTS), Lt. John Cox (MSABS), and the Rev. A. Brown (BFSFSBU).

340. Cf. published reports of the various seamen's mission societies through the 1820's (and those of the NMBS from the preceding decade). Note especially: SML 1820, pp 22-6; 1827, pp. 150, 279. NMBS *Report* 1826, pp. 11-2.

341. Lewis 1965, pp. 68-9, 87. Cf. Penn 1957, p. 32.
342. NMBS *Report* 1837, pp. 27-8. Cf. SML 1825, p. 318; 1827, pp. 55-6.
343. Marks (NY) 1843, p. 245.
344. E.g., NMBS *Report* 1832, p. 30.
345. Infra, pp. 540-6, 551-3.

PART III — NOTES

1. Lloyd 1968, pp. 285-6, 289.
2. Infra, pp. 543-4.
3. Infra, p. 546. Cf. Foster, 1960, pp. 67, 102.
4. Supra, p. 83.
5. Canton Vol. 1, 1904, p. 123.
6. Ibid., p. 126.
7. Supra, p. 83.
8. Infra, p. 592.
9. Edinburgh Bible Society *Report* 1810, p. 2. (MS) Knight n.d., p. 10. RTS *Proceedings* 1820, pp. 96, 106-7, and passim.
10. E.g., Seierstad 1923, pp. 219-20. Cadbury 1926, pp. 66-71.
11. In a letter reporting on his activities, Allen refers to the commission he received from a BFBS sub-committee appointed for maritime distribution in 1811. (MS) BFBS *Home Corresp.*, letter from Samuel Allen to Joseph Reyner, March 25, 1815. The letter also lists others who were active in Scripture distribution among foreign seamen in London, including a Wapping shopkeeper, a Mr. Boon. Cf. (MS) BFBS *Minutes*, April 29, May 6, 1816.
12. BFBS *Reports* 1805-10, pp. 138-9, 158-9; 1811-13, pp. 177-8. Canton Vol. 1, 1904, p. 9.
13. BFBS *Reports* 1811-13, pp. 177-8. Owen 1816, Part II, pp. 567-8.
14. Canton Vol. 1, 1904, pp. 128-42. Kathleen J. Cann, BFBS Archivist, personal interview, June 1970. The designation "agent afloat" is used by Captain Francis Reynalds in a letter to Joseph Tarn, June 24, 1813. (MS) BFBS *Home Corresp.* Many of these naval and merchant captains were in touch with "the Hon. Mrs. Grey" (e.g., Captain Francis Reynalds in a letter to Joseph Tarn, June 24, 1813. [MS] BFBS *Home Corresp.;* also, Captain Gourly, [MS] BFBS *Minutes*, Nov. 6, 1809.) Eventually, this form of foreign distribution was actually incorporated in organizational regulations (cf. Dudley 1821, p. 317).
15. RTS 1820, e.g., pp. 287-8, 336.
16. (MS) BFBS *Home Corresp.*, letters from Francis Reynalds, 1810-17. Cf. BFBS *Reports* 1816-17, pp. 91-2.
17. (MS) BFBS *Home Corresp.*, letter from Francis Reynalds to Joseph Tarn, Sept. 2, 1811.

18. Ibid., letters from George Orton, 1812-31. Cf. BFBS *Reports* 1811-13, pp. 416-7.

19. (MS) BFBS *Home Corresp.* 1825-31. Cf. SML 1820, p. 23; 1821, pp. 94-5, 144. Re. Captain Reynalds' post-war involvement, see infra, p. 229.

20. Infra, p. 413.

21. Landers elaborates, in a letter to Joseph Tarn, Oct. 4, 1816, in (MS) BFBS *Home Corresp.*, on how he had left a large quantity of Sunday School books with "a Public Spirited Lady" in New York, and returned to find she had "fill'd the City with Sunday Schools." Presumably, the lady referred to was Mrs. Divie Bethune (cf. Foster 1960, p. 162). For the complete text of Captain Landers' fascinating letter, see transcript in Appendix No. 3 (pp. 620-21).

22. (MS) BFBS *Home Corresp.*, letter from Anthony Landers to Joseph Tarn, Oct. 4, 1816.

23. Ibid.

24. Landers 1815, See also infra, pp. 576-7.

25. (MS) BFBS *Home Corresp.*, accompanying the letter from Anthony Landers to Joseph Tarn, Oct. 4, 1816. SML 1822, pp. 196-8; cf. 1837, pp. 157-9. Also, infra, pp. 242-3.

26. Canton Vol. 1, 1904, pp. 59-62, 351-3.

27. Dudley 1821, pp. 203-4.

28. Ibid., p. 204.

29. (MS) Southwark Auxiliary Bible Society *Minutes,* May 12, 1813.

30. Supra, pp. 127-8.

31. (MS) Southwark Auxiliary Bible Society *Minutes,* July 14, 1813. Dudley 1821, p. 294. BFBS *Reports* 1814-15, pp. 201-2.

32. Ibid. The By-Laws, subsequently adopted, provide for the division of the General Committee into four District Committees, consisting of the members of each of the cooperating auxiliaries, and each given charge of the depositories within their respective districts (Dudley 1821, p. 295).

33. Dudley 1821, pp. 33-4 of the Appendices (No. XI).

34. Ibid., pp. 295-6. (MS) *Home Corresp.*, copy of resolution, May 11, 1815, of the Thames Union Bible Committee, enclosed with letter from Samuel Allen to Joseph Reyner, March 25, 1815; also, letter from Joseph Shewell to Joseph Tarn, Dec. 6, 1815.

35. Dudley 1821, pp. 296-7. A circular letter of appeal to auxiliaries in Southern England and the Midlands resulted in a promising initial response, especially from Cambridge and Norwich. This source was soon closed, however, since—as the Parent Committee pointed out—such application of auxiliary funds was incompatible with the principle of centralization of non-local responsibilities. (Dudley 1821, p. 297. Cf. [MS] BFBS *Minutes:* June 6, 1814; July 4, 1814; Oct. 3, 1814. Also, [MS] BFBS *Correspondence Books* No. 6, 1813-14, pp. 165, 300.

36. (MS) Southwark Auxiliary Bible Society *Minutes,* July 12, 1815. Dudley 1821, p. 297.

37. (MS) BFBS Home *Corresp.,* letter from Francis Reynalds to Joseph Tarn, June 24, 1813. Dudley 1821, pp. 327-8. (Here, the name is incorrectly spelt "Reynolds," and the month of founding given as "July.")

38. Canton Vol. 1, 1904, pp. 49, 53-6. Cf. NSM 1857, p. 103.

39. Dudley 1821, pp. 327, 329; also, pp. 34-5 of the *Appendices* (No. XI).

40. Owen 1816, Part II, pp. 586-7. Dudley 1821, p. 329.

41. Dudley 1821, p. 328. (Edinburgh Bible Society *Report* 1815, p. 55, also Canton Vol. 1, 1904, pp. 119-20, are examples of sources which ignore Captain Reynald's original version. Cf. supra, p. 140.)

42. (MS) Southwark Auxiliary Bible Society *Minutes,* July 12, 1815.

43. Ibid., Feb. 14, 1816. At this stage, "C.L." of Bermondsey published his conviction that waterfront Bible Associations should still be able to undertake merchant navy distribution "without the formation of another Society for this express object" (EM 1916, pp. 92-3).

44. (MS) Southwark Auxiliary Bible Society *Minutes:* March 12, 1817; Oct. 8, 1817. MSABS *Address* 1818, p. 1. Dudley 1821, pp. 297-8, 307-9. (The Jerusalem Coffee House, Cornhill, became for years the headquarters of the new Society.)

45. MSABS *Address* 1818, pp. 1-4. Cf. supra, pp. 540-54.

46. Ibid., p. 3.

47. Ibid., p. 1. MSABS *Prospectus and Regulations* 1818, pp. 20-1. BFBS *Reports* 1855-57, p. ccxxxviii.

48. MSABS *Prospectus and Regulations* 1818, p. 21.

49. Ibid., pp. 9, 12-3, 24.

50. (MS) Southwark Auxiliary Bible Society *Minutes,* Jan. 14, 1818.

51. Canton Vol. 1, 1904, p. 329.

52. Cf. BFBS *Monthly Extracts,* Jan. 31, 1819, p. 69.

53. Dudley 1821, pp. 310-11, 338. At its first Annual Meeting, the Society was compelled to report that circular letters to owners, ship's husbands and captains of all vessels entered out at the Custom House, during an experimental period of three months, "did not produce a single application for Bibles at the Society's depository in London," and that all similar efforts had met with only "total and absolute failure . . ." (Ibid., p. 310.) Again, in their *Annual Report* for 1820, the Committee voiced "the regret and disappointment they have felt at the backwardness which has been shown by the merchants and shipowners *in general* to promote the society's objectives . . ." (Ibid., p. 338).

54. Dudley 1821, p. 311. MSABS *AR* 1826, p. 24.

55. (MS) Southwark Auxiliary Bible Society *Minutes,* March 12, 1817.

56. (MS) BFBS *Home Corresp.,* letter from John Cox to Joseph Reyner, June 4, 1806. (An extract is quoted in BFBS *Reports* 1805-10, pp. 156-7.)

57. (MS) BFBS *Home Corresp.,* Letters from John Cox, 1808-9. Cf. letter from the Rev. L. Vaughan, Dec. 2, 1811.

58. Ibid., letter from John Cox to Joseph Tarn, June 30, 1809.

59. BFBS *Reports* 1818-19, pp. 263-5 (quoting from MSABS *AR* 1819).

60. Ibid. Of the 24,765 men on ships supplied during the Society's first year, 3,094 were apparently unable to read (p. 265).

61. Ibid., pp. 264-71. BFBS *Monthly Extracts* No. 20, 1819, pp. 77-8. Cf. extracts in BFBS *Reports* and *Monthly Extracts* for succeeding years, also quoted in various religious periodicals. In the USA, see e.g., Bible Society of Philadelphia *AR* 1819, pp. 50-2; also, ABS *AR* 1820, pp. 171-4.

62. BFBS *Reports* 1818-19, pp. 266-8.

63. Ibid., pp. 268-70.

64. MSABS *AR* 1826, p. 15.

65. BFBS *Reports* 1818-19, pp. 265-6.

66. MSABS *AR* 1826, pp. 30, 35. BFBS *Monthly Extracts* No. 186, 1833, p. 675. The BFBS had, from the start, realistically stated, "it would be happy to receive such an Auxiliary, although it might require that the whole of its Funds should be expended in the purchase of Bibles." ([MS] BFBS *Minutes,* Jan. 5, 1818).

67. Note the different situations with W.H. Angas and Ward Stafford, respectively (infra. pp. 251-60, 418-24).

68. (MS) BFBS *Minutes,* July 16, 1816. Dudley 1821, p. 297. BFBS *Monthly Extracts* No. 95, 1825, pp. 17-8; No. 117, 1827, p. 114; No. 139, 1829, p. 214.

69. Dudley 1821, pp. 305-6. Note the concern of the Sunderland Auxiliary Bible Society for Scripture "destitution" among the 500 vessels trading from that port, and the rapid response of the Edinburgh Bible Society, 1810-11 (Canton Vol. 1, 1904, pp. 96-7).

70. Dudley 1821, p. 298.

71. BFBS *Reports* 1818-19, p. 290 (footnote). Dudley 1821, pp. 298-302.

72. Captain Reynalds had been appointed acting secretary of the Provisional Committee, and had written to London in advance to obtain a copy of the rules and regulations of the Thames Marine Bible Association Committee. (MS) BFBS *Home Corresp.,* letter from Francis Reynalds to Joseph Tarn, Feb. 1, 1817. (MS) BFBS *Minutes,* March 3, 1817. Dudley 1821, pp. 302-4. Cf. BFBS *Reports* 1814-15, p. 506.

73. Dudley 1821, pp. 304-5.

74. By 1821, these three societies had sold to seamen 3,771 Bibles and Testaments, remitted a gift of £113.9.3 to the Parent Society, and reported a total of 25 Marine Bible Associations formed on ships from their respective ports. The corresponding data from the London MSABS was: 3,053 copies sold (with 9,100 gratuitously distributed), £1,500 received from the Parent Society, and not one Marine Bible Society yet reported. Dudley 1821, pp. 337-8.

75. Dudley 1821, pp. 299-305, 321-2.

76. Ibid., pp. 299-305, 336-7.

77. Ibid., p. 305. Information on Methodist influence supplied by Dr. Deryck W. Lovegrove at Author's disputation, June 2, 1984.

78. Weibust 1969, pp. 42-3, 214-5.

79. Edinburgh Bible Society *Report* 1819, pp. 14, 53-5. SML 1820, pp. 305-8. Dudley 1821, pp. 317-9. Information on Baptist and Independent influence supplied by Dr. Deryck W. Lovegrove at Author's disputation, June 2, 1984.

80. BFBS Monthly *Extracts* No. 18, 1819, p. 69. BFBS *Reports* 1818-19, p. 255. Dudley 1821, pp. 316-7.

81. SML 1820, p. 344; cf. p. 353. Dudley 1821, pp. 306-7.

82. Dudley 1821, pp. 341-2. SML 1822, pp. 109-10. The Association was, in 1818, united with the West London Auxiliary Bible Society (Dudley 1821, p. 341). Cf. infra. pp.300-2.

83. Edinburgh Bible Society *Report* 1819, p. 14.

84. Supra, p. 146.

85. Infra, pp. 412-7.

86. Svenska Bibel-Sällskapet 1816, pp. 42-3. BFBS *Reports* 1816-17, p. 19. BFBS *Monthly Extracts* No. 21, 1819, p. 82. Edinburgh Bible Society *Report* 1820, pp. 53-4. Canton Vol. 1, 1904, p. 448. Cf. Dudley's different dating (1821, p. 340).

87. Svenska Bibel-Sällskapet 1819, p. 23; 1820, pp. 20-1; 1821, pp. 35-6; 1822, pp. 29-30. BFBS *Reports* 1818-19, p. 319; cf. ABS *AR* 1820, pp. 159-61. BFBS *Monthly Extracts* 1828, pp. 175-6. Canton Vol. 1, 1904, pp. 217, 448.

88. BFBS *Reports* 1816-17, pp. 268-9. NMBS *Report* 1818, pp. 11-2. Canton Vol. 1, 1904, pp. 407-8. The work of the Auxiliary was later supplemented by Dr. J. Pinkerton, when visiting hospitalized seamen and prisoners in hulks in Cronstadt, 1820 (BFBS *Reports* 1820-21, pp. 54-5).

89. Bibelselskabet i Danmark *Maanedlige Efterretninger* No. 6, 1820, cc. 73-80; *Sjette Beretning* 1821, p. 35; *Syvende Beretning* 1822, pp. 33-4. BFBS *Reports* 1820-21, pp. xl, 110.

90. BFBS *Reports* 1814-15, p. 505; 1818-19, p. 293. Canton Vol. 1, 1904, p. 202. There were, a few years later, also reports of a Prussian Marine Bible Society, and a Royal Marine Bible Society of Berlin ([MS] Knight, Part I, n.d., pp. 73-4).

91. BFBS *Reports* 1820-21, p. xxiii; 1822-23, pp. xxvi-xxvii. (Based on contents of the 6th and 7th *Reports* of the United Netherlands Bible Society.)

92. Captain Reynalds found, during a call at Cronstadt earlier in 1816, that there was a great dearth of Scriptures among "thousands of Poor Russians (Sailors especially) . . . as well as . . . numbers of Natives of other countrys resident there." He encouraged the local English minister, the Rev. Mr. Marshall, to cooperate in meeting these needs. ([MS] BFBS *Home Corresp.,* letter from Francis Reynalds to Joseph Tarn, Oct. 30, 1816.) The annual distribution lists of BFBS *Reports* during and immediately after the Napoleonic War give numerous examples of such endeavors.

93. Infra, p. 595.

94. Dudley 1821, pp. 336-7.

95. Supra, pp. 71-90.

96. Infra, pp. 152-6.

97. Supra, p. 137.

98. The BFBS recognized the validity of this reasoning, and only a Corresponding Committee was then formed. This proved eminently active, however, not least among this shipping, with the zealous support of its secretary, Lt. J.W. Bailey, RN, and local Methodists. (The quotation is from a letter by Dr. Michael Parker, Royal Artillery, Sept. 28, 1820, in [MS] Cann 1969.)

99. Re. this so-called "Hopeless Charge," see supra, pp. 51-2, and infra, pp. 539-40.

100. NSM 1828, pp. 385-6. New Schaff-Herzog Vol. 10, 1911, p. 316, states incorrectly that "a Methodist clergyman, George Charles Smith, established prayer-meetings for seamen on the Thames at London."

101. G.C. Smith, who worked closely with Zebedee Rogers from 1817 on, and eventually buried him, uses the first name "Zebedee" consistently. This is also the name referred to in (MS) PLS *Minutes,* April 14 and 21, 1818. (Only in his earliest published allusion to him does Smith refer to him anonymously as "A—," cf. Bethel, pp. 4-5.) The name of the "maritime" tribe of Israel, "Zebulon," has been generally adopted by American sources dealing with the Thames Revival (e.g., *Quarterly Christian Spectator* 1831, p. 256; SMNY 1830-31, p. 235; Warren 1858, p. 4; ASFS AR 1860, p. 6; *The Encyclopædia of Missions* Vol. 2, 1891, p. 317). SML 1836, then under the BFSS, has a third variant, "Zachariah," on p. 153. Cf. Heasman 1962, p. 248.

102. Canute's Dyke, built (according to the Saxon Chronicle) by the invading Danes in order to bypass London Bridge with their ships of war, is traditionally believed to have begun at the southeastern end of Rotherhithe, where the Howland Great Wet Dock was eventually constructed. (The latter, later known as Greenland Dock, was completed around the year 1700, and is claimed to be the oldest wet dock in the country.) During the early part of the 19th century, large dock systems were developed on the marshlands of the Rotherhithe peninsula, making this the center of London's timber trade (ultimately amalgamated as the Surrey Commercial Docks). Walford 1878, p. 134. Wheatley 1891, pp. 174-5. Beck 1907, pp. 1-2, 15-6, 174, 200-1, 226-8. Besant Vol. 3, 1912, pp. 135-6. Broodbank 1912, pp. 53-6. Wilson 1966, pp. 5-9, 47-9. Cf. Kvale 1981.

103. SML 1820, p. 7. SMNY 1856-57, p. 354. G.C. Smith *Bethel* n.d., p. 4. Cf. MSABS *AR,* p. 22. Matthews 1911, p. 185. Concerning Rogers' family origin, Smith states elsewhere: "Z.R. was a native, I believe, of *Rochester;* I know he was a freeman, as I have seen him frequently go down to Rochester respecting the privilege he enjoyed as freeman" (NSM 1837, p. 876).

104. The narrative was "handed in by Z.R. as his own account of the commencement of those important prayer-meetings afloat," included in a general account of Bethel Meetings drawn up by G.C. Smith, and read at a meeting commemorating the thirteenth anniversary of their origin, June 22, 1827. (SMNY 1828-29, p. 227.) Purporting to be originally prepared by Rogers himself, this narrative implies greater authenticity than Smith's own, slightly variant account in *Bethel* 1819, pp. 4-5, and SML 1820, pp. 7-8 (although this, too, was, in the main, endorsed by Captain Simpson himself, cf. SML 1825, Suppl. p. 16). Many inconsistencies are dectectable in Smith's much later account in NSM 1861, pp. 189-90.

105. SML 1820, p. 226. SMNY 1828-29, p. 227. NSM 1829, Part II, pp. 343-4.

106. SML 1821, p. 321.

107. Smith states that Captain Simpson had "heard a sermon" at a Methodist chapel in his home town of North Shields before sailing for London. This had already produced "soul-affecting convictions, but not conversion," before he made his way to the Silver-Street Chapel in Rotherhithe. (NSM 1861, p. 189.) In the meantime, Captain Simpson's spiritual quest had been intensified as a result of another chapel visit; according to a personal statement published in

NSM 1839, Suppl. *St. George's Wesleyan Chapel, East London,* p. 3, Captain Simpson had, while anchored at Blackwall waiting for access to discharge in the Pool, attended a Sunday evening service at St. George's Wesleyan Chapel, East London, and there become personally "convinced of sin." Following his conversion, there is evidence that Captain Simpson continued his connection with the Methodists at home (cf. NSM 1829, Part II, pp. 302-3).

108. *Captain David Simpson:* Besides actively cooperating in the expanding Bethel Prayer Meetings in the Lower and Upper Pools of the Thames, Captain Simpson offered public prayers at the first annual meeting of the BFSFBU in 1820, and at the memorable joint Coronation Day Service on the *Ark,* July 19, 1821. After 1825, he is mentioned as having taken part with both prayer and preaching at public services at the London Mariners' Church in Wellclose Square. His pioneer efforts abroad included innovative shipboard services under the Bethel Flag at both Memel and Archangel. He is listed as a member of the committee of the Stepney and Wapping Bethel Mission Society (in cooperation with Zebedee Rogers) in the early 1820's, and that of the BFSSFS in the late 1820's. On a preaching mission to Tyneside in May 1838, G.C. Smith made a point of once more visiting his "old, and excellent, and faithful friend, Captain Simpson," at North Shields, and was "much affected at his weakness, as he was . . . one of the most worthy of all." (SML 1820, pp. 226, 457; 1821, p. 306; 1826, pp. 119-20, 441. NSM 1828, pp. 205, 234; 1832, pp. 152-4; 1838 Suppl. *Greenwich Fair and Hospital,* p. 9. Cf. *The Evangelical Magazine* 1821, pp. 342-3. Also, G.C. Smith *The Press Gang,* n.d., p. 12.)

109. SML 1820, pp. 7-8. G.C. Smith *The British Ark* 1823, p. 8; *Bethel* n.d., pp. 4-6. (SMNY 1830-31, p. 336, states incorrectly that these meetings in 1814-16 were "chiefly confined to the Friendship.")

110. Note, for example, the dark picture drawn by a "coal meter" of the type of seaman he could remember from his work on the Thames. (MSABS *AR* 1826, p. 22. Cf. Runciman 1926, pp. 40ff.)

111. SML 1824, p. 376; 1825 Suppl. p. 6.

112. E.g., BFBS *Monthly Extracts* No. 95, 1825, pp. 17-8. Cf. Matthews 1911, p. 185. Runciman 1926, pp. 106-8. It seems significant that the coastal districts of Yorkshire and Northumberland had been the scene of particularly strong revival movements in recent times. Torial Joss was a classical example of what could result (supra, pp. 9, 16).

113. Note especially SML 1820, p. 208; 1826, p. 442. NSM 1828, p. 189.

114. Here was the scene of the life-labors of that forceful Puritan divine, Thomas Gataker (1574-1654). (Beck 1907, pp. 44-5, 164. DNB Vol. 21, 1890, pp. 60-2.) Here, too, was the Nonconformist meeting-house of that intrepid 17th-century seamen's preacher, James Janeway (supra, p. 16).

115. Southwark Park Wesleyan Chapel n.d., pp. 1-3.

116. NSM 1828, p. 187; 1861, p. 190.

117. SML 1820, p. 52. Wilson 1966, p. 29.

118. *Samuel Jennings:* although there are also scattered references elsewhere in his magazines, G.C. Smith's article on Mr. Jennings of Rotherhithe in NSM 1828, pp. 187-9, gives important data in a more coherent form. *The Wesleyan Methodist Magazine* April 1828, in an obituary on Jenning's death at Rotherhithe, Jan. 26, 1828, gives the following summary of his spiritual

standpoint: "He had very humble views of himself; but exalted views of the Saviour" (p. 285). E.P. Harris has recorded the result of his research into the exact extent of the property acquired by Jennings from 1811 onwards on the Rotherhithe riverside (see Harris, 1935). In (MS) PLS *Minutes* 1818-28, p. 126, Jennings' address is shown as "Near the Horse ferry Rotherhithe." An *Indenture* dated August 28, 1855, concerning a subsequent conveyance of the property, contains the name of his wife, Sarah Jennings, and six surviving children ([MS] Indenture 1855). Where sources refer to the first name, it is given as "Samuel." (The initial "J" in NSM 1828, p. 125, is, therefore, incorrect.) Re. Mr. Jennings' Sunday School, see also Wilson 1966, pp. 29-30; cf. Lewis 1883.

119. NSM 1828, p. 125; 1838, pp. 299-300.
120. NSM 1838, pp. 299-300; 1857, p. 84.
121. NSM 1828, pp. 187-9. It is stated that Jennings had "*one hundred and twenty-five members* in his classes at one time." It is not clear, however, whether any organized "Class-Meeting" was ever restricted to seamen alone, although this is assumed in SMNY 1828-29, p. 228. (Cf. SML 1820, p. 9; 1825, p. 248. NSM 1837, p. 186; 1838, pp. 299-300.)
122. NSM 1828, p. 203.
123. Ibid., p. 188. The Rev. Joseph Sutcliffe (d. 1856) served the Deptford Circuit in 1816-17. He is represented as having been "a very eminent minister in his day," renowned for his biblical scholarship. After G.C. Smith had become heavily involved in public controversy, Sutcliffe, in 1832, sent him a donation, affirming that his heart and soul were still "with Mr. Smith and the sailor's cause." (NSM 1832, p. 81. Hill 1853, p. 182. *Minutes of the Methodist Conferences* 1859, pp. 211-2.)
124. SMNY 1828-29, p. 228. A youthful local preacher from the Deptford Circuit, William Munro, is also mentioned as one who came to the aid of Rogers at his meetings in the Lower Pool. (Cf. Milne 1851, p. 6.)
125. NSM 1828, p. 189.
126. Ibid., pp. 187-9. "The School-Room" is, in 1820, described as "about 40 feet long, neatly papered, and filled with forms," with Jennings himself having his customary place "at his desk." At the early Sunday meeting, G.C. Smith notes the hymns and prayers were *short,* the tunes *lively,* "and the whole very refreshing. . . ." (SML 1820, p. 209).
127. NSM 1828, p. 188. Cf. SML 1825, p. 248. Supra, Note No. 121.
128. SML 1820, p. 9. NSM 1828, pp. 188-9; 1837, p. 876. Estimates of the number of seamen who might attend at the School-Room vary in the sources quoted, from 50 to 70.
129. NSM 1828, p. 187.
130. NSM 1838, p. 299. Cf. infra, p. 158.
131. NSM 1828, p. 189. For his full name, see SML 1838, p. 114.
132. NSM 1837, p. 876; 1858, p. 414.
133. SML 1820, pp. 147-8. This account must, from its close proximity to the events, be considered more authentic than his retrospect in 1841, which contains several deviating details, some of which are quite manifestly incorrect (SML 1841, pp. 133-6).

134. SML 1841, p. 133.

135. SML 1820, p. 147; 1841, p. 133. Captain Mortin, evidently overwhelmed at the sight of his own cabin boy engaging in public prayer, cried repeatedly, "Lord, bless this lad—Lord, bless the lad!" According to Wilkins, both experienced conversion.

136. SML 1820, p. 147. From Captain Wilkins' own earliest account, little more than three years after the event, it seems that the *Happy Return* was the first ship on which the lantern signal for prayer-meetings was hoisted. G.C. Smith implies that is was from the top-gallant masthead of the *Thomas* of North Shields. (*Bethel* n.d. p. 5. SML 1820, p. 8.) Since Captain Wilkins, in his 1841 retrospect, refers to the peak-end (or outer extremity of a gaff) as the first position of the lantern signal, and "shortly after" — the top-gallant masthead, it is conceivable that these two positions refer to the *Happy Return* and the *Thomas* respectively. (SML 1841, p. 133.)

137. NSM 1828, pp. 188-9; 1861, p. 190.

138. SML 1820, pp. 147-8.

139. Ibid., p. 148; 1841, p. 133. Cf. Port of Dublin Society *Report* 1823, p. 6.

140. NSM 1861, pp. 190-1. Kingsford 1947, pp. 157-8.

141. Note, for example, SMNY 1834-5, p. 348, on the presentation of a British Bethel Flag in New York (in 1821), as the condition for "Bethel operations" commencing in the USA.

142. NSM 1828, p. 189; 1837, p. 876. SMNY 1828-29, p. 228. SML 1841, p. 133. Note: In 1821, however, G.C. Smith publicly introduced a seaman by the name of Peter Craig, whom he then believed to be the one who "put the first letters together." (SML 1821, pp. 456-7. Cf. G.C. Smith *The Press Gang* n.d., p. 12.)

143. G.C. Smith *Bethel* n.d., p. 6. SML 1820, p. 8. SMNY 1828-29, p. 228. Captain Hindhulph's initial and the spelling of his surname are based on the official list of committee members of the Stepney and Wapping Bethel Mission Society (G.C. Smith *The Press Gang* n.d., p. 12). The *Zephyr* is, in NSM 1837, p. 877, described as being registered in North Shields.

144. SML 1820, p. 395. NSM 1828, p. 189.

145. SML 1841, p. 134.

146. E.g., SML 1821, p. 480. CC 1882, p. 17. Webster 1932, p. 43.

147. The entry in (MS) BFSFSBU *Minutes,* Sept. 17, 1822, includes the star and the dove in the original composition. (See transcription, infra, Note No. 160.) See CC 1914, p. 55, for a reproduction of the standard version of the Bethel Flag. The cover of the October number of SMNY 1839 provides an American example of the same (here with a white border along the top and base).

148. E.g., SML 1825, p. 242. CC 1913, p. 110.

149. Both the word "Bethel" and the star are described in early version as having been in red, on a blue background. (G.C. Smith *The British Ark* 1823, pp. 3-4. G.C. Smith *Bethel* n.d., p. 5. Cf. SML 1837, p. 17.) This juxtaposition of the colors was contrary to usage in heraldry, however. (*Encyclopædia Britannica* 1968, Vol. 9, p. 398.) The star is also represented as being yellow. (SML 1820, pp. 456, 478-9. NSM 1828, p. 200.) An improvised version in Leeds, with the dove in green, and the background in crimson, was deemed "not

right." (NSM 1828, pp. 215-6.) A border in white met with approval, however. (NSM 1828, pp. 127, 231, 262; 1832, p. 341.) In the 1820's the word "Union" was occasionally added to the word "Bethel," to underscore the bond of fellowship for which the emblem stood. (Cf. Matthews 1911, p. 83.)

150. Matthews 1911, p. 186.

151. Examples of the standard interpretation are: SML 1820, pp. 478-9; 1821, p. 499; 1823, p. 134; 1827, p. 148. The Scriptural allusions for "Bethel," the star, and the dove, are found in: Gen. 28:16-19, Matt. 2:2, Gen. 8:11, respectively. The Rev. Edward W. Matthews, himself converted under the Bethel Flag as a seaman in 1863, became, as senior secretary of the BFSS, an eager proponent of a Trinitarian interpretation. Seeing "Bethel," the star and the dove as symbolic of the Father, Son, and Holy Spirit, he solves the problem of the olive branch in the following fascinating manner: "The Dove [depicts] . . . 'The Spirit of God descending as a Dove.' But in the mouth of the Dove the sailor put an olive branch, pointing back to when the earth was wrecked, and the few saved were saved in a ship! Looking forward, he said within himself, if Nations and Tribes are to be saved, Christianized, civilized, there is no new way, it must still be by *ships!*" (CC 1913, p. 130.) Nevertheless, the tradition of Christian symbolism is quite unequivocal on this score: The dove carrying an olive-branch points to the wrath of God assuaged, *not* the third person in the Trinity. (The Scottish Sailors' and Soldiers' Bethel Flag Union *AR*, p. 32. Cf. Ursin 1965, pp. 105-7, 229-30. Kverndal 1965, pp. 421-2.) The star of the Bethel Flag was, as the Star of Bethlehem, normally five-pointed (although there were exceptions). It is noteworthy that where, in Roman Catholic tradition, the Virgin Mary is seen as "Stella Maris," it is the *five*-pointed star which has been most frequently used (Ursin 1965, pp. 191-2; cf. infra, p. 403). An early (1822) *American* interpretation of the Bethel Flag describes it as "the standard of the Prince of Peace [which] invites all who seek rest and peace to come, and when the shades of evening are thickening . . . , the symbol of the evening star reminds them of the Babe of Bethlehem" (SMNY 1835-36, p. 266).

152. NSM 1833, p. 160.

153. This has, understandably, been particularly the case with the BSS (who still retain the star and dove in their official emblem). Other examples of institutional emblems with elements of the Bethel Flag: SML 1821, p. 376; 1822, p. 383; 1823, p. 308; 1841, p. 81. Green 1828, pp. 153-5. The Scottish Sailors' and Soldiers' Bethel Flag Union *AR* 1836, p. 32. CC 1886, pp. 116-7. ASFS *The Acts* 1908, pp. 108-9.

154. Infra, pp. 265-79.

155. *Zebedee Rogers:* After years of voluntary promotion of prayer-meetings on the Thames, Rogers was employed by the BFSFSBU, as superintendent of the Bethel Meetings in the Lower Pool; in 1822, he fell into disfavor with the committee and resigned, although he continued to be warmly defended by G.C. Smith. His health gave reason for anxiety at this time, having "suffered greatly by severe colds, caught in the service of the Society." ([MS] BFSFSBU *Minutes,* November 13 and 27, 1822, cf. March 19 and 26, 1823. SML 1824, p. 427. NSM 1837, p. 878; 1844, p. 257.) He was later engaged by Smith as Agent of the BFSSFS for the Lower Pool. (NSM 1829, pp. 344-5; 1830, pp 252-3.) Finally he served as a "Steward" of the Sailors' Rest Asylum in Cannon-Street Road. (NSM 1831, pp. 134, 226, 235; 1833, pp. 212, 470; 1855, p. 230.)

156. See c.g., SML 1820, pp. 65, 147-8, 453, 478. NSM 1858, p. 414. G.C. Smith *The Press Gang* n.d., p. 12. In 1826, he is recorded as having preached for G.C. Smith at the Mariner's Church on more than one occasion (SML 1826, pp. 441, 479).

157. Re. the background of the foundation of the British and Foreign Sailors' Society (1833), see Part IV. Captain Wilkins heads the list of 100 "Bethel Captains" endorsing the BFSS in an 1837 *Bethel Covenant*, quoted in *A Voice from the Ocean*. (SML 1838, p. 114. Cf. SML 1840, pp. 402-4. NSM 1838, p. 10.) Infra, p. 368.

158. Early examples of such vacillating official statments of origin are: BFSS *What are Bethel Meetings?* n.d., p. 3. BFSS *Lord Gambier and the Bethel Flag* n.d., pp. 2-3. SML 1840, p. 402. BFSS *AR* 1851, p. 2. The climax was reached on the eve of the First World War: at the 95th Annual Meeting of the BFSS, May 19, 1913, it was decided to launch a massive £20,000 Bethel Flag Centenary Fund, thereby turning to promotional purposes the supposed invention of the flag by Captain Wilkins and his wife in 1814. Small silk replicas of the Bethel Flag were sent to Queen Alexandra and the heads of state of maritime nations throughout the world. (At the "Centennial Year" Annual Meeting, May 4, 1814, the Kaiser himself was, through his naval attaché, among those who promised a personal contribution.) A scheme was also started for supplying every day-school and Sunday-school throughout the British Empire with a Bethel Flag banner, containing the following inscription: "This Sailor's Flag, emblem of the ever-blessed Trinity was designed in 1814 by a sailor (Captain Wilkins) as a signal of Divine service for the Brotherhood of the Sea, culminating in the foundation of the above Society in 1818, which extended its stations to bless sailors socially, morally and spiritually of all nations, 'The sea is His.' " Many such banners had already been distributed before the outbreak of war. (CC 1913, pp. 109-11, 130-1, 1914, pp. 55-6, 91-102.) Examples of works into which the "Wilkins Version" has found its way: Timpson 1856, pp. 42-3; Luke 1868, p. 35; Hodder 1891, p. 57-8; Pike 1897, pp. 36-7; Matthews 1911, pp. 185-6; Riddle 1915, p. 18; Waltari 1925, p. 71; Anson 1964, p. 109; (MS) Schepen 1971, p. 6. (Kverndal 1965, p. 422, was also written before other sources became available to the Author.) American works have more consistently kept to the "Rogers Version." E.g.: SMNY 1828-9, pp. 227-8; 1830-31, pp. 235-6; Warren 1858, p. 4; Langley 1967, pp. 48-9.

159. The following are examples of the erroneous assumption that the word "Bethel" was used of Thames prayer-meetings *before* the invention of the Bethel Flag: BFSS *Lord Gambier and the Bethel Flag* n.d., p. 2. SMNY 1839-40, p. 89. Langley 1967, pp. 48-9.

160. SMNY 1828-29, p. 230. Cf. SML 1823, p. 354. Note: The (MS) BFSFSBU *Minutes* for Sept. 17, 1822, contain the following entry, "Resolved—That Mr. Van be informed that the Flag adopted by this Society, be that originally instituted being made of blue bunting with the word Bethel, a Star and Dove in the corners at the head & that Mr. Van be requested to inform Captains & others applying, that this is the Flag recommended by the Society."

161. NSM 1833, p. 470. Note: G.C. Smith's warm reaction against later attempts to "rob a poor man of the honour of being an instrument of so much good" (NSM 1841, Supplement, p. 35).

162. On the contrary, cf. SML 1820, p. 148; 1841, p. 133.

163. Abroad, Captain Wilkins' pioneering Bethel services in Memel and Hamburg were particularly noteworthy. (NSM 1832, pp. 204-6. SML 1840, pp. 402-4.) He died, "after long and faithful service in his Master's cause," in March 1851. (BFSS *AR* 1851, p. 2.)

164. G.C. Smith *Bethel* n.d., p. 8.

165. Ibid.

166. E.g., SML 1822, p. 189; 1841, pp. 133-4. *The Christian Guardian* 1826, p. 173.

167. NSM 1860, p. 69. Cf. supra, pp. 107-11.

168. SML 1841, p. 133.

169. Ibid.

170. G.C. Smith *The Custom House* n.d., p. 26.

171. SML 1841, pp. 133-4. Cf. 1820, p. 353.

172. G.C. Smith *The Custom House* n.d., pp. 26-8. Note Smith's statement that, to commemorate this event, seamen said, "Now we must have a Dove in the [Bethel] Flag, for we shall have peace" (NSM 1860, p. 71).

173. Trevelyan 1959, p. 466. Cf. SMNY 1876, p. 131. Also, Woodward 1938, pp. 60-2.

174. Cf. RTS 1820, pp. 295-6.

175. G.C. Smith *Bethel* n.d., pp. 8-9.

176. Cf. SML 1841, p. 134.

177. Thompson 1829, pp. 22, 40. Cf. SML 1822, p. 465. NSM 1857, p. 78. (G.C. Smith's spelling is inconsistent, however.)

178. (MS) BFBS *Home Corresp.*, letters from Thomas Phillips, Nov. 4, 1816, etc. Phillips' office is in 1817 described as located at Botolph Wharf, and in the 1820's as being at Cox's Quay, Lower Thames Street. (Cf. SML 1822, p. 470. NSM 1857, p. 78.)

179. (MS) BFBS Home Corresp., letter from Thomas Phillips, Nov. 4, 1816.

180. Ibid., letters from Thomas Phillips, 1816-30. (See especially March 31, 1818; March 14, 1822; Sept. 23, 1830.)

181. Phillips' letter describing his discovery of the Bethel prayer-meetings was published by the RTS in their *Reports* (cf. RTS 1820, p. 383). It was republished in: G.C. Smith Bethel, n.d., pp. 6-8; SML 1820, pp. 8-9; Thompson 1829, pp. 22-3. The last-mentioned source openly identifies *Onesiphorus,* the anonymous author of this and similar reports, with Thomas Phillips (cf. 2 Tim. 1:16, 4:19). Phillips' informant was Joseph Valentine, "a Deacon of the Rev. George Clayton's Church at Walworth" (Thompson 1829, p. 22).

182. G.C. Smith *Bethel* n.d., p. 6. SML 1825, p. 198.

183. G.C. Smith *Bethel* n.d., pp. 6-8. The captain in question was apparently Anthony Wilkins again, and the ship the *Hannah* (cf. SML 1841, p. 135).

184. G.C. Smith *Bethel* n.d., pp. 6-17. Cf. SML 1820, pp. 8-11, 50-4. CH 1820-21, p. 402.

185. Supra, pp. 135-48.

186. RTS 1820, pp. 43, 45, 68, 110, 161, 217, 287-8.

187. E.g., Ryther 1803, Janeway 1806 and 1810, Flavel 1808. Cf. supra, pp. 12, 16.

188. E.g., *The Seaman's Confidence* n.d., Clark 1801, Young 1810. The Rev. George Young of Whitby was known for his early concern for seafarers. His sermon preached to Greenland ships, on the eve of departure, March 10, 1816, was also published. (CC 1879, pp. 39-40, 81; 1901, p. 209.) Noteworthy too, were the new editions of John Newton's *Narrative,* e.g., the 9th London edition, 1799; and of the naval surgeon James Meikle's *Solitude Sweetened* 1803 and *The Traveller* 1805.

189. DNB Vol. 20, 1889, pp. 24-5. Forster 1814. Newton 1799, Meikle 1803 and 1805.

190. *The Evangelical Magazine* 1806, pp. 508-9.

191. RTS 1820, pp. ix-xiv. Hewitt 1949, pp. 32-3.

192. *The Evangelical Magazine* 1807, pp. 22-5. Griffin 1818; *James Covey* n.d. RTS 1820, pp. ix-xiv. CHSM 1824, p. 771. SML 1826, p. 273. The Rev Charles Williamson (chaplain to the Levant Company's "Factory" in Smyrna, 1817-20) even managed to negotiate a translation into modern Greek at the press of the Ecumenical Patriarchate in Constantinople, 1818. (MS) BFBS *Foreign Corresp.,* letter from Charles Williamson to the Rev. C.F.A. Steinkopff, Sept. 21, 1818. Clogg 1968, passim. Cf. early Swedish and Danish translations, infra, p. 595.

193. RTS 1820, pp. 337, 369, 417. *The Christian Guardian* 1826, pp. 173-4. Marks *Retrospect* 1843, p. 245. Marsden 1847, pp. 37-8.

194. RTS 1820, p. 337.

195. RTS 1820, p. 369. Marks 1823. Cf. Marks 1818, p. iii; 1826, Preface. Smith 1874, pp. 4-5.

196. G.C. Smith *Bethel* n.d., pp. 16-17.

197. Ibid, pp. 10-3, 16-7. SML 1820, p. 347.

198. G.C. Smith *Bethel* n.d., p. 17. Cf. SML 1822, p. 266.

199. NSM 1829, p. 82.

200. G.C. Smith *The Custom House* n.d., pp. 37-8.

201. SML 1820, p. 24; 1824, p. 320. NSM 1857, pp. 79-80. Lt. Francis Collins was active in the founding of the BFSFSBU and its first committee. (SML 1821, p. 494; 1824, pp. 423-4. G.C. Smith *English Sailors* n.d., pp. 30, 32.)

202. NSM 1857, pp. 101-2.

203. G.C. Smith *The Scilly Islands* 1828, p. 5. NSM 1857, pp. 102-3. Matthews 1960, pp. 124-8. Graham, 1964, p. 31.

204. The year of the first arrival of Smith and Jeffery is given as 1815, in a petition to the BFBS from a public meeting in Trescow School-Room, May 9, 1818. Here, the inhabitants gratefully acknowledge the aid of these two in providing preaching, and founding "Sabbath and week-day Schools." They humbly request a new gratuitous shipment of Scriptures, as they have "for many months been in the greatest distress for lack of bread." ([MS] BFBS *Home Corresp.,* encl. with letter from G.C. Smith, May 17, 1818.) Smith simul-

taneously requests a supply of foreign Testaments for French, Danish, Swedish and Welsh ships, which "very often" call at the Scilly Islands, and whose crews then come into contact with the Rev. Mr. Jeffery. (NSM 1857, pp. 102-3. Cf. G.C. Smith *The Scilly Islands* 1828, pp. 4-5.) Jeffery was, at this time, the pioneer agent of the Baptist Missionary Society, founded that same year—1815. (Information supplied by Dr. Dereck V. Lovegrove, at Author's disputation, June 2, 1984.)

205. Matthews 1960, pp. 126-7.

206. G.C. Smith *The Scilly Islands* 1828, pp. 5-16. NSM 1857, pp. 98, 102-3. Matthews 1960, pp. 126-31.

207. G.C. Smith *The Scilly Islands* 1828, pp. 9, 11-4. NSM 1832, p. 98; 1857, p. 103; 1859, p. 441.

208. G.C. Smith *The Scilly Islands* 1828, p. 12. A suggestion in Matthews 1960, p. 127, that Smith should himself have provided the flag in advance, appears altogether too far-fetched. Smith doubtless had something of a "showman" in him; but he was no blackguard.

209. G.C. Smith *The Scilly Islands* 1828, p. 9.

210. Ibid., pp. 14-6, 64-6. Cf. Thompson 1829, pp. 14-5.

211. E.g., infra, pp. 356-8. Cf. NSM 1858, p. 465.

212. NSM 1857, p. 126; 1858, p. 543; 1861, pp. 106, 191. Cf. Boase and Courtney Vol. 2, 1882, p. 664. Boase Vol. 3, 1965, c. 628.

213. NSM 1834, p. 228; 1857, p. 103; 1861, pp. 191, 535.

214. NSM 1857, p. 104.

215. G.C. Smith *The Floating Chapel* n.d., p. 24. Matthews 1911, p. 197. Smith's published works include several tracts written in vehement protest against the interference of officialdom with open-air preaching. He was adamant against police action on this score to the last. (Cf., e.g., NSM 1858, p. 407.)

216. Thompson used Smith's North Devon journal as the basis of appeals in founding the new society in 1819. (G.C. Smith *The Scilly Islands* 1828, pp. 4-5. Thompson 1829, p. 20. NSM 1833, p. 223; 1834, p. 229; 1857, pp. 102-4. Luke 1868, pp. 36-7, 41-2, 228. Mee 1947, pp. 174-5.) "The Christian Education Society" was presumably founded in 1825 (Brown 1961, pp. 338, 340).

217. E.g., BFBS *Minutes,* April 7, 1817. BFBS *Reports* 1816-17, p. 334. RTS 1820, pp. 141, 165, 342.

218. G.C. Smith *British Villages* n.d., pp. 2-3, 6-7. Cf. infra, pp. 212-7.

219. Infra, pp. 327-39.

220. NSM 1857, pp. 100-3.

221. NSM 1861, p. 535.

222. G.C. Smith Bethel n.d., p. 9. G.C. Smith *The British Ark* 1823, p. 3. Thompson 1829, pp. 22-3. NSM 1856, p. 270; 1857, pp. 58-9, 78.

223. G.C. Smith *The British Ark* 1823, pp. 3-9. Cf. G.C. Smith *Bethel* n.d., p. 9. NSM 1837, pp. 876-7; 1861, p. 192.

224. G.C. Smith *The British Ark* 1823, pp. 4-5.

225. Ibid., pp. 5-9.

226. The text of the sermon was the same as on the *Dolphin* in 1809, and at Carter Lane in 1812: Jonah 1:6, applied to "the long sleep of sin." (G.C. Smith *The British Ark* 1823, pp. 9-12. G.C. Smith *Bethel* n.d., p. 9. Thompson 1829, p. 23.) The statement in Warren 1858, p. 5, that Smith first preached on the *John* is inconsistent with other sources.

227. Thompson 1829, p. 23. NSM 1837, p. 877; 1858, p. 412; 1861, pp. 192, 219.

228. Supra, pp. 127-8.

229. G.C. Smith *Bethel* n.d., p. 9. G.C. Smith *The British Ark* 1823, pp. 12-3. SML 1821, pp. 471-2. NSM 1832, p. 212; 1837, p. 877; 1857, pp. 77-8; 1858, p. 412; 1860, pp. 363-4; 1861, p. 192. Captain Thomas Hill of 77 Wapping Wall became, in 1818, a member of the Founding Committee of the Port of London Society, whose floating chapel was to be moored in precisely the same part of the Thames as the *Agenoria*. ([MS] PLS *Minutes* 1818. SML 1821, pp. 471-2.) Captain Posgate went on to become an active Bethel Captain, before he finally perished by shipwreck. (SML 1824, p. 419. NSM 1838, pp. 11-2.) The impact of the *Agenoria* service was such, that a commemoration service on the same ship four years later also attracted "an immense congregation." (SML 1821, p. 472. G.C. Smith *The Custom House* n.d., pp. 28-9.)

230. G.C. Smith *The British Ark* 1823, pp. 12-3. SML 1821, pp. 471-2. NSM 1857, p. 78.

231. G.C. Smith *The British Ark* 1823, p. 13.

232. Ibid., pp. 13-4. G.C. Smith *The Custom House* n.d., p. 28.

233. G.C. Smith *The British Ark* 1823, pp. 14-5.

234. Ibid., pp. 17-8. Cf. G.C. Smith *Bethel* n.d., p. 9. SML 1820, p. 166.

235. NSM 1858, p. 465 (quoting *The Christian World,* Sept. 10, 1858). Cf. ASFS *AR* 1860, p. 7.

236. NSM 1856, p. 63. *The Revival,* No. 179, 1862, p. 303; No. 181, 1863, p. 23. DNB Vol. 53, 1898, p. 42. The precise origin of this title is obscure. It is certain that Smith was never a boatswain himself (cf. NSM 1833, pp. 407-8). The boatswain's mate in his famous tract series was Bob; James, who more closely reflected Smith's own life, was a quartermaster. However, there was probably much about Smith's general manner which corresponded with the popular conception of a boatswain (cf. NSM 1838, p. 16). The assumption in CC 1879, p. 146, that he was "in the boatswain department" is as incorrect as that article's uncertainty of Smith's earlier midshipman's status (cf. supra, p. 116).

237. NSM 1833, pp. 190-1; 1837, p. 877. SML 1841, p. 134. Captain Wilkin's estimate of "about August" cannot be depended upon, however. Cf. his quite incorrect dating of Jennings' death.

238. Ryther 1806, pp. v-vi. DNB Vol. 50, 1897, p. 70. There were other similarities; Ryther and Smith, both born of Yorkshire stock, were both more than once placed under arrest on account of their preaching activities.

239. Cf. NSM 1828, p. 395. Warren 1858, p. 5.

240. Cf. CC 1879, pp. 47-8. Matthews 1911, p. 189.

241. NSM 1857, pp. 78, 300-1; cf. 1837, p 877; 1838, pp. 11-2. Smith compares the way in which this plan pervaded his thoughts, "waking and sleeping," with the situation of Wilberforce (SML 1820, pp. 166-7).

242. SML 1820, pp. 343-4.

243. *The Evangelical Magazine* 1812, pp. 345-6.

244. SML 1820, p. 162. Highmore 1822, pp. 812-3. The Marine Society *213th AR*, p. 1.

245. G.C. Smith *The British Ark* 1823, pp. 14-5, 17. G.C. Smith *The Log-Book* n.d., Vol. 1, p. 8. NSM 1857, p. 104.

246. G.C. Smith *The British Ark* 1823, pp. 15-6.

247. Ibid., p. 17.

248. Ibid., p. 15. G.C. Smith *The Custom House* n.d., pp. 50-4.

249. G.C. Smith *The British Ark* 1823, pp. 16-7.

250. SML 1820, p. 167. NSM 1857, p. 78.

251. SML 1820, p. 167. G.C. Smith *The Custom House* n.d., pp. 36-7.

252. SML 1820, p. 167. G.C. Smith *The British Ark* 1823, pp. 18-9. NSM 1857, p. 79.

253. *Robert Humphrey Marten,* who died December 11, 1839, is described in a memorial sermon preached by the Rev. William Temple, as "of a sanguine temperament," prone to become both "too warm" and, at times, deeply depressed. He is represented as having been manly in his avowal of Christian principles, and honest about his own shortcomings, deploring what he detected as a "love of human applause." (SML 1840, pp. 33-40. Cf. NSM 1857, p. 79.) Although other benevolent causes received his frequent support, he devoted himself, as from his 1817 meeting with G.C. Smith, principally to the Seamen's Cause, serving for fifteen years as treasurer of the PLS and subsequently the PLBUS. During this period of mounting controversy between his own societies and those of G.C. Smith, Marten does not, from available records, appear to have taken any part in public polemics, at least not under his own name (cf. infra, pp. 199-208).

254. SML 1820, p. 167.

255. Ibid., pp. 167-8. G.C. Smith *The British Ark* 1823, p. 19. NSM 1837, p. 877; 1857, pp. 79-80. Luke 1868, pp. 32-3.

256. SML 1820, pp. 168-9, 212. Matthews 1911, pp. 191-3.

257. *The Evangelical Magazine* Dec. 1817, pp. 479-80. Cf. G.C. Smith *The British Ark 1823,* pp. 21-4.

258. SML 1820, p. 212. G.C. Smith *The British Ark* 1823, Cf. SML 1820, footnote p. 88.

259. SML 1820, p. 212. Cf. NSM 1857, p. 80.

260. SML 1820, p. 212. Cf. *The Evangelical Magazine* Feb. 1818, p. 77. G.C. Smith *The British Ark* 1823, p. 18. CC 1879, pp. 48-9.

261. Supra, pp. 141-2.

262. *The Evangelical Magazine* Jan. 1818, p. 79. Port of Dublin Society *Report* 1823, p. 6. NSM 1833, p. 152. Cf. Woodward 1938, p. 60.

263. *Lieutenant James Edward Gordon, R.N.,* emerges from a variety of sources as an intense, eloquent, militantly Protestant participant in a wide range of religious, social, and political activity. At one time, he was M.P. for Dundalk. He played a leading role in the BFBS "Tests Controversy," also in the founding of both the Trinitarian Bible Society and the Protestant Reformation

Society. (NSM 1832, p. 188; 1833, p. 158. Canton Vol. 1, 1904, pp. 357-8, 406.) His involvement in seamen's mission activities seems to have begun with the Naval Awakening. (As a "pious lieutenant" on the *Valiant,* 74, he was, in 1812, on Lady Mary Grey's correspondence list.) He became a leader in the Scilly Islands Charity, Life Governor of the NMBS, committee member of the MSABS, secretary of the EFCS. (NMBS *Report* 1817, pp. 25-6, 60-9; 1819, p. 40. MSABS *Prospectus* 1818, p. 26. G.C. Smith *The Scilly Islands* 1828, p. 8. SML 1825, p. 320; 1826, p. 258. NSM 1830, p. 272; 1833, p. 152; 1857, pp. 98, 103. O'Byrne 1849, p. 410.

264. *The Gentlemen's Magazine* Jan. 1818, p. 79. SML 1823, p. 301; 1824, pp. 423-4. NSM 1833, p. 152; 1838, p. 107. Cf. Palmer 1973, p. 58.

265. Ibid. See also (MS) BFBS *Home Corresp.,* letter from J.E. Gordon, Jan. 12, 1818. BFBS *Reports* 1818-19, p. 293. *The Gentlemen's Magazine* Feb. 1818, pp. 155-6. SML 1820, p. 162; 1821, pp. 96-7. Port of Dublin Society *Report* 1823, pp. 7-8. G.C. Smith *The British Ark* 1823, p. 20.

266. Dennis Jeffery 1818 (1st and 2nd editions), passim.

267. NSM 1833, p. 152. Infra, pp. 336-7.

268. SML 1821, pp. 96-7. Cf. infra, p. 324.

269. SML 1821, p. 97. Port of Dublin Society *Report* 1823, p. 6. Cf. Highmore 1822, p. 63.

270. SML 1820, p. 212. NSM 1837, pp. 877-8.

271. *The Evangelical Magazine* Feb. 1818, p. 77; March 1818, p. 127. SML 1820, p. 212. Note: E.W. Matthews, one-time secretary and historian of the BFSS, assumes that the Provisional Committee was formed on Feb. 12, 1818, evidently misled by the fact that the first *Minute Book* of the PLS begins at this date, without alluding to the preliminary meeting on Feb. 5, 1818. (CC 1879, p. 77. Matthews 1911, pp. 193-4.) Warren 1858, p. 6, has, likewise incorrectly, Feb. 15, 1818 as the date.

272. *The Evangelical Magazine* 1818, p. 127; 1821, p. 118. Cf. SML 1820, pp. 212-3. Infra, pp. 283-94.

273. (MS) PLS *Minutes,* Feb. 12 to March 18, 1818. SML 1820, p. 213 (quoting from R.H. Marten's tract *The Sequel of the British Ark*).

274. (MS) PLS *Minutes,* Feb. 12 and 17, 1818. Cf. infra, pp. 186-7, 200, 218, 378.

275. (MS) PLS *Minutes,* March 4, 1818. SML 1820, pp. 213, 218. The *Speedy* had been made a receiving ship in 1811, and was then sold to a Mr. Warwick in July 1817, for £950, according to (MS) BSS *Note* (an undated typescript summary of results of research on the origin of the *Ark*). *The Nautical Magazine* 1833, pp. 590-1, states (erroneously) that the *Ark* was formerly HMS *Swift.* Further particulars of H.M. Sloop-of-war *Speedy:* "16 guns, purchased 1803 into RN. In March 1818 BSS Ship. Built at Newcastle 1803. Length Gun Deck 101.5 ft. Beam 29.4 ft. 379 tons." ([MS] Naish 1972.)

276. (MS) PLS *Minutes,* 4, 10 (?) March 1818.

277. (MS) PLS *Minutes,* 10 (?) March 1818; June 13, 1820. SML 1820, pp. 213, 218. Cf. NSM 1858, p. 413, where the amount is incorrectly stated to have been £300.

278. SML 1820, pp. 213-6. Cf. 1821, pp. 388-9. Hodder 1891, p. 32.

279. (MS) PLS *Minutes,* Feb. 24, 1818.

280. SML 1820, pp. 213-6.

281. (MS) PLS *Minutes,* Feb 24, 1818.

282. Ibid., March 18, 1818. SML 1820, pp. 216-7. The temporary title, adopted by the Provisional Committee, had been: "Society for Promoting the Religious Instruction of British Seamen" ([MS] PLS *Minutes,* Feb. 12, 1818. Founded in 1818, this first comprehensive seamen's mission organization thus shared its birth-year with the Queen whose name would be linked with the greater part of the century. Benjamin Shaw, M.P., was well-known as an active Baptist businessman (Brown 1961, pp. 351-2).

283. (MS) PLS *Minutes,* March 18, 1818. SML 1820, p. 217.

284. (MS) PLS *Minutes,* March 18, 1818. *The Evangelical Magazine* April 1818, p. 168.

285. (MS) PLS *Minutes,* March 18, 1818. Cf. supra, p. 34.

286. (MS) PLS *Minutes,* March 4 and 18, 1818.

287. (MS) PLS *Minutes,* March 18, 1818. Cf. SML 1820, pp. 160-3; 1839, pp. 129-31. It is misleading to state that, "The Church of England started mission work among seafarers in co-operation with Nonconformists in 1818, when the *British and Foreign Sailors' Society* was formed in London" (Anson 1955, p. 109).

288. SML 1820, pp. 216-7. The event was also recorded across the Atlantic (e.g., *Religious Remembrancer,* June 27, 1818, p. 1741). *The Times* for March 19, 1818 records that "a gentleman of the Jewish persuasion," passing through the house to a royal charity dinner just before the meeting, "liberally subscribed" through R.H. Marten. With such an example before them, said the Treasurer amidst "great applause," in his subsequent speech, what was the duty of *Christians*?

289. SML 1820, p. 213; 1822, pp. 506-7. NSM 1857, p. 132.

290. SML 1820, p. 218. Highmore 1822, p. 51.

291. (MS) PLS *Minutes,* April 14, 1818. SML 1820, p 213. Highmore 1822, p. 53; cf. p. 58 (where the author assumes that the name of the *Ark* originated with seamen themselves).

292. (MS) PLS *Minutes,* March 10 (?); April 14, 21, 28; May 19, 26, 1818; Highmore 1822, p. 52.

293. (MS) PLS *Minutes,* May 26, 1818.

294. Ibid., May 5; June 9, 1818.

295. Ibid., Feb. 12, 17, 24; March 4; April 28, 1818. (Cf. Elliott-Bins 1964, p. 30.)

296. Ibid., Feb. 17, 1818.

297. Ibid., Dec. 8, 1818.

298. Ibid., May 5, 1818.

299. Highmore 1822, p. 52. SML 1839, p. 130.

300. (MS) PLS *Minutes,* May 19, 1818. Highmore 1822, p. 53.

301. (MS) PLS *Minutes,* March 10 (?), 31, 1818.

302. Ibid., March 31; April 7, 21, 1818. Zebedee Rogers was among the original candidates, but his name was, for some unspecified reason withdrawn (ibid., April 21, 1818).

303. (MS) PLS *Minutes,* April 7, 14; May 5, 1818. One Thursday evening in August 1818, "some irregularity" resulted in five ministers appearing at once (ibid., Aug. 25, 1818). Vacancy problems were, however, more frequent. In a subsequent report, in reply to various complaints, the sub-committee stressed that, despite everything, they have "decidedly preferred" resorting to students rather than lay preachers, in meeting emergencies (ibid., Feb. 9, 1819, appended report, pp. 120-1).

304. *Religious Remembrancer,* July 18, 1818, p. 188. SML 1820, p. 218. Highmore 1822, p. 51.

305. (MS) PLS *Minutes,* Feb. 12; April 28, 1818. *Religious Remembrancer,* July 18, 1818, p. 188. SML 1820, pp. 99, 218; 1826, p. 269; 1828, pp. 4-5. Highmore 1822, p. 51. Warren 1858, p. 6. CC 1913, p. 130. Wapping Stairs was a well-known landing place for both wares and people. Adjoining them was the old Thames-side tavern called "The Town of Ramsgate" (formerly frequented by Ramsgate fishermen after landing their catch at the Stairs). A manuscript still displayed at this ancient inn states that it was here that the notorious Judge Jeffreys was discovered in 1688, and dragged off to the Tower. Thus, as Pike puts it in his history of the BFSS, it was at Wapping, just where this "arch-criminal 'Lord Chief Justice' " sought in vain for refuge from the fury of the mob, that sailors were now called to seek a surer refuge "from the wrath to come" (Pike 1897, p. 70). Note: The location of the *Ark* was later referred to as the "Middle Pool" (NSM 1858, p. 491). Thomas Phillips contended, in 1828, that this location between the two Pools (the Upper and the Lower) meant that the *Ark* could serve neither quite satisfactorily. (NSM 1833, p. 219. Cf. SML 1825, p. 199.)

306. (MS) PLS *Minutes,* April 7, 14; May 5, 1818. *Religious Remembrancer,* July 18, 1818, p. 188. SML 1820, p. 218; 1839, p. 131. Highmore 1822, pp. 51-2. CC 1879, pp. 81-3.

307. Written by the Rev. Edward Walter Matthews, himself a former seafarer, and, for a whole generation, (General) Secretary of the BFSS (Matthews 1911, p. 187).

308. ASFS *AR* 1860, p. 6. Cf. Middleton 1819, p. 75.

309. Supra, pp. 152-3.

310. SML 1820, p. 148.

311. Milne 1851, pp. 2-3, 9. Cf. ASFS *AR* 1860, pp. 5-6.

312. E.g., SML 1821, p. 488.

313. Supra, pp. 130-2.

314. Marks 1826, pp. 220-1.

315. Supra, pp. 134-67. There was, by 1818, a tradition of tract distribution on the Tyne as well as the Thames (cf. RTS 1820, pp. 130-1, 295-6, 370).

316. Supra, pp. 152-3.

317. Supra, pp. 73-5.

318. Supra, pp. 130-2.

319. NMBS *AR* 1820, p. 45. Milne 1851, pp. 4-5. Cf. Lewis 1965, p. 176.

320. *The Christian Guardian* 1826, p. 174.

321. Pascoe 1901, p. 4.

322. EM 1818, p. 336.

323. CC 1879, pp. 175-6.

324. Translated from Waltari 1925, p. 71.

325. Milne 1851, pp. 7-8.

326. E.g., SML 1820, pp. 441-4; 1821, pp. 486-8.

327. Quoting from Psalm 102:13. NSM 1839, p. 447. Cf. SML 1820, pp. 312, 443.

Part IV — Notes

1. SML 1820, pp. 173, 444. Dudley 1821, p. 307. Lewis 1965, p. 66. Cf. G.C. Smith *The British Ark* n.d., p. 16. The aggregate number for vessels of the British Empire was given as 173,609 for the year 1818 (*Second Report* 1847-48).

2. PLS *Proceedings* 1821, pp. 18, 53. SML 1821, p. 97; 1827, p. 41.

3. Cf. (MS) PLS *Minutes*, Feb. 9, 1819. A capacity congregation was, even late 1818, quite exceptional (e.g., *Minutes*, Nov. 24, 1818.

4. Dennis 1818 (2nd ed.), p. 86.

5. (MS) PLS *Minutes*, June 23, Aug. 11, 1818; Feb. 9, 1819. EM 1819, p. 33. SML 1821, pp. 97-8. Thompson 1829, pp. 24-5.

6. PLS *Proceedings* 1823, pp. 40, 44, 48. SML 1821, pp. 97-8.

7. NSM 1837, p. 878.

8. G.C. Smith *Bethel* n.d., p. 19.

9. SML 1820, p. 458.

10. G.C. Smith *Bethel* n.d., pp. 14-6. SML 1820, p. 226; 1821, p. 489. *Captain Foster*, who persevered as a zealous coadjutor in the Upper Pool Bethel Meetings until his death in 1824, also became a pioneer of the Bethel Cause in Hull (SML 1824, pp. 279, 424-5). Note Smith's frank admission in *Blackheath* n.d., p. 46: ". . . when we talked of establishing the Bethel Flag in the Upper Pool, he [Mr. Phillips] . . . shot ahead of me, and got it done." Captain Wilkins, who cooperated in the Upper Pool extension, confirms Phillips' central role, but dates his superintendance of "our district" from early in the spring of 1818. His dating at this period of his life is not consistently correct, however (SML 1841, p. 135).

11. SML 1825, p. 198.

12. SML 1820, pp. 53, 208, 210.

13. Infra, pp. 272-4.

14. NSM 1857, pp. 132-3; 1861, p. 193.

15. NSM 1837, pp. 878-9; 1857, pp. 132-3; 1861, p. 193.

16. G.C. Smith *Bethel* n.d., pp. 13-6. NSM 1860, p. 66.

17. Supra, p. 155.

18. Thompson 1829, pp. 28-30. NSM 1837, p. 878-9; 1857, pp. 132-3. An indication of the height to which feelings ran is the language used by Thomas Phillips, a member of the PLS Committee at the time. He refers to the action

of the Floating Chapel Committee as an "inquisitorial proceeding" which was "worthy the dark ages of the 15th and 16th centuries" (Thompson 1829, p. 28). Smith states that Tanner and Francis won over three of the most active ministerial committee members at that time: Charles Hyatt, George Evans and Henry Lacey (NSM 1858, p. 17). He also charges the two managers with trying to promote commercial influence with owners and captains through a sort of religious hegemony on the River (NSM 1857, 132-3). Such allegations must be seen in the light of previous accusations, leveled by the PLS against Smith, for having been motivated by greed and vanity when founding the new Society in 1819 (PLBUS 1829, p. 40). In 1820, the PLS transferred their Thursday evening meeting to Wednesday, but reverted to Thursday in 1822 ([MS] *Minutes*, Aug. 8, 1820, Nov. 22, 1822).

19. NSM 1837, p. 879; 1857, pp. 133-4; 1858, p. 18; 1861, p. 193. An indication of the popularity of Smith's 1819 preaching on the *Ark* is the fact that advance enquiries were made from Watermen's Hall about his sermon engagements, in order to ensure a sufficiently numerous supply of boats (NSM 1837, p. 879).

20. NSM 1860, p. 72.

21. BFSSFS 1829, p. 2.

22. Thompson 1829, p. 29. NSM 1857, p. 133.

23. SML 1820, p. 78.

24. Ibid. SML 1822, p. 2. *The Christian Guardian* 1826, p. 174. Cf. G.C. Smith *Bethel* n.d., p. 17.

25. SML 1820, p. 319. Referring later to "the old dissenting formalists" that managed the Floating Chapel in 1818-19, Smith exclaims: "What, stop prayer meetings! I would as soon stop a man's breath, for only while we pray we live" (NSM 1839, pp. 211-2).

26. CHSM 1823, p. 24. NSM 1837, pp. 878-9; 1857, p. 133; 1858, p. 18.

27. NSM 1858, pp. 18, 413; 1861, p. 193.

28. SML 1822, pp. 232-3. Thompson 1829, p. 28. NSM 1837, p. 878; 1857, pp. 132-4; 1860, p. 66.

29. NSM 1857, p. 133; 1858, p. 18.

30. NSM 1858, p. 18. Cf. G.C. Smith *Injustice and Cruelty* n.d., pp. 5-6. Also, CHSM 1823, pp. 24-5.

31. Thompson 1829, p. 30. NSM 1837, p. 879. Smith offers the following definition of a *Bethel Union* in its basic sense: "The congregating of two or more persons for religious purposes in any place appropriated to the worship of God" (NSM 1833, p. 160). The concept of *union*, however, applied not only to the seamen themselves, but evidently also to their friends ashore (e.g., SML 1822, p. 322). At all events, a spirit of fellowship across denominational lines was considered an indispensable feature (SML 1821, p. 93). "The Seamen's Union" was, in fact, occasionally used as an abbreviation during earlier years (e.g., SML 1820, p. 26). By 1825, however, the latter term had been appropriated by the incipient coastal trade union movement (SML 1825, pp. 193-4). Cf. CHSM 1823, pp. 25.

32. G.C. Smith *Bethel* n.d., p. 23. SML 1820, p. 444.

33. G.C. Smith *Bethel* n.d., p. 23.

34. G.C. Smith *English Sailors* n.d., pp. 26-36. NSM 1837, p. 879; 1858, p. 18.

35. G.C. Smith *English Sailors* n.d., pp. 26-8. SML 1820, pp. 444-5. NSM 1857, p. 134. For Minutes of these crucial meetings, see Appendix No. 6.

36. G.C. Smith *English Sailors* n.d., pp. 29-30. SML 1820, pp. 184-5.

37. G.C. Smith *English Sailors* n.d., pp. 26-36. The *Robert and Margaret's* feat was made the subject of a tract, entitled *The Life Boat* (SML 1822, p. 39; cf. 1820, pp. 230-1). Cf. G.C. Smith *The Press Gang* n.d., p. 11 (where presumably the same seamen's first name is given as "Cuthbert"). Cf. supra, p. 153.

38. EM 1819, p. 519. SML 1820, pp. 25-6, 445. NSM 1837, p. 879; 1857, pp. 134-5; 1858, pp. 19, 414. (Re. Ward's involvement in seamen's missions, see SML 1824, pp. 422-3.) Cf. *The Baptist Magazine* 1820, pp. 118-9.

39. Ibid. DNB Vol. 1, 1885, p. 413. Hodder 1891, pp. iii-iv, 23, 50-64. Among the amazing series of achievements in the long life of *George Fife Angas*, were also his foundation of the first Sunday School Union in the North of England, his powerful promotion of both foreign and seamen's missions, and his successful sponsorship of persecuted Prussian Lutherans to South Australia. One of the leading philanthropists of the century, he is also credited with having produced, in 1823, the first practical proposal of a ship-canal through the Isthmus of Darien (Hodder 1891, pp. iii-iv, 38-41). Note: Hodder's account of the origin of early metropolitan seamen's mission societies contains several misstatements (see especially pp. 57-9). Cox 1834, pp. 49-50, credits W.H. Angas (not G.F. Angas) with the "water-line" remark.

40. Officially adopted at Committee Meeting, Oct. 6, 1820 (SML 1820, pp. 426-7).

41. Brown 1961, p. 327.

42. E.g., Jonas Hanway *The Seaman's Christian Friend*, London, 1779. Richard Marks *The Seaman's Friend*, London, 1817-1818. An anonymous and undated tract called *The Sailor's Friend* was published as Tract No. 34 by the Glasgow Religious Tract Society.

43. SML 1823, p. 219. G.C. Smith was evidently the "originator" of the "Bethel Union" combination (cf. NSM 1844, p. 1123). The "Seamen's Friend" combination (whoever first proposed its new use) had already been adopted in Greenock, Leith and Bristol before October 1820, when it became official in London (SML 1820, pp. 426-7). In the USA, the "Seamen's Friend" designation has continued in New York, Boston, Norfolk and New Haven. In England, there is still the Seamen's Christian Friend Society, and in Scotland there are the Glasgow and Dundee Seamen's Friend Societies. Cf. CHSM 1823, p. 26.

44. See Appendix No. 6.

45. SML 1820, pp. 426, 445.

46. SML 1821, p. 420. Cf Weibust 1969, pp. 211-4, 232.

47. G.C. Smith *English Sailors* n.d., p. 35. Cf SML 1820, p. 426; 1821, p. 240; 1825, p. 199. SMNY 1835-36, pp. 170 ff. (article on "Communion of Seamen").

48. SML 1820, p. 26. Cf. Highmore 1822, p. 70.

49. SML 1820, p. 445.

50. Jones 1850, p. 48. Cf. CC 1879, p. 176.

51. G.C. Smith *Bethel* n.d., pp. 22-3. SML 1820, pp. 25-6, 426-7, 445.

52. G.C. Smith *Bethel* n.d., p. 23. Note also the quotation, on p. 23, of the PLS Committee's expectation that others, too, "may enter the extensive field. . . .")

53. G.C. Smith *English Sailors* n.d., p. 28.

54. As Thompson (later) found reason to admit, "On the surface all was friendship; beneath bitterness itself" (Thompson 1829, p. 9). Note: Where subsequent reference is made to charges against the Rev. G.C. Smith in Dr. John Styles' tract on behalf of the Committee of the PLBUS, entitled *An Appeal* (1829), these statements must be read in light of the corresponding passages in the most convincing *Refutation*, written (also in 1829) by the two late honorary secretaries of this Society, Thomas Thompson and Thomas Phillips.

55. SML 1820, p. 444. NSM 1837, p. 879; 1839, p. 470; 1857, p. 134.

56. (MS) PLS *Minutes*, April 25, 1820, June 13, 1820. SML 1820, p. 444; 1822, pp. 420-1. Thompson 1829, p. 29. Smith published the communications between the two societies, held in 1820, in a pamphlet entitled *Tarbucket*, under the pseudonym Capsicum (Boase & Courtney Vol. 2 1882, p. 665).

57. (MS) PLS *Minutes*, Nov 9, 1819. G.C. Smith *Aldermanbury* n.d., p. 5. Thompson 1829, pp. 8-9. 29. NSM 1837, p. 879. Cf. PLBUS 1829, pp. 12 ff.

58. Thompson 1829, p. 8. PLBUS 1829, p. 12.

59. SML 1820, p. 148. Thompson 1829, p. 29. NSM 1857, pp. 134-5; 1858, p. 414.

60. Smith had, during the summer of 1818, supplied the pulpit of the *Ark* on the same gratuitous basis as other ministers, but far oftener and with far greater response. John Francis, as one of the managers, eventually insisted on Smith (as an out-of-town minister) accepting a one-guinea remuneration when a *collection* sermon was preached. Some of the other ministers took exception to this, it seems. Smith's position is convincingly vindicated by Thomas Phillips. (Thompson 1829, pp. 9, 24-8. Cf. PLBUS 1829, pp. 36-9.)

61. G.C. Smith *Aldermanbury* n.d., p. 4. SML 1825, pp. 307-8. PLBUS 1829, pp. 40-3. On a print of the *Ark*, published Sept 1, 1819, and subsequently used for P.R. purposes, the artist, J. Gendall, inscribed the following: "Dedicated to R.H. MARTEN, ESQR. FOUNDER AND TREASURER. . . ." Exaggerated statements of Marten's role were also carried in *The New Times*, July 21, 1825 (SML 1825, pp. 307-8). However, on *this* score, Thompson while quite aware of the historicity of Smith's originator role, was less disposed to justify his wrath. Phillips, too, refused to dwell on this issue. (Thompson 1829, pp. 19, 30.)

62. Again, in true Nelson tradition (Cf. Watson 1960, p. 428).

63. G.C. Smith *Aldermanbury* n.d., passim. Cf. Thompson 1829, pp. 9, 28-30.

64. Hence the justification for a detailed analysis of the origin of the controversy. Cf. G.C. Smith *Aldermanbury* n.d., p. 5. NSM 1858, p. 19.

65. Dr. John Styles is the author of these formulations (in PLBUS 1829, pp. 11, 41). His charges of vanity and greed as dominating motives in Smith's promotion of the new Society are roundly refuted by Thompson and Phillips. (See especially their *Refutation* 1829, pp. 11, 30.) There is no reason to doubt that why R.H. Marten (and several leading members of the PLS Committee) felt so "seriously prejudiced" against Smith and fellow-founders of the Bethel Union, was a genuine apprehension that the new Society would "injure the

Port of London Society" (G.C. Smith *The Floating Chapel*, n.d., p. 23). A second metropolitian *interdenominational* society was seen in a quite different light from a prospective metropolitan *Anglican* society (Cf. SML 1825, p. 294).

66. Luke 2:34.

67. (MS) BFSFSBU *Minutes* 1822-27, give constant examples of such terminological identification. PECMSS *AR* 1849, p. 12, provides an instance of unstinted approbation of the Bethel Movement by Americans (Cf. *The Christian Guardian* 1826, pp. 174-5.)

68. SML 1822, pp. 419-21.

69. SML 1820, p. 20. *The Christian Guardian* 1826, p. 174.

70. Ibid. With G.C. Smith, this was an incessant theme (e.g., SML 1824, p. 403).

71. NSM 1858, p. 543. Boase Vol. 3, 1965, c. 628.

72. SML 1820-27, also (MS) BFSFSBU *Minutes* 1822-27, contain copious source materials on Smith's activities in the Bethel Cause during this period (Cf. NSM 1858, p. 414). The Society's offices (which remained those of this Society and its successor, the PLBUS) were located in the former residence of the notorious Judge Jeffreys. (SML 1828, pp. 2-3. Cf. Part III, Note No. 305.)

73. Cf. NSM 1858, p. 18.

74. (MS) BFSFSBU *Minutes* 1822-27. (E.g., June 18, 1823.)

75. In 1820, W.H. Angas is listed as joint foreign secretary. SML 1820, p. 427; 1821, pp. 493-4. See list of officers in Appendix No. 6.

76. SML 1820, p. 472; 1821, pp. 412-6, 494; 1822, pp. 466-7; 1823, p. 425; 1824, pp. 427-8; 1825, Supplement pp. 13-5; 1827, p. 9. Cf. (MS) BFSFSBU *Minutes*, Aug. 21, 1822. It was, in fact, the BFSFSBU which first "brought into active usefulness" naval officers in general, in the field of seamen's mission activities (SML 1825, p. 119). Note also the addition of five further admirals as vice-presidents (SML 1826, pp. 464-5).

77. SML 1820, pp. 230, 427 (and successive BFSFSBU *Annual Retrospects*); 1827, p. 197. Milne 1851, p. 11. Cf. NSM 1828, p. 433. Also, Thompson 1829, p. 38, which contains a warm appraisal of the Rev. A. Brown's maritime ministry: "Constantly at his post in all weathers, and breaking the bread of life to his perishing *brother Sailors*, he was honoured of God in being made the instrument of conversion of many. . . ."

78. SML 1820, pp. 26, 77-9, 209-10; 1821, pp. 489, 492; 1824, p. 402. NSM 1828, pp. 127, 234. (MS) BFSFSBU *Minutes*, Jan 28, 1824. Cf. SML 1825, pp. 276-8.

79. SML 1824, pp. 430-1.

80. SML 1820, p. 56.

81. Ibid.

82. SML 1820, p. 207; 1821, p. 463. G.C. Smith *The Custom House* n.d., p. 38.

83. SML 1820, p. 211.

84. Ibid.

85. Ibid., pp. 210-1, 458-9.

86. Ibid., pp. 208, 211.

87. E.g., (MS) BFSFSBU *Minutes* 182-27, Dec. 18, 1822.

88. SML 1820, pp. 208-9, 279, 434-5; 1821, pp. 320-1. Special signals were agreed by which vessels might be recognized. Thus, "a small blue flag, with a yellow star in the centre," or (at night) "a lantern hoisted to the top of a boat hook," distinguished a *Signal Boat*; "a long broad blue pendant, with a red flag, and, in the centre, seven stars," were hoisted by a *Receiving Ship.* The first vessel appointed as Receiving Ship was the *Isabella*, South Shields, owned by Christopher Warne, known as a particularly enthusiastic supporter of efforts to "promote the eternal welfare of seamen" (SML 1820, p. 209). Note also the coordinative activity of *Signal Joe*, a youthful employee of the BFSFSBU in 1829, charged with securing ships for evening Bethel Meetings and inviting to these (NSM 1829, Pt. II, p. 343).

89. SML 1820, p. 317; 1821, pp. 320-1.

90. Infra, pp. 552-3.

91. SML 1820, pp. 25, 54-5, 279, 382; 1822, pp. 211-2.

92. SML 1820, p. 54.

93. SML 1821, pp. 297, 489. G.C. Smith *The Press Gang* n.d., p. 2. Hall 1859, pp. 473-4. Note: *The Press Gang*, though undated, must have been published between Oct. 1821 (Cf. p. 10) and March 1822 (Cf. SML 1822, p. 220).

94. SML 1821, pp. 35-6, 297-8. G.C. Smith *The Press Gang* n.d., p. 3.

95. G.C. Smith *The Press Gang* n.d., pp. 2-3.

96. The Bethel Mission-house at Stepney was evidently most strategically situated, in Old Road, close to a particularly notorious sailors' brothel. Generally, Bethel Meetings ashore would also be held at the Mission-house on *Wednesday* evenings. (SML 1821, pp. 35-6, 297-300, 313-4, 341-5; 1822, pp. 212, 322-4. G.C. Smith *The Press Gang* n.d., pp. 3-10.)

97. SML 1821, pp. 297-300, 341-5. G.C. Smith *The Press Gang* n.d., pp. 4-8.

98. G.C. Smith *The Press Gang* n.d., pp. 5-6.

99. Ibid., p. 9.

100. Ibid., pp. 4-5, 8. SML 1821, pp. 343-5. Cf. 1822, pp. 192-3, 212. A comical case of friendly coercion is quoted by Smith: An intemperate tar became terrified at the sight of the Bethel Flag suspended from the window, when conducted to the Mission-house. He was only prevented from bolting, when it was explained to him that this was *not*, as he had assumed, a naval impress rendez-vous! (SML 1821, p. 300.)

101. SML 1821, pp. 343-5. G.C. Smith *The Press Gang* n.d., p. 8.

102. SML 1821, pp. 297, 300, 488-9. G.C. Smith *The Press Gang* n.d., pp. 10-2.

103. SML 1820, p. 443; 1821, pp. 297, 488-9.

104. The Blackwall, Poplar, and Limehouse Auxiliary, too, working in close conjunction with the Stepney Mission, resolved in May 1822 that the Bethel Flag should be hoisted at all chapels ashore, when Sailors' Meetings were scheduled, whether for prayer or preaching, "in order to direct Seamen thereto" (SML 1822, p. 324).

105. Infra, pp. 579-81.

106. Infra, p. 553.

107. SML 1820, p. 26.

108. SML 1820, pp. 26, 445-6; 1821, pp. 38-9; 1824, p. 404; 1825, pp. 119-20; 1826, p. 462; 1827, pp. 396-7. Note a former *Victory* seaman hailing ladies to turn to in the Bethel Cause (SML 1821, pp. 303-4).

109. SML 1820, pp. 26, 65, 396, 428, 446; 1821, pp. 93, 488; 1822, pp. 148-50, 426-7; cf. 1826, p. 462.

110. SML 1823, pp. 120, 127-9; 1824, p. 404; 1825, p. 304; 1826, p. 463; 1827, p. 73. EM 1824, p. 207.

111. SML 1825, Supplement p. 3. NSM 1829, Pt. I, p. 210. Cf. EM 1802, p. 467.

112. SML 1821, pp. 162-3, 201, 239, 297-8, 313-4, 489; 1822, pp. 322-4. G.C. Smith *The Press Gang* n.d., pp. 3-4. (MS) BFSFSBU *Minutes*, May 15 & 22, 1822 (cf. entries for Jan. 17 & Feb. 5, 1823, indicating that the spiritual needs of seamen and waterman about the East and West India Docks, as well as the London Docks, were nevertheless far from adequately met).

113. SML 1821, pp. 38, 117, 198, 443; 1822, pp. 99, 424, 489; 1823, pp. 197-9; 1824, p. 405; 1825, pp. 354-5; 1826, pp. 259-60. (MS) BFSFSBU *Minutes*, Feb. 4, 1824. Re.: early *soldiers' missions*, see infra, pp. 297-8.

114. SML 1822, p. 247; 1823, p. 398; 1825, pp. 41-7, 355-6; Supplement p. 3; 1826, p. 462.

115. SML 1820, pp. 318-9, 358-9, 446-7, 467-8; 1843, p. 27. EM 1820, p. 343.

116. Ibid. Highmore 1822, p. 293, gives the erroneous impression that the activities of "The Cambrian Union Society" were a function of "The Maritime Cambrian Society," founded in 1805, as a mutual benefit society for Cambrian shipmasters (cf. supra, p. 16-7).

117. SML 1820, pp. 397, 446-7, 456-7, 478-9; 1821, p. 281. EM 1820, pp. 521-2.

118. SML 1822, pp. 128-9, 381. Cf. North Shields Seamen's Chapel (infra, p. 235).

119. SML 1822, pp. 126-7, 330-1, 381-2. The Cambrian Chapel was ultimately transferred to the London Mariners' Church Society (Thompson 1829, pp. 36-7).

120. SML 1820, pp. 396, 446-7. *Benjamin Tanner* (of the PLS) cooperated at one point in the meetings among the Scotch smacks (SML 1821, p. 488). Despite SML 1822, p. 129, Cambrian Union Flags do not appear to have been extensively used outside the Port of London. Even in *Welsh* ports, it was generally the traditional Bethel Flag which was reported to have been hoisted (e.g.: SML 1821, pp. 35, 363-4, 400; 1822, pp. 246, 369-70).

121. Supra, pp. 146, 166-7.

122. Infra, pp. 305-13.

123. CHSM 1823, p. 26. Supra, p. 203.

124. The service was conducted principally by seafarers, and the shipmaster's address was "replete with such manly eloquence and genuine professional feeling, that few persons could listen to it unmoved." The *Robert*, on which the first Bethel Flag was thus hoisted at Greenock, was lost by shipwreck shortly afterwards. (SML 1820, pp. 105-6, 184-5, 443, 460-1; 1821, pp. 274-5. Cf. Matthews 1911, pp. 210-1.)

125. SML 1820, pp. 185-6, 443, 460-1. SMR 1820, pp. 124-7. The indispensable exertions of "some excellent and pious females" at the formation of the Society was given warm recognition (SML 1821, p. 141).

126. SML 1821, pp. 176-7.

127. SML 1821, pp. 175-80. SMR 1821, pp. 48-50; 1822, pp. 46-8; 1829, pp. 106-9; 1830, pp. 250-2; 1834, pp. 57-9.

128. SML 1820, pp. 169-80, 446. SMR 1820, p. 80.

129. SMR 1821, p. 47. Cf. SML 1821, p. 374. As "Extraordinary Directors," were elected the magistrates and ministers "of all denominations," both in Edinburgh and Leith, besides the Master and Assistants of the Trinity House of Leith (ibid.).

130. SMR 1821, pp. 46-8, 372-3; 1833, p. 9. SML 1820, p. 435; 1821, pp. 375-8, 395-6. The series of shipboard Sunday services was inaugurated Sept. 17, 1820, by the Rev. W. Henry, preaching to a crowded congregation under a huge awning on the *Westmoreland* of Hull (SML 1821, p. 375). The Leith Society's flag consisted of "a swallow-tailed white pendant, 28 feet long, with a Union [clasped hands] in the corner, and 'SEAMAN'S FRIEND,' inscribed in large blue characters, in the centre of the pendant, surmounted by a guilded dove, bearing the olive branch" (SML 1821, pp. 376-7). A detailed description of the accommodation and fittings of the Leith Floating Chapel is contained in SML 1821, pp. 394-5. The Lord Provost of Edinburgh secured the Society both an ideal mooring and exemption from dock dues (SML 1821, p. 376).

131. SMR 1827, p. 256; 1830, p. 298; 1833, pp. 9, 379.

132. SMR 1821, pp. 674-5; 1823, pp. 487-8; 1826, pp. 566-7; 1827, pp. 258, 293-8; 1829, pp. 204-6; 1830, pp. 298-9; 1833, pp. 8-9, 380-1. The Society's Home Missionary, Matthew Kirkland, who took up his duties Jan. 31, 1830, was a licenciate of the Church of Scotland, appointed with the approval of the parish minister of North Leith (SMR 1830, p. 299). Cf. Infra, pp. 324.

133. SML 1824, p. 468. MM 1825, p. 270.

134. NSM 1861, p. 535. Supra, p. 171.

135. EM 1818, p. 213. An opening service is reported to have been performed May 10, 1818, under a "large flag, inscribed with the word 'Ark'" (*The Religious Remembrancer* 1818, p. 196). The pioneering efforts of "a respectable merchant" and "Methodist Preachers" are recognized in an introduction to the 1822 *Report* of the Bristol Seamen's Friend Society (SML 1823, p. 52).

136. Supra, p. 147.

137. SML 1820, pp. 351-6, 373-4; 1821, pp. 240-1, 423-4, 496. See also EM 1820, p. 389. G.C. Smith *The Custom House* n.d., p. 42. NSM 1855, pp. 235-6.

138. SML 1821, 423-4, 461, 498-9; 1823, pp. 52-4, 452-3; 1824, pp. 406-7; 1825, pp. 25-6, 415; 1826, pp. 255, 302. EM 1823, pp. 508-9. G.C. Smith *The Custom House* n.d., p. 42. *The Pilot* 1835, pp. 227-9. NSM 1857, p. 407. The expense of fitting up the Floating Chapel totaled £520, tradesmen and others having donated several items of equipment (SML 1821, pp. 424, 499). The opening date was, according to the *Bristol Mercury* (Sept. 1, 1821, p. 3, c. 2) definitely Aug. 29, 1821. The reference to Sept. 20, 1821 in SML 1821, p. 425, is, therefore, erroneous. Re. Bristol's Sailortown (near the Grove) see Hugill 1967, pp. 34-6.

139. SML 1820, p. 352; 1823, p. 55; 1824, p. 157; 1825, p. 27. The Bristol Marine School Society, founded on board the Bristol Floating Chapel, opened its School House at 33 Queen Square in January 1824, with a Day School for sea-boys, and an Evening School for adults and apprentices (Bristol Marine School Society *Report* 1825; *Proceedings* 1827).

140. SML 1820, pp. 373-5; 1821, pp. 24-6, 499-500.

141. SML 1820, pp. 356, 373. In SML 1821, pp. 465-6, apparently the same person is referred to as "the Rev. Mr. Parker" (cf. SML 1822, p. 346; 1823, p. 332; 1826, p. 96). In NSM 1829, Pt. II, Smith refers to a lay Wesleyan coadjutor in Bristol named Hugh Roberts, with a similar background.

142. SML 1820, p. 374; 1823, pp. 54-5; 1824, pp. 156, 407; 1825, p. 26.

143. SML 1823, pp. 331-7, 366, 384-7, cf. Supplement pp. 6-7. Provided that the date of the preliminary meeting is correctly quoted as "Wednesday, August 15th," the date of the general meeting was presumably Wednesday, Sept. 19, 1823 (not Sept. 10, as stated p. 385, cf. p. 331). As resident honorary secretaries, were elected *Lieutenant J.E. Mogridge, R.N.*, whose concern for a local tract depot contributed to the founding of the Society, and *Mr. J.S. Parker* (SML 1823, pp. 384, 386; 1826, p. 96). The constitution of the new Society shows objects and means to have been in general conformity with trends now becoming traditional for Seamen's Friend Societies and Bethel Unions (SML 1823, pp. 331-2). Pulpit supply was based on the so-called *Tabernacle Plan*, with "a minister from a distance every six weeks" (SML 1824, p. 260).

144. SML 1823, p. 384; 1824, pp. 258-60; 1826, pp. 96, 255. On the *Clifton Ark*, unsightly cross-beams were eliminated, and the middle deck was removed, to permit inclining galleries. A "very handsome" gallery was constructed abaft the pulpit, "entirely for respectable visitors" (i.e. shipowners, merchants, officers, and their families). These, it was assumed, the common sailor with his wife and children, seated in the body of the chapel below, would be gratified to behold "worshiping the same God on board the same ship" (SML 1824, pp. 258-9).

145. SML 1824, pp. 260, 397; 1826, p. 98. Among individual contributors were, besides G.C. Smith's early patron, Opie Smith of Bath, a "pious lady of Aston" (Mrs. Weare), who virtually consolidated the project with gifts totaling £150 (SML 1823, p. 386; 1824, p. 407).

146. Supra, p. 147.

147. Supra, pp. 183-4. Cf. SML 1825, p. 107.

148. A large proportion of Philip's hearers were evidently fishermen and their families (*The Baptist Magazine* 1824, p. 83). Philip is also credited with having formed a Marine Society during his ministry at Newington Chapel. He was ultimately (1852) honored with a D.D. degree by Dartmouth College, USA. (SML 1821, p. 393; 1823, p. 86; 1825, p. 107. Philip 1823, Advertisement. DNB Vol. 45 1896, pp. 158-9.) Cf. infra, p. 310.

149. SML 1821, pp. 383, 490; 1823, pp. 83-4, 86; 1825, pp. 106-7. Cf. PLS *Proceedings* 1823, p. 41.

150. SML 1823, p. 84.

151. SML 1821, p. 383; 1823, p. 84. DNB Vol. 47 1896, p. 160. G.C. Smith confirms Aug. 28, 1921 as the date of the *Merope* service (NSM 1828, p. 70).

152. SML 1821, pp. 383-4; 1823, p. 84. SMR 1822, p. 14; 1823, p. 15. The Society is still active, but changed its title from "Liverpool Seamen's Friend Society and Bethel Union" to "Liverpool Seamen and Emigrants' Friend Society," then "Liverpool Seamen's Friend Society", and (now) "Gordon Smith Institute for Seamen (Incorporated)." The erroneous year of foundation

(1820) was incorporated in the Liverpool Seamen's Friend Society's *Historical Sketch of the Work of the Society* [1900], p. 6, after having appeared in previous *Annual Reports* (e.g., the 74th, for 1895, pp. 4-5). The error has been repeated in more recent works, too, such as Kingsford 1957, p. 11; Whittington-Egan 1955, p. 34.

153. SML 1821, pp. 384, 386; 1823, pp. 81-5. SMR 1823, pp. 14-5.

154. SML 1821, pp. 384, 390-1; 1825, p. 108. *Nicholas Hurry*, a manager of Dr. Raffles' Chapel, was Smith's host during his 1821 visit to Liverpool, and became from the first one of his most enthusiastic coadjutors (NSM 1861, pp. 535-6). Re. *Samuel Hope*, see also supra, p. 184.

155. SML 1821, pp. 384, 390-1; 1823, p. 82. Infra, pp. 287-9.

156. SML 1821, pp. 386-8; 1823, pp. 84-5.

157. SML 1821, p. 939. G.C. Smith *The Custom House* n.d., pp. 41-2.

158. SML 1821, pp. 491-2; 1823, pp. 81, 85. SMR 1823, pp. 14-5. NSM 1833, pp. 144-55. DNB Vol. 44 1895, pp. 266-70. Canton Vol. 1 1904, p. 383. Infra, p. 101.

159. SML 1823, p. 199. NSM 1860, p. 66. DNB Vol. 29, 1892, pp. 355-63.

160. SML 1821, p. 393; 1823, pp. 81, 86; 1825, p. 107; 1826, p. 257; 1827, pp. 102-4. Philip 1823, Advertisement. *The Baptist Magazine* 1824, p. 83. DNB Vol. 55 1896, pp. 158-9. Infra, p. 310.

161. SML 1823, pp. 19, 82, 92, 456; 1824, pp. 465-8; 1825, p. 108. In sailor-like manner, Kirkpatrick could make light of the fact that, during his naval service, he had "lost one of his fins" by enemy cannon-shot (SML 1823, p. 489).

162. SML 1821, pp. 386, 391-3; 1823, pp. 81, 87, 92; 1825, pp. 103, 107.

163. SML 1823, p. 85. Cf. (MS) BFSFSBU *Minutes*, June 15, 1825.

164. SML 1822, p. 477; 1823, p. 86.

165. SML 1822, p. 477; 1823, pp. 86-7. EM 1822, p. 113. SMR 1823, pp. 15-6. The *William* is stated by A.C. Wardle to have been launched by John Sutton in Liverpool, March 2, 1775, for Richard Kent (*Sea Breezes* Vol. 1, 1946, p. 281). She was bought by the Society for £940 (SML 1823, p. 86; see also p. 93 for a complete statement, including cost of fitting up). In later publications of the Liverpool Seamen's Friend Society, the Floating Chapel (i.e. the former merchantman *William*) was confused with the Mariners' Church (the former man-of-war *Tees,* opened as a Church of England venture in 1827, and moored in the George's Dock). See, for example, Liverpool Seamen's Friend Society *79th Annual Report* for 1900, p. 11, and their *Historical Sketch* [1900], p. 96. Cf. erroneous statements in *Sea Breezes* Vol. 1 1946, p. 174; Whittington-Egan 1955, p. 34; Hugill 1967, p. 96. Re. the Liverpool Mariners' Church (ex *Tees*), see infra, pp. 287-9.

166. SML 1825, p. 414; 1828, p. 34. Whittington-Egan 1955, p. 34. Hugill 1967, pp. 95, 98, 104-5, 111. According to A.C. Wardle in *Sea Breezes* Vol. 1 1946, p. 281, the Floating Chapel remained in the King's Dock until about 1850, having by then incurred dock dues totaling £1,277. The Liverpool Society was, in this regard, less fortunate than its counterpart in Leith (SML 1825, p. 502; cf. supra, p. 223).

167. SML 1822, pp. 396-9; 1823, pp. 85, 87-8, 456-7; 1824, p. 497; 1825, pp. 102-4, Supplement p. 5; 1828, pp. 36-7. SMR 1823, pp. 18-9. (MS) BFSFSBU *Minutes*, June 21, 1825.

168. Two such sermons, held February 25, 1810 and February 17, 1811, by the Rev. Thomas Boscher at the Bethel Chapel, Bridge Street, have been published. (Port of Hull Society 1907, pp. 8-9. Cf. SML 1820, p. 468.)

169. Supra, p. 146.

170. G.C. Smith *The Custom House* n.d., p. 41. Cf. supra, pp. 199, 202.

171. SML 1821, p. 489. Cf. supra, pp. 136, 140.

172. SML 1821, p. 118.

173. SML 1821, p. 339; 1822, pp. 496-7. (SML 1838, p. 149, has incorrectly 1831.)

174. William Rust, a goldsmith by profession, also wrote a promotional tract (*The Floating Chapel*) at the request of the Society. Captain Francis Reynalds was still traveling for the Society in the late 1820's. (NSM 1828, pp. 474-5; cf. 1831, pp. 469-70.) As joint secretaries with Reynalds, were elected the Rev. Thomas Thonger, a Baptist, and George Locker, a ship and insurance broker. (Port of Hull Society 1907, pp. 20-7. Mitchell 1961, pp. 15-8.) Re. Dykes, see infra, p. 289.

175. SML 1821, p. 118. Cf. PLS *Proceedings* 1821, pp. 38-40.

176. SML 1821, p. 339; 1822, pp. 497-8. Port of Hull Society 1907, pp. 20-1, 28-9, 31.

177. The ship had been bought for £450, and fitted up at Dykes' yard. (SML 1821, p. 489; 1822, pp. 497-8, cf. p. 36. Port of Hull Society 1907, pp. 28-32.)

178. Exact dimensions of the transformed Floating Chapel are quoted in SML 1822, p. 515. Otherwise, see Port of Hull Society 1907, pp. 28-30. Re. attendance, see PHS *Annual Reports*, passim. Cf. SML 1826, p. 455.

179. SML 1822, p. 499. Cf. Mitchell 1961, p. 20.

180. Port of Hull Society 1907, pp. 30-1. Mitchell 1961, p. 20.

181. SML 1822, p. 36; 1823, pp. 457-8, 489-91; 1825, p. 358, Supplement p. 6. NSM 1828, p. 473. Cf. Port of Hull Society 1907, p. 87.

182. SML 1822, p. 499; 1824, pp. 49-50. PHS *AR* 1823, pp. 10-1.

183. SML 1823, p. 365; 1824, p. 50; 1825, pp. 147-8; 1826, p. 455. PHS *AR* 1823, pp. 11-2. Mitchell 1961, pp. 22-3.

184. SML 1822, p. 12.

185. See SML 1820-27, passim.

186. The officer referred to was evidently D. M'Crery (the Society's early secretary). The original title was the *Bethel Seamen's Union Society, established at Portsmouth.* The Rev. F. Mitchell was engaged as minister in 1823. The Chapel premises were transferred in 1825 from East Street to Bath Square. (SML 1820, pp. 279, 318; 1821, pp. 15-21, 466; 1822, p. 167; 1825, pp. 343-5; 1826, pp. 136-9; 1827, pp. 23-4.)

187. Besides Commissioner Creyke as Patron, the Plymouth Society included four admirals as subscribers. (SML 1820, pp. 186-9; 1821, pp. 22-3, 36, 212-5; 1822, pp. 10-7, 90-9; 1823, pp. 16-21; 1824, pp. 51-5; 1825, pp. 96-102.)

188. SML 1820, pp. 436-9; 1824, pp. 493-5. Cf. SML 1822, pp. 98-9; 1825, p. 343. Supra, pp. 218-9.

189. Supra, pp. 221-2.

190. SML 1820, p. 468.

191. E.g., SML 1821 pp. 383, 385 (in the case of *Liverpool*).

192. SML 1822, pp. 354-5.

193. Infra, pp. 251-60.

194. SML 1822, pp. 346-7. Cf. Cox 1834, pp. 68-75. Angas had himself, in a letter dated Dec. 2, 1819, recommended to the new Society that "a deputation of chiefly sea-faring characters of respectability and address" be sent to all sea-ports in the kingdom in order to form societies (SML 1820, p. 64).

195. SML 1822-23 carried a series of reports from W.H. Angas himself, as well as local correspondents, concerning the efforts made at different ports included in his tour (1822, pp. 286-7, 324-9, 346-54, 404-10, 444-5, 521, 523;1823, pp. 116-9, 159-60, 197, 514). Cox 1834, p. 78, also includes Carlisle and Lancaster among West Coast towns visited. Re. preparatory work at Newcastle, see also SML 1822, p. 207. Early in 1823, a Bethel Room was engaged here, and fitted up "contageous to the Quayside" (SML 1823, p. 118).

196. Ibid. As to North Shields, the early Bethel pioneers of this port had established a "North Shields Auxiliary Seamen's Friend Society" on Nov. 24, 1820, and fitted up "a large sail loft, down Shepherd's Quay," as their "Seamen's Chapel." It was, in April 1821, reported to be capable of holding "about 400," and constantly "crowded" (SML 1821, pp. 198-9). At Great Yarmouth, a shipowner (W.D. Palmer, Sr.) had furnished and fitted up a small sloop as an *Ark*, with which he zealously promoted a local seamen's ministry (SML 1822, pp. 168, 325, 487). At Sunderland, a Mariners' Church was opened 16 May 1828 in Robinson's Lane, in connection with the BFSSFS (NSM 1828, pp. 260-2, 277-8, 283).

197. SML 1822, p. 521. At Sunderland and Whitby, both on the North Country "Bethel Coast," the ground had been prepared by earlier Marine Bible Societies, local RTS activity, and Bethel Meetings. At Sunderland, the Rev. Thomas Stratten (of the Bethel New Chapel) had already been preaching regularly to seamen; and at Whitby, the Rev. George Young (the well-known Presbyterian divine) had done the same. (SML 1822, pp. 406-8, 521. NSM 1828,pp. 277-80.) Cf. supra, p. 146.

198. SML 1822, pp. 497-8. NSM 1828, pp. 474-5. Port of Hull Society 1907, pp. 28-9; cf. pp. 50-1.

199. SML 1823, p. 495; 1824, pp. 408-9; 1825, pp. 109, 497-502, Supplement pp. 7-8. NSM 1860, pp. 73-4.

200. SML 1823, pp. 460-2.

201. SML 1822, pp. 368-9; 1823, pp. 413, 460; 1825, pp. 158-60. SMR 1823, pp. 208-10. The title of the institution varied: in 1829, it is referred to as the "[Aberdeen] Bethel Seamen's Friend Society" (SMR 1829, pp. 398-401; cf. Bethel Seamen's Friend Society *Report* 1829). In S.W. England, a "Sailor's Chapel" (or "Seamen's Chapel") at Newlyn, Cornwall, was in 1821 referred to as having been erected "for some time"; this was presumably the chapel built by local Baptists for the benefit of the resident community, who in this typical sea-port would be largely associated with seafaring. (SML 1820, p. 104; 1821, p. 161; 1824, p. 207. "Vindicator," 1824, pp. 42-3.)

202. SML 1823, p. 462. The Editor of *The Sailor's Magazine* refers, in 1824, to the journal of a *Lieutenant Calder*, in connection with the progress of the Seamen's Cause in Scotland (SML 1824, p. 283). He also quotes a Rev. Donaldson of Dundee, writing in April 1823, both about a local society

("formed in the year 1820") promoting regular preaching for seamen in the Seamen's Fraternity Hall, and about the recent acquisition of a "Seamen's Reading Room."

203. SML 1822, pp. 248, 367-8; 1823, pp. 238-40, 416-20, 462; 1825, p. 280. SMR 1825, pp. 343-4. The later *plural* form of the title was not used in the Society's first published *Regulations* (Glasgow Seamen's Friend Society 1822, pp. 1, 3). The worship services instituted on the brig *Morning Star* were transferred first to the Riding School, York Street, thence (from November 1822) to an apartment in the old Delftfield, James Watt Street, (SML 1823, pp. 417-8). The Seamen's Chapel at 11 Brown Street, now known as the "Seamen's Bethel," was reconstructed in 1860, and again in 1908, following a fire (Glasgow Seamen's Friend Society 1923, p. 6). See also SML 1823, p. 277.

204. SML 1822, pp. 210-1; 1826, pp. 260-1.

205. SML 1820, p. 27; 1821, pp. 364, 400; 1822, pp. 246-7, 488.

206. SML 1822, p. 369.

207. SML 1824, p. 407; 1825, pp. 144-5; Supplement p. 7.

208. SML 1820, p. 447; 1821, pp. 157, 492-3; 1822, pp. 519-20; 1823, p. 76; 1827, pp. 10-7. The Rev. William Cooper, Sr., of Plunket Street Chapel, was evidently zealous in assisting from the outset. The Seamen's Missionary is referred to as the Rev. George *Silly*, by the correspondent in SML 1822, pp. 519-20.

209. SML 1822, pp. 521-2. Cf. BFBS *Reports* 1820-21, p. 260. The very first sermon under the Bethel Flag in Belfast was delivered in the summer of 1822, on board a Welsh brig, by a naval lieutenant, on the initiative of "the mate of a Belfast trader." The mate's wife had made the flag. (SML 1822,pp. 431-2.)

210. SML 1820, p. 447; 1822, pp. 428, 519; 1824, p. 407. Cf. NSM 1830, pp. 421-2.

211. SML 1820, p. 396; 1822, p. 519; 1823, p. 398.

212. Bethel Flag services in the Shetlands were carried on by the Wesleyan Rev. Dunn in 1823 (SML 1824, p. 50). After earlier preaching under the Bethel Flag, a "Jersey Seamen's Friend Society and Bethel Union" was formed at St. Helen's, June 11, 1824, shortly after which a "Seamen's Chapel" was opened ashore. Similar steps were taken on Guernsey (SML 1822, pp. 194-6; 1823, pp. 398-9; 1824, pp. 117, 356-7; 1825, pp. 116-7, 140-4).

213. In this way, local societies might well speak of themselves as the Parent Institution's "different dependencies." (SML 1824, p. 158. Cf. Warren 1858, p. 37.)

214. SML 1822, p. 446. Organizational conformity with the London Society would, of course, vary with the degree of prior communication in each case.

215. G.C. Smith *The Custom House and the Bethel Flag* n.d. (1st ed. 1823). Cf. SML 1822, pp. 370-1; 1823, pp. 24-6, 257-61. NSM 1860, pp. 66-8.

216. Supra, p. 204.

217. Supra, pp. 135-6.

218. Infra, pp. 307, 312.

219. E.g.: SML 1822, pp. 78-9; 1824, p. 397.

220. SML 1820, p. 26; 1823, pp. 115, 371; 1824, pp. 422-3; 1825, p. 526. The BFBS cooperated closely with the LMS and the "Lascar Committee," in ministering to Asian seamen in London, as early as in 1815 (BFBS *Reports* 1814-15, p. 506; 1816-17, pp. 270, xcviii). Infra, pp. 246, 378.

221. SML 1820, p. 64; 1822, pp. 347-8; 1826, p. 117.

222. SML 1825, pp. 314, 396-8, 431-2, 449, 489-90. Cf. Green 1828, pp. 145-7. The Continental Society *Extracts* 1827, p. 5. The allusion in SML 1847, p. 2, to cooperation with the PLS is misleading, since this Society did not amalgamate with the BFSFSBU (with whom von Bülow was, in fact, associated) until 1827. Infra, pp. 260-2.

223. SML 1825, p. 356; 1826, pp. 133, 455; 1827, pp. 518-9. SMR 1826, 567; 1827, p. 257. Green 1828, pp. 147-8. It was Captain H.I. Waterburg, of the *Four Brothers*, Groningen, who preached to his Dutch compatriots, in the Hull Floating Chapel, on Sunday, May 8 and 15, 1825 (MMNY 1825, pp. 297-8).

224. SML 1820, p. 426.

225. SML 1822, p. 355; 1823, p. 354. (MS) BFSFSBU *Minutes*, May 26, 1824. Cf. supra, p. 161.

226. (MS) BFSFSBU *Minutes*, Dec. 18, 1822. SML 1823, pp. 34-5.

227. (MS) BFSFSBU *Minutes*, July 30, 1823.

228. Weibust 1969, pp. 347-8, 354.

229. Infra, pp. 308-12.

230. SML 1821, pp. 178-9; 1826, p. 455; 1837, p. 158. SMR 1827, p. 297.

231. Ibid. Cf. Weibust 1969, pp. 162, 269-70.

232. PLS *Proceedings* 1821, pp. 16-7.

233. SML 1825, p. 444; Supplement p. 10. Another typical case of improvisation is related from a South American port, where a captain's wife resolved her husband's predicament by pulling a sheet out of a drawer and getting him to inscribe "BETHEL" with lamp-black (SML 1825, p. 380).

234. SMR 1827, p. 297. Infra, pp. 250-1.

235. PHS *AR* 1823, p. 11. NSM 1828, pp. 237-8; 1832, pp. 152-4, 204-6. Cf. SML 1836, pp. 153-6.

236. NSM 1828, pp. 237-8.

237. SML 1837, pp. 157-9.

238. SML 1824, p.463. See also SML 1820, p. 460; 1823, pp. 379, 400; 1825, p. 279. Cf. *Bud og Hilsen*, April 1866, p. 17. *Bud fra Havet*, No. 3-4 1981, pp. 12-13.

239. Lewis 1959, p. 167.

240. E.g.: SML 1821, pp. 337-9; 1827, pp. 77-8, 148-9. Eliza Morrison 1839 Vol. 1, pp. 108-26. Cf. supra, pp. 510-11.

241. Infra, pp. 551-3.

242. SML 1820, p. 449, Cf. SML 1820, p. 188; 1821, pp. 337-9.

243. (MS) BFSFSBU *Minutes*, May 15, 1822. W.H. Angas undertook to forward these materials to the BMS. Another committee member undertook to contact the LMS.

244. SML 1824,pp. 20-1, 419.

245. Infra, pp. 245-8.

246. E.g.: SML 1822, p.429; 1824, p. 415. Cf. Seierstad 1947, pp. 170-4.

247. E.g.: SML 1820, pp. 188-9; 1824, pp. 413, 462-3.

248. E.g.: SML 1821, p. 456; 1822, p.167; 1826, pp. 38-9.

249. E.g., (MS) BFSFSBU *Minutes*, Jan 17, Feb. 19, April 2, June 25, Sept. 24, 1823. Cf. NSM 1829, Pt. II, p. 346.

250. E.g., (MS) BFSFSBU *Minutes*, Jan 17, 1823.

251. E.g., SML 1824, p. 360. MM 1825, p. 300.

252. SML 1822, pp.167, 288-90, 429, 479-80; 1823, pp. 235-6; 1824, pp. 34-6, 78-9, 519-20; 1825, pp. 38-9. (MS) BFSFSBU *Minutes*, May 28, 1823. Zealous coadjutors were also the assistant secretary, a Peter Hepburn ("appointed to H.M. dockyard at Gibraltar"), and—afloat— especially the merchant captains John Oakley and John Hague. Lt. Bailey, besides being treasurer of the local Bethel Society, became the highly efficient secretary of the BFBS "Gibraltar Correspondence Committee," formed about the same time. With his colleague, he ensured that both British and foreign shipping was well supplied with Scriptures and tracts. On transferring to the Isle of Wight in 1825, he forthwith promoted a Port of Cowes Society there. ([MS], BFBS *Foreign Corresp.*, letters from J. W. Bailey, April 27, Oct. 25, 1821; *Home Corresp.*, Sept. 21, Dec. 6, 1825. [MS] BFSFSBU *Minutes*, May 28, 1823. BFBS *Reports* 1822-24, p. lviii. [MS] Cann 1969.)

253. (MS) BFSFSBU *Minutes*, July 14, Aug. 25, 1824; Sept. 7, Dec. 14, 1825. SML 1824, pp. 317-8, 415-6; 1825, p. 489; 1826, pp. 38-9. BFBS *Reports* 1825-27, pp. xl-xli.

254. SML 1822, p. 429; 1823, p. 370; 1824, pp. 415-6; 1825, pp. 29, 357, 444-5, Supplement pp. 9-10; 1826, pp. 38, 487.

255. Howse 1960, p. 94. Cf. supra, pp. 204, 239.

256. (MS) BFSFSBU *Minutes*, Feb. 19, March 5, 1823. SML 1823, pp. 115-6, 371; 1824, pp. 56, 359-60, 414-5; 1825, pp. 335-7, 526-7; Supplement p. 11; 1826, pp. 347-8. The Society was accorded early official recognition by the acquisition of Commodore Hayes, the Master Attendant, as president, and the Governor himself, the Marquis of Hastings, as patron (SML) 1825, p. 336).

257. SML 1824, pp. 277, 359-60. Cf. infra, pp. 379-80.

258. SML 1825, pp. 311, 337, Supplement p. 11.

259. Calcutta Seamen's Friend Society *AR* 1842, p. 13; cf. 1838, pp. 15-21.

260. Ibid., *ARs* 1838-42.

261. (MS) BFSFSBU *Minutes*, April 2, 1823. SML 1824, pp. 133-9, 415; 1825, Supplement p. 11. Cf. NMBS *Report* 1817, pp. 34, 65.

262. BFBS *Monthly Extracts* No. 168, 1831, pp. 507-8. Bombay Seamen's Friend Association *Reports* 1831, 1838, 1840.

263. (MS) BFSFSBU *Minutes*, 30 April 1823. SML 1823, p. 371; 1824, p. 415; 1825, Supplement p. 11.

264. Infra, pp. 464-7.

265. *The Sydney Gazette* Sept. 27, 1822. NSM 1831, pp. 15-6. Cf. *Chambers's Encyclopedia* Vol. 1 1950, p. 807.

266. Ibid. SML 1824, p. 413. One Wesleyan missionary, a Rev. Erskine, had been so impressed with what he had witnessed of the efforts of the Calcutta Bethel Society, while in transit to New South Wales, that he declared his determination to "hoist the Bethel Flag in that distant port of the world as soon as he arrived" (SML 1824, pp. 360, 415). In 1823, a series of *Reports* and a print of the Thames Floating Chapel were sent by the Committee of the PLS to the secretary of the Society which was understood to be evolving in Sydney ([MS] PLS *Minutes*, July 22, 1823). At the public meeting finalizing the founding of the Sydney Society, it was the Rev. Samuel Marsden who presided (SML 1824, p. 413).

267. SML 1824, p. 413. NSM 1831, pp. 14-7. Re. further Australian developments, see infra, pp. 380, 476.

268. (MS) BFSFSBU *Minutes*, Feb. 19, Sept. 24, 1823; Jan. 31, 1827. SML 1823, pp. 368-9; 1824, pp. 412-3; 1825, p. 359, Supplement p. 11. Cf. (MS) PLS *Minutes*, March 11, 1823, July 12, 1825. Also, SML 1823, pp. 135-6.

269. SML 1825, pp. 429-31.

270. SML 1823, p. 369; 1825, pp. 67-8, 147-8; 1826, pp. 193-4. Cf. (MS) BFSFSBU *Minutes*, April 15, 1823. Captain William Scoresby was particularly active as Bethel Captain in these waters (infra, p. 287).

271. SML 1820, pp. 188-9, 448. Cf. infra, pp. 428-30.

272. SML 1821, p. 37; 1822, p. 428.

273. SML 1823, p. 368. The flag at Quebec was stated to have been left by "Capt. Hindaugh of the *Zephyrus* . . .with some friends of the Society" ([MS] BFSFSBU *Minutes*, April 21, 1824).

274. (MS) BFSFSBU *Minutes*, Aug. 3 & 10, 1825. Cf. (MS) BFSS *Minutes*, March 20, 1829. Under 1827, the Rev. Osgood is listed as Agent of the "Montreal Sailors' and Strangers' Society," in connection with a temporary Bethel on the Canal Side, described as Montreal's "first modern Sailor Service" (Atherton 1935, p. 6).

275. (MS) BFBS *Home Corresp.*, letter from William Cooke, Jan. 21, 1825. SML 1825, pp. 279-80; 1826, pp. 212-3. Cf. (MS) PLS *Minutes*, Jan. 11, 1825, Feb. 28, 1826.

276. SML 1822, p. 429.

277. SML 1820, pp. 440, 449; 1821, p. 39.

278. SML 1822, p. 429. (MS) BFSFSBU *Minutes*, Jan. 17, 1823.

279. The Berbice correspondent, the Rev. John Wray (a missionary of the LMS), had, previous to this, already commenced a personal ministry to seamen. ([MS] BFSFSBU *Minutes*, May 1, 1822, Jan. 17, 1823. SML 1822, pp. 205-6, 429.) The Anglican clergyman at neighboring Demarara, the Rev. Mr. Austin, evidently showed sympathy with the BFSFSBU. (SML 1824, pp. 462-3. Cf. [MS] BFSFSBU *Minutes*, Jan. 17, 1823.)

280. SML 1822, p. 429; 1823, p. 368. Cf. infra, p. 433.

281. SML 1821, p. 456; 1822, pp. 371, 429; 1826, pp. 222-3. Hodder 1891, pp. 59-60. In 1829, it was reported: "The service is generally conducted by two British merchants, residents there, viz. Messrs. M'Kay and Thornton, who constantly attend, with others, from the shore. . . ." (NSM 1830, pp. 47-8).

282. In Montevideo, Captain Richard Ainsley was concerned, despite the attendance of merchants from shore, over not finding any with whom he could entrust the

flag on leaving (SML 1823, pp. 434-6). At Buenos Ayres, "one of the American Independent Missionaries" there undertook to continue Sunday shipboard preaching, with the support of an active residential Anglo-American group (SML 1825, pp. 445-6, Supplement p. 11-2).

283. SML 1824, p. 412; cf. 1825, pp. 345-7. The BFSFSBU were able to send out many of its publications via Cornish miners bound for Chili from Falmouth (SML 1825, Supplement p. 11).

284. SML 1823, pp. 367-8. Cf. infra, pp. 476-7.

285. Hodder 1891, pp. 21-3, 28-38, 59-61. After the passing of the Honduras Bill (resulting in the emancipation, 1824, of 200-300,000 natives), G.F. Angas sought to multiply the fruits accruing from his experiment with Christian captains and agents, by publishing, in 1825, a prospectus for "The Society for Promoting Christianity and Civilization through the Medium of Commercial, Scientific, and Professional Agency." However, the project foundered during the great commercial panic of 1825-26 (ibid., pp. 64-7).

286. E.g.: SML 1820,p. 440; 1823, p. 436. Also, Hodder 1891, pp. 59-61.

287. *William Henry Angas* Valuable primary sources of biographical data are contained in his own narrative in the "Account of the Ordination of the Rev. Wm. Henry Angas to the Work and Office of a Missionary to Seafaring Men . . ." (SML 1822, pp. 283-6), as well as in numerous letters from his pen, published in the early volumes of *The Sailor's Magazine* (London). In his biography of 1834, F.A. Cox had access not only to these sources, but also to copious family correspondence. The Rev. E.W. Matthews includes data from Cox in his *Historic Glances* in CC 1879, pp. 143-8. In *The King's Brotherhood* 1911, pp. 1-173, he includes the whole of Cox's text. In his far later biography of G.F. Angas, Edwin Hodder includes a biographical summary of his brother, William Henry (Hodder 1891, pp. 23-8, 47-63). Note the biographical sketch in Timpson 1856, pp. 64-7. DNB Vol. 1 1885, has only a brief notice (p. 413). The Author had the benefit, in May 1970, of consulting with the Rev. Norman J. Parkes (then Senior Chaplain, BSS Scottish Branch, Glasgow), who had engaged in a detailed research of the life of W.H. Angas.

288. SML 1822, pp. 283-4. Cox 1834, pp. i-xi, 1-7. It was W.H. Angas' grand-father who, for unknown reasons, changed the spelling from "Angus" to "Angas" (Cox 1834, p. i). W.H. Angas was given a solid education, being sent first to boarding school at Catterick, Yorkshire, then to the Rev. W. Turner's school at Barrass Bridge (Cox 1834, pp. 3-6).

289. Supra, pp. 115-6.

290. SML 1822, pp. 284-5. Cox 1834, pp. 7-30. W.H. Angas had, at the age of nine or ten, received the "first serious impressions" he could remember. A "pious grandfather" aroused in the boy a vivid fear of hell. The concept of salvation by works, reinforced at his first school, continued to terrify him until, under his parents' minister (the Rev. Mr. Skinner), he was led to see that salvation was "entirely of grace." Now, by basing his faith instead on the Lord's "pardoning love," he found "peace of conscience." Although these impressions "gradually wore off" during ensuing years at sea, they were evidently never altogether extinguished (SML 1822, pp. 284-6).

291. SML 1822, pp. 284-5. Cox 1834, pp. 15-29. Caleb Angas, a "truly exemplary character," traveled with his younger brother as supercargo. Among books he handed to William, John Newton's *Life* engrossed the latter especially (SML 1822, p. 285).

292. SML 1822, p. 285. Cf. Cox 1834, pp. 64-6.

293. Cox 1834, p. 32. Cf. Hodder 1891, p. 48.

294. SML 1822, p. 285. Cox 1834, pp. 30, 36-45.

295. SML 1820, pp. 64-5; 1822, p. 285. F.A. Cox credits W.H. Angas with agitating for a widening of the scope of the BSU, to include world-wide foreign operations. (Cox 1834, pp. 49-50.) Significantly, Cox ignores (in 1834) the role of G.C. Smith; Hodder repeats the omission in 1891 (Hodder 1891, pp. 57-9).

296. Cox 1834, pp. 51-63. W.H. Angas' dedication to his original call is evidenced by his rejection, in 1819, of a position of exceptional "emolument and honour," as residential minister in Berbice (pp. 45-8). Of historical interest is the fact that W.H. Angas, also in 1819, shortly before the founding of the BSU, broached the possibility of the "Baptist Missionary Society" taking up his seamen's mission plans (pp. 47-8).

297. SML 1822, pp. 283-5. Note: The Rev. W.H. Angas' fellow-Baptist biographer takes care to distinguish, prior to the ordination, between the church's call in 1817 to the Christian ministry, and its call in 1822 to "the office of a Missionary to Seafaring Men" (Cox 1834, pp. 41, 67).

298. Supra, p. 244.

299. SML 1820, pp. 77-9. The article, signed *Aristarchus*, refers to the offer of twenty guineas toward such an appointment already made by "A friend to Sailors" through G.C. Smith (p. 26). The appointment of a full-time *stationary* minister to seamen was, in the British religious press, not yet under discussion. Cf. infra, pp. 269-70.

300. SML 1822, p. 285.

301. SML 1823, p. 219. Cox 1834, pp. 65-6.

302. Supra, pp. 234-5.

303. SML 1822, p. 407.

304. SML 1821, p. 281; 1822, p. 445. Cf. Hugill 1967, pp. 136-42.

305. Thun 1959, p. 12. Deutsche Seemannsmission in Hamburg R.V. 1966, pp. 136-42.

306. SML 1821, pp. 117, 281-2.

307. SML 1821, pp. 318-9. Cf. NMBS *Report* 1819, p. 24.

308. EM 1822, p. 158.

309. SML 1822, pp. 445-6, 512-3, 219-26, 370. Cox 1834, pp. 75-7, 108, 130. The *Hope* of Greenock and the *Admittance* of Boston (Mass.) were for weeks especially useful to Angas, being the most spacious ships in port, and readily offered. (SML 1823, 153-5, 219-26. Cox 1834, p. 77.) Before the Hamburg Senate's approval of local floating chapel plans, an incipient interest in this method of ministry had already been aroused in Germany. The King of Saxony had, on Nov. 6, 1820, presented £25 through his ambassador toward the London Floating Chapel, together with a letter expressing his "interest in the welfare of seamen." Amongst other simultaneous contributions were 100 Saxon Thallers "from the Burgo Master and Magistrates of Leipzig." It was reported shortly afterwards that a sermon preached by the Rev. J.A. James at the 1820 Anniversary of the PLS had been translated into German at Leipzig, and published in aid of the Society. (PLS *Proceedings* 1821, pp. 33-4. Cf. SML 1820, pp. 479-80.) Besides Angas' publishing activities, *The Boatswain's*

Mate and several others of G.C. Smith's tracts were, in the 1823 *Retrospect* of the BFSFSBU, reported to have been translated and circulated in Germany "by a zealous Burgo-master" (SML 1823, p. 370; 1824, p. 294).

310. SML 1822, pp. 512-3; 1823, p. 223. Cox 1834, pp. 76-8. Not all merchants were equally negative. A Mr. Becket of Jackson & Becket personally took part with Angas in the meetings afloat (SML 1823, pp. 153, 219; cf. 1822, p. 445).

311. SML 1822, p. 445; 1824, pp. 18-9, 21, 293-7, 416. "By way of a change," the highest window of Matthews' house, which was visible from the shipping, was made available to Angas for hoisting the Bethel Flag (SML 1823, p. 225).

312. *J.G. Oncken*, who was born in Varel, Oldenburg, Jan. 26, 1800, had been brought to Scotland as a youth, and spoke fluent English. When sent by The Continental Society to Hamburg in December 1823, he had become deeply influenced by Congregational circles. A subsequent leaning toward Baptist views culminated in his baptism by Dr. Barnas Sears, April 22, 1834. From 1828-29, and for fifty years to come, he was the zealous agent of the Edinburgh Bible Society, later the National Bible Society of Scotland. (Hodder 1891, p. 63. Brun 1902, pp. 163-7, 170-1. KLN Vol. 3, 1911, p. 433. [MS] Knight n.d., pp. 72-3.) Re. "The Continental Society," see infra, p. 261.

313. SML 1824, pp. 294-7, 360; 1825, pp. 57-60; Supplement p. 9.

314. SML 1824, p. 319; 1826, p. 260. NSM 1832, p. 191. Re. Matthew's U.K. fund-raising tour, see (MS) BFSFSBU *Minutes*, October 13, 1824. See also SML 1825, p. 105.

315. NSM 1831, p. 299; 1832, p. 191. Cox 1834, 129-30. Official restrictions (with which Bethel pioneers so frequently had to contend in Hamburg) continued to harass in 1831 (NSM 1832, p. 191).

316. Cox 1834, pp. 47, 58, 64, 67-8, 78-98. Cf. SML 1824, p. 21.

317. SML 1824, pp. 19-20, 419: cf. 1821, p. 472.

318. SML 1824, pp. 21, 116, 360. A Mr. Martens (a "pious and principal merchant" of Antwerp) proved particularly helpful to Angas (SML 1824, p. 360).

319. SML 1825, pp. 399-400; Supplement p. 8. Cox 1834, pp. 104-5.

320. SML 1825, pp. 356-7, 399-400; Supplement p. 8. Cox 1834, pp. 105-7.

321. Supra, pp. 149. Dutch seafarers had already gained a reputation for responsiveness to the Gospel in British seamen's mission circles of the early 1820's. (E.g.: SML 1821, p. 296. PLS *Proceedings* 1821, p. 34.) Cf. supra, Part IV, Note No. 223.

322. SML 1825, pp. 356-7, 399-400; Supplement p. 8. (MS) BFSFSBU *Minutes*, August 10, 1825. Cox 1834, pp. 106, 121.

323. Cox 1834, pp. 111-30. During a brief but important mission for the BMS to Jamaica in 1830-31, Angas successfully established his system of "seamen's Bible-classes" during the sea-voyage, confirming his conviction of this as a fundamental condition for the evangelization of seamen. (Cox 1834, pp. 155-7. Cf. the "Ministering Seafarers' Program," [MS] Eckhoff 1979. See also infra, p. 581.)

324. Cox 1834, pp. 159-63. (Cf. Canton Vol. 1, 1904, pp. 362-3.) In the words of Angas' biographer, "he was perhaps surprised, but neither alarmed nor

unprepared," because his lamp was "ready trimmed" (Ibid., pp. 160-1). The following day, he was buried at Westgate Hill Cemetery, Newcastle, where a warm tribute is inscribed over his grave. (Ibid., pp. 163-4. Hodder 1891, pp. 62-3.)

325. Up to 1826, the relationship between G.C. Smith and W.H. Angas appears to have been one of only mutual warmth and respect. After the eruption of organizational warfare in 1827, however, an estrangement developed. (SML 1822, p. 513; 1823, p. 219; 1826, p. 117. Cf. NSM 1829, pp. 210, 216; 1837, p. 880.) On the other hand, E.W. Matthews' comparison between the two pioneer figures is far from impartial (CC 1879, pp. 146-7). Whatever may otherwise be said of Angas' rhetorical abilities, a collection of striking "Nautical Aphorisms" included in Cox's biography (pp. 173-214) certainly evince a gift which must have served him well in his ministry to seamen.

326. Cf. SML 1820, pp. 77-9; 1823, pp. 214, 245: 1824, p. 403.

327. SML 1823, pp. 222-3. Although by nature conciliatory and ecumenically liberal, Angas was, for his own part, firmly evangelical (see, for example, Cox 1834, pp. 48, 106-7).

328. Hodder 1891, pp. 56, 61-2. Matthews 1911, p. xvi.

329. Richter 1896, p. 87. Cf. (MS) Hirsch n.d., p. 356. *Carlos* was used both of and by von Bülow, during his employment with The Continental Society. (E.g.: The Continental Society 1827, pp. 1, 3. [MS] BFBS *For. Corresp.*, letters from Carlos von Bülow 1827-28.) Later, as BFSS Missionary to Foreign Sailors, he is again referred to as *Carl* (SML 1846, p. 256; 1847, p. 1).

330. SML 1846, pp. 256-7; 1847, pp. 1-4. The latter contains a hitherto little-known presentation of von Bülow's life and doctrinal position. Cf. Thrap 1906, p. 549. KLN Vol. 4 1921, p. 99. Haaland 1956, pp. 146-7. Where occasionally referred to as *Baron* von Bülow (e.g.: SML 1826, p. 455; SMR 1827, p. 257; BFBS *Reports* 1828-30, p. xlix), this may also have been due to a confusion with the Baron von Bülow who was Prussian Chargé d'Affairs in London about this time ([MS] BFBS *Home Corresp.*, letters from *Baron* von Bülow, 1819-20. SML 1823, p. 45.) The father of Carl von Bülow, Johan Hartvig Victor Carl von Bülow, himself a cavalry officer, remained in Norway, as postmaster in Drammen 1789-1810, thence retiring to nearby Holmestrand until his death, 1823 (Haaland 1956, p. 147). Carl von Bülow held the rank of *Lieutenant-Colonel* at the end of the war.

331. BFBS *Reports* 1818-19, p. 320. SML 1825, p. 398. The Continental Society 1827, p. 4. Jones 1850, pp. 322-4. Thrap 1906, pp. 549-50. KLN Vol. 4, 1929, p. 999. Danbolt 1947, pp. 211-2. Haaland 1956, p. 147. (MS) Knight Pt. I, n.d., p. 40.

332. Before leaving Scotland (for the second time in 1819), von Bülow married Helen Hay Inglis, daughter of an Edinburgh solicitor. She accompanied him both now and on his later missions to Norway. (KLN Vol. 4, 1929, p. 999. Cf. The Continental Society 1827, pp. 6, 44.)

333. SML 1825, pp. 314, 396-9. Green 1828, pp. 144-7. Haaland 1956, pp. 147-8. On Dec. 1, 1824, the Committee of the BFSFSBU discussed the offer of "a Foreign Preacher," and a suggestion that the Danish Church in Wellclose Square could be obtained for the purpose of "regular preaching to the Foreign Seamen." A decision was deferred, however ([MS] BFSFSBU *Minutes*, Dec.

1, 1824). Examples of von Bülow's cooperation with G.C. Smith at this stage: SML 1825, pp. 11, 348; also, Port of London Society 1829, pp. 68-9. Von Bülow's 1846 statement that, on his arrival in London in 1824, he "volunteered to the Port of London Society to visit the foreign vessels," presumably refers to the BFSFSBU, which three years later merged with the PLS to form the PLBUS (SML 1847, p. 2).

334. SML 1825, pp. 314, 396.

335. The official object of the Society was "to assist local Native Ministers in preaching the Gospel, and in distributing Bibles, Testaments, and religious publications over the Continent of Europe; but without the design of establishing any distinct sect or party" (The Continental Society 1819, p. 13). Cf. *The Baptist Magazine* 1820, p. 282. Also, Highmore 1822, pp. 120-32. In the mid-1830's, the Society changed its name to "The European Missionary Society."

336. SML 1825, pp. 314, 396-9. In America, it was erroneously assumed that here was a "Seamen's Continental Society," specifically formed "for the diffusion of religious knowledge among seamen over the continent of Europe, by aid of native preachers" (MMNY 1825-26, pp. 307-8).

337. (MS) BFSFSBU *Minutes*, Jan. 11, 1826. (Ten guineas were voted for the purpose.)

338. This tour was expressly "to promote the funds for a mission to the Sailors of Norway, Sweden, and Denmark" (SML 1825, pp. 489-90; Supplement p. 9).

339. The Continental Society 1827, pp. 6-47. SML 1827, pp. 107-8; 1847, p. 2. Faber 1915, pp. 144-5. Haaland 1956, pp. 149-52. Seierstad 1923, pp. 200-6, Nome 1942, pp. 145-70, and Danbolt 1947, pp. 211-20, deal in detail with von Bülow's general activities in Norway, but their presentations do not specifically concern themselves with his ministry to *seafarers* there.

340. The Continental Society 1827, pp. 6, 43, 47. *The World*, May 19, 1827 (under "Continental Society"). SML 1846, p. 257; 1847, pp. 2-3. KLN Vol. 4, 1929, p. 999. Haaland 1956, p. 152. Cf. (MS) BFBS *For. Corresp.*, letters from von Bülow, Feb. 19, March 12, 1827.

341. The Continental Society stood by their embattled emissary, who now—for some years—transferred his activities to Denmark, North Germany, and Prussia (The Continental Society 1829, pp. 7-8, 12). *The Missionary Register* 1831, p. 268. SML 1847, p. 3.) Seierstad 1923, pp. 200-6, Nome 1942, pp. 163-70, and Danbolt 1947, pp. 211-20, provide details of von Bülow's controversies with Norwegian officialdom.

342. Seierstad 1923, p. 205. KLN Vol. 4, 1929, pp. 999-1000. Nome 1942, pp. 149-50, 159-63, 170, 175. Danbolt 1947, pp. 217-20. Cf. Seierstad 1947, pp. 174-5. Aarflot 1967, p. 333.

343. As an experiment, a yacht was evidently employed in the summer of 1821, in order to stimulate Bethel operations on the West Coast of England; but it is not clear whether this vessel could actually accommodate meetings *on board* (SML 1822, pp. 88-9). Cf. infra, pp. 385-6.

344. Infra, pp. 477-8, 596.

345. SML 1823, p. 369.

346. SML 1822, p. 507.

347. Ibid., p. 39.

348. SML 1822, pp. 430, 507-8; 1823, pp. 369, 394; 1824, pp. 57, 416; 1825, Supplement pp. 9, 16. (MS) BFSFSBU *Minutes*, June 25, 1823. SMR 1827, pp. 296-7. Henderson 1859, pp. 277-81. Canton, Vol. 1 1904, pp. 414-8. The Rev. R. Knill, a Congregational "missionary," stationed at St. Petersburg, also provided zealous support for the Bethel Cause at Cronstadt (SML 1822, p. 430; 1823, p. 394).

349. SML 1821, pp. 441-2; 1823, pp. 36-7; 1826, pp. 79-80, 167-8. (MS) BFSFSBU *Minutes*, June 25, 1823. There were, in 1821, plans for a "Riga Bethel Society" (SML 1821, p. 442; cf. 1826, p. 168).

350. SML 1824, pp. 416, 436-8; 1826,pp. 117-8, 120. NSM 1829 Pt. I, pp. 114-5; 1832, pp. 204-6. SML 1836, p. 155. Cf. Part III, Notes Nos. 108, 163.

351. SML 1821, p. 318.

352. At *Hamburg*, both Matthews and Oncken had (in vain) pointed to the acute need for full-time workers, both for English-language and native seafarers (SML 1824, p. 293; 1825, p. 59). Not before 1831 was the modest beginning of a "Seamen's Friend Society" made at *Le Havre*, by the BFSSFS (infra, p. 470).

353. SML 1822, p. 463.

354. SML 1824, p. 397.

355. SML 1824, pp. 49, 57; 1825, pp. 199, 277, 317. *The Christian Guardian* 1826, pp. 175-6. *The Baptist Magazine* 1826, p. 334.

356. G.C. Smith *Bethel* n.d., p. 23. SML 1820, pp. 57, 359, 397, 447-8.

357. (MS) BFSFSBU *Minutes*, Aug. 12, 1822; March 5, Sept. 23, 1823. SML 1822, pp. 338-40, 424-5; 1823, pp. 446-9, 464-6.

358. SML 1822, pp. 339-40; 1824, p. 232; 1825, pp. 181, 199, 294. Cf. Timpson 1856, p. 56.

359. SML 1822, p. 339; 1825, p. 199.

360. SML 1822, p. 425; 1823, p. 363; 1824, p. 403; 1825, p. 199. Cf. infra, pp. 291-2.

361. SML 1823, p. 448; 1825, pp. 176-85, 241-51. Cf. infra, pp. 305, 582.

362. (MS) BFSFSBU *Minutes*, Dec. 1, 1824. G.C. Smith *Blackheath* n.d., p. 45. Green 1828, pp. 137-8. BFSSFS *Decision* 1829, pp. 3-4. Cf. Faber 1915, p. 143. Note: Philadelphia Mariners' Church *Report* 1826, pp. 12-7, had already reproduced the letter from G.C. Smith, quoted in Green 1828, pp. 136-43.

363. SML 1825, pp. 426-8. G.C. Smith *Blackheath* n.d., p. 44. Green 1828, p. 138.

364. (MS) BFSFSBU *Minutes*, Aug. 24 & 31, 1825. G.C. Smith *Blackheath* n.d., pp. 44-50. Faber 1915, p. 143; 1926, pp. 67-8. Henry Ashley, Esq., "a respectable solicitor," together with "another friend," agreed to share legal responsibility with Smith (*Blackheath*, p. 50). Cf. infra, p. 358.

365. SML 1825, pp. 184-5, 356, 371-9. G.C. Smith *Blackheath* n.d., pp. 49-50. The Society could also, until 1827, be referred to as the "London Mariners' Church and Rivermen's Bethel Union Society," or simply the "(London) Mariners' Society" (e.g.: SML 1826, pp. 478, 482; 1827, p. 26).

366. SML 1825, pp. 184-5, 356, 377; 1826, pp. 1-2.

367. SML 1825, p. 426. G.C. Smith *Blackheath* n.d., pp. 44, 59.

368. NSM 1828, pp. 64-5. G.C. Smith *Blackheath* n.d., p. 50.

369. Ibid., p. 57. Cf. SML 1826, p. 22. Plans for a similar, south-bank establishment for the Deptford-Greenwich area, at Creek Bridge, did not materialize,
however. (SML 1825, pp. 368-72. G.C. Smith *Blackheath* n.d., pp. 20-1.)

370. SML 1826, pp. 52, 116-7. Green 1828, p. 138. NSM 1829 Pt. I, p. 132;
1858, p. 115. The church had been built and decorated by the Danish-born
sculptor *Caius Gabriel Cibber*, in the Renaissance style of Wren — in red
brick and Portland stone, as used at Hampton Court (Faber 1926, pp. 63-7).
Barnes 1967, pp. 179-82.

371. SML 1825, p. 246. Green 1828, p. 139. NSM 1829 Pt. I, pp. 132-4. Faber
1915, pp. 42-3, 139, 188; 1926, pp. 61-2, 67. Hugill 1967, p. 118. The name
"Well Close," thought to have been derived from a *well* located in this *close*,
or field, had by 1694 given way to "Marine Square"; this was in the 18th
century supplanted by "Wellclose Square." (Harben 1918, p. 618. *The
Copartnership Herald* 1934, p. 36.) The continuing notoriety of the Sailortown
surrounding Wellclose Square was, forty years later, used as an argument
against placing a "Scandinavian" Seamen's Church there (BH 1867, p. 19).

372. SML 1825, p. 246. NSM 1829 Pt. II, p. 134.

373. SML 1823, pp. 446-9, 464-6; 1825, pp. 162-3, 376-7; 1826, pp. 65-72, 116-
7.

374. Infra, pp. 315-40.

375. Supra, pp. 199-202.

376. SML 1820, p. 464.

377. E.g., PLBUS *Appeal* 1829, pp. 1-3, 7, 50, 53.

378. G.C. Smith *Blackheath* n.d., pp. 6-7, 11-2, 21-2. Cf. SML 1825, pp. 242-3.
NSM 1837, p. 880.

379. SML 1824, p. 492; 1825, pp. 162, 358-9. G.C. Smith *Blackheath* n.d., pp.
11-2, 21-2.

380. G.C. Smith *Aldermanbury* n.d., p. 12. Cf. PLBUS *Appeal* 1829, p. 70.

381. SML 1825, pp. 246-7, 370. Allegations of "trickery and falsehood" on the
part of G.C. Smith in obtaining possession of the Danish Church (PLBUS
Appeal 1829, pp. 65-78) were roundly refuted in Thompson 1829 (pp. 12, 30,
36-7). Cf. G.C. Smith *Blackheath* n.d., pp. 44-50.

382. SML 1826, pp. 263-4. G.C. Smith *Blackheath* n.d., pp. 18, 57-8. Cf. NSM
1834, p. 211; 1839, p. 449; 1858, pp. 547-8.

383. SML 1824, p. 335. Cf. NSM 1858, p. 114.

384. SML 1825, p. 376. G.C. Smith *Blackheath* n.d., pp. 49-50. Thompson 1829,
p. 12.

385. SML 1825, p. 429; 1826, pp. 22, 207.

386. (MS) BFSFSBU *Minutes*, May 10, 1826. SML 1826, pp. 263-4.

387. Ibid. Although the exact circumstances surrounding Smith's resignation are
somewhat differently represented, it seems certain that some degree of pressure
was exerted by the Committee of the BFSFSBU. ([MS] BFSFSBU *Minutes*,
April 12 & 19, 1826. PLBUS *Appeal* 1829, pp. 87-99. G.C. Smith *Blackheath*
n.d., pp. 62-3. NSM 1837, p. 880.)

388. (MS) BFSFSBU *Minutes*, Jan 10, 1827; see also indications of mounting
friction throughout the entries for 1826, e.g.: May 3, 10 & 24, June 21, July 5,

Aug. 9, Nov. 29, Dec. 27. PLBUS *Appeal* 1829, pp. 87-135. Thompson 1829, pp. 11-2, 15, 30-1. BFSSFS *Decision* 1829,p. 5. *The Revival* 1863, p. 23. Cf. infra, p. 308.

389. (MS) PLS *Minutes*, Oct. 11, Nov. 22, Dec. 20, 1825; Aug. 22, Sept. 26, 1826. SML 1826, p. 269. Thompson 1829, pp. 29-30, 38-9.

390. E.g., (MS) *Minutes*, March 8, April 26, Nov. 8, 1825. By 1825, the Society's annual receipts had fallen to £283, not even *one percent* of those, for example, of the London Missionary Society (MR 1825, pp. 212-3).

391. E.g., (MS) PLS *Minutes*, Nov. 12, 1822. (Cf. SML 1822, pp. 419-21.) (MS) PLS *Minutes*, May 24, 1825. Timpson 1856, p. 56. The Joint Coronation Day Service, July 19, 1821, was a complete exception (SML 1821, pp. 283-4, 306).

392. G.C. Smith *Blackheath* n.d., pp. 11-2, 20-2. Thompson 1829, pp. 36-7. NSM 1833, p. 191.

393. (MS) BFSFSBU *Minutes*, Sept. 26, Nov. 1, 15, 29, Dec. 6, 1826. (MS) PLS *Minutes*, Nov. 28, 1826.

394. (MS) BFSFSBU *Minutes*, Dec. 19, 1826. Cf. (MS) PLS *Minutes*, Dec. 26, 1826.

395. SML 1827, pp. 41-4, 95-101, 131-2, 201-5, 313. (P. 231 contains a list of the officers of the new Society, drawn from its two components.) Cf. SML 1820, p. 461.

396. (MS) PLS *Minutes*, Jan. 31, 1827. (MS) BFSFSBU *Minutes*, Jan. 31, 1827.

397. SML 1827, p. 202. Cf. BFSS *Report* 1857, p. 1.

398. Thompson 1829, pp. 28-9.

399. SML 1827, p. 42.

400. PLBUS *Appeal* 1829, p. 44. Although Smith was still officially Editor of *The Sailor's Magazine* until his dismissal on Jan. 10, 1827, a proposal for new editorship is significantly mentioned among assumptions for the agreed merger, in (MS) PLS *Minutes*, Dec. 26, 1826. Smith himself felt, from 1819 to 1825, "incessantly opposed and persecuted by the Port Society" (NSM 1829 Pt. II, Supplement: *The Thames*, p. 2).

401. NSM 1833, p. 333.

402. NSM 1829 Pt. II, p. 417.

403. NSM 1828, pp. 64-5, 341-2; 1831, pp. 135, 246. Cf. G.C. Smith *Blackheath* n.d., p. 64.

404. NSM 1828, pp. 64, 231; 1833, p. 313; 1837, p. 880.

405. SML 1827, p. 132. MR 1827, p. 237. NSM 1833, p. 192. G.C. Smith *The Floating Chapel* n.d., pp. 8-12.

406. *Dr. John Styles* of Holland Chapel, North Brixton, was elected to the Committee of the BFSFSBU in July 1825, but also preached "an excellent discourse" at the Anniversary of the MCS in July 1826. It was in March 1827, that the PLBUS appointed him editor of *The Sailor's Magazine*. In July 1828, he was also appointed traveling secretary. ([MS] BFSFSBU *Minutes*, July 6, 1825. SML 1826, p. 370. [MS] PLBUS *Minutes*, March 14, 1827. Thompson 1829, p. 17. Cf. NSM 1828, pp. 374-6; 1829 Pt I, p. 249; 1833, p. 334; 1835, pp. 304-5.)

407. SML 1827, p. 203. NSM 1828, p. 375; 1829 Pt. I, pp. 249-50.

408. G.C. Smith *The Floating Chapel* n.d., p. 12. NSM 1828, p. 417. Cf. BFSSFS *Decision* 1829, p. 5.

409. The following tracts, written by G.C. Smith in 1827-28, all concern the controversy between Smith/BFSSFS and Styles/PLBUS: *Aldermanbury* (1827), *The Floating Chapel* (1827?), *Injustice and Cruelty* (1827?), *Common Honesty* (1828), *Chichester* (1828), *Blackheath* (1828), *Brixton* (1828), *Spa Fields* (1828), *Birmingham* (1828). Cf. BFSSFS *Decision* 1829, p. 5.

410. (MS) BFSFSBU *Minutes*, Feb. 26, March 11, 18, 22, 28, 1828. PLBUS *Appeal* 1829, pp. iii-iv, 144. NSM 1829 Pt. I, pp. 257-9; Pt. II, p. 426; 1831, p. 364; 1833, p. 192; 1835, pp. 304-5; 1838, pp. 9-10. G.C. Smith *Persecution* 1829, p. 46.

411. G.C. Smith *The Thames* 1829, pp. 4-12. Thompson 1829, pp. 17-8. BFSSFS *Decision* 1829, p. 5. Cf. NSM 1828, pp. 300-1, 380-4, 432-5.

412. The charge of rapacity, as imputed against Smith in the *Appeal*, is warmly refuted in Thompson 1829, pp. 11-3, 24-8, 30-1.

413. Thompson 1829, p. 20.

414. NSM 1828, p. 374; 1829 Pt. I, pp. 82, 251-3; 1834, p. 59. G.C. Smith *Persecution* 1829, p. 35. Cf. Styles 1829, pp. 3-4.

415. NSM 1828, p. 382; 1829 Pt. I, p. 250. Cf. EM 1829, p. 259.

416. NSM 1829 Pt. I, pp. 217-32, 250; Supplement p. 11; Pt. II, p. 425.

417. NSM 1828, pp. 347-8; 1858, pp. 113, 119.

418. (MS) PLBUS *Minutes*, June 6, Oct. 23 & 25, Nov. 20, 1827, April 28, 1828. NSM 1828, p. 233; 1829, pp. 229, 333-4; 1829, Supplement: *The Sailor's Steam Ship*, pp. 34-5. G.C. Smith *Freemasons' Hall 1829, pp. 9-11. G.C. Smith Persecution* 1829, p. 17.

419. NSM 1829 Pt. I, p. 234. Cf. supra, p. 174.

420. NSM 1829 Pt. II, pp. 415-9, 518-24; 1832, p. 322; 1857, p. 136. G.C. Smith *Freemason's Hall* 1829, pp. 8-12. G.C. Smith *Persecution* 1829, pp. 12-3, 21-2, 35-8, 46-8. The author, whose identity could evidently not be concealed indefinitely (cf. NSM 1838, p. 157), proved to be the sender of those "inflammatory circulars" from the PLBUS, which were intended to warn the country against the MCS as early as in 1827 (NSM 1833, p. 192). Attempts by the Committee of the PLBUS to absolve themselves from complicity were vehemently contested by Smith. (G.C. Smith *Persecution* 1829, pp. 35-9. NSM 1829 Pt. II, pp. 521-2; 1833, p. 193.)

421. G.C. Smith *Freemasons' Hall* 1829, pp. 11-2. NSM 1831, pp. 251, 518; 1832, pp. 316, 336-7, 464; 1833, pp. 194-5; 1834, p. 59. Mead 1831, passim.

422. The Rev. J. Sibree continued the contest into 1832, publishing in that year *A Voice from Coventry* against Smith and the BFSSFS (NSM 1831, pp. 516-25; 1832, pp. 163-70, 316, 378-9, 464). Another "discarded agent," S.H. Mace, supported Sibree in *A Signal Gun* 1832 (cf. NSM 1832, pp. 209-10, 316). Even the Rev. R. Marks became estranged from Smith after reading Mead's *Voice* (NSM 1832, pp. 464, 466). A powerful refutation of allegations by Mead and Sibree was published by the Secretary of the Coventry Auxilliary of the BFSSFS, J. Weigham, in *Truth from Coventry*, 1832 (NSM 1832, pp. 254-6, cf. pp. 78-9).

423. NSM 1832, pp. 74, 163, 197, 316, 378-9; 1833, p. 194.

424. NSM 1831, pp. 249, 363-7, 435-7, 462-3, 496-7; 1832, pp. 120, 316, cf. pp. 534-7. The Lord Mayor, Sir John Key, Bart., was both president of the BFSSFS and at the same time its chief creditor (NSM 1832, pp. 89, 393).

425. NSM 1832, pp. 74-82, 118-25, 163, 291-3, 379, 464. A recommendation to reduce the Society's traveling agency was rejected by Smith as utterly suicidal (NSM 1832, p. 163).

426. NSM 1832, pp. 291-7, 309-17, 379-97. Cf. DNB Vol. 11 1887, p. 15; Vol. 12 1888, p. 411.

427. NSM 1832, pp. 397-405, 429-31.

428. Ibid., p. 447, 1833, p. 335. *The Soldiers' Magazine* 1832, pp. 465-6.

429. Ibid.

430. NSM 1833, pp. 197-8.

431. NSM 1828, pp. 296, 382-3, 433; 1832,p. 253; 1858, p. 114. Thompson 1829, pp. 38-9. G.C. Smith *The Thames* 1829, pp. 14, 37, 39. Cf. MR 1828, p. 228; 1832, p. 213. See also supra, p. 274.

432. G.C. Smith *Blackheath* n.d., pp. 59-60. NSM 1832, p. 253.

433. NSM 1832, pp. 200-3, 253, 398-400, 427-31, 537-8; 1833, pp. 195-8, 333-7; 1834, p. 59.

434. From available sources, it is difficult to understand how Clayton and his colleagues could ever have expected Smith to be able to run an independent so-called "Mariners' Church Department" without some form of promotional framework. (Cf. NSM 1832, pp. 398-401, 447. G.C. Smith *An Humble Christian Remonstrance* 1835, pp. 3-6.) NSM 1832, pp. 394, 399, 405; 1833, p. 198.

435. NSM 1831, pp. 455-6.

436. NSM 1832, pp. 398, 400-1, 434-5.

437. Ibid., pp. 442-8, 464.

438. Ibid., pp. 464-5, 498-500. *The Soldiers' Magazine* 1832, p. 465.

439. Ibid. NSM 1832, pp. 448, 482, 534-7; 1833, p. 335.

440. NSM 1833, pp. 335-6, 342-3, 345-6: 1834, p. 59. A "Birmingham Sailors' and Soldiers' Bethel Flag Union" had been formed as early as Oct. 16, 1832. Similar auxiliaries were planned elsewhere (*The Soldiers' Magazine* 1832, pp. 421-3, 465-6). The addition "or London Mariners' Church Society" could occasionally be made to the title of the Parent Society (e.g., NSM 1834, pp. 219-21). In 1836, the Parent Society reassumed the title "British and Foreign Seamen and Soldiers' Friend Society" (NSM 1836, pp. 146, 151).

441. NSM 1828, p. 233; 1830, p. 247; 1832, pp. 430-1; 1837, p. 415. Supra, p. 276.

442. NSM 1834, p. 303; 1836, p. 153. Hodder 1891, pp. 63-4.

443. (MS) BFSS *Minutes*, May 6, 1833. MR 1833, p. 226. NSM 1833, p. 337; 1834, p. 303. BFSS *Report* 1834, p. 7. SML 1839, p. 200.

444. (MS) BFSS *Minutes*, May 6, 1833.

445. Ibid., May 16, 20, 31, June 4, 10, 21, 28, 1833. NSM 1833, pp. 272, 337; 1834, p. 235; 1837, p. 881. SML 1839, p. 200. Hodder 1891, p. 64.

446. (MS) BFSS *Minutes*, June 21, 24, 1833. EM 1833, pp. 358-9. MR 1833 pp. 521-2. NSM 1833, pp. 313-4, 337-8. BFSS *Report* 1834, pp. 7-8. Cox 1834,

p. 50. Hodder 1891, p. 64. Re. Lord Healey, see DNB Vol. 16 1888, p. 361, Moorman 1953, p. 347. R.H. Marten was subsequently elected a vice-president (BFSS *Report* 1835, p. iii). John Pirie (like G.F. Angas) later made his mark in Australian history (Matthews 1911, p. 212).

447. Re. the Sailors' Society, see (MS) BFSS *Minutes*, May 6, 1833; also MR 1833, p. 226. Re. the BFSS, see (MS) BFSS *Minutes* June 28, 1833; EM 1833, pp. 358-9; Cox 1834, pp. 50-3; Matthews 1911, pp. 60-4. Cf. SML 1839, p. 200; also 1852, p. 35 (where the 1833 merger is erroneously represented as the PLBUS simply having "assumed the name of the BFSS").

448. (MS) BFSS *Minutes*, May 20, 31, 1833. Cf. BFSS *Report* 1834, pp. 9-10; 1835, p. 2. NSM 1833, p. 272.

449. The 2nd Annual Report of the BFSS (1835) is, on its title-page, represented as the 17th from the Society's "First Establishment" (cf. NSM 1858,p. 25). In 1968, the British Sailors' Society celebrated its "Sesquicentennial Anniversary."

450. CC 1879, pp. 44-9; 1901, p. 208; Spring No. 1960, p. 3. Pike 1897, p. 38. BSS *Report* 1967, p. 1.

451. Strong criticism was leveled against the BFSS for virtually "assuming" the name of the British and Foreign Sailors' and Soldiers' Bethel Flag Union (NSM 1833, pp. 313-4; 1834, pp. 60, 235). From this time on, the name of Smith's own Society went through wide variations (cf. p. 356; also p. 357, *illus.*).

PART V — NOTES

1. Cf. supra, pp. 28-35. Also infra, p. 381.

2. *The Christian Observer* 1805, pp. 338-40, 726-7. Cf. supra, pp. 101-2.

3. SML 1820, pp. 160-3, 412-4; cf. p. 319.

4. Russel 1915, p. 58. Balleine 1951, pp. 152-3. Cf. Brown 1961, p. 264.

5. Supra, pp. 181-2. SML 1820, p. 162; 1821, pp. 212-3; 1823, p. 300; 1825, p. 282.

6. From a sermon preached at St. Ann's, Blackfriar's, before the BFSFSBU, 1826, by the Rev. Thomas Webster, late Fellow of Queen's College, Cambridge. (*The Christian Guardian* 1826, pp. 449-56. SML 1827, pp. 1-10.) Similar sentiments were expressed by the Rev. Richard Marks (*The Christian Guardian* 1826, pp. 485-6; cf. 1827, pp. 209-10). See also SML 1822, pp. 466-7; Scoresby 1831, p. vii.

7. Foster 1960, p. 81.

8. Cf. SML 1827, pp. 150, 279. (Otherwise, SML and NSM for 1820-30 provide constant examples.)

9. NMBS *Report* 1825, p. 11.

10. E.g.: SML 1820, pp. 352, 426; 1821, p. 496.

11. SML 1820, p. 319; 1823, pp. 300-3; 1825, p. 317; 1826, p. 443. Cf. *The Christian Guardian* 1825, p. 315; 1826, pp. 485-6. Well might a Rowland Hill exclaim: "If a Clergyman of the Church of England were to preach in a chapel, it would not occasion an earthquake." Nevertheless, the principle remained the same (SML 1821, p. 464).

12. NSM 1828, p. 73. SML 1828, p. 72.

13. SML 1820, p. 161; 1825, p. 282; 1826, p. 149; 1827, p. 307; 1828, pp. 71-2. *The Christian Guardian* 1826, pp. 485-6, 501.

14. *The Christian Guardian* 1823, pp. 355-6. Port of Dublin Society 1823, pp. 4, 11. A corresponding, interdenominational "Dublin Mariners' Bethel Union" was not formed by the Dissenters until 1826 (SML 1827, pp. 10-7).

15. Evangelical societies were considered an important adjunct in "rescuing" the Irish from Roman Catholicism (Brown 1961, p. 343). Cf. Moorman 1953, p. 385; Overton 1906, p. 347.

16. SML 1822, pp. 310-1; 1823, pp. 303-10. Port of Dublin Society *Report* 1823, pp. 8-12. Cf. PLS *Proceedings* 1821, p. 38.

17. SML 1823, pp. 303-10, 366; 1824, pp. 217-8; 1825, pp. 282, 310; 1826, pp. 442-4. NSM 1829 Pt. II, pp. 513-4; 1833, p. 247. Port of Dublin Society *Report* 1823, pp. 2-12. *The Christian Guardian* 1823, pp. 355-6; 1825, p. 315.

18. *The Christian Guardian* 1826, pp. 8-14, 49-52, 89-94, 129-36, 169-76. Marks 1843, pp. 245-6. The series was reproduced in SML 1826, with enthusiastic comments by G. C. Smith, who regretted that Marks had not been "settled in London over a Seamen's Church, where he might form a sort of rallying point for his . . . brethren of the establishment," for example, in the neglected but strategically important district between Whitechapel and Limehouse (pp. 51-2).

19. *The Christian Guardian* 1826, pp. 337-40, 410-2, 484-6; 1827, pp. 140-2, 209-15. This series, too, was quoted in SML. Cf, SML 1826, p. 458. Mariners' Church, Philadelphia, *Reports* 1826, pp. 16-7; 1827, pp. 15-6. Green 1828, pp. 141-3.

20. *The Christian Guardian* 1826, pp. 485-6.

21. Ibid. Marks did, however, find reason to deplore the "spirit of persecution" exhibited by certain "Anti-Saints," including fellow-clergymen, concerning Evangelical support for nondenominational seamen's mission endeavours (*The Christian Guardian* 1827, pp. 209-10). Cf. SML 1825, p. 135 (quoting an assertion that "the only object of the Bethel Society was to pull down the Church of England").

22. *The Christian Guardian* 1826, pp. 340, 410-2, 484-6.

23. Ibid., p.486.

24. SML 1825, pp. 413-5. Peet 1913, pp. 3-5.

25. NSM 1828, pp. 466, 505. Cf. supra, p. 182.

26. NSM 1828, pp. 466-7.

27. Ibid., pp. 70-4, 464-7. SML 1828, p. 34. DNB Vol. 12, 1893, pp. 1086-8. Russel 1915, p. 59. *Sea Breezes* Vol. 1, 1946, pp. 4-6 (cf. pp. 174, 281). Kingsford 1957, pp. 10-2. Whittington-Egan 1955, p. 35. Cf. Chapter IV, Note No. 165.

28. Cf. SML 1825, p. 413.

29. SML 1821, p. 383; 1823, p. 82; 1826, p. 223. NSM 1828, p. 70; 1852, p. 572. Scoresby-Jackson 1861, passim. DNB Vol. 51, 1897, pp. 6-8. Kingsford 1957, pp. 9-14. His father, *William Scoresby the Elder* (1760-1829), also achieved considerable (if somewhat less) renown as an Arctic navigator (DNB Vol. 51, 1897, pp. 5-6). The conversion of *William Scoresby the Younger* (1789-1857) is linked by his biographer to the accumulated influence of the

prayers and personal piety of both his mother and his first wife, also the preaching and subsequent friendship of the Evangelical clergyman at Whitby, the Rev. Dr. Holloway (Scoresby-Jackson 1861, pp. 249-59. Kingsford 1957, pp. 10-3. Stamp 1976, passim).

30. NSM 1828, p. 467. Scoresby-Jackson 1861, pp. 244-8. DNB Vol. 51, 1897, pp. 7-8. Kingsford 1957, p. 10.

31. NSM 1828, pp. 1-3, 45-7, 70-4, 464-8, 504-5. Scoresby 1831, pp. vii-ix; 1835, pp. 178-9; 1837, passim. Scoresby-Jackson 1861, pp. 249-59. Kingsford 1957, pp. 10-3.

32. Scoresby-Jackson 1861, pp. 259-62.

33. (MS) PLS *Minutes,* October 13, 1824. SML 1826, p. 223, Scoresby-Jackson 1861, pp. 177-8, 203-4.

34. Scoresby 1831, pp. ix-x. Scoresby-Jackson 1861, p. 250.

35. Scoresby 1835, pp. vii-x; 1850, pp. v-viii. Dr. Scoresby died at Torquay, March 21, 1857, after serving as voluntary ship's chaplain on a round trip to Australia, undertaken in 1856, in order to make a series of scientific observations on magnetism. His epitaph at Upton Church makes the glaring omission of ignoring his pioneering role in Anglican seamen's missions. (Scoresby-Jackson 1861, pp. 385, 398-9. DNB Vol. 51, 1897, p. 8. Kingsford 1957, pp. 13-4.)

36. *Sea Breezes* 1946, Vol. 2, p. 253. Kingford 1957, pp. 12, 14-5; Appendix, pp. vi-vii.

37. SML 1822, p. 498; 1824, p. 405. NSM 1828, pp. 122-5, 473-4; 1842, pp. 484-5. DNB Vol. 16, 1888, pp. 292-3. *Lifebelt and Anchor* 1907, pp. 24-5. Allison 1969, p. 213. Cf. King 1849, passim.

38. NSM 1831, pp. 247-8; 1842, pp. 484-5.

39. NSM 1828, pp. 122-5. SML 1838, p. 151. The inscription at the present Missions to Seamen Club (900 Hedon Road, Hull) has "1927" as the year of the Society's foundation. The Hon. Captain Vernon, R.N., son of the Archbishop of York, is credited with giving a "decisive impulse" to the final founding of the Society (NSM 1828, p. 123; 1829 Pt. II, p. 481). From the first, the Corporation of the local Trinity House played a prominent supportive role (NSM 1828, pp. 123-4).

40. NSM 1828, pp. 123-5. Cf. 1842, pp. 484-5.

41. NSM 1828, pp. 123-5. SML 1838, p. 151. Sheahan 1866, p. 528. Allison 1969, 213.

42. NSM 1828, pp. 473-4. *Lifebelt and Anchor* 1907, p. 25. Cf. NSM 1828, p. 34.

43. NSM 1833, pp. 526-7. SML 1838, p. 151. Sheahan 1866, pp. 428-9. Allison 1969, p. 213.

44. SML 1826, pp. 472-3. NSM 1828, p. 74. Scoresby 1831, p. vii. Cf. SML 1822, pp. 98-9. Supra, p. 232.

45. NSM 1830, pp. 421-2. Scoresby 1831, p. vii. Cf. supra, p.238.

46. Pascoe 1901, pp. 479, 1828. Supra, p. 246.

47. Bombay Seamen's Friend Association *Address* 1831, p. 5; *Report* 1838, p. 12. NSM 1831, pp. 287-8. Meanwhile, the Bombay Seamen's Friend Association continued under Anglican patronage. Supra, p. 247.

48. Supra, p. 266. Cf. BFSFSBU *Minutes*, May 28, 1823.

49. (MS) PLS *Minutes*, July 26, 1825 (incl. appended *Prospectus* for what was prior to July 20, 1825 known as the Episcopal Floating *Chapel* Society. SML 1825, pp. 315-6, 392; 1827, pp. 147-8. *The Christian Guardian* 1825, p. 315. G.C. Smith *Blackheath* n.d., p. 6. *Viscount Melville* (1771-1851) was First Lord of the Admiralty 1812-27, 1828-30 (DNB Vol. 6, 1885-86, pp. 195-6).

50. (MS) PLS *Minutes*, July 26, 1825 (incl. appended newspaper cutting). SML 1825, pp. 316-20. MR 1825, pp. 309-10. *The Christian Guardian* 1825, p. 315. Cf. Timpson 1856, p. 59.

51. SML 1825, pp. 199, 315-20. *The Christian Guardian* 1825, p. 315.

52. SML 1824, p. 232; 1825, pp. 314-5, 320, 428; 1838, p. 284. There are indications that the *manner* in which the work was transferred caused mixed feelings. (SML 1825, pp. 292-3. NSM 1831, pp. 290-1; 1832, p. 336.)

53. SML 1825, pp. 315-20, 392, 489. Canton Vol. 1, 1904, p. 324.

54. Walrond 1904, p. xiii. Cf. Montagu 1832, p. 1. Also, NSM 1833, p. 129.

55. SML 1825, p. 320; 1826, pp. 258-9, 442-4; 1827, p. 9. *Lt. J.E. Gordon* had also played an active role in the origin of the Society. (NSM 1830, p. 272, 1838, p. 284. G.C. Smith *Blackheath* n.d., p. 6.) For further biographical data on Lt. Gordon, see supra, pp. 169,179-80.

56. NSM 1828, pp. 83, 125, 128, 382-3, 433; 1831, pp. 248, 291; 1858, p. 415. *The Christian Guardian* 1829, p. 198. MR 1835, p. 186. DNB Vol. 21, 1889-90, pp. 328-9. Gates 1931, p. 198. Re. Captains Gambier and Elliot, see infra, pp. 325-40.

57. G.C. Smith was instrumental in negotiating this apparently advantageous place of mooring (NSM 1828, pp. 125, 128, 382-3; 1831, p. 291; 1838, p. 284).

58. *The Christian Guardian* 1829, p. 198. NSM 1829, Pt. I, Supplement p. 79. Timpson 1856, p. 60. The BFSS periodical SML 1839 refers to the Episcopal Floating Church as having been opened in 1826 (p. 199). This error recurs in Walrond 1904, p. xiii; Kingsford 1947, p. 125; Cuthbertson 1966, p. [1].

59. E.g.: MR 1829, pp. 198, 218-9; 1834, p. 218; 1840, p. 268. NSM 1834, pp. 259-60. *The Christian Observer* 1830, p. 645. *The Christian Guardian* 1836, p. 279.

60. G.C. Smith *Persecution* 1829, p. 19. NSM 1830, p. 64; 1831, pp. 289-91; 1838, pp. 281-5. SMNY 1830-31, p. 362. MR 1832, p. 218; 1836, p. 237; 1837, p. 233; 1838, p. 242. SML 1836, p. 237.

61. NSM 1832, p. 360. Gribble 1849, p. 29.

62. MR 1834, p. 218; 1835, p. 186. The vessel thus arrived at length at the station originally contemplated, adjoining the Receiving Ship *Perseus* (NSM 1828, p. 83).

63. NSM 1831, p. 290. MR 1834, p. 218; 1835, pp. 186-7; 1837, p. 233; 1838, p. 242. SMNY 1835-36, p. 373.

64. NSM 1831, pp. 289-93; 1832, pp. 188-91, 360; 1834, pp. 259-60; 1838, pp. 281-5. Cf. infra, pp. 335-40.

65. Apart from the scantily-attended Sunday services on their own ship, chaplains could hold relatively well-attended week-day "Meetings for Instruction and

Prayer" on board vessels in different parts of the river (MR 1832, p. 218; 1835, p. 186). Cf. infra, pp. 395-8.

66. E.g., supra, pp. 145, 253, 270.

67. Canton Vol. 1, 1904, pp. 57-62. Cf. Dudley 1821, Chapter VII.

68. SML 1821, pp. 303-4. Cf. G.C. Smith in NSM 1829 Pt. I, pp. 7-9, 134.

69. This Glasgow pioneer society had a brief but brave career (NMBS *Reports* 1817, pp. 26, 68-9; 1819, pp. 12, 23, 26, 42; 1820, pp. 73, 90; 1821, pp. 38-9, 66; 1824, p. 27). A "Ladies' Association in Aid of the Edinburgh Auxiliary Naval and Military Bible Society" followed shortly afterwards, and managed to persevere (NMBS *Reports* 1820, pp. 75-6; 1830, p. 57).

70. This Society was later renamed the "Ladies' Association for the Promotion of Religious Knowledge among Seamen" (NMBS *Reports* 1822, pp. 39-40; 1828, p. 11).

71. Infra, p. 341.

72. E.g.: (MS) BFSFSBU *Minutes*, May 15, 22, 1822. SML 1824, p. 157; 1825, p. 117; 1826, p. 215. NSM 1828, pp. 478-9. SMR 1826, pp. 566-7; 1833, p. 10.

73. E.g., SML 1824, pp. 356-7, 518-9.

74. SML 1820, p. 457; 1821, pp. 413-5.

75. Infra, p. 356.

76. SML 1821, pp. 161, 491.

77. NSM 1835, pp. 191, 255-6.

78. SML 1820, pp. 25-6.

79. SML 1822, p. 426; 1823, pp. 365-6.

80. E.g.: SML 1821, pp. 410-1. NSM 1829 Pt. I, pp. 217-8. Smith 1967, passim. Cf. infra, pp. 313,341-2.

81. Bullock 1963, p. 173.

82. Early reports of the SPCK, RTS, and BFBS show that all three became quite naturally involved in both seamen's *and* soldiers' work. In the case of the SPCK, this dual involvement goes back as far as the year 1701 (Allan 1898, p. 456).

83. SML 1820, p. 437. Supra, pp. 128-9.

84. SML 1820, pp. 426, 447. Supra, p. 232.

85. SML 1822, p. 424; 1823, p. 365; 1824, p. 419; 1826, p. 462. Supra, p. 232.

86. SML 1822, p. 424. Heasman 1962, pp. 258-9.

87. Cf. SML 1820, p. 470. From 1828-36, Smith published concurrently a *separate* periodical for soldiers' missions, entitled *The Soldier's Magazine and Military Chronicle* (1828-32), and *The Mariners' Church Soldiers' Magazine and Military Chronicle* (1833-36).

88. NSM 1829, Pt. II, pp. 283-4; 1830, p. 66; 1831, pp. 138-9; 1861, p. 291. Smith 1874, p. 12. Heasman 1962, p. 259.

89. BFBS *Reports* 1811-33. Scripture supplied to "Convicts embarking" is recorded as early as 1808. (Canton Vol. 1, 1904, pp. 122-3. See also the BFBS Distribution Lists of various *Reports*, including 1831-33, p. 59, as well as *Monthly Extracts* 1832, p. 668.) (MS) BFBS *Home Corresp.*, letter from Edward Suter to Joseph Tarn, August 1, 1818. *The Christian Guardian*

1828, p. 343. Brown 1961, p. 76. (MS) Knight n.d., pp. 18-9. Cf. NSM 1829, Pt. I, p. 115. Where naval surgeons, charged with medical welfare on board transports, also assumed pastoral and educational responsibilities, remarkable results could be achieved, as attested in the widely-read works of Dr. Colin A. Browning: *England's Exiles* 1842, and *The Convict Ship* 1844. Cf. Canton Vol. 2, 1904, pp. 412-3.

90. Timpson 1847, pp. 118-24, 257. Bateson 1969, pp. 65-6, 77. BFBS *Reports*, from 1827 on, record Scripture distribution by the "Committee for the Reformation of Female Prisoners" ("for the use of Convicts preceeding on their respective voyages"). Cf. Distribution Lists of BFBS *Reports* 1828-33.

91. Concerning conditions in general on board convict transports, see Nicol 1822, pp. 108 ff., and especially C. Bateson's monograph, *The Convict Ships 1787-1868*, 1969. (The latter, however, shows little or no appreciation for the spiritual needs of transportees, or for the many genuine efforts to meet them. Cf. p. 77.)

92. BFBS *Reports* 1816-17, p. 334; 1818-19, p. 293.

93. (MS) BFBS *Home Corresp.*, letter from Edward Suter to Joseph Tarn, September 24, 1819.

94. BFBS *Reports* 1818-33. See the Society's Distribution Lists, and especially its Reports for 1832, p. xcv, and for 1833, pp. xcii-xciii. Note also SML 1820, pp. 175-6, and NSM 1834, p. 197. PBHS *Proceedings* 1828-33; re. 1830-31, p. 48; re. 1832-33, p. 89.

95. Pascoe 1901, pp. 818-20. Concerning British 19th century emigration in general, see Carrothers 1929, Guillet 1963, and Coleman 1972.

96. SML 1820, pp. 346-7; 1821, pp. 470-1; 1822, pp. 379-82, 468-70. Cf. NSM 1829, pt. I p. 246; 1831, p. 223. PBHS *Proceedings* 1829, p. 40; 1833, pp. 91-2. (MS) Coombs 1960, pp. 126-8. Boatmen were included in the terms "rivermen" and "canalmen," all according to which waters they were navigating. As to their spiritual self-assessment, one converted boatman described his former conviction thus: "The Lord's mercy could not be for me because I was a Boatman" (SML 1822, p. 234).

97. Supra, pp. 147-8.

98. SML 1820, pp. 346-7; 1821, p. 492; 1822, pp. 168, 355-6, 379-89, 424. (MS) BFSFSBU *Minutes*, August 7, 1822. SMR 1822, pp. 417-8. A confirmatory general meeting of the new Society was planned before the end of the year (SML 1822, pp. 389, 424).

99. Of the 30,000 "rivermen," about 9,000 were estimated to be "watermen" and "lightermen." SML 1822, pp. 356, 386. Cf. (MS) BFSFSBU *Minutes*, August 7, 1822.

100. SML 1822, pp. 126-7, 379-89; 1823, p. 363, 468-9; 1824, p. 418. (MS) BFBS *Home Corresp.*, letters from Charles Lucey of Cox's Quay (as secretary of the Society), dated November 24, 1823, April 25, 1824, and September 17, 1827. The last of these letters, referring to the collapse of the Society as already factual, contradicts Theophilus Smith 1874, p. 8. Cf. supra, p. 220.

101. Supra, pp. 268.

102. NSM 1828, pp. 118-20, 392, 533-4; cf. 1829 Pt. I, pp. 225-6; Pt. II, pp. 283-4; 1830, p. 460; 1831, pp. 138-9.

103. SML 1821, pp. 480-1; 1822, p. 381; cf. 1823, p. 331. Supra, p. 236.

104. Supra, p. 236.

105. NSM 1829 Pt. II, pp. 27-9; Supplement pp. 30-1, 36-40; 1831, pp. 141, 223-4, 259-61.

106. NSM 1831, p. 452. Cf. NMBS *Report* 1830, p. 24.

107. PBHS *Proceedings* 1829, p. 40.

108. Supra, pp. 146-7. cf. p. 248. BFS *Monthly Extracts* 1821-27, pp. 34-5.

109. Infra, pp. 468-70.

110. SML 1821, pp. 156-7, 489.

111. E.g.: SML 1822, pp. 356, 386. NSM 1829 Pt. II, p. 284.

112. Founded in 1828, the Society opened a *Bethel Loft* the same year (NSM 1829 Pt. I, pp. 42-3, 142-5; 1831, pp. 223, 225).

113. The first hundred years of the mission are recorded in Pritchard 1980. However, more detailed records of its origins are found in Mather 1887 and Gordon 1890. The history of mission among fishing communities in the late 19th and early 20th centuries is currently the subject of Ph.D. dissertation research at the University of Leeds by Stephen Friend ([MS] Friend, 1985). Infra, p. 398.

114. BFBS *Reports* 1805-10, pp. 396-7; 1811-13, p. 178; 1825-27, p. 54. (MS) BFBS *Minutes*, October 16, 1809. SML 1824, p. 417. Cf. supra, p. 83.

115. NSM 1829 Pt. I, pp. 58-9. PBHS *Proceedings* 1833, p. 92. MR 1833, p. 390.

116. SML 1824, p. 418.

117. E.g. SML 1822, p. 449.

118. Infra, pp. 323-4, 341. Cf. supra, p. 223.

119. "The Care of Seafarers' Families" has, since 1969, become a cardinal concern of ICMA. (Cf. *The Flying Angel* No. 5, 1972, pp. 4-5. Frayne 1972, pp. 7-16. Vincent 1975, pp. 14-26. Wulff 1982, pp. 40-5.)

120. Cf. NMBS *Report* 1826, p. 11.

121. SML 1821, pp. 425-6.

122. SML 1820, p. 259; 1823, pp. 469, 490-1; 1827, p. 176. RTS 1820, pp. 26-7. NMBS *Report* 1831, p. 12. Jones 1850, pp. 245-6. Hewitt 1949, pp. 15-6. Brown 1961, pp. 71, 428-9.

123. NMBS *Reports* 1817, pp. 11, 25-6, 60-9; 1830, pp. 2, 8. Supra, p. 87.

124. NMBS *Reports* 1824, p. 27; 1825, pp. 8, 19-20, 24-6, 32.

125. NMBS *Reports* 1817, pp. 61, 65-6; cf. 1816, pp. 42-3. NSM 1829, Pt. II, pp. 453-4. Allen 1898, p. 456. Supra, pp. 101.

126. NMBS *Report* 1825, p. 32.

127. The BFBS found it necessary to protect the interests of its own Auxiliary (the MSABS) by excepting distribution on the Thames from its Scripture grants to the NMBS for foreign seamen in British ports. ([MS] BFBS *Home Corresp.*, letters from Captain Bazalgette, dated August 11, 1828, and February 6, 1829. [MS] BFBS *Minutes*, October 3, 1828; January 5, February 9, March 23, June 22, 1829.) On the other hand, the Parent Society found it impracticable to "interfere" in response to complaints by agents of the MSABS of underselling by the NMBS amongst British seamen in London. ([MS] BFBS *Home Corresp.*, letter from Edward Suter October 12, 1829. [MS] BFBS *Minutes*, December 21, 1829.)

128. NMBS *Report* 1831, pp. 17-35. McCarthy 1861, pp. 53-67. Canton Vol. 1, 1904, p. 354. The Rev. Edward Irving's endorsement of the Society at its 1831 Annual Meeting is significant on the background of allegations of his influence among leaders of the NMBS at this time. (NMBS *Report* 1831, pp. 26-8. *The Soldiers' Magazine* 1832, pp. 188-90. Infra, p. 335.)

129. NMBS *Reports* 1826, pp. 17-8; 1828, pp. 18-20, 26-7; 1829, pp. 18-20; 1830, p. 13. Cf. McCarthy 1861, pp. 45-6, 49-50, 52.

130. NMBS *Reports* 1827-33.

131. NMBS *Report* 1830, p. 34.

132. MSABS *Report* 1826, p. 24. Supra, pp. 142-6.

133. E.g.: MSABS *Reports* 1821, pp. 19-21; 1826, pp. 14-28. NSM 1830, pp. 9-12. BFBS *Monthly Extracts* 1821-27, August 1823, p. 43; 1827-33, January 1833, pp. 675-6.

134. NSM 1830, p. 10.

135. E.g.: BFBS *Reports* 1822-24, p. lxv of 1823 *Report*; 1828-30, p. xc of 1829 *Report*.

136. (MS) Knight Pt. I, n.d., pp. 72-4. Supra, pp. 256-7. Cf. SMR 1830, p. 163.

137. Cf. supra, pp. 166-7.

138. RTS 1820, p. 417. *The Christian Guardian* 1826, pp. 173-4. Supra, pp. 108,167.

139. Burder 1822. *The Baptist Magazine* 1822, p. 153. SML 1822, pp. 245-6. (MS) PLS *Minutes*, May 23, June 27, 1826. NSM 1829, Pt. I, p. 12. SML 1836, pp. 121-2. DNB Vol. 3, 1885, pp. 294-5. Hewitt 1949, p. 20. Note: Jones 1850, p. 130, erroneously dates the *Sea Sermons* post-1825.

140. E.g: PLS 1821, p. 36. SML 1824, p. 418. (MS) PLBUS *Minutes*, March 18, 1828. SMR 1830, p. 298. Cf. (MS) BFSS *Minutes*, October 16, 1855.

141. E.g.: SML 1820, p. 426; 1821, p. 385, 395.

142. E.g.: (MS) PLS *Minutes*, June 24, 1823. (MS) BFSFSBU *Minutes*, October 28, 1823.

143. E.g.: SML 1824, pp. 55-9, 108-11. (MS) BFSFSBU *Minutes*, August 25, 1824. Cf. EM 1818, p. 169.

144. NMS 1858, p. 567. Supra, p. 206.

145. SML 1820, pp. iii-iv, 146-8; 1821, pp. iii-iv; 1822, pp. 421, 423; 1823, p. 160; 1824, p. 463. Cf. NSM 1830, p. 277; 1831, pp. 227-8; 1858, p. 567. (MS) BFSFSBU *Minutes* contain constant cases of gratuitous grants of sets of magazines for expanding the work (e.g.: May 1, July 31, 1822; November 19, 1823; February 4, 1824; February 8, 1826).

146. SML 1827, pp. iii-v. BFSS *Report* 1870, p. 12. Matthews 1911, pp. 355-6. Cf. supra, pp. 270-1,277

147. Supra, pp. 271. Infra, p. 354. Concerning confusing changes of title of *The Sailor's Magazine* (London), and *New Sailor's Magazine*, see Bibliography.

148. Supra, pp. 11-2, 166.

149. (MS) PLS *Minutes*, December 8, 1818. PLS *Proceedings* 1821, pp. 38-9, 41, 47-8. Highmore 1822, pp. 59-60. SML 1823, pp. 135, 138; 1825, p. 444.

150. SML 1821, pp. 37, 284, 484; 1822, p. 423. G.C. Smith *The Coaster's and Sailor's Hymn Book* 1824. CC 1881, pp. 2-3. BFSS *Our Sailor's Hymn-Book* 1881. Moorman 1953, pp. 334-5.

151. SML 1827, pp. 324, 424.

152. EM 1832, pp. 393-4.

153. supra, pp.167, 289.

154. Philip 1823 (see especially *Advertisement*). Liverpool Seamen's Friend Society *Report* 1895, p. 24. Supra, p. 226.

155. *The Christian Mariner's Journal* 1829, pp. iii-iv. NSM 1832, p. 53.

156. Supra, pp. 101-2.

157. PBHS *Proceedings* 1824, pp. 62-3; 1825, p. 34. MR 1824, pp. 489-90. SML 1825, pp. 510-12; Supplement p. 6. It is not impossible that Scoresby's *Seaman's Prayer Book* of 1822 provided additional incentive (supra, p. 289). Shortly afterwards, an Anglican clergyman produced *A Few Helps to Devotion to Seamen* (SML 1826, pp. 463-4).

158. PBHS *Proceedings* 1825, pp. 34-41. MR 1825, pp. 385-6. SML 1825, pp. 510-2. PBHS *Occasional Papers* No. 8 (1831), p. 101.

159. PBHS *Proceedings* 1813, p. xi; 1830, pp. 37-8. *The Christian Guardian* 1825, pp. 116-7.

160. SML 1825, pp. 366-8. *The Christian Guardian* 1825, pp. 116-7.

161. *The Soldier's Magazine* 1829 Pt. I, p. 140. Cf. PBHS *Proceedings* 1829, pp. 36-8. NMBS *Report* 1845, pp. 25-6.

162. In 1825-26, among 1,261 ships visited, 1,604 Prayer-books, and 19 copies of the Book of Homilies, were sold to seamen at reduced prices; nearly 1,500 copies of the Book of Select Homilies were given for the use of various crews (*The Christian Guardian* 1826, p. 501). MR 1828, p. 372. (MS) PLBUS *Minutes*, August 22, 1827. *The Soldier's Magazine* 1829 Pt. I, p. 140.

163. PBHS *Proceedings* 1830, p. 38.

164. Ibid. 1831, p. 74; cf. 1829, pp. 36-8. Also, MR 1828, pp. 372-3.

165. MR 1824, p. 491. PBHS *Proceedings* 1830, p. 52; 1831, p. 47.

166. MR 1825, p. 386; 1828, p. 372. NSM 1828, pp. 364-5. PBHS *Occasional Papers* No. 7 (1830), p. 52; 1832, pp. 54-5.

167. E.g.: MR 1824, p. 490; 1827, pp. 353-4; 1832, p. 469; 1833, p. 390. PBHS *Proceedings* 1833, pp. 91-2.

168. Cf. supra, pp. 101-2.

169. (MS) PRO ADM 12 Ind. 4999 Section 22. *The Navy List* 1827, p. 185. NSM 1828, p. 473. Timpson 1847, pp. 214-5. Smith 1961, p. 92. Taylor 1978, pp. 224-5, 249-51. The order was allegedly linked to the Duke's shocking discovery (on a visit to Portsmouth and Plymouth shortly before) "that [evangelical] religion had entered some of our ships in the royal navy" (NSM 1857, pp. 98-9; 1858, pp. 534, 537).

170. SML 1827, p. 357.

171. *The Christian Guardian* 1827, p. 320. SML 1828, p. 57.

172. NSM 1828, p. 27; 1829 Pt I, pp. 131, 177, 217; Pt. II, pp. 346-8, 390; 1861, p. 370. G.C. Smith *Windsor* n.d., passim.

173. E.g.: NSM 1828, p. 27; 1829 Pt. II, pp. 390, 441-55; 1830, p. 64. SML 1828, p. 45; 1838, pp. 4-6. A relaxing of the Duke's attitude evidently followed his succession to the throne in 1830 (NSM 1857, p. 99; 1858, p. 537).

174. Infra, pp. 341-2.

175. Infra, pp. 19-22, 50-1, 179-80, 222-4.

176. Braaten 1972, p. 37.

177. SML 1821, p. 177. Supra, p. 222. Cf. Hope 1969, p. 20.

178. A "Seaman's Library" on the London *Ark* was evidently not satisfactorily organized until 1823. (EM 1821, p. 430. [MS] PLS *Minutes*, March 25, 1823.)

179. SML 1822, pp. 1-3; 1823, pp. 261-2, 371, 401, cf. 490; 1824, p. 423. (MS) BFSFSBU *Minutes*, February 24, April 13, July 13, 1824; January 11, 1825. Cf. supra, pp. 125-6.

180. SML 1826, p. 67. NSM 1829 Pt. I, p. 161; 1830, pp. 460-1. Such maritime Christian media depositories were not uncommon (e.g., NSM 1828, p. 283), and would naturally provide library opportunities.

181. SML 1823, pp. 486-7. SMR 1827, p. 258.

182. Robinson 1894, pp. 142-3. Kealey 1905, p. 28.

183. Supra, p. 107.

184. Cox 1834, pp. 113, 117-8, 126-7. Supra, p. 258.

185. SML 1823, pp. 486-7, cf. 490; 1827, p. 519. SMR 1827, p. 258.

186. E.g.: EM 1821, p. 430. (MS) PLS *Minutes*, November 12, 1823. SML 1824, pp. 217, 357; 1825, p. 28; 1827, pp. 116, 151. (MS) BFSFSBU *Minutes*, February 8, 1826.

187. E.g.: SML 1823, p. 487; 1827, pp. 519-20. SMR 1827, p. 258.

188. SML 1821, pp. 379, 396, 501; 1822, p. 170.

189. SML 1821, p. 177.

190. SML 1826, p. 455. Cf. NSM 1828, p. 474.

191. SML 1823, pp. 462-3. The Committee of the Dundee Seamen's Friend Society were, like their colleagues in Leith, pained at the sight of seamen during the long winter evenings "roaming in the streets, exposed to temptations, and, at all events, removed from improving exercises." Hence, a reading-room was rented for their use during the winter of 1823-24, where they could find "books fitted to advance their religious and intellectual culture" (SML 1824, p. 284).

192. SML 1823, p. 401: 1826, p. 67. NSM 1830, p. 460.

193. NSM 1828, pp. 175-8; 1829 Pt. I, pp. 17, 132; 1830, p. 98.

194. E.g., infra, pp. 338-9.

195. Moorman 1953, pp. 324-5. Young 1956, pp. 13-4. Halévy 1964, pp. 529-34.

196. Infra, pp. 563-71.

197. Smith 1961, pp. 142, 153-4. Cf. NMBS *Report* 1818, pp. 96, 100; SML 1826, p. 48.

198. SML 1820, pp. 251-2; 1823, p. 422; 1824, pp. 126-30; 1825, p. 177. *The Marine Society* n.d., p. 9.

199. SML 1823, p. 482; 1824, pp. 129-30. Bristol Marine School Society *Report* 1825, p. 15. G.C. Smith *The Royal Brunswick* [1828], p. 20. Cf. NSM 1831, p. 106. Harris 1837 (transl. Oxehufwud), p. 165.

200. SML 820, pp. 249-50; 1823, p. 447; 1825, p. 472.

201. Supra, p. 33.

202. *The New Schaff-Herzog Encyclopedia* Vol. II, 1911, p. 154. Whiteley 1938, pp. 330-3. Foster 1960, pp. 78-80.

203. E.g.: SML 1820, p. 435; 1821, pp. 383, 396; 1824, p. 197; 1826, p. 201; 1827, pp. 114-5.

204. SML 1821, p. 501; 1823, p. 55.

205. SML 1822, p. 329; 1825, p. 94. Cox 1834, pp. 76, 128-9. Cf. supra, p. 258.

206. SML 1820, pp. 249-53; cf. 1822, pp. 449-50; 1824, p. 47; 1825, pp. 471-2. Note the earlier attempt by "a Naval Institution" at Brighton to educate 500 boys, "chiefly the children of sea-faring men," on Dr. Bell's system (EM 1813, p. 311).

207. Thompson 1829, p. 37. Despite their 1818 resolution "especially to promote the Religious instruction of Boys training to a Seafaring Life," the PLS failed to establish even a successful Sunday-School aboard the *Ark* ([MS] PLS *Minutes*, March 18, September 22, November 11, 1818).

208. Supra, p. 218. Cf. SML 1822, p. 422; 1823, p. 364.

209. (MS) PLBUS *Minutes*, August 29, 1827. SML 1827, pp. 394-5. MR 1828, p. 228; 1833, p. 225.

210. NSM 1828, pp. 236-7; 1829 Pt. I, pp. 132, 225-6, 230; 1831, p. 224; 1832, p. 91. As schoolmaster, Smith secured the services of one *George Woolcott*, a veteran naval seaman, converted while in prison at Arras shortly before Amiens, wounded under Nelson on the *Victory* at Trafalgar, and latterly an ardent agent of the BFSSFS. ([MS] Woolcott 1814-29. SML 1822, pp. 321-2. [MS] BFSFSBU *Minutes*, January 8, 1823. NSM 1828, pp. 1-4, 10-2, 294; 1829 Pt. II, p. 342; cf. 1832, pp. 536-7; 1834, p. 216.)

211. Supra, p. 226.

212. For example Leith (see SML 1825, p. 487; 1827, p. 517).

213. SML 1823, p. 331; 1824, p. 197.

214. SMR 1827, p. 295.

215. SML 1823, p. 486; 1825, pp. 486-7; 1827, pp. 520-1. Cf. SMR 1829, p. 205.

216. Supra, p. 225 and Part IV, Note 139. Although run by a distinct society, the Marine School remained closely affiliated with the local Seamen's Friend Society.

217. Port of Hull Society *Report* 1823, pp, 12-3; 1836, p. 10; 1834, p. 8 SML 1825, p. 149; 1826, p. 456. NSM 1828, p. 474; 1831, p. 469.

218. SML 1823, p. 486. Bristol Marine School Society *Report* 1825, pp. 10, 13-4.

219. SMR 1826, p. 566; 1827, pp. 295-6.

220. NSM 1831, pp. 237-41.

221. (MS) PLBUS *Minutes*, April 18,Aug. 29, Sept. 5, Oct. 25, Dec. 26, 1827; Jan. 2, 1828. SML 1827, pp. 322-3, 395-6, 509-13; 1828, pp. 31-2. Cf. Thompson 1829, p. 37. Also, cf. NSM 1829 Pt. II, p. 465; *The Nautical Magazine* 1833, pp. 590-5; Low 1862, p. 242.

222. NSM 1829 Pt. I, pp. 169-72, 207; Pt. II, pp. 303-4; Supplement pp. 3-4; 1831, pp. 237-41, 348-9; 1838, p. 3 Cf. NSM 1832, pp. 482, 500; Low 1850, p. 304.

223. NMBS *Report* 1830, p. 24. Low 1850, pp. 303-4. This institution eventually absorbed the "Female Orphan Home." (Low 1861, p. 242. Cf. NSM 1840, Supplement pp. 2-3.)

224. Supra, p. 16-7.

225. Young 1956, p. 10. Trevelyan 1959, p. 414. Halévy 1961, pp. 325-30. Heasman 1962, pp. 6-7.

226. *The Christian Guardian* 1827, pp. 213-4. NSM 1828, pp. 260-2, 277-80; 1829 Pt. I, Supplement p. 98. MR 1829, p. 216. So-called "Seamen's Loyal Standard Associations" were active in other North Country ports, too, for example in North Shields, South Shields, and Hull (NSM 1829 Pt. II, Supplement pp. 15-6; 1831, p. 31). Cf. the "Benevolent Fund" of Leith seafarers (SML 1827, p. 521). Cf. also NSM 1831, p. 106.

227. SML 1825, p. 14; cf. 1826, p. 8.

228. SML 1824, pp. 130-6, 216, 410; 1825, pp. 6-7. King George's Fund for Sailors 1954, p. 64. Warner 1974, passim.

229. (MS) BFSFSBU *Minutes*, December 1, 1824. SML 1825, pp. 1-15, 199-200; 1826, pp. 6-22, 37-8. Cf. Highmore 1822, p. 293. Smith 1874, p. 8. King George's Fund 1954, pp. 84-5.

230. E.g.: SML 1824, p. 356. SMR 1827, p. 298.

231. SMR 1829, pp. 204-5; 1830, pp. 299-300; 1833, pp. 9, 380-2.

232. NSM 1829 Pt. I, Supplement pp. 5-10; Pt. II, pp. 23, 330-1; 1840, p. 424. Carr 1829, p. 32.

233. NSM 1829 Pt. I, p. 208; cf. 1831, p. 76.

234. NSM 1840, p. 409.

235. Supra, pp. 179-80.

236. NSM 1858, pp. 22-3; cf. 1840, pp. 409-10.

237. Ibid.

238. NSM 1828, p. 28; 1829 Pt. I, Supplement p. 22; 1840, pp. 408-9; 1858, pp. 20-1. Gribble 1849, pp. 19-20. Cf. O'Byrne 1849, pp. 334, 386-7.

239. Destitute Sailors' Asylum *Report* 1830, pp. 7-9. See also NSM 1828, pp. 231-5; 1829 Pt. I, Supplement pp. 22-3; 1838, p. 122; 1840, p. 410; 1858, pp. 23-4. Examples of the erroneous dating of the Asylum are: Low 1850, p. 137; The Sailors' Home and Red Ensign Club 1955, p. 1.

240. Smith and the BFSSFS constantly gave publicity, collected clothes, and provided preaching for the Asylum in this period (see "Asylum Journal" in NSM 1828 and 1829 Pt. I).

241. Carr 1829, p. 31. NSM 1831, pp. 26, 247. Gribble 1849, p. 20. Cf. infra, p. 335.

242. Carr 1829, pp. 29-30. NSM 1829 Pt. II, p. 516; 1830, p. 240; 1831, pp. 39-40.

243. Carr 1829, pp. 30-2. NSM 1829 Pt. II, pp. 532-4; 1830, pp. 139-41, 240-1, 273-4; 1831, pp. 28-9, 33-40. BFSSFS *The Managers* . . . 1831, p. 1. Cf. Destitute Sailors' Asylum *Report* 1831, p. 12.

244. MR 1833, p. 226. NSM 1833, pp. 201-2, 500; 1838, pp. 368-71; 1840, p. 410. Supra, p. 276. Shipwrecked and Distressed Sailors' Asylum *Letters* . . . 1838, pp. 5-6.

245. Destitute Sailors' Asylum *Reports* 1830, etc. These sources show clearly how a deep-sea sailor's home parish frequently refused all responsibility where home ties had not been maintained (cf. NSM 1831, pp. 36-7, 66-7).

246. Destitute Sailors' Asylum *Reports* 1830, pp. 6-7; 1831, pp. 7-8; 1834, pp. 5-6. Cf. G.C. Smith *Royal Brunswick Theatre* n.d., p. 68.

247. NSM 1829 Pt. I, Supplement p. 23; 1831, pp. 37, 68, 90, 247. Cf. Smith 1874, p. 16.

248. Infra, pp. 567-8.

249. Smith devoted much of his magazines in 1829 and 1831 to details of crimping as currently practiced in London (see especially NSM 1829 Pt. I, Supplement pp. 17-23, 37-48, 53-7, 69-74, 85-106; 1831, pp. 45-68, 89-96). Cf. Hohman 1952, pp. 270-1; Hugill 1967, pp. 82-9; (MS) Dixon 1981.

250. E.g.: NSM 1829 Pt. I, pp. 21-2, Supplement pp. 16-8; 1831, pp. 68-9, 72, 89-91.

251. E.g.: SML 1821, pp. 252-4; 1824, pp. 326-47

252. SML 1820, p. 426. Cf. G.C. Smith *The Press Gang* n.d., p. 12.

253. SML 1821, pp. 253-4; 1822, p. 425. (MS) BFSFSBU *Minutes*, various entries April 3, 1822 to April 2, 1823 (cf. July 16 and August 20, 1823, June 28, 1826). NSM 1832, p. 544.

254. SML 1821, p. 385; 1822, pp. 89, 494; 1824, pp. 497-8; 1828, p. 35.

255. SML 1820, pp. 174, 186, 435; 1821, p. 379, 501; 1822, p. 323; 1827, p. 520. Cf. SMR 1827, pp. 293-4. The text of the Edinburgh and Leith Society's circular to inbound captains is quoted in SML 1821, pp. 395-6. Cf. (MS) Kennerley 1984.

256. E.g., G.C. Smith *The First Sailors' Home* [1861], passim. Cf. Gribble 1849, pp. 20-2.

257. SML 1825, p. 216, 1826, pp. 201-2, 256. NSM 1828, pp. 148-9; 1840, pp. 415-7. Gribble 1849, pp. 22-3. Wheatley 1891 Vol. 1, p. 288; Vol. 3, p. 189. Cf. Halévy 1961, pp. 486, 502-5.

258. NSM 1828, pp. 148-9; 1829 Pt. I, Supplement pp. 91-2; 1838, p. 121; 1840, p. 420. G.C. Smith *A Correct View* 1853, p. 1. Wheatley 1891 Vol. 1, p. 288.

259. NSM 1828, pp. 148-9; 1829 Pt. I, Supplement p. 110; 1838, p. 157; 1840, p. 418; 1857, p. 120. G.C. Smith *Site of the Late Brunswick Theatre* [1828], pp. 1-2; *A Correct View* 1853, p. 1; *The First Sailors' Home* [1861], pp. 1-3.

260. NSM 1828, pp. 149-50, 167, 413-23; 1829 Pt. I, Supplement pp. 1-4, 109; Pt II, p. 414; Supplement p. 33; 1838, pp. 121-2; 1840, pp. 418-22. G.C. Smith *The First Sailors' Home* [1861], pp. 1-10; *Royal Brunswick Theatre* No. 5, n.d., pp. 65-6.

261. MR 1829, pp. 216-7. NSM 1829 Pt. I, Supplement passim; Pt. II, p. 414; Supplement pp. 33, 92-3; 1840, pp. 422-4. The 6th Chapter of Nehemiah was read during a service with the workers on the site, before the first brick was laid on June 22; similar services were repeated every morning. (NSM 1829 Pt. II, Supplement pp. 6-7. Gribble 1849, p. 24.) Examples of the erroneous dating of the institution are: The Sailors' Home and Red Ensign Club *AR* 1955, p. 1; *Its History and Activities* 1955, p. 1.

262. NSM 1828, p. 150; 1829, Pt. I, Supplement p. 24; cf. p. 4; 1840, pp. 418, 422.

263. Note, for example, the glaring omission of Smith's contribution in the following accounts: Parry 1855, pp. 56-63; Stuart 1856, pp. 13-5; also, the commemorative plaque inside the present structure (listing only others as founders). Cf. G.C. Smith *Persecution* 1829, pp. 17-8.

264. G.C. Smith *The Royal Brunswick* [1828], pp. 10, 21-2. NSM 1829, Pt. I, Supplement pp. 1-2, 95-9.

265. Ibid. Cf. NSM 1829, Pt. II, Supplement p. 10.

266. SML 1825, p. 487; 1827, p. 521. SMR 1826, p. 567; 1827, p. 293; cf. 1829, p. 206. From its very origin, in 1820, the Greenock Seamen's Friend Society encouraged seamen to deposit their savings in the local "Provident Bank" (SML 1820, p. 186). A proposal for a general "Mariners' Savings Bank" was published in 1822 (SMR 1822, pp. 436-7). Cf. Smith in SML 1823, pp. 401, 447, 465; 1824, pp. 336-7, 426; 1825, p. 163; 1826, p. 68. Warren 1858, p. 12, erroneously gives *Liverpool* pride of place in this field (cf. SML 1824, p. 498). Infra, p. 522.

267. G.C. Smith *The Royal Brunswick* [1828], pp. 10-1, 20. NSM 1828, p. 416; 1829 Pt. I, Supplement pp. 37-8, 72, 96.

268. SML 1823, pp. 359-60, 383, 401 447, 465, 483, 490; 1824, pp. 421, 426, 498; 1826, p. 68. SMR 1827, p. 295. Cf. NSM 1831, p. 64. Infra, pp. 346-50.

269. G.C. Smith *The Royal Brunswick* [1828], pp. 20-1. NSM 1829 Pt. I, Supplement p. 1; cf. Pt. II, pp. 530-4; 1830, pp. 97-8, 339-40.

270. G.C. Smith *The Royal Brunswick* [1828], pp. 11-20. NSM 1829 Pt. I, Supplement pp. 1, 96-7; 1830, pp. 99-100; 1831, pp. 98-107. Cf. SML 1826, p. 369.

271. G.C. Smith *The Royal Brunswick* [1828], pp. 11, 19-20. NSM 1829 Pt. I, p. 161; Supplement pp. 1-2, 72-97.

272. NSM 1829 Pt. II, pp. 405-6; Supplement pp. 1-2, 33-5. G.C. Smith *Freemasons' Hall* 1829, pp. 1-12; *Persecution* 1829, pp. 1-48.

273. SML 1823, p. 277. In 1828-29, Irving frequently preached at the "Destitute Sailors' Asylum" (e.g.: NSM 1829, Pt. II, Supplement pp. 13, 32-3, 49, 61). DNB Vol. 10, 1887, pp. 489-93. Elliott-Binns 1946, pp. 51, 54. Brown 1961, pp. 48-9. In contrast to the more moderate "post-millennialism" of the Evangelicals and Dissenters, Irving was an avowed "pre-millenarian" (Berg 1956, p. 122). Both in appearance and effect, early Irvingism evidently had much in common with the modern "Charistmatic Movement" (Latourette 1953, pp. 1184-5).

274. NSM 1829 Pt. I, pp. 14-6; Pt. II, Supplement p. 33. G.C. Smith *Freemasons' Hall* 1829, pp. 1-8; *Persecution* 1829, pp. 1-7, 26-7. As these sources indicate, Gambier gave Smith little hope on Christ's return: "As to you, you will be burnt in Smithfield." Smith himself readily accepted the doctrine of the Second Coming as such, but eschewed alarmism. As he put it: "The Lord can come, and will come, when he pleases . . . and my business is to be found . . . working for his glory, when he does come."

275. NSM 1829, Pt. II, pp. 384-5, 405-26, 482-3, 515-24; Supplement pp. 1-2, 9-11, 33-5; 1830, pp. 34-6, 145. G.C. Smith *Freemasons' Hall* 1829, pp. 6-12; *Persecution* 1829, pp. 7-48. Smith 1874, pp. 10-2. Whatever Gambier, or for that matter Elliot, may have felt about Smith and his fund-raising, these

sources give no indication of the slightest complicity on their part in the "Philo-Veritas" scandal (see supra, p. 275).

276. The thirteen trustees to whom the property was transferred in November 1829 included William Wilberforce (NSM 1830, p. 35). Although building operations had already been commenced a year previously, the foundation stone was not officially laid until June 10, 1830 (*The Christian Guardian* 1830, p. 398.) Irving was invited to preach, and was escorted to Well Street by Elliott and his friends as late as in 1832, the year Irving was deposed by his own church in London; and Henry Drummond, zealous co-founder of the Irvingite "Catholic Apostolic Church," remained a director of the Sailors' Home until 1834 (NSM 1832, p. 517; 1833, p. 379; 1834, p. 259). See also NSM 1830, p. 489; 1831, pp. 26-7, 248, 292-3, 353-9, 427-30; 1832, pp. 515-9; 1833, p. 381. *The Soldiers' Magazine* 1832, pp. 188-90. Montagu 1832, pp. v-vi, 61-80. Gribble 1849, pp. 24-30. Cross 1971, pp. 251, 423, 702-3. Infra, p. 340.

277. Supra, p. 326.

278. NSM 1830, pp. 97-103; 1832, p. 517.

279. SML 1821, pp. 96-7; 1822, pp. 413-8; 1823, p. 19; 1824, pp. 135, 160; 1825, pp. 177, 470; 1826, pp. 68-9; 1827, pp. 117-8; 1851, p. 118. Seamen's Hospital Society *First Report* 1822, pp. 1-19. Highmore 1822, pp. 397-40. Low 1850, pp. 20-1. The *Dromedary*, one of the original seven receiving ships, had been retained until 1820 as a temporary hospital ship, thus proving the need for a permanent solution (Highmore 1822, p. 398). Viscount Melville himself was the Society's first president; Admiral Gambier, William Wilberforce, and Zachary Macaulay were among its earliest promoters. In 1873, the hospital moved ashore into the infirmary of Greenwich Hospital, where it continued until recently as the "Dreadnought Seamen's Hospital" (Lloyd 1961, pp. 16-7). Supra, p. 180.

280. SML 1823, p. 19; 1825, p. 470. NSM 1829 Pt. I, Supplement p. 110; 1830, pp. 99, 141, 145-6; 1831, p. 107. Destitute Sailors' Asylum *Reports* 1831, p. 17; 1833, pp. 6-7; 1835, p. 7.

281. SML 1825,pp. 5-6. G.C. Smith *The Royal Brunswick* [1828], p. 20. NSM 1829 Pt. II, Supplement p. 16; 1830, pp. 101-2, 342-4; 1831, pp. 327-9; 1832, p. 519. Cf. Destitute Sailors' Asylum *Report* 1834, pp. 3-4.

282. NSM 1829 Pt. II, Supplement p. 16; 1830, pp. 101-3, 146, 342-4; 1831, pp. 107, 327-9; 1832, p. 519; 1833, pp. 185-9; 1840, pp. 412-3. In North Shields, the local "Seamen's Loyal Standard Benefit Society" built, in 1829, an "Asylum" expressly intended for their own "aged seafaring members" (NSM 1829, Pt. II, Supplement pp. 15-6).

283. NSM 1829, Pt. II, pp. 482, 523; 1830, pp. 34-6, 91-3, 97-8, 145, 339-40; 1831, pp. 91-7, 327; 1833, pp. 185-6. So as not to "interfere" with the original Sailors' Home (while there still seemed good prospects of its completion), the Sailors' Rest project at first only envisaged, for sea-going seamen, an implementation of Smith's 1826 "Snug Harbour" plan, viz. society-recommended boarding-houses. (SML 1826, p. 68. NSM 1829 Pt. II, pp. 515-6.) A temporary "New Sailors' Home" was, in fact, started (for fifty seamen), in connection with the Cannon-Street Road Asylum (NSM 1832, pp. 90-1).

284. NSM 1829, Pt. II, pp. 515-6, Supplement p. 10.

285. NSM 1829, Pt. I, Supplement pp. 20-1; Pt. II, p. 347; Supplement p. 10; cf. 1838, pp. 124-5. Destitute Sailors' Asylum *Report* 1831, p. 13.

286. NSM 1831, p. 104; 1833, pp. 185-6. Cf. infra, p. 371.

287. NSM 1833, p. 297.

288. This "Providence Institution, or Sailors' Boarding House" had, it was claimed, a potential capacity for 200 residents. (*The Soldiers' Magazine* 1832, p. 440. NSM 1832, pp. 543-5; 1833, pp. 54-8, 380.)

289. G.C. Smith *Freemasons' Hall* 1829, pp. 1, 7. NSM 1830, pp. 91-2; 1833, pp. 296-9. MR 1833, p. 226. SML 1835, pp. 250-1; 1839, pp. 199-200. SMNY 1835-36, pp. 105-7. Gribble 1849, pp. 24-30. This historic maritime residential institution by Wellclose Square continued to serve seafarers for many years. Eventually, the Sailors' Home on Well Street (now Ensign Street) extended its premises to the rear, acquiring an impressive new frontage on Dock Street. Rebuilt after World War II, and known as the "Red Ensign Club," Dock Street, its usefulness declined with the closing of the local docks, and it was itself finally closed on December 31, 1974. Since 1975, a "Sailors' Home Trust and Destitute Sailors' Fund," symbolizing the close association between the Destitute Sailors' Asylum and the Sailors' Home over the years, has been administered by The Marine Society (The Marine Society *ARs*, 1975, 1976).

290. G.C. Smith *The Royal Brunswick* 1828, p. 8. NSM 1829, Pt. I, Supplement pp. 69-71; 1831, pp. 358-9.

291. NSM 1829, Pt. I, Supplement pp. 69-72; Pt. II, p. 364; Supplement pp. 9-15; 1830, pp. 41, 71-8.

292. NSM 1830, pp. 72-8, 113-4, 141-4, 461; 1831, pp. 32, 75-6, 177-81, 211, 225, 348, 491; 1832, pp.. 82, 91, 291, 482, 500; 1833, p. 446; 1839, pp. 420-1; 1840, pp. 455-6. The *immediate* result of the prostitute preaching in the London Mariners' Church was the formation of the "Metropolitan Female Asylum," under the leadership of Abraham Booth Jr.; since this was established at Hackney, and sought to embrace prostitutes from *all* parts of the Metropolis, the need was felt for a Sailortown refuge specifically for "sea harlots."

293. SML 1822, p. 449. NSM 1829 Pt. I, Supplement pp. 73, 85-91; 1858, p. 145. Supra, p. 213.

294. *A Collection* 1768, pp. 671-4. SML 1820, p. 438; 1822, 15-6; 1824, pp. 370-6; 1826, pp. 48-9, 63, 464; 1827, pp. 217-8. NSM 1828, pp. 260, 287-8; 1829, Pt. I, pp. 217-8; Pt. II, pp. 371-6, 382-3; 1839, pp. 430-2; 1840, pp. 410-2. Brown 1961, pp. 21-2. Baynham 1969, pp. 93-4, 129-31. Kemp 1970, pp. 36-7. With varying success, evangelical commanders would, by insisting on the production of marriage licenses, or by other means, seek to prevent the access of prostitutes on board. (SML 1821, p. 408; 1826, pp. 101, 464. NSM 1828, p. 34.)

295. G.C. Smith *Portsmouth* 1828. NSM 1828, pp. 372, 532-3; 1829, Pt. I, pp. 131, 217-8; Pt. II, pp. 359-60; 1830, pp. 397-8; 1838, p. 432. Smith discounted Admiral Penrose's mild critique (Penrose 1824, pp. 51-66), as well-intentioned but quite ineffectual. (G.C. Smith *The Devonport Ark* 1825, passim. SML 1826, pp. 46-51, 58-63, 100-7. NSM 1830, p. 321.)

296. SML 1821, pp. 365-70, 405-9, 445-52, 566-7; 1822, pp. 39, 389-96; 1823, pp. 252-7; 1824, pp. 372-6. *The Christian Guardian* 1822, pp. 345-51, 400; 1826, p. 451; 1827, pp. 212-3, 230. Marks 1823, pp. 13-5. Lloyd 1968, pp. 245-7. Kemp 1970, pp. 168-70. Cf. NSM 1837, pp. 52-3.

297. NSM 1856, p. 63; 1860, p. 186. A major reason why the Admiralty finally did away with the practice was no doubt the fact that eventually it was found feasible to grant sailors shore leave when in port (Kemp 1970, p. 172).

298. E.g., Flavel 1760, pp. 155-74, 193-210.

299. Infra, pp. 565-7.

300. Marks 1823, pp. 8-11. Baynham 1969, pp. 95, 129-31. Kemp 1970, p. 45. This was an age when *alcoholism* had not yet been identified as distinct from "alcohol abuse," much less recognized as a disease. (See J.I.F. 1947, pp. 498-505; Rose 1961, p. 37; [MS] Ruth Kverndal 1981, passim; ICMA 1982, pp. 29-30. Cf. Backhaus 1982, pp. 46-56; Blume 1984, p. 37.)

301. Scoresby 1831, pp. 248-9. NSM 1833, p. 94; 1844, pp. 329-37; 1859, p. 140.

302. NSM 1832, pp. 344-5, 503; 1833, pp. 93-103, 289-95; 1837, pp. 416-9; 1838, pp. 126-31, 455-8; 1858, pp. 358-9; 1859, pp. 140-2. In the provinces, the Greenock Seamen's Friend Society was especially zealous in temperance efforts (SMR 1834, p. 59; cf. 1827, p. 293). Cf. SMNY 1829-30, pp. 368-70.

303. Whiteley 1938, p. 254.

304. *A Collection* 1768, pp. 67-4. SML 1820, pp. 135, 300; 1822, pp. 15-6; 1825, p. 265; 1826, p. 158. Marks 1823, p. 12. NSM 1829 Pt. II, pp. 373-4; 1831, pp. 7-8. Cf. Flavel 1760, pp. 175-92.

305. NSM 1828, p. 34; 1829 Pt. II, p. 359. Cf. Marks 1821, pp. 118-9. Matthews 1911, p. 201. Thompson 1951, pp. 28-9. Lewis 1960, p. 75.

306. E.g.: RTS *The Swearer's Prayer* n.d., pp. 1-4. SML 1820, p. 137; 1822, pp. 499-500. Marks 1823, pp. 11-3. Pascoe 1901, p. 10. Hewitt 1949, pp. 18-9.

307. BFBS *Monthly Extracts* 1822, p. 58.

308. NSM 1831, pp. 142-3. Cf. SMR 1827, p. 298.

309. SML 1852.

310. SML 1820, pp. 138-9. Marks 1821, pp. 95-6. Jones 1972, p. 429.

311. SML 1824, pp. 381-2; 1827, pp. 366, 480-2. Cf. infra, p. 355.

312. SML 1820, pp. 138; 1824, pp. 378-82.

313. Scoresby 1831, pp. 201-24; 1835, passim.

314. (MS) PLS *Minutes*, April 11, 1820; Sept. 11, 1821. SML 1821, p. 109, 306-8; 1822, pp. 99-103, 191; 1823, pp. 501-2; 1824, pp. 291-2; 1826, p. 368; 1827, pp. 365-9, 405-9, 434-5, 480-2, 521-2. NSM 1829 Pt. II, pp. 325-6, 510-1; 1833, pp. 14, 523-6. SMR 1829, p. 206.

315. SML 1827, p. 434. NSM 1833, pp. 523-6.

316. SML 1827, p. 368.

317. SML 1827, pp. 480, 522. Howse 1952, pp. 122-4. Relief from "oppression *seven* days a week," became historically the precondition for both popular education and the Trade Union Movement.

318. Supra, pp. 19-22, 48-51.

319. SML 1824, p. 326; 1825, pp. 288-9. NSM 1833, pp. 103-6, 182, 300-1, 389-91, 408, 511, 530-9. Lloyd 1968, pp. 267-70. Jones 1972, pp. 430-2. Those who campaigned against impressment would also, on occasion, agitate for an international outlawing of *privateering*. Such "legalizing of merchant sea plunder" must never again be allowed to "demoralize and brutify Sailors." (SML 1825, p. 291. NSM 1833, pp. 182-3.)

320. Robinson 1909, p. 54. Laffin 1969, p. 60.

321. SML 1825, pp. 281-8. NSM 1830, pp. 441-5, 453-6, 1831, pp. 1-14, 64, 171; 1832, pp. 65-6; 1833, pp. 187, 299-301, 346-7, 516. Cf. Biden 1830, passim. Clarkson 1845, passim. G. C. Smith also sought official curbs on the

cruelty and avarice evidenced in *wrecking*. (NSM 1833, p. 187. Cf. G.C. Smith *The Wreckers* 1818, passim.) For a historic overview of the subject, including the effect of the Acts of 1835, 1850, and especially 1854, see Ministry of Transport 1956, pp. 60-3.

322. NSM 1830, pp. 454-5; 1831, pp. 36, 70-1; 1833, pp. 103-7. Jones 1972, pp. 432-3. An able seaman on an East Indiaman received about 35 shillings per month at this time, on a free-trader 45-55 shillings (NSM 1831, p. 61).

323. NSM 1831, p. 12.

324. Webb 1965, p. 93.

325. Ibid., pp. 93-112. Marriott 1954, pp. 61-2.

326. SML 1825, pp. 193-4, 487; 1827, pp. 315-6. SMR 1827, p. 299. Cf. NSM 1831, p. 9. The contemporary identification of trade unions with sedition and infidelity was quite evidently shared by men like Richard Marks (*The Christian Guardian* 1827, p. 214), and G.C. Smith (cf. his insistence that the new "Seamen's Union" had "no reference to the Bethel Union," SML 1825, p. 193). See also Hennell 1960, p. 59. Supra, p. 202.

327. Dillon 1961, pp. 300-16. Axtell n.d., pp. 57, 171-80, 221. Healey n.d., passim. Cf. Stott 1975, p. 30.

328. Foster 1951, p. 49; 1960, p. 76. Hennell 1960, p. 59. Supra, pp. 223-4.

329. Gray 1908, p. 315. Cf. Elliott-Binns 1946, p. 249.

330. E.g., Whittington-Egan 1955, p. 34. Cf. Elliot-Binns 1946, p. 249.

331. NSM 1831, p. 247. Cf. Stott 1975, pp. 25-8.

332. II Cor. 5:14. Cf. Infra, p. 547.

PART VI — NOTES

1. Matthews 1911, p. 212.

2. NSM 1828, p. 338; 1832, p. 377; 1833, p. 194; 1834, pp. 223-4. Canton Vol. 1, 1904, pp. 333-50, 354-61.

3. Whiteley 1938, p. 25. Nevertheless, even then there were limits (see, for example, Balleine 1951, p. 163).

4. SML 1826, p. 264. G.C. Smith *The Thames* 1829, p. 12. NSM 1831, pp. 250-1, 497; 1833, p. 118; 1839, pp. 209-10.

5. Cf. supra, pp. 294, 339.

6. The American adoption of responsibility in Canton (1830) and Le Havre (1832) are both significant cases in point (infra, pp. 466-8, 470-2). Cf. NSM 1832, p. 201; 1833, p. 248. CC 1879, pp. 34-5.

7. G.C. Smith *Freemasons' Hall* 1829, pp. 9-10. NSM 1830, pp. 109, 111. Cf. PLBUS *Appeal* 1829, pp. 2-3.

8. Cf. infra, pp. 356-9.

9. Supra, p. 308.

10. NSM 1834, p. 247. Cf. 1835, pp. 531-2.

11. A "Steamers' Church Ship" moored in the Upper Pool, an itinerant "Steamers' Ark," and a "Steamers' Orphan Asylum" were among the objects projected

(NSM 1838, pp. 351-3, Supplement. *The Steamers' Church Ship Prospectus*, pp. 1-4; 1844, pp. 389-93).

12. NSM 1835, pp. 225-7, 259; 1839, p. 298. Smith 1874, p. 13.

13. NSM 1830, p. 197; 1835, pp. 81-8, 259; 1839, p. 356; 1841, p. 307; 1859, pp. 138-47. Here, J.S. Buckingham, M.P., chairman of the Select Committee, collaborated closely with Smith and his eldest son (NSM 1837, pp. 416-9; 1838, pp. 126-30; 1859, pp. 142-4). Although in the Royal Navy grog was not finally abolished until 1970, Smith did live to see the reduction of the daily allowance by a half. (NSM 1856, p. 63. Lloyd 1968, pp. 256, 273.) Smith also involved himself in the *Anti-Smoking Movement* of his day (NSM 1855, facing p. 1; 1861, pp. 534-5). Cf. supra, pp. 342-3.

14. NSM 1844, pp. 332-4; 1857, p. 515.

15. NSM 1838, pp. 72-5; 1840, pp. 267-8; 1842, pp. 310-3.

16. NSM 1840, pp. 1-4; 1841, p. 518.

17. NSM 1840, pp. 88-102; 1841, pp. 515-20.

18. NSM 1836, pp. 32-8.

19. NSM 1838, pp. 9-14, 36.

20. NSM 1838, pp. 161-7, 201-9, 241-8; 1839, pp. 361-79.

21. NSM 1836, pp. 146, 151.

22. NSM 1833, pp. 234, 313-4, 339; 1834, pp. 56-61, 221-51, 416, 434-5; 1835, pp. 51-4; 1836, pp. 123, 133, 308; 1837, p. 903; 1839, pp. 36-7, 209-10, 227, 230; 1842, p. 158. The assumption in Harms 1909, p. 8, regarding relations between the two societies, is quite erroneous.

23. NSM 1835, p. 27; 1838, p. 113; 1839, pp. 465-7; 1840, pp. 437-9; 1844, pp. 91-4. Smith published charges that certain persons within the leadership of the BFSS actually purchased "a great quantity" of *G.C.S. Unmasked* and "circulated them freely through the country" (NSM 1839, p. 466; 1844, p. 92).

24. NSM 1836, pp. 215-6, 310; 1839, pp. 465-7; 1840, pp. 236-8, 266-7, 469; 1844, pp. 91-3, 233, 245, 372-3; 1852, p. 225; 1855, pp. 104-5, 229-30; 1857, pp. 104-5, 514-6; 1838, p. 233. Smith's writings are replete with instances of arrests for open-air preaching; but these never led to long-term incarceration.

25. NSM 1836, pp. 241, 271; 1857, pp. 514-6; cf. 1830, p. 315. Named after the 18th century pioneer of prison reform, John Howard, the endeavor was significant in a day when ministers in general "held aloof" from prison visitation, even though the Society never realized its declared goal of seeing the Bethel Flag unfurled over convict transports, prison hulks, and jails ashore (cf. Traill Vol. 5, 1904, pp. 656-8).

26. NSM 1852, p. 400; 1855, pp. 84-5; 1857, pp. 105, 516; 1858, p. 233. Faber 1915, pp. 143, 145, 149; 1926, pp. 67-8. Smidt 1927, pp. 61, 64. Polak 1968, pp. 115, 121. Supra, p. 277.

27. MR 1833, p. 521. NSM 1834, p. 56. Cf. NSM 1829, Pt. II, p. 8; 1832, pp. 468, 481; 1835, pp. 51-4.

28. NSM 1832, pp. 379, 467-8, 499; 1834, pp. 430, 435; 1835, p. 27, 135; 1836, p. 308; 1837, p. 904. Trestrail 1879, pp. 107-8.

29. NSM 1852, pp. 225, 253-5; 1855, pp. 104-6; 1857, p. 516; 1858, p. 119.

30. *The Baptist Magazine* 1848, pp. 293, 563, 690. NSM 1852, p. 429; 1855, pp. 464-5; 1856, p. 192; 1857, pp. 516-7; 1859, pp. 124-5. In 1834, many members had seceded, and in 1836 opened a "Clarence Street Baptist Church." This church is still active, and holds the minute-records of Jordan Chapel. ([MS] Jordon Chapel *Minutes*. NSM 1857, pp. 126-7; 1858, pp. 545-6. Rees 1956, p. 43.)

31. Lack of privacy had made Smith's house in Wellclose Square "a thoroughfare," rather than a home. Also, a chronic lack of funds had compelled his family to borrow, "even for the necessities of life." (G.C. Smith *Persecution* 1829, pp. 20-1. NSM 1834, p. 435.)

32. NSM 1861, pp. 497-9.

33. NSM 1841, pp. 584-5; 1844, pp. 303-4; 1855, inside of front cover of No. 1; 1856, p. 303; 1859, p. 310. While in prison, Smith received significant support not only from fellow-seafarers (NSM 1840, p. 469), and his Penzance "home-base" (NSM 1836, p. 215; 1844, pp. 190-1), but even from ministers connected with the BFSS (1840, pp. 470-4).

34. After the Danish Church in Wellclose Square was thus incorporated into the Anglo-Catholic "St. George's Mission," under the local parish church of St. George's-in-the-East, it became the scene of some of the more spectacular anti-liturgical riots of the day. In 1859, the 77-year old Smith was himself at the center of such scenes, when escorted out of his former church for loudly protesting against "Popery in a protestant church." (NSM 1857, pp. 230-4, 329-30; 1858, p. 293; 1859, pp. 310-6; 1860, pp. 181-3. Faber 1915, pp. 156-8; 1926, p. 68.) The famous edifice was finally torn down in 1869, after being bought by the Bishop of London's Fund, and transferred to St. Paul's Church, Dock Street, which then erected day-schools for seamen's children on the site. (Faber 1915, pp. 183-8; 1926, p. 69. Wheatley Vol. 3, 1891, p. 458.)

35. NSM 1855, p. 157. However, Smith was able to renew in modified form his earlier Naval Correspondence Mission (NSM 1856, pp. 38-41, 60-1).

36. NSM 1857, pp. 113-5; 1858, pp. 321-7; 1859, pp. 149-56, 159-68, 199-201, 387-8; 1861, pp. 31, 126-7. No doubt the veteran of the Battle of Copenhagen had also planned to press home his previous petitions to the King and Government of Denmark for the restoration of the Danish Church in London to his use (cf. NSM 1852, pp. 417-23, 437-41; 1856, pp. 233-7).

37. NSM 1858, pp. 486-7; 1859, pp. 302-3. Sweet 1950, pp. 310-1. Cf. 1832, p. 209; 1844, pp. 509-10. Infra, pp. 531-2.

38. NSM 1858, pp. 209-11, 231; 1860, pp. 535-6; 1861, pp. 31-2, 126-7, 134-6, 146-7, 221-3, 271-6, 321-36, 361-75, 387-8, 534-5, 398-401. SMNY 1860-61, p. 368; 1861-62, pp. 9-10, 52-3; 1862-63, p. 208. Through his own intensive ministry to fellow-passengers and crew members during the crossing, Smith sought to alert others to this neglected area of outreach (NSM 1861, p. 334). The silver commemorative medal is in the possession of the "Seamen's Christian Friend Society," England. Chaplain Jones was at this time the eminently successful minister of the New York Mariners' Church (infra, pp. 530-2).

39. *The Revival* 1862, p. 303; 1863, pp. 23, 45-6. *The Times* January 15, 1863, p. 12. *The Gentleman's Magazine* 1863, pp. 260, 390-1. SMNY 1862-63, p. 208. Boase 1882, p. 664. DNB Vol. 53, 1898, p. 43. Smith 1874, p. 14, erroneously gives Smith's age at his death as eighty-two.

40. NSM 1840, p. 175. *The Revival* 1863, pp. 23, 46. The close of Smith's life was also in striking harmony with the text at his ordination: Matthew 24:46. (SMNY 1876, p. 130. Supra, p. 119.)

41. *The Revival* 1863, p. 46. Boase 1882, p. 664. According to SMNY 1862-63, p. 208, the number of mourners was one thousand. Cf. DNB Vol. 53, 1898, p. 43. The statement in *Chart and Compass* 1879, p. 147, that Smith "went down to his grave unmourned," is utterly erroneous. The tombstone marking Smith's grave contains an inscription which includes the following incorrect claims: "He [George Charles Smith] was the first who advocated the claims of Sailors on Christian sympathy. . . . He instituted prayer meetings for Sailors in 1819, and opened the Bethel Floating Chapel on the River Thames" ([MS] Richards 1967). See infra, Note No. 49, for full inscription.

42. Chaplain Jones, himself a London-born former seafarer, identified closely with Smith, and systematically sought to piece together a fuller and fairer picture of his life and work. (SMNY 1876, pp. 107-11, 129-34, 193-7; 1878, pp. 205-7. Cf. CC 1879, pp. 145-7, 326.) The statement designating Smith as "the Morning Star of the Sailor's Reformation" was originally made by the Rev. James Sherman (later of Surrey Chapel), during a public meeting in support of the BFSSFS, at Reading Town Hall, July 22, 1828 (NSM 1828, 395-6; 1860, pp. 552-3).

43. SML 1820, p. 365. NSM 1828, p. 395; cf. pp. 423-5. PLBUS *Appeal* 1829, p. 88. Matthews 1911, pp. 188-9. Cf. Lord Nelson's advice: "No captain can do very wrong if he places his ship alongside that of an enemy" (Mathew 1943, p. 36).

44. Smith was not bereft of self-criticism (NSM 1833, pp. 198-9, p. 472). But he abhorred restriction, and refused to be rebuffed (NSM 1829, Pt. II, p. 366; 1832, pp. 491-2). In railery over rivals with "grand collegiate distinctions," he adopted in later years the letters "B.B.U." after his name, signifying "Burning Bush Unconsumed," cf. Exodus 3:2 (NSM 1840, pp. 296-8; 1844, pp. 402-4; 1861, pp. 247, 531). Supra, p. 277.

45. SML 1827, 474. NSM 1839, p. 472. CC 1879, p. 146. Faber 1915, p. 143.

46. The Editor, Joshua Leavitt, acknowledges that: "It does not become us in America to take part in the controversies in which Mr. Smith seems to be continually engaged." However, he adds, "we may be permitted to express our hope that one so useful will not appear to have done any thing worthy of death or of bonds." (NSM 1830-31, pp. 268-9. Cf. CC 1879, p. 326.)

47. CC 1879, pp. 176-7; 1901, pp. 208-9; 1902, p. 46; 1960, Spring No., p. 3. Pike 1897, pp. 38-40. Matthews 1911, pp. 188-9, 196-7. BFSS *The Glory* . . . 1918, p. 15. BSS *ARs* 1967, 1968. By appropriating Smith's arguments and ideas, the BFSS had long since indirectly, too, endorsed his pioneering role. (Cf. NSM 1841, pp. 288-9. BFSS *AR* 1851, p. 2.)

48. SML 1820, pp. 466-7. NSM 1841, pp. 356-7; 1855, pp. 454-5. *The Revival* 1863, p. 23. SMNY 1862-63, p. 208. People still living, who had personal links with Smith's contemporaries, confirm his prophet-like demeanor. In an interview with the Author in July, 1967, *Leonard Martin Richards* of Madron, Penzance (a direct descendant of Hannibal Curnoe, who in 1809 involved the Baptist Pastor of Penzance in the Naval Awakening), gave it as his conclusion, after long local research, that G.C. Smith must have been "a real firebrand, reminiscent of the Old Testament prophets." In another interview with the Author, also in July 1967, *Violet Maud Rosier*, of 34 Kensington Park

Gardens, London (a great granddaughter of G.C. Smith), recalled family stories of her great grandfather's powerful frame and thundering voice.

49. One (Nordic) seamen's mission leader credits G.C. Smith with the unique accomplishment of having saved the Seamen's Revival from disintegration, for lack of follow-up and coordination. (Waltari 1925, p. 71. Cf. CC 1879, pp. 176-7. Orädd 1951, pp. 54-5.) The inscription on Smith's tombstone reads, as far as can be discerned, as follows:

> Sacred to the memory of the Rev. George Charles Smith, born in London 1782, died at Penzance Jan. 1863. He served in the Royal Navy from 1796 to 1803. He was converted to God at Reading in 1803, studied for the Christian Ministry in 1804 and became Pastor of the Church worshipping at the Jordan Chapel, Penzance in 1807, where he successfully laboured for many years. He was the first who advocated the claims of Sailors on Christian Sympathy, commencing with his ministrations to Seamen on board His Majesty's Revenue Cutter *DOLPHIN,* in 1809. He instituted prayer meetings for Sailors in 1819, and opened the Bethel Floating Chapel on the River Thames. He founded the first Mariners' Church in Wellclose Sq., London, and established Asylums for Sailors and others, as well as Orphan Homes for the destitute (children?) of Seamen and others.

The inscription was recorded with local help from Leonard M. Richards. However, as will be noted, the original contains many errors of fact (cf. supra, Note No. 41.

50. BFSS *AR* 1842, p. 31. Clark 1971, p. 426.

51. Supra, p. 354. Cf. BFSS *AR* 1834, p. 20. (MS) BFSS *Minutes,* July 23, 1839. Timpson 1856, p. 124.

52. There was, during these years, certainly none with the dimensions of a G.C. Smith.

53. SML 1839, p. 181. Shortly afterwards, G.F. Angas resigned his treasureship in the Society, owing to disagreement with its policies ([MS] BFSS *Minutes,* January 17, 1840).

54. NSM 1838, pp. 269-70, 1841, p. 281. Not before 1849 did the Society's annual income reach £3,000 (BFSS *AR* 1849, last page; cf. 1844, p. 21).

55. (MS) BFSS *Minutes,* August 14, November 20, December 18, 1833; January 15, February 19, 1834. BFSS *AR* 1834, pp. 9, 15. The last service on board the Floating Chapel was held May 25, 1834. She was sold in 1835 for £150 to a "Mr. Castle." ([MS] BFSS *Minutes,* April 30, 1834, June 3, 1835. Cf. BFSS *AR* 1836, p. 43.)

56. (MS) BFSS *Minutes,* February 26, March 12, April 9, 23, 30, 1834. BFSS *ARs* 1834-46, passim. SML 1839, pp. 132, 181; 1844, p. 64. Timpson 1856, p. 111.

57. (MS) BFSS *Minutes,* 1833, etc. BFSS *AR* 1837, p. 39; 1839, p. 29; 1846, pp. 8, 13. Cf. NSM 1835, p. 261; 1837, pp. 532-4, 755-6.

58. E.g.: SML 1820, pp. 26, 77-9. NSM 1829, Pt. II, Supplement p. 18.

59. EM 1833, p. 358. Timpson 1856, pp. 100-2.

60. SML 1822, pp. 206-7; 1824, pp. 437, 463; 1835, pp. 112-8. Timpson 1856, passim.

61. NSM 1830, pp. 297-301, 379-81; 1831, pp. 200-1; 1832, pp. 115-6, 190-3, 538-9. G.C. Smith found it very hard to forget how his rivals "took" Captain Prynn from him, in his view (at that time) the "only man worth a straw" among them (NSM 1833, p. 339; 1836, p. 153; 1839, p. 339).

62. BFSS *ARs* 1834-56, passim. SML 1835, pp. 112-8. Timpson 1856, passim. (The Rev. Thomas Timpson, author of Prynn's biography, *The "Living-House"; or, Memoirs of Captain B. Prynn*, was a secretary of the BFSS during its first six years, 1833-39.) See also Pike 1897, pp. 72-4.

63. BFSS *ARs* 1834-46, passim. (MS) BFSS *Minutes*, March 1, 1837.

64. (MS) BFSS *Minutes*, 1833-49, passim. BFSS *ARs* 1834-47, passim. Among such voluntary collaborators, a Mr. Hague ("formerly an English commander") served with great tenacity and devotion in the Prussian port of Memel. The Society provided him with a Bethel Cutter for use in the harbor, helped obtain Government permission for the erection of a chapel, but was unable to support financially. Nevertheless, Mr. Hague is listed as still active in that port as late as in 1847. From the late 1830's, Bethel Flags and Christian literature were also sent to local contacts in Hamburg and Bremerhaven.

65. (MS) BFSS *Minutes*, November 14, 1837, October 10, 1838, February 27, 1839. BFSS *AR* 1838, pp. 33-4; 1839, pp. 33-4; 1840, p. 28.

66. (MS) BFSS *Minutes*, 1834-56, passim. BFSS *ARs* 1834-56, passim. For details on developments in Cronstadt, Le Havre, Sydney and Amsterdam (another port where both the BFSS and ASFS were involved), see infra, pp. 470-2, 475-6.

67. BFSS *AR* 1854, p. 3; 1859, p. 22.

68. Supra, p. 244. Cf. infra, p. 463.

69. BFSS *AR* 1834, pp. 20-2. Cf. SML 1835, pp. 51-2.

70. BFSS *ARs* 1834-40, passim. (MS) BFSS *Minutes*, 1834-40, passim. Cf. SML 1835, pp. 325-8; 1845, pp. 33-5. Supra, pp. 240-8.

71. BFSS *AR* 1836, pp. 4, 35-9.

72. SML 1835, pp. 191-6, 301-2, 414-5; 1836, pp. 55-6. BFSS *AR* 1837, pp. 8, 43; 1838, pp. 5, 13-4, 45-6.

73. BFSS *AR* 1836, pp. 36, 38; 1840, p. 29. At the LMS station at Apua, in the Samoan Islands, a harbor which became a focal point for British and American whalers, after the French annexation of Tahiti, the BFSS supported the erection of a prefabricated iron Seamen's Chapel, sent out with the missionary ship *John Williams* in 1847, and completed in 1849. ([MS] BFSS *Minutes*, July 23 & October 8, 1847, April 25 and May 23, 1849. SML 1847, pp. 201-3, 267; 1849, pp. 170-1; 1850, pp. 86-7. BFSS *AR* 1848, pp. 3-4.)

74. BFSS *AR* 1837, pp. 41-2.

75. Supra, pp. 242-3.

76. SML 1837, pp. 169-70, 350-1. Cf. SML 1835, pp. 332-4; 1837, pp. 8-12, 156-9. BFSS *AR* 1838, pp. 16-7.

77. Infra, p. 456.

78. SML 1838, pp. 109-16. BFSS *AR* 1838, p. 40.

79. BFSS *ARs*, 1838-45, passim. SML 1840, pp. 51-2, 57-61, 395. Pre-1838 statistics of Bethel Captains appear to have been overstated (BFSS *AR* 1836, p. 42; 1837, p. 48; cf. 1844, p. 8). Particular publicity was accorded the

dedication of departing *missionary ships* as Bethel Ships, for example the *Camden*, the *John Williams* and the *Dove* (BFSS *AR* 1838, pp. 13, 45-6; 1845, pp. 48-9). A striking example of the spirit of these Bethel Captains was the successful establishment of a Bethel Chapel in the lazarette in Odessa, through the cooperation of the Russian authorities during the winter of 1839-40. (SML 1840, pp. 143-4, 321-3. BFSS *AR* 1840, pp. 14-5; 1841, pp. 64-5; 1845, p. 7. Cf. Pike 1877, p. 97.).

80. SML 1840, p. 402. For the further development of the concept of Christian seafarers' associations, see infra, pp. 580-1.

81. SML 1837, pp. 109-18, 126. BFSS *AR* 1842, pp. 22-3; 1843, p. 24. SML 1842, pp. 257, 350. Cf. infra, p. 581.

82. (MS) BFSS *Minutes*, February 7 & 28, May 2, 1845. SML 1845, pp. 49-51, 65-6. Cf. supra, p. 358.

83. Trevelyan 1959, p. 481. Cf. Clark 1971, pp. 431-2.

84. BFSS *ARs* from 1843 on, passim.

85. BFSS *AR* 1836, p. 41; 1839, p. 11. (MS) BFSS *Minutes*, March 29, 1837. SML 1837, pp. 7-8, 73-7, 126-7. Cf. Timpson 1856, p. 143. Harris (London, Boston and Stockholm editions), 1837. Some saw *Britannia* as basically an assortment of arguments advocated by G.C. Smith "for years" (NSM 1841, pp. 288-9; cf. 1837, p. 398).

86. BFSS *AR* 1855, p. 8; 1857, p. 2. Although Fieldwick at first had hoped to expand the facilities of the Wellclose Square Sailors' Church, negotiations with the trustees of the property failed ([MS] BFSS *Minutes* 1849-54).

87. (MS) BFSS *Minutes*, July 23, 1939, July 4, 1849. SML 1848, pp. 209-16. One of the Society's directors claimed he knew the names of no less than twenty illicit collectors, connected with five alleged "pseudo-sailor societies" (SML 1853, pp. 36-9).

88. (MS) BFSS *Minutes*, July 4, 1849. SML 1849, pp. 233-4. BFSS *AR* 1850, p. 1.

89. (MS) BFSS *Minutes*, July 4 to December 12, 1849. SML 1849, pp. 233-7; 1850, pp. 1-17. BFSS *AR* 1850, pp. 1-2; 1851, pp. 3-4. Up to 1849, the BFSS *ARs* reproduced a "Constitution" which contained no statement of object whatsover (cf. EM 1833, p. 358).

90. SML 1849, p. 233; 1850, p. 2. BFSS *AR* 1850, p. 2; 1856, p. 8. Cf. infra, p. 556. The Society's Minute Books, Annual Reports, and Magazines, during the period 1833-49, provide ample evidence of early educational and social endeavors. However, a *stronger* concern for the vocational and social ameliora-tion of seafarers is apparent from such examples as "lobbying" by leaders of the BFSS during the passing of the Merchant Service bills of 1850 (SML 1850, pp. 73-4).

91. Harris (London) 1837, pp. 115-7. PHS *AR* 1843, pp. 8-9. (MS) BFSS *Minutes*, July 4, 1849, April 25 & May 24, 1854. Mitchell 1961, p. 36. *Ashore and Afloat*, April 1971, p. 22. Supra, pp. 335-9.

92. (MS) BFSS *Minutes*, 1854-58, passim. BFSS *ARs* 1854-58, passim. SML 1854-58, passim. *Illustrated Times* November 10, 1855, p. 373. Low 1862, pp. 270-80.

93. Harris 1837, p. 115. NSM 1841, pp. 362-4. Riddle 1915, pp. 23-4. Parallel with the establishment of the Sailors' Institute, Annual Reports reveal how,

under Fieldwick, the Society's system of Auxiliary Associations and Provincial Auxiliaries around the British Isles underwent significant expansion. With the opening of vast dock systems downriver, and with the expiration of the lease of the Mercers' Street site, the original Sailors' Institute was succeeded in 1903 by the "Sailors' Palace" (popularly known as "Jack's Palace"), erected east of Shadwell, at 680 Commercial Road, Limehouse. This building, later known as the "Mariners' Hotel," remained until recently the address of the Society's head office. (Matthews 1911, pp. 398-410. BFSS *Glory* . . . 1918, pp. 91-3. BSS *AR* 1968.) Cf. Infra, p. 573.

94. A ministry which was, in practice, closely identified with that of the foreign-language Thames Missionaries, and which went back to the earliest years of the Society, was that of its metropolitan *Missionaries to Welsh Seamen.* (Following the pioneer work of the Rev. J.T. Rowland, one Evan Evans maintained this ministry for decades.) Infra, pp. 598-9.

95. (MS) BFSS *Minutes*, April 12, 1837. BFSS *AR* 1837, pp. 24-5; 1838, pp. 25-6, 58-9; 1839, p. 17. SML 1837, pp. 206-8; 1838, pp. 309-11. Hodder 1891, pp. 156-95. As it proved, effective organization of *German seamen's missions* did not come before some fifty years after Kavel's commencement. Standard versions of German seamen's mission history have hitherto omitted any mention of this early organizational initiative. (E.g.: *Realencyklopädie* Vol. 18, 1906, pp. 317-8. Münchmeyer 1912, pp. 90-209. Thun 1959, pp. 11-32. *Die Religion in Geschichte und Gegenwart* Vol. 5, 1961, cc. 1647-8.)

96. Supra, pp. 240, 260-2.

97. (MS) BFBS *Foreign Corresp.*, letters from von Bülow, July 12, 1832, October 17, 1837. SML 1846, pp. 214-8, 256-8; BFSS *ARs* 1846-50. Von Bülow eventually died in London, October 19, 1867. (KLN Vol. 4, 1929, pp. 999-1000. Haaland 1956, p. 159.)

98. (MS) BFSS *Minutes*, January 14, April 11, 1851. BFSS *AR* 1851, p. 17.

99. (MS) BFSS *Minutes*, May 18, 1852, etc. BFSS *ARs* 1852-55, passim. Cf. (MS) BFBS River Colportage Sub-Committee *Minutes*, July 9, 1855.

100. (MS) BFSS *Minutes*, June 22, 1857, June 21, 1858. (MS) BFSS *Minutes*, March 16, 1858, March 22, 1859. BFSS *AR* 1857, p. 7. The Association seems to have flourished for decades, helping also to lay the foundation of German seamen's missions in the UK, before dissolving around the turn of the century (BFBS *Reports*, up to 1897, passim). Cf. BH 1870, pp. 55-6. Harms 1909, pp. 12, 31. Münchmeyer 1912, p. 93.

101. (MS) BFSS *Minutes* 1860-62, passim. BFSS *ARs* 1861-63, passim. SML 1861, pp. 7-8, 14-5; 1862, pp. 15-7, 58-61, 81-3; 1863, p. 204. *Folkevennen* 1861, pp. 101-19, 369-77. *Norsk Kirketidende* 1861, cc. 253-6, 279-85, 382-4, 412-3, 463, 623, 713, 736, 812-4; 1862, cc. 94-6, 284-5, 407-8. Folkestad 1887, pp. 1-2. Schartum 1910, pp. 20-30. Waltari 1925, p. 77. Kverndal (Bergen) 1978, pp. 114-6. Infra, pp. 398-9.

102. The so-called "Rotherhithe Institute" was opened first at 39 Lower York Street, in the summer of 1861, but shortly afterwards removed to 7 Thames Street. ([MS] BFSS *Minutes*, June 25, 1961. BFSS *AR* 1862, passim.) Pending the appointment of a successor to Thiemann, who left for Sweden, the Institute was led by one Andrew H. Darling, an independent seamen's missionary from Bristol. ([MS] BFSS *Minutes* Dec. 30, 1862, Jan. 27, 1863. *The Revival* 1863, pp. 146-8, 161-3.)

103. (MS) BFSS *Minutes*, Dec. 29, 1863; Dec. 27, 1864. BFSS *ARs* 1864-71, passim. SML 1863, pp. 251-3. BH 1866, No. 3, p. 29. From London, Schelling left for Havana, where he died at his post (from yellow fever) after barely two years of devoted ministry to seafarers in that port (Folkestad 1887, pp. 5-6).

104. Infra, p. 601.

105. BFSS *AR* 1859, p. 21. (MS) BFSS *Minutes*, May 29, 1860. SML 1860, pp. 75-6.

106. BFSS *AR* 1867.

107. BFSS *ARs* 1868-74, passim.

108. *The Rev. Edward W. Matthews* (also known as "Father Neptune") succeeded to the secretaryship in 1878, and remained at the helm until the First World War. (Matthews 1911, pp. 259-68, 352-4. Webster 1932, p. 53.) In response to the nationalistic sentiment of the times, the name of the Society was, from the year 1925, shortened to the "British Sailors' Society" (BSS *AR* 1926).

109. (MS) SCFS *Minutes*, Jan. 14, 1846. NSM 1852, pp. 307-8. SCFS *100th Report* 1946, p. 2. The Society wished, in the words of the original *Minutes*, to be "considered as having grown out of the operations of a Society established in the Year 1819 and known as the 'Port of London & Bethel Union' Society." This statement (which was repeated on the title-page of the Society's earlier Annual Reports) calls for clarification. The PLBUS was, as previously noted, established in 1827, not 1819, and then as a merger of two societies, the PLS and the BFSFSBU, dating back to 1818 and 1819, respectively. Again, the PLBUS merger was effected entirely independently of G.C. Smith and his organization at that time (cf. supra, p. 271). The title of the Society was changed from "The Seamen and Soldiers' Evangelical Friend Society" in 1846, to "The Seamen's Evangelical Society" in 1847, and again to "The Seamen's Christian Friend Society" in 1848 ([MS] SCFS *Minutes* 1846-48, passim). The Society holds, at its head office, several significant relics of G.C. Smith, attesting to the Society's close ties with him and his family.

110. (MS) SCFS *Minutes* 1846-49, 1851-65, passim. *The Seamen and Soldiers' Evangelical Magazine* 1846, pp. 1-15. SCFS *Annual Reports* 1847-92, 1946, 1971, passim. At the outset, the Society had to contend with being confused, by over-zealous directors of the BFSS, with the so-called "Counterfeit Seamen's Societies." (NSM 1852, pp. 242-4. [MS] BFSS *Minutes*, April 30, 1861. Cf. supra, p. 370.) From 1922, the Society, through a separate Hospital Trust, assumed administrative responsibility for the "King George V Merchant Seamen's Memorial Hospital," Malta (SCFS *100th Report* 1946, pp. 3, 23-32).

111. (MS) LCM *Minutes* 1835-37, passim. *The City Mission Magazine* 1836, pp. 130-1. LCM *AR* 1837, p. iv. Low 1850, p. 388. NSM 1855, p. 256. Weylland 1884, pp. 183-99.

112. NMBS *Reports* 1834-1905, passim. NSM 1857, pp. 201-4. (MS) Fowler 1852, passim. Scripture Gift Mission 1961, p. 66. *Naval, Military and Air Force Bible Society* (a brochure current in 1970). (MS) Joseph M. Smith *Interview* 1970.

113. BFBS *Reports* 1834-65, passim. (MS) BFBS *Minutes*, March 26, April 9, 27, May 14, 1855. (MS) BFBS River Colportage Sub-Committee *Minutes*, July 9, 20, 23, August 6, 1855.

114. NSM 1835, pp. 357-75, 476; 1837, p. 398. Scottish Sailors' and Soldiers' Bethel Flag Union *Reports* 1836-43, passim.

115. These missions were launched largely through the instrumentality of a deeply dedicated Presbyterian student of theology, Thomas Rosie, born in the Orkneys in 1825, died as Missionary to the Bombay Harbour Mission, 1860. The Scottish Coast Missions ultimately merged with the BFSS, with which they had early associations. (BFSS *Report* 1853, p. 16. [MS] BFSS *Minutes* July 26, 1864. Dodds 1863, passim. BH April 1866, pp. 15-6; 1886, 1st Supplement pp. 4-12.)

116. Ample documentation is available in the reports of the respective societies, as well as in the SML and NSM, for these years. In Liverpool, the work of the Liverpool Seamen's Friend Society has been carried on in the name of the "Gordon Smith Institute for Seamen" (opened November 26, 1900).

117. NSM 1838, pp. 362, 366. For details on the continuing history of the Sailors' Home and the Destitute Sailors' Asylum, see Part V, Note No. 289.

118. The same year (1841), Trinity Congregational Chapel was opened close by, built by Green, partly to serve the needs of the Home. On the death of Green's son, Richard, the Home was transferred to the Board of Trade as a Mercantile Marine Office; it has since been used by the Dept. of Health & Social Security. (SML 1841, p. 281. BFSS *Report* 1842, p. 22. NSM 1857, p. 340; 1858, p. 415; 1861, pp. 413-4. Stuart 1856, pp. 28-32, 46. *Tower Hamlets News*, Dec. 1969, p. 2.)

119. The promoters of the Coloured Sailors' Home project had first applied to the Sailors' Home in Well Street, as well as others, but were told that this was "impracticable," and that a "separate" institution would be required, compatible with "their customs, habits, and language." (NSM 1857, pp. 249-52; 1861, pp. 413-4. Low 1862, p. 99. Weylland 1884, pp. 190-2.)

120. U.K. ports in which there existed sailors' homes in 1856 were: London (2), Newcastle, Sunderland, Liverpool, Bristol, Falmouth, Devonport, Plymouth, Portsmouth, Folkestone, Dover, Dublin, Belfast, Cork, Queenstown, Glasgow, Greenock, Stornoway, Leith. Under preparation in: North Shields, Cardiff, Sheerness, Chatham, Woolwich, Limerick, Waterford. (Stuart 1856, pp. 47, 53-4, 60-1. NSM 1857, pp. 428-33; 1858, Supplement pp. 1-14. *Sailors' Homes* 1865, pp. 1-23. Toynbee 1866, p. 2. Kingsford 1947, pp. 138-9. Jones 1972, p. 433.) The Merchant Shipping Acts of the early 1850's paid a compliment to sailors' homes by making it possible to open *Mercantile Marine Offices* there. (G.C. Smith *A Correct View* 1853, passim. The Sailors' Home *Its History* 1855, passim. Stuart 1856, p. 122.) Some of these early sailors' homes were established in typical naval ports; but it was not until the advent of Agnes Weston and her *Sailors' Rests* in the 1870's that shore facilities for naval seamen became available on a more satisfactory scale. (Weston 1911, passim. Heasman 1962, pp. 254-5. Cf. NSM 1844, p. 450;]MS[Kennerley 1984.)

121. Calcutta Seamen's Friend Society *Reports* 1838, pp. 15-6; 1842, pp. 12-4, 31-2. Bombay Seamen's Friend Association *Reports* 1838, pp. 5-9; 1840, pp. 5-8. NSM 1838, pp. 123-6; 1841, pp.110-7. BFSS *AR* 1840, pp. 31, 75-7; 1841, p. 10; 1845, pp. 20-1.

122. The fact that the Bethel Cause in Sydney had not completely capitulated during the preceding decade was largely attributable to the efforts of a "Baptist Missionary" there, the Rev. John Saunders, who arrived in 1834, and served

as voluntary "Agent and Foreign Director" of the BFSS for Sydney. It was in response to Saunders' appeal in 1836, and that of Dr. John D. Lang (Principal of the Australian College) in 1840, that the Americans sent Chaplain Adam. From 1841, Adam secured the use of an old whaling vessel, the *Sir William Wallace*, as a floating chapel. In 1844, the Society succeeded in building its first Mariners' Church ashore, at the foot of Erskine Street. Relevant sources: BFSS *AR* 1835, p. 22; 1836, pp. 37-8; 1837, pp. 42-3; 1859, p. 23. SMNY 1836-37, pp. 356-57; 1840-41, pp. 94-5; 1841-42, pp. 94-5. ASFS *AR* 1838, pp. 14-5; 1841, p. 11. SML 1840, pp. 210-2; 1841, pp. 318-9; 1856, pp. 37-8. *The Colonial Observer* (Sydney), March 15, 1843. NSM 1844, pp. 1123-30. *Evening News* (Sydney), March 27, 1909. Matthew 1911, p. 486. The Missions to Seamen. NSW, *Annual Report for 1974*, p. 8. Re. Chaplain M. T. Adam and the "Sydney Case," see infra, p. 476.

123. SMNY 1840-41, pp. 291-2 (quoting *The Sydney Herald*); 1857-58, p. 26. SML 1846, pp. 18-9.

124. Barclay obtained in 1840 the use of the *Lady Wellington* as a supplementary "preaching station." (BFSS *ARs* 1838, 1839, 1841, passim. SML 1839, pp. 29-31. SMNY 1840-41, pp. 291-2.)

125. SML 1857, pp. 193-5, 214-6; 1863, pp. 239-41. Victorian Bethel Union *AR* 1859, pp. 1-10. BFSS *AR* 1859, pp. 22-3. It is interesting to note that the Governor's Residence of that day ("Toorak House") has, since 1956, served as a Scandinavian Seamen's Center in Melbourne.

126. (MS) BFSS *Minutes*, Oct. 11, 1844. BFSS *AR* 1859, p. 21. SML 1860, pp. 43-4.

127. Trevelyan 1946, p. 512.

128. *The Christian Observer* 1833, p. iii. Trevelyan 1946, pp. 509-17. Elliott-Binns 1946, pp. 65-75. Moorman 1953, pp. 147, 329-60. Warren 1965, p. 17. Webb 1969, pp. 224-33. The *third* ("Broad Church") party emerging during this period, following Frederick D. Maurice' 1838 publication of *The Kingdom of Christ*, with its powerful advocacy of "Christian Socialism," was destined to have less immediate influence on seamen's missions. However, a trend of the times with more manifest implications for seamen's mission organization was the movement away from the hitherto predominatly "subjective" type of agency toward a more diversified scene, with the emergence of an "objective" type, too, emphasizing ecclesiastical integration and confessional loyalty (see Myklebust 1976, pp. 318-20). Cf. Younggren (1981, pp. 38-9) on "parachurch" agencies.

129. Supra, pp. 293-4.

130. Hence the title of a widely-circulated booklet, *From the Bristol Channel to the Seven Seas*, written for the Society by C.A.J. Nibbs [1935].

131. *Mission to British Seamen* April 1853, p. 77. This publication's "History of the Mission" (pp. 77-81) is the earliest version of the origin of Ashley's work which has been accessible to the Author. It is quoted in *The Word on the Waters* 1858, pp. 8-12, in an article entitled "Origin of the Mission to Seamen." See also BH 1877, 4th Supplement pp. 52-5; Walrond 1904, pp. 21-2.

132. Ibid. The version incorporating the clergyman's son is reproduced in Walrond 1904, pp. 21-2; Gollock 1930, p. 56; Nibbs 1935, p. 2; Strong 1956, p. 18; Jacob 1973, p. 19. Cf. M.R. Kingsford's critique in his 1957 publication, pp. 139-40.

133. *Mission to British Seamen* April 1853, p. 78.

134. Ibid., pp. 78-80. Walrond 1904, pp. 25-41.

135. Ibid.

136. Ibid. (MS) Bristol Channel Mission *Chaplain's Journal* 1841-43, passim.

137. *Mission to British Seamen* April 1853, p. 79. Cf. BH 1877, 4th Supplement pp. 54-5.

138. Ibid. Walrond 1904, pp. 38-41.

139. Dr. Ashley was, as late as in 1853, still listed as *Chaplain* of the Bristol Channel Seamen's Mission (*Mission to British Seamen* April 1853, p. 77).

140. *Mission to British Seamen* April 1853, p. 80. WW 1858, p. 12. Walrond 1904, p. 46. Nibbs 1935, p. 4.

141. The Missions to Seamen *Report* for 1856-57, pp. 12-3. WW 1858, pp. 12-3, 146. Walrond 1904, pp. 45-53. Kingsford 1947, pp. 59, 62-3, 67, 129-33. In early 1856, the revived Bristol Society appointed the Rev. Clement D. Strong (a lineal descendant of Sir Francis Drake) as Dr. Ashley's successor in the Bristol Channel. (The Missions to Seamen *Report* for 1856-57, pp. 13-4. Walrond 1904, pp. 54-66, Cf. Kingsford 1957, pp. 138-9.) Infra, pp. 391-2.

142. Kingston 1857, pp. IX, XXIII. Walrond 1904, p. 53. Kingsford 1947, pp. 132-3.

143. Kingston 1857, pp. I-II. MTS *Report* for 1859-60, p. 6. Walrond 1904, pp. 71-2. WW 1906, p. 99 states that the February 20 meeting was convened "in Fenchurch Street" (*not*, as stated in Kingsford 1957, p. 18, in Kingston's Blackheath home).

144. Walrond 1904, pp. 85-91, 96-106, 122-37. The object of the Society was ultimately given the wording it still retains: "The spiritual, moral and physical well-being of seafarers of all races at home and overseas."

145. Kingston 1857, pp. I-VI. Kingsford 1947, pp. 133-44.

146. Kingston 1857, pp. I-XVIII. MTS *Report* for 1857-58, pp. 10-3. Walrond 1904, pp. 74-85. Kingsford 1947, pp. 133-50; 1957, pp. 17-21. To the Elbe station, support was for some years sent by this *Anglican* Society for the ministrations of a *Lutheran* Chaplain (William Stoeber) to English-speaking sailors. (*Report* for 1856-57, pp. 10-1; 1861-62, p. 11. Nibbs 1935, p. 17.)

147. MTS *Report* for 1856-57, p. 4; for 1857-58, pp. 2, 4, 14. (MS) MTS *Committee Book*, May 19, 1858. WW 1858, pp. 145-51. BH 1877, 4th Supplement pp. 55-8. Kingsford 1947, pp. 149-50; 1957, pp. 138-9. Presumably, local loyalties and the deeply emotional issue of "firsts" both contributed to early tension. Kingston saw the early resignation of Chaplain Childs as "very much owing to the misunderstanding of the two Societies." He also states that it was "in consequence of its [the Bristol Society's] debts," that the London Society "refused to date their origin from the Bristol Society," electing instead to maintain the year 1856 for this purpose (Kingston 1857, p. XXIII). However, the united Society readily acknowledged the Bristol Mission as in actual fact "the parent of all the rest" (WW 1860, p. 73).

148. Kingston 1857, pp. XXIV, XXVI. Walrond 1904, p. 72. Kingsford 1947, pp. 156-8. Cf. SML 1827, p. 307 (an early introduction of the *Flying Angel* motif).

149. Kingsford 1947, pp. 153-6; 1957, pp. 136-40. Note the minimal mention of Kingston in Nibbs 1935, p. 5.

150. Supra, p. 279.

151. Cf. WW 1906, pp. 98-9. Kingsford 1947, p. 154.

152. Roadstead missions were attempted off the Downs and the Isle of Wight in the early 1820's (SML 1820, pp. 436, 447; 1821, p. 403; 1823, p. 120). W.H. Angas was also involved in this work in the 1820's (Cox 1834, pp. 112-3, 118-9). Cf. von Bülow's Norway Missions, supra, pp. 260-2.

153. A typical overstatement at the outset was: "Seamen's chapels have generally proved a failure, from the simple fact, that the great majority of sailors cease to exercise the power of volition the moment they put their feet on shore" (WW 1856, pp. 1-7).

154. MTS *Report* for 1863-64, pp. 7-8. Walrond 1904, pp. 122-37, 155-207. WW 1906, pp. 102-4. Nibbs 1935, p. 11. Strong 1956, pp. 33-8. Jacob 1973, pp. 32-4. The first rudimentary Anglican "Institute" in point of time seems to have been the reading-room established at Deal, Oct. 1, 1861, by the Society's President, Lord Shaftesbury, and a few friends (Walrond 1904, pp. 122-3).

155. Kingston 1857, pp. XXI-XXII. WW 1859, pp. 215-22; 1868, pp. 44-9; 1906, pp. 104-5. Church of England 1878, p. 7. Gollock 1930, pp. 59-60. Kingsford 1947, p. 143. (MS) Coombs 1960, pp. 111-2. The list of officers in the Society's first *Report*, p. 1, contains three Archbishops as vice-patrons; sixteen Domestic Bishops and eight Overseas Bishops are listed as vice-presidents.

156. WW 1859, pp. 219-20. Strong 1956, p. 40. Cf. infra, p. 581.

157. MTS *Report* for 1974, p. 22. *Flying Angel News* No. 1, 1975, p. 4.

158. Kingsford 1947, p. 142. Anson 1955, p. 109. An exception was the school for sailor-boys and home for elderly seamen set up by the "Sisters of Mercy," organized in Plymouth in 1848. Cf. The Order of St. Paul, founded in 1889 (Anson 1955, pp. 106-21).

159. Walrond 1904, pp. 52-3. Strong 1956, p. 32. Kingsford 1957, pp. 29-30.

160. SAWCM *Report* 1869, p. 9. Scarth 1889, pp. 22-65, 118-22.

161. SAWCM *Report* 1869, p. 11; 1914, p. 10. Scarth 1889, pp. 122-7, 132. Kingsford 1957, pp. 29-32. The Missions to Seamen, and other Anglican organizations subscribing to "that system of a society monopolising a particular class," were branded before the world as "irresponsible." (SAWCM *Report* 1874, p. 19. Church of England 1888, pp. 101-3.)

162. Church of England 1888, pp. 110-1. Kingsford 1957, pp. 30-2. The issue is familiar from other fields, too (e.g., military, institutional and industrial chaplaincy in general).

163. Lower House of the Convocation of Canterbury, 1878, pp. 8-9. Scarth 1889, passim. SAWCM *Report* 1914, pp. 2-3. The Mission developed strong ties with the independent Anglican "Mediterranean Mission to Seamen," begun by the Bishop of Gibraltar in the 1880's. (Scarth 1889, pp. 78-87. Gollock 1930, pp. 225-9.)

164. Kingsford 1957, pp. 32-3. *The Encylopedia of Modern Christian Missions* 1967, pp. 168, 446. An Interconfessional Conference of Seafarers' Chaplains

at Bangkok, 1974, affirmed the "need for the maritime apostolate to be recognized as an integral part of the mission of the local churches" (*Flying Angel News* No. 1, 1975, p. 8).

165. Supra, pp. 293-4.

166. Kingston 1857, p. XXIII. Walrond 1904, p. 46. WW Jan. 1906, p. 101.

167. Ibid. (MS) TCM *Minutes*, February 23, 1844, etc. NSM 1858, p. 492. *Havnen*, Jan. 1886, pp. 17-8.

168. Ibid. (MS) National Maritime Museum *Summary*, April 4, 1972. Supra, p. 340.

169. (MS) TCM *Minutes*, May 3, 1844, etc. TCM *Report* 1847, passim. NMBS *Report* 1848, p. 22. Low 1850, pp. 389-90; 1862, p. 279. Parry 1855, pp. 34-5. NSM 1858, pp. 491-6. *Havnen* Jan. 1886, pp. 17-21; Jan. 1887, pp. 8-18; Mather 1887, passim. G.C. Smith *The Boatswain's Mate* 1888; Gordon 1890, pp. 56-83. Pritchard 1980, pp. 13-22.

170. (MS) MTS *Index*, especially Resolution 2, 477, 529, 612, 1708 and 2042. WW 1858, p. 14; 1906, p. 101. MTS *Report* for 1864-65, p. 8. Strong 1956, pp. 174-5. The Missions to Seamen continued the Thames Church Mission ministry on the river right up to the early 1970's, with the *John Ashley III* (dedicated 1971) as the last of a long line of mission ships on the Thames (MTS *TSMY John Ashley III* 1971).

171. MR 1836, p. 237. SML 1846, p. 270. NMBS *Report* 1846, p. 25; 1848, p. 27. Gribble 1849, p. 29. Cuthbertson 1966, n.p.

172. NSM 1829, p. 124; 1858, pp. 231, 239-40, 415. Parry 1855, p. 31. SAWCM *Report* 1914, pp. 16-7. *The Pilot*, Aug. 1962, n.p. Cuthbertson 1966, n.p.

173. Champneys 1875, pp. 10-2. (MS) Coombs 1960, pp. 112-6.

174. SML 1837, pp. 217-30. Lea 1859, passim. Cf. Whalley 1909. Balleine 1951, pp. 138-44. (MS) Coombs 1960, pp. 126-34, 143. Chadwick 1966, p. 446. A Mariners' Chapel was erected in Worcester in 1840, a Floating Chapel was established on the Worcester-Birmingham Canal in 1842, and in 1849 a Mariners' Chapel was raised in Gloucester, for the special benefit of the overseas shipping there.

175. From mid-century on, the *Colonial Church Chronicle* makes frequent reference to this form of ministry. Cf. Balleine 1951, pp. 137-8. It was largely thanks to Mayers that a Sailors' Home could be opened in Marseilles in Oct. 1854 (Stuart 1856, p. 52).

176. Pascoe 1901, pp. 736-9. Cf. SPG *Provision* 1851. (MS) BFSS *Minutes*, Nov. 21, 1854. Thompson 1951, p. 470.

177. E.g.: *The Christian Guardian* 1838, p. 34. MR 1843, 440-1. NMBS *Report* 1845, pp. 25-6.

178. Allen 1898, pp. 402-12. Kingsford 1947, p. 130; 1957, p. 16. *The Encyclopedia of Modern Christian Missions* 1967, pp. 594-5.

179. King George's Fund 1954, pp. 65-6. Anson 1948, pp. 43-4.

180. G.C. Smith urged the formation of a British "Baptist Sailors' Society," but in vain (NSM 1844, pp. 377-9). The Presbyterians produced no denominational seamen's mission organization in England; by this time, many English Presbyterians had turned Unitarian (Latourette 1953, p. 1180).

181. E.g.: NSM 1828, p. 189; 1838, pp. 88-90.

182. WSM *Reports* from 1847, passim, 1870, pp. 5-6. SMNY 1865-66, pp. 198-9. Sanders n.d., pp. 13-35.

183. WSM *Reports*, passim. *The Quarterly Plea* April 1858, pp. 1-4. Sanders n.d., pp. 21-8. From 1864, the reading-room was kept open daily.

184. *The Quarterly Plea* Oct. 1860, pp. 1-4. WSM *Reports* 1861 etc., passim. Sanders n.d., pp. 35-8. "Bible Women" had recently been introduced in the "poor districts of the city" in general (WSM *Report* 1862, p. 11).

185. WSM *Reports* 1861 etc. Supra, pp. 368-9.

186. The building is located on the site of "The Magnet," until the 1880's one of the most notorious public houses in Sailortown, strategically situated in Jeremiah Street, immediately opposite the (former) Mercantile Marine Office in "Green's" Sailors' Home. (Bullen 1901, pp. 3-15. Sanders n.d., pp. 56-7.) The Society is now known as "The Seamen's Mission of the Methodist Church."

187. (MS) BFSS *Minutes*, Jan. 2, 1839, July 13, 1849, April 26, 1859.

188. Anson 1948, pp. 40-6.

189. Ibid., pp. 38-9.

190. Ibid., pp. 63-4. *Stella Maris* (Star of the Sea), as a title of the Virgin Mary, has deep roots in the Roman Catholic Church. It has been attributed to St. Jerome, and is linked by St. Bernard of Clairvaux to the Messianic prophecy in Numbers 24:17. "Our Lady, Star of the Sea" is portrayed in the emblem of the National Catholic Conference for Seafarers in the USA. (Anson 1948, pp. 31-2. Ursin 1965, pp. 191-2. *Catholic Maritime News*, August 1979. Cf. supra, p. 15.)

191. The 1890's saw the formation of a Seamen's Branch of the "Apostleship of Prayer," a Seamen's Committee of the "Catholic Truth Society," and the adoption of seamen's work by the "Society of St. Vincent de Paul." As a result, beginnings were made not only in the UK, but also in France, Italy, Canada and the USA. (The first Roman Catholic center for merchant seafarers in the modern sense was opened in Montreal, May 18, 1893.) In 1894, the "Société des Oeuvres de Mer" was successfully founded in France by the Augustinians of the Assumption, as a counterpart to the Royal National Mission to Deep Sea Fishermen. (Anson 1948, pp. 38-85; 1970, pp. 46-53.)

192. Co-founders with Peter Anson were Arthur Gannon and Daniel Shields (a Jesuit Brother). Anson designed the well-known badge of the Apostleship; Shields contributed the name; and Gannon became the persevering organizing secretary. In 1922, Pius XI issued a Papal Brief, giving the enterprise his warm approbation. (Some date the founding of the organization from this event. E.g., *Brockhaus Enzyklopädie* 1973 Vol. 18, p. 233.) In 1970, Apostolatus Maris, with over one hundred International Stella Maris Clubs in major ports around the world, and a further fifty smaller centers caring for national and local seafarers, was integrated into the new "Pontifical Commission for the Pastoral Care of Migrants and Itinerant Peoples." Migrants and itinerant peoples are also collectively referred to as: "People on the Move," or, in German "Menschen Unterwegs." (Martindale 1938, pp. 2-5. Anson 1948, pp. 86-106. Gannon 1965, pp. 1-4. McGuiness 1975, pp. 7-15. Frayne n.d., passim; 1972, pp. 33-34.) Infra, pp. 552-3.

PART VII — NOTES

1. Paine 1919, pp. 107-16. Sprout 1946, pp. 61-3. Perkins 1961, pp. 150-83. Morison, 1972, Vol. 2, pp. 97-110. Mitchell 1967, p. 81.

2. Morison 1921, passim. Writers' Program (Massachusetts) 1941, pp. 86-7.

3. Sweet 1950, pp. 240-2; 1963, pp. 190-4. Burr 1961, pp. 219-33. Hudson 1965, pp. 113-4. Dunstan 1966, pp. 6-8.

4. For an exhaustive and authoritative study on Tuckerman's life and work, see Daniel T. McColgan's dissertation on *Joseph Tuckerman: Pioneer in American Social Work* (Washington D.C., 1940). See also Channing 1843, pp. 111-46; Carpenter 1851, pp. 31-135; Sprague 1865, pp. 345-56; Eliot 1935, pp. 1-32; DAB Vol. 19 1936, p. 46. Cf. Ahlstrom 1975 Vol. 2, p. 82.

5. Channing 1834, pp. 112-3. Cf. Tuckerman 1838, p. 173. Brooks 1940, pp. 53-4.

6. Supra, p. 12-14.

7. BSRMIS *Address* 1812, pp. 3-4. Spooner 1879, p. 81.

8. BSRMIS *Address* 1812, pp. 4-6. The *Panoplist* 1812 (May), pp. 564-5. *The Christian Disciple* 1813, p. 94.

9. The name of Captain *Gamaliel Bradford*, like that of his fellow-officers, is listed in *The Panoplist* 1812, pp. 564-5. For biographical data, see Massachusetts Historical Society 1825, pp. 202-9; *New England Historical and Genealogical Register* 1850; Bradford 1958, pp. 29-40.

10. Captain *Jonathan Chapman* became known as an ardent advocate of the Temperance Cause, especially among the young (Chapman 1832, passim).

11. Captain *Tristam Barnard* was at times whaling master (Federal Writers 1838, p. 48), merchant captain, and shipowner (Survey 1942, pp. 124-5).

12. Examples of biographies of *William Ellery Channing*: Furness 1851, Peabody 1880, DAB Vol. 4 1930, pp. 4-7, Brown 1956 & 1961.

13. For biography of the Rev. *Joseph S. Buckminster*, see: MHS 1838, pp. 271-4.

14. Biographies of the Rev. *Charles Lowell*: MHS 1862, pp. 427-40; DAB 1872, pp. 565-6; Appleton's Vol. 4, 1888, pp. 42-3.

15. Biographies of the Rev. *Horace Holley*: Pierpoint 1827; Caldwell 1828.

16. For biography of *Richard Sullivan*, see: *New England Historical and Genealogial Register* 1862 (April), pp. 185-6.

17. BSRMIS *Address* 1812, pp. 6-12. Cf. SMNY 1835-36, pp. 48-9.

18. BSRMIS *Address* 1812, p. 5. Cf. supra, pp. 17-18.

19. Channing Vol. 4, 1917, pp. 346-454. Morison 1941, pp. 184-98; 1969 Vol. 1, pp. 357-65. Selement 1973, pp. 409-17.

20. *The Christian Disciple* 1813, pp. 94-6.

21. Ibid. MHS 1825, p. 203. Tuckerman 1838, p. 173 (quoted in Carpenter 1851, pp. 44-5). DAB Vol. 19, 1936, p. 46. The degree to which the Society was identified with this function is evidenced by the fact that it became known as "the tract society for sailors" (BSRMIS *Tracts*, No. 9, p. 4). See the

Bibliography under "BSRMIS" for list of ten tracts traced by the Author (including locations).

22. BSRMIS *Tracts*, Nos. 7 and 8. Re. Captain Bradford's sea career, see supra, Note 9.

23. Tuckerman 1838, p. 173.

24. BSRMIS *Address* 1812, p. 2. *The Christian Disciple* 1813, pp. 94-6. Warren 1858, p. 8.

25. BSRMIS *Tracts*, no. 5, p. 4. Channing 1843, p. 113. McColgan 1940, p. 37. Sweet 1963, p. 192. A study of the contents of the BSRMIS *Tracts* reveals several references to the soteriological role of Christ. The Unitarian leanings of the Society's leadership, however, is reflected in the tracts' predominant ethical emphasis. (Cf. Tyler 1944, p. 28.)

26. Tuckerman 1838, p. 173. Channing 1843, p. 144. McColgan 1940, pp. 36-7.

27. Channing 1843, p. 113. McColgan 1940, pp. 36-7.

28. BSRMIS *Address* 1812, p. 2. *The Christian Disciple* 1813, pp. 94-6. MHS 1825, p. 205. Tuckerman 1838, p. 173. Cf. Deems 1975, p. 2. A dismissal of the Society's tracts as nothing but "cold, proselytizing propaganda" (McColgan 1940, p. 37, see also Langley 1967, p. 51) seems altogether too harsh. The tracts were still in demand "nearly twenty years after" (SMNY 1835-36, p. 48; cf. 1864, p. 84).

29. SMNY 1864, p. 84. Cf. McColgan 1940, p. 37.

30. E.g.: MMNY 1825, pp. 265, 268; SMNY 1830-31, p. 337.

31. Supra, p. 71.

32. Channing's statement that his friend Tuckerman (in 1812) knew "little or nothing" of the seafarer whom he wished to serve is, to say the least, debatable (Channing 1843, p. 113). Of his *continuing* concern (and understanding), there are clear indications, such as: Tuckerman *Diary*, Nov. 10 - Dec. 15, 1819 (quoted in McColgan 1940, pp. 49-50), and Tuckerman 1838, pp. 31-2, 173.

33. Supra, pp. 135-48.

34. Supra, p. 93.

35. Tyler 1944, pp. 41-5. Sweet 1950, pp. 243-4, 264. Foster 1951, pp. 48-50; 1960, pp. vii-viii, 101-18. Smith Vol. 1 1960, pp. 519-20; Vol. 2 1963, pp. 10-2, 66-7. Hudson 1965, pp. 145-6.

36. Massachusetts Bible Society *Report* 1814, pp. 5-6, 19-24; *The First Hundred Years* 1909, pp. 14-7. BFBS *Reports* 1814-15, pp. 36-7, 120-23. Cf. Foster 1960, pp. 105-7.

37. Burr 1961, p. 159. Sweet 1963, pp. 237-8. Hudson 1965, pp. 131-57. Gaustad 1966, pp. 154-78.

38. BFBS *Reports* 1811-13, pp. 25-6. Browne Vol. 2 1859, pp. 297-305. Canton Vol. 1 1904, pp. 241-8. Dwight 1916, pp. 8-9. Foster 1951, p. 53.

39. The early reports of Bible Societies in Philadelphia, New York, Boston and Charleston provide numerous examples.

40. (MS) Bible Society of Salem *Records*, Oct. 20, 1813. BFBS *Reports* 1816-17, p. 38 (quoting Louisiana Bible Society *Report*, 1815). SMNY 1828-29, p. 323. Cf. *An Oration* 1815; also Kverndal "A Voice from the Prison Hulks" 1978, pp. 142-3. Supra, p. 136.

41. E.g.: *The Massachusetts Missionary Magazine* 1807, pp. 230-1; 1808, pp. 386-7. *Boston Recorder* April 17, 1816, July 22, 1817. BFBS *Report* 1814-15, pp. 201-2. Supra, pp. 140-1.

42. (MS) BFBS *Foreign Corresp.*, letter from Robert Ralston to Josiah Roberts, March 8, 1816. SML 1822, p. 107. Cf. (MS) Paul 1965, pp. 7-9. Appleton's Vol. 5 1888, p. 164, gives a brief biography of Robert Ralston.

43. Bible Society of Philadelphia *Report* 1816, pp. 17-23, 48.

44. Ibid. *Reports* 1817-21, passim.

45. RR, June 21, 1817, p. 172. Bible Society of Philadelphia *Report* 1818, p. 8. Re. Commodore Dale, see infra, pp. 442-3.

46. New York Bible Society *Annual Reports* 1810-17, passim (see especially 1816, pp. 8-9). Fant 1965, p. 80.

47. CH 1816-17, pp. 412-4; 1817-18, p. 82. MBSNY *Constitution* 1817, pp. 3-4. Warren 1858, p. 9.

48. MBSNY *Constitution* 1817, Supplement pp. 1-6.

49. MBSNY *AR* 1818, pp. 9-10, 18; 1821, pp. 6, 13-4.

50. Stafford 1817, pp. 33-4. MBSNY *AR* 1818, p. 5. Cf. infra, pp. 580-1.

51. MBSNY *Constitution* 1817, p. 4; *AR* 1819, pp. 5-7. ASFS *AR* 1832, p. 4. SMNY 1831-32, p. 253; 1852-53, p. 372. Captain Prince "performed a large proportion of the distribution with his own hand . . . till a short time before his death in 1832" (SMNY 1835-36, p. 31).

52. MBSNY *Constitution* 1817, p. 4. Stafford 1817, pp. 4, 33-4. ABS *AR* 1821, pp. 114-9. SMNY 1830-31, p. 337. Dwight 1916, p. 93. (MS) *ABS History* Vol. 3 Pt. I, Essay 14, p. 29. Ward Stafford graduated at Yale in 1812 (*Catalogue* 1924, p. 147).

53. MBSNY 1818, pp. 12-3, 23-4; 1820, pp. 8-9. MBS Charleston *AR* 1820, pp. 7-11; 1821, 6-7. ABS *AR* 1822, pp. 212-3.

54. Dudley 1821, pp. 338-40. SML 1821, p. 317; 1822, pp. 107-8. SMNY 1828-29, pp. 121-2. (MS) *ABS History* Vol. 4 Pt. III, Essay 14, pp. 132-4. The MBSNY was, in 1840, merged into the NYBS, where a "Marine Department" is still active (Fant 1965 pp. 16, 80-9).

55. SMNY 1830-31, p. 337; cf. 1831-32, p. 33.

56. E.g., Jackman 1964, p. 110.

57. McColgan 1940, p. 37.

58. Female Missionary Society 1818, p. 7. Foster 1951, pp. 47-52; 1960, pp. 115, 156-8.

59. Stafford 1817, pp. 1-55. Female Missionary Society 1818, p. 7. Foster 1951, p. 52.

60. Stafford 1817, pp. 4, 8, 32.

61. Stafford 1817, pp. 32-6.

62. Certainly, Stafford's proposals can hardly have had any bearing on the origin of marine schools and libraries in *Great Britain*. Supra, pp. 135-48, 315-6.

63. Supra, pp. 412-7.

64. Stafford 1817, pp. 34-6, 46-7. Cf. supra, pp. 14, 244.

65. Stafford *Extracts* n.d., p. 8. SMNY 1830-31, p. 337.

66. SMNY 1844-45, p. 161; 1852-53, p. 372. Greenleaf 1846, pp. 302-3. Cf. Stafford 181, p. 6.

67. Cf. supra, pp. 12-13.

68. SMNY 1832-33, pp. 378-9. Webster 1932, pp. 2-5. Farr 1943, pp. 2-3. Savage 1949, pp. 118-9. ASFS 124th *AR* (1952), n. pag.

69. Ibid. DAB Vol. 17 1935, pp. 479-80. Dr. Gardiner Spring even authored a seamen's devotional, entitled *The Bethel Flag* 1848.

70. SMNY 1830-31, p. 337; 1831-32, p. 253; 1863-64, p. 368. Warren 1858, pp. 8-9. The statement in Seymour 1976, p. 42, that "a few sailors in 1816 suggested to Dr. Spring . . . that he arrange special services for seamen," is not substantiated by primary source material available to the Author.

71. Stafford preached "in a room kindly furnished by the Messrs. Browns," to audiences of "usually about 300" (Stafford 1817, p. 4).

72. Stafford 1817, p. 36; 1818, p. 6. SMNY 1830-31, p. 337. Warren 1858, p. 9.

73. Stafford 1817 (2nd ed.); *Important to Seamen* n.d. *The Pamphlist and Missionary Magazine* 1817, pp. 311-7. (Quoted also in SML 1820, pp. 273-5, 310-2.)

74. Stafford 1817, pp. 34-6. *Note:* For more detailed quotations, see Appendix No. 4.

75. Stafford 1818, p. 1. SML 1821, pp. 41-7. Warren 1858, p. 9. TR55,TR56,CD65,TR51

76. Stafford's *The Mariners' Church* 1818 (12 pp.) is notable for its early, broad and systematic presentation of motives for maritime mission.

77. NYPS *Report* 1843, p. 8. Warren 1858, p. 9.

78. Supra, p. 184.

79. Jackman 1964, p. 110.

80. Supra, p. 43; infra p. 583.

81. Supra, pp. 419-20.

82. Supra, p. 419.

83. SML 1821, p. 266.

84. The first to recognize the independent origin of the NYPS was G.C. Smith, in SML 1820, p. 272; cf. 1821, p. 399. SMNY 1830-31, p. 337. NYPS *Report* 1843, p. 7. Warren 1858, p. 8. ASFS *AR* 1860, p. 6. Infra, p. 426.

85. Paine 1919, pp. 136-41. Albion 1938, passim. Writers' Program (N.Y.) 1941, pp. 142-4, 153. Davidson 1951, pp. 325-7. Mitchell 1967, pp. 81-4.

86. NYPS *Report* 1821, pp. 6-7. He had first obtained another school-room (in James Street), but this became "too strait." The larger hall could be entered also from Roosevelt Street, and was situated at the rear of the future Mariners' Church. (SMNY 1835-36, p. 49. NYPS *Report* 1843, p. 8. Warren 1858, p. 9.)

87. Griffin 1819, pp. 19-21. NYPS *Report* 1821, p. 7. NYBU *Report* 1822, p. 4. CHSM 1823, p. 186. SMNY 1830-31, p. 337; 1832-3, pp. 142-3. Warren 1858, p. 9.

88. NYPS *Report* 1821, p. 7; 1843, p. 9. EM 1820, pp. 386-7; 1822, p. 199. SMNY 1844-45, p. 162. Warren 1858, pp. 9-10.

89. NYPS *Report* 1821, p. 7. SMNY 1830-31, pp. 337-8. Warren 1858, p. 10. The ecumenical character of the church was evidenced also by the fact that it became the natural venue of the city's monthly interdenominational prayer-meeting (NYPS *Report* 1821, p. 7.)

90. EM 1820, 386-7.

91. NYPS *Report* 1821, pp. 8-9. Cf. supra, p. 226; also p. 187 *illus.*.

92. SML 1821, pp. 316-7. NYPS *Report* 1843, p. 9. The "Bowery Church" was completed in 1822; in 1828, Stafford resigned his charge (Greenleaf 1844, pp. 154-5). During the 1830's, he served as pastor of a Presbyterian church at Youngstown, Ohio; in 1843, he served as teacher in the Presbytery of Brooklyn, N.Y.; and from 1844 until his death, March 26, 1851 (at the age of 60), he was affiliated "without charge" to the Presbytery of Newark, residing at Bloomfield, N.J. ([MS] The Presbyterian Church *Extracts*, 1821-51. [MS] Newark Presbytery *Records*, 1843-56, p. 54.) In an obituary by a colleague here, his "impaired health" and recent death are attributed to his "almost indomitable energy" in pursuing purposes to which he sensed himself called ([MS] Newark Presbytery *Records*, 1843-56, pp. 267-8).

93. NYPS *Reports* 1821, pp. 9-10, 25; 1822, p. 8. SML 1821, pp. 261-2, 316-7; 1822, p. 18. CH 1820-21, p. 768. CHSM 1821-22, pp. iii-iv. Infra, p. 458; see also p. 429 *illus.*

94. Although Smith refers to W.H. Angas and Henry Chase in this connection (SML 1823, p. 214), he was well aware of Stafford's precedence (cf. SML 1820, p. 272; 1821, p. 316). Whereas W.H. Angas was the *first to be ordained a missionary to seamen*, Ward Stafford was, before that, the *first ordained missionary to seamen*. Cf. Lt. John Cox, supra, pp. 143-5.

95. NYPS *Report* 1821, pp. 7-8, 10, 17-8; 1822, p. 6. Cf. CHSM 1821-22, p. 544. Seaman 1892, pp. 207-8. The Rev. Charles Walker of the Theological Seminary at Andover, Mass., was invited to assist in the ministry of the Mariners' Church for a few weeks during the autumn of 1821 (NYPS *Report* 1843, p. 10).

96. CHSM 1821-22, p. 544. NYPS *Report* 1822, pp. 7-8; 1843, p. 10.

97. (MS) The Otsego Presbytery, pp. 40, 66-7, 91, 99. Swinnerton 1876, pp. 19-20. Oneida Presbytery, a few years after Truair's departure from those parts, became the center of a sensational revival under the preaching of Charles G. Finney (*A Narrative* 1826).

98. CHSM 1821-22, pp. 29-30. NYPS *Report* 1821, p. 25. NSM 1834, p. 229. Cf. supra, p. 427.

99. CHSM 1821-22, p. 30. SMNY 1834-35, pp. 348-9; 1835-36, pp. 10-1; 1839-40, pp. 89-90. Cf. SML 1836, pp. 73-4.

100. Ibid. Cf. supra, p. 425.

101. Supra, pp. 248-9.

102. SML 1821, pp. 261-2, 317-8. CHSM 1821-22, 64, 95-6. NYBU *Report* 1822, pp. 4ff. Among other British correspondents who conveyed encouragement and early information were Thomas Phillips, Captain Charles Allen, and Humphrey Marten. (CH 1820-21, pp. 401-5, 524-5. NYPS *Report* 1821, pp. 26-8) *Divie Bethune* (1771-1824), born in Dingwall, Scotland, and described as one of New York's evangelical "merchant princes" of the day, "was at the foundation of many, and took an active part in most of the charitable and

religious institutions in this city." (*American Missionary Register* 1824, pp. 327-6. NYBU *Report* 1825, pp. 74-5. Foster 1960, pp. 138-9.)

103. CHSM 1821-22, p. 128. NYBU *Report* 1822, pp. 5-6. Warren 1858, p. 11. The berth of the *Cadmus* was very near the present South Street Seaport.

104. CHSM 1821-22, p. 255. NYBU *Report* 1822, p. 8. Warren 1858, p. 11.

105. CHSM 1821-22, pp. 96, 315. NYBU *Report* 1822, p. 13.

106. NYPS *Report* 1821, pp. 8-9. CHSM 1821-24, passim. NYBU *Report* 1822, p. 4. SMNY 1835-36, pp. 32-5.

107. MMNY 1825-26, p. 95. Burr 1961, p. 161. Supra, pp. 210-2.

108. CHSM 1821-24, passim. SML 1823, p. 320. Sprague 1861, p. 476.

109. Milnor 1822. NYPS *Report* 1821, pp. 26-7; 1822, p. 9; 1843, p. 11. CHSM 1822-23, pp. 480, 539-40, 637. Stone 1848, passim, Foster 1960, pp. 141-2. Infra, p. 488.

110. E.g., CHSM 1822-23, p. 90.

111. CHSM 1821-24, passim. SML 1821, p. 318. Miller 1962, passim. ATS *ARs* 1826 etc. passim. Foster 1960, pp. 107-8.

112. CHSM 1821-24, passim. NYBU *Reports* 1822-25, passim.

113. Supra, pp. 272-9.

114. E.g.: CHSM 1821-22, p. 286. Warren 1858, pp. 11-2. From 1826, Bethel Meetings on shore were transferred to the Mariners' Church, and after 1830 no further shipboard Bethel Meetings appear to have been held in New York (SMNY 1835-36, pp. 34-35).

115. CHSM 1822-23, p. 480. Infra, p. 456.

116. SML 1822, p. 428; 1823, pp. 224-5. CHSM 1822-23, pp. 94, 567.

117. Cogswell 1833, p. 345.

118. E.g.: ASFS *AR* 1841, p. 11. SMNY 1871, p. 238. BSFS *AR* 1878, pp. 6-7.

119. *The Record*, Aug. 11, 1818, p. 131.

120. BSMRIP *AR* 1817, p. 1; 1916, pp. 11-2. Foster 1951, pp. 52-3; 1960, p. 163. Dunstan 1966, p. 14. The preaching ministries already established in Rotherhithe (London) and New York refute the claim (for example, in BSFS *AR* 1875, p. 7) that the Seamen's Meeting on Central Wharf, Boston, was "the first regular preaching to seamen on shore in the world."

121. BSMRIP *AR* 1916, pp. 10-3. Dunstan 1966, pp. 6-22. Cf. Olmstead 1961, p. 75. Brooks 1940, p. 64.

122. BSFS *AR* 1864, p. 10.

123. Tuckerman 1838, p. 173.

124. Dunstan 1966, pp. 18, 27.

125. MHS *Proceedings*, Jan. 1868, pp. 106-12. (MS) MHS *William Jenks' Papers*, miscellaneous correspondence. Hill 1890 Vol. 2, pp. 412-3. DAB Vol. 10 1933, pp. 54-5. Dunstan 1966, pp. 28-9. Supra, p. 40.

126. (MS) MHS *William Jenks' Papers*, to the Rev. Joshua Huntington, Oct. 20, 1818 (reproduced in BSMRIP *AR* 1818, pp. 16-8).

127. BSMRIP *ARs* 1818-26, passim. Bethel Meetings in Boston were "more in the manner of an ordinary lecture than of a meeting for prayer"; hence the dependence on Jenks and clerical colleagues. From 1824, the meetings were

transferred ashore to the chapel in Charter Street and the Society's own Bethel Boarding House (ibid.).

128. BSMRIP *AR* 1822, pp. 24-5, 29; 1825, pp. 23-6. Infra, pp. 468-9.

129. BSMRIP *AR* 1822, pp. 25-6; 1824, p. 19. Infra, pp. 464-6.

130. BSMRIP *AR* 1824, pp. 14-5. Kverndal 1971, p. 82. Infra, p. 476.

131. BSMRIP *ARs* 1821-26, passim. SMNY 1835-36, p. 51. Cf. (MS) MHS *William Jenks' Papers*, to the Rev. B.B. Wisner, Dec. 29, 1825.

132. BSMRIP *AR* 1823, pp. 24-6; 1825, pp. 15, 22-3; 1827, p. 23. *American Sailors' Magazine* 1824, pp. 29-31. Angas' original letter, dated Antwerp, Dec. 26, 1824, is preserved with the *William Jenks' Papers*, MHS.

133. Infra, pp. 454-60.

134. BSMRIP *AR* 1824, p. 16; 1827, pp. 23-4; 1828, p. 25. BSFS *Address* 1828, p. 11. SMNY 1835-36, p. 53. It was on Dec. 13, 1827, at a meeting called in Dr. Lyman Beecher's church in Hanover Street. "to consider the propriety of forming a distinct society," that a motion to that effect was made and agreed upon (BSFS *AR* 1875, p. 7; 1878, pp. 6-7). The Society adopted this year (1827) as the basis for its sesquicentennial celebrations in 1977. (Deems 1975, pp. 11-3. *The Sea Breeze* 1977, no. 2, p. 3; no. 3, p. 6.) However, p. 4 of the *First Annual Report* of the new Society, presented Jan. 1, 1829, and published that same year, states that it was only "in January last" that the Society was "ultimately" formed. Subsequent annual reports continued for many years to be dated from the year 1828 (e.g., BSFS *Fiftieth Annual Report* 1878). See also SMNY 1831-32, p. 33; 1835-36, p. 53; 1871, p. 238.

135. Infra, p. 513 *illus.*

136. BSFS *AR* 1829, pp. 3-4.

137. CHSM 1821-22, p. 446. BSMRIP *AR* 1822, p. 24. Jenks felt no need of "descending to the cant phraseology of sailors," in order to gain their attention (NYPS *Report* 1821, p. 19).

138. BSMRIP *AR* 1824, pp. 15-6; 1826, pp. 21-2. Infra, p. 511.

139. It was during his long Green Street pastorate that Dr. Jenks wrote his famous *Comprehensive Commentary on the Holy Bible* (6 Vols., 1835-38). However, he continued his concern for the seafarer all his life; at 85, armed as usual with his "huge ear-trumpet," he took an active part in the 36th Anniversary of the BSFS. (BSFS *AR* 1864, p. 11. DAB Vol. 10 1933, p. 54.)

140. Green 1828, pp. 2, 115. Ashbel Green's biography of Eastburn is summarized in SMNY 1830-31, pp. 198-206.

141. Green 1828, pp. 3-4, cf. pp. 183-208. Robert Eastburn, born in England in 1701 "of a strict Quaker family," came to America with his parents when four years old, and eventually became what Whitefield called "his first fruit in America," and a dedicated deacon of Second Presbyterian Church, Philadelphia. Supra, p. 39-41.

142. Green 1828, pp. 5-16. SMNY 1875, pp. 304-5.

143. Green 1828, pp. 13-33. SMNY 1875, p. 305.

144. (MS) Presbytery of Philadelphia *Minutes*, May 14, 1805, pp. 423-7. Green 1828, pp. 33-46. Joseph Eastburn was rebaptized by immersion in the Baptist Church in Southampton around 1788, reportedly "to satisfy a scrupulous conscience." However, he never formally joined the Baptists, and for the future kept his convictions on the subject private (Green 1828, pp. 24-6, 45).

145. Green 1828, pp. 114-5. Eastburn was even attributed a doctorate of divinity in the Philadelphia *Directory* for 1819 ([MS] Paul 1958, p. 6).

146. Green 1828, pp. 46-72. Cf. (MS) Paul 1958, pp. 6-7. A dramatic example of Eastburn's effectiveness as chaplain is how, on the insistence of the celebrated Dr. Benjamin Rush, he preached to the "insane" at the Hospital, with the result that several of them were, through the years, "restored to lost reason, and converted to the Lord" (SMNY 1838-39, pp. 276-7).

147. Green 1828, pp. 20-2, 51, 72, 76, 113. Dashiell 1828, p. 12.

148. BSMRIP *AR* 1819, p. 17. Supra, pp. 435-8.

149. *Poulson's American Daily Advertiser*, Oct. 23, 1819, p. 2. *The United States Gazette and True American*, Oct 23, 1819, p. 2. CHSM 1821-22, p. 62. According to (MS) Paul 1958, p. 1, the sail-loft was located at Bickley's Wharf. Eastburn states that the opening was delayed "on account of the alarm of the fever" (CHSM 1821-22, p. 220). The date Oct. 17, 1819, or "the third Sabbath," must be erroneous, if the contemporary press is to be presumed to have been correct.

150. Ibid.

151. Supra, p. 414.

152. SMNY 1830-31, p. 335. Keen 1880, pp. 494-500. DAB Vol. 5 1930, pp. 32-3. (MS) Paul 1965, pp. 5-6.

153. DAB Vol. 1 1928, p. 341. (MS) Paul 1965, pp. 6-7.

154. Green 1828, p. 113.

155. CHSM 1821-22, p. 220. *The Mariner's Church, Philadelphia*, 1824, pp. 3-5 (also in CHSM 1824, pp. 665-7). SMNY 1835-36, pp. 74-8. (MS) Paul 1958, pp. 1-2, 7. According to Paul, p. 2, the site corresponded to present numbers 129-133 South Water Street.

156. Ibid. The Mariners' Church, Philadelphia *Reports* 1825-27, passim.

157. CHSM 1821-22, pp. 32, 63, 127, 507; 1822-23, pp. 29-30. (MS) BFSFSBU *Minutes*, May 22, 1822. Green 1828, pp. 86, 153-4. SMNY 1835-36, pp. 75-6. Note spelling "Mariner Church" on emblem in contemporary illustration in Presbyterian Historical Society, showing Father Eastburn preaching in the sail-loft.

158. CHSM 1821-22, pp. 62, 220. SML 1821, pp. 160, 258-61, 317, 399-400; 1823, pp. 284-90. The Mariners' Church, Philadelphia, *Report* 1826, pp. 12-7. NSM 1828, p. 233. Green 1828, pp. 132-43.

159. CHSM 1821-22, p. 220. Dashiell 1828, p. 19. Green 1828, pp. 107-13. SMNY 1875, p. 306. The Mariners' Church, Philadelphia, *Report* 1826, has this to say: "The sum and substance of his preaching is, repent, or perish—believe in the Lord Jesus Christ, and be saved. Gospel simplicity is well suited to his audience . . ." (p. 5, see also p. 6). As to the effect, many would "come in the close of the meeting with tears flowing, to speak of their soul's concern, and entreating to be remembered in prayer" (Green 1828, p. 131).

160. E.g.: CHSM 1821-22, pp. 126, 220, 250-2; 1824, pp. 744-5. Green 1828, pp. 113, 143-4, 150. Cf. supra, pp. 436-7.

161. Green 1828, pp. 107-15. SMNY 1875, p. 304. Eastburn's immense prestige also earned him the title "the old Commodore" (SMNY 1835-36, p. 141).

162. CHSM 1821-22, p. 32.

163. NYPS *Report* 1821, p. 19. The chief magistrate could confirm that the Police Office was "no longer a seat of justice, as it formerly was, for pronouncing judgment upon mariners brought there in a state of intoxication..." (*The Christian Guardian* 1827, p. 142).

164. CHSM 1821-22, pp. 254-55. Green 1828, pp. 88-9, 94, 103. Cf. SMNY 1875, p. 304.

165. *The United States Gazette*, Feb. 4, 1828, p. 2. Dashiell 1828, pp. 28-9. Green 1828, p. 116. "The cortege filled the streets from his [Eastburn's] home at 224 Vine Street, to the cemetery, and prevented all other traffic" ([MS] Paul 1958, p. 11). The Mariners' Church Sunday School (dating back to 1819) had, in 1827, an enrollment of 300 (The Mariners' Church, Philadelphia, *Report* 1827, p. 9).

166. SMNY 1835-36, p. 76.

167. SMNY 1875, p. 307.

168. MBS Charleston *AR* 1820, pp. 9-10; 1821, pp. 5-6. SML 1821, pp. 266-7. Howe 1883, pp. 228, 402-3. SMNY 1835-36, p. 112, dates these meetings to "as early as the year 1818." Cf. Yates 1851, pp. 8-9, where the Society is linked to Charleston's historic Circular Congregational Church, and the pioneering role of the Rev. Jonas King is underscored.

169. MBS Charleston *AR* 1820, p. 10; 1821, p. 6. CHSM 1821-22, p. 640. SMNY 1835-36, p. 112. Yates 1851, pp. 8-10. Palmer 1822 reproduces the Opening Day Sermon.

170. CPS *AR* 1824, pp. 6-8, 15. SMNY 1835-36, p. 112. Yates 1851, p. 10. Chichester 1885, pp. 7-8. Brown had already preached for seamen as city missionary with the Female Domestic Missionary Society (Howe 1883, pp. 402-3). Infra, p. 458.

171. CBU *AR* 1824, pp. 7-8. The quotation of G.C. Smith (SML 1821, p. 490) is erroneously attributed to Lord Gambier (in 1822) by Yates 1851, p. 10.

172. CBU *AR* 1824, pp. 15-21. SMNY 1835-36, pp. 111-2. The strict Sabbath observance of Charleston packet owners indicates a successful approach to that class, too (CHSM 1822-23, p. 123).

173. CBU *AR* 1824, pp. 15-7.

174. E.g.: SML 1823, pp. 359-60, 383. CHSM 1822-23, pp. 697-9; 1824, p. 31. BSMRIP *AR* 1824, pp. 15-16. Green 1828, pp. 160-3.

175. CBU *AR* 1824, pp. 19-20; 1827, p. 24. MMNY 1825-26, pp. 53-4. Although register offices were already reported "in some ports in Europe" (CBU *AR* 1824, p. 16), these appeared as yet to have been only in the planning stage (SML 1823, p. 490). As late as March 1825, a query from Charleston drew only an embarrassed admission from New York that nothing had so far been done with a register office there (MMNY 1825-26, p. 40). Cf. supra, p. 334.

176. CBU *AR* 1824, pp. 18-9; 1827, pp. 7-9, 16-20, 24. MMNY 1825-26, pp. 54-5. SMNY 1835-36, p. 113. This was, however, not the first such establishment in the *world* (cf. supra, pp. 329-30).

177. CHSM 1822-23, p. 159. One reason for selecting the *Union* was apparently that "one of the under officers ... was a pious man" (ibid.). For a summary of early seamen's missions in Baltimore, see "Forgjengerne" and "A Summary in English" in Nilsen 1969, pp. 13-5, and 58-60, respectively.

178. CHSM 1822-23, p. 159.

179. Ibid., pp. 159-60; 1824, p. 96. SUBSB *ARs* 1824, 1825, passim. Henshaw 1826, p. 26. SMNY 1828-29, p. 93; 1835-36, pp. 136-41. The prominent position of the word "Union" in the title of the Society reflects the significance attached to its ecumenical basis.

180. SMNY 1835-36, pp. 137, 139, 141. Henshaw 1826, passim. Dwight 1916, p. 22.

181. ABS *AR* 1821, pp. 117-8. Goold 1886, p. 288. Supra, p. 417.

182. Payson 1821, title-page. BFBS *Reports* 1823-24, p. 138. BSMRIP *AR* 1824, p. 15. SMNY 1835-36, p. 176. Willis 1865, pp. 660-1. Goold 1886, pp. 287-8. Cummings n.d., pp. 313-7 et passim.

183. For others of Payson's published seamen's sermons, see Bibliography.

184. CHSM 1824, p. 160. MMNY 1825-26, pp. 345-7. SMNY 1835-36, pp. 176-7.

185. SMNY 1828-36, passim. Willis 1865, p. 679.

186. SMNY 1828-29, p. 187. Willis 1865, pp. 679-80. Infra, p. 484.

187. New Orleans Port Society *AR* 1838, pp. 14-5. Boudraux 1961, pp. 1-2. Hugill 1967, pp. 183-6.

188. CHSM 1823, pp. 190-2. To be precise, that first mid-March meeting took place on March 16, 1823, "in Fouberg, St. Mary" (see p. 190).

189. *The Louisiana Gazette*, March 11, 1825.

190. MMNY 1825-26, pp. 405-6. SML 1826, pp. 74-6, 107-11. Boudraux 1961, p. 360. It was hoped that a mariners' church in New Orleans would also provide a Protestant ministry to the unchurched, the stranger, and the sick, besides serving as a strategic staging area for Scripture distribution in several recently-liberated Latin-American states (SML 1826, pp. 75-6, 109-11).

191. SMNY 1829-30, pp. 167-8; 1835-36, pp. 231-2.

192. Infra, p. 482.

193. *The Georgian*, Jan. 18, 1822. Georgian Historical Society *Will Book "G"*, entry for Penfield, Josiah. SMNY 1835-36, pp. 209-10. (Note that this latter source also mentions meetings on shipboard in Savannah harbor during the 1820's. (MS) Savannah Port Society *Minutes*, 1834-73, passim. Gamble 1900, p. 215. Kverndal 1981, pp. 3-7.

194. SMNY 1835-36, pp. 264-7.

195. MMNY 1825-26, p. 15 (quoting from *Rel. Chron.*). Infra, p. 456, cf. 454.

196. MMNY 1825-26, pp. 15-6. SMNY 1835-36, p. 348; 1871, pp. 236-7; 1876, pp. 97-104. Cf. *Memorial* n.d., pp. 3-4.

197. CHSM 1822-23, p. 224. SMNY 1828-29, p. 320; 1829-30, pp. 67-8, 84-7, 128; 1835-36, p. 348. Seymour 1976, pp. 43-6, 50, 62-3, 89.

198. MBS Salem and Beverly 1820, pp. 1-4. *Essex Register*, Sept. 20, 1820. BSMRIP *AR* 1824, p. 15. SMNY 1835-36, pp. 304-5.

199. SMNY 1835-36, pp. 305-7. Miller 1891 I, p. 125. (MS) Holmes n.d., p. 45.

200. SMNY 1835-36, pp. 225-7, 267, 845-8. Infra, pp. 482-6.

201. CHSM 1823, p. 26. Supra, pp. 202-6.

202. CHSM 1822-23, pp. 224, 287-8, 384, 443-47. Cf. SML 1822, p. 447.

203. CHSM 1823, p. 26. Cf. SMNY 1828-29, p. 5.

204. MMNY 1825-26, pp. 1-4.

205. Ibid., p. 168. (Webster 1932, p. 10, has erroneous dating.)

206. Ibid., pp. 2, 151, 165, 171, 175, 191, 270-1. SMNY 1828-29, pp. 5-6. Among American national societies of the 1820's were: The American Sunday School Union (1824), the American Tract Society (1825), the American Home Missionary Society (1826) the American Society for Promoting Temperance (1826). See Sweet 1963, pp. 262-3. Also, Foster 1960, p. 144.

207. MMNY 1825-26, pp. 237-42, 248-51, 256-60. Cf. SML 1826, pp. 81-3. Re. Truair's ecumenicity, see Truair 1820, passim; also MMNY 1825-26, p. 191.

208. MMNY 1825-26, pp. 272-5, 301-6. "October 1828" in Davis 1979, p. 46, is presumably a misprint for "October 1825."

209. MMNY 1825-26, pp. 369-74.

210. Ibid., p. 369.

211. See, for example, Stott 1975, pp. 25-8. Cf. infra, pp. 555-7.

212. SMNY 1828-29, p. 3; 1830-31, p. 339. Cf. Truair 1826, pp. 19-20. Supra, p. 268.

213. MMNY 1825-26, pp. 385-94, 408. Truair 1826, passim. SMNY 1828-29, p. 3. The contents of the *Call* are strongly reminiscent of a series of articles written under the pseudonyms "The Friend of Seamen" and "The Seaman's Friend," taken into CHSM 1823 and 1824 by Truair; together, they constitute a significant early vision of a *maritime missiology*.

214. ASFS *The Acts* 1909, p. 7.

215. ASFS *AR* 1829, pp. 9, 19. SMNY 1836-37, p. 75. Warren 1858, p. 15. The "saturation campaign" with which the Evangelical United Front sought to meet the challenge of the "stampede to the West" (including the 1826 founding of the American Home Missionary Society) doubtless helped to divert attention away from seafarers. (Sweet 1950, p. 250, Hudson 1965, p. 154.)

216. Examples of Truair's caustic criticism of New York and American efforts hitherto: MBSNY *AR* 1822, p. 5; MMNY 1825-26, pp. 2, 151, 171, 175, 270-1. On the impact of Truair's resignation, see: SMNY 1828-29, p. 6; 1830-31, p. 339. *The Rev. John Truair* was, from 1828, pastor of the so-called "Union Church," a group which in that year had seceded from the Congregational Church of Westhampton, Massachusetts. His role was considered "divisive" and therefore "improper" by members of the Hampshire Central (Ministerial) Association, who in 1829 withdrew fellowship from him, and prevailed on his own Presbytery of New York to depose him (which they did in 1831). Truair himself vigorously defended his action in an *Appeal*, published in 1829. He returned some years later to the scene of his ordination in 1810: Cambridge, Vermont. Here he is said to have "agitated" the church for a time, and died "about 1845." (Truair 1829, passim. Memorial 1866, p. 81. [MS] Davis 1930, Vol. 1, pp. 243-4. [MS] Gillette, 1970.)

217. SMNY 1828-29, pp. 1-7, 68; 1830-31, p. 339; 1835-36, p. 75; 1876, p. 98. ASFS *AR* 1829, pp. 7-8. Warren 1858, p. 15. Webster 1932, pp. 17-25.

218. SMNY 1828-29, pp. 1-2.

219. ASFS *AR* 1829, p. 5. Cf. Webster 1932, p. 17. Also, ASFS *AR* 1953, p. 7.

220. Cole 1954, pp. 13, 75-7. Foster 1960, pp. 179, 210. Smith Vol. 2 1963, pp. 12-5, Hudson 1965, p. 154. Supra, p. 42-3.

221. At this period, there were an estimated number of 45,000 U.S. seamen in foreign trade, of a total of more than 100,000 (ASFS *AR* 1832, p. 11). During the 25-year period prior to the Civil War, U.S. overseas tonnage trebled itself, surpassing 2,500,000 by 1861 (Brooks 1899, pp. 179, 181). Supra, p. 425, incl. Note 85. In commemoration of the historic Atlantic crossing of the S.S. *Savannah,* her departure date from Savannah, Georgia, May 22nd, has become "National Maritime Day" in the USA. (Rev. A. Dale Umbreit, International Seamen's House, Savannah.)

222. SMNY 1828-29, p. 67, 217; cf. 1840-41, pp. 94, 98, 362-3.

223. Truair 1826, pp. 10-1. SMNY 1840-41, pp. 363-7. ASFS *AR* 1845, p. 12. Cf. Stafford 1817, pp. 36, 46-7. Also SML 1825, pp. 162-3. Supra, p. 419.

224. SMNY 1828-29, pp. 65-9, 89.

225. Foster 1960, pp. 64, 209-10. Cf. Olmstead 1960, pp. 280-83.

226. SMNY 1828-29, p. 217. Warren 1858, p. 16.

227. Supra, pp. 255-8, 260-2.

228. SMNY 1828-29, pp. 65-6, 69, 89. ASFS *AR* 1829, p. 8; 1832, p. 20. Warren 1858, pp. 15-6. Webster 1932, pp. 17-25. DAB Vol. 11 1933, pp. 84-5, Cole 1954, pp. 39-43. Smith Vol. 2 1963, pp. 36-7. Leavitt's course was continued by his successors, first briefly by the Rev. Joseph Brown, before his health gave way (1832-33), then by the Rev. Jonathan Greenleaf of the Boston Seaman's Friend Society (1833-41). (ASFS *ARs* 1834-41, passim. Warren 1858, pp. 19-20. SMNY 1865-66, 54.)

229. Bible Society of Philadelphia *AR* 1817, p. 43. SML 1824, pp. 29-20; 1825, pp. 163, 321-4; Suppl. pp. 15-6; 1826, p. 233; 1827, pp. 225-7, 241-4. (MS) BFSFSBU *Minutes,* April 26, 1826. MMNY 1825, p. 325. Morrison 1826, passim. SMNY 1828-29, pp. 30, 234-8, 266-70. Morrison 1839, passim. Broomhall 1924, passim. Kverndal 1969, pp. 222-4. Dr. Morrison's *Tract, Addressed to Sailors* (Canton, Sept. 22, 1822), and *Proposal for Bettering the Morals and Condition of Sailors in China* (Canton, Sept. 25, 1822) are reproduced in both Morrison 1826 and Morrison 1839 Vol. 2. It was Dr. Morrison's benefactor, D.W.C. Olyphant, missionary-minded Presbyterian merchant and shipowner of New York, who "prepared" the first Bethel Flag for his friend in Canton. (Morrison 1826, pp. 2, 370. Morrison 1839 Vol. 2, p. 167. Broomhall 1924, p. 193.) Supra, p. 247.

230. SMNY 1828-29, pp. 234-8, 266-70. ASFS *AR* 1829, pp. 17-8; 1830, pp. 6-7. ABCFM *AR* 1829, p. 96. Warren 1858, pp. 16-7. Supra, p. 149.

231. SMNY 1829-30, pp. 37-40, 74-82; 1830-31, passim. ASFS *AR* 1829, pp. 17-8; 1830, pp. 6-7. Abeel 1834, passim. Williamson 1848, passim. ASFS *The Acts* 1909, pp. 8-12. DAB Vol. 1, 1928, pp. 26-7. (MS) Poppen 1959, passim. These sources show it was Dr. Morrison's shipowning friend, D.W.C. Olyphant, who contacted Abeel on behalf of the ABCFM and the ASFS, and shortly afterwards arranged for his gratuitous passage to Canton, together with the Rev. Elijah C. Bridgman (pioneer ABCFM missionary to China) on one of his company's ships.

232. SMNY 1830-31, pp. 325-8. ASFS *AR* 1831, pp. 3-5. Williamson 1848, passim. (MS) Poppen 1959, p. 49.

233. ASFS *AR* 1832, pp. 8-9. Warren 1858, pp. 18-9. Cf. infra, p. 606.

234. SMNY 1831-32, pp. 328-31; 1837-38, pp. 114-20. ASFS *ARs* 1832-40, passim.

235. CHSM 1822-23, pp. 413-4. SMNY 1830-31, pp. 130-1; 1831-32, pp. 290-1; 1837-8, pp. 343-46. NSM 1830, pp. 397-8; 1832, pp. 323-4. ASFS *AR* 1832, p. 12. Harris 1837, pp. 73-81, 174-7. Dodge 1965, pp. 140-4. Kverndal 1969, pp. 8-9; 1980, pp. 6-8. Bullen n.d., pp. 164-5. Robotti 1962, pp. 149-50, is a more recent example of negative literary reaction to the moral code of the missionaries. Cf. supra, p. 248.

236. SMNY 1832-33, pp. 48-50, 121-2. ASFS *AR* 1832, pp. 16-9. *Advocate and Friend*, July 31, 1843, p. 36. Strong 1910, pp. 65-6. Dodge 1965, pp. 113-26.

237. SMNY 1832-38, passim. ASFS *ARs* 1832-38, passim. The exact site was at the west corner of King Street, and what came to be called Bethel Street. On May 12, 1837, a nondenominational, covenant-type "Oahu Bethel Church" was constituted by nine resident Christians, designating Diell as their pastor. When the "Bethel Church," as it came to be called, was burned down in the big fire of 1886, the congregation joined in forming famous "Central Union Church" of Honolulu, now located at the corner of Beretania and Punahou Streets, and affiliated with the United Church of Christ. (SMNY 1837-38, pp. 188-91. Damon 1883, pp. 5-8. Matthews 1911, pp. 507-8. Hawaiian Mission Children's Society 1969, p. 4.)

238. SMNY 1834-35, pp. 3-4.

239. SMR 1823, p. 539. Supra, pp. 103, 135-6.

240. (MS) PLBUS *Minutes*, Sept. 5, 1827. NSM 1929 Pt. II, p. 469; 1831, pp. 113-4. SMR 1829, p. 428. SMNY 1828-29, pp. 217-8. Cf. (MS) BFBS *Home Corresp.*, letter from Miss Alicia D'Arcy, dated Dec. 3, 1831. Kverndal 1972, p. 34, gives a Norwegian-language summary of early maritime mission in Le Havre.

241. NSM 1831, pp. 113-7. The reading-room in Le Havre was dubbed "Prynne's Chapel" in his honor (Timpson 1856, p. 73).

242. NSM 1829 Pt. II, p. 467-71; 1830, p. 316; 1831, passim (especially pp. 208-10); 1855, pp. 194-5. Cf. (MS) BFBS *Home Corresp.* from G.C. Smith, Sept. 13, 1818; from M. Moore, March 28, 1831. Also, supra, p. 129.

243. SMNY 1831-32, passim. ASFS *ARs* 1832-38, passim. *The Soldiers' Magazine* 1832, p. 345. NSM 1833, p. 474. Re. *Sawtell*, see also Sawtell 1860, passim, and *General Catalogue* 1909, p. 102.

244. ASFS *AR* 1837, p. 9. SMNY 1836-37, passim.

245. SMNY 1831-32, p. 355; 1835-38, passim (see especially 1837-38, pp. 149-52). ASFS *AR* 1836, p. 9; 1837, p. 10. Supra, p. 250.

246. SMNY 1833-8, passim. ASFS *ARs* 1833-37, passim. Cf. supra, pp. 245-8.

247. SMNY 1836-38, passim (see especially 1837-38, pp. 82-4). ASFS *ARs* 1837-38, passim.

248. SMNY 1847-48, pp. 93-4; 1848-49, pp. 60-1.

249. A small beginning was also made in Japan, with appropriations to foreign missionaries at Kanagawa (in 1862) and Yokohama (from 1864). SMNY 1847-65, passim. ASFS *ARs* 1847-65, passim.

250. SMNY 1841-65, passim; 1885, pp. 101-5. ASFS *ARs* 1842-65, passim. *The Friend* 1843-85, passim.

251. SMNY 1836-43, 1855-64, passim. Sawtell 1860, passim.

252. At Marseilles, the Rev. M. John Mayers ministered for years at the English Church, as well as at the Sailors' Home (which he had himself established). At Bordeaux, a zealous "evangelical Moravian minister," J.L. Schiep, also served Scandinavian and Russian seafarers. (ASFS *ARs* 1848-64, passim.) Infra, p. 592.

253. ASFS *AR* 1829, p. 17. Sources do not indicate to what extent such prospects may have been impaired by deteriorating Anglo-American political relations around 1840 (see Klose, Vol. 1 1965, p. 202).

254. SMNY 1836-43, passim. ASFS *ARs* 1837-43, passim. (MS) BFSS *Minutes* 1836-42, passim. SML 1837-42, passim. The BFSS sponsored a brief chaplaincy by John K. Stallybrass, in 1847 (BFSS *AR* 1847, pp. 15-6; 1848, p. 22). Supra, p. 149.

255. BFSS *ARs* 1841-45, passim. SML 1842-45, passim. SMNY 1842-44, passim. ASFS *ARs* 1842-44, passim.

256. In 1862, the ASFS "adopted" a veteran Belgian "sailor missionary," H. Vosskamp, a man who had already worked the waterfront for 12 years (as colporteur for "Le Comité pour la Mission Intérieure"). After sending their own chaplain and enlisting the support of the BFSS, the ASFS eventually (1872) turned the station over to the BFSS. (SMNY 1861-72, passim. ASFS *ARs* 1862-72, passim. BFSS *ARs* 1867-72, passim. Supra, p. 257.)

257. Supra, p. 380.

258. The original plan called for co-sponsorship of Chaplain Adam, with the ASFS, the BFSS, and the Sydney Bethel Union each raising one third of his salary. For reasons not specified in available sources, the BFSS did not follow through, a fact which caused temporary tension between the British and American societies, and drew spirited comment in the Sydney press. (SML 1840, pp. 200-1, 210-2; 1841, pp. 318-21. [MS] BFSS *Minutes* Oct. 20, 1840, April 5, Sept. 13, 1842, June 27, 1843, Aug. 21, Oct. 16, 1855, March 18, 1856. ASFS *AR* 1841, p. 11; 1845, p. 10. *The Colonial Observer*, March 15, 1843, p. 1.) G.C. Smith, who at this time was serving one of his prison terms, proposed, on the strength of this particular press article, that a provisional committee should peaceably invite the BFSS "entirely to dissolve" (NSM 1844, pp. 1123-30). Supra, pp. 356-8.

259. SMNY 1837-66, passim. ASFS *ARs* 1837-66, passim.

260. Ibid. About Dr. Turnbull's unique contribution, see ASFS *The Acts* 1909, pp. 17-20.

261. SMNY 1835-66, passim. ASFS *ARs* 1835-66, passim. In their 1851 *AR*, pp. 9-10, the ASFS, whose early flag bore the Bethel peace emblem of the dove with the olive-branch, commented thus on conditions in Havana: "The seamen . . . are demanding to know why they may not enjoy unrestricted in a Roman Catholic port, such religious privileges as the Roman Catholics not only enjoy in Protestant ports, but have protected to them by law."

262. SMNY 1851-66, passim. ASFS *ARs* 1851-66, passim. ASFS *ARs* 1851-66, passim. These sources also show how, after the completion of the railroad (in 1855), one chaplain took over both termini, 1856-58; from 1862 on, the Society instead sent an appropriation to a chaplain appointed by the Railroad Company. See also articles on the Panama Canal area in *Encyclopedia Americana* 1967, Vols. 2, p. 519, 7 p. 291, and 21 pp. 234ff.

263. ASFS *The Acts* 1909, pp. 21-7.

264. SMNY 1845-46, p. 257. ASFS *AR* 1861, pp. 17-8; cf. 1860, p. 16, referring to that "Northern hive from which multitudes of our best sailors come." (Gjerset 1928, pp. 1-15; 1933, pp. 66-71. Cf. Kverndal [Chicago] 1976, p. C. 50.)

265. E.g.: SMNY 1844-45, p. 371; 1871, pp. 340-1. Cf. WW 1860, p. 246.

266. SMNY 1837-38, pp. 390-1; 1840-41, p. 321. ASFS *AR* 1850, pp. 9-10. Westin 1929, pp. 1-4, 521-3; 1956, pp. 11-49. Hunter 1965, pp. 38-9. Infra, p. 600.

267. SMNY 1840-54, passim. ASFS *ARs* 1842-52, passim, also 1864, pp. 18-9, and 1867, pp. 15-6. Westin 1929, pp. 550-663. For biographical material on *F.O. Nelson*, see Byström 1910, passim; Backlund 1942, passim; Weltzer 1952, pp. 19-20. Stephenson 1932, p. 76, is at error in referring to Nelson as "a Lutheran" until 1845.

268. SMNY 1848-68, passim. ASFS *ARs* 1848-68, passim; also 1871, pp. 340-3. Much manuscript material on *Ljungberg's* approximately 40-year waterfront ministry is available at Stockholm's Stadsarkiv ("EFS arkiv"); see also Lundmark 1969, p. 11, and Carlzon 1969, p. 168. Additional sources on *Rymker's* activities: Rymker's *Journals* 1850-70; *Den danske Evangelist* 1857-62, passim; Stiansen 1933, pp. 66-82, Weltzer 1952, pp. 16-9; Lundmark 1969, p. 11. Bloch-Hoell 1973, pp. 222-3. Although the ASFS did retain sailor missionaries in Scandinavia until as late as World War I, more stringent, American-oriented qualifications as from 1878 resulted in somewhat reduced representation (ASFS *ARs* 1869-1917, passim).

269. See especially SMNY 1871, pp. 340-1. Also, for example, *Luthersk Kirketidende* Sept. 1867, pp. 122-3; BH Sept. 1867, p. 169, and Sept. 1868, p. 5; ASFS *AR* 1880, pp. 20-1; Westin 1929, p. 617; Rygnestad 1955, pp. 31-3; Hassing 1974, pp. 3-4; Kverndal 1977, pp. 231-3. Cf. infra, pp. 596-9.

270. *Encyclopedia Americana* 1967, Vols. 5, pp. 484-5, and 23, p. 139. Morison 1972, Vol. 2, pp. 135-6.

271. MMNY 1825-26, pp. 264, 278. ASFS *AR* 1830, p. 11; 1860, p. 67. *The Quarterly Christian Spectator* 1831, p. 263. Supra, p. 461.

272. CHSM 1824, p. 224. MMNY 1825-26, p. 269. SMNY 1829-30, pp. 362-3; 1835-36, pp. 368-73; 1844-45, pp. 129-30. ASFS *ARs* 1829-36, passim. Warren 1858, pp. 18-9.

273. American Bethel Society *ARs* 1836-47, 1860, passim. Warren 1858, pp. 39-40. In the early 1850's, there were also canal missionaries, employed by the "Philadelphia Sabbath Association," and a "Boatmen's Church" at St. Louis, Missouri, built by the Rev. Charles J. Jones for the "Western Boatmen's Union." (ASFS *AR* 1851, p. 14. Jones 1884, pp. 80ff.)

274. SMNY 1835-36, pp. 372-5. Western Seamen's Friend Society *ARs*, 1848-61, passim. Warren 1858, p. 40. ASFS *AR* 1860, p. 67.

275. Western Seamen's Friend Society *ARs* 1848 etc., passim. Pierce Vol. 1 1937, p. 261; Vol. 2 1940, pp. 368-9, 376, 436, 445. A "Chicago Bethel Association" was founded in 1843. (SMNY 1843-44, p. 197. Kverndal 1976, p. C. 52.)

276. See especially ASFS *AR* 1860, pp. 78-9; 1863, p. 59.

277. ASFS *AR* 1829, p. 19. Cf. ASFS *The Acts* 1909, pp. 83-4.

278. BSFS *AR* 1830, pp. 14-5; 1831, pp. 4-7. Deems 1975, pp. 16, 60-2. Early chaplains who made significant contributions were: Jonathan Greenleaf (1829-33), Daniel M. Lord (1834-48), and Elijah Kellogg (1855-65). Deems also deals in detail with the various relocations of the Society's facilities through 150 years. Supra, p. 438.

279. Warren 1858, pp. 38-9. NYPS *AR* 1856, pp. 9-10.

280. Available sources by no means justify the statement that the NYPS was only "marginal" in scope and support (cf. Davis 1979, pp. 45-6). NYPS *ARs* 1827-54, passim. Warren 1858, p. 10. Sprague 1861, pp. 475-8. SMNY 1853-54, pp. 23-5. Haven 1871, pp. 210-1. The General Conference of the Methodist Episcopal Church made an interesting exception in the case of "preachers who were laboring for the spiritual good of seamen, and allowed Chase to be retained uninterruptedly in the New York Conference" (Bangs 1953, pp. 306-7). Supra, p. 428.

281. The "new" Mariners' Church (at 46 Madison Street) was a former Methodist Episcopal church, originally erected by the Fourth Presbyterian Congregation (Seaman 1892, p. 336.)

282. SMNY 1854-64, passim. NYPS *ARs* 1855-64, passim. SML 1862, p. 231. NYPS *The Record*, March 1868, pp. 2-7. *Charles J. Jones*, born just by the shipyards of Deptford (then in the County of Kent), went to sea not yet 13 years of age on a British man-of-war. After some 10 years on board British convict-transports and American merchantmen, replete with bouts of "drunkenness and debauchery," he relates how, in early 1841, he came under the pulpit of Father Taylor and the Rev. Daniel Lord in Boston, was counseled by Captain Joshua Buffam at the Fort Hill Sailors' Home, and finally "gave himself to Jesus" just after putting to sea again. Sponsored by the Female Seamen's Friend Society of Philadelphia, he prepared for the ministry. After 6 years as chaplain to Mississippi boatmen at St. Louis, Missouri (1848-54), Jones served eight and a half years at the New York Mariners' Church. The record of his intensive pastoral ministry there makes incredible reading. Finally, his health broken by incessant toil, he was given the chaplaincy of Sailors' Snug Harbor, Staten Island, in 1863. (CC 1880, passim. Jones 1884, passim. [MS] BFSS *Minutes*, May 19 & 26, 1863.)

283. Infra, p. 602.

284. Infra, pp. 530-3.

285. ASFS *ARs* from 1829. SMNY from 1829-30 (especially 1835-36, pp. 232-5; 1836-37, p. 193; 1837-38, pp. 360-1). Warren 1858, pp. 18, 22, 42. Webster 1922, p. 66. Powell 1940, passim. Rose 1940, passim.

286. SMNY 1835-61, passim. ASFS *ARs* 1836-61, passim. The ministry of the Rev. Alexander McGlashan at Mobile during these years was especially outstanding. (Warren 1858, p. 39. Delaney 1968, pp. 108-9. Cf. BSMRIP *AR* 1819, p. 18.) In Mobile's eastern neighbor, Pensacola, regular work only began in 1869 (Kverndal 1979, pp. 8-9).

287. ASFS *ARs* 1830-64, passim. Warren 1858, p. 37. Cummings 1864, pp. 679-80. Supra, pp. 449-50.

288. The Missionary Society 1799, p. lxxxviii. ASFS *ARs* 1849-64, passim. SMNY 1851-65, passim. Dillon 1961, passim (especially Chapter 2). A local "Ladies' Seamen's Friend Society" (founded in June 1856) came to Davis' support, and succeeded in opening San Francisco's first "Sailors' Home" in February 1857.

289. ASFS *AR* 1849, pp. 11-2. Kverndal 1980, pp. 3-5 (based largely on sources in the Local History Section of the Tacoma Public Library).

290. ASFS *ARs* 1829-34, passim. The YMCA, too, was cooperating with the ASFS in seamen's work as early as in the 1850's (Seymour 1976, pp. 62-3).

291. For extensive details of the marine distribution of the American Bible Society, see the Society's typescript essays on *ABS History* n.d., passim. Cf. supra, p. 417. For further information about the seamen's work of the American Tract Society, see ATS *ARs* from 1826, passim. (Cf. Illustrated Seamen's Narratives n.d., and Foster 1960, pp. 107-8, 145.) Pioneer tract work on the New York waterfront, both among seamen and immigrants, should be credited to the "New York Religious Tract Society" (today the New York City Mission Society), founded as early as in 1812. (SMNY 1828-29, pp. 77, 336-9. Miller 1962, passim.) Following Milnor 1822, and Leavitt 1830, examples of American devotional aids for seamen are: ASFS 1843; Spring 1848; Cheever 1852; Macduff 1859; Bonney 1862; ATS 1863; Spaulding 1865. See also Webster 1932, p. 33. Supra, p. 432.

292. Concerning the role of the magazine, see ASFS *AR* 1829, pp. 7-10. "A Seamen's Communion" is a particular subject of debate in MMNY 1825-26, passim. Also SMNY 1835-36, passim. Note similar sentiments in the U.K.: SML 1825, pp. 487-8; 1837, pp. 109-18. There were, during the early 19th century, various "Christian Church" movements in America, claiming to restore "the true New Testament idea of the Church" (Smith Vol. 2 1963, p. 66).

293. SMNY from 1830-31. ASFS *ARs* from 1830. Supra, pp. 470, 472.

294. Foster 1951, pp. 64-5; 1960, pp. 223, 249-52. Smith Vol. 2 1963, pp. 66-74. Hudson 1965, pp. 158-67, 197-203. Ahlstrom 1975 Vol. 2 chapters 36-40, passim. Sweet speaks of the new church divisions becoming "denominationally conscious, to an exaggerated degree" (Sweet 1950, p. 305; cf. pp. 258-9). See also Myklebust 1976, pp. 110-1, 318-20. In maritime literary media work, mounting denominationalism manifested itself around mid-century in the production of seamen's tracts, devotional aids, etc. through *denominational* publishing agencies. Examples of such publications are: The Protestant Episcopal Tract Society 1839, Berrian 1844, Milner 1848 (Episcopal), Presbyterian Board of Publication 1847, Rockwell 1864 (Presbyterian), Stowe 1858, Cushman n.d. (Baptist), Lorrain 1852 (Methodist).

295. SMNY 1844-45, pp. 125, 292. Greenleaf 1846, pp. 300-1. Bangs 1853, p. 307. Seaman 1892, p. 336. Barclay 1949, p. 266. Mead 1970, p. 219. Ahlstrom 1975 Vol. 2, p. 288.

296. For a more detailed study and documentation of the Bethel ship Mission, see the Author's monograph: "The Bethel Ship 'John Wesley': A New York Ship Saga from the Mid-1800's with Reverberations on Both Sides of the Atlantic Ocean," in *Methodist History* (Lake Junaluska, N.C.), July 1977, pp. 211-33. Principal primary source materials used: *The Sailor's Magazine*, New York, The Missionary Society of the Methodist Episcopal Church *Annual Reports*, New York. Secondary source materials of significance: Reid 1882, Norelius 1890, Haagensen 1894, Witting 1902, Eltzholtz 1903, Bethelskib 1924, Thunstrom 1935, (MS) Lawson 1937, (MS) Whyman 1937, Rygg 1941, Hagen 1961, Andersen 1962, Hassing 1974, Terdal 1974.

297. Irrefutable evidence of June 8, 1845 as the correct date for Hedstrom's opening service is to be found in *Christian Advocate and Journal*, June 18, 1845, and Oct. 1, 1845.

298. For a history of both the *Bethel Ship John Wesley I* (in service 1844-57), and her successor, the *Bethel Ship John Wesley II* (former bark *Carrier Pigeon*, in service 1857-79), see Kverndal 1977, pp. 215-6, 224, 228.

299. For a Norwegian-language presentation of this aspect of *missiological* motivation, see Kverndal (Oslo) 1969. Cf. Bloch-Hoell 1973, pp. 218-23.

300. Kverndal 1977, pp. 230-2; (Bergen) 1978, pp. 110-6, 132; (New York) 1978, pp. 15-7, 24.

301. Lednum 1859, pp. 431-2. Methodist Episcopal Mariners' Bethel *AR* 1882, pp. 14-8. (MS) Bradley 1899, pp. 1-4. Captain *Thomas Webb*, the colorful British-born pioneer of Methodism in America, began in Philadelphia in the late 1760's by holding meetings in a sail-loft on the south-east corner of Dock Creek and the Delaware River. It must be assumed that seafarers and their families were among his hearers (Lednum 1859, pp. 39-41). Before 1841, the designation varied from "Mariners' Bethel" to "Southwark Mission" ([MS] The Philadelphia Conference of the Methodist Episcopal Church *Minutes* 1835-40, passim).

302. *The Christian Advocate*, March 20, 1844, p. 125. Warren 1858, p. 41. *The Baltimore American*, April 24, 1910. Kverndal (Bergen) 1969, p. 14.

303. See back cover of September issue of SMNY 1846-47, and succeeding issues.

304. SMNY 1828-29, pp. 123, 318-9. Haven 1871, pp. 106-7. Examples of the erroneous (1829) dating are: DAB Vol. 17 1946, p. 321, and Campbell 1977, p. 255.

305. The standard biographical source has been the hastily compiled volume by Gilbert Haven and Thomas Russell, *Father Taylor, the Sailor Preacher*, Boston, 1871. However, a carefully researched but hitherto little known essay by David L. Holmes, Jr., entitled *The Early Career of Father Taylor* (submitted as an M.A. thesis to the Faculty of Philosophy at Columbia University, New York), sheds significant new light on the famous sailor-preacher's crucial years of preparation for his life-work (1793-1828). Holmes has a valuable 3-page bibliography of sources on Father Taylor (pp. 56-8). In addition to these, the following sources have also been consulted in compiling the brief sketch of Father Taylor's life in this and ensuing paragraphs: *The Sailor's Magazine*, New York, from 1828-29, passim (see especially 1871, pp. 260-2; 1875, pp. 247-8; 1891, pp. 136-9, 330-1). Boston Port Society, later Boston Port and Seamen's Aid Society *AR's*. Calcutta Seamen's Friend Society *AR* 1842, pp. 38-9. CC 1879, pp. 294-304, 326-30. *The Mariners' Advocate*, August-September 1915, pp. 4-6.

306. On another occasion, Taylor added the following elaboration on the event (referring to the powerful preaching of the new pastor of the Bromfield Street Church, and the lay exhorter who noted the young sailor's distressed reaction, and encouraged him to commit himself at the closing altar-call): "I was dragged through the lubber-hole, brought down by a broadside from the seventy-four, Elijah Hedding, and fell into the arms of Thomas W. Tucker." (Haven 1871, p. 30. [MS] Holmes 1960, pp. 13-5.)

307. Holmes quotes convincing evidence (p. 21), disputing the fact that Taylor was ever transferred to Dartmoor Prison in England, as held by Haven (p. 35).

308. Nevertheless, as late as in its January 1838 issue, *The Sailor's Magazine* of New York was still (erroneously) listing the Boston Port Society's Bethel as the "Methodist Mariner's Bethel." "Father Matthews" of the BFSS sums matters up with typical bluntness: "They [the rich Unitarian Merchants] found the money and the Methodists found the men. Better this way than the reverse!" (CC 1879, p. 295. Cf. Seamen's Aid Society *AR* 1839, p. 19.)

309. During a dramatic description of a storm, for example, Taylor's hearers could cry quite impulsively: "Out with the long-boat!" (Haven 1871, p. 150. Collyer 1906, pp. 39-40. Macdonald 1935, p. 311.) But though he spoke without notes, Taylor did not slight his task. He compared getting ready for the pulpit to *fermentation*, the culmination of much careful preparation.

310. Of the records left of these celebrated visitors, the best known is probably that of Charles Dickens in his *American Notes* (see especially p. 68). Cf. Walt Whitman in Haven 1871, pp. lxvii-lxxi; Kaplan 1980, p. 253; Brooks 1940, p. 269. For examples of Father Taylor's rhetorical genius, see Appendix No. 7.

311. Infra, pp. 520-1.

312. The Bethel Temperance Society was reported upon in 1836 (Haven 1871, p. 449).

313. *Debora Taylor* (1797-1869) had been awakened as a twelve-year-old, under the preaching of Taylor's later friend and colleague, Enoch Mudge (Haven 1871, p. 74). Infra, p. 499. Father Taylor's famous *Bethel* proved too big for his successors to fill, Italian immigrants moved into the North Square area, and in 1884 the Bethel was sold. The Mariners' House, with its own chapel (to which Father Taylor's original pulpit was transferred) became the center of the Society's operations. The former Bethel is still in use, as the Sacred Heart (Roman Catholic) Church.

314. Dana 1929, p. 138.

315. Bartol 1872, p. 325.

316. (MS) New Bedford Port Society *Minutes*, from May 17, 1830. New Bedford Port Society *ARs*, 1831 etc., passim. SMNY 1835-36, pp. 306-7. Macdonald 1935, p. 317. Melville 1964, pp. 49-61. (MS) Holmes 1960, pp. 45-6. Dahl 1977, pp. 234-50, throws interesting new light on the life of "Father Mudge." Supra, pp. 454, 494.

317. Sweet 1950, passim. Gaustad 1962, p. 12; 1966, p. 189. Hudson 1965, pp. 166-7. Ahlstrom 1975 Vol. 1, pp. 535-8.

318. SMNY 1831-32, pp. 58-60; 1835-36, p. 80. See also listings on back cover of Pennsylvania Seamen's Friend Society *ARs*, through the 1880's and 1890's.

319. Greenleaf 1846, pp. 269-70. SMNY 1863-64, p. 370. Putnam 1868, passim. Schroeder 1898, passim. Byström 1910, passim. Stiansen 1933, pp. 66-8. Backlund 1942, passim. Bloch-Hoell 1973, pp. 222-23. Supra, pp. 491-2. During the 1850's, the First Baptist Mariners' Church was located on Cherry Street, between Pike and Rutgers, only a short distance above the New York Sailors' Home. However, the site was found to be unsuitable, and sold prior to moving to Oliver Street in 1863. (See also American Baptist Mariners' Society, *Its Origin — First Annual Meeting*, 1857, p. 5.)

320. Denison 1846, passim. (In this book, published under the auspices of an "Independent Bethel Union of the Port of Boston," organized in January 1846, Denison vehemently defends himself against allegations which, in 1845, brought about his departure from the original Society.) Cooke 1874, passim.

Cf. SMNY 1844-45, p. 207. Much of the work begun by Stowe still continues, from what is now known as the "Bethel Christian Center," 332 Hanover Street, serving the mixed population of Boston's North End, under the auspices of the Boston Baptist Bethel City Mission Society.

321. (MS) Paul *The Mariners' Church* n.d. (MS) Third and Scots Presbyterian Church *Bulletins*, Nov. 8 & 22, 1959. Kverndal (Duluth) 1976, pp. 26-7. The original Mariners' Church or "Eastburn Mariners' Church," as it came to be called, moved in 1868 to new premises on the southwest corner of Front and Union (now Delancey) Streets. In 1963, the building was gutted by fire (*The Philadelphia Inquirer*, June 24, 1963).

322. SMNY 1864-65, pp. 212, 249-50; 1865-66, pp. 220-1. ASFS *AR* 1866, p. 48. Brückbauer n.d., passim. From 1937 and for the following ten years, the Baptist "Mariners' Temple" was merged for missionary purposes with the Presbyterian "Church of the Sea and Land" (Miller 1962, p. 168). In 1972, the building was ceded to "The First Chinese Presbyterian Church."

323. This Norwegian congregation of 1866 (now "Our Saviour's Lutheran Church" of Brooklyn) can actually trace its beginnings back to the "Scandinavian Lutheran Congregation in New York," founded in 1860 (*Kirkelig Maanedstidende* 1866, pp. 130-1). For a general history of the origins of the Norwegian Seamen's Church in New York, see Kverndal (New York) 1978, pp. 5-26.

324. Deems 1975, pp. 98-118. Supra, pp. 434-8.

325. *A Statement* 1817. SMR 1828, pp. 185-8. Sweet 1950, pp. 210-2, 247-8, 359-60. Hudson 1965, pp. 147-8. (MS) Loetscher 1970. Supra, pp. 41, 45.

326. (MS) *Records* 1829. Supra, p. 436.

327. (MS) *Records* 1829, passim. ASFS *AR* 1832, pp. 8-9. Before finishing at Princeton, John Diell studied two years at Andover (SMNY 1832-33, p. 121). The *Records* also show "Bro. Dana" to have been a member of the Seaman's Committee (e.g., Entry for Nov. 28, 1831). Supra, pp. 469-70.

328. ASFS *AR* 1832, pp. 8-9. Cf. SMNY 1831-32, p. 350. Female Seamen's Friend Society of Philadelphia 1843, *Appendix*. Infra, p. 522.

329. SMNY 1831-32, p. 307. Supra, p. 467.

330. Sweet 1950, pp. 263-7. Gaustad 1962, pp. 66-7. Smith Vol. 2, 1963, pp. 75-6. Hobart held the bishopric 1811-30. To him, Episcopal agencies were indispensable, since they denied "the validity of a nonepiscopal ministry" (Hudson 1965, p. 172).

331. SMNY 1834-35, p. 32. As early as in 1823, G.C. Smith had called on "Episcopalians of North America" to take up the challenge. (SML 1823, p. 310. Cf. Anderson 1920, p. 333.) Supra, p. 249.

332. PECMSS *AR* 1846, pp. 11-3. (MS) Nook n.d., pp. 44-52. (MS) Healey 1940, pp. 13-4. Nook and Healey were able to benefit by the rediscovery of the records of the Society of 1834 (stated in PECMSS *AR* 1846, p. 4, to have been lost), including the Rev. B.C.C. Parker's *Journal*. (Cf. [Nook] n.d., p. 44. *The Lookout*, Sept. 1959, p. 3.) Kelley, in his valuable article (1940, p. 350) is in conflict with original source materials when he refers to the reorganized society of 1842 as "The Young Men's Church and Missionary Society for Seamen in the City and Port of New York." See also infra, Note No. 337.

333. (MS) Nook n.d., pp. 52-7. (MS) Healey 1940, pp. 14-5. From the sources quoted, it transpires that attempts by the City Mission Society to attract seamen to their first mission church on Vandewater Street, from 1831 on, were

"none too successful." Nor had that Society's resolution in 1841, to establish a separate Mariners' Church, so far materialized.

334. PECMSS *AR* 1859, pp. 37-43. (MS) Healey 1940, pp. 16-7.

335. PECMSS *ARs* 1845-59, passim. (MS) Nook n.d., passim. (MS) Healey 1940, passim. Kelley 1940, pp. 350-1.

336. SMNY 1843-44, pp. 65-7, 162, 263-4; 1844-45, pp. 163-4. Berrian 1844, p. 121. PECMSS *AR* 1845, pp. 5-8; 1853, p. 16. For a *negative* view of floating sanctuaries, see SMNY 1865-66, pp. 198-9. Cf. NSM 1829 Pt. I, Suppl. p. 10, and supra, p. 266.

337. PECMSS *AR* 1846, pp. 13-4. Kelley 1940, pp. 350-1. The Seamen's Church Institute of New York has, in later years, adopted the year of founding of the Young Men's Auxiliary Education and Missionary Society (1834) as its own year of origin. However, to state (as for example on the inside cover of *The Lookout* in recent years) that the Institute was "first established in 1834 as a floating chapel in New York harbor," is at variance with the primary source materials quoted in this study.

338. Berrian 1844, p. 121. (MS) Healey 1940, pp. 22-3. *The Lookout*, Sept. 1964, pp. 10-1.

339. It had, from the outset, been a declared object of the PECMSS to provide as many sanctuaries for seamen in New York as they might "deem proper" (PECMSS *AR* 1845, p. 6, cf. p. 9; 1846, pp. 4-6; 1847, pp. 3-4; 1869, p. 7). (MS) Healey 1940, pp. 24-6. Kelley 1940, pp. 351-2.

340. PECMSS *ARs* 1853, etc., passim. Cf. Healey 1936, pp. 132-3. (MS) Healey 1940, pp. 35-6.

341. PECMSS *ARs* 1845-69, passim. Kelley 1940, pp. 352-3. A *second* "Floating Church of Our Saviour" served on the East River station 1869-1910, where-upon it was towed to Staten Island, and became, on land, "All Saints' Church" (Kelley 1940, p. 353).

342. The name was changed to "Seamen's Church Institute of New York" in 1906, and the various shore stations were consolidated in one huge, new thirteen-story building at 25 South Street in 1913, under the outstanding leadership of Dr. Archibald R. Mansfield ([MS] Healey 1940, passim. Kelley 1940, pp. 353-5. *The Lookout*, Sept. 1959, pp. 2-3.) The Institute moved into a magnificent new skyscraper building at 15 State Street in 1968, and has since augmented its title to "Seamen's Church Institute of New York and New Jersey." Due to changing needs, however, the Institute sold this building in 1985, and moved into temporary facilities at 50 Broadway. For fascinating insights into the most recent developments and projections for the future of the Institute, see (MS) Whittemore 1985.

343. PECMSS *AR* 1848, pp. 11-2; 1849, p. 6 CMAS *Appeal* 1848, passim. Potter 1848, pp. 10-2. SMNY 1848-49, pp. 184-5. Protestant Episcopal Church in the Diocese of Pennsylvania *Journal* 1848-51, passim. CMAS *ARs* 1849-55, passim. CMAS *Constitution* 1885, pp. 4-6. Seamen's Church Institute of Philadelphia *The Dedication* 1925, pp. 7-10. (MS) Healey 1940, pp. 33-4. *The Crow's Nest*. Summer 1967, pp. 6-7. The original structure was destroyed by fire in 1870 (*The Crow's Nest,* Summer 1967, p. 2). Reorganized and incorporated in 1920 as the *Seamen's Church Institute of Philadephia*, the Society became interdenominational in the composition of its Board, and, under the conspicuous leadership of Dr. Percy R. Stockman, virtually "The successor of the work for seamen previously done by the Episcopal, Baptist, and the Methodist Churches." (Kelly 1940, pp. 356-7. *The Crow's Nest*, Summer

1968, p. 4.) Since 1974, the Institute has operated from a "Merchant Seamen's Center" at 249 Arch Street. (Secor 1985.)

344. The Marine Mission at Large *ARs* 1849, etc., passim.

345. SMNY 1845-46, p. 76. Free Church of St. Mary for Sailors *ARs* 1857 & 1858, passim. Cf. Kelley 1940, pp. 358-60.

346. PECMSS *AR* 1848, pp. 11-2.

347. SMNY 1846-47, back cover of issue for Sept. 1846. ASFS *AR* 1858, p. 26; 1859, pp. 42-3; 1860, p. 49 (where the name appears as "St. Paul's Church"); cf. 1869, p. 54.

348. Thomas 1957, pp. 694-7. The Charleston Port Society meanwhile reaped the benefit of the 46-year term of Chaplain Joseph Brown's outstanding successor, the Rev. W.B. Yates, 1836-82 (Chichester 1885, p. 11). See also Kelley 1940, p. 358.

349. Kelley 1940, pp. 358-67. Gaustad 1962, pp. 68-9. Ahlstrom 1975, Vol. 2, pp. 113-4. Illustrative of the bond between the two church bodies, is the case of San Francisco. Founded in 1893 by the storied "Fell of 'Frisco" (Chaplain James Fell [1869-1923], the man who bodily beat up the crimping fraternity of San Francisco), the station was in 1914 transferred by the (British) Missions to Seamen to the Prostestant Episcopal Church of America, to become the "Seamen's Church Institute of San Francisco." (Kelley 1940, pp. 360-4. Strong 1956, pp. 48-52. Kingsford 1957, pp. 47-54.)

350. Morison 1941, p. 260. Tyler 1944, p. 45. Straus 1950, pp. 9-11. Cole 1954, p. 7.

351. SML 1826, p. 458. Truair 1826, pp. 19-21. SMNY 1828-29, pp. 123, 157. Seamen's Aid Society *AR* 1839, p. 17. Warren 1858, pp. 32-3. Dillon 1961, passim. Hugill 1967, passim. Crimping continued to be a major problem in waterfront ministry after the Civil War, and even into the 20th century. (See also SMNY 1866-67, pp. 173-5. ASFS *The Acts* 1909, pp. 99-100.) Supra, pp. 327-9.

352. Supra, pp. 446-7.

353. Truair 1826, p. 21. Supra, pp. 457-8.

354. ASFS *AR* 1829, pp. 11-2; 1830, pp. 9-10. SMNY 1829-30, p. 292. Supra, p. 330.

355. ASFS *AR* 1850, p. 13.

356. ASFS *ARs* 1836-45, passim, also, 1857, p. 28. Warren 1858, pp. 34-6. Jewell 1874, pp. 74-6. Campbell 1977, pp. 181-4. (The texts to the illustrations of the homes in New York and Portland on pp. 180 and 183, respectively, have been misplaced in Campbell's article. See, for example, Warren 1858, pp. 36-7; also, front cover of Vol. 24, SMNY 1851-52.)

357. For an overview, see Warren 1858, pp. 37-43. For details, see *Reports* of the individual societies involved; also, SMNY and ASFS *ARs* from the 1830's to the 1860's. In New York, the Episcopalians sought to emulate the non-denominational ASFS by opening their own New Sailors' Home at 338 Pearl Street, in 1854. (SMNY 1854-55, p. 189. Kelley 1940, p. 352.) Register offices were also maintained in connection with seamen's *churches*, for example in New Bedford and New Orleans (see inside cover, SMNY Sept. 1839). Later, the Episcopalians' New York Seamen's Church Institute maintained for years a successful shipping office, in open competition with the crimps (Kelley 1940, p. 354).

358. *Encyclopedia of Social Reform* 1897, p. 1320. Foster 1951, p. 64; 1960, pp. 167-77. Cole 1954, pp. 116-25. Ahlstrom 1975, Vol. 1, pp. 516-7.

359. Supra, p. 342.

360. (MS) *William Jenks' Papers*, letter from Levi Chamberlain dated Honolulu, Jan. 12, 1825, BSMRIP *AR* 1825, pp. 23-5. Cf. SML 1825, p. 431.

361. SMNY 1829-30, p. 367.

362. SMNY 1831-32, pp. 35-6; 1832-33, pp. 219-21. Sprague 1861, p. 477.

363. SMNY 1832-33, p. 220.

364. SMNY 1833-61, passim. ASFS *ARs* 1834-61, passim. SML 1837, p. 40. Warren 1858, pp. 35, 41, 45. Cf. *Sheet Anchor* 1843, p. 51.

365. Cf. Rockwell 1842, Vol. 2, pp. 396-7.

366. Cf. McGavran 1956, pp. 1-7. Weibust 1969, pp. 442-50.

367. Langley 1967, p. 214.

368. Morris Vol. 2 1900, passim. Society for Seamen's Children 1947, n.p.

369. Straus 1950, pp. 22-48. Williams 1951, pp. 29-42.

370. SMNY 1828-29, pp. 153, 210-2; 1830-31, pp. 291-2, 331; 1837-38, pp. 73-4. AFSF *ARs* 1831 etc., passim. Morris Vol. 2 1900, pp. 423-4. An "avalanche of appeals" during the 1830's resulted in several new marine hospitals, especially in the South and West, bringing the total to 27 by 1861. But much of their history was marred by abuse, and many were short-lived (Straus 1950, pp. 47-58). However, "Marine Hospital" on Staten Island continued to fill important and expanding needs, more recently as a "United States Public Health Service Hospital."

371. SMNY 1833-34, pp. 1-3, 25, 214, 1875, pp. 297-300. Sailors' Snug Harbor *ARs* 1832 etc., passim. Morris Vol. 2 1900, pp. 412-22. DAB Vol. 15 1935, pp. 348-9. In his will (reportedly drawn up by his friend, Alexander Hamilton) Randall originally directed that the asylum should be built on his Manhattan farmland, but this rose so rapidly in value, as New York City expanded, that his trustees obtained the State Legislature's approval of a Staten Island location instead. With the soaring lease of the land in the city, Sailors' Snug Harbor soon became one of the richest charities in the nation. (SMNY 1842-43, pp. 282-4. *Copy* 1876, pp. 3-18.) For an excellent comprehensive history, see Shepherd 1979. The institution has recently been transferred to more modern facilities at Sealevel, North Carolina (1976).

372. Sailors' Snug Harbor of Boston *Report*, 1960.

373. See, for example, front cover of Mariners' Family Home *AR* 1957.

374. SMNY 1832-33, pp. 283-4. Female Bethel Association *Constitution* 1836, passim. Mariners' Family Industrial Society *Records* 1865, pp. 5-6.

375. Seaman's Aid Society *ARs* 1834-66, passim. Like her husband, "Mother Taylor" was, from the start, closely involved with the Seaman's Aid Society. (The Society changed its name from "Seaman's" to "Seamen's" as from its *AR* of 1840.) The Society's store was first located "under the Seamen's Bethel," but was moved to the new "Mariners' House" after this was dedicated March 24, 1847. (A recent letter-head makes the conflicting statement that the home was "founded in 1829.") In 1867, the Society merged with the Boston Port Society, to form the "Boston Port and Seamen's Aid Society." "Mariners' House" has continued its ministry until today, under the auspices of this joint Society. Supra, p. 497.

376. SMNY 1843-44, pp. 228-9; 1855-56, p. 125; 1862-63, pp. 203-4. Mariners' Family Industrial Society *Records* 1865, passim. Morris Vol. 2, 1900, pp. 425-6. SMNY 1852-53, p. 373, gives (in error) 1853 as the year of the Home's dedication. The "Short History" in recent Mariners' Family Home *ARs* (e.g., for 1957, p. 5) contains an erroneous date for the commencement of the Society's "Charity of Wages" (adopted in 1843, not 1832).

377. Society for the Relief of Destitute Children of Seamen *ARs* 1847 etc., passim. (MS) Society for the Relief of Destitute Children of Seamen *Minutes*, 1848-57, passim. Morris Vol. 2, 1900, pp. 426-8. In 1925, "institutional care" was superseded by "individual care," by means of foster homes; and in 1937, the Society's name was shortened to "Society for Seamen's Children" (Society for Seamen's Children 1946, passim).

378. Supra, p. 17.

379. MMNY 1825-26, p. 369. ASFS *ARs* 1829-59, passim. Hopkins 1980, pp. 38-45. The Merchant Marine School of the Seamen's Church Institute of NY & NJ, and the Education Program of the Woman's Seamen's Friend Society of Connecticut, are more modern manifestations of the same concern. Supra, pp. 453, 506.

380. Supra, pp. 446, 506. Cf. PECMSS *AR* 1853, pp. 11-2.

381. SMNY 1828-29, pp. 58, 219. ASFS *AR* 1837, p. 12; 1838, pp. 19-20, etc. Timpson 1856, p. 136. ASFS *Ship's Libraries* 1880, passim. Seymour 1976, p. 45. Note the corresponding purpose of the current-day "Ministering Seafarers' Program" ([MS] Eckhoff 1979). Infra, p. 581.

382. SMNY 1828-29, p. 153. Cf. supra, p. 60.

383. SMNY 1828-29, pp. 135-7, 153, 288, 317-8, 361-4. ASFS *AR* 1829, p. 13; 1830, p. 6. *New York Standard*, Feb. 4, 1831. Manchester 1929, passim. Healey 1936, p. 127. Supra, p. 223, 334, 457.

384. Suffolk 1933, passim. (The bank adopted its present name in 1842: "The Suffolk Savings Bank for Seamen and Others.") Cf. SMNY 1839-40, inside cover.

385. Female Seamen's Friend Society of Philadelphia *AR* 1846. SMNY 1852-53, pp. 221-2. Cooke 1874, pp. 26-7. Cf. supra, p. 338.

386. Boston Port and Seamen's Aid Society 1904, p. 450.

387. SMNY 1828-29, etc., passim. *Sheet Anchor* 1844, p. 162. Coan 1846, passim. For an early and interesting theological debate on the subject, see Captain Obadiah Congar and Dr. Thomas Scott's correspondence in 1817 (Cheever 1851, pp. 174-81). Cf. supra, pp. 9-10.

388. SMNY 1828-29, etc., passim. (See especially comments in *The American Jurist*, SMNY 1839-40, pp. 340-1.) Ames 1830, pp. 35-6. Claflin 1857, n.pp. Codman 1860, p. 2. Sawtell 1860, "Book II," passim (first published as four letters in SMNY 1855-56, 1857-58). Dana 1929 and 1937, passim. DAB Vol. 5 1930, p. 60. Langley 1967, p. 157. Even at the close of the 19th century, allegations like the following were still being made: "If the laws now on our statute were enforced, a large majority of American captains and mates would be sent to the penitentiary and not a few to the electric chair. . . ." (Johnson 1899, p. 4). Cf. supra, p. 55-6.

389. SMNY 1828-29, etc., passim. Cf. Rensselaer 1854, pp. 9-18. PECMSS *AR* 1854, pp. 16-7. Supra, p. 54.

390. ASFS *AR* 1854, pp. 5-8; 1856, pp. 5-12. Cf. SMNY 1861-62, pp. 82-7. Healey 1936, pp. 61-7.

391. E.g.: SMNY 1829-30, p. 377; (MS) Nook n.d., pp. 73-7.

392. SMNY 1828-29, passim. *Remarks* 1845, passim. Stuart 1856, p. 50. Langley 1967, passim (especially chs. 4-5). Cf. Andersen 1962, p. 46.

393. SMNY 1845-46, pp. 382-3; 1862-63, pp. 200-1. ASFS *ARs* 1840-65, passim. Langley 1967, pp. 92-5. *William P. Powell*, himself a black, remained superintendent of the "Home for Colored Seamen" in New York for a whole generation, from its first commencement at 70 John Street in 1839. However, a "Boarding House for Colored Seamen," run by one Thomas Jenkins, also a black, at 59 (later 79) Ann Street, was listed among Society-recommended boarding-houses in SMNY from 1834 on. Likewise, around mid-century a "Home for Colored Seamen" was provided in New Bedford (corner of 6th and Bedford Streets). An "American Seamen's Protective Union Association" for black seamen (many of whom would sail as cook or steward in the days of sail) was reported founded in New York in 1863, with Prince Loveridge as chaplain. (SMNY 1862-63, p. 200. ASFS *AR* 1865, p. 38.) Note the official segregation practiced at Sailors' Snug Harbor, New York, too, in earlier years; here, in 1875, the men were still eating in "the ordinary mess, the blind mess, the colored mess, etc." (SMNY 1875, p. 299).

394. Langley 1967, pp. 116, 154, quoting from McNally 1839.

395. ASFS *AR* 1833, pp. 10-1. Dension 1944, pp. 187-9. The condition of American naval seamen was characterized by Truair in 1822 as "awful" (CHSM 1822-23, p. 477). Eventually, the ASFS would confine its activities to the merchant service (Webster 1932, p. 98). The Society's initial involvement with the Navy was, during the first decade, symbolized by the title of its magazine: *The Sailor's Magazine, and Naval Journal*. Cf. Langley 1967, p. 64.

396. ASFS *AR* 1829, p. 26. Cf. ASMBUM 1824, pp. 131-2. Also, ASFS *AR* 1830-31, p. 342.

397. SMNY 1830-31, p. 164. Webster 1932, p. 98. Langley 1967, p. 64.

398. SMNY 1830-31, pp. 223-4. ASFS *AR* 1830, pp. 11-2.

399. SMNY 1830-31, pp. 342-3. Drury Vol. 1 1949, pp. 33-92. Langley 1967, pp. 35-8. Cf. NSM 1829 Pt. I, p. 218. That American naval chaplaincy, even during the Civil War, still left much to be desired both quantitively and qualitatively, is attested by such sources as SMNY 1862-63, pp. 161-2, and Jones 1884, pp. 391-2. Cf. ASFS *AR* 1864, pp. 38-9.)

400. Langley 1967, pp. 131-9, 209-14. Cf. Henry Baynham's review in MM 1968, pp. 320-2.

401. SMNY 1829-30, p. 223. Supra, p. 526.

402. SMNY 1830-31, p. 361.

403. E.g.: SMNY 1832-33, p. 293; 1861-62, pp. 362-3. Also, ASFS *AR* 1833, p. 11.

404. Langley 1967, pp. 226-41.

405. Ibid., pp. 131-20; cf. pp. 89-92. Whereas Herman Melville's *White Jacket* only appeared in 1850, William McNally's *Evils and Abuses in the Naval and Merchant Service Exposed* (1839) was published early enough to produce a powerful long-term effect (see pp. 87, 106, 128, on flogging). Concerning the degree of Melville's influence, see Chapel 1982, pp. 57-65.

406. SMNY 1859-60, pp. 116-7; 1861-62, pp. 363-4. ASFS *AR* 1855, p. 15. Langley 1967, pp. 242-69. *Dueling* in the Navy had already become punishable in 1820 (Langley 1967, pp. 24, 124.)

407. Langley 1967, pp. 183-5, 278. Denison 1944, p. 194.

408. Supra, pp. 411-12.

409. ABS *ARs* 1818-65, passim (see especially 1818, p. 24; 1821, p. 16). Drury Vol. 1 1949, p. 88; cf. p. 71. (MS) ABS Archives, letter from Smith Thompson to ABS, Nov. 15, 1820. The original grant to the *John Adams* was commemorated by the donation of the fifty millionth copy of the Scriptures (in the Society's armed forces distribution) to the Polaris Submarine USS *John Adams* on the high seas ([MS] ABS *News Release*, Jan. 15, 1968).

410. ATS *ARs* 1826-65, passim.

411. NYBU *Report* 1821, p. 8. MMNY 1825-26, p. 271.

412. ASFS *AR* 1830, pp. 12-3; 1831, pp. 12-3; 1832, p. 10; 1833, pp. 10-1. Drury Vol. 1 1949, p. 71, quoting from Melville's *White Jacket.*

413. Langley 1967, pp. 194, 201-2, 266.

414. ASFS *AR* 1859, p. 57. Jones 1884, pp. 299-307.

415. Jones 1884, pp. 300-5. Morris is described as big and benevolent-looking; yet "bold as a lion" in standing up for what he saw to be right. Before he died, in February 1863, only 51 years old, he had achieved certification as a ship's captain (pp. 299-301, 419).

416. Jones 1884, pp. 299-301. Supra, p. 482.

417. Jones 1884, pp. 305, etc. Cf. NYPS *AR* 1859, p. 9.

418. ASFS *AR* 1859, pp. 57-8; 1861, p. 52. Jones 1884, pp. 307-13, 329, 341-51. Drury Vol. 1 1949, p. 36. Langley 1967, pp. 147, 279-80. Supra, pp. 482, 490, 500.

419. Jones 1884, pp. 325-62.

420. Ibid., pp. 299, 346-400, 411, 469-502.

421. Jones combined *individual pastoral letters* with the occasional dispatch of *general "lithographed" mailings* to all sea-going members of the Mariners' Church. (Jones 1884, pp. 308, 503-12, 525-7. Cf. SMNY 1862-63, p. 149.) Supra, pp. 122-30.

422. SMNY 1859-65, passim. ASFS *ARs* 1859-65, passim. Jones 1884, p. 308.

423. ASFS *AR* 1859, p. 58. Jones 1884, p. 309. Supra, pp. 491-2.

424. Jones 1884, pp. 391-2, 395. Infra, p. 542.

425. Ibid., p. 353.

426. ASFS *AR* 1861, p. 52. Jones 1884, p. 341.

427. Supra, p. 111.

428. CHSM 1822-23, p. 247.

429. Morison 1965, p. 400.

430. For this use of the word "firsts," see, for example, George Morgan, *The City of Firsts*, Philadelphia, 1926. Some examples of erroneous statements on origins: MMNY 1825-26, pp. 265, 273. PLBUS *Appeal* 1829, p. 23. SMNY 1830-31, p. 337; 1876, p. 47. *The Friend* 1846, pp. 84-5. BFSS *AR* 1851, p. 2. Yates 1851, pp. 6-7. Parry 1855, pp. 28-9. Timpson 1856, pp. 38-69. *Havnen* 1883, p. 150. Pike 1897, p. 2. *Salomonsens* Vol. 22 1927, p. 1014.

KLN Vol. 4 1929, p. 477. *Illustrert* Vol. 3 1950, p. 371. Svensk Uppslagsbok Vol. 26 1957, c. 81. *Nordisk* 1957, cc. 546-7. Jackman 1964, p. 110. Wasberg 1964, p. 29. Henningsen 1967, pp. 16-7. Langley 1967 pp. 46-9. Seymour 1976, p. 40. Under the mounting pressure of attacks from his enemies, G.C. Smith's assessments became increasingly subjective. (E.g.: Smith *Decision* 1829, p. 2. NSM 1842, p. 600; 1852, p. 274; 1861, p. 219. Cf. SML 1820, p. 214.)

431. Infra, pp. 555-61.

432. Supra, pp. 71, 90.

433. Supra, pp. 407-12.

434. Supra, p. 139.

435. Supra, pp. 182-90.

436. Supra, pp. 418-28.

437. Supra, pp. 197-208, 253, 308.

438. Timpson 1856, pp. 51-5.

439. Supra, p. 43. The facts do not, therefore, justify the statement that American efforts were inspired "mainly" by groups in Great Britain (Davis 1979, p. 45).

440. MBSNY *AR* 1821, p. 16.

441. Pascoe 1901, p. 734. The minute-books, magazines, and reports of early British and American seamen's mission societies are replete with examples.

442. E.g.: RTS *Proceedings* 1820, p. 287. SML 1821, p. 160; 1825, p. 26. (MS) BFSFSBU *Minutes*, Oct. 28, 1823.

443. PLS *Proceedings* 1821, p. 41. Cf. NSM 1830, p. 536.

444. Every volume of these magazines carries copious examples.

445. Smith *The Custom House* 1823, p. 19.

446. E.g.: SML 1820, p. 374; 1821, p. 26: 1822, p. 429; 1823, pp. 224-5; 1824, p. 519. CHSM 1822-23, p. 94. MMNY 1825-26, pp. 340-1. Also, supra, pp. 451, 472-6.

447. Smith *Freemasons' Hall* 1829, pp. 9-10. NSM 1830, pp. 109, 111. SMNY 1830-31, p. 278.

448. CHSM 1822-23, p. 384. NSM 1833, p. 332.

449. Supra, p. 111.

450. MMNY 1825-26, pp. 267-71. NSM 1828, pp. 151-2. Timpson 1856, p. 52. SMNY 1878, p. 207. Cf. Foster 1960, p. viii. Supra, p. 456.

451. Cf. Burr 1961, p. 113. Hudson 1865, pp. 3-5, 16-22.

452. Scoresby 1831, p. vi. BFSS *AR* 1840, p. 30. SML 1846, pp. 126-7. Cf. SMNY 1882, p. 25. Supra, p. 354.

453. SML 1820, pp. 272-3; 1823, p. 320. NSM 1828, p. 493; 1832, p. 309; 1833, p. 332. SMNY 1876, p. 194. Supra, pp. 360, 427, 444, 454-7.

454. Supra, pp. 360-2.

455. Paine 1919, pp. 176-9. Gjerset 1933, pp. 79-81. Writers' 1941, pp. 186-7. Ahlstrom 1975 Vol. 2, p. 91.

456. Kverndal (Bergen) 1978, p. 118. Infra, pp. 591-610.

PART VIII — NOTES

1. At all events, maritime ministry represents a valid and early form of *industrial chaplaincy* ([MS] Uittenbosch 1977, pp. 9-10). Cf. supra, pp. 170-1.

2. Supra, pp. 18-9, 246.

3. Supra, pp. 4, 244, 468-70. Infra, pp. 551-3, 589-90. Cf. Berg 1956, p. 84.

4. Crews of rapidly rising Communist bloc and Third World merchant fleets present a powerful current missionary challenge (cf. Kverndal 1969, p. 14).

5. These components are found in studies of missiology from Gustav Warneck's pioneering work, *Evangelische Missionslehre* 1892-1903, to the present era (e.g.: Linsell 1955, Syrdal 1967). Cf. Bavinck 1960, pp. 6-7. Also, *Concise Dictionary* 1970 (under individual entries). For a discussion of the origin and current understanding of the term "missiology," see Verkuyl 1978, pp. 1-17.

6. Latourette 1953, pp. 65-108. Allen 1962, pp. 6-17, 143-4. Scherer 1964, pp. 41-2. Myklebust 1970, pp. 24-5; 1976, pp. 279-80.

7. Supra, pp. 190-2.

8. *Encyclopedia of Missions* 1904, pp. 551-7. Cf. Beaver 1970, p. 26.

9. Infra, p. 572.

10. E.g.: SML 1823, p. 122. SMR 1830, p. 252; 1834, p. 57. Cf. BH 1869, pp. 70-1.

11. SMNY 1831-32, p. 291. Cf. Henshaw 1826, pp. 8-9.

12. SML 1820, p. 448; 1821, pp. 387-8; 1823, pp. 121-3; 1826, p. 299. NSM 1828, pp. 451-2. Cf. Marks 1826, pp. 214-20.

13. Ames 1832, e.g. p. 47. Supra, pp. 210-2.

14. MSABS *AR* 1821, p. 31. SML 1823, pp. 124-5. Cf. *The Christian Mariner's Journal* 1829, pp. 36-7.

15. Marks 1826, pp. 216-8. Cf. SML 1822, p. 245; 1827, p. 145. Lloyd 1968, pp. 237-8. Supra, p. 51.

16. SML 1820, p. 470; 1823, p. 122; 1825, p. 385; 1827, p. 276. Cf. SMNY 1829-30, p. 168. Mitchell 1961, p. 15. Supra, pp. 197, 422.

17. CBU *Report* 1822, p. 5. Cf. SML 1821, pp. 267, 390, 462-3; 1826, p. 208; 1827, pp. 365-66. SMNY 1830-31, p. 334. SUBSB *AR* 1837, pp. 3-4. Calcutta Seamen's Friend Society *AR* 1842, p. 36. CMAS *AR* 1850, p. 9. Sullivan 1853, p. 29.

18. Truair 1826, pp. 3-4. SMNY 1831-32, p. 291. Norborg 1932, pp. 152, 166. Weltzer 1952, p. 32. Cf. SML 1826, p. 142. Supra, pp. 58-9, 64-7.

19. SML 1821, p. 342. Supra, pp. 111, 131.

20. PLS *Proceedings* 1821, p. 45. SML 1821, p. 379. Truair 1826, p. 3. Henshaw 1826, pp. 8-9. Calcutta Seamen's Friend Society *AR* 1842, p. 32. SMNY 1843-44, p. 37. PECMSS *AR* 1851, p. 8. Supra, p. 65. Infra, p. 547-8.

21. Truair 1826, pp. 5-6. PECMSS *AR* 1849, p. 12. Yates 1851, pp. 13-4. Cf. SML 1821, pp. 99, 299; 1822, p. 349; 1823, p. 88. Reports of both British

and American societies are replete with accounts of the conversion of seafarers, as encouragement for further support. Infra, p. 586-7.

22. NMBS *AR* 1818, p. 18; 1844, p. 25. PLS *Proceedings* 1821, pp. 8-9. SML 1823, pp. 122, 277; 1825, p. 199; 1826, p. 458; 1827, p. 41. Marks 1826, pp. 228-33. NSM 1828, p. 73; 1833, p. 150.

23. NMBS *AR* 1818, pp. 5-6; 1820, pp. 24-9. SML 1821, pp. 146-7.

24. BSRMIS *Address* 1815, pp. 3-16.

25. SML 1821, pp. 426-7.

26. E.g.: G. C. Smith *The Boatswain's Mate* n.d. Pt. V, p. 16. Cf. BH No. 4, 1866, pp. 21-2. Brun 1879, p. 200. Infra, pp. 543-5.

27. NMBS *AR* 1818, p. 28; 1832, p.30; 1836, pp. 23-4. SML 1820, pp. 135, 319; 1821, p. 46; 1824, p. 234; 1825, p. 318; 1827, pp. 55-6. PLS *Proceedings* 1821, pp. 45-6. Marks 1821, pp. 84-5. MSABS *AR* 1826, p. 20. NSM 1828, pp. 193-4. Harris 1837, pp. 134-8. Bechervaise 1847, pp. 25-8. Parry 1855, p. 19. Smith 1961, p. 127. Cf. supra, pp. 188, 514. Infra, pp. 586-7.

28. SML 1826, p. 52.

29. Many of Johannes van den Berg's conclusions in his outstanding study of the motives of the great missionary awakening in Great Britain are also applicable to the early advocacy of seamen's missions. As to the issues of purity and priority of motives, see, for example, Berg 1956, pp. 144-9. Cf. Warren 1965, p. 45. Verkuyl 1978, pp. 162-4, 168.

30. Berg 1956, p. 144. Beaver 1968, p. 118.

31. SML 1824, p. 428. Cf. SML 1825, p. 199. NSM 1833, p. 105.

32. Lloyd 1936, p. 131. Cf. SML 1821, p. 462.

33. SML 1822, p. 93. Cf. NMBS *AR* 1818, p. 8. PLS *Proceedings* 1821, p. 6.

34. SML 1820, pp. 156, 229; 1821,p. 149; 1825, pp. 193-4. PLS *Proceedings* 1821, p. 47. G.C. Smith *The Boatswain's Mate* n.d. Pt. III, p. 22. Finch 1831, p. 3. Kealey 1905, pp. 29-30. Cf. supra, p. 57, infra, p. 569.

35. *The Christian Guardian* 1839, p. 317. Cf. supra, pp. 524-5.

36. MMNY 1825-26, pp. 165, 171, 175. SML 1826, pp. 1-2. WW 1858, pp. 169-70. Cf. Beaver 1968, pp. 114, 140.

37. SML 1820, p. 374; 1822, pp. 305-6. MR 1825, p. 212. CC 1913, p. 147; 1918, pp. 118, 168. For an interesting example of how Bethel Meetings could promote the integration of blacks and whites, see SML 1821, pp. 18-9. Cf. supra, pp. 412-3.

38. Stafford 1818, pp. 7-8, 10. Griffin 1819, pp. 13-4. CH 1820-21, p. 699. SML 1821, p. 241; 1826, p. 459. Dudley 1821, p. 392. Spencer 1836, pp. 16-7. SMNY 1860-61, p. 274; 1865-66, p. 221. Cf. Montagu 1832, p. 50. Verkyl 1978, pp. 172-3.

39. Stafford 1818, p. 7. Griffin 1819, pp. 14-5. SML 1820, pp. 347-8; 1821, p. 149; 1825, p. 502. Marks 1821, p. 205. SMR 1829, pp. 399-400. SAS *AR* 1839, p. 18. SUBS AR 1843, p. 6. PECMSS *AR* 1845, p. 10. Dewey 1845, pp. 12-3. (MS) BFSS *Minutes*, May 17, 1853. BFSS *AR* 1859, pp. 1-2. Cf. Straus 1950, pp. 1-3, 15-6. Infra, pp. 569-71.

40. E.g.: NMBS 1824, p. 30. NSM 1828, p. 215; Thompson 1951, p. 448. Cf. infra, pp. 552-3.

41. Marks 1821, pp. 180-4. SML 1823, p. 81; 1825, pp. 92-3. MMNY 1825-26, p. 144. Supra, p. 8.

42. Berg 1956, pp. 150-1. Beaver 1968, pp. 119-21. Cf. Griffin 1819, p. 13. SMNY 1865-66, p. 221.

43. NSM 1829 Pt. I, Suppl. p. 2. Marine Hospitals Service *AR* 1873, pp. 131-2. PECMSS *AR* 1882, pp. 8-9. Kolmodin 1889, pp. 5-6, 22-4. Cf. SML 1820, p. 355; 1821, pp. 39, 99, 251-3. Henshaw 1826, pp. 112-4. Scoresby 1831, pp. v-vi. Bullen 1901, pp. vii-xii. *Flying Angel News* July-August 1976, p. 1.

44. PLS *Proceedings* 1821, p. 9. SML 1826, p. 90. NSM 1829 Pt. I, Suppl. p. 29. G. C. Smith *The Boatswain's Mate* n.d. Pt. III, pp. 22-3. For an American example, see Henshaw 1826, pp. 112-4.

45. NMBS *AR* 1818, p. 22. SML 1820, pp. 247-8; 1826, p. 87; 1828, pp. 456-7. SMNY 1836-37, p. 248; 1861-62, p. 193. Cf. Foster 1960, p. 213.

46. SML 1820, p. 175; 1821, p. 462; 1825, p. 14. NSM 1835, p. 247; 1861, p. 20. Calcutta Seamen's Friend Society *AR* 1842, pp. 17-8. *Flying Angel News* July-August 1976, p. 1.

47. Griffin 1819, p. 15. SML 1820, pp. 158, 175; 1821, p. 389; 1822, pp. 91, 224; 1823, p. 489, 1824, pp. 335, 339; 1825, p. 84. Highmore 1822, p. 62. Truair 1826, p. 23. SMNY 1831-32, pp. 135-6. NSM 1834, p. 428. Huntington 1862, p. 11. (MS) Curry 1956, p. 110. Cf. supra, p. 5.

48. Griffin 1819, p. 13. MMNY 1825-26, p. 191. SML 1826, p. 53. NMBS *AR* 1820, p. 28; 1829, p. 21. Harris 1837, p. 107. Gollock 1930, pp. 51-3. Lloyd 1949, p. xiii. Weltzer 1952, p. 23.

49. Berg 1956, p. 152. Stott 1975, pp. 25-37. Cf. SML 1825, p. 317. Supra, pp. 34-5. Infra, pp. 555-6.

50. SMNY 1830-31, p. 334. Elliott-Binns 1946, p. 399. Berg 1956, pp. 153-5. Smith Vol. I 1960, pp. 119-20. Watson 1960, p. 534. Cf. Foster 1960, pp. 42-3, 212-3. Ahlstrom 1975, Vol. 2, p. 22. Elements of a romantic impulse have already been identified in early marine Scripture distribution, as well as in the choice of early overseas stations (supra, pp. 135, 464, 488). For other early examples, see: NMBS *AR* 1818, p. 40. CHSM 1824, p. 95.

51. SML 1825, pp. 294-6, 319. Cf. Berg 1956, pp. 94, 147-9. Beaver 1964, pp. 13-4; 1968, pp. 133-9. Warren 1965, pp. 41-4; 1967, pp. 86-91. Myklebust 1976, p. 185. Verkuyl 1978, pp. 171-2.

52. SML 1825, pp. 340-3. BFSS *AR* 1838, p. 13. Berg 1956, pp. 29, 61, 94, 147.

53. SML 1821, pp. 251, 389; 1825, p. 14, 1826, p. 88. NMBS *AR* 1827, p. 17.

54. SML 1820, pp. 229, 355. *Establishment* 1844, pp. 8-9. SMNY 1865-66, p. 221. Cf. infra, p. 551.

55. Wesleyan Seamen's Mission *AR* 1872, p. 5. Lindsell 1955, pp. 47-8. Berg 1956, pp. 61-2. Warren 1967, p. 91. Cf. infra, pp. 557, 583-4.

56. SML 1823, p. 239. International Social Christian Institute 1930, p. 7. Berg 1956, pp. 63, 99, 147.

57. Griffin 1819, pp. 6-7. Henshaw 1826, pp. 11-2. Marks 1826, pp. 228-30. *The Christian Mariner's Journal* 1829, pp. 41-6. NSM 1838, p. 286. *Encyclopedia of Missions* 1904, p. 512. Cf. Lindsell 1955, pp. 43-4. Berg 1956, pp. 99-100, 147-9, 156-8, 211. Sundkler 1966, pp. 44-6. Stott 1975, pp. 29-30. Verkuyl 1978, p. 165.

58. Infra, pp. 555-7.

59. Lindsell 1955, pp. 46-7. Berg 1956, pp. 100, 156-9. Beaver 1968, pp. 126-7. Cf. Foster 1960, pp. 212-3. Trueblood 1972, passim. According to Kraemer 1938, pp. 292-3, although "altruistic and humane ideals" might have their "own peculiar value and necessity," they all "labour under an overt or covert relativistic subjectivism" (compared with the Bible-based "apostolic motive" of confronting the world with the Gospel of Jesus Christ, and building up a community of those who respond).

60. PLS *Proceedings* 1821, p. 27. Berg 1956, p. 100. Stott 1975, pp. 29-30. Cf. SML 1821, pp. 100, 146; 1824, p. 426. PLS *Proceedings* 1821, p. 20. WSM *AR* 1859, p. 5.

61. (MS) BFBS *Home Corresp.*, printed letter to captains, p. 2 (accompanying letter from Anthony Landers to Joseph Tarn, Oct. 4, 1816). SML 1820 pp. 168-9; 1822, p. 447; 1827, pp. 96-8. *The Sydney Gazette*, Sept. 27, 1822. SUBS *AR* 1843, p. 6. SMNY 1845-46, p. 62. *The Seamen and Soldiers' Evangelical Magazine* 1846, pp. 1-3. Huntington 1862, p. 11. Cf. infra, p. 555-7.

62. SML 1824, pp. 381-2, 464; 1825, p. 489; 1826, p. 435. PLS *Proceedings* 1821, pp. 10-1, 21, 51-2. SMNY 1831-32, p. 303. Spencer 1836, pp. 3-11. Hodder 1891, pp. 56-7. Confronted by the criticism of the cautious, G.C. Smith voiced his personal sense of urgency with typical directness and defiance: "I will not suffer souls to plunge headlong to hell, because a select few must not be offended . . ." (NSM 1842, p. 465).

63. Marks 1826, pp. 236-7; Cf. 1818, pp. 168-9.

64. Berg 1956, pp. 101, 194.

65. Ibid., p. 164. Carey 1961, pp. 7-13. Cf. *Encyclopedia of Missions* 1904, p. 512. Verkuyl 1978, p. 164.

66. Matthew 28:19-20. Luke 24:47. John 20:21. Acts 1:8. Cf. Mersey Missions to Seamen *AR* 1963, p. 5. Stott 1975, pp. 22-3. (MS) Kverndal, *The Great Commission . . . ,* 1984, pp. 1, 12.

67. SML 1820, p. 467; 1824, p. 171. MMNY 1825-26, pp. 210-1. NSM 1828, pp. 121, 449-50.

68. Griffin 1819, pp. 6-7. Berg 1956, p. 196. (MS) Schepen 1971, pp. 1-4. Stott 1975, pp. 28-31. Warren 1976, p. 13.

69. Marks 1826, p. 221. In this context, it would be appropriate to speak of "the constraining love of Christ" (2 Cor. 5:14) in the *objective* genitive sense, of love *for* the Lord. (PHS 1823, p. 13. Berg 1956, pp. 194-200. Beaver 1964, p. 6; 1968, pp. 141-5. Cf. John 14:15.) As already noted, G.C. Smith consistently made this motive his main defence, when arrested for open-air preaching (supra, p. 170).

70. Berg 1956, pp. 29, 155-6, 101, 155-6. Miller 1961, pp. 78-9. Beaver 1968, p. 121. Verkuyl 1978, pp. 165-6.

71. Marks 1821, p. 176.

72. Calcutta Seamen's Friend Society *AR* 1842, p. 27.

73. Marks 1826, p. 238. Concern for the glory of God was, of course, closely connected with the missiological motive (e.g., Truair 1826, p. 12). Infra, pp. 551-3.

74. Cf. Ex. 20:10, 23:9; Num. 15:14-16; Dt. 10:18-19, 26:11-12, 31:12; Mt. 25:35. Chaplain Jan Wristers of New Orleans points out how the normal attitude of officialdom (for example customs officers) to seamen and other "strangers within the gates" is still one of protecting the interests of *the host country*, not those of *the visitor*. The only exception to this rule, he says, is the Mosaic Law, which expressly ordains protection and care for the stranger. For the Christian, this obligation is reinforced by Christ himself, "he who became in a unique sense 'The Alien' when he came to this earth, and who died for aliens, for sojourners, for the poor and the ignored and the forgotten..." (Wristers 1979, p. 14).

75. Dennis 1893, pp. 157-8. Berg 1956, pp. 101-2, 159, 203-4. Miller 1961, p. 79. Andersen 1961, p. 304. Myklebust 1976, pp. 101-6.

76. SML 1821 pp. 160, 252-3, 503; 1822, p. 245. Henshaw 1826, pp. 10-1. SMR 1834, p. 57. PHS *AR* 1836, p. 7. WW 1866, p. 69. Cf. supra, pp. 169-71. As the westward wave of uprooted Europeans increased, a corresponding challenge was presented by the immigrant (supra, pp. 491-2).

77. SML 1826, p. 368. Scoresby 1831, p. vii. Calcutta Seamen's Friend Society *Report* 1842, p. 29. SMNY 1845-46, p. 62. WW 1858, pp. 26-37; 1907, pp. 201-1. NSM 1860, p. 134. Scarth n.d., p. 126. BH No. 4, 1866, pp. 21-2; No. 10, 1867, p. 18. Allen 1898, p. 411. Kverndal 1971, p. 77; (Bergen) 1978, pp. 110-6. State church-promoted protectionism may show little recognition of the realities of secularization (cf. Bergmark 1974, pp. 184-5). See also Verkulyl 1978, pp. 173-4, on "ecclesiastical colonialism."

78. MMNY 1825-26, pp. 161-2. Cf. Stafford 1817, p. 47; 1818, p. 10. SML 1821, p. 197. Truair 1826, pp. 15-6. ASFS *AR* 1859, p. 30.

79. SML 1821, p. 420. G. C. Smith *The Boatswain's Mate* n.d. Pt. VII, p. 12. Bristol Marine School Society *Report* 1825, p. 10. Truair 1826, p. 16. Dewey 1845, p. 13. Pennsylvania Seamen's Friend Society *AR* 1846, pp. 20-1. NYPS *AR* 1865, p. 13. SMNY 1878, p. 234. The quotation is from the first stanza of F.W. Faber's hymn, "There's a Wideness in God's Mercy." Cf. supra, pp. 205, 284.

80. CHSM 1824, p. 219. Truair 1826, p. 16. NYPS *AR* 1865, p. 13. SMNY 1876, p. 175. ASFS *The Acts* 1909, p. 104.

81. SML 1820, p. 397; 1821, pp. 93, 392, 420, 460, 502; 1822, pp. 305-6; 1827, pp. 458-9; 1849, p. 154. Truair 1826, p. 16. SMR 1827, p. 297. Calcutta SFS *AR* 1842, pp. 26-7. Supra, p. 238.

82. SMNY 1863-64, p. 186. Supra, pp. 381, 488.

83. Örner 1971, pp. 395-40. Kerfoot 1972, pp. 108-23. Kverndal 1973, pp. 31-4; (Bergen) 1978, pp. 103-4. Gracida 1979, pp. 38-41. Cooperation with Catholics (or "Papists" as they were then called) would have been unthinkable during the period of this study (cf. McCulgan 1951, p. 220). A concurrent feature of the present-day Ecumenical Phase of the work is a renewed "denominationalism," the purpose of which is not to enlist seafarers into the various denominations, but to promote awareness of, and support for, seamen's mission work within each individual denomination. (See *Watermarks* 1981, no. 2-3, pp. 1-2). Common *social endeavor* was listed as a third ecumenical impetus in maritime mission (besides the nature of the seafarer's *pluralistic world* and his *itinerant vocation*), by Dr. Nils E. Bloch-Hoell, at the Author's Disputation, June 2, 1984. It remains to be seen whether modern-day maritime

ecumenism will lead to the renewal of a richer, more genuinely biblical concept of mission, or succumb to the temptation of reductionism (Cf. Myklebust 1976, pp. 249-50. Seymour 1976, pp. 54-60.)

84. BFSS *AR* 1838, p. 7. It might, especially in the early years of the ASFS, appear as if the Society were primarily seeking to "enlist the seamen of America and the world in the foreign mission enterprise" (ASFS *The Acts* 1909, p. 30). There is, however, no reason to believe that concern for the welfare of the seafarer himself was not the overriding motive. Supra, pp. 367, 419, 463.

85. NSM 1828, p. 158. Cogswell 1833, p. 194. BFSS *AR* 1839, pp. 70-1. Kverndal 1969, p. 3.

86. Forster 1814, pp. 15-6. SML 1820, p. 468; 1822, p. 2; 1823, p. 334; 1826, p. 303; 1835, pp. 191-3; 1839, pp. 3-4. Truair 1826, pp. 8-12. MRL 1826, pp. 239, 354. NSM 1828, pp. 29, 158-9; 1829 Pt. I, Suppl. p. 88; 1833, p. 289; 1838, pp. 128-9, 161-8, 241-8. Scoresby 1831, p. 93. Montagu 1832, p. 51. Harris 1837 pp. 73-81, 174-7. SMNY 1837-38, pp. 343-6. BFSS *AR* 1840, pp. 34-5. Warren 1858, pp. 48-51. Kverndal 1969, pp. 3-9. Cf. Kemp 1970, p. 41.

87. NSM 1829 Pt. I, pp. 107-12. SMR 1831, pp. 254-5. Potter 1848, p. 22. Davies 1961, pp. 229-31. Dodge 1965, pp. 140-4. Kverndal 1969, p. 9. Supra, p. 468.

88. Stafford 1817, p. 6. CHSM 1821, p. iv. NSM 1828, pp. 158-9. *The Christian Intellegencer* 1839, p. 37. Allen 1898, pp. 258-9. Kverndal 1969, pp. 6, 10. Bloch-Hoell 1975, pp. 137, 140. Cf. *Occasional Bulletin* No. 1, 1978, passim.

89. SML 1825, p. 14. SMNY 1840-41, p. 1. NSM 1852, pp. 288-93. ASFS *AR* 1888, p. 31. NYPS 1893, p.7.

90. Stafford 1817, pp. 46-7. ASFS *AR* 1842, p. 12.

91. SML 1820, pp. 171, 461; 1827, p. 366. PLS *Proceedings* 1821, p. 52. NMBS *AR* 1825, pp. 21-2. MMNY 1825-26, pp. 178-9, 375. SMNY 1845-46, pp. 262-3. NYPS *AR* 1856, p. 31. Cf. BFSS *AR* 1887, p. 22. Schartum 1933, pp. 97-111.

92. SML 1820, p. 24; 1835, p. 196. CHSM 1821, p. iv. *American Missionary Register* 1824, p. 260. Truair 1826, pp. 12-3. ASFS *AR* 1832, p. 14. Tuckerman 1838, pp. 31-2. SMNY 1845-6, p. 62; 1875, pp. 1-11. BH 1873, Nos. 7-8, pp. 118-25. Note also the crucial role of seamen in enforcing the abolition of the Slave Trade (e.g., Wilson 1851, passim).

93. SML 1821, pp. 131-3; 1823, pp. 311, 368-9; 1824, pp. 58, 462; 1825, pp. 429-31; 1826, pp. 417-9; 1837, pp. 8-12. Cogswell 1833, p. 193. BFSS *AR* 1845, pp. 48-50. Warren 1858, pp. 51-5. Horne 1894, p. 32. Cf. Dowley 1977, p. 562. Supra, pp. 136-8, 242, 414.

94. SML 1827, p. 76. Green 1828, pp. 549-51. NSM 1831 p. 76. SMR 1832, pp. 190-2. SMNY 1828-29, p. 89; 1832-33, p. 142. Jones 1884, p. 446. Pike 1897, p. 295. ASFS *The Acts* 1909, pp. 100-4. Cf. Beaver 1964, p. 6. Supra, p. 107-11, 210-7.

95. SML 1820, p. 460; 1821, pp. 292-4; 1823, pp. 27-8, 196. MMNY 1825-26, pp. 116, 375. SMR 1830, p. 251. Warren 1858, pp. 53-5. SMNY 1861-62, pp. 68-9. Among evangelicals, there was deep concern for the witness of

seafaring coadjutors to port-cities of nominally Roman Catholic countries. (SML 1823, p. 239. Warren 1858, pp. 53-5. Foster 1960, p. 213.) Supra, pp. 212-7, 250, 544.

96. MMNY 1825-26, p. 162. SML 1826, p. 299. Green 1828, pp. 550-1. SMNY 1840-41, p. 367; 1845-46, pp. 262-3.

97. Berg 1956, p. 182.

98. Berg 1956, pp. 104-5, 119-22, 182-5, 207-10. Smith 1963 Vol. 2, pp. 12, 18. Gaustad 1966, pp. 151-3. Schorzman 1970, pp. 191-2. Brauer 1971, pp. 551-3. Ahlstrom 1975 Vol. 1, p. 579. Cf. SML 1820 p. 441. Beaver 1968, p. 124.

99. The Scottish Sailors' and Soldiers' Bethel Flag Union AR 1836, p. 35. BFSS AR 1841, p. 31. SMNY 1872, pp. iii-iv. Cf. Barth 1961, p. 64.

100. G.C. Smith English Sailors n.d., passim. Other examples of prophecies quoted in connection with seafarers and the sea: Psalm 68:31 (SMNY 1862-63, p. 200). Psalm 72:8 (NMBS AR 1816, pp. 38-9). Psalm 89:25 (NSM 1839, p. 257). Isaiah 60:5 (SML 1822, pp. 150, 501; 1824, p. 57). Isaiah 60:8-9 (Cogswell 1833, p. 192). Zechariah 9:10 (NSM 1839, p. 257).

101. SMNY 1872, pp. iii-iv. Cf. SML 1821, p. 501.

102. Brauer 1971, pp. 551-2.

103. Berg 1956, pp. 207-10. Cf. Sundkler 1966, p. 38.

104. Ibid. Cf. Lindsell 1955, p. 45. Beaver 1968, p. 131. Myklebust 1976, p. 31. Verkuyl 1978, pp. 166-7.

105. Cf. Cook 1954, pp. 59-64. Bavinck 1960, pp. 155-90. For an incisive, more comprehensive treatment of missionary objectives, see, for example, Verkuyl 1978, pp. 176-204. For a valuable, innovative, sociological study of the particular relationship between evangelistic and social concern in maritime ministry, see (MS) Oxenford 1983.

106. SML 1827, pp. 96-8. NSM 1828, p. 2; 1831, p. 78. BFSS AR 1850, pp. 1-2. WW 1859, p. 25. Uittenbosch 1969, pp. 3-8: (MS) 1977, pp. 11-3. McGavran 1970, p. 596. Cf. Steensness 1964. Also, Bishop of Llandaff in Flying Angel News Sept./Oct. 1976. Quoting paragraphs of the 1974 Lausanne Covenant, that "in the church's mission of sacrificial service evangelism is primary," John Stott puts the position of current-day evangelicalism as follows: "Anything which undermines human dignity should be an offence to us. But is anything so destructive of human dignity as alienation from God through ignorance or rejection of the gospel? And how can we seriously maintain that political and economic liberation is just as important as eternal salvation?" (Stott 1975, pp. 35-6, Cf. p. 57). Commenting on an occasional negative response to evangelistic enthusiasm, Strong states (1956, p. 31): "Too much zeal undid many of the pioneers." More likely, it could have been a lack of accompanying discernment (cf. Romans 10:2).

107. Supra, p. 423.

108. SML 1820, p. 352. For a modern-day example, see Seamen's Mission of the Methodist Church AR 1980, inside cover.

109. Henshaw 1826, passim. For a modern-day example, see Michaelsen 1979, pp. 15-24.

110. Cogswell 1833, pp. 194-6.

111. The (Church of England) Missions to Seamen, for example, saw their object as no less than "the glory of our triune God, the dissemination of the pure Gospel of Jesus Christ, and the gathering in of the sheep of the Redeemer into His everlasting fold" (WW 1858, pp. 149-50). Cf. Bavinck 1960, p. 158. Beaver 1964, p. 6. (MS) Uittenbosch 1977, p. 11. See also McGavran 1976, p. 14, on discipling as making "dependable members of his [Christ's] church."

112. E.g.: SML 1825, p. 317. BFSS *AR* 1839, p. 23. WW 1858, p. 149; 1859, p. 25.

113. Kraemer 1938, pp. 292-3. Pierard 1976, p. 975. Cf. Hohman 1952, p. 283. Heasman 1962, pp. 19-20. Lindsell 1966, p. 193. Stott 1975, p. 16. Myklebust 1976, p. 207.

114. (MS) PLS *Minutes*, March 18, 1818. SML 1820, p. 217.

115. Southwark Auxiliary Bible Society *Minutes*, March 12, 1817 (pp. 139-40).

116. SML 1822, p. 417. NSM 1833, pp. 151-2. Cf. SML 1825, p. 14. NSM 1841, pp. 137-41. Supra, pp. 350.

117. The quotation is from the constitution of the Leith Seamen's Friend Society (SML 1820, p. 175). Cf. SML 1822, p. 323. Glasgow Seaman's Friend Society *AR* 1823, p. 1. The (Church of England) Missions to Seamen at first referred only to "the spiritual welfare of the seafaring classes at home and abroad," as their official object. However, it was made clear that this would not prevent the Society from also using "such means as might better his [the seaman's] temporal position." (Missions to Seamen *Report* 1860, p. 6. Walrond 1904, p. 96.)

118. The point is not whether pioneer advocates of seamen's mission saw social concern as a means of promoting receptivity to the verbalized Gospel. (This was just as legitimate and necessary then as now.) The point is whether they saw social concern *only* as a means to an end, or whether it had an *inherent* validity, too. (Jaeger 1965, p. 17. Cf. PHS *AR* 1836, p. 7. SAS *AR* 1839, pp. 17-8.) Hohman (1952, p. 283) makes the undocumented statement that the seaman's physical welfare was originally regarded as *only* a means to the "higher goal" of spiritual salvation. Supra, pp. 349-50.

119. Henshaw 1826, pp. 11-2. NSM 1838, p. 286. Ladies' Seamen's Friend Society of the port of San Francisco *Report* 1868, p. 6. Cf. Hocking 1932, p. 326. See also the Bishop of Grantham in *Flying Angel News* No. 3, 1977, and (MS) Uittenbosch 1977, p. 13.

120. E.g., NSM 1831, p. 78. SMNY 1843-44, p. 357.

121. Cf. Myklebust 1976, p. 208. Supra, pp. 161, 349-50, 355, 392, 464, 474, 519-24. Infra, pp. 584-5.

122. NSM 1829 Pt. II, p. 517.

123. Indications of the onset of secularism: SMNY 1898, pp. 363-6; 1907, pp. 83-4. ASFS *The Acts* 1909, pp. 99-104. Cf. Hocking 1932, pp. 325-9. Hohman 1952, pp. 283-4, 291-3. Current-day examples of subjectivism and secularism in goal-setting: Mitchell 1961, p. 10. Uittenbosch 1969, pp. 32-7. Hill 1969 pp. 48-55. Seymour 1976, p. 42. (MS) Ratcliffe 1976, pp. 2, 7, 8; Cf. (MS) Kverndal *Comments* on same 1977, p. 1. Dowell 1984, pp. 32-3. Note on the other hand the highly relevant observation of Uittenbosch, in 1969, pp. 13-23. Cf. Kraemer 1938, pp. 292-5. (MS) Schepen 1971, pp. 10-1. Beyerhaus 1974, pp. 74-5.

124. Stott 1875, pp. 29-30. Some (like [MS] Mansfield n.d.) might see the revised object of the ASFS as an early inauguration of "secular welfare." However, the Society's *Annual Reports* and *The Sailor's Magazine*, New York, evidence consistent concern, through the century, for the evangelization of the seafarer as a primary objective. Cf. Uittenbosch 1969, p. 5. Supra, p. 555.

125. Supra, p. xxv.

126. Harms 1909, p. 4. Supra, p. xxv.

127. Supra, p. 253.

128. CHSM 1823, p. 320.

129. ASFS *AR* 1830, p. 5. The term "Sea Missions" was later applied to the ship's libraries of the ASFS (AR 1859 p. 58).

130. For examples of such exceptions, see: Snow 1963, passim. Goldsmith-Carter 1966, pp. 80-2. Lloyd 1968, pp. 245-6, 272.

131. Supra, pp. 295-304. Cf. Harms 1909, p. 3. Healey 1936, pp. 6-10. Hohman, who tends to see seamen's missions as only involved with "port welfare," excludes activities concerned with "would-be seamen" and "ex-seamen" (1952, p. 286).

132. Frayne 1972, p. 33.

133. Kverndal (Bergen) 1978, pp. 103-33. An *expanding* area of ministry has been to Nordic nationals resident abroad. (Ibid., p. 129. [MS] Bondevik 1974, pp. 2-22.) Infra, p. 610. Cf. The Marine Society [1976], p. 6.

134. E.g.: Brun 1879, pp. 1-2. Harms 1890, pp. 3-5. Cf. Kverndal 1971, p. 77.

135. Cf. Myklebust 1971, p. 13.

136. Anderson 1970, p. 594. Stott 1975, pp. 23-5, 30, 35. Cf. Myklebust 1971, pp. 12-25; 1976, p. 14.

137. Harms 1890, pp. 2-3. *Realencyklopädie* Vol. 18 1906, p. 145. Münchmeyer 1912, p. 91. *Die Religion im Geschichte und Gegenwart* Vol. 5 1961, cc. 1647-8. Cf. *Lexikon für Theologie und Kirche* Vol. 9 1964 c. 588. The assertion that *seamen's* chaplaincy grew out of *industrial* chaplaincy is contrary to the historical facts ("Industrial Chaplaincy," 1980, p. 2). Infra, pp. 563-9.

138. E.g., *Concise Dictionary of Religious Knowledge and Gazeteer* 1891, p. 847. *The Encyclopedia of Missions* Vol. 2 1891, pp. 317-20. *The New Schaff-Herzog* Vol. 10 1910, pp. 316-9. *A Dictionary of Religion and Ethics* 1921, p. 403. *Salmonsens* Vol. 22 1927, p. 1014. *Kirkeleksikon for Norden* Vol. 4 1929, pp. 477-8. *An Encyclopedia of Religion* 1945, pp. 698-9. *Svensk Uppslagsbok* Vol. 26 1953, cc. 81-2. *The Twentieth Century Encyclopedia of Religious Knowledge* 1955, pp. 1007-8. *Der Grosse Brockhaus* Vol. 10 1956, p. 606. *Evangelisches Kirchenlexikon* Vol. 3 1959, cc. 914-5.

139. Another matter is that a statement of objective(s) would, in practice, frequently include a specification of methods by which such objective(s) would be promoted (e.g., Kingsford 1857, Appendix). Cf. Stott 1975, pp. 38-40.

140. This obligation might well form the title of a discourse, as in Huntington 1862, and Jones n.d. Cf. Sundkler 1966, p. 40. Neill 1970, p. 110. Glazik 1970, pp. 388-9. Anderson 1970, p. 594. Stott 1975, p. 56. Myklebust 1976, pp. 15-29.

141. E.g.: *The Christian Observer* 1830. SML 1835, pp. iii-iv. Cf. Ward 1970, pp. 378-80. Stott 1975, pp. 40-1, 56-7. Supra, pp. 97-8, 102. Infra, p. 575.

142. Supra, pp. 370, 557.
143. Cf. Anson 1947, p. xiii. Neill 1970, p. 12. *The Lausanne Covenant* 1975, pp. 30-1.
144. Cf. Kraemer 1938, pp. 292-3. McGavran 1970, p. 34. *The Lausanne Covenant* 1975, pp. 20, 25, 30. Stott 1975, pp. 35, 56-57. Verkuyl 1978, pp. 197-204. Supra, pp. 558-9.
145. For examples of a more detailed treatment of such impediments, see Griffin 1819, pp. 8-9; CHSM 1823, pp. 473-5; 1824, pp. 153-5; ASFS *AR* 1854, pp. 6-8; Warren 1858, pp. 43-4; McCarthy 1861, Ch. 5; Oehlkers 1897, passim.
146. Calcutta Seamen's Friend Society *Report* 1842, p. 28.
147. Stafford 1817, p. 2. Cf. (MS) Powell 1940, p. 12. Straus 1950, pp. 12-4. Dillenburg 1980, pp. 2-5.
148. NMBS *AR* 1818, p. 26. SML 1823, p. 83. Warren 1858, pp. 43-4. Even today, the seafarer must be classified as a "temporarily dislocated" worker in an "industrial complex," characterized by the fact that it has "institutional" attributes, where one both works and lives. ([MS] Uittenbosch 1977, pp. 1, 10. Cf. Frayne 1972, pp. 7-16. CC Christmas 1975, pp. 11-2.)
149. NMBS *AR* 1826, p. 13. PECMSS *AR* 1848, Appendix p. 6. NSM 1860, pp. 111-2. Cf. Weibust 1969, pp. 213, 418-9. Sherar 1973, pp. 18, 20, 22. (MS) Ratcliffe 1976, p. 8.
150. SML 1820, pp. 171-2; 1821, p. 146. Cf. Grönseth 1958, passim.
151. Weibust 1969, pp. 214-5.
152. Straus 1950, pp. 12-4. Cf. ASFS *AR* 1854, p. 8. Closely connected with the seafarer's loneliness and social privation was (and still is) his susceptibility to *boredom*, with all its attendant ills (Sorenson 1979, pp. 42-6).
153. Straus 1950, pp. 9, 12, Cf. CHSM 1824, p. 155. SMNY 1834-35, pp. 298-9. Supra, p. 57.
154. SML 1823, p. 83. Cf. SMNY 1828-29, p. 3. Straus 1950, p. 12. Sherar 1973, p. 35.
155. Weibust 1969, pp. 429-30. Cf. SML 1821, pp. 333-5.
156. World Health Organization 1959, passim. Ström 1960, pp. 1237-40. Sundby 1960, pp. 1240-3. Otterland 1960, passim. Brun-Gulbrandsen 1964, p. 162 & passim. Arner 1970, passim. (MS) Daasvand 1982, p. 83.
157. ASFS *AR* 1854, p. 8.
158. Weibust 1969, for example, deals at length with the seafarer's varied physical, mental and emotional needs (pp. 407-36), only not his *spiritual* needs. The same may be said of Sherar 1973. Cf. Sundby 1964, p. 1240, where the author lists lack of provision for seamen's spiritual needs as one of ten "disintegrating enviromental factors" on shipboard strongly predisposing to psychiatric illness. Supra, p. 63-4.
159. SML 1821, p. 146; 1826, p. 54. NMBS *AR* 1826, p. 13. NSM 1831, pp. 98-9; 1833, p. 187. WSM *AR* 1872, p. 5.
160. Clap 1738, pp. 72-3.
161. SML 1821, pp. 252-3; 1827, p. 14. Supra, p. 422.
162. SML 1821, p. 316. NYPS *AR* 1822, p. 10. American Bethel Society *AR* 1843, p. 17.

163. SMNY 1834-35, p. 373. SAS *AR* 1839 pp. 19-20. BH Oct./Nov. 1868, pp. 20-1. Cf. Lindsell 1955, p. 258. Neill 1970, pp. 496-7. Supra, pp. 95-8, 272-8.

164. Supra, pp. 370.

165. Undue emphasis on shipowners' "self-interest" in advocating seamen's missions might well create a suspicion of partiality. Hence, the importance of such social action and ministry as could *counter* "cross-social" communication barriers. Cf. Healey 1936, pp. 131-4. Supra, pp. 200, cf. 524.

166. SML 1821, pp. 252-3. Cf. Romans 3:23-24.

167. SML 1820, p. 462; 1825, pp. 92-3. SMNY 1840-41, pp. 362-3. Calcutta Seamen's Friend Society *AR* 1842, p. 28. Cf. Matthew 12:43-45. Also supra, p. 328. Although an inmate of a total institution would not necessarily be a "deviant" on entry, he would soon be labeled as such. Here, the sailor was no exception.

168. Goffman 1961, pp. 1-124. Cf. Straus 1950, pp. 12-4. Weibust 1958, passim; 1969, pp. 211-33, 429. Aubert 1959, pp. 200-19; 1969, pp. 156-65. Zurcher 1965, passim. (MS) Fricke 1972, passim. Ritzer 1979, passim. Of particular relevance is Zurcher's 1965 study, where he shows the significance of superstitions, initiations, and traditions, in assuring that a new sailor shall be "squared away," and transformed into a "salt," in other words — an accepted member of the "informal organization" of the shipboard society, adjusted to the role expectations of that particular community (pp. 395-400).

169. Ibid. Dudley 1821, pp. 307-8. McColgan 1940, pp. 49-50. Cf. Backhaus 1968, pp. 11-2, Weibust 1969, pp. 442-50. Fricke 1973, pp. 1-6. Sherar 1973, pp. 18-23, 41-6. Dillenburg 1980, pp. 3-5.

170. Faced with phenomena like the "hyperbolic sentiment of group solidarity" with which Christian mission among Islamics has to contend, it is recognized that "spiritual reproduction" will normally be facilitated where "social solidarity" has not been impaired (Kraemer 1938, p. 1297. Pickett 1956, pp. 98-100. Neill 1970, pp. 110-1.)

171. BSRMIS *An Address* 1812, p. 5; *Home* 1816, pp. 14, 16. (MS) Currey 1956, p. 111. Weibust 1969, pp. 207-10. Sherar 1973, p. 35. Ritzer 1979, pp. 166-93. Maddocks 1981, pp. 94-5. Supra, pp. 107-11, 531-2.

172. SMNY 1878, p. 201; Cf. 1837-38, p. 170. See also Marks 1821, pp. 69, 78-83. CHSM 1822-23, p. 536. G.C. Smith *The Boatswain's Mate* n.d., passim. SML 1824, pp. 126, 292-3; 1825, pp. 67-8; 1826, pp. 233-4. NSM 1841, pp. 179-80; 1859, p. 162. Baynham 1969, pp. 139-41. Villiers 1970, p. 187. Supra, pp. 123, 129.

173. BSRMIS *True Friendship* 1812, pp. 8-9. SML 1820, pp. 106, 173, 202-4, 355; 1821, pp. 121-3, 252, 314; 1823, p. 239. EM 1826, pp. 346-7. *The Christian Mariner's Journal* 1829, pp. 42-4. BFSS *AR* 1842, p. 19. Warren 1858, p. 44. Smith 1961, pp. 38-9, 113-5, 146. Backhaus 1968, passim. Baynham 1969, p. 91. Laffin 1969, p. 113. Sherar 1977, pp. 36-7. On "yarning," see SML 1826, p. 55. On the other forms of "maritime vice," see The Marine Society *Bye-laws* 1809, pp. 107-16. On the relatively low level of *homosexuality* at sea, see Backhaus 1968, pp. 17, 166-7.

174. For an incisive study of the sociological factors coming into play as soon as a sailor "hits the beach," when the informal organization of the shipboard

society would be replaced by a new set of ("liberty hound") role expectations, see Zurcher 1965, p. 398. Cf. Charlton 1980, pp. 38-9. Supra, pp. 327-8.

175. Destitute Sailors' Asylum *Report* 1849, p. 5. Cf. SML 1821, p. 252. Dudley 1821, pp. 307-8. NMBS *AR* 1834, pp. 27-8. PECMSS *AR* 1855, pp. 6-7. Straus 1950, p. 9. Hohman 1956, p. 8. Backhaus 1968, passim.

176. Healey 1936, p. 53. Cf. Sherar 1973, p. 35.

177. SML 1823, p. 127; 1849. pp. 49-52. Calcutta Seamen's Friend Society *AR* 1842, p.28. Warren 1858, p. 33. Smith 1925, passim. Straus 1950, p. 10. Hugill 1967, pp. 33, 72-4, & passim. Weibust 1969, pp. 154-5. Jones 1972, pp. 432-3.

178. WSM *AR* 1873, pp. 5-6. Cf. Sorenson 1979, p. 44.

179. Sherar 1973, pp. 20-2. Cf. Straus 1950, pp. 9-14. Supra, pp. 342-3.

180. Sherar 1973, pp. 30-2. 35, 37. Cf. Healey 1936, pp. 67-70. Hugill 1967, pp. 75-7. Weibust 1969, p. 155. Supra, pp. 340-1.

181. Griffin 1819, pp. 8-9. ASFS *AR* 1854, p. 8. PECMSS *AR* 855, pp. 6-7. However, from personal observation, both as seaman and subsequent seamen's chaplain, the Author does not share Healey's deterministic disregard for the option of *sublimation*. (Healey 1936, pp. 67-70. Cf. Kverndal 1971, pp. 38-9.)

182. ASFS *The Acts* 1908, p. 97. Matthews 1911, p. 283. Cf. Hohman 1952, p. 274. Strong 1956, pp. 26-7, 33-8. Jones 1972, pp. 433-7. Sherar 1973, pp. 23, 37. Hugill 1967, pp. 318, 339-42. (MS) Dixon 1981.

183. G. C.Smith *The Royal Brunswick* 1828, p. 8. NSM 1829 Pt. I, Suppl., p. 41. Supra, p. 7.

184. Woodward 1723, pp. 67-75. (An 1812 edition is contained in SPCK *Religious Tracts* 1815.) Mather 1723, passim. EM 1810, p. 411. SML 1820, pp. 148-9, 221-2, 308, 347-9; 1822, pp. 442-4; 1823, p. 64. MMNY 1825-26, pp. 11-4. *The Christian Guardian* 1826, pp. 132-3. Herbert 1879, passim. Gill 1913, passim. Whiteley 1938, pp. 224-5. Gosse 1946, passim. Carse 1957, passim. Dugan 1966, passim. Wright 1967, pp. 117-8. Cf. Kemp 1976, pp. 570, 650-1. Supra, p. 93.

185. SML 1824, p. 411; 1825, p. 291. NSM 1833, pp. 182-5. Cf. Beck 1973, p. 315. Kemp 1976, p. 670. Garitee 1977, passim. Botting 1978, passim.

186. SML 1821, pp. 149, 180-6, 218-21, 315; 1823, pp. 107-11; 1826, p. 234. *The Christian Guardian* 1823, pp. 356-7. *American Missionary Register* 1824, p. 248. Truair 1826, p. 11. NSM 1831, pp. 74-5. *The Encyclopedia of Social Reform* 1897, p. 1258. Dow 1927, pp. v, xxvii. Lloyd 1949, pp. 3, 7, 24. Birkeli 1952, p. 443. Pope-Hennessy 1968, passim. Ward 1969, passim. Morison 1972, Vol. 3, pp. 140, 367-70. Between 1640 and 1807, Great Britain was alleged to have transported 15,000,000 slaves (NSM 1829, p. 235). John Newton could testify from personal experience how the necessity of treating human beings like cattle gradually brought a "numbness upon the heart" (Laing 1974, p. 230). Another significant link between slaving and piracy is the fact that prime pirate recruits were all too often sailors suitably hardened in the Slave Trade (Botting 1978, p. 15). Supra, pp. 46-50.

187. Whiteley 1938, pp. 223-4. Cameron 1961, pp. 55-6. Carse 1970, passim. Kemp 1976, p. 812.

188. EM 1819, p. 292. RTS *Proceedings* 1820, p. 417. NSM 1829 Pt. I, pp. 42-3. Matthews 1911, p. 118. Supra, pp. 28, 168-9, 258.

189. NSM 1855, pp. 443-4; 1856, back cover of July Number. Cf. Thompson 1951, pp. 440-1. Latourette 1953, pp. 1323-4.

190. EM 1818, p. 564. SML 1820, pp. 104, 189-90. Marks 1826, p. 2. Chase 1965, pp. 75-83. Wright 1967, pp. 15-7, 115-6. Murphy 1970, pp. 3-4. Kemp 1976, p. 945. Cf. supra. pp. 7, 28.

191. See NSM 1829 Pt. II, Suppl., and Strong 1956, p. 51, for examples of desertion due to crimp enticements and inhuman treatment on board, respectively.

192. Supra, pp. 3, 56-7, 568.

193. Straus 1950, pp. 6-7. That seafarers are still, especially on ships flying "flags of convenience," not infrequently deprived of basic human rights, is forcibly attested in Chapman 1981, passim. Supra, p. 542. Infra, p. 588.

194. Infra, p. 588.

195. Supra, pp. 54, 348.

196. Plimsoll 1872, passim. Hohman 1956, pp. 7, 21-2. Course 1963, p. 203.

197. Jewell 1874, passim. Cf. Clarkson 1845, pp. 11-7; Postscript pp. 6-19. ASFS *AR* 1854, pp. 6-7. *Seafarers and Their Ships* 1956, pp. 30-2. Jackson 1964, p. 118. Supra, pp. 347-8, 474, 524.

198. Straus 1950, pp. 11-2. Cf. Jewell 1874, p. 14. On the contemporary scene, structural change in the shipping industry has, while bringing undoubted advantages from a technical and economical viewpoint, increased such dehumanizing factors as social isolation and vocational stress. (Uittenbosch 1969, pp. 10-3. Sherar 1973, passim. Sorenson 1979, pp. 42-6.) The International Christian Maritime Association has, since its foundation in 1969, devoted much of its attention to the continuing exploitation of crews, largely from Third World countries, on ships under "open registry" (flags of convenience). See CC Christmas 1975, p. 11; Vincent 1976, pp. 14-26; (MS) Uittenbosch 1977, p. 10; 1979, p. 47; Chapman 1981, passim; (MS) 1981, Appendix A; (MS) 1983 passim; *ICMA News,* Summer 1981, pp. 299-30; (MS) ICMA *Standing Committee Report* 1981, pp. 5-6; ICMA 1982, pp. 17-8, 25-8; ICMA 1985, passim.

199. Supra, pp. 540-2.

200. PHS *AR* 1836, p. 7.

201. Riddle 1915, p. 33. Cf. BFSS *AR* 1841, p. 57.

202. Supra, pp. 204, 326, 332, 371.

203. For examples of summarized maritime methodologies of mission, see: SML 1822, p. 247. Truair 1826, pp. 16-25. SMR 1828, pp. 63-5. Cogswell 1833, pp. 194-7. BFSS *AR* 1841, p. 57. (MS) BFSS *Minutes,* July 13, 1849. Cf. Gollock 1930, pp. 51-2. Cf. supra, pp. 206, 268, 336-9, 418-9, 457-9. Infra, p. 636.

204. Supra, pp. 12, 45-6, 71, 99-103, 135-50, 407-17.

205. NMBS *AR* 1826, p. 11. BFSS *AR* 1837, p. 11. Calcutta Seamen's Friend Society *AR* 1842, p. 36.

206. SML 1821, pp. 425-6.

207. EM 1798, pp. 467-8; 1817, pp. 208-10. MBSNY *Constitution* 1817, p. 7. SML 1820, pp. 355-6; 1821, p. 293. Henshaw 1826, pp. 16-8. Morrison 1839, pp. 297-8. Supra, pp. 81, 135-50, 305-7, 412-7.

208. G.C. Smith *Bethel* 1819, p. 17. SML 1820, pp. 53-4, 259; 1821, p. 308; 1822, p. 266; 1823, pp. 490-1. RTS *Proceedings* 1820, pp. 68-9. Truair 1826, p. 17. SMNY 1834-35, p. 11. Supra, pp. 99-103, 165-7, 307, 409-11.

209. SML 1822, pp. 245-6; 1823, p. 65. For a modern example, see Dresselhuis 1978. Supra, pp. 12-4, 101-2, 308-12, 488.

210. NYPS *AR* 1900, pp. 16, 21. Cf. SMNY 1876, p. 211. Kverndal 1971, p. 82. (MS) Eckhoff 1979. *Watermarks* 1979, no. 3, pp. 8, 13. *Flying Angel News* 1980 no. 3, p. 8. Supra, pp. 122-30, 332. Infra, p. 581.

211. SML 1820, pp. iii-iv; 1824, p. 190. MMNY 1825-26, p. 300. SMNY 1829-30, p. 122. NSM 1830, p. 68. CC 1879, pp. iii-3. Supra, pp. 308, 427.

212. ASFS *Ship's Libraries* 1880, passim. Supra, pp. 315-6, 521-2.

213. PLS *Proceedings* 1821, pp. 31-2. Cf. CHSM 1824, pp. 441-2.

214. NSM 1830, p. 270.

215. CHSM 1824, pp. 442-3. Cf. supra, pp. 192, 422, 568.

216. SMNY 1834-35, pp. 8-9.

217. Marks 1821, pp. 49-51; 1823, pp. 18-20. Cf. SML 1821, p. 502; 1823, p. 332; 1824, p. 479; 1825, pp. 314-20. Cf. Fenton 1966, p. 479.

218. Smith 1961, pp. 90-1, 142-58. Cf. The Marine Society *Bye-laws* 1809, pp. 110-1. Laffin 1969, pp. 118-9. Supra, pp. 62-3, 97-8.

219. Marks 1823, pp. 18-21. Cf. G.C. Smith *The Boatswain's Mate* n.d. Pt. 6, p. 7. NSM 1859, p. 437.

220. Supra, pp. 151-73, 342, 513-6.

221. Montagu 1832, pp. 55-6. SMNY 1832-33, p. 50; 1834-35, pp. 4-5. Cf. supra, pp. 551-3.

222. E.g., Landers 1815, passim. Philip 1823, p. 103. NSM 1833, p. 360. Raffles 1837, passim.

223. Landers 1815, pp. 21-2. CHSM 1822-23, p. 57. Marks 1823, pp. 8-15. SML 1825, p. 180. Cf. Smith 1961, pp. 151, 154. Supra, pp. 60, 340-6.

224. E.g., Ames 1832, pp. 40-8. Cf. SML 1821, p. 180; 1822, p. 483.

225. SML 1821, p. 424. CHSM 1824, p. 441. See also Marks 1818, pp. 182-7. SML 1821, p. 333. NSM 1855, p. 456.

226. SML 1820, pp. 99, 128-9, 476; 1821, pp. 274-5; 1826, p. 461. Philip 1823, pp. 179-86. NSM 1828, pp. 78-80; 1830, pp. 497-507. Green 1828, p. 139.

227. E.g.: Marks 1823, pp. 17-8. Philip 1823, pp. 1-6, 75-88. SML 1820, pp. 400-1. Cf. Stott 1975, pp. 69-70, on the place of *elenctics* in world mission. Supra, pp. 4, 540-2.

228. Seamen's magazines and devotionals are replete with examples (e.g., SML 1820, pp. 47-9, 196-9, 202-7, 287-92, 332-3). For a remarkable, modern-day *systematization* of sea-related Bible-texts, see Wristers 1978. Cf. Kverndal 1971, pp. 129-31.

229. SML 1822, p. 246. CHSM 1824, pp. 443-4. NSM 1833, p. 218. Smith 1961, pp. 134, 150. Jackman 1964, p. 117. Eastburn would say, somewhat facetiously, "Jack is acquainted with one *ism,* that is, the rheumatism" (SMNY 1834-35, pp. 6-7). However, he would be the last to insinuate that seamen were simpletons. (Cf. SML 1820, p. 323; 1822, pp. 417-8. SMNY 1834-35, p. 5.)

230. SMNY 1832-33, p. 49; 1834-35, p. 9; 1840-41, p. 98; 1856-57, pp. 325-6. Cf. *The Christian Guardian* 1826, pp. 173-4. NSM 1828, p. 69.

231. Ibid. Fortunately, a misapplication, too, could occasionally be "improved" (e.g., MMNY 1825-26, pp. 318-9). Scriptural examples of nautical imagery: Micah 7:19, Matthew 4:19, 1 Timothy 1:18-19, Hebrews 6:17-20, James 3:4, 1 Peter 3:18-21.

232. Landers 1815, p. 21. G.C. Smith *The Boatswain's Mate* n.d., passim. SML 1862, pp. 235-6. Haven 1871, pp. 168-83. Cf. Marks 1818, *Preface*. SML 1820, p. 471. SAS *AR* 1839, p. 21. Matthews 1911, pp. 73-5. Healey 1936, pp. 133-4. Kingsford 1957, p. 10. Supra, pp. 494-6.

233. SML 1820, pp. 355, 472. NSM 1829 Pt. II, pp. 529-30. Cf. Dana 1929, p. 62. Smith 1961, pp. 138-9, 190.

234. CHSM 1824, pp. 441-2. SMNY 1832-33, p. 49. Fenton 1966, p. 479. Cf. 2 Corinthians 5:20. Ephesians 5:14.

235. SML 1821, pp. 179-80; 1822, pp. 248-9, 307. CHSM 1822-23, pp. 476-7; 1824, pp. 443-4. SMNY 1832-33, p. 49; 1834-35, pp. 6-9. Colton 1851, pp. 81-3. Cf. Matthew 9:37. John 4:35. An additional reason for forcefulness in presenting the message was the strong streak of *fatalism* in the seaman's religiosity (Williamson 1848, pp. 72-3). Supra, p. 63.

236. CHSM 1824, pp. 445-6. See also G.C. Smith *The Log-Book* n.d. Pt. I, pp. 20-1. CC 1879, p. 32. Cf. 2 Timothy 4:2.

237. CHSM 1824, p. 186.

238. None were more outspoken in this regard than G.C. Smith. (E.g.: SML 1820, p. 78; 1822, p. 246; 1824, p. 403. NSM 1855, pp. 195-6.) Cf. NSM 1860, p. 163. WW 1860, pp. 41, 45. Esping 1870, pp. 168-78. Supra, pp. 170-1, 208-17.

239. Uittenbosch 1969, p. 1; (MS) 1971, pp. 2, 4-13. Cf. Kverndal 1970, pp. 43-4.

240. SML 1821, p. 178; 1825, p. 428. MSABS *AR* 1826, p. 24.

241. Periodicals and reports from the early decades of the work constantly quote cases of maritime conversational evangelism. (E.g.: SML 1823, pp. 18, 220-4; 1824, pp. 96-7, 138, 340-7. NSM 1828, pp. 327-9; 1860, p. 133. SMNY 1842-43, p. 63. Marks 1843, p. 152. WW 1861, pp. 207-19. Matthews 1911, pp. 84, 113-4.) The classical example is that of G.C. Smith *The Boatswain's Mate* n.d. This form of dialogue is certainly a far cry from the non-directive, "presence"-oriented, anthropocentric counseling model against which the Lausanne Covenant argues (Stott 1975, pp. 58-60, 73, 80-1). Supra, pp. 109-10.

242. E.g.: Landers 1815, p. 7. Woodward 1723, p. 37. Hawker 1980 Pt. II, pp. 141-2. SML 1820, pp. 102, 183. NSM 1845, pp. 121-4. WW 1861, pp. 209-10. G.C. Smith *The Boatswain's Mate* n.d., passim. Supra, pp. 425, 531.

243. CHSM 1823, pp. 160, 186.

244. Supra, pp. 9-111, 151-67, 197-220.

245. SML 1820, p. 56. Cf. Lazareth 1965, pp. 1964-6. Warren 1967, p. 95. Neill 1970, p. 110. McGavran 1970, pp. 200, 286-7. Massey 1975, pp. 56-7. Down 1979, p. 29. *Watermarks* 1980, no. 2, p. 11. It is interesting to note how "modern" William Carey was in his understanding of the principles of "Church Growth," advocating the training at the earliest possible moment of

an indigenous ministry (Yamamori 1975, p. 28, cf. pp. 167-9). Cf. Verkuyl 1978, pp. 189-92. Supra, pp. 565-7.

246. *Flying Angel News* Sept./Oct. 1976 (quoting John Poole-Hughes, Bishop of Landaff). Cf. Riddle 1915, p. 33. Scherer 1964, p. 86. Neill 1970, pp. 472-3.

247. SML 1820, pp. 163-4. Jones 1884, p. 36. Beaver 1964, p. 6. Supra, p. 553.

248. Supra, p. 208. Cf. SML 1842, p. 252.

249. E.g., Matthews 1911, pp. 17-26. ICMA *Report* 1972, p. 5. Spong 1973, p. 25.

250. E.g., SML 1820, pp. 15, 323-6. Marks 1821, pp. 111-3. (MS) BFSFSBU *Minutes*, May 1, 1826. Harris 1837, pp. 122-5.

251. SML 1821, pp. 178-9; 1822, p. 248; 1825, pp. 122, 279. NSM 1830, p. 442. WW 1860, p. 279. Cf. Weibust 1969, p. 162.

252. Andersen 1961, p. 312. Bonhoeffer 1976, pp. 17-9.

253. (MS) Bloomquist 1985, pp. 175-205. Supra, pp. 190-3.

254. Supra, p. 456.

255. Supra, p. 368.

256. CC 1886, pp. 115-8; 1900 Title Page of January Number.

257. ASFS *The Acts* 1909, pp. 107-10. Matthews 1911, pp. xv, 537. Prior to 1908, there were precursors in America, too, bearing such names as the "Windward Society" (ASFS *AR* 1832, p. 19), the "Floating Society of Christian Endeavor" (SMNY 1891, pp. 13-6), the "Hold Fast Brotherhood" (*The Sea Breeze*, July 1961, p. 7). Cf. supra, p. 552.

258. G.C. Smith, who himself zealously promoted shipboard Christian fellowship groups, underscored their "more than ordinary obligation" to counteract suspicions of disloyalty or hypocrisy by scrupulous diligence and friendliness in relation to superiors and peers, respectively (SML 1820, p. 15). Strong denominationalists would show understandably little interest in *nondenominational* associations; but they might well withold support for *denominational* fellowships, too, pointing to the "peril" of small groups creating divisiveness, and becoming "ecclesiolae in ecclesia." (*Sjömansvännen* 1896, p. 180; 1910, pp. 188-90. Norwegian 1903. Bullock 1963, passim. Cf. Verkuyl 1978, p. 192.) It could also be a very real temptation for members to think they "had a certain pull over other seamen with Chaplains" ([MS] Kerfoot 1964, p. 3).

259. The involvement of the British (and Foreign) Sailor's Society was, from 1917, centered in the "International Sailors' Brotherhood" (CC 1918, p. 95; Autumn 1955, p. 2); this was, from 1955, reorganized as the "Seafarers' Christian Fellowship" (CC Christmas 1955, p. 16). Meanwhile, concurrently with the founding of the nondenominational "Seamen's Christian Brotherhood" in 1908, an Anglican counterpart called the "Seamen's Guild" was launched by the Church of England Men's Society, in collaboration with the Missions to Seamen; this was eventually succeeded by the "Flying Angel Fellowship." ([MS] Kerfoot 1964, pp. 1-5. *Flying Angel News* Sept./Oct. 1973, pp. 4-5.) In 1968, the Seafarers' Christian Fellowship and the Flying Angel Fellowship were merged into one, multi-denominational organization, "The Seafarers' Fellowship." (MMS *AR* 1968, p. 6. CC Summer 1973, p. 10.) There also exists a strongly evangelical, British-based "Merchant Navy Christian Fellowship," inaugurated in 1959, and reinforced by a 1962 merger with the "Merchant Navy Christian Officers' Association" of 1907. (Merchant Navy Christian Fellowship *Report* 1959. [MS] Christian Witness to Seafarers

1962.) For several years, the International YMCA sponsored a "Seamen's Christian Association," with affiliates in Scandinavia. (*Havnen* 1895, pp. 65-71, 135-9. Sjömaends Kristelige Forening *To-aarsberetning* 1899, passim. Webster 1932, pp. 129-30.) Independent Scandinavian Christian seamen's associations were organized from the year 1884, and are still active. See histories in Johansen 1949, Ljungberg 1959, Helle 1960, 1985. For a notable example of a modern-day Scandinavian Bethel Captain, see Kverndal (Stavanger) 1970, pp. 164-70.

260. McDonough 1972, pp. 58-9. (MS) *East Asian Regional Conference* 1972, pp. 7-9. Spong 1973, pp. 22-5. Kverndal 1973, pp. 34-5; (MS) 1985, pp. 5-7. Down 1979, p. 29. (MS) Eckhoff 1979; (MS) 1981, Appendix B. ICMA 1982, pp. 19, 28-9. See also Part VIII, Note No. 210.

261. Cf. Beaver 1970, p. 285.

262. SML 1820, p. 396; 1821, p. 487; 1825, passim. SMR 1827, p. 296. NSM 1828, pp. 272-3. G.C. Smith *English Sailors* n.d., p. 27. A mother's prayers for her seafaring son would always be highly valued (e.g., SML 1852, p. 29). For want of biblical justification, however, Protestant seamen and seamen's friends did not, as a rule, practice prayer for the dead (cf. Warburg 1884, pp. 146-52). Supra, pp. 107-11, 152-67.

263. NSM 1833, pp. 497-8; 1844, p. 10.

264. SMNY 1831-32, pp. 290, 317; 1845-46, p. 156. General Association of Massachusetts *Minutes* 1832, p. 7. BSFS *AR* 1838, p. 7. Cf. NSM 1833, p. 332. SML 1840, pp. 61, 377-8. (MS) BFSS *Minutes*, July 26, 1853. Kverndal (Bellevue) 1979, pp. 4-5.

265. SML 1820, pp. 332, 335, 448; 1821, pp. 98, 148 9, 160, 396; 1825, pp. 315-6, 414; 1826, pp. 54, 59-60. PLS *Proceedings* 1821, pp. 5-6, 44, 48. SMR 1823, p. 18; 1827, p. 47. EM 1824, p. 267. Henshaw 1826, pp. 19-20. Landsmen would, however, frequently participate enthusiastically as members of mariners' churches. Supra, pp. 437, 472, 497, 506. Cf. Kverndal (Bergen) 1978, p. 129.

266. SML 1820, pp. 168, 218, 319, 435-6; 1821, pp. 99, 160, 379; 1822, pp. 327-8; 1823, pp. 296, 316-7, 448; 1824, p. 236, 357; 1825, pp. 183-5; 1826, pp. 1-2. SMR 1821, p. 48; 1830, pp. 298, 380. Cf. Highmore 1822, pp. 55-56, 61-2. SMNY 1865-6, pp. 198-9. Supra, pp. 175-6, 198, 505.

267. Supra, pp. 165 172. Continental seamen's missions have, in their physical facilities, pursued a "home-from-home" rather than "institutional" concept, with greater success than others. Cf. Gulbrandsen 1941, pp. 51-3. *Evangelisches Kirchenlexikon* Vol. 3 1962, c. 915. Kverndal (Bergen) 1978, p. 130.

268. The Rev. T.C. Childs spoke of a literally "moveable church" (NSM 1860, pp. 13-5). Cf. *Port Exchange* No. 2, 1971, p. 11. Article: "Shipping Changes Demand Highly Mobile Mission" in *Flying Angel News* No. 3, 1977. Supra, pp. 385-91.

269. *The Christian Guardian* 1827, p. 141. SMNY 1832-33, pp. 48-50. (MS) BFSS *Minutes*, January 17, 1854. PECMSS *AR* 1857, p. 20. WW 1861, pp. 230-1. NSM 1856, p. 410. Matthews 1911, pp. vii-viii.

270. SML 1823, p. 85. Howse 1960, p. 113. Cf. Kerfoot 1973, pp. 26-32. Supra, pp. 32, 34, 43.

271. Supra, pp. 550-1.

272. Supra, pp. 272-9.

273. SML 1825, p. 184. SMNY 1834-35, p. 11. *Evangelisk Ugeskrift* 1858, No. 1-2, p. 29. Supra, pp. 230, 497.

274. Supra, pp. 378, 525-6.

275. Supra, pp. 317-21, 419, 520-1. In addition to its popular Merchant Marine School, the Seamen's Church Institute of NY & NJ has, since 1973, offered innovative evening courses for *shore-based* maritime personnel, too (SCI of NY & NJ 1981, p. 7).

276. Kverndal 1971, p. 83; (Bergen) 1978, pp. 130-1. Hough 1972, pp. 6, 41-4. (MS) ICMA *International Labour Conference 62nd (Maritime) Session — Geneva 1976,* 1976, pp. 5-6. *ICOSA Newsletter* Summer 1977, pp. 13-4.

277. Goodsell 1959, p. 82. Cf. Boyd 1970, pp. 182-3.

278. Myklebust 1970, p. 301; 1976, p. 23. Stott 1975, pp. 22-36. Supra, pp. 555-7.

279. SAS *AR* 1839, pp. 17-8.

280. *Encyclopædia Britannica* Vol. 15 1964, p. 599. Stott 1975, p. 40.

281. Cf. International Social Christian Institute 1930, pp. 6-8. Cf. Jackman 1964, p. 117.

282. Supra, pp. 19-22, 46-50.

283. Supra, pp. 327-40, 378-80, 511-3.

284. If seamen were to turn from "frolic" to listen to the "sacred truths" of the Christian religion, the "commonest provision for their comfort and convenience" could not be ignored. Devotion and recreation, "the altar and the fireside," belonged together in seamen's mission (New Bedford Port Society *AR* 1867, pp. 7-8).

285. Supra, pp.'57, 557. Cf. Hope, 1969 & 1974, passim.

286. Supra, pp. 303-4, 321-4, 519-21. Cf. Frayne 1973, pp. 7-16.

287. Supra, pp. 322-7, 334-9, 516-23.

288. Supra, pp. 19-22, 46-50, 168-9, 327-50, 355, 510-28. Cf. Elliott-Binns 1964, p. 26. Stott 1975, pp. 28-34. Chapman 1981; (MS) 1981; (MS) 1983. Windley 1982. (MS) Whittemore 1985.

289. Cf. supra, pp. 346-50, 524. In the early years of maritime trade unionism, tensions developed which led some to believe that, between unions and voluntary seamen's mission societies, there existed an "institutional incompatibility." This early union movement saw voluntary agencies for seamen's welfare as "charity" and "paternalism," essentially hostile to a fighting spirit of independence and self-help in the seafarer himself, and a "delaying influence" in the evolution of shoreside facilities run by (not only for) the seafarer. (Healey 1936, pp. 131-5. Hohman 1952, pp. 291-7. Cf. Dillon 1961, p. 65.)

290. SMNY 1843-44, p. 247.

291. *The Church and the Sailor* 1935, p. 117. Straus 1950, p. 127. Jackson 1964, p. 118. Cf. supra, p. 54, 571.

292. Supra, pp. 339, 346-50, 524-8. For an overview of American Seamen's Mission facilities and certain physical statistics, see Appendix No. 8, pp. 640-1.

293. E.g., (MS) PLS *Minutes,* June 24, 1823. Truair 1826, pp. 27-9.

294. PLS *Proceedings* 1821, pp. 42-3. SML 1821, p. 316. Warren 1858, pp. 43-4.

295. NMBS *Report* 1818, p. 13. SML 1820, p. 52; 1821, pp. 443-44; 1823, pp. 155-6; 1824, p. 496; 1825, p. 317; 1827, pp. 148-9. PLS *Proceedings* 1821, p. 25. Highmore 1822, pp. 58-9. EM 1824, p. 267; 1826, p. 346. SMR 1827, pp. 298-9. SMNY 1833-34, p. 192; 1878, pp. 207-8. ASFS *AR* 1842, p. 13; 1845, p. 7. Marks 1843, pp. 245-6. The stereotype statement that the seafarers of the day were "more interested in booze and women than in tracts and salvation" does justice neither to seafarers nor to those ministering to them (Dillon 1961, p. 12; see also pp. 65, 224-46).

296. SML 1820, pp. 5, 1823, p. 493. CHSM 1822-23, p. 159. MMNY 1825-26, p. 271. PECMSS *AR* 1847, p. 11. WW 1860, p. 194. Cf. NMBS *Report* 1832, pp. 28-9. Supra, pp. 144-6, 215, 430, 504, 553.

297. MMNY 1825-26, pp. 144, 270-1. Truair 1826, p. 5. Henshaw 1826, p. 26. Charleston Port Society *AR* 1826, p. 13. NSM 1828 p. 194. BSFS *AR* 1884, p. 6. Cf. SML 1820, p. 144.

298. Luke 10:42. Warren 1858, pp. 43-4. BSFS *AR* 1884, p. 8. Seymour 1976, pp. 55-6. Davis 1979, pp. 56-7, does scant justice to the presuppositions and purposes of the pioneers; it seems especially questionable to criticize those pioneers for not becoming what they never intended to be—simply a social reform front.

299. Marks 1821, pp. 116-7. *The Encyclopedia of Missions* 1904, p. 512. ASFS *The Acts* 1909, p. 104. Stott 1975, pp. 38-41. Cf. (MS) Sorenson 1978, passim.

300. Quotation from remarks by a seafarer during the Author's waterfront ministry.

301. Cf. Warren 1858, p. 44. Wesleyan Seamen's Mission *AR* 1859, pp. 4-5.

302. Matthew 16:26. SMNY 1898, pp. 363-6; 1907, pp. 83-4. ASFS *The Acts* 1909, pp. 99-104. Uittenbosch 1969, pp. 13-23. Stott 1975, pp. 19-20, 35-7. Cf. Wright 1971, p. 85. *ICMA News* 1979 no. 4, p. 27. ICMA 1982, pp. 21-3. Supra, p. 555-7.

303. Uittenbosch 1969, pp. 10, 21-5. ILO 1971 passim. USS (1972), pp. 2-4. ICMA *Report* 1972, pp. 3-6, 47. Sherar 1973, pp. 58-61, 66-7. Cf. Kverndal (Bergen) 1978, pp. 129-30. On Jan. 17, 1986, representatives of the International Christian Maritime Association and the International Transport Workers' Federation agreed to form an "ICMA/ITF Liaison Committee," in order to "promote all aspects of seafarers' welfare and to combat abusive practices in the shipping industry." The event is a natural outcome of the wide communality of concern between international maritime ministry and international trade unionism, and represents an historic new departure as the first instance of formalized cooperation between these two. (*ICMA Bulletin,* No. 11, Feb. 1986.)

304. SML 1826, p. 142. Cf. Beaver 1964, pp. 6-7. Aardal 1973, pp. 17-21.

305. (MS) *East Asian Regional Conference* 1972. Frayne 1978, pp. 40-6. *Watermarks* 1980, No. 2, passim. Kverndal 1983, p. 3; 1985, pp. 8-11; (MS) 1985, passim. Dillenburg 1985, passim. Adeney 1985, pp. 73-85. Krug 1985, passim.

306. Supra, p. 551-3.

307. See especially supra, pp. 553, 579-81.

308. Hebrews 12:2, 13:8. Warren 1858, pp. 46-7. (MS) Kverndal 1985, passim.
309. Potter 1848, p. 22. Trumble 1967, p. 1. Kverndal 1969, p. 14. Warren 1970, pp. 449-50. Webster 1970, p. 411. Bloch-Hoell 1975, p. 137. Myklebust 1976, p. 55. *Watermarks* 1980, No. 4, p. 7. Cf. ASFS *AR* 1853, p. 13. NSM 1856, p. 263.
310. *Watermarks* 1980, no. 2, p. 14.

ADDENDUM — NOTES

1. Much of the contents of this addendum forms part of an English-language article by the Author included as pp. 103-34 in the 1977 *Norwegian Yearbook of Maritime History,* published in 1978 by the Maritime Museum of Bergen, Norway. The article, entitled "The Origin and Nature of Nordic Missions to Seamen," has subsequently been distributed as an offprint by the International Christian Maritime Association, with funding from the four Nordic Seamen's Missions.
2. Supra, pp. 5-14. For a highly commended study and bibliography on Norse maritime heritage, see Eriksen 1968, passim.
3. Kverndal (Bergen) 1978, pp. 106-7. See also, concerning "Sint Olofs Kerk," supra, p. 15.
4. BFBS, NMBS, RTS, and SPCK *Reports* for these years contain copious evidence of this activity. See also Cadbury 1926, pp. 60 ff.; 1941, pp. 14 ff.
5. (MS) Paterson 1858, Vol. 2, p. 5. Supra, pp. 167, 595.
6. Quoted from SML 1823, p. 468. See *Reports* of societies mentioned in Note 4 above for examples of activities of "Agents Afloat" in Nordic waters. Supra, p. 136-8, 242-3.
7. Supra, pp. 148-9.
8. Supra, p. 101-2, 310-2.
9. It is not generally known that both in Gothenburg and Stockholm a local mutual "Sjömannasällskap" (Marine Society) adopted the Bethel Flag tradition in modified form as early as 1838. (Primary source materials in archives of the Maritime Museums of Gothenburg and Stockholm, also the Royal Library, Stockholm.) A pioneer advocate of the Swedish version of the Bethel Movement was that colorful naval officer Adolph Göran Oxehufwud (1799-1852), who did much to acquaint Scandinavians with the British Bethel Movement, and British seamen's mission activity in general, by translating John Harris' prize-winning essay: *Britannia: or, the Moral Claims of Seamen Stated and Enforced,* London, 1837. (Swedish version: *Britannia, eller Sjömäns Moraliska Anspraak, framställde af Rev. John Harris . . . ,* Stockholm, 1837.) Cf. Helle 1960, passim. Supra, pp. 162, 242-3, 366, 581.
10. Supra, pp. 260-3.
11. Supra, pp. 477-8.
12. Kverndal 1977, pp. 211-33. Supra, pp. 490-2.
13. Supra, pp. 374-5.
14. BFSS *Minutes* and *Annual Reports,* as well as SML, for the years 1860-63, contain numerous references to Thiemann's Scandinavian ministry. See also *Folkevennen* 1861, pp. 101-19, 369-77. Likewise, *Norsk Kirketidende,* 1861-62, passim. Cf. Aarflot 1965, pp. 116-21.

15. *Norsk Kirketidende* 1861, cc. 812-14; 1862, cc. 94-6, 780; 1863, cc. 190-1. See also SML 1862, pp. 15-6.

16. It was conceded that well might visiting emissaries stir the slumbering; but they must refer such "awakened souls" to the teaching and pastoral care of the State Church. *Norsk Kirketidende* 1862, cc. 284-5.

17. Cf. Molland 1961, p. 231.

18. The German-born Thames Missionary found in Storjohann one who was himself of German extract (on his father's side), and who was just then serving part-time at the German-language St. Mary's Church in Bergen. Their 1861 meeting is included in Waltari 1925, p. 77, quoting from a paper by Storjohann at a Nordic Seamen's Chaplains' Conference in Copenhagen, 1896.

19. For biographical sketches of Storjohann, see *Menneskevennen* 1881, pp. 205-9; *Stille Stunder* 1914, pp. 73-4; Schartum 1932, pp. 11-74; Molland 1966, pp. 50-5; 1979, passim; Tronsen 1974, pp. 4-6. See also obituary in *Morgenbladet*, April 24, 1914. For a Norwegian-language study of Storjohann's contribution to a "Maritime Pastoral Theology," see (MS) Kverndal, *Storjohann*, 1984.

20. The traditional version has it that Storjohann first sensed the call to initiate a ministry to seafarers through the instrumentality of this conscience-stricken mariner. As already seen, it would be more correct to designate this an affirmation of the call originally transmitted through Thiemann.

21. The major source for this and the following paragraphs on the further development of Norwegian maritime ministry is volumes of *Bud og Hilsen,* from 1865, as supplemented by the archives of the Norwegian Seamen's Mission in Bergen, Norway. See also (MS) Daasvand 1982, and (MS) Brekne 1983, passim.

22. Scottish ministers were conspicuous for their helpfulness (as in the case of the Rev. John Thomson, who provided hospitality in the Mariners' Church, Leith, and the Rev. Alexander Campbell, who had begun a ministry to Scandinavian seamen in Montrose and vicinity even before 1864). See, for example, *Bud og Hilsen*, January 1866, pp. 10-11; April 1866, p. 14. Cf. Macfarlane 1864, pp. 24-7.

23. *Bud og Hilsen*, September 1867, pp. 15-9. *Luthersk Kirketidende* 1867, pp. 265-7.

24. The Norwegian Seafarers' Fellowship ("Den norske Broderkrets paa Havet") was founded in 1885; the Danish ("Den danske Broderkreds paa Havet") in 1889; and the Swedish ("Svenska Betelföreningen") in 1884. See histories: Helle 1960 and 1985; Johansen 1948; and Ljungberg 1959, respectively.

25. *Almindelig Kirketidende* 1865, pp. 69-76; 1867, pp. 145-50. *Kirkeligt Maanedsblad* 1867, pp. 261-8. *Bud og Hilsen*, September 1867, pp. 28-9. The Society's own magazine *Havnen* (from 1871), and Henningsen 1967, provide the continuing narrative of Danish ministry to seafarers overseas.

26. Larsen 1945, pp. 7-9. Weltzer 1952, pp. 23-4. *Redningsbaaden* Oct. 1974, pp. 3-5; Dec. 1981, pp. 4-5.

27. Lundborg evidently had much in common with Storjohann, including strong stimuli from theological research in Scotland. Sources relevant to this and the following two paragraphs: (MS) Evangeliska Fosterlands-Stiftelsen 1856. *Missions-Tidning*, especially 1869, pp. 75-6; 1894, pp. 161-3. Renström 1926. Hofgren 1969. *Ute och Hemma*, No. 6-7, 1969. Bergmark 1974. Re.

Swedish-origin maritime ministry in New York, see (MS) Foelsch 1973 and Sahlberg 1974.

28. Ekman 1895, pp. 570-8. Engvall 1914, passim. Smidt 1927, pp. 105-6. Lindskog 1929, passim. Cedarleaf 1980. Helle 1985, pp. 11-13. The Scandinavian Seamen's Mission in San Francisco, a combined ministry of Nordic and American Baptist churches, is an example of continuing modern-day Nordic free-church concern for mission to seafarers.

29. The gradual "emancipation" of the Church of Sweden's ministry to seafarers from the Mission Board of the National Church is dealt with in depth in Bergmark 1974.

30. Basic sources relative to the evolution of the Finnish Seamen's Mission are: (MS) Finska Sjömansmissionssällskapet *Minutes,* from 1875. *Sjömansvännen* (from 1882). *Missions-Tidning för Finland,* 1870-75 (see especially 1870, pp. 73-8). Waltari 1925. Hytönen 1950.

31. *Havnen,* Nov.-Dec. 1980, pp. 93-5.

32. See, for example, Brun 1879, pp. 1-2.

33. Kverndal (Bergen) 1978, p. 129; 1983, p. 24; 1984-85, passim; 1985, pp. 8-11. (MS) Ekvik 1983, pp. 1-13. Krug 1983, pp. 1-3. Re. the status of Norwegian resident communities abroad, see Stöylen 1958; Kverndal 1968; (MS) Bondevik 1974; (MS) Brekne 1983. On the initiative of LAMM, the Lutheran World Federation, at its 7th World Assembly in Budapest 1984, expressly included, for the first time since its founding in 1947, seafarers of the world as an outreach responsibility of the LWF (*Lutheran Maritime News,* No. 2, 1984; No. 3, 1985. See also Kverndal 1985).

Bibliography

A. Published Materials

Aardal, Johannes.
"Ethnic and Religious Groups," *Report of First Plenary Conference, London ... 1972.* ICMA, London [1973], pp. 17-21.

Aarflot, Andreas.
"Til belysning av Den norske Sjömannsmisjons forhistorie" (Toward a Clarification of the Prior History of the Norwegian Seamen's Mission), *Luthersk Kirketidende* (Oslo), 1965, pp. 114-21.
Norsk Kirkehistorie (Norwegian Church History), Vol. 2. Oslo, 1967.

Abbot, Abiel.
The Mariner's Manual. Salem (Massachusetts), 1804.
Sermons to Mariners. Boston (Massachusetts), 1812.

Abeel, David.
Journal of a Residence in China, and the Neighboring Countries, from 1829 to 1833. New York, 1834.

Adeney, Miriam.
"Those to Whom We Minister," *Proceedings,* James E. Dillenburg, 1985, pp. 73-85.

Advocate and Friend. Honolulu.

Ahlstrom, Sydney E.
A Religious History of the American People. 2 Vols. New York, 1975.

Aiken, John, Thomas Morgan, and William Johnston.
General Biography. Vols. 4 & 5. London, 1803 & 1804.

Albion, Robert G.
Square-Riggers on Schedule. Princeton (New Jersey), 1938.

Allen, Garner.
Our Navy and the Barbary Corsairs. Boston (Massachusetts), 1905.

Allen, Roland.
The Spontaneous Expansion of the Church. Grand Rapids (Michigan), 1962.

Allen, W.O.B., and Edmund McClure.
Two Hundred Years: The History of the Society for Promoting Christian Knowledge, 1698-1898. London, 1898.

Allison, K.J. (Ed.)
A History of the County of York East Riding. Vol. 1. London, 1969.

Almindelig Kirketidende. Aarhus (Denmark).

American Baptist Mariners' Society.
Its Origin: First Annual Meeting. New York, 1857.

American Bethel Society.
Annual Reports. Buffalo (New York).

American Bible Society.
Annual Reports. New York.

American Board of Commissioners for Foreign Missions.
Annual Reports. Boston (Massachusetts).

The American Missionary Register. New York.

The American Neptune. Salem (Massachusetts).

The American Sailor's Magazine and Bethel Messenger. New York.
Note: Published as Vol. 1 in 12 monthly numbers through 1824, with virtually the same contents as "The Seaman's Magazine" section of *The Christian Herald and Seaman's Magazine* (q.v.).

American Seamen's Friend Society.
Seamen's Hymns and Devotional Assistant. New York, 1843.
Ship's Libraries. New York [1880].
The Acts of the Apostles of the Sea. New York, 1909.
Annual Reports. New York.
American Seamen: A Review. New York.

American Tract Society.
Hymns and Tunes for the Army and Navy. New York, 1863.

[Ames, Nathaniel.]
A Mariner's Sketches. Providence (Rhode Island), 1830.

Ames, Nathaniel.
Nautical Reminiscences. Providence (Rhode Island), 1832.

Andersen, Arlow W.
The Salt of the Earth: A History of Norwegian-Danish Methodism in America. Nashville (Tennessee), 1962.

Andersen, Rasmus.
Den danske Kirke og Episkopalkirken (The Church of Denmark and the Episcopal Church). Brooklyn (New York), 1920.

Andersen, Wilhelm.
Towards a Theology of Mission. London, 1955.
"Further toward a Theology of Mission," *The Theology of the Christian Mission,* Gerald H. Anderson (Ed.), New York, 1961, pp. 300-13.

Anderson, Gerald H. [Ed.].
The Theology of the Christian Mission. New York, 1961.
"Theology of Mission," *Concise Dictionary of the Christian World Mission,* London, 1970, pp. 594-5.

Andrea, Alfred J.
"The Relationship of Sea Travellers and Excommunicated Captains Under Thirteenth Century Canon Law," *The Mariner's Mirror,* 1982, pp. 203-9.

Andrew, John A.
Rebuilding the Christian Commonwealth: New England Congregationalism and Foreign Missions, 1800-1830. Lexington (Kentucky), 1976.

Andrews, Kenneth R.
"The Elizabethan Seaman," *The Mariner's Mirror,* 1982, pp. 245-62.

The Annual Biography and Obituary. London.

Anson, Peter F.
The Church and the Sailor: A Survey of the Sea-Apostolate Past and Present. London, 1948.
Christ and the Sailor: A Study of the Maritime Incidents in the New Testament. London, 1954.
The Call of the Cloister: Religious Communities and Kindred Bodies of the Anglican Communities. London, 1955.
"A.M. History: 50th Anniversary of the Foundation of Apostolatus Maris," *Apostolatus Maris—Information,* No. 38, Rome, 1970, pp. 46-53.

Apostleship of the Sea. *XII International Congress of the Apostleship of the Sea.* Rome, 1951.

Appleton's Cyclopaedia of American Biography. New York, 1888.

Armstrong, Anthony.
The Church of England: The Methodists and Society 1700-1850. Totowa (New Jersey), 1973.

Arner, Oddvar.
Dödsulykker blant sjomenn (Mortality among Seamen). Oslo, 1970.

Aspinall, A.
The Early English Trade Unions. London, 1949.

Atherton, William H.
History of the Harbour Front of Montreal. Montreal, 1935.

Atken, Mary Cage.
Paul Cuffe and the African Promised Land. Nashville (Tennessee), 1977.

Atkinson, John.
The Beginnings of the Wesleyan Movement in America and the Establishment therein of Methodism. New York, 1896.

Aubert, Vilhelm.
Sosiologi. Oslo, 1969.

Aubert, Vilhelm, and Oddvar Arner.
"On the Social Structure of the Ship," *Acta Sociologica* (Oslo), 1959, pp. 200-19.

Axtell, Silas B. (Ed.).
A Symposium on Andrew Furuseth. New Bedford (Massachusetts), n.d.

Backhaus, Arnold.
Sozialhygienische Erhebungen zur Problematik der Freizeit der Zeeleute. D.Med. Dissertation, University of Hamburg, 1968.
"Alcohol: Joy and Danger to Mankind," *Report of Fourth Plenary Conference, Berlin . . . 1981,* ICMA, London [1982], pp. 46-56.

Backlund, Jonas O.
A Pioneer Trio: Fredrik Olaus Nilsson, Gustaf Palmquist, Anders Wiberg. Chicago, 1942.

Balleine, G.R.
A History of the Evangelical Party in the Church of England. London, 1951.

The Baltimore American. Baltimore.

Bangs, Nathan.
   History of the Methodist Episcopal Church. New York, 1853.
   A History of the Methodist Episcopal Church. Vol. 3. New York, 1853
   (3rd ed.).

Bankers' Trust Company.
   America's Merchant Marine. New York, 1920.

The Baptist Magazine. London.

Barclay, Wade C.
   Early American Methodism, 1769-1844. (Vol. 1 of *History of Methodist
   Missions.*) New York, 1949.
   Widening Horizons, 1845-95. (Vol. 3 of ditto.) New York, 1957.

Barnes, Michael.
   "A Short History of the Norwegian Church in London," *Vaar Arv: Streif fra
   norsk kirke-og kulturhistorie i London* (Our Heritage: Glimpses from Norwegian Church and Cultural History in London), Leif Frivold (Ed.), London,
   1967, pp. 179-96.

Barth, Karl.
   "An Exegetical Study of Matthew 28:16-20," *The Theology of the Christian
   Mission,* Gerald H. Anderson (Ed.), New York, 1961, pp. 55-71.

Bartol, Cyrus A.
   "Genius: Father Taylor," *Radical Problems* (Boston), 1872.

Basset, Fletcher S.
   Legends and Superstitions of the Sea and of Sailors. Chicago, 1885.

Bateson, Charles.
   The Convict Ships 1787-1868. Glasgow, 1969. (1st ed. 1959.)

Bavinck, John H.
   An Introduction to the Science of Missions. Philadelphia, 1960.

Baynham, Henry.
   "Social Reform in the United States Navy, 1798-1862. By Harold D.
   Langley." (Review), *Mariner's Mirror* (London), 1968, pp. 320-2.
   From the Lower Deck: The Old Navy, 1780-1840. London, 1969.

Beaver, R. Pierce.
   From Missions to Mission. New York, 1964.
   "Missionary Motivation through three Centuries," *Reinterpretation in Ameri-
   can Church History,* J.C. Brauer (Ed.). Chicago, 1968, pp. 113-51.
   "The Anti-missionary Movement," *Concise Dictionary of the Christian World
   Mission,* London 1970, p. 26.

Béchervaise, John.
   A Farewell to My Old Shipmates and Messmates. Portsea, 1847.
   Thirty-six Years of a Seafaring Life, by an Old Quarter Master. Portsea,
   1839.

Beck, Edward Josselyn.
   Memorials to Serve for a History of the Parish of St. Mary, Rotherhithe.
   Cambridge, 1907.

Beck, Horace.
   Folklore and the Sea. Middletown (Connecticut), 1973.

Berg, Johannes van den.
Constrained by Jesus' Love: An Inquiry into the Motives of the Missionary Awakening in Great Britain in the Period between 1698 and 1815. Kampen (Netherlands), 1956.
"Missionary Motives," *Concise Dictionary of the Christian World Mission,* London, 1970, pp. 425-26.

Bergmark, Ingemar.
Kyrka och sjöfolk: En studie i Svenska kyrkans sjömansvaard 1911-1933 (Church and Seamen: A Study of the Church of Sweden's Care for Seamen 1911-1933. With a Summary in English). Uppsala, 1974.

Berrian, William.
The Sailor's Manual of Devotion. New York, 1844.

Besant, Walter.
Great Survey of London (Vol. 3 of *London South of the Thames*). London, 1912.

Bethel Seamen's Friend Society.
Seventh Report. Aberdeen, 1829.

Bethelskib Norske Methodistmenighet.
Bethelskib Kirkens Femti Aars Jubilaeum (Bethelship Church Fiftieth Anniversary). New York, 1924.

Beyerhaus, Peter.
Missions: Which Way? Humanization or Redemption. Grand Rapids (Michigan).

Bibelselskabet i Danmark.
Maanedlige Efterretninger fra Bibelselskabet for Danmark. Copenhagen.
... *Beretning fra Bibelselskabet i Danmark.* Copenhagen.

Bible Society of Philadelphia.
Reports. Philadelphia (Pennsylvania).

Bibliotheca Cornubiensis. 3 Vols. London, 1882.

Biden, Christopher.
Naval Discipline. London, 1830.

Birkeli, Fridtjov.
Politikk og misjon (Politics and Mission). Oslo, 1952.

Blackwood's Edinburgh Magazine. Edinburgh.

Bloch-Hoell, Nils Egede.
The Pentecostal Movement. Oslo, 1964.
"The Impact in Norway of American Religious Dissent," *Contagious Conflict: The Impact of American Dissent on European Life* (A.N.J. den Hollander, Ed.), Leiden, 1973, pp. 214-32.
"Misjonsteologi i en ny tid" (Theology of Mission in a New Age), *Norsk Tidsskrift for Misjon* (Oslo), 1975, pp. 135-145.

Blume, Kenneth J.
"The Hairy Ape Reconsidered," *The American Neptune,* Winter 1984, pp. 33-47.

Boase, Frederic.
Modern English Biography. 2nd imp. London, 1965.

Boase, George Clement.
Collectanea Cornubiensia. N.p., 1904.

Bombay Seamen's Friend Association.
   Address to Seamen Frequenting the Port of Bombay. Bombay, 1831.
   Reports. Bombay, 1838, 1840.

Bonhoeffer, Dietrich.
   Life Together. New York, 1976.

Bonney, S.W.
   The Seamen's Compass and Chart; for Daily Use, Afloat and Ashore.
   Canton (China) [1862].

Boston Port and Seamen's Aid Society.
   Life of Father Taylor, the Sailor Preacher. (Incl. reprint of Gilbert Haven and
   Thomas Russell, *Father Taylor, the Sailor Preacher,* 1871.) Boston, 1904.
   Annual Reports. Boston.

Boston Port Society.
   Annual Reports. Boston.

Boston Seaman's Friend Society.
   Address of the Directors to the Christian Public. Boston, 1828.
   Annual Reports. Boston.

Boston Society for the Moral and Religious Instruction of the Poor. (From 1841:
   City Missionary Society.)
   Annual Reports. Boston.

The Boston Society for the Religious and Moral Improvement of Seamen.
   *An Address to the Masters of Vessels on the Objects of the Boston Society for
   the Moral and Religious* (sic) *Improvement of Seamen.* Boston, 1812.
   Tracts, published in Boston, 1812-17, listed here with their respective
   repositories, due to the rarity and significance of these sources:
   — *True Friendship, Distinguished from that which Is False, in a Short
      Narrative of Jack Saunders.* No. 1, 1812. (Boston Athenaeum).
   — *A Sailor's Tribute of Gratitude to Two Virtuous Women.* No. 2, 1812.
      (Boston Public Library).
   — *The Adventures of a Bible.* In Three Parts. No. 4, 1813. (American
      Antiquarian Society.)
   — *Handsome Jack, an Example for Sailors.* No. 5, 1813. (Massachusetts
      Historical Society.)
   — *The Duty and Reasonableness of Prayer, Suggested by the Loss of the
      Lady Hobart Packet*... No. 6, 1814. (American Antiquarian Society.)
   — *Address to a Master of a Vessel, Intended to Accompany a Book of
      Prayers. Prepared for the Use of Seamen.* No. 7, 1815. (American
      Antiquarian Society.)
   — *Prayers, Social and Private, to Be Used at Sea.* No. 8, 1815. (Boston
      Athenaeum.)
   — *The Sailor's Life Boat.* No. 9, 1816. (Boston Athenaeum.)
   — *Home, or a Short Account of Charles Grafton.* No. 10, 1816. (Boston
      Athenaeum.)
   — *The Seaman's Friend.* No. 11, 1817. (American Antiquarian Society.)

[Boswell, James.]
   Boswell's Life of Johnson. London, 1953.

Botting, Douglas.
   The Pirates. Alexandria (Virginia), 1978.

Boudreaux, Julianna L.
A History of Philanthropy in New Orleans 1835-1862. New Orleans, 1961.

Boyd, A.J.
"Education as Missionary Method," *Concise Dictionary of the Christian World Mission,* London, 1970, pp. 182-83.

Braaten, Carl E.
"Theology and Welfare," *Lutheran Social Concern* (New York), 1972, Vol. 12, no. 3.

Bradford, Gersham.
"Captain Gamaliel Bradford, Soldier and Privateersman," *Old-Time New England,* Vol. 49, no. 2, n.p., 1958.

Brauer, Jerald C. (Ed.)
The Westminster Dictionary of Church History. Philadelphia, 1971.

Brautewaite, William C.
The Second Period of Quakerism. Cambridge, 1961.

Bready, J. Wesley.
England: Before and after Wesley. London, 1938.

Briggs, J.H.Y.
"The First Industrial Nation," *Eerdman's Handbook to the History of Christianity,* Tim Dowley (Ed.), Grand Rapids (Michigan), 1977, pp. 510-33.

Bristol Channel Seamen's Mission.
Mission to British Seamen on the Coasts of England and Wales, in the Bristol Channel. January 1851, April 1853.

Bristol Marine School Society.
Report of the First Anniversary Meeting. . . . Bristol, 1825.
Proceedings of the Third Anniversary Meeting. . . . Bristol, 1827.

The Bristol Mercury. Bristol.

British and Foreign Bible Society.
Reports of the British and Foreign Bible Society, with Extracts of Correspondence, &c. Vol. 1 (1805-10), 2 (1811-13), 3 (1814 etc.). London.

British and Foreign Sailors' Society.
Our Sailors' Hymn-Book. London, 1881.
Glory of the Sea. One Hundred Years of Service for the Sailor. London, 1918.
Annual Reports. London.
What are Bethel Meetings? What are Bethel Captains? London, n.d. (Bound with BFSS *AR* 1836, in BSS Archives.)
Admiral Lord Gambier and the Bethel Flag. London, n.d. (Bound with BFSS *AR* 1836, in BSS Archives.)

British and Foreign Seamen and Soldiers' Friend Society.
Decision. London, 1829. (Bound with NSM 1829 Pt. II.)
The Managers of the Sailor's Rest. . . . London [1831].

Brockham Enzyklopädie. Wiesbaden, 1973.

Broodbank, J.G.
"The Howland Great Wet Dock," *The Mariner's Mirror* 1912, pp. 53-6.

Brooke, Richard.
Liverpool as It Was during the Last Quarter of the Eighteenth Century, 1775-1800. Liverpool, 1853.

Brooks, Elbridge S.
The American Sailor. Boston, 1899.

Brooks, Van Wyck.
The Flowering of New England 1815-1865. New York, 1940.

Broomhall, Marshall.
Robert Morrison: A Master-builder. London, 1924.

Brown, Andrew.
A Sermon on the Dangers and Duties of the Seafaring Life. Boston, 1793.

Brown, Arthur W.
Always Young for Liberty. Syracuse (New York), 1956.
William Ellery Channing. New York, 1961.

Brown, Colin.
"Reason and Unreason," *Eerdman's Handbook to the History of Christianity,* Tim Dowley (Ed.), Grand Rapids (Michigan), 1977, pp. 479-98.

Brown, Ford K.
Fathers of the Victorians: The Age of Wilberforce. Cambridge, 1961.

Browne, George.
The History of the British and Foreign Bible Society. 2 Vols. London, 1859.

Browning, Colin Arrott.
England's Exiles. . . . London, 1842.
The Convict Ship. . . . London, 1844. (An 1855 New York edition was published from the 4th London ed.)

Brückbauer, Frederick.
The Kirk on Rutgers Farm. N.p., n.d.

Brun, Christen.
Baptismens Historie. Bergen, 1902.

Brun-Gulbrandsen, Sverre, and Olav Irgens-Jensen.
Alkoholmisbruk blant unge norske sjömenn (The Misuse of Alcohol among Young Norwegian Seamen). Oslo, 1964.

Brun, Johan N.
Den norske Sömandsmissions Historie (History of the Norwegian Seamen's Mission). Kristiania (Oslo), 1879.

Bud fra Havet. Gjeving (Norway).
Note: Published by Den norske Broderkrets paa Havet (The Norwegian Christian Brotherhood of the Ocean).

Bud og Hilsen. Bergen (Norway).
Note: Published by the Norwegian Seamen's Mission.

Bullen, Frank T.
With Christ in Sailor Town: What the Seamen's Mission is Doing. London, 1901.
The Way of the Sea. London, 1904.
The Cruise of the Cachalot. Philadelphia, n.d.

Bullock, F.W.B.
Voluntary Religious Societies, 1520-1799. St. Leonards-on-Sea, 1963.

Burder, George.
Sea Sermons. London, n.d. (1st ed. 1821.)

Burr, Nelson R.
A Critical Bibliography of Religion in America. Princeton (New Jersey), 1961.

Burwash, Dorothy.
English Merchant Shipping 1460-1540. Toronto, 1947.

Byström, J.
En frikyrklig banbrytare, eller F.O. Nilssons lif och verksamhet (A Free Church Pioneer, or the Life and Work of F.O. Nilsson). Stockholm, 1910.

Cadbury, Henry J.
"The Norwegian Quakers of 1825," *Studies and Records,* Norwegian-American Historical Association, Minneapolis, Vol. 1, 1926.
"First Norwegian Contact with Quakerism," *Harvard Theological Review.* Cambridge (Massachusetts), Vol. 3, 1941, pp. 14 ff.

Calcutta Sailors' Home.
12th & 19th Reports. Calcutta, 1850, 1857.

Calcutta Seamen's Friend Society.
Annual Reports. Calcutta.

Caldwell, Charles.
A Discourse on the Genius and Character of the Rev. Horace Holley, LL.D. Boston, 1828.

Callender, Geoffrey.
The Naval Side of British History. London, 1934.

Cameron, Richard M.
Methodism and Society in Historical Perspective. Nashville (Tennessee), 1961.

Campbell, George D.
"Father Taylor: The Seamen's Apostle," *Methodist History* (Lake Junaluska, North Carolina), pp. 251-60.

Canright, Stephen.
"The Black Man and the Sea," *South Street Reporter,* Winter, 1973-74, pp. 5-7.

Canton, William.
A History of the British and Foreign Bible Society. 4 Vols. London, 1904-10.

Carey, William.
An Enquiry into the Obligations of Christians to Use Means for the Conversion of the Heathens.... London, 1961. (Facsimile of 1st ed., 1792.)

Carlisle, Rodney.
"Black-Owned Shipping Before Marcus Garvey," *The American Neptune,* 1975, pp. 197-206.

Carlzon, Lars.
" 'Saa laangt som havets bölja gaar . . . ' Glimtar ur Sjömanskyrkans historia" (As far as the Ocean Wave rolls . . . Glimpses from the History of the Seamen's Church), *Ute och Hemma,* 1969, pp. 164-75.

Carpenter, Mary.
"Memoir of Joseph Tuckerman," *American Unitarian Biography,* William Ware (Ed.), Vol. 2, Boston, 1851, pp. 31-135. (First published separately, London, 1849.)

Carr, Robert.
  Sailors at the Police Office, or the Sailors' Asylum .... London, 1829.
Carroll, Mary T.
  The Man Who Dared to Care: The Story of James Edward Oglethorpe. New York, 1942.
Carrothers, W.A.
  Emigration from the British Isles. London, 1929.

Carse, Robert.
  The Age of Piracy. New York, 1957.
  The Book of Smugglers. New York, 1970.
Catalogue of the Officers and Graduates of Yale University .... New Haven, 1924.
Cathcart, William (Ed.)
  The Baptist Encyclopædia .... Vol. 2. Philadelphia, 1881.
Catholic Maritime News. Pensacola (Florida), later Corpus Christi (Texas).
  Note: Newsletter of the Apostleship of the Sea in the United States.

Cedarleaf, Wallace (Ed.).
  Under Full Sail 1880-1980: Boston Seamen's Mission Inc. Boston, 1980.
  Note: Later changed to "New England Seamen's Mission Inc."
Chadwick, Owen.
  The Victorian Church. London, 1966.
Chamberlain, Mellen.
  A Documentary History of Chelsea, 1624-1824. 2 Vols. Boston, 1908.
Chambers's Encyclopædia. London, 1950.
Channing, Edward.
  A History of the United States. 6 Vols. New York, 1905-25.
Channing, William Ellery.
  "Discourse on the Life and Character of the Rev. Dr. Tuckerman," *The Works of William E. Channing, D.D.,* Vol. 6, Boston, 1843, pp. 111-46. (First published separately, Boston, 1841.)
Chapel, Robert B.
  "The Word against the Cat: Melville's Influence on Seamen's Rights," *The American Neptune,* 1982, pp. 57-65.

[Chapman, Jonathan.]
  Address of the Young Men's Temperance Society to the Young Men of Boston. Boston, 1832.
Chapman, Paul K.
  Human Rights for Seafarers. New York, 1981.
Charlton, Harold W.
  "Hi Jack!—Hijack!" *Nautical Magazine,* 1980, pp. 38-39.
The Chart and Compass, Sailors' Magazine. London.
  Note: From 1879, published by the British and Foreign Sailors' Society, as a continuation of *The Sailor's Magazine* (q.v.).
Chase, Mary E.
  The Story of Lighthouses. New York, 1965.

Cheever, Henry T.
The Autobiography and Memorials of Captain Obadiah Cougar, for Fifty Years Mariner and Shipmaster from the Port of New York. New York, 1851.
A Reel in a Bottle, for Jack in the Doldrums. New York, 1852.

Chichester, C.E.
Historical Sketch of the Charleston Port Society.... Charleston (South Carolina), 1885.

Chidsey, Donald B.
The Wars in Barbary: Arab Piracy and the Birth of the United States Navy. New York, 1971.

The Christian Advocate. Philadelphia.

The Christian Advocate and Journal. New York.

The Christian Disciple. Boston.

The Christian Guardian. London.

The Christian Herald. New York.
Note: Commenced March 1816 in order to provide "information concerning the progress of Christianity" (in general), Vols. 1-7, 1816-1821.
Continued from May 1821 as The Christian Herald and Seaman's Magazine, under the patronage of the "Port of New-York Society for Promoting the Gospel among Seamen," with twice-monthly numbers, Vols. 8-11, 1821-1824.

The Christian Intelligencer. Calcutta.

The Christian Mariner's Journal. London, 1829.

The Christian Observer. London.

Church, Leslie F.
Oglethorpe: A Study of Philanthropy in England and Georgia. London, 1932.

The Church of England.
Church Work Amongst Sailors in 64 Home Ports. (Paper read in the Lower House of the Convocation of Canterbury.) London, 1878.
The Duty of the Church to Merchant Seamen. (Paper read at the Church Congress at Manchester, October 2, 1888.) [London, 1888].

The Churchman. London.

Churchmen's Missionary Association for Seamen of the Port of Philadelphia.
Appeal of the Churchmen's Missionary Association for Seamen of the Port of Philadelphia. Philadelphia, 1848.
Constitution of the Churchmen's Missionary Society... and a Historical Sketch of the Association. Philadelphia, 1885.
Annual Reports. Philadelphia.

The City Mission Magazine. London, 1836.

Claflin, George.
An Account of the Voyage of the Ship Ann E. Hooper: A Tale of Cruelty and Suffering. n.p. [1857].

Clap, Nath.
Zebulun Advised: Serious and Suitable Counsels for them that Go to Sea, and for All that Mind the Good of their Souls. Newport (Rhode Island), 1738.

Clark, Elmer T. (Ed.)
The Journal and Letters of Francis Asbury. Vol. 1. London, 1958.

Clark, George.
English History. A Survey. Oxford, 1971.

Clarkson, Thomas.
An Essay on the Slavery and Commerce of the Human Species, Particularly the African. London, 1786.
An Essay on the Impolicy of the African Slave Trade. London, 1788.
History of the Rise, Progress and Accomplishment of the Abolition of the African Slave Trade, by the British Parliament. London, 1808.
The Grievances of Our Mercantile Seamen, a National and Crying Evil. London, 1845.

Clogg, Richard.
"Some Protestant Tracts Printed at the Press of the Ecumenical Patriarchate in Constantinople: 1818-1820," *Eastern Churches Review*, Vol. 2, No. 2, 1968.

Coast Missions: A Memoir of the Rev. Thomas Rosie. London, 1862.

Codman, John.
A Letter to Hon. Charles Sumner of the United States Senate, on the Condition and Requirements of the American Mercantile Marine. Washington D.C., 1860.

Cogswell, William.
The Harbinger of the Millennium. Boston, 1833.

Cole, Charles C., Jr.
The Social Ideas of the Northern Evangelists 1826-1860. New York, 1954.

Coleman, Terry.
Going to America. New York, 1972.

A Collection of the Statutes Relating to the Admiralty, Navy, Ships of War, and Incidental Matters . . . . London, 1768.

Collyer, Robert.
Father Taylor. Boston, 1906.

The Colonial Observer. Sydney, N.S.W.

Concise Dictionary of the Christian World Mission. (Eds.: Stephen Neill, Gerald H. Anderson, John Goodwin.) London, 1970.

Concise Dictionary of Religious Knowledge and Gazeteer. Vol. 2. New York, 1891.

The Continental Society.
Extracts from Letters Received by the Committee of the Continental Society . . . London, 1819.
Extracts from the Journal of the Rev. Carlos Von Bülow, Agent to the Continental Society; Employed on the Norway Mission, from April 13, 1826, to January 17, 1827. London, 1827.

Cook, Harold R.
An Introduction to the Study of Christian Missions. Chicago, 1954.

Cooke, Henry A.
Phineas Stowe, and Bethel Work. Boston, 1874.

The Copartnership Herald. London.

Copy of the Last Will and Testament of the Late Robert Richard Randall, Esq. . . . . New York, 1876.

Corbett, J.S.
Drake and the Tudor Navy. Vol. 1. London, 1899.

The Corporation of Trinity House.
Trinity House London. London, n.d.

Coupland, Reginald.
Wilberforce: A Narrative. Oxford, 1923.
The British Anti-Slavery Movement. London, 1933.

Course, A.G.
The Merchant Navy: A Social History. London, 1963.

Cowan, Henry.
John Knox, the Hero of the Scottish Reformation. New York, 1905.

Cox, F.A.
Memoirs of the Rev. William Henry Angas, Ordained a "Missionary to Seafaring Men," May 11, 1822. London, 1834.

Coxere, Edward.
Adventures by Sea of Edward Coxere: A Relation of the Several Adventures by Sea with the Dangers, Difficulties, and Hardships I Met for Several Years. . . . Ed.: E.H.W. Meyerstein. Oxford, 1945.

Cragg, G.R.
The Church and the Age of Reason: 1648-1789. London, 1962.

Creighton, Mandell.
Memoirs of Sir George Grey, Bart., G.C.B. London, 1901. (1st ed. Newcastle, 1884.)

Cross, F.L. (Ed.).
The Oxford Dictionary of the Christian Church. London, 1971. (1st ed. 1957.)

Crow, Hugh.
Memoirs of the Late Captain Hugh Crow of Liverpool. . . . Liverpool, 1830.

The Crow's Nest. (Seamen's Church Institute of Philadelphia.) Philadelphia.

Cummings, Asa.
A Memoir of the Rev. Edward Payson, D.D., Late of Portland, Maine. New York [n.d.].

Currey, E. Hamilton.
Sea-Wolves of the Mediterranean. New York, 1910.

Cushman, R.W.
The Anchor for the Soul, Addressed to Seamen. Philadelphia, n.d.

Cuthbertson, Hugh S.
The Story of St. Paul's, Dock Street. London, 1966.

Daae, Ludvig.
Nordmaends Udvandringer til Holland og England i nyere Tid (The Emigration of Norwegians to Holland and England in Recent Times). Christiania (Oslo), 1880.

Dahl, Curtis.
"Three Fathers, Many Sons," *Methodist History,* 1977, pp. 234-50.

Damon, Samuel C.
A Jubilee Sermon, Preached in The Bethel, Honolulu, Dec. 2d, 1883. [Honolulu, 1883.]

Dana, Richard H., Jr.
   Two Years before the Mast: A Personal Narrative. Boston, 1929.
   Cruelty to Seamen: Being the Case of Nichols & Couch. Berkeley (California),
   1937.

Danbolt, Erling.
   Misjonstankens gjennombrudd i Norge (The Emergence of the Missionary
   Idea in Norway). Vol. 1, Oslo, 1947.
   "Den ukjente Egede" (The Unknown Egede), *Tidsskrift for Teologi og Kirke,*
   1973, No. 1.

Dashiell, Alfred H.
   *Barnabas; or, the Son of Consolation; Exemplified in the Life and Character
   of the Rev. Joseph Eastburn....* Philadelphia, 1828.

Davidson, Marshall B.
   Life in America. Vol. 1. Boston, 1951.

Davis, Hugh H.
   "The American Seamen's Friend Society and the American Sailor 1828-
   1838," *The American Neptune,* 1979, pp. 45-57.

Davis, J.K.
   The Seamen's and Boatmen's Manual. New York, 1847.

Davies, John.
   The History of the Tahitian Mission 1799-1830. Cambridge, 1961.

Davis, Ralph.
   The Rise of the English Shipping Industry in the 17th and 18th Centuries.
   London, 1962.

Defoe, Daniel.
   *Some Considerations on the Reasonableness and Necessity of Encreasing
   and Encouraging Seamen....* London, 1728.

Delaney, Caldwell.
   Craighead's Mobile. Mobile, 1968.

Den danske Evangelist. Odense (Denmark).

Denison, A.C.
   America's Maritime History. New York, 1944.

Denison, Charles W.
   *Defence of Rev. Charles W. Denison, from the Slander of the Boston Baptist
   Bethel Society and First Baptist Church....* Boston, 1846.

Dennis, James. S.
   Foreign Missions after a Century. New York, 1893.

[Dennis, Jeffery.]
   *An Address to the Honourable Committee for the Relief of Distressed
   Seamen... By the Merchant Seaman's Friend.* London (1st ed., February),
   1818.

Dennis, Jeffery.
   *An Address to the Honourable Committee for the Relief of Distressed
   Seamen....* London (2nd ed., November), 1818.

Destitute Sailors' Asylum.
   Reports. London. Note: Later, "Destitute Sailors' Fund." (Reports were
   eventually published jointly with the Sailors' Home and Red Ensign Club.)

Deutsche Seemannsmission in Hamburg R.V.
75 Jahre: Deutsche Seemannsmission in Hamburg R.V. 1891-1966. Hamburg, 1966.

Dewey, Orville.
The Character and Claims of Sea-faring Men. New York, 1845.

A Dialogue between a Member of Parliament, and a Commander of a Ship, about Encouraging the Seamen of Great Britain, and the Speedy Manning the Navy without Impressing. London, 1709.

Dickens, Charles.
American Notes for General Circulation. (Vol. 11 in The Works of Charles Dickens.) London, n.d.

Dictionary of American Biography. New York.

Dictionary of National Biography. London.

A Dictionary of Religion and Ethics. New York, 1921.

Dillenburg, James E.
"What is Loneliness?" Catholic Maritime News, September, 1980, pp. 3-5.
"Catechesis of Seafarers in a USA Ecumenical Context," On the Move, no. 37, Vatican City (Rome), 1983, pp. 76-79.

Dillenburg, James E. (Ed.).
Proceeding of the Annual Convention: ICOSA and NCCS, Seattle, Washington, October 4, 1984. Corpus Christi (Texas), 1985.

Dillon, Richard H.
Shanghaiing Days. New York, 1961.

Distad, N. Merrill.
"Jonas Hanway and the Marine Society," The Nautical Magazine, 1973, pp. 156-60.

Dixon, Conrad.
"The Rise and Fall of the Crimp," British Shipping and Seamen, 1630-1960: Some Studies. Stephen Fisher (Ed.). Exeter, 1984, pp. 49-66.

Dodge, Ernest S.
New England and the South Seas. Cambridge (Massachusetts), 1965.

Dow, George F.
Slave Ships and Slaving. Salem (Massachusetts), 1927.

Dowell, David A., Cheryl Krichmar, and Mabel Miramen.
A Study of the Needs of Seafarers in the Port of Los Angeles. Sponsored by the Seamen's Church Institute, San Pedro, California. [Long Beach 1984.].

Dowley, Tim (Ed.).
Eerdman's Handbook to the History of Christianity. Grand Rapids (Michigan), 1977.

Down, William J.D.
"Evangelisation and Pastoral Care of Seafarers, with Particular Reference to the 'Self-Sufficient Seafarer,'" Third Plenary Conference New York 1978: Papers and Addresses, ICMA, [1979], pp. 25-32.

Downey, Joseph T.
The Cruise of the Portsmouth, 1845-1847. New Haven (Connecticut), 1958.

Dresselhuis, J.E.F.
Chart and Compass: Prayers, Songs and Thoughts for Seafarers. Vancouver B.C., 1978.

Drury, Clifford M.
The History of the Chaplain Corps, United States Navy. Vol. 1: 1778-1939. Washington D.C., 1949.

Dudley, C.S.
An Analysis of the System of the Bible Society. London, 1821.

Dugan, James.
The Great Mutiny. London, 1966.

Dunstan, J. Leslie.
A Light to the City: 150 Years of the City Missionary Society of Boston, 1816-1966. Boston, 1966.

Dwight, Henry O.
The Centennial History of the American Bible Society. New York, 1916.

Eckhoff, Ray.
"Ministering Seafarers," *4th Triennial Conference: Standing Committee Report,* ICMA, London, 1981, Appendix B.

Edinburgh Bible Society.
Reports. Edinburgh.

Ekman, E.J.
Illustreret Missionshistorie (Illustrated Mission History). Kristiansund N. (Norway), 1895.

Elias, Frank.
Heaven and the Sea. London, 1912.

Eliot, Christopher R.
"Joseph Tuckerman: Pioneer in Scientific Philanthropy," *Proceedings,* Unitarian Historical Society, Boston, 1935, pp. 1-32.

Ellacott, Samuel E.
The Seaman. 2 Vols. New York 1971.

Elliott-Binns, L.E.
Religion in the Victorian Era. London, 1946.

Elmes, James.
Thomas Clarkson: A Monograph. London, 1854.

Eltzholtz, Carl F.
Livsbilleder af Pastor O.P. Petersen (A Biographic Portrayal of the Rev. O.P. Petersen). Chicago, 1903.

Emerson, Joseph.
A Chart for Seamen. Salem (Massachusetts), 1804.

Encyclopaedia of the Social Sciences. New York.

Encyclopaedia Britannica. Chicago, 1964.

The Encyclopaedia of Missions. (1st edition.) New York, 1891.

The Encyclopedia Americana. (International edition.) New York, 1967.

The Encyclopedia of Missions. (2nd edition.) New York, 1904.

The Encyclopedia of Modern Christian Missions. Camden (New Jersey), 1967.

An Encyclopedia of Religion. New York, 1945.

The Encyclopedia of Social Reform. New York, 1897.

Engvall, C.J.
*Vaar Sjömansmission: Naagot om Svenska Missionsförbundets arbete bland
sjöfolket* (Our Seamen's Mission: Something about the Swedish Mission
Federation's Work among Seafarers). Stockholm, 1914.

Erickson, Arvel B., and Martin J. Havran.
England: Prehistory to the Present. New York, 1968.

Eriksen, Erling.
Vaar gamle sjöfartskultur (Our Old Maritime Culture). Oslo, 1968.

Esping, Julius L.
Adrift and at Anchor. Boston, 1870.

Esquiros, Alphonse.
English Seamen and Divers. London, 1868.

The Essex Register. Salem (Massachusetts).

Establishment of a Sailors' Home.... Liverpool, 1844.

Ettinger, Amos A.
James Edward Oglethorpe: Imperial Idealist. Oxford, 1936.

The Evangelical Magazine, London.

Evangelisches Kirchenlexikon. Vol. 3. Göttingen, 1959.

The Evening News. Sydney, N.S.W.

Evjen, John O.
Scandinavian Immigrants in New York 1630-1674. Minneapolis, 1916.

Faber, Harald.
Danske og Norske i London og deres Kirker (Danes and Norwegians in
London and Their Churches). Copenhagen, 1915.
Caius Gabriel Cibber, 1630-1700: His Life and Work. Oxford, 1926.

Fairburn, William A.
Merchant Sail. 6 Vols. Center Lovell (Maine), 1945-55.

Fant, David J.
The Bible at Work in New York. New York, 1965.

Farr, James McCullough.
A Short History of the Brick Presbyterian Church... 1768-1943. New York,
1943.

The Federal Writers' Project of Massachusetts.
Whaling Masters. New Bedford (Massachusetts), 1938.

Female Bethel Association of New-York.
Constitution, By-laws, and Address.... New York, 1836.

Female Missionary Society for the Poor of the City of New-York and its Vicinity.
Second Anniversary Report. New York, 1818.

Female Seamen's Friend Society of Philadelphia.
Annual Reports. Philadelphia.

Fenton, Horace L.
"Debits and Credits—The Wheaton Congress," *International Review of
Missions* (Geneva), October 1966.

Field, C.
Old Times Afloat: A Naval Anthology. London, 1932.

Finch, John.
    A Statement . . . . Liverpool, 1831.
"The First Bible Society," *The Sunday at Home*, Dec. 5, 1874, pp. 772-5.
Flavel, John.
    The Seaman's Companion. London, 1676.
    Navigation Spiritualiz'd; or, a New Compass for Seamen, Consisting of XXXII Points . . . . London, 1760. (1st ed.: 1671. American ed.: Newbury-port, Massachusetts, 1796.)
    The Seaman's Monitor. London, 1799.
The Flying Angel. London.
    Note: Newsletter of the Missions to Seamen. Continued as *Flying Angel News.*
Folkestad, Abraham.
    "Sömandsmisjonens Forlöbere" (The Seamen's Mission's Precursors), *Bud og Hilsen*, 1887, 2nd Suppl., pp. 1-9.
Folkevennen. Kristiania (Oslo).
Foner, Philip S.
    History of the Labor Movement in the United States. New York, 1947.
Forster, William.
    A Christian Exhortation to Sailors, and Persons Engaged in a Sea-faring Life. London, 1814. (1st ed., 1813.)
Foster, Charles I.
    "The Urban Missionary Movement," *The Pennsylvania Magazine of History and Biography* (Philadelphia), 1951, pp. 47-65.
    An Errand of Mercy: The Evangelical United Front, 1790-1837. Chapel Hill (North Carolina), 1960.
Fournier, Georges.
    Hydrographie. Paris, 1677.
Frayne, Francis S.
    What is the Apostleship of the Sea? Liverpool, n.d.
    "The Care of Seafarers' Families" *Report of First Plenary Conference, London* . . . *1972*, ICMA [1973], pp. 7-16.
    "The Present Situation of the Apostleship of the Sea," *On the Move*, no. 4, Vatican City (Rome), 1972, pp. 33-41.
    "The New Situation in the Maritime World," *On the Move*, no. 21, Vatican City (Rome), 1978, pp. 40-46.
Free Church of St. Mary for Sailors.
    Annual Reports. Boston, 1857, 1858.
    Constitution and By-laws of Sailors' Aid Society. Boston, 1862.
Fricke, Peter H.
    "Seafarer and Community," *Seafarer and Community: Towards a Social Understanding of Seafaring*, Peter H. Fricke (Ed.), London, 1973, pp. 1-7.
The Friend. Honolulu.
Frivold, Leif (Ed.).
    Vaar arv: Streif fra norsk kirke- og kulturhistorie i London (Our Heritage: Glimpses from Norwegian Church and Cultural History in London). London, 1967.

Froude, James A.
English Seamen in the Sixteenth Century. London, 1926.

Furness, William H.
"Memoir of William Ellery Channing," *American Unitarian Biography,* William Ware (Ed.) Boston, 1851.

Gamble, Thomas Jr.
A History of the City Government of Savannah, Ga., from 1790 to 1901. Savannah, 1900.

Gannon, Arthur.
Apostolatus Maris 1920-1960. New Orleans, 1965.

Garitee, Jerome R.
The Republic's Private Navy. Middletown (Connecticut), 1977.

Garstin, Crosbie.
An Eighteenth Century Seaman. New York, 1925.

Gates, William G.
Illustrated History of Portsmouth. Portsmouth, 1900.
History of Portsmouth: A Naval Chronology. Portsmouth, 1931.

Gaustad, Edwin S.
Historical Atlas of Religion in America. New York, 1962.
A Religious History of America. New York, 1966.

Gautier, Anita M.
"The Black Whalers of Nantucket," *The Lookout,* New York, August 1983, pp. 24-27.

The General Association of Massachusetts.
Minutes of the General Association of Massachusetts. Boston, 1832.

General Catalogue of the Theological Seminary, Andover, Massachusetts 1808-1908. Boston, 1909.

The Gentleman's Magazine. London.

The Georgian. Savannah.

Georgian Historical Society.
Will Book "G." Savannah, n.d.

Gill, Conrad.
The Naval Mutinies of 1797. Manchester, 1913.

Gjerset, Knut.
Norwegian Sailors on the Great Lakes. Northfield (Minnesota), 1928.
Norwegian Sailors in American Waters. Northfield (Minnesota), 1933.

Glasgow Seaman's Friend Society.
Seaman's Friend Society. [Glasgow, 1822.]
Annual Reports. Glasgow, 1823 etc.

Glasgow Seamen's Friend Society.
1822-1922: Centenary Report. Glasgow, 1923.

Glazik, Josef.
"Missiology," *Concise Dictionary of the Christian World Mission,* 1970, pp. 387-89.

Goffman, Erving.
"On the Characteristics of Total Institutions," *Asylums* (Garden City, New York), 1961, pp. 1-124.

Goldberg, Joseph P.
The Maritime Story. Cambridge (Massachusetts), 1958.

Goldsmith-Carter, George.
Sailors, Sailors. London, 1966.

Gollock, G.A.
At the Sign of the Flying Angel. London, 1930.

Goold, William.
Portland in the Past. Portland (Maine), 1886.

Gordon, Alexander C.
What Cheer O? Or, the Story of the Mission to Deep Sea Fishermen. London, 1890.

Gosse, Philip.
The History of Piracy. London, 1932.
The History of Piracy. New York, 1946.

Gracida, Rene H.
"Evangelisation of Seafarers," *Third Plenary Conference, New York 1978: Papers and Addresses,* ICMA, 1979, pp. 38-41.

Graham, Frank.
Smuggling in Cornwall. Newcastle-upon-Tyne, 1964.

Granberg, Gunnar (Ed.).
Svenska Kyrkan i New York 100 Aar (The Swedish Church in New York 100 Years). New York, 1974.

Gray, B. Kirkman.
A History of English Philanthropy. London, 1905.
Philanthropy and the State, or Social Politics. London, 1908.

Green, Ashbel.
Memoirs of the Rev. Joseph Eastburn. Philadelphia, 1828.

Greenleaf, Jonathan.
A History of the Churches ... in the City of New York. New York, 1846.

Gribble, Charles B.
The Naval Officer; a New Creature in Christ Jesus, Exemplified in the Living and Dying of Captain Robert James Elliot, R.N. London, 1849.

Griffin, Clifford S.
Their Brothers' Keepers: Moral Stewardship in the United States, 1800-1865. New Brunswick (New Jersey), 1960.

Griffin, Edward D.
The Claims of Seamen. New York, 1819.

[Griffin, John.]
An Account of the Bravery & Happy Death of James Covey, a British Seaman. London, n.d.

Griggs, Earl L.
Thomas Clarkson: The Friend of Slaves. London, 1936.

Grönseth, E., and P. Tiller.
"Father Absence in Sailor Families ... ," *Nordisk Psykologi* (Monograph Series, No. 9: Oslo), 1958.

Der Grosse Brockhaus. Vol. 10. Wiesbaden, 1956.

Guillet, Edwin C.
The Great Migration: The Atlantic Crossing by Sailing-ship since 1770. Toronto, 1963.

Gulbrandsen, Leif T.
"The Three Homes," *American Seamen: A Review,* 1941, no. 1, Vol. 1, pp. 51-53.

Gummere, Amelia M. (Ed.).
The Journal and Essays of John Woolman. New York, 1922.

Haagensen, Andrew.
Den norsk-danske Methodismes Historie paa begge Sider Havet (History of Norwegian-Danish Methodism on Both Sides of the Ocean). Chicago, 1894.

Haaland, Erling.
"Carl Gustav von Bülows opphold og virke i Norge" (Carl Gustav von Bülow's Residence and Activities in Norway.), *Tidsskrift for Teologi og Kirke,* 1956, pp. 146-60.

Hagen, Odd.
Preludes to Methodism in Northern Europe. Oslo, 1961.

Hakluyt, Richard.
Principal Navigations. Extra Series. Glasgow, 1903.

Halévy, Elie.
England in 1815. London, 1961. (1st ed. in French 1913.)

Hansen, Thorkild.
The Way to Hudson Bay: The Life and Times of Jens Munk. New York, 1970.

Hanway, Jonas.
Motives for the Establishment of the Marine Society. "By a Merchant" [Jonas Hanway] London, 1757.
An Account of the Marine Society . . . . London, 1759.
The Seaman's Faithful Companion. London [1763].
The Sea Lad's Trusty Companion. London, 1778.
The Seaman's Christian Friend; Containing Moral and Religious Advice to Seamen. London, 1779.
Prudential Instruction to the Poor Boys Fitted Out by the Corporation of the Marine Society. London, 1788.

Harben, Henry A.
A Dictionary of London. London, 1918.

Hardy, Aage.
O.P. Petersen, Metodistkirkens grunnlegger i Norge: En livsskildring (O.P. Petersen, Founder of the Methodist Church in Norway: A Biography). Oslo, 1953.

Hardy, E.J.
"The Religion of Soldiers and Sailors," *Good Words.* [London], 1892.

Harms, F.M.
Die Seemannsmission. (In "Zimmers Handbibliothek der praktischen Theologie.") Gotha, 1890.
Die Geschichte der deutschen evangelischen Seemannsmission. Stettin [1909]. Note: Also published as pp. 90-209 in Reinhard Münchmeyer, *Handbuch der deutschen evangelischen Seemannsmission,* Stettin, 1912.

Harper, Edyth.
"They Sailed in Biblical Times," *The Nautical Magazine,* 1972, pp. 20-23.
"Off-shore Saints," *The Nautical Magazine,* 1975, pp. 293-94.

Harris, E.P.
"Then and Now," *ENTO Journal* (H.J. Enthoven & Sons, Ltd., Rotherhithe Street, London), Christmas, 1935.

Harris, John.
Britannia; or, the Moral Claims of Seamen Stated and Enforced. London, 1837.
Zebulon; or, the Moral Claims of Seamen Stated and Enforced. (Revised American ed.) Boston, 1837.
Britannia, eller Sjömäns Moraliska Ansprak. . . . (Britannia, or the Moral Claims of Seamen . . .). Transl.: A.G. Oxehufwud. Stockholm, 1837.

Haven, Gilbert, and Thomas Russel.
Father Taylor, the Sailor Preacher. Boston, 1871.

Havnen. Copenhagen.
Note: Published by the Danish Seamen's Church in Foreign Ports.

Hawaiian Mission Children's Society.
Missionary Album. Honolulu, 1969.

Healey, James C.
Foc's'le and Glory-Hole: A Study of the Merchant Seaman and His Occupation. New York, 1936.
A Symposium on Andrew Furuseth. New Bedford, n.d.

Heasman, Kathleen.
Evangelicals in Action: An Appraisal of Their Social Work in the Victorian Era. London, 1962.

Heimert, Alan, and Perry Miller.
The Great Awakening: Documents Illustrating the Crisis and its Consequences. Indianapolis and New York, 1967.

Heitman, Johan H.
Besvaerede Soë-Maends söde Siele-Roe . . . (Troubled Seamen's Sweet Peace of Soul . . .), Copenhagen, 1793 (1st ed.: 1730).

Helle, Kaare, and Roald Kverndal.
Broderkretsen paa Havet 1885-1960 (The Christian Brotherhood of the Ocean 1885-1960). Bergen 1960.

Helle, Kaare (Ed.).
Broderkretsen paa Havet 1885-1985 (The Christian Brotherhood of the Ocean). Kristiansand S. (Norway), 1985.

Hennell, Michael M.
"A Little-Known Social Revolution," *The Church Quarterly Review* (London), 1947, pp. 189-207.
"England in 1804: The Historical Setting of the Bible Society Movement in England," *Bulletin of the United Bible Societies* (London), 1954, pp. 16-24.
"Evangelism and Social Class," *The Christian Graduate* (London), 1960, pp. 58-62.
"The Evangelicals," *Eerdman's Handbook to the History of Christianity,* Tim Dowley (Ed.), Grand Rapids (Michigan), 1977, pp. 512-14.

Henningius, Tilemannus.
    En liden ny Skibsbog udaff den hellige Bibelske Schrifft (A Small New
    Ship's Book, Based on the Holy Scriptures). Rostock, 1580.

Henningsen, Henning.
    Kirkeskibe og kirkeskibsfester (Church Ships and Church Ship Festivals).
    Elsinore, 1950.
    "Ship-Models in Danish Churches," *The Mariner's Mirror*, 1952, pp. 294-
    300.
    Crossing the Equator: Sailors' Baptism and Other Initiation Rites. (Ph.D.
    Thesis at University of Copenhagen.) Copenhagen, 1961.
    "Jonas—profet og ulykkesfugl," *Handels- og Söfartsmuseet paa Kronborg:
    Aarbok for 1966* (Commercial and Maritime Museum at Kronborg: Yearbook
    for 1966), Copenhagen, 1966.
    "Kvinder, praester og Jonas'er om bord" (Women, Clergymen and Jonah's on
    Shipboard), *Jul i havn og paa hav* (Copenhagen), 1967, pp. 5-10.
    Sömand og Sömandskirke: Dansk Sömandskirke i fremmede Havne (Seaman
    and Seaman's Church: Danish Seamen's Church in Foreign Ports). Copen-
    hagen, 1967.
    "Sömandsliv paa langfart og i hjemlige farvande" (Seamen's Life in Deep Sea
    and Domestic Trades), *Dagligliv i Danmark 1620-1790*, Axel Steensberg
    (Ed.), Copenhagen, 1969.

Henshaw, John P.K.
    A Plea for Seamen . . . . Baltimore, 1826.

Herbert, David.
    Great Historical Mutinies. Edinburgh, 1879.

Hewitt, Gordon.
    *Let the People Read: A Short History of the United Society for Christian
    Literature.* London, 1949.

Highmore, Anthony.
    Philanthropia Metropolitana. London, 1822.

Hill, Hamilton A.
    History of the Old South Church. 2 Vols. Boston, 1890.

Hill, William.
    An Alphabetical Arrangement of All the Wesleyan-Methodist Ministers. . . .
    London, 1853. (7th ed.)

Hoare, Prince.
    Memoirs of Granville Sharp, Esq. London, 1820. (A second edition in 2
    Vols., 1828.)

Hobsbaum, E.J.
    Industry and Empire. London, 1968.

Hocking, William E. (Ed.).
    Re-thinking Missions. New York, 1932.

Hodder, Edwin.
    George Fife Angas: Father and Founder of South Australia. London, 1891.

Hodgson, Peter C. (Ed.).
    Ferdinand Christian Baur on the Writing of Church History. New York,
    1968.

Hofgren, Allan (Ed.).
Svensk sjömanskyrka 100 ar 1869-1969 (Swedish Seamen's Church 100 Years 1869-1969). Klippan (Sweden), 1969.

Hogg, William R.
"The Rise of Protestant Missionary Concern, 1517-1914," *The Theology of Christian Mission,* Gerald H. Anderson (Ed.), 1961, pp. 95-111.

Hohman, Elmo P.
Seamen Ashore: A Study of the United Seamen's Service and of Merchant Seamen in Port. New Haven (Connecticut), 1952.
History of American Merchant Seamen. Hamden (Connecticut), 1956.

Hollander, A.N.J. den (Ed.).
Contagious Conflict: The Impact of American Dissent on European Life. Leiden, 1973.

Holmes, Thomas J.
Cotton Mather: A Bibliography of his Works. Cambridge (Massachusetts), 1940.

Hope, Ronald.
In Cabined Ships at Sea: Fifty Years of the Seafarers' Education Service. London, 1969.
Spare Time at Sea. London, 1974.

Hopkins, Fred.
"From Warship to School Ship: The History of U.S.S. Ontario, America's First Floating School," *The American Neptune,* 1980, pp. 38-45.

Hough, John.
"The Ministry of Christian Seafarers' Organizations During Maritime Training," *Report of First Plenary Conference... London, 1972,* ICMA [1973], pp. 41-44.

Howard, Thomas.
Black Voyage: Eyewitness Accounts of the Atlantic Slave Trade. Boston, 1971.

Howe, George.
History of the Presbyterian Church in South Carolina. Vol. 2. Columbia (South Carolina), 1883.

Howse, Ernest M.
Saints in Politics: The "Clapham Sect" and the Growth of Freedom. London, 1960.

Hoxse, John.
The Yankee Tar. Northampton (Massachusetts), 1840.

Hudson, Winthrop S.
Religion in America. New York, 1965.

Hugill, Stan.
Sailortown. London, 1967.

Hunter, Leslie S. (Ed.).
Scandinavian Churches. Minneapolis, 1965.

Huntington, F.D.
An Address Delivered May 28, 1862 before the Boston Seaman's Friend Society.... Boston, 1862.
Our Duty, As Christian Citizens, to the Sailor. Boston, 1862.

Hutchinson, J.R.
The Press-Gang Afloat and Ashore. New York, 1914.

Hytönen, Paavo (Ed.).
Bortom havet (Beyond the Ocean). Helsingfors, 1950.

ICMA Bulletin. Felixstowe (England).
Note: Newsletter of the International Christian Maritime Association from 1982.

ICMA News. London.
Note: Newsletter of the same until 1981.

Illustrated Seamen's Narratives: By Various Authors. (Published by the American Tract Society.) [New York], n.d.

Illustrert Religionsleksikon. Vol. 3. Odense (Denmark), 1950.

"Industrial Chaplaincy, the Other Five Days," *ACTS* (The American Lutheran Church: Minneapolis), May 1980, p. 2.

International Christian Maritime Association (ICMA).
Report of First Plenary Conference, London, 31st July-4th August 1972. London [1973].
Report of the Second Plenary Conference, Denmark, 7th-11th July 1975. London [1976].
Report of the Third Plenary Conference, New York, 9th-13th October 1978. London [1979].
Third Plenary Conference New York 1978: Papers and Addresses. London [1979].
Report of the Fourth Plenary Conference, Berlin, 12th-18th July 1981. London [1982].
Report of the Fifth Plenary Conference, the Philippines, 15th-21st April 1985. Felixstowe (England) [1985].

International Labour Organisation (ILO).
Winds of Change: On the High Seas and in the World's Ports and on the Inland Waterways. Geneva, 1971.

International Review of Mission(s). London/Geneva.

International Social Christian Institute.
The Churches and the Welfare of Seamen. Geneva, 1930.

Ireland, J. de Courcy.
"The Corsairs of North Africa," *The Mariner's Mirror,* 1976, pp. 271-83.

Israel, Herman.
"Some Religious Factors in the Emergence of Industrial Society in England," *American Sociological Review* (Albany, New York) 1966, pp. 589-99.

Jackman, Eugene T.
"Efforts Made before 1825 to Ameliorate the Lot of the American Seaman: With Emphasis on his Moral Regeneration," *The American Neptune,* 1964, pp. 109-18.

Jacob, Michael.
The Flying Angel Story. London & Oxford, 1973.

Jaeger, Dorothea, and Leo W. Simmons.
Woman's Seamen's Friend Society of Connecticut: Background—Survey—Recommendations. New Haven (Connecticut), 1965.

Janeway, James.
    A Token for Mariners.... London 1708. (1st edition: 1674.)
    The Mariners Divine Mate: Or, Spiritual Navigation Improved. (Boston, 1715.) Note: Authorship evidenced by initials "J.J."
    An Address to Seamen. Greenock, 1810. Note: Published anonymously, but authorship endorsed by "W.F." in *The Evangelical Magazine*, 1806, p. 508.
    The Heavenly Pilot: Or, the Mariner's Sure Guide to the Best Port.... (No. 3 in "The Cottage Library of Christian Knowledge".) N.p., n.d.

Jenkins, Lawrence W.
    The Marine Society at Salem in New England. Salem (Massachusetts), 1952.

Jewell, J. Grey.
    Among Our Sailors. New York, 1874.

J.I.F.
    "Alcoholism: An Occupational Disease of Seamen . . . ," *Quarterly Journal of Studies on Alcohol,* Dec. 1947, pp. 498-505.

Johansen, Frederik.
    Broderkredsen paa Havet 1899-1949 (The Christian Brotherhood of the Ocean, 1899-1949). Korsor (Denmark) [1949].

Johnson, T. Augustus.
    The American Sailor: An Address Delivered at the National Conference of Seamen's Aid Societies at Boston, Mass., Oct. 26 1899. New York, [1899].

Johnson, W.B.
    The English Prison Hulks. London, 1970 (2nd ed.).

Jones, Charles J.
    From the Forecastle to the Pulpit: Fifty Years among Sailors. New York, 1884.
    The Duty of the Church to the Men of the Sea. New York, n.d.

Jones, Stephen.
    "Blood Red Roses: The Supply of Merchant Seamen in the Nineteenth Century," *The Mariner's Mirror,* 1972, pp. 429-42.

Jones, William.
    The Jubilee Memorial of the Religious Tract Society. London, 1850.

Kaplan, Justin.
    Walt Whitman: A Life. New York, 1980.

[Kealey, A.G.]
    Chaplains of the Royal Navy, 1626-1903. Portsmouth [1905].

Keen, Gregory B.
    "The Descendants of Jöran Kyn . . . ," *The Pennsylvania Magazine of History and Biography* (Philadelphia), 1880, vol. 4, pp. 494-500.

Kelley, Harold H.
    "The Early History of the Church's Work for Seamen in the United States," *Historical Magazine of the Protestant Episcopal Church,* Dec. 1940, pp. 349-67.

Kemp, Peter.
    The British Sailor: A Social History of the Lower Deck. London, 1970.

Kemp, Peter (Ed.).
    The Oxford Companion to Ships and the Sea. London, 1976.

Kennedy, Gavin.
Bligh. London, 1978.

Kerfoot, T.P.
"Finance and the Well-Being of Seafarers: The Financing of Seafarers' Welfare Facilities," *Report of First Plenary Conference London ... 1972*, ICMA [1973], pp. 26-32.
"Interconfessional Collaboration," *On the Move*, No. 4, December 1972, pp. 108-23.
Note: Also editor of First to Fourth *ICMA Plenary Conference Reports* and *ICMA News*.

King George's Fund for Sailors.
Nautical Benevolent and Welfare Organisations. London, 1954.

King, John.
Memoirs of the Rev. Thomas Dykes. London, 1849.

Kingsford, Maurice Rooke.
The Life, Work and Influence of William Henry Giles Kingston. Toronto, 1947.
The Mersey Mission to Seamen 1856-1956. Abingdon, 1957.

Kingston, William H.G.
A Cruise on the Mersey... with an Account of the Late Proceedings of the Society for Promoting Missions to Seamen Afloat at Home and Abroad, and a Sketch of the Intended Operations of the Committee. London, 1857. (Reprinted as an addendum, pp. I-XXVI, to *The Mersey Mission to Seamen, 1856-1956*, M.R. Kingsford, Abingdon, 1957.)

Kirke-Leksikon for Norden (Church Encyclopedia for the Nordic Nations). 4 Vols. Copenhagen, 1900-29.

Kirkelig Maanedstidende. Madison (Wisconsin).

Kirkeligt Maanedsblad. Fredericia (Denmark).

Kirke og Kultur (Church and Culture). Kristiania/Oslo.

Klose, Nelson.
American History. Vol. 1. Woodbury, New York, 1965.

Knox, Dudley W.
A History of the United States Navy. New York, 1948.

Kolmodin, A.
"Naagra ord om Den Svenska Sjömans-Missionen" (About the Swedish Seamen's Mission), *Missions-Bibliotek för Folket*, Pt. IV, Stockholm, 1889.

Kraemer, Hendrik.
The Christian Message in a Non-Christian World. New York, 1938.

Kvale, Dagfinn.
"Maiblomsten" ("The Mayflower"), *Maanedsbladet* (London), May 1981 (n. pag.). Note: Newsletter of the Norwegian Seamen's Church, London.

Kverndal, Roald.
Broderkretsen paa Havet 1885-1960 (The Christian Brotherhood of the Ocean 1885-1960). Co-authored with Kaare Helle, Bergen, 1960.
"Styrmannen som ga stötet" (The Chief Mate who gave the Impulse), *Bud og Hilsen*, 1964, pp. 292-5.
"Et sjömannsemblem som aldri maa dö" (A Seamen's Emblem which must never Die), *Bud og Hilsen*, pp. 421-5.

"Sjömannskirken i London som kolonikirke" (The Norwegian Seamen's Church in London as Church for Resident Norwegians), *Kirke og Kultur,* 1968, pp. 346-54.

"Mötet mellom sjöfolk og ikke-kristne folkeslag som motiv for de eldste sjömannsmisjonsbestrebelser" (The Encounter between Seamen and Non-Christian Peoples as a Motivation for Early Missions to Seamen), *Norsk Tidsskrift for Misjon,* 1969, pp. 220-35.

"Forgjengerne" (The Forerunners), *Se Deg om i glede: Sjömannskirken i Baltimore 50 aar 1919-1969* (Look around you with Joy: 50th Anniversary of the Seamen's Church in Baltimore 1919-1969). Asbjörn Nilsen (Ed.), Bergen, 1969, pp. 13-5.

"How Do We Approach Ship Visitation in the Norwegian Seamen's Mission?" *Port Exchange* (New York), March 1970, pp. 43-4. Note: Newsletter of the American Seamen's Friend Society.

"Broderkretskapteinen Arthur Kildahl" (The Bethel Captain Arthur Kildahl), *En sjöens adelsmann. Fra kaptein Arthur G. Kildahls liv,* Sverre Norborg (Ed.), Stavanger, 1970, pp. 164-70.

Sjömannsetikk: Haandbok i yrkesetikk og livssynsorientering (Maritime Ethics: A Manual in Vocational Ethics and Faith Guidance). Oslo, 1971.

"Naadens Havn: 100 aar siden den förste norske sjömannsmisjonsstasjon ble opprettet pa fransk jord" (Haven of Grace: 100 Years since the First Norwegian Seamen's Mission Station was Established on French Soil), *Sjömannsmisjonens julehefte* (Bergen), 1972, pp. 34-38.

"Internasjonal sjömannsmisjon: Opprinnelse og förste fremvekst" (International Seamen's Mission: Origin and Early Growth), *Forskningsnytt* (Oslo), 1972, pp. 38-41.

"Sjömannsmisjon og ökumenikk" (Seamen's Missions and Ecumenics), *Norsk Tidsskrift for Misjon,* 1973, pp. 31-36.

"Den förste nordiske sjömannsmisjon: Blad fra 'Bethelskipets' saga, i nittende-aarhundrets New York" (The First Nordic Seamen's Mission: Pages from the Bethelship Saga in Nineteenth Century New York), *Kirke og Kultur,* 1974, pp. 630-4.

"Sörlendinger og sjöfart i den Nye Verden" (Southern Norwegians and Seafaring in the New World), *Aarbok for Agder Bispedömme* (Kristiansand, Norway), 1975, pp. 45-51.

"Memoirs of the Founder of Seamen's Missions in 1801," *The Mariner's Mirror,* 1976, pp. 47-51.

"The Origin of the Maritime Ministry in the Port of Philadelphia," *The ICOSA Newsletter* (Duluth, Minnesota), November 1976, pp. 20-7.

"Serving the Seafarer: The Ministry to Mariners from Norway in the Port of Chicago," *From Fjord to Prairie,* Lawrence M. Nelson (Ed.), Chicago, 1976, c., pp. 50-5.

"The Bethel Ship 'John Wesley': A New York Ship Saga from the Mid-1800's with Reverberations on Both Sides of the Atlantic Ocean," *Methodist History,* July 1977, pp. 211-33.

"A Voice from the Prison-Hulks: Speech by 'An American Seaman' at Chatham, England, 4 July 1814," *The American Neptune,* April 1978, pp. 142-43.

"The Origin and Nature of Nordic Missions to Seamen," *Sjöfartshistorisk Aarbok 1977* (Norwegian Yearbook of Maritime History 1977), Bergen, 1978, pp. 103-34.

"Pionerspor i verdenshavnen: Fra norsk sjömannsmisjons forhistorie og grunnleggelse i New York" (Pioneer Tracks in the World Port: From the Prehistory and Foundation of Norwegian Seamen's Mission in New York), *Norsk sjömannsmisjon i New York 1878-1978 100 aar* (Norwegian Seamen's Mission in New York 1878-1978 100 Years), Sigurd Daasvand (Ed.), New York, 1978, pp. 5-26.

"The 200th Anniversary of Organized Seamen's Missions, 1779-1979," *The Mariner's Mirror,* 1979, pp. 255-63.

"Pensacola: The Pioneer Period of its Ministry to Seafarers," *Watermarks,* 1979, No. 2, pp. 8-9.

"Prayers for Seafarers: A Historical Perspective—With Presentday Promise," *Watermarks,* 1979, No. 3, pp. 4-5.

"Tacoma Seamen's Friends: A Heritage and a Challenge," *Watermarks,* 1980, No. 2, pp. 3-5.

"Captain Cook, Seamen's Missions—and Hawaii," *Nautical Magazine,* 1980, pp. 6-8.

"How Seamen's Work Started in Savannah," *Watermarks,* 1981, No. 2-3, pp. 3-7.

Enhanced Lutheran Outreach to Seafarers: A Report with Recommendations on Maritime Ministry in U.S. Port Cities. Published by Lutheran Council in the USA. New York, 1983.

Hva er sjömannsmisjon? (What is Mission to Seafarers?). A 12-part series in *Bud og Hilsen,* Bergen (Norway), 1984-85.

"Mission to Seafarers: A 'New' Frontier of World Mission and a Lutheran Response," *Mission Notes,* Geneva, Oct. 1985, pp. 8-11.

Kverndal, Roald (Ed.).
Bud fra Havet (q.v.), 1958-61, 1963-67.
Lutheran Maritime News (q.v.), from 1982.
Watermarks (q.v.), from 1979.

Ladies' Seamen's Friend Society of the Port of San Francisco.
Reports. San Francisco.

Laffin, John.
Jack Tar: The Story of the British Sailor. London, 1969.

Laing, Alexander.
The American Heritage History of Seafaring America. New York, 1974.

Landers, Anthony.
Sailors Wanted! Officers and Men, on a Voyage with the Captain of Our Salvation; Bound from the Harbour of Destruction to the Haven of Eternal Rest. New York, 1815.

Lane, Arthur.
Illustrated Notes on English Church History. London, 1900.

Langley, Harold D.
Social Reform in the United States Navy, 1798-1862. Chicago, 1967.

Larrouy, Maurice.
   Le Marin. Paris, 1927.
Lascelles, E.C.P.
   Granville Sharp and the Freedom of Slaves in England. Oxford, 1928.
Latimer, John.
   The Annals of Bristol in the 18th Century. Bristol, 1893.
Latourette, Kenneth Scott.
   "Research and Christian Missions," *The International Review of Missions*
   (London), 1932, pp. 532-46.
   A History of Christianity. New York, 1953.
   A History of the Expansion of Christianity. 7 Vols. Grand Rapids (Michigan),
   1970.
The Lausanne Covenant. (John Stott, Ed.). Minneapolis, 1975.
Lazareth, William H.
   "Priest and Priesthood," *The Encyclopedia of the Lutheran Church,* Minne-
   apolis, 1965, Vol. 3, pp. 1964-66.
Lea, George.
   Memoir of the Rev. John Davies . . . . London, 1859.
Leavitt, Joshua [Ed.].
   *Seamen's Devotional Assistant and Mariners' Hymns: Prepared under
   Direction of the American Seamen's Friend Society.* New York, 1830.
Lecky, William E.H.
   A History of England in the Eighteenth Century. London, 1921.
Lednum, John.
   A History of the Rise of Methodism in America . . . . Philadelphia, 1859.
Leech, Samuel.
   A Voice from the Main Deck. Boston (Massachusetts), 1843.
Lehane, Brendan.
   The Northwest Passage. Alexandria (Virginia), 1981.
Lensch, Friedrich.
   " 'Christliche Seefahrt' im Mittelalter," *75 Jahre Deutsche Seemannsmission
   in Hamburg R.V. 1891-1966,* Hamburg, 1966, pp. 27-32.
Lewis, J.G.
   Fifty Years of Sunday School Work. London, 1883.
Lewis, Michael.
   England's Sea-Officers: The Story of the Naval Profession. London, 1948a.
   The Navy of Britain: A Historical Portrait. London, 1948b.
   The History of the British Navy. London, 1959. (1st ed. 1957).
   A Social History of the Navy, 1793-1815. London, 1960.
   The Navy in Transition, 1814-1864: A Social History. London, 1965.
The Life and Labors of Adam Clarke, LL.D. London, 1834.
Lindsay, W.S.
   History of Merchant Shipping and Ancient Commerce. 4 Vols. London,
   1874-76.
Lindsell, Harold.
   Missionary Principles and Practice. Old Tappan (New Jersey), 1955.
   The Church's Worldwide Mission. Waco (Texas), 1966.

Lindskog, J.
Agnes Welin och hennes livsverk (Agnes Welin and Her Life's Work). Stockholm, 1929.

Littell, Franklin H.
"The Free Church View of Mission," *The Theology of the Christian Mission.* Gerald H. Anderson (Ed.), 1961, pp. 112-21.

Liverpool Seamen's Friend Society.
Historical Sketch of the Work of the Society. Liverpool [1900].
Annual Reports, 1895-1906.

Ljungberg, Enoch.
Svenska Betelföreningen 1884-1959. (Swedish Bethel Union 1884-1959.) Klippan (Sweden), 1959.

Lloyd, Christopher.
The British Seaman 1200-1860: A Social Survey. London, 1968.

London City Mission.
Annual Reports. London.

The Lookout. New York (New York).
Note: Published by Seamen's Church Institute of New York and New Jersey.

Lorrain, Alfred M.
The Square-Rigged Cruiser; or, Lorrain's Sea-Sermons. Cincinnati (Ohio), 1852.

The Louisiana Gazette. New Orleans.

Low, Sampson.
The Charities of London. London, 1850.
The Charities of London in 1861. London, 1862.

Luke, Jemima.
Sketches of the Life and Character of Thomas Thompson. London, 1868.

Lundmark, Gustaf.
"Evangeliska Fosterlands-Stiftelsens sjömannsmission genom 100 aar" (The Evangelical National Missionary Society's Seamen's Mission during 100 Years), *Svensk sjömanskyrka 100 aar, 1869-1969,* Allan Hofgren (Ed.), Stockholm, 1969.

Lurting, Thomas.
The Fighting Sailor Turned Peaceable Christian: Manifested in the Convincement and Conversion of Thomas Lurting . . . . Leeds, 1816.

Lutheran Maritime News. Bellevue/Seattle (Washington).
Note: Newsletter of the Lutheran Association for Maritime Ministry (LAMM).

Lutheran World Information. (Geneva).
Note: Weekly newsletter of the Lutheran World Federation.

Luthersk Kirketidende. Christiania/Kristiania/Oslo.

Lydenberg, Harry M.
Crossing the Line. New York, 1957.

Macdonald, Allan.
"A Sailor among the Transcendentalists," *The New England Quarterly* 1935, pp. 307-19.

McDonough, Thomas A.
"Christian Animation of Shipboard Communities," *On the Move,* no. 4, Vatican City (Rome), 1972, pp. 158-9.

Macduff, J.R.
The Sailor's Text-book. Boston [1859].

Mace, S.H.
A Signal Gun... Containing the Substance of the Letter of the Rev. J. Sibree... to the World Newspaper.... London, 1832.

Macfarlane, George.
Biographical Sketches of the Leith Clergy. Leith, 1864.

Maddocks, Melvin.
The Atlantic Crossing. Alexandria (Virginia), 1981.

Madoxe, John.
A Learned and a Godly Sermon, to Be Read of All Men; but Especially for All Marryners, Captaynes, and Passengers, which Travell the Seas.... Weymouth, 1581.

Manchester, Herbert.
A Century of Service: The Seamen's Bank for Savings 1829-1929. New York, 1929.

Mannix, Daniel.
Black Cargo: A History of the Atlantic Slave Trade, 1619-1862. Stanford, 1963.

Manwaring, G.E. (Ed.).
The Diary of Henry Teonge: Chaplain on Board H.M.'s Ships Assistance, Bristol, and Royal Oak, 1675-1679. London, 1927.

The Marine Bible Society, Charleston (South Carolina).
Annual Reports. Charleston (South Carolina).

The Marine Bible Society for the District of Salem and Beverly.
Marine Bible Society. Salem (Massachusetts), 1820.

The Marine Bible Society of New-York.
Constitution of the Marine Bible Society of New-York, Auxiliary to the American Bible Society; together with an Address to Merchants and Masters of Vessels, and an Address to Seamen. New York, 1817.
Annual Reports. New York.

Marine-Hospital Service.
Annual Report of the Supervising Surgeon of the Marine-Hospital Service of the United States. Washington, 1873.

Marine Hospital Service.
Annual Reports. Washington, D.C.

The Marine Mission at Large.
Annual Reports. Boston, 1849, etc.

The Marine Society.
The Bye-laws and Regulations.... London, 1809.
Annual Reports (213th-218th). London, 1970-75.
The Marine Society. London, n.d.

The Mariners' Advocate. Boston.

The Mariner's Church, Philadelphia. Philadelphia, 1824.

The Mariners' Church, Philadelphia.
   Reports. Philadelphia.

Mariners' Family Industrial Society.
   Records of Benevolent Efforts .... New York, 1865.
   Annual Reports. New York.
   Note: Name changed to: "Mariners' Family Asylum," and again to: "Mariners' Family Home."

The Mariners' Magazine. New York.
   Note: Published as Vol. 1 in 52 weekly numbers, March 5, 1825–February 25, 1826, under the patronage of the "[Port of New-York] Society for Promoting the Gospel among Seamen" and the "Bethel Union of New-York," and under the editorship of the Rev. John Truair.

The Mariner's Mirror. (The Society for Nautical Research.) London.

Mariners' Pilot. Philadelphia.

Marks, Richard.
   Nautical Essays; or, a Spiritual View of the Ocean and Maritime Affairs ....
   London, 1818.
   The Reprospect; or, Review of Providential Mercies. (Pseudonym: *Aliquis.*)
   Philadelphia, 1821. (From 4th London ed., 1st ed.: London, 1816.)
   Ditto. New York, 1843. (3rd American ed., from 17th London ed.) Note: As from 15th London ed., enlarged with 9 additional chapters.
   The Seamen's Friend .... Hartford (Connecticut), 1823. (1st ed. London, n.d.)
   The Ocean, Spiritually Reviewed .... London, 1826. (1st ed. 1824.)
   Sea Sermons .... London, 1843.
   The Smugglers. London, n.d.
   The Wreckers, or, a View of What Sometimes Passes on Our Sea Coast.
   London, n.d.

Marriott, J.A.R.
   England since Waterloo. London, 1954. (1st ed. 1913.)

Marryat, Frederick.
   Mr. Midshipman Easy. London, 1836.

Marsden, J.B.
   Two Sermons on the Life, Ministry and Death of the Rev. Richard Marks.
   London, 1847.

Martin, Bernhard.
   John Newton: A Biography. London, 1950.

Martindale, C.C.
   The Sea and its Apostolate. London, (Revised ed.) N.d.

Martingale, Hawser (J.S. Sleeper).
   Tales of the Ocean, and Essays for the Forecastle. Boston (Massachusetts), 1856.

Marty, Martin E.
   A Short History of Christianity. Cleveland (Ohio), 1975.

Marvin, Winthrop.
   The American Merchant Marine: In History and Romance from 1620 to 1902. New York, 1910.

Massachusetts Bible Society.
The First Hundred Years... 1809-1909. Boston, [1909].
Reports. Boston (Massachusetts).

Massachusetts Historical Society.
"Memoir of Gamaliel Bradford, Esq.," *Collections,* Boston, 1825, pp. 202-9.
"Memoir of the Late Rev. J.S. Buckminster," *Collections,* Boston, 1838, pp. 271-4.
"Memoir of the Rev. Charles Lowell, D.D.," *Proceedings,* Feb., 1862, Boston, pp. 427-440.
"Memoir of William Jenks, D.D., L.L.D.," *Proceedings,* Jan. 1868, Boston, pp. 106-12.

The Massachusetts Missionary Magazine. Boston.

Massey, Craig.
"Peer Groups Need Your Witness," *Moody Monthly* (Chicago), October 1975, pp. 56-60.

Mather, Cotton.
The Religious Marriner.... Boston, 1700.
The Sailours Companion and Counsellour: An Offer of Considerations for the Tribe of Zebulun. Boston, 1709.
The Thankful Christian... Address'd... Especially unto them, who after Good Successes of a Whaling Season, Would Express their Gratitude unto God.... Boston, 1717.
Useful Remarks... A Sermon on the Tragical End, unto which the Way of Twenty-Six Pirates Brought them. New London (Connecticut), 1723.
Religious Societies: Proposals for the Revival of Dying Religion, by Well-ordered Societies for that Purpose.... Boston, 1724.

Mather, Ebenezer J.
Nor'ard of the Dogger.... London, 1887.

Mathew, David.
British Seamen. London, 1943.

Matthews, Edward Walter.
Belaying-Pin Gospel. London, 1885.
The King's Brotherhood. London, 1911.

Matthews, Gordon Forrester.
The Isles of Scilly. London, 1960.

McCarthy, Charles P.
The Word and the Sword: Being the Substance of a Lecture Delivered in London, and in Various Towns, on the Progress of Religion amongst the Soldiers and Seamen of England. London, 1861.

McColgan, Daniel T.
Joseph Tuckerman: Pioneer in American Social Work. Washington, D.C., 1940.
A Century of Charity. Milwaukee (Wisconsin), 1951.

McGavran, Donald A.
"The People Movement Point of View," *Church Growth and Group Conversion,* J.W. Pickett, A.L. Warnhuis, G.H. Singh and D.A. McGavran. Lucknow, 1956, pp. 1-7.

"Theory of Mission," *Concise Dictionary of the Christian World Mission.* London, 1970, pp. 595-96.

Understanding Church Growth. Grand Rapids (Michigan), 1970.

McGuinness, Denis.
Apostleship of the Sea. London, 1975.

McNally, William.
Evils and Abuses in the Naval and Merchant Service, Exposed: With Proposals for Their Remedy and Redress. Boston, 1839.

McPherson, Charles.
Life on Board a Man-of-War. Glasgow, 1829.

Mead, Frank S.
Handbook of Denominations in the United States. Nashville (Tennessee), 1970.

Mead, Joseph.
A Voice from Wellclose Square: . . . Containing a Complete Exposure of the Conduct of the Rev. G.C. Smith . . . . London [1831].

Mead, Sidney E.
The Lively Experiment: The Shaping of Christianity in America. New York, 1963.

Mee, Arthur (Ed.).
The King's England: Cornwall. London, 1947.

Meikle, James.
Solicitude Sweetened . . . . Edinburgh, 1803.
The Traveller . . . . Edinburgh, 1811. (1st ed., 1805.)

Melville, Herman.
White Jacket: Or, the World in a Man-of-War. Boston, 1892.
Moby Dick: Or, the White Whale. New York, 1964.

Memorial of the Norfolk Seamen's Friend Society. (Doc. No. 68, presented to the Legislature of the State of Virginia.) N.p., n.d.

Memorial of the Reunion of the Natives of Westhampton, Mass., Sept. 5, 1866. Waltham, 1866.

Menneskevennen. Kristiania (Oslo).

Merchant Navy Christian Fellowship.
Report of the Inaugural Meeting held at Southport . . . 1959. N.p., 1959.

Merchant Seamen's Auxiliary Bible Society.
Prospectus and Regulations. London, 1818.
Annual Reports. London.

Mersey Mission to Seamen.
Annual Reports. Liverpool.

Methodist History. Lake Junaluska (North Carolina).

Methodist Episcopal Mariner's Bethel.
Annual Report. Philadelphia, 1882.

Michaelsen, Oddvar M.
"Evangelisation and Pastoral Care in Relation to Seafarers," *Third Plenary Conference, New York 1978: Papers and Addresses* (ICMA), 1979, pp. 15-24.

[Middleton, Robert.]
  Memoirs of Mr. George Cussons of London. London, 1819.

Miller, Amos C.
  "John Syms, Puritan Naval Chaplain," *The Mariner's Mirror,* 1974.

Miller, Bennetts C. (Ed.)
  Souvenir History of the New England Southern Conference. Nantasket (Massachusetts), 1891.

Miller, Donald G.
  "Pauline Motives for the Christian Mission," *The Theology of the Christian Mission* Gerald H. Anderson (Ed.), 1961.

Miller, Kenneth and Ethel.
  The People Are the City. New York, 1962.

Miller, Perry.
  Errand into the Wilderness. New York, 1964.

Miller, Russel.
  The East Indiamen. Alexandria (Virginia), 1980.

Millington, E.C.
  Seamen in the Making. London, 1935.

Milne, James.
  Maritime Piety: Being a Sketch of the Life and Labours of Jeremiah Taylor . . . . With a Sketch of the Rise and Progress of Religion among Seamen. London, 1851.

Milner, Joseph.
  An Affectionate Admonition to Seamen. Boston, 1848.

Milnor, James.
  The Seaman's Devotional Assistant. New York, 1822.

The Ministry of Transport and Civil Aviation, and the Central Office of Information.
  Seafarers and Their Ships: The Story of a Century of Progress in the Safety of Ships and the Wellbeing of Seamen. New York, 1956.

Minutes of the Methodist Conferences. London.

Mission Notes. Geneva.
  Note: Newsletter of the Lutheran World Federation, Department of Church Cooperation.

Mission to British Seamen. Bristol, April, 1853.
  Note: Published by the Bristol Channel Seamen's Mission, and quoted in *The Word on the Waters* (London, 1858, pp. 8-12), under the title "Origin of the Mission to Seamen."

The Missionary Advocate. New York.

The Missionary Register. London.

The Missionary Society.
  A Missionary Voyage to the Southern Pacific Ocean: Performed in the Years 1796, 1797, 1798, in the Ship Duff, Commanded by Captain James Wilson. London, 1799.

The Missionary Society of the Methodist Episcopal Church.
  Annual Reports. New York.

The Missions to Seamen.
T S M Y John Ashley III. London, 1971.
Annual Reports. London.

Missions-Tidning. (Evangeliska Fosterlands-Stiftelsen.) Stockholm.

Missions-Tidning för Finland. (Finska Missionssällskapet.) Helsingfors.

Mitchell, C. Bradford.
"Pride of the Seas," *American Heritage* (New York), 1967, Vol. 19, no. 1,
pp. 64-88.

Mitchell, Charles.
The Long Watch: A History of the Sailors' Children's Society 1821-1961.
[Hull], 1961.

Molland, Einar.
Konfesjonskunnskap (Symbolics). Oslo, 1961.
"Storjohann, Johan Cordt Harmens," *Norsk biografisk Leksikon.* Vol. 15.
Oslo, 1966, pp. 50-5.
Norges kirkehistorie i det 19. aarhundre (Norway's Church History in the
19th Century). 2 Vols. Oslo, 1979.

Montagu, Horatio.
*Zebulon under the Law and Zebulon under the Gospel: A Sermon, on Behalf
of the Bristol Seamen's Friend Society.* Bristol, 1832.

Montgomery, D.H.
The Leading Facts of American History. Boston, 1902.

Moorman, John R.H.
A History of the Church in England. London, 1953.

Morgan, George.
The City of Firsts. Philadelphia, 1926.

Morgenbladet. Oslo.

Morison, Samuel Eliot.
Maritime History of Massachusetts, 1783-1860. Boston, 1921. (Another ed.:
Boston 1941).
The Oxford History of the American People. New York 1965, also 1972.

Morris, Ira K.
Morris's Memorial History of Staten Island. Vol. 2. Staten Island (New
York), 1900.

[Morrison, Eliza.]
Memoirs of the Life and Labours of Robert Morrison, D.D. 2 Vols. London,
1839.

Morrison, Robert.
A Parting Memorial.... London, 1826.

Moyse-Bartlett, H.
A History of the Merchant Navy. London, 1937.

Münchmeyer, Rienhard.
Handbuch der deutschen evangelischen Seemannsmission. Stettin, 1912.

Murphy, Abbie M.
"Ever Heard of Mooncussers?" *The Lookout,* October 1970, pp. 3-4.

Muscat, Joseph.
"An Altar from the Galleys of the Order of St. John: The Celebration of Mass at Sea," *The Mariner's Mirror,* 1984, pp. 389-95.

Myklebust, Olav G.
"Encyklopediske synspunkter med hensyn paa misjonsvitenskapen" (Encyclopedic Considerations in Connection with the Science of Missions) in *Tidsskrift for Teologi og Kirke,* 1946, pp. 118-31.
Misjon i en ny tid (Mission in a new age). Oslo, 1971.
Misjonskunnskap: En innföring (The Science of Mission: An Introduction). Oslo, 1976.

A Narrative of the Revival of Religion . . . . Particularly in the Bounds of the Presbytery of Oneida, in the Year 1826. Utica (New York), 1826.

Nasty-face, Jack.
Nautical Economy: Or, Forecastle Recollections of Events during the Last War . . . . London, 1836.

Nautical Magazine. Glasgow.

Nautical Magazine. London.

The Naval Chronicle. London.

Naval and Military Bible Society.
An Account of the Naval and Military Bible Society from its Institution in 1780 to Lady-Day 1804. London, 1804.
Appeal in Behalf of the Naval and Military Bible Society. London, 1834.
Annual Reports. London.

Naval, Military and Air Force Bible Society. (Undated brochure current in 1970.)

The Navy List. London.

The Negro Almanac. New York, 1976.

Neill, Stephen.
A History of Christian Missions. London, 1964.
Anglicanism. London, 1965.
"Aim of Missions," *Concise Dictionary of the Christian World Mission.* London, 1970, p. 12.
"Church Growth," *ditto,* pp. 110-1.
"Paternalism," *ditto,* pp. 472-73.
"Problems of Missionaries," *ditto,* pp. 496-7.

Nerhus, Hans.
"Sjymain'n" (The Seaman), *For kirke og kultur,* 1941, pp. 467-81, 553-62.

New Bedford Port Society.
Annual Reports. New Bedford (Massachusetts).

The New Bible Dictionary. Grand Rapids (Michigan), 1974.

New Catholic Encyclopedia. New York, 1967.

New England Historical and Genealogical Register. Boston (Massachusetts).

New Orleans Port Society.
Annual Reports. New Orleans.

Newton, John.
An Authentic Narrative . . . . London, 1799. (1st ed., 1764.)

The New Sailor's Magazine. London.
    Note: Commenced 1827 as: *The New Sailor's Magazine and Naval Chronicle.*
    Editor (until his death in 1863): The Rev. George Charles Smith. Published
    under the auspices of the British and Foreign Seamen and Soldier's Friend
    Society, and the other societies with which the Editor was successively
    affiliated. Volume designation is not consistent, but eventually reverts to an
    enumeration from 1820. Titles vary as follows:
    — From 1833: *The Mariners' Church Society Sailors' Magazine and Naval
       Chronicle.*
    — From 1836: *The Mariners' Church Soldiers' and Sailors' Magazine.*
    — From 1839: *The Mariners' Church Temperance Soldiers' and Sailors'
       Magazine.*
    — From 1842: *The Mariners' Church Gospel Temperance Soldiers' and
       Sailors' Magazine.*
    — From 1853: *The Soldiers' and Sailors' Magazine.*
    — From 1856: *The Evangelical Christian Soldiers' and Sailors' Temperance
       Magazine.*
    — From 1860: *The Mariners' Church Gospel Temperance Sailors' and
       Soldiers' Magazine.*

The New Schaff-Herzog Encyclopedia of Religious Knowledge. New York, 1906-12.

New York Bethel Union.
    Reports. New York.

New York Bible Society.
    Annual Reports. New York.

New York Port Society.
    Note: Original title: "Society for Promoting Gospel among Seamen in the Port
    of New-York."
    Reports. New York.
    The Record. New York.

New York Standard. New York.

[Nibbs, C.A.J.]
    From the Bristol Channel to the Seven Seas. London [1935] (12th ed., 1962).

Nicol, John.
    The Life and Adventures of John Nicol, Mariner. London, 1822.

Nilsen, Asbjörn (Ed.)
    Se deg om i glede. Sjömannskirken i Baltimore 50 aar: 1919-1969 (Look
    Around You with Joy: the]Norwegian[Seaman's Church in Baltimore During
    50 Years: 1919-69). Bergen, 1969.

Nome, John.
    Demringstid i Norge: Fra misjonsinteresse til misjonsselkap. (Early Dawn in
    Norway, From Missionary interest to Missionary Society.) Stavanger, 1942.

Norborg, Sverre.
    Sjömenn og sjöliv (Seamen and Sea Life). Oslo, 1932.

Norborg, Sverre (Ed.).
    En sjöens adelsmann: Fra kaptein Arthur G. Kildahls liv (A Nobleman of
    the Sea: From the Life of Captain Arthur G. Kildahl). Stavanger, 1970.

Nordisk Familjebok (Nordic Family Book). Malmö (Sweden), 1963. (4th edition.)

Nordisk Teologisk Uppslagsbok (Nordic Theological Encyclopedia). Lund (Sweden), 1957.

Norelius, Eric.
De svenska luterska församlingarnas och svenskarnas historie i America (History of the Swedish Lutheran Congregations and the Swedes in America). Rock Island (Illinois), 1890.

Norsk Kirketidende. Christiania (Oslo).

Norsk Tidsskrift for Misjon (Norwegian Journal of Mission). Oslo.
Note: Published by the Egede Institute of Missionary Study and Research.

Norwegian Seamen's Mission.
Rundskriv til Foreningens Udsendinger (Circular to the Society's Representatives). Bergen (Norway), January, 1903.

O'Byrne, William Richard.
A Naval Biographical Dictionary. London, 1849.

Oehlkers, P.
Bestand, Ziele, Hindernisse der deutschen evangelischen Seemannsmission (Situation, Aims, Impediments of the German Evangelical Seamen's Mission). Bremen, 1897.

[Oglethorpe, James E.]
The Sailors Advocate. London, 1728. (Also, a 7th Edition in 1777, with Granville Sharp contributing to the "Introduction.")

Olán, Eskil.
Sjörövarna paa Medelhavet och Levantiska Compagniet (The Pirates in the Mediterranean and the Levantine Company). Stockholm, 1921.

Olmstead, Clifton E.
History of Religion in the United States. Englewood Cliffs (New Jersey), 1960.
Religion in America Past and Present. Englewood Cliffs (New Jersey), 1961.

On the Move. See "Pontificia Commissio."

"On the Probable Influence of Moral and Religious Instruction on the Character and Situation of Seamen" (by "E."), *Blackwood's Edinburgh Magazine* (Edinburgh), 1821, pp. 414-21, 531-40, 363-71, and 514-24.

Orädd, Daniel.
Sjöfolkets bästa bedrift (Seafarers' Finest Accomplishment). Helsingfors, 1951.

An Oration: Delivered by Permission on Board the Nassau Prison-ship by Chatham, England, on the Fourth July, 1814: By an American Seaman, Prisoner of War. Boston, 1815.

Orchard, Ronald K., and Stephen Neill.
"Mission Boards and Societies, Great Britain," *Concise Dictionary of the Christian World Mission.* London, 1970.

Örner, Jan.
"Missions to Seamen," *International Review of Mission* (Geneva), 1971, pp. 395-400.

Otterland, Anders.
A Sociomedical Study of the Mortality in Merchant Seafarers. Gothenburg, 1960.

Overton, John H.
The Evangelical Revival in the Eighteenth Century. London, 1886.

Overton, John H., and Frederic Relton.
The English Church: From the Accession of George I. to the End of the Eighteenth Century. London, 1906.

Owen, John.
The History of the Origin and First Ten Years of the British and Foreign Bible Society. 2 parts. London, 1816.

Page, Samuel.
Divine Sea-service: Containing Sundry Necessary and Usefull Formes of Prayer and Thanksgiving for the Helpe of Such as Travaile by Sea, Fitted to their Severall Necessities. London, 1616.

Paine, Ralph D.
The Old Merchant Marine: A Chronicle of American Ships and Sailors. New Haven (Connecticut), 1919.

Palmer, Roy (Ed.).
The Valiant Sailor . . . . Cambridge, 1973.

Palmer, Benjamin M.
Claims of Seamen on Christian Benevolence . . . . Charleston (South Carolina), 1822.

The Pamphleteer. London.

The Panoplist and Missionary Magazine. Boston.

Parkinson, C. Northcote.
Portsmouth Point: The British Navy in Fiction 1793-1815. Cambridge (Massachusetts), 1949.

Parry, William Edward.
A Lecture . . . . London, 1855.

Pascoe, C.F.
Two Hundred Years S.P.G.: An Historical Account of the Society for the Propagation of the Gospel in Foreign Parts 1701-1900. London, 1901.

Paterson, John.
The Book for every Land. London, 1858.

Paulding, Hiram.
Journal of a Cruise of the United States Schooner Dolphin. New York, 1831.

Payson, Edward.
An Address to Seamen . . . . Portland (Maine), 1821.
The Oracles of God . . . . Portland (Maine), 1824.
Jesus Christ, Anchor of the Soul. Philadelphia, 1858. (New Edition.)
The Seamen's Chart . . . . New York [n.d.].

Peabody, Elizabeth P.
Reminiscences of Rev. W. Ellery Channing, D.D. Boston, 1880.

Peet, Henry.
St. Nicholas's Church, Liverpool. Liverpool, 1913.

Penn, Geoffrey.
Snotty: The Story of the Midshipman. London, 1957.

Pennsylvania Seamen's Friend Society.
Annual Reports. Philadelphia.

Penrose, Charles V.
    Observations on Corporal Punishment, Impressment, and Other Matters....
    Bodmin, 1824.

Perkins, Bradford.
    Prologue to War: England and the United States, 1804-1812. Berkeley
    (California), 1961.

Pfeiffer, Edward.
    Mission Studies. Columbus (Ohio), 1920.

The Philadelphia Inquirer. Philadelphia.

Philip, Robert.
    The Bethel Flag, or Sermons to Seamen. Liverpool, 1823.

Phillips, Clifton J.
    *Protestant America and the Pagan World: The First Half Century of the
    American Board of Commissioners for Foreign Missions, 1810-1860.*
    Cambridge (Massachusetts), 1969.

Phillips, John.
    The Briton's Bulwark, or, the Sailor's Friend. Liverpool, 1766.

Pickett, J.W., A.L. Warnshuis, G.H. Singh, and D.A. McGavran.
    Church Growth and Group Conversion. Lucknow, 1956.

Pierard, Richard V.
    "Social Concern in Christian Missions," *Christianity Today* (Washington,
    D.C.), 1976, pp. 975-8.

Pierce, Bessie Louise.
    A History of Chicago. Vols. 1-2. New York, 1937, 1940.

Pierpoint, John.
    A Discource... [on] *Horace Holley LL.D.* Boston, 1827.

Pike, G. Holden.
    Among the Sailors: During the Life and Reign of the Queen. London, 1897.

The Pilot. (St. Paul's Church for Seamen.) London.

The Pilot, or Sailors' Magazine. (British and Foreign Sailors' Society).
    Note: See *The Sailor's Magazine,* London.

Plimsoll, Samuel.
    Our Seamen. London, 1872.

Polak, Ada.
    Wolffs & Dorville. Oslo, 1968.

Polley, Jane (Ed.)
    American Folklore and Legend. Pleasantville (New York), 1978.

Pontificia Commissio de Spirituali Migratorum atque Itinerantium Cura.
    On the Move. Vatican City (Rome). Note: A review published by the Pontifical
    Commission for the Pastoral Care of Migrants and Itinerant Peoples (which
    includes "Apostolatus Maris").

Pope, Dudley.
    The Great Gamble: Nelson at Copenhagen, a Definitive Account. New York,
    1972.

Pope-Hennessy, James.
    Sins of the Fathers: A Study of the Atlantic Slave Traders 1441-1807. New
    York, 1968.

Port of Dublin Society.
Report of the Proceedings at a Public Meeting . . . 14th of March, 1823. Dublin, 1823.

Port of Hull Society.
Annual Reports. Hull.
Lifebelt and Anchor: The Story of the Port of Hull Society and Sailors' Orphan Homes. Hull [1907].

Port of London Society.
Proceedings at the Third Anniversary . . . . London, 1821.

Port of London Society and Bethel Union [sic], Committee of the.
An Appeal to the Public, Being an Answer to the Misrepresentations and Calumnies of the Rev. G. C. Smith . . . ." London, 1829.
Note: Referred to in Notes under standard abbreviation—PLBUS. Written for the Committee by their Secretary, the Rev. John Styles, D.D. (See also Thompson and Phillips *Refutation,* 1829, a reply to the above.)

Potter, Alonzo.
A Sermon before the Churchmen's Missionary Association for Seamen of the Port of Philadelphia. Philadelphia, 1848.

Poulsen's American Daily Advertiser. Philadelphia.

Powell, Isabel G.
"Naval Chaplains in the Early Stuart Period," *Mariner's Mirror,* 1922, pp. 290-96.

Pratt, Fletcher.
The Navy: A History. Garden City (New York), 1941.

Prayer Book and Homily Society.
Proceedings. London.
Annual Reports. London.
Occasional Papers. London.

Presbyterian Board of Publication.
A Manual of Devotion for Soldiers and Sailors. Philadelphia, 1847.

Pritchard, Stanley.
Fish and Ships: Royal National Mission to Deep Sea Fishermen 1881-1981. London, 1980.

Proctor, Francis, and Walter H. Frere.
A New History of the Book of Common Prayer. London, 1951. (1st ed. by Francis Proctor: 1855.)

The Protestant Episcopal Church Missionary Society for Seamen, in the City and Port of New York.
Annual Reports. New York, 1845 etc.

The Protestant Episcopal Church, Diocese of Pennsylvania.
Journal of the Proceedings of the Protestant Episcopal Church in the Diocese of Pennsylvania. Philadelphia.

Putnam, Mrs. C.H.
A Concise History of the Origin, Organization, and Progress of the First Baptist Mariners' Church, New York. New York, 1868.

The Quarterly Christian Spectator. New Haven (Connecticut).

The Quarterly Plea for the Wesleyan Seamen's Missionary Society. London.

Rappaport, Angelo S.
Superstitions of Sailors. London, 1928.

Raskin, Bernard.
On a True Course: The Story of the National Maritime Union of America, AFL-CIO. [New York], 1967.

Rawson, Geoffrey.
Ships and Seamen. London, 1934.

Ray, William.
The American Tars in Tripolitan Slavery. (Reprint of 1808 edition.) New York, 1911.

Realencyklopädie für protestantische Teologi und Kirche. Vol. 5. Leipzig, 1906.

The Record. Boston.

Redningsbaaden (The Life Boat).
Note: Published by the Danish Domestic-Port Seamen's Mission.

Rees, Edgar A.
Old Penzance. Penzance, 1956.

Reid, John M.
Missions and Missionary Society of the Methodist Episcopal Church. New York, 1882. (1st ed. 1879.)

Die Religion in Geschichte und Gegenwart. Tübingen, 1961.

The Religious Remembrancer. Philadelphia.

The Religious Society of Friends.
An Exposition of the African Slave Trade, from the Year 1840, to 1850, Inclusive. Philadelphia, 1851.

Religious Tract Society.
Proceedings of the First Twenty Years. London, 1820.
The First Series Tracts. Vol. 1. London, 1828.
The Iniquity of the Slave Trade. London, n.d.

Remarks on the Scarcity of American Seamen, and the Remedy . . . . New York, 1845.

Renström, Carl.
I hamnar och storstader (In Harbors and Big Cities). Stockholm, 1926.

The Revival. London.

Richter, V.
Den danske Landmilitaeretat 1801-94 (Danish Military Forces on Land 1801-94). Pt. I. Copenhagen, 1896.

Riddle, T. Wilkinson.
For Flag and Empire: The Story of the British and Foreign Sailors' Society in Peace and War. London, 1915.

Ritzer, George, Kenneth C.W. Kammeyer and Norman R. Yetman.
Sociology: Experiencing a Changing Society. Boston, 1979.

Robinson, Charles N.
The British Fleet: The Growth, Achievements and Duties of the Navy of the Empire. London, 1894.
The British Tar in Fact and Fiction. New York, 1909.

Robinson, George L.
"Ship," *Dictionary of the Apostolic Church,* Edinburgh, 1918, pp. 474-76.

Robotti, Frances D.
Whaling and Old Salem. New York, 1962.

Rockwell, Charles.
Sketches of Foreign Travel and Life at Sea. 2 Vols. Boston, 1842.

Rockwell, Stanley.
The Sheet Anchor. Philadelphia, 1864.

Rogers, Stanley.
Sea-Lore. London, 1934.

Rose, Harry K., and M.M. Glatt.
"A Study of Alcoholism as an Occupational Hazard of Merchant Seamen,"
Journal of Mental Science, 1961, pp. 18-30.

Rose, R. Barrie.
"A Liverpool Sailors' Strike," *Transactions of the Lancashire and Cheshire
Antiquarian Society* (Manchester), 1958, pp. 85-92.

Runciman, Walter.
Collier Brigs and Their Sailors. London, 1926.

Russell, George W.E.
A Short History of the Evangelical Movement. London, 1915.

Rygg, Andrew N.
Norwegians in New York. New York, 1941.

Rygnestad, Knut.
Dissentarspörsmaalet i Noreg fraa 1845 til 1891 (The Question of the
Dissenters in Norway from 1845 to 1891). Oslo, 1955.

Ryther, John.
*The Seaman's Preacher: Consisting of Nine Short and Plain Discourses on
Jonah's Voyage.* Cambridge (Massachusetts), 1806. (First English edition:
1675.)

Sahlberg, Björn.
"100 aars Svensk Kyrkohistoria i New York" (100 years' Swedish Church
History in New York), *Svenska Kyrkan i New York 100 Aar* (The Swedish
Church in New York 100 Years), Gunnar Granberg (Ed.). New York [1974].

Sailors' Children's Society.
Ashore and Afloat. Hull. Note: Magazine of the former Port of Hull Society.

The Sailors' Home and Red Ensign Club.
Its History and Activities. London, 1955.
Annual Reports. London.

Sailors' Homes: Their Origin and Progress. London, 1865.

The Sailor's Magazine. London.
Notes:
— Commenced January 1820, London, as: *The Sailor's Magazine, and Naval
Miscellany.* (Until 1827, under British and Foreign Seamen's Friend
Society and Bethel Union, with the Rev. George Charles Smith as Editor.
From March 1827, under the Port of London and Bethel Union Society.)
— Recommenced from 1835 as: *The Pilot, or Sailors' Magazine* (under the
British and Foreign Sailors' Society).

— Continued from 1839 as: *The Sailors' Magazine and Nautical Intelligencer* (under the same).
— Continued from 1854 as: *The Sailors' Magazine and Monthly Reporter* (under the same).
— Continued from 1858 as: *The Sailors' Magazine and Quarterly Reporter* (under the same).
— Recommenced from 1879 as: *The Chart and Compass, Sailors' Magazine* (under the same).

The Sailor's Magazine. New York.
Note: Published monthly by the American Seamen's Friend Society, as yearly volumes from September to August, 1828-67; Volume 40 includes 16 numbers, Sept. 1867 to Dec. 1868; from 1869, yearly volumes, January to December. Titles vary as follows:
— From 1828-29 (Vol. 1) to 1855-56 (Vol. 28): *The Sailor's Magazine and Naval Journal.*
— From 1856-57 (Vol. 29) to 1857-58 (Vol. 30): *The Sailor's Magazine.*
— From 1858-59 (Vol. 31): *The Sailor's Magazine and Seamen's Friend.*

Sailors' Snug Harbor.
Annual Reports of the Trustees.... New York.

Sailors' Snug Harbor of Boston.
Report. Boston, 1960.

St. Andrew's Waterside Church Mission.
Reports. London.

Salmonsens Konversations Leksikon. Vol. 22. Copenhagen, 1927.

Sampson, Abel.
The Wonderful Adventures of Abel Sampson. Lawrence City (Massachusetts), 1847.

Sanders, C.J.O.
Carest these not? Facts and Incidents in the History of the Seamen's Mission. London, n.d.

Savage, Theodore F.
The Presbyterian Church in New York City. New York, 1949.

Sawtell, Eli N.
Treasured Memories.... London, 1860.

Scarth, John.
Into All the World. London [1889].

Schartum, Sven.
"For 50 Aar siden: August Thiemann - Eilert Sundt" (50 Years Ago: August Thiemann - Eilert Sundt), *Bud og Hilsen,* Dec. 1910, pp. 20-30.
Sjöfolk: Fortellinger fra livet derute (Seafarers: Tales from Life out there). Bergen (Norway), 1933.

Scherer, James A.
Missionary, Go Home! Englewood Cliffs (New Jersey), 1964.

Schorzmann, Artur.
"Eschatology and Mission," *Concise Dictionary of the Christian World Mission,* London, 1970, pp. 191-92.

Schroeder, Gustavus W.
History of the Swedish Baptists in Sweden and America. New York, 1898.

Scoresby, William (the Younger).
   Discourses to Seamen. London, 1831.
   Memorials of the Sea . . . . London, 1835; 2nd enlarged ed.: London, 1850.
   Memorials of F.R.H. Scoresby. London, 1837.
Scoresby-Jackson, R.E.
   The Life of William Scoresby, M.A., D.D., F.R.S.S.L. & E. . . . London,
   1861.
The Scottish Missionary (and Philanthropic) Register. Edinburgh.
The Scottish Sailors' and Soldiers' Bethel Flag Union.
   Reports. Edinburgh.

Scripture Gift Mission.
   Publishing Salvation: The Story of the Scripture Gift Mission. London,
   1961.
The Sea Breeze. Boston. Note: Published by the Boston Seaman's Friend Society.
Sea Breezes. Liverpool.
*Seafarers and Their Ships: The Story of a Century of Progress in the Safety of
   Ships and the Well-Being of Seamen.* New York, 1956.
Seaman, Samuel A.
   Annals of New York Methodism. New York, 1892.
Seaman's Aid Society.
   Annual Reports. Boston (Massachusetts), 1834-39.
The Seaman's Confidence: Dialogue between Two Seamen after a Storm. (Anony-
   mous.) London, n.d.
The Seamen and Soldiers' Evangelical Magazine. London, 1846.
Seamen's Aid Society.
   Annual Reports. Boston (Massachusetts), 1840, etc.

Seamen's Christian Friend Society.
   Annual Reports. London.
   100th Report. London, 1947.
   Note: Title of Society changed from "The Seamen and Soldiers' Evangelical
   Friend Society" (1846), to "The Seamen's Evangelical Society" (1847), and
   again to "The Seamen's Christian Friend Society" (1848).
Seamen's Church Institute of New York and New Jersey.
   The Professional Challenge: Maritime Education for the 80's. Vol. 5, No. 1.
   New York, 1981.
Seamen's Church Institute of Philadelphia.
   The Dedication of the Chapel of the Redeemer . . . . Philadelphia, 1925.
Seamen's Hospital Society.
   First Report. London, 1822.
Seamen's and Landsmen's Aid Society.
   Annual Reports. Philadelphia.
The Seamen's Mission of the Methodist Church (Formerly "Wesleyan Seamen's
   Mission").
   Annual Reports. London.
Seamen's Union Bethel Society of Baltimore.
   Annual Reports. Baltimore (Maryland).

"Second Report from the Select Committee of the House of Lords appointed to inquire into the Policy and Operation of the Navigation Laws . . . ," *Reports from Committees, 1847-48.* Vol. 20, Pt. II, London [1848].

Secor, Neale A. (Ed.)
Seamen's Church Institute: Five Year Plan 1986-1990. Philadelphia, 1985.

Seierstad, Andreas.
Kyrkjelegt reformarbeid i Norig i nittande hundreaaret. Vol. 1. Bergen, 1923.
"Norsk misjonsverksemd i 1820-aara" (Norwegian Missionary Activity in the 1820's), *Tidsskrift for teologi og kirke,* 1947, pp. 164-81.

Selement, George.
"Impressment & the American Merchant Marine 1782-1812," *Mariner's Mirror,* 1973, pp. 409-17.

Seymour, Jack M.
Ships, Sailors and Samaritans: The Women's Seamen's Friend Society of Connecticut 1859-1976. New Haven (Connecticut), 1976.

Sharp, Granville.
An Address to the People of England Being the Protest of a Private Person Against Every Suspension of Law that Is Liable to Injure or Endanger Personal Security. London, 1778.

Shay, Frank.
A Sailors' Treasury. New York, 1951.

Sheahan, James Joseph.
History of the Town and Port of Kingston-Upon-Hull. Hull, 1866.

Seymour, Jack M.
Ships, Sailors and Samaritans: The Women's Seamen's Friend Society of Connecticut 1859-1976. New Haven (Connecticut), 1976.

Sharp, Granville.
An Address to the People of England Being the Protest of a Private Person Against Every Suspension of Law that Is Liable to Injure or Endanger Personal Security. London, 1778.

Shay, Frank.
A Sailors' Treasury. New York, 1951.

Sheahan, James Joseph.
History of the Town and Port of Kingston-Upon-Hull. Hull, 1866.

Sheet Anchor. Boston.

Shepherd, Barnett.
Sailors' Snug Harbor, 1801-1976. New York, 1979.

Sherar, Miriam G.
Shipping Out: A Sociological Study of the American Merchant Seaman. Cambridge (Maryland), 1973

Shillibeer, John.
A Narrative of the Briton's Voyage to Pitcairn's Island . . . . Taunton, 1817.

Shipwrecked and Distressed Sailors' Asylum.
Letters between 1836 and 1838 . . . . London, 1838.

Sjömansvännen. Helsingfors.

Sjömaends Kristelige Forening.
To-aarsberetning for Sjömaends Kristelige Faellesforening.... (Biennial Report of the Seamen's Christian Joint Association). Tönsberg (Norway), 1899.

Smidt, Johannes.
Fotefar; Spor av norsk kristenliv i London för Olavskirkens indvielse June 26, 1927. (Footprints; Traces of Norwegian Christianity in London before the Dedication of the Church of St. Olav, June 26, 1927.) Bergen (Norway), 1927.

Smith, C. Fox.
Ship Alley: Story of Sailortowns. New York, 1925.

Smith, George Charles.
The Wreckers. London, 1818.
The British Ark; Being a Brief Narrative of Facts, Leading, by Divine Providence, to an Attempt to Obtain a Floating Place of Worship, for the Use of Religious Seamen in the Port of London. London, 1823. (1st ed.: 1817.) Note: Also published in SML 1820, pp. 88 ff.
The Coaster's and Sailor's Hymn Book. London, 1824. (1st ed.: 1822.)
The Devonport Ark. London, 1825.
The Scilly Islands, and the Famine Occasioned by the Legal Prevention of Smuggling with France.... London, 1828.
Common Honesty: In Three Parts. London, 1828.
Portsmouth;...Concerning the... Admission of Unmarried Females into British Ships of War.... London, 1828.
Windsor, ... Respecting an Order of the Duke of Clarence Prohibiting the Circulation of Religious Tracts in the British Navy.... London, 1828.
Birmingham, or No Preaching.... London, 1828.
Chichester, or... Reflections on the Evil Effects of Prejudice.... London, 1828.
Spa Fields.... London [1828].
Site of the Late Brunswick Theatre. London [1828].
The Royal Brunswick. London [1828].
Intemperance.... London, 1829.
The Thames. London, 1829. Note: Also included as a *Supplement,* NSM 1829 Pt. II.
Persecution. London, 1829.
Note: Also included as a *Supplement,* NSM 1829 Pt. II.
Freemasons' Hall: Errors of Judgement. London, 1829. Note: Also included as a *Supplement,* NSM 1829 Pt. II.
Common Justice.... Sheffield, 1831.
An Humble Christian Remonstrance. London, 1835.
A Correct View of the Brunswick Theatre Ruins.... London, 1853.
The First Sailors' Home in the World, at Well Street, East London. London [1861].
The Boatswain's Mate: or, an Interesting Dialogue between Two British Seamen. 7 Parts. London, n.d. (1st ed. from 1817.) Note: Pts. I-II originally published jointly in the *Instructor* newspaper, 1811-12.

English Sailors: or, Britain's Best Bulwarks: Being the Substance of Various Addresses to Seamen. . . . London, n.d. (1st ed. 1819.) Note: Also published in SML 1820, pp. 3 ff.

Bethel: or, the Flag Unfurled: Containing, a Correct Statement of Interesting Facts Respecting the Prayer Meetings on the River Thames. London, n.d. (1st ed. 1819.) Note: Also published in SML 1820, pp. 6 ff.

The Log-Book. 2 Parts. London, n.d.

The Custom House and the Bethel Flag: or, the Minehead and Watchet Officers. London, n.d. (1st ed. 1823.)

The Press Gang: or, War Proclaimed by the Prince of Peace, against the Prince of Darkness. London, n.d.

Aldermanbury: or, an Address to Mr. Thos. Phillips, Containing Anecdotes of the Port of London and the Bethel Union Societies' proceedings during the last nine years. . . . London, n.d. (1st ed. 1827.)

Injustice and Cruelty: or, a Brief History of the Sailor's Magazine and a Statement of the proceedings of the Port of London and Bethel Union Society in Wresting the Copyright from the Late Editor. . . . London, n.d. (1st ed. 1827?)

The Floating Chapel, and the Sixteen Thousand Hearers, with Cursory Remarks on . . . Slanderous Imputations, in "The Report". . . . London, n.d. (1st ed. 1827?)

British Villages: or, Tales of the Nineteenth Century. London, n.d.

Blackheath: Being a Brief Historical Review of Some Leading Circumstances Connected with Seamen's Societies, since a Residence on Blackheath in 1825. London, n.d. (1st ed. 1828?)

A Sailor's Visit to Surrey Chapel: or, Interesting Recollections in Early Life, on Shore and at Sea. London, n.d.

The History of a Sunderland Cabin Boy . . . . London, n.d.

Royal Brunswick Theatre. No. 5. London, n.d.

Smith, H.S., R.T. Handy, and L.A. Loetscher.
  American Christianity. Vols. 1-2. New York, 1960, 1963.

Smith, J.
  The Voyage and Shipwreck of St. Paul. London, 1880.

Smith, Philip C.F.
  "The Salem Marine Society, 1766-1966," *The American Neptune,* 1966, pp. 272-79.

Smith, Thomas.
  A Practical Discourse to Sea-Faring Men. Boston, 1771.

Smith, Theophilus.
  The Great Moral Reformation of Sailors . . . . Richmond, Surrey, 1874.

Smith, Toulmin J.&L. (Eds.)
  English Gilds. London 1870.

Smith, Waldo E.L.
  The Navy and its Chaplains in the Days of Sail. Toronto, 1961.
  The Navy Chaplain and His Parish. Ottawa, 1967.

Snow, Edward R.
  Women of the Sea. London, 1963.

The Society for Promoting Christian Knowledge.
Religious Tracts Dispersed by the Society for Promoting Christian Knowledge.
Vol. 13, London, 1815.
Reports. London.

The Society for the Propagation of the Gospel in Foreign Parts.
Provision for the Spiritual Destitution of British Seamen. London [1851].

Society for the Relief of Destitute Children of Seamen.
Annual Reports. New York.
Note: Name changed in 1937 to: "Society for Seamen's Children."

Society for Seamen's Children.
Our First Hundred Years, 1846-1946. New York, 1946.

The Soldier's Magazine. London.
Note: Published under the editorship of the Rev. George Charles Smith as follows:
— From 1828 (separately) as *The Soldier's Magazine and Military Chronicle.*
— From July 1836 until January 1863 jointly with the *New Sailor's Magazine* (q.v.), under varying titles.

Sorenson, Robert C.
"Catching up with Social Change in Seafaring," Third Plenary Conference, New York 1978: Papers and Addresses, ICMA, 1979, pp. 42-6.

South Street Reporter. New York.

Southwark Auxiliary Bible Society.
Minutes. London, 1817.

Southwark Park Wesleyan Chapel.
Southwark Park Wesleyan Chapel, Lower Road, Rotherhithe: Report of a Building Fund. London, n.d.

Spaulding, J.
The Sabbath at Sea. New York, 1865.

Spears, John R.
The Story of the American Merchant Marine. New York, 1910.

Spencer, Ichabod S.
The Claims of Seamen. New York, 1836.

Spong, Bernard.
"Leaders and Animators aboard Ship," Report of the First Plenary Conference London ... 1972, ICMA [1973], pp. 22-25.

Spooner, Nath'l.
Gleanings from the Records of the Boston Marine Society through its First Century 1742-1842. Boston, 1879.

Sprague, William B.
Annals of the American Methodist Pulpit. New York, 1861.
Unitarianism. (Vol. 8, in *Annals of the American Pulpit.*) New York, 1865, pp. 345-56.

Spring, Gardiner.
The Bethel Flag: a Series of Short Discourses to Seamen. New York, 1848.

Sprout, Harold and Margaret.
The Rise of American Naval Power, 1776-1918. Princeton (New Jersey), 1946.

Stackpole, Edouard A. (Ed.)
 Those in Peril on the Sea. New York, 1962.
Stafford, Ward.
 New Missionary Field: a Report to the Female Missionary Society for the Poor of the City of New-York, and its Vicinity. New York, 1817. (A 2nd ed., also in 1817.)
 Important to Seamen: Extracts from a Report Entitled New Mission Field. New York, n.d.
[Stafford, Ward.]
 The Mariners' Church: Resolutions and Address at a Meeting for the Purpose of Establishing the Mariners' Church. New York, 1818. Note: Authorship deduced from Warren 1858, p. 9.
Stamp, Tom and Cordelia.
 William Scoresby, Arctic Scientist. Whitby, 1976.
A Statement of the Origin, Progress, and Present Design of the Society of Inquiry respecting Missions, of the Theological Seminary Established at Princeton, New Jersey. Trenton (New Jersey), 1817.
Steensnaes, Hans.
 "Glött i Den norske Sjömannsmisjons loggbok over de hundre aars seilas" (Glimpses of the Norwegian Seamen's Mission's Logbook during its Hundred Year Voyage), *Med norsk sjömannsmisjon i hundre aar 1864-1964*, Gunnar C. Wasberg, Bergen, 1964, pp. 310-23.
Stephenson, George M.
 The Religious Aspects of Swedish Immigration. Minneapolis, 1932.
Stiansen, Peder.
 History of the Baptists in Norway. Chicago, 1933.
 Stille Stunder. Volda (Norway).
Stone, John S.
 A Memoir of the Life of James Milnor, D.D. . . . New York, 1848.
Storey, Arthur.
 Trinity House of Kingston-upon-Hull. Kingston-upon-Hull, 1967.
Storli, Magne.
 "Sjömennenes kirke för Sjömannskirken?" (A Church for Seamen before the Seamen's Church?), *Sjömannsmisjonens paaskehefte*, Bergen, 1971.
Stott, John R.W.
 Christian Mission in the Modern World. Downers Grove (Illinois), 1975.
Stowe, Phineas.
 Ocean Melodies and Seamen's Companion. Boston, 1858.
Stöylen, Kaare.
 Claus Frimann: Almuens sanger 1746-1829 (Claus Frimann: Poet of the People 1746-1829). Bergen, 1955.
 "Den norske kirke i utlandet" (The Church of Norway Abroad), *Arv og ansvar* (Heritage and Responsibility). Oslo, 1958, pp. 136-76.
Stranks, C.J.
 Anglican Devotion: Studies in the Spiritual Life of the Church of England between the Reformation and the Oxford Movement. London, 1961.

Straus, Robert.
Medical Care for Seamen: The Origin of Public Medical Service in the United States. New Haven (Connecticut), 1950.

Ström, Harald.
"Psykiatriske lidelser hos sjömenn: Praktiske erfaringer" (Psychiatric Disorders among Seamen: Practical Experience), *Tidsskrift for Den norske laegeforening.* Oslo 1964, pp. 1237-40.

Strong, L.A.G.
Flying Angel: The Story of The Missions to Seamen. London, 1956.

Strong, William E.
The Story of the American Board. Boston, 1910.

Stuart, Thomas.
A Nautical Essay. Cork, 1856.

Styles, John.
A Letter to Thomas Thompson, Esq. Occasioned by his Refutation.... London, 1829. Note: For Styles' original 1829 tract *An Appeal ...*, see under "Port of London Society and Bethel Union [sic], Committee of the."

Suffolk Savings Bank for Seamen and Others.
One Hundred Years of the Suffolk Savings Bank for Seamen and Others. Boston, 1933.

[Sullivan, Thomas V.]
Scarcity of Seamen: Report of the Marine Mission at Large. Boston, 1853.

The Sunday at Home. London.
Note: Published by the Religious Tract Society, as "a Family Magazine for Sabbath Reading."

Sundby, Per.
"Psykiatriske lidelser hos sjömenn: Sosialpsykiatriske undersökelser" (Psychiatric Disorders among Seamen: Socio-psychiatric Studies, *Tidsskrift for Den norske laegeforening,* Oslo, 1964, pp. 1240-43, 1289.

Sundkler, Bengt.
The World of Mission. Grand Rapids (Michigan), 1966.

The Survey of Federal Archives.
Ship Registers and Enrollments of Boston and Charlestown. Vol. 1. Boston, 1942.

Svenska Bibel-Sällskapet.
Berättelse och Redovisning af Svenska Bibel-Sällskapets Comité för aar.... Stockholm.

Svensk Uppslagsbok (Swedish Encyclopedia). Malmö (Sweden), 1957.

Sweet, William W.
Revivalism in America. New York, 1944.
The Story of Religion in America. New York, 1950.
Religion in the Development of American Culture 1765-1840. Gloucester (Massachusetts), 1963.

Swinnerton, H.U.
An Historical Account of the Presbyterian Church at Cherry Valley, N.Y. Cherry Valley (New York), 1876.

The Sydney Gazette. Sydney (N.S.W.).

Syrdal, Rolf A.
To the End of the Earth: Mission Concept in Principle and Practice.
Minneapolis, 1967.

Taylor, Gordon.
The Sea Chaplains: A History of the Chaplains of the Royal Navy. Oxford,
1978.

Taylor, James S.
*Jonas Hanway, Founder of the Marine Society: Charity and Policy in
Eighteenth-Century Britain.* London & Berkeley, 1985.

Teonge, Henry.
The Diary of Henry Teonge. London & New York, 1927.

Terdal, Harriet (Ed.).
Bethelship Norwegian United Methodist Church: 100th Anniversary. New
York, 1974.

Thames Church Mission.
Reports. London.

Thomas, Albert S.
*A Historical Account of the Protestant Episcopal Church in South Carolina,
1820-1957.* [Columbia (South Carolina), 1957].

Thompson, H.P.
*Into All Lands: The History of the Society for the Propagation of the Gospel
in Foreign Parts 1701-1950.* London, 1951.

Thompson, Lawrance.
Melville's Quarrel with God. Princeton (New Jersey), 1952.

Thompson, Thomas, and Thomas Phillips.
Refutation: Being a Reply to the "Appeal" of the Port of London Society.
London, 1829.

Thrap, D.
*"Fra norske Menigheder i 1820-Aarene" (From Norwegian Congregations in
the 1820's), For Kirke og Kultur,* 1906, pp. 545-57.

Thue, Johannes B.
"Bergen og sjöfarten II 1800-1860" (Bergen and Seafaring, Pt. II, 1800-
1860), *Sjöfartshistorisk aarbok 1979* (Norwegian Yearbook of Maritime
History 1979), Bergen, 1980, pp. 9-231.

Thun, R.W.
Werden und Wachsen der Deutschen Evangelischen Seemannsmission.
Bremen/Hamburg-Altona, 1959.

Thunström, Carl.
Olof Gustaf Hedström. Stockholm, 1935.

Tidsskrift for teologi og kirke (Journal of Theology and Church). Oslo.

The Times. London.

Timpson, Thomas.
Memoirs of Mrs. Elizabeth Fry. London, 1847.
The Living Light-house: or, Memoirs of Captain B. Prynn.... London,
1856.

Toynbee, Arnold.
Toynbee's Industrial Revolution. London, 1969.

Toynbee, Henry.
The Social Condition of Seamen. [London, 1866.]

Traill, H.D., and J.S. Mann (Eds.).
Social England. Vols. 1-6. London, 1901-4.

Trestrail, Frederick.
Reminiscences of College Life in Bristol. London [1879].

Trevelyan, George M.
English Social History. London, 1946.
A Shortened History of England. London, 1959.

Trinterud, L.J.
The Forming of an American Tradition. Philadelphia, 1949.

Tronsen, Tron.
"Storjohann, en byggmester i Guds rike" (Storjohann: A Master-builder in God's Kingdom), *Sjömannsmisjonens julehefte,* Bergen (Norway), 1974, pp. 4-6.

Truair, John.
Plain Truth, on Christian Baptism, and Communion. Utica (New York), 1820.
Call from the Ocean, or an Appeal to the Patriot and the Christian. New York, 1826.
An Appeal to the Churches of Christ, and to the Public, on a Document from the Hampshire Central Association, Withdrawing Ministerial Fellowship from the Author. Northampton (Massachusetts), 1829.

Trueblood, Elton.
The Validity of the Christian Mission. New York, 1972.

Trumble, Frank M.
"A Letter from the General Secretary," *The Helmsman* (Seamen's Christian Friend Society and Hospital Trust) No. 215, London, 1967.

Tuckerman, Joseph.
The Principles and Results of the Ministry at Large in Boston. Boston, 1838.
The Twentieth Century Encyclopedia of Religious Knowledge. Grand Rapids (Michigan), 1955.

Tyler, Alice F.
Freedom's Ferment: Phases of American Social History to 1860. Minneapolis, 1944.

Uittenbosch, Hans.
"The Sea Is His, and He Made It . . . ," *Third Plenary Conference, New York, 1978: Papers and Addresses,* ICMA, 1979, pp. 47-52.

Uittenbosch, Hans (Ed.).
Shipvisiting: A Collection of Essays Presented Under the Auspices of the International Council of Seamen's Agencies Inc. [Montreal], 1969.

United Bible Societies.
Bulletins of the United Bible Societies. London.

United Seamen's Service.
  The Maritime Industrial Revolution and the Modern Seafarer. New York
  [1972].
The United States Gazette and True American. Philadelphia.
Urquart, Thomas.
  "Substance of a Letter to Lord Viscount Melville, Written in May, 1815, with
  the Outlines of a Plan . . . to Do Away with the Evils of Impressment, and
  Man Our Ships Effectually with Mercantile Seamen," *The Pamphleteer,*
  London, 1824, pp. 464-76.
  "A Letter to W. Wilberforce, Esq., M.P. on the Subject of Impressment,
  Calling on Him and the Philanthropists of This Country to Prove Those
  Feelings of Sensibility They Expressed in the Cause of Humanity on Negro
  Slavery, by Acting with the Same Ardour and Zeal in the Cause of British
  Seamen," written in January, 1816, and published in *The Pamphleteer,*
  London, 1824, pp. 384-402.
Ursin, J.
  Kristne symboler: En haandbok (Christian Symbols: A Manual). Oslo, 1965.
Ute och Hemma. Stockholm, later Uppsala.
  Note: Published by the Swedish Seamen's Church, now "Svenska kyrkan i
  utlandet" (The Swedish Church Abroad).
Verkuyl, Johannes.
  Contemporary Missiology: An Introduction. Grand Rapids (Michigan), 1978.
The Victorian Bethel Union and Sailors' Mission at Melbourne.
  Annual Reports. Melbourne.
Vidler, Alec R.
  The Church in an Age of Revolution. London, 1961.
Villiers, Alan.
  Captain James Cook. New York, 1967.
  The Way of a Ship. New York, 1970.
Vincent, Bernard.
  "The Personal and Family Implications of Being a Seafarer from the Third
  World," *Report of Second Plenary Conference, Denmark . . . 1975,* ICMA
  [1976], pp. 14-26.
"Vindicator" (Pseud.)
  An Impartial View of the State of Religion, in Penzance and its Vicinity.
  Penzance, 1824.
  *Vinland the Good: The Saga of Leif Eiriksson and the Viking Discovery of
  America.* (With a Preface by Helge Ingstad.) Oslo, 1970.
Virginia Evangelical and Literary Magazine. Richmond (Virginia).
Walford, Edward.
  Old and New London. Vol. 6. London, 1878.
Walls, A.F.
  "Outposts of Empire," *Eerdman's Handbook to the History of Christianity.*
  Tim Dowley (Ed.), Grand Rapids (Michigan), 1977, pp. 546-68.
  "Societies for Mission," Ditto, pp. 549-53.
Walrond, Mary L.
  Launching out into the Deep: or, the Pioneers of a Noble Effort. London,
  1904.

Waltari, Toivo.
Finska Sjömansmissionen 1875-1925. (The Finnish Seamen's Mission 1875-1925.) Helsingfors, 1925.

Warburg, L.A.
Söndagsbog tilsös (Sunday Book at Sea). Copenhagen, 1884.

Ward, Edward.
The Wooden World. London, 1929. (First published 1707.)

Ward, Marcus.
"Message of the Missionary," *Concise Dictionary of the Christian World Mission,* London, 1970. pp. 378-80.

Ward, W.E.F.
The Royal Navy and the Slavers: The Suppression of the Atlantic Slave Trade. New York, 1969.

Warneck, Gustav.
Evangelische Missionslehre. Vols. 1-5. Gotha, 1892-1903.
Outline of a History of Protestant Missions. Edinburgh, 1901.

Warner, Oliver.
The Life-boat Service: A History 1824-1974. London, 1974.

Warner, Wellman J.
The Wesleyan Movement in the Industrial Revolution. London, 1930.

Warren, Israel P.
The Seamen's Cause: Embracing the History, Results, and Present Condition, of the Efforts for the Moral Improvement of Seamen. New York [1858]. Note: Also published in *The Sailors' Magazine* (N.Y.), Vols. 29 (1856-57) and 30 (1857-58).

Warren, Max.
The Missionary Movement from Britain in Modern History. London, 1965.
Social History and Christian Mission. London, 1967.
"Non-Professional Missionary," *Concise Dictionary of the Christian World Mission,* London, 1970, pp. 449-50.
I Believe in the Great Commission. Grand Rapids (Michigan), 1976.

Wasberg, Gunnar Christie.
Med norsk sjömannsmisjon i hundre aar 1864-1964. (A Century of Norwegian Seamen's Missions 1864-1964.) Bergen, 1964.

Watermarks. Bellevue/Seattle (Washington).
Note: Quarterly newsletter of the International Council of Seamen's Agencies (ICOSA).

Watson, J. Steven.
The Reign of George III, 1760-1815. Oxford, 1960.

Watson, Richard.
The Adventures of a Greenwich Pensioner. Newcastle, 1827.

Webb, R.K.
Modern England: From the Eighteenth Century to the Present. New York and Toronto, 1969.

Webb, Sidney and Beatrice.
The History of Trade Unionism. (Reprint of 1894 edition.) New York, 1965.

Webster, Douglas.
  "The Missionary," *Concise Dictionary of the Christian World Mission*, London, 1970, pp. 410-11.
Webster, George S.
  The Seamen's Friend: A Sketch of the American Seamen's Friend Society. New York, 1932.
Weedfald, Arthur A.
  Personnel Handling on Merchant Ships. New York, 1956.
Weibust, Knut.
  The Crew as a Social System. Oslo, 1958.
  Deep Sea Sailors: A Study in Maritime Ethnology. Stockholm, 1969.
Weltzer, Carl.
  Bölger der baerer. (Waves which Carry). Copenhagen, 1952.
Wesley Historical Society.
  Proceedings. London.
The Wesleyan Methodist Magazine, London.
Wesleyan Seamen's Mission (Originally "Wesleyan Seamen's Missionary Society").
  Reports. London.
Westerman, Adam.
  Groote Christelyke Zeevaart. . . . (Great Christian Navigation). Amsterdam, 1635.
Western Seamen's Friend Society.
  Annual Reports. Cleveland (Ohio), etc.
Westin, Gunnar.
  George Scott och hans verksamhet i Sverige. (George Scott and His Activities in Sweden). Stockholm, 1929.
  Den kristna friförsamlingen i Norden. (The Christian Free Church in the Nordic Countries). Stockholm, 1956.
Weston, Agnes.
  My Life among the Bluejackets. London, 1911.
Weylland, John M.
  These Fifty Years, Being the Jubilee Volume of the London City Mission. London [1884].
Whalley, W.A.
  The Mariners' Chapel, Gloucester. London, 1909.
Wheatley, Henry B.
  London Past and Present. London, 1891.
Whiteley, J.H.
  Wesley's England: A Survey of XVIIIth Century Social and Cultural Conditions. London, 1938.
Whittington-Egan, Richard.
  Liverpool Colonnade. Liverpool, 1955.
Williams, Peter Jr.
  A Discourse Delivered on the Death of Capt. Paul Cuffee, before the New-York African Institution. New York, 1818.
Williams, Ralph C.
  The United States Public Health Service, 1798-1950. Washington D.C., 1951.

Williamson, G.R.
    Memoir of the Rev. David Abeel, D.D. New York, 1848.

Williamson, J.A.
    The Ocean in English History. Oxford, 1941.
    Cook and the Opening of the Pacific. London, 1946.

Willis, William.
    The History of Portland, from 1832 to 1864.... Portland (Maine), 1865.

Wilson, Derek A.
    Sail and Steam, 1794-1901. London, 1973.

Wilson, John L.
    The British Squadron on the Coast of Africa: The Anti-Slavery Squadron.
    London, 1851.

Wilson, F. Mary.
    Between Bridgers. London [1966].

Winchester, John.
    The Life of John Wesley. New York, 1966.

Windley, Carlyle.
    "S.C.I. Establishes Center for Seafarers' Rights," *The Lookout,* June/July
    1982, pp. 10-12.

Witting, Victor.
    Minnen fraan mitt lif. (Memories from my Life). Worcester (Massachusetts),
    1902.

Wolfe R.B.
    *English Prisoners in France ... during Nine Years' Residence in the Depots
    of Fontainebleau, Verdun, Givet and Valencienne.* London, 1830.

Wood, A. Skevington.
    "Awakening," *Eerdman's Handbook to the History of Christianity.* Grand
    Rapids (Michigan), 1977, pp. 434-55.

Wood, John.
    *The True Honour of Navigation and Navigators: Or, Holy Meditations for
    Sea-men.* London, 1618.

Woodward, E.L.
    "The Age of Reform, 1815-1870." (In *The Oxford History of England.*)
    Oxford, 1938.

Woodward, Josiah.
    *The Seaman's Monitor: or, Advice to Sea-faring Men, with Reference to their
    Behaviour before, in, and after their Voyage....* London, 1723. (1st ed.:
    1705.)
    An Account of the Societies in the City of London, &c. Liverpool, 1935. (1st
    ed. 1697).

The Word on the Waters. London.
    Note: Published from 1858 by The Missions to Seamen.

The World. London.

Wright, Kenyon E.
    "Urban-Industrial Mission: Humanization or Evangelization," *International
    Review of Mission,* (Geneva), 1971.

Wright, Louis B.
   Gold, Glory and the Gospel: The Adventurous Lives and Times of the Renaissance Explorers. New York, 1970.
Wright, R.F.
   "The High Seas and the Church in the Middle Ages," *The Mariner's Mirror,* 1967, pp. 3-31, 115-35.
Wright, Robert.
   A Memoir of General James Oglethorpe, One of the Earliest Reformers of Prison Discipline in England, and the Founder of Georgia, in America. London, 1867.
Wristers, Jan.
   Here is the Sea: Meditations, Songs, Prophesies and History Written by Prophets, Psalmists, Evangelists and Apostles. Hong Kong, 1978.
   "Seamen's Agencies as 'Mercy Missions'?" *Watermarks* 1979, No. 2, p. 14.
Writers' Program (State of Massachusetts).
   Boston Looks Seaward: The Story of the Port, 1630-1940. Boston, 1941.
Writers' Program (New York City).
   A Maritime History of New York. New York, 1941.
Wulff, Jurgen.
   "Seafarers and Their Families: Wishes and Anxieties," *Report of Fourth Plenary Conference, Berlin... 1981,* ICMA [1982], pp. 40-5.
Yamamori, Tetsunao, and E. LeRoy Lawson.
   Introducing Church Growth: A Textbook in Missions. Cincinnati (Ohio), 1975.
Yarham, E.R.
   "Blessing the Waters," *The Nautical Magazine,* 1972, pp. 214-16.
Yates, William B.
   An Historical Sketch of the Rise and Progress of Religious and Moral Improvement among Seamen.... Charleston (South Carolina), 1851.
Yexley, Lionel.
   The Inner Life of the Navy. London, 1908.
Young, A.F., and E.T. Ashton.
   British Social Work in the Nineteenth Century. London, 1956.
Youngren, J. Alan.
   "Parachurch Proliferation: The Frontier Spirit Caught in Traffic," *Christianity Today* (Carol Stream, Illinois), November 1981, pp. 38-41.
Zurcher, Louis A.
   "The Sailor Aboard Ship: A Study of Role Behavior in a Total Institution," *Social Forces,* Chapel Hill (North Carolina), 1965, pp. 389-400.

B. Unpublished Materials

American Bible Society.
   ABS History, Typescript Essays. n.d. (Archives of the ABS, N.Y.)
   News Release, Jan. 15, 1968. (Code 68-02).
Bible Society of Salem and Vicinity.
   Records of the Bible Society of Salem and Vicinity, Instituted August 22, 1810.... (Essex Institute, Salem, Massachusetts.)

Bloomquist, Daniel R.
   The Contribution of the Lutheran Bible Institute of Seattle to Missions.
   Unpublished D. Miss. Dissertation, Trinity Evangelical Divinity School,
   Deerfield (Illinois), 1985.

Bondevik, Halfdan.
   Kirkelig omsorg for landsmenn i utlandet. (The Ministry of the Church to
   Fellow-nationals Abroad). Mimeographed typescript, Oslo, 1974. (Archives
   of Norwegian Seamen's Mission, Bergen, Norway.)

Bradley, William N.
   Historical Sketch of M.E. Mariners Bethel. Typescript. Philadelphia, 1899.
   (Old St. George's United Methodist Church Archives, Philadelphia.)

Brekne, Abraham D.
   *The Norwegian Seamen's Mission — Agency or Church? The Problem and
   Consequences as to Ministry, Related to This Question.* Unpublished Ph.D.
   Dissertation, California Graduate School of Theology, Glendale (California),
   1983.

Bristol Channel Mission.
   Chaplain's Journal. November 12, 1841 - February 11, 1843, February 11,
   1843 - July 2, 1843. (The Missions to Seamen Archives, London.)

British and Foreign Bible Society.
   Correspondence Books. (BFBS Archives, London.)
   Foreign Correspondence. (Ditto.)
   Home Correspondence. (Ditto.)
   Minutes. (Ditto.)
   Minutes of Southwark Auxiliary Bible Society. (Ditto.)
   Minutes of Sub-Committees. (Ditto.)

British and Foreign Sailor's Society.
   Minutes, 1833-37. (BSS Archives, London.)
   Minutes, 1837-43. (Ditto.)
   Minutes, 1843-50. (Ditto.)
   Summary of Annual Reports, 1861-69. (Ditto.)

British and Foreign Seamen's Friend Society and Bethel Union.
   Minutes, 1822-27. (BSS Archives, London.)

Cann, Kathleen.
   The Distribution of the Scriptures from Gibraltar in the 19th Century.
   Typescript. London, 1969. (BFBS Archives, London.)

Chapman, Paul.
   "Human Rights for Seafarers: A Project of the Seamen's Church Institute of
   New York and New Jersey," (MS) *4th Trennial Conference: Standing
   Committee Report,* ICMA, London, 1981, Appendix A.
   Human Rights for Seafarers. Unpublished D. Min. Dissertation, New York
   Theological Seminary, New York (N.Y.), 1983.

Christian Witness to Seafarers.
   (A mimeographed orientation prepared by the Merchant Navy Officers'
   Christian Association and Merchant Navy Christian Fellowship in unison.)
   N.p., 1962.

Coombs, Peter B.
   A History of the Church Pastoral-Aid Society 1836-1861. Unpublished M.A.
   Thesis, University of Bristol, 1960.

Curry, James.
    English Sea-Chaplains in the Royal Navy, 1577-1684. Unpublished M.A.
    Thesis, University of Bristol, 1956.

Daasvand, Paul O.
    *The Norwegian Seamen's Mission: History, Analysis, Evaluation, and
    Contemporary Ministry.* Unpublished D. Min. Dissertation, School of
    Theology of University of the South. Sewanee, Tennessee, 1982.

Davis, Emerson.
    Biographical Sketches of the Congregational Pastors of New England. Vol.
    1. Typescript [1930]. (Congregational Library, Boston.)

Dixon, Conrad.
    The Rise and Fall of the Crimp, 1840-1914. Paper read to the University of
    Exeter Maritime History Seminar, October 24-25, 1984.

East Asian Regional Conference....
    (Participants: The Missions to Seamen, Apostleship of the Sea, and Norwegian
    Seamen's Mission.) Mimeographed Report. Hong Kong, 1972. (Archives of
    the Missions to Seamen, London.)

Eckhoff, Ray.
    Ministering Seafarers. Mimeographed Report by the Chaplain-Director,
    Tacoma Seamen's Center, to the International Council of Seamen's Agencies,
    dated Tacoma, Washington, October 23, 1979. (ICOSA Archives, Bellevue/
    Seattle, Washington.)

Ekvik, Steinar.
    Untitled Study on Cooperation between Lutheran Church Bodies in America
    and the Norwegian Seamens' Mission. (Archives of the American Lutheran
    Church D.S.M.A.)

Evangeliska Fosterlands-Stiftelsen (The Evangelical National Missionary Society).
    EFS arkiv. (Stockholms Stadsarkiv, Stockholm.)

Finska Sjömansmissionssällskapet.
    Minutes, from 1875. Helsingfors. (Finnish Seamen's Mission Archives.)

Foelsch, Charles B.
    Seamen and International House: 100 Years of Christian Concern. [New
    York, 1973.]

Fowler, William A.
    The Naval and Military Bible Society. Manuscript in seven parts, 1952.
    (Scripture Gift Mission Archives, London.)

Fricke, Peter H.
    *The Social Structure of the Crews of British Dry-Cargo Merchant Ships: A
    Study of the Organization and Environment of an Occupation.* Unpublished
    Ph.D. Dissertation, University of Durham, 1972.

Friend, Stephen.
    Letter, dated Leeds, July 31, 1985, to the Author.

Gillette, Gerald W.
    (Research Historian, Presbyterian Historical Society, Philadelphia.) Letter,
    dated Philadelphia, January 22, 1970, to the Author.

Hassing, Arne.
    Methodism and Society in Norway, 1853-1918. Unpublished Ph.D. Disserta-
    tion, Northwestern University. Evanston, Illinois, 1974.

Healey, James C.
The Life of Archibald Romaine Mansfield, Apostle to Seamen, and Review of a Century of Service of the Seamen's Church Institute of New York. Typescript. New York, 1940. (Archives of Seamen's Church Institute of N.Y. and N.J., New York.)

Hirsch, J.C.W. and K.
Danske og norske Officerer 1648-1814. (Danish and Norwegian Officers, 1648-1814). Copenhagen, n.d. (Rigsarkivet, Copenhagen.)

Holmes, David L. (Jr.).
The Early Career of Father Taylor. Unpublished M.A. Thesis, Faculty of Philosophy, Columbia University, New York, 1960.

Indenture, dated August 28, 1855. (H.J. Enthoven & Sons, Ltd., Rotherhithe Street, London.)

International Christian Maritime Association.
International Labour Conference 62nd (Maritime) Session — Geneva 1976. Mimeographed Report. London, 1976. (ICMA Secretariat, London.)
4th Triennial Conference: Standing Committee Report. Mimeographed Report by Prebendary T.P. Kerfoot, General Secretary. London, 1981. (ICMA Secretariat, London.)

Jordan Chapel, Penzance.
Minutes, 1802-39. (Archives of Clarence Street Baptist Church, Penzance.)

Kennerley, Alston.
Seamen's Welfare Organizations: An Overview with Some Reference to the South West. Paper read to the University of Exeter Maritime History Seminar, Dartington Hall, October 20-21, 1984.

Kerfoot, T.P.
Letter, dated London, May 25, 1964, to the Author, setting forth a history of the Flying Angel Fellowship, written when Deputy General Secretary of The Missions to Seamen, London.

Kjeldal, Ragnar.
Religious Work among Seamen. Unpublished MST Thesis, Lutheran Theological Seminary, Philadelphia, 1940.

Knight, G.A. Frank.
The History of the National Bible Society of Scotland: Part I, 1809-1900. Typescript. [Edinburgh] n.d. (Archives of National Bible Society of Scotland, Edinburgh.)

Kverndal, Julian.
Letter, dated Harefield (Middlesex), June 1, 1976, to the Author.

Kverndal, Roald.
Comments on "Seafarers Services in the Ports of Tacoma and Seattle . . . by Allen W. Ratcliffe, Ph.D. Typescript. Chicago, 1977. (Archives of the American Lutheran Church, North Pacific District, Seattle.)
The Great Commission: Matthew 28:18-20. Unpublished Trial Lecture delivered at the University of Oslo, June 1, 1984.
Storjohann som sjömannsprest, med saerlig henblikk paa hans bidrag til en maritim pastoralteologi. (Storjohann as Seamen's Pastor: With Particular Reference to his Contribution to a Maritime Pastoral Theology.) Unpublished Trial Lecture delivered at the University of Oslo, June 1, 1984.

Report to the Lutheran World Federation's Department of Church Cooperation on Maritime Ministry Consultations held in East Asia in April, 1985. Bellevue/Seattle, 1985.

Kverndal, Ruth L.

Alcohol and the Seafarer. Unpublished paper for Alcohol Studies Program of Seattle University, Winter Quarter 1981. Seattle, 1981. (ICMA Archives, London.)

Lawson, Evald B.

The Origins of Swedish Religious Organizations in the United States, with Special Reference to Olof Gustaf Hedstrom and the Early Structure of Swedish Methodism. Unpublished Th.D. Dissertation, Biblical Seminary in New York, April 1937.

Lingren, Charlotte H.

The Common Seaman in Nineteenth Century American Fiction. Unpublished Ph.D. Dissertation, Boston University Graduate School. Boston, 1961.

Loetscher, Lefferts A.

Letter, dated Princeton, New Jersey, Jan. 19, 1970, to the Author.

London City Mission.

Minutes, 1835-37. (LCM Archives, London.)

Lovegrove, Deryck W.

The Practice of Itinerant Evangelism in English Calvinistic Dissent 1780-1830. Unpublished Ph.D. Dissertation, Cambridge University, 1981.

The Missions to Seamen.

Index to Committee Resolutions, 1856-91 (The Missions to Seamen Archives, London.)

Committee Book, 1858-68. (Ditto.)

National Maritime Museum, London.

Summary of Information from Navy Lists and Admiralty Progress Books, dated April 4, 1972. (Notes supplied to the Author by George P.B. Naish, Hon. Secretary, Society for Nautical Research.)

Nederlandsch Historisch Scheepvaart Museum.

Letter, dated Amsterdam, July 1970, to the Author, enclosing reprint of Museum Library Catalogue, listing titles under: "Verzorging van zeevarenden" (Care of seafarers).

Newark Presbytery.

Records . . . Oct. 18, 1843 - Feb. 14, 1856. (Presbyterian Historical Society Archives, Philadelphia.)

New Bedford Port Society.

Constitution and Minutes. (Old Dartmouth Historical Society's Whaling Museum, New Bedford, Massachusetts.)

Nook, Jay (Ed.).

Dr. Mansfield's Biography. Typescript. New York, n.d. (Archives of Seamen's Church Institute of N.Y. and N.J., New York.)

The Otsego Presbytery (N.Y.).

Minutes . . . 1819-1830. (Presbyterian Historical Society Archives, Philadelphia.)

Oxenford, Douglas R.
Ideology, Ecclesiastics and the Seafarer: A Pilot Study. Unpublished M.A. Thesis, Ohio State University, Columbus (Ohio), 1983.

Paterson, John.
Memoirs of John Paterson. Vol. 2. (BFBS Archives, London.)

Paul, Lester E.
Joseph Eastburn—Preacher to Mariners. Typescript. Chester (Pennsylvania), 1958. (Presbyterian Historical Society, Philadelphia.)
The Founders of the Mariners' Church. Typescript. Chester (Pennsylvania), 1965. (Ditto.)
The Mariners' Church. Undated handwritten notes. (Ditto.)

The Philadelphia Conference of the Methodist Episcopal Church.
Minutes, 1835-40. (Old St. George's United Methodist Church Archives, Philadelphia.)

Poppen, Alvin J.
The Life and Work of David Abeel. Unpublished MST Thesis, Union Theological Seminary, New York, 1959.

Port of London Society.
Minutes, 1818-28. (BSS Archives, London.)

Powell, Vera P.
A Study of the Seamen's Bethel of New Orleans, Louisiana. Unpublished MSW Thesis, School of Social Work, Tulane University, New Orleans (Louisiana), 1940.

The Presbytery of Philadelphia.
Minutes . . . . (Presbyterian Historical Society Archives, Philadelphia.)

The Presbyterian Church in the United States of America.
Extracts from the Minutes of the General Assembly . . . . (Presbyterian Historical Society Archives, Philadelphia.)

Public Record Office, London.
PRO Adm. 107/30. ff. 32-3. (Richard Marks: *Lieutenant's Passing Certificate,* and *Baptismal Certificate.*)
PRO ADM 12 Ind. 4999 Section 22. (Circular concerning Dr. Samuel Cole, and the issue of religious books to the Fleet.)

Ratcliffe, Allen W.
Seafarers Services in the Ports of Tacoma and Seattle. Mimeographed report. N.p., 1976. (Archives of the American Lutheran Church, North Pacific District, Seattle.)

Richards, Leonard M.
Portion of Inscription on Tombstone [of George Charles Smith], Penzance Cemetery. Typescript, Madron, nr. Penzance, 1967.

Rose, Ruth C.
A Survey of Five Programs for Seamen in New Orleans. Unpublished MSW Thesis, School of Social Work, Tulane University, New Orleans (Louisiana), 1940.

Rymker, F.L.
Rymkers Dagbog. Vols. 1-12, 1850-70. (Baptistsamfunnets Arkiv, Copenhagen.)

Savannah Port Society.
  Minutes. Savannah, 1843-73. (Archives of Savannah Port Society, Savannah,
  Georgia.)

Schepen, John van.
  *Sing a New Song to the Lord . . . You that sail the Sea: A Discussion on the
  Mission among Seamen.* Unpublished Thesis for "Doctoraal" examination in
  Theology, Vrije Universiteit, Amsterdam, 1971.

Seamen's Christian Friend Society.
  Minutes, 1846-49, 1851-65. (SCFS Archives, Manchester.)

Secor, Neale A.
  Seamen's Church Institute: Five Year Plan 1986-1990. Philadelphia, 1985.

Smith, Joseph Mighell.
  Record of interview, April 27, 1970, with the Author. (J. Mighell Smith, since
  1969, Secretary of the Scripture Gift Mission, London, was Secretary of the
  NMBS from 1938.)

Society of Inquiry Respecting Missions.
  "Records of the Seaman's Committee Instituted August 1829," *Papers of the
  Society of Inquiry Respecting Missions,* 1811, etc. (Andover-Newton Theo-
  logical School Library, Newton Center, Massachusetts.)

The Society for Promoting Christian Knowledge.
  Minutes. (SPCK Archives, London.)

Society for the Relief of Destitute Children of Seamen.
  Minutes of the Board of Managers . . . New York, 1848-1857. (Archives of
  the Society for Seamen's Children, Staten Island, New York.)

Thames Church Mission.
  Minutes 1844-47. London. (The Missions to Seamen Archives, London.)

Third and Scots Presbyterian Church, Philadelphia.
  Church Bulletins, Morning Worship Service, November 8 & 22, 1959.
  (Presbyterian Historical Society Archives, Philadelphia.)

Thompson, Smith.
  Letter, dated November 15, 1820, to the American Bible Society. (ABS
  Archives, New York.)

Uittenbosch, Hans.
  *Shipvisiting II: A Paper Read at the 1971 Meeting of the International
  Council of Seamen's Agencies . . . .* Mimeographed report. Montreal, 1971.
  (ICOSA Archives, Bellevue/Seattle, Washington.)
  Industrial Chaplaincy: An Inquiry. Mimeographed study. [Montreal], 1977.
  (ICOSA Archives, Bellevue/Seattle, Washington.)

Whittemore, James. R.
  Seamen's Church Institute: 150 Years and Beyond. Unpublished D.Min.
  Dissertation, New York Theological Seminary, New York, 1985.

Whyman, Henry C.
  *The Conflict and Adjustment of Two Religious Cultures, the Swedish and the
  American, as Found in the Swede's Relation to American Methodism.*
  Unpublished Ph.D. Dissertation, New York University, New York, 1937.

William Jenks' Papers.
  (Manuscript Collection of Massachusetts Historical Society, Boston.)

Woolcott, George.
   Diary 1814-29. Typescript of extracts. (BSS Archives, London.)
World Health Organization.
   Health and Welfare of Seafarers. Mimeographed typescript report of a con-
   ference organized by the Regional Office for Europe of the World Health
   Organization. Marseilles, 1959.

Index

"I think I have now, by God's help, discharged my obligation in writing this large work. Let those who think I have said too little, or those who think I have said too much, forgive me; and let those who think I have said just enough join me in giving thanks to God. Amen."

Last paragraph of Augustine's *City of God.*